MANAGEMENT

14E

GE

MANAGEMENT

14E

GE

Stephen P. Robbins
San Diego State University

Mary Coulter
Missouri State University

With contributions by

Joseph J. Martocchio
University of Illinois

Lori K. Long
Baldwin Wallace University

Harlow, England • London • New York • Boston • San Francisco • Toronto • Sydney • Dubai • Singapore • Hong Kong
Tokyo • Seoul • Taipei • New Delhi • Cape Town • Sao Paulo • Mexico City • Madrid • Amsterdam • Munich • Paris • Milan

Vice President, Business Publishing: Donna Battista
Director of Portfolio Management: Stephanie Wall
Portfolio Manager: Kris Ellis-Levy
Associate Acquisitions Editor, Global Edition: Ishita Sinha
Associate Project Editor, Global Edition: Paromita Banerjee
Assistant Editor, Global Edition: Tahnee Wager
Editorial Assistant: Hannah Lamarre
Vice President, Product Marketing: Roxanne McCarley
Director of Strategic Marketing: Brad Parkins
Strategic Marketing Manager: Deborah Strickland
Product Marketer: Becky Brown
Field Marketing Manager: Lenny Ann Kucenski
Product Marketing Assistant: Jessica Quazza
Vice President, Production and Digital Studio, Arts and Business: Etain O'Dea
Director of Production, Business: Jeff Holcomb
Managing Producer, Business: Ashley Santora
Senior Manufacturing Controller, Global Edition: Trudy Kimber
Content Producer, Global Edition: Purnima Narayanan
Content Producer: Claudia Fernandes
Operations Specialist: Carol Melville
Creative Director: Blair Brown
Manager, Learning Tools: Brian Surette
Content Developer, Learning Tools: Lindsey Sloan
Managing Producer, Digital Studio, Art and Business: Diane Lombardo
Digital Studio Producer: Monique Lawrence
Digital Studio Producer: Alana Coles
Media Production Manager, Global Edition: Vikram Kumar
Full-Service Project Management and Composition: Cenveo® Publisher Services
Interior Designer: Cenveo® Publisher Services
Cover Image: Comaniciu Dan/Shutterstock

Acknowledgments of third-party content appear on the appropriate page within the text.

Pearson Education Limited
KAO Two
KAO Park
Harlow
CM17 9NA
United Kingdom

and Associated Companies throughout the world

Visit us on the World Wide Web at: www.pearsonglobaleditions.com

Authorized adaptation from the United States edition, entitled Management, 14th Edition, ISBN 978-0-13-452760-4 by Stephen P. Robbins and Mary Coulter, published by Pearson Education © 2018.

ISBN 10: 1-292-21583-6
ISBN 13: 978-1-292-21583-9

British Library Cataloguing-in-Publication Data
A catalogue record for this book is available from the British Library

10 9 8 7 6 5 4 3 2 1

Typeset in Times NR MT Pro by Cenveo® Publisher Services
Printed in Malaysia (CTP-VVP)

To my wife, Laura
Steve

To my husband, Ron
Mary

About the Authors

STEPHEN P. ROBBINS received his Ph.D. from the University of Arizona. He previously worked for the Shell Oil Company and Reynolds Metals Company and has taught at the University of Nebraska at Omaha, Concordia University in Montreal, the University of Baltimore, Southern Illinois University at Edwardsville, and San Diego State University. He is currently professor emeritus in management at San Diego State.

Dr. Robbins's research interests have focused on conflict, power, and politics in organizations, behavioral decision making, and the development of effective interpersonal skills. His articles on these and other topics have appeared in such journals as *Business Horizons*, the *California Management Review, Business and Economic Perspectives, International Management, Management Review, Canadian Personnel and Industrial Relations*, and *The Journal of Management Education.*

Dr. Robbins is the world's best-selling textbook author in the areas of management and organizational behavior. His books have sold more than 7 million copies and have been translated into 20 languages. His books are currently used at more than 1,500 U.S. colleges and universities, as well as hundreds of schools throughout Canada, Latin America, Australia, New Zealand, Asia, Europe, and the Arab World.

Dr. Robbins also participates in masters track competition. Since turning 50 in 1993, he's won 23 national championships and 14 world titles. He was inducted into the U.S. Masters Track & Field Hall of Fame in 2005.

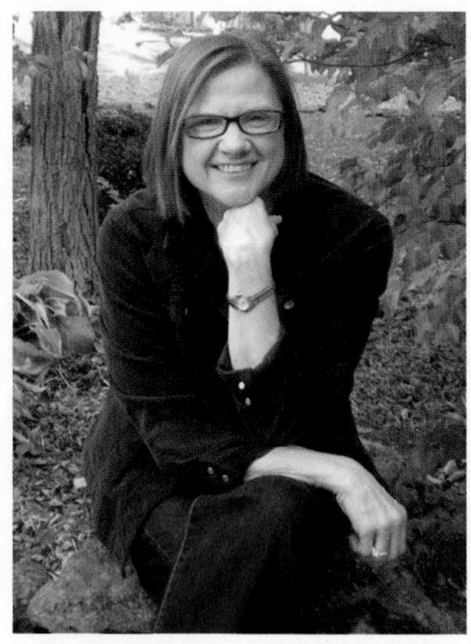

MARY COULTER received her Ph.D. from the University of Arkansas. She held different jobs including high school teacher, legal assistant, and city government program planner before completing her graduate work. She has taught at Drury University, the University of Arkansas, Trinity University, and Missouri State University. She is currently professor emeritus of management at Missouri State University. In addition to *Management*, Dr. Coulter has published other books with Pearson including *Fundamentals of Management* (with Stephen P. Robbins), *Strategic Management in Action*, and *Entrepreneurship in Action.*

When she's not busy writing, Dr. Coulter enjoys puttering around in her flower gardens, trying new recipes, reading all different types of books, and enjoying many different activities with husband Ron, daughters and sons-in-law Sarah and James, and Katie and Matt, and most especially with her two grandkids, Brooklynn and Blake, who are the delights of her life!

Brief Contents

Contents

Part 6 Controlling 630

Preface

The book you have before you is one of the world's most popular introductory management textbooks. It's used by several hundred U.S. colleges and universities; it's translated into Spanish, French, Russian, Dutch, Bahasa, Korean, and Chinese; and there are adapted editions for Australia, Canada, India, and the Arab World.

For a textbook first published in 1984—in a crowded market where there are currently several dozen choices, why has Robbins/Coulter *Management* been so popular and enduring? We believe there are three characteristics that set us apart: contemporary topic coverage, readability, and relevance.

Contemporary Topic Coverage

We have always prided ourselves on bringing the latest management issues and research to this book. In preparing each edition, we carefully comb the academic journals and business periodicals to identify topics that students need to be current on. For instance, prior editions of this book were the first to discuss self-managed teams, emotional intelligence, open-book management, sustainability, social entrepreneurship, stretch goals, the contingent workforce, self-managed careers, wearable technology, big data, and design thinking.

This current edition continues the tradition by including a new section on disruptive innovation. No topic appears to be more current or important to students today than dealing with major structural changes taking place in industries as varied as automobiles, hotels, banking, TV networks, or book publishing. In fact, there are few industries that aren't being threatened by disruptive innovation. In Chapter 6, we define disruptive innovation; explain why it's important; describe who is vulnerable; and discuss implications for entrepreneurs, corporate managers, and your career planning.

Key Changes to the 14th Edition

- Chapter 6 on managing change has been expanded to include a discussion of disruptive innovation as an important driver of change.
- The Part 2 module on creating and leading entrepreneurial ventures has become a separate chapter (Chapter 10). We've expanded our discussion, added end-of-chapter applications, and acknowledged the importance of entrepreneurship by giving it its own chapter.
- The two chapters on organizational design have been merged into one chapter (Chapter 11) in response to comments by users and reviewers. But we've retained the key concepts that students need to know.
- The addition of "Workplace Confidential" pages throughout the book which address common frustrations and challenges that employees face in the workplace.
- Current and timely topics—including the Internet of things, real-time feedback, and choosing appropriate communication media, among others—have been added.
- Dozens of current examples illustrating management practices and challenges in start-up and established organizations, small and large organizations, and manufacturing, service and technology organizations have been added.

Readability

Every author claims his or her books are highly readable. The reality is that few actually are. From the first edition of this book, we were determined to make the field of management interesting and engaging for the reader. How did we do it? First, we committed to a conversational writing style. We wanted the book to read like normal people talk. Second, we relied on an extensive use of examples. As your senior author learned early in his teaching career, students don't remember theories but they do remember stories. So you'll find a wealth of current examples in this book.

A well-written book should be able to be used successfully at all levels of higher education, from community colleges to graduate programs. And over its 30+ years of life, this book has done just that. You'll find this book is used in community colleges, at for-profit colleges, by undergraduate students at both regional and land-grant universities, and in numerous graduate programs.

Relevance

Students are unlikely to be motivated if they think a course and its textbooks aren't relevant to their career goals. We've responded to this challenge in a number of ways. Our latest inclusion is an important new feature—the *Workplace Confidential* pages—that's designed to make this book more meaningful to non-management majors. We also want to highlight four additional features that have helped build this book's reputation for practicality.

Providing value to non-management students. New to this edition are in-chapter pages entitled *Workplace Confidential.* This unique feature marks a distinct break from what typically has been included in the traditional introductory management text.

Your authors have long heard a common complaint about the introductory management course from students in majors such as accounting, finance, and marketing. As summed up by one accounting student: "Why do I need to take a management course? I have no interest in pursuing a career in management!" Even though that accounting student might some day lead an audit team or manage an office of a major CPA firm, we understand those non-management majors who question the relevance of this course to their career goals. We've listened and responded.

We've made the contents of this 14th edition relevant to any student who plans to work in an organization. Regardless of whether an organization employs three people or 300,000, there are common challenges that every employee encounters. We've researched those challenges and identified the nearly dozen-and-a-half most frequent. Then we looked at providing students with guidance for dealing with these challenges. The result is the *Workplace Confidential* features that you'll find throughout this book. For instance, you'll find suggestions for dealing with organizational politics, job stress, coping with an uncommunicative or abusive boss, and responding to an unfair performance review.

Insights from real managers. One feature that has differentiated Robbins/Coulter for more than 15 years is our "real" managers. Student feedback tells us that they appreciate learning from real managers in their everyday jobs. In *Let's Get Real* boxes, actual managers respond to problem scenarios. In *Leader Making a Difference* boxes, you'll meet a variety of global executives whose knowledge and skills significantly influenced organizational outcomes.

Focus on skills. Today's students need both knowledge (knowing) and skills (doing). Students want to leave class knowing what management is all about but also with the skills necessary to help them succeed in today's workplaces. In response, you'll find several features in this book that are designed to build skill expertise. *It's Your Career* chapter openers cover skills ranging from managing time and being self aware to being a pro at giving feedback and being change ready. These chapter openers include information about the skill and are reinforced with a *Pearson MyLab Management* component that tests students' comprehension of the skill. Also, at the end of each chapter, you'll find more skill exercises, where we provide a thorough discussion of additional skills and give students opportunities to practice these skills.

Looking ahead. Students are going to spend most of their future work life in a setting that's likely to look very different from today. To help students prepare for that future, we have included *Future Vision* boxes throughout the book that look at how management and organizations might change over the next 15 to 20 years. Although no one has a perfectly accurate view into the future, certain trends in place today offer insights into what tomorrow's work world might look like. We draw from recent research and forecasts to consider this future.

Pearson MyLab Management Suggested Activities

Making assessment activities available online for students to complete before coming to class will allow you, the instructor, more discussion time during the class to review areas that students are having difficulty in comprehending. The activities below are available in Pearson MyLab Management and are integrated into the textbook.

Watch It

Recommends a video clip that can be assigned to students for outside classroom viewing or that can be watched in the classroom. The video corresponds to the chapter material and is accompanied by multiple-choice questions that reinforce students' comprehension of the chapter content.

Try It

Recommends a mini simulation that can be assigned to students as an outside classroom activity or be done in the classroom. As the students watch the simulation they will be asked to make choices based on the scenario presented in the simulation. At the end of the simulation the student will receive immediate feedback based on the answers they gave. These simulations reinforce the concepts of the chapter and the students' comprehension of those concepts.

Talk About It

These are discussion-type questions that can be assigned as an activity within the classroom.

Write It

Students can be assigned these broad-based, critical-thinking discussion questions that will challenge them to assimilate information that they've read in the chapter.

Personal Inventory Assessments (PIA)

Students learn better when they can connect what they are learning to their personal experience. PIA (Personal Inventory Assessments) is a collection of online exercises designed to promote self-reflection and engagement in students, enhancing their ability to connect with concepts taught in principles of management, organizational behavior, and human resource management classes. Assessments are assignable by instructors who can then track students' completions. Student results include a written explanation along with a graphic display that shows how their results compare to the class as a whole. Instructors will also have access to this graphic representation of results to promote classroom discussion.

Assisted Graded Writing Questions

These are short essay questions that the students can complete as an assignment and submit to you, the professor, for grading.

Chapter-by-Chapter Changes

Chapter 1

- New *FYI* features
- New *Workplace Confidential*: Dealing with Organizational Politics
- New *Watch It* Pearson MyLab Management recommended video assignments
- New *Let's Get Real*
- New *Ethics Dilemma*

- New examples
- New *Working Together* and *My Turn to Be a Manager* activities
- New Case Application on the ALS Ice Bucket Challenge

Chapter 2
- New *Workplace Confidential*: Making Good Decisions
- New examples
- New *Future Vision*: Crowdsourcing Decisions
- New *FYI* features
- New *Watch It* Pearson MyLab Management recommended video assignments
- New *Ethics Dilemma*
- Updated Skills Exercise, new *Working Together* and *My Turn to Be a Manager* activities
- New Case Application on Card Connection's business model to decide on franchisee locations
- New Case Application on Manchester City Football Club's use of big data in game strategies

Chapter 3
- Updated *It's Your Career* opener and Pearson MyLab Management component: Developing Your Global Perspective: Jump-start Your Cultural Intelligence
- Updated *Future Vision*: Communicating in a Connected World
- New *Leader Making a Difference*: Lucy Peng (Alibaba)
- New *FYI* features
- New *Watch It* Pearson MyLab Management recommended video assignments
- New examples
- New *Ethics Dilemma*
- Updated Skills Exercise, new *Working Together* and *My Turn to Be a Manager* activities
- New Case Application on expanding internationally at Tableau, a technology company

Chapter 4
- New *Future Vision*: Diversity of Thought
- New *FYI* features
- New examples
- New *Watch It* Pearson MyLab Management recommended video assignments
- New *Let's Get Real*
- New *Workplace Confidential*: Dealing with Diversity
- New *Ethics Dilemma*
- Updated Skills Exercise, new *Working Together* and *My Turn to Be a Manager* activities
- New Case Application on ethical management at Albergo Etico

Chapter 5
- New *FYI* features
- New *Workplace Confidential*: Balancing Work and Personal Life
- New examples
- New *Watch It* Pearson MyLab Management recommended video assignments
- New *Let's Get Real*
- New *Ethics Dilemma*
- Updated Skills Exercise, new *Working Together* and *My Turn to Be a Manager* activities
- New Case Application on ethical problems at Volkswagen

Chapter 6
- New *It's Your Career* opener and Pearson MyLab Management component: Learning to Manage Your Stress
- New *Future Vision*: The Internet of Things
- New *FYI* features
- New *Workplace Confidential*: Coping with Job Stress

- New Examples
- New *Watch It* Pearson MyLab Management recommended video assignments
- New *Let's Get Real's*
- New *Working Together* and *My Turn to Be a Manager* activities
- New Case Application on the iPhone as a technology disruptor

Chapter 7
- New *Leader Making a Difference*: Indra Nooyi (Pepsi)
- New *FYI* features
- New *Watch It,* Pearson MyLab Management recommended video assignments
- New *Let's Get Real*
- New *Workplace Confidential*: Adjusting to a New Job or Work Team
- New examples
- Updated Skills Exercise, new *Working Together* and *My Turn to Be a Manager* activities
- New Case Application on organizational culture at Tesco
- New Case Application on Amazon's use of drone technology

Chapter 8
- New *Future Vision*: Using Social Media for Environmental Scanning
- New *FYI* features
- New *Watch It* Pearson MyLab Management recommended video assignments
- New *Workplace Confidential*: When You Face a Lack of Clear Directions
- New examples
- New *Let's Get Real*
- New *Ethics Dilemma*
- New *Working Together* and updated *My Turn to Be a Manager* activities
- New Case Application on shipping challenges at Hermès

Chapter 9
- New *Leader Making a Difference*: Mary Barra (GM)
- New *FYI* features
- New *Watch It* Pearson MyLab Management recommended video assignments
- New *Workplace Confidential*: Developing a Career Strategy
- New examples
- New *Let's Get Real*
- New *Ethics Dilemma*
- New *Working Together* and *My Turn to Be a Manager* activities
- New Case Application on Costco's strategy

Chapter 10
- New *It's Your Career* opener and Pearson MyLab Management component: Being Entrepreneurial Even If You Don't Want to Be an Entrepreneur
- New *Leader Making a Difference*: Mark Zuckerberg (Facebook)
- New *Future Vision*: The Growth of Social Businesses
- New *FYI* features
- New *Watch It,* Pearson MyLab Management recommended video assignments
- New *Let's Get Real's*
- New *Workplace Confidential*: Dealing with Risks
- New examples
- New *Ethics Dilemma*
- New *Personal Inventory Assessment*
- New *Working Together* and *My Turn to Be a Manager* activities
- New Skills Exercise: Developing Grit
- New Case Applications on Jamie Oliver's unique social business at Fifteen

Chapter 11
- New *FYI* features
- New *Workplace Confidential*: Coping with Multiple Bosses

- New examples
- New *Working Together* activity

Chapter 12

- New *Leader Making a Difference*: Dr. Dara Richardson-Heron (YWCA USA)
- New *FYI* features
- New *Watch It* Pearson MyLab Management recommended video assignments
- New *Let's Get Real*
- New *Workplace Confidential*: Handling Difficult Coworkers
- New examples
- Updated *Ethics Dilemma*
- Updated Skills Exercise, new *Working Together* and *My Turn to Be a Manager* activities
- New Case Application on self-directed teams at W.L. Gore and Associates

Chapter 13

- New *It's Your Career* opener and Pearson MyLab Management component: Negotiating Your Salary
- New *Future Vision*: Gamification of HR
- New *FYI* features
- New *Watch It* Pearson MyLab Management recommended video assignments
- New *Let's Get Real*
- New *Workplace Confidential*: Job Search
- New examples
- Updated statistics
- Updated Skills Exercise, new *Working Together* and *My Turn to Be a Manager* activities
- New Case Application on Maersk and the HR management challenges in China
- New Case Application on BAE Systems making use of schedule based working

Chapter 14

- New *It's Your Career* opener and Pearson MyLab Management component: I'm Listening
- New *Future Vision*: No Longer Lost in Translation
- New *Leader Making a Difference*: Angela Ahrendts (Apple)
- New *FYI* features
- New *Workplace Confidential*: An Uncommunicative Boss
- New examples
- New *Let's Get Real*
- New Skills Exercise: Developing Your Presentation Skills
- New *Working Together* and *My Turn to Be a Manager* activities
- New Case Application on performance feedback at Amazon

Chapter 15

- New *Leader Making a Difference*: Carolyn McCall (easyJet)
- New *FYI* features
- New *Watch It* Pearson MyLab Management recommended video assignments
- New *Let's Get Real*
- New *Workplace Confidential*: An Abusive Boss
- New examples
- New *Ethics Dilemma*
- New *Working Together* and *My Turn to Be a Manager* activities
- New Case Application on the Tencent Holdings, China

Chapter 16

- New *Leader Making a Difference*: Dr. Delos "Toby" Cosgrove (Cleveland Clinic)
- New *FYI* features
- New *Watch It* Pearson MyLab Management recommended video assignments
- New *Workplace Confidential*: A Micromanaging Boss

- New examples
- New *Let's Get Real*
- New *Working Together* and *My Turn to Be a Manager* activities
- New Case Application on PepsiCo's Indra Nooyi imbibing qualities of an inspirational leader

Chapter 17
- New *Leader Making a Difference*: Susan Wojcicki (YouTube)
- New *FYI* features
- New *Workplace Confidential*: Feelings of Unfair Pay
- New examples
- New *Watch It* Pearson MyLab Management recommended video assignments
- New *Let's Get Real*
- Updated Skills Exercise, new *Working Together* and *My Turn to Be a Manager* activities
- New Case Application on Hong Kong Disneyland's HR programs to motivate employees
- New Case Application on John Lewis Partnership balancing success and happiness

Chapter 18
- New *Future Vision*: Real-time Feedback
- New *FYI* features
- New *Watch It* Pearson MyLab Management recommended video assignments
- New *Let's Get Real*
- New *Workplace Confidential*: Responding to an Unfair Performance Review
- New examples
- New *Ethics Dilemma*
- Updated Skills Exercise, new *Working Together* and *My Turn to Be a Manager* activities
- New Case Applications on Chipotle's food contamination problems and Bring Your Own Device programs

For Students Taking a Management Course:

What This Course Is About and Why It's Important

This course and this book are about management and managers. Managers are one thing that all organizations—no matter the size, kind, or location—need. And there's no doubt that the world managers face has changed, is changing, and will continue to change. The dynamic nature of today's organizations means both rewards *and* challenges for the individuals who will be managing those organizations. Management is a dynamic subject, and a textbook on it should reflect those changes to help prepare you to manage under the current conditions. We've written this 14th edition of *Management* to provide you with the best possible understanding of what it means to be a manager confronting change and to best prepare you for that reality.

But not every student aspires to a career in management. And even if you do, you may be five or ten years away from reaching a managerial position. So you might rightly feel that taking a course in management now may be getting ahead of the game. We hear you. In response to these concerns, we've added new material to this book that is important and relevant to everyone working in an organization—manager and non-manager alike. Our "Workplace Confidential" pages identify, analyze, and offer suggestions for dealing with the major challenges that surveys indicate frustrate employees the most. You should find these pages valuable for helping you survive and thrive in your workplace. Surprisingly, this topic has rarely been addressed in business programs. Inclusion in an introductory management course appeared to us to be a logical place to introduce these challenges and to provide guidance in handling them.

Instructor Resources

At the Pearson's catalog, https://www.pearsonglobaleditions.com/Robbins, instructors can easily register to gain access to a variety of instructor resources available with this text in downloadable format. If assistance is needed, our dedicated technical support team is ready to help with the media supplements that accompany this text. Visit https://support.pearson.com/getsupport for answers to frequently asked questions and toll-free user support phone numbers.

The following supplements are available with this text:

- Instructor's Resource Manual
- Test Bank
- TestGen® Computerized Test Bank
- PowerPoint Presentation

This title is available as an eBook and can be purchased at most eBook retailers.

Acknowledgments

Every author relies on the comments of reviewers, and ours have been very helpful. We want to thank the following people for their insightful comments and suggestions:

Michael Alleruzzo, *St. Joseph University, PA*

Matthias Bollmus, *Carroll University, WI*

Brione Burrows, *Central Georgia Tech, GA*

M. Suzanne Clinton, *University of Central Oklahoma, OK*

Dana J. Frederick, *Missouri State University, MO*

Julia M. Fullick, *Quinnipiac University, CT*

Karl Giulian, *Atlantic Cape Community College, NJ*

Dan Morrell, *Middle Tennessee State University, TN*

L. Renee Rogers, *Forsyth Technical Community College, NC*

Global Edition Acknowledgments

We want to thank the following people for their contributions:

John Opute, *London South Bank University*

Andrew Richardson, *University of Leeds*

Marcello Russo, *University of Bologna*

Jon and Diane Sutherland, *Freelance Writers*

Ken Wong, *Hong Kong Polytechnic University*

Yong Wooi Keong, *Sunway University*

Marian B. Wood, *Freelance Writer*

We would also like to thank the following people for reviewing the Global Edition and sharing their insightful comments and suggestions:

Caroline Akhras, *Notre Dame University–Louaize*

Azim Khan Aminuddin, *United Arab Emirates University*

Lindos Daou, *Holy Spirit University of Kaslik*

Evangelos Dedousis, *American University of Dubai*

Suresh George, *Coventry University*

Richard Jefferies, *The University of the West of Scotland*

J. C. Santora, *International School of Management, Paris*

Vimala Venugopal, *Taylor's University Malaysia*

Our team at Pearson has been amazing to work with, as always! This team of editors, production experts, technology gurus, designers, marketing specialists, sales representatives, and warehouse employees works hard to turn our files into a bound textbook and a digital textbook and sees that it gets to faculty and students. We couldn't do this without all of you! Our sincere thanks to the people who made this book "ready to go," including Stephanie Wall, Kris Ellis-Levy, Claudia Fernandes, Hannah Lamarre, and Nancy Moudry, as well as Kathy Smith and the team at Cenveo. All of you are consummate professionals who truly are committed to publishing the best textbooks! We're glad to have you on our team!

Finally, Steve and Mary would like to thank Joe Martocchio at the University of Illinois and Lori Long at Baldwin Wallace University for helping with this revision. They were instrumental in updating the research, examples, boxes, skill exercises, and cases. This revision could never have been done without your assistance. We thank you so much!

Chapter 1 Managers and You in the Workplace

It's Your Career

Source: valentint/Fotolia

A key to success in management and in your career is having good time management skills.

The ABC's of Managing Your Time

Are you BUSY? Do you always seem to have a lot to do and never seem to get it done, or done on time, or are things done at the last minute under a lot of pressure and stress? If you're like most people, the answer to these questions is YES! Well, maybe in a management textbook we need to do something about that by focusing on one aspect of management that can be tremendously useful to you . . . TIME MANAGEMENT! Time is a unique resource and one of your most valuable resources. Time is also a limited resource. First, if it's wasted, it can never be replaced. People talk about saving time, but time can never actually be saved. Second, unlike resources such as money or talent, which are distributed unequally in the world, time is an equal-opportunity resource. Each one of us gets exactly the same amount of time: 24 hours per day or 168 hours each week. But as you have undoubtedly observed, some people are a lot more efficient in using their allotment. It is not uncommon to hear others say that they need additional hours to get everything done, but that is simply wishful thinking. Commit to improving your ability to manage those 168 hours so you can be more efficient and effective—in your career and in your personal life! Here are some suggestions to help you better use your time:

*1. **Make and keep a list of all your current, upcoming, and routine goals.** Know what needs to be done daily, weekly, and monthly.*

*2. **Rank your goals according to importance.** Not all goals are of equal importance. Given the limitations on your time, you want to make sure you give highest priority to the most important goals.*

*3. **List the activities/tasks necessary to achieve your goals.** What specific actions do you need to take to achieve your goals?*

*4. **Divide these activities/tasks into categories using an A, B, and C classification.** The A's are important and urgent. B's are either important or urgent, but not both. C's are routine—not important nor urgent, but still need to be done.*

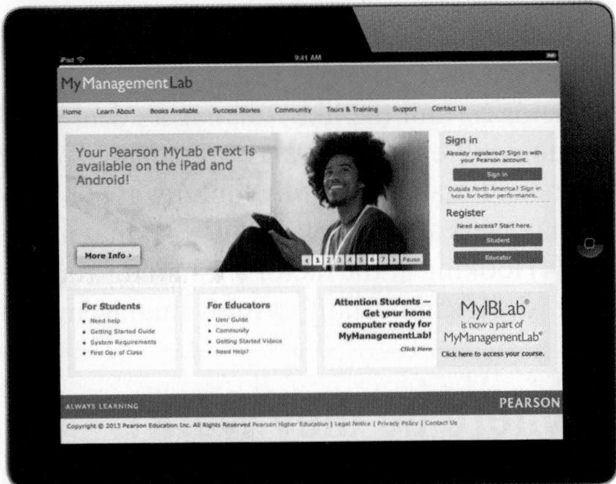

Pearson MyLab Management®

✪ Improve Your Grade!

When you see this icon, visit **www.mymanagementlab.com** for activities that are applied, personalized, and offer immediate feedback.

Learning Objectives

• SKILL OUTCOMES

1.1 Tell *who managers are and where they work.*

- **Know how to** *manage your time.*

1.2 Explain *why managers are important to organizations.*

1.3 Describe *the functions, roles, and skills of managers.*

- **Develop your skill** *at being politically aware.*

1.4 Describe *the factors that are reshaping and redefining the manager's job.*

1.5 Explain *the value of studying management.*

5. Schedule your activities/tasks according to the priorities you've set. *Prepare a daily plan. Every morning, or at the end of the previous workday, make a list of the five or so most important things you want to do for the day. Then set priorities for the activities listed on the basis of importance and urgency.*

6. Plan your to-do list each day so that it includes a mixture of A, B, and C activities/tasks. *And it's best to spread the three types of tasks throughout your day so you're not lumping together all your demanding tasks. Also, be realistic about what you can achieve in a given time period.*

7. Recognize that technology makes it too easy to stay connected. *Just think for a moment how many phone calls, e-mails, texts, postings on social media, and unscheduled visitors you receive on a typical day. Some are essential to the tasks at hand, while others are distractions that do not require immediate attention. Prioritize the importance of this information.*

8. Realize that priorities may change as your day or week proceeds. *New information may change a task's importance or urgency. As you get new information, reassess your list of priorities and respond accordingly.*

9. Remember that your goal is to manage getting your work done as efficiently and effectively as you can. *It's not to become an expert at creating to-do lists. Find what works best for you and use it!*

Like many students, you've probably had a job (or two) at some time or another while working on your degree. And your work experiences, regardless of where you've worked, are likely to have been influenced by the skills and abilities of your manager. What are today's successful managers like and what skills do they need in dealing with the problems and challenges of managing in the twenty-first century? This text is about the important work that managers do. The reality facing today's managers—and that might include you in the near future—is that the world is changing. In workplaces of all types—offices, stores, labs, restaurants, factories, and the like—managers deal with changing expectations and new ways of managing employees and organizing work. In this chapter, we introduce you to managers and management by looking at (1) who managers are and where they work, (2) why managers are important, and (3) what managers do. Finally, we wrap up the chapter by (4) looking at the factors reshaping and redefining the manager's job and (5) discussing why it's important to study management.

WHO **are managers and where do they work?**

LO1.1 Managers may not be who or what you might expect! Managers can range in age from 18 to 80+. They run large corporations, medium-sized businesses, and entrepreneurial start-ups. They're also found in government departments, hospitals, not-for-profit agencies, museums, schools, and even nontraditional organizations such as political campaigns and music tours. Managers can also be found doing managerial work in every country on the globe. In addition, some managers are top-level managers while others are first-line managers. And today, managers are just as likely to be women as they are men; however, the number of women in top-level manager positions remains low—only 24 (4%) women were CEOs of Fortune 500 companies in 2014.[1] Similarly, only 20 (4%) were minorities. Even in government leadership roles, women are far outnumbered by men in the U.S. Senate and House of Representatives, representing approximately 20 percent of these total elected officials.[2] But no matter where managers are found or what gender or race they are, managers have exciting and challenging jobs!

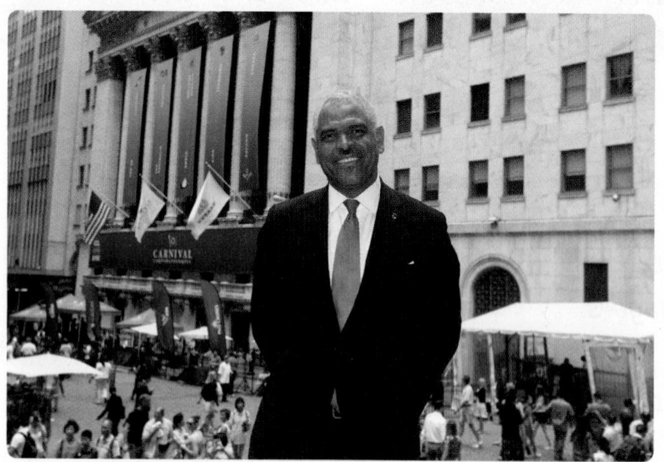

Carnival Corporation's CEO Arnold Donald is the top manager of the world's largest cruise line, with over 100,000 employees from different cultures and countries, 10 cruise line brands, and 100 ships. His challenging job involves making decisions and developing plans that help Carnival achieve its goal "to show our guests the kind of fun that memories are made of."
Source: Jason DeCrow/AP Images for Carnival Corporation

Who Is a Manager?

It used to be fairly simple to define who managers were: They were the organizational members who told others what to do and how to do it. It was easy to differentiate *managers* from *nonmanagerial employees*. Now, it isn't quite that simple. In many organizations, the changing nature of work has blurred the distinction between managers and nonmanagerial employees. Many traditional nonmanagerial jobs now include managerial activities.[3] For example, the gaming company Valve does not award job titles, and there is little formal supervision. Virtually any employee is free to start a project as long as the employee obtains funding and assembles a project team.[4] Or consider an organization like Morning Star Company, the world's largest tomato processor, where no employees are called managers—just 400 full-time employees who do what needs to be done and who together "manage" issues such as job responsibilities, compensation decisions, and budget decisions.[5] Sounds crazy, doesn't it? But it works—for this organization. (See Case Application 2 at the end of the chapter to see how another business—Zappos—has gone bossless!)

manager
Someone who coordinates and oversees the work of other people so organizational goals can be accomplished

So, how *do* we define who managers are? A **manager** is someone who coordinates and oversees the work of other people so organizational goals can be accomplished. A manager's job is not about *personal* achievement—it's about helping *others* do their work. That may mean coordinating the work of a departmental group, or it might mean supervising a single person. It could involve coordinating the work activities of a team with people from different departments or even people outside the organization such as temporary employees or individuals who work for the organization's suppliers. Keep in mind that managers may also have work duties not related to coordinating and overseeing others' work. For example, an insurance claims supervisor might process claims in addition to coordinating the work activities of other claims clerks.

How can managers be classified in organizations? In traditionally structured organizations (often pictured as a pyramid because more employees are at lower

Exhibit 1-1
Levels of Management

organizational levels than at upper organizational levels), managers can be classified as first-line, middle, or top. (See Exhibit 1-1.) At the lowest level of management, **first-line (or frontline) managers** manage the work of nonmanagerial employees who typically are involved with producing the organization's products or servicing the organization's customers. These managers often have titles such as *supervisors* or even *shift managers, district managers, department managers*, or *office managers*. **Middle managers** manage the work of first-line managers and can be found between the lowest and top levels of the organization. They may have titles such as *regional manager, project leader, store manager*, or *division manager*. Middle managers are mainly responsible for turning company strategy into action. At the upper levels of the organization are the **top managers**, who are responsible for making organization-wide decisions and establishing the plans and goals that affect the entire organization. These individuals typically have titles such as *executive vice president, president, managing director, chief operating officer,* or *chief executive officer*.

first-line (frontline) managers
Managers at the lowest level of management who manage the work of nonmanagerial employees

middle managers
Managers between the lowest level and top levels of the organization who manage the work of first-line managers

top managers
Managers at or near the upper levels of the organization structure who are responsible for making organization-wide decisions and establishing the goals and plans that affect the entire organization

Not all organizations are structured to get work done using a traditional pyramidal form, however. Some organizations, for example, are more loosely configured, with work done by ever-changing teams of employees who move from one project to another as work demands arise. For instance, Atlassian, a global software company based in Australia, forms employee teams with the skills and experience needed for each work project. When a project is complete, the team disbands and its members join new teams. Because team members may be in separate buildings or even in separate countries, Atlassian emphasizes clear and constant communication.[6] Although it's not as easy to tell who the managers are in these organizations, we do know that someone must fulfill that role—that is, someone must coordinate and oversee the work of others, even if that "someone" changes as work tasks or projects change or that "someone" doesn't necessarily have the title of manager.

Where Do Managers Work?

It's obvious that managers work in organizations. But what is an **organization**? It's a deliberate arrangement of people to accomplish some specific purpose. Your college or university is an organization; so are fraternities and sororities, government departments, churches, Google, your neighborhood grocery store, the United Way, the St. Louis Cardinals baseball team, and the Mayo Clinic. All are considered organizations and have three common characteristics. (See Exhibit 1-2.)

organization
A deliberate arrangement of people to accomplish some specific purpose

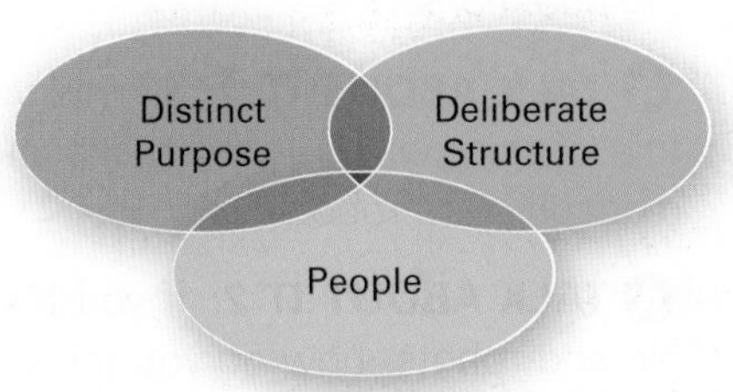

Exhibit 1-2
Characteristics of Organizations

- Frontline managers directly supervise some 93 percent of all nonsupervisory employees.
- 9.3 million managers and executives were in the U.S. workforce in 2014.
- 6.9 million middle managers were in the U.S. workforce
- 2.4 million top executives were in the U.S. workforce.[7]

First, an organization has a distinct purpose typically expressed through goals the organization hopes to accomplish. Second, each organization is composed of people. It takes people to perform the work that's necessary for the organization to achieve its goals. Third, all organizations develop a deliberate structure within which members do their work. That structure may be open and flexible, with no specific job duties or strict adherence to explicit job arrangements. For instance, most big projects at Google (at any one time, hundreds of projects are in process simultaneously) are tackled by small, focused employee teams that set up in an instant and complete work just as quickly.[8] Or the structure may be more traditional—like that of Procter & Gamble or General Electric or any large corporation—with clearly defined rules, regulations, job descriptions, and some members identified as "bosses" who have authority over other members. In the military, there is a well-defined hierarchy. In the U.S. Air Force, the General of the Air Force is the highest ranking officer and Second Lieutenant is the lowest ranking officer. Between the two are nine officer ranks.

Many of today's organizations are structured more like Google, with flexible work arrangements, employee work teams, open communication systems, and supplier alliances. In these organizations, work is defined in terms of tasks to be done. And workdays have no time boundaries since work can be—and is—done anywhere, anytime. However, no matter what type of approach an organization uses, some deliberate structure is needed so work can get done, with managers overseeing and coordinating that work.

FUTURE VISION Is It Still Managing When What You're Managing Are Robots?

While this text presents a fairly accurate description of today's workplace, you're going to spend most of your work life in the future. What will that work life look like? How will it be different from today? The workplace of tomorrow is likely to include workers that are faster, smarter, more responsible—and who just happen to be robots.[9] Are you at all surprised by this statement? Although robots have been used in factory and industrial settings for a long time, it's becoming more common to find robots in the office, and it's bringing about new ways of looking at how work is done and at what and how managers manage. So what *would* the manager's job be like managing robots? And even more intriguing is how these "workers" might affect how human coworkers interact with them.

As machines have become smarter, researchers have been looking at human-machine interaction and how people interact with the smart devices that are now such an integral part of our professional and personal lives. One conclusion is that people find it easy to bond with a robot, even one that doesn't look or sound anything like a real person. In a workplace setting, if a robot moves around in a "purposeful way," people tend to view it, in some ways, as a coworker. People name their robots and can even describe the robot's moods and tendencies. As telepresence robots become more common, the humanness becomes even more evident. For example, when Erwin Deininger, the electrical engineer at Reimers Electra Steam, a small company in Clear Brook, Virginia, moved to the Dominican Republic when his wife's job transferred her there, he was able to still be "present" at the company via his VGo robot. Now "robot" Deininger moves easily around the office and the shop floor, allowing the "real" Deininger to do his job just as if he were there in person. The company's president, satisfied with how the robot solution has worked out, has been surprised at how he acts around it, feeling at times that he's interacting with Deininger himself.

There's no doubt that robot technology will continue to be incorporated into organizational settings. The manager's job will become even more exciting and challenging as humans and machines work together to accomplish an organization's goals.

If your professor has chosen to assign this, go to ***www.mymanagementlab.com*** *to discuss the following questions.*

TALK ABOUT IT 1: What's your response to the title of this box: Is it still managing when what you're managing are robots? Discuss.

TALK ABOUT IT 2: If you had to "manage" people and robots, how do you think your job as manager might be different than what the chapter describes?

WHY **are managers important?**

LO1.2 What can a great boss do?

- Inspire you professionally and personally
- Energize you and your coworkers to accomplish things together that you couldn't get done by yourself
- Provide coaching and guidance with problems
- Provide you feedback on how you're doing
- Help you to improve your performance
- Keep you informed of organizational changes
- Change your life[10]

If you've worked with a manager like this, consider yourself lucky. Such a manager can make going to work a lot more enjoyable and productive. However, even managers who don't live up to such lofty ideals and expectations are important to organizations. Why? Let's look at three reasons.

The first reason why managers are important is because *organizations need their managerial skills and abilities* more than ever in uncertain, complex, and chaotic times. As organizations deal with today's challenges—changing workforce dynamics, the worldwide economic climate, changing technology, ever-increasing globalization, and so forth—managers play an important role in identifying critical issues and crafting responses. For example, BlackBerry Limited introduced software for autonomous cars. The company's vehicle-to-vehicle software will enable cars to communicate with each other to prevent collisions and improve traffic flow.[11] Teams of talented scientists and engineers create the hardware and software to make this possible. But it takes more than that to be successful. There has to be a focus on commercial potential. For example, Virgin Galactic and Xcor Aerospace are working toward creating a new industry—space tourism for civilians. These companies possess the technological and scientific know-how and resources to make this a reality; however, the fare for a suborbital flight around Earth is expected to be about $100,000 per passenger.[12] Most people will not have the discretionary funds to take these flights. That's why, behind the scenes, you'd also find a team of managers who scrutinize ideas and focus on the question: *Is there a sustainable market?* These managers realize what is critical to success. The opposite "types" have worked together and created a successful business.[13]

Another reason why managers are important to organizations is because *they're critical to getting things done.* For instance, Philips has thousands of general managers who supervise the work of 113,000 employees worldwide.[14] These managers deal with all kinds of issues as the company's myriad tasks are carried out. They create and coordinate the workplace environment and work systems so that others can perform those tasks. Or, if work isn't getting done or isn't getting done as it should be, they're the ones who find out why and get things back on track. And these managers are key players in leading the company into the future.

Finally, *managers do matter* to organizations! How do we know that? The Gallup Organization, which has polled millions of employees and tens of thousands of managers, has found that the single most important variable in employee productivity and loyalty isn't pay or benefits or workplace environment—it's the quality of the relationship between employees and their direct supervisors.[15] In addition, global consulting firm Towers Watson found that the way a company manages and engages its people can significantly affect its financial performance.[16] Companies that hire managers based on talent realize a 48 percent increase in profitability, a 22 percent increase in productivity, a 30 percent increase in employee engagement scores, a 17 percent increase in customer engagement scores, and a 19 percent decrease in turnover.[17] That's scary considering another study by the Gallup Organization found that leadership is the single largest influence on employee engagement.[18] In yet another study by different researchers, 44 percent of the respondents said their supervisors strongly increased engagement.[19] However, in this same study, 41 percent of respondents also said their supervisors strongly decreased engagement. And, a different study of organizational performance found that managerial ability was important in creating organizational value.[20] So, as you can see, managers can and do have an impact—positive and negative. What can we conclude from such reports? Managers are important—and they *do* matter!

WHAT do managers do?

LO1.3 Simply speaking, management is what managers do. But that simple statement doesn't tell us much, does it? Let's look first at what management is before discussing more specifically what managers do.

management
Coordinating and overseeing the work activities of others so their activities are completed efficiently and effectively

Management involves coordinating and overseeing the work activities of others so their activities are completed efficiently and effectively. We already know that coordinating and overseeing the work of others is what distinguishes a managerial position from a nonmanagerial one. However, this doesn't mean that managers or their employees can do what they want anytime, anywhere, or in any way. Instead, management involves ensuring that work activities are completed efficiently and effectively by the people responsible for doing them, or at least that's what managers should be doing.

efficiency
Doing things right, or getting the most output from the least amount of inputs

Efficiency refers to getting the most output from the least amount of inputs or resources. Managers deal with scarce resources—including people, money, and equipment—and want to use those resources efficiently. Efficiency is often referred to as "doing things right," that is, not wasting resources. For instance, Southwest Airlines has achieved operating efficiency through a variety of practices, which include using one aircraft model (Boeing 737) throughout its fleet. Using one model simplifies scheduling, operations, and flight maintenance, and the training costs for pilots, ground crew, and mechanics are lower because there's only a single aircraft to learn.[21] These efficient work practices paid off, as Southwest has made a profit for 42 consecutive years![22]

effectiveness
Doing the right things, or doing those work activities that will result in achieving goals

It's not enough, however, just to be efficient. Management is also concerned with employee effectiveness. **Effectiveness** is often described as "doing the right things," that is, doing those work activities that will result in achieving goals. Besides being efficient, Southwest Airlines' mission is "dedication to the highest quality of Customer Service delivered with a sense of warmth, friendliness, individual pride, and Company Spirit."[23] Two of the many reasons cited for the airlines' effectiveness are permitting two checked bags for free and permitting a change in itinerary without incurring a penalty.[24] Whereas efficiency is concerned with the *means* of getting things done, effectiveness is concerned with the *ends*, or attainment of organizational goals (see Exhibit 1-3). In successful organizations, high efficiency and high effectiveness typically go hand in hand. Poor management (which leads to poor performance) usually involves being inefficient and ineffective or being effective but inefficient.

★ It's Your Career

Time Management—If your instructor is using Pearson MyLab Management, log onto **www.mymanagementlab.com** and test your *time management knowledge*. **Be sure to refer back to the chapter opener!**

Now let's take a more detailed look at what managers do. Describing what managers do isn't easy. Just as no two organizations are alike, no two managers' jobs are alike. In spite of this, management researchers have developed three approaches to describe what managers do: functions, roles, and skills.

Exhibit 1-3
Efficiency and Effectiveness in Management

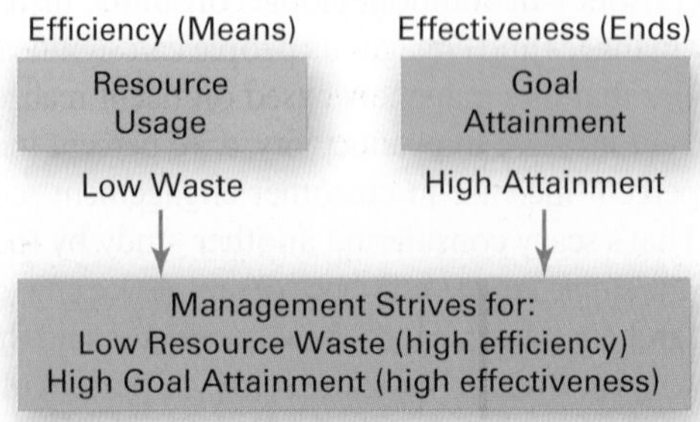

Exhibit 1-4
Four Functions of Management

Planning	Organizing	Leading	Controlling	Lead to
Setting goals, establishing strategies, and developing plans to coordinate activities	Determining what needs to be done, how it will be done, and who is to do it	Motivating, leading, and any other actions involved in dealing with people	Monitoring activities to ensure that they are accomplished as planned	Achieving the organization's stated purposes

Management Functions

According to the functions approach, managers perform certain activities or functions as they efficiently and effectively coordinate the work of others. What are these functions? Henri Fayol, a French businessman in the early part of the twentieth century, suggested that all managers perform five functions: planning, organizing, commanding, coordinating, and controlling.[25] (See Management History Module for more information.) Today, we use four functions to describe a manager's work: planning, organizing, leading, and controlling (see Exhibit 1-4). Let's briefly look at each.

If you have no particular destination in mind, then any road will do. However, if you have someplace in particular you want to go, you've got to plan the best way to get there. Because organizations exist to achieve some particular purpose, someone must define that purpose and the means for its achievement. Managers are that someone. As managers engage in **planning**, they set goals, establish strategies for achieving those goals, and develop plans to integrate and coordinate activities.

Managers are also responsible for arranging and structuring work that employees do to accomplish the organization's goals. We call this function **organizing**. When managers organize, they determine what tasks are to be done, who is to do them, how the tasks are to be grouped, who reports to whom, and where decisions are to be made.

Every organization has people, and a manager's job is to work with and through people to accomplish goals. This is the **leading** function. When managers motivate subordinates, help resolve work group conflicts, influence individuals or teams as they work, select the most effective communication channel, or deal in any way with employee behavior issues, they're leading.

The final management function is **controlling**. After goals and plans are set (planning), tasks and structural arrangements are put in place (organizing), and people are hired, trained, and motivated (leading), there has to be an evaluation of whether things are going as planned. To ensure goals are met and work is done as it should be, managers monitor and evaluate performance. Actual performance is compared with the set goals. If those goals aren't achieved, it's the manager's job to get work back on track. This process of monitoring, comparing, and correcting is the controlling function.

Just how well does the functions approach describe what managers do? Do managers always plan, organize, lead, and then control? Not necessarily. What a manager does may not always happen in this sequence. However, regardless of the order in which these functions are performed, managers do plan, organize, lead, and control as they manage.

Leading is an important function of The Container Store manager Jaimie Moeller (left). She influences the behavior of employees by leading them in a team huddle before they begin their work day. Coaching employees to succeed in the store's team-selling environment helps Moeller achieve the store's sales performance and customer service goals.
Source: ZUMA Press Inc/Alamy

planning
Management function that involves setting goals, establishing strategies for achieving those goals, and developing plans to integrate and coordinate activities

organizing
Management function that involves arranging and structuring work to accomplish the organization's goals

leading
Management function that involves working with and through people to accomplish organizational goals

controlling
Management function that involves monitoring, comparing, and correcting work performance

If your professor has assigned this, go to **www.mymanagementlab.com** to complete the *Simulation: **What Is Management?*** and see how well you can apply the ideas of planning, organizing, leading, and controlling.

Although the functions approach is a popular way to describe what managers do, some have argued that it isn't relevant.[26] So let's look at another perspective.

let's get REAL

The Scenario:

Micah, one of your best employees, was just promoted to a managerial position. You invited him to lunch to celebrate and to see what was on his mind about his new position. Waiting for your food to arrive, you asked him if he had any concerns or questions about being a manager. Looking straight at you, Micah said, "How is being a manager going to be different? What will I do as a manager?"

How would you respond?

Being a manager means that you have a greater responsibility to consider, and keep in mind big-picture organizational goals and how your work and that of your staff contribute to those goals. As a manager you also have a responsibility to think about development opportunities for any team members who may now report to you. How will you help to put them on a path toward growth and success?

Maribel Lara
Director, Account Management

Source: Maribel Lara

Mintzberg's Managerial Roles and a Contemporary Model of Managing

Henry Mintzberg, a well-known management researcher, studied actual managers at work. In his first comprehensive study, Mintzberg concluded that what managers do can best be described by looking at the managerial roles they engage in at work.[27] The term **managerial roles** refers to specific actions or behaviors expected of and exhibited by a manager. (Think of the different roles you play—student, employee, student organization member, volunteer, sibling, and so forth—and the different things you're expected to do in these roles.) When describing what managers do from a roles perspective, we're not looking at a specific person per se, but at the expectations and responsibilities associated with the person in that role—the role of a manager.[28] As shown in Exhibit 1-5, these 10 roles are grouped around interpersonal relationships, the transfer of information, and decision making.

managerial roles
Specific actions or behaviors expected of and exhibited by a manager

The **interpersonal roles** involve people (subordinates and persons outside the organization) and other ceremonial and symbolic duties. The three interpersonal roles include figurehead, leader, and liaison. The **informational roles** involve collecting, receiving, and disseminating information. The three informational roles include monitor, disseminator, and spokesperson. Finally, the **decisional roles** entail making decisions or choices and include entrepreneur, disturbance handler, resource allocator, and negotiator. As managers perform these roles, Mintzberg proposed that their activities included both reflection (thinking) and action (doing).[29]

interpersonal roles
Managerial roles that involve people and other duties that are ceremonial and symbolic in nature

informational roles
Managerial roles that involve collecting, receiving, and disseminating information

decisional roles
Managerial roles that revolve around making choices

A number of follow-up studies have tested the validity of Mintzberg's role categories, and the evidence generally supports the idea that managers—regardless of the type of organization or level in the organization—perform similar roles.[30] However, the emphasis that managers give to the various roles seems to change with organizational level.[31] At higher levels of the organization, the roles of disseminator, figurehead, negotiator, liaison, and spokesperson are more important; while the leader role (as Mintzberg defined it) is more important for lower-level managers than it is for either middle or top-level managers.

Exhibit 1-5
Mintzberg's Managerial Roles

Source: Based on H. Mintzberg, *The Nature of Managerial Work* (New York: Prentice Hall, 1983).

So which approach is better, managerial functions or Mintzberg's propositions? Although each does a good job of depicting what managers do, the functions approach still seems to be the generally accepted way of describing the manager's job. "The classical functions provide clear and discrete methods of classifying the thousands of activities managers carry out and the techniques they use in terms of the functions they perform for the achievement of goals."[32] However, Mintzberg's role approach and additional model of managing do offer us other insights into managers' work.

Management Skills

UPS is a company that understands the importance of management skills.[33] The company's new on-road supervisors are immersed in a new manager orientation where they learn people and time management skills. The company started an intensive eight-day offsite skills training program for first-line managers as a way to improve its operations. What have supervisors learned from the skills training? Some things they mentioned learning were how to communicate more effectively and important information about safety compliance and labor practices.

What types of skills do managers need? Robert L. Katz proposed that managers need three critical skills in managing: technical, human, and conceptual.[34] (Exhibit 1-6 shows the relationships of these skills to managerial levels.) **Technical skills** are the job-specific knowledge and techniques needed to proficiently perform work tasks. These skills tend to be more important for first-line managers

technical skills
Job-specific knowledge and techniques needed to proficiently perform work tasks

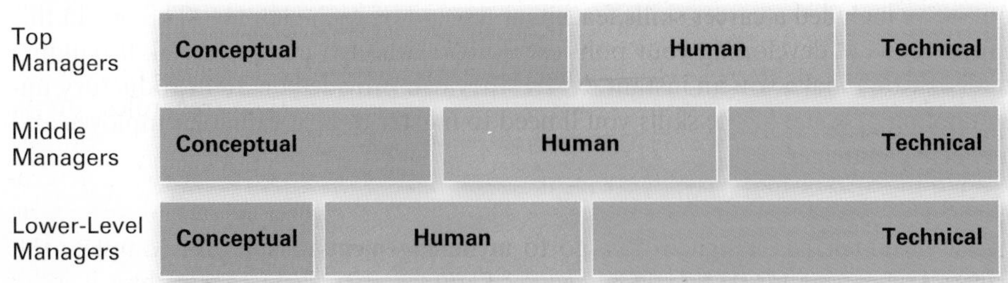

Exhibit 1-6
Skills Needed at Different Managerial Levels

Exhibit 1-7
Important Managerial Skills

Source: Based on *Workforce Online*; J. R. Ryan, *Bloomberg BusinessWeek Online*; In-Sue Oh and C. M. Berry; and R. S. Rubin and E. C. Dierdorff.

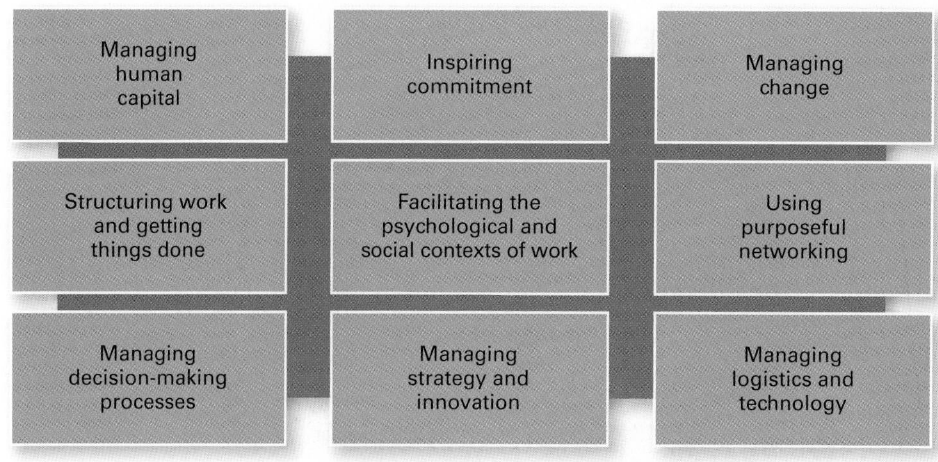

because they typically manage employees who use tools and techniques to produce the organization's products or service the organization's customers. Often, employees with excellent technical skills get promoted to first-line manager. For example, Dean White, a production supervisor at Springfield Remanufacturing, started as a parts cleaner. Now, White manages 25 people in six departments. He noted that at first it was difficult to get people to listen, especially his former peers. "I learned I had to gain respect before I could lead," White said. He credits mentors—other supervisors whose examples he followed—with helping him become the type of manager he is today.[35] Dean is a manager who has technical skills, but also recognizes the importance of **interpersonal skills**, which involve the ability to work well with other people both individually and in a group. Because all managers deal with people, these skills are equally important to all levels of management. Managers with good human skills get the best out of their people. They know how to communicate, motivate, lead, and inspire enthusiasm and trust. Finally, **conceptual skills** are the skills managers use to think and to conceptualize about abstract and complex situations. Using these skills, managers see the organization as a whole, understand the relationships among various subunits, and visualize how the organization fits into its broader environment. Managers then can effectively direct employees' work. For example, Ian McAllister, general manager at Amazon, indicates that a successful general manager understands the whole business. With this understanding, managers can get everyone on the same page. In turn, employees will make a substantial number of decisions in support of the company's vision.[36] These skills are most important to top managers.

interpersonal skills
The ability to work well with other people individually and in a group

conceptual skills
The ability to think and to conceptualize about abstract and complex situations

Other important managerial skills that have been identified are listed in Exhibit 1-7. In today's demanding and dynamic workplace, employees who want to be valuable assets must constantly upgrade their skills, and developing management skills can be particularly beneficial. We feel that understanding and developing management skills is so important that we've included a skills activity component for each chapter's *It's Your Career* opener. You'll find that activity at www.mymanagementlab.com. In addition, we've included a career skills feature at the end of each chapter. (The one in this chapter looks at developing your political skills.) Although completing skill-building exercises won't make you an instant expert, they can provide you an introductory understanding of some of the skills you'll need to master to be a valuable employee and an effective manager.

★ Write It!

If your professor has assigned this, go to **mymanagementlab.com** and complete the **Writing Assignment *MGMT 1: Management Skills.***

let's get REAL

The Scenario:

After three years as a lead customer service representative for an Internet-based clothing company, Jane is eager to apply for a team supervisor position. She has good relationships with the employees in her department, but she is not sure what skills she needs to have to be considered for the promotion. At her performance appraisal meeting with her manager, she asks, "What can I do to build my skills to prepare me to become a supervisor?"

Source: Whitney Portman

Whitney Portman
Senior Marketing Communications Manager

What advice can you give Jane on developing her skills?

As you advance in your career, the biggest shift in your skill set will be going from the "doer" to the "delegator." Instead of getting all the work done, you'll become air traffic control and act as more of a guide for your employees. You can hone these leadership skills before ever actually getting the role. Try to approach each new project as if you were leading the team responsible for it. Think more strategically and consider the broader business objectives versus just the details of the tasks at hand. Your manager will start to notice this shift in your mindset and it will become clear that you're ready to seamlessly take on the new responsibilities.

HOW is the manager's job changing?

LO1.4 In today's world, managers are dealing with global economic and political uncertainties, changing workplaces, ethical issues, security threats, and changing technology. For example, as annual sales surge past 500,000 vehicles, a major challenge for Jaguar Land Rover is staffing its UK assembly plants to meet demand. The Halewood plant near Liverpool has tripled its workforce during the past six years and is always seeking qualified employees. To attract a large and diverse pool of job candidates, managers created apprenticeships for recent graduates. They also launched "Young Women in the Know," a program in which Jaguar Land Rover's women engineers and managers conducted factory tours to get girls and women interested in manufacturing. At the same time, these managers are facing decisions in an uncertain environment now that the United Kingdom has voted to exit the European Union.[37] It's likely that more managers *will* have to manage under such demanding circumstances, and the fact is that *how* managers manage is changing. Exhibit 1-8 shows some of the most important changes facing managers. Throughout the rest of this text, we'll discuss these and other changes and how they affect the way managers plan, organize, lead, and control. We want to focus on six of these changes: customers, technology, social media, innovation, sustainability, and the employee.

Focus on the Customer

John Legere, CEO of T-Mobile, likes to listen to customers. "My business philosophy is listen to your employees, listen to your customers. Shut up and do what they tell you. And each of our Un-carrier moves and the way I run my company is completely aligned with that."[38] This manager understands the importance of customers and clearly believes that focusing on customers is essential to success. Without them, most organizations would cease to exist. Yet, focusing on the customer has long been thought to be the responsibility of marketing types. "Let the marketers worry about the customers" is

Exhibit 1-8
Changes Facing Managers

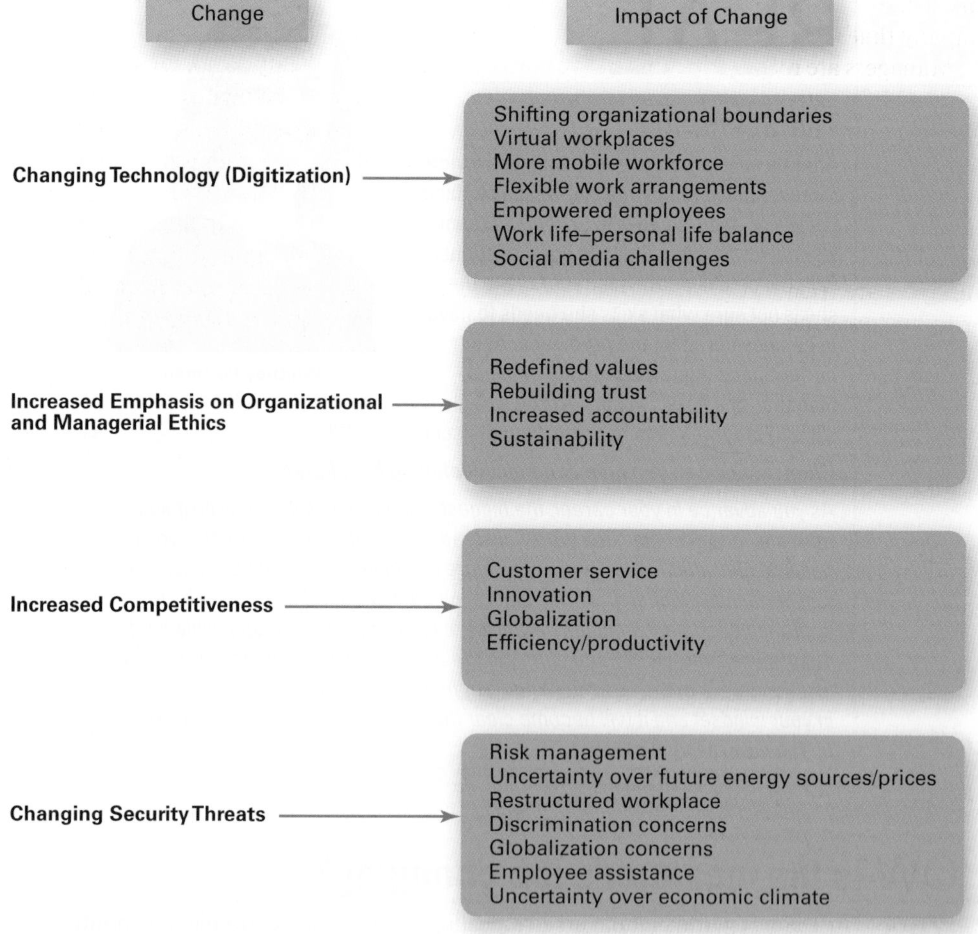

how many managers felt. That sentiment is out of date. At Banana Republic, the customer experience manager position is responsible for ensuring that customers enjoy a high-quality in-store experience. This manager is also responsible for staffing and training as well as supporting the implementation of product placement, marketing, and promotional strategies.[39] We're discovering, however, that employee attitudes and behaviors play a big role in customer satisfaction and a return on investment. The J.D. Power 2015 North American Airline Satisfaction Study supports this idea. According to J.D. Power's global travel and hospitality practice leader, Rich Garelick, building customer satisfaction creates "better customer advocates for the airline."[40] Successful airlines such as Alaska Airlines and Jet Blue Airways treat passengers well by putting forward friendly announcements to inform them on the ground or in the air about flight status and offering amenities such as in-flight entertainment.

With the growing popularity of tourism in the Dominican Republic, a large percentage of the labor force works in service jobs for resorts, attractions, and tourist-related activities such as the aerobics instructor shown here leading a class on the beach for tourists. To succeed in the service industry, managers must create a customer-responsive organization.
Source: Ellen McKnight/Alamy

Today, the majority of employees in developed countries work in service jobs. For instance, almost 80 percent of the U.S. labor force is employed in service industries.[41] In Australia, 75 percent work in service industries, and in Canada, 76 percent do. In the United Kingdom, Germany, and Japan, the percentages are 83, 74, and 71, respectively. Even in developing countries such as Colombia, Dominican Republic, Vietnam, and Bangladesh, we find 62 percent, 65 percent, 31 percent, and 40 percent of the labor force employed in service jobs.[42] Examples of service jobs include technical support representatives, food servers or fast-food counter workers, sales clerks, custodians and housekeepers, teachers, nurses, computer repair technicians, front-desk clerks, consultants, purchasing agents, credit representatives, financial planners, and bank tellers. The odds are pretty good that when you graduate, you'll go to work for a company that's in a service industry, not in manufacturing or agriculture.

Managers are recognizing that delivering consistent, high-quality customer service is essential for survival and success in today's competitive environment. Good customer care pays off. A recent study found that nearly all customers (92%) whose issue was resolved during first contact with customer service would likely continue using the company.[43] That number drops to about half (51%) for customers whose issue was not resolved during first contact. Employees are an important part of that equation.[44] The implication is clear: managers must create a customer-responsive organization where employees are friendly and courteous, accessible, knowledgeable, prompt in responding to customer needs, and willing to do what's necessary to please the customer.[45] We'll look at customer service management in other chapters.

If your professor has assigned this, go to **www.mymanagementlab.com** to watch a video titled ***Zane's Cycles: The Management Environment*** and to respond to questions.

★ Watch It 1!

Focus on Technology

Managers increasingly face challenges in their work because technology has been changing how things get done. Cloud computing, social media, and robotics are examples of technology. Getting employees on board presents a challenge to many managers. Managers must work with employees to understand why new technology is an improvement over present ways of conducting business. According to Didier Bonnet, coauthor of *Leading Challenge*, "The job of a manager is to help people cross the bridge—to get them comfortable with the technology, to get them using it, and to help them understand how it makes their lives better."[46]

It is a myth that social skills have become less important because there is more technology in the workplace. Take robotic technology. Software programming can systemize human decision making and physical tasks, which can be carried out by machinery. However, technological advances have fallen short of replicating human interactions and technology falls short of substituting human judgment. Particularly in team settings, workers rely on each other's expertise, and they are able to adapt to changing circumstances than is made possible by software.[47] As a result, managers are continually challenged to oversee team building and problem solving. Management expert Henry Mintzberg, however, warns that "wonderful as they are in enhancing communication, [technological devices] can have a negative effect on collaboration unless they are carefully managed. An electronic device puts us in touch with a keyboard, that's all."[48] Therein lies a significant challenge for managers. Social media technology adds further challenges to the mix.

Focus on Social Media

You probably can't imagine a time when employees did their work without smart devices, e-mail, or Internet access. Yet, some 25 years ago, as these tools were becoming more common in workplaces, managers struggled with the challenges of providing guidelines for using the Internet and e-mail in their organizations. Today, the new frontier is **social media**, forms of electronic communication through which users create online communities to share ideas, information, personal messages, and other content. And employees don't just use these on their personal time, but also for work purposes. That's why managers need to understand and manage the power and peril of social media. For instance, all 143,000 workers in the Singapore Civil Service are being encouraged to use a workplace chat function provided by Facebook for internal conversations. The idea is to reduce reliance on email and instead enable real-time collaboration among employees.[49] More businesses are turning to social media as a way to connect with customers. Increasingly, many companies encourage employees to use social media to become employee activists. For this purpose, employee activists draw visibility to their workplace, defend their employers from criticism, and serve as advocates, both online and off.[50]

social media
Forms of electronic communication through which users create online communities to share ideas, information, personal messages, and other content

But the potential peril is in how it's used. CEO of Berkshire Hathaway, Warren Buffet, has said that, "It takes 20 years to build a reputation and five minutes to ruin it."[51] Internally, social media also becomes problematic when it becomes a way for boastful employees to brag about their accomplishments, for managers to publish one-way messages to employees, or for employees to argue or gripe about something or someone they don't like at work—then it has lost its usefulness. To avoid this, managers need to remember that social media is a tool that needs to be managed to be beneficial. At SuperValu, about 9,000 store managers and assistant managers use the social media system. Although sources say it's too early to draw any conclusions, it appears that managers who actively make use of the system are having better store sales revenues than those who don't.

In the remainder of the book, we'll look at how social media is impacting how managers manage, especially in the areas of human resource management, communication, teams, and strategy. For example, a particular question is whether human resource managers should use social media to screen potential employees.

★ Watch It 2!

If your professor has assigned this, go to **www.mymanagementlab.com** to watch a video titled ***CH2M Hill: Emotions and Moods*** and to respond to questions.

Focus on Innovation

Success in business today demands innovation. Innovation means exploring new territory, taking risks, and doing things differently. And innovation isn't just for high-tech or other technologically sophisticated organizations. Innovative efforts can be found in all types of organizations. For instance, the manager of the Best Buy store in Manchester, Connecticut, clearly understood the importance of being innovative, a task made particularly challenging because the average Best Buy store is often staffed by young adults in their first or second jobs who aren't always committed long term to a retail career. Yet, the increasingly sophisticated products carried by the store required a high level of employee training. The store manager tackled this challenge by getting employees to suggest new ideas. One idea—a "team close," in which employees scheduled to work at the store's closing time closed the store together and walked out together as a team—had a remarkable impact on employee attitudes and commitment.[53] As you'll see throughout the book, innovation is critical throughout all levels and parts of an organization. It's so critical to today's organizations and managers that we also address this topic in other chapters.

LEADER making a DIFFERENCE

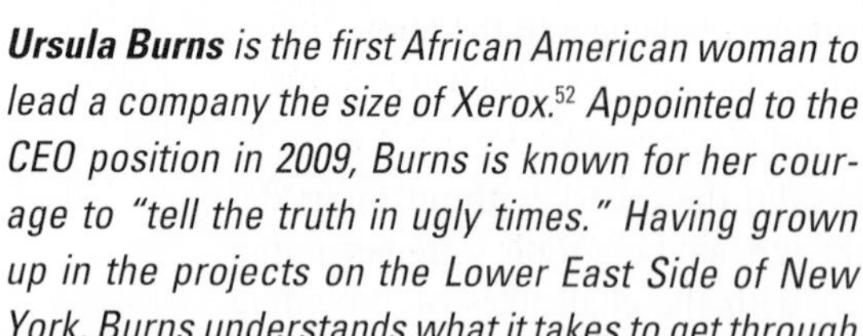

Source: Jemal Countess/Getty Images Entertainment/Gettyimages.com

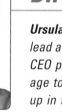

***Ursula Burns** is the first African American woman to lead a company the size of Xerox.[52] Appointed to the CEO position in 2009, Burns is known for her courage to "tell the truth in ugly times." Having grown up in the projects on the Lower East Side of New York, Burns understands what it takes to get through those uncertainties. With her aptitude for math, Burns went on to earn a mechanical engineering degree from Polytechnic Institute of New York. After a summer engineering internship at Xerox, she was hooked. At Xerox, Burns was mentored by individuals who saw her potential. Throughout her more than 30-year career at Xerox, Burns had a reputation for being bold. As a mechanical engineer, she got noticed because she wasn't afraid to speak up bluntly in a culture that's known more for being polite, courteous, and discreet than for being outspoken. Although Burns is still radically honest and direct, she has become more of a listener, calling herself a "listener-in-chief."* What can you learn from this leader making a difference?

Focus on Sustainability

Microsoft Corporation generated $93.6 billion in software sales and $12.1 billion in profits, and it had a workforce of 118,000 in 2015. We all know Microsoft for its development and sales of software such as Windows, Skype, and Xbox Live. And Microsoft is probably the last company that you'd think about in a section describing sustainability. However, Microsoft invests in a variety of sustainability projects. Management funds these projects through taxes levied on its business units' energy consumption that contributes to environmentally unfriendly carbon emissions. The responsibility for savings falls on division managers. Microsoft's efforts have paid off. In a recent three-year period, the company has reduced its emissions by 7.5 metric tons of carbon dioxide.[54] According to the U.S. Environmental

Protection Agency, this level of emissions is the equivalent of removing more than 1.5 million cars from the road for a year."[55] This corporate action affirms that sustainability and green management have become mainstream issues for managers.

What's emerging in the twenty-first century is the concept of managing in a sustainable way, which has had the effect of widening corporate responsibility not only to managing in an efficient and effective way, but also to responding strategically to a wide range of environmental and societal challenges.[56] Although "sustainability" means different things to different people, the World Business Council for Sustainable Development describes a situation where all the earth's inhabitants can live well with adequate resources.[57] From a business perspective, **sustainability** has been described as a company's ability to achieve its business goals and increase long-term shareholder value by integrating economic, environmental, and social opportunities into its business strategies.[58] Sustainability issues are now moving up the agenda of business leaders and the boards of thousands of companies. We'll examine sustainability and its importance to managers in other places throughout the book.

sustainability
A company's ability to achieve its business goals and increase long-term shareholder value by integrating economic, environmental, and social opportunities into its business strategies

Focus on the Employee

In 2015, more than 75 percent of organizations worldwide indicated that they would follow a strategy of building talent from within their organizations rather than recruiting talent from the external labor force.[59] Also, progressive companies recognize the importance of treating employees well not only because it's simply the right thing to do, but also because it is good business. Well-treated employees are more likely to go the extra mile when performing their jobs. Every year, *Fortune* magazine publishes the list titled Great Places to Work. In 2015, outdoor retailer L.L. Bean was among the top 10 retail companies, and it ranked first for an outdoor retailer. L.L. Bean president and CEO Chris McCormick maintains that L.L. Bean's strong leadership makes it an employer of choice. According to McCormick, "It reflects the work our leadership has done to develop a culture that helps ensure employees feel trusted to do a good job, take pride in their work, and feel that their contributions are truly valued."[60]

Successful managers regularly provide performance feedback that serves as an evaluation of an employee's performance and provides the foundation for discussing developmental opportunities. Effective performance appraisal outcomes depend on clearly communicating performance expectations and the resources available to help employees perform well and providing feedback on how well expectations were met. Also, conversations about an employee's career aspirations in the context of past performance serve a developmental role that will motivate workers to strive for excellence. When performance appraisal works in these ways, the company stands to build a strong talent base. Developmental practices also can support a structure on which to base rewards. Effective managers strive to reward employees with competitive base wages or salary and pay raises that recognize past performance and future potential.

Successful managers often embrace work-life practices and provide encouragement to employees who wish to use them. Such behavior expresses the value the manager and company leadership place on the well-being of employees. The company stands to benefit through higher employee satisfaction, talent retention, and higher employee engagement.[61]

WHY **study management?**

LO1.5 You may be wondering why you need to study management. If you're majoring in accounting or marketing or any field other than management, you may not understand how studying management is going to help your career. We can explain the value of studying management by looking at three things: the universality of management, the reality of work, and the rewards and challenges of being a manager.

The Universality of Management

Just how universal is the need for management in organizations? We can say with absolute certainty that management is needed in all types and sizes of organizations, at all organizational levels and in all organizational work areas, and in all organizations, no matter where they're located. This is known as the **universality of management**.

universality of management
The reality that management is needed in all types and sizes of organizations, at all organizational levels, in all organizational areas, and in organizations no matter where located

Exhibit 1-9
Universal Need for Management

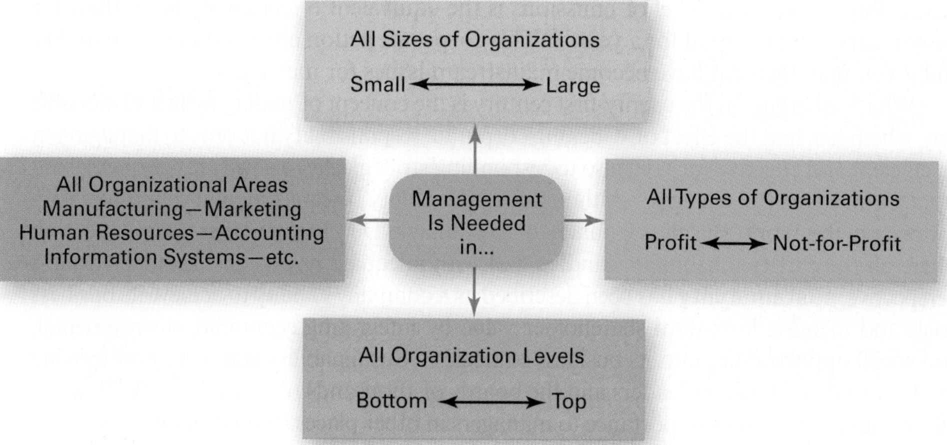

(See Exhibit 1-9.) In all these organizations, managers must plan, organize, lead, and control. However, that's not to say that management is done the same way. What a supervisor in an applications testing group at Twitter does versus what the CEO of Twitter does is a matter of degree and emphasis, not function. Because both are managers, both will plan, organize, lead, and control. How much and how they do so will differ, however.

Management is universally needed in all organizations, so we want to find ways to improve the way organizations are managed. Why? Because we interact with organizations every single day. Organizations that are well managed—and we'll share many examples of these throughout the text—develop a loyal customer base, grow, and prosper, even during challenging times. Those that are poorly managed find themselves losing customers and revenues. By studying management, you'll be able to recognize poor management and work to get it corrected. In addition, you'll be able to recognize and support good management, whether it's in an organization with which you're simply interacting or whether it's in an organization in which you're employed.

If your professor has assigned this, go to **www.mymanagementlab.com** to complete ***Simulation: Managing Your Career*** and get a feel for your career goals.

The Reality of Work

Another reason for studying management is the reality that for most of you, once you graduate from college and begin your career, you will either manage or be managed. For those who plan to be managers, an understanding of management forms the foundation upon which to build your management knowledge and skills. For those of you who don't see yourself managing, you're still likely to have to work with managers. Also, assuming that you'll have to work for a living and recognizing that you're very likely to work in an organization, you'll probably have some managerial responsibilities even if you're not a manager. Our experience tells us that you can gain a great deal of insight into the way your boss (and fellow employees) behave and how organizations function by studying management. Our point is that you don't have to aspire to be a manager to gain something valuable from a course in management.

Rewards and Challenges of Being a Manager

We can't leave our discussion here without looking at the rewards and challenges of being a manager. (See Exhibit 1-10.) What *does* it mean to be a manager in today's workplace?

First, there are many challenges. It can be a tough and often thankless job. In addition, a portion of a manager's job (especially at lower organizational levels) may entail duties that are often more clerical (compiling and filing reports, dealing with bureaucratic procedures, or doing paperwork) than managerial.[62] Managers also spend significant amounts of time in meetings and dealing with interruptions, which can be time

Exhibit 1-10
Rewards and Challenges of Being a Manager

Rewards	Challenges
• Create a work environment in which organizational members can work to the best of their ability • Have opportunities to think creatively and use imagination • Help others find meaning and fulfillment in work • Support, coach, and nurture others • Work with a variety of people • Receive recognition and status in organization and community • Play a role in influencing organizational outcomes • Receive appropriate compensation in the form of salaries, bonuses, and stock options • Good managers are needed by organizations	• Do hard work • May have duties that are more clerical than managerial • Have to deal with a variety of personalities • Often have to make do with limited resources • Motivate workers in chaotic and uncertain situations • Blend knowledge, skills, ambitions, and experiences of a diverse work group • Success depends on others' work performance

consuming and sometimes unproductive.[63] Managers often have to deal with a variety of personalities and have to make do with limited resources. It can be a challenge to motivate workers in the face of uncertainty and chaos. And managers may find it difficult to successfully blend the knowledge, skills, ambitions, and experiences of a diverse work group. Finally, as a manager, you're not in full control of your destiny. Your success typically is dependent on others' work performance.

Despite these challenges, being a manager *can* be rewarding. You're responsible for creating a work environment in which organizational members can do their work to the best of their ability and thus help the organization achieve its goals. You help others find meaning and fulfillment in their work. You get to support, coach, and nurture others and help them make good decisions. In addition, as a manager, you often have the opportunity to think creatively and use your imagination. You'll get to meet and work with a variety of people—both inside and outside the organization. Other rewards may include receiving recognition and status in your organization and in the community, playing a role in influencing organizational outcomes, and receiving attractive compensation in the form of salaries, bonuses, and stock options. Finally, as we said earlier in the chapter, organizations need good managers. It's through the combined efforts of motivated and passionate people working together that organizations accomplish their goals. As a manager, you can be assured that your efforts, skills, and abilities are needed.

Gaining Insights into Life at Work

A good number of students regularly remind your authors that they are not planning a career in management. These students' career goals are to be accountants or financial analysts or marketing researchers or computer programmers. They ask us: Why do I need to take a management course? Our answer is: Because understanding management concepts and how managers think will help you get better results at work and enhance your career. And who knows, you may become a manager someday. Oftentimes, successful employees are promoted to managerial roles. For example, you may begin your career as an auditor with a major accounting firm and find, a few years later, you're overseeing an audit team or you're a partner thrust into managing a regional office.

For instance, throughout this book you'll encounter pages that we call "Workplace Confidential." This feature will introduce you to challenges you're likely to face at work—like organizational politics, an uncommunicative boss, or an unfair performance review—and offer you specific suggestions on how to deal with these challenges.

If you expect to work with others—whether it's in a Fortune 100 corporation or in a three-person start-up—studying Management can pay demonstrable dividends.

WORKPLACE CONFIDENTIAL Dealing with Organizational Politics

In an ideal world, the good guys always win, everyone tells the truth, and job promotions and generous pay raises go to the most deserving candidate. Unfortunately, we don't live in such an ideal world. The world we live in is a political one.

Politics is a fact of life in organizations. People who ignore this fact do so at their own peril. But why, you may wonder, must politics exist? Isn't it possible for an organization to be politics free? It's possible, but most unlikely.

Organizations are made up of individuals and groups with different values, goals, and interests. This sets up the potential for conflict over resources. Departmental budgets, office allocations, project responsibilities, promotion choices, and salary adjustments are just a few examples of the resources about whose allocation organizational members will disagree.

Resources in organizations are also limited, which turns potential conflict into real conflict. If resources were abundant, then all the various constituencies within the organization could satisfy their goals. But because they are limited, not everyone's interests can be provided for. Furthermore, whether true or not, gains by one individual or group are often perceived as being at the expense of others within the organization. These forces create a competition among members for the organization's limited resources.

Maybe the most important factor leading to politics within organizations is the realization that most of the facts that are used to allocate the limited resources are open to interpretation. What, for instance, is good performance? What's an adequate improvement? What constitutes an unsatisfactory job? One person's team player is another's "yes man." So it is the large and ambiguous middle ground of organizational life—where the facts don't speak for themselves—that politics flourish.

The above explains why some people in the workplace lie, misrepresent, conceal, backstab, play favorites, scheme, pass the buck, deny responsibility, form alliances, or engage in similar political actions.

If you want to improve your political skills at work, we offer the following suggestions:

- ***Frame arguments in terms of organizational goals.*** People whose actions appear to blatantly further their own interests at the expense of the organization are almost universally denounced, are likely to lose influence, and often suffer the ultimate penalty of being expelled from the organization. Challenges to your actions are not likely to gain much support if your actions appear to be in the best interests of the organization.
- ***Develop the right image.*** Make sure you understand what your organization wants and values from its employees—in terms of dress, associates to cultivate and those to avoid, whether to appear to be a risk taker or risk averse, the importance of getting along with others, and so forth. Because the assessment of your performance is rarely a fully objective process, you need to pay attention to style as well as substance.
- ***Gain control of organizational resources.*** The control of organizational resources that are scarce and important is a source of influence. Knowledge and expertise are particularly effective resources to control. These resources make you more valuable to the organization and, therefore, more likely to gain security, advancement, and a receptive audience for your ideas.
- ***Make yourself appear indispensable.*** You don't have to be indispensable as long as key people in your organization believe that you are. If the organization's prime decision makers believe there is no ready substitute for what you bring to the organization, your job is likely safe and you're likely to be treated well.
- ***Be visible.*** If you have a job that brings your accomplishments to the attention of others, that's great. However, if not—without creating the image of a braggart—you'll want to let others know what you're doing by giving progress reports to your boss and others, having satisfied customers relay their appreciation to higher-ups, being seen at social functions, being active in your professional associations, and developing powerful allies who can speak positively about your accomplishments.
- ***Develop powerful allies.*** It is often beneficial to have friends in high places. Network by cultivating contacts with potentially influential people above you, at your own level, and in the lower ranks. These allies often can provide you with information that's otherwise not readily available and provide you with support if and when you need it. Having a mentor in the organization who is well respected is often a valuable asset.
- ***Avoid "tainted" members.*** In almost every organization, there are fringe members whose status is questionable. Their performance and/or loyalty are suspect. Or they have strange personalities. Keep your distance from such individuals. Given the reality that effectiveness has a large subjective component, your own effectiveness might be called into question if you're perceived as being too closely associated with tainted members.
- ***Support your boss.*** Your immediate future is in the hands of your current boss. Because that person evaluates your performance, you'll typically want to do whatever is necessary to have your boss on your side. You should make every effort to help your boss succeed, make her look good, support her if she is under siege, and spend the time to find out the criteria she will use to assess your effectiveness. Don't undermine your boss. And don't speak negatively of her to others.

Based on D. Krackhardt, "Assessing the Political Landscape: Structure, Cognition, and Power in Organizations," *Administrative Science Quarterly*, June 1990, pp. 342–369; G. R. Ferris, S. L. Davidson, and P.L. Perrewé, *Political Skill at Work: Impact on Work Effectiveness* (Mountain View, CA: Davies-Black Publishing, 2005); and J. Bolander, "How to Deal with Organizational Politics," *The Daily MBA*, February 28, 2011.

Chapter 1 PREPARING FOR: Exams/Quizzes

CHAPTER SUMMARY by Learning Objectives

LO1.1 TELL who managers are and where they work.

Managers coordinate and oversee the work of other people so that organizational goals can be accomplished. Nonmanagerial employees work directly on a job or task and have no one reporting to them. In traditionally structured organizations, managers can be first-line, middle, or top. In other more loosely configured organizations, the managers may not be as readily identifiable, although someone must fulfill that role.

Managers work in an organization, which is a deliberate arrangement of people to accomplish some specific purpose. Organizations have three characteristics: They have a distinctive purpose, they are composed of people, and they have a deliberate structure. Many of today's organizations are structured to be more open, flexible, and responsive to changes.

LO1.2 EXPLAIN why managers are important to organizations.

Managers are important to organizations for three reasons. First, organizations need their managerial skills and abilities in uncertain, complex, and chaotic times. Second, managers are critical to getting things done in organizations. Finally, managers contribute to employee productivity and loyalty; the way employees are managed can affect the organization's financial performance, and managerial ability has been shown to be important in creating organizational value.

LO1.3 DESCRIBE the functions, roles, and skills of managers.

Broadly speaking, management is what managers do and involves coordinating and overseeing the efficient and effective completion of others' work activities. Efficiency means doing things right; effectiveness means doing the right things.

The four functions of management include planning (defining goals, establishing strategies, and developing plans), organizing (arranging and structuring work), leading (working with and through people), and controlling (monitoring, comparing, and correcting work performance).

Mintzberg's managerial roles include interpersonal, which involve people and other ceremonial/symbolic duties (figurehead, leader, and liaison); informational, which involve collecting, receiving, and disseminating information (monitor, disseminator, and spokesperson); and decisional, which involve making choices (entrepreneur, disturbance handler, resource allocator, and negotiator).

Katz's managerial skills include technical (job-specific knowledge and techniques), interpersonal (ability to work well with people), and conceptual (ability to think and express ideas). Technical skills are most important for lower-level managers, while conceptual skills are most important for top managers. Interpersonal skills are equally important for all managers. Some other managerial skills identified include managing human capital, inspiring commitment, managing change, using purposeful networking, and so forth.

LO1.4 DESCRIBE the factors that are reshaping and redefining the manager's job.

The changes impacting managers' jobs include global economic and political uncertainties, changing workplaces, ethical issues, security threats, and changing technology. Managers must focus on customer service because employee attitudes and behaviors play a big role in customer satisfaction. Managers must focus on technology as it impacts how things get done in organizations. Managers must focus on social media because these forms of communication are important and valuable tools in managing. Managers must focus on innovation because it is important for organizations to be competitive. Managers must also focus on sustainability as business goals are developed. And finally, managers must focus on employees in order for them to be more productive.

LO1.5 EXPLAIN the value of studying management.

It's important to study management for three reasons: (1) the universality of management, which refers to the fact that managers are needed in all types and sizes of organizations, at all organizational levels and work areas, and in all global locations; (2) the reality of work—that is, you will either manage or be managed; and (3) the awareness of the significant rewards (such as creating work environments to help people work to the best of their ability, supporting and encouraging others, helping others find meaning and fulfillment in work, etc.) and challenges (having to work hard, sometimes having more clerical than managerial duties, interacting with a variety of personalities, etc.) in being a manager.

Pearson MyLab Management

Go to **mymanagementlab.com** to complete the problems marked with this icon .

REVIEW AND DISCUSSION QUESTIONS

1-1. What are the three main roles performed by a manager?

1-2. Why are managers important to organizations? What are their key responsibilities in an organization?

1-3. Mintzberg suggested that specific actions or behaviors expected of and exhibited by a manager comprise of three specific roles. Briefly explain them.

1-4. In your opinion, is management still relevant as a course of study today? Explain using relevant examples.

1-5. It is sometimes said that management is a tough and thankless job. Do you think this is true?

1-6. Is the task of seeking innovative processes really a manager's job?

1-7. Discuss how managers define organizational purpose. How would the managerial functions help in achieving that purpose?

1-8. Henri Fayol suggested that all managers perform the five functions of planning, organizing, commanding, coordinating, and controlling. Was he correct?

Pearson MyLab Management

If your professor has assigned these, go to **mymanagementlab.com** for the following Assisted-graded writing questions:

1-9. Is there one best "style" of management? Why or why not?

1-10. Christine Porath, together with the Harvard Business Review and Tony Schwartz, examined the views of 20,000 employees regarding commitment and engagement. The one thing that the employees could agree on was that they wanted respect from their leaders. Is management as simple as this? What other areas do you consider important?

PREPARING FOR: My Career

✪ PERSONAL INVENTORY ASSESSMENTS

Time Management Assessment

Take a look at how well *you* manage time. This PIA will help you determine how skillfully you do that.

✪ ETHICS DILEMMA

Mintzberg suggests that managerial roles should encompass interpersonal, decisional, and informational roles. Clearly this is an idealized vision of the manager. They are encouraged to encompass all of these characteristics but this is an unattainable goal. A manager can never be all these things at once.

1-11. To what extent is it unethical to expect a manager to have such a broad base of skills and abilities?

1-12. Do managerial models like this reflect the reality of day-to-day management? Explain.

SKILL EXERCISE Developing Your Political Skill

About the Skill

Research has shown that people differ in their political skills.[64] Political skill can be defined as the ability to understand and influence others for the benefit of the individual or the organization.[65] Those who are politically skilled are more effective in their use of influence tactics. Politically skilled individuals are able to exert their influence without others detecting it, which is important in being effective so that you're not labeled political. A person's political skill is determined by his or her networking ability, interpersonal influence, social astuteness, and apparent sincerity.

Steps in Practicing the Skill

- *Develop your networking ability.* A good network can be a powerful tool. You can begin building a network by getting to know important people in your work area and the organization and then developing relationships with individuals in positions of power. Volunteer for committees or offer your help on projects that will be noticed by those in positions of power. Attend important organizational functions so that you can be seen as a team player and someone who's interested in the organization's success. Utilize a professional networking site such as LinkedIn to connect with those you meet. Then, when you need advice on work, use your connections and network with others throughout the organization.
- *Work on gaining interpersonal influence.* People will listen to you when they're comfortable and feel at ease around you. Work on your communication skills so that you can communicate easily and effectively with others. Work on developing good rapport with people in all areas and at all levels of your organization. Be open, friendly, and willing to pitch in. The amount of interpersonal influence you have will be affected by how well people like you.
- *Develop your social astuteness.* Some people have an innate ability to understand people and sense what they're thinking. If you don't have that ability, you'll have to work at developing your social astuteness by doing things such as saying the right things at the right time, paying close attention to people's facial expressions, and trying to determine whether others have hidden agendas.
- *Be sincere.* Sincerity is important to getting people to want to associate with you. Be genuine in what you say and do. And show a genuine interest in others and their situations.

Practicing the Skill

Select each of the components of political skill and spend one week working on it. Write a brief set of notes describing your experiences—good and bad. Were you able to begin developing a network of people throughout the organization or did you work at developing your social astuteness, maybe by starting to recognize and interpret people's facial expressions and the meaning behind those expressions? What could you have done differently to be more politically skilled? Once you begin to recognize what's involved with political skills, you should find yourself becoming more connected and politically adept.

WORKING TOGETHER Team Exercise

All of us have an idealized view of the skills and characteristics that a manager should possess. Often managers excel in certain areas, but fail in others. They may be quick-witted and decisive; however, they may lack the communication skills to disseminate their decisions and ideas. The fact is that managers who have a good grasp of the full range of skills are rare. In some cases this will cause problems, either internally or externally, in an organization. Do you think managers should be fully rounded individuals? What skills might be less critical than others? Form small groups with 3–4 other class members and be prepared to share your lists with the rest of the class. Can you agree on a list of critical and non-critical skills?

MY TURN TO BE A MANAGER

- Use the most current *Occupational Outlook Handbook* (U.S. Department of Labor, Bureau of Labor Statistics) to research three different categories of managers. For each, prepare a bulleted list that describes the following: the nature of the work, training and other qualifications needed, earnings, and job outlook and projections data.
- Get in the habit of reading at least one current business periodical (*Wall Street Journal, Bloomberg BusinessWeek, Fortune, Fast Company, Forbes*, etc.). Sign up to follow a few of these publications on Twitter.
- Explore the social media presence of your favorite company. Like their Facebook page and follow them on Twitter, Instagram, and/or any other social media outlet the company uses.
- Interview two different managers and ask them the following questions: What are the best and worst parts about being a manager? What's the best management advice you ever received? Type up the questions and their answers to turn in to your professor.
- Accountants and other professionals have certification programs to verify their skills, knowledge, and professionalism. What about managers? Two certification programs for managers include the Certified Manager (Institute of Certified Professional Managers) and the Certified Business Manager (Association of Professionals in Business Management). Research each of these programs. Prepare a bulleted list of what each involves.
- If you have work experience, consider managers who you have encountered. Did you work with any good managers? Did you work with any bad managers? Based on your experience, create a list of traits or skills that good managers possess.

CASE APPLICATION 1 The Power of Social Media

In the summer of 2014, the ALS Association (ALSA) learned first-hand about the power of social media.[66] In just a little over a month, more than 17 million people dumped buckets of ice water over their heads, raising more than $115 million for the ALSA in what became known as the Ice Bucket Challenge. To put that number in perspective, the organization raised just $23 million in the entire previous year.

The ALSA is a nonprofit organization that supports the fight against amyotrophic lateral sclerosis (ALS), a disease that affects nerve cells in the brain and spinal cord. Often referred to as Lou Gehrig's disease, ALS affects about 20,000 people in the United States. As this number is far lower than other diseases such as cancer, ALS researchers do not receive as much federal funding, making ALSA's fundraising pivotal for the fight against the disease. In addition to supporting scientific research, the ALSA works to provide compassionate care for ALS patients and advocates for public policies that benefit people living with the disease.

How did the ALSA convince so many people to get involved in this fundraising success? Surprisingly, the organization had very little to do with it. The Ice Bucket Challenge was initiated by Chris Kennedy, a professional golfer whose brother-in-law has ALS. The challenge took off after reaching Pete Frates, a former Boston College baseball player, and his friend Pat Quinn, who both suffer from ALS. From there, the challenge became a worldwide sensation and attracted millions of participants including influential people such as Bill Gates, Mark Zuckerberg, and even President Barack Obama.

The Ice Bucket Challenge spread quickly due to the power of viral videos. Once challenged, individuals recorded themselves getting a bucket of ice water dumped on them and then challenged some friends to do the same. Videos were posted on Facebook and friends were tagged do the challenge. If challenged, you could donate to the ALSA, or get dumped on. However, many people ended up doing the challenge and still donating. Why were people so willing to engage in this unpleasant experience? Carrie Munk, an ALS spokesperson, asked this question of many participants and reported that most people said they did it because they were asked.

Interestingly, many of those friends who were asking knew little about ALS. The movement went well beyond those who already were impacted by the disease. Barbara Newhouse, the CEO of ALSA, did admit the organization helped catalyze the movement with one e-mail to 60,000 on their mailing list, but otherwise it took off on its own. And thus the organization not only had its most successful fundraiser in history, but it also built international awareness of the disease.

Can the Ice Bucket Challenge become a sustainable source of funding for the ALSA? The organization is hoping that it can, initiating a campaign in 2015 to make it an annual event. However, the attempt to repeat the challenge the following year did not see the same results, raising only about 500,000 dollars in the same time frame. This was not a big surprise for the organization. ALSA leadership knew that because of the nature of the giving, the funding would not be sustainable at the same level. Many gave with little awareness, and that does not usually lead to repeat donations. Brian Frederick, ALSA's chief of staff, acknowledged they can't recreate the phenomenon but suggested they can build on the momentum of the 2014 events by making it an annual event.

DISCUSSION QUESTIONS

1-13. Why is it important for the ALSA management team to understand the importance of social media in their work?

1-14. Do you think the ALSA can continue to rely on the Ice Bucket Challenge to support the organization's fundraising efforts? Why or why not?

1-15. Do you think the Ice Bucket Challenge would have had the same success if the management at ALSA initiated the challenge?

1-16. What can the ALSA learn from this experience to help the organization take advantage of the power of social media in the future?

CASE APPLICATION 2 Who Needs a Boss?

"Holacracy."[67] That's the word of the day at Zappos, the Nevada-based online shoe and apparel retailer. During a four-hour, year-end employee meeting in 2013, CEO Tony Hsieh announced that he was eliminating the company's traditional managerial and structural hierarchy to implement a holacracy. What is a holacracy, you ask? In a nutshell, it's an organizational system with no job titles, no managers, and no top-down hierarchy with upper, middle, or lower levels where decisions can get hung up. The idea behind this new type of arrangement is to focus on the work that needs to be done and not on some hierarchical structure where great ideas and suggestions can get lost in the channels of reporting. The holacracy concept was dreamed up by Brian Robertson, the founder of a Pennsylvania software start-up. Its name comes from the Greek word *holos,* a single, autonomous, self-sufficient unit that's also dependent on a larger unit.[68] A simple explanation of Robertson's vision of a holacracy is workers as partners, job descriptions as roles, and partners organized into circles.[69] (It might help in grasping this idea by thinking of these employee circles as types of overlapping employee groups but with more fluid membership and individual roles and responsibilities.)

In these circles, employees can take on any number of roles, and the expectation is that each employee will help out wherever he or she can. Without titles or a hierarchy, anyone can initiate a project and implement innovative ideas. The hope is that circle members will pool ideas and watch out for each other. The goal is radical transparency and getting more people to take charge. Yet, trusting individuals who probably know the details of the job better than any manager to work conscientiously, creatively, and efficiently is good as long as there is a way to keep standards high. The last thing Zappos wants is for a slacker mentality to take hold.

Hsieh has always approached leading his business in unique and radical ways. He strongly believes in the power of the individual and has created a highly successful organization (which is now part of Amazon) that's known for its zany culture, where corporate values are matched with personal values and where "weirdness and humility" are celebrated.[70] However, as the company moves away from the traditional work model to this new system, it may face some challenges. Both Zappos and Robertson caution that while a holacracy might eliminate the traditional manager's job, there is still structure and accountability. Poor performers will be obvious because they won't have enough "roles" to fill their time, or a circle charged with monitoring the company's culture may decide they're not a good fit. Also, just because there are no traditional managers doesn't mean that leaders won't emerge. But it will be important to watch for dominant personalities emerging as authority figures, which could potentially cause other employees to be resentful or to rebel. Zappos says that it will not be leaderless. Some individuals will have a bigger role and scope of purpose, but leadership is also distributed and expected in each role. "Everybody is expected to lead and be an entrepreneur in their own roles, and holacracy empowers them to do so."[71] Also, there will be some structure arrangement where "the broadest circles can to some extent tell subgroups what they're accountable for doing."[72] But accountability, rather than flowing only up, will flow throughout the organization in different paths. Other challenges they're still trying to figure out include who has the ultimate authority to hire, fire, and decide pay. The hope is that eventually the authority for each of these roles will be done within the holacratic framework as well. So, if no one has a title and there are no bosses, is Tony Hsieh still the CEO? So far, he hasn't publicly commented about how his own role is impacted.

DISCUSSION QUESTIONS

1-17. What is a holacracy?

1-18. What benefits do you see to an organization where there are no job titles, no managers, and no hierarchy?

1-19. What challenges does a holacratic approach have?

1-20. Discuss why you would or would not like to work in an organization like this.

ENDNOTES

1. A. Swanson, "The Number of Fortune 500 Companies Led by Women Is at an All-Time High: 5 Percent," *The Washington Post* online, washingtonpost.com, June 4, 2015.
2. Pew Research Center, "Women and Leadership," www.pewsocialtrends.org/2015/01/14/women-and-leadership/, January 14, 2015.
3. D. J. Campbell, "The Proactive Employee: Managing Workplace Initiative," *Academy of Management Executive*, August 2000, pp. 52–66.
4. J. Morgan, "The 5 Types of Organizational Structures: Part 3, Flat Organizations," *Forbes* online, www.forbes.com, July 13, 2015.
5. "Interaction: First, Let's Fire All the Managers," *Harvard Business Review*, March 2012, pp. 20–21; and G. Hamel, "First, Let's Fire All the Managers," *Harvard Business Review*, December 2011, pp. 48–60.
6. Simon Thomsen, "The Atlassian CEOs Have a Detailed, Philosophical View on the Role of Teams in Humanity's Progress," *Business Insider Australia*, November 11, 2016, http://www.businessinsider.com.au/the-atlassian-ceos-have-a-detailed-philosophical-view-on-the-role-of-teams-in-humanitys-progress-2016-11; Adam Lashinsky, "What's Atlassian's Secret Sauce? Teamwork," *Fortune*, December 11, 2015, http://fortune.com/2015/12/11/atlassians-secret-sauce/.

7. U.S. Bureau of Labor Statistics, "Occupational Employment and Wage Estimates–May 2015," (USDL-16-0661), March 30, 2016.
8. Q. Hardy, "Google Thinks Small," *Forbes*, November 14, 2005, pp. 198–202.
9. Future Vision box based on M. Saltsman, "The Employee of the Month Has a Battery," *Wall Street Journal,* January 30, 2014, p. A13; L. Weber, "Robots Need Supervisors Too," *Wall Street Journal,* August 8, 2013, p. B5; S. Grobart, "Robot Workers: Coexistence Is Possible," *Bloomberg BusinessWeek Online,* December 13, 2012; and D. Bennett, "I'll Have My Robots Talk to Your Robots," *Bloomberg BusinessWeek,* February 21–27, 2011, pp. 52–62.
10. J. Welch and S. Welch, "An Employee Bill of Rights," *Bloomberg BusinessWeek*, March 16, 2009, p. 72.
11. B. Dummett, "BlackBerry Launches New Software for Driverless Cars," *Wall Street Journal* online January 6, 2016.
12. T. Dinerman, "2016 Could Be the Year Space Tourism Takes Off," *Observer* online, September 22, 2015.
13. R. Goffee and G. Jones, "Creating the Best Workplace on Earth," *Harvard Business Review,* May 2013.
14. "Five-Year Overview 2015," Philips Group Annual Report, https://www.annualreport.philips.com/#!/five-year-overview, November 21, 2016.
15. R. Beck and J. Harter, "Why Great Managers Are So Rare," *Gallup Business Journal,* businessjournal.gallup.com, March 25, 2014; E. Frauenheim, "Managers Don't Matter," *Workforce Management Online*, April 2010; and K. A. Tucker and V. Allman, "Don't Be a Cat-and-Mouse Manager," The Gallup Organization, www.brain.gallup.com, September 9, 2004.
16. "Work USA 2008/2009 Report: Driving Business Results through Continuous Engagement," Watson Wyatt Worldwide, Washington, DC.
17. A. Adkins, "Report: What Separates Great Managers from the Rest," The Gallup Organization, May 12, 2015.
18. "The New Employment Deal: How Far, How Fast and How Enduring? Insights from the 2010 Global Workforce Study," Towers Watson, Washington, DC.
19. R. R. Hastings, "Study: Supervisors Drive Employee Engagement," *HR Magazine*, August 2011, p. 22.
20. T. R. Holcomb, R. M. Holmes, Jr., and B. L. Connelly, "Making the Most of What You Have: Managerial Ability as a Source of Resource Value Creation," *Strategic Management Journal*, May 2009, pp. 457–485.
21. M. Srinivasan, "Southwest Airlines Operations—A Strategic Perspective," Airline Industry Articles, http://airline-industry.malq.net/, September 11, 2014.
22. Southwest, "Southwest Corporate Fact Sheet," http://www.swamedia.com/channels/Corporate-Fact-Sheet/pages/corporate-fact-sheet, January 10, 2016.
23. From "The Mission of Southwest Airlines," January 5, 2016. https://www.southwest.com/html/about-southwest/index.html?clk=GFOOTER-ABOUT-ABOUT. Copyright (c) 2016 Southwest Airlines.
24. D. Landsel, "11 Reasons Why Southwest Is the Best Airline You're Probably Not Flying," *Airfarewatchdog* (website), www.airfarewatchdog.com, April 20, 2015.
25. H. Fayol, *Industrial and General Administration* (Paris: Dunod, 1916).
26. For a comprehensive review of this question, see C. P. Hales, "What Do Managers Do? A Critical Review of the Evidence," *Journal of Management*, January 1986, pp. 88–115.
27. J. T. Straub, "Put on Your Manager's Hat," *USA Today Online*, www.usatoday.com, October 29, 2002; and H. Mintzberg, *The Nature of Managerial Work* (New York: Harper & Row, 1973).
28. E. C. Dierdorff, R. S. Rubin, and F. P. Morgeson, "The Milieu of Managerial Work: An Integrative Framework Linking Work Context to Role Requirements," *Journal of Applied Psychology*, June 2009, pp. 972–988.
29. H. Mintzberg and J. Gosling, "Educating Managers Beyond Borders," *Academy of Management Learning and Education*, September 2002, pp. 64–76.
30. See, for example, M. J. Martinko and W. L. Gardner, "Structured Observation of Managerial Work: A Replication and Synthesis," *Journal of Management Studies*, May 1990, pp. 330–357; A. I. Kraut, P. R. Pedigo, D. D. McKenna, and M. D. Dunnette, "The Role of the Manager: What's Really Important in Different Management Jobs," *Academy of Management Executive*, November 1989, pp. 286–293; and C. M. Pavett and A. W. Lau, "Managerial Work: The Influence of Hierarchical Level and Functional Specialty," *Academy of Management Journal*, March 1983, pp. 170–177.
31. Pavett and Lau, "Managerial Work."
32. S. J. Carroll and D. J. Gillen, "Are the Classical Management Functions Useful in Describing Managerial Work?" *Academy of Management Review*, January 1987, p. 48.
33. K. Tyler, "Train Your Front Line," *HR Magazine,* December 2013, pp. 43–45.
34. See, for example, J. G. Harris, D. W. DeLong, and A. Donnellon, "Do You Have What It Takes to Be an E-Manager?" *Strategy and Leadership*, August 2001, pp. 10–14; C. Fletcher and C. Baldry, "A Study of Individual Differences and Self-Awareness in the Context of Multi-Source Feedback," *Journal of Occupational and Organizational Psychology*, September 2000, pp. 303–319; and R. L. Katz, "Skills of an Effective Administrator," *Harvard Business Review*, September/October 1974, pp. 90–102.
35. K. Fivecoat-Campbell, "Up the Corporate Ladder," *Springfield, Missouri, Business Journal*, March 12–18, 2012, pp. 9+.
36. I. McAllister, "What Does It Take to Be a Great General Manager for a Web Company?" *Forbes* online, www.forbes.com, October 22, 2013.
37. Francesca Fitzsimmons, "Jaguar Land Rover Warns Potential New Brexit Taxes Could Be 'Huge Challenge'," *Liverpool Echo*, November 18, 2016, http://www.liverpoolecho.co.uk/news/business/jaguar-land-rover-warns-potential-12194456; Tom Belger, "Look Inside Jaguar Land Rover's Halewood Factory, Where a Car Is Rolled Out Every 80 Seconds," *Liverpool Echo*, January 1, 2016, http://www.liverpoolecho.co.uk/news/liverpool-news/look-inside-jaguar-land-rovers-10673386; Tom Belger, "Fancy Working for Jaguar Land Rover? The Halewood Plant Is Looking for Apprentices," *Liverpool Echo*, November 6, 2016, http://www.liverpoolecho.co.uk/news/liverpool-news/jlr-jaguar-halewood-work-jobs-12134930.
38. A. Stevenson, "T-Mobile CEO to Cramer: 'Shut Up and Listen'," *CNBC.Com*, April 28, 2015.
39. "Customer Experience Manager – Banana Republic Rockefeller Center," https://www.linkedin.com/jobs/view/161542983, accessed August 1, 2016.
40. J.D. Power and Associates, "Airlines: A Transportation or Hospitality Business?" jdpower.com, May 13, 2015.

41. U.S. Bureau of Labor Statistics, "The Employment Situation—December 2015," (USDL-16-0001), January 8, 2016.
42. Data from *The World Factbook 2015*, https://www.cia.gov/library/publications/resources/the-world-factbook/.
43. C. J. Grimm, "Good Customer Care Pays Off," *CX Act 2014 Touch Point Study,* https://hbr.org/visual-library/2015/05/good-customer-care-pays-off, May 19, 2015.
44. C. B. Blocker, D. J. Flint, M. B. Myers, and S. F. Slater, "Proactive Customer Orientation and Its Role for Creating Customer Value in Global Markets," *Journal of the Academy of Marketing Science*, April 2011, pp. 216–233; D. Dougherty and A. Murthy, "What Service Customers Really Want," *Harvard Business Review*, September 2009, p. 22; and K. A. Eddleston, D. L. Kidder, and B. E. Litzky, "Who's the Boss? Contending with Competing Expectations from Customers and Management," *Academy of Management Executive*, November 2002, pp. 85–95.
45. See, for instance, D. Meinert, "Aim to Serve," *HR Magazine*, December 2011, p. 18; D. M. Mayer, M. G. Ehrhart, and B. Schneider, "Service Attribute Boundary Conditions of the Service Climate-Customer Satisfaction Link," *Academy of Management Journal*, October 2009, pp. 1034–1050; M. Groth, T. Hennig-Thurau, and G. Walsh, "Customer Reactions to Emotional Labor: The Roles of Employee Acting Strategies and Customer Detection Accuracy," *Academy of Management Journal*, October 2009, pp. 958–974; J. W. Grizzle, A. R. Zablah, T. J. Brown, J. C. Mowen, and J. M. Lee, "Employee Customer Orientation in Context: How the Environment Moderates the Influence of Customer Orientation on Performance Outcomes," *Journal of Applied Psychology*, September 2009, pp. 1227–1242; B. A. Gutek, M. Groth, and B. Cherry, "Achieving Service Success through Relationships and Enhanced Encounters," *Academy of Management Executive*, November 2002, pp. 132–144; Eddleston, Kidder, and Litzky, "Who's the Boss? Contending with Competing Expectations from Customers and Management"; S. D. Pugh, J. Dietz, J. W. Wiley, and S. M. Brooks, "Driving Service Effectiveness through Employee-Customer Linkages," *Academy of Management Executives*, November 2002, pp. 73–84; S. D. Pugh, "Service with a Smile: Emotional Contagion in the Service Encounter," *Academy of Management Journal*, October 2001, pp. 1018–1027; W. C. Tsai, "Determinants and Consequences of Employee Displayed Positive Emotions," *Journal of Management*, vol. 27, no. 4, 2001, pp. 497–512; Naumann and Jackson, Jr., "One More Time: How Do You Satisfy Customers?"; and M. D. Hartline and O. C. Ferrell, "The Management of Customer-Contact Service Employees: An Empirical Investigation," *Journal of Marketing*, October 1996, pp. 52–70.
46. R. Knight, "Convincing Skeptical Employees to Adopt New Technology," *Harvard Business Review*, online https://hbr.org, March 19, 2015.
47. I. Wladawsky-Berger, "The Growing Value of Social Skills in the Age of Automation," (blog) *The Wall Street Journal* online, wsj.com, November 27, 2015.
48. H. Mintzberg, "We Need Both Networks and Communities," *Harvard Business Review* online, https://hbr.org, October 5, 2015.
49. Eileen Yu, "Singapore civil servants to be on Facebook Workplace by March 2017," *ZDNet*, November 10, 2016, http://www.zdnet.com/article/singapore-civil-servants-to-be-on-facebook-workplace-by-march-2017/.
50. K. Higginbottom, "Social Media Ignites Employee Activism," *Forbes* online, www.forbes.com, April 14, 2014.
51. A. Goodman, "To 40 Buffet-isms: Inspiration to Become a Better Investor," *Forbes* online, www.forbes.com, September 25, 2015.
52. Leader Making a Difference box based on C. Hymowitz, "Ursula Burns," *Bloomberg BusinessWeek,* August 12–25, 2013, pp. 56–58; "What Do CEOs Admire?" *Fortune*, March 19, 2012, p. 143; N. Kolakowski, "Ursula Burns: Focused on the Core," *eWeek*, February 13, 2012, pp. 10–13; E. McGert, "Fresh Copy," *Fast Company*, December 2011/January 2012, pp. 132–138; and D. Mattioli, "Xerox Chief Looks Beyond Photocopiers Toward Services," *Wall Street Journal*, June 13, 2011, p. B9.
53. R. Wagner, "One Store, One Team at Best Buy," *Gallup Brain,* http://brain.gallup.com/content/, August 12, 2004.
54. D. Gelles, "Microsoft Leads Movement to Offset Emissions with Internal Carbon Tax," *The New York Times* online, www.nyt.com, September 26, 2015.
55. U.S. Environmental Protection Agency, "Greenhouse Gas Emissions from a Typical Passenger Vehicle," EPA-420-F-14-040a, May 2014.
56. KPMG Global Sustainability Services, *Sustainability Insights*, October 2007, www.kpmg.com.
57. WBCSD, *Vision 2050* Report, Overview, www.wbcsd.org/vision2050.aspx.
58. *Symposium on Sustainability—Profiles in Leadership*, New York, October 2001.
59. WorldatWork, "Companies Look to 'Build From Within' for Success," *Newsline* online, December 28, 2015.
60. "L.L. Bean Named to the 2015 Fortune 100 Best Companies to Work for List," *Globe Newswire*, March 5, 2015, http://www.prweb.com/releases/2015/03/prweb12563945.htm.
61. WorldatWork Alliance for Work-Life Progress, "Flexibility in the Workplace Remains Flat, Managers Continue to Get on Board," *Newsline*, October 6, 2015.
62. R. E. Silverman, "Where's the Boss? Trapped in a Meeting," *Wall Street Journal*, February 14, 2012, pp. B1+; and J. Sandberg, "Down over Moving Up: Some New Bosses Find They Hate Their Jobs," *Wall Street Journal*, July 27, 2005, p. B1.
63. Silverman, "Where's the Boss? Trapped in a Meeting."
64. S. Y. Todd, K. J. Harris, R. B. Harris, and A. R. Wheeler, "Career Success Implications of Political Skill," *Journal of Social Psychology*, June 2009, pp. 179–204; G. R. Ferris, D. C. Treadway, P. L. Perrewé, R. L. Brouer, C. Douglas, and S. Lux, "Political Skill in Organizations," *Journal of Management*, June 2007, pp. 290–329; K. J. Harris, K. M. Kacmar, S. Zivnuska, and J. D. Shaw, "The Impact of Political Skill on Impression Management Effectiveness," *Journal of Applied Psychology*, January 2007, pp. 278–285; and G. R. Ferris, D. C. Treadway, R. W. Kolodinsky, W. A. Hochwarter, C. J. Kacmar, C. Douglas, and D. D. Frink, "Development and Validation of the Political Skill Inventory," *Journal of Management*, February 2005, pp. 126–152.
65. J. Leslie, "Why You Have to Be a Politician at Your Job," *Forbes* online, www.forbes.com, May 26, 2010.
66. C. Zillman, "A Different #icebucketchallenge: How Will the ALS Association Spend All That Money?" *Fortune* online, www.fortune.com, August 22, 2014; M. Tirrell, "Ice Bucket

Challenge: 6 Months Later," www.cnbc.com, February 15, 2015; "How Will ALS Ice Bucket Challenge Money Be Spent," *PBS NewsHour* interview by Judy Woodruff, www .pbs.org, August 22, 2014; Diamond, D., "OK, the ALS Ice Bucket Challenge Worked. Now Where Will the Dollars Go?," *Forbes* online, www.forbes.com, August 18, 2014; E. Wolff-Mann, "Remember the Ice Bucket Challenge? Here's What Happened to the Money," *Time Magazine—Money* online, www.time.com/money, August 21, 2015; A. Nordrum, "Ice Bucket Challenge 2015: Can the ALS Association Turn Last Year's Viral Phenomenon into an Annual Fundraiser?," *International Business Times* online, www.ibtimes.com, August 26, 2015; www.alsa.org.

67. E. Kampf, "Can You Really Manage Engagement Without Managers?," *Gallup Business Journal*, businessjournal.gallup.com, April 24, 2014; "Holacracy," *T&D,* March 2014, p. 17; S. Helgesen, "An Extreme Take on Restructuring: No Job Titles, No Managers, No Politics," *Strategy + Business,* www.strategy-business.com, February 11, 2014; R. Trikha, "Zappos Says Bye to Managers—What If You Had No Boss?," www.cybercoders.com/insights/, January 7, 2014; G. Anders, "No More Bosses for Zappos (A Cautionary Tale)," jobs.aol.com/articles/, January 7, 2014; M. Wohlsen, "The Next Big Thing You Missed: Companies That Work Better without Bosses," www.wired.com/business/, January 7, 2014; C. Sweeney and J. Gosfield, "No Managers Required: How Zappos Ditched the Old Corporate Structure for Something New," www.fastcompany.com, January 6, 2014; J. McGregor, "Zappos Says Goodbye to Bosses," (blog), www.washingtonpost.com/blogs/on-leadership/, January 3, 2014; J. Edwards, "Zappos Is Getting Rid of All Job Titles and Managers, But Some Bosses Will Still Decide Who Gets Paid What," www.businessinsider.com/, January 2, 2014; A. Groth, "Zappos Is Going Holacratic: No Job Titles, No Managers, No Hierarchy," qz.com/, December 30, 2013; R. E. Silverman, "Managers? Who Needs Those?" *Wall Street Journal,* August 7, 2013, pp. B1+; M. Shaer, "The Boss Stops Here," nymag.com/news/features/, June 16, 2013; S. Wagreich, "A Billion Dollar Company with *No* Bosses? Yes, It Exists," www.inc.com/, March 14, 2013; R. E. Silverman, "Who's the Boss? There Isn't One," *Wall Street Journal,* June 20, 2012, pp. B1+; G. Hamel, "First, Let's Fire All the Managers"; and J. Badal, "Can a Company Be Run as a Democracy?," *Wall Street Journal*, April 23, 2007, p. B1.
68. C. Sweeney and J. Gosfield, "No Managers Required: How Zappos Ditched the Old Corporate Structure for Something New."
69. Ibid.
70. D. Richards, "At Zappos, Culture Pays," www.strategy-business.com/article, August 24, 2010.
71. A. Groth, "Zappos is Going Holacratic: No Job Titles, No Managers, No Hierarchy," qz.com, December 30, 2013.
72. G. Anders, "No More Bosses for Zappos (A Cautionary Tale)," jobs.aol.com/articles, January 7, 2014.

Management History *Module*

Henry Ford once said, "History is more or less bunk." Well, he was wrong! History is important because it can put current activities in perspective. In this module, we're going to take a trip back in time to see how the field of study called management has evolved. What you're going to see is that today's managers still use many elements of the historical approaches to management. Only through reflection can we fully appreciate the effects of the past on present thought and action. Use this knowledge to become effective managers by learning from past mistakes and successes. For now, focus on the following learning objectives as you read and study this module.

Learning Objectives

MH1.1 ***Describe*** *some early management examples.*

MH1.2 ***Explain*** *the various theories in the classical approach.*

MH1.3 ***Discuss*** *the development and uses of the behavioral approach.*

MH1.4 ***Describe*** *the quantitative approach.*

MH1.5 ***Explain*** *various theories in the contemporary approach.*

3000 BC - 1776	1911 - 1947	Late 1700s - 1950s	1940s - 1950s	1960s - present
Early Management	Classical Approach	Behavioral Approach	Quantitative Approach	Contemporary Approaches

MH1.1 EARLY Management

Management has been practiced a long time. Organized endeavors directed by people responsible for planning, organizing, leading, and controlling activities have existed for thousands of years. Let's look at some of the most interesting examples.

Source: Stephen Studd/The Image Bank/Getty Images

The Egyptian pyramids and the Great Wall of China are proof that projects of tremendous scope, employing tens of thousands of people, were completed in ancient times.[1] It took more than 100,000 workers some 20 years to construct a single pyramid. Who told each worker what to do? Who ensured there would be enough stones at the site to keep workers busy? The answer is *managers.* Someone had to plan what was to be done, organize people and materials to do it, make sure those workers got the work done, and impose some controls to ensure that everything was done as planned.

In 1776, Adam Smith published *The Wealth of Nations*, in which he argued the economic advantages that organizations and society would gain from the **division of labor** (or **job specialization**)—that is, breaking down jobs into narrow and repetitive tasks. Using the pin industry as an example, Smith claimed that 10 individuals, each doing a specialized task, could produce about 48,000 pins a day among them. However, if each person worked alone performing each task separately, it would be quite an accomplishment to produce even 10 pins a day! Smith concluded that division of labor increased productivity by increasing each worker's skill and dexterity, saving time lost in changing tasks and creating labor-saving inventions and machinery. Job specialization continues to be popular. For example, think of the specialized tasks performed by members of a hospital surgery team, meal preparation tasks done by workers in restaurant kitchens, or positions played by players on a football team.

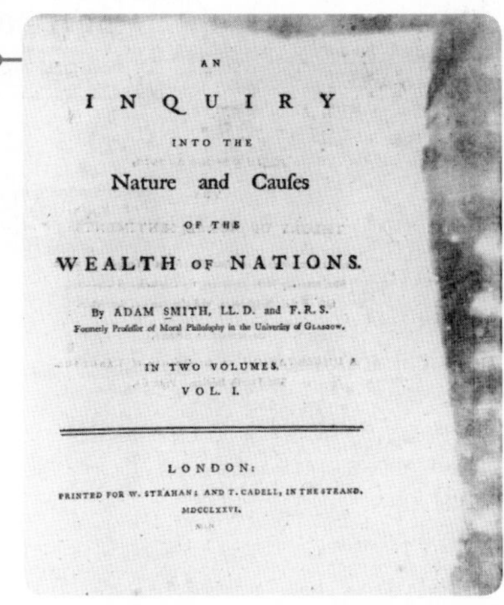
AN
INQUIRY
INTO THE
Nature and Caufes
OF THE
WEALTH OF NATIONS.
By ADAM SMITH, LL.D. and F.R.S.
Formerly Profeffor of Moral Philofophy in the Univerfity of Glasgow.
IN TWO VOLUMES.
VOL. I.
LONDON:
PRINTED FOR W. STRAHAN; AND T. CADELL, IN THE STRAND.
MDCCLXXVI.

Source: Fotosearch/Archive Photos/Getty Images

Starting in the late eighteenth century when machine power was substituted for human power, a point in history known as the **industrial revolution**, it became more economical to manufacture goods in factories rather than at home. These large, efficient factories needed someone to forecast demand, ensure that enough material was on hand to make products, assign tasks to people, direct daily activities, and so forth. That "someone" was a manager. These managers would need formal theories to guide them in running these large organizations. It wasn't until the early 1900s, however, that the first steps toward developing such theories were taken.

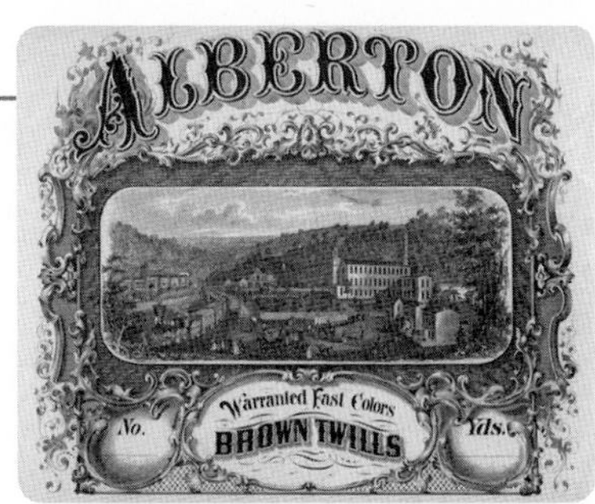

Source: Transcendental Graphics/Archive Photos/Getty Images

In this module, we'll look at four major approaches to management theory: classical, behavioral, quantitative, and contemporary. (See Exhibit MH-1.) Keep in mind that each approach is concerned with trying to explain management from the perspective of what was important at that time in history and the backgrounds and interests of the researchers. Each of the four approaches contributes to our overall understanding of management, but each is also a limited view of what it is and how to best practice it.

division of labor (job specialization)
The breakdown of jobs into narrow and repetitive tasks

industrial revolution
A period during the late eighteenth century when machine power was substituted for human power, making it more economical to manufacture goods in factories than at home

Exhibit MH-1
Major Approaches to Management

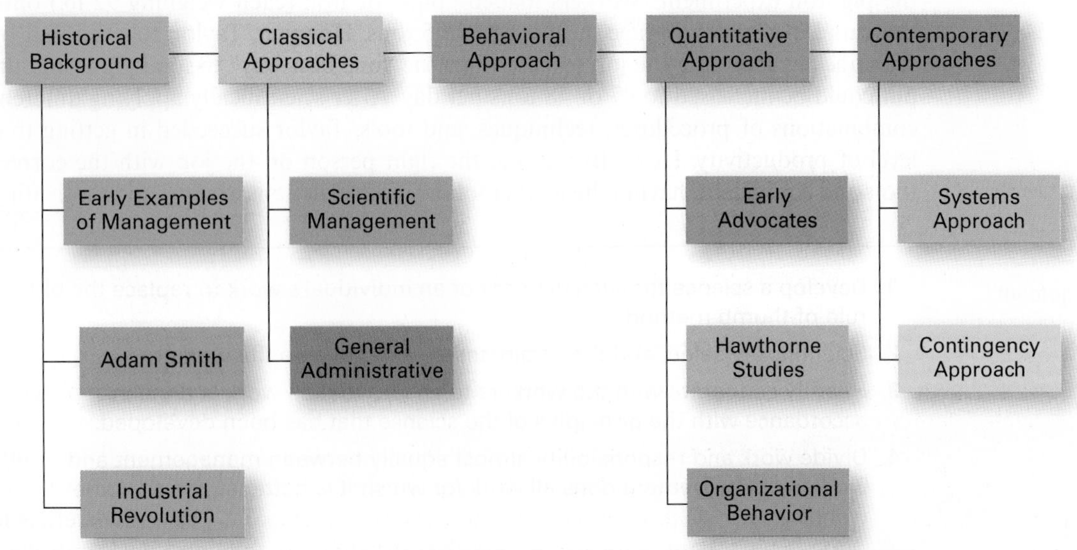

MH1.2 CLASSICAL **Approach**

Although we've seen how management has been used in organized efforts since early history, the formal study of management didn't begin until early in the twentieth century. These first studies of management, often called the **classical approach**, emphasized rationality and making organizations and workers as efficient as possible. Two major theories compose the classical approach: scientific management and general administrative theory. The two most important contributors to scientific management theory were Frederick W. Taylor and the husband-wife team of Frank and Lillian Gilbreth. The two most important contributors to general administrative theory were Henri Fayol and Max Weber. Let's take a look at each of these important figures in management history.

classical approach
First studies of management, which emphasized rationality and making organizations and workers as efficient as possible

Scientific Management

Source: Jacques Boyer/The Image Works

If you had to pinpoint when modern management theory was born, 1911 might be a good choice. That was when Frederick Winslow Taylor's *Principles of Scientific Management* was published. Its contents were widely embraced by managers around the world. Taylor's book described the theory of **scientific management**: the use of scientific methods to define the "one best way" for a job to be done.

scientific management
An approach that involves using the scientific method to find the "one best way" for a job to be done

Taylor worked at the Midvale and Bethlehem Steel Companies in Pennsylvania. As a mechanical engineer with a Quaker and Puritan background, he was continually appalled by workers' inefficiencies. Employees used vastly different techniques to do the same job. They often "took it easy" on the job, and Taylor believed that worker output was only about one-third of what was possible. Virtually no work standards existed, and workers were placed in jobs with little or no concern for matching their abilities and aptitudes with the tasks they were required to do. Taylor set out to remedy that by applying the scientific method to shop-floor jobs. He spent more than two decades passionately pursuing the "one best way" for such jobs to be done.

Taylor's experiences at Midvale led him to define clear guidelines for improving production efficiency. He argued that these four principles of management (see Exhibit MH-2) would result in prosperity for both workers and managers.[2] How did these scientific principles really work? Let's look at an example.

Probably the best known example of Taylor's scientific management efforts was the pig iron experiment. Workers loaded "pigs" of iron (each weighing 92 lb.) onto rail cars. Their daily average output was 12.5 tons. However, Taylor believed that by scientifically analyzing the job to determine the "one best way" to load pig iron, output could be increased to 47 or 48 tons per day. After scientifically applying different combinations of procedures, techniques, and tools, Taylor succeeded in getting that level of productivity. How? By putting the right person on the job with the correct tools and equipment, having the worker follow his instructions exactly, and motivating

Exhibit MH-2
Taylor's Scientific Management Principles

1. Develop a science for each element of an individual's work to replace the old rule-of-thumb method.
2. Scientifically select and then train, teach, and develop the worker.
3. Heartily cooperate with the workers to ensure that all work is done in accordance with the principles of the science that has been developed.
4. Divide work and responsibility almost equally between management and workers. Management does all work for which it is better suited than the workers.

Source: F. W. Taylor, *Principles of Scientific Management* (New York: Harper, 1911).

the worker with an economic incentive of a significantly higher daily wage. Using similar approaches for other jobs, Taylor was able to define the "one best way" for doing each job. Overall, Taylor achieved consistent productivity improvements in the range of 200 percent or more. Based on his groundbreaking studies of manual work using scientific principles, Taylor became known as the "father" of scientific management. His ideas spread in the United States and to other countries and inspired others to study and develop methods of scientific management. His most prominent followers were Frank and Lillian Gilbreth.

A construction contractor by trade, Frank Gilbreth gave up that career to study scientific management after hearing Taylor speak at a professional meeting. Frank and his wife Lillian, a psychologist, studied work to eliminate inefficient hand-and-body motions. The Gilbreths also experimented with the design and use of the proper tools and equipment for optimizing work performance.[3] Also, as parents of 12 children, the Gilbreths ran their household using scientific management principles and techniques. In fact, two of their children wrote a book, *Cheaper by the Dozen*, which described life with the two masters of efficiency.

Source: Bettmann/Getty Images

Frank is probably best known for his bricklaying experiments. By carefully analyzing the bricklayer's job, he reduced the number of motions in laying exterior brick from 18 to about 5, and in laying interior brick from 18 to 2. Using Gilbreth's techniques, a bricklayer was more productive and less fatigued at the end of the day.

The Gilbreths invented a device called a microchronometer that recorded a worker's hand-and-body motions and the amount of time spent doing each motion. Wasted motions missed by the naked eye could be identified and eliminated. The Gilbreths also devised a classification scheme to label 17 basic hand motions (such as search, grasp, hold), which they called **therbligs** (Gilbreth spelled backward with the *th* transposed). This scheme gave the Gilbreths a more precise way of analyzing a worker's exact hand movements.

therbligs
A classification scheme for labeling basic hand motions

HOW TODAY'S MANAGERS USE SCIENTIFIC MANAGEMENT Many of the guidelines and techniques Taylor and the Gilbreths devised for improving production efficiency are still used in organizations today. When managers analyze the basic work tasks that must be performed, use time-and-motion study to eliminate wasted motions, hire the best-qualified workers for a job, or design incentive systems based on output, they're using the principles of scientific management. Nowadays, adaptive robotics can help boost worker efficiency. By freeing workers from repetitive tasks, one study revealed that workers could complete essential tasks requiring manual dexterity 25 percent faster.[4] At ABB, a Swiss energy and automation company, the use of adaptive robots reduced workers' idle time by 85 percent.[5]

general administrative theory
An approach to management that focuses on describing what managers do and what constitutes good management practice

General Administrative Theory

General administrative theory focused more on what managers do and what constituted good management practice. We introduced Henri Fayol in Chapter 1 because he first identified five functions that managers perform: planning, organizing, commanding, coordinating, and controlling.[6]

Source: Jacques Boyer/The Image Works

Fayol wrote during the same time period as Taylor. While Taylor was concerned with first-line managers and the scientific method, Fayol's attention was directed at the activities of *all* managers. He wrote from his personal experience as the managing director of a large French coal-mining firm.

Fayol described the practice of management as something distinct from accounting, finance, production, distribution, and other typical business functions. His belief that management was an activity common to all business endeavors, government, and

Exhibit MH-3
Fayol's 14 Principles of Management

1. **Division of work.** Specialization increases output by making employees more efficient.
2. **Authority.** Managers must be able to give orders, and authority gives them this right.
3. **Discipline.** Employees must obey and respect the rules that govern the organization.
4. **Unity of command.** Every employee should receive orders from only one superior.
5. **Unity of direction.** The organization should have a single plan of action to guide managers and workers.
6. **Subordination of individual interests to the general interest.** The interests of any one employee or group of employees should not take precedence over the interests of the organization as a whole.
7. **Remuneration.** Workers must be paid a fair wage for their services.
8. **Centralization.** This term refers to the degree to which subordinates are involved in decision making.
9. **Scalar chain.** The line of authority from top management to the lowest ranks is the scalar chain.
10. **Order.** People and materials should be in the right place at the right time.
11. **Equity.** Managers should be kind and fair to their subordinates.
12. **Stability of tenure of personnel.** Management should provide orderly personnel planning and ensure that replacements are available to fill vacancies.
13. **Initiative.** Employees allowed to originate and carry out plans will exert high levels of effort.
14. **Esprit de corps.** Promoting team spirit will build harmony and unity within the organization.

Source: Based on Henri Fayol's 1916 Principles of Management, "Administration Industrielle et Générale," translated by C. Storrs, *General and Industrial Management* (London: Sir Isaac Pitman & Sons, London, 1949).

even the home led him to develop 14 **principles of management**—fundamental rules of management that could be applied to all organizational situations and taught in schools. These principles are shown in Exhibit MH-3.

principles of management
Fundamental rules of management that could be applied in all organizational situations and taught in schools

Source: Hulton Archive/Getty Images

Max Weber (pronounced VAY-ber) was a German sociologist who studied organizations.[7] Writing in the early 1900s, he developed a theory of authority structures and relations based on an ideal type of organization he called a **bureaucracy**—a form of organization characterized by division of labor, a clearly defined hierarchy, detailed rules and regulations, and impersonal relationships. (See Exhibit MH-4.) Weber recognized that this "ideal bureaucracy" didn't exist in reality. Instead, he intended it as a basis for theorizing about how work could be done in large groups. His theory became the structural design for many of today's large organizations.

bureaucracy
A form of organization characterized by division of labor, a clearly defined hierarchy, detailed rules and regulations, and impersonal relationships

Bureaucracy, as described by Weber, is a lot like scientific management in its ideology. Both emphasized rationality, predictability, impersonality, technical competence, and authoritarianism. Although Weber's ideas were less practical than Taylor's, the fact that his "ideal type" still describes many contemporary organizations attests to their importance.

HOW TODAY'S MANAGERS USE GENERAL ADMINISTRATIVE THEORY Several of our current management ideas and practices can be directly traced to the contributions of general administrative theory. For instance, the functional view of the manager's job can be attributed to Fayol. In addition, his 14 principles serve as a frame of reference from which many current management concepts—such as managerial authority, centralized decision making, reporting to only one boss, and so forth—have evolved.

Exhibit MH-4
Characteristics of Weber's Bureaucracy

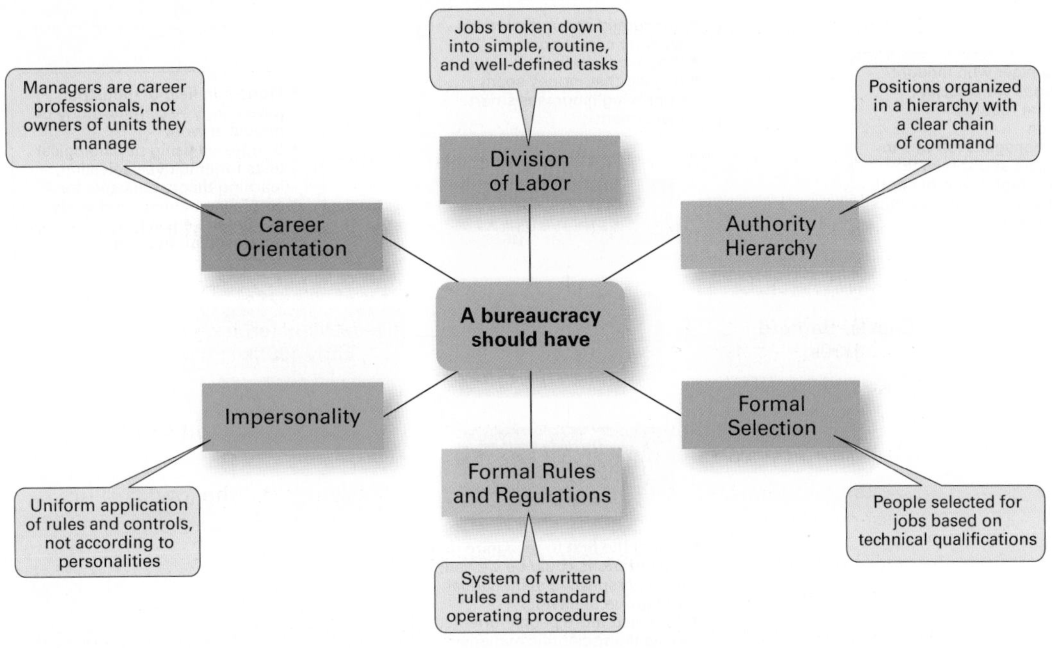

Source: Based on *Essays in Sociology* by Max Weber, translated, edited, and introduced by H. H. Gerth and C. Wright Mills (New York: Oxford University Press, 1946).

Weber's bureaucracy was an attempt to formulate an ideal prototype for organizations. Although many characteristics of Weber's bureaucracy are still evident in large organizations, his model isn't as popular today as it was in the twentieth century. Many managers feel that a bureaucratic structure hinders individual employees' creativity and limits an organization's ability to respond quickly to an increasingly dynamic environment. However, even in flexible organizations of creative professionals—such as Google, Samsung, General Electric, or Cisco Systems—bureaucratic mechanisms are necessary to ensure that resources are used efficiently and effectively. In some organizations, such as the U.S. Food and Drug Administration, bureaucracy has been a double-edged sword. Back in the 1960s, the FDA carefully scrutinized thalidomide, which was marketed to women in Europe for morning sickness. Thalidomide was not approved for this purpose because much evidence showed that it was causing profound birth defects. At times, the FDA's bureaucracy may not serve the public interest. The FDA's bureaucracy delayed the release of a vaccine for meningitis B for several months without explanation after a serious outbreak across college campuses.

3000 BC - 1776	1911 - 1947	Late 1700s - 1950s	1940s - 1950s	1960s - present
Early Management	Classical Approach	Behavioral Approach	Quantitative Approach	Contemporary Approaches

BEHAVIORAL **Approach**

As we know, managers get things done by working with people. This explains why some writers have chosen to look at management by focusing on the organization's people. The field of study that researches the actions (behavior) of people at work is called **organizational behavior (OB)**. Much of what managers do today when managing people—motivating, leading, building trust, working with a team, managing conflict, and so forth—has come out of OB research.

organizational behavior (OB)
The study of the actions of people at work

Exhibit MH-5
Early OB Advocates

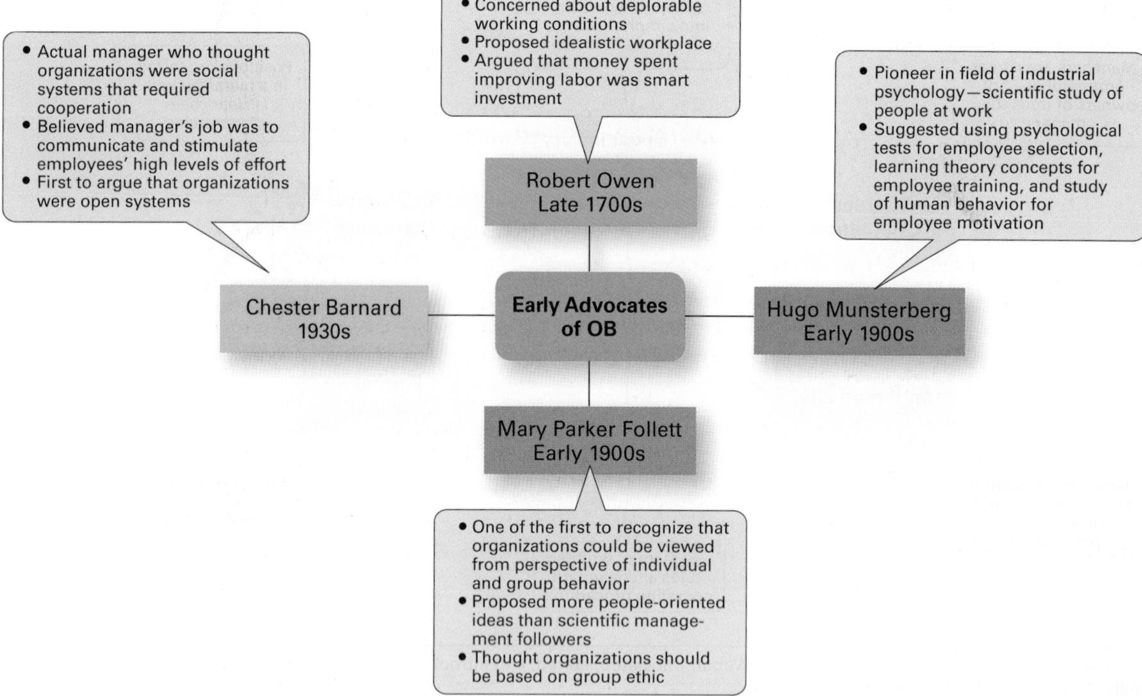

• Concerned about deplorable working conditions
• Proposed idealistic workplace
• Argued that money spent improving labor was smart investment
Robert Owen Late 1700s
• Actual manager who thought organizations were social systems that required cooperation
• Believed manager's job was to communicate and stimulate employees' high levels of effort
• First to argue that organizations were open systems
Chester Barnard 1930s
Early Advocates of OB
• Pioneer in field of industrial psychology—scientific study of people at work
• Suggested using psychological tests for employee selection, learning theory concepts for employee training, and study of human behavior for employee motivation
Hugo Munsterberg Early 1900s
Mary Parker Follett Early 1900s
• One of the first to recognize that organizations could be viewed from perspective of individual and group behavior
• Proposed more people-oriented ideas than scientific management followers
• Thought organizations should be based on group ethic

Although a number of individuals in the early twentieth century recognized the importance of people to an organization's success, four stand out as early advocates of the OB approach: Robert Owen, Hugo Munsterberg, Mary Parker Follett, and Chester Barnard. Their contributions were varied and distinct, yet all believed that people were the most important asset of the organization and should be managed accordingly. Their ideas provided the foundation for such management practices as employee selection procedures, motivation programs, and work teams. Exhibit MH-5 summarizes each individual's most important ideas.

Source: Hawthorne Works Museum of Morton College

Hawthorne Studies
A series of studies during the 1920s and 1930s that provided new insights into individual and group behavior

Without question, the most important contribution to the OB field came out of the **Hawthorne Studies**, a series of studies conducted at the Western Electric Company Works in Cicero, Illinois. These studies, which started in 1924, were initially designed by Western Electric industrial engineers as a scientific management experiment. They wanted to examine the effect of various lighting levels on worker productivity. Like any good scientific experiment, control and experimental groups were set up, with the experimental group exposed to various lighting intensities, and the control group working under a constant intensity. If you were the industrial engineers in charge of this experiment, what would you have expected to happen? It's logical to think that individual output in the experimental group would be directly related to the intensity of the light. However, they found that as the level of light was increased in the experimental group, output for both groups increased. Then, much to the surprise of the engineers, as the light level was decreased in the experimental group, productivity continued to increase in both groups. In fact, a productivity decrease was observed in the experimental group *only* when the level of light was reduced to that of a moonlit night. What would explain these unexpected results? The engineers weren't sure, but concluded that lighting intensity was not directly related to group productivity and that something else must have contributed to the results. They weren't able to pinpoint what that "something else" was, though.

In 1927, the Western Electric engineers asked Harvard professor Elton Mayo and his associates to join the study as consultants. Thus began a relationship that would last through 1932 and encompass numerous experiments in the redesign of jobs, changes in workday and workweek length, introduction of rest periods, and individual versus group wage plans.[8] For example, one experiment was designed to evaluate the effect of a group piecework incentive pay system on group productivity. The results indicated that the incentive plan had less effect on a worker's output than group pressure, acceptance, and security. The researchers concluded that social norms or group standards were the key determinants of individual work behavior.

Scholars generally agree that the Hawthorne Studies had a game-changing impact on management beliefs about the role of people in organizations. Mayo concluded that people's behavior and attitudes are closely related, that group factors significantly affect individual behavior, that group standards establish individual worker output, and that money is less a factor in determining output than group standards, group attitudes, and security. These conclusions led to a new emphasis on the human behavior factor in the management of organizations.

HOW TODAY'S MANAGERS USE THE BEHAVIORAL APPROACH The behavioral approach has largely shaped how today's organizations are managed. From the way managers design jobs to the way they work with employee teams to the way they communicate, we see elements of the behavioral approach. Much of what the early OB advocates proposed and the conclusions from the Hawthorne Studies have provided the foundation for our current theories of motivation, leadership, group behavior and development, and numerous other behavioral approaches. It is important that managers embrace the lessons from the behavioral approach. The Gallup Organization's survey on employee engagement revealed an alarming statistic—87 percent of global employees are disengaged.[9] According to one CEO, "It's no wonder most employees are disengaged. We isolate people and put them in standardized, uniform work settings that reinforce the idea that your unique wants and needs are not of importance to us."[10]

3000 BC - 1776	1911 - 1947	Late 1700s - 1950s	1940s - 1950s	1960s - present
Early Management	Classical Approach	Behavioral Approach	Quantitative Approach	Contemporary Approaches

QUANTITATIVE Approach

Although passengers bumping into each other when trying to find their seats on an airplane can be a mild annoyance for them, it's a bigger problem for airlines because lines get backed up, slowing down how quickly the plane can get back in the air. Based on research in space-time geometry, one airline innovated a unique boarding process called "reverse pyramid" that has saved at least two minutes in boarding time.[11] This is an example of the **quantitative approach**, which is the use of quantitative techniques to improve decision making. This approach also is known as *management science.*

quantitative approach
The use of quantitative techniques to improve decision making

The quantitative approach evolved from mathematical and statistical solutions developed for military problems during World War II. After the war was over, many of these techniques used for military problems were applied to businesses. For example, one group of military officers, nicknamed the Whiz Kids, joined Ford Motor Company in the mid-1940s and immediately began using statistical methods and quantitative models to improve decision making.

Source: Bert Hardy/Hulton Archive/Getty Images

What exactly does the quantitative approach do? It involves applying statistics, optimization models, information models, computer simulations, and other quantitative techniques to management activities. Linear programming, for instance, is a technique that managers use to improve resource allocation decisions. Work scheduling can be more efficient as a result of critical-path scheduling analysis. The economic order quantity model helps managers determine optimum inventory levels. Each of these is an example of quantitative techniques being applied to improve managerial decision making. Another area where quantitative techniques are used frequently is in total quality management.

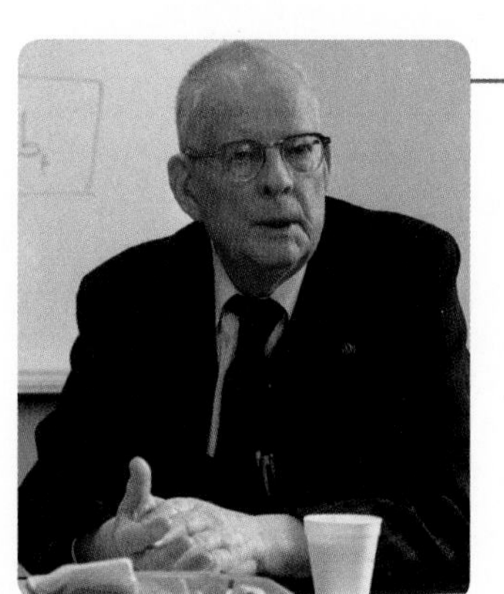

Source: Richard Drew/AP Images

A quality revolution swept through both the business and public sectors in the 1980s and 1990s.[12] It was inspired by a small group of quality experts, the most famous being W. Edwards Deming (pictured at left) and Joseph M. Juran. The ideas and techniques they advocated in the 1950s had few supporters in the United States but were enthusiastically embraced by Japanese organizations. As Japanese manufacturers began beating U.S. competitors in quality comparisons, however, Western managers soon took a more serious look at Deming's and Juran's ideas, which became the basis for today's quality management programs.

Total quality management, or **TQM**, is a management philosophy devoted to continual improvement and responding to customer needs and expectations. (See Exhibit MH-6.) The term *customer* includes anyone who interacts with the organization's product or services, internally or externally. It encompasses employees and suppliers, as well as the people who purchase the organization's goods or services. *Continual improvement* isn't possible without accurate measurements, which require statistical techniques that measure every critical variable in the organization's work processes. These measurements are compared against standards to identify and correct problems.

total quality management (TQM)
A philosophy of management that is driven by continuous improvement and responsiveness to customer needs and expectations

HOW TODAY'S MANAGERS USE THE QUANTITATIVE APPROACH No one likes long lines, especially residents of New York City. If they see a long checkout line, they often go somewhere else. However, at Whole Foods' first gourmet supermarkets in Manhattan, customers found something different—that is, the longer the line, the shorter the wait. When ready to check out, customers are guided into serpentine single lines that feed into numerous checkout lanes. Whole Foods, widely known for its organic food selections, can charge premium prices, which allow it the luxury of staffing all those checkout lanes. And customers are finding that their wait times are shorter than expected.[13] The science of keeping lines moving is known as queue management. And for Whole Foods, this quantitative technique has translated into strong sales at its Manhattan stores.

The quantitative approach contributes directly to management decision making in the areas of planning and control. For instance, when managers make budgeting, queuing, scheduling, quality control, and similar decisions, they typically rely on quantitative techniques. Specialized software has made the use of these techniques less intimidating for managers, although many still feel anxious about using them.

Exhibit MH-6
What Is Quality Management?

1. **Intense focus on the customer.** The customer includes outsiders who buy the organization's products or services and internal customers who interact with and serve others in the organization.
2. **Concern for continual improvement.** Quality management is a commitment to never being satisfied. "Very good" is not good enough. Quality can always be improved.
3. **Process focused.** Quality management focuses on work processes as the quality of goods and services is continually improved.
4. **Improvement in the quality of everything the organization does.** This relates to the final product, how the organization handles deliveries, how rapidly it responds to complaints, how politely the phones are answered, and the like.
5. **Accurate measurement.** Quality management uses statistical techniques to measure every critical variable in the organization's operations. These are compared against standards to identify problems, trace them to their roots, and eliminate their causes.
6. **Empowerment of employees.** Quality management involves the people on the line in the improvement process. Teams are widely used in quality management programs as empowerment vehicles for finding and solving problems.

3000 BC – 1776	1911 – 1947	Late 1700s – 1950s	1940s – 1950s	1960s – present
Early Management	Classical Approach	Behavioral Approach	Quantitative Approach	Contemporary Approaches

CONTEMPORARY **Approaches**

MH1.5

As we've seen, many elements of the earlier approaches to management theory continue to influence how managers manage. Most of these earlier approaches focused on managers' concerns *inside* the organization. Starting in the 1960s, management researchers began to look at what was happening in the external environment *outside* the boundaries of the organization. Two contemporary management perspectives—systems and contingency—are part of this approach. Systems theory is a basic theory in the physical sciences, but had never been applied to organized human efforts. In 1938, Chester Barnard, a telephone company executive, first wrote in his book, *The Functions of an Executive,* that an organization functioned as a cooperative system. However, it wasn't until the 1960s that management researchers began to look more carefully at systems theory and how it related to organizations.

A **system** is a set of interrelated and interdependent parts arranged in a manner that produces a unified whole. The two basic types of systems are closed and open. **Closed systems** are not influenced by and do not interact with their environment. In contrast, **open systems** are influenced by and do interact with their environment. Today, when we describe organizations as systems, we mean open systems. Exhibit MH-7 shows a diagram of an organization from an open systems perspective. As you can see, an organization takes in inputs (resources) from the environment and transforms or processes these resources into outputs that are distributed into the environment. The organization is "open" to and interacts with its environment.

Source: Frederic J. Brown/AFP/Getty Images/Newscom

How does the systems approach contribute to our understanding of management? Researchers imagined organizations as complex systems comprised of many components, including individuals, groups, structure, goals, status, and authority. What this means is that as managers coordinate work activities in the various parts of the organization, they ensure that all these parts are working together so the organization's goals can be achieved. For example, the systems approach recognizes that, no matter how efficient the production department, the marketing department must anticipate changes in customer tastes and work with the product development department in creating products customers want—or the organization's overall performance will suffer.

In addition, the systems approach implies that decisions and actions in one organizational area will affect other areas. For example, if the purchasing department

system
A set of interrelated and interdependent parts arranged in a manner that produces a unified whole

closed systems
Systems that are not influenced by and do not interact with their environment

open systems
Systems that interact with their environment

Exhibit MH-7
Organization as an Open System

Environment
Organization

Inputs	Transformation Process	Outputs
Raw Materials Human Resources Capital Technology Information	Employees' Work Activities Management Activities Technology and Operations Methods	Products and Services Financial Results Information Human Results

Feedback
Environment

doesn't acquire the right quantity and quality of inputs, the production department won't be able to do its job.

Finally, the systems approach recognizes that organizations are not self-contained. They rely on their environment for essential inputs and as outlets to absorb their outputs. No organization can survive for long if it ignores government regulations, supplier relations, or the varied external constituencies on which it depends.

How relevant is the systems approach to management? Quite relevant. Consider, for example, a shift manager at a Starbucks restaurant who must coordinate the work of employees filling customer orders at the front counter and the drive-through windows, direct the delivery and unloading of food supplies, and address any customer concerns that come up. This manager "manages" all parts of the "system" so that the restaurant meets its daily sales goals.

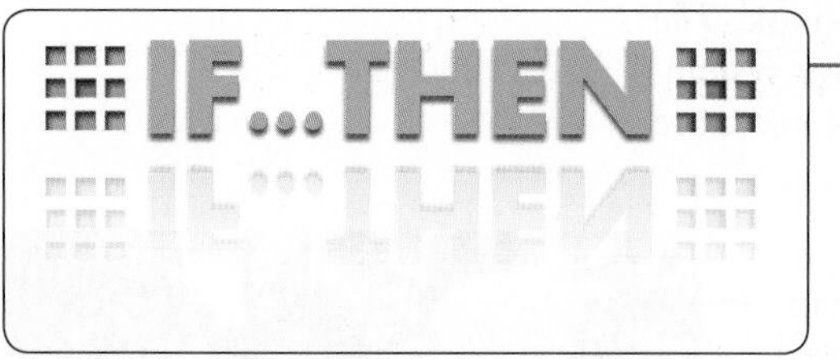

The early management theorists came up with management principles they generally assumed to be universally applicable. Later research found exceptions to many of these principles. For example, division of labor is valuable and widely used, but jobs can become *too* specialized. Bureaucracy is desirable in many situations, but in other circumstances, other structural designs are *more* effective. Management is not (and cannot be) based on simplistic principles to be applied in all situations. Different and changing situations require managers to use different approaches and techniques. The **contingency approach** (sometimes called the *situational approach*) says that organizations are different, face different situations (contingencies), and require different ways of managing.

contingency approach
A management approach that recognizes organizations as different, which means they face different situations (contingencies) and require different ways of managing

A good way to describe contingency is "if, then." *If* this is the way my situation is, *then* this is the best way for me to manage in this situation. It's intuitively logical because organizations and even units within the same organization differ—in size, goals, work activities, and the like. It would be surprising to find universally applicable management rules that would work in *all* situations. But, of course, it's one thing to say that the way to manage "depends on the situation" and another to say what the situation is. Management researchers continue working to identify these situational variables. Exhibit MH-8 describes four popular contingency variables. Although the list is by no means comprehensive—more than 100 different variables have been identified—it represents those most widely used and gives you an idea of what we mean by the term *contingency variable.* The primary value of the contingency approach is that it stresses there are no simplistic or universal rules for managers to follow.

So what do managers face today when managing? Although the dawn of the information age is said to have begun with Samuel Morse's telegraph in 1837, dramatic changes in information technology that occurred in the latter part of the twentieth century and

Exhibit MH-8
Popular Contingency Variables

Organization Size. As size increases, so do the problems of coordination. For instance, the type of organization structure appropriate for an organization of 50,000 employees is likely to be inefficient for an organization of 50 employees.

Routineness of Task Technology. To achieve its purpose, an organization uses technology. Routine technologies require organizational structures, leadership styles, and control systems that differ from those required by customized or nonroutine technologies.

Environmental Uncertainty. The degree of uncertainty caused by environmental changes influences the management process. What works best in a stable and predictable environment may be totally inappropriate in a rapidly changing and unpredictable environment.

Individual Differences. Individuals differ in terms of their desire for growth, autonomy, tolerance of ambiguity, and expectations. These and other individual differences are particularly important when managers select motivation techniques, leadership styles, and job designs.

continue through today directly affect the manager's job. Managers now may manage employees who are working from home or working halfway around the world. An organization's computing resources used to be mainframe computers locked away in temperature-controlled rooms and only accessed by the experts. Now, practically everyone in an organization is connected—wired or wireless—with devices no larger than the palm of the hand. Just like the impact of the industrial revolution in the 1700s on the emergence of management, the information age has brought dramatic changes that continue to influence the way organizations are managed.

Source: Image Source/Getty Images

Management History *Module*

PREPARING FOR: Exams/Quizzes

CHAPTER SUMMARY by Learning Objectives

MH1.1 DESCRIBE **some early management examples.**

Studying history is important because it helps us see the origins of today's management practices and recognize what has and has not worked. We can see early examples of management practice in the construction of the Egyptian pyramids and the Great Wall of China. One important historical event was the publication of Adam Smith's *Wealth of Nations*, in which he argued the benefits of division of labor (job specialization). Another was the industrial revolution, where it became more economical to manufacture in factories than at home. Managers were needed to manage these factories, and these managers needed formal management theories to guide them.

MH1.2 EXPLAIN **the various theories in the classical approach.**

Frederick W. Taylor, known as the "father" of scientific management, studied manual work using scientific principles—that is, guidelines for improving production efficiency—to find the one best way to do those jobs. The Gilbreths' primary contribution was finding efficient hand-and-body motions and designing proper tools and equipment for optimizing work performance. Fayol believed the functions of management were common to all business endeavors but also were distinct from other business functions. He developed 14 principles of management from which many current management concepts have evolved. Weber described an ideal type of organization he called a bureaucracy—characteristics that many of today's large organizations still have. Today's managers use the concepts of scientific management when they analyze basic work tasks to be performed, use time-and-motion study to eliminate wasted motions, hire the best qualified workers for a job, use adaptive robotics to boost worker efficiency, and design incentive systems based on output. They use general administrative theory when they perform the functions of management and structure their organizations so that resources are used efficiently and effectively.

MH1.3 DISCUSS **the development and uses of the behavioral approach.**

The early OB advocates (Robert Owen, Hugo Munsterberg, Mary Parker Follett, and Chester Barnard) contributed various ideas, but all believed that people were the most important asset of the organization and should be managed accordingly. The Hawthorne Studies dramatically affected management beliefs about the role of people in organizations, leading to a new emphasis on the human behavior factor in managing. The behavioral approach has largely shaped how today's organizations are managed. Many current theories of motivation, leadership, group behavior and development, and other behavioral issues can be traced to the early OB advocates and the conclusions from the Hawthorne Studies.

MH1.4 DESCRIBE **the quantitative approach.**

The quantitative approach involves applications of statistics, optimization models, information models, and computer simulations to management activities. Today's managers use the quantitative approach, especially when making decisions, as they plan and control work activities such as allocating resources, improving quality, scheduling work, or determining optimum inventory levels. Total quality management—a management philosophy devoted to continual improvement and responding to customer needs and expectations—also makes use of quantitative methods to meet its goals.

MH1.5 EXPLAIN **the various theories in the contemporary approach.**

The systems approach says that an organization takes in inputs (resources) from the environment and transforms or processes these resources into outputs that are distributed into the environment. This approach provides a framework to help managers understand how all the interdependent units work together to achieve the organization's goals and that decisions and actions taken in one organizational area will affect others. In this way, managers can recognize that organizations are not self-contained, but instead rely on their environment for essential inputs and as outlets to absorb their outputs.

The contingency approach says that organizations are different, face different situations, and require different ways of managing. It helps us understand management because it stresses there are no simplistic or universal rules for managers to follow. Instead, managers must look at their situation and determine that *if* this is the way my situation is, *then* this is the best way for me to manage.

Pearson MyLab Management

Go to **mymanagementlab.com** to complete the problems marked with this icon .

REVIEW AND DISCUSSION QUESTIONS

MH-1. Explain why studying management history is important.

MH-2. What is the significance of the industrial revolution?

MH-3. What is a bureaucracy? Do bureaucracies still exist today?

MH-4. What did the early advocates of OB contribute to our understanding of management?

MH-5. Why were the Hawthorne Studies so critical to management history?

MH-6. Explain what the quantitative approach has contributed to the field of management.

MH-7. Describe total quality management.

MH-8. How has technology impacted how managers use the quantitative approach in today's workplace?

MH-9. How do systems theory and the contingency approach make managers better at what they do?

MH-10. How do societal trends influence the practice of management? What are the implications for someone studying management?

PREPARING FOR: My Career

MY TURN TO BE A MANAGER

- Conduct research and identify a new or emerging management theory. Do you think the new theory will have an impact on future management practices?
- Can scientific management principles help you be more efficient? Choose a task you do regularly (such as laundry, fixing dinner, grocery shopping, studying for exams, etc.).

Analyze it by writing down the steps involved in completing that task. See if any activities could be combined or eliminated. Find the "one best way" to do this task. And the next time you have to do the task, try the scientifically managed way! See if you become more efficient (keeping in mind that changing habits isn't easy to do).

- How do business organizations survive for 100+ years? Obviously, they've seen a lot of historical events come and go. Choose one of these companies and research their history: Coca-Cola, Procter & Gamble, Avon, or General Electric. How has it changed over the years? From your research on this company, what did you learn that could help you be a better manager?
- Pick one historical event from this century and do some research on it. Write a paper describing the impact this event might be having or has had on how workplaces are managed.
- Come on, admit it, you multitask, don't you? And if not, you probably know people who do. Multitasking is also common in the workplace. But does it make employees more efficient and effective? Pretend you're the manager in charge of a loan-processing department. Describe how you would research this issue using each of the following management approaches or theories: scientific management, general administrative theory, quantitative approach, behavioral approach, systems theory, and contingency theory.

ENDNOTES

1. C. S. George, Jr., *The History of Management Thought*, 2d ed. (Upper Saddle River, NJ: Prentice Hall, 1972), p. 4.
2. F. W. Taylor, *Principles of Scientific Management* (New York: Harper, 1911), p. 44. For other information on Taylor, see S. Wagner-Tsukamoto, "An Institutional Economic Reconstruction of Scientific Management: On the Lost Theoretical Logic of Taylorism," *Academy of Management Review*, January 2007, pp. 105–117; R. Kanigel, *The One Best Way: Frederick Winslow Taylor and the Enigma of Efficiency* (New York: Viking, 1997); and M. Banta, *Taylored Lives: Narrative Productions in the Age of Taylor, Veblen, and Ford* (Chicago: University of Chicago Press, 1993).
3. See, for example, F. B. Gilbreth, *Motion Study* (New York: Van Nostrand, 1911); and F. B. Gilbreth and L. M. Gilbreth, *Fatigue Study* (New York: Sturgis and Walton, 1916).
4. "Smarter, Smaller, Safer Robots," *Harvard Business Review* online, https://hbr.org, November 2015.
5. W. Knight, "How Human-Robot Teamwork Will Upend Manufacturing," *MIT Technology Review* online, http://www.technologyreview.com, September 16, 2015.
6. H. Fayol, *Industrial and General Administration* (Paris: Dunod, 1916).
7. M. Weber, *The Theory of Social and Economic Organizations*, ed. T. Parsons, trans. A. M. Henderson and T. Parsons (New York: Free Press, 1947); and M. Lounsbury and E. J. Carberry, "From King to Court Jester? Weber's Fall from Grace in Organizational Theory," *Organization Studies*, vol. 26, no. 4, 2005, pp. 501–525.
8. E. Mayo, *The Human Problems of an Industrial Civilization* (New York: Macmillan, 1933); and F. J. Roethlisberger and W. J. Dickson, *Management and the Worker* (Cambridge, MA: Harvard University Press, 1939).
9. S. Crabtree, "Worldwide, 13% of Employees Are Engaged at Work," Gallup online, http://www.gallup.com, October 8, 2013.
10. J. Keane, "Meaningful Work Should Be Every CEO's Top Priority," *Harvard Business Review* online, https://hbr.org, November 5, 2015.
11. N. Zamiska, "Plane Geometry: Scientists Help Speed Boarding of Aircraft," *Wall Street Journal*, November 2, 2005, p. A1+.
12. See, for example, J. Jusko, "Tried and True," *IW*, December 6, 1999, pp. 78–84; T. A. Stewart, "A Conversation with Joseph Juran," *Fortune*, January 11, 1999, pp. 168–170; J. R. Hackman and R. Wageman, "Total Quality Management: Empirical, Conceptual, and Practical Issues," *Administrative Science Quarterly*, June 1995, pp. 309–342; T. C. Powell, "Total Quality Management as Competitive Advantage: A Review and Empirical Study," *Strategic Management Journal*, January 1995, pp. 15–37; R. K. Reger, L. T. Gustafson, S. M. Demarie, and J. V. Mullane, "Reframing the Organization: Why Implementing Total Quality Is Easier Said Than Done," *Academy of Management Review*, July 1994, pp. 565–584; C. A. Reeves and D. A. Bednar, "Defining Quality: Alternatives and Implications," *Academy of Management Review*, July 1994, pp. 419–445; J. W. Dean, Jr. and D. E. Bowen, "Management Theory and Total Quality: Improving Research and Practice through Theory Development," *Academy of Management Review*, July 1994, pp. 392–418; B. Krone, "Total Quality Management: An American Odyssey," *The Bureaucrat*, Fall 1990, pp. 35–38; and A. Gabor, *The Man Who Discovered Quality* (New York: Random House, 1990).
13. M. Barbaro, "A Long Line for a Shorter Wait at the Supermarket," *New York Times* online, www.nyt.com, June 23, 2007.

Chapter 2 Decision Making

It's Your Career

Source: Zudy and Kysa/Shutterstock

A key to success in management and in your career is knowing how to be an effective problem-solver.

Problem Solving—Not A Problem

Every day you're faced with problems to solve—what class assignment should I focus on first? What am I going to eat for dinner? What's the quickest way for me to get to work (or school) today since I'm running behind schedule? And when you're done with school and employed by an organization, you are going to be expected to show that you're a good problem solver.

And having good problem-solving skills is important if you're going to be successful in your career. What can you do to develop and improve your problem-solving skills? Let's look at some suggestions.

*1. **Define the problem**. This might seem self-evident but you'd be surprised at how many people try to jump in with a quick and easy solution without having spent time to first understand and then define the problem. When you do that, you might come up with a solution... to the wrong problem! Instead, spend some time in asking questions. Lots of questions! But don't get so caught up in defining the problem that you ignore solving the problem. Another precautionary note when defining the problem is, as we describe in the chapter, making sure you don't confuse problems with symptoms of problems. For instance, supposed you've applied for several jobs, but have not received any interview invites. The problem isn't the lack of interview invites... that's only a symptom of a problem. There's some reason you're not getting asked in for an interview. Before you can "solve" this situation, you need to define the problem. So, ask questions. Is it your résumé? Is it your cover letter? Are you applying for jobs you're not suited for?*

*2. **Look at the problem from different perspectives and generate multiple solutions.** A good problem-solver (and a good decision-maker)*

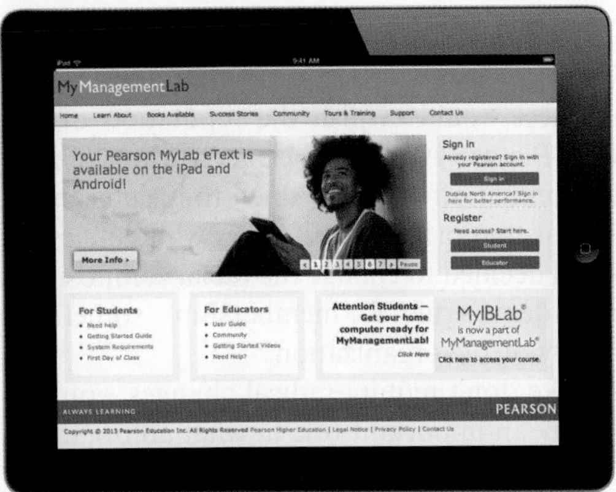

Pearson MyLab Management®

Improve Your Grade!

When you see this icon, visit **www.mymanagementlab.com** for activities that are applied, personalized, and offer immediate feedback.

Learning Objectives

SKILL OUTCOMES

2.1 Describe *the eight steps in the decision-making process.*

- **Develop your skill** at being creative.

2.2 Explain *the four ways managers make decisions.*

2.3 Classify *decisions and decision-making conditions.*

2.4 Describe *how biases affect decision making.*

- **Know how to** recognize when you're using decision-making errors and biases and what to do about it.

2.5 Identify *effective decision-making techniques.*

has an open mind and attempts to be as creative as possible in coming up with solutions to a problem.

3. Evaluate the ideas or possible solutions. *Evaluate your ideas carefully and thoroughly by how they would impact the problem. But it's also critical to look at the constraints of time and money. Can your solutions lead to successful results in the time frame and the budget constraints you face?*

4. Implement your solution. *A problem doesn't get solved without implementing your solution. Think through the "how's" of your solution. If you don't execute this step well, the problem is likely to still be there or even get worse.*

5. Re-examine your solution. *Has the problem been resolved or at least gotten better? If not, you'll have to determine if it is still the right solution or what additional actions might be needed.*

Decision making is the essence of management. It's what managers do (or try to avoid). And all managers would like to make good decisions because they're judged on the outcomes of those decisions. In this chapter, we examine the concept of decision making and how managers make decisions.

THE **decision-making process**

LO2.1 In 2016, actor Will Smith, director Spike Lee, and others publicly announced that they would boycott the Academy Awards ceremony. Their protest came on the heels of the announcement of the Oscar nominations, which did not include any African

American filmmakers or actors. Such protest would tarnish the reputation of the award's sponsor, the Academy of Motion Picture Arts and Sciences. Management promptly analyzed the root cause of the nomination process, which they determined to be a homogenous membership base, consisting primarily of older, white males. In response, the Academy's management board decided to change the racial composition of the Academy by radically altering the Academy's rules for membership—something that had not been done in the 90-year history of the organization.

Although most decisions managers make don't require radical changes, you can see that decisions—choices, judgments—play an important role in what an organization has to do or is able to do.

decision
A choice among two or more alternatives

Managers at all levels and in all areas of organizations make **decisions**. That is, they make choices. For instance, top-level managers make decisions about their organization's goals, where to locate manufacturing facilities, or what new markets to move into. Middle- and lower-level managers make decisions about production schedules, product quality problems, pay raises, and employee discipline. Our focus in this chapter is on how *managers* make decisions, but making decisions isn't something that just managers do. All organizational members make decisions that affect their jobs and the organization they work for.

Although decision making is typically described as choosing among alternatives, there's more to it than that! Why? Because decision making is (and should be) a process, not just a simple act of choosing among alternatives.[1] Even for something as straightforward as deciding where to go for lunch, you do more than just choose burgers or pizza or hot dogs. Granted, you may not spend a lot of time contemplating your lunch decision, but you still go through the process when making that decision. Exhibit 2-1 shows the eight steps in the decision-making process. This process is as relevant to personal decisions as it is to corporate decisions. Let's use an example—a manager deciding what laptop computers to purchase—to illustrate the steps in the process.

Step 1: Identify a Problem

problem
An obstacle that makes it difficult to achieve a desired goal or purpose

Your team is dysfunctional, your customers are leaving, or your plans are no longer relevant.[2] Every decision starts with a **problem**, a discrepancy between an existing and a desired condition.[3] Let's work through an example. Amanda is a sales manager whose reps need new laptops because their old ones are outdated and inadequate for doing their job. To make it simple, assume it's not economical to add memory to the old computers and it's the company's policy to purchase, not lease. Now we have a problem—a disparity between the sales reps' current computers (existing condition) and their need to have more efficient ones (desired condition). Amanda has a decision to make.

How do managers identify problems? In the real world, most problems don't come with neon signs flashing "problem." When her reps started complaining about their computers, it was pretty clear to Amanda that something needed to be done, but few problems are that obvious. Managers also have to be cautious not to confuse problems with symptoms of the problem. Is a 5 percent drop in sales a problem? Or are declining sales merely a symptom of the real problem, such as poor-quality products, high prices, bad advertising, or shifting consumer preferences?[4] For example, McDonald's Corporation has fallen on hard times in recent years as its sales have declined substantially.[5] Also, keep in mind that problem identification is subjective. One possibility for McDonald's sales decline is the different preferences of younger generations compared to the older generations who "grew up" eating McDonald's hamburgers and french fries. One manager might consider this to be the problem, but another manager might not. In addition, a manager who resolves the wrong problem perfectly is likely to perform just as poorly as the manager who doesn't even recognize a problem and does nothing. For instance, what if McDonald's management were to attribute sales declines exclusively to its advertising campaign rather than to changing consumer preferences? As you can see, effectively identifying problems is important, but not easy.[6]

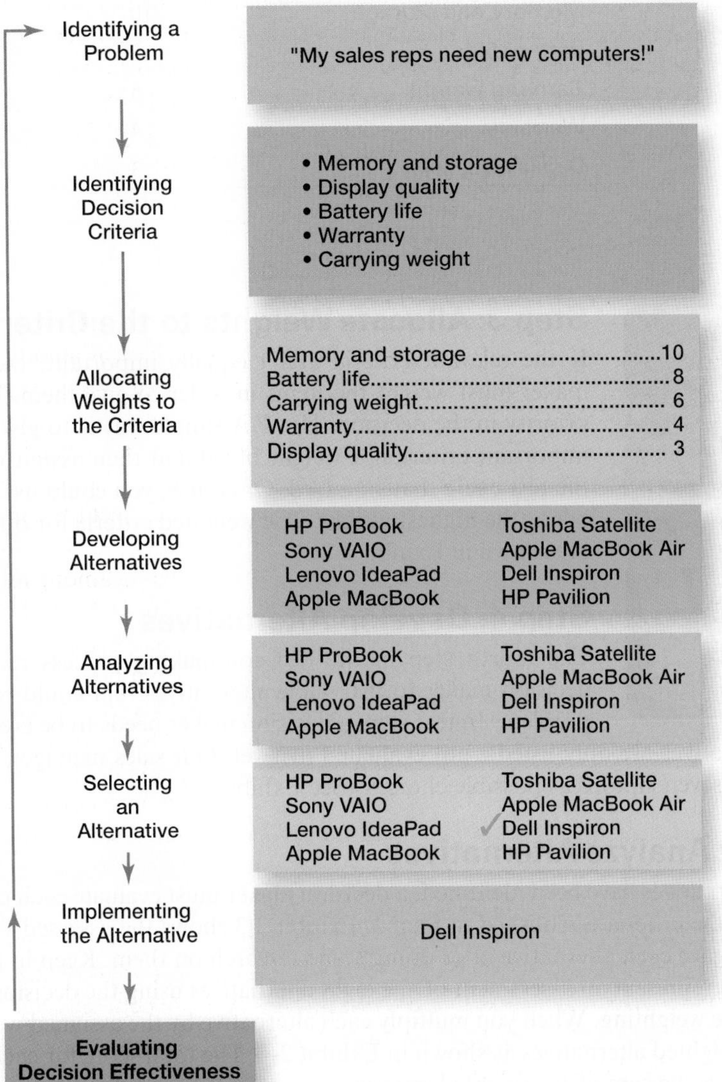

Exhibit 2-1
Decision-Making Process

Step 2: Identify Decision Criteria

Once a manager has identified a problem, he or she must identify the **decision criteria** important or relevant to resolving the problem. Every decision maker has criteria guiding his or her decisions even if they're not explicitly stated. In our example, Amanda decides after careful consideration that memory and storage capabilities, display quality, battery life, warranty, and carrying weight are the relevant criteria in her decision.

decision criteria
Criteria that define what's important or relevant to resolving a problem

Sometimes, decision criteria change. For instance, considering the demographics, interests, and preferences of consumers were essential criteria in making advertising decisions. Nowadays, many companies realize that those criteria in making advertising choices are not sufficient because consumers are more multifaceted.[7] We work, read books for pleasure, take vacations, enjoy eating out, and so forth. Understanding the psychology of consumers at different moments is shown to be more effective than relying exclusively on demographics and interests.[8] Mobile technology enables consumers to be influenced by companies with ease and when consumers need it most. For example, restaurants that want to attract travelers and locals who seek new eating experiences are signing up with mobile apps like RoundMenu. Based in the United Arab Emirates, RoundMenu understands that consumers routinely rely on apps for everyday needs like finding a restaurant. Therefore, the RoundMenu app makes it easy for users to browse restaurant listings and menus, reserve a table, or order meals for home delivery.[9]

Exhibit 2-2
Important Decision Criteria

Memory and storage	10
Battery life	8
Carrying weight	6
Warranty	4
Display quality	3

The eight-step decision-making process begins with identifying a problem and ends with evaluating the result of the decision. After identifying the need to buy new laptop computers for her sales reps, the manager must identify relevant criteria such as price, display quality, and memory that will help guide her final decision.
Source: Alex Segre/Alamy Stock Photo

Step 3: Allocate Weights to the Criteria

If the relevant criteria aren't equally important, the decision maker must weight the items in order to give them the correct priority in the decision. How? A simple way is to give the most important criterion a weight of 10 and then assign weights to the rest using that standard. Of course, you could use any number as the highest weight. The weighted criteria for our example are shown in Exhibit 2-2.

Step 4: Develop Alternatives

The fourth step in the decision-making process requires the decision maker to list viable alternatives that could resolve the problem. In this step, a decision maker needs to be creative, and the alternatives are only listed—not evaluated just yet. Our sales manager, Amanda, identifies seven laptops as possible choices. (See Exhibit 2-3.)

Step 5: Analyze Alternatives

Once alternatives have been identified, a decision maker must evaluate each one. How? By using the criteria established in Step 2. Exhibit 2-3 shows the assessed values that Amanda gave each alternative after doing some research on them. Keep in mind that these data represent an assessment of the eight alternatives using the decision criteria, but *not* the weighting. When you multiply each alternative by the assigned weight, you get the weighted alternatives as shown in Exhibit 2-4. The total score for each alternative, then, is the sum of its weighted criteria.

Sometimes a decision maker might be able to skip this step. If one alternative scores highest on every criterion, you wouldn't need to consider the weights because that alternative would already be the top choice. Or if the weights were all equal, you could evaluate an alternative merely by summing up the assessed values for each one. (Look again at Exhibit 2-3.) For example, the score for the HP ProBook would be 36, and the score for the Apple MacBook Air would be 35.

Exhibit 2-3
Possible Alternatives

	Memory and Storage	Battery Life	Carrying Weight	Warranty	Display Quality
HP ProBook	10	3	10	8	5
Lenovo IdeaPad	8	5	7	10	10
Apple MacBook	8	7	7	8	7
Toshiba Satellite	7	8	7	8	7
Apple MacBook Air	8	3	6	10	8
Dell Inspiron	10	7	8	6	7
HP Pavilion	4	10	4	8	10

Exhibit 2-4
Evaluation of Alternatives

	Memory and Storage	Battery Life	Carrying Weight	Warranty	Display Quality	Total
HP ProBook	100	24	60	32	15	231
Lenovo IdeaPad	80	40	42	40	30	232
Apple MacBook	80	56	42	32	21	231
Toshiba Satellite	70	64	42	32	21	229
Apple MacBook Air	80	24	36	40	24	204
Dell Inspiron	100	56	48	24	21	249
HP Pavilion	40	80	24	32	30	206

Step 6: Select an Alternative

The sixth step in the decision-making process is choosing the best alternative or the one that generated the highest total in Step 5. In our example (Exhibit 2-4), Amanda would choose the Dell Inspiron because it scored higher than all other alternatives (249 total).

Step 7: Implement the Alternative

In Step 7 in the decision-making process, you put the decision into action by conveying it to those affected and getting their commitment to it. We know that if the people who must implement a decision participate in the process, they're more likely to support it than if you just tell them what to do. Another thing managers may need to do during implementation is reassess the environment for any changes, especially if it's a long-term decision. Are the criteria, alternatives, and choices still the best ones, or has the environment changed in such a way that we need to reevaluate? For instance, businesses that offer goods and services with an online component must secure private customer data, such as passwords and payment details. However, even companies that have taken steps to protect customer data are rethinking their criteria and alternatives because of a dramatic increase in cybercrime. VTech Holdings, a Hong Kong company that makes tech-enabled toys, is a case in point. After a VTech website for children was hacked, the company was criticized for being slow to confirm the breach and notify parents to change passwords. After investigating, VTech's executives hired a cybersecurity consulting firm to strengthen online defenses. Later, they relaunched the website with updated terms of use disclosing the potential problems, saying no company can offer a 100 percent guarantee that it won't be hacked.[10]

Step 8: Evaluate Decision Effectiveness

The last step in the decision-making process involves evaluating the outcome or result of the decision to see whether the problem was resolved. If the evaluation shows that the problem still exists, then the manager needs to assess what went wrong. Was the problem incorrectly defined? Were errors made when evaluating alternatives? Was the right alternative selected but poorly implemented? For example, following BP's catastrophic Deepwater Horizon oil spill in the Gulf of Mexico, CEO Tony Hayward (now former) issued an apology to the public that was poorly conceived and executed. In response to the spill, Hayward said: "We are sorry for the massive disruption it's caused their lives. There's no one who wants this thing over more than I do. I'd like my life back."[11] Indeed, it was the right decision to issue an apology to the victims. But Hayward's decision to include himself as a victim was poorly conceived. The answers to the questions asked as a result of evaluating the outcome might lead you to redo an earlier step or might even require starting the whole process over. In this particular case, Hayward did not have this opportunity because he resigned in the wake of public outcry.

- Decision making is the essence of management.[12]

APPROACHES to decision making

LO2.2 Although everyone in an organization makes decisions, decision making is particularly important to managers. As Exhibit 2-5 shows, it's part of all four managerial functions. That's why managers—when they plan, organize, lead, and control—are called *decision makers*.

The fact that almost everything a manager does involves making decisions doesn't mean that decisions are always time-consuming, complex, or evident to an outside observer. Most decision making is routine. For instance, every day of the year you make a decision about what to eat for dinner. It's no big deal. You've made the decision thousands of times before. It's a pretty simple decision and can usually be handled quickly. It's the type of decision you almost forget *is* a decision. And managers also make dozens of these routine decisions every day; for example, which employee will work what shift next week, what information should be included in a report, or how to resolve a customer's complaint. Keep in mind that even though a decision seems easy or has been faced by a manager a number of times before, it still is a decision. Let's look at four perspectives on how managers make decisions.

Rationality

rational decision making Describes choices that are logical and consistent and maximize value

We assume that managers will use **rational decision making**; that is, they'll make logical and consistent choices to maximize value.[13] After all, managers have all sorts of tools and techniques to help them be rational decision makers. What does it mean to be a "rational" decision maker?

ASSUMPTIONS OF RATIONALITY A rational decision maker would be fully objective and logical. The problem faced would be clear and unambiguous, and the decision maker would have a clear and specific goal and know all possible alternatives and consequences. Finally, making decisions rationally would consistently lead to selecting

Exhibit 2-5
Decisions Managers May Make

Planning
- What are the organization's long-term objectives?
- What strategies will best achieve those objectives?
- What should the organization's short-term objectives be?
- How difficult should individual goals be?

Organizing
- How many employees should I have report directly to me?
- How much centralization should there be in an organization?
- How should jobs be designed?
- When should the organization implement a different structure?

Leading
- How do I handle employees who appear to be unmotivated?
- What is the most effective leadership style in a given situation?
- How will a specific change affect worker productivity?
- When is the right time to stimulate conflict?

Controlling
- What activities in the organization need to be controlled?
- How should those activities be controlled?
- When is a performance deviation significant?
- What type of management information system should the organization have?

the alternative that maximizes the likelihood of achieving that goal. These assumptions apply to any decision—personal or managerial. However, for managerial decision making, we need to add one additional assumption—decisions are made in the best interests of the organization. These assumptions of rationality aren't very realistic and managers don't always act rationally, but the next concept can help explain how most decisions get made in organizations.

Bounded Rationality

Despite the unrealistic assumptions, managers are *expected* to be rational when making decisions.[14] They understand that "good" decision makers are supposed to do certain things and exhibit good decision-making behaviors as they identify problems, consider alternatives, gather information, and act decisively but prudently. When they do so, they show others that they're competent and that their decisions are the result of intelligent deliberation. However, a more realistic approach to describing how managers make decisions is the concept of **bounded rationality**, which says that managers make decisions rationally, but are limited (bounded) by their ability to process information.[15] Because they can't possibly analyze all information on all alternatives, managers **satisfice**, rather than maximize. That is, they accept solutions that are "good enough." They're being rational within the limits (bounds) of their ability to process information. Let's look at an example.

bounded rationality
Decision making that's rational, but limited (bounded) by an individual's ability to process information

satisfice
Accept solutions that are "good enough"

Suppose you're a finance major and upon graduation you want a job, preferably as a personal financial planner with a minimum salary of $55,000 and within 100 miles of your hometown. You accept a job offer as a business credit analyst—not exactly a personal financial planner but still in the finance field—at a bank 50 miles from home at a starting salary of $47,500. If you had done a more comprehensive job search, you would have discovered a job in personal financial planning at a trust company only 25 miles from your hometown and starting at a salary of $55,000. You weren't a perfectly rational decision maker because you didn't maximize your decision by searching all possible alternatives and then choosing the best. But because the first job offer was satisfactory (or "good enough"), you behaved in a bounded-rationality manner by accepting it.

Most decisions that managers make don't fit the assumptions of perfect rationality, so they satisfice. However, keep in mind that their decision making is also likely influenced by the organization's culture, internal politics, power considerations, and by a phenomenon called **escalation of commitment**, an increased commitment to a previous decision despite evidence that it may have been wrong.[16] The *Challenger* space shuttle disaster is often used as an example of escalation of commitment. Decision makers chose to launch the shuttle that day even though the decision was questioned by several individuals who believed it was a bad one. Why would decision makers escalate commitment to a bad decision? Because they don't want to admit that their initial decision may have been flawed. Rather than search for new alternatives, they simply increase their commitment to the original solution.

escalation of commitment
An increased commitment to a previous decision despite evidence it may have been wrong

Netflix CEO Reed Hastings relies on what he calls "informed intuition" in the development of original programming, which plays a major role in the company's international growth. Although Netflix invests heavily in data analytics, Hastings says that intuition is as important as data in making final decisions. *Source: Tobias Hase/picture alliance / dpa/ Newscom*

Intuition

When managers at stapler-maker Swingline saw the company's market share declining, they used a logical scientific approach to address the issue. For three years, they exhaustively researched stapler users before deciding what new products to develop. However, at Accentra, Inc., founder Todd Moses used a more intuitive decision approach to come up with his line of unique PaperPro staplers.[17]

Exhibit 2-6
What Is Intuition?

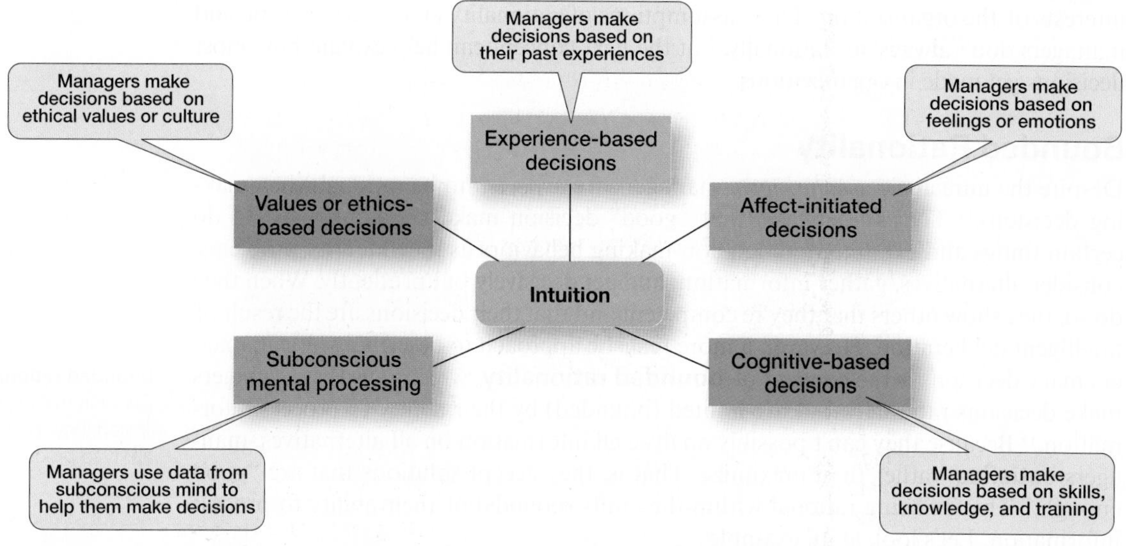

Source: Based on L. A. Burke and M. K. Miller, "Taking the Mystery Out of Intuitive Decision Making," *Academy of Management Executive*, October 1999, pp. 91–99.

intuitive decision making
Making decisions on the basis of experience, feelings, and accumulated judgment

Like Todd Moses, managers often use their intuition to help their decision making. What is **intuitive decision making**? It's making decisions on the basis of experience, feelings, and accumulated judgment. Researchers studying managers' use of intuitive decision making have identified five different aspects of intuition, which are described in Exhibit 2-6.[18] How common is intuitive decision making? One survey found that almost half of the executives surveyed "used intuition more often than formal analysis to run their companies."[19]

Intuitive decision making can complement both rational and bounded rational decision making.[20] First of all, a manager who has had experience with a similar type of problem or situation often can act quickly with what appears to be limited information because of that past experience. In addition, a recent study found that individuals who experienced intense feelings and emotions when making decisions actually achieved higher decision-making performance, especially when they understood their feelings as they were making decisions. The old belief that managers should ignore emotions when making decisions may not be the best advice.[21]

★ Watch It 1!

If your professor has assigned this, go to **www.mymanagementlab.com** to watch a video titled *CH2MHill Decision Making* and to respond to questions.

Evidence-Based Management

Sales associates at the cosmetics counter at department store Bon-Ton Stores, Inc. had the highest turnover of any store sales group. Using a data-driven decision approach, managers devised a more precise pre-employment assessment test. Now, not only do they have lower turnover, they actually have better hires.[22]

Suppose you were exhibiting some strange, puzzling physical symptoms. In order to make the best decisions about proper diagnosis and treatment, wouldn't you want your doctor to base her decisions on the best available evidence? Now suppose you're a manager faced with putting together an employee recognition program. Wouldn't you want those decisions also to be based on the best available evidence?

let's get REAL

The Scenario:

Juan Hernandez is a successful business owner. His landscaping business is growing, and a few months ago he decided to bring in somebody to manage his office operations since he had little time to keep on top of that activity. However, this individual can't seem to make a decision without agonizing about it over and over and on and on.

What could Juan do to help this person become a better decision maker?

Juan could give his office assistant a more complete picture of the tasks at hand for the day/week/month as well as timelines for each. It would force his decision to be made within a certain timeframe as well as give him a bigger-picture view of the workload. It would make him realize that there are many more tasks to accomplish.

Prudence Rufus
Business Owner/Photographer

Source: Prudence Rufus

"Any decision-making process is likely to be enhanced through the use of relevant and reliable evidence, whether it's buying someone a birthday present or wondering which new washing machine to buy."[23] That's the premise behind **evidence-based management (EBMgt)**, the "systematic use of the best available evidence to improve management practice."[24]

evidence-based management (EBMgt)
The systematic use of the best available evidence to improve management practice

EBMgt is quite relevant to managerial decision making. The four essential elements of EBMgt are (1) the decision maker's expertise and judgment; (2) external evidence that's been evaluated by the decision maker; (3) opinions, preferences, and values of those who have a stake in the decision; and (4) relevant organizational (internal) factors such as context, circumstances, and organizational members. The strength or influence of each of these elements on a decision will vary with each decision. Sometimes, the decision maker's intuition (judgment) might be given greater emphasis in the decision; other times it might be the opinions of stakeholders; and at other times, it might be ethical considerations (organizational context). The key for managers is to recognize and understand the mindful, conscious choice as to which elements are most important and should be emphasized in making a decision.

TYPES of decisions and decision-making conditions

LO2.3 Restaurant managers in Portland make routine decisions weekly about purchasing food supplies and scheduling employee work shifts. It's something they've done numerous times. But now they're facing a different kind of decision—one they've never encountered: how to adapt to a new law requiring that nutritional information be posted.

- The more trust employees have in their managers, the more likely the employees are to expect organizational outcomes to be favorable and the more likely they are to expect that the procedures used by authorities to plan and implement decisions will be fair.[25]

Types of Decisions

Such situations aren't all that unusual. Managers in all kinds of organizations face different types of problems and decisions as they do their jobs. Depending on the nature of the problem, a manager can use one of two different types of decisions.

STRUCTURED PROBLEMS AND PROGRAMMED DECISIONS Some problems are straightforward. The decision maker's goal is clear, the problem is familiar, and information about the problem is easily defined and complete. Examples might include when a customer returns a purchase to a store, when a supplier is late with an important delivery, a news team's response to a fast-breaking event, or a college's handling of a student wanting to drop a class. Such situations are called **structured problems** because they're straightforward, familiar, and easily defined. For instance, a server spills a drink on a customer's coat. The customer is upset and the manager needs to do something. Because it's not an unusual occurrence, there's probably some standardized routine for handling it. For example, the manager offers to have the coat cleaned at the restaurant's expense. This is what we call a **programmed decision**, a repetitive decision that can be handled by a routine approach. Because the problem is structured, the manager doesn't have to go to the trouble and expense of going through an involved decision process. The "develop-the-alternatives" stage of the decision-making process either doesn't exist or is given little attention. Why? Because once the structured problem is defined, the solution is usually self-evident or at least reduced to a few alternatives that are familiar and have proved successful in the past. The spilled drink on the customer's coat doesn't require the restaurant manager to identify and weight decision criteria or to develop a long list of possible solutions. Instead, the manager relies on one of three types of programmed decisions: procedure, rule, or policy.

structured problems
Straightforward, familiar, and easily defined problems

programmed decision
A repetitive decision that can be handled by a routine approach

A **procedure** is a series of sequential steps a manager uses to respond to a structured problem. The only difficulty is identifying the problem. Once it's clear, so is the procedure. For instance, a purchasing manager receives a request from a warehouse manager for 15 tablets for the inventory clerks. The purchasing manager knows how to make this decision by following the established purchasing procedure.

procedure
A series of sequential steps used to respond to a well-structured problem

A **rule** is an explicit statement that tells a manager what can or cannot be done. Rules are frequently used because they're simple to follow and ensure consistency. For example, rules about lateness and absenteeism permit supervisors to make disciplinary decisions rapidly and fairly.

rule
An explicit statement that tells managers what can or cannot be done

The third type of programmed decisions is a **policy**, a guideline for making a decision. In contrast to a rule, a policy establishes general parameters for the decision maker rather than specifically stating what should or should not be done. Policies typically contain an ambiguous term that leaves interpretation up to the decision maker. Here are some sample policy statements:

policy
A guideline for making decisions

- The customer always comes first and should always be *satisfied.*
- We promote from within, *whenever possible*.
- Employee wages shall be *competitive* within community standards.

Notice that the terms *satisfied, whenever possible*, and *competitive* require interpretation. For instance, the policy of paying competitive wages doesn't tell a company's human resources manager the exact amount he or she should pay, but it does guide the manager in making the decision.

Decision Making, Part 1—If your instructor is using Pearson MyLab Management, log onto **mymanagementlab.com** and test your *decision-making knowledge*. **Be sure to refer back to the chapter opener!**

UNSTRUCTURED PROBLEMS AND NONPROGRAMMED DECISIONS Not all the problems managers face can be solved using programmed decisions. Many organizational situations involve **unstructured problems**, new or unusual problems for which information is ambiguous or incomplete. After more than 50 years of separation between the United States and Cuba, how the United States

unstructured problems
Problems that are new or unusual and for which information is ambiguous or incomplete

Characteristic	Programmed Decisions	Nonprogrammed Decisions
Type of problem	Structured	Unstructured
Managerial level	Lower levels	Upper levels
Frequency	Repetitive, routine	New, unusual
Information	Readily available	Ambiguous or incomplete
Goals	Clear, specific	Vague
Time frame for solution	Short	Relatively long
Solution relies on...	Procedures, rules, policies	Judgment and creativity

Exhibit 2-7
Programmed Versus Nonprogrammed Decisions

government builds economic ties with Cuba is an example of an unstructured problem. So, too, is the problem facing American HR professionals who must decide how to modify their health insurance plans to comply with the Patient Protection and Affordable Care Act. When problems are unstructured, managers must rely on nonprogrammed decision making in order to develop unique solutions. **Nonprogrammed decisions** are unique and nonrecurring and involve custom-made solutions.

nonprogrammed decisions
Unique and nonrecurring decisions that require a custom-made solution

Exhibit 2-7 describes the differences between programmed and nonprogrammed decisions. Lower-level managers mostly rely on programmed decisions (procedures, rules, and policies) because they confront familiar and repetitive problems. As managers move up the organizational hierarchy, the problems they confront become more unstructured. Why? Because lower-level managers handle the routine decisions and let upper-level managers deal with the unusual or difficult decisions. Also, upper-level managers delegate routine decisions to their subordinates so they can deal with more difficult issues.[26] Thus, few managerial decisions in the real world are either fully programmed or nonprogrammed. Most fall somewhere in between.

If your professor has assigned this, go to **www.mymanagementlab.com** to complete the Writing Assignment *MGMT 8: Decision Making.*

Decision-Making Conditions

When making decisions, managers may face three different conditions: certainty, risk, and uncertainty. Let's look at the characteristics of each.

CERTAINTY The ideal situation for making decisions is one of **certainty**, a situation where a manager can make accurate decisions because the outcome of every alternative is known. For example, entrepreneurs and business managers in Sweden can be certain they will receive prompt payment for goods and services when they decide to allow customers to make purchases through financial services apps like iZettle and Trustly. As you might expect, the outcomes of most managerial decisions are not as certain.[27]

certainty
A situation in which a manager can make accurate decisions because all outcomes are known

RISK A far more common situation is one of **risk**, conditions in which the decision maker is able to estimate the likelihood of certain outcomes. Under risk, managers have historical data from past personal experiences or secondary information that lets them assign probabilities to different alternatives. Let's do an example.

risk
A situation in which the decision maker is able to estimate the likelihood of certain outcomes

Suppose you manage a Colorado ski resort, and you're thinking about adding another lift. Obviously, your decision will be influenced by the additional revenue that the new lift would generate, which depends on snowfall. You have fairly reliable weather data from the last 10 years on snowfall levels in your area—three years of heavy snowfall, five years of normal snowfall, and two years of light snow. And you have good information on the amount of revenues generated during each level of snow. You can use this information to help you make your decision by calculating expected value—the expected return from each possible outcome—by multiplying expected revenues by snowfall probabilities. The result is the average revenue you can expect over time if the given probabilities hold. As Exhibit 2-8 shows, the expected revenue from adding a new ski lift is $687,500. Of course, whether that's enough to justify a decision to build depends on the costs involved in generating that revenue.

UNCERTAINTY The general manager and employees of the Fukushima Daini nuclear power plant in Japan faced a crisis because of the damage that resulted from an earthquake and tsunami. A strong possibility existed for a catastrophic nuclear meltdown and explosion at the power plant. Many possible factors could

FUTURE VISION Crowdsourcing Decisions

The Hershey Co. needs to find a way to keep their chocolates cool when shipping during the summer months or in warmer climates.[28] To meet this challenge, Hershey is turning to the crowd. Instead of looking for a solution within the company, management is using a crowdsourcing innovation competition to solve this supply chain management problem. Anyone can submit an idea, and the contest winner gets $25,000 in development funds and the opportunity to collaborate with Hershey to develop the proposed solution.

Finding innovative solutions to problems is one of several uses of crowdsourcing in organizations. Crowdsourcing can help managers gather insights from customers, employees, or other groups to help make decisions such as what products to develop, where they should invest, or even who to promote. Powered by the collective experiences and ideas of many, crowdsourcing can help managers make better informed decisions by getting input from the front line and beyond.

Crowdsourcing is not new in the business world. One of the first examples of a business using crowdsourcing occurred in 1916 when Planters Peanuts held a contest to create its logo. However, today's Internet connectivity provides businesses quick and easy access to insights from customers and employees, effectively tapping into their cumulative wisdom. This connectivity, coupled with new software applications that facilitate crowdsourcing, gives it the potential to significantly impact the future of organizational decision making.

The ability of crowdsourcing to help organizations make decisions and solve problems will depend on management's ability to effectively harness the power of the crowd. Harvard Business School Professor Karim Lakhani suggests that organizations must find the right people and create appropriate incentives to motivate them to contribute. Effective crowdsourcing must draw a diversity of opinions that are independent of one another. Organizations must also have a mechanism to aggregate individual responses into a collective opinion in order to support the use of crowdsourcing in decision making.

Crowdsourcing could be a game changer for making decisions in organizations if used strategically. We could see a shift from the traditional model of decision making led from the top of the hierarchy to more effective decisions driven by customers, employees, or others. This revolution in the decision-making process could challenge conventional management practices, requiring new skills from managers.

*If your professor has chosen to assign this, go to **www.mymanagementlab.com** to discuss the following questions.*

TALK ABOUT IT 1: How can crowdsourcing help managers make better decisions?

TALK ABOUT IT 2: What are some risks in using crowdsourcing to make decisions?

Event	Expected Revenues	×	Probability	=	Expected Value of Each Alternative
Heavy snowfall	$850,000		0.3		$255,000
Normal snowfall	725,000		0.5		362,500
Light snowfall	350,000		0.2		70,000
					$687,500

Exhibit 2-8
Expected Value

have led to these outcomes, including whether vital systems damaged in the quake could be repaired and whether aftershocks would further destabilize the nuclear reactors. What happens if you face a decision where you're not certain about the outcomes and can't even make reasonable probability estimates? We call this condition **uncertainty**. Managers face decision-making situations of uncertainty. Under these conditions, the choice of alternatives is influenced by the limited amount of available information and by the psychological orientation of the decision maker. An optimistic manager will follow a *maximax* choice (maximizing the maximum possible payoff); a pessimist will follow a *maximin* choice (maximizing the minimum possible payoff); and a manager who desires to minimize his maximum "regret" will opt for a *minimax* choice. Let's look at these different choice approaches using an example.

uncertainty
A situation in which a decision maker has neither certainty nor reasonable probability estimates available

A marketing manager at Visa has determined four possible strategies (S_1, S_2, S_3, and S_4) for promoting the Visa card throughout the West Coast region of the United States. The marketing manager also knows that major competitor MasterCard has three competitive actions (CA_1, CA_2, and CA_3) it's using to promote its card in the same region. For this example, we'll assume that the Visa manager had no previous knowledge that would allow her to determine probabilities of success of any of the four strategies. She formulates the matrix shown in Exhibit 2-9 to show the various Visa strategies and the resulting profit, depending on the competitive action used by MasterCard.

In this example, if our Visa manager is an optimist, she'll choose strategy 4 (S_4) because that could produce the largest possible gain: $28 million. Note that this choice maximizes the maximum possible gain (maximax choice).

If our manager is a pessimist, she'll assume that only the worst can occur. The worst outcome for each strategy is as follows: S_1 = $11 million; S_2 = $9 million; S_3 = $15 million; S_4 = $14 million. These are the most pessimistic outcomes from each strategy. Following the *maximin* choice, she would maximize the minimum payoff; in other words, she'd select S_3 ($15 million is the largest of the minimum payoffs).

In the third approach, managers recognize that once a decision is made, it will not necessarily result in the most profitable payoff. There may be a "regret" of profits given up—*regret* referring to the amount of money that could have

Visa Marketing Strategy (in millions of dollars)	MasterCard's Competitive Action		
	CA_1	CA_2	CA_3
S_1	13	14	11
S_2	9	15	18
S_3	24	21	15
S_4	18	14	28

Exhibit 2-9
Payoff Matrix

Exhibit 2-10
Regret Matrix

Visa Marketing Strategy (in millions of dollars)	MasterCard's Competitive Action		
	CA_1	CA_2	CA_3
S_1	11	7	17
S_2	15	6	10
S_3	0	0	13
S_4	6	7	0

LEADER making a DIFFERENCE

Source: Kristoffer Tripplaar/ Sipa USA (Sipa via AP Images)

He's not your typical CEO. In fact, some might call him a little crazy, except for the fact that his track record at turning crazy ideas into profitable ventures is pretty good. We're talking about ***Elon Musk.***[29] *In 2002, he sold his second Internet startup, PayPal, to eBay for $1.5 billion. (His first company, a Web software firm, was acquired by Compaq.) Currently, Musk is CEO of Space Exploration Technologies (SpaceX) and Tesla Motors, and chairman and largest shareholder of SolarCity, an energy technology company. SpaceX, which builds rockets for companies and countries to put satellites in space, was the first private company to deliver cargo to the International Space Station. It's reigniting interest in space exploration. Tesla Motors is the world's most prominent maker of electric cars and is proving that electric cars can be green, sexy, and profitable. SolarCity is now the leading provider of domestic solar panels in the United States. Each of these ventures has transformed (or is transforming) an industry: PayPal—Internet payments; Tesla—automobiles; SpaceX—aeronautics; and SolarCity—energy. As a decision maker, Musk deals mostly with unstructured problems in risky conditions. However, like other business innovators, Musk is comfortable with that and in pursuing what many might consider "crazy" idea territory. His genius has been compared to that of the late Steve Jobs. And* Fortune *magazine named him the 2013 Businessperson of the Year.* What can you learn from this leader making a difference?

been made had a different strategy been used. Managers calculate regret by subtracting all possible payoffs in each category from the maximum possible payoff for each given event, in this case for each competitive action. For our Visa manager, the highest payoff—given that MasterCard engages in CA_1, CA_2, or CA_3—is $24 million, $21 million, or $28 million, respectively (the highest number in each column). Subtracting the payoffs in Exhibit 2-9 from those figures produces the results shown in Exhibit 2-10.

The maximum regrets are S_1 = $17 million; S_2 = $15 million; S_3 = $13 million; and S_4 = $7 million. The *minimax* choice minimizes the maximum regret, so our Visa manager would choose S_4. By making this choice, she'll never have a regret of profits given up of more than $7 million. This result contrasts, for example, with a regret of $15 million had she chosen S_2 and MasterCard had taken CA_1.

Although managers try to quantify a decision when possible by using payoff and regret matrices, uncertainty often forces them to rely more on intuition, creativity, hunches, and "gut feel."

If your professor has assigned this, go to **www.mymanagementlab.com** to watch a video titled *Gaviña Gourmet Coffee: Organizational Behavior* and to respond to questions.

DECISION-MAKING **biases and errors**

LO2.4 When managers make decisions, they may use "rules of thumb," or **heuristics**, to simplify their decision making. Rules of thumb can be useful because they help make sense of complex, uncertain, and ambiguous information.[30] Even though managers may use rules of thumb, that doesn't mean those rules are reliable. Why? Because they may lead to errors and biases in processing and

heuristics
Rules of thumb that managers use to simplify decision making

Exhibit 2-11
Common Decision-Making Biases

evaluating information. Exhibit 2-11 identifies 12 common decision errors of managers and biases they may have. Let's look at each.[31]

When decision makers tend to think they know more than they do or hold unrealistically positive views of themselves and their performance, they're exhibiting the *overconfidence bias.* The *immediate gratification bias* describes decision makers who tend to want immediate rewards and to avoid immediate costs. For these individuals, decision choices that provide quick payoffs are more appealing than those with payoffs in the future. The *anchoring effect* describes how decision makers fixate on initial information as a starting point and then, once set, fail to adequately adjust for subsequent information. First impressions, ideas, prices, and estimates carry unwarranted weight relative to information received later. When decision makers selectively organize and interpret events based on their biased perceptions, they're using the *selective perception bias*. This influences the information they pay attention to, the problems they identify, and the alternatives they develop. Decision makers who seek out information that reaffirms their past choices and discounts information that contradicts past judgments exhibit the *confirmation bias.* These people tend to accept at face value information that confirms their preconceived views and are critical and skeptical of information that challenges these views. The *framing bias* occurs when decision makers select and highlight certain aspects of a situation while excluding others. By drawing attention to specific aspects of a situation and highlighting them, while at the same time downplaying or omitting other aspects, they distort what they see and create incorrect reference points. The *availability bias* happens when decision makers tend to remember events that are the most recent and vivid in their memory. The result? It distorts their ability to recall events in an objective manner and results in distorted judgments and probability estimates. When decision makers assess the likelihood of an event based on how closely it resembles other events or sets of events, that's the *representation bias.* Managers exhibiting this bias draw analogies and see identical situations where they don't exist. The *randomness bias* describes the actions of decision makers who try to create meaning out of random events. They do this because most decision makers have difficulty dealing with chance even though random events happen to everyone, and there's nothing that can be done to predict them. The *sunk costs error* occurs when decision makers forget that current choices can't correct the past. They incorrectly fixate on past expenditures of time, money, or effort in assessing choices rather than on future consequences. Instead of ignoring sunk costs, they can't forget them. Decision makers who are quick to take credit for their successes and to blame failure on outside factors are exhibiting the *self-serving bias.* Finally, the *hindsight bias* is the tendency

- When managers reduced the effects of bias in their decision making, their organizations' performance returns were 7 percent higher.[32]

for decision makers to falsely believe that they would have accurately predicted the outcome of an event once that outcome is actually known.

Managers avoid the negative effects of these decision errors and biases by being aware of them and then not using them! Fortunately, some research shows that training can successfully engage employees to recognize particular decision-making biases and reduce subsequent biased decision making with a long-lasting effect.[33] Beyond that, managers also should pay attention to "how" they make decisions and try to identify the heuristics they typically use and critically evaluate the appropriateness of those heuristics. Finally, managers might want to ask trusted individuals to help them identify weaknesses in their decision-making style and try to improve on those weaknesses. For example, Christopher Cabrera, founder and CEO of Xactly, did just that. "I had a seasoned boss who was a wonderful mentor, and he really helped me with hiring and understanding how to create diverse teams. The company was growing quickly, and hiring was a big part of my job."[34]

Decision Making, Part 2—If your instructor is using Pearson MyLab Management, log onto **mymanagementlab.com** and test your *decision-making knowledge.* **Be sure to refer back to the chapter opener!**

Overview of Managerial Decision Making

Exhibit 2-12 provides an overview of managerial decision making. Because it's in their best interests, managers *want* to make good decisions—that is, choose the "best" alternative, implement it, and determine whether it takes care of the problem, which is the reason the decision was needed in the first place. Their decision-making process is affected by four factors: the decision-making approach, the type of problem, decision-making conditions, and certain decision-making errors and biases. So whether a decision involves addressing an employee's habitual tardiness, resolving a product quality problem, or determining whether to enter a new market, it has been shaped by a number of factors.

Exhibit 2-12
Overview of Managerial Decision Making

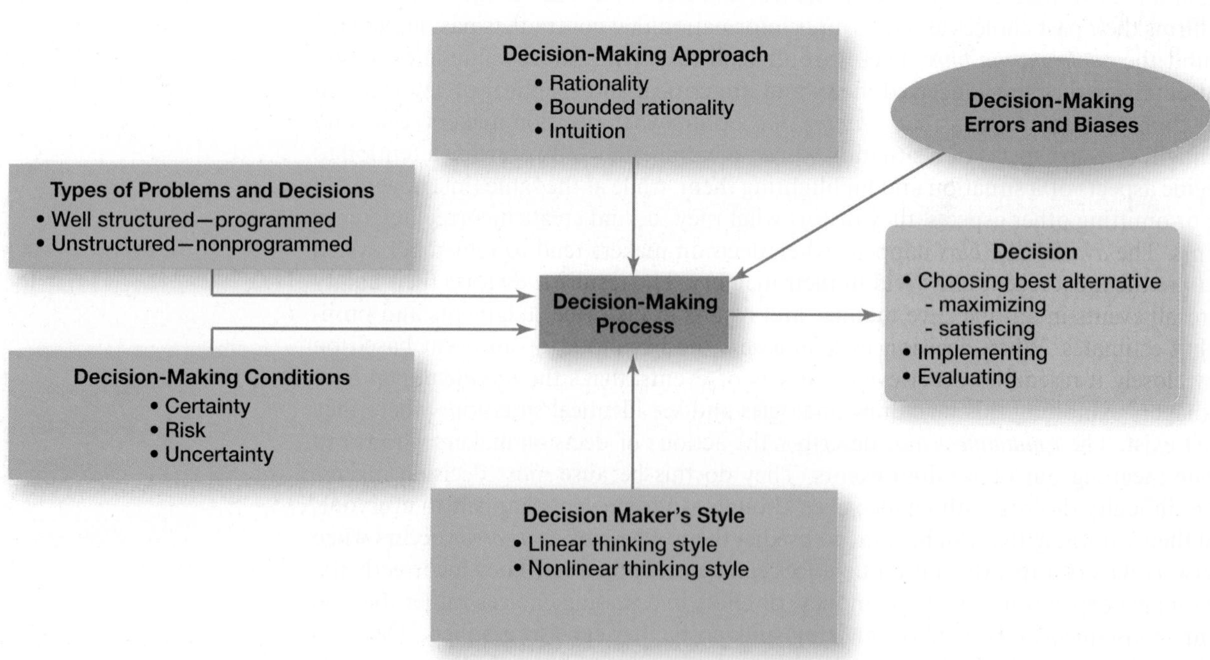

WORKPLACE **CONFIDENTIAL** Making Good Decisions

Life comes with tough decisions. And so do jobs. The tough decisions start with choosing whether to accept an initial job offer. They often continue with deciding who to befriend and trust at work, whether or not to join a new work team or accept a promotion to a new city, how to respond to a situation that might compromise your ethics, or how to relay bad news to your boss.

Let's begin with the basic tenet that you can't avoid tough decisions by ignoring them. The decision to do nothing *is still a decision.* It's a decision to maintain the status quo.

You can maintain the status quo by following either of two paths—one active and the other passive. You can rationally assess your current situation, identify your options, carefully review the strengths and weaknesses of these options, and conclude that no new alternative is superior to the path you're currently taking. This active approach is fully consistent with rational decision making. Our concern here, however, is with the passive approach—where the current path is followed only because you fail to consider your other options. You don't, for instance, want to find yourself regretting having spent 20 years in a go-nowhere job that you disliked because you avoided looking for other opportunities.

How do you counter the nondecision decision? The first step is awareness. You can't opt out of decisions by ignoring them. To do so is merely choosing to continue along the path you're on. That path may be the one you want, but the astute decision maker recognizes that there are costs associated with maintaining the status quo as well as with change. You also need to directly challenge the status quo. It's not merely enough to know that doing nothing is a decision. You also need to occasionally justify why you *shouldn't* pursue another path that's different from the one you're currently following. Why aren't you looking for other job opportunities? Are the stocks, bonds, and mutual funds in your retirement plan properly aligned to recent changes in the economy? Finally, consider the costs of inaction. Too often we focus only on the risks associated with change. You're less likely to get caught up in decision inaction if you also address the risks related to doing nothing.

We should also take a look at arguably the three most critical errors you're likely to make in your decision making: overconfidence, a short-term focus, and the confirmation bias. While each is briefly mentioned in this chapter, let's take a closer look at them. Conquer these three and you'll go a long way toward improving the quality of your decisions.

It has been said that no problem in judgment and decision making is more prevalent and more potentially catastrophic than overconfidence. Almost all of us suffer from it. When we're given factual questions and asked to judge the probability that our answers are correct, we tend to be far too optimistic. In general, we overestimate our knowledge, undervalue risk, and overestimate our ability to control events.

Studies have found that when people say they're 65 percent to 70 percent confident that they're right, they're actually correct only about 50 percent of the time. And when they say they're 100 percent sure, they tend to be only 70 percent to 85 percent correct.

To reduce overconfidence, begin by recognizing this tendency, and expect it to most likely surface when your confidence is extremely high or when accurate judgments are difficult to make. Next, adjust your confidence awareness to reflect your level of expertise on an issue. You're most likely to be overconfident when you're considering issues outside your expertise. Finally, directly address this bias by challenging yourself to look for reasons why your predictions or answers might be wrong.

A lot of us suffer from the tendency to want to grab for immediate rewards and avoid immediate costs. If it feels good, we want to do it now; if it implies pain, we want to postpone it. This immediate gratification bias explains why it's so hard to diet, quit smoking, avoid credit card debt, or save for retirement. Each comes with an immediate reward—tasty food, an enjoyable cigarette, an immediate purchase, or extra disposable money to spend. And each delays its costs to some nebulous future.

If you see yourself as vulnerable to the immediate gratification bias, what can you do? First, set long-term goals and review them regularly. This can help you focus on the longer term and help you to justify making decisions whose payoff may be far into the future. If you don't know where you want to be in 10 or 20 years, it's easier to discount your future and live for the moment. Second, pay attention to both rewards *and costs.* Our natural tendency is to inflate immediate rewards and underplay future costs. For instance, think about what it would be like to be retired, having no savings and trying to live on a $1200-a-month Social Security check. Or look around for examples of people who didn't plan for their future and now are suffering the consequences.

Finally, the rational decision-making process assumes that we objectively gather information. But we don't. We *selectively* gather information so it confirms our current beliefs, and we dismiss evidence that challenges those beliefs. We also tend to accept at face value information that confirms our preconceived views, while being critical and skeptical of information that challenges these views.

Overcoming this confirmation bias begins by being honest about your motives. Are you seriously trying to get information to make an informed decision, or are you just looking for evidence to confirm what you'd like to do? If you're serious about this, then you need to purposely seek out contrary or disconfirming information. That means you have to be prepared to hear what you don't want to hear. You'll also need to practice skepticism until it becomes habitual. In the same way that a defense attorney seeks contradictory evidence to disprove a plaintiff's case, you have to think of reasons why your beliefs might be wrong and then aggressively seek out evidence that might prove them to be so.

Based on S. P Robbins, *Decide & Conquer: The Ultimate Guide for Improving Your Decision Making*, 2nd ed. (Upper Saddle River, NJ: Pearson Education, 2015).

Korean carmaker Hyundai decided to take the design thinking approach in testing the durability and quality of its i30 hatchback family car by letting a group of 40 safari park baboons examine it for 10 hours. Hyundai hopes that the lessons learned from the excessive wear-and-tear test of the car's parts and interior can be applied to the research and development of future cars.
Source: REX Features/AP Images

EFFECTIVE **decision making in today's world**

LO2.5 Per Carlsson, a product development manager at IKEA, "spends his days creating Volvo-style kitchens at Yugo prices." His job is to take the "problems" identified by the company's product-strategy council (a group of globe-trotting senior managers that monitors consumer trends and establishes product priorities) and turn them into furniture that customers around the world want to buy. One "problem" identified by the council: the kitchen has replaced the living room as the social and entertaining center in the home. Customers are looking for kitchens that convey comfort and cleanliness while still allowing them to pursue their gourmet aspirations. Carlsson must take this information and make things happen. There are a lot of decisions to make—programmed and nonprogrammed—and the fact that IKEA is a global company makes it even more challenging. Comfort in Asia means small, cozy appliances and spaces, while North American customers want oversized glassware and giant refrigerators. His ability to make good decisions quickly has significant implications for IKEA's success.[35] Similarly, hotel giant Hilton Worldwide Holdings plans to diversify its portfolio by establishing a newly branded hotel. The brand, Tru by Hilton, is being established to meet the preferences of a millennial mind-set, regardless of age. CEO Christopher Nassetta is positioning the new brand to people who "are united by a millennial mind-set—a youthful energy, a zest for life and a desire for human connection."[36]

Today's business world revolves around making decisions, often risky ones, usually with incomplete or inadequate information and under intense time pressure. Making good business decisions in today's rapid-paced and messy world isn't easy. Things happen too fast. Customers come and go in the click of a mouse or the swipe of a screen. Market landscapes can shift dramatically overnight along several dimensions. Competitors can enter a market and exit it just as quickly as they entered. Thriving and prospering under such conditions means managerial decision making must adapt to these realities. Most managers make one decision after another; and as if that weren't challenging enough, more is at stake than ever before. Bad decisions can cost millions. What do managers need to do to make effective decisions in today's fast-moving world? First, let's look at some suggested guidelines. Then, we'll discuss an interesting new line of thinking that has implications for making effective decisions—especially for business types—called design thinking.

★ Try It!

If your professor has assigned this, go to **www.mymanagementlab.com** to complete the Simulation: *Decision Making* and see how well you can apply the ideas behind the decision-making process.

Guidelines for Effective Decision Making

Decision making is serious business. Your abilities and track record as an effective decision maker will determine how your organizational work performance is evaluated and whether you'll be promoted to higher and higher positions of responsibility. Here are some additional guidelines to help you be a better decision maker.

- *Understand cultural differences.* Managers everywhere want to make good decisions. However, is there only one "best" way worldwide to make decisions? Or does the "best way depend on the values, beliefs, attitudes, and behavioral patterns of the people involved?"[37] Getting work done is less likely when individuals from one culture are tone deaf to cultural norms elsewhere. For example, L'Oréal's decision-making culture encourages open debate, which management maintains generates creativity.[38] However, that style probably does not fit well with cultural differences in other countries. For example, the company's confrontational approach is inconsistent with the cultural values in Southeast Asia, a region in which they conduct business. An Indonesian employee said, "To an Indonesian person, confrontation in a group setting is extremely negative because it makes the other person lose face. So it's something that we try strongly to avoid in any open manner."[39]

- *Create standards for good decision making.* Good decisions are forward-looking, use available information, consider all available and viable options, and do not create conflicts of interest.[40] The Bill & Melinda Gates Foundation expect employees not to engage in decision making that could create a conflict of interest. "Foundation employees are obligated to avoid and disclose ethical, legal, financial, or other conflicts of interest involving the foundation, and remove themselves from a position of decision-making authority with respect to any conflict situation involving the foundation."[41]
- *Know when it's time to call it quits.* When it's evident that a decision isn't working, don't be afraid to pull the plug. For instance, only months after Steve Rowe became CEO of UK-based Marks & Spencer, he decided to close dozens of stores domestically and abroad in a major move to boost the retailer's profitability. Although the previous CEO had reestablished large stores in and around Paris after a decade of not operating in France, Rowe reversed that decision as a way to significantly reduce costs.[42] However, as we said earlier, many decision makers block or distort negative information because they don't want to believe their decision was bad. They become so attached to a decision that they refuse to recognize when it's time to move on. In today's dynamic environment, this type of thinking simply won't work.
- *Use an effective decision-making process.* Experts say an effective decision-making process has these six characteristics: (1) it focuses on what's important; (2) it's logical and consistent; (3) it acknowledges both subjective and objective thinking and blends analytical with intuitive thinking; (4) it requires only as much information and analysis as is necessary to resolve a particular dilemma; (5) it encourages and guides the gathering of relevant information and informed opinion; and (6) it's straightforward, reliable, easy to use, and flexible.[43]
- *Develop your ability to think clearly* so you can make better choices at work and in your life.[44] Making good decisions doesn't come naturally. You have to work at it. Read and study about decision making. Keep a journal of decisions in which you evaluate your decision-making successes and failures by looking at the process you used and the outcomes you got.

- 77 percent of managers say the number of decisions they make during a typical day has increased.[45]

Design Thinking and Decision Making

The way managers approach decision making—using a rational and analytical mindset in identifying problems, coming up with alternatives, evaluating alternatives, and choosing one of those alternatives—may not be the best, and is certainly not the only, choice in today's environment. That's where design thinking comes in. **Design thinking** has been described as "approaching management problems as designers approach design problems."[46] More organizations are beginning to recognize how design thinking can benefit them.[47] PepsiCo embraces the importance of design thinking. For example, the company designers created the Pepsi Spire, which is a high-tech beverage dispensing machine with a futuristic design. PepsiCo CEO Indra Nooyi had this to say about the company's design approach: "Other companies with dispensing machines have focused on adding a few more buttons and combinations of flavors. Our design guys essentially said that we're talking about a fundamentally different interaction between consumer and machine."[48]

design thinking
Approaching management problems as designers approach design problems

While many managers don't deal specifically with product or process design decisions, they still make decisions about work issues that arise, and design thinking can help them be better decision makers. What can the design thinking approach teach managers about making better decisions? Well, it begins with the first step of identifying problems. Design thinking says that managers should look at problem identification collaboratively and integratively, with the goal of gaining a deep understanding of the situation. They should look not only at the rational aspects, but also at the emotional elements. Then invariably, of course, design thinking would influence how managers identify and evaluate alternatives. "A traditional manager (educated in a business school, of course) would take the options that have been presented and analyze them based on deductive reasoning and then select the one with the highest net present value. However, using design thinking, a manager would say, 'What is something completely new that would be lovely if it existed but doesn't now?' "[49] Design thinking means opening up your perspective and gaining insights by using observation and inquiry skills and not relying simply on rational analysis. We're not saying that rational analysis isn't needed; we are saying that there's more needed in making effective decisions, especially in today's world. Just a heads up: Design thinking also has broad implications for managers in other areas, and we'll be looking in future chapters at its impact on innovation and strategies.

Big Data and Decision Making

- China's Alibaba, the world's largest online retailer, profits from its technology to personalize customer offers and handle 175,000 purchases per second.[50]
- At Etihad Airways, based in Abu Dhabi, managers rely on extensive data analysis for a variety of business decisions. They considered the financial services and technological resources of 14 different banks before choosing two banks capable of providing the necessary data, in the necessary detail and software format, for key decisions about managing the airline's money.[51]
- It's not just businesses that are exploiting big data. Thanks to improved data collection and analysis techniques, including new software for modeling supply and demand, managers at the National Blood Authority in Australia can make better decisions about distributing blood products to medical facilities—saving a lot of lives and a lot of money.[52]

Yes, there's a ton of information out there—100 petabytes here in the decade of the 2010s, according to experts. (In bytes, that translates to 1 plus 17 zeroes, in case you were wondering!)[53] And businesses—and other organizations—are finally figuring out how to use it. So what is **big data**? It's the vast amount of quantifiable information that can be analyzed by highly sophisticated data processing. One IT expert described big data with "3V's: high volume, high velocity, and/or high variety information assets."[54]

big data
The vast amount of quantifiable information that can be analyzed by highly sophisticated data processing

What does big data have to do with decision making? A lot, as you can imagine. With this type of data at hand, decision makers have very powerful tools to help them make decisions. However, experts caution that collecting and analyzing data for data's sake is wasted effort. Goals are needed when collecting and using this type of information. As one individual said, "Big data is a descendant of Taylor's 'scientific management' of more than a century ago."[55] While Taylor used a stopwatch to time and monitor a worker's every movement, big data is using math modeling, predictive algorithms, and artificial intelligence software to measure and monitor people and machines like never before. But managers need to really examine and evaluate how big data might contribute to their decision making before jumping in with both feet. Why? Because big data, no matter how comprehensive or well analyzed, needs to be tempered by good judgment. For instance, a recent government report states: "Companies should remember that while big data is very good at detecting correlations, it does not explain which correlations are meaningful."[56] Credit companies have generally established a correlation between credit score and repayment history (lower scores are associated with lower payment histories). However, it is certainly not the case that every person with a low credit score will fail to pay credit cards. When making decisions, it is important to remember that correlation does not equate with cause and effect.

Chapter 2 PREPARING FOR: Exams/Quizzes

CHAPTER SUMMARY by Learning Objectives

LO2.1 DESCRIBE the eight steps in the decision-making process.

A decision is a choice. The decision-making process consists of eight steps: (1) identify the problem; (2) identify decision criteria; (3) weight the criteria; (4) develop alternatives; (5) analyze alternatives; (6) select alternative; (7) implement alternative; and (8) evaluate decision effectiveness.

LO2.2 EXPLAIN the four ways managers make decisions.

The assumptions of rationality are as follows: the problem is clear and unambiguous; a single, well-defined goal is to be achieved; all alternatives and consequences are known; and the final choice will maximize the payoff. Bounded rationality says that managers make rational decisions but are bounded (limited) by their ability to process information. Satisficing happens when decision makers accept solutions that are good enough. With escalation of commitment, managers increase commitment to a decision even when they have evidence it may have been a wrong decision. Intuitive decision making means making decisions on the basis of experience, feelings, and accumulated judgment. Using evidence-based management, a manager makes decisions based on the best available evidence.

LO2.3 CLASSIFY decisions and decision-making conditions.

Programmed decisions are repetitive decisions that can be handled by a routine approach and are used when the problem being resolved is straightforward, familiar, and easily defined (structured). Nonprogrammed decisions are unique decisions that require a custom-made solution and are used when the problems are new or unusual (unstructured) and for which information is ambiguous or incomplete. Certainty is a situation in which a manager can make accurate decisions because all outcomes are known. Risk is a situation in which a manager can estimate the likelihood of certain outcomes. Uncertainty is a situation in which a manager is not certain about the outcomes and can't even make reasonable probability estimates. When decision makers face uncertainty, their psychological orientation will determine whether they follow a maximax choice (maximizing the maximum possible payoff); a maximin choice (maximizing the minimum possible payoff); or a minimax choice (minimizing the maximum regret—amount of money that could have been made if a different decision had been made).

LO2.4 DESCRIBE how biases affect decision making.

The 12 common decision-making errors and biases include overconfidence, immediate gratification, anchoring, selective perception, confirmation, framing, availability, representation, randomness, sunk costs, self-serving bias, and hindsight. The managerial decision-making model helps explain how the decision-making process is used to choose the best alternative(s), either through maximizing or satisficing and then implementing and evaluating the alternative. It also helps explain what factors affect the decision-making process, including the decision-making approach (rationality, bounded rationality, intuition), the types of problems and decisions (well structured and programmed or unstructured and nonprogrammed), and the decision-making conditions (certainty, risk, uncertainty).

LO2.5 IDENTIFY effective decision-making techniques.

Managers can make effective decisions by understanding cultural differences in decision making, creating standards for good decision making, knowing when it's time to call it quits, using an effective decision-making process, and developing their ability to think clearly. An effective decision-making process (1) focuses on what's important; (2) is logical and consistent; (3) acknowledges both subjective and objective thinking and blends both analytical and intuitive approaches; (4) requires only "enough" information as is necessary to resolve a problem; (5) encourages and guides gathering relevant information and informed opinions; and (6) is straightforward, reliable, easy to use, and flexible.

Design thinking is "approaching management problems as designers approach design problems." It can be useful when identifying problems and when identifying and evaluating alternatives. Using big data, decision makers have power tools to help them make decisions. However, no matter how comprehensive or well analyzed the big data, it needs to be tempered by good judgment.

> **Pearson MyLab Management**
> Go to **mymanagementlab.com** to complete the problems marked with this icon ✪.

✪ REVIEW AND DISCUSSION QUESTIONS

2-1. Explain how good decision making is a skill that can be learned and improved.

2-2. Where in the eight-step decision-making process are the likely problem areas for managers?

2-3. What role does intuition play in decision making? Discuss.

2-4. Is satisficing a desirable way of making managerial decisions?

2-5. Most managers adopt particular styles to simplify their decision making. This helps them make sense of information. Why do you think these styles are unreliable?

2-6. What should a good manager do if it becomes apparent that a decision that has already been made is clearly not working or solving the situation?

2-7. What do you understand by personalization technologies? How does big data fit into decision-making processes?

> **Pearson MyLab Management**
> If your professor has assigned these, go to **www.mymanagementlab.com** for the following Assisted-graded writing questions:
>
> **2-8.** How might an organization's culture influence the way managers make decisions?
>
> **2-9.** Efe has looked at last year's sales figures and incorporated a 20 percent growth for his year. He figures that his business can cut costs by at least 15 percent with little effort. Identify his biases and the mistakes he might be making.

PREPARING FOR: My Career

✪ PERSONAL INVENTORY ASSESSMENTS

Solving Problems Analytically and Creatively

Making decisions is all about solving problems. Do this PIA and find out about your level of creativity and innovation in problem solving.

✪ ETHICS DILEMMA

In the United Kingdom, the National Health Service employs 1.7 million people.[57] It is the world's largest publicly funded health service. There are cases when employees have found themselves "victimized" by management for one reason or another. A prime example is that of a senior consultant, around 50 years old, working for a London hospital. She was suspended on full pay for three years after raising concerns over staffing levels in her clinic. Shortly before her suspension, a major case of child abuse implicating the hospital hit the headlines. As the hospital had failed to pick up on these problems, the consultant became a whistle-blower and exposed staffing concerns. Deeply concerned, the hospital promptly offered her money with a gagging clause as part of the agreement. She turned it down. It took the support of hundreds of colleagues for her to eventually return to work. Petitions that received great support from former patients had added to the call. However, she would never work for that hospital again. Since the incident, the consultant has been instrumental in trying to bring about changes to the support and protection of whistle-blowers in service.

2-10. Was the hospital's decision to suspend the consultant correct? Explain why or why not.

2-11. If you were the consultant's line manager, how would you have dealt with the situation?

SKILLS EXERCISE Developing Your Creativity Skill

About the Skill

Creativity is a frame of mind. You need to open your mind to new ideas. Every individual has the ability to be creative, but many people simply don't try to develop that ability. Developing your creative skills can help you become a better problem-solver and contributor in the workplace. Dynamic environments and managerial chaos require that managers look for new and innovative ways to attain their goals as well as those of the organization.[58]

Steps in Practicing the Skill

- ***Think of yourself as creative.*** Although it's a simple suggestion, research shows that if you think you can't be creative, you won't be. Believing in yourself is the first step in becoming more creative.
- ***Pay attention to your intuition.*** Every individual's subconscious mind works well. Sometimes answers come to you when least expected. For example, when you are about to go to sleep, your relaxed mind sometimes whispers a solution to a problem you're facing. Listen to that voice. In fact, most creative people keep a notepad near their bed and write down those great ideas when they occur. That way, they don't forget them.
- ***Move away from your comfort zone.*** Every individual has a comfort zone in which certainty exists. But creativity and the known often do not mix. To be creative, you need to move away from the status quo and focus your mind on something new.
- ***Engage in activities that put you outside your comfort zone.*** You not only must think differently; you need to do things differently and thus challenge yourself. Learning to play a musical instrument or learning a foreign language, for example, opens your mind to a new challenge.

- ***Seek a change of scenery.*** People are often creatures of habit. Creative people force themselves out of their habits by changing their scenery, which may mean going into a quiet and serene area where you can be alone with your thoughts.
- ***Find several right answers.*** In the discussion of bounded rationality, we said that people seek solutions that are good enough. Being creative means continuing to look for other solutions even when you think you have solved the problem. A better, more creative solution just might be found.
- ***Play your own devil's advocate.*** Challenging yourself to defend your solutions helps you to develop confidence in your creative efforts. Second-guessing yourself may also help you find more creative solutions.
- ***Believe in finding a workable solution.*** Like believing in yourself, you also need to believe in your ideas. If you don't think you can find a solution, you probably won't.
- ***Brainstorm with others.*** Being creative is not a solitary activity. Bouncing ideas off others creates a synergistic effect.
- ***Turn creative ideas into action.*** Coming up with ideas is only half the process. Once the ideas are generated, they must be implemented. Keeping great ideas in your mind or on paper that no one will read does little to expand your creative abilities.

Practicing the Skill

Developing your creative skills is similar to building your muscles through exercise; it requires effort over time. Every week pick a new activity to develop your creative skills. Try something new, take an art class, practice brainstorming, or spend some time with a new group of people. Keep a journal of creative ideas or insights.

WORKING TOGETHER Team Exercise

Just how do you make decisions? Researchers suggest that the way we make decisions greatly depends on our individual thinking style. It is all about the sources of information we use and how we process that information. The researchers have categorized the numerous ways of thinking into two distinct styles: linear and nonlinear. Create a group of three or four and discuss how you source and process information. Which of you are linear and which are nonlinear? Share your findings with the rest of the class. Can you arrive at an agreement as to whether one method is better, faster, or more accurate than the other? Is it possible to change from linear to nonlinear or vice versa?

MY TURN TO BE A MANAGER

- Consider a big decision that you have made. Write a description of the decision using the steps in the decision-making process as your guide. What could you have done differently in the process to improve your decision?
- Write a procedure, a rule, and a policy for your instructor to use in your class. Be sure that each one is clear and understandable. And be sure to explain how it fits the characteristics of a procedure, a rule, or a policy.
- Find three examples of managerial decisions described in any of the popular business periodicals (*Wall Street Journal, BusinessWeek, Fortune*, etc.). Write a paper describing each decision and any other information, such as what led to the decision, what happened as a result of the decision, etc. What did you learn about decision making from these examples?
- Interview two managers and ask them for suggestions on what it takes to be a good decision maker. Write down their suggestions and be prepared to present them in class.
- Do a Web search on the phrase "101 dumbest moments in business." Get the most current version of this end-of-year list. Pick three of the examples and describe what happened. What's your reaction to the examples? How could the managers have made better decisions?
- Visit the Mindtools website (www.mindtools.com) and find the decision-making toolkit. Explore the decision-making tools suggested and select one tool to use the next time you need to make a decision.

CASE APPLICATION 1 On The Cards: Decision Making

Card Connection is one of the United Kingdom's largest card publishers and a market leader in the franchise distribution of greeting cards in the United Kingdom and the Republic of Ireland (ROI). Established in 1992, it is regarded as one of the Britain's best-run franchise operations and has been a member of the British Franchise Association since 1995.

Its franchisees don't operate under a standard retail format and, instead, act as intermediaries in supplying cards to a range of retail outlets in allocated franchise areas. Typically, its franchise holders supply products to post offices, convenience stores, gas stations, and other retailers. Given this customer base, Card Connection's management takes advantage of a business model that requires it to place its products in the outlets on a "consignment" basis—customers don't buy the stock and only pay for what they sell. This proved to be a success. At the beginning of 2017, there were 63 franchises across Britain and around 12,000 retail outlets using its services in ROI. At any given time, the management of Card Connection looks for potential franchisees—a mix of new and unexplored territories and replacement franchisees.

To decide which areas to allocate to which franchise holder, Card Connection analyzes several data sources. The primary data drivers are demographic, a combination of raw population figures and number of households. The decision makers must also analyze the number of potential stockists, competitors in the area, the average income of the population, and other elements. While the initial process of dividing the United Kingdom and the ROI into equal portions is simple, as the franchises develop and with changes in demographics, regional and local economics, and other criteria, the value of each area changes.

Each franchise holder has a discrete and exclusive territory that only they can supply to. It is because of this that Card Connection's decision-making process regarding territories often revolves around geography. In most cases, this is how franchise areas are determined and how territories derived. A major problem arises when a franchisee attracts business from a customer outside of its franchise area. The franchisor needs to be clear about these instances. Some franchise agreements allow the franchisor to change the territory, should the circumstance arise. This is an indicator of changes in the demographics within a territory, a development in technology, or a rise in the demand for the product or service being offered within the franchise system.[59]

DISCUSSION QUESTIONS

2-12. What ongoing decisions are necessary about the size of franchise areas?

2-13. What factors should you consider when deciding to acquire a franchise?

2-14. How might globalization impact the decision-making process for Card Connection?

CASE APPLICATION 2 Manchester City: Football Big Data Champions

In most football teams, the minutes before the match are spent in the locker room where the coach provides last minute tips and delivers a motivational speech to the players. However, for Manchester City Football Club the ritual is a bit different. The team spends 15 minutes before each match meeting the club's performance analyst team, discussing things they had done well or wrong in previous matches. For instance, the defense examines several factors—the number of crosses, effective or ineffective tackles, balls lost or recovered, the relationship with midfield, and movements in protecting their penalty area.

The day after the match, the analysis team, headed by Gavin Fleig, gives each player a detailed and personalized report of all their movements during the match, thus, enabling each player to get an accurate feedback on improvements required. In a 2012 interview released to Forbes, Fleig declared that the goal of the performance analysis unit is both to help the club make smarter decisions by relying on objective and more informative data, and to enhance players' performance by helping them to become more reflective and aware of their unique features, actions, and movements on the pitch.

To illustrate how the performance analysis team helps better the team's performance, let's look at Manchester City's performance and the set-piece goals scored in the 2010–11 season.

According to the analyst team, City was underperforming more than any other club in Premier League with only one set-piece goal scored over 21 matches. To understand what led to the goals scored across several European leagues, the analyst team studied more than 500 corner kicks. The players were then presented with videos illustrating the best tactics and movements applied by other teams. This helped City to score 9 goals in the first 15 matches of the next season from corners, which represents a tremendous improvement in their performance.

Data analysis is a critical decision-making support tool for Manchester City's managers at all levels, including for youth teams. For example, future young players are helped in understanding their strengths and weaknesses within the different formation plays and what aspects they need to focus on to develop their talent. It is important to note that big data is just a means to facilitate the achievement of Manchester City's strategic goals concerning youth team development, which is to integrate young homegrown-talents into the first team's formation. The performance analysts have helped the team to become very successful—Manchester City got the best defensive records for two consecutive years since 2012, and it won the title in the seasons 2011–12 and 2013–14 after more than four decades of no wins. Of course, big data is not the only factor behind these successes, but it was very important.

To continue being a leader in football big data, in 2016, Manchester City organized a global Hackathon, with more than 400 applications received from all over the world, where data and football experts created algorithms and simulations using data from real players that have never before been available to external actors. The challenge was to create algorithms that could help identify new movements, passes, runs and pressure to be more effective on the pitch. The winning team, who received a cash prize of £7000 and the promise to collaborate with the performance analysis team, created a learning machine algorithm that tracks decision-making during games.[60]

DISCUSSION QUESTIONS

2-15. What types of decisions are made by football managers? Would you characterize these decisions as structured or unstructured problems? Explain.

2-16. Describe how big data can help football managers to make better decisions and how this has an effect on the decision-making process.

2-17. What type(s) of conditions are more likely to influence the performance analyst team's work: certainty, uncertainty, or risks? Explain.

2-18. Do you think it is appropriate for football managers to use only quantitative information to evaluate their players' performance during a season? Why or why not?

2-19. How can big data transform football decisions in the future?

ENDNOTES

1. S. Minter, "The Season of Snap Judgments," *Industry Week*, May 2010, p. 6; and D. A. Garvin and M. A. Roberto, "What You Don't Know About Making Decisions," *Harvard Business Review*, September 2001, pp. 108–116.
2. "A Bold Alternative to the Worst 'Best' Practices," *BusinessWeek Online*, www.businessweek.com, September 15, 2009.
3. W. Pounds, "The Process of Problem Finding," *Industrial Management Review*, Fall 1969, pp. 1–19.
4. J. Jargon, "McDonald's Faces 'Millennial' Challenge," *The Wall Street Journal*, www.wsj.com, August 24, 2014.
5. C. Dulaney, "McDonald's January Sales Fall 1.8%," *The Wall Street Journal*, www.wsj.com, February 9, 2015.
6. R. J. Volkema, "Problem Formulation: Its Portrayal in the Texts," *Organizational Behavior Teaching Review*, 11, No. 3 (1986–1987), pp. 113–126.
7. S. Gupta, "In Mobile Advertising, Timing is Everything," *Harvard Business Review* online, https://hbr.org, November 4, 2015.
8. Ibid.
9. Jessica Holland, "Big Appetite for UAE Restaurant Locator Start-ups," *The National (UAE)*, March 15, 2016, http://www.thenational.ae/business/the-life/big-appetite-for-uae-restaurant-locator-start-ups (accessed December 2, 2016).
10. James Titcomb, "VTech Says It Is Not Responsible for Security after Hack Exposed Children's Details," *The Telegraph (UK)*, February 10, 2016, http://www.telegraph.co.uk/technology/2016/02/10/vtech-says-it-is-not-responsible-for-security-after-hack-exposed/ (accessed December 7, 2016); Anjie Zheng, "Regulators to Tighten Cyberdefenses as Attacks in Asia Increase," *Wall Street Journal*, June 14, 2016, http://www.wsj.com/articles/regulators-to-tighten-cyberdefenses-as-attacks-in-asia-increase-1465899792 (accessed December 7, 2016).
11. E. Shogren, "BP: A Textbook Example of How Not to Handle PR," *NPR*, online, May 13, 2011.
12. T. A. Stewart, "Did You Ever Have to Make Up Your Mind?" *Harvard Business Review*, January 2006, p. 12; and E. Pooley, "Editor's Desk," *Fortune*, June 27, 2005, p. 16.
13. See A. Langley, "In Search of Rationality: The Purposes Behind the Use of Formal Analysis in Organizations," *Administrative Science Quarterly*, December 1989, pp. 598–631; and H. A. Simon, "Rationality in Psychology and Economics," *Journal of Business*, October 1986, pp. 209–224.
14. J. G. March, "Decision-Making Perspective: Decisions in Organizations and Theories of Choice," in *Perspectives on Organization Design and Behavior*, ed. A. H. Van de Ven and W. F. Joyce (New York: Wiley-Interscience, 1981), pp. 232–233.
15. See P. Hemp, "Death by Information Overload," *Harvard Business Review*, September 2009, pp. 82–89; D. Heath and C. Heath, "The Gripping Statistic," *Fast Company*, September 2009, pp. 59–60; D. R. A. Skidd, "Revisiting Bounded Rationality," *Journal of Management Inquiry*, December 1992, pp. 343–347; B. E. Kaufman, "A New Theory of Satisficing," *Journal of Behavioral Economics*, Spring 1990, pp. 35–51; and N. M. Agnew and J. L. Brown, "Bounded Rationality: Fallible Decisions in Unbounded Decision Space," *Behavioral Science*, July 1986, pp. 148–161.
16. See, for example, G. McNamara, H. Moon, and P. Bromiley, "Banking on Commitment: Intended and Unintended Consequences of an Organization's Attempt to Attenuate Escalation of Commitment," *Academy of Management Journal*, April 2002, pp. 443–452; V. S. Rao and A. Monk, "The Effects of Individual Differences and Anonymity on Commitment to Decisions," *Journal of Social Psychology*, August 1999, pp. 496–515; C. F. Camerer and R. A. Weber, "The Econometrics and Behavioral Economics of Escalation of Commitment: A Re-examination of Staw's Theory," *Journal of Economic Behavior and Organization*, May 1999, pp. 59–82; D. R. Bobocel and J. P. Meyer, "Escalating Commitment to a Failing Course of Action: Separating the Roles of Choice and Justification," *Journal of Applied Psychology*, June 1994, pp. 360–363; and B. M. Staw, "The Escalation of Commitment to a Course of Action," *Academy of Management Review*, October 1981, pp. 577–587.
17. W. Cole, "The Stapler Wars," *Time Inside Business*, April 2005, p. A5.
18. See E. Dane and M. G. Pratt, "Exploring Intuition and Its Role in Managerial Decision Making," *Academy of Management Review*, January 2007, pp. 33–54; M. H. Bazerman and D. Chugh, "Decisions Without Blinders," *Harvard Business Review*, January 2006, pp. 88–97; C. C. Miller and R. D. Ireland, "Intuition in Strategic Decision Making: Friend or Foe in the Fast-Paced 21st Century," *Academy of Management Executive*, February 2005, pp. 19–30; E. Sadler-Smith and E. Shefy, "The Intuitive Executive: Understanding and Applying 'Gut Feel' in Decision Making," *Academy of Management Executive*, November 2004, pp. 76–91; and L. A. Burke and M. K. Miller, "Taking the Mystery Out of Intuitive Decision Making," *Academy of Management Executive*, October 1999, pp. 91–99.
19. C. C. Miller and R. D. Ireland, "Intuition in Strategic Decision Making: Friend or Foe," vol. 19 no. 1, February 1, 2005, p.20.
20. J. L. Risen and D. Nussbaum, "Believing What You Don't Believe," *The New York Times* online, www.nytimes.com, October 30, 2015; T. Chamorro-Premuzic, "The Intuitive Manager: A Threatened Species?," *Forbes* online, www.forbes.com, April 24, 2014; and E. Sadler-Smith and E. Shefy, "Developing Intuitive Awareness in Management Education," *Academy of Management Learning & Education*, June 2007, pp. 186–205.
21. M. G. Seo and L. Feldman Barrett, "Being Emotional During Decision Making—Good or Bad? An Empirical Investigation," *Academy of Management Journal*, August 2007, pp. 923–940.
22. B. Roberts, "Hire Intelligence," *HR Magazine*, May 2011, p. 63.
23. R. B. Briner, D. Denyer, and D. M. Rousseau, "Evidence-Based Management: Concept Cleanup Time?" *Academy of Management Perspective*, November 2009, p. 22.
24. J. Pfeffer and R. Sutton, "Trust the Evidence, Not Your Instincts," *New York Times* online, www.nytimes.com, September 3, 2011; and T. Reay, W. Berta, and M. K. Kohn, "What's the Evidence on Evidence-Based Management?" *Academy of Management Perspectives*, November 2009, p. 5.

25. M. Seifert, J. Brockner, E. C. Bianchi, and H. Moon, "How Workplace Fairness Affects Employee Commitment," *Sloan Management Review* online, Winter 2016.
26. K. R. Brousseau, M. J. Driver, G. Hourihan, and R. Larsson, "The Seasoned Executive's Decision-Making Style," *Harvard Business Review*, February 2006, pp. 111–121.
27. Eeva Haaramo, "Disrupting IT in the Nordics, from Banks to Taxis," *ComputerWeekly*, April 28, 2016, http://www.computerweekly.com/news/450294201/Disrupting-IT-in-the-Nordics-from-banks-to-taxis (accessed December 7, 2016).
28. Future Vision box based on B. Power, "Improve Decision-making with Help from the Crowd," *Harvard Business Review* online, www.hbr.org, April 8, 2014; "The Biggest Challenge to the Future of Crowdsourcing in Business," *Harvard Business School Digital Initiative*, www.digital.hbs.edu, September 17, 2015; P. Galagan, "Headstrong," *TD Magazine*, November, 2015, pp. 22–25; D. Lacombe, "Crowdsourcing Taps Public for Work, Ideas," www.crowdsourcing.org, May 5, 2012; and "Hershey Launches Innovative Technology Contest to Solve Summertime Shipping Dilemma," Business Wire, www.businesswire.com, January 14, 2016.
29. Leader Making a Difference box based on J. Weisenthal, "Here's Why Elon Musk Built Tesla Even Though He Thought It Was Probably Going to Fail," www.businessinsider.com, March 30, 2014; M. Adamo and C. Leahey, "The List: 2013's Top People in Business," *Fortune*, December 9, 2013, pp. 90–91; A. Vandermey, "Businessperson of the Year," *Fortune*, December 9, 2013, pp. 98–108; T. Hessman, "The World According to Elon Musk," *Industry Week*, October 2013, pp. 12–17; and A. Vance, "Electric Company," *Bloomberg BusinessWeek*, July 22, 2013, pp. 48–52.
30. P. Johnson, "Avoiding Decision Paralysis in the Face of Uncertainty," *Harvard Business Review* online, https://hbr.org, March 11, 2015; E. Teach, "Avoiding Decision Traps," *CFO*, June 2004, pp. 97–99; and D. Kahneman and A. Tversky, "Judgment Under Uncertainty: Heuristics and Biases," *Science* 185 (1974), pp. 1124–1131.
31. Information for this section taken from D. Kahneman, D. Lovallo, and O. Sibony, "Before You Make That Decision . . .," *Harvard Business Review*, June 2011, pp. 50–60; and S. P. Robbins, *Decide & Conquer* (Upper Saddle River, NJ: Financial Times/Prentice Hall), 2004.
32. D. Kahneman, D. Lovallo, and O. Siboney, "Before You Make That Big Decision," *Harvard Business Review*, June 2011, pp. 50–60.
33. C. K. Morewedge, "How a Video Game Helped People Make Better Decisions," *Harvard Business Review* online, https://hbr.org, October 13, 2015.
34. A. Bryant, "Christopher Cabrera of Xactly: Learning to Stay Above the Drama," *The New York Times* online, www.nytimes.com, January 9, 2016.
35. L. Margonelli, "How IKEA Designs Its Sexy Price Tags," *Business 2.0*, October 2002, p. 108.
36. A. Steele, "Hilton to Offer Value Brand Aimed at Younger Guests," *The Wall Street Journal* online, www.wsj.com, January 25, 2016.
37. P. C. Chu, E. E. Spires, and T. Sueyoshi, "Cross-Cultural Differences in Choice Behavior and Use of Decision Aids: A Comparison of Japan and the United States," *Organizational Behavior & Human Decision Processes*, vol. 77, no. 2 (1999), pp. 147–170.
38. E. Meyer, "When Culture Doesn't Translate," *Harvard Business Review*, October 2015, p. 6.
39. Ibid.
40. D. Ariely, "Good Decisions. Bad Outcomes," *Harvard Business Review*, December 2010, p. 40.
41. Bill & Melinda Gates Foundation, "Conflict of Interest Policy," Revised April 8, 2015, http://www.gatesfoundation.org/Jobs/Conflict-of-Interest.
42. Harry Yorke, "The Full List of Marks & Spencer Stores Potentially Facing Closure," *The Telegraph (UK)*, November 14, 2016, http://www.telegraph.co.uk/business/2016/11/14/the-full-list-of-marks--spencer-stores-potentially-facing-closur/ (accessed December 2, 2016); Zoe Wood, "M&S to Close 30 UK Stores and Cut Back on Clothing," *The Guardian (UK)*, November 8, 2016, https://www.theguardian.com/business/2016/nov/08/m-and-s-marks-spencer-close-80-stores-major-overhaul (accessed December 2, 2016).
43. J. S. Hammond, R. L. Keeney, and H. Raiffa, *Smart Choices: A Practical Guide to Making Better Decisions* (Boston, MA: Harvard Business School Press, 1999), p. 4.
44. R. Dobelli, *The Art of Thinking Clearly* (New York: HarperCollins), 2013; and *Decisive: How to Make Better Choices in Life and Work* (New York: Random House/Crown Business, 2013).
45. J. MacIntyre, "Bosses and Bureaucracy," *Springfield Business Journal*, August 1–7, 2005, p. 29.
46. D. Dunne and R. Martin, "Design Thinking and How It Will Change Management Education: An Interview and Discussion," *Academy of Management Learning & Education*, December 2006, p. 512.
47. M. Korn and R. E. Silverman, "Forget B-School, D-School Is Hot," *Wall Street Journal*, June 7, 2012, pp. B1+; R. Martin and J. Euchner, "Design Thinking," *Research Technology Management*, May/June 2012, pp. 10–14; T. Larsen and T. Fisher, "Design Thinking: A Solution to Fracture-Critical Systems," *DMI News & Views*, May 2012, p. 31; T. Berno, "Design Thinking versus Creative Intelligence," *DMI News & Views*, May 2012, p. 28; J. Liedtka and Tim Ogilvie, "Helping Business Managers Discover Their Appetite for Design Thinking," *Design Management Review*, no. 1, 2012, pp. 6–13; and T. Brown, "Strategy by Design," *Fast Company*, June 2005, pp. 52–54.
48. A. Ignatius, "How Indra Nooyi Turned Design Thinking into Strategy," *Harvard Business Review*, September 2015, p. 4.
49. D. Dunne and R. Martin, "Design Thinking and How It Will Change Management Education," p. 514.
50. Declan Kearney, "Alibaba Set to Break Records Again for 11.11 with $5bn in Sales in First Two Hours," *The Drum (UK)*, November 11, 2016, http://www.thedrum.com/opinion/2016/11/11/alibaba-set-break-records-again-1111-with-5bn-sales-first-two-hours (accessed December 2, 2016); Glenda Korporaal, "Alibaba Extends Global Cloud Push, Opens Arm in Australia," *The Australian*, November 28, 2016, http://www.theaustralian.com.au/business/technology/alibaba-extends-global-cloud-push-opens-arm-in-australia/news-story/987f7092a5c49fed9d32b6edf55340bf (accessed December 2, 2016).
51. "How Etihad Airways Selected Its Transactional Banking Partners," *Treasury Today*, March 2016, http://treasurytoday

.com/2016/03/how-etihad-airways-selected-its-transactional-banking-partners-ttti (accessed December 2, 2016).

52. David Braue, "How Data Saves Lives in Australia's Hospitals," *Computer Weekly*, June 10, 2016, http://www.computerweekly.com/news/450298093/How-data-saves-lives-in-Australias-hospitals (accessed December 2, 2016).
53. M. Kassel, "From a Molehill to a Mountain," *Wall Street Journal*, March 11, 2013, p. R1.
54. D. Laney, "The Importance of 'Big Data': A Definition," www.gartner.com/it-glossary/big-data/, March 22, 2013.
55. S. Lohr, "Sure, Big Data Is Great. But So Is Intuition," *New York Times* online, www.nytimes.com, December 29, 2012.
56. U.S. Federal Trade Commission, "Big Data: A Tool for Inclusion or Exclusion," January 2016, p. 29.
57. Patrick Butler, "Great Ormond Street Hospital Issues Apology to Baby P Whistleblower," *The Guardian*, June 14, 2011; James Meikle, "NHS Whistleblowers are Being Gagged, says Consultant Pediatrician," *The Guardian*, December 13, 2011, www.ajustnhs.com/case-histories-of-victimised-nhs-staff/.
58. Developing Your Creative Skill exercise based on S. P. Robbins, *Essentials of Organizational Behavior*, 8th ed. (Upper Saddle River, NJ: Prentice Hall, 2004); C. W. Wang and R. Y. Horng, "The Effects of Creative Problem Solving Training on Creativity, Cognitive Type, and R & D Performance," *R&D Management* (January 2002), pp. 35–46; S. Caudron, "Creativity 101," *Workforce* (March 2002), pp. 20, 24; and T. M. Amabile, "Motivating Creativity in Organizations," *California Management Review* (Fall 1997), pp. 42–52.
59. "About Card Connection-The UK's Leading Greeting Card Franchise," *Card Connection*, http://card-connection.co.uk (accessed on February 3, 2017); Lucy Smith, "Card Connection: Robin Brisbourne," *Startups* online, http://startups.co.uk (accessed November 29, 2012); and "Card Connection Franchisee Grows Business by 18%," *Irish Franchise Association*, http://www.irishfranchiseassociation.com/card-connection-1 (accessed May 16, 2016).
60. Andy Hunter, "Manchester City to Open the Archive on Player Data and Statistics," *The Guardian*, www.theguardian.com (accessed August 16, 2012); Zach Slaton, "The Analyst Behind Manchester City's Rapid Rise," *Forbes*, August 16, 2012, www.forbes.com; "Set-piece Marking," *BBC News*, http://news.bbc.co.uk/sport2/hi/football/rules_and_equipment/4685580.stm; and B. Curtis, "Manchester City's First Football Data Hackathon A Roaring Success," *SportTechie*, https://www.sporttechie.com/manchester-citys-first-football-data-hackathon-a-roaring-success/ (accessed August 1, 2016).

PART 1 Management Practice

A Manager's Dilemma

Selina Lo loves her job as the manager of a toy store in San Francisco. She loves the chaos and the excitement of kids as they wander around the store searching for their favorite toys. Teddy bears pulled off the shelves and toy trucks left on the floor are part and parcel of managing a toy store. Yet, her biggest challenge, which is a problem faced by many retailers, is employee turnover. Many of her employees leave after just a few months on the job because of hectic schedules and long work hours. Selina is always looking for new ways to keep her employees committed to their jobs. She also takes care of customers' requests and complaints and tries to address them satisfactorily. This is what Selina's life as a manager is like. However, retailers are finding that people with Selina's skills and enthusiasm for store management are few and far between. Managing a retail store is not the career that most college graduates aspire to. Attracting and keeping talented managers continues to be a challenge for all kinds of retailers.

Suppose you're a recruiter for a large retail chain and want to get college graduates to consider store management as a career option. Using what you learned in Part 1, how would you do that?

Global Sense

Who holds more managerial positions worldwide: women or men? Statistics tell an interesting story. In the United States, women held 50 percent of all managerial positions and 15 percent were members of the senior leadership team, but only 4 percent of the Fortune 500 CEO spots. In the United Kingdom, only 1.8 percent of the FTSE 500 companies' top positions are held by women. In Germany, women hold 35.6 percent of all management positions, but only 3 percent of women are executive board members. Asian countries have a much higher percentage of women in CEO positions. In Thailand, 30 percent of female managers hold the title of CEO, as do 18 percent in Taiwan. In China, 19 percent of the female workforce are CEOs. Even in Japan, 8 percent of senior managers are women. A census of Australia's top 200 companies listed on the Australian Stock Exchange showed that 11 percent of company executive managers were women. Finally, in Arab countries, the percentage of women in management positions is less than 10 percent.

As you can see, companies across the globe have a large gender gap in leadership. Men far outnumber women in senior business leadership positions. These circumstances exist despite efforts and campaigns to improve equality in the workplace. The situation may be slowly changing in Europe. Many countries there require corporations to allocate a specified percentage of board seats to women. For example, 100 of the largest German corporations award at least 30 percent of board seats to women. The remaining German companies were required to establish quotas sometime in 2016. One company—Deutsche Telekom—has chosen to aggressively tackle the problem head-on. It says it intends to "more than double the number of women who are managers within five years." One action the company is taking is to improve and increase the recruiting of female university graduates. The company's goal: to have at least 30 percent of the places in executive development programs held by women. Other steps taken by the company revolve around the work environment and work-family issues. Deutsche's chief executive René Obermann said, "Taking on more women in management positions is not about the enforcement of misconstrued egalitarianism. Having a greater number of women at the top will quite simply enable us to operate better."

Discuss the following questions in light of what you learned in Part 1:

- *What issues might Deutsche Telekom face in recruiting female university graduates?*
- *How could it address those issues?*
- *What issues might it face in introducing changes in work-family programs, and how could it address those issues?*
- *What do you think of Obermann's statement that having a greater number of women at the top will enable the company to operate better?*
- *What could other organizations around the globe learn from Deutsche Telekom?*

Sources: P. Dwyer, "German Boards Need Women, Not Quotas," Bloomberg View online, www.bloombergview.com, March 10, 2015; M. Egan, "Still Missing: Female Business Leaders," money.cnn.com, March 24, 2015; A. Swanson, "The Number of Fortune 500 Companies Led by Women Is at an All-Time High: 5 Percent, The Washington Post *online, washingtonpost.com, June 4, 2015; "Nearly 20 percent of Female Chinese Managers Are CEOs," www.fastcompany.com, March 8, 2011; S. Doughty, "Cracking the Glass Ceiling: Female Staff Have the Same Chance as Men of Reaching the Top, Figures Reveal," www.dailymail.co.uk, March 4, 2011; G. Toegel, "Disappointing Statistics, Positive Outlook," Forbes.com, February 18, 2011; E. Butler, "Wanted: Female Bosses for Germany," www.bbc.co.uk, February 10, 2011; S. P. Robbins, M. Coulter, Y. Sidani, and D. Jamali,* Management: Arab World Edition *(London: Pearson Education Limited, 2011), p. 5; "Proportion of Executive Managers and Board Directors of ASX 200 Companies Who Are Women," Australian Bureau of Statistics, www.abs.gov.au, September 15, 2010; Stevens and J. Espinoza, "Deutsche Telekom Sets Women-Manager Quota,"* Wall Street Journal *online, www.wsj.com, March 22, 2010; J. Blaue, "Deutsche Telekom Launches Quota for Top Women Managers," www.german-info.com/business_shownews; and N. Clark, "Goal at Deutsche Telekom: More Women as Managers,"* New York Times *online, www.nytimes.com, March 15, 2010.*

Continuing Case

Starbucks—Introduction

Community. Connection. Caring. Committed. Coffee. Five Cs that describe the essence of Starbucks Corporation—what it stands for and what it wants to be as a business.

Beginning in 1971 as a coffee shop in Seattle's Pike's Place Market, Starbucks has grown to become the world's top specialty coffee retailer with shops in more than 62 countries and an expanded product line including merchandise, beverages and fresh food, global consumer products, and a Starbucks card and consumer rewards program. Starbucks' first store, shown here today, retains its original look with signs and other items bearing the company's first logo.
Source: ZUMA Press, Inc./Alamy

With more than 31,000 stores in 70 countries, Starbucks is the world's number one specialty coffee retailer. The company also owns Seattle's Best Coffee, Teavana, Tazo Tea, Starbucks VIA, Starbucks Refreshers, Evolution Fresh, La Boulange, and Verismo brands. It's a company that truly epitomizes the challenges facing managers in today's globally competitive environment. To help you better understand these challenges, we're going to take an in-depth look at Starbucks through these continuing cases, which you'll find at the end of every part in the textbook. Each of these six part-ending continuing cases will look at Starbucks from the perspective of the material presented in that part. Although each case "stands alone," you'll be able to see the progression of the management process as you work through each one.

The Beginning

"We aren't in the coffee business, serving people. We're in the people business, serving coffee." That's the philosophy of Howard Schultz, chief executive officer of Starbucks. It's a philosophy that has shaped—and continues to shape—the company.

The first Starbucks, which opened in Seattle's famous Pike Place Market in 1971, was founded by Gordon Bowker, Jerry Baldwin, and Zev Siegl. The company was named for the coffee-loving first mate in the book *Moby Dick*, which also influenced the design of Starbucks' distinctive two-tailed siren logo. Schultz, a successful New York City businessperson, first walked into Starbucks in 1981 as a sales representative for a Swedish kitchenware manufacturer. He was hooked immediately. He knew that he wanted to work for this company, but it took almost a year before he could persuade the owners to hire him. After all, he *was* from New York and he hadn't grown up with the values of the company. The owners thought Schultz's style and high energy would clash with the existing culture. But Schultz was quite persuasive and was able to allay the owners' fears. They asked him to join the company as director of retail operations and marketing, which he enthusiastically did. Schultz's passion for the coffee business was obvious. Although some of the company's employees resented the fact that he was an "outsider," Schultz had found his niche and he had lots of ideas for the company. As he says, "I wanted to make a positive impact."

About a year after joining the company, while on a business trip to Milan, Schultz walked into an espresso bar and right away knew that this concept could be successful in the United States. He said, "There was nothing like this in America. It was an extension of people's front porch. It was an emotional experience. I believed intuitively we could do it. I felt it in my bones." Schultz recognized that although Starbucks treated coffee as produce, something to be bagged and sent home with the groceries, the Italian coffee bars were more like an experience—a warm, community experience. That's what Schultz wanted to recreate in the United States. However, Starbucks' owners weren't really interested in making Starbucks big and didn't really want to give the idea a try. So Schultz left the company in 1985 to start his own small chain of espresso bars in Seattle and Vancouver called *Il Giornale*. Two years later when Starbucks' owners finally wanted to sell, Schultz raised $3.8 million from local investors to buy them out. That small investment has made him a very wealthy person indeed!

Company Facts

Starbucks' main product is coffee—more than 30 blends and single-origin coffees. In addition to fresh-brewed coffee, here's a sampling of other products the company also offers:

- **Handcrafted beverages:** Hot and iced espresso beverages, coffee and noncoffee blended beverages, Tazo® teas, and smoothies
- **Merchandise:** Home espresso machines, coffee brewers and grinders, premium chocolates, coffee mugs and coffee accessories, compact discs, and other assorted items
- **Fresh food:** Baked pastries, sandwiches, salads, hot breakfast items, and yogurt parfaits
- **Global consumer products:** Starbucks Frappuccino® coffee drinks, Starbucks Iced Coffee drinks, Starbucks Liqueurs, and a line of super-premium ice creams
- **Starbucks card and My Starbucks Rewards® program:** A reloadable stored-value card and a consumer rewards program
- **Brand portfolio:** Starbucks Entertainment, Ethos™ Water, Seattle's Best Coffee, and Tazo® Tea

At the end of 2015, the company had more than 235,000 full- and part-time partners (employees) around the world. Howard Schultz is the chair, president, and CEO of Starbucks. Some of the other "interesting" executive positions include chief operating officer; global chief marketing officer; chief creative officer; executive vice president of partner resources and chief community officer; executive vice president, global supply chain; executive vice president, global coffee; learning business partner; and international partner resource coordinator.

Decisions, Decisions

One thing you may not realize is that after running the show for 15 years at Starbucks, Howard Schultz, at age 46, stepped out of the CEO job in 2000 (he remained as chairman of the company) because he was "a bit bored." By stepping down as CEO—which he had planned to do, had prepared for, and had no intention of returning to—essentially he was saying that he agreed to trust the decisions of others. At first the company thrived, but then the perils of rapid mass-market expansion began to set in and customer traffic began to fall for the first time ever. As he watched what was happening, there were times when he felt the decisions being made were not good ones. Schultz couldn't shake his gut feeling that Starbucks had lost its way. In fact, in a memo dubbed the "espresso shot heard round the world," he wrote to his top managers explaining in detail how the company's unprecedented growth had led to many minor compromises that when added up led to a "watering down of the Starbucks experience." Among his complaints: sterile "cookie cutter" store layouts, automatic espresso machines that robbed the "barista theater" of roasting and brewing a cup of coffee, and flavor-locked packaging that didn't allow customers to inhale and savor that distinctive coffee aroma. Starbucks had lost its "cool" factor, and Schultz's criticism of the state of the company's stores was blunt and bold. There was no longer a focus on coffee but only on making the cash register ring. Within a year of the memo (and eight years after he left the CEO gig), Schultz was back in charge and working to restore the Starbucks experience. His goals were to fix the troubled stores, to reawaken the emotional attachment with customers, and to make long-term changes like reorganizing the company and revamping the supply chain. The first thing he did, however, was to apologize to the staff for the decisions that had brought the company to this point. In fact, his intention to restore quality control led him to a decision to close all (at that time) 7,100 U.S. stores for one evening to retrain 135,000 baristas on the coffee experience ... what it meant, what it was. It was a bold decision, and one that many "experts" felt would be a public relations and financial disaster. But Schultz felt doing so was absolutely necessary to revive and reenergize Starbucks. Another controversial decision was to hold a leadership conference with all store managers (some 8,000 of them) and 2,000 other partners—all at one time and all in one location. Why? To energize and galvanize these employees around what Starbucks stands for and what needed to be done for the company to survive and prosper. Schultz was unsure about how Wall Street would react to the cost, which was around $30 million total (airfare, meals, hotels, etc.), but again he didn't care because he felt doing so was absolutely necessary and critical. And rather than gathering together in Seattle, where Starbucks is headquartered, Schultz chose New Orleans as the site for the conference. Here was a city still recovering from Hurricane Katrina, which had totally devastated it five years earlier in 2005. Talk about a logistical nightmare—and it was. But the decision was a symbolic choice. New Orleans was in the process of rebuilding itself and succeeding, and Starbucks was in the process of rebuilding itself and could succeed, too. While there, Starbucks partners volunteered some 50,000 hours of time, reinforcing to Schultz and to all the managers that despite all the problems, Starbucks had not lost its values. Other decisions, like closing 800 stores and laying off 4,000 partners, were more difficult. Since that transition time, Schultz has made lots of decisions. Starbucks has again come back even stronger in what it stands for, achieving in 2015 phenomenal record financial results, and it is on track to continue those record results.

So we're beginning to see how Starbucks epitomizes the five Cs—community, connection, caring, committed, and coffee. In this Continuing Case in the Management Practice section at the end of Parts 2–6, you'll discover more about Starbucks' unique and successful ways of managing. As you work on these remaining continuing cases, keep in mind that there may be information included in this introduction you might want to review.

Discussion Questions

P1-1. What management skills do you think would be most important for Howard Schultz to have? Why? What skills do you think would be most important for a Starbucks store manager to have? Why?

P1-2. How might the following management theories/approaches be useful to Starbucks: scientific management, organizational behavior, quantitative approach, systems approach?

P1-3. Choose three of the current trends and issues facing managers and explain how Starbucks might be impacted. What might be the implications for first-line managers? Middle managers? Top managers?

P1-4. Give examples of how Howard Schultz might perform the interpersonal roles, the informational roles, and the decisional roles.

P1-5. Look at Howard Schultz's philosophy of Starbucks. How will this affect the way the company is managed?

P1-6. Go to the company's website, www.starbucks.com, and find the list of senior officers. Pick one of those positions and describe what you think that job might involve. Try to envision what types of planning, organizing, leading, and controlling this person would have to do.

P1-7. Look up the company's mission and guiding principles at the company's website. What do you think of the mission and guiding principles?

Describe how these would influence how a barista at a local Starbucks store does his or her job. Describe how these would influence how one of the company's top executives does his or her job.

P1-8. Starbucks has some pretty specific goals it wants to achieve (look ahead to Part 3 on p. 379 for these company goals). Given this, do you think managers would be more likely to make rational decisions, bounded rationality decisions, or intuitive decisions? Explain.

P1-9. Give examples of decisions that Starbucks managers might make under conditions of certainty. Under conditions of risk. Under conditions of uncertainty.

P1-10. What kind of decision maker does Howard Schultz appear to be? Explain your answer.

P1-11. How might biases and errors affect the decision making done by Starbucks executives? By Starbucks store managers? By Starbucks partners?

P1-12. How might design thinking be important to a company like Starbucks? Do you see any indication that Starbucks uses design thinking? Explain.

Notes for the Part 1 Continuing Case

Information from company website, www.starbucks.com, including 2015 Annual Report; "Starbucks on the *Forbes* World's Most Innovative Companies List," *Forbes* online, www.forbes.com, August 19, 2015; H. Schultz (with J. Gordon), *Onward: How Starbucks Fought for Its Life Without Losing Its Soul* (New York: Rodale, 2011); J. Cummings, "Legislative Grind," *Wall Street Journal*, April 12, 2005, pp. A1+; A. Serwer and K. Bonamici, "Hot Starbucks to Go," *Fortune*, January 26, 2004, pp. 60–74; R. Gulati, Sarah Huffman, and G. Neilson, "The Barista Principle," *Strategy and Business*, Third Quarter 2002, pp. 58–69; B. Horovitz, "Starbucks Nation," *USA Today*, May 29–31, 2006, pp. A1+; and H. Schultz and D. Jones Yang, *Pour Your Heart into It: How Starbucks Built a Company One Cup at a Time* (New York: Hyperion, 1997).

Chapter 3 Global Management

It's Your Career

Source: Irina Nartova/Shutterstock

Developing Your Global Perspective—Working with People from Other Cultures

- *Nearly 70 percent of executives and management professionals say that developing global competencies is very important or extremely important to the future success of their companies.*[1]
- *The five most important attitudes, knowledge, skills, and abilities for effective global leadership include:*

Multicultural sensitivity/awareness
Communicates effectively
Strategic thinking
Leadership, influences others
Respect for differences[2]

A key to success in management and in your career is becoming comfortable with cultural differences and recognizing how to be more culturally aware so you can learn to respond appropriately in different situations. Know that becoming culturally competent is a process during which time you will likely make mistakes. Remember that to err is human. Develop a forgiveness strategy and show others that you are sincere in your desire and efforts to learn.

You can be certain that during your career you will work with individuals who were born in a different country than you were. Their first language is likely to be different from yours. And they will probably exhibit habits and customs that differ significantly from those familiar to you. You may find it hard to understand some of those people's behaviors, and you may find your differences make it difficult to communicate and work together. Welcome to the twenty-first century! That's why it's important for you to develop your global perspective—especially your cultural intelligence! As you develop your global competence, start with the perspective that "I am different from the rest," rather than "They are different from me."

So what can you do to increase your ability to work with people from different cultures?[3]

*1. **Become aware of your own level of openness to and confidence in cross-cultural experiences.** Some people just aren't as open to and comfortable with new and different experiences as others are. For instance, do you try new foods with unfamiliar or exotic ingredients? Are you comfortable with class project teams that have individuals from other countries? Do you dread having to communicate with individuals who don't speak your native language? If you're one of those who isn't comfortable with new and different experiences, try to overcome your fear and reluctance by*

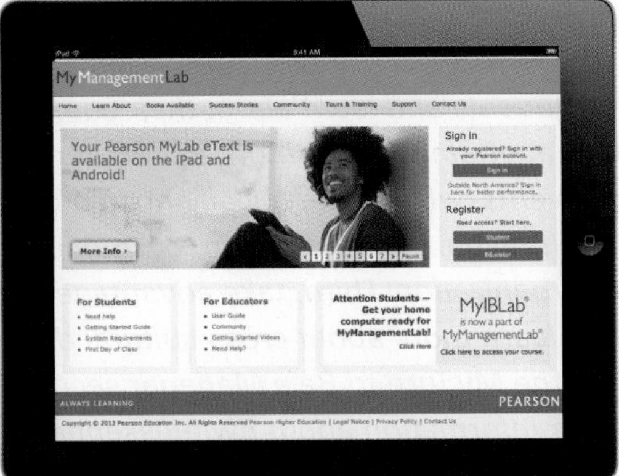

Pearson MyLab Management®

Improve Your Grade!

When you see this icon, visit **www.mymanagementlab.com** for activities that are applied, personalized, and offer immediate feedback.

Learning Objectives

• SKILL OUTCOMES

3.1 ***Contrast*** *ethnocentric, polycentric, and geocentric attitudes toward global business.*

- **Develop your skill** at collaborating in cross-cultural settings.

3.2 ***Discuss*** *the importance of regional trading alliances and global trade mechanisms.*

3.3 ***Describe*** *the structures and techniques organizations use as they go international.*

3.4 ***Explain*** *the relevance of the political/legal, economic, and cultural environments to global business.*

- **Know how** to be culturally aware.

starting small. Practice listening closely to those who struggle with your language. Maybe try a new and unusual menu item or get to know individuals in your classes who are from other cultures. Your goal should be expanding your comfort zone.

2. ***Assume differences until similarity is proven.*** *Most of us have a tendency to assume people are like us until proven otherwise. Try to think the reverse. Assume that individuals from different cultures will interpret communication or behaviors differently. Carefully observe how individuals from other cultures relate to each other and how those interactions differ from how people within your culture relate. Then, you can try interacting with individuals with those observations in mind. This approach will help avoid embarrassing situations.*

3. ***Emphasize description rather than interpretation or evaluation.*** *Delay making judgments until you have observed and interpreted the situation from the perspectives of all cultures involved. Description emphasizes observation. Some customs may be different from what you're used to, but different doesn't make them wrong or inferior.*

4. ***Show empathy.*** *When trying to understand the words, motives, and actions of a person from another culture, try to interpret them from the perspective of that culture rather than your own. This will also encourage you to read up on various cultures to learn their customs and practices.*

5. ***Treat your initial interpretations as working hypotheses.*** *Check with people from other cultures to make sure that your evaluation of a behavior is accurate if you're in doubt. Treat your first interpretations as working hypotheses rather than facts, and pay careful attention to feedback in order to avoid serious miscommunications and resulting problems.*

6. ***Educate yourself on cross-cultural issues and approaches.*** *Although we trust that you're learning a great deal in your classes (and from your textbooks!) about cross-cultural norms, practices, and behaviors, you can learn even more in at least three additional ways! How? First, get international experience through traveling. Invest in short-term study trips abroad. Maybe do an entire semester abroad where you can immerse yourself in a different culture and perhaps even get some overseas work experience, depending on your semester-abroad program. You could also participate in international volunteer programs. If the expense of these kinds of trips is an insurmountable obstacle, you're not off the hook! Second, right where you are, take the initiative to get to know other international students and learn about their countries. Consider attending one or more cultural or multicultural events, which are typically hosted by a single cultural (maybe, Latin American) or multicultural student organization. Third, take advantage of online tools to learn more about cross-cultural differences. (See the MyTurn to Be a Manager section on page 137 for information about Kwintessential.) And at the very least, you can start paying attention to global news stories.*

7. ***Make a good first impression.*** *Greetings differ among cultures. In the United States, the handshake is used while hugs and cheek-kisses are commonly demonstrated in some other countries in Europe and South America. In Japan, present your business card with two hands.*

Going global is something that most organizations want to do. A study of U.S. manufacturing firms found that companies operating in multiple countries had twice the sales growth and significantly higher profitability than strictly domestic firms.[4] There are many contributing factors to success. Among them is an innate global bias. That is, some American companies with strong performance in international markets are led by executives who are foreign-born or first generation American.[5] For example, Facebook's Eduardo Saverin is Brazilian. Other research has found additional evidence that multinational business increases the value of U.S. companies.[6] However, if managers don't closely monitor changes in the global environment or don't consider specific location characteristics as they plan, organize, lead, and control, they may find limited global success. In this chapter, we're going to discuss the issues managers face as they manage in a global environment.

WHO owns what?

One way to see how global the marketplace has become is to consider the country of origin for some familiar products. You might be surprised to find that many products you thought were made by U.S. companies aren't! Take the following quiz[7] and then check your answers at the end of the chapter on page 140.

1. Tombstone and DiGiorno frozen pizzas are products of a company based in:
   a. Italy **b.** United States **c.** Canada **d.** Switzerland
2. Transportation network company Uber Technologies is a company based in:
   a. Poland **b.** United Kingdom **c.** United States **d.** Germany
3. Rajah spices are products of a company based in:
   a. United States **b.** Brazil **c.** India **d.** Switzerland
4. Dos Equis, Tecate, and Sol beer products are owned by a company based in:
   a. The Netherlands **b.** Mexico **c.** United States **d.** Colombia
5. The *America's Got Talent* show is a part of a franchise based in:
   a. United States **b.** United Kingdom **c.** Italy **d.** Spain
6. Chobani Greek yogurt is owned by a company based in:
   a. Japan **b.** France **c.** United States **d.** India
7. The manufacturer of the Swatch watch is based in:
   a. Germany **b.** United States **c.** Switzerland **d.** Brazil

8. The British newspaper the *Independent* is owned by a company based in:
   a. Russia **b.** United Kingdom **c.** South Africa **d.** Canada
9. Spotify is owned by a company located in:
   a. Sweden **b.** United Kingdom **c.** United States **d.** Canada
10. The *Candy Crush Saga* mobile video game was developed by a company based in:
   a. United States **b.** Sweden **c.** France **d.** Japan

How well did you do on the quiz? Were you aware of how many products we use every day that are made by companies not based in the United States? Probably not! Most of us don't fully appreciate the truly global nature of today's marketplace.

WHAT'S **your global perspective?**

LO3.1 It's not unusual for Germans, Italians, or Indonesians to speak three or four languages. In China, a large majority of children learns English in school. On the other hand, most U.S. children study only English in school—only a small percentage are studying Chinese.[8] At schools—elementary through college—large numbers of students will *not* have the opportunity to study a foreign language as courses and programs are reduced or cut. For decades, there has been a steady decline in the availability of foreign language courses, and many colleges and universities have eliminated completion of one or more courses as a degree requirement altogether.[9] Not surprisingly, experts note that there is a "foreign language deficit" in the United States,[10] including a U.S. Secretary of Education who lamented that "The United States is a long way from being the multilingual society that so many of our economic competitors are."[11] Americans tend to think of English as the only international business language and don't see a need to study other languages. This could lead to future problems, as a major research report commissioned by the British Council says that relying only on English hurts the future competitive abilities of both Britain and the United States.[12] Foreign language proficiency is essential for successful business transactions. For instance, many languages such as Italian, French, and Spanish include two versions of the word *you*—one is considered to be formal and the other informal. In Italy, it is appropriate to use the formal *lei* when conducting business discussions and the informal *tu* when holding conversations with friends.

- Between 18 and 27 percent of Americans say they can converse in more than one language.[13]

Monolingualism is one sign that a nation suffers from **parochialism**—viewing the world solely through one's own eyes and perspectives.[14] People with a parochial attitude do not recognize that others have different ways of living and working. They ignore others' values and customs and rigidly apply an attitude of "ours is better than theirs" to foreign cultures. This type of narrow, restricted attitude is one approach that managers might take, but it isn't the only one.[15] In fact, there are three possible global attitudes. Let's look at each more closely.

parochialism
Viewing the world solely through your own perspectives, leading to an inability to recognize differences between people

First, an **ethnocentric attitude** is the parochial belief that the best work approaches and practices are those of the *home* country (the country in which the company's headquarters are located). Managers with an ethnocentric attitude believe that people in foreign countries don't have the needed skills, expertise, knowledge, or experience to make business decisions as well as people in the home country do. They don't trust foreign employees with key decisions or technology.

ethnocentric attitude
The parochial belief that the best work approaches and practices are those of the home country

Next, a **polycentric attitude** is the view that employees in the *host* country (the foreign country in which the organization is doing business) know the best work approaches and practices for running their business. Managers with this attitude view every foreign operation as different and hard to understand. Thus, they're likely to let employees in those locations figure out how best to do things.

polycentric attitude
The view that the managers in the host country know the best work approaches and practices for running their business

The final type of global attitude managers might have is a **geocentric attitude**, a *world-oriented* view that focuses on using the best approaches and people from around the globe. Managers with this type of attitude have a global view and look for the best approaches and people regardless of origin. For instance, Carlos Ghosn, CEO of Nissan and Renault, was born in Brazil to Lebanese parents, educated in France, and

geocentric attitude
A world-oriented view that focuses on using the best approaches and people from around the globe

speaks four languages fluently. He could very well be the "model of the modern major corporate leader in a globalized world bestraddled by multinational companies."[16] Ghosn's background and perspective have given him a much broader understanding of what it takes to manage in a global environment—something characteristic of the geocentric attitude. Another Renault management veteran in the geocentric mold is Carlos Tavares, who was recently named CEO of PSA Peugeot Citroen.[17] He also speaks four languages and has run auto operations in Japan, Europe, North America, and South America. A geocentric attitude requires eliminating parochial attitudes and developing an understanding of cross-cultural differences. That's the type of approach successful managers will need in today's global environment.[18]

- Ranked no. 1 on a list of three skills every twenty-first-century manager needs: GLOBAL MIND SET.[19]

UNDERSTANDING **the global trade environment**

LO3.2 One important feature of today's global environment is global trade, which, if you remember history class, isn't new. Countries and organizations have been trading with each other for centuries.[20] And it continues strong today, as we saw in the chapter-opening quiz. Global trade today is shaped by two forces: regional trading alliances and trade mechanisms that ensure that global trade can happen.

Regional Trading Alliances

Global competition once was considered country against country—the United States versus Japan, France versus Germany, Mexico versus Canada, and so on. Now, global competition and the global economy are shaped by regional trading agreements, including the European Union (EU), North American Free Trade Agreement (NAFTA), and the Association of Southeast Asian Nations (ASEAN), which we review here. A comprehensive list of trading alliances is available on the U.S. federal government's International Trade Administration website (www.trade.gov). More than 200 countries participate in at least one regional trade agreement.[21] The United States alone has agreements with 75 countries.[22]

Countries enter into regional trading alliances for a variety of political and national security reasons. Mainly, countries choose to participate with the goal of stimulating economic growth. Reducing trade barriers such as tariffs or taxes imposed upon imported goods opens new markets for companies in participating countries. For example, U.S. automobile manufacturers Ford and General Motors have benefited tremendously from participation in a variety of regional trade blocs. NAFTA, which we describe later in this chapter, has provided an economic boost to U.S. automobile manufacturers, including Ford and General Motors. These companies have been able to establish manufacturing facilities in Mexico where labor costs are lower than in the United States. The NAFTA agreement also permits the companies to sell those vehicles in the United States without restrictive tariffs.

European Union (EU)
A union of 28 European nations created as a unified economic and trade entity

THE EUROPEAN UNION The **European Union (EU)** is an economic and political partnership of 28 democratic European countries. (See Exhibit 3-1.) Five countries (Albania, the former Yugoslav Republic of Macedonia, Turkey, Montenegro, and Serbia) are candidates to join the EU. Two countries are potential candidates to join the EU (Bosnia and Herzegovina and Kosovo).[23] Before they are allowed to join, however, the countries must meet the criteria, which include democracy, rule of law, a market economy, and adherence to the EU's goals of political and economic union. When the 12 original members formed the EU in 1992, the primary motivation was to reassert the region's economic position against the United States and Japan. Before then, each European nation had border controls, taxes, and subsidies; nationalistic policies; and protected industries. These barriers to travel, employment, investment, and trade prevented European companies from developing economic efficiencies. Now, with these barriers removed, the economic power represented by the EU is considerable. Its current membership covers a population base of more than half a billion people (7 percent of the world population)[24] and accounts for approximately 16 percent of the

Exhibit 3-1
European Union Map

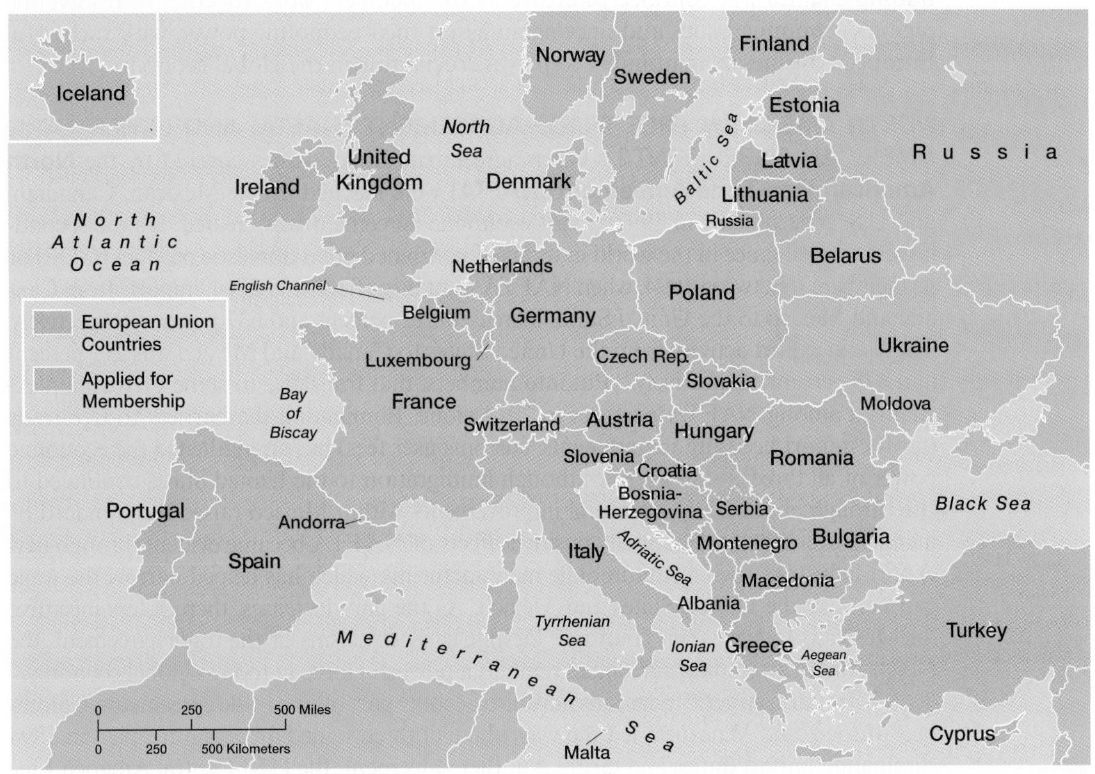

Source: Data based on: "EU Member Countries on the Road to EU Membership", www.europa.eu

world's global exports and imports.[25] In June 2016, the citizens of the United Kingdom (U.K.) voted to remove themselves from the EU because they felt that their needs and interests were being shifted to the greater EU. Conflicts have arisen over immigration, legal, and economic policies. The U.K. decided that its interests would be better served as an independent entity. While the U.K.'s transition will take a few years to complete, this vote holds significance for both the U.K. and other EU countries. The fact that the U.K. will no longer be part of the EU opens the door for other countries to vote themselves out, which could eventually lead to the demise of the EU.

Another step toward full unification occurred when the common European currency, the **euro**, was adopted. The euro is currently in use in 18 of the 28 member states, and all new member countries must adopt the euro. Only Denmark, the United Kingdom, and Sweden have been allowed to opt out of using the euro.[26] Another push in unification has been attempts to develop a unified European constitution. EU leaders struggled for nearly a decade to enact a treaty designed to strengthen the EU and give it a full-time president. The so-called Lisbon Treaty (or Reform Treaty), which was ratified by all 28 member states, provides the EU with a common legal framework and the tools to meet the challenges of a changing world, including climatic and demographic changes, globalization, security, and energy. And backers feel the new structure will help strengthen the EU's common foreign policy. Many believe that a more unified Europe could have more power and say in the global arena. As the former Italian prime minister and European Commission president said, "Europe has lost and lost and lost weight in the world."[27]

euro
A single common European currency

The last couple of years were difficult economically for the EU and its members, as they were for many global regions. However, things are looking up. The economic recovery, which began mid-2013, is expected to continue spreading across countries and gaining strength. Europe's economies are benefiting from many factors. Oil prices remain relatively low, global growth is steady, and the euro has continued to depreciate.[28]

The euro zone is a larger economic unit than the United States or China and is a major source of world demand for goods and services. The importance of this regional trading alliance will continue to evolve as EU members work together to resolve the region's economic issues and once again assert their economic power, with successful European businesses continuing to play a crucial role in the global economy.

North American Free Trade Agreement (NAFTA)
An agreement among the Mexican, Canadian, and U.S. governments in which barriers to trade have been eliminated

NORTH AMERICAN FREE TRADE AGREEMENT (NAFTA) AND OTHER LATIN AMERICAN AGREEMENTS When agreements in key issues covered by the **North American Free Trade Agreement (NAFTA)** were reached by the Mexican, Canadian, and U.S. governments in 1992, a vast economic agreement was created. It's the second-largest trade alliance in the world in terms of combined gross domestic product (GDP) of its members.[29] Between 1994, when NAFTA went into effect, and 2014, imports from Canada and Mexico to the United States increased 212 percent and 637 percent, respectively. The rise in export activity from the United States to Canada and Mexico was 211 percent and 478 percent, respectively.[30] Put into numbers, that translates to some $1.1 trillion exchanged among NAFTA partners in 2014 alone. Eliminating the barriers to free trade (tariffs, import licensing requirements, customs user fees) has strengthened the economic power of all three countries. Even though immigration to the United States continued to rise through about 2005, structural improvements within Mexico raised the standard of living.[31] After 2005, substantially positive effects of NAFTA became evident through new export industries such as automobile manufacturing, which has helped narrow the wage gap between the United States and Mexico. As the gap decreases, there is less incentive for Mexicans to leave their country.[32] Despite early criticisms of the trade agreement, the North American trading agreement remains a powerful force in today's global economy.[33]

Association of Southeast Asian Nations (ASEAN)
A trading alliance of 10 Southeast Asian nations

Other Latin American nations have also become part of free trade agreements. Colombia, Mexico, and Venezuela led the way when all three signed an economic pact in 1994 eliminating import duties and tariffs. Another agreement, the U.S.–Central America Free Trade Agreement (CAFTA-DR), promotes trade liberalization between the United States and five Central American countries: Costa Rica, El Salvador, Guatemala, Honduras, and Nicaragua as well as the Dominican Republic. The CAFTA-DR region was the third-largest export market in Latin America behind Mexico and Brazil, as well as the thirteenth largest in the world.[34] The United States also signed a trade deal with Colombia that is said to be the "largest Washington has concluded with a Latin American country since signing" NAFTA.[35] Upon the U.S.–Colombia Trade Promotion Agreement (TPA) going into effect in 2012, over 80 percent of U.S. industrial goods exports to Colombia became duty-free.[36] Another free trade agreement of 10 South American countries known as the Southern Common Market or Mercosur already exists. Some South Americans see Mercosur as an effective way to combine resources to better compete against other global economic powers, especially the EU and NAFTA.

NAFTA has made it easier for Mexican-based commercial baking company Grupo Bimbo to operate throughout the United States. Since NAFTA, Grupo's subsidiary Bimbo Bakeries USA has grown to become the largest U.S. baking company with 22,000 employees, 11,000 sales distribution routes, and more than 60 bakeries, including the tortilla plant shown here.
Source: Owen Brewer/ZUMA Press/Newscom

ASSOCIATION OF SOUTHEAST ASIAN NATIONS (ASEAN) The **Association of Southeast Asian Nations (ASEAN)** is a trading alliance of 10 Southeast Asian nations. (See Exhibit 3-2.) The ASEAN region has a population of more than 625 million with a combined GDP of US $2.4 trillion.[37] In addition to these 10 nations, leaders from a group dubbed ASEAN+3, which include China, Japan, and South Korea, have met to discuss trade issues. Also, leaders from India, Australia, and New Zealand have participated in trade talks with ASEAN+3 as well. The main issue with creating a trade agreement of all 16 nations has been the lack of any push toward regional integration. Despite the Asian culture's emphasis on consensus building, "ASEAN's biggest problem is that individual members haven't been willing to sacrifice for the common good."[38] Although Southeast Asian leaders agree that closer regional integration would help economic growth, the large differences in wealth among ASEAN members have made it "difficult to create

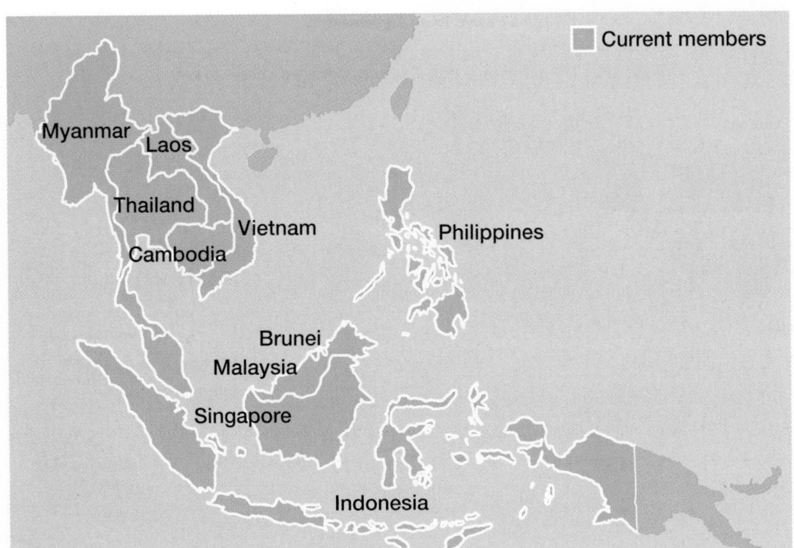

Exhibit 3-2
ASEAN Map

Source: This infographic was first published for IBA Global Insight online news analysis, 30 July 2013, [available at www.ibanet.org] and is reproduced by kind permission of the International Bar Association, London, UK. © International Bar Association.

common standards because national standards remain so far apart."[39] However, the challenges brought on by the recent worldwide recession, which adversely affected many countries in this region, triggered greater interest in pushing for integration. In fact, on January 1, 2010, China and ASEAN launched an ambitious free trade agreement, making it the world's third-largest trade agreement.[40]

Despite the barriers and challenges, progress toward regional integration continues. This fast-growing region means ASEAN and other Asian trade alliances will be increasingly important globally with an impact that eventually could rival that of both NAFTA and the EU.

OTHER TRADE ALLIANCES Other regions around the world have also developed regional trading alliances. For instance, the 54-nation African Union (AU), which came into existence in 2002, seeks to "build an integrated, prosperous and peaceful Africa, an Africa driven and managed by its own citizens and representing a dynamic force in the international arena."[41] Members of this alliance have created an economic development plan to achieve greater unity among Africa's nations. Like members of other trade alliances, these countries hope to gain economic, social, cultural, and trade benefits from their association. Such cooperation couldn't be more important as Africa's economic output is booming like never before, and trade relations with China have been particularly robust.[42] GDP growth rates have been averaging 4.8 percent, the highest rate outside Asia, with most of that growth coming domestically. In addition, Africa has been experiencing a "virtually unprecedented period of political stability with governments steadily deregulating industries and developing infrastructure."[43]

Five east African nations—Burundi, Kenya, Rwanda, Tanzania, and Uganda—have formed a common market called the East African Community (EAC).[44] Under this agreement, goods can be sold across borders without tariffs. The next step for the EAC will be monetary union, although that will take time to implement.

The South Asian Association for Regional Cooperation (SAARC), composed of eight member states (India, Pakistan, Sri Lanka, Bangladesh, Bhutan, Nepal, the Maldives, and Afghanistan), began eliminating tariffs in 2006.[45] Its aim, like all the other regional trading alliances, is to allow free flow of goods and services, and it continues to negotiate tariff reduction agreements with countries throughout the region.[46]

Finally, in 2015, 12 countries forged the terms of a trade alliance called the Trans-Pacific Partnership (TPP).[47] The countries involved in the agreement include the United States, Canada, Mexico, Japan, Australia, and seven other countries around the Pacific region, excluding China. (See Exhibit 3-3.) If the agreement goes into effect, it will influence about two-thirds of world economic input, making it among the largest trade alliances of all time. Among its provisions is the elimination of more than 18,000 tariffs that make cross-national trade relationships costly.

Exhibit 3-3
TPP Map

Source: Data based on AFL-CIO, www.aflcio.org, October 16, 2015./AFL-CIO

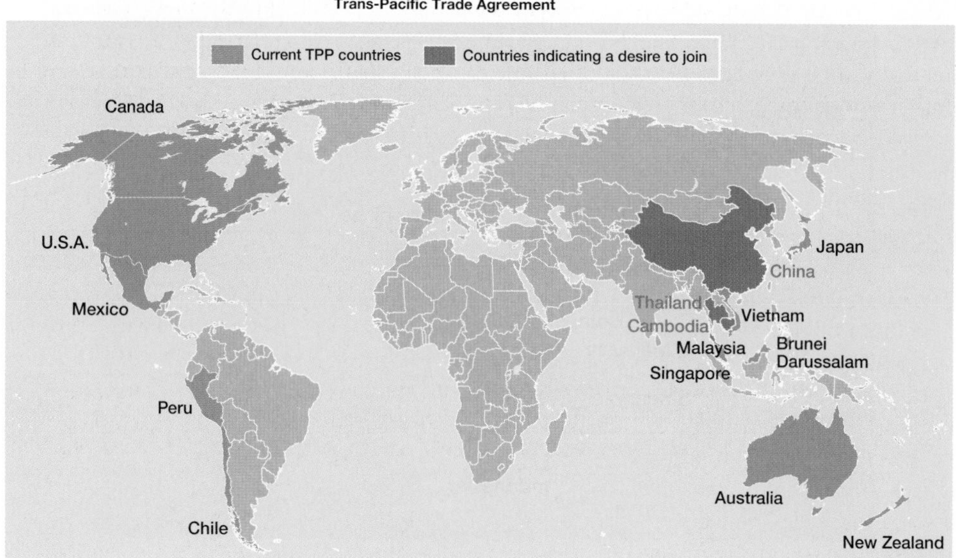

The preceding discussion indicates that global trade is alive and well. Regional trade alliances continue to be developed in areas where member countries believe it's in their best interest economically and globally to band together and strengthen their economic position.

Global Trade Mechanisms

Global trade among nations doesn't just happen on its own. As trade issues arise, global trade systems ensure that trade continues efficiently and effectively. Indeed, one of the realities of globalization is the interdependence of countries—that is, what happens in one can impact others, good or bad. For example, the financial crisis that started in the United States in 2008 threw the global economy into a tailspin. Although things spiraled precariously out of control, it didn't completely collapse. Why? Because governmental interventions and trade and financial mechanisms helped avert a potential crisis. We're going to look at four important global trade mechanisms: the World Trade Organization, the International Monetary Fund, the World Bank Group, and the Organization for Economic Cooperation and Development.

World Trade Organization (WTO)
A global organization of 161 countries that deals with the rules of trade among nations

WORLD TRADE ORGANIZATION The **World Trade Organization (WTO)** is a global organization of 161 countries (as of April 2015) that deals with the rules of trade among nations.[48] Formed in 1995, the WTO evolved from the General Agreement on Tariffs and Trade (GATT), a trade agreement in effect since the end of World War II. Today, the WTO is the only *global* organization that deals with trade rules among nations. Its membership consists of 161 member countries and 24 observer governments (which have a specific time frame within which they must apply to become members). The goal of the WTO is to help countries conduct trade through a system of rules. Although critics have staged vocal protests against the WTO, claiming that global trade destroys jobs and the natural environment, it appears to play an important role in monitoring, promoting, and protecting global trade. For instance, the WTO ruled that the European plane maker Airbus received improper European Union subsidies for the A380 super jumbo jet and several other airplanes, hurting its American rival, Boeing.[49] Airbus has the right to appeal the ruling, but even after appealing, any member ultimately found to have provided improper subsidies is obliged to bring its policies into compliance with global trade rules. Failure to comply could bring trade sanctions. In another news story, the U.S. government is weighing whether to file a WTO complaint against China's Internet censorship.[50] There is one last example worth mentioning. President Barack Obama announced that the United States, the European Union, and Japan filed a challenge with the World Trade Organization against China's export restrictions on minerals that are an essential ingredient in the production of numerous high-tech devices.[51] Examples of these devices include smartphones, hybrid car batteries, and wind turbines. The case seeks to force China to lift export limits on rare earths, which are the particular essential minerals. China produces nearly all of these minerals. With continued restrictions, the long-term viability of companies in the United States, the European Union, and Japan is at risk. According to the WTO, China agreed to lift these restrictions in 2015.[52] These examples illustrate the types of trade issues with which the WTO deals. Such issues are best handled by an organization such as the WTO, and it has played, without a doubt, an important role in promoting and protecting global trade.

INTERNATIONAL MONETARY FUND AND WORLD BANK GROUP Two other important and necessary global trade mechanisms include the International Monetary Fund and the World Bank Group. The **International Monetary Fund (IMF)** is an organization of 188 countries that promotes international monetary cooperation and provides member countries with policy advice, temporary loans, and technical assistance to establish and maintain financial stability and to strengthen economies.[54] During the global financial turmoil of the last few years, the IMF was on the forefront of advising countries and governments in getting through the difficulties.[55] The **World Bank Group** is a group of five closely associated institutions, all owned by its member countries, that provides vital financial and technical assistance to developing countries around the world. The goal of the World Bank Group is to promote long-term economic development and poverty reduction by providing members with technical and financial support.[56] For instance, during the recent global recession, financial commitments by the World Bank Group reached $100 billion as it helped nations respond to and recover from the economic downturn.[57] Both entities have an important role in supporting and promoting global business and often collaborate to achieve these goals.

International Monetary Fund (IMF)
An organization of 188 countries that promotes international monetary cooperation and provides advice, loans, and technical assistance

World Bank Group
A group of five closely associated institutions that provides financial and technical assistance to developing countries

ORGANIZATION FOR ECONOMIC COOPERATION AND DEVELOPMENT (OECD) The forerunner of the OECD, the Organization for European Economic Cooperation, was formed in 1947 to administer American and Canadian aid under the Marshall Plan for the reconstruction of Europe after World War II. Today, the **Organization for Economic Cooperation and Development (OECD)** is a Paris-based international economic organization whose mission is to help its 34 member countries achieve sustainable economic growth and employment and raise the standard of living in member countries while maintaining financial stability in order to contribute to the development of the world economy.[58] When needed, the OECD gets involved in negotiations with OECD countries so they can agree on "rules of the game" for international cooperation. One current focus is combating small-scale bribery in overseas commerce. The OECD says such "so-called facilitation payments are corrosive…particularly on sustainable economic development and the rule of law."[59] In 2015, a group of finance ministers from several countries expressed support for a plan that provides governments with solutions for closing the gaps in existing international rules. The long-standing laws have allowed corporate profits to be artificially shifted to low-/no-tax environments, where little or no economic activity takes place.[60] With a long history of facilitating economic growth around the globe, the OECD now shares its expertise and accumulated experiences with more than 80 developing and emerging market economies.

Organization for Economic Cooperation and Development (OECD)
An international economic organization that helps its 34 member countries achieve sustainable economic growth and employment

LEADER making a DIFFERENCE

Source: Bao fan - Imaginechina/AP Images

*The China-based online retailing giant Alibaba made history in 2014 with the largest global initial public offering (IPO) of all time.[53] A key leader behind the IPO and the company's overall success is founding partner **Lucy Peng**, number 33 on Forbes 2015 list of the world's most powerful women. Peng created and now leads Alibaba's human resources department as their chief people officer. She also serves as the CEO of Ant Financial Services, a stand-alone financial services company that serves about 615 million customers. A former economics teacher, Peng was a founding leader of the company in 1999. She is credited with creating the family-like organizational culture at The Alibaba Group, which has helped the company grow to become the world's largest online marketplace with nearly 35,000 employees. While she is known for being funny and down-to-earth, her strong values of humility and passion create the foundation for her success at Alibaba.* What can you learn from this leader making a difference?

DOING business globally

LO3.3 Daimler, Nissan Motor, and Renault are part of a strategic partnership that shares small-car technology and powertrains—an arrangement that all three automakers say will allow them to better compete in an environment where cutting costs is crucial. Convenience store operator 7-Eleven, a subsidiary of Japan-based Seven & iHoldings, has created a profitable niche in Jakarta by adapting its stores to Indonesian ways. Procter & Gamble Company relocated the top executives from its global skin, cosmetics, and personal-care unit from its Cincinnati headquarters to Singapore. Reckitt Benckiser, the U.K.-based maker of consumer products (Lysol, Woolite, and French's mustard are just a few of its products), has operations in more than 60 countries, and its top 400 managers represent 53 different nationalities. The Missouri State Employees' Retirement System pays retirement benefits to recipients in 20 countries outside the United States.[61] As these examples show, organizations in different industries and from different countries do business globally. But *how* do they do so?

FYI

- The world's 500 largest companies generated $31.2 trillion in revenues and $1.7 trillion in profits in 2014. Together, this year's Fortune Global 500 employ 65 million people worldwide and are represented by 36 countries.[62]

Different Types of International Organizations

Companies doing business globally aren't new. DuPont started doing business in China in 1863. H.J. Heinz Company was manufacturing food products in the United Kingdom in 1905. Ford Motor Company set up its first overseas sales branch in France in 1908. By the 1920s, other companies, including Fiat, Unilever, and Royal Dutch/Shell, had gone international. But it wasn't until the mid-1960s that international companies became quite common. Today, few companies don't do business internationally. However, there's not a generally accepted approach to describe the different types of international companies; different authors call them different things. We use the terms *multinational, multidomestic, global,* and *transnational.*[63] A **multinational corporation (MNC)** is any type of international company that maintains operations in multiple countries.

multinational corporation (MNC)
A broad term that refers to any and all types of international companies that maintain operations in multiple countries

One type of MNC is a **multidomestic corporation**, which decentralizes management and other decisions to the local country. This type of globalization reflects the polycentric attitude. A multidomestic corporation doesn't attempt to replicate its domestic successes by managing foreign operations from its home country. Instead, local employees typically are hired to manage the business, and marketing strategies are tailored to that country's unique characteristics. For example, Switzerland-based Nestlé is a multidomestic corporation. With operations in almost every country on the globe, its managers match the company's products to its consumers. In parts of Europe, Nestlé sells products that are not available in the United States or Latin America. Another example is Frito-Lay, a division of PepsiCo, which markets a Dorito chip in the British market that differs in both taste and texture from the U.S. and Canadian version. Even the king of retailing, Walmart, has learned that it must "think locally to act globally" as it tailors its inventories and store formats to local tastes.[64] Many consumer product companies organize their global businesses using this approach because they must adapt their products to meet the needs of local markets.

multidomestic corporation
An MNC that decentralizes management and other decisions to the local country

Another type of MNC is a **global company**, which centralizes its management and other decisions in the home country. This approach to globalization reflects the ethnocentric attitude. Global companies treat the world market as an integrated whole and focus on the need for global efficiency and cost savings. Although these companies may have considerable global holdings, management decisions with company-wide implications are made from headquarters in the home country. Some examples of global companies include Sony, Deutsche Bank AG, Starwood Hotels, and Merrill Lynch.

global company
An MNC that centralizes management and other decisions in the home country

Other companies use an arrangement that eliminates artificial geographical barriers. This type of MNC is often called a **transnational, or borderless, organization**

transnational or borderless organization
An MNC in which artificial geographical barriers are eliminated

and reflects a geocentric attitude.[65] For example, IBM CEO Ginni Rometty is initiating the largest global reorganization in IBM's history. The goal is to create a vibrant future. "Multiple sources told us senior managers were this week informed about the changes that will see IBM try to shed the dusty hardware, software and services silo structure."[66] The main units are expected to include Research, Sales & Delivery, Global Technology Services, Cloud, Security, Commerce, and Analytics. Ford Motor Company is pursuing the second generation of what it calls the One Ford concept as it integrates its operations around the world and has achieved efficiencies by reducing the number of vehicle platforms from 27 to 9.[67] Another company, Thomson SA (renamed to Technicolor SA), which is legally based in France, has eight major locations around the globe. The CEO said, "We don't want people to think we're based anyplace."[68] Managers choose this approach to increase efficiency and effectiveness in a competitive global marketplace.[69]

If your professor has assigned this, go to **www.mymanagementlab.com** to complete the Writing Assignment *MGMT 5: The Global Marketplace.*

How Organizations Go International

When organizations do go international, they often use different approaches. (See Exhibit 3-4.) Managers who want to get into a global market with minimal investment may start with **global sourcing** (also called global outsourcing), which is purchasing materials or labor from around the world wherever it is cheapest. The goal: take advantage of lower costs in order to be more competitive. For instance, Massachusetts General Hospital uses radiologists in India to interpret CT scans.[70] Although global sourcing may be the first step in going international for many companies, they often continue to use this approach because of the competitive advantages it offers. Each successive stage of going international beyond global sourcing, however, requires more investment and thus entails more risk for the organization.

global sourcing
Purchasing materials or labor from around the world wherever it is cheapest

The next step in going international may involve **exporting** the organization's products to other countries—that is, making products domestically and selling them abroad. In addition, an organization might do **importing**, which involves acquiring products made abroad and selling them domestically. Both usually entail minimal investment and risk, which is why many small businesses often use these approaches to doing business globally.

exporting
Making products domestically and selling them abroad

importing
Acquiring products made abroad and selling them domestically

Exhibit 3-4
How Organizations Go Global

Global Investment	
Significant	Foreign Subsidiary
	Strategic Alliance – Joint Venture
	Franchising
	Licensing
	Exporting and Importing
Minimal	Global Sourcing

licensing
An organization gives another organization the right to make or sell its products using its technology or product specifications

franchising
An organization gives another organization the right to use its name and operating methods

Managers also might use **licensing** or **franchising**, which are similar approaches involving one organization giving another organization the right to use its brand name, technology, or product specifications in return for a lump sum payment or a fee usually based on sales. The only difference is that licensing is primarily used by manufacturing organizations that make or sell another company's products and franchising is primarily used by service organizations that want to use another company's name and operating methods. For example, Chicago consumers can enjoy Guatemalan Pollo Campero fried chicken, South Koreans can indulge in Dunkin' Donuts coffee, Hong Kong residents can dine on Shakey's Pizza, and Malaysians can consume Schlotzky's deli sandwiches—all because of *franchises* in these countries. On the other hand, Anheuser-Busch InBev has *licensed* the right to brew and market its Budweiser beer to brewers such as Kirin in Japan and Crown Beers in India.

If your professor has assigned this, go to **www.mymanagementlab.com** to watch a video titled *Domino's Pizza: Franchising* and to respond to questions.

strategic alliance
A partnership between an organization and foreign company partner(s) in which both share resources and knowledge in developing new products or building production facilities

joint venture
A specific type of strategic alliance in which the partners agree to form a separate, independent organization for some business purpose

foreign subsidiary
Directly investing in a foreign country by setting up a separate and independent production facility or office

When an organization has been doing business internationally for a while and has gained experience in international markets, managers may decide to make more of a direct foreign investment. One way to increase investment is through a **strategic alliance**, which is a partnership between an organization and a foreign company partner or partners in which both share resources and knowledge in developing new products or building production facilities. For example, Honda Motor and General Electric teamed up to produce a new jet engine. A specific type of strategic alliance in which the partners form a separate, independent organization for some business purpose is called a **joint venture**. For example, Hewlett-Packard has had numerous joint ventures with various suppliers around the globe to develop different components for its computer equipment. British automaker Land Rover and Chinese automaker Chery created a joint venture, which aims to combine the experience of Britain's luxury vehicle manufacturer with Chery's deep understanding of the Chinese markets and customer preferences. These partnerships provide a relatively easy way for companies to compete globally.

Finally, managers may choose to directly invest in a foreign country by setting up a **foreign subsidiary** as a separate and independent facility or office. This subsidiary can be managed as a multidomestic organization (local control) or as a global organization (centralized control). As you can probably guess, this arrangement involves the greatest commitment of resources and poses the greatest amount of risk. For instance, United Plastics Group of Houston, Texas, built two injection-molding facilities in Suzhou, China. The company's executive vice president for business development said that level of investment was necessary because "it fulfilled our mission of being a global supplier to our global accounts."[71]

China's Lenovo CEO Yang Yuanqing (left) and Japan's NEC President Nobuhiro Endo formed a strategic alliance to create a new joint venture called NEC Lenovo Japan Group to sell personal computers in Japan. The joint venture gives the two electronics firms the opportunity to expand their business in Japan, the third-largest PC market in the world.
Source: Kyodo/AP Images

MANAGING **in a global environment**

LO3.4 Assume for a moment that you're a manager going to work for a branch of a global organization in a foreign country. You know that your environment will differ from the one at home, but how? What should you look for?

Any manager who finds himself or herself in a new country faces challenges. In this section, we'll look at some of these challenges. Although our discussion is presented through the eyes of a U.S. manager, this framework could be used by any manager, regardless of national origin, who manages in a foreign environment.

The Political/Legal Environment

The growing complexity of the political and legal landscapes in the global environment is one of the most important trends affecting global business. Managers working for global businesses contend with a growing tide of employment legislation that cuts across national boundaries. Legal and political forces are unique to each country, and sometimes the laws of one contradict those of another, or are ignored altogether. For instance, Americans may encounter laws that are routinely ignored by host countries, creating somewhat of a dilemma. The laws in some countries that require a minimum age for factory workers are often not enforced. A U.S. Department of Labor report revealed continued child labor abuses in the apparel and textile industries.[72]

U.S. managers are accustomed to a stable legal and political system. Changes tend to be slow, and legal and political procedures are well established. Elections are held at regular intervals, and even when the political party in power changes after an election, it's unlikely that anything too radical will happen. The stability of laws allows for accurate predictions. However, this certainly isn't true for all countries. Managers must stay informed of the specific laws in countries where they do business. For instance, the president of Zimbabwe is pushing ahead with plans to force foreign companies to sell majority stakes to locals.[73] Such a law would be a major barrier to foreign business investment. In China, foreign businesses are finding a less-than-welcoming climate as government policies are making it more difficult to do business there.[74] U.S. companies find that China provides preferential treatment to protect and promote domestic firms and state-owned companies.[75]

Also, some countries have risky political climates. For instance, BP could have warned Exxon about the challenges of doing business in Russia. During its long involvement in the country, BP has "had so many police run-ins that its stock price often nudges up or down in response to raids or the arrests of employees." However, almost a quarter of BP's output comes from Russian oil and natural gas, so the company has learned to live with the disruptions. Recently, not long after Exxon formed a strategic alliance with Russia's state-owned oil company, armed commandos raided BP's offices in "one of the ritual armed searches of white-collar premises that are common here." These incidents are so common that they've been "given a nickname: masky shows (so-called because of the balaclavas—ski masks—the agents often wear)." The episode was sure to "send a signal that when it comes to dealing with the state-run business world of Prime Minister Vladimir V. Putin, Exxon wasn't in Texas anymore."[76]

Risks are part of doing business globally. Those risks encompass political ones as well as security, kidnap, and maritime situations. The 2014 annual report by Control Risks maps the trends that multinational companies need to track.[77] Managers of businesses in countries with higher risk levels face dramatically greater uncertainty. In addition, political interference is a fact of life in some regions, especially in some Asian countries such as China.[78] In other nations, however, the legal and political systems are much less stable. Some governments are subject to coups, dictatorial rule, and corruption, which can substantially alter both the business and legal environments. Legal systems can also become unstable, with contracts suddenly becoming unenforceable because of internal politics.

Keep in mind that a country's political/legal environment doesn't have to be risky or unstable to be a concern to managers. Just the fact that it differs from that of the home country is important. Managers must recognize these differences if they hope to understand the constraints and opportunities that exist.

The Economic Environment

Strange as it may sound, 17,000 tons of Parmesan cheese, with an estimated value of $187 million, were held in the vaults of Italian bank Credito Emiliano. The cheese was collateral from Italian cheese makers struggling through the recent recession.[79] Such an example of an economic factor of business may seem peculiar for those of us in the United States, but it's not all that unusual for Italian businesses.

A global manager must be aware of economic issues when doing business in other countries. First, it's important to understand a country's type of economic system. The two major types are a free market economy and a planned economy. A **free market economy** is one

free market economy
An economic system in which resources are primarily owned and controlled by the private sector

FUTURE VISION | Communicating in a Connected World

The United Nations International Telecommunication Union estimates that 3.2 billion people use the Internet.[80] To put this into perspective, the world population is just over 7.2 billion. These figures translate into nearly 45 percent! About 2 billion of those connections are in the developing world. With all these people on the Internet, one of the challenges—as it is in the physical realm—is the many different languages spoken by Internet users. In fact, there are nearly 800 languages spoken in India alone! The top 10 languages used on the Internet are as seen in the graph.[81]

Top Ten Languages in the Internet in millions of users

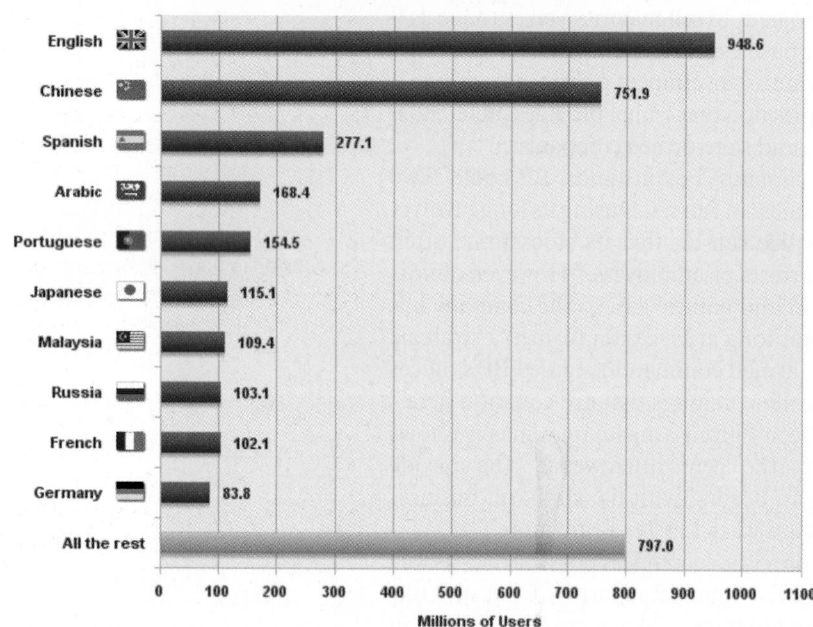

Source: Internet World Stats, "Estimated total Internet Users Are 3,366,260,056," www.internetworldstats.com/stats7.htm, November 30, 2015, Copyright 2016, Miniwatts Marketing Group.

The diversity of Internet users creates challenges for the increasing number of companies expanding operations globally. One of the challenges for companies is to find a common language to ensure effective communication and shared understanding across cultures. Today's workplace often includes geographically dispersed teams, creating a need to overcome these communication challenges.[82] When teams address conceptual matters such as consumer preferences, there is a significant risk that team members will have different interpretations of a particular idea or concept.[83] The growing availability of translation software is making it easier to communicate across language differences. For example, Skype now offers real-time translation services between seven of the world's most used languages for video discussions.[84] Skype also provides translation of more than fifty languages through their text chat service. However, cultural differences still create communication concerns. As the number of Internet users continues to grow, so will challenges for companies working with international employees as well as customers.

If your professor has chosen to assign this, go to ***www.mymanagementlab.com*** *to discuss the following questions.*

TALK ABOUT IT 1: How can a manager improve communication between employees in different international locations?

TALK ABOUT IT 2: How can companies learn more about their customers with different cultural backgrounds?

planned economy
An economic system in which economic decisions are planned by a central government

in which resources are primarily owned and controlled by the private sector. A **planned economy** is one in which economic decisions are planned by a central government. Let's consider the United States and China, respectively, as examples of these types of economies. The U.S. economy is based on the idea of *capitalism*. Under capitalism, the government does not possess ownership of all land, businesses, or natural resources. This economic system relies on market forces in which supply and demand for products, services, and labor determine monetary value. China's political and economic systems are tightly intertwined and are founded on *communism*. Communism draws on the principle of community ownership. That is, all property, businesses, and natural resources are community owned, but these items are controlled by the single political party (Communist Party). Also, in communist societies, the government provides basic necessities based on need. In principle, citizens elect individuals to serve in the Communist Party, but that is rarely the case. In recent decades, China's economy has become more diverse. While maintaining communist control, economic growth has been fueled by market forces and capitalism. As a result, a growing segment of the population has gained considerable wealth and is adopting lifestyles similar to those in the United States. Actually, no economy is purely free market or planned. Why would managers need to know about a country's economic system? Because it, too, has the potential to constrain decisions. Other economic issues managers need to understand include (1) *currency exchange rates*, (2) *inflation rates*, and (3) diverse *tax policies*.

1. An MNC's profits can vary dramatically, depending on the strength of its home currency and the currencies of the countries in which it operates. For instance, prior to the overall global economic slowdown, the rising value of the euro against both the dollar and the yen had contributed to strong profits for German companies.[85] Any currency exchange revaluations can affect managers' decisions and the level of a company's profits.
2. Inflation means that prices for products and services are increasing, but it also affects interest rates, exchange rates, the cost of living, and the general confidence in a country's political and economic system. Country inflation rates can, and do, vary widely. The *World Bank* shows rates ranging from a negative 18.7 percent in South Sudan to a positive 48.6 percent in Venezuela.[86] Managers need to monitor inflation trends so they can anticipate possible changes in a country's monetary policies and make good business decisions regarding purchasing and pricing.
3. Finally, tax policies can be a major economic worry. Some countries' tax laws are more restrictive than those in an MNC's home country. Others are more lenient. About the only certainty is that they differ from country to country. For instance, U.S. companies have been unable to move profits from Venezuela and are buying up commercial real estate in Caracas, the capitol.[87] Managers need accurate information on tax rules in countries in which they operate to minimize their business's overall tax obligation.

If your professor has assigned this, go to **www.mymanagementlab.com** to complete the Simulation: *Managing in the Global Environment.*

The Cultural Environment

One year, the entire senior leadership team at Starwood Hotels relocated to Shanghai, China, for five weeks. Why? Because clearly China is a huge growth market and "working closely with people from a different culture helps you to see pitfalls and opportunities in a very different way."[88]

Managing today's talented global workforce can be a challenge![89] Consider the cultural challenges faced by Sodexo, a multinational corporation based in France, with more than 400,000 employees working at facilities in 80 countries. Businesses, hospitals, universities, and other organizations contract with Sodexo for on-site catering, cleaning, reception, and other services. Clients often ask for services in two different nations, as happened when Sodexo handled maintenance for the headquarters of the French space agency as well as for the agency's base in Guyana. When supervising employees in such situations, Sodexo's managers must be sensitive to the client's management practices, not just to differing cultural norms and communication preferences. Another management challenge is posed by the range of ages within the workforce. In the United Kingdom, Sodexo created a program to improve cross-generational collaboration by highlighting generational similarities, not just differences, and by demonstrating the benefits of teamwork among employees of all ages.[90]

Most often, cross-cultural challenges are described between countries that speak different languages, and these language differences can result in conflict or misunderstandings. Perhaps surprisingly, misunderstanding can occur between two countries that share the same language, such as is the case for the United States and the United Kingdom. For instance, Martin Brooks, Production and Export Manager of pet nutrition company Hilton Herbs, considers the U.S. as one of the most challenging. "As an example, we had a product for older horses and dogs called 'Veteran,'" he says.[91] Sales were lackluster until the company replaced the word "veteran" with "senior," which is the way people in the United States refer to older pets and animals. Veteran is a commonplace descriptor in the United Kingdom. If such a large cultural divide can exist between two countries that share a common mother tongue, how much wider must the chasm be between nations that speak different languages?

Top executives of French car manufacturer PSA Peugeot Citroen participate in a Hindu puja ritual during a ceremony celebrating the firm's plan to re-enter the Indian market with the construction of a new plant. The spiritual ritual is an integral part of India's national culture, which research shows has a greater effect on employees than an organization's culture.
Source: Sam Panthaky/AFP/Getty Images

As we know from Chapter 7, organizations have different cultures. Countries have cultures, too. **National culture** includes the values and attitudes shared by individuals from a specific country that shape their behavior and their beliefs about what is important.[92] National culture is steeped in a country's history, and we can describe it based on a society's social traditions, political and economic philosophy, and legal system.

Which is more important to a manager—national culture or organizational culture? For example, is an IBM facility in Germany more likely to reflect German culture or IBM's corporate culture? Research indicates that national culture has a greater effect on employees than their organization's culture.[93] German employees at an IBM facility in Munich will be influenced more by German culture than by IBM's culture.

Legal, political, and economic differences among countries are fairly obvious. The Japanese manager who works in the United States or his or her American counterpart who works in Japan can get information about laws or tax policies without too much effort. Getting information about cultural differences isn't quite that easy! The primary reason? It's difficult for natives to explain their country's unique cultural characteristics to someone else. For instance, if you were born and raised in the United States, how would you describe U.S. culture? In other words, what are Americans like? Think about it for a moment and see which characteristics in Exhibit 3-5 you identified.

national culture
The values and attitudes shared by individuals from a specific country that shape their behavior and beliefs about what is important

HOFSTEDE'S FRAMEWORK FOR ASSESSING CULTURES Geert Hofstede developed one of the most widely referenced approaches to helping managers better understand differences between national cultures. His research found that countries vary on five dimensions of national culture.[94] These dimensions are described in Exhibit 3-6, which also shows some of the countries characterized by those dimensions.

If your professor has assigned this, go to **www.mymangementlab.com** to watch a video titled *Impact of Culture on Business: Spotlight on China* and to respond to questions.

Exhibit 3-5
What Are Americans Like?

- Americans are *very informal.* They tend to treat people alike even when great differences in age or social standing are evident.
- Americans are *direct.* They don't talk around things. To some foreigners, this may appear as abrupt or even rude behavior.
- Americans are *competitive.* Some foreigners may find Americans assertive or overbearing.
- Americans are *achievers.* They like to keep score, whether at work or at play. They emphasize accomplishments.
- Americans are *independent and individualistic.* They place a high value on freedom and believe that individuals can shape and control their own destiny.
- Americans are *questioners.* They ask a lot of questions, even of someone they have just met. Many may seem pointless ("How ya' doin'?") or personal ("What kind of work do you do?").
- Americans *dislike silence.* They would rather talk about the weather than deal with silence in a conversation.
- Americans *value punctuality.* They keep appointment calendars and live according to schedules and clocks.
- Americans *value cleanliness.* They often seem obsessed with bathing, eliminating body odors, and wearing clean clothes.

Sources: Based on M. Ernest, ed., *Predeparture Orientation Handbook: For Foreign Students and Scholars Planning to Study in the United States* (Washington, DC: U.S. Information Agency, Bureau of Cultural Affairs, 1984), pp. 103–105; A. Bennett, "American Culture Is Often a Puzzle for Foreign Managers in the U.S.," *Wall Street Journal*, February 12, 1986, p. 29; "Don't Think Our Way's the Only Way," *The Pryor Report*, February 1988, p. 9; and B. J. Wattenberg, "The Attitudes Behind American Exceptionalism," *U.S. News & World Report*, August 7, 1989, p. 25.

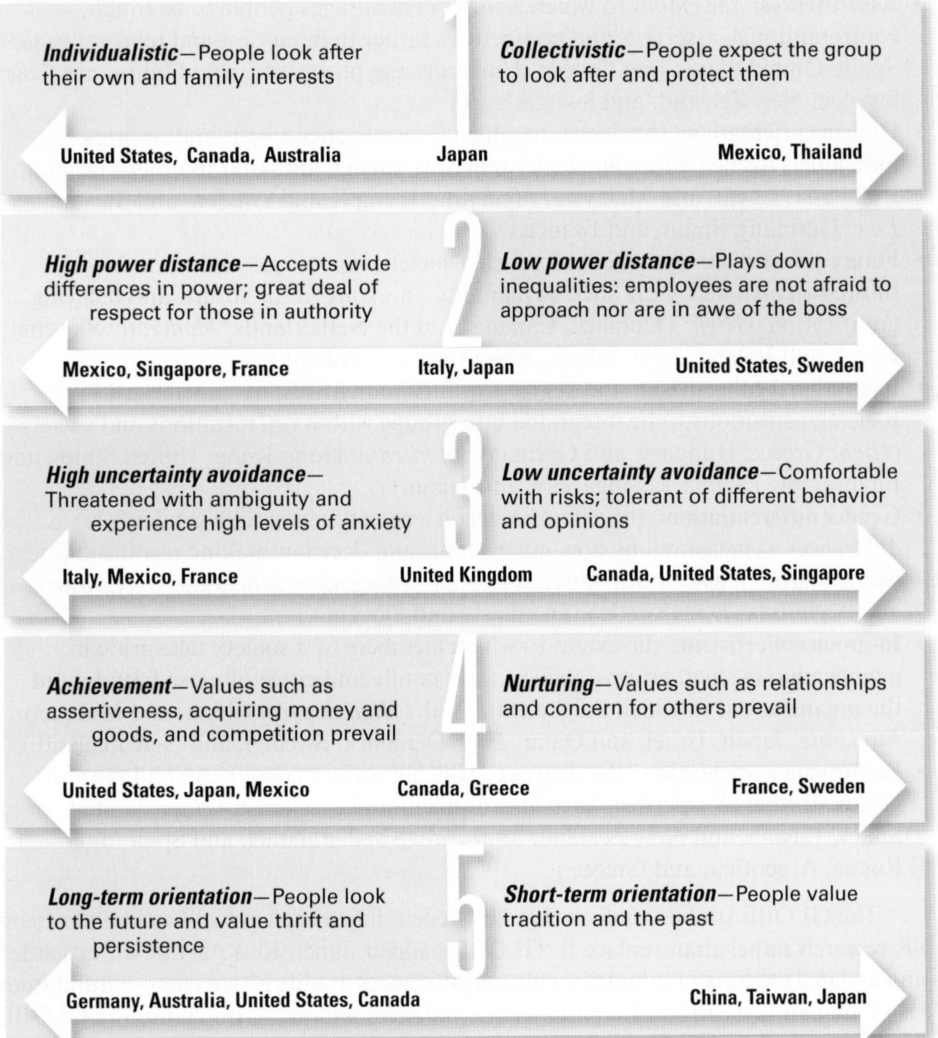

Exhibit 3-6
Hofstede's Five Dimensions of National Culture

Source: Based on Hofstede, Geert, *Culture's Consequences: International Differences in Work-Related Values,* © Geert Hofstede, 1980 (Newbury Park: SAGE Publications, Inc., 1980).

THE GLOBE FRAMEWORK FOR ASSESSING CULTURES The **Global Leadership and Organizational Behavior Effectiveness (GLOBE)** program is an ongoing research program that extended Hofstede's work by investigating cross-cultural leadership behaviors and giving managers additional information to help them identify and manage cultural differences. Using data from more than 18,000 managers in 62 countries, the GLOBE research team (led by Robert House) identified nine dimensions on which national cultures differ.[95] Two dimensions (power distance and uncertainty avoidance) fit directly with Hofstede's. Four are similar to Hofstede's (assertiveness, which is similar to achievement-nurturing; humane orientation, which is similar to the nurturing dimension; future orientation, which is similar to long-term and short-term orientation; and institutional collectivism, which is similar to individualism-collectivism). The remaining three (gender differentiation, in-group collectivism, and performance orientation) offer additional insights into a country's culture. Here are descriptions of these nine dimensions. For each of these dimensions, we have indicated which countries rated high, which rated moderate, and which rated low.

Global Leadership and Organizational Behavior Effectiveness (GLOBE) program
The research program that studies cross-cultural leadership behaviors

- **Power distance:** the extent to which a society accepts that power in institutions and organizations is distributed unequally. (*High:* Russia, Spain, and Thailand. *Moderate:* England, France, and Brazil. *Low:* Denmark, the Netherlands, and South Africa.)
- **Uncertainty avoidance:** a society's reliance on social norms and procedures to alleviate the unpredictability of future events. (*High:* Austria, Denmark, and Germany. *Moderate:* Israel, United States, and Mexico. *Low:* Russia, Hungary, and Bolivia.)

- **Assertiveness:** the extent to which a society encourages people to be tough, confrontational, assertive, and competitive rather than modest and tender. (*High:* Spain, United States, and Greece. *Moderate:* Egypt, Ireland, and Philippines. *Low:* Sweden, New Zealand, and Switzerland.)
- **Humane orientation:** the degree to which a society encourages and rewards individuals for being fair, altruistic, generous, caring, and kind to others. (*High:* Indonesia, Egypt, and Malaysia. *Moderate:* Hong Kong, Sweden, and Taiwan. *Low:* Germany, Spain, and France.)
- **Future orientation:** the extent to which a society encourages and rewards future-oriented behaviors such as planning, investing in the future, and delaying gratification. (*High:* Denmark, Canada, and the Netherlands. *Moderate:* Slovenia, Egypt, and Ireland. *Low:* Russia, Argentina, and Poland.)
- **Institutional collectivism:** the degree to which individuals are encouraged by societal institutions to be integrated into groups within organizations and society. (*High:* Greece, Hungary, and Germany. *Moderate:* Hong Kong, United States, and Egypt. *Low:* Denmark, Singapore, and Japan.)
- **Gender differentiation:** the extent to which a society maximizes gender role differences as measured by how much status and decision-making responsibilities women have. (*High:* South Korea, Egypt, and Morocco. *Moderate:* Italy, Brazil, and Argentina. *Low:* Sweden, Denmark, and Slovenia.)
- **In-group collectivism:** the extent to which members of a society take pride in membership in small groups, such as their family and circle of close friends, and the organizations in which they're employed. (*High:* Egypt, China, and Morocco. *Moderate:* Japan, Israel, and Qatar. *Low:* Denmark, Sweden, and New Zealand.)
- **Performance orientation:** the degree to which a society encourages and rewards group members for performance improvement and excellence. (*High:* United States, Taiwan, and New Zealand. *Moderate:* Sweden, Israel, and Spain. *Low:* Russia, Argentina, and Greece.)

The GLOBE studies confirm that Hofstede's dimensions are still valid and extend his research rather than replace it. GLOBE's added dimensions provide an expanded and updated measure of countries' cultural differences. It's likely that cross-cultural studies of human behavior and organizational practices will increasingly use the GLOBE dimensions to assess differences among countries.[96] While indeed Hofstede's dimensions are still valid, it is also important to recognize that our interactions with individuals from the same culture may differ because a variety of factors, such as personality, influence how people interact with each other. For example, we previously described Americans as being proactive. Indeed, this is a fair characterization of most Americans. But, by nature, some may not fulfill this expectation because they are inherently introverted. Introverted people tend to be focused more on internal thoughts, feelings, and moods rather than on seeking out interactions with others. Personality variables are measured on a continuum. Introversion is typically considered as part of a continuum along with extraversion, or individuals who generally seek out interactions with others.

★ It's Your Career!

Cultural Intelligence—If your instructor is using Pearson MyLab Management, log onto **mymanagementlab.com** and test your *cultural intelligence knowledge*. **Be sure to refer back to the chapter opener!**

Global Management in Today's World

Doing business globally today isn't easy! As we look at managing in today's global environment, we want to focus on two important issues. The first issue involves the challenges associated with globalization, especially in relation to the openness that's part of being global. The second issue revolves around the challenges of managing a global workforce.

THE CHALLENGE OF OPENNESS The push to go global has been widespread. Advocates praise the economic and social benefits that come from globalization, but globalization also creates challenges because of the openness that's necessary for it

let's get REAL

The Scenario:

Renata Zorzato, head of new product development for a global recruiting company, is preparing to move from Saõ Paulo to San Diego to head up a team of executive recruiters. Her newly formed team will include company employees from Berlin, London, Shanghai, Mexico City, Kuala Lumpur, New York, and San Diego. The team will be designing and launching an innovative new global executive recruiting tool. But first, Renata has to get the team members all working together, each bringing his or her unique strengths and perspectives to the project.

What's the best way for Renata to get this culturally diverse team up and running?

I would organize an off-site luncheon; food is a universal language. While at the luncheon, I would have each team member go around the room and introduce themselves, and being that the group is from all over the world, I would have each person speak a little about where they are from. After the lunch I would have an interactive game of some sort that requires the team to slowly begin working together—the idea would be for them to have more fun as opposed to work and get to know each other.

Katie Pagan
Accounting & HR Manager

Source: Katie Pagan

to work. One challenge is the increased threat of terrorism by a truly global terror network. Globalization is meant to open up trade and to break down the geographical barriers separating countries. Yet, opening up means just that—being open to the bad as well as the good. In a wide range of countries, from the Philippines and the United Kingdom to Israel and Pakistan, organizations and employees face the risk of terrorist attacks. Another challenge from openness is the economic interdependence of trading countries. As we saw over the last couple of years, the faltering of one country's economy can have a domino effect on other countries with which it does business. So far, however, the world economy has proved to be resilient. And as we discussed earlier, structures that are currently in place, such as the World Trade Organization and the International Monetary Fund, help to isolate and address potential problems.

The far more serious challenge for managers in the openness required by globalization comes from intense underlying and fundamental cultural differences—differences that encompass traditions, history, religious beliefs, and deep-seated values. Managing in such an environment can be extremely complicated. Even though globalization has long been praised for its economic benefits, some individuals think that globalization is simply a euphemism for "Americanization"—that is, the way U.S. cultural values and U.S. business philosophy are said to be slowly taking over the world.[97] At its best, proponents of Americanization hope others will see how progressive, efficient, industrious, and free U.S. society and businesses are and want to emulate that way of doing things. However, critics claim that this attitude of the "almighty American dollar wanting to spread the American way to every single country" has created many problems.[98] Although history is filled with clashes between civilizations, what's unique now is the speed and ease with which misunderstandings and disagreements can erupt and escalate. The Internet, television and other media, and global air travel have brought the good and the bad of American entertainment, products, and behaviors to every corner of the globe. For those who don't like what Americans do, say, or believe, this exposure can lead to resentment, dislike, distrust, and even outright hatred.

Challenges of Managing a Global Workforce

- Cross-cultural work teams can have many benefits, but conflicts can arise due to differences in work methods, pay levels, and language barriers.[99]

- Global companies with multicultural work teams are faced with the challenge of managing the cultural differences in work-family relationships. The work-family practices and programs appropriate and effective for employees in one country may not be the best solution for employees in other locations.[100]

These examples indicate challenges associated with managing a global workforce. As globalization continues to be important for businesses, it's obvious that managers need to understand how to best manage that global workforce. Some researchers have suggested that managers need **cultural intelligence** or cultural awareness and sensitivity skills.[101] Cultural intelligence encompasses three main dimensions: (1) knowledge of culture as a concept—how cultures vary and how they affect behavior; (2) mindfulness—the ability to pay attention to signals and reactions in different cross-cultural situations; and (3) behavioral skills—using one's knowledge and mindfulness to choose appropriate behaviors in those situations.

cultural intelligence
Cultural awareness and sensitivity skills

Other researchers have said that what effective global leaders need is a **global mind-set**, attributes that allow a leader to be effective in cross-cultural environments.[102] Those attributes have three components, as shown in Exhibit 3-7.

global mind set
Attributes that allow a leader to be effective in cross-cultural environments

Leaders who possess such cross-cultural skills and abilities—whether cultural intelligence or a global mind-set—will be important assets to global organizations. Successfully managing in today's global environment will require incredible sensitivity and understanding. Managers from any country will need to be aware of how their decisions and actions will be viewed, not only by those who may agree, but more importantly, by those who may disagree. They will need to adjust their leadership styles and management approaches to accommodate these diverse views, and at the same time be as efficient and effective as possible in reaching the organization's goals.

Exhibit 3-7
A Global Mind Set

Intellectual capital:	Knowledge of international business and the capacity to understand how business works on a global scale	
Psychological capital:	Openness to new ideas and experiences	
Social capital:	Ability to form connections and build trusting relationships with people who are different from you	

Source: Based on M. Javidan, M. Teagarden, and D. Bowen, "Making It Overseas," *Harvard Business Review,* April 2010, and J. McGregor, ed., "Testing Managers' Global IQ," *Bloomberg BusinessWeek,* September 28, 2009.

Chapter 3 PREPARING FOR: Exams/Quizzes

CHAPTER SUMMARY by Learning Objectives

LO3.1 CONTRAST ethnocentric, polycentric, and geocentric attitudes toward global business.

Parochialism is viewing the world solely through your own eyes and perspectives and not recognizing that others have different ways of living and working. An ethnocentric attitude is the parochial belief that the best work approaches and practices are those of the home country. A polycentric attitude is the view that the managers in the host country know the best work approaches and practices for running their business. And a geocentric attitude is a world-oriented view that focuses on using the best approaches and people from around the globe.

LO3.2 DISCUSS the importance of regional trading alliances and global trade mechanisms.

Countries enter regional trading alliances for a variety of reasons, mainly to stimulate economic growth. The European Union consists of 28 democratic countries with 5 countries having applied for membership. NAFTA continues to help Canada, Mexico, and the United States strengthen their global economic power. In Latin America, CAFTA-DR promotes trade liberalization between the United States and 5 Central American countries, and another free trade agreement of 10 South American countries known as the Southern Common Market or Mercosur is seen as an effective way to combine resources to better compete against other global economic powers. ASEAN is a trading alliance of 10 Southeast Asian nations—a region that remains important in the global economy. Other trade alliances include the African Union (AU), the East African Community (EAC), the South Asian Association for Regional Cooperation (SAARC), and the Trans-Pacific Partnership (TPP). To counteract some of the risks in global trade, the World Trade Organization (WTO) plays an important role in monitoring and promoting trade relationships. The International Monetary Fund (IMF) and the World Bank Group are two entities that provide monetary support and advice to their member countries. The Organization for Economic Cooperation and Development assists its member countries with financial support in achieving sustainable economic growth and employment.

LO3.3 DESCRIBE the structures and techniques organizations use as they go international.

A multinational corporation is an international company that maintains operations in multiple countries. A multidomestic organization is an MNC that decentralizes management and other decisions to the local country (the polycentric attitude). A global organization is an MNC that centralizes management and other decisions in the home country (the ethnocentric attitude). A transnational organization (the geocentric attitude) is an MNC that has eliminated artificial geographical barriers and uses the best work practices and approaches from wherever. Global sourcing is purchasing materials or labor from around the world wherever it is cheapest. Exporting is making products domestically and selling them abroad. Importing is acquiring products made abroad and selling them domestically. Licensing is used by manufacturing organizations that make or sell another company's products and use the company's brand name, technology, or product specifications. Franchising is similar but is usually used by service organizations that want to use another company's name and operating methods. A global strategic alliance is a partnership between an organization and foreign company partners in which they share resources and knowledge to develop new products or build facilities. A joint venture is a specific type of strategic alliance in which the partners agree to form a separate, independent organization for some business purpose. A foreign subsidiary is a direct investment in a foreign country that a company creates by establishing a separate and independent facility or office.

LO3.4 EXPLAIN the relevance of the political/legal, economic, and cultural environments to global business.

The laws and political stability of a country are issues in the global political/legal environment with which managers must be familiar. Likewise, managers must be aware of a country's economic issues such as currency exchange rates, inflation rates, and tax policies. Geert Hofstede identified five dimensions for assessing a country's culture, including individualism-collectivism, power distance, uncertainty avoidance, achievement-nurturing, and long-term/short-term orientation. The GLOBE studies identified nine dimensions for assessing country cultures: power distance, uncertainty avoidance, assertiveness, humane orientation, future orientation, institutional collectivism, gender differentiation, in-group collectivism, and performance orientation. The main challenges of doing business globally in today's world include (1) the openness associated with globalization and the significant cultural differences between countries and (2) managing a global workforce, which requires cultural intelligence and a global mind-set.

Pearson MyLab Management

Go to **mymanagementlab.com** to complete the problems marked with this icon ✪.

✪ REVIEW AND DISCUSSION QUESTIONS

3-1. A monolingual, parochial, and ethnocentric organization is bound to fail. Discuss.

3-2. The European Union (EU) is an economic and political partnership of countries. What are the practical implications of this union?

3-3. Discuss the role of the World Trade Organization (WTO).

3-4. What are the characteristics of a multidomestic corporation?

3-5. Is learning a foreign language essential for managers?

3-6. What clarity of perspective would the GLOBE framework, as presented in this chapter, offer to local managers to help them understand their employees better?

3-7. What makes the Association of Southeast Asian Nations (ASEAN) different from the European Union (EU) as a trade alliance? Can those differences impair ASEAN's effectiveness as a trade alliance compared to the EU?

3-8. How many ways can an organization go global? What is the primary driver for the organization to choose a particular path toward going global?

Pearson MyLab Management

If your professor has assigned these, go to **mymanagementlab.com** for the following Assisted-graded writing questions:

3-9. What are the main challenges of global business and how would you suggest handling them?

3-10. Is globalization good for business? For consumers? Discuss.

PREPARING FOR: My Career

✪ PERSONAL INVENTORY ASSESSMENTS

PERSONAL INVENTORY ASSESSMENT

Intercultural Sensitivity Scale

Managing in a global environment absolutely demands being sensitive to other country's cultures. Use this PIA to determine your level of cultural sensitivity.

✪ ETHICS DILEMMA

In 2013, a clothing factory in Bangladesh collapsed, killing 1,138 people.[103] Some 27 global brands, including Walmart and Benetton, were using the factory. One year on, these two corporations were among 22 of the 27 yet to contribute toward a compensation fund created for this cause. Factories in developing countries face similar problems all the time, but such instances may go unreported. Bangladesh alone houses around 5,000 garment factories. Many of these factories are converted to residential buildings, with no fire escapes or alarms. The scale of the problem means reforms may well take time.

3-11. Do you think that corporations that outsource to developing countries have a responsibility of care to the workers on those sites?

3-12. What can be done globally to ensure that employees working under such conditions are protected?

SKILLS EXERCISE Developing Your Collaboration Skill

About the Skill

Collaboration is the teamwork, synergy, and cooperation used by individuals when they seek a common goal. In many cross-cultural settings, the ability to collaborate is crucial. When all partners must work together to achieve goals, collaboration is critically important to the process. However, cultural differences can often make collaboration a challenge.

Steps in Practicing the Skill

- ***Look for common points of interest.*** The best way to start working together in a collaborative fashion is to seek commonalities that exist among the parties. Common points of interest enable communications to be more effective.
- ***Listen to others.*** Collaboration is a team effort. Everyone has valid points to offer, and each individual should have an opportunity to express his or her ideas.
- ***Check for understanding.*** Make sure you understand what the other person is saying. Use feedback when necessary.
- ***Accept diversity.*** Not everything in a collaborative effort will "go your way." Be willing to accept different ideas and different ways of doing things. Be open to these ideas and the creativity that surrounds them.
- ***Seek additional information.*** Ask individuals to provide additional information. Encourage others to talk and more fully explain suggestions. This brainstorming opportunity can assist in finding creative solutions.
- ***Don't become defensive.*** Collaboration requires open communications. Discussions may focus on things you and others may not be doing or need to do better. Don't take the constructive feedback as personal criticism. Focus on the topic being discussed, not on the person delivering the message. Recognize that you cannot always be right!

Practicing the Skill

Interview individuals from three different nationalities about the challenges of collaborating with individuals from different cultures. What challenges do different cultures create? How have they dealt with these challenges? What advice do they have for improving collaboration across cultural differences? Based on your interviews, what are some general ideas you learned to improve your ability to collaborate?

WORKING TOGETHER Team Exercise

Moving to a foreign country isn't easy, no matter how many times you've done it or how receptive you are to new experiences. Successful global organizations are able to identify the best candidates for global assignments, and one of the ways they do this is through individual assessments prior to assigning people to global facilities. Form groups of three to five individuals. Your newly formed team, the Global Assignment Task Force, has been given the responsibility for developing a global aptitude assessment form for Yum Brands (the largest food operator in the world whose units include Taco Bell, Pizza Hut, KFC, Long John Silver's, and A&W). Because Yum is expanding its global operations significantly, it wants to make sure it's sending the best possible people to the various global locations. Your team's assignment is to come up with a rough draft of a form to assess people's global aptitude. Think about the characteristics, skills, attitudes, and so on that you think a successful global employee would need. Your team's draft should be at least half a page, but not lengthier than one page. Be prepared to present your ideas to your classmates and professor.

MY TURN TO BE A MANAGER

- Find two current examples of each of the ways that organizations go international. Write a short paper describing what these companies are doing.
- The U.K.-based company Kwintessential has several cultural knowledge "quizzes" on its website (www.kwintessential.co.uk/resources/culture-tests.html). Go to the website and try two or three of them. Were you surprised at your score? What does your score tell you about your cultural awareness?
- On this website, you'll also find Intercultural Management Guides (www.kwintessential.co.uk/intercultural/management/guide.html). Pick two countries to study (from different regions), and compare them. How are they the same? Different? How would this information help a manager?
- Interview two or three professors or students at your school who are from other countries. Ask them to describe what the business world is like in their country. Write a short paper describing what you found out.
- Take advantage of opportunities you might have to travel to other countries, either on personal trips or on school-sponsored trips.
- Sign up for a foreign language course.

- Suppose you were sent on an overseas assignment to another country (you decide which one). Research that country's economic, political/legal, and cultural environments. Write a report summarizing your findings.
- If you don't have your passport yet, go through the process to get one. (The current fee in the United States is $140.)
- It is important to understand basic etiquette when traveling internationally for business (e.g., how does one greet someone new, and is a handshake appropriate?). Identify three countries that you would like to travel to and conduct research to learn about business etiquette for those countries. Summarize your findings.
- Identify a company that operates internationally and has locations in more than two different countries. Explore the "Career" page of the company's website. Write a brief report about the career opportunities available at the company and the required qualifications of applicants.

CASE APPLICATION 1 Dirty Little Secret

Money. Secrecy. Foreign officials. "Greasing palms." Bribery. That's the dirty little secret about doing business globally that managers at multinational companies don't want to talk about. Although 39 countries worldwide have signed up for the OECD Anti-Bribery Convention to outlaw bribery and corruption, the problem is far from gone. Take Greece, for example, which has been censored by the OECD for failing in its promise to crack down on corruption. The practice of political favouritism and passing "fakelaki"—envelopes stuffed with cash—in return for services is as prevalent today as it ever was. Indeed, since the country joined the European Community, more than 150 scandals have come to light, and it is thought that part of the blame for the country's €367 billion ($486 billion) debt is down to an epidemic of corruption. From needless jobs to a refusal to give receipts, through tax evasion and then on to high-level bribery, it is estimated that Greek citizens spent nearly €1.62 billion ($2.15 billion) in 2012 on bribes. Foreign companies looking toward Greece are aware that this is often the cost of doing business there. In August 2012, the German group Siemens AG, reached a €330 million ($438 billion) settlement with the Greek government over long-running allegations that Siemens AG used bribery to secure a raft of contracts for the Athens Olympic Games in 2004. In an earlier case, two managers from another German company, industrial firm Ferrostaal, were convicted of paying bribes in Greece and ordered to pay fines.[104]

DISCUSSION QUESTIONS

3-13. What's your reaction to the events mentioned in the case? Are you surprised that bribery is illegal? Why do you think bribery takes place? Why do you think it needs to be outlawed?

3-14. Research whether other countries outlaw bribery. (Hint: look at the Organization for Economic Cooperation and Development.)

3-15. We've said it's important for managers to be aware of external environmental forces, especially in global settings. Discuss this statement in light of the events described.

3-16. What might the managers at Siemens AG have done differently? Explain.

3-17. Siemens AG is not the only company to be linked to bribery. Find at least three other examples and describe them briefly.

CASE APPLICATION 2 The Power of Presence

How do you successfully manage a growing international company? CEO Christian Chabot of Seattle-based Tableau now believes being there physically is an important piece in the often complex puzzle of international management.[105] International growth is nothing new for Tableau, which was founded in 2004. As a leading provider of analytics and business intelligence software solutions, the company has more than 35,000 clients in over a dozen countries.

Tableau provides software tools and interactive dashboards that allow users to generate useful business insights through the analysis and visualization of data. The company is on the cutting edge of data-imaging solutions for end-users, creating products such as Elastic, which allows users to create graphics from spreadsheets. Despite tough competition in the market for business intelligence from software giants such as Microsoft, Tableau has continued to maintain its share of the marketplace, and the company's value continues to grow with a 64 percent increase in revenue over last year. Much of the company's growth is attributed to the company's expansion into international markets, with an 86 percent increase in revenue last year from international markets, which now account for a quarter of the company's total revenues.

With plans to hire about 1,000 more employees in the next year, the company's projected continued success is evident. While more than half of their current 2,800 employees work in the company's Seattle headquarters, Tableau has 14 locations around the world in places such as Shanghai, Singapore, Sydney, and London. About 400 of the new employees will be hired outside of the Seattle headquarters, and Tableau's expansion will include opening new international offices.

International growth creates many challenges for companies, particularly as they open and staff branch locations in different countries. Cultural differences, time differences, and simply the geographic distance can make it difficult to sustain the same management practices at home and abroad. How has Chabot managed the quick growth of this international company? One strategy was to spend almost a year abroad working in the company's London office. His focused time at that location helped grow regional sales, but also provided the CEO with valuable insights to support further international expansion.

Chabot reported that the time he spent in London highlighted the importance of managing culture and people. Prior to the trip he did not have a true understanding of the challenges of international employees working for a U.S.-based company. He found that many working in international branch offices did not feel like they were taken seriously by those at the home office. Geographically remote workers can feel disconnected from a global company, particularly when they report to management they have never met in person at headquarters.

Chabot's time working in London was valuable for employees in all locations of the company, as his actions sent the message that he feels employees outside of headquarters are important. While he spent time only in London, the fact that he spent a year away from the home office emphasized his belief that locations beyond Seattle are important for the company's success. Chabot's experience is having such a profound impact on the company's success, Tableau is now encouraging other executives to spend time at international offices.

DISCUSSION QUESTIONS

3-18. Tableau staffs its international offices primarily with host country nationals. What are the advantages and disadvantages of this staffing strategy?

3-19. Do you agree with Chabot that the company will benefit if more executives spend time in international offices? Why or why not?

3-20. As Tableau executives get ready to spend time in the company's international offices, how can they prepare for the cultural differences they will encounter?

3-21. What are some of the challenges Tableau will face as it hires 1,000 new employees in one year?

ANSWERS TO "WHO OWNS WHAT" QUIZ

1. **d. Switzerland**
   Nestlé SA bought both the Tombstone and DiGiorno frozen-pizza brands from Kraft Foods in 2009.
2. **c. United States**
   Uber Technologies, LLC is a U.S. company based in San Francisco, California, established in 2009.
3. **a. United States**
   Rajah Spices are products of the Lea & Perrins sauce division, which the H.J. Heinz Company acquired in June of 2005.
4. **a. The Netherlands**
   Mexico's second-largest beer producer was acquired by Heineken N.V. in January 2010.
5. **b. United Kingdom**
   The television show *America's Got Talent* premiered in June 2006, and it is a part of the British franchise *Got Talent*, owned by SYCOtv company.
6. **c. United States**
   Chobani, LLC is a U.S. company that manufactures and distributes Greek yogurt, and prior to 2012, was named Agro-Farma, Inc.
7. **c. Switzerland**
   The Swatch Group Ltd. was established through the merger of two Swiss watch companies—ASUAG and SSIH, in 1983.
8. **a. Russia**
   Russian tycoon Alexander Lebedev acquired the *Independent* in March 2010.
9. **a. Sweden**
   Spotify is a service of Spotify AB, which was established in 2008.
10. **b. Sweden**
    Interactive game company King Digital Entertainment was established in 2003.

ENDNOTES

1. B. Leonard, "Study Examines the Importance of Globally Competent Leaders," *SHRM Online,* www.shrm.org/hrdisciplines/businessleadership/articles/pages/global-leadership-study.aspx., May 21, 2015.
2. "Compete and Connect: Developing Globally Competent Leaders," Human Capital Institute Report, Kenan-Flagler Business School Executive Development, University of North Carolina, www.execdev.unc.edu, 2015.
3. J. Eisenberg, H-J. Lee, F. Bruck, B. Brenner, M-T. Claes, J. Mironski, and R. Bell, "Can Business Schools Make Students Culturally Competent? Effects of Cross-Cultural Management Courses on Cultural Intelligence," *Academy of Management Learning & Education,* December 2013, pp. 603–621; M. E. Mendenhall, A. A. Arnardottir, G. R. Oddou, and L. A. Burke, "Developing Cross-Cultural Competencies in Management Education via Cognitive-Behavior Therapy," *Academy of Management Learning & Education,* September 2013, pp. 436–451; B. D. Blume, T. T. Baldwin, and K. C. Ryan, "Communication Apprehension: A Barrier to Students' Leadership, Adaptability, and Multicultural Appreciation," *Academy of Management Learning & Education,* June 2013, pp. 158–172; P. Caligiuri, "Develop Your Cultural Agility," *T&D,* March 2013, pp. 70+; M. Li, W. H. Mobley, and A. Kelly, "When Do Global Leaders Learn Best to Develop Cultural Intelligence? An Investigation of the Moderating Role of Experiential Learning Style," *Academy of Management Learning & Education,* March 2013, pp. 32–50; N. Jesionka, "Why Knowing About the World Can Help Your Career," www.thedailymuse.com, June 14, 2013.
4. G. Koretz, "Things Go Better with Multinationals—Except Jobs," *BusinessWeek*, May 2, 1994, p. 20.
5. N. Kelly, "7 Traits of Companies on the Fast Track to International Growth," *Harvard Business Review* online, https://hbr.org, March 6, 2015.
6. M. Palmquist, "Measuring the Value of Going Global," *Strategy + Business Online,* Spring 2012.
7. The idea for this quiz was adapted from R. M. Hodgetts and F. Luthans, *International Management*, 2d ed. (New York: McGraw-Hill, 1994).
8. A. R. Carey and V. Bravo, "Proficiency in Foreign Languages," *USA Today,* December 3, 2013, p. 1A.
9. D. Skorton and G. Altschuler, "America's Foreign Language Deficit," www.forbes.com, August 21, 2012.
10. Based on Reuters Limited, *USA Today* online, www.usatoday.com, February 21, 2006; D. Graddol, "Indian English Challenge Hurts Bahrain," *The Telegraph* (Calcutta, India), February 22, 2006; and "Learning the Lingo," *USA Today,* January 26, 2006, p. 1A.
11. U.S. Department of Education, "Education and the Language Gap: Secretary Arne Duncan's Remarks at the Foreign Language Summit," press release, http://www.ed.gov/news/speeches/education-and-language-gap-secretary-arne-duncans-remarks-foreign-language-summit, December 8, 2010.

12. D. Skorton and G. Altschuler, "America's Foreign Language Deficit," *Forbes* online, www.forbes.com, August 21, 2012.
13. R. Lederer, "We Americans Need to Improve Our Basic Verbal Skills," *The San Diego Union-Tribune* online, http://www.sandiegouniontribune.com/news/2014/jan/11/we-americans-need-to-improve-our-basic-verbal, January 11, 2014.
14. N. Adler, *International Dimensions of Organizational Behavior*, 5th ed. (Cincinnati: South-Western, 2008).
15. M. R. F. Kets De Vries and E. Florent-Treacy, "Global Leadership From A to Z: Creating High Commitment Organizations," *Organizational Dynamics,* Spring 2002, pp. 295–309; P. R. Harris and R. T. Moran, *Managing Cultural Differences,* 4th ed. (Houston: Gulf Publishing Co., 1996); R. T. Moran, P. R. Harris, and W. G. Stripp, *Developing the Global Organization: Strategies for Human Resource Professionals* (Houston: Gulf Publishing Co., 1993); Y. Wind, S. P. Douglas, and H. V. Perlmutter, "Guidelines for Developing International Marketing Strategies," *Journal of Marketing*, April 1973, pp. 14–23; and H. V. Perlmutter, "The Tortuous Evolution of the Multinational Corporation," *Colombia Journal of World Business*, January–February 1969, pp. 9–18.
16. T. K. Grose, "When in Rome, Do as Roman CEOs Do," *U.S. News & World Report,* November 2009, pp. 38–41.
17. M. Ramsey, "The Next Model of Auto Boss," *Wall Street Journal,* December 21, 2012, pp. B1+.
18. "Developing Global-Minded Leaders to Drive High Performers," American Management Association, http://www.amanet.org/training/articles/Developing-Global-minded-Leaders-to-Drive-High-Performance.aspx, June 19, 2015.
19. C. Davidson, "3 Skills Every 21st-Century Manager Needs," *Harvard Business Review,* January–February 2012, pp. 138–143.
20. S. Kotkin, "The World as an Imperfect Globe," *New York Times* online, www.nytimes.com, December 2, 2007.
21. K. Kpodar and P. Imam, "Does a Regional Trade Agreement Lessen or Exacerbate Growth Volatility? An Empirical Investigation" (working paper, International Monetary Fund (IMF), Washington, DC, WP/15/177, 2015).
22. Office of the United States Trade Representative Countries and Regions, website, www.ustr.gov, October 14, 2015.
23. European Union, "EU Member Countries and on the Road to EU Membership," www.europa.eu/, October 14, 2015.
24. European Union, "Population and Population Change Statistics," www.ec.europa.eu/, October 14, 2015.
25. European Union, "EU Position in World Trade," www.ec.europa.eu, October 14, 2015.
26. European Union, "The Euro," www.europa.eu/, March 10, 2014.
27. European Union, "Treaty of Lisbon: Taking Europe into the 21st Century," www.europa.eu/, March 10, 2014.
28. European Union, "Spring 2015 Economic Forecast: Tailwinds Support Recovery," ec.europa.eu, Spring 2015, October 14, 2015.
29. Central Intelligence Agency, *CIA World Factbook*, https://www.cia.gov/library/publications/resources/the-world-factbook/, 2012.
30. M. A. Villarreal and I. F. Fergusson, "The North American Free Trade Agreement (NAFTA)," Congressional Research Service, www.crs.gov, April 16, 2015.
31. D. Cave, "Better Lives for Mexicans Cut Allure of Going North," *New York Times* online, www.nytimes.com, July 6, 2011.
32. J. M. Krogstad and J. S. Passel, "5 Facts about Illegal Immigration in the U.S.," Pew Research Center, www.pewresearch.org, July 24, 2015; and Editorial Board, "The Receding Tide of Illegal Immigrants from Mexico," *New York Times* online, www.nytimes.com, April 28, 2012.
33. M. A. O'Grady, "NAFTA at 20: A Model for Trade Policy," *Wall Street Journal,* January 6, 2014, p. A11; and G. P. Shultz, "The North American Global Powerhouse," *Wall Street Journal,* July 12, 2013, p. A13.
34. Dominican Republic-Central America-United States Free Trade Agreement (CAFTA-DR), www.export.gov, October 14, 2015.
35. J. Forero, "U.S. and Colombia Reach Trade Deal after 2 Years of Talks," *New York Times* online, www.nytimes.com, February 28, 2006.
36. U.S. Trade Information Center, "The U.S.-Columbia Trade Promotion Agreement," www.ustr.gov, October 15, 2015.
37. ASEAN, *Statistical Yearbook*, www.asean.org, July 2015.
38. J. Hookway, "Asian Nations Push Ideas for Trade," *Wall Street Journal,* October 26, 2009, p. A12; and Bloomberg News, "Southeast Asian Nations Talk of Economic Union," *New York Times* online, www.nytimes.com, March 2, 2009.
39. "Asia's Never-Closer Union," *Economist,* February 6, 2010, p. 48; "East Asia Summit: Regional Unity Decades Away," *Business Monitor International*, www.asia-monitor.com, 2009/2010; and Bloomberg News, "Southeast Asian Nations Talk of Economic Union."
40. "China-ASEAN FTA: Winners and Losers," *China & North East Asia,* February 2010, p. 2.
41. "2014–2017 Strategic Plan," *African Union Commission's Strategic Plan,* http://www.au.int/en/auc/strategic-plan-2014-2017; and D. Kraft, "Leaders Question, Praise African Union," *Springfield News-Leader,* July 10, 2002, p. 8A.
42. C. Gower, "What Is the African Union and Has It Been Successful?," *The Telegraph* online, www.telegraph.co.uk, July 28, 2015.
43. J. Guo, "Africa Is Booming Like Never Before," *Newsweek,* March 1, 2010, p. 6.
44. "It Really May Happen," *Economist,* January 2, 2010, p. 36; and "Five into One?," *Business Africa,* December 1, 2009, p. 1.
45. SAARC Official website, www.saarc-sec.org; and N. George, "South Asia Trade Zone in Works," *Springfield News-Leader,* January 4, 2004, p. 1E+.
46. "Note by the Secretariat on Economic and Financial Cooperation," SAARC Official website, www.saarc-sec.org, January 22, 2015.
47. W. Mauldin, "At a Glance: Trans-Pacific Partnership," *The Wall Street Journal* online, www.wsj.com, October 5, 2015.
48. This section is based on materials from the World Trade Organization Web site [www.wto.org]; "What's Up at the WTO?" *Industry Week,* February 2010, p. 20; and D. A. Irwin, "GATT Turns 60," *Wall Street Journal,* April 9, 2007, p. A13.
49. J. W. Miller and M. Dalton, "WTO Finds EU Aid to Airbus Is Illegal," *Wall Street Journal,* March 24, 2010, p. A10; and C. Drew and N. Clark, "WTO Affirms Ruling of Improper Airbus Aid," *New York Times* online, www.nytimes.com, March 23, 2010.
50. "Internet Censorship: Showdown at the WTO?," *Bloomberg BusinessWeek,* March 15, 2010, p. 12.
51. CNN Wire Staff, "Obama Announces WTO Case against China over Rare Earths," *CNN* online, www.cnn.com, March 13, 2012.
52. World Trade Organization, "China—Measures Related to the Exportation of Rare Earths, Tungsten and Molybdenum," www.wto.org, October 15, 2015.

53. Leader Making a Difference Box based on R. Mac, "Alibaba Claims Title for Largest Global IPO Ever with Extra Share Sales," *Forbes* online, www.forbes.com, September 22, 2014; E. Howard, "The World's 100 Most Powerful Women 2015," *Forbes* online, www.forbes.com, May 26, 2015; S. Cendrowski, "Alibaba's Maggie Wu and Lucy Peng: The Dynamic Duo behind the IPO," *Fortune* online, www.fortune.com, September 17, 2014; "Women in Finance, Lucy Peng," www.financeasia.com, August 5, 2015.
54. International Monetary Fund website, www.imf.org, October 15, 2015.
55. S. Johnson, "Can the I.M.F. Save the World?," *New York Times* online, www.nytimes.com, September 22, 2011; and Associated Press, "IMF Warns Global Instability Demands Strong Policies," *USA Today,* September 21, 2011, p. 3B.
56. World Bank Group website, www.worldbank.org, October 15, 2015.
57. News Release, "World Bank Group: Record US $100 Billion Response Lays Foundation for Recovery from Global Economic Crisis," www.worldbank.org, April 7, 2010.
58. Organization for Economic Cooperation and Development website, www.oecd.org, October 15, 2015.
59. D. Searcey, "Small-Scale Bribes Targeted by OECD," *Wall Street Journal,* December 10, 2009, p. A4.
60. "OECD/G20 Base Erosion and Profit Shifting Project Forwarded to G20 Heads of State in November," www.oecd.org, September 10, 2015.
61. S. Schonhardt, "7-Eleven Finds a Niche by Adapting to Indonesian Ways," *New York Times* online, www.nytimes.com, May 28, 2012; E. Glazer, "P&G Unit Bids Goodbye to Cincinnati, Hello to Asia," *Wall Street Journal,* May 11, 2012, p. B1; D. Jolly, "Daimler, Nissan, and Renault Unveil Partnership," *New York Times* online, www.nytimes.com, April 7, 2010; B. Becht, "Building a Company without Borders," *Harvard Business Review,* April 2010, pp. 103–106; and "Statistical Information," www.mosers.org, March 15, 2010.
62. "Fortune Global 500," *Fortune* online, www. http://fortune.com/global500/, October 16, 2015.
63. C. A. Bartlett and S. Ghoshal, *Managing Across Borders: The Transnational Solution,* 2d ed. (Boston: Harvard Business School Press, 2002); and N. J. Adler, *International Dimensions of Organizational Behavior,* 4th ed. (Cincinnati, OH: South-Western, 2002), pp. 9–11.
64. M. Bustillo, "After Early Errors, Wal-Mart Thinks Locally to Act Globally," *Wall Street Journal,* August 14, 2009, pp. A1+.
65. P. F. Drucker, "The Global Economy and the Nation-State," *Foreign Affairs,* September–October, 1997, pp. 159–171.
66. P. Kunert, "IBM Ushers in Biggest Ever Re-Org for the Cloud Era, Say Insiders," *Forbes* online, www.forbes.com, January 9, 2015.
67. J. Henry, "One Ford, Part Two; Tweaking the Master Plan," *Forbes* online, www.forbes.com, August 30, 2015.
68. P. Dvorak, "Why Multiple Headquarters Multiply," *Wall Street Journal,* November 19, 2007, pp. B1+.
69. B. Becht, "Building a Company without Borders"; D. A. Aaker, *Developing Business Strategies,* 5th ed. (New York: John Wiley & Sons, 1998); and J. A. Byrne et al., "Borderless Management," *BusinessWeek*, May 23, 1994, pp. 24–26.
70. B. Davis, "Migration of Skilled Jobs Abroad Unsettles Global-Economy Fans," *Wall Street Journal,* January 26, 2004, p. A1.
71. J. Teresko, "United Plastics Picks China's Silicon Valley," *Industry Week,* January 2003, p. 58.
72. U.S. Department of Labor, *Findings on the Worst Forms of Child Labor,* September 30, 2015.
73. F. Mutsaka and P. Wonacott, "Mugabe Presses Law Requiring Foreign Entities to Cede Control," *Wall Street Journal,* February 19, 2010, p. A9.
74. D. Roberts, "Closing for Business," *Bloomberg BusinessWeek,* April 5, 2010, pp. 32–37; and A. Browne and J. Dean, "Business Sours on China," *Wall Street Journal,* March 17, 2010, pp. A1+.
75. U.S. Department of State, "China: Investment Climate Statement 2015," www.state.gov, May 2015.
76. W. Mauldin, "Russians Search BP Office Second Day," *Wall Street Journal*, September 2, 2011, p. B6; and A. E. Kramer, "Memo to Exxon: Business with Russia Might Involve Guns and Balaclavas," *New York Times* online, www.nytimes.com, August 31, 2011.
77. M. Moran, "Political Risk on the Rise: The Peril of Emerging Markets," http://www.forbes.com/sites/riskmap/2014/01/17/political-risk-on-the-rise-the-peril-of-emerging-markets/, March 10, 2014.
78. U.S. Department of State, "China: Investment Climate Statement 2015,"; Roberts, "Closing for Business"; and Browne and Dean, "Business Sours on China."
79. "Leading Indicator," *Newsweek,* September 14, 2009, p. 14.
80. British Broadcasting Corporation, "Internet Used by 3.2 Billion People in 2015," bbc.com, May 26, 2015.
81. Internet World Users by Language: Top 10 Languages," www.internetworldstats.com, October 15, 2015.
82. R. Knight, "How to Manage Remote Direct Reports," *Harvard Business Review* online, www.hbr.org, June 27, 2013, February 10, 2015.
83. M. Watkins, "Making Virtual Teams Work: Ten Basic Principles," *Harvard Business Review* online, www.hbr.org, June 27, 2013.
84. P. Hernandez, "Skype Translator Now Available for All Windows Users," www.eweek.com, January 16, 2016.
85. M. Landler, "Germany's Export-Led Economy Finds Global Niche," *New York Times* online, www.nytimes.com, April 13, 2007.
86. The World Bank, "Inflation, GDP Deflator (Annual %)," http://data.worldbank.org/, October 15, 2015.
87. S. S. Munoz, "Escape for Cash Trapped in Caracas," *Wall Street Journal,* September 4, 2013, p. B8.
88. "Working Remotely," *Harvard Business Review,* May 2013, p. 12; D. M. Airoldi, "Starwood Studies Abroad," *CFO,* September 2011, pp. 29–30; A. Sheivachman, "Starwood Puts Priority on Chinese Development," *Hotel Management,* August 1, 2011, p. 15; and A. Berzon, "Frits Van Paasschen: Starwood CEO Moves to China to Grow Brand," *Wall Street Journal,* June 6, 2011, p. B6.
89. J. McGregor and S. Hamm, "Managing the Global Workforce," *Bloomberg BusinessWeek,* January 28, 2008, pp. 34–51.
90. Katie Jacobs, "Sodexo's Natalie Bickford on Diversity, Engagement, and Mobility," *HR Magazine (UK)*, February 23, 2015, http://www.hrmagazine.co.uk/article-details/sodexos-natalie-bickford-on-diversity-engagement-and-mobility (accessed December 13, 2016); Erin McGuire, "Communication Crucial for Generation Game," *Irish Times*, October 16, 2015 (accessed December 13, 2016); Michel Landel, "Sodexo's CEO on Smart Diversification," *Harvard Business Review*, March 2015, https://hbr.org/2015/03/sodexos-ceo-on-smart-diversification (accessed December 13, 2016).

91. J. Hirschkorn, "Business Etiquette: The Importance of Cultural Sensitivity," *The Telegraph* online, www.telegraph.co.uk, January 30, 2014.
92. See G. Hofstede, *Culture's Consequences: International Differences in Work-Related Values,* 2d ed. (Thousand Oaks, CA: Sage Publications, 2001), pp. 9–15.
93. S. Bhaskaran and N. Sukumaran, "National Culture, Business Culture and Management Practices: Consequential Relationships?," *Cross Cultural Management: An International Journal,* vol. 14, no. 7, 2007, pp. 54–67; G. Hofstede, *Culture's Consequences;* and G. Hofstede, "The Cultural Relativity of Organizational Practices and Theories," *Journal of International Business Studies,* Fall 1983, pp. 75–89.
94. M. Minkov and G. Hofstede, "The Evolution of Hofstede's Doctrine," *Cross Cultural Management,* February 2011, pp. 10–20.
95. R. R. McCrae, A. Terracciano, A. Realo, and J. Allik, "Interpreting GLOBE Societal Practices Scale," *Journal of Cross-Cultural Psychology,* November 2008, pp. 805–810; J. S. Chhokar, F. C. Brodbeck, and R. J. House, *Culture and Leadership Across the World: The GLOBE Book of In-Depth Studies of 25 Societies* (Philadelphia: Lawrence Erlbaum Associates, 2007); and R. J. House, P. J. Hanges, M. Javidan, P. W. Dorfman, and V. Gupta, *Culture, Leadership, and Organizations: The GLOBE Study of 62 Societies* (Thousand Oaks, CA: Sage Publications, 2004).
96. For instance, see D. A. Waldman, M. S. de Luque, and D. Wang, "What Can We Really Learn About Management Practices across Firms and Countries?," *Academy of Management Perspectives,* February 2012, pp. 34–40; A. E. Munley, "Culture Differences in Leadership," *IUP Journal of Soft Skills,* March 2011, pp. 16–30; and R. J. House, N. R. Quigley, and M. S. de Luque, "Insights from Project GLOBE: Extending Advertising Research Through a Contemporary Framework," *International Journal of Advertising,* 29, no. 1 (2010), pp. 111–139.
97. D. Yergin, "Globalization Opens Door to New Dangers," *USA Today,* May 28, 2003, p. 11A; K. Lowrey Miller, "Is It Globaloney?," *Newsweek,* December 16, 2002, pp. E4–E8; L. Gomes, "Globalization Is Now a Two-Way Street—Good News for the U.S.," *Wall Street Journal*, December 9, 2002, p. B1; J. Kurlantzick and J. T. Allen, "The Trouble With Globalism," *U.S. News and World Report,* February 11, 2002, pp. 38–41; and J. Guyon, "The American Way," *Fortune,* November 26, 2001, pp. 114–120.
98. Guyon, "The American Way," p. 114.
99. Based on H. Seligson, "For American Workers in China, a Culture Clash," *New York Times* online, www.nytimes.com, December 23, 2009.
100. G. N. Powell, A. M. Francesco, and Y. Ling, "Toward Culture-Sensitive Theories of the Work-Family Interface," *Journal of Organizational Behavior,* July 2009, pp. 597–616.
101. "Why You Need Cultural Intelligence (And How to Develop It)," *Forbes* online, www.forbes.com, March 24, 2015; J. S. Lublin, "Cultural Flexibility in Demand," *Wall Street Journal,* April 11, 2011, pp. B1+; S. Russwurm, L. Hernández, S. Chambers, and K. Chung, "Developing Your Global Know-How," *Harvard Business Review,* March 2011, pp. 70–75; "Are You Cued in to Cultural Intelligence?" *Industry Week,* November 2009, p. 24; M. Blasco, "Cultural Pragmatists? Student Perspectives on Learning Culture at a Business School," *Academy of Management Learning & Education,* June 2009, pp. 174–187; and D. C. Thomas and K. Inkson, "Cultural Intelligence: People Skills for a Global Workplace," *Consulting to Management,* vol. 16, no. 1, pp. 5–9.
102. M. Javidan, M. Teagarden, and D. Bowen, "Making It Overseas," *Harvard Business Review,* April 2010, pp. 109–113.
103. Jason Burke, "Rana Plaza: One Year on from the Bangladesh Factory Disaster," *The Guardian*, April 19, 2014.
104. OECD Web site, www.oecd.org/greece, November 2012.
105. T. Soper, "Tableau Software Set to Hire Another 1,000 Employees in 2016; CEO Says Business 'Flourishing,'" www.geekwire.com, December 14, 2015; N. Ungerleider, "What Tinder Did for Dating, Tableau Wants to Do for Spreadsheets." *Fast Company* online, www.fastcompany.com, February 24, 2015; "Tableau's Q3 Earnings: International Expansion & New Products Drive Top-Line Growth," *Forbes* online, www.forbes.com, November 11, 2015; "Tableau's Entry into China a Good Move as Company Targets International Growth," *Forbes* online, www.forbes.com, August 21, 2015; T. Soper, " How to Lead a Global Company: What Tableau's CEO Learned During His Year in London," www.geekwire.com, December 25, 2015.

Chapter 4

Valuing a Diverse Workforce

It's Your Career

Source: MNSKumar/Shutterstock

A key to success in management and in your career is knowing how to find a great sponsor/ mentor and how to be a great protégé.

Find a Great Sponsor/ Mentor—Be a Great Protégé

What do you want from your career? If your goal is to "move up the organizational ladder" to higher and more challenging positions of responsibility, then consider finding influential people who believe in you and will work with you to help you get ahead. These individuals—called sponsors or mentors—can be a wonderful source of career support. How? By advocating for your career path/ promotion; assisting you in dealing with problems/ conflicts; expanding your perception of what you can do; helping you "connect" with senior executives and other influential people; and advising you on "how" to be promotable. Now that you know what they're called... what are you called? The term for the other person in this relationship is protégé, *which comes from a French word meaning to protect. As someone with a lot of knowledge and experience, the sponsor/mentor "protects" the protégé by helping prepare (groom) that person for more challenging job responsibilities. Here's what you need to know to have active and effective sponsor/protégé relationships:*

*1. **Absolutely, positively, always DO GREAT WORK.** Be sure that your work performance is stellar. Demonstrate that you can and will deliver outstanding performance. Realize that doesn't mean that you won't ever make mistakes. But if you do make mistakes, learn quickly from those mistakes. Seek out new challenges and be enthusiastic when you get them. And remember, doing great work **is** absolutely essential!*

*2. **TRUSTWORTHINESS and LOYALTY and DEPENDABILITY are absolutely critical.** Sponsors/mentors want to know that you can be trusted in all ways and in all things. Be loyal. Keep your sponsor "in the know." Your sponsor wants to know that you can be depended on totally to do the right thing. Make your sponsor look good and look smart for taking you on as a protégé. Ideally, you and your sponsor(s) should work together to*

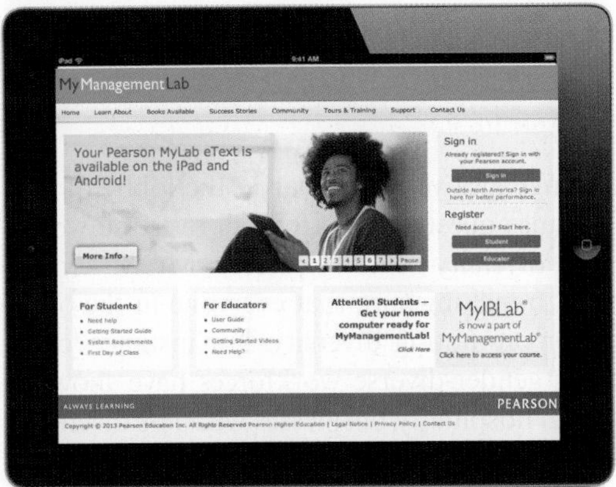

Pearson MyLab Management®

Improve Your Grade!

When you see this icon, visit **www.mymanagementlab.com** for activities that are applied, personalized, and offer immediate feedback.

Learning Objectives

• SKILL OUTCOMES

4.1 ***Define*** *workplace diversity and explain why managing it is so important.*

- **Develop your skill** at valuing and working with diverse individuals and teams.

4.2 ***Describe*** *the changing workplaces in the United States and around the world.*

4.3 ***Explain*** *the different types of diversity found in workplaces.*

4.4 ***Discuss*** *the challenges managers face in managing diversity.*

4.5 ***Describe*** *various workplace diversity management initiatives.*

- **Know how** to find a great sponsor/mentor and be a great protégé.

accomplish results that can help each of you fast track your careers. A mentor/protégé relationship can—and should—be mutually beneficial.

*3. **BE SELECTIVE in seeking out your sponsor(s)/mentor(s).** Look for individuals who are compatible and complement your work style/approach and who can help you reach your goals. Although you may start off with just one, don't be content with that. Target leaders (inside and outside your organization) whose expertise and networks you think you learn from. It's helpful to think of these individuals as your own personal "board of advisors" who are helping you develop your skills and abilities.*

*4. **NURTURE the relationship.** Have regular meetings—face-to-face, by phone, or by e-mail. Prove that you were worth the investment by meeting deadlines, exceeding targets, and advancing the organization's mission. Look for ways to support your sponsors and help them build their careers. Also, remember at some point to become a sponsor/mentor yourself. When you harness and help develop other talent, that's a great demonstration of leadership!*

Although many companies have a goal of cultivating a diverse workforce, there's still a lot of work to be done by organizations around the globe. For instance, only seven women are CEOs of the United Kingdom's FTSE 100 companies, leading major firms like GlaxoSmithKline, Whitbread, and easyJet. Few corporations in South Korea and Japan have female CEOs. In Australia, only about 18 percent of CEOs are women. This is why some nations, including Germany, Norway, and Malaysia, now set minimum standards for the number of women on corporate boards. Other minorities are also underrepresented in top management. Tidjane Thiam of Credit Suisse Group is the first black CEO of a leading European bank. Antonio Simões of HSBC Bank is among the relatively few openly gay chief executives.[1] Clearly, the issue of moving beyond a homogeneous workforce remains important. This chapter will look at managing diversity in the workplace.

DIVERSITY 101

LO4.1 It's amazing all the different languages you can hear in the lobby of one of MGM Mirage's hotels. Because guests come from all over the world, the company is committed to reflecting that diversity in its workforce. MGM Mirage has implemented a program that is devoted to making sure that everyone in the organization feels included. There are payoffs for promoting diversity. For instance, companies in the hospitality business that boast gender-diverse workforces have shown a 19 percent higher average quarterly profit than hospitality businesses with less diversity.[2]

Such diversity—and inclusion—can be found in many organizational workplaces domestically and globally.[3] Sodexo, provider of quality of life services, is an example. The company offers "Spirit of Inclusion" training sessions for employees who work throughout Europe, including their locations in Finland, Germany, and Luxembourg.[4] Managers in those workplaces are looking for ways to value and develop that diversity, as you'll see through the various examples throughout this chapter. However, before we look at what it takes to manage diversity, we first have to know what workplace diversity is and why it's important.

What Is Workplace Diversity?

Look around your classroom (or your workplace). You're likely to see young/old, male/female, tall/short, blonde hair, blue-eyed/dark hair, brown-eyed, any number of races, and any variety of dress styles. You'll see people who speak up in class and others who are content to keep their attention on taking notes or daydreaming. Have you ever noticed your own little world of diversity where you are right now? Many of you may have grown up in an environment around diverse individuals, while others may not have had that experience. We want to focus on *workplace* diversity, so let's look at what it is. By looking at various ways that diversity has been defined, you'll gain a better understanding of it.

Diversity has been "one of the most popular business topics over the last two decades. It ranks with modern business disciplines such as quality, leadership, and ethics. Despite this popularity, it's also one of the most controversial and least understood topics."[5] With its basis in civil rights legislation and social justice, the word *diversity* often invokes a variety of attitudes and emotional responses in people. Diversity has traditionally been considered a term used by human resources departments, associated with fair hiring practices, discrimination, and inequality. But diversity today is considered to be so much more. Exhibit 4-1 illustrates a historical overview of how the concept and meaning of workforce diversity has evolved.

workforce diversity
The ways in which people in an organization are different from and similar to one another

We're defining **workforce diversity** as the ways in which people in an organization are different from and similar to one another. Notice that our definition not only focuses on the differences, but also the similarities of employees. This reinforces our belief that managers and organizations should view employees as having qualities in common as well as differences that separate them. It doesn't mean that those differences are any less important, but that our focus as managers is in finding ways to develop strong relationships with and engage our entire workforce.

surface-level diversity
Easily perceived differences that may trigger certain stereotypes, but that do not necessarily reflect the ways people think or feel

We want to point out one final thing about our description of "what" workforce diversity is:[6] The demographic characteristics that we tend to think of when we think of diversity—age, race, gender, ethnicity, and so on—are just the tip of the iceberg. These demographic differences reflect **surface-level diversity**, which includes easily perceived differences that may trigger certain stereotypes but don't necessarily reflect the ways people think or feel. Such surface-level differences in characteristics can affect the way people perceive others, especially when it comes to assumptions or stereotyping. The Time Warner Corporation works diligently to turn surface-level diversity into an advantage. According to Chief Diversity Officer Lisa Garcia Quiroz, "our success as a business is directly correlated to our ongoing efforts to attract talent and maintain a progressive and inclusive environment where employees can thrive regardless of gender, race, ethnicity or sexual orientation."[7]

Exhibit 4-1
Timeline of the Evolution of Workforce Diversity

1960s to 1970s	**Focus on complying with laws and regulations:** Title VII of Civil Rights Act; Equal Employment Opportunity Commission; affirmative action policies and programs
Early 1980s	**Focus on assimilating minorities and women into corporate setting:** Corporate programs developed to help improve self-confidence and qualifications of diverse individuals so they can "fit in"
Late 1980s	**Concept of workforce diversity expanded from compliance to an issue of business survival:** Publication of *Workforce 2000* opened business leaders' eyes about the future composition of workforce—that is, more diverse; first use of term *workforce diversity*
Late 1980s to Late 1990s	**Focus on fostering sensitivity:** Shift from compliance and focusing only on women and minorities to include everyone; making employees more aware and sensitive to the needs and differences of others
New Millennium	**Focus on diversity and inclusion for business success:** Workforce diversity seen as core business issue; important to achieve business success, profitability, and growth

Source: Based on "The New Global Mindset: Driving Innovation Through Diversity" by Ernst & Young, January 27, 2010.

As people get to know one another, these surface-level differences become less important and **deep-level diversity**—differences in values, personality, and work preferences—becomes more important. At Nielsen, Angela Talton, Senior Vice President of Global Diversity & Inclusion, endorses this idea: "By diversity, we mean far more than the diversity you can see; we value diversity of thought, experiences, skills and backgrounds. It is our ability to create a culture of inclusion—whereby we value, encourage and promote the various thoughts, opinions and insights of our diverse workforce—that enables us to grow and continuously provide clients with innovative solutions."[8] These deep-level differences can affect the way people view organizational work rewards, communicate, react to leaders, negotiate, and generally behave at work.

deep-level diversity
Differences in values, personality, and work preferences

Why Is Managing Workforce Diversity So Important?

Ranked on *Diversity Inc.*'s list of top 50 companies for diversity, financial services company Wells Fargo recognizes the powerful benefits of diversity. The company's chief diversity officer says, "With more than 264,000 team members, we know there is power in mobilizing our global organization around common diversity and inclusion goals and priorities. By doing so, we will create a sustainable culture that is accepting of differences, open to new ideas, and able to create a competitive advantage in the marketplace."[9] Another example is KeyBank, which is "committed to supplier diversity through business strategy and community access. We support diverse business enterprises and our Supplier Diversity team in our Corporate Responsibility group provides accountability."[10] Many companies besides Wells Fargo and KeyBank are experiencing the benefits that diversity can bring. In this section, we want to look at *why* workforce diversity is so important to organizations. The benefits fall into three main categories: people management, organizational performance, and strategic. (See Exhibit 4-2.)

Exhibit 4-2
Benefits of Workforce Diversity

People Management

- Better use of employee talent
- Increased quality of team problem-solving efforts
- Ability to attract and retain employees of diverse backgrounds

Organizational Performance

- Reduced costs associated with high turnover, absenteeism, and lawsuits
- Enhanced problem-solving ability
- Improved system flexibility

Strategic

- Increased understanding of the marketplace, which improves ability to better market to diverse consumers
- Potential to improve sales growth and increase market share
- Potential source of competitive advantage because of improved innovation efforts
- Viewed as moral and ethical; the "right" thing to do

Sources: Based on Ernst & Young, "The New Global Mindset: Driving Innovation Through Diversity," EYGM Limited, 2010; M. P. Bell, M. L. Connerley, and F. K. Cocchiara, "The Case for Mandatory Diversity Education," *Academy of Management Learning & Education*, December 2009, pp. 597–609; E. Kearney, D. Gebert, and S. C. Voelpel, "When and How Diversity Benefits Teams: The Importance of Team Members' Need for Cognition," *Academy of Management Journal*, June 2009, pp. 581–598; J. A. Gonzalez and A. S. DeNisi, "Cross-Level Effects of Demography and Diversity Climate on Organizational Attachment and Firm Effectiveness," *Journal of Organizational Behavior*, January 2009, pp. 21–40; O. C. Richard, "Racial Diversity, Business Strategy, and Firm Performance: A Resource-Based View," *Academy of Management Journal*, April 2000, pp. 164–177; and G. Robinson and K. Dechant, "Building a Business Case for Diversity," *Academy of Management Executive*, August 1997, pp. 21–31.

- Racial and ethnic diversity are 35 percent more likely to have financial returns above national industry medians.
- Currently 97 percent of U.S. companies fail to have senior leadership teams that reflect the country's ethnic labor force.[11]

PEOPLE MANAGEMENT When all is said and done, diversity *is*, after all, about people, both inside and outside the organization. The people management benefits that organizations get because of their workforce diversity efforts revolve around attracting and retaining a talented workforce. Organizations want a talented workforce because it's the people—their skills, abilities, and experiences—who make an organization successful. Positive and explicit workforce diversity efforts can help organizations attract and keep talented diverse people and make the best of the talents those individuals bring to the workplace. In addition, another important people management benefit is that as companies rely more on employee teams in the workplace, those work teams with diverse backgrounds often bring different and unique perspectives to discussions, which can result in more creative ideas and solutions. However, recent research has indicated that such benefits might be hard to come by in teams performing more interdependent tasks over a long period of time. Such situations also present more opportunities for conflicts and resentments to build.[12] But, as the researchers pointed out, that simply means that those teams may need stronger team training and coaching to facilitate group decision making and conflict resolution.

★ Watch It 1!

If your professor has assigned this, go to **www.mymanagementlab.com** to watch a video titled: *Verizon: Diversity* and to respond to questions.

ORGANIZATIONAL PERFORMANCE The performance benefits that organizations get from workforce diversity include cost savings and improvements in organizational functioning. The cost savings can be significant when organizations that cultivate a diverse workforce reduce employee turnover, absenteeism, and the chance of lawsuits.

let's get REAL

Source: Leya Gaynor

Leya Gaynor
HR Business Partner

The Scenario

As the district manager for a region of retail discount clothing stores, Henry Banks is preparing for a quarterly meeting with all of the store managers in his district. As part of a presentation about company hiring practices, he plans to stress the importance of diversity. He knows the company needs a diverse workforce to meet the needs of the company's diverse customer base; however, he is not sure how to convey this to the group of store managers.

What do you think Henry should say in his presentation?

Henry should take this opportunity to review the company's values and to consider how diversity is a critical aspect of a dynamic culture. He could provide data that indicate that diverse companies perform better than less diverse companies, overall. With a diverse customer base, Henry should provide real-life examples of situations in which diversity helped with a customer's shopping experience or increased a sale, as well as examples in which lack of diversity had a negative impact on the business. Lastly, Henry should explain how the store managers' incentives are tied to the overall performance of the store; the better the store performs, the greater incentive opportunity they have.

For instance, the Royal Canadian Mounted Police recently agreed to a very costly settlement in cases of sexual discrimination and harassment brought by hundreds of female Mounties.[13] Women in China are increasingly speaking out against sexual discrimination, not just to attain management positions but also for the right to work in jobs that traditionally have been held by men.[14] In the United Kingdom, employees file more than 3,000 complaints about racial discrimination every year. One organization was ordered to pay more than £162,000 for racial discrimination, an amount that can seriously affect the bottom line. According to a U.K. study, job applicants from ethnic minorities tend to receive fewer employer responses than non-minority applicants.[15] In addition to gender and race, discrimination on the basis of age, disability, or sexual orientation also causes employees to file complaints (and, often, to find work elsewhere).[16] In Hong Kong, for example, one in three employees surveyed by the Equal Opportunities Commission said they had faced age discrimination, and one in four had been denied promotions due to age.[17] However, from the positive side, organizational performance *can be* enhanced through workforce diversity because of improved problem-solving abilities and system flexibility. An organization with a diverse workforce can tap into the variety of skills and abilities represented, and just the fact that its workforce is diverse requires that processes and procedures be more accommodative and inclusive. The benefits of promoting diversity are worthwhile. According to Professor Christine Riordan, "inclusion also has the promise of many positive individual and organizational outcomes such as reduced turnover, greater altruism, and team engagement. When employees are truly being included within a work environment, they're more likely to share information, and participate in decision-making."[18]

STRATEGIC Organizations also benefit strategically from a diverse workforce. You have to look at managing workforce diversity as the key to extracting the best talent, performance, market share, and suppliers from a diverse country and world. One important strategic benefit is that with a diverse workforce, organizations can better anticipate and respond to changing consumer needs. Diverse employees bring a variety of points of view and approaches to opportunities, which can improve how the organization markets to diverse consumers. For instance, as the Hispanic population has grown, so have organizational efforts to market products and services to that demographic group. Organizations have found their Hispanic employees to be a fertile source of insights that would otherwise not have been available. Food service companies, retailers, financial services companies, and automobile manufacturers are just a few of the industries that have seen sales and market share increases because they paid attention to the needs of diverse consumers using information from employees. It is important to remember that a diverse workforce is not a magic pill: "Diversity does not produce better results automatically, through a sort of multicultural magic. It does so only if it is managed well."[19]

A diverse workforce also can be a powerful source of competitive advantage, primarily because innovation thrives in such an environment. A report by Ernst & Young stated that "cultural diversity offers the flexibility and creativity we need to re-create the global economy for the twenty-first century."[21] Innovation is never easy, but in a globalized world, it's even more challenging. Tapping into differing voices and viewpoints can be powerful factors in steering innovation. Companies that want to lead their industries have to find ways to "stir the pot"—to generate the lively debate that can create those new ideas. And research shows that diverse viewpoints can do that. "Diversity powers innovation, helping businesses generate new products and services."[22]

Companies with diverse leadership are:[20]

- 45 percent more likely to report a growth in market share over the previous year
- 70 percent more likely to have captured a new market

Finally, from an ethical perspective, workforce diversity and effectively managing diversity is the right thing to do. Although many societies have laws that say it's illegal to treat diverse people unfairly, many cultures also exhibit a strong ethical belief that diverse people should have access to equal opportunities and be treated fairly and justly. Businesses do have an ethical imperative to build relationships that value and enable all employees to be successful. Managers need to view workforce diversity as a way to bring different voices to the table and to build an environment based on trusting relationships. If they can do that, good things can happen, as we've noted.

★ Watch It 2!

If your professor has assigned this, go to **www.mymanagementlab.com** to watch a video titled: *Rudi's Bakery: Diversity* and to respond to questions.

THE CHANGING **workplace**

LO4.2 An African American serving as the chief executive of the United States. A woman heading up the Federal Reserve. A Latina sitting on the nation's highest court. Even at the highest levels of the political arena, we see a diverse workplace. In the business world, the once predominantly white male managerial workforce has given way to a more gender-balanced, multiethnic workforce. But it's a workforce still in transition as the overall population changes. In this section, we want to look at some of those changes, focusing on demographic trends by looking first at the characteristics of the U.S. population and then at global diversity trends. These trends will be reflected in a changing workplace, thus making this information important for managers to recognize and understand.

Characteristics of the U.S. Population

Of all the babies born in the United States recently, less than half are whites of European ancestry—a significant demographic milestone that will affect the country's political, economic, and labor force characteristics.[23] Statistics from the latest U.S. Census reports are reinforcing what we've already seen happening—America is changing.[24] We are an increasingly diverse society with some major readjustments occurring that will dramatically change the face of America by the year 2050. Let's look at some of the most dramatic of these changes.[25]

WORKPLACE **CONFIDENTIAL** Dealing with Diversity

This chapter looks at diversity from the standpoint of management: Specifically, what can *management* do to create a workplace that welcomes and appreciates differences—such as gender, age, race, religion, sexual orientation, disabilities, or social class? But this chapter doesn't offer *you* direct guidance on how to deal with coworker diversity. While management and the organization are largely responsible for fostering an inclusive culture that values diversity, you play a vital part.

Let's begin with the realization that many individuals have difficulty accepting others who are different from themselves. Human nature is such that we tend to be attracted to and feel more comfortable with people who are like us. It's not by chance, for example, that new immigrants gravitate to communities where there is a sizeable population of people from their country of origin. But "embracing differences" has become an unquestioned goal in most advanced economies and a mantra within organizations. It's increasingly difficult to survive in today's workplace if you can't accept differences and function effectively with a diverse workforce.

As described in this chapter, a strong argument can be made for a diverse workforce. From your standpoint, that argument would include being part of more effective work groups through a broader perspective in decision making; gaining a better understanding of diverse markets and customer preferences; improved ability to work comfortably with others in your workplace; and promoting fairness for individuals from underrepresented groups. Furthermore, we would be naïve to ignore that supporting diversity is, for lack of a better term, "politically correct." Today's workplace is sensitive to appearances of prejudice or unfairness. If you expect to be a valued and accepted member of today's labor force, you need to recognize that supporting diversity is the ethical and morally right thing to do.

Research tells us that we all have biases. Demographics mostly reflect surface-level diversity and can lead you to perceive others through stereotypes and assumptions. In contrast, when you get to know others, you become less concerned about demographic differences if you can see yourself sharing more important, deeper-level characteristics. Let's elaborate on the difference between surface- and deep-level diversity.

Most of us typically define diversity in terms of surface-level characteristics. Surface-level diversity relates to those characteristics that are easily noticeable; the things we initially see in people. This includes gender, age, skin color, language, and the presence or absence of a physical disability. So when a 20-year-old sees someone who's 70 and quickly classifies him as "old," that person is operating at a surface level. In contrast, deep-level diversity refers to characteristics that are not easily noticeable. They're communicated through verbal and nonverbal behaviors. Examples of deep-level differences would include personality, moods, attitudes, values, and beliefs. As you get to know a person, especially someone you like and bond with, you tend to forget surface differences and focus on your deeper commonalities.

An interesting illustration of the difference between these two types of diversity is the typical college campus. For more than 40 years, most college admissions' personnel have actively sought to expand surface diversity by considering race or ethnicity in their decision criteria. In addition, other factors such as gender, sexual orientation, socioeconomic status, or geographic background might also be applied to expand diversity. When these other factors can be visibly assessed by the way someone looks, dresses, or talks, then they are also surface-level variables. But here's the interesting observation: While college administrators try to increase diversity through admission selection, students themselves tend to undermine surface diversity by gravitating to others like themselves. Fraternities and sororities choose members who are like themselves. And friends tend to be those with similar majors, or living in the same dorm wing, or belonging to a common on-campus affinity group. So what we find is that campuses do a very good job at promoting surface-level diversity through admission decisions, but this breaks down once students are on campus. Natural student groupings tend to be defined more by deep-level characteristics.

So what can you do to more effectively deal with coworker diversity? At the surface level, start by confronting your biases and assumptions about others. You can't deal with your prejudices unless you recognize them. Then consider the positives of diversity. As we noted in the chapter, a diverse workforce has numerous pluses. You need to recognize, accept, and value the unique contributions of those who are different from you in terms of appearance, culture, skills, experiences, and abilities.

At the deep level, the good news is that as we get to know people, most of us look beyond the surface to find common bonds. Specifically, the evidence shows that the longer individuals work together, the less the effects of surface diversity. So your first reaction might be to assume you have nothing in common with a colleague who is 30 years older, or raised in a different country, or whose first language is different from yours. But start with the basics. You're both working for the same employer. That alone suggests a common bond. Both of you saw something in your employing organization that drew you to it. Then, if you're having trouble dealing with someone's differences, look beyond the surface and try to get to know the individual's personality, interests, and beliefs. You're likely to be pleasantly surprised. You might initially think someone isn't like you or won't understand you, but as you dig deeper and spend more time with the person, you'll often find common bonds.

In addition to working one-on-one with a diverse set of coworkers, you'll likely have to deal with diversity within work teams. Occasionally, diversity within teams can create problems known as "faultlines." Faultlines are subgroups that develop naturally within teams, typically along various demographic lines. The behavior of the team leader and way in which she structures the leadership role is essential for promoting communication and cohesiveness across the subgroups and for rallying the membership to meet a common cause.

Source: Based on D. A. Harrison, K. H. Price, and M. P. Bell, "Beyond Relational Demography: Time and the Effects of Surface- and Deep-Level Diversity on Work Group Cohesion," *Academy of Management Journal*, February 1998, pp. 96–107; D. C. Lau and J. K. Murnighan, "Demographic Diversity and Faultlines: The Compositional Dynamics of Organizational Groups," *Academy of Management Review*, April 1998, pp. 325–340; L. F. Pendry, D. M. Driscoll, and S. C. T. Field, "Diversity Training: Putting Theory into Practice," *Journal of Occupational Psychology*, March 2007, pp. 27–50; and M-E. Roberge, E. Petrov, and W-R. Huang, "Students' Perceptions of Their Attitudes and Behaviors Toward Different Cultures/Ethnicities Before and After a Diversity Training Program," *Journal of Business Diversity*, August 2014, pp. 80–90.

Exhibit 4-3
Changing Population Makeup of the United States

	2015	2050
Foreign-born	14%	19%
Racial/Ethnic Groups		
White*	72%	47%
Hispanic	12%	29%
Black*	12%	13%
Asian*	4%	9%

*= Non-Hispanic

American Indian/Alaska Native not included.

Sources: Based on "Population Density by County," U.S. Census Bureau, www.census.gov, accessed February 24, 2016; H. El Nasser, "U.S. Hispanic Population to Triple by 2050," *USA Today*, February 12, 2008; and J. Passel and D. Cohn, "U.S. Population Projections: 2005–2050," Pew Research Center, February 11, 2008.

The total population of the United States is projected to increase to 438 million by the year 2050, up from 322 million in 2015; 82 percent of that increase will be due to immigrants and their U.S.-born descendants. Nearly one in five Americans will be an immigrant in 2050, compared with one in eight in 2015. In addition to total population changes, the components of that population are projected to change as well. Exhibit 4-3 provides the projected population breakdown. As the projections show, the main changes will be in the percentages of the Hispanic and white population. But the data also indicate that the Asian population will be more than double. Also, as a nation, the population of the United States is aging. According to the CIA World Factbook, the median age stands at 37.8 years, up from 36.2 years in 2001.[26] By 2050, one in every five persons will be age 65 or over. The most populous group would be those age 80 and over.[27]

Such population trends are likely to have a major impact on U.S. workplaces. The reality of these trends for businesses is that they'll have to accommodate and embrace such workforce changes. Although America historically has been known as a "melting pot," where people of different nationalities, religions, races, and ethnicities have blended together to become one, that perspective is no longer relevant.[28] Organizations must recognize that they can't expect employees to assimilate into the organization by adopting similar attitudes and values. Instead, there's value in the differences that people bring to the workplace. It's not been easy. The ability of managers and organizations to effectively manage diversity has not kept pace with these population changes, creating challenges for minorities, women, and older employees. But many businesses are excelling at managing diversity, and we'll discuss some of their workplace diversity initiatives in a later section of this chapter.

Global Population Trends and the Changing Global Workforce

Right now, we share our planet with more than 7.4 billion people, a number projected to increase to nearly 10 billion by 2050.[29] That's a worldwide population increase of more than one-third, with much of this future growth occurring in Africa and Asia. What are some of the key population trends and what do they mean for the global workplace?

Age Trends. First, as life spans increase, some areas will have a higher proportion of older people. Europe currently has a higher percentage of people over 60 than any other region, followed by North America. At the country level, Japan's population is the oldest, with a median age over 46 and a low birth rate. Germany, Italy, and Portugal have a median age over 44. By 2050, China's median age is projected to be 56, and Singapore's will be 53.[30] Management challenges will increase as large numbers of workers retire and businesses will need to fill many open positions to maintain operations. On the other hand, this trend creates business opportunities for entrepreneurs and companies that can fill the needs of an aging population.

In comparison, some countries have particularly young populations with high birth rates. Niger is the world's youngest country, with a median age just below 15. Although that median age is expected to increase to nearly 18 by 2050, analysts project that Niger will remain the youngest country for decades to come. In fact, Africa is currently the continent with the largest percentage of the population younger than 15. One benefit of a younger population is having a youthful workforce that contributes to productivity as well as economic growth. The challenge here is to provide education, employment opportunities, and welfare services to these young workers.[31]

Gender, Gender Identity, and Sexual Orientation. In today's global population, there are slightly more males than females overall. Individual countries, however, can have vastly different proportions of males and females in the population. Russia, for example, has fewer than 90 men for every 100 women. In contrast, India has 107 men for every 100 women. Looking ahead to 2050, when there will be slightly more females than males in the overall world population, how will traditional gender roles and cultural norms affect the ability of companies to attract and retain a motivated workforce? Also while some countries are legalizing equal rights for the LGBTQ community, preventing discrimination and harassment on the basis of gender identity or sexual orientation will remain an important issue for organizations.

Migration and Movement. Strife and violence in certain regions are increasing pressures on migration, which leads to changes in national and regional policies on immigration that affect the ability of businesses to hire people from other countries. Migration also affects the ethnic (and sometimes the religious) composition of the local population, which global businesses must bear in mind. Managers must also consider where jobs and workers are located. In Europe, for instance, much of the working-age population is concentrated in urban areas, which is a consideration for companies deciding where to open new facilities. With managers recognizing that many jobs can only be performed in person, should workplaces be moved to areas with an abundance of skilled labor and other valued resources, or should workers be expected to move to take advantage of career opportunities?

These trends indicate the real urgency for improving diversity in the workplace. Businesses are increasingly concerned about being able to attract more workers, from the domestic or international population, regardless of gender, ethnicity, religion, or age. Organizations that actively recruit across national borders, seeking to fill specialized jobs or address competitive issues, are paying close attention to how government policies regarding migration and work permits are changing. To prepare for the future, managers must understand the current realities of the global workforce and the many dimensions of workplace diversity.[32]

How much do *you* know about global aging? (Our guess is . . . probably not much!) Take the quiz in Exhibit 4-4—no peeking at the answers beforehand—and see how well you scored. Were you surprised by some of the answers?

At 90, Bill Dudley, Europe's oldest McDonald's employee, works as a part-time member of the customer care team at a restaurant in Wales. McDonald's values its older employees for their strong work ethic, reliability, loyalty, mentoring skills that help younger co-workers, and friendly and helpful service that results in high customer satisfaction.
Source: Peter Byrne/PA Wire/AP Images

TYPES **of workplace diversity**

LO4.3 As we've seen so far, diversity is a big issue, and an important issue, in today's workplaces. What types of dissimilarities—that is, diversity—do we find in those workplaces? Exhibit 4-5 shows several types of workplace diversity. Let's work our way through the different types.

Age

The Marriott hotel group, headquartered in Bethesda, Maryland, employs more than 100,000 employees in the United States. What's interesting is that 43 percent of those employees are age 45 and older, and 18 percent are 55 and older.[33] To make it easier for older workers, company managers are redesigning tasks that require bending, stretching, lifting, pushing, and pulling. For instance, an older employee may be paired with a younger one, and tasks such as bending to clean under beds are shared.

Exhibit 4-4

Global Aging: How Much Do You Know?

1. True or False: At age 65, life expectancy is expected to be an additional 20 years.
2. The world's older population (60 and older) is expected to change from 841 million in 2013 to _____ people in 2050?
   a. decrease to 500 million
   b. decrease to 750 million
   c. increase to 1.5 billion
   d. increase to 2 billion
3. Which of the world's continents has the highest percentage of older people (age 60 or older)?
   a. North America
   b. Latin America
   c. Europe
   d. Asia
4. True or False: The worldwide median age was 27 in 2015.
5. Which country had the world's highest percentage of older people in 2013?
   a. Sweden
   b. Japan
   c. China
   d. Italy

Answers to quiz:

1. ***True.*** At age 60, people worldwide can expect to live an additional 20 years. That number is smaller in least developed countries (17 years) and higher in more developed countries (23 years). According to the United Nations, African countries and Asian countries (excluding Japan) are examples of least developed countries. The United States and Sweden are examples of more developed countries.
2. ***d.*** The number of older people is expected to be approximately 2 billion people in 2050.
3. ***c.*** Four of the top five countries with the greatest percentage of older people (age 60 or older) are located on the European continent: Italy (26.9%), Germany (26.8%), and Bulgaria and Finland (26.1%).
4. ***False.*** The worldwide median age was estimated to be about 30 in 2015. That age was 24 in 1950, and it is expected to reach 36 by 2050.
5. ***b.*** Japan, with 32 percent of its population aged 60 or over, has supplanted Italy as the world's oldest major country.

Sources: Based on CIA *World Factbook*, www.cia.gov/library/publications/the-world-factbook/, 2016; "World Population Ageing," by Department of Economic and Social Affairs Population Division, from United Nations, 2013.

Exhibit 4-5

Types of Diversity Found in Workplaces

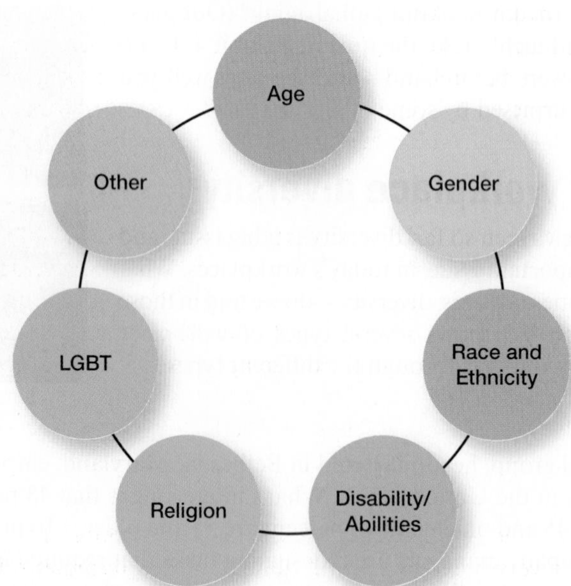

As we saw in the last section, the aging population is a major critical shift taking place in the workforce. Many people over 50 are enthusiastic and productive workers, contrary to the sometimes negative stereotypes. To accommodate the aging workforce, more organizations are changing their approach to mandatory retirement, and government policies are also being adjusted. In South Korea, where more than 20 percent of the population will be 65 or older by 2026, the country has increased the official retirement age from 55 to 60. Yet age discrimination remains a major concern for employees and employers, as well as a legal and regulatory challenge. Australia is one of many nations strengthening plans to encourage older workers to remain in the workforce while vigorously enforcing laws against discrimination.[34]

One issue with older workers is the perception that people have of those workers. Perceptions such as they're sick more often and they can't work as hard or as fast as younger employees—perceptions that are inaccurate. Employers have mixed feelings about older workers.[35] On the positive side, they believe that older workers bring a number of good qualities to the job, including experience, judgment, a strong work ethic, and a commitment to doing quality work. Also, some companies recognize the value of these attributes. For instance, global bank Barclays launched an internship program for persons age 50 or older. The bank's management believes that the real life experience of older workers will benefit their business.[36]

Although the Barclays example shows promise for utilizing the knowledge, skills, and experience of older workers, there remain many employers who also view older workers as not being flexible or adaptable and being more resistant to new technology. The challenge for managers is overcoming those misperceptions of older workers and the widespread belief that work performance and work quality decline with age.

Another issue that also supports the need for effectively managing workplace age diversity is that when Baby Boomers do retire, experts point out that some industries will face severe shortages of qualified employees. "Many of today's growth industries require a higher level of technical competence in quantitative reasoning, problem solving, and communication skills...and the United States simply does not have enough students who are getting solid math and science education."[37] Organizations that do not plan for such a future may find themselves struggling to find a competent workforce, diverse or not.

Finally, the aging population is not the only age-related issue facing organizations. Some 50 million Generation Xers juggle work and family responsibilities. And now some 76 million members of Generation Y (often referred to as Millennials) are either already in or poised to enter the workforce.[38] These Gen Yers will make up about 75 percent of the global workforce by 2025.[39] Having grown up in a world where they've had the opportunity to experience many different things, Gen Y workers bring their own ideas and approaches to the workplace. For instance, one study revealed that Millennials are 71 percent more likely to focus on teamwork, 28 percent more likely to focus on business impact, and 22 percent more likely to focus on a culture of connection. In contrast, non-Millennials are 31 percent more likely to focus on equity; 28 percent more likely to focus on acceptance, tolerance and fairness of opportunity; and 26 percent more likely to focus on integration.[40] Given these differences, managers face the challenges of creating and maintaining a culture of inclusivity. According to this study, "unfortunately, millennials are currently less engaged than members of older generations because organizations are falling short in these areas."[41] Managers need to ensure that they take into account differing norms between generations. Effectively managing an organization's diverse age groups can lead to their working well with each other, learning from each other, and taking advantage of the different perspectives and experiences that each has to offer. It can be a win-win situation for all.

Gender

Women (49.5%) and men (50.5%) now each make up almost half of the workforce.[42] Yet gender diversity issues are still quite prevalent in organizations. Take the gender pay gap. The latest information shows that women's median earnings were

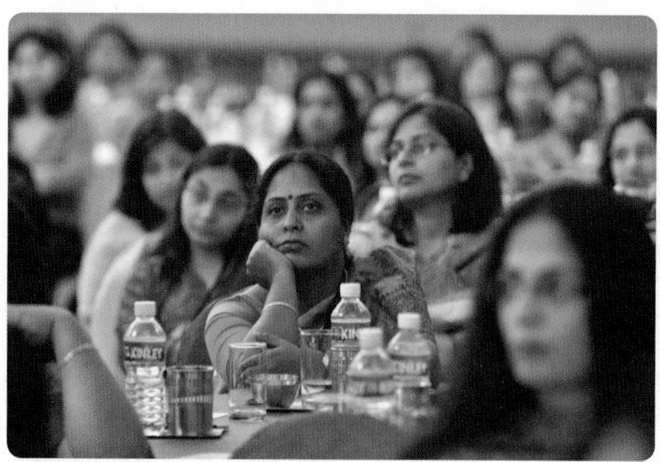

IBM India staged a leadership conference to encourage its female employees in the workplace and to enhance their leadership and networking skills. IBM's key diversity efforts in the advancement of women focuses on mentoring and coaching programs that help them develop their careers and on creating an environment that balances their professional and personal needs.
Source: Aijaz Rahi/AP Images

83 percent of male full-time wage and salary workers.[43] *The Wall Street Journal* cites a recent study which determined that about 8 percent of the wage gap cannot be explained by job-related factors, concluding that discrimination may be the reason.[44] Other issues involve career start and progress. Research by Pew Research Center shows that young women now place more importance on having a high-paying career or profession than do young men.[45] Yet, although 57 percent of today's college students are women, and women now collect nearly 60 percent of four-year degrees and are just as likely to have completed college and hold an advanced degree, inequities persist.[46] Research by Catalyst found that men start their careers at higher levels than women. And after starting out behind, women don't ever catch up. Men move up the career ladder further and faster as well.[47] A study by Mercer revealed that women make up only 35 percent of the average company's workforce at the professional level and above.[48] A study by the Pew Research Center found that more women are not in executive positions because they are held to higher standards.[49] However, leaving women behind may be to companies' detriment. One study found some support that having more women in executive positions improves firm performance.[50] Finally, misconceptions, mistaken beliefs, and unsupported opinions still exist about whether women perform their jobs as well as men do. You can see why gender diversity issues are important to attend to. So what *do* we know about differences between men and women in the workplace?

- Most regions of the world continue to face challenges in increasing women's representation at all levels: Asia is expected to have the lowest representation of women in 2025.[52]

First of all, few, if any, important differences between men and women affect job performance.[51] No consistent male-female differences exist in problem-solving ability, analytical skills, competitive drive, motivation, sociability, or learning ability. Psychological research has found minor differences: Women tend to be more agreeable and willing to conform to authority, while men are more aggressive and more likely to have expectations of success.

Another area where we also see differences between genders is in preference for work schedules, especially when the employee has preschool-age children. To accommodate their family responsibilities, working mothers are more likely to prefer part-time work, flexible work schedules, and telecommuting. They also prefer jobs that encourage work-life balance.

One question of much interest as it relates to gender is whether men and women are equally competent as managers. Research evidence indicates that a "good" manager is still perceived as predominantly masculine.[53] But the reality is that women tend to use a broader, more effective range of leadership styles to motivate and engage people. They usually blend traditional masculine styles—being directive, authoritative, and leading by example—with more feminine ones that include being nurturing, inclusive, and collaborative. Men tend to rely primarily on masculine styles.[54] Another study showed that women managers were significantly more likely than their male counterparts to coach and develop others and to create more committed, collaborative, inclusive, and, ultimately, more effective teams. This study also found that women were more likely to foster genuine collaboration while males were far more likely to view negotiations and other business transactions as zero-sum games.[55] A recent Gallup survey concluded, "Organizations should hire and promote more female managers. Female managers in the U.S. exceed male managers at meeting employees' essential workplace requirements. And female managers themselves are more engaged at work than their male counterparts."[56] Despite this, according to another Gallup survey, Americans—male and female—still prefer a male boss, although 41 percent of the respondents said they had no preference.[57]

What should you take away from this discussion? Not that either women or men are the superior employees, but rather a better appreciation for why it's important for organizations to explore the strengths that both women and men bring to an organization and the barriers they face in contributing fully to organizational efforts. And it's important to note that many companies *are* "grooming more women for the corner office." The pool of highly qualified women continues to grow as those who have received advanced degrees and worked in the corporate world are moving up through the ranks. In fact, research by McKinsey & Co. found that 24 percent of senior vice presidents at 58 big companies are women.[58]

If your professor has assigned this, go to **www.mymanagementlab.com** to complete the *Simulation: HR & Diversity* and get a better understanding of the challenges of diversity in organizations.

★ Try It 1!

Race and Ethnicity

Roll the calendar back to the year 2000. The Coca-Cola Company has just agreed to an enormous settlement of $192.5 million for a class-action racial discrimination lawsuit.[59] Court documents describe a company atmosphere in which black employees "formed informal networks to provide 'sanity checks' and diversity efforts were not considered a high priority by senior management." Also, as the number of African American hires declined, a "number of highly educated and trained African-Americans at the company noted receiving unfavorable treatment, thus creating the impression that Coke was a high-risk environment for high-potential and aggressive African-Americans." Now, fast-forward to 2013. The Coca-Cola Company is named by *Diversity Inc.* magazine as number 2 on the list of Top 10 Companies for blacks and number 10 on the Top 10 Companies for Latinos. How did the company make such a drastic turnaround?

Since being sued for racial discrimination, Coca-Cola has made considerable strides in its diversity efforts at all levels and in all areas. Commitment from top executives became and remains a cornerstone for managing diversity at the company. CEO Muhtar Kent (who was not CEO at the time of the discrimination problems) says, "Building a diverse and inclusive workforce is central to our 2020 Vision, which calls for us to 'achieve true diversity' throughout our business." Kent also personally signs off on executive compensation tied to diversity goals and actions. Coca-Cola's chief diversity officer, Steve Bucherati, has managed the company's diversity programs for years. He has been described as a strong and devoted advocate for inclusion and routinely provides Coke's board of directors with reports about diversity initiatives and outcomes. Coca-Cola has recognized that diversity can greatly benefit the company in many ways. CEO Kent says, "The real power of diversity is the synergies that are created when different people and cultures come together united behind a common goal of winning and creating shared value. Extraordinary things truly happen."

Many other companies have had similar racial issues. There's a long and controversial history in the United States and in other parts of the world over race and how people react to and treat others of a different race.[60] Race and ethnicity are important types of diversity in organizations. We're going to define **race** as the biological heritage (including physical characteristics such as one's skin color and associated traits) that people use to identify themselves. Most people identify themselves as part of a racial group. Such racial classifications are an integral part of a country's cultural, social, and legal environments. The racial and ethnicity choices in the most recent U.K. Census included 16 classifications: white (with choices such as British or Irish), mixed/multiple ethnic group (choices such as white and black Caribbean or white and Asian), Asian/Asian British (such as Indian, Pakistani, Bangladeshi, Chinese, and other Asian), Black/African/Caribbean/Black British (African, Caribbean, other black), and choices in an "other ethnic group" category. However, these categories may change in the next U.K. Census as the government tests ways to allow people to more accurately describe their racial and ethnic backgrounds.[61] **Ethnicity** is related to race, but it refers to social traits—such as one's cultural background or allegiance—that are shared by a human population.

race
The biological heritage (including skin color and associated traits) that people use to identify themselves

ethnicity
Social traits (such as cultural background or allegiance) that are shared by a human population

As we saw earlier in Exhibit 4-3, the racial and ethnic diversity of the U.S. population is increasing at an exponential rate. We're also seeing this same effect in the composition of the workforce. Most of the research on race and ethnicity as they relate to the workplace has looked at hiring decisions, performance evaluations, pay, and workplace discrimination.[62] However, much of that research has focused on the differences in attitudes and outcomes between whites and African Americans. Minimal study has been done on issues relevant to Asian, Hispanic, and Native American populations. Let's look at a few key findings.

One finding is that individuals in workplaces tend to favor colleagues of their own race in performance evaluations, promotion decisions, and pay raises. Although such effects are small, they are consistent. Next, research shows substantial racial differences in attitudes toward affirmative action, with African Americans favoring such programs to a greater degree than whites. Other research shows that African Americans generally do worse than whites in decisions related to the workplace. For instance, in employment interviews, African Americans receive lower ratings. In the job setting, they receive lower job performance ratings, are paid less, and are promoted less frequently. However, no statistically significant differences between the two races are observed in absenteeism rates, applied social skills at work, or accident rates. As you can see, race and ethnicity issues are a key focus for managers in effectively managing workforce diversity.

Disability/Abilities

According to the U.S. Census Bureau, people with disabilities are the largest minority in the United States. Estimates vary, but it's believed that there are some 19.8 million working-age Americans with disabilities. And that number continues to increase as military troops return from Iraq and Afghanistan.[63]

The year 1990 was a watershed year for persons with disabilities. That was the year the Americans with Disabilities Act (ADA) became law. The ADA prohibits

let's get REAL

The Scenario

Katie Harris is a manager in a branch office of a large insurance claims company. She manages a diverse team of 15 people. One of her team members stopped in to tell her that "several of them were upset that other team members were talking in their native language throughout the day." Their complaint? They felt it was "rude" for coworkers to speak another language at work, and it made the other team members feel excluded and uncomfortable.

What should Katie do to resolve this issue?

Katie should have a conversation with the team members who were speaking in their native language to understand why they were speaking in their native language throughout the day. She should provide them with feedback that there are some coworkers who feel uncomfortable with this situation. Katie should definitely ask them for a solution on how to avoid this in the future. She should express that, as long as the conversation is work related, all coworkers need to be involved as communication is key in a work environment. Any other type of conversations can be spoken in their native language offstage; for example, at lunch or breaks.

Claudia Gutierrez
Service Manager

Source: Claudia Gutierrez

discrimination against an individual who is "regarded as" having a disability and requires employers to make reasonable accommodations so their workplaces are accessible to people with physical or mental disabilities and enable them to effectively perform their jobs. With the law's enactment, individuals with disabilities became a more representative and integral part of the U.S. workforce.

One issue facing managers and organizations is that the definition of disability is quite broad. The U.S. Equal Employment Opportunity Commission classifies a person as disabled if he or she has any physical or mental impairment that substantially limits one or more major life activities. For instance, deafness, chronic back pain, AIDS, missing limbs, seizure disorder, schizophrenia, diabetes, and alcoholism would all qualify. However, since these conditions have almost no common features, it's been difficult to study how each condition affects employment. It's obvious that some jobs cannot be accommodated to a disability. For instance, the law recognizes that a visually impaired person could not be an airline pilot, a person with severe cerebral palsy could not be a surgeon, and a person with profound mobility constraints could not be a firefighter. However, computer technology and other adaptive devices have shattered many employment barriers for other employees with disabilities.

A survey by the Society for Human Resource Management found that 61 percent of the HR professionals responding said that their organizations now include disabilities in their diversity and inclusion plans. However, only 47 percent said that their organizations actively recruit individuals with disabilities. And 40 percent said that their senior managers demonstrate a strong commitment to do so.[64] Even after 20-plus years of the ADA, organizations and managers still have fears about employing disabled workers. A survey by the U.S. Department of Labor looked at these unfounded fears.[65] Exhibit 4-6 describes some of those fears as well as the reality; that is, what it's really like. Let's look at one company's experience. Walgreens has hired individuals with mental and physical disabilities to work at its distribution center in Anderson, South Carolina.[66] These employees work in one of three departments: case check-in (where merchandise initially comes in), de-trash (where merchandise is unpacked), or picking (where products are sorted into tubs based on individual store orders). Using an innovative approach that included job coaches, automated processes, and comprehensive training, Walgreens now has a capable and trusted workforce. The company's senior vice president of distribution said, "One thing we found is they (the disabled employees) can all

Exhibit 4-6

Employers' Fears About Disabled Workers

Sources: Based on R. Braum, "Disabled Workers: Employer Fears Are Groundless," *Bloomberg BusinessWeek,* October 2, 2009; and "Survey of Employer Perspectives on the Employment of People with Disabilities," U.S. Department of Labor/Office of Disability Employment Policy, November 2008.

FEAR: Hiring people with disabilities leads to higher employment costs and lower profit margins	***REALITY:*** Absentee rates for sick time are virtually equal between employees with and without disabilities; workers' disabilities are not a factor in formulas calculating insurance costs for workers' compensation
FEAR: Workers with disabilities lack job skills and experience necessary to perform as well as their abled counterparts	***REALITY:*** Commonplace technologies such as the Internet and voice-recognition software have eliminated many of the obstacles for workers with disabilities; many individuals with disabilities have great problem-solving skills from finding creative ways to perform tasks that others may take for granted
FEAR: Uncertainty over how to take potential disciplinary action with a worker with disabilities	***REALITY:*** A person with a disability for whom workplace accommodations have been provided has the same obligations and rights as far as job performance
FEAR: High costs associated with accommodating disabled employees	***REALITY:*** Most workers with disabilities require no accommodation but for those who do, more than half of the workplace modifications cost $500 or less

Omar Troy is one of a team of baristas employed by Asbury Automotive to staff coffee cafes for customers at its car dealerships. The program, called Café Blends: Blending Autism into the Workplace, focuses on hiring and training autistic young adults and on educating other employees about the disability and ways they can help integrate the baristas in the workplace.
Source: Robin Nelson/ZUMA Press/Alamy

do the job. What surprised us is the environment that it's created. It's a building where everybody helps each other out."

Increasingly, there are companies that specialize in preparing the disabled for employment. For instance, Specialisterne, a Danish company, focuses on training and placing autistic individuals for high-tech careers. Computer Aid is one of the companies that has hired autistic individuals who were trained by Specialisterne. Ernie Dianastasis, the managing director of Computer Aid, maintains, "The individuals I've hired are phenomenal. People on the autism spectrum are loyal, reliable, and have a high degree of accuracy in their work."[67]

In effectively managing a workforce with disabled employees, managers need to create and maintain an environment in which employees feel comfortable disclosing their need for accommodation. Those accommodations, by law, need to enable individuals with disabilities to perform their jobs but they also need to be perceived as equitable by those not disabled. That's the balancing act that managers face.

Religion

In her sophomore year at college, Umme-Hani Khan worked for three months as a stock clerk at a Hollister clothing store in San Francisco.[68] One day, she was told by her supervisors to remove the head scarf that she wears in observance of Islam (known as a *hijab*) because it violated the company's "look policy" (which instructs employees on clothing, hair styles, makeup, and accessories they may wear to work). She refused on religious grounds and was fired one week later. Like a number of other Muslim women, she filed a federal job discrimination complaint. A spokesperson for Abercrombie & Fitch (Hollister's parent company) said, "If any Abercrombie associate identifies a religious conflict with an Abercrombie policy . . . the company will work with the associate in an attempt to find an accommodation." Although that's a step in the right direction, Abercrombie & Fitch was found guilty of religious discrimination in another case when it chose not to hire a Muslim job applicant because she wore a hijab.[69]

Title VII of the Civil Rights Act prohibits discrimination on the basis of religion (as well as race/ethnicity, country of origin, and sex). Today, it seems that the greatest religious diversity issue in the United States revolves around Islam, especially after 9/11.[70] Islam is one of the world's most popular religions, and over 2 million Muslims live in the United States. For the most part, U.S. Muslims have attitudes similar to those of other U.S. citizens. However, there are real and perceived differences. For instance, nearly 4 in 10 U.S. adults admit they harbor negative feelings or prejudices toward U.S. Muslims, and 52 percent believe U.S. Muslims are not respectful of women.

Religious beliefs also can prohibit or encourage work behaviors. Many conservative Jews believe they should not work on Saturdays. Some Christians do not want to work on Sundays. Religious individuals may believe they have an obligation to express their beliefs in the workplace, making it uncomfortable for those who may not share those beliefs. Some pharmacists have refused to give out certain kinds of contraceptives on the basis of their beliefs. Similarly, in 2015, Kentucky state clerk Kim Davis refused to issue marriage licenses to same-sex couples until she was directed by court order not to interfere with same-sex couples' constitutional rights to marriage. Ms. Davis refused to issue same-sex marriage licenses because homosexuality is not supported by her religion.

As you can see, religion and religious beliefs can generate misperceptions and negative feelings. The latest EEOC statistics showed that 3,502 religious-based complaints were filed in 2015.[71] In accommodating religious diversity, managers need to recognize and be aware of different religions and their beliefs, paying special attention to when certain religious holidays fall. Try to accommodate, when at all possible, employees who have special needs or requests, but do so in such a way that other employees don't view it as "special treatment."

LGBT: Sexual Orientation and Gender Identity

The acronym LGBT—which refers to lesbian, gay, bisexual, and transgender people—relates to the diversity of sexual orientation and gender identity.[72] Sexual orientation has, in fact, been called the "last acceptable bias."[73] We want to emphasize that we're not condoning this perspective, but what the comment refers to is that most people understand that racial and ethnic stereotypes are off-limits. Still, it's not unusual to hear derogatory comments about gays or lesbians—in fact, negative attitudes toward LGBT are not uncommon.[74] How many LGBT people are in the overall population? It's difficult to know, exactly. Some governments are actually trying to find out by including questions about sexual identity on national census forms. Already, some estimates are becoming available. For instance, the Office for National Statistics reports that 1.7 percent of the U.K. population identifies as lesbian, gay, or bisexual; of those people, most were in the age category of 16 to 24.[75]

A growing number of nations are adopting laws banning discrimination against LGBT people. For example, in the European Union, the Employment Equality Directive requires all member states to introduce legislation making it unlawful to discriminate on grounds of sexual orientation.[76] Despite the progress, much more needs to be done. One study found more than 40 percent of gay and lesbian employees indicated they had been unfairly treated, denied a promotion, or pushed to quit their job because of their sexual orientation.[77] Another study found that "closeted" LGBTs who felt isolated at work were 73 percent more likely to leave their job within three years than "out" workers.[78] This statistic is not surprising based on the results of a third study: More than one-third of LGBT workers felt they had to lie about their personal lives at work, and about the same percentage felt exhausted from the time and energy needed to hide their gender identity.[79]

Employers take differing approaches to employing LGBT people. Sometimes companies band together to push for change as a group, as happened recently in Japan. Thirty businesses, including Panasonic, Sony, and Dai-ichi Life Insurance, jointly developed standards that individual firms can copy or adapt as policies for making LGBT employees more welcome in Japanese workplaces.[80] Another approach is to take the initiative by setting goals for increasing the number of LGBT people employed, as part of the drive for diversity and inclusion in the workplace. The British Broadcasting Corporation (BBC), for example, has pledged to meet a target of having LGBT employees comprise 8 percent of its workforce within a few years. The BBC's other diversity targets include increasing the percentage of women to 50 percent of its workforce and the percentage of disabled people to 8 percent.[81] Other businesses are showing support for LGBT employees through personnel policies and practices. Not only does the Swedish communications tech giant Ericsson promote equal opportunity in employment and professional development for LGBT people, it encourages the formation of LGBT networking groups to foster a deeper sense of connection. The company has a global diversity council with representatives from each geographic region, plus local diversity councils in each area where Ericsson operates. These councils include LGBT employees in programs aimed at improving inclusion and understanding, as well as reducing unconscious biases within the workforce.[82]

As with most of the types of diversity we've discussed in this section, managers need to look at how best to meet the needs of their LGBT employees. They need to respond to employees' concerns while also creating a safe and productive work environment for all.

Other Types of Diversity

As we said earlier, diversity refers to *any* dissimilarities or differences that might be present in a workplace. Other types of workplace diversity that managers might confront and have to deal with include socioeconomic background (social class and income-related factors), team members from different functional areas or organizational units, physical attractiveness, obesity/thinness, job seniority, or intellectual abilities. Each of these types of diversity also can affect how employees are treated in the workplace. Again, managers everywhere need to ensure that all employees—no matter the similarities or dissimilarities—are treated fairly and given the opportunity and support to do their jobs to the best of their abilities.

FUTURE VISION Diversity of Thought

What does diversity mean to you? Your response might depend on when you were born.[83] According to a recent study from Deloitte and the Billie Jean King Leadership Initiative, those born between about 1980 and 2000, known as the Millennial generation, may have a different definition of diversity than do older generations. Instead of thinking of diversity as those surface-level differences including demographic characteristics such as gender or race, the Millennial generation focuses more on deep-level differences, quickly taking to this expanded view of diversity. The researchers suggest that unlike Baby Boomers and Generation X, the Millennials are already comfortable with diversity in the traditional sense and don't necessarily see the need for organizational efforts to build awareness around diversity. However, they do see the value in a different kind of diversity that directly impacts business outcomes. Millennials believe in what is often called diversity of thought. People join organizations with a wide range of experiences that shape how they think. People attend different schools and grow up in different parts of the world. They come to the workplace with different backgrounds, cultural experiences, and personalities. All of these experiences and traits develop cognitive viewpoints that are wide and varied. Diversity of thought creates significant potential value to organizations if effectively cultivated. Diverse thinkers in an organization can help guard against groupthink and give organizations an advantage through more innovation and creative problem solving. Given that Millennials will make up nearly 75 percent of the workforce by the year 2025, it seems that organizations need to look more closely at this deep-level definition of diversity. Valuing diversity means openness to different perspectives, and those coming to the workplace with varied experiences can bring with them this diversity of thought.

If your professor has chosen to assign this, go to **www.mymanagmentlab.com** *to discuss the following questions.*

TALK ABOUT IT 1: Do you agree that diverse cognitive viewpoints benefit organizations? What kind of challenges could diverse thinking create for organizations?

TALK ABOUT IT 2: How can managers cultivate diversity of thought?

CHALLENGES in managing diversity

LO4.4 Nooses, racist graffiti, and Confederate battle flags should have been enough to warrant action. However, the discovery that he was paid less as a painter than white workers is what finally prompted an African American employee to complain to his employer, Texas-based Turner Industries Group LLC.[84] Soon after filing the complaint, he was fired. His complaints, along with those of seven other employees, "have led the federal government to conclude there was evidence of racial discrimination." Despite the benefits that we know workforce diversity brings to organizations, managers still face challenges in creating accommodating and safe work environments for diverse employees. In this section, we're going to look at two of those challenges: personal bias and the glass ceiling.

Personal Bias

Women drivers. Smokers. Working mothers. Football players. Blondes. Female president of the United States. Hispanic. Blue-collar worker. What impressions come to mind when you read these words? Based on your background and experiences, you probably have pretty specific ideas and things you would say, maybe even to the point of characteristics you think that all smokers or all working mothers or all Hispanics share. Each of us has biases—often hidden from others.[85] Employees can and do bring such ideas about various groups of people with them into the workplace. Such ideas can lead to prejudice, discrimination, and stereotypes—all of which shape and influence our personal biases. And research is pointing to a troubling fact: Eliminating bias is a lot more difficult than previously thought.[86]

bias
A tendency or preference toward a particular perspective or ideology

Bias is a term that describes a tendency or preference toward a particular perspective or ideology. It's generally seen as a "one-sided" perspective. Our personal biases cause us to have preconceived opinions about people or things. Such preconceived opinions can create all kinds of inaccurate judgments and attitudes. Let's take a look at how our personal biases affect the way we view and respond to diversity.

One outcome of our personal biases can be **prejudice**, a preconceived belief, opinion, or judgment toward a person or a group of people. Our prejudice can be based on all the types of diversity we discussed: race, gender, ethnicity, age, disability, religion, sexual orientation, or even other personal characteristics.

prejudice
A preconceived belief, opinion, or judgment toward a person or a group of people

A major factor in prejudice is **stereotyping**, which is judging a person on the basis of one's perception of a group to which he or she belongs. For instance, "married persons are more stable employees than single persons" is an example of stereotyping. Keep in mind, though, that not all stereotypes are inaccurate. For instance, asking someone in accounting about a budgeting problem you're having would be an appropriate assumption and action. However, many stereotypes—red-haired people have a bad temper, elderly drivers are the most dangerous, working mothers aren't as committed to their careers as men are, and so forth—aren't factual and distort our judgment.

stereotyping
Judging a person based on a perception of a group to which that person belongs

Both prejudice and stereotyping can lead to someone treating others who are members of a particular group unequally. That's what we call **discrimination**, which is when people act out their prejudicial attitudes toward people who are the targets of their prejudice. You'll find in Exhibit 4-7 definitions and examples of different types of discrimination. Many of these actions are prohibited by law, so you won't find them discussed in employee handbooks or organizational policy statements. However, you can still see these actions in workplaces. "As discrimination has increasingly come under both legal scrutiny and social disapproval, most overt forms have faded, which may have resulted in an increase in more covert forms like incivility or exclusion."[87]

discrimination
When someone acts out their prejudicial attitudes toward people who are the targets of their prejudice

Discrimination, whether intentional or not, can lead to serious negative consequences for employers, as illustrated by the example we discussed at the beginning of this chapter and section. But it's not just the potential financial consequences organizations and managers face for discriminatory actions. It's the reduced employee productivity, negative and disruptive interpersonal conflicts, increased employee turnover, and overall negative climate that can lead to serious problems for managers. Even if an organization has never had an employment discrimination lawsuit filed against it, managers need to aggressively work to eliminate unfair discrimination.

Glass Ceiling

Pretend you've just finished your MBA degree. It's not been easy. Your graduate classes were challenging, but you feel well-prepared for and excited about that first post-MBA job. If you're female, that first job for 60 percent of you will be an entry-level position. However, if you're male, only 46 percent of you would start out in an entry-level position.[89] And 2 percent of women would make it to the CEO or senior executive position, although 6 percent of men would. "Although entry into occupations such as accounting, business, and law happens at about the same rate for men and women, evidence is mounting that women's and men's career paths begin to divide soon after."[90] This issue can be seen with minorities as well. Only a small percentage of both male and female Hispanics and African Americans have made it into management positions in the United States. What's going on here? After all these years of "equal opportunity," why do we still see statistics like these?

LEADER making a DIFFERENCE

Source: Juan Manuel Vargas/AP Images

Dr. Rohini Anand, *senior vice president and global chief diversity officer at Sodexo, says her job is to carry out the vision that "diversity and inclusion would result in Sodexo being able to identify and develop the best talent and create an environment where employees could thrive and deliver outstanding service solutions to clients and customers."[88] Anand, who grew up in India, was "surrounded by others who looked like me, but had variation by socioeconomic status or religion." It was when she moved to the United States that she was first perceived as a minority, which led her to the work she does today. After earning her PhD from the University of Michigan, Anand worked in various corporate and government positions and came to Sodexo in 2003. Under her intelligent and compassionate leadership, the company is consistently in the top two or three on* DiversityInc's *Top Companies for Diversity list. And it's easy to see why. From the CEO down, there is a strong commitment to integrating diversity and inclusion throughout the organization.* What can you learn from this leader making a difference?

Exhibit 4-7
Forms of Discrimination

Type of Discrimination	Definition	Examples from Organizations
Discriminatory policies or practices	Actions taken by representatives of the organization that deny equal opportunity to perform or unequal rewards for performance	Older workers may be targeted for layoffs because they are highly paid and have lucrative benefits.[a]
Sexual harassment	Unwanted sexual advances and other verbal or physical conduct of a sexual nature that create a hostile or offensive work environment	Salespeople at one company went on company-paid visits to strip clubs, brought strippers into the office to celebrate promotions, and fostered pervasive sexual rumors.[b]
Intimidation	Overt threats or bullying directed at members of specific groups of employees	African American employees at some companies have found nooses hanging over their work stations.[c]
Mockery and insults	Jokes or negative stereotypes; sometimes the result of jokes taken too far	Arab Americans have been asked at work whether they were carrying bombs or were members of terrorist organizations.[d]
Exclusion	Exclusion of certain people from job opportunities, social events, discussions, or informal mentoring; can occur unintentionally	Many women in finance claim they are assigned to marginal job roles or are given light workloads that don't lead to promotion.[e]
Incivility	Disrespectful treatment, including behaving in an aggressive manner, interrupting the person, or ignoring his or her opinions	Female lawyers note that male attorneys frequently cut them off or do not adequately address their comments.[f]

Notes:
a. J. Levitz and P. Shishkin, "More Workers Cite Age Bias After Layoffs," *Wall Street Journal*, March 11, 2009, pp. D1–D2.
b. W. M. Bulkeley, "A Data-Storage Titan Confronts Bias Claims," *Wall Street Journal*, September 12, 2007, pp. A1, A16.
c. D. Walker, "Incident with Noose Stirs Old Memories," *McClatchy-Tribune Business News*, June 29, 2008; and D. Solis, "Racial Horror Stories Keep EEOC Busy," *Knight-Ridder Tribune Business News*, July 30, 2005, p. 1.
d. H. Ibish and A. Stewart, *Report on Hate Crimes and Discrimination Against Arab Americans: The Post-September 11 Backlash, September 11, 2001–October 11, 2001* (Washington, DC: American-Arab Anti-Discrimination Committee, 2003).
e. A. Raghavan, "Wall Street's Disappearing Women," *Forbes*, March 16, 2009, pp. 72–78.
f. L. M. Cortina, "Unseen Injustice: Incivility as Modern Discrimination in Organizations."

Source: S. Robbins and T. Judge, *Organizational Behavior*, 15th ed., Prentice Hall, p. 43.

glass ceiling
The invisible barrier that separates women and minorities from top management positions

First used in a *Wall Street Journal* article in the 1980s, the term **glass ceiling** refers to the invisible barrier that separates women and minorities from top management positions.[91] The idea of a "ceiling" means something is blocking upward movement and the idea of "glass" is that whatever's blocking the way isn't immediately apparent. Many biases and stereotypes about women reinforce the glass ceiling. For instance, "[a male's] interaction with a woman comes with a reputation risk that can damage careers—'there's more than just a professional relationship between the two.'"[92]

Research on the glass ceiling has looked at identifying the organizational practices and interpersonal biases that have blocked women's advancement. Findings from those studies have ranged from lack of mentoring to sex stereotyping, views that associate masculine traits with leader effectiveness, and bosses' perceptions of family-work conflict.[93]

- 57 percent of women feel that unconscious bias is the greatest barrier they face in the workplace.[94]

Another perspective on why there are so few top women leaders in many fields was offered by a highly successful woman—Sheryl Sandberg, former vice president of Google and currently the chief operating officer of Facebook. In her book, *Lean In*,

Sandberg suggests that there's a "leadership ambition gap"—that is, women don't get top jobs because they don't really want to.[95] She suggests that women "lean in" and be as assertive as men are in pushing forward their careers.[96]

Whatever is believed to be the reason why so few women reach the executive level, and as others have said, it's time to shatter the glass ceiling for all employees. *Every* employee should have the opportunity to work in a career in which they can use their skills and abilities and to have a career path that allows them to progress as far as they want to go. Getting to that end, however, isn't going to be easy. As we'll see in the next section, there are a number of workplace diversity initiatives that organizations can implement to work toward that end.

WORKPLACE **diversity initiatives**

LO4.5 Marriott International takes diversity seriously. A company spokesperson said that "we leverage our core values to embed diversity and inclusion so deeply that it is integral to how we do business globally."[97] Arne Sorenson, the company's president and CEO, is a visible force and advocate for diversity both in the company and externally. For instance, he publically spoke against Indiana's anti-LGBT Religious Freedom Restoration Act, saying: "This is just plain wrong and . . . and we will not stand for it . . . the notion that you can tell businesses that somehow they are free to discriminate is not right."[98] The company also has mandatory diversity training every month and a number of employee resource groups that provide input and advice. Their diversity management efforts have earned the company the number 13 spot on the Top 50 Companies for Diversity list for 2015.

As the Marriott example shows, some businesses *are* effectively managing diversity. In this section, we look at various workplace diversity initiatives; however, before we start discussing these, we first look at the legal framework within which diversity efforts take place.

The Legal Aspect of Workplace Diversity

Would workplaces have evolved to the level of diversity that currently exists without federal legislation and mandates?[99] Although it's an interesting question, the fact is that federal laws *have* contributed to some of the social change we've seen over the last 50-plus years. Exhibit 4-8 describes the major equal employment opportunity laws with which organizations must comply. Failure to do so, as we have seen in some of the examples we've described, can be costly and damaging to an organization's bottom line and reputation. It's important that managers know what they can and cannot do legally and ensure that all employees understand as well.

However, effectively managing workplace diversity needs to be more than understanding and complying with federal laws. Organizations that are successful at managing diversity use additional diversity initiatives and programs. We're going to look at four of these: top management commitment, mentoring, diversity skills training, and employee resource groups.

Top Management Commitment to Diversity

Today's increasingly competitive marketplace underscores the reality that creating a diverse workplace has never been more important. It's equally important to make diversity and inclusion an integral part of the organization's culture. "A sustainable diversity and inclusion strategy must play a central role in decision making at the highest leadership level and filter down to every level of the company."[100] How do organizational leaders do that?

One of the first things to do is make sure that diversity and inclusion are part of the organization's purpose, goals, and strategies. Look back at our chapter opener. That's one of the things that the Coca-Cola Company does. Even during economically challenging times, an organization needs a strong commitment to diversity and inclusion programs. Diversity needs to be integrated into every aspect of the business—from the

- 67 percent of mid- to senior-level businesswomen said mentorship was highly important in helping advance and grow their careers.
- 63 percent have never had a formal mentor.[101]

Exhibit 4-8
Major Equal Employment Opportunity Laws

Year	Law or Ruling	Description
1963	Equal Pay Act	Prohibits pay differences for equal work based on gender
1964 (amended in 1972)	Civil Rights Act, Title VII	Prohibits discrimination based on race, color, religion, national origin, or gender
1967 (amended in 1978)	Age Discrimination in Employment Act	Prohibits discrimination against employees 40 years and older
1973	Rehabilitation Act	Prohibits discrimination against a qualified person with a disability in the federal government as well as retaliation against a person who complained about discrimination
1978	Pregnancy Discrimination Act	Prohibits discrimination against women in employment decisions on the basis of pregnancy, childbirth, and related medical decisions
1990	Americans with Disabilities Act	Prohibits discrimination against individuals who have disabilities or chronic illnesses; also requires reasonable accommodations for these individuals
1991	Civil Rights Act of 1991	Reaffirms and tightens prohibition of discrimination and gives individuals right to sue for punitive damages
1993	Family and Medical Leave Act	Gives employees in organizations with 50 or more employees up to 12 weeks of unpaid leave each year for family or medical reasons
2008	Genetic Information Nondiscrimination Act	Prohibits discrimination against employees or applicants because of genetic information (one's own or family members' genetic tests)
2009	Lilly Ledbetter Fair Pay Act	Changes the statute of limitations on pay discrimination to 180 days from each paycheck

Source: U.S. Equal Employment Opportunity Commission, www.eeoc.gov.

workforce, customers, and suppliers to products, services, and the communities served. Policies and procedures must be in place to ensure that grievances and concerns are addressed immediately. Finally, the organizational culture needs to be one where diversity and inclusion are valued, even to the point where, like Marriott International, individual performance is measured and rewarded on diversity accomplishments.

Mentoring

One of the consequences of having few women and minorities in top corporate leadership positions is that lower-level diverse employees lack someone to turn to for support or advice. That's where a mentoring program can be beneficial. **Mentoring** is a process whereby an experienced organizational member (a mentor) provides advice and guidance to a less-experienced member (a protégé). Mentors usually provide two unique forms of mentoring functions: career development and social support.[102]

mentoring
A process whereby an experienced organizational member (a mentor) provides advice and guidance to a less experienced member (a protégé)

Andrea Jung, former CEO of Avon Products, the first woman to hold that job in the female-oriented products company, said her male mentor (previous CEO James Preston) had the most influence on her career.[103] A study by Catalyst of male mentors to women found that men who impeded or who were indifferent to the progress of women viewed the workplace as a zero-sum game where promotion of women came at

Exhibit 4-9

What a Good Mentor Does

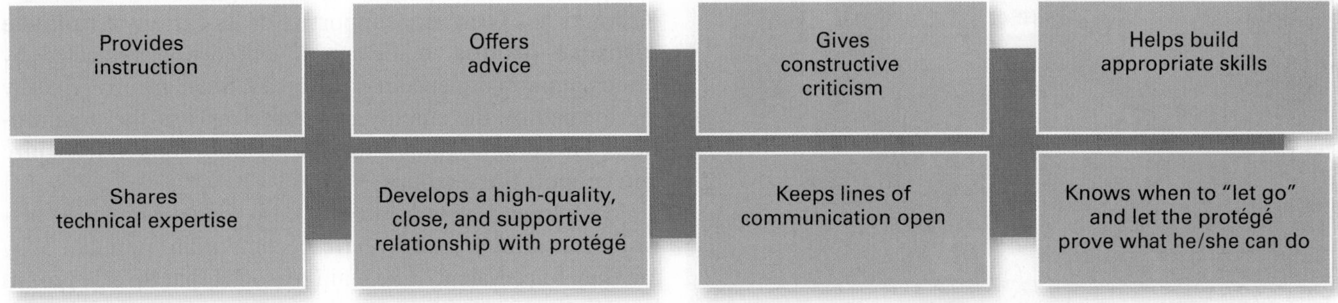

Sources: Based on J. Prime and C. A. Moss-Racusin, "Engaging Men in Gender Initiatives: What Change Agents Need to Know," *Catalyst,* www.catalyst.org, 2009; T. J. DeLong, J. J. Gabarro, and R. J. Lees, "Why Mentoring Matters in a Hypercompetitive World," *Harvard Business Review,* January 2008, pp. 115–121; S. N. Mehta, "Why Mentoring Works," *Fortune,* July 9, 2001, p. 119; and D. A. Thomas, "Race Matters: The Truth About Mentoring Minorities," *Harvard Business Review,* April 2001, pp. 99–107.

the expense of men. However, one thing that stood out among men who championed women was a strong sense of fairness.[104]

A good mentoring program would be aimed at all employees with high potential to move up the organization's career ladder. Exhibit 4-9 looks at what a good mentor does. If an organization is serious about its commitment to diversity, it needs to have a mentoring program in place.

Mentors and Protégés—If your instructor is using Pearson MyLab Management, log onto **mymanagementlab.com** and test your *mentor-protégé knowledge.* **Be sure to refer back to the chapter opener!**

Diversity Skills Training

"The only thing in human DNA is to discriminate. It's a part of normal human tribal behavior."[105] In a chapter on managing diversity, you might be surprised to find a statement like this. However, it reflects reality. Our human nature is to not accept or approach anyone who is different from us. But it doesn't make discrimination of any type or form acceptable. And we live and work in a multicultural context. So the challenge for organizations is to find ways for employees to be effective in dealing with others who aren't like them. That's where **diversity skills training**—specialized training to educate employees about the importance of diversity and teach them skills for working in a diverse workplace—comes in. Millions of dollars are spent on this effort annually, much of it on training.[106]

diversity skills training
Specialized training to educate employees about the importance of diversity and teach them skills for working in a diverse workplace

Most diversity skills training programs start with *diversity awareness training.* During this type of training, employees are made aware of the assumptions and biases they may have. Once we recognize that, we can look at increasing our sensitivity and openness to those who are different from us. Sounds simple, but it's not. However, if people can be taught to recognize that they're prejudging people and to consciously address that behavior, then the diversity awareness training has been successful. The next step is *diversity skills training*, in which people learn specific skills on how to communicate and work effectively in a diverse work environment. At Sodexo, the food services/facilities management company, employee diversity training is an important part of its diversity management program.

Employee Resource Groups

Kellogg Company, the cereal corporation, is a pioneer in workplace diversity. More than 100 years ago, company founder W. K. Kellogg employed women in the workplace and reached across cultural boundaries. That commitment to diversity continues

A gospel choir employee resource group at Nissan's automotive plant in Canton, Mississippi, brings together a diverse group of employees, from technicians to salaried workers, who all share a love of singing. Nissan's top managers are committed to employee diversity initiatives that also include mentoring and skills training.
Source: Rogelio V. Solis/AP Images

today. The company's CEO attributes much of the company's success to the wide variety of histories, experiences, ideas, and perspectives employees have brought to the business.[107] Kellogg's has been very supportive of its various **employee resource groups**, made up of employees connected by some common dimension of diversity. Such groups typically are formed by the employees themselves, not the organizations. However, it's important for organizations to recognize and support these groups.

Employee resource groups (also called employee networks or affinity groups) have become quite popular. Why are they so prevalent? The main reason is that diverse groups have the opportunity to see that their existence is acknowledged and that they have the support of people within and outside the group. Individuals in a minority often feel invisible and not important in the overall organizational scheme of things. Employee resource groups provide an opportunity for those individuals to have a voice. For instance, Prudential, a financial services and insurance company, has seven employee resource groups—some are Abled & Disabled Associates Partnering Together (ADAPT); Prudential Military Veterans Network (VETNET); Employee Association of Gay Men, Lesbians, Bisexual, Transgender & Allies (EAGLES); and the newest—Generations—which focuses on generational diversity. These groups demonstrate a commitment to empowering, leveraging, and fostering the development of the individual members of the resource group. Through these employee resource groups, those in a minority find they're not alone—and that can be a powerful means of embracing and including all employees, regardless of their differences.

employee resource groups
Groups made up of employees connected by some common dimension of diversity

Chapter 4 PREPARING FOR: Exam/Quizzes

CHAPTER SUMMARY by Learning Objectives

LO4.1 DEFINE workplace diversity and explain why managing it is so important.

Workplace diversity is the ways in which people in an organization are different from and similar to one another. Managing workforce diversity is important for three reasons: (1) people management benefits—better use of employee talent, increased quality of team problem-solving efforts, and ability to attract and retain diverse employees; (2) organizational performance benefits—reduced costs, enhanced problem-solving ability, and improved system flexibility; and (3) strategic benefits—increased understanding of a diverse marketplace, potential to improve sales and market share, and competitive advantage.

LO4.2 DESCRIBE the changing workplaces in the United States and around the world.

The main changes in the workplace in the United States include the total increase in the population; the changing components of the population, especially in relation to racial/ethnic groups; and an aging population. The most important changes in the global population include the total world population and the aging of that population.

LO4.3 EXPLAIN the different types of diversity found in workplaces.

The different types of diversity found in workplaces include age (older workers and younger workers), gender (male and female), race and ethnicity (racial and ethnic classifications), disability/abilities (people with a disability that limits major life activities), religion (religious beliefs and religious practices), sexual orientation and gender identity (gay, lesbian, bisexual, and transgender), and other (for instance, socioeconomic background, team members from different functional areas, physical attractiveness, obesity, job seniority, and so forth).

LO4.4 DISCUSS **the challenges managers face in managing diversity.**

The two main challenges managers face are personal bias and the glass ceiling. Bias is a tendency or preference toward a particular perspective or ideology. Our biases can lead to prejudice, which is a preconceived belief, opinion, or judgment toward a person or a group of people; stereotyping, which is judging a person on the basis of one's perception of a group to which he or she belongs; and discrimination, which is when someone acts out prejudicial attitudes toward people who are the targets of that person's prejudice. The glass ceiling refers to the invisible barrier that separates women and minorities from top management positions.

LO4.5 DESCRIBE **various workplace diversity management initiatives.**

It's important to understand the role of federal laws in diversity. Some of these laws include Title VII of the Civil Rights Act, the Americans with Disabilities Act, and Age Discrimination in Employment Act. Workplace diversity management initiatives include top management commitment to diversity; mentoring, which is a process whereby an experienced organizational member provides advice and guidance to a less experienced member; diversity skills training; and employee resource groups, which are groups made up of employees connected by some common dimension of diversity.

Pearson **MyLab** Management

Go to **mymanagementlab.com** to complete the problems marked with this icon ✪.

✪ REVIEW AND DISCUSSION QUESTIONS

4-1. How has workforce diversity changed since the 1960s, particularly in the West?

4-2. Identify the three main challenges of having workforce diversity in an organization.

4-3. Which countries experience a "demographic dividend," and what does this mean? Is it sustainable or not?

4-4. Do you think religion can affect work behaviors?

4-5. Look around you and summarize the different forms of diversity you can find at your university.

4-6. Different ethnicity causes problems associated with diversity management. Discuss.

4-7. Are laws, federal or otherwise, necessary for supporting diversity initiatives?

4-8. Who is responsible for doing more to break the glass ceiling barrier for women and minorities?

Pearson **MyLab** Management

If your professor has assigned these, go to **mymanagementlab.com** for the following Assisted-graded writing questions:

4-9. What is workforce diversity, and why is managing it so important?

4-10. What would you include in a diversity training program? Justify your suggestions.

PREPARING FOR: My Career

✪ PERSONAL INVENTORY ASSESSMENTS

Multicultural Awareness Scale

It's highly likely that you'll be employed in an organization with a diverse workforce. How aware are you of other cultures and other cultural contexts? Complete this PIA and find out.

✪ ETHICS DILEMMA

An unexpected ethical issue arose when Hungary, Romania, and Bulgaria joined the European Union (EU). The start of the free movement of workers across the EU meant that workers from these countries could effectively undercut the domestic workforce. Wages in Eastern Europe were considerably lower than its Western counterparts, but recruitment agencies actively hired to help businesses drive down their salary and wage bills. With unemployment being relatively high in France, the United Kingdom, and Spain, for example, recruiters offered high-quality workers a fraction of the domestic rates. Locals were being priced out of the job market.

4-11. Do you think the Eastern Europeans were being exploited by the recruitment agencies?

4-12. Should a country ever adopt a "locals first" policy in terms of employment opportunity? Does legal migration only imply flooding lucrative job markets?

SKILLS EXERCISE Developing Your Valuing Diversity Skill

About the Skill

Understanding and managing people who are similar to us can be challenging—but understanding and managing people who are dissimilar from us and from each other can be even tougher.[108] The diversity issues a manager might face are many. They may include issues such as communicating with employees whose familiarity with the language may be limited; creating career development programs that fit the skills, needs, and values of a particular group; helping a diverse team cope with a conflict over goals or work assignments; or learning which rewards are valued by different groups.

Steps in Practicing the Skill

- ***Fully accept diversity.*** Successfully valuing diversity starts with each individual accepting the principle of diversity. Accept the value of diversity for its own sake—not simply because it's the right thing to do. And it's important that you reflect your acceptance in all you say and do.
- ***Recruit broadly.*** When you have job openings, work to get a diverse applicant pool. Although referrals from current employees can be a good source of applicants, that source tends to produce candidates similar to the present workforce.
- ***Select fairly.*** Make sure the selection process doesn't discriminate. One suggestion is to use job-specific tests rather than general aptitude or knowledge tests. Such tests measure specific skills, not subjective characteristics.
- ***Provide orientation and training for diverse employees.*** Making the transition from outsider to insider can be particularly difficult for a diverse employee. Provide support either through a group or through a mentoring arrangement.
- ***Sensitize nondiverse employees.*** Not only do you personally need to accept and value diversity, as a manager you need to encourage all your employees to do so. Many organizations do this through diversity training programs. In addition, employees can also be part of ongoing discussion groups whose members meet monthly to discuss stereotypes and ways of improving diversity relationships. The most important thing a manager can do is show by his or her actions that diversity is valued.
- ***Strive to be flexible.*** Part of valuing diversity is recognizing that different groups have different needs and values. Be flexible in accommodating employee requests.
- ***Seek to motivate individually.*** Motivating employees is an important skill for any manager; motivating a diverse workforce has its own special challenges. Managers must strive to be in tune with the background, cultures, and values of employees.
- ***Reinforce employee differences.*** Encourage individuals to embrace and value diverse views. Create traditions and ceremonies that promote diversity. Celebrate diversity

by accentuating its positive aspects. However, also be prepared to deal with the challenges of diversity such as mistrust, miscommunication, lack of cohesiveness, attitudinal differences, and stress.

Practicing the Skill

Read through the following scenario. Write down some notes about how you would handle the situation described. Be sure to refer to the eight behaviors described for valuing diversity.

Scenario

You have recently taken over the management of a team assigned to implement a new information technology system at your company. Read through the descriptions of the following employees who are on your team. Consider the steps you can take to ensure that your team successfully works together. What types of employee issues might you face as the team's manager? How can you ensure your team works together successfully and benefits from the diversity of the team? Make some notes of your plans on how you will manage your new team.

Lester. Lester is 57 years old, a college graduate, and has been with the company for more than 20 years. His two children are married, and he is a grandparent of three beautiful grandchildren. He lives in a condo with his wife, who does volunteer work and is active in their church. Lester is healthy and likes to stay active, both physically and mentally.

Sanjyot. Sanjyot is a 30-year-old who joined the company after she came to the United States from Indonesia 10 years ago. She completed high school after moving to the United States and has begun to attend evening classes at a local community college. Sanjyot is a single parent with two children under the age of 8. Although her health is excellent, one of her children suffers from a severe learning disability.

Yuri. Yuri is a recent immigrant from one of the former Soviet republics and is new to the company. He is 42 and his English communication skills are quite limited. He is unmarried and has no children but feels obligated to send much of his paycheck to relatives back in his home country. As a result, he is willing to work extra hours to increase his pay.

Beth. Beth joined the company two years ago when she graduated from college. She is recently married and is very involved in the local community, volunteering with several local nonprofit organizations when she is not at work. She grew up in a nearby community and also has responsibility for caring for her aging parents who have recently developed several health problems.

WORKING TOGETHER Team Exercise

A challenge for organizations in managing diversity is how to recruit and hire a diverse workforce. In groups of three or four students, discuss opportunities to identify and attract a diverse job applicant pool for an organization. Consider the different types of diversity and generate a list of ideas of where a company could publicize job openings in order to target more diverse applicants. Be prepared to share your ideas with the class.

MY TURN TO BE A MANAGER

- Describe your experiences with people from other backgrounds. What challenges have you faced? What have you learned that will help you in understanding the unique needs and challenges of a diverse workplace?
- Go to DiversityInc.com (www.diversityinc.com) and find the latest list of Top 50 Companies for Diversity. Select three companies from this list. Describe and evaluate what they're doing as far as workplace diversity is concerned.
- Think of times when you may have been treated unfairly because of stereotypical thinking. What stereotypes were being used? How did you respond to the treatment?
- The Job Accommodation Network is a free resource for employers to identify ways to provide work accommodations to allow disabled workers to be productive and hold a wider variety of jobs. Visit www.askjan.org and search the accommodation database to find examples of accommodations for specific disabilities.
- Assume you are designing a mentoring program for an organization. Conduct some research on mentoring programs that currently exist in different organizations and identify characteristics of an effective mentoring program.
- Pick one of the laws listed in Exhibit 4-8. Research that law looking for these elements: Whom does the law cover? What does the law prohibit? What are the consequences for violating the law?

CASE APPLICATION 1 An Ethical Hotel where Disabled People Can Find Their Way

In 2015, the Albergo Etico (Ethical Hotel), located in Asti, Norther Italy, opened its doors to the public and has quickly become a case of excellence in the management of disabled workers in the hospitality industry. The main characteristic of this hotel is that disabled workers represent a large part of the company's workforce. The hotel's management ensures that the employees are mentored throughout their tenure with the company and are supported in developing their personal and professional abilities.

This successful diversity management initiative began in 2006 with a project called "download." This was created by a group of friends who wanted to do something to improve the society they lived in and, particularly, to help Niccolò, a young man with Down syndrome, to complete work experience to validate his diploma in hospitality management. Niccolò began his internship working in the hotel and its restaurant, performing all core activities completed by the hotel staff, including working in the back and front offices and serving clients during meals. Through the hotel's support, Niccolò's development in his work and personal life were significant. He has reached a considerable degree of autonomy, now having his own key to the restaurant, serving as a mentor for newcomers to the business, and living independently.

Today, with help from charities like the Vodafone Foundation, the download project has implemented structured training and has seen more disabled workers joining Alberto Etico following Niccolò's example. The hotel hosts an Academy of Independence within its premises, allowing disabled people to work, learn, and live together for the entire duration of the three-year program. The hotel staff guides the trainees through all the different hotel functions to help build their skills. A fundamental moment of each day in training is the lunch where trainees and mentors take time to reflect on challenges of the morning. They also find time to relax and develop their relationships. The camaraderie between employees is incredibly strong and contributes in creating a unique climate of trust, respect, and collaboration that enable the workers to learn all the necessary skills to work in the hotel in a safe environment. Trainees are also encouraged to use these skills in their personal life, to strengthen their independence.

However, working in the hospitality industry is not always easy as the responsibilities and clients can be demanding. Therefore, hotel managers take into serious account the physical and mental well-being of their collaborators, especially of the disabled workers who need to strengthen their musculature to be able to perform all required tasks. To achieve this goal, the hotel's direction has decided to develop partnerships with local sport centers to let disabled workers practice regular sport and massage therapy to relax and reinforce their musculature. Disabled workers are initiated to jogging or Nordic walking who are sports particularly suitable for them as can be practiced with graduation and enable them to correct posture and body balance. Another suitable sport is the Judo that enables disabled workers to improve their equilibrium, movements, and coordination.

With organizations across the world recognizing the need to hire more differently abled people in their verticals, and envisaging business development in which they also play an important part, Albergo Etico is an illustrative example of how a company can be profitable and socially responsible at the same time. It was able to achieve this by not just hiring and training its staff, but by also providing a barrier-free and disabled-friendly work environment. Its efforts have received recognition from the President of the Italian Republic, the European Parliament, and Pope Francis, to name a few. The experience of Albergo Etico is a best practice in diversity management demonstrating that managing employees belonging to minority groups can follow traditional performance imperative exactly as other employees rather than the logics of compassion or compliance with laws and regulations, with positive repercussion on the entire organization, diverse workers, and the social community.[109]

DISCUSSION QUESTIONS

4-13. What challenges could a manager face in the long-term management of disabled workers?

4-14. What are the hotel's advantages of having its workforce being comprised largely of disabled workers? What are the potential drawbacks?

4-15. In your opinion, would a performance imperative approach or a compassionate approach be applicable to the management of disabled workers?

4-16. What do you think managers can do to let disabled workers find the "right place" in an organization? How can disabled employees help in this process? Explain.

4-17. How can other companies be sensitized to recruit more disabled workers? According to you, how would Albergo Etico inspire them? Explain.

CASE APPLICATION 2 Women in Management at Deutsche Telekom

Companies across Europe have a problem—a large gender gap in leadership.[110] Men far outnumber women in senior business leadership positions. This dismal picture of sexism in Europe exists despite efforts and campaigns to try and ensure equality in the workplace. But one European company is tackling the problem head-on. Deutsche Telekom, Europe's largest telecommunication company, says it intends to "more than double the number of women who are managers within five years." In addition, it plans to increase the number of women in senior and middle management to 30 percent by the end of 2015. With this announcement, the company becomes the first member of the DAX 30 index of blue-chip German companies to introduce a gender quota. Deutsche's chief executive René Obermann said, "Taking on more women in management positions is not about the enforcement of misconstrued egalitarianism. Having a greater number of women at the top will quite simply enable us to operate better." In addition to its plans to intensify recruiting of female university graduates, Deutsche Telekom will need to make changes in its corporate policies and practices to attract and keep women in management positions. So what is Deutsche Telekom doing to achieve its goal of bringing more women into management positions? One action the company is taking is to increase and improve recruiting of female university graduates. In fact, the company has committed to having at least 30 percent of the places in executive development programs held by women. Other steps being taken by the company revolve around the work environment and work–family issues. The company plans to expand its parental-leave programs and introduce more flexible working hours for managers. Right now, less than 1 percent of the company's managers work part time. In addition, the company plans to double the number of available places in company child-care programs. The company also has realized it needs to become more transparent in its selection and appointment processes and to monitor whether recruiting and retention goals have been reached. Despite its efforts, Deutsche Telekom and other German companies have struggled with gender goals. In 2012, only 4 percent of senior executives at Germany's top 200 companies were female.

DISCUSSION QUESTIONS

4-18. What do you think of the "quota" approach that Deutsche Telekom is pursuing? What benefits and drawbacks does such an approach have?

4-19. What issues might Deutsche Telekom face in recruiting female university graduates? How could they address these issues?

4-20. What issues might the company face in introducing changes in work–family programs? How can these issues be addressed?

4-21. What workplace diversity initiatives, discussed in the chapter, might be appropriate for Deutsche Telekom? What would be involved in implementing these initiatives?

ENDNOTES

1. Claire Cohen, "Just Who Are the 7 Women Bosses of the FTSE 100?" *The Telegraph (UK)*, September 20, 2016, http://www.telegraph.co.uk/women/work/just-who-are-the-7-women-bosses-of-the-ftse-100/ (accessed December 14, 2016); Anthony Fensom, "Asia's Boards: Where Are the Women?" *The Diplomat*, March 16, 2016, http://thediplomat.com/2016/03/asias-boards-where-are-the-women/ (accessed December 14, 2016); Jon Menon, "Thiam's Rise to Become First Black CEO of European Bank: Timeline," *Bloomberg*, March 10, 2015, https://www.bloomberg.com/news/articles/2015-03-10/prudential-ceo-s-route-to-top-job-at-credit-suisse-timeline (accessed December 14, 2016); Eilidh Macleod, "Out at Work: The Top 50 List of LGBT Executives," *The Telegraph (UK)*, January 16, 2015, http://www.telegraph.co.uk/finance/11349808/Out-at-Work-The-top-50-list-of-LGBT-executives.html (accessed December 14, 2016).
2. S. Bharadwaj Badal, "How Hiring a Gender-Diverse Workforce Can Improve A Company's Bottom Line," www.gallup.com/businessjournal/, January 20, 2014.
3. V. Hunt, D. Layton, and S. Prince, "Why Diversity Matters," www.mckinsey.com, January 2015.
4. "Sodexo Training Programs for Diversity & Inclusion," www.sodexo.com, February 2016.
5. R. Anand and M. Frances Winters, "A Retrospective View of Corporate Diversity Training from 1964 to the Present," *Academy of Management Learning & Education,* September 2008, pp. 356–372.
6. This section is based on S. P. Robbins and T. A. Judge, *Organizational Behavior,* 15th ed. (Upper Saddle River, NJ: Pearson Prentice Hall, 2013), p. 42.
7. "The 2015 DiversityInc Top 50 Companies for Diversity," DiversityInc.com, April 23, 2015.
8. Ibid.
9. "The 2013 DiversityInc Top 50 Companies for Diversity," DiversityInc.com, April 23, 2013; and "Top 50 Companies for Diversity," *Diversity Inc.,* May/June 2009, p. 42.
10. "Supplier Diversity," www.key.com/about/supplier-information/key-supplier-diversity.jsp. Copyright © KeyBank.
11. R. Tulshyan, "Racially Diverse Companies Outperform Industry Norms by 35%," *Forbes*, www.forbes.com, January 30, 2015.
12. A. Joshi and H. Roh, "The Role of Context in Work Team Diversity Research: A Meta-Analytic Review," *Academy of Management Journal,* June 2009, pp. 599–627.
13. Jessica Murphy, "Mounties Reach Multi-Million Sexual Harassment Settlement," *BBC News*, October 6, 2016, http://www.bbc.com/news/world-us-canada-37578859 (accessed December 14, 2016).
14. Jonathan Kaiman, "In China, Feminism Is Growing—and So Is the Backlash, *Los Angeles Times*, June 15, 2016, http://www.latimes.com/world/asia/la-fg-china-feminist-activists-20160614-snap-story.html (accessed December 14, 2016).
15. Emma Thelwell, "Are Race Discrimination Laws Still Needed in the Workplace?" *BBC News*, March 12, 2015, http://www.bbc.com/news/uk-31856147 (accessed December 14, 2016).
16. Stephen Simpson, "When Workplace Nicknames Lead to Discrimination," *Personnel Today*, March 11, 2016, http://www.personneltoday.com/hr/workplace-nicknames-lead-discrimination/ (accessed December 14, 2016).
17. York Chow, "Hong Kong Must End Age Discrimination in the Workplace," *South China Morning Post*, January 7, 2016, http://www.scmp.com/comment/insight-opinion/article/1898376/hong-kong-must-end-age-discrimination-workplace (accessed December 14, 2016).
18. C. M. Riordan, "Diversity is Useless Without Inclusivity," *Harvard Business Review* online, www.hbr.org, June 5, 2014.
19. "Diversity Fatigue," *The Economist* online, www.economist.com, February 13, 2016.
20. S. A. Hewlett, M. Marshall, and L. Sherbin, "How Diversity Can Drive Innovation," *Harvard Business Review,* December 2013, p. 30.
21. Ernst & Young, "The New Global Mindset: Driving Innovation Through Diversity," EYGM Limited, 2010, p. 1.
22. Ibid.
23. Based on C. Dougherty and M. Jordan, "Minority Births Are New Majority," *Wall Street Journal,* May 17, 2012, p. A4; and S. Tavernise, "Whites Account for Under Half of Births in U.S.," *New York Times* online, May 17, 2012.
24. H. El Nasser and P. Overberg, "1990–2010: How America Changed," *USA Today,* August 10, 2011, pp. 1A+; and D. Meinert, "Census Data Reflect Older, More Diverse U.S. Workforce," *HR Magazine,* July 2011, pp. 18–19.
25. Information in this section from: H. El Nasser, "U.S. Hispanic Population to Triple by 2050," *USA Today* online, www.usatoday.com, February 12, 2008; "U.S. Population Projections: 2005–2050," Pew Research Center, www.pewhispanic.org/reports/, February 11, 2008; U.S. Department of Labor, The Bureau of Labor Statistics,

"Report of the Taskforce on the Aging of the American Workforce", www.bls.gov, 2008; and L. B. Shrestha, "The Changing Demographic Profile of the United States," *Congressional Research Service/The Library of Congress,* May 5, 2006.
26. CIA *World Factbook*, www.cia.gov/library/publications/the-world-factbook/, 2016.
27. "The Changing Demographic Profile of the United States," Congressional Research Service. March 31, 2011, pg. 16.
28. U.S. Bureau of Labor Statistics, "Labor Force Projections to 2024: The Labor Force Is Growing, But Slowly," *Monthly Labor Review* online, www.bls.gov, December 2015.
29. "Statistical Yearbook, 2016 Edition," *United Nations Department of Economic and Social Affairs*, 2016, pp. 1–8; "World Population Prospects 2015," *United Nations Department of Economic and Social Affairs*, 2015, pp. 1–12; and "Population and Population Change Statistics," *Eurostat*, July 2016, http://ec.europa.eu/eurostat (accessed December 14, 2016).
30. "Profile of the Global Workforce: Present and Future," *The Economist Intelligence Unit*, 2015, http://futurehrtrends.eiu.com/report-2015/ (accessed December 14, 2016).
31. "International Data Base, World Population by Age and Sex," *U.S. Census Bureau*, September 27, 2016, https://www.census.gov/population/international/data/idb/worldpop.php (accessed December 14, 2016).
32. Julia Smirnova and Weiyi Cai, "See Where Women Outnumber Men Around the World (and Why)," *Washington Post*, August 19, 2015, https://www.washingtonpost.com/news/worldviews/wp/2015/08/19/see-where-women-outnumber-men-around-the-world-and-why/?utm_term=.e6592f65ce34 (accessed December 14, 2016).
33. K. Gurchiek, "Options for Older Workers," *HR Magazine,* June 2012, p. 18.
34. Lee Sang Ok and Tan Teck Boon, "South Korea's Demographic Dilemma," *East Asia Forum*, March 25, 2016, http://www.eastasiaforum.org/2016/03/25/south-koreas-demographic-dilemma/ (accessed December 15, 2016); Jackie Keast, "Government Needs National Strategy to Address Age Discrimination in the Workplace: Report," *Australian Aging Agenda*, May 6, 2016, http://www.australianageingagenda.com.au/2016/05/06/ggovernment-needs-national-strategy-to-address-age-discrimination-in-the-workplace-report/ (accessed December 15, 2016).
35. R. J. Grossman, "Invest in Older Workers," *HR Magazine,* August 2013, pp. 20–25; and T. W. H. Ng, "Stereotypes and the Older Worker," www.strategy-business.com, March 1, 2013. Other material in this section adapted from Robbins and Judge, *Organizational Behavior,* 15th ed., p. 44.
36. H. Ruthven, "Barclays Shifts Perception by Rolling Out Apprenticeship Scheme for Those Over 50," http://realbusiness.co.uk, February 9, 2015.
37. L. Wolgemuth, "How to Stand Out from the Crowd and Kick-Start Your Own Recovery," *U.S. News & World Report,* May 2010, pp. 14–16.
38. R. B. Williams, "Generation Y Poised to Dominate the Workplace", network.nationalpost.com/np/blogs, June 13, 2009.
39. "Most Common Gen Y Job Titles Today," *T&D,* April 2012, p. 23; and P. Ketter, "Value Proposition? Oh, Yes!" *T&D,* November 2011, p. 10.
40. C. Smith and S. Turner, "The Radical Transformation of Diversity and Inclusion: The Millennial Influence," Deloitte University, The Leadership Center for Inclusion, 2015.
41. Ibid.
42. U.S. Bureau of Labor Statistics, "The Employment Situation—January 2016," (USDL-16-0210), February 5, 2016.
43. U.S. Bureau of Labor Statistics, "Women's Earnings Compared to Men's Earnings in 2014," *The Economics Daily* online, www.bls.gov, accessed February 20, 2016.
44. L. Weber, "What Women—and Men—Say About the Gender Wage Gap—Real Time Economics," *The Wall Street Journal* online, February 25, 2016.
45. C. Rampell, "Young Women are More Career-Driven than Men," *New York Times* online, April 19, 2012.
46. "Postbaccalaureate Enrollment," National Center for Education Statistics, http://nces.ed.gov, May 31, 2015; "Fast Facts: Back to School Statistics," National Center for Education Statistics,, http://nces.ed.gov/fastfacts/display.asp?id=372, March 15, 2014; and A. Fisher, "Boys vs. Girls: What's Behind the College Grad Gender Gap," cnnmoney.com, March 27, 2013.
47. "Postbaccalaureate Enrollment," National Center for Education Statistics, http://nces.ed.gov, May 31, 2015; N. M. Carter and C. Silva, "Women in Management: Delusions of Progress," *Harvard Business Review,* March 2010, pp. 19–21.
48. "When Women Thrive, Businesses Thrive," Mercer, www.mercer.com, 2016.
49. "Women and Leadership: Public Says Women are Equally Qualified, but Barriers Persist," The Pew Research Center, January 14, 2015.
50. M. Noland, T. Moran, and B. Kotschwar, "Is Gender Diversity Profitable? Evidence from a Global Survey," Peterson Institute for International Economics, February 2016.
51. Material in this section adapted from Robbins and Judge, *Organizational Behavior,* 14th ed., pp. 45–46.
52. "When Women Thrive, Businesses Thrive," Mercer, www.mercer.com, 2016
53. G. N. Powell, D. A. Butterfield, and J. D. Parent, "Gender and Managerial Stereotypes: Have the Times Changed?" *Journal of Management,* vol. 28 (2), 2002, pp. 177–193.
54. "Women Leaders: The Hard Truth About Soft Skills," *Bloomberg BusinessWeek* online, February 16, 2010; and A. Bryant, "No Doubts: Women Are Better Managers," *New York Times* online, July 26, 2009.
55. "Women Leaders: The Hard Truth About Soft Skills."
56. V. Lipman, "Are Women Really, As This Major Research Says, Better Managers than Men?" *Forbes* online, www.forbes.com, April 16, 2015.
57. F. Newport and J. Wilke, "Americans Still Prefer a Male Boss," www.gallup.com/poll/, November 11, 2013.
58. Lublin and Eggers, "More Women Are Primed to Land CEO Roles."
59. "Global Diversity: Our Strategy Framework," Coca-Cola Web site, May 25, 2012; "The 2012 DiversityInc Top 10 Companies for Blacks," *DiversityInc.com*, April 24, 2012; J. J. Sapolek, "Coca-Cola Division Refreshes Its Talent With Diversity Push on Campus," *Workforce Management Online,* March 24, 2011; J. Lewis Jr., "The Ground Up," *Inside Counsel,* August 2010, p. 10; R. Hastings, "Diversity Speakers Encourage Innovation, Global Mindset," *HR Magazine,* January 2009, p. 85; J. Wiscombe, "Corporate America's Scariest Opponent," *Workforce,* April 2003, pp. 34–39; and B. McKay, "Coca-Cola Concedes Its Diversity Efforts Have

Been Slow, Says It Will Do Better," *Wall Street Journal,* February 10, 2000, p. A11.

60. A. M. Carton and A. S. Rosette, "Explaining Bias Against Black Leaders: Integrating Theory on Information Processing and Goal-Based Stereotyping," *Academy of Management Journal,* December 2011, pp. 1141–1156; and "I Didn't Get the Job Because I'm Black," *DiversityInc.,* diversityinc.com/legal-issues/didnt-get-job/, June 2011.
61. Nora Fakim and Nomia Iqbal, "Identity in the UK: Who Ticks the British Box on the National Census Form?" *BBC*, August 13, 2015, http://www.bbc.co.uk/newsbeat/article/33860433/identity-in-the-uk-who-ticks-the-british-box-on-the-national-census-form (accessed December 15, 2016).
62. Material in this section adapted from Robbins and Judge, *Organizational Behavior,* 14th ed., p. 47.
63. J. L. S. Wittmer, "Take a Walk in Our Shoes," *T&D,* November 2011, pp. 57–59.
64. D. Meinert, "Opening Doors," *HR Magazine,* June 2012, pp. 55–57.
65. U.S. Department of Labor/Office of Disability Employment Policy, "Survey of Employer Perspectives on the Employment of People with Disabilities", www.dol.gov/odep/documents/survey_report_jan_09.doc, November 2008.
66. A. Merrick, "Erasing 'Un' From 'Unemployable'; Walgreen Program Trains the Disabled to Take on Regular Wage-Paying Jobs," *Wall Street Journal,* August 2, 2007, pp. B1+.
67 L. Federico-O'Murchu, "Tapping the Talents of Disabled Workers," www.cnbc.om, July 25, 2014.
68. M. Trottman, "Religious-Discrimination Claims on the Rise," *Wall Street Journal,* October 28, 2013, pp. B1+; and M. Bello, "Controversy Shrouds Muslim Women's Head Coverings" *USA Today,* April 15, 2010.
69. U.S. Equal Employment Opportunity Commission, "Supreme Court Rules in Favor of EEOC in Abercrombie Religious Discrimination Case," press release, www.eeoc.gov, June 1, 2015.
70. Material in this section adapted from Robbins and Judge, *Organizational Behavior,* 15th ed., pp. 50–51; S. Greenhouse, "Muslims Report Rising Discrimination at Work," *New York Times* online, September 23, 2010; and S. Ghumman and L. Jackson, "The Downside of Religious Attire: The Muslim Headscarf and Expectations of Obtaining Employment," *Journal of Organizational Behavior,* January 2010, pp. 4–23.
71. "Religion-Based Charges, FY 1997–FY 2015," *U.S. Equal Opportunity Employment Commission*, http://www1.eeoc.gov/eeoc/statistics/enforcement/religion.cfm?renderforprint=1, February 24, 2016.
72. P. Wang and J. L. Schwartz, "Stock Price Reactions to GLBT Nondiscrimination Policies," *Human Resource Management*, March–April 2010, pp. 195–216; "A Broken Bargain," Center for American Progress, http://www.americanprogress.org/issues/lgbt/report/2013/06/04/65133/a-broken-bargain/ (accessed June 4, 2013).
73. L. Sullivan, "Sexual Orientation—The Last 'Acceptable' Bias," *Canadian HR Reporter*, December 20, 2004, pp. 9–11.
74. Mona Chalabi, "Anti-LGBT Views Still Prevail, Global Survey Finds," *The Guardian (UK)*, May 17, 2016, https://www.theguardian.com/world/2016/may/17/global-lgbt-rights-new-survey-ilga (accessed December 15, 2016).
75. "Statistical Bulletin: Sexual Identity, UK: 2015," *Office for National Statistics* (UK), 2015, https://www.ons.gov.uk/peoplepopulationandcommunity/culturalidentity/sexuality/bulletins/sexualidentityuk/2015 (accessed December 15, 2016).
76. F. Colgan, T. Wright, C. Creegan, and A. McKearney, "Equality and Diversity in the Public Services: Moving Forward on Lesbian, Gay and Bisexual Equality?" *Human Resource Management Journal*, vol. 19, no. 3, 2009, pp. 280–301.
77. J. Hempel, "Coming Out in Corporate America," *BusinessWeek*, December 15, 2003, pp. 64–72.
78. S. A. Hewlett and K. Sumberg, "For LGBT Workers, Being 'Out' Brings Advantages," *Harvard Business Review*, July/August, 2011.
79. "The Cost of the Closet and the Rewards of Inclusion," Human Rights Campaign Foundation, www.hrc.org, May 2014.
80. Kentaro Todo and Kunio Endo, "Japanese Workplaces Inching toward LGBT Inclusion," *Nikkei Asian Review*, June 22, 2016, http://asia.nikkei.com/Business/Trends/Japanese-workplaces-inching-toward-LGBT-inclusion (accessed December 15, 2016).
81. "BBC Pledges Half of Workforce Will Be Women by 2020," *BBC*, April 23, 2016, www.bbc.com/news/entertainment-arts-36120246 (accessed December 15, 2016).
82. Namrata Singh, "We Are Trying to Get People to Think about Unconscious Bias: Maria Angelica Pérez," *The Times of India*, November 19, 2016, http://timesofindia.indiatimes.com/business/india-business/We-are-trying-to-get-people-to-think-about-unconscious-bias-Maria-Angelica-Prez/articleshow/55516351.cms (accessed December 15, 2016); www.ericsson.com.
83. Future Vision box based on G. White, "The Weakening Definition of Diversity," *The Atlantic* online, www.theatlantic.com, May 13, 2015; C. Smith & S. Turner, "The Radical Transformation of Diversity and Inclusion: The Millennial Influence," Deloitte University Leadership Center for Inclusion and the Billie Jean King Leadership Initiative, May 27, 2015; S. Rezvani, "Five Trends Driving Workplace Diversity in 2015," *Forbes* online, www.forbes.com, February 3, 2015; A. Griswold, "Why 'Thought Diversity' is the Future of the Workplace," *Business Insider* online, www.businessinsider.com, September 27, 2013.
84. L. Eaton, "Black Workers' Complaints Advance," *Wall Street Journal,* April 16, 2010, p. B4.
85. J. S. Lublin, "Do You Know Your Hidden Work Biases?" *Wall Street Journal,* January 10, 2014, pp. B1+.
86. T. Henneman, "You, Biased? No, It's Your Brain," *Workforce,* February 2014, pp. 28+.
87. Robbins and Judge, *Organizational Behavior,* 15th ed., p. 42.
88. Leader Making a Difference box based on R. Anand, "How Diversity and Inclusion Drives Employee Engagement," *DiversityInc,* Winter 2013, p. 20; N. Rigoglioso, "Steering the No. 1 Company for Diversity: 5 Minutes with Rohini Anand," Diversitywoman.com, February 6, 2012; "Sodexo," *DiversityInc,* Summer 2011, p. 34; "Case Study No. 1: Sodexo," *DiversityInc,* Early Fall 2011, pp. 48–50; DiversityInc Staff, "Sodexo's Rohini Anand: Breaking Gender Barriers and Creating Change," *DiversityInc,* June 7, 2010; and "Rohini Anand: Leading Sodexho's Commitment to a Globally Diverse Workforce," *Nation's Restaurant News,* February 10, 2003, p. 24.
89. Catalyst, "Workforce Metrics: Level of First Position," Workforce Management Online, www.workforce.com, April 8, 2010.

90. J. M. Hoobler, S. J. Wayne, and G. Lemmon, "Bosses' Perceptions of Family-Work Conflict and Women's Promotability: Glass Ceiling Effects," *Academy of Management Journal,* October 2009, pp. 939–957.
91. C. Hymowitz and T. D. Schellhardt, "The Glass Ceiling," *Wall Street Journal: A Special Report—The Corporate Woman,* March 24, 1986, pp. D1+.
92. S. Charas, L. L. Griffeth, & R. Malik, "Why Men Have More Help Getting to the C-Suite," *Harvard Business Review,* online, www.hbr.org, November 16, 2015.
93. Hoobler, Wayne, and Lemmon, "Bosses' Perceptions of Family-Work Conflict and Women's Promotability: Glass Ceiling Effects."
94. L. O'Conor, "A Third of Working Women Say They're Discriminated Against," *The Guardian* online, www .theguardian.com, June 3, 2015.
95. C. Allen, "Do As I Do, Not As I Say," *Wall Street Journal,* March 13, 2013, p. A13.
96. L. McDermott, "Women, Seize Your Leadership Role," *T&D,* March 2014, pp. 28–33.
97. "Top 50 Companies for Diversity: Marriott International," DiversityInc, April 23, 2016, p. 39.
98. Ibid.
99. K. A. Cañas and H. Sondak, *Opportunities and Challenges of Workplace Diversity,* 2nd ed. (Upper Saddle River, NJ: Pearson Prentice Hall, 2011), p. 26.
100. "Leaders Create Sustainable Approaches to Diversity," *DiversityInc,* February 2010, p. 20.
101. "Study: Mentoring Still Not Happening for Women at Work," talentmgt.com, March 18, 2014.
102. K. E. O'Brien, A. Biga, S. R. Kessler, and T. D. Allen, "A Meta-Analytic Investigation of Gender Differences in Mentoring," *Journal of Management,* March 2010, pp. 537–554.
103. D. Jones, "Often, Men See Women to the Top," *USA Today,* August 5, 2009, pp. 1B+.
104. J. Prime and C. A. Moss-Racusin, "Engaging Men in Gender Initiatives: What Change Agents Need to Know," *Catalyst,* www.catalyst.org, 2009.
105. L. Visconti, "Diversity Is Not in Your DNA, Says White Guy," *DiversityInc* online, www.diversityinc.com, March 3, 2010.
106. D. Meinert, "Tailoring Diversity Practices Produces Different Results," *HR Magazine,* July 2013, p. 16.
107. Kellogg Company, "Our Commitment to Diversity," www .kelloggcompany.com, April 22, 2010.
108. Based on P. L. Hunsaker, *Training in Management Skills* (Upper Saddle River, NJ: Prentice Hall, 2009); C. Harvey and J. Allard, *Understanding and Managing Diversity: Readings, Cases, and Exercises,* 3rd ed. (Upper Saddle River, NJ: Prentice Hall, 2005); and J. Greenberg, *Managing Behavior in Organizations: Science in Service to Practice,* 2nd ed. (Upper Saddle River, NJ: Prentice Hall, 1999).
109. Francesca Carli, "Inaugurato ad Asti il primo Albergo Etico Gestito Direttamente Da Personale Con La Sindrome Di Down [Asti Opens its First Ethics Hotel Directly Managed by People with Down Syndrome]," *LaFame*, July 27, 2015, http://lafame.net/albergo-etico-asti/; Independence Academy, Albergo Etico, http://www.albergoetico.it/progetti/accademia-indipendenza/, accessed November 2016. Independence Academy, Albergo Etico, http://www.albergoetico.asti.it/accademia.php, accessed November 2016. Benessere (Wellness), Albergo Etico, http://www.albergoetico.it/progetti/benessere/, accessed November 2016.
110. J. S. Lublin and T. Francis, "Women Gain Board Seats—Abroad," *Wall Street Journal*, February 5, 2014, p. B6; A. Webb, "Siemens Warming to Quotas Underscores Germany's Gender Gap," www.bloomberg.com/news/, December 4, 2013; R. Rayasam, "Do More Women on the Board Mean Better Results?" www.newyorker.com/online, November 19, 2013; K. Gurchiek, "The Global Battle for Female Talent," *HRMagazine*, June 2012, pp. 48–52; T. Sattleberger, "HR Report 2010/2011: Facts and Figures," Deutsche Telekom [www.e-paper.telekom.com/hrreport-2010-2011/epaper/HR2010_11_eng. pdf], June 2012; N. Clark, "Deutsche Telekom Struggles With Gender Goal," *New York Times Online*, October 2, 2011; K. Bennhold, "Women Nudged Out of German Workforce," *New York Times Online*, June 28, 2011; L. Stevens and J. Espinoza, "Deutsche Telekom Sets Women-Manager Quota," *Wall Street Journal Online*, March 22, 2010; J. Blaue, "Deutsche Telekom Launches Quota for Top Women Managers" [www.german-info.com/business_shownews]; N. Clark, "Goal at Deutsche Telekom: More Women as Managers," *New York Times Online*, March 15, 2010; R. Foroohar and S. H. Greenberg, "Working Women Are Poised to Become the Biggest Economic Engine the World Has Ever Known," *Newsweek*, November 2, 2009, pp. B2–B5; News Release, "Women Still Hold Less Than a Quarter of Senior Management Positions in Privately Held Businesses," *Grant Thornton International* [www.gti.org], March 5, 2009; and Catalyst Research Report, "Different Cultures, Similar Perceptions: Stereotyping of Western European Business Leaders" *Catalyst* [www.catalyst.org], 2006.

Chapter 5 Socially-Conscious Management

It's Your Career

Source: Cattallina/Shutterstock.

A key to success in management and in your career is knowing how to make good decisions about ethical dilemmas.

How to Be Ethical When No One Else Seems to Be

You make choices every day: Your boss asks you to do something questionable; you see a colleague doing something that violates a company rule or policy; you think about calling in sick because it's a beautiful day, and boy oh boy do you need a day off; you need to make copies of some personal documents and the company copier isn't monitored by anyone; you need to get some bills paid online and your boss is in meetings all day. Choices, choices, choices. What do you do?

When an ethical dilemma occurs at work—the place where you spend the vast majority of your week and the source of your income that pays your bills and provides benefits—it can be challenging to decide what to do. In addition to the chapter suggestions (see Exhibit 5-8), here are some ideas that might help nudge you to be ethical when no one else seems to be:

1. Make sure you have all the information you need to make a decision. *Sometimes, ethical "dilemmas" at work turn out to be nothing more than rumors or speculation about worst-case scenarios. "You can only do the right thing when you're not looking at things all wrong."[1] Get the facts, but use your discretion, patience, and common sense. Seek out advice from someone you trust and who you think is knowledgeable and wise.*

2. Recognize that we don't always act the way we think we're going to act when faced with an ethical dilemma.[2] *Most of us would say that we know we should be fair, be respectful, be trustworthy, be responsible, treat others as we want to be treated, etc. We have a set of values we want—and strive—to live by. What happens, though, is that when faced with an ethical dilemma, our "I" self rationalizes by saying: I don't want to lose my job, I don't want to be punished, I don't want to look foolish, etc. And so when something happens that we know is ethically questionable or even wrong, we "know" we should*

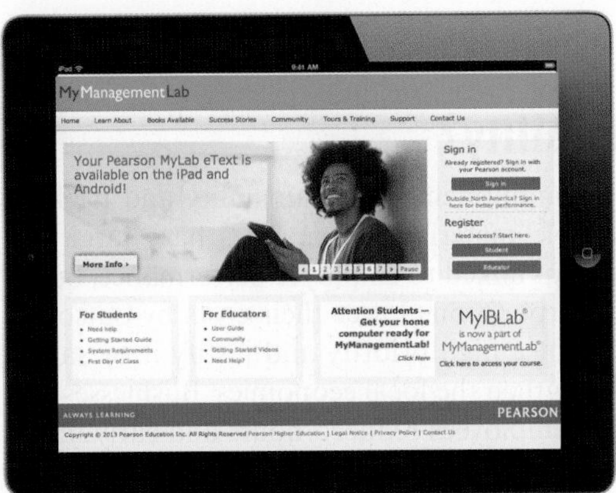

Pearson MyLab Management®

Improve Your Grade!

When you see this icon, visit **www.mymanagementlab.com** for activities that are applied, personalized, and offer immediate feedback.

Learning Objectives

• SKILL OUTCOMES

***5.1 Discuss** what it means to be socially responsible and what factors influence that decision.*

***5.2 Explain** green management and how organizations can go green.*

***5.3 Discuss** the factors that lead to ethical and unethical behavior.*

- **Develop your skill at** creating trust in work groups.

***5.4 Describe** management's role in encouraging ethical behavior.*

- **Know how** to make good decisions about ethical dilemmas.

***5.5 Discuss** current social responsibility and ethics issues.*

---

speak up or make it right. But we can't quite figure out how to do that, and then we explain it away by saying that it's okay that we acted the way we did. So, be aware of the way you "fool" yourself. Don't ignore or downplay ethical dilemmas.

***3. TEST yourself.** When faced with an ethical dilemma, use these "tests:"*[3]

- *The Golden Rule Test: Would I want people to do this to me?*
- *The Truth Test: Does this action represent the whole truth and nothing but the truth?*
- *The Stench Test: Does this action "stink" when I contemplate doing it?*
- *The What-If-Everybody-Did-This Test: Would I want everyone to do this? Would I want to live in that kind of world?*
- *The Family Test: How would my parents/spouse/significant other/children feel if they found out I did this?*
- *The Conscience Test: Does this action go against my conscience? Will I feel guilty afterwards?*
- *The Consequences Test: Might this action have bad consequences? Might I regret doing this?*
- *The Front Page/Social Media Test: How would I feel if this action was reported on the front page of my hometown newspaper or splashed across social media outlets for all to see?*

Deciding how ethical and socially responsible an organization needs to be and when raises complicated issues managers may have to address as they plan, organize, lead, and control. As managers manage, these issues can and do influence their actions. Let's see what we can learn about social responsibility and ethics.

WHAT is social responsibility?

LO5.1 Organizations profess their commitment to sustainability and package their products in nonrecyclable materials. Companies have large pay inequities; however, the difference is often not linked to employee performance, but to entitlement and "custom." Large global corporations lower their costs by outsourcing to countries where human rights are not a high priority and justify it by saying they're bringing in jobs and helping to strengthen the local economies. Businesses facing a difficult economic environment offer employees reduced hours and early retirement packages. Are these companies being socially responsible? Managers regularly face decisions that have a dimension of social responsibility in areas such as employee relations, philanthropy, pricing, resource conservation, product quality and safety, and doing business in countries that devalue human rights. What does it mean to be socially responsible?

From Obligations to Responsiveness to Responsibility

The concept of *social responsibility* has been described in different ways. For instance, it's been called "profit making only," "going beyond profit making," "any discretionary corporate activity intended to further social welfare," and "improving social or environmental conditions."[4] We can understand it better if we first compare it to two similar concepts: social obligation and social responsiveness.[5] **Social obligation** is when a firm engages in social actions because of its obligation to meet certain economic and legal responsibilities. The organization does what it's obligated to do and nothing more. This idea reflects the **classical view** of social responsibility, which says that management's only social responsibility is to maximize profits. The most outspoken advocate of this approach is economist and Nobel laureate Milton Friedman. He argued that managers' primary responsibility is to operate the business in the best interests of the stockholders, whose primary concerns are financial.[6] He also argued that when managers decide to spend the organization's resources for "social good," they add to the costs of doing business, which have to be passed on to consumers through higher prices or absorbed by stockholders through smaller dividends. Friedman doesn't say that organizations shouldn't be socially responsible, but his interpretation of social responsibility is to maximize profits for stockholders—a view still held by some today. An advisory firm that works with major corporations says, "Companies would achieve more social good by simply focusing on the bottom line rather than social responsibility programs."[7]

social obligation
When a firm engages in social actions because of its obligation to meet certain economic and legal responsibilities

classical view
The view that management's only social responsibility is to maximize profits

The other two concepts—social responsiveness and social responsibility—reflect the **socioeconomic view**, which says that managers' social responsibilities go beyond making profits to include protecting and improving society's welfare. This view is based on the belief that corporations are *not* independent entities responsible only to stockholders, but have an obligation to the larger society. An example is Laureate Education, which is a for-profit educational company. Laureate claims that its objective is to have a "positive effect for society and students by offering diverse education programs both online and at campuses around the world."[8] Organizations around the world have embraced this view, as shown by a survey of global executives in which 84 percent said that companies must balance obligations to shareholders with obligations to the public good.[9] But how do these two concepts differ?

socioeconomic view
The view that management's social responsibility goes beyond making profits to include protecting and improving society's welfare

Social responsiveness is when a company engages in social actions in response to some popular social need. Managers are guided by social norms and values and make practical, market-oriented decisions about their actions.[10] For instance, Ford Motor Company became the first automaker to endorse a federal ban on sending text messages while driving. A company spokesperson explained that research has found that activities, such as text messaging, distract a drivers' eyes from watching the road and traffic and contribute to an increased risk of getting in an accident.[11] By supporting this ban, company managers "responded" to what they felt was an important social need. After Hurricane Katrina, Procter & Gamble sent mobile laundromats to

social responsiveness
When a firm engages in social actions in response to some popular social need

New Orleans. Employees and volunteers washed and folded laundry for residents whose homes were destroyed. In 2014, Boeing arranged 10 flights transporting more than 54,000 pounds of medical supplies and equipment to patients in Ethiopia, Kenya and Thailand; educational books and computers to schools in Ethiopia; toys to orphans in Iraq; and winter clothing, blankets and quilts to the displaced and needy in Bangladesh, Iraq and Thailand.[12]

A socially *responsible* organization views things differently. It goes beyond what it's obligated to do or chooses to do because of some popular social need and does what it can to help improve society because it's the right thing to do. We define **social responsibility** as a business's intention, beyond its legal and economic obligations, to do the right things and act in ways that are good for society.[13] Our definition assumes that a business obeys the law and cares for its stockholders, but adds an ethical imperative to do those things that make society better and not to do those that make it worse. A socially responsible organization does what is right because it feels it has an ethical responsibility to do so. For example, according to our definition, home builder Prime Five Homes in Los Angeles, California, would be described as socially responsible. Prime Five Homes builds environmentally friendly homes, which they sell for profit. The company directs a portion of these proceeds to its nonprofit organization named Dream Builders Project. Dream Builders Project supports a variety of social causes including anti–human trafficking campaigns. CEO Mayer Dahan says: "The Dream Builders Project is setting new standards for the nonprofit industry, and acting as a seamless link for individuals and corporations to give back."[14]

Pfizer Consumer Healthcare employees volunteered with Habitat of Humanity in response to the needs of residents who lost their homes during Hurricane Sandy on the U.S. East Coast. This disaster-relief effort of rebuilding homes destroyed by the storm is part of Pfizer's Advil Relief in Action initiative that celebrates volunteers who work to improve the lives of others.
Source: Diane Bondareff/Invision for Pfizer Consumer Healthcare/AP Images

social responsibility
A business's intention, beyond its legal and economic obligations, to do the right things and act in ways that are good for society

So how should we view an organization's social actions? A U.S. business that meets federal pollution control standards or that doesn't discriminate against employees over the age of 40 in job promotion decisions is meeting its social obligation because laws mandate these actions. However, when it provides on-site childcare facilities for employees or packages products using recycled paper, it's being socially responsive. Why? Working parents and environmentalists have voiced these social concerns and demanded such actions.

For many businesses, their social actions are better viewed as socially responsive, rather than socially responsible (at least according to our definition). However, such actions are still good for society. For example, Unilever recently met its "zero waste" target for operations in 600 factories, warehouses, and offices in 70 countries, using recycling and recovery techniques to keep all waste from landfills. France's Sodexo will switch to using cage-free eggs only in all food operations by 2025.[15] These types of actions are in response to societal concerns.

If your professor has assigned this, go to **www.mymanagementlab.com** to watch a video titled: *Honest Tea: Corporate Social Responsibility* and to respond to questions.

★ Watch It 1!

Should Organizations Be Socially Involved?

Other than meeting their social obligations (which they *must* do), should organizations be socially involved? One way to look at this question is by examining arguments for and against social involvement. Several points are outlined in Exhibit 5-1.[16]

Numerous studies have examined whether social involvement affects a company's economic performance.[17] Although most found a small positive relationship, no generalizable conclusions can be made, because these studies have shown that relationship is affected by various contextual factors such as firm size, industry, economic conditions, and regulatory environment.[18] Another concern was causation. If a study showed that social involvement and economic performance were positively related,

Exhibit 5-1
Arguments For and Against Social Responsibility

FOR	AGAINST
Public expectations Public opinion now supports businesses pursuing economic and social goals.	**Violation of profit maximization** Business is being socially responsible only when it pursues its economic interests.
Long-run profits Socially responsible companies tend to have more secure long-run profits.	**Dilution of purpose** Pursuing social goals dilutes business's primary purpose—economic productivity.
Ethical obligation Businesses should be socially responsible because responsible actions are the right thing to do.	**Costs** Many socially responsible actions do not cover their costs and someone must pay those costs.
Public image Businesses can create a favorable public image by pursuing social goals.	**Too much power** Businesses have a lot of power already; if they pursue social goals, they will have even more.
Better environment Business involvement can help solve difficult social problems.	**Lack of skills** Business leaders lack the necessary skills to address social issues.
Discouragement of further governmental regulation By becoming socially responsible, businesses can expect less government regulation.	**Lack of accountability** There are no direct lines of accountability for social actions.
Balance of responsibility and power Businesses have a lot of power and an equally large amount of responsibility is needed to balance against that power.	
Stockholder interests Social responsibility will improve a business's stock price in the long run.	
Possession of resources Businesses have the resources to support public and charitable projects that need assistance.	
Superiority of prevention over cures Businesses should address social problems before they become serious and costly to correct.	

this correlation didn't necessarily mean that social involvement *caused* higher economic performance—it could simply mean that high profits afforded companies the "luxury" of being socially involved.[19] Such methodological concerns can't be taken lightly. In fact, one study found that if the flawed empirical analyses in these studies were "corrected," social responsibility had a neutral impact on a company's financial performance.[20] Another found that participating in social issues not related to the organization's primary stakeholders was negatively associated with shareholder value.[21] A reanalysis of several studies concluded that managers can afford to be (and should be) socially responsible.[22]

social screening
Applying social criteria (screens) to investment decisions

Another way to view social involvement and economic performance is by looking at socially responsible investing (SRI) funds, which provide a way for individual investors to support socially responsible companies. Typically, these funds use some type of **social screening**; that is, they apply social and environmental criteria to investment decisions. For instance, SRI funds usually will not invest in companies involved in liquor, gambling, tobacco, nuclear power, weapons, price fixing, fraud, or in companies that have poor product safety, employee relations, and environmental track records. The number of socially screened mutual funds has grown from 55 to 205, and assets in these funds have grown to more than $10.6 trillion—an amount that equals the combined GDPs of Brazil and India.[23] But more important than the total amount invested in these funds is that the Social Investment Forum reports that the performance of most SRI funds is comparable to that of non-SRI funds.[24]

So what can we conclude about social involvement and economic performance? It appears that a company's social actions *don't hurt* its economic performance. Given political and societal pressures to be socially involved, managers probably need to take social issues and goals into consideration as they plan, organize, lead, and control.

GREEN **management and sustainability**

LO5.2 Nike Inc. launched an app called Making, which allows its design engineers to see the environmental effects of their material choices on water, energy and waste, and chemistry.[25] The Fairmont Hotel chain generated a lot of buzz over its decision to set up rooftop beehives to try to help strengthen the population of honeybees, which have been mysteriously abandoning their hives and dying off by the millions worldwide. This Colony Collapse Disorder could have potentially disastrous consequences since one-third of the food we eat comes from plants that depend on bee pollination. At Toronto's Fairmont Royal York, six hives are home to some 360,000 bees that forage in and around the city *and* produce a supply of award-winning honey.[26] The hotel chain now maintains beehives at 16 of its hotels. Bee honey is an ingredient in some of the menu items, including honey walnut bread, and in the *Beetini*, the hotel's house cocktail.[27] Did you know that planning a driving route with more right-hand turns than left can save you money? UPS does. That's just one of many stats the global logistics leader can quote about how research-based changes in its delivery route design contribute to the sustainability of the planet.[28] Being green is in!

- 75 percent of workplaces have at least one green technology practice.[29]

Until the late 1960s, few people (and organizations) paid attention to the environmental consequences of their decisions and actions. Although some groups were concerned with conserving natural resources, about the only reference to saving the environment was the ubiquitous printed request "Please Don't Litter." However, a number of environmental disasters brought a new spirit of environmentalism to individuals, groups, and organizations. Increasingly, managers have begun to consider the impact of their organization on the natural environment, which we call **green management**. What do managers need to know about going green?

green management
Managers consider the impact of their organization on the natural environment

How Organizations Go Green

Managers and organizations can do many things to protect and preserve the natural environment.[30] Some do no more than what is required by law; that is, they fulfill their social obligation. However, others have radically changed their products and production processes. For instance, the Swedish packaging company Tetra Pak is pioneering a new technique for using bioplastic materials in its shelf-stable packaging. This breakthrough is helping the company reduce its carbon footprint and reduce the use of traditional fossil fuel-derived plastics as it produces more than 180 billion packages yearly. Emirates Airlines isn't simply investing in solar power and special lighting to reduce energy use and emissions, it's explaining its efforts in a yearly environmental sustainability report.[31] Although interesting, these examples don't tell us much about how organizations go green. One model uses the terms *shades of green* to describe the different environmental approaches that organizations may take.[32] (See Exhibit 5-2.)

The first approach, the *legal (or light green) approach,* is simply doing what is required legally. In this approach, which illustrates social obligation, organizations exhibit little environmental sensitivity. They obey laws, rules, and regulations without legal challenge and that's the extent of their being green.

Exhibit 5-2
Green Approaches

Source: Based on R. E. Freeman, J. Pierce, and R. Dodd, *Shades of Green: Business Ethics and the Environment* (New York: Oxford University Press, 1995).

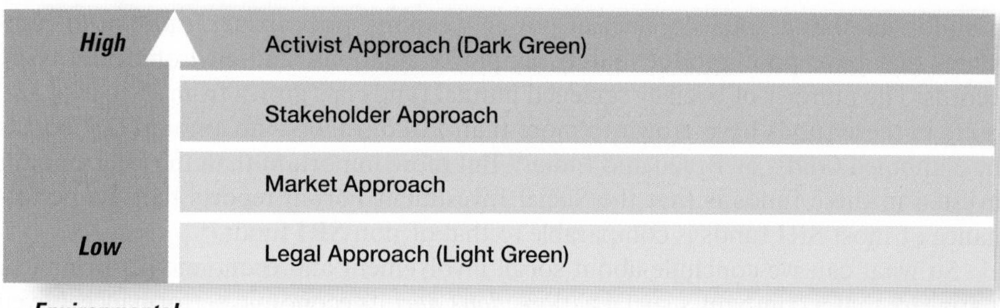

LEADER making a DIFFERENCE

Source: Brad Barket/Getty Images

***Yvon Chouinard** is a self-taught blacksmith who, in 1957, started crafting mountain-climbing pitons he and other climbing enthusiasts used as anchors on risky climbs.*[33] *His hardware became so popular that he would go on to found the outdoor-clothing company Patagonia. As his company grew, Chouinard realized that everything his company did had an effect—mostly negative—on the environment. Today, he defines the company's mission in eco-driven terms: "To use business to inspire and implement solutions to the environmental crisis." Chouinard has put environmental activism at the forefront of his company. Since 1985, Patagonia has donated 1 percent of its annual sales to grassroots environmental groups and has gotten more than 1,300 companies to follow its lead as part of its "1% for the Planet" group. He recognizes that "every product, no matter how much thought goes into it, has a destructive impact on Earth." But nonetheless, he keeps doing what he does because "it's the right thing to do."* What can you learn from this leader making a difference?

As an organization becomes more sensitive to environmental issues, it may adopt the *market approach* and respond to environmental preferences of customers. Whatever customers demand in terms of environmentally friendly products will be what the organization provides. For example, SC Johnson Company collaborated with a European company to develop an environmentally friendly alternative to the original formulation of Saran Wrap, which had come under criticism for containing polyvinyl chloride (PVC). Even though the reformulated Saran Wrap product does not work as well as the original in keeping food odors within the wrapping, S. C. Johnson decided not to return to the original formulation despite consumer preferences. S. C. Johnson's CEO Fisk Johnson III based this decision on the belief that trustworthiness is the most important quality that any company has.[34] This is a good example of social responsiveness, as is the next approach.

In the *stakeholder approach*, an organization works to meet the environmental demands of multiple stakeholders such as employees, suppliers, or community. For instance, Hewlett-Packard and Panasonic have several corporate environmental programs in place for their supply chain (suppliers), product design and product recycling (customers and society), and work operations (employees and community).

Finally, if an organization pursues an *activist (or dark green) approach*, it looks for ways to protect the earth's natural resources. The activist approach reflects the highest degree of environmental sensitivity and illustrates social responsibility. For example, Belgian company Ecover produces ecological cleaning products in a near-zero-emissions factory. This factory (the world's first ecological one) is an engineering marvel with a huge grass roof that keeps things cool in summer and warm in winter and a water treatment system that runs on wind and solar energy. The company chose to build this facility because of its deep commitment to the environment.

Evaluating Green Management Actions

As businesses become "greener," they often release detailed reports on their environmental performance. More than 7,500 companies around the globe now voluntarily report their efforts in promoting environmental sustainability using the guidelines developed by the Global Reporting Initiative (GRI). These reports, which can be found on the GRI website (www.globalreporting.org), describe the numerous green actions of these organizations. A recent study revealed that 90 percent of the world's 250 largest companies reported information about their corporate responsibility initiatives.[35] Also, 154 U.S. companies voluntarily signed the American Business Act on Climate Pledge to demonstrate their additional commitment to promoting environmental sustainability.[36] Among the companies signing the pledge, Berkshire Hathaway Energy promised to retire more than 75 percent of its coal-fueled generating capacity in Nevada by 2019.

Another way organizations show their commitment to being green is through pursuing standards developed by the nongovernmental International Organization for Standardization (ISO). Although ISO has developed more than 18,000 international standards, it's probably best known for its ISO 9000 (quality management) and ISO 14000 (environmental management) standards. Organizations that want to become ISO 14000 compliant must develop a total management system for meeting environmental challenges. In other words, it must minimize the effects of its activities on the environment and continually improve its environmental performance. If an organization can meet these standards, it can state that it's ISO 14000 compliant—an accomplishment achieved by organizations in over 155 countries.

One final way to evaluate a company's green actions is to use the Global 100 list of the most sustainable corporations in the world (www.corporateknights.com).[37] To be named to this list—announced each year at the renowned World Economic Forum in Davos, Switzerland—a company has displayed a superior ability to effectively manage environmental and social factors. In 2016, European companies led the list with 53 Global 100 companies representing a variety of industries.[38] North American companies

let's get REAL

The Scenario:

Carol Borg is concerned about the waste at the coffee shop where she works as the assistant manager. She has made suggestions to the store manager on how the store could have less of a negative impact on the environment by taking steps such as encouraging customers to recycle their paper cups or by using ceramic cups for customers who aren't taking their coffee to go. However, the store manager insists that these ideas are too costly and refuses to invest in new recycling bins or ceramic cups.

What can Carol say to convince her manager that these are worthwhile investments?

Change is never easy, but a well-researched cost-benefit analysis that details the achievable cost savings and risk management strategy can change the challenge to "Go Green" into a positive opportunity.

Knowing the numbers is important: provide specifics on how much money the company would save, statistics on what competitors have done (are you a leader or behind the curve?), what—if any—government benefits are available, and how the change will be positive for the company's reputation and marketing opportunities in the community. Proposing a pilot program to test the green options will also allow for a practical comparative analysis of both practices and demonstrate that there's proof in the pudding—or coffee!

Karen Heger
Manager, Organizational Development and Training

Source: Karen S. G. Heger

followed with 27. The remaining 20 spots were earned by companies from Asia, Africa, and Australia. The top three spots were taken by BMW (Germany), Dassault Systemes (France), and Outoec (Finland). Other companies on the 2016 list included Marks & Spencer Group (United Kingdom) and Coca-Cola Enterprises (USA).

MANAGERS and ethical behavior

LO5.3 One hundred fifty years. That was the maximum prison sentence handed to financier Bernard Madoff, who stole billions of dollars from his clients, by a U.S. district judge who called his crimes "evil." In Britain, which has been characterized by some critics as a "nanny state because of its purported high level of social control and surveillance," a controversy arose over the monitoring of garbage cans. Many local governments have installed monitoring chips in municipally distributed trash cans. These chips match cans with owners and can be used to track the weight of the bins, leading some critics to fear that the country is moving to a pay-as-you-go system, which they believe will discriminate against large families. A government report says that Iceland, hit hard by both the global economic meltdown and a pesky volcano, was "victimized by politicians, bankers, and regulators who engaged in acts of extreme negligence."[39] When you hear about such behaviors—especially after the high-profile financial misconduct at Enron, WorldCom, Lehman Brothers, and other organizations—you might conclude that businesses aren't ethical. Although that's not the case, managers—at all levels, in all areas, in all sizes and kinds of organizations—do face ethical issues and dilemmas. For instance, is it ethical for a pharmaceutical sales representatives to provide doctors with lavish gifts as an inducement to buy? Would it make a difference if the bribe came out of the sales rep's commission? Is it ethical for someone to use a company car for private use? How about using company e-mail for personal correspondence or using the company phone to make personal phone calls? As an employee, would it be all right to award a lucrative contract to a company in which you hold significant financial interest? What if you managed an employee who worked all weekend on an emergency situation and you told him to take off two days sometime later and mark it down as "sick days" because your company had a clear policy that overtime would not be compensated for any reason?[40] Would that be okay? How will you handle such situations? As managers plan, organize, lead, and control, they must consider ethical dimensions.

ethics
Principles, values, and beliefs that define what is right and wrong behavior

What do we mean by **ethics**? We're defining it as the principles, values, and beliefs that define right and wrong decisions and behavior.[41] Many decisions managers make require them to consider both the process and who's affected by the result.[42] To better understand the ethical issues involved in such decisions, let's look at the factors that determine whether a person acts ethically or unethically.

Factors That Determine Ethical and Unethical Behavior

Whether someone behaves ethically or unethically when faced with an ethical dilemma is influenced by several things: his or her stage of moral development and other moderating variables, including individual characteristics and the organization's structural design, which we will discuss in a later section of the chapter, and the intensity of the ethical issue. (See Exhibit 5-3.) People who lack a strong moral sense are much less likely to do the wrong things if they're constrained by organizational rules or job descriptions that disapprove of such behaviors. Conversely, intensely moral individuals can be corrupted by an organizational structure that permits or encourages unethical practices.[43] Let's look more closely at these factors.

STAGE OF MORAL DEVELOPMENT Research divides moral development into three levels, each having two stages.[44] At each successive stage, an individual's moral judgment becomes less dependent on outside influences and more internalized.

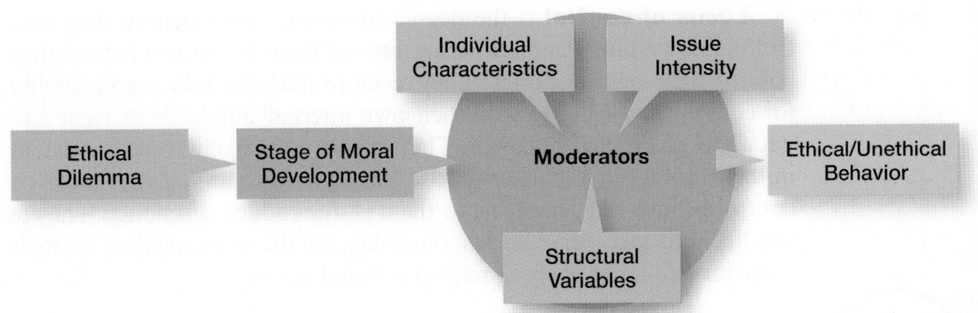

Exhibit 5-3
Factors That Determine Ethical and Unethical Behavior

At the first level, the *preconventional* level, a person's choice between right and wrong is based on personal consequences from outside sources, such as physical punishment, reward, or exchange of favors. At the second level, the *conventional* level, ethical decisions rely on maintaining expected standards and living up to the expectations of others. At the *principled* level, individuals define moral values apart from the authority of the groups to which they belong or society in general. The three levels and six stages are described in Exhibit 5-4.

What can we conclude about moral development?[45] First, people proceed through the six stages sequentially. Second, there is no guarantee of continued moral development. Third, the majority of adults are at stage four: They're limited to obeying the rules and will be inclined to behave ethically, although for different reasons. A manager at stage three is likely to make decisions based on peer approval; a manager at stage four will try to be a "good corporate citizen" by making decisions that respect the organization's rules and procedures; and a stage five manager is likely to challenge organizational practices that he or she believes to be wrong.

INDIVIDUAL CHARACTERISTICS Two individual characteristics—values and personality—play a role in determining whether a person behaves ethically. Each person comes to an organization with a relatively entrenched set of personal **values**, which represent basic convictions about what is right and wrong. Our values develop from a young age based on what we see and hear from parents, teachers, friends, and others. Thus, employees in the same organization often possess very different values.[46] Although *values* and *stage of moral development* may seem similar, they're not. Values are broad and cover a wide range of issues; the stage of moral development is a measure of independence from outside influences.

values
Basic convictions about what is right and wrong

Two personality variables have been found to influence an individual's actions according to his or her beliefs about what is right or wrong: ego strength and locus of control. **Ego strength** measures the strength of a person's convictions. People with high ego strength are likely to resist impulses to act unethically and instead follow their convictions. That is, individuals high in ego strength are more likely to do what they think is right and be more consistent in their moral judgments and actions than those with low ego strength.

ego strength
A personality measure of the strength of a person's convictions

- An organization devoted to global ethics says that societies share five core moral values—honesty, respect, responsibility, fairness, and compassion.[47]

Level	Description of Stage
Principled	6. Following self-chosen ethical principles even if they violate the law
	5. Valuing rights of others and upholding absolute values and rights regardless of the majority's opinion
Conventional	4. Maintaining conventional order by fulfilling obligations to which you have agreed
	3. Living up to what is expected by people close to you
Preconventional	2. Following rules only when doing so is in your immediate interest
	1. Sticking to rules to avoid physical punishment

Exhibit 5-4
Stages of Moral Development

Source: L. Kohlberg, "Moral Stages and Moralization: The Cognitive-Development Approach," in *Moral Development and Behavior: Theory, Research, and Social Issues*, ed. T. Lickona (New York: Holt, Rinehart & Winston, 1976), pp. 34–35.

Juliana Rotich has high ego strength. A native of Kenya, she believes in the transformational power of technology to address social problems. Determined to speed up the digital revolution in Africa, Rotich and her team of innovators have developed open disaster-mapping software, formed a technology hub in Nairobi, and created a new Internet connectivity device to overcome problems of poor reception and power outages in Africa. *Source: Robert Schlesinger/Picture Alliance/ Robert Schles/Newscom*

locus of control
A personality attribute that measures the degree to which people believe they control their own fate

Locus of control is the degree to which people believe they control their own fate. People with an *internal* locus of control believe they control their own destinies. They're more likely to take responsibility for consequences and rely on their own internal standards of right and wrong to guide their behavior. They're also more likely to be consistent in their moral judgments and actions. People with an *external* locus of control believe what happens to them is due to luck or chance. They're less likely to take personal responsibility for the consequences of their behavior and more likely to rely on external forces.[48]

STRUCTURAL VARIABLES An organization's structural design can influence whether employees behave ethically. Those structures that minimize ambiguity and uncertainty with formal rules and regulations and those that continuously remind employees of what is ethical are more likely to encourage ethical behavior. Other structural variables that influence ethical choices include goals, performance appraisal systems, and reward allocation procedures.

Although many organizations use goals to guide and motivate employees, those goals can create some unexpected problems. One study found that people who don't reach set goals are more likely to engage in unethical behavior, even if they do or don't have economic incentives to do so. The researchers concluded that "goal setting can lead to unethical behavior."[49] Examples of such behaviors abound—from companies shipping unfinished products just to reach sales goals or "managing earnings" to meet financial analysts' expectations, to schools excluding certain groups of students when reporting standardized test scores to make their "pass" rate look better.[50]

An organization's performance appraisal system also can influence ethical behavior. Some systems focus exclusively on outcomes, while others evaluate means as well as ends. When employees are evaluated only on outcomes, they may be pressured to do whatever is necessary to look good on the outcomes and not be concerned with how they got those results. Research suggests that "success may serve to excuse unethical behaviors."[51] The danger of such thinking is that if managers are more lenient in correcting unethical behaviors of successful employees, other employees will model their behavior on what they see.

Closely related to the organization's appraisal system is how rewards are allocated. The more that rewards or punishment depend on specific goal outcomes, the more employees are pressured to do whatever they must to reach those goals—perhaps to the point of compromising their ethical standards. New doctors take the Hippocratic Oath, which pledges that they will do no harm and they will follow ethical standards. However, in recent years, the news has been filled with stories about surgeons who have performed unnecessary surgeries. Dr. John Santa indicated that financial considerations explain why many unnecessary surgeries take place: "Doctors' income can hinge largely on the number of surgeries they do—and the revenue those procedures generate."[52] Tragically, unnecessary surgeries cause many patients to sustain major injuries or death.

ISSUE INTENSITY A student who would never consider breaking into an instructor's office to steal an accounting exam doesn't think twice about asking a friend who took the same course from the same instructor last semester what questions were on an exam. Similarly, a manager might think nothing about taking home a few office supplies, yet be highly concerned about the possible embezzlement of company funds. These examples illustrate the final factor that influences ethical behavior: the intensity of the ethical issue itself.[53]

As Exhibit 5-5 shows, six characteristics determine issue intensity or how important an ethical issue is to an individual: greatness of harm, consensus of wrong, probability of harm, immediacy of consequences, proximity to victim(s), and concentration of effect. These factors suggest that:

- the larger the number of people harmed
- the more agreement that the action is wrong
- the greater the likelihood that the action will cause harm
- the more immediately the consequences of the action will be felt

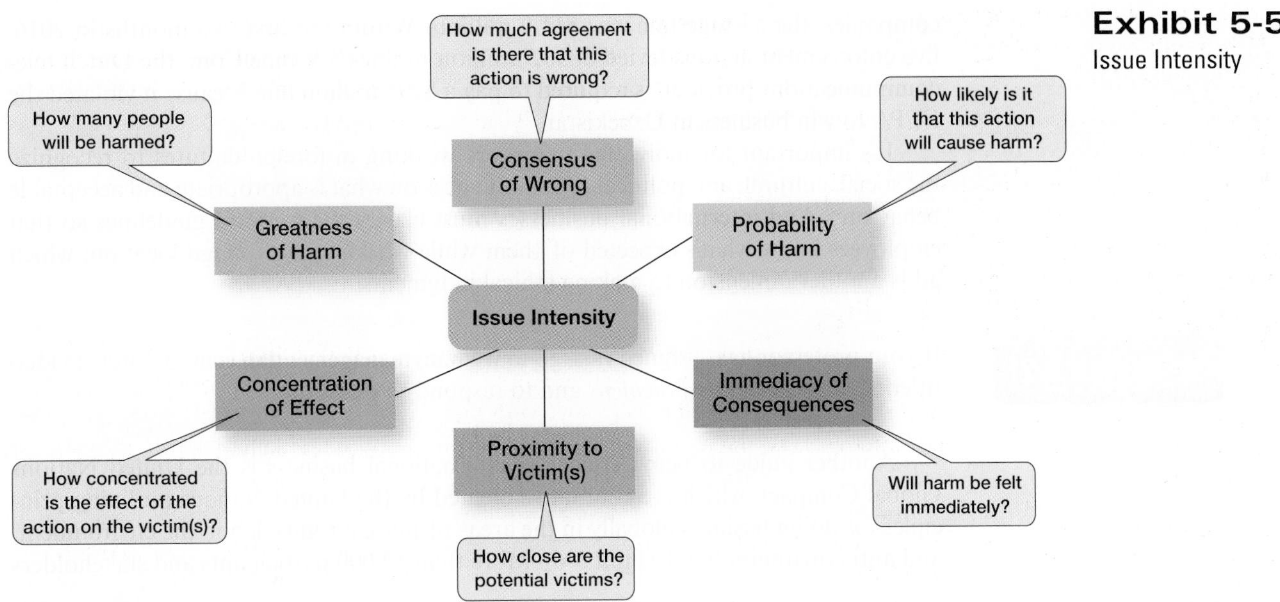

Exhibit 5-5
Issue Intensity

- the closer the person feels to the victim(s)
- the more concentrated the effect of the action on the victim(s)...

the greater the issue intensity or importance. When an ethical issue is important, employees are more likely to behave ethically.

Ethics—If your instructor is using Pearson MyLab Management, log onto **mymanagementlab.com** and test your *knowledge about being ethical.* **Be sure to refer back to the chapter opener!**

★ It's Your Career

Ethics in an International Context

Are ethical standards universal? Although some common moral beliefs exist, social and cultural differences between countries are important factors that determine ethical and unethical behavior.[54]

Should Coca-Cola employees in Saudi Arabia adhere to U.S. ethical standards, or should they follow local standards of acceptable behavior? If Airbus (a European company) pays a "broker's fee" to an intermediary to get a major contract with a Middle Eastern airline, should Boeing be restricted from doing the same because such practices are considered improper in the United States? (Note: In the United Kingdom, the Law Commission, a governmental advisory body, has said that bribing officials in foreign countries should be a criminal offense. It said that claims of "it's local custom" should not be a reason for allowing it.[55]) British defense giant BAE, which has been the target of various bribery and corruption allegations, was ordered to "submit to the supervision of an ethics monitor and pay nearly $500 million to resolve the corruption allegations."[56]

In the case of payments to influence foreign officials or politicians, U.S. managers are guided by the Foreign Corrupt Practices Act (FCPA), which makes it illegal to knowingly corrupt a foreign official. However, even this law doesn't always reduce ethical dilemmas to black and white. In some countries, government bureaucrat salaries are low because custom dictates that they receive small payments from those they serve. Payoffs to these bureaucrats "grease the machinery" and ensure that things get done. The FCPA does not expressly prohibit small payoffs to foreign government employees whose duties are primarily administrative or clerical *when* such payoffs are an accepted part of doing business in that country. Any action other than this is illegal. In 2013 (latest numbers available), the U.S. Department of Justice brought 12 FCPA enforcement actions, collecting approximately $143.1 million in fines.[57] Among the 12 companies, the average fine was $11.9 million. Within the first two months in 2016, five enforcement actions levied $838.7 million in fines.[58] VimpelCom, the Dutch telecommunications provider, is required to pay a $795 million fine because it violated the FCPA to win business in Uzbekistan.[59]

It's important for individual managers working in foreign cultures to recognize the social, cultural, and political-legal influences on what is appropriate and acceptable behavior.[60] And international businesses must clarify their ethical guidelines so that employees know what's expected of them while working in a foreign location, which adds another dimension to making ethical judgments.

★ Watch It 2!

If your professor has assigned this, go to **www.mymanagementlab.com** to watch a video titled: *Global Ethics and Siemens* and to respond to questions.

Another guide to being ethical in international business is the United Nations Global Compact, which is an initiative created by the United Nations outlining principles for doing business globally in the areas of human rights, labor, the environment, and anti-corruption (see Exhibit 5-6). More than 12,000 participants and stakeholders

Exhibit 5-6

The Ten Principles of the United Nations Global Compact

The UN Global Compact asks companies to embrace, support, and enact, within their sphere of influence, a set of core values in the areas of human rights, labor standards, the environment, and anti-corruption:

Human Rights

Principle 1:	Business should support and respect the protection of internationally proclaimed human rights within their sphere of influence; and
Principle 2:	Make sure they are not complicit in human rights abuses.

Labor Standards

Principle 3:	Business should uphold the freedom of association and the effective recognition of the right to collective bargaining;
Principle 4:	The elimination of all forms of forced and compulsory labor;
Principle 5:	The effective abolition of child labor; and
Principle 6:	The elimination of discrimination in respect to employment and occupation.

Environment

Principle 7:	Business should support a precautionary approach to environmental challenges;
Principle 8:	Undertake initiatives to promote greater environmental responsibility; and
Principle 9:	Encourage the development and diffusion of environmentally friendly technologies.

Anti-Corruption

Principle 10:	Business should work against corruption in all its forms, including extortion and bribery.

Source: United Nations Global Compact (www.unglobalcompact.org). Copyright © 2012 United Nations Global Compact.

from over 170 countries have committed to the UN Global Compact, making it the world's largest voluntary corporate citizenship initiative.[61] The goal of the UN Global Compact is a more sustainable and inclusive global economy. Organizations making this commitment do so because they believe that the world business community plays a significant role in improving economic and social conditions. In addition, the Organization for Economic Co-operation and Development (OECD) has made fighting bribery and corruption in international business a high priority. The centerpiece of its efforts is the Anti-Bribery Convention (or set of rules and guidelines), which was the first global instrument to combat corruption in cross-border business deals. To date, significant gains have been made in fighting corruption in the 41 countries that have ratified it.[62]

ENCOURAGING **ethical behavior**

LO5.4 The City of Los Angeles, California is suing Wells Fargo Bank based on allegations that the company has engaged in unlawful and fraudulent conduct: Bank employees routinely opened customer accounts without their authorization, and those accounts came with monthly fees. Los Angeles City Attorney Michael Feuer maintains that bank management was regularly "abusing employees and telling them 'to do whatever it takes' to reach quotas on the number of new accounts they must open."[63] You have to wonder what the firm's managers were thinking or doing while such ethically questionable decisions and actions were taking place, when they could have reconsidered whether sales targets were realistic.

Managers can do a number of things if they're serious about encouraging ethical behaviors—hire employees with high ethical standards, establish codes of ethics, lead by example, and so forth. By themselves, such actions won't have much of an impact. But if an organization has a comprehensive ethics program in place, it can potentially improve an organization's ethical climate. The key variable, however, is *potentially*. There are no guarantees that a well-designed ethics program or publically espoused values will lead to the desired outcome. For instance, Enron, often referred to as the "poster child" of corporate wrongdoing, outlined values in its final annual report

let's get REAL

Source: Justin Kidwell

Justin Kidwell
Management Consultant

The Scenario

All through university, Finlay Roberts wasn't sure what he really wanted to do. But now he had found what he thought was a great job, one where he could enhance his leadership skills in a competitive environment with teams of employees who sold security systems over the phone. What he soon discovered, though, was that competing to meet sales goals often led to unethical actions. After learning about ethics in pretty much every management class he took, Finlay wanted to show his employees that he was committed to an ethical workplace.

What advice would you give Finlay?

One of the cornerstones to professional success is to maintain and demonstrate strong ethics—often by exceeding the standards set by the organization. One potential path for Finlay is to remember that damaging the company's brand can risk destroying his career, but missing sales/performance targets will only impede his career. Over the long run, professionals with strong reputations will outlast those with questionable character.

that most would consider ethical—communication, respect, integrity, and excellence. Yet the way top managers behaved didn't reflect those values at all.[64] Here's another example: A recent study of United States Army management practices describes a "culture where deceptive information is both accepted and commonplace" where "officers become ethically numb."[65] It's quite disturbing and inconsistent with one of the organization's values: "Do what's right, legally and morally. Integrity is a quality you develop by adhering to moral principles. It requires that you do and say nothing that deceives others."[66] Now let's look at some specific ways that managers can encourage ethical behavior and create a comprehensive ethics program.

Employee Selection

Wanting to reduce workers' compensation claims, Hospitality Management Corp. did preemployment integrity testing at one hotel to see if the tests could "weed out applicants likely to be dishonest, take dangerous risks or engage in other undesirable behaviors." After six months, claims were down among new hires.[67]

The selection process (interviews, tests, background checks, and so forth) should be viewed as an opportunity to learn about an individual's level of moral development, personal values, ego strength, and locus of control.[68] However, a carefully designed selection process isn't foolproof, and even under the best circumstances, individuals with questionable standards of right and wrong may be hired. That means having other ethics controls in place.

- 70 percent of middle managers' performance is based, in part, on ethics and compliance.[69]

We learned in Chapter 7 that an organization's culture consists of the shared organizational values. These values reflect what the organization stands for and what it believes in as well as create an environment that influences employee behavior ethically or unethically. When it comes to ethical behavior, a culture most likely to encourage high ethical standards is one that's high in risk tolerance, control, and conflict tolerance. Employees in such a culture are encouraged to be aggressive and innovative, are aware that unethical practices will be discovered, and feel free to openly challenge expectations they consider to be unrealistic or personally undesirable.

values-based management
The organization's values guide employees in the way they do their jobs

Because shared values can be powerful influences, many organizations are using **values-based management**, in which the organization's values guide employees in the way they do their jobs. For instance, Timberland is an example of a company using values-based management. With a simple statement, "Make It Better," employees at Timberland know what's expected and valued; that is, they find ways to "make it better"—whether it's creating quality products for customers, performing community service activities, designing employee training programs, or figuring out ways to make the company's packaging more environmentally friendly. As it says on the company's website, "Everything we do at Timberland grows out of our relentless pursuit to find a way to make it better." At Corning, Inc. one of the core values guiding employee behavior is integrity. Employees are expected to work in ways that are honest, decent, and fair. Timberland and Corning aren't alone in their use of values-based management. A survey of global companies found that a large number (more than 89 percent) said they had a written corporate values statement.[70] This survey also found that most of the companies believed their values influenced relationships and reputation, the top-performing companies consciously connected values with the way employees did their work, and top managers were important to reinforcing the importance of the values throughout the organization. Middle management plays an important role as well. One survey revealed that more than 98 percent of middle management is somewhat or extremely active in ensuring that daily business decisions and behaviors are in line with company values.[71]

Thus, an organization's managers do play an important role here. They're responsible for creating an environment that encourages employees to embrace the culture and the desired values as they do their jobs. In fact, research shows that the behavior of managers is *the single most important influence* on an individual's decision to act ethically or unethically.[72] People look to see what those in authority are doing and use that as a benchmark for acceptable practices and expectations.

But establishing an ethics culture is not an easy task. After the financial crisis in 2008, which resulted largely because of unethical practices of financial services companies, U.S. government regulators set out to change the compliance culture in those firms. Compliance with rules is expected to promote ethical practices. Despite good intentions, regulators have made little progress because there has been little agreement on what composes a culture of compliance or how to measure it. Susan Devers from LRN Advisory Services Group, an ethics and compliance consulting firm, said: "A lot of people think [culture] is another checklist item."[73] In addition, she endorses regulators' efforts, saying "it's good that regulators are focused on it ... because it shows they are moving beyond checklists."[74]

Finally, as we discussed in Chapter 7, a strong culture exerts more influence on employees than does a weak one. If a culture is strong and supports high ethical standards, it has a powerful and positive influence on the decision to act ethically or unethically. For example, IBM has a strong culture that has long stressed ethical dealings with customers, employees, business partners, and communities.[78] To reinforce the importance of ethical behaviors, the company developed an explicitly detailed set of guidelines for business conduct and ethics. And the penalty for violating the guidelines? Disciplinary actions, including dismissal. IBM's managers continually reinforce the importance of ethical behavior and reinforce the fact that a person's actions and decisions are important to the way the organization is viewed.

Codes of Ethics and Decision Rules

George David, former CEO and chairman of Hartford, Connecticut–based United Technologies Corporation (UTC), believed in the power of a code of ethics. That's why UTC has always had one that was quite explicit and detailed. Employees know the company's

FUTURE VISION Building an Ethical Culture That Lasts

Let's start off with the bad news about the state of ethics in the U.S. workplace:

- 60 percent of misdeeds reported by workers involved someone with managerial authority.
- 24 percent of those observed misdeeds involved senior managers.
- In organizations with weak ethical cultures, 88 percent of workers reported seeing misconduct.[75]

Now, how about some better news:

- In organizations with strong ethical cultures, only 20 percent of workers reported seeing misconduct.[76]
- Companies on Ethisphere's World's Most Ethical Companies list had 20 percent greater profits and 6 percent better shareholder returns than did other companies.[77]

Ethics *is* a part of an organization's culture. And it's becoming ever more critical for businesses to "do things around here" ethically. Society expects it. Customers demand it. And with the speed and spread of news globally—bad and good—you can't hide! So what are the critical aspects of an ethical culture? Certainly, they encompass things like whether an organization's employees are trustworthy, reliable, fair, honest, compassionate, and respectful in dealings with customers, peers, and other stakeholders. But it's also whether managers at all levels talk about ethics and model appropriate behavior. Is ethical behavior reinforced? However, the responsibility for doing things ethically isn't just on managers' backs. In ethical cultures, organizational colleagues support one another in making ethical decisions and in doing ethical work. It can be an infectious type of atmosphere in which good people do good and the organization where they work prospers by achieving those greater profits and better shareholder returns. A win-win in anyone's book! This vision of an ethical workplace isn't just for the future; it's also important for today.

If your professor has chosen to assign this, go to ***www.mymanagementlab.com*** *to discuss the following questions.*

TALK ABOUT IT 1: Why do you think organizations with *weak* ethical cultures have four times as many workers witnessing misconduct?

TALK ABOUT IT 2: "Society expects it (ethical practices). Customers demand it." Discuss why you agree or disagree with this.

behavioral expectations, especially when it comes to ethics. UBS AG, the Swiss bank, also has an explicit employee code crafted by the CEO that bans staff from helping clients cheat on their taxes.[79] However, not all organizations have such explicit ethical guidelines.

code of ethics
A formal statement of an organization's primary values and the ethical rules it expects its employees to follow

Uncertainty about what is and is not ethical can be a problem for employees. A **code of ethics**, a formal statement of an organization's values and the ethical rules it expects employees to follow, is a popular choice for reducing that ambiguity. Research shows that 97 percent of organizations with more than 10,000 employees have a written code of ethics. Even in smaller organizations, nearly 93 percent have one.[80] And codes of ethics are becoming more popular globally. Research by the Institute for Global Ethics says that shared values such as honesty, fairness, respect, responsibility, and caring are pretty much universally embraced.[81] In addition, a survey of businesses in 22 countries found that 78 percent have formally stated ethics standards and codes of ethics; and more than 85 percent of *Fortune* Global 200 companies have a business code of ethics.[82]

What should a code of ethics look like? It should be specific enough to show employees the spirit in which they're supposed to do things, yet loose enough to allow for freedom of judgment. A survey of companies' codes of ethics found their content tended to fall into three categories, as shown in Exhibit 5-7.[83]

Unfortunately, codes of ethics may not work as well as we think they should. A survey of employees in U.S. businesses found that 41 percent of those surveyed had

Exhibit 5-7
Codes of Ethics

Cluster 1. Be a Dependable Organizational Citizen

1. Comply with safety, health, and security regulations.
2. Demonstrate courtesy, respect, honesty, and fairness.
3. Illegal drugs and alcohol at work are prohibited.
4. Manage personal finances well.
5. Exhibit good attendance and punctuality.
6. Follow directives of supervisors.
7. Do not use abusive language.
8. Dress in business attire.
9. Firearms at work are prohibited.

Cluster 2. Do Not Do Anything Unlawful or Improper That Will Harm the Organization

1. Conduct business in compliance with all laws.
2. Payments for unlawful purposes are prohibited.
3. Bribes are prohibited.
4. Avoid outside activities that impair duties.
5. Maintain confidentiality of records.
6. Comply with all antitrust and trade regulations.
7. Comply with all accounting rules and controls.
8. Do not use company property for personal benefit.
9. Employees are personally accountable for company funds.
10. Do not propagate false or misleading information.
11. Make decisions without regard for personal gain.

Cluster 3. Be Good to Customers

1. Convey true claims in product advertisements.
2. Perform assigned duties to the best of your ability.
3. Provide products and services of the highest quality.

Source: From "An Empirical Study of Codes of Business Ethics: A Strategic Perspective," by F.R. David, paper presented at the 48th Annual Academy of Management Conference, Anaheim, California, August 1988. Copyright © 1988 Fred David.

Exhibit 5-8
A Process for Addressing Ethical Dilemmas

Step 1: What is the **ethical dilemma**?
Step 2: Who are the **affected stakeholders**?
Step 3: Which **personal, organizational,** and **external factors** are important in this decision?
Step 4: What are possible **alternatives**?
Step 5: What is my **decision** and how will I act on it?

observed ethical or legal violations in the previous 12 months, including such things as conflicts of interest, abusive or intimidating behavior, and lying to employees. And 37 percent of those employees didn't report observed misconduct.[84] Does this mean that codes of ethics shouldn't be developed? No. However, in doing so, managers should use these suggestions:[85]

1. Organizational leaders should model appropriate behavior and reward those who act ethically.
2. All managers should continually reaffirm the importance of the ethics code and consistently discipline those who break it.
3. The organization's stakeholders (employees, customers, and so forth) should be considered as an ethics code is developed or improved.
4. Managers should communicate and reinforce the ethics code regularly.
5. Managers should use the five-step process (see Exhibit 5-8) to guide employees when faced with ethical dilemmas.

Leadership at the Top

In 2011, Tim Cook was named CEO of Apple Inc. Although it's an extremely successful company, Apple is viewed by some as the epitome of greedy capitalism with no concern for how its products are manufactured. Cook, who was named one of the 100 Most Influential People in Business Ethics by *Ethisphere*, has increased the company's focus on supply chain ethics and compliance issues. It was the first technology company to join the Fair Labor Association, which means that organization can now review the labor practices within the company's supply chain. In addition, at a recent annual stockholders' meeting with investors and journalists, Cook, who was challenged by a spokesperson from a conservative think tank to explain how the company's sustainability efforts were in the best interests of shareholders, bluntly and clearly said that Apple wasn't just about making a profit and that "We want to leave the world better than we found it."[86]

Doing business ethically requires a commitment from managers at all levels, but especially the top level. Why? Because they're the ones who uphold the shared values and set the cultural tone. They're role models in terms of both words and actions, though what they *do* is far more important than what they *say*. If top managers, for example, take company resources for their personal use, inflate their expense accounts, or give favored treatment to friends, they imply that such behavior is acceptable for all employees.

Top managers also set the tone by their reward and punishment practices. The choices of whom and what are rewarded with pay increases and promotions send a strong signal to employees. As we said earlier, when an employee is rewarded for achieving impressive results in an ethically questionable manner, it indicates to others that those ways are acceptable. When an employee does something unethical, managers must punish the offender and publicize the fact by making the outcome visible to everyone in the organization. This practice sends a message that doing wrong has a price and it's not in employees' best interests to act unethically!

Job Goals and Performance Appraisal

Employees in three Internal Revenue Service offices were found in the bathrooms flushing tax returns and other related documents down the toilets. When questioned, they openly admitted doing it, but offered an interesting explanation for their behavior. The employees' supervisors had been pressuring them to complete more work in less time. If the piles of tax returns weren't processed and moved off their desks more quickly, they were told their performance reviews and salary raises would be adversely affected. Frustrated by few resources and an overworked computer system, the employees decided to "flush away" the paperwork on their desks. Although these employees knew what they did was wrong, it illustrates how powerful unrealistic goals and performance appraisals can be.[87] Recall the allegations about Wells Fargo management putting undue pressure on employees to meet lofty sales quotas. Under the stress of unrealistic goals, otherwise ethical employees may feel they have no choice but to do whatever is necessary to meet those goals. Also, goal achievement is usually a key issue in performance appraisal. If performance appraisals focus only on economic goals, ends will begin to justify means. To encourage ethical behavior, both ends *and* means should be evaluated. For example, a manager's annual review of employees might include a point-by-point evaluation of how their decisions measured up against the company's code of ethics as well as how well goals were met.

- 81 percent of companies provide ethics training.[88]

Ethics Training

More organizations are setting up seminars, workshops, and similar ethics training programs to encourage ethical behavior. Such training programs aren't without controversy, as the primary concern is whether ethics can be taught. Critics stress that the effort is pointless because people establish their individual value systems when they're young. Proponents note, however, that several studies have shown that values can be learned after early childhood. In addition, they cite evidence that shows that teaching ethical problem solving can make an actual difference in ethical behaviors;[89] that training has increased individuals' level of moral development;[90] and that, if nothing else, ethics training increases awareness of ethical issues in business.[91]

How can ethics be taught? Let's look at an example involving global defense contractor Lockheed Martin, one of the pioneers in the case-based approach to ethics training.[92] Lockheed Martin's employees take annual ethics training courses delivered by their managers. The main focus of these short courses features department or job-specific issues. In each department, employee teams review and discuss the cases and then apply an "Ethics Meter" to "rate whether the real-life decisions were ethical, unethical, or somewhere in between." For example, one of the possible ratings on the Ethics Meter, "On Thin Ice," is explained as "bordering on unethical and should raise a red flag." After the teams have applied their ratings, managers lead discussions about the ratings and examine why the company's core ethics principles were or were not applied in the cases. In addition to its ethics training, Lockheed Martin has a widely used written code of ethics, an ethics helpline that employees can call for guidance on ethical issues, and ethics officers based in the company's various business units.

An innovative training video called "Ethics Idol" teaches Cisco Systems' employees how to deal with ethical problems at work. Featured on Cisco's intranet, the video presents ethical scenarios from Cisco's Code of Business Conduct that are evaluated by judges, asks employees questions related to which judge's answer they agree with, and then shows the official Cisco answer.
Source: AP Photo/Paul Sakuma

Independent Social Audits

The fear of being caught can be an important deterrent to unethical behavior. Independent social audits, which evaluate decisions and management practices in terms of the organization's code of ethics, increase that likelihood. Such audits can be regular evaluations or they can occur randomly with no prior announcement. An effective ethics program probably needs both. To maintain integrity, auditors should be responsible to the company's board of directors and present their findings directly to the board. This arrangement gives the auditors clout and lessens the opportunity for retaliation from those being audited. Because the Sarbanes-Oxley Act holds businesses to more rigorous standards of financial disclosure and corporate governance, more organizations are finding the idea of independent social audits appealing. As the publisher of *Business Ethics* magazine stated, "The debate has shifted from *whether* to be ethical to *how* to be ethical."[93]

If your professor has assigned this, go to **www.mymanagementlab.com** to complete the Writing Assignment MGMT 4: Ethics.

SOCIAL **responsibility and ethics issues in today's world**

LO5.5 Today's managers continue to face challenges in being socially responsible and ethical. Next, we examine three current issues: managing ethical lapses and social irresponsibility, social entrepreneurship, and promoting positive social change.

Managing Ethical Lapses and Social Irresponsibility

Even after public outrage over the Enron-era misdeeds, irresponsible and unethical practices by managers in all kinds of organizations haven't gone away, as you've observed with some of the questionable behaviors that took place at financial services firms such as Goldman Sachs and Lehman Brothers. But what's more alarming is what's going on "in the trenches," in offices, warehouses, and stores. One survey reported that among 5,000 employees 45 percent admitted falling asleep at work; 22 percent said they spread a rumor about a coworker; 18 percent said they snooped after hours; and 2 percent said they took credit for someone else's work.[94] Another study revealed that employee theft accounts for 43 percent of revenue loss in retail stores in the United States and 28 percent worldwide.[95] In the United States, that amounts to an annual loss of about $18 billion. The report also lists the reasons why there is so much employee theft. Key reasons include ineffective preemployment screening, less employee supervision, and easy sale of stolen merchandise.

Some interesting recent research suggests that men are more likely to act unethically than women in situations where failure could harm their sense of masculinity.[96] The researchers suggest that the reason is that losing a "battle, particularly in contexts that are highly competitive and historically male oriented, presents a threat to masculine competency. To ensure victory, men will sacrifice moral standards if doing so means winning."

Unfortunately, it's not just at work that we see such behaviors; they're prevalent throughout society. Studies show that most teenagers lie to their parents on more than 20 issues.[97] This activity is prevalent in many countries, including the United States, Chile, the Philippines, Italy, and Uganda. In China, the government is testing the use of drones to detect whether students are cheating on their college entrance exams.[98] Students feel extreme pressure to do well since performance on these exams determines the quality of university that Chinese students can enter. What do such statistics say about what managers may have to deal with in the future? It's not too far-fetched to say that organizations may have difficulty upholding high ethical standards when their future employees so readily accept unethical behavior.

What can managers do? Two actions seem particularly important: ethical leadership and protecting those who report wrongdoing.

ETHICAL LEADERSHIP Managers at Alibaba, the world's largest e-commerce company, recently discovered that four software engineers had created a program to get more than their fair share of an employee perk. The company gives each employee a free box of holiday mooncakes, and then sells leftover boxes at cost to employees. But after the engineers rigged the system to buy more than 100 boxes at the special low price, Alibaba managers fired them, saying it was "another reminder to our staff that every game comes with rules."[99] As this example illustrates, managers must provide ethical leadership. As we said earlier, what managers *do* has a strong influence on employees' decisions whether to behave ethically.[100] When managers cheat, lie, steal, manipulate, take advantage of situations or people, or treat others unfairly, what kind of signal are they sending to employees (or other stakeholders)? Probably not the one they want to send. Exhibit 5-9 gives some suggestions on how managers can provide ethical leadership.

Exhibit 5-9
Being an Ethical Leader

- Be a good role model by being ethical and honest.
  - Tell the truth always.
  - Don't hide or manipulate information.
  - Be willing to admit your failures.
- Share your personal values by regularly communicating them to employees.
- Stress the organization's or team's important shared values.
- Use the reward system to hold everyone accountable to the values.

PROTECTION OF EMPLOYEES WHO RAISE ETHICAL ISSUES What would you do if you saw other employees doing something illegal, immoral, or unethical? Would you step forward? Many of us wouldn't because of the perceived risks. That's why it's important for managers to assure employees who raise ethical concerns or issues that they will face no personal or career risks. These individuals, often called **whistle-blowers**, can be a key part of any company's ethics program. For example, Sherron Watkins, who was a vice president at Enron, clearly outlined her concerns about the company's accounting practices in a letter to chairman Ken Lay. Her statement that, "I am incredibly nervous that we will implode in a wave of accounting scandals" couldn't have been more prophetic.[101] However, surveys show that most observers of wrongdoing don't report it, and that's the attitude managers have to address.[102] One of the reasons employees give for not blowing the whistle include the fear it might damage someone's career. This is a difficult position for an employee to be in. A U.S. Senate report stated that "Whistle-blowers often face the difficult choice between telling the truth and the risking of committing career suicide."[103] Other reasons include fear that it would make it harder to work with that individual, fear that he/she (the whistle-blower) wouldn't be taken seriously, fear of not having enough proof, thought someone else would report it, and fear of losing job or other retaliation.[104] So, how can employees be protected so they're willing to step up if they see unethical or illegal things occurring?

whistle-blower
Individual who raises ethical concerns or issues to others

One way is to set up toll-free ethics hotlines. For instance, Dell has an ethics hotline that employees can call anonymously to report infractions that the company will then investigate.[105] In addition, managers need to create a culture where bad news can be heard and acted on before it's too late. Michael Josephson, founder of the Josephson Institute of Ethics (www.josephsoninstitute.org) said, "It is absolutely and unequivocally important to establish a culture where it is possible for employees to complain and protest and to get heard."[106] Even if some whistle-blowers have a personal agenda they're pursuing, it's important to take them seriously. Another way is to have in place a "procedurally just process," which means making sure the decision-making process is fair and that employees are treated respectfully about their concerns.[107] Backlash against whistle-blowers can be costly. For instance, Walter Tamosaitis, a former employee of Aecom (a contractor involved in the Hanford nuclear-weapons cleanup project) received a $4.1 million settlement of a lawsuit in which he claimed that the employer had punished him for speaking up.[108] Finally, federal legislation offers some legal protection. According to the Sarbanes-Oxley Act, any manager who retaliates against an employee for reporting violations faces a stiff penalty: a 10-year jail sentence.[109] Antiretaliation protections against whistle-blowers have been strengthened by the more recent Dodd-Frank Wall Street Reform Act. Unfortunately, despite this protection, fewer than two of every three employees felt they would be protected from retaliation, and about the same proportion fear losing their jobs if they do not meet performance targets.[110] At the present time, it's not a perfect solution, but it is a step in the right direction.

If your professor has assigned this, go to **www.mymanagementlab.com** to complete the Simulation: *Management and Ethics* and get a better understanding of the challenges of managing ethically in organizations.

Social Entrepreneurship

Social entrepreneur Saba Gul (left), founder of the high-end handbag company Popinjay, created an organization that provides opportunities for impoverished women in her home country of Pakistan to transform their lives. She trains, employs, and pays artisan women a fair wage to embroider silk designs that are incorporated in Popinjay handbags.
Source: Rex Features/AP Images

The world's social problems are many and viable solutions are few. But numerous people and organizations are trying to do something. For instance, take John Schoch, the CEO of Profile Products, which is a profitable manufacturer and distributor of products for soil and water management. He decided to invest some of the company's resources to help address a global crisis—a lack of clean water. He established a nonprofit subsidiary of Profile Products that put millions of dollars into research and development of a product called ProCleanse, which is a water filtration device. Schoch has chosen to pursue a purpose as well as a profit.[111] He is an example of a **social entrepreneur**, an individual or organization who seeks out opportunities to improve society by using practical, innovative, and sustainable approaches.[112] "What business entrepreneurs are to the economy, social entrepreneurs are to social change."[113] Social entrepreneurs want to make the world a better place and have a driving passion to make that happen. For example, Microsoft Corporation announced that it would donate $1 billion in cloud services to nonprofits and university researchers. Microsoft's goal is to provide the same computing tools that have allowed business firms to become more agile and tackle substantial technical challenges.[114] Also, social entrepreneurs use creativity and ingenuity to solve problems. For instance, Seattle-based PATH (Program for Appropriate Technology in Health) is an international nonprofit organization that uses low-cost technology to provide needed health-care solutions for poor, developing countries. By collaborating with public groups and for-profit businesses, PATH has developed simple life-saving solutions such as clean birthing kits, credit card–sized lab test kits, and disposable vaccination syringes that can't be reused. PATH has pioneered innovative approaches to solving global medical problems.[115]

social entrepreneur
An individual or organization that seeks out opportunities to improve society by using practical, innovative, and sustainable approaches

What can we learn from these social entrepreneurs? Although many organizations have committed to doing business ethically and responsibly, perhaps there is more they can do, as these social entrepreneurs show. Maybe, as in the case of PATH, it's simply a matter of business organizations collaborating with public groups or nonprofit organizations to address a social issue. Or maybe, as in the case of Microsoft, it's providing services where needed. Or it may involve nurturing individuals who passionately and unwaveringly believe they have an idea that could make the world a better place and simply need the organizational support to pursue it.

Businesses Promoting Positive Social Change

Since 1946, Target has contributed 5 percent of its annual income to support community needs, an amount that adds up to more than $3 million a week. And it's not alone in those efforts. "Over the past two decades, a growing number of corporations, both within and beyond the United States, have been engaging in activities that promote positive social change."[116] Businesses can do this in a couple of ways: through corporate philanthropy and through employee volunteer efforts.

CORPORATE PHILANTHROPY Corporate philanthropy can be an effective way for companies to address societal problems.[117] For instance, the breast cancer "pink" campaign and the global AIDS Red campaign (started by Bono) are ways that companies support social causes.[118] Many organizations also donate money to various causes that employees and customers care about. In 2014 (latest numbers available), the sum of corporate giving totaled over $18 billion in cash and products.[119] Other corporations have funded their own foundations to support various social issues. For example, Google's foundation—called DotOrg by its employees—supports five areas: develop-

Pierre Andre Senizergues, CEO and founder of the action sports footwear and apparel firm Sole Technology, hands out new shoes to homeless people and at-risk children during an annual Los Angeles Mission event. Aimed at making our world a better place, the firm's philanthropy includes giving time, money, shoes, and apparel to charities and supporting disaster relief efforts.
Source: David McNew/Getty Images

ing systems to help predict and prevent disease pandemics, empowering the poor with information about public services, creating jobs by investing in small and midsized businesses in the developing world, accelerating the commercialization of plug-in cars, and making renewable energy cheaper than coal. Each year, DotOrg donates $100 million in grants, 80,000 hours to its charitable causes, and $1 billion in products.[120]

EMPLOYEE VOLUNTEERING EFFORTS Employee volunteering is another popular way for businesses to be involved in promoting social change. For instance, Dow Corning sent a small team of employees to rural India helping women "examine stitchery and figure out prices for garments to be sold in local markets."[122] PCL Construction holds Habitat for Humanity home-building projects. And, for the past 30 years, it has sponsored volunteer days for participation in the Brother's redevelopment Paint-A-Thon. PricewaterhouseCoopers employees renovated an abandoned school in Newark, New Jersey. Every VMWare employee is given five paid days off from work each year to volunteer in his or her community. Other businesses are encouraging their employees to volunteer in various ways. The Committee to Encourage Corporate Philanthropy says that more than 90 percent of its members had volunteer programs and almost half encouraged volunteerism by providing paid time off or by creating volunteer events. More than half of the companies provided a company-wide day of service domestically, and 30 percent offered a day of service internationally.[123] Many businesses have found that such efforts not only benefit communities, but enhance employees' work efforts and motivation.

North American companies made philanthropic contributions totaling $1.04 billion to companies located on the following continents:[121]

- $88.37 million to Africa
- $374.47 million to Asia
- $410.23 million to Europe
- $168.36 million to Latin America and the Caribbean

WORKPLACE CONFIDENTIAL Balancing Work and Personal Life

Several business critics have proposed that business firms have a social responsibility to help employees balance their work demands with their family and personal commitments. A number of companies, usually large ones and often in high-tech industries, have responded by making work-life balance an important corporate goal. They've introduced flexible work hours; offered paid leaves for both new dads and moms; built on-site childcare facilities, and introduced similar policies that make it easier for employees to balance their personal life and work. But such workplace benefits are probably more the exception than the rule. Unfortunately, most of us face situations more accurately described as work-life imbalance.

If you're going to achieve balance, responsibility is most likely to fall largely on your own shoulders. So what can you do?

In an ideal world, you would seek a progressive employer that sees the benefits of providing its employees with the flexibility to balance work and personal responsibilities. As we've noted, there are such firms. *Fortune* magazine publishes an annual list of the 100 best companies to work for. Many of these companies make the *Fortune* list in large part because of their progressive human resource policies that include options to facilitate work-life balance.

Our next suggestion asks you to assess your priorities. What trade-offs are you prepared to make between your work and personal life? Keep in mind that the answer to this question often changes over time. At age 25, your career might be your highest priority and working 70 hours a week might be a price you're willing to pay to move up the career ladder. At 35, you might not feel the same way. There is nothing wrong with going "all in" on your job. Just realize that there are trade-offs. If you have high career aspirations, just recognize that you will need to make personal sacrifices. Consider where you want to be in 5, 10, 20, and even 30 years. If you decide that pursuing a rich personal life outside of work is important to you, consider this fact when seeking a job. And per Chapter 7, choose an organization whose culture is compatible with your values. If your non-work activities are your highest priority, choose an organization and a job where your preference will be honored.

Take a look back at the opening of Chapter 1. It provides a brief summary of time-management techniques. To successfully manage conflicts that might arise between your work and non-work life, few activities are more valuable than effective use of your time.

As noted in Chapter 1, time is a unique resource in that, if it's wasted, it can never be replaced. Importantly, every one of us is allotted the same 24 hours a day, seven days a week. Some people just use their allotments better than others. That is, they do a better job of managing their time. For instance, you can reduce work-life conflicts by prioritizing both work and personal activities by importance and urgency. Besides prioritizing activities, here are three addition time-management suggestions:

Follow the 10-90 principle. Most of us produce 90 percent of our results using only 10 percent of our time. It's easy to get caught in an activity trap and confuse actions with accomplishments. Those who use their time well make sure that the crucial 10 percent gets highest priority.

Know your productivity cycle. Each of us has a daily energy cycle that influences when we feel most productive or unproductive. Some of us are morning people, while others are late-afternoon or evening people. Don't fight your natural cycle. Understand it and use it to your advantage. Handle your most demanding problems during the high part of your energy cycle, when you are most alert and productive. Relegate routine and undemanding tasks to your low periods.

Group less important activities together. Set aside a regular time period each day to make phone calls, respond to e-mails, do follow-ups, and perform other kinds of "busy work." Ideally, this should be during your low cycle. This avoids duplication, waste, and redundancy; it also prevents trivial matters from crowding out high-priority tasks.

The following are a few additional practices that can help you balance your work-life commitments.

- ***Set specific time targets for leaving work***. Make it a habit to leave work at a set time each day. As this pattern is established, colleagues will become increasingly aware of your schedule and learn to interact with you during your specific work hours.
- ***Separate work and personal cell phones.*** Use two separate cell phones or cell accounts. Respond to your work number during working hours and your personal number at other times. Turn off your business phone when you're outside your work hours.

  Avoid checking e-mails or responding to work-related texts outside work hours. Don't let your work hours become 24/7. In our digital world, it's increasingly common for people to assume we're always available. Make clear to others that you separate your personal life from your work. In reality, most "urgent" messages aren't urgent. Most replies can be delayed 10 or 12 hours with minimal effects.
- ***Our final suggestion recognizes that working for others always requires giving up some degree of control.*** No matter how progressive your employer, the employment agreement implies a trade-off: You give up some of your freedom in return for compensation. You can potentially maximize control of your work-life conflicts by becoming your own boss. While this rarely lessens demands on your time, it can allow you to dictate how you will spend your time. You may end up working longer hours than you would if you worked for someone else, but that decision will be yours rather than someone else's. You'll be able to prioritize your commitments as you best see fit.

Based on M. A. O'Connor, "Corporate Social Responsibility for Work/Family Balance," *St. John's Law Review*, Fall 2005, pp. 1193–1220; T. Kalliath and P. Brough, eds., "Achieving Work-Life Balance," *Journal of Management and Organization*, Special Issue, July 2008, pp. 224–327; and B. Tracy, *Time Management* (New York: AMACOM, 2014).

Chapter 5 PREPARING FOR: Exams/Quizzes

CHAPTER SUMMARY by Learning Objective

LO5.1 DISCUSS what it means to be socially responsible and what factors influence that decision.

Social obligation, which reflects the classical view of social responsibility, is when a firm engages in social actions because of its obligation to meet certain economic and legal responsibilities. Social responsiveness is when a firm engages in social actions in response to some popular social need. Social responsibility is a business's intention, beyond its economic and legal obligations, to pursue long-term goals that are good for society. Both of these reflect the socioeconomic view of social responsibility. Determining whether organizations should be socially involved can be done by looking at arguments for and against it. Other ways are to assess the impact of social involvement on a company's economic performance and evaluate the performance of SRI funds versus non-SRI funds. We can conclude that a company's social responsibility doesn't appear to hurt its economic performance.

LO5.2 EXPLAIN green management and how organizations can go green.

Green management is when managers consider the impact of their organization on the natural environment. Organizations can "go green" in different ways. The light green approach is doing what is required legally, which is social obligation. Using the market approach, organizations respond to the environmental preferences of their customers. Using the stakeholder approach, organizations respond to the environmental demands of multiple stakeholders. Both the market and stakeholder approaches can be viewed as social responsiveness. With an activist or dark green approach, an organization looks for ways to respect and preserve the earth and its natural resources, which can be viewed as social responsibility.

Green actions can be evaluated by examining reports that companies compile about their environmental performance, by looking for compliance with global standards for environmental management (ISO 14000), and by using the Global 100 list of the most sustainable corporations in the world.

LO5.3 DISCUSS the factors that lead to ethical and unethical behavior.

Ethics refers to the principles, values, and beliefs that define right and wrong decisions and behavior. The factors that affect ethical and unethical behavior include an individual's level of moral development (preconventional, conventional, or principled), individual characteristics (values and personality variables—ego strength and locus of control), structural variables (structural design, use of goals, performance appraisal systems, and reward allocation procedures), and issue intensity (greatness of harm, consensus of wrong, probability of harm, immediacy of consequences, proximity to victims, and concentration of effect).

Since ethical standards aren't universal, managers should know what they can and cannot do legally as defined by the Foreign Corrupt Practices Act. It's also important to recognize any cultural differences and to clarify ethical guidelines for employees working in different global locations. Finally, managers should know about the principles of the Global Compact and the Anti-Bribery Convention.

LO5.4 DESCRIBE management's role in encouraging ethical behavior.

The behavior of managers is the single most important influence on an individual's decision to act ethically or unethically. Some specific ways managers can encourage ethical behavior include paying attention to employee selection, creating an organizational culture that positively influences ethical behavior, having and using a code of ethics, recognizing the important ethical leadership role they play and how what they do is far more important than what they say, making sure that goals and the performance appraisal process don't reward goal achievement without taking into account how those goals were achieved, and using ethics training and independent social audits.

LO5.5 DISCUSS current social responsibility and ethics issues.

Managers can manage ethical lapses and social irresponsibility by being strong ethical leaders and by protecting employees who raise ethical issues. The example set by managers has a strong influence on whether employees behave ethically. Ethical leaders also are honest, share their values, stress important shared values, and use the reward system appropriately. Managers can protect whistle-blowers (employees who raise ethical issues or concerns) by encouraging them to come forward, by setting up toll-free ethics hotlines, and by establishing a culture in which employees can complain and be heard without fear of reprisal. Social entrepreneurs play an important role in solving social problems by seeking out opportunities to improve society by using practical, innovative, and sustainable approaches. Social entrepreneurs want to make the world a better place and have a driving passion to make that happen. Businesses can promote positive social change through corporate philanthropy and employee volunteering efforts.

Pearson **MyLab** Management

Go to **mymanagementlab.com** to complete the problems marked with this icon ✪.

✪ REVIEW AND DISCUSSION QUESTIONS

5-1. Give reasons why you think an organization might not value social responsibility.

5-2. Many organizations around the world claim they are green. What criteria would you consider to objectively evaluate their green credentials?

5-3. How might the moral development of an individual affect their ethical stance?

5-4. How can internal and external locus of control influence work behaviors?

5-5. In April 2010, the Deepwater Horizon oil spill in the Gulf of Mexico caused the largest oil spill in history, at an estimated 4.9 million barrels of oil. Initial efforts to cap the well were declared successful; however, subsequent independent reports of continued oil leaks were ignored by BP (British Petroleum) and the NOAA (National Oceanic and Atmospheric Administration) until it was verified a month later. Did employees in BP and NOAA behave ethically in ignoring the reports?

5-6. What kind of protection can be afforded to whistle-blowers? Are these protective steps sufficient to encourage such actions in future?

5-7. "Ethical leaders are honest, share their values, stress important shared values, and use the reward system appropriately." Observe your college professors. Would you consider them to be ethical leaders? Discuss.

5-8. What can an organization do to encourage ethical behaviour?

Pearson **MyLab** Management

If your professor has assigned these, go to **mymanagementlab.com** for the following Assisted-graded writing questions:

5-9. What is green management and how can organizations go green?

5-10. What would you include in an ethics training workshop?

PREPARING FOR: My Career

PERSONAL INVENTORY ASSESSMENTS

PERSONAL INVENTORY ASSESSMENT

Ethical Leadership Assessment

Organizations need ethical leadership from all employees, but especially from managers. In this PIA, you'll see how much thought and effort goes into your being ethical in your workplace behavior.

ETHICS DILEMMA

A coworker takes credit for the excellent job you've performed. Frustrating! It's probably happened to you or someone you know. How did it happen? Perhaps you shared an idea with a coworker and then hear her present it as her own in a meeting. Or perhaps you worked during the weekend to ensure that a project report is completed on time and your coworker takes credit for your initiative. Or maybe you resolved a conflict with a customer, but your department head reports the resolution as his own.

5-11. What are some of the possible reasons for others taking credit for your work? Are any of the reasons justifiable? Why or why not?

5-12. Do you think that those who take credit for your work know that what they're doing is wrong?

5-13. How would you respond to your coworker or boss? Explain.

SKILLS EXERCISE Developing Your Building Trust Skill

About the Skill

Trust plays an important role in the manager's relationships with his or her employees.[124] Given the importance of trust in setting a good ethical example for employees, today's managers should actively seek to develop it within their work group.

Steps in Practicing the Skill

- ***Practice openness***. Mistrust comes as much from what people don't know as from what they do. Being open with employees leads to confidence and trust. Keep people informed. Make clear the criteria you use in making decisions. Explain the rationale for your decisions. Be forthright and candid about problems. Fully disclose all relevant information.
- ***Be fair***. Before making decisions or taking actions, consider how others will perceive them in terms of objectivity and fairness. Give credit where credit is due. Be objective and impartial in performance appraisals. Pay attention to equity perceptions in distributing rewards.
- ***Speak your feelings***. Managers who convey only hard facts come across as cold, distant, and unfeeling. When you share your feelings, others will see that you are real and human. They will know you for who you are and their respect for you is likely to increase.
- ***Tell the truth***. Being trustworthy means being credible. If honesty is critical to credibility, then you must be perceived as someone who tells the truth. Employees are more tolerant of hearing something "they don't want to hear" than of finding out that their manager lied to them.
- ***Be consistent***. People want predictability. Mistrust comes from not knowing what to expect. Take the time to think about your values and beliefs, and let those values and beliefs consistently guide your decisions. When you know what's important to you, your actions will follow, and you will project a consistency that earns trust.
- ***Fulfill your promises***. Trust requires that people believe that you are dependable. You need to ensure that you keep your word. Promises made must be promises kept.
- ***Maintain confidences***. You trust those whom you believe to be discreet and those on whom you can rely. If people open up to you and make themselves vulnerable by telling you something in confidence, they need to feel assured you won't discuss it with others or betray that confidence. If people perceive you as someone who leaks personal confidences or someone who can't be depended on, you've lost their trust.
- ***Demonstrate competence***. Develop the admiration and respect of others by demonstrating technical and professional ability. Pay particular attention to developing and displaying your communication, negotiation, and other interpersonal skills.

Practicing the Skill

Building trust in teams you work on for class projects is a great way to practice your skills in building trust. It's important to quickly develop trust among your teammates if the project is to succeed. Using the steps above, create a plan that you can use to more quickly build and maintain trust in team projects. Make a list of steps you can take at the beginning of the project to begin building trust. Next, make a list of behaviors you are willing to commit to during the team project in order to continue to build and maintain trust. For example, you may want to commit to responding to your teammates' communications within a certain time period. Implement your plans with your next team project.

WORKING TOGETHER Team Exercise

Around half of all businesses in the United Kingdom have between 1 and 9 percent of their employees donating toward charities from their salaries. Only 10 percent reported between 10 and 24 percent of their employees doing this. In the United Kingdom, charitable donations attract a like-for-like payment from the government, making such donations twice as valuable. It has been estimated that around 735,000 employees donated to charities directly from their pay. Working together in groups of three or four, consider ways in which an employer could encourage their workers to make charitable donations. How can the schemes be run? Create a series of suggestions and share your ideas with the rest of the class. While there are proven ways to promote this kind of giving, is it reasonable to expect employees to get involved?

MY TURN TO BE A MANAGER

- Go to the Global Reporting Initiative website (www.globalreporting.org) and choose three businesses from the list that have filed reports. Look at those reports and describe/evaluate what's in them. In addition, identify the stakeholders who might be affected and how they might be affected by the company's action.
- Identify three companies that are known for being socially responsible. List and compare the types of socially responsible behavior that each company engages in.
- Research careers in sustainability. Visit the Occupational Information Network (O*Net) at www.onetcenter.org and search for careers using the terms "sustainability" or "green management." Create a list of the types of jobs or careers you can pursue. Identify the skills and abilities that are required for a career in sustainability.
- Find five different examples of organizational codes of ethics. Using Exhibit 5-7, describe what each contains. Compare and contrast the examples.
- Using the examples of codes of ethics you found, create what you feel would be an appropriate and effective organizational code of ethics. In addition, create your own *personal code of ethics* you can use as a guide to ethical dilemmas.
- Over the course of two weeks, see what ethical "dilemmas" you observe. These could be ones you face personally, or they could be ones that others (friends, colleagues, other students talking in the hallway or before class, and so forth) face. Write these dilemmas down and think about what you might do if faced with that dilemma.
- Interview two different managers about how they encourage their employees to be ethical. Write down their comments and discuss how these ideas might help you be a better manager.

CASE APPLICATION 1 A Novel Wellness Culture

Menssana in corporesano. The one-thousand-year-old Latin saying represents the core idea of The Wellness Foundation, launched by Nerio Alessandri, founder of Italian wellness company Technogym. The goal is as simple as it is challenging: promoting a novel style of living in society, grounded in creating a perfect balance between physical, mental, and social components. In Europe, only 9 percent of the population participate in regular physical activity. The sedentary lifestyle is responsible for harmful effects such as an increase in the number of chronic pathologies, a huge deficit in governments' health budgets, and work absenteeism. The Wellness Foundation intends to address these problems by promoting scientific research, education, and tangible projects and by encouraging people of all generations to engage in regular physical activity. "Play Wellness," for example, is one of the most important projects promoted by the foundation. It is geared toward 10,000 children between 3 and 9 years of age in the city of Cesena (Emilia Romagna, Italy). It consists of 2,700 hours of physical activity at school with professional instructors, training for school teachers on the benefits of physical activity for children's growth, and the realization of end products detailing the benefits of physical activity for children.

The project is financially supported by Technogym, the official supplier of gym equipment for the Olympic Games as well as for major luxury hotel chains in the world such as the Mandarin Oriental and Four Seasons. The company employs more than 2,000 employees and counts the Real Madrid football players among its clients as well as celebrities such as Madonna and George Clooney. The goodness of this initiative has gained international recognition through its involvement with the "Let's Move!" campaign.[125]

DISCUSSION QUESTIONS

5-14. How can Technogym balance being socially responsible and focused on profits?

5-15. Would you describe Nerio Alessandri's approach as a social obligation, social responsiveness, or social responsibility? Explain.

5-16. It's time to think like a manager. Corporate social responsibility is wonderful, though often criticized as purely rhetorical and laden with subtle profit goals. How can a manager emphasize genuineness of corporate social responsibilities and activities in society?

5-17. Do you think the Wellness Foundation can boost Technogym's turnover? Why or why not?

CASE APPLICATION 2 Defeating the System: Ethics at Volkswagen

In one of the worst business ethics scandals in history, the world learned in 2015 that Volkswagen intentionally circumvented government exhaust emission tests for years by installing so called "defeat devices" on their clean diesel vehicles.[126] This revelation was a shock to many given the company's long-standing success in the auto industry. Volkswagen, one of the world's most recognized brands, was founded in 1937. The company is headquartered in Germany but employs more than half a million people around the world.

Researchers at West Virginia University (WVU) first discovered the violation when they started studying clean diesel engines. When they tested the performance of Volkswagen vehicles, they were surprised to find that on the road emissions exceeded government allowances by almost 40 times. Further investigation by the U.S. Environmental Protection Agency (EPA) found that the vehicles were actually equipped with software that could essentially trick emission testing systems. The diesel engines could detect when they were being tested for emissions and changed the vehicle's performance to improve testing results. Once on the road, the vehicle would switch out of the test mode, emitting excessive nitrogen oxide pollutants, as the WVU researchers found.

The EPA's finding covered about 500,000 cars sold in the United States only. But Volkswagen later admitted that about 11 million cars worldwide were fitted with this software. It will be a long time before Volkswagen realizes all of the damage of this ethical blunder. There will be legal sanctions from governments, private lawsuits, and consumer bans that will impact the company for a long time to come.

How could such a blatant ethical violation occur? It may take years to sort out who is to blame. CEO Martin Winterkorn, who resigned in response to the scandal, initially claimed not to know about the devices. While many high-ranking executives were suspended, no one is sure who knew about or authorized the software. In fact, some believe that the driven, performance-based culture may be more to blame than any individual.

Winterkorn, who reinforced the unique culture, has been described as a hard-driving perfectionist who was committed to securing the top spot among global car manufacturers. He was known to criticize employees publically, and this generated both fear among employees and the commitment to do whatever necessary to ensure the company's success. The company's culture has been described as "confident, cutthroat, and insular." It is possible that arrogance led Volkswagen managers to assume that U.S. government or other officials wouldn't discover the misleading emissions tests.

What's more problematic is Volkswagen's response to the scandal. The company first suggested a technical problem with the cars, but finally admitted the software devices were designed to cheat the system. Initially, the company reported only a limited number of cars were affected; however, as more details were uncovered, the company admitted more cars were fitted with the device and that these actions occurred over a longer period of time than originally reported. The company's faulty initial response to the scandal has clearly made the road ahead a bigger challenge for them. In fact, a recent poll of Americans' attitude toward 100 large companies put Volkswagen in last place.

DISCUSSION QUESTIONS

5-18. Are you surprised that an organization as large as Volkswagen was caught engaging in such unethical behavior? Do you agree that the organization's culture could have encouraged this behavior?

5-19. Are there structural variables that may have influenced the unethical behavior at Volkswagen?

5-20. Evaluate Volkswagen's actions based on the factors in Exhibit 5-5. How would you describe the issue intensity of Volkswagen's actions?

5-21. Moving forward, what do you think Volkswagen needs to do to avoid such an ethical lapse in the future?

ENDNOTES

1. S. Welch, "The Uh-Oh Feeling: Sticky Situations at Work," www.oprah.com/money/, from the November 2007 issue of *O, the Oprah Magazine*.
2. A. Tugend, "In Life and Business, Learning to Be Ethical," *New York Times* online, www.nytimes.com. January 10, 2014.
3. A. Goodman, "The Dilemma: Addicted & Conflicted About Laughing at the Afflicted," www.globalethics.org/newsline, June 3, 2013; and T. Lickona, *Character Matters: How to Help Our Children Develop Good Judgment, Integrity, and Other Essential Virtues* (New York: Touchstone Publishing, 2004).
4. M. L. Barnett, "Stakeholder Influence Capacity and the Variability of Financial Returns to Corporate Social Responsibility," *Academy of Management Review*, July 2007, pp. 794–816; A. Mackey, T. B. Mackey, and J. B. Barney, "Corporate Social Responsibility and Firm Performance: Investor Preferences and Corporate Strategies," *Academy of Management Review*, July 2007, pp. 817–835; and A. B. Carroll, "A Three-Dimensional Conceptual Model of Corporate Performance," *Academy of Management Review*, October 1979, p. 499.
5. See K. Basu and G. Palazzo, "Corporate Social Performance: A Process Model of Sensemaking," *Academy of Management Review*, January 2008, pp. 122–136; and S. P. Sethi, "A Conceptual Framework for Environmental Analysis of Social Issues and Evaluation of Business Response Patterns," *Academy of Management Review*, January 1979, pp. 68–74.
6. M. Friedman, *Capitalism and Freedom* (Chicago: University of Chicago Press, 1962); and Friedman, "The Social Responsibility of Business Is to Increase Profits," *New York Times Magazine*, September 13, 1970, p. 33.
7. V. Vermaelen, "An Innovative Approach to Funding CSR Projects," *Harvard Business Review*, June 2011, p. 28; S. Strom, "To Be Good Citizens, Report Says Companies Should Just Focus on Bottom Line," *New York Times* online, www.nytimes.com, June 14, 2011; and A. Karnani, "The Case Against Social Responsibility," *Wall Street Journal*, August 23, 2010, pp. R1+.
8. D. Gelles, "For Start-Ups, Altruism as an Alternative to Acquisition or I.P.O.," *New York Times* online, www.nytimes.com, November 4, 2015.
9. S. Lohr, "First, Make Money. Also, Do Good," *New York Times* online, www.nytimes.com, August 13, 2011; and S. Liebs, "Do Companies Do Good Well?" *CFO*, July 2007, p. 16.
10. See, for example, D. J. Wood, "Corporate Social Performance Revisited," *Academy of Management Review*, October 1991, pp. 703–708; and S. L. Wartick and P. L. Cochran, "The Evolution of the Corporate Social Performance Model," *Academy of Management Review*, October 1985, p. 763.
11. N. Bunkley, "Ford Backs Ban on Text Messaging by Drivers," *New York Times* online, www.nytimes.com, September 11, 2009.
12. "Building Better Communities Worldwide," The Boeing Company 2014 Corporate Citizenship Report, 2015, p. 52.
13. See, for example, R. A. Buchholz, *Essentials of Public Policy for Management*, 2d ed. (Upper Saddle River, NJ: Prentice Hall, 1990).
14. "Mayer Dahan: Where One Man's Care & Dedication Sets a Clear Path for a Better Tomorrow," *U&C Lifestyle Magazine*, www.upandcomingonline.com, January 2, 2016.

15. Fiona Briggs, "Unilever Announces New Global Zero Waste to Landfill Achievement," *Retail Times*, February 9, 2016, http://www.retailtimes.co.uk/43948-2/ (accessed December 16, 2016); Karin Brulliard, "The Movement to Free Hens from Cages May Be Going Global," *Washington Post*, July 25, 2016, https://www.washingtonpost.com/news/animalia/wp/2016/07/25/the-movement-to-free-hens-from-cages-may-be-going-global/?utm_term=.03750da90cd6 (accessed December 16, 2016).
16. This section is based on J. D. Margolis and J. P. Walsh, "Misery Loves Companies: Rethinking Social Initiatives by Business," *Administrative Science Quarterly*, vol. 48, no. 2, 2003, pp. 268–305; K. Davis and W. C. Frederick, *Business and Society: Management, Public Policy, Ethics*, 5th ed. (New York: McGraw-Hill, 1984), pp. 28–41; and R. J. Monsen Jr., "The Social Attitudes of Management," in *Contemporary Management: Issues and Views*, ed. J. M. McGuire (Upper Saddle River, NJ: Prentice Hall, 1974), p. 616.
17. See, for instance, J. Surroca, J. A. Tribo, and S. Waddock, "Corporate Responsibility and Financial Performance: The Role of Intangible Resources," *Strategic Management Journal*, May 2010, pp. 463–490; R. Garcia-Castro, M. A. Ariño, and M. A. Canela, "Does Social Performance Really Lead to Financial Performance? Accounting for Endogeneity," *Journal of Business Ethics*, March 2010, pp. 107–126; J. Peloza, "The Challenge of Measuring Financial Impacts from Investments in Corporate Social Performance," *Journal of Management*, December 2009, pp. 1518–1541; J. D. Margolis and H. Anger Elfenbein, "Do Well by Doing Good? Don't Count on It," *Harvard Business Review*, January 2008, pp. 19–20; M. L. Barnett, "Stakeholder Influence Capacity and the Variability of Financial Returns to Corporate Social Responsibility," 2007; D. O. Neubaum and S. A. Zahra, "Institutional Ownership and Corporate Social Performance: The Moderating Effects of Investment Horizon, Activism, and Coordination," *Journal of Management*, February 2006, pp. 108–131; B. A. Waddock and S. B. Graves, "The Corporate Social Performance–Financial Performance Link," *Strategic Management Journal*, April 1997, pp. 303–319; J. B. McGuire, A. Sundgren, and T. Schneeweis, "Corporate Social Responsibility and Firm Financial Performance," *Academy of Management Journal*, December 1988, pp. 854–872; K. Aupperle, A. B. Carroll, and J. D. Hatfield, "An Empirical Examination of the Relationship Between Corporate Social Responsibility and Profitability," *Academy of Management Journal*, June 1985, pp. 446–463; and P. Cochran and R. A. Wood, "Corporate Social Responsibility and Financial Performance," *Academy of Management Journal*, March 1984, pp. 42–56.
18. Peloza, "The Challenge of Measuring Financial Impacts from Investments in Corporate Social Performance."
19. B. Seifert, S. A. Morris, and B. R. Bartkus, "Having, Giving, and Getting: Slack Resources, Corporate Philanthropy, and Firm Financial Performance," *Business & Society*, June 2004, pp. 135–161; and McGuire, Sundgren, and Schneeweis, "Corporate Social Responsibility and Firm Financial Performance."
20. A. McWilliams and D. Siegel, "Corporate Social Responsibility and Financial Performance: Correlation or Misspecification?," *Strategic Management Journal*, June 2000, pp. 603–609.
21. A. J. Hillman and G. D. Keim, "Shareholder Value, Stakeholder Management, and Social Issues: What's the Bottom Line?," *Strategic Management Journal*, vol. 22, 2001, pp. 125–139.
22. M. Orlitzky, F. L. Schmidt, and S. L. Rynes, "Corporate Social and Financial Performance," *Organization Studies*, vol. 24, no. 3, 2003, pp. 403–441.
23. "Performance & SRI," The Forum for Sustainable and Responsible Investment, www.ussif.org, February 27, 2016.
24. "Sustainable & Responsible Mutual Fund Chart," The Forum for Sustainable and Responsible Investment, www.ussif.org, February 27, 2016.
25. "Sustainability: Just Do It," *Industry Week*, February 2014, pp. 22–23.
26. "Hive Mentality," *Body + Soul*, December 2009, p. 26.
27. A. Zipkin, "Hotels Embrace Sustainability to Lure Guests and Cut Costs," *The New York Times* online, www.nytimes.com, April 27, 2015.
28. S. Rosenbush and L. Stevens, "At UPS, the Algorithm Is the Drive," *The Wall Street Journal* online, www.wsj.com, February 16, 2015; "The Total Package," *Bloomberg BusinessWeek*, March 19–March 25, 2012, p. 6.
29. J. Yang and P. Trap, "Applying Green Tech at Work," *USA Today*, May 13, 2013, p. 1B.
30. D. A. Lubin and D. C. Esty, "The Sustainability Imperative," *Harvard Business Review*, May 2010, pp. 42–50; J. Pfeffer, "Building Sustainable Organizations: The Human Factor," *Academy of Management Perspectives*, February 2010, pp. 34–45; R. Nidumolu, C. K. Prahalad, and M. R. Rangaswami, "Why Sustainability Is Now the Key Driver of Innovation," *Harvard Business Review*, September 2009, pp. 56–64; A. A. Marcus and A. R. Fremeth, "Green Management Matters Regardless," *Academy of Management Perspectives*, August 2009, pp. 17–27; D. S. Siegel, "Green Management Matters Only If It Yields More Green: An Economic/Strategic Perspective," *Academy of Management Perspectives*, August 2009, pp. 5–16; and A. White, "The Greening of the Balance Sheet," *Harvard Business Review*, March 2006, pp. 27–28.
31. Terry Slavin, "Tetra Pak Makes Pioneering Foray into Bioplastics," *Ethical Corporation Magazine*, December 9, 2016, http://www.ethicalcorp.com/tetra-pak-makes-pioneering-foray-bioplastics (accessed December 14, 2016); "Emirates Group Releases Sixth Annual Environmental Report," *Gulf Times*, December 15, 2016, http://www.gulf-times.com/story/524873/Emirates-Group-releases-sixth-annual-environmental (accessed December 16, 2016).
32. The concept of shades of green can be found in R. E. Freeman, J. Pierce, and R. Dodd, *Shades of Green: Business Ethics and the Environment* (New York: Oxford University Press, 1995).
33. Leader Making a Difference box based on "Questions for Rick Ridgeway," *Fortune*, September 16, 2013, p. 25; C. Winter, "Patagonia's Latest Product: A Venture Fund," *Bloomberg BusinessWeek*, May 13–19, 2013, pp. 23–24; One Percent for the Planet, http://www.onepercentfortheplanet.org/en/, June 12, 2012; S. Stevenson, "Patagonia's Founder Is America's Most Unlikely Business Guru," *Wall Street Journal Magazine*, May 2012; "Responsible Company," *Wall Street Journal* online, www.nytimes.com, April 25, 2012; T. Henneman, "Patagonia Fills Payroll with People Who Are Passionate," *Workforce Management Online*, November 4, 2011; M. J. Ybarra, "Book Review: The Fun Hog Expedition Revisited," *Wall Street Journal*, February 19, 2010, p. W8; K. Garber, "Not in the Business of Hurting the Planet," *US News & World Report*, November 2009, p. 63; and T. Foster, "No Such Thing as Sustainability," *Fast Company*, July/August 2009, pp. 46–48.
34. F. Johnson, "SC Johnson's CEO on Doing the Right Thing, Even When It Hurts Business," *Harvard Business Review*, www.hbr.org, April 2015.
35. "Currents of Change: The KPMG Survey of Corporate Responsibility Reporting," KPMG, www.kpmg.com, 2015.
36. "White House Announces Additional Commitments to the American Business Act on Climate Package," White House, www.whitehouse.gov, December 1, 2015.
37. The Global 100 list is a collaborative effort of Corporate Knights Inc. and Innovest Strategic Value Advisors. Information from Global 100 website, www.global100.org, January 22, 2014.
38. "Spotlight on the 2016 Global 100," Corporate Knights, www.corporateknights.com, January 20, 2016.

39. C. Hausman, "Financial News Focuses on Questions of Ethics," *Ethics Newsline*, www.globalethics.org/newsline, April 20, 2010; C. Hausman, "Privacy Issues Prominent in Week's Tech News," *Ethics Newsline*, www.globalethics.org/newsline, March 9, 2010; and H. Maurer and C. Lindblad, "Madoff Gets the Max," *Bloomberg BusinessWeek*, July 13 and 20, 2009, p. 6.
40. This last example is based on J. F. Viega, T. D. Golden, and K. Dechant, "Why Managers Bend Company Rules," *Academy of Management Executive*, May 2004, pp. 84–90.
41. K. Davis and W. C. Frederick, *Business and Society*, p. 76.
42. F. D. Sturdivant, *Business and Society: A Managerial Approach*, 3rd ed. (Homewood, IL: Richard D. Irwin, 1985), p. 128.
43. M. C. Gentile, "Keeping Your Colleagues Honest," *Harvard Business Review*, March 2010, pp. 114–117; J. R. Edwards and D. M. Cable, "The Value of Value Congruence," *Journal of Applied Psychology*, May 2009, pp. 654–677; G. Weaver, "Ethics and Employees: Making the Connection," *Academy of Management Executive*, May 2004, pp. 121–125; V. Anand, B. E. Ashforth, and M. Joshi, "Business as Usual: The Acceptance and Perpetuation of Corruption in Organizations," *Academy of Management Executive*, May 2004, pp. 39–53; J. Weber, L. B. Kurke, and D. W. Pentico, "Why Do Employees Steal?," *Business & Society*, September 2003, pp. 359–380; V. Arnold and J. C. Lampe, "Understanding the Factors Underlying Ethical Organizations: Enabling Continuous Ethical Improvement," *Journal of Applied Business Research*, Summer 1999, pp. 1–19.
44. L. K. Treviño, G. R. Weaver, and S. J. Reynolds, "Behavioral Ethics in Organizations: A Review," *Journal of Management*, December 2006, pp. 951–990; T. Kelley, "To Do Right or Just to Be Legal," *New York Times*, February 8, 1998, p. BU12; J. W. Graham, "Leadership, Moral Development, and Citizenship Behavior," *Business Ethics Quarterly*, January 1995, pp. 43–54; L. Kohlberg, *Essays in Moral Development: The Psychology of Moral Development*, vol. 2 (New York: Harper & Row, 1984); and L. Kohlberg, *Essays in Moral Development: The Philosophy of Moral Development*, vol. 1 (New York: Harper & Row, 1981).
45. See, for example, J. Weber, "Managers' Moral Reasoning: Assessing Their Responses to Three Moral Dilemmas," *Human Relations*, July 1990, pp. 687–702.
46. W. C. Frederick and J. Weber, "The Value of Corporate Managers and Their Critics: An Empirical Description and Normative Implications," in *Business Ethics: Research Issues and Empirical Studies*, ed. W. C. Frederick and L. E. Preston (Greenwich, CT: JAI Press, 1990), pp. 123–144; and J. H. Barnett and M. J. Karson, "Personal Values and Business Decisions: An Exploratory Investigation," *Journal of Business Ethics*, July 1987, pp. 371–382.
47. K. Strom-Gottfried, "A Personal Take on Global Ethics," *Ethics Newsline*, globalethics.org, March 25, 2013; and "Creating Value Skeptics," *Ethics Newsline*, globalethics.org, August 13, 2012.
48. M. E. Baehr, J. W. Jones, and A. J. Nerad, "Psychological Correlates of Business Ethics Orientation in Executives," *Journal of Business and Psychology*, Spring 1993, pp. 291–308; and L. K. Treviño and S. A. Youngblood, "Bad Apples in Bad Barrels: A Causal Analysis of Ethical Decision-Making Behavior," *Journal of Applied Psychology*, August 1990, pp. 378–385.
49. M. E. Schweitzer, L. Ordonez, and B. Douma, "Goal Setting as a Motivator of Unethical Behavior," *Academy of Management Journal*, June 2004, pp. 422–432.
50. M. C. Jensen, "Corporate Budgeting Is Broken—Let's Fix It," *Harvard Business Review*, June 2001, pp. 94–101.
51. R. L. Cardy and T. T. Selvarajan, "Assessing Ethical Behavior Revisited: The Impact of Outcomes on Judgment Bias," paper presented at the Annual Meeting of the Academy of Management, Toronto, 2000.
52. P. Eisler and B. Hansen, "Doctors Perform Thousands of Unnecessary Surgeries," *USA Today* online, www.usatoday, June 20, 2013.
53. T. Barnett, "Dimensions of Moral Intensity and Ethical Decision Making: An Empirical Study," *Journal of Applied Social Psychology*, May 2001, pp. 1038–1057; and T. M. Jones, "Ethical Decision Making by Individuals in Organizations: An Issue-Contingent Model," *Academy of Management Review*, April 1991, pp. 366–395.
54. W. Bailey and A. Spicer, "When Does National Identity Matter? Convergence and Divergence in International Business Ethics," *Academy of Management Journal*, December 2007, pp. 1462–1480; and R. L. Sims, "Comparing Ethical Attitudes Across Cultures," *Cross Cultural Management: An International Journal*, vol. 13, no. 2, 2006, pp. 101–113.
55. BBC News Online, "Legal Review of Overseas Bribery," November 29, 2007.
56. C. Hausman, "British Defense Giant BAE Must Hire Ethics Monitor and Pay Huge Penalties Under Corruption Settlement," *Ethics Newsline*, www.globalethics.org, February 15, 2010.
57. "FCPA Digest," www.fcpaprofessor.com, January 2016.
58. "SEC Enforcement Actions: FCPA Cases," U.S. Securities and Exchange Commission, www.sec.gov, accessed February 28, 2016.
59. "VimpelCom to Pay $795 Million in Global Settlement for FCPA Violations," Securities and Exchange Commission (press release 2016-34), www.sec.gov, February 18, 2016.
60. L. Paine, R. Deshpande, J. D. Margolis, and K. E. Bettcher, "Up to Code: Does Your Company's Conduct Meet World-Class Standards?," *Harvard Business Review*, December 2005, pp. 122–133; G. R. Simpson, "Global Heavyweights Vow 'Zero Tolerance' for Bribes," *Wall Street Journal*, January 27, 2005, pp. A2+; A. Spicer, T. W. Dunfee, and W. J. Bailey, "Does National Context Matter in Ethical Decision Making? An Empirical Test of Integrative Social Contracts Theory," *Academy of Management Journal*, August 2004, pp. 610–620; J. White and S. Taft, "Frameworks for Teaching and Learning Business Ethics Within the Global Context: Background of Ethical Theories," *Journal of Management Education*, August 2004, pp. 463–477; J. Guyon, "CEOs on Managing Globally," *Fortune*, July 26, 2004, p. 169; A. B. Carroll, "Managing Ethically with Global Stakeholders: A Present and Future Challenge," *Academy of Management Executive*, May 2004, pp. 114–120; and C. J. Robertson and W. F. Crittenden, "Mapping Moral Philosophies: Strategic Implications for Multinational Firms," *Strategic Management Journal*, April 2003, pp. 385–392.
61. United Nations Global Compact, website, http://www.unglobalcompact.org/ParticipantsAndStakeholders/index.html, February 28, 2016.
62. Organization for Economic Cooperation and Development, "OECD Convention on Combating Bribery of Foreign Public Officials in International Business Transactions," www.oecd.org, April 21, 2014.
63. P. Rudegeair, "Los Angeles Sues Wells Fargo Over Sales Tactics," *The Wall Street Journal* online, www.wsj.com, May 5, 2015.
64. Enron example taken from P. M. Lencioni, "Make Your Values Mean Something," *Harvard Business Review*, July 2002, p. 113;.
65. B. Starr, "Army Officers Routinely Lie and Deceive, Study Finds," www.cnn.com, February 2, 2015.
66. "The United States Army–Army Values," www.army.mil/values/, accessed February 21, 2016.
67. B. Roberts, "Your Cheating Heart," *HR Magazine*, June 2011, pp. 55–60.
68. J. R. Edwards and D. M. Cable, "The Value of Value Congruence," *Journal of Applied Psychology*, May 2009, pp. 654–677; and Treviño and Youngblood, "Bad Apples in Bad Barrels," p. 384.

69. "LRN Global Ethics Survey," March 6, 2015 to March 11, 2015.
70. P. Van Lee, L. Fabish, and N. McCaw, "The Value of Corporate Values," *Strategy & Business,* Summer 2005, pp. 52–65.
71. "LRN Global Ethics Survey," March 6, 2015 to March 11, 2015.
72. F. O. Walumba and J. Schaubroeck, "Leader Personality Traits and Employee Voice Behavior: Mediating Roles of Ethical Leadership and Work Group Psychological Safety," *Journal of Applied Psychology,* September 2009, pp. 1275–1286; G. Weaver, "Ethics and Employees: Making the Connection," May 2004; G. Weaver, L. K. Treviño, and P. L. Cochran, "Integrated and Decoupled Corporate Social Performance: Management Commitments, External Pressures, and Corporate Ethics Practices," *Academy of Management Journal*, October 1999, pp. 539–552; G. R. Weaver, L. K. Treviño, and P. L. Cochran, "Corporate Ethics Programs as Control Systems: Influences of Executive Commitment and Environmental Factors," *Academy of Management Journal*, February 1999, pp. 41–57; R. B. Morgan, "Self- and Co-Worker Perceptions of Ethics and Their Relationships to Leadership and Salary," *Academy of Management Journal*, February 1993, pp. 200–214; and B. Z. Posner and W. H. Schmidt, "Values and the American Manager: An Update," *California Management Review*, Spring 1984, pp. 202–216.
73. S. Dockery, "Regulators' Emphasis on 'Culture' Spurs Hunt to Measure It," *The Wall Street Journal* online, www.wsj.com, February 4, 2016.
74. Ibid.
75. National Business Ethics Survey of the U.S. Workforce, 2013, *Ethics Resource Center*, www.ethics.org, March, 2014.
76. Ibid.
77. S. Watkins, "Set Example, Train Employees to Build Ethical Culture," investors.com, February 28, 2013.
78. IBM Corporate Responsibility Report, 2007, www.ibm.com; and A. Schultz, "Integrating IBM," *CRO,* March/April 2007, pp. 16–21.
79. K. Bart, "UBS Lays Out Employee Ethics Code," *Wall Street Journal* online, www.wsj.com, January 12, 2010; J. L. Lunsford, "Transformer in Transition," *Wall Street Journal,* May 17, 2007, pp. B1+; and J. S. McClenahen, "UTC's Master of Principle," *Industry Week,* January 2003, pp. 30–36.
80. M. Weinstein, "Survey Says: Ethics Training Works," *Training,* November 2005, p. 15.
81. J. E. Fleming, "Codes of Ethics for Global Corporations," *Academy of Management News,* June 2005, p. 4.
82. "Corporate Codes of Ethics Spread," *Ethics Newsline*, www .globalethics.org, October 12, 2009; "Global Ethics Codes Gain Importance as a Tool to Avoid Litigation and Fines," *Wall Street Journal*, August 19, 1999, p. A1; and J. Alexander, "On the Right Side," *World Business*, January/February 1997, pp. 38–41.
83. F. R. David, "An Empirical Study of Codes of Business Ethics: A Strategic Perspective," paper presented at the 48th Annual Academy of Management Conference, August 1988, Anaheim, California.
84. National Business Ethics Survey of the U.S. Workforce, 2013, *Ethics Resource Center*, www.ethics.org, March, 2014.
85. J. B. Singh, "Determinants of the Effectiveness of Corporate Codes of Ethics: An Empirical Study," *Journal of Business Ethics,* July 2011, pp. 385–395; P. M. Erwin, "Corporate Codes of Conduct: The Effects of Code Content and Quality on Ethical Performance," *Journal of Business Ethics,* April 2011, pp. 535–548; "Codes of Conduct," Center for Ethical Business Cultures, www.cebcglobal.org, February 15, 2006; L. Paine, R. Deshpande, J. D. Margolis, and K. E. Bettcher, "Up to Code: Does Your Company's Conduct Meet World-Class Standards"; and A. K. Reichert and M. S. Webb, "Corporate Support for Ethical and Environmental Policies: A Financial Management Perspective," *Journal of Business Ethics,* May 2000.
86. L-M. Eleftheriou-Smith, "Apple's Tim Cook: 'Business Isn't Just About Making Profit,'" *Independent* online, www.independent. co.uk, March 2, 2014; and P. Elmer-Dewitt, "Apple's Tim Cook Picks a Fight with Climate Change Deniers," *Fortune* online www .tech.fortune.com, March 1, 2014.
87. V. Wessler, "Integrity and Clogged Plumbing," *Straight to the Point,* newsletter of VisionPoint Corporation, Fall 2002, pp. 1–2.
88. National Business Ethics Survey of the U.S. Workforce, 2013, Ethics Resource Center, www.ethics.org/nbes, 2014.
89. T. A. Gavin, "Ethics Education," *Internal Auditor*, April 1989, pp. 54–57.
90. L. Myyry and K. Helkama, "The Role of Value Priorities and Professional Ethics Training in Moral Sensitivity," *Journal of Moral Education,* 2002, vol. 31, no. 1, pp. 35–50; W. Penn and B. D. Collier, "Current Research in Moral Development as a Decision Support System," *Journal of Business Ethics*, January 1985, pp. 131–136.
91. J. A. Byrne, "After Enron: The Ideal Corporation," *Business Week,* August 19, 2002, pp. 68–71; D. Rice and C. Dreilinger, "Rights and Wrongs of Ethics Training," *Training & Development Journal,* May 1990, pp. 103–109; and J. Weber, "Measuring the Impact of Teaching Ethics to Future Managers: A Review, Assessment, and Recommendations," *Journal of Business Ethics*, April 1990, pp. 182–190.
92. E. White, "What Would You Do? Ethics Courses Get Context," *Wall Street Journal,* June 12, 2006, p. B3; and D. Zielinski, "The Right Direction: Can Ethics Training Save Your Company," *Training,* June 2005, pp. 27–32.
93. G. Farrell and J. O'Donnell, "Ethics Training as Taught by Ex-Cons: Crime Doesn't Pay," *USA Today,* November 16, 2005, p. 1B+.
94. "Survey Reveals How Many Workers Commit Office Taboos," *Ethics Newsline*, www.globalethics.org, September 18, 2007.
95. A. Fisher, "U.S. Retail Workers Lead the World in Theft from Employers," *Fortune* online, www.fortune.com, January 26, 2015.
96. C. Hausman, "Men Are Less Ethical than Women, Claims Researcher," *Ethics Newsline,* www.globaletehics.org/newsline, June 25, 2012; and C. May, "When Men Are Less Moral than Women," ScientificAmerican.com, June 19, 2012.
97. N. Darling, "Why You Lied to Your Parents (and What They Really Knew)," *Psychology Today*, www.psychologytoday.com, April 19, 2015.
98. "China Uses Drone to Catch Cheaters on College Entrance Exams," CBS News online, www.cbsnews.com, June 8, 2015.
99. Pei Li and Alyssa Abkowitz, "Over the Moon: Alibaba Engineers Fired for Mooncake Hacking." *Wall Street Journal*, September 14, 2016, http://blogs.wsj.com/chinarealtime/2016/09/14/over-the-moon-alibaba-engineers-fired-for-mooncake-hacking/ (accessed December 16, 2016); "Alibaba Fires Employees for Mooncake Fraud," *AsiaOne*, September 14, 2016, http://news.asiaone.com/news/asia/alibaba-fires-employees-mooncake-fraud (accessed December 16, 2016).
100. S. S. Wiltermuth and F. J. Flynn, "Power, Moral Clarity, and Punishment in the Workplace," *Academy of Management Journal,* August 2013, pp. 1002–1023; M. Crossnan, D. Mazutis, G. Seijts, and J. Gandz, "Developing Leadership Character in Business Programs," *Academy of Management Learning and Education,* June 2013, pp. 285–305; D. M. Mayer, K. Aquino, R. L. Greenbaum, and M. Kuenze, "Who Displays Ethical Leadership, and Why Does It Matter? An Examination of Antecedents and Consequences of Ethical Leadership," *Academy of Management Journal,* February 2012, pp. 151–171; and F. O. Walumbwa, D. M. Mayer, P. Wang, H. Wang, K. Workman, and A. L. Christensen,

"Linking Ethical Leadership to Employee Performance: The Roles of Leader-Member Exchange, Self-Efficacy, and Organizational Identification," *Organizational Behavior & Human Decision Processes,* July 2011, pp. 204–213.

101. W. Zellner, "A Hero—and a Smoking-Gun Letter," *Business Week,* January 28, 2002, pp. 34–35.
102. *National Business Ethics Survey* (Arlington, VA: Ethics Resource Center, 2007).
103. J. B. Stewart, "He Was a JPMorgan Chase Whistle-Blower. Then Came the Blowback," *New York Times* online, www.nytimes.com, December 1, 2015.
104. R. Bell, "Blowing the Whistle, Blowing Your Career?," *Workforce,* December 2013, p. 12; and A. Fredin, "The Unexpected Cost of Staying Silent," *Strategic Finance,* April 2012, pp. 53–59.
105. S. Armour, "More Companies Urge Workers to Blow the Whistle," *USA Today,* December 16, 2002, p. 1B.
106. J. Wiscombe, "Don't Fear Whistleblowers," *Workforce,* July 2002, pp. 26–27.
107. "ERC Releases New Research: Reporting Improves with a Procedurally Just Process," Ethics Resource Center, www.ethics .org, May 30, 2013.
108. J. R. Emshwiller, "Settlement Reached in Hanford Whistleblower Suit," *Wall Street Journal* online, www.wsj.com, August 13, 2015.
109. T. Reason, "Whistle Blowers: The Untouchables," *CFO,* March 2003, p. 18; and C. Lachnit, "Muting the Whistle-Blower?," *Workforce,* September 2002, p. 18.
110. R. Warner, "The 'Do Whatever It Takes' Attitude Gone Wrong," *Huffington Post* online, www.huffingtonpost.com, July 20, 2015.
111. K. Flynn, "A New Pursuit for Social Entrepreneurship: Profits," *Forbes* online, www.forbes.com, June 20, 2014.
112. This definition based on P. Tracey and N. Phillips, "The Distinctive Challenge of Educating Social Entrepreneurs: A Postscript and Rejoinder to the Special Issue on Entrepreneurship Education," *Academy of Management Learning & Education,* June 2007, pp. 264–271; Schwab Foundation for Social Entrepreneurship, www.schwabfound.org, February 20, 2006; and J. G. Dees, J. Emerson, and P. Economy, *Strategic Tools for Social Entrepreneurs* (New York: John Wiley & Sons, Inc., 2002).
113. P. Margulies, "Linda Rottenberg's High-Impact Endeavor," *Strategy + Business Online,* Spring 2012; S. Moran, "Some Ways to Get Started as a Social Entrepreneur," *New York Times* online, www.nytimes.com, June 22, 2011; P. A. Dacin, M. T. Dacin, and M. Matear, "Social Entrepreneurship: Why We Don't Need a New Theory and How We Move Forward From Here," *Academy of Management Perspective,* August 2010, pp. 37–57; and D. Bornstein, *How to Change the World: Social Entrepreneurs and the Power of New Ideas* (New York: Oxford University Press, 2004), inside cover jacket.
114. N. Wingfield, "Microsoft to Donate $1 Billion in Cloud Services to Nonprofits and Researchers," *New York Times* online, www .nytimes.com, January 19, 2016.
115. K. H. Hammonds, "Now the Good News," *Fast Company,* December 2007/January 2008, pp. 110–121; C. Dahle, "Filling the Void," *Fast Company,* January/February 2006, pp. 54–57; and see PATH, website, www.path.org.
116. R. J. Bies, J. M. Bartunek, T. L. Fort, and M. N. Zald, "Corporations as Social Change Agents: Individual, Interpersonal, Institutional, and Environmental Dynamics," *Academy of Management Review,* July 2007, pp. 788–793.
117. "The State of Corporate Philanthropy: A McKinsey Global Survey," *The McKinsey Quarterly* online, www.mckinsey.com, February 2008.
118. R. Nixon, The Associated Press, "Bottom Line for (Red)," *New York Times* online, www.nytimes.com, February 6, 2008; and G. Mulvihill, "Despite Cause, Not Everyone Tickled Pink by Campaign," *Springfield News-Leader,* October 15, 2007, p. 2E.
119. Giving in Numbers: 2015 Edition, Committee Encouraging Corporate Philanthropy, http://cecp.co/research.html.
120. "A Better World, Faster," Google.org, website, https://www .google.org, accessed February 28, 2016.
121. "Giving Around the World: 2015 Edition," CECP, http://cecp.co/.
122. A. Tergesen, "Doing Good to Do Well," *Wall Street Journal,* January 9, 2012, p. B7.
123. *Giving in Numbers: 2015 Edition*, Committee Encouraging Corporate Philanthropy, available at http://cecp.co/research.html.
124. Skills Exercise based on F. Bartolome, "Nobody Trusts the Boss Completely—Now What?," *Harvard Business Review*, March–April 1989, pp. 135–142; and J. K. Butler Jr., "Toward Understanding and Measuring Conditions of Trust: Evolution of a Condition of Trust Inventory," *Journal of Management*, September 1991, pp. 643–663.
125. Case written by Marcello Russo, Assistant Professor, Rouen Business School, France; Saiqa Chaudhari, "Horwich school gets new state-of-the-art gym," *The Bolton News*, November 18, 2014; "The Wellness Foundation" Web site, [www.wellnessfoundation. it]; Data: Special Eurobarometer 334, conducted by TNS Opinion & Social, survey co-ordinated by Directorate General Communication; "Sport and Physical Activity," European Commission, March 2010 [http://ec.europa.eu/public_opinion/ archives/ebs/ebs_334_en.pdf]

Chapter 6 Managing Change

It's Your Career

Source: 13ree.design/Shutterstock

A key to success in management and in your career is knowing how to manage your stress.

Learning to Manage Your Stress

Are you stressed? Frequently stressed? With all the projects, deadlines, and pressure to get good grades, school can be an obvious source of stress. But the workplace can be (and will be!) just as stressful. Here are some statistics about workplace stress that will make you sit up and take notice: The average employee has 30 to 100 projects going on simultaneously; employees are interrupted seven times an hour and are distracted some 2.1 hours in a workday; and 40 percent of adults say that stressful events keep them awake at night.[1] It's no wonder we feel continually stressed. However, as you'll see later in this chapter, too much stress can have adverse consequences on your physical, emotional, and psychological well-being. That's why learning how to manage your stress is an important skill. Here are some suggestions for managing your stress:

*1. **Know your stress triggers.** What produces the stress you face? Keep a record for a couple of weeks of situations, events, and people linked to the stress you're feeling. What's causing the most stress and how are you responding to it? Is it someone who continually changes deadlines or expectations? Is it someone who doesn't do what they had promised to do? Is it continual interruptions or persistent noise? Examining your stress triggers may expose obvious sources of stress and may also highlight subtle but persistent causes of stress. Keeping a record of this can help you identify patterns and similarities in your stressors and how you react to them.*

*2. **Develop healthy responses.** Reduce stress by making healthy choices when you feel stress coming on. Alcohol, fast food, smoking, or continual snacking may help you feel better temporarily, but are probably not the healthiest choices you can make. Likewise, working long hours to finish a project might make you feel in control, but sleep deprivation can leave you vulnerable to even more stress. Also, when you're stressed by*

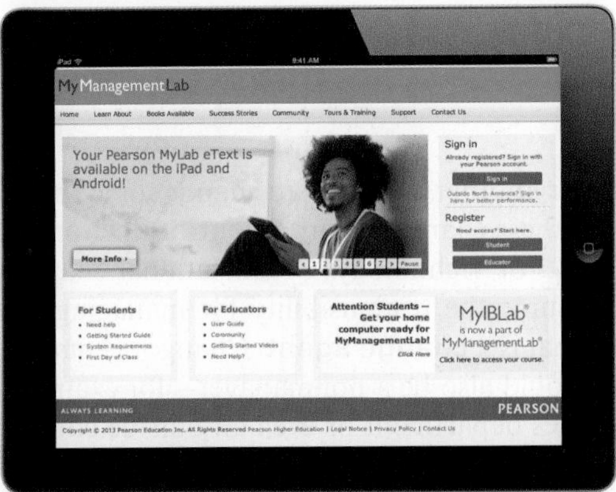

Pearson MyLab Management®

Improve Your Grade!

When you see this icon, visit **www.mymanagementlab.com** for activities that are applied, personalized, and offer immediate feedback.

Learning Objectives

• SKILL OUTCOMES

***6.1 Describe** making the case for change.*

***6.2 Compare** and contrast views on the change process.*

***6.3 Classify** areas of organizational change.*

***6.4 Explain** how to manage change.*

- **Know how** to be change ready by overcoming your resistance to change.

***6.5 Discuss** contemporary issues in managing change.*

- **Develop your skill** in change management so you can serve as a catalyst for change.

***6.6 Describe** techniques for stimulating innovation.*

***6.7 Explain** why managing disruptive innovation is important.*

---

time constraints, it's easy to skip physical activity (exercise), but regular exercise is a powerful stress reliever. Even short periods of exercise, which might be easier to fit into your schedule, can be beneficial.

***3. Establish boundaries.** Our 24/7 digital world can be—and is—overwhelming. That's why you have to really fight the urge to keep checking your devices. But it's important to establish those boundaries if you're trying to manage your stress so you can be at your optimum best, whatever you're doing. Commit to perhaps not checking your email from home in the evening or putting your phone on silent while spending time with your friends or partner. Create some boundaries between your work (or school) life and your personal life.*

***4. Improve time management skills.** Take a look back at Chapter 1's* It's Your Career *chapter opener. Improving your time management skills can help you feel less overwhelmed and out of control.*

In today's world, big companies and small businesses, universities and colleges, state and city governments, and even the military are forced to be innovative. Although innovation has always been a part of the manager's job, it has become even more important in recent years. In this chapter, we'll describe why innovation is important, how managers can manage innovation, and the impact of disruptive innovation. Because innovation is often closely tied to an organization's change efforts, let's start by looking at change and how managers manage change.

THE CASE for change

organizational change
Any alteration of people, structure, or technology in an organization

change agent
Someone who acts as a catalyst and assumes the responsibility for managing the change process

LO6.1 Most managers, at one point or another, will have to change some things in their workplace. We classify these changes as **organizational change**, which is any alteration of people, structure, or technology. Organizational changes need someone to act as a catalyst and assume the responsibility for managing the change process, as our opener described—that is a **change agent**. Change agents can be a manager within the organization but could also be a nonmanager—for example, a change specialist from the human resources department or even an outside consultant.[2] For major changes, an organization often hires outside consultants to provide advice and assistance. Because they're from the outside, they can provide an objective perspective that insiders may lack. But outside consultants have a limited understanding of the organization's history, culture, operating procedures, and people. They're also more likely to initiate drastic change than insiders because they don't have to live with the repercussions after the change is implemented. In contrast, internal managers may be more thoughtful, but possibly overcautious, because they must live with the consequences of their decisions.

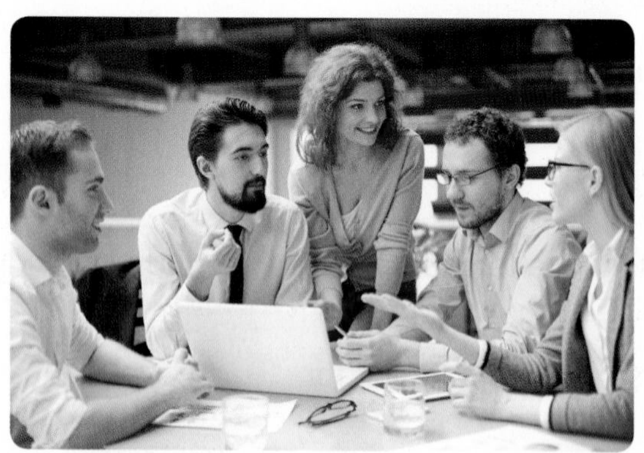

Managers serve as effective change agents because they have a good understanding of their organization's history, culture, procedures, employees, and customers. They act as catalysts in initiating change, lead and manage the change process, and develop plans to implement change.
Source: Pressmaster/Shutterstock

Managers at the Ford Motor Company are taking on the role of change agent. Making changes has become necessary as peoples' needs and preferences for travel are shifting. The company recently conducted a series of experiments to better understand customers' and prospective customers' needs and preferences.[3] Ford's experiments revealed differences in how members of the younger generation prefer to get around compared to members of older generations. As a result, Ford is broadening its scope from selling cars and trucks to include car-sharing services, offering foldable electric bikes that can be charged while in the vehicle, and an app that determines the best mode of transportation to a destination (for example, driving part of the way, then, riding a bike for the remainder). Needless to say, the company has had to make some organizational changes as it has entered into the business of providing alternative transportation modes. Ford's managers are doing what managers everywhere must do—implementing change.

If it weren't for change, a manager's job would be relatively easy. Planning would be simple because tomorrow would be no different from today. The issue of effective organizational design would also be resolved because the environment would not be uncertain and there would be no need to redesign the structure. Similarly, decision making would be dramatically streamlined because the outcome of each alternative could be predicted with almost certain accuracy. But that's not the way it is. Change is an organizational reality.[4] Organizations face change because external and internal factors create the forces for change (see Exhibit 6-1). Let's review major external and internal factors associated with change.

Exhibit 6-1
External and Internal Forces for Change

External

- Changing consumer needs and wants
- New governmental laws
- Changing technology
- Economic changes

Internal

- New organizational strategy
- Change in composition of workforce
- New equipment
- Changing employee attitudes

External Factors

CHANGING CONSUMER NEEDS AND WANTS Ford Motor Company understands the importance of being responsive to its customers. The company's experiments will also enable them to attract a new breed of customers, helping to secure the company's future. But sometimes a company may make changes that fail to meet customer preferences. Burger King recently learned that lesson by rapidly expanding its menu with items that were not popular with its customers. It had to drop its lower calorie fries called "Satisfries" and its apple cranberry salads after one year because of poor sales. Burger King's president Jose Cil admitted "it's not what our guests were looking for."[5]

NEW GOVERNMENTAL LAWS Government laws require changes in how managers must conduct business. Five broad categories of governmental laws include truth-in-advertising, employment and labor fair practices, environmental protection, privacy, and safety and health. For example, in Singapore, where some employers have difficulty filling jobs because of legal restrictions on foreign workers, the government offers subsidies for testing robots in the workplace. Now the Chilli Padi Nonya Café is one of several restaurants to test a robot in the dining room. In China, businesses managers must pay close attention to changing employment laws affecting the minimum wage and open-ended labor contracts, among other factors.[6]

CHANGING TECHNOLOGY What do the Chevrolet Volt and the Tesla Motors Model S have in common? Both are examples of electric-powered vehicles. Compared to gas-powered vehicles, electric cars have shorter driving ranges; however, ongoing research and development into improving battery capacity to extend their range is a high priority. While most electric vehicles rely on lithium-ion batteries, Toyota and Volkswagen are considering alternatives, including solid state batteries, in order to extend driving ranges.[8]

- 78 percent of U.S. chief executive officers are concerned that overregulation represents threats to their companies' growth prospects.[7]

ECONOMIC CHANGES Managers must respond to changes in economic forces. Consider the impact of an economic recession. According to the U.S. Bureau of Labor Statistics, recessions are characterized by a general slowdown in economic activity, a downturn in the business cycle, and a reduction in the amount of goods and services produced and sold.[9] The so-called Great Recession (2007–2009) was considered to be one of the more severe recessions felt worldwide. In the United States, the unemployment rate jumped from 5 percent to 10.8 percent. In response, executives in many organizations sought to protect profits by cutting costs, which often included mass employee layoffs. Although unavoidable, these management practices contributed to the severity of the recession because unemployed individuals are less able to purchase discretionary goods and services. Ironically, the increase in unemployment and subsequent drop in sales often led management to implement further cost-cutting practices.

Economic changes, of course, are not limited to the U.S. context. Forecasts for slower economic growth in China have prompted China's Labor Ministry to call for "steady and cautious control" over minimum wage increases.[10] The rationale behind this practice is to help companies manage rising labor costs. With these actions come long-term risks: Chinese consumers' ability to purchase many goods and services will likely diminish and companies will have to consider additional cost-cutting methods such as reductions in hiring.

Internal Factors

NEW ORGANIZATIONAL STRATEGY For decades, Walgreens' strategy focused on increasing its number of retail stores. In most cities, you can find multiple Walgreens stores located just a couple of miles apart. The costs of maintaining so many stores are substantial, putting downward pressures on profit levels. Company management reconsidered its strategy of adding stores. In its place, the company refocused its strategy to improving the customer service experience and providing more competitive product pricing. The latter became necessary particularly as large retailers like Walmart offer prescription medication and similar nonprescription items at a price advantage.

CHANGE IN COMPOSITION OF WORKFORCE Through the decades, the U.S. workforce has become more diverse. In Chapter 3, we saw the challenges managers face when managing a workforce that is diverse based on surface-level variables, including age and race, as well as deep-level variables, including differences in values, personality, and work preferences. A key challenge entails orchestrating these differences to maintain an inclusive culture that focuses on productivity.

Architectural design firms benefit from new 3-D printing equipment by dramatically reducing the time it takes to create hand-made building models. Invented by Charles Hull, the equipment produces accurate, highly detailed, and full-color physical 3-D models printed from digital data that help architects, contractors, and clients envision building projects.
Source: MBI/Alamy Stock Photo

NEW EQUIPMENT In 1983, American engineer Charles Hull invented the first three-dimensional (3D) printer, which is based on the technology of transforming liquid polymers into solid objects.[11] Only recently has this technology become highly refined. Now, more and more companies are using 3D printers to create product prototypes. For example, the medical industry more easily creates customized prosthetics and implants.[12] And, Apple uses 3D printer technology to create the casings for its laptops.

Technological changes are particularly making their marks on health care. These technologies include advances in genomics, biotechnology, robotics, connected care, and artificial intelligence. Advances in robotic technology, for example, is changing how surgeons perform some surgical procedures. As a case in point, the world-renowned Cleveland Clinic offers robotically assisted heart surgery. This technology enables cardiothoracic surgeons to use computer consoles to control surgical instruments and minimize the invasiveness of some surgeries.

CHANGING EMPLOYEE ATTITUDES A recent survey revealed that the attitudes of employees at organizations going through significant changes tend to be less favorable than at more stable companies.[13] Where change is happening, the largest differences are in attitudes toward company leadership and company image. But, not all employees in changing organizations have less favorable attitudes. Those who prefer stability are less likely to try new technology or embrace change than employees who are open to change. Changing attitudes challenge managers to adopt methods to support employees through organizational changes.

THE CHANGE **process**

LO6.2 Two very different metaphors can be used to describe the change process.[14] One metaphor envisions the organization as a large ship crossing a calm sea. The ship's captain and crew know exactly where they're going because they've made the trip many times before. Change comes in the form of an occasional storm, a brief distraction in an otherwise calm and predictable trip. In this calm waters metaphor, change is seen as an occasional disruption in the normal flow of events. In another metaphor, the organization is seen as a small raft navigating a raging river with uninterrupted white-water rapids. Aboard the raft are half a dozen people who have never worked together before, who are totally unfamiliar with the river, who are unsure of their eventual destination, and who, as if things weren't bad enough, are traveling at night. In the white-water rapids metaphor, change is normal and expected and managing it is a continual process. These two metaphors present very different approaches to understanding and responding to change. Let's take a closer look at each one.

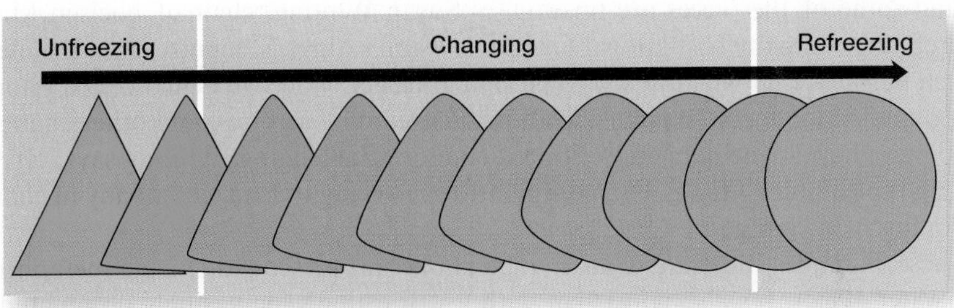

Exhibit 6-2
The Three-Step Change Process

Calm Waters Versus White-Water Rapids Metaphors

THE CALM WATERS METAPHOR At one time, the calm waters metaphor was fairly descriptive of the situation managers faced. It's best understood by using Kurt Lewin's three-step change process.[15] (See Exhibit 6-2.)

According to Lewin, successful change can be planned and requires *unfreezing* the status quo, *changing* to a new state, and *refreezing* to make the change permanent. The status quo is considered equilibrium. To move away from this equilibrium, unfreezing is necessary. Unfreezing can be thought of as preparing for the needed change. It can be done by increasing the *driving forces,* which are forces pushing for change; by decreasing the *restraining forces*, which are forces that resist change; or by combining the two approaches.

Once unfreezing is done, the change itself can be implemented. However, merely introducing change doesn't ensure that it will take hold. The new situation needs to be *refrozen* so that it can be sustained over time. Unless this last step is done, there's a strong chance that employees will revert back to the old equilibrium state—that is, the old ways of doing things. The objective of refreezing, then, is to stabilize the new situation by reinforcing the new behaviors.

Lewin's three-step process treats change as a move away from the organization's current equilibrium state. It's a calm waters scenario where an occasional disruption (a "storm") means planning and implementing change to deal with the disruption. Once the disruption has been dealt with, however, things continue on under the new changed situation. This type of environment isn't what most managers face today. Still, we can find some illustrations of the calm water metaphor, for instance, the 2015 Germanwings Airlines plane crash. The copilot of a Germanwings international flight from Barcelona–El Prat Airport in Spain to Düsseldorf Airport in Germany intentionally crashed the plane into a mountain, killing all passengers and crew members. The captain left the cockpit for a short period. When he tried to re-enter the cockpit using a security code, he quickly learned that the copilot disabled this security measure using cockpit controls. Civil aviation authorities in several countries, including Australia, Germany, and New Zealand, responded to this tragic disruption by implementing new rules that require two crewmembers to be present in the cockpit of commercial aircraft at all times. Germanwings immediately complied with this ruling and continued to operate flights.

David Newman is the director of the new Target Technology Innovation Center in San Francisco. Target competes in a white-water rapids environment where major changes in technology and shopping behavior continue to reshape retailing. Newman and his team of innovators study evolving technologies and interactive devices to improve Target's performance and customers' shopping experiences online and in stores.
Source: Jeff Chiu/AP Images

WHITE-WATER RAPIDS METAPHOR An expert on weather patterns has said, "There are some times when you can predict weather well for the next 15 days. Other times, you can only really forecast a couple of days. Sometimes you can't predict the next two hours." Today's business climate is turning out to be a lot like that two-hour weather scenario. "The pace of change in our economy and our culture is accelerating and our visibility about the future is declining."[16]

As senior vice president and general manager of Connected Energy, a unit of Cisco, Laura Ipsen's company works on developing energy ecosystems for the smart-grid market. She describes her job as follows, "My job is like having to put together a 1,000-piece puzzle, but I don't have the box top with the picture of what it looks like, and some of the pieces are missing."[17] Susan Whiting, chair of Nielsen Media Research, the company best known for its television ratings, recognizes that the media research business isn't what it used to be. The Internet, video on demand, cell phones, iPads, digital video recorders, music and news streaming services, and other changing technologies have made data collection much more challenging. Whiting says, "If you look at a typical week I have, it's a combination of trying to lead a company in change in an industry in change."[18]

These examples illustrate what change is like in our second change metaphor—white-water rapids. It's also consistent with a world that's increasingly dominated by information, ideas, and knowledge.[19]

Here's what managing change might be like for you in a white-water rapids environment. The college you're attending has the following rules: Courses vary in length. When you sign up, you don't know how long a course will run. It might go for 2 weeks or 15 weeks. Furthermore, the instructor can end a course at any time with no prior warning. If that isn't challenging enough, the length of the class changes each time it meets: Sometimes the class lasts 20 minutes; other times it runs for 3 hours. And the time of the next class meeting is set by the instructor during this class. There's one more thing: All exams are unannounced, so you have to be ready for a test at any time. To succeed in this type of environment, you'd have to respond quickly to changing conditions. Students who are overly structured or uncomfortable with change wouldn't succeed.

Increasingly, managers are realizing that their job is much like what a student would face in such a college. The stability and predictability of the calm waters metaphor don't exist. Disruptions in the status quo are not occasional and temporary, and they are not followed by a return to calm waters. Many managers never get out of the rapids.

Is the white-water rapids metaphor an exaggeration? Probably not! Although you'd expect a chaotic and dynamic environment in high-tech industries, even organizations in non-high-tech industries are faced with constant change. Take the case of Dunkin' Donuts. You might think that the food and beverage industry couldn't be all that complex—after all, coffee and baked goods such as donuts and bagels appear to be fairly uncomplicated—but that impression would be wrong. Dunkin' Donuts management has had several challenges to confront.[20] First, there's the challenge of developing products that will appeal to a wide range of global customers. For instance, the company has had to adjust its menu to appeal to its customers in other countries. For example, you can get a kai young donut in Thailand, which is a donut topped with dried, shredded chicken and Thai chili paste. Second, the company is struggling with increased operating costs due to the rising minimum wage in some parts of the United States, particularly in New York City where the rate is rising from $10.50 to $15.00 in 2018. This increase will translate into a 71 percent increase in the cost of employee compensation.[21] Third, slow customer service has been a concern. Management has responded by organizing prep stations to be more efficient to meet on-the-go morning schedules.[22]

Today, any organization that treats change as the occasional disturbance in an otherwise calm and stable world runs a great risk. Too much is changing too fast for an organization or its managers to be complacent. It's no longer business as usual. And managers must be ready to efficiently and effectively manage the changes facing their organization or their work area.

Reactive versus Proactive Change Processes

As students, you have taken many tests. Now think about a difficult course that you have taken and the experiences of your classmates taking the same class. Most students find the material to be difficult and they're concerned about performing poorly on the midterm exam. We might see two types of behavior patterns emerge. One group might go through the course struggling with the material in silence. They do nothing about it and later perform poorly on the midterm exam. Only after receiving the poor grade do they ask their professor for guidance to help them prepare for the final exam. These students are *reacting* to a situation (difficult course material).

Another group of students takes the initiative right away when they realize the material is difficult to master. These students visit the professor during her office hours, participate in a study group, and work on practice problem sets together. This group of students has initiated preparation well ahead of the midterm exam, and represents an example of a *proactive* change process. We can find these same patterns in organizations. The civil aviation authorities illustrate a reactive change process in direct response to the Germanwings crash, and the Ford Motor Company's experiments describe a proactive change process.

AREAS **of change**

LO6.3 Have you seen (or used) the 3M Co.'s Command picture-hanging hooks (which can actually be used to hang many different items)? They're an easy-to-use, relatively simple product consisting of plastic hooks and sticky foam strips. The manufacturing process, however, was far from simple. The work used to be done in four different states and take 100 days. However, a couple of years ago, the company's former CEO decided to start "untangling its hairballs" by streamlining complex and complicated production processes. Needless to say, a lot of changes had to take place. Today, those Command products are produced at a consolidated production "hub" in a third less time.[23] 3M Co. was up for the "hairball" challenge and focused its change efforts on its people and processes.

Managers face four main areas of change: strategy, structure, technology, and people (see Exhibit 6-3). Changing *strategy* signifies a change in how managers ensure the success of the company. Changing *structure* includes any change in structural variables such as reporting relationships, coordination mechanisms, employee empowerment, or job redesign. Changing *technology* encompasses modifications in the way work is performed or the methods and equipment that are used. Changing *people* refers to changes in attitudes, expectations, perceptions, and behavior of individuals or groups.

Exhibit 6-3
Four Types of Change

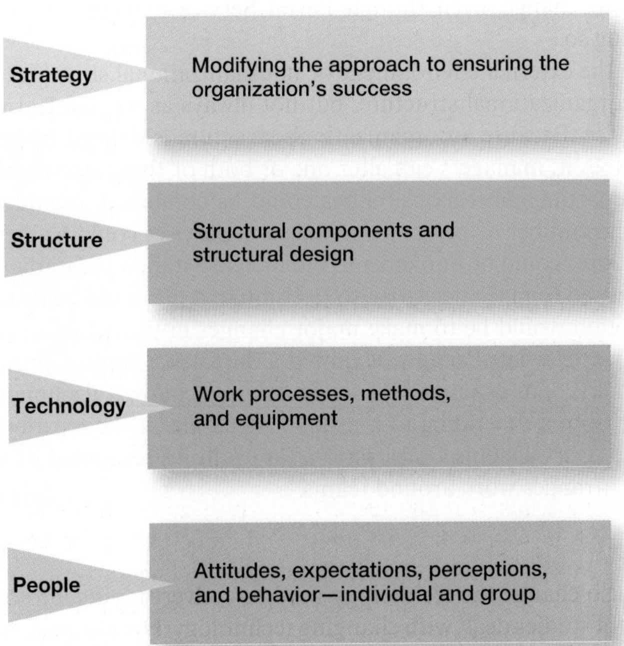

Strategy

Failure to change strategy when circumstances dictate could undermine a company's success. Let's consider the example of Ryanair, which is a regional airline based in Europe. Just more than 30 years old, the airline started out with a strategy to differentiate itself from the competition by offering low-cost airfares. Lower fares came with spartan cabin décor, hefty fees for baggage handling, snacks, and the use of the restroom facilities while onboard. The airline developed a poor reputation for customer service. It was a case of the customer almost never being right! Through the years, this strategy proved to undermine the airline's reputation and financial performance because of competitors who didn't skimp on amenities. With new, aggressive competitors, the company realized that a change in strategy was essential. At the center of the new strategy was raising customer service quality, including cutting out many extra fees. Michael O'Leary, Ryanair's CEO admitted: "If I had only known that being nicer to our customers was good for business I would have done it years ago."[24] Had the company maintained its original strategy, Ryanair probably would no longer exist.

Structure

Jin Zhiguo, chairman of China's Tsingtao Brewery, understands how important structural change can be. When the company shifted from a government-run company to a market-led company, many changes had to take place. He says, "Having worked for a state-owned enterprise, our people weren't used to competing for jobs or to being replaced for performance."[25] The change from a bureaucratic and risk-averse company to one that could compete in a global market required structural changes such as decentralizing decision making.

Unfortunately, not all bureaucratic organizations can change easily. For instance, the U.S. Postal Service has been losing substantial amounts of money for years. In fiscal year 2015, the Postal Service reported a $5.1 billion loss, which extends the losing streak to the last nine years. There are many reasons for the Postal Service's poor performance, including the growth of e-mail, competition from package delivery services such as FedEx, and the rapidly growing costs of providing health care to its retirees. The Postal Service's leadership recognizes the need to grow the business, but that's easier said than done. Postmaster General Megan Brennan said, "...we will also need the enactment of legislation that makes our retiree health benefit system affordable and that provides for increased pricing and product flexibility."[26] The influence of labor unions and various government regulations have created an organizational structure that is difficult to change, even though Postal Service management recognizes the necessity of doing so.

Changes in the external environment or in organizational strategies often lead to changes in the organizational structure, but not always as we just learned about the U.S. Postal Service. Because an organization's structure is defined by how work gets done and who does it, managers can alter one or both of these *structural components*. For instance, departmental responsibilities could be combined, organizational levels eliminated, or the number of persons a manager supervises could be increased. More rules and procedures could be implemented to increase standardization. Or employees could be empowered to make decisions so decision making could be faster.

Another option would be to make major changes in the actual *structural design*. For instance, when Hewlett-Packard acquired Compaq Computer, product divisions were dropped, merged, or expanded. Structural design changes also might include, for instance, a shift from a functional to a product structure or the creation of a project structure design. Avery-Dennis Corporation, for example, revamped its structure to a new design that arranges work around teams.

Technology

Managers can also change the technology used to convert inputs into outputs. Most early management studies dealt with changing technology. For instance, scientific management techniques involved implementing changes that would increase production efficiency. Today, technological changes usually involve the introduction of new equipment, tools, or methods; automation; or computerization.

For example, software company Visia Solutions developed a quality assurance program for Ford Motor Company. Assembly workers in Ford's Valencia, Spain, manufacturing facility wear a small device on their wrists that enables them to ensure that vehicle specifications are correct. According to Ford of Europe's manufacturing vice president, "The ability to simply consult a smartphone screen to check any aspect of a vehicle's quality and specification helps to guarantee highest levels of product quality, and improves work processes and manufacturing efficiency."[27]

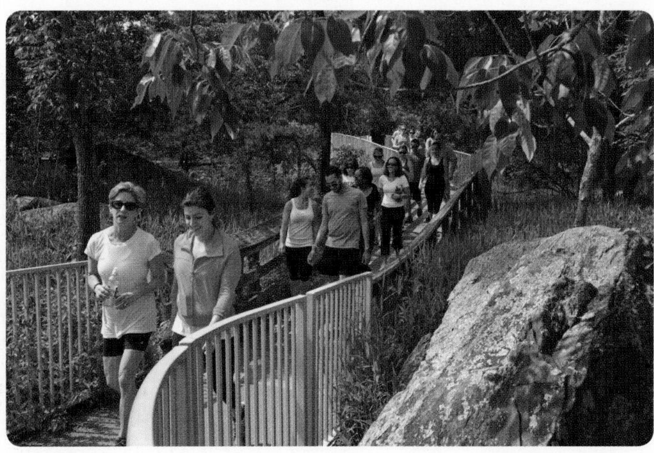

Managers of Wellness Corporate Solutions use employee hikes and group office exercises as organizational development methods to bring about changes in employee attitudes and behaviors regarding physical fitness, nutrition, and mental health. The OD methods help employees learn how other employees think and work and improve the quality of their interpersonal work relationships.
Source: Chikwendiu/The Washington Post/ Getty Images

Automation is a technological change that replaces certain tasks done by people with tasks done by machines. Robotic technology has been incorporated in many business settings. For instance, FANUC America Corporation has developed robotic devices for use in many settings, including manufacturing and warehouse product distribution. Walk through any large home improvement store such as the Home Depot. Did you think that workers piled those dozens of 50-pound bags of cement onto the pallets? Probably not. Robotic equipment placed those bags onto pallets in preparation for shipment to the stores.

The most visible technological changes have come from computerization. Most organizations have sophisticated information systems. For instance, supermarkets and other retailers use scanners that provide instant inventory information and many are starting to accept mobile payments such as Apple Pay and PayPal. Also, most offices are computerized. At BP p.l.c., for example, employees had to learn how to deal with the personal visibility and accountability brought about by an enterprise-wide information system. The integrative nature of this system meant that what any employee did on his or her computer automatically affected other computer systems on the internal network.[28] At the Benetton Group SpA, computers link its manufacturing plants outside Treviso, Italy, with the company's various sales outlets and a highly automated warehouse. Now, product information can be transmitted and shared instantaneously, a real plus in today's environment.[29]

People

Changing people involves changing attitudes, expectations, perceptions, and behaviors—something that's not easy to do. **Organizational development (OD)** is the term used to describe change methods that focus on people and the nature and quality of interpersonal work relationships.[30] The most popular OD techniques are described in Exhibit 6-4. Each seeks to bring about changes in the organization's people and make them work together better. For example, executives at Scotiabank, one of Canada's Big Five banks, knew that the success of a new customer sales and service strategy depended on changing employee attitudes and behaviors. Managers used different OD techniques during the strategic change, including team building, survey feedback, and intergroup development. One indicator of how well these techniques worked in getting people to change was that every branch in Canada implemented the new strategy on or ahead of schedule.[31]

organizational development (OD)
Change methods that focus on people and the nature and quality of interpersonal work relationships

Much of what we know about OD practices has come from North American research. However, managers need to recognize that some techniques that work for U.S. organizations may not be appropriate for organizations or organizational divisions based in other countries.[32] For instance, a study of OD interventions showed that "multirater [survey] feedback as practiced in the United States is not embraced in Taiwan" because the cultural value of "saving face is simply more powerful than the value of receiving feedback from subordinates."[33] What's the lesson for managers? Before using the same OD techniques to implement behavioral changes, especially across different countries, managers need to be sure they've taken into account cultural characteristics and whether the techniques "make sense for the local culture."

Exhibit 6-4
Popular OD Techniques

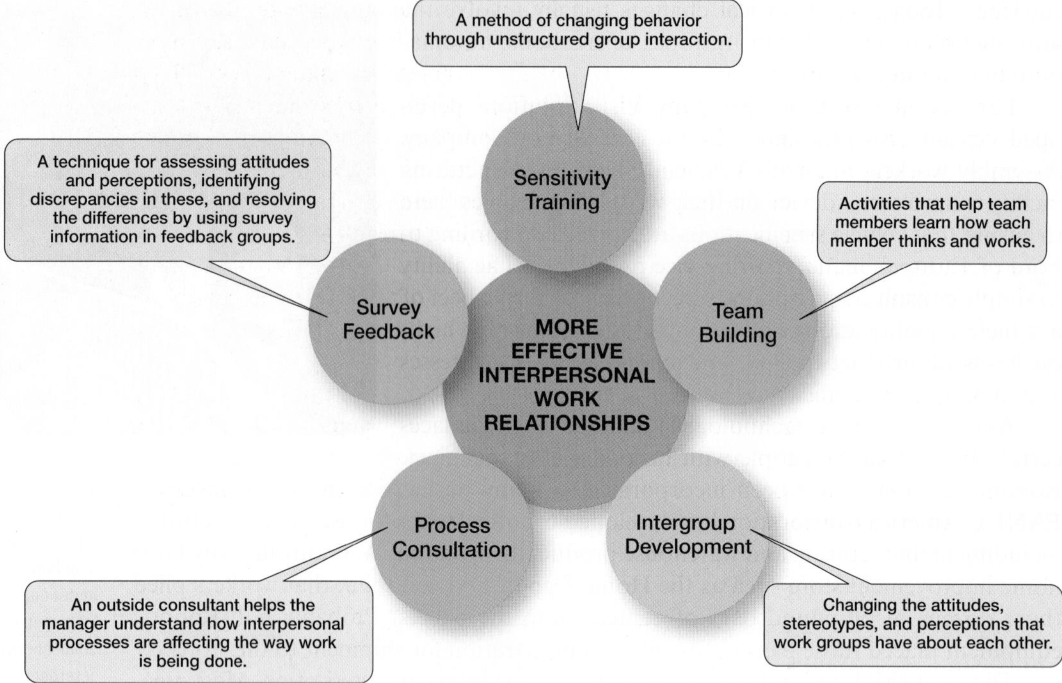

MANAGING change

LO6.4 We know it's better for us to eat healthy and to be active, yet few of us follow that advice. We resist making changes in our lifestyle. Volkswagen Sweden and ad agency DDB Stockholm did an experiment to see if they could get people to change their behavior and take the healthier option of using the stairs instead of riding an escalator.[34] How? They put a working piano keyboard on a stairway in a Stockholm subway station to see if commuters would use it. The experiment was a resounding success as stair traffic rose 66 percent. The lesson—people can change if you make the change appealing.

Change can be a threat to people in an organization. Organizations can build up inertia that motivates people to resist changing their status quo, even though change might be beneficial. Why do people resist change, and what can be done to minimize their resistance?

Why Do People Resist Change?

It's often said that most people hate any change that doesn't jingle in their pockets. This resistance to change is well documented.[35] Why *do* people resist change? The main reasons include uncertainty, habit, concern over personal loss, and the belief that the change is not in the organization's best interest.[36]

Change replaces the known with uncertainty. No matter how much you may dislike attending college, at least you know what's expected of you. When you leave college for the world of full-time employment, you'll trade the known for the unknown. Employees in organizations are faced with similar uncertainty. For example, when quality control methods based on statistical models are introduced into manufacturing plants, many quality control inspectors have to learn the new methods. Some may fear that they will be unable to do so and may develop a negative attitude toward the change or behave poorly if required to use them.

Another cause of resistance is that we do things out of habit. Every day when you go to school or work, you probably go the same way, if you're like most people. We're creatures of habit. Life is complex enough—we don't want to have to consider the full range of options for the hundreds of decisions we make every day. To cope with this complexity, we rely on habits or programmed responses. But when confronted with change, our tendency to respond in our accustomed ways becomes a source of resistance.

The third cause of resistance is the fear of losing something already possessed. Change threatens the investment you've already made in the status quo. The more people have invested in the current system, the more they resist change. Why? They fear the loss of status, money, authority, friendships, personal convenience, or other economic benefits they value. Consider what happened when Commonwealth Bank in Australia introduced an "activity-based" workplace to improve teamwork. The company replaced the traditional arrangement of permanent desk assignments with desks and meeting spaces assigned as needed from day to day. Recognizing that employees might feel disconnected from colleagues in this new work environment, bank managers laid the groundwork a year in advance with informational meetings and communications. After the changeover, managers continued to offer "settling in" support while employees became accustomed to the new workspace arrangement.[37]

A final cause of resistance is a person's belief that the change is incompatible with the goals and interests of the organization. For instance, an employee who believes that a proposed new job procedure will reduce product quality can be expected to resist the change. This type of resistance actually can be beneficial to the organization if expressed in a positive way.

Techniques for Reducing Resistance to Change

When managers see resistance to change as dysfunctional, what can they do? Several strategies have been suggested in dealing with resistance to change. These approaches

let's get REAL

The Scenario:

Jayden Hunter doesn't understand why it is so difficult for the dispatchers to adapt to the new company tracking system. Jayden is a manager at a trucking company and about six months ago the company implemented a new software system to track transportation assignments. However, he has found that the dispatchers aren't using the new system, reverting back to the paper tracking system they used in the past because they say it is easier.

What can Jayden do to convince his staff to give the new system a chance?

Systems changes require a planned process as well as transparent and frequent communication. It is imperative that those who are most affected by the change—the users of the system—understand why the change is happening, how the change will benefit their roles and responsibilities (WIIFM—What's In It For Me), and most importantly, how they are a part of the process. Since the change has already happened, opening communication about these three items is important and can be done through town hall meetings, which encourage discussion and provide answers, and focus groups, which can get to the heart of issues and determine solutions together rather than in a silo. When it's clear employees are not on the same page as management, listening is half the battle to the solution, and then the rubber must hit the road: Enact agreed-upon solutions in a timely manner that allow for an effective and successful transition to the new system.

Karen Heger
Manager, Organizational Development and Training

Source: Karen S. G. Heger

Exhibit 6-5
Techniques for Reducing Resistance to Change

Technique	When Used	Advantage	Disadvantage
Education and communication	When resistance is due to misinformation	Clear up misunderstandings	May not work when mutual trust and credibility are lacking
Participation	When resisters have the expertise to make a contribution	Increase involvement and acceptance	Time-consuming; has potential for a poor solution
Facilitation and support	When resisters are fearful and anxiety ridden	Can facilitate needed adjustments	Expensive; no guarantee of success
Negotiation	When resistance comes from a powerful group	Can "buy" commitment	Potentially high cost; opens doors for others to apply pressure too
Manipulation and co-optation	When a powerful group's endorsement is needed	Inexpensive, easy way to gain support	Can backfire, causing change agent to lose credibility
Coercion	When a powerful group's endorsement is needed	Inexpensive, easy way to gain support	May be illegal; may undermine change agent's credibility

include education and communication, participation, facilitation and support, negotiation, manipulation and co-optation, and coercion. These tactics are summarized here and described in Exhibit 6-5. Managers should view these techniques as tools and use the most appropriate one, depending on the type and source of the resistance.

Education and communication can help reduce resistance to change by helping employees see the logic of the change effort. This technique, of course, assumes that much of the resistance lies in misinformation or poor communication. The use of social media might be useful as part of an overall communication plan. A recent study found that 55 percent of participants who had experienced change in the workplace expressed a desire that their employer provide more social media engagement.[38] In addition, 42 percent preferred having more face-to-face communication. These findings suggest that both the use of technology and conventional methods in communicating change should be part of a plan to deliver information about change.

Participation involves bringing those individuals directly affected by the proposed change into the decision-making process. Their participation allows these individuals to express their feelings, increase the quality of the process, and increase employee commitment to the final decision.

Facilitation and support involve helping employees deal with the fear and anxiety associated with the change effort. This help may include employee counseling, therapy, new skills training, or a short paid leave of absence.

Negotiation involves exchanging something of value for an agreement to lessen the resistance to the change effort. This resistance technique may be quite useful when the resistance comes from a powerful source.

Manipulation and co-optation refer to covert attempts to influence others about the change. It may involve distorting facts to make the change appear more attractive.

Finally, *coercion* can be used to deal with resistance to change. Coercion involves the use of direct threats or force against the resisters.

★ It's Your Career

Change Readiness—If your instructor is using Pearson MyLab Management, log onto **mymanagementlab.com** and test your *change readiness knowledge.* **Be sure to refer back to the chapter opener!**

CONTEMPORARY issues in managing change

LO6.5 Change occurs in most workplaces. The pace of change varies substantially from place to place, and frequent change can create a stressful environment for employees. That's why Todd Thibodeaux, president and CEO of CompTIA, has furnished offices and conference rooms with game consoles. He encourages employees to play games, which he views as having few, if any, drawbacks. Thibodeaux maintains: "It's an amazing team-building mechanism, particularly when people from around the company gather around a console in a single room."[39] And, Thibodeaux credits gaming for stress relief, which helps boost employee performance. Employee stress is one of the major critical concerns for managers today. In this section, we're going to discuss stress and two other critical concerns—effectively implementing and leading change and creating a culture for change. Let's look first at leading organizational change.

FYI

- Only 43 percent of change initiatives achieved the desired goal.[41]

Leading Change

Organizational change is an ongoing daily challenge. In a global study of organizational changes in more than 2,000 organizations in Europe, Japan, and the United States, 82 percent of the respondents had implemented major information systems changes; 74 percent had created horizontal sharing of services and information; 65 percent had implemented flexible human resource practices; and 62 percent had introduced decentralized operational decisions.[40] Each of these major changes entailed numerous other changes in structure, technology, and people. When changes are needed, who makes them happen? Who manages them? Although you may think it's just top-level managers, actually managers at *all* organizational levels should be involved in the change process.

Even with the involvement of all levels of managers, change efforts don't always work the way they should. In fact, a global study of organizational change concluded that "hundreds of managers from scores of U.S. and European companies [are] satisfied with their operating prowess... [but] dissatisfied with their ability to implement change."[42]

How can managers make change happen successfully? They can (1) make the organization change capable, (2) understand their own role in the process, and (3) give individual employees a role in the change process. Let's look at each of these suggestions.

In an industry where growth is slowing and competitors are becoming stronger, United Parcel Service (UPS) prospers. How? By embracing change! Managers spent a decade creating new worldwide logistics businesses because they anticipated slowing domestic shipping demand. They continue change efforts in order to exploit new opportunities.[43] UPS is what we call a *change-capable organization*. What does it take to be a change-capable organization? Exhibit 6-6 summarizes the characteristics.

The second component of making change happen successfully is for managers to recognize their own important role in the process. Managers can, and do, act as change agents. But their role in the change process includes more than being catalysts for change; they must also be change leaders. When organizational members resist change, it's the manager's responsibility to lead the change effort. But even when there's no resistance to the change, someone has to assume leadership. That someone is managers.

The final aspect of making change happen successfully revolves around getting all organizational members involved. Successful organizational change is not a one-person job. Individual employees are a powerful resource in identifying and addressing change issues. "If you develop a program for change and simply hand it to your people, saying, 'Here, implement this,' it's unlikely to work. But when people help to build something, they will support it and make it work."[44] Managers need to encourage employees to be change agents—to look for those day-to-day improvements and changes that individuals and teams can make. For instance, a study of organizational

Exhibit 6-6
Change-Capable Organizations

- ***Link the present and the future.*** Think of work as more than an extension of the past; think about future opportunities and issues and factor them into today's decisions.
- ***Make learning a way of life.*** Change-friendly organizations excel at knowledge sharing and management.
- ***Actively support and encourage day-to-day improvements and changes.*** Successful change can come from the small changes as well as the big ones.
- ***Ensure diverse teams.*** Diversity ensures that things won't be done like they've always been done.
- ***Encourage mavericks.*** Because their ideas and approaches are outside the mainstream, mavericks can help bring about radical change.
- ***Shelter breakthroughs.*** Change-friendly organizations have found ways to protect those breakthrough ideas.
- ***Integrate technology.*** Use technology to implement changes.
- ***Build and deepen trust.*** People are more likely to support changes when the organization's culture is trusting and managers have credibility and integrity.
- ***Couple permanence with perpetual change.*** Because change is the only constant, companies need to figure out how to protect their core strengths during times of change.
- ***Support an entrepreneurial mindset.*** Many younger employees bring a more entrepreneurial mindset to organizations and can serve as catalysts for radical change.

change found that 77 percent of changes at the work group level were reactions to a specific, current problem or to a suggestion from someone outside the work group, and 68 percent of those changes occurred in the course of employees' day-to-day work.[45]

★ Try It!

If your professor has assigned this, go to **www.mymanagementlab.com** to complete the Simulation: *Change* and get a better understanding of the challenges of managing change in organizations.

Creating a Culture for Change

Korean Air CEO Cho Yang-Ho had a challenging change situation facing him. He wanted to transform his airline's image of an accident-prone airline from a developing country to that of a strong international competitor.[46] His main focus was on improving safety above all else, which meant making significant changes to the organization's culture. What made his task even more challenging was Korea's hierarchical culture that teaches Koreans to be deferential toward their elders and superiors. Cho says, "It (the hierarchical culture) exists in all Oriental culture." His approach to changing his company's culture involved implementing a "systems approach aimed at minimizing the personality-driven, top-down culture that is a legacy of Korean business managers who place emphasis on intuition and responding to orders." The cultural change must have worked. Korean Air is now one of the world's largest commercial cargo carriers, and it has earned a four-star rating (out of five possible stars) from a London aviation firm that rates airlines on quality.

The fact that an organization's culture is made up of relatively stable and permanent characteristics tends to make it very resistant to change.[47] A culture takes a long time to form, and once established it tends to become entrenched. Strong cultures are particularly resistant to change because employees have become so committed to them. For instance, IBM was not amenable to change because it had developed an entrenched culture based on tradition. It didn't take long for Lou Gerstner, who was CEO of IBM from 1993 to 2002, to discover the power of a strong culture. Gerstner, the first outsider to lead IBM, needed to overhaul the ailing, tradition-bound company if it was going to regain its role as the dominant player in the computer industry. However, accomplishing that feat in an organization that prided itself on its long-standing culture was Gerstner's biggest challenge. He said, "I came to see in my decade at IBM that culture isn't just one aspect of the game—it *is* the game."[48] Over time, if a certain culture becomes a handicap, a manager might be able to do little to change it, especially in the short run. Even under the most favorable conditions, cultural changes have to be viewed in years, not weeks or even months.

UNDERSTANDING THE SITUATIONAL FACTORS What "favorable conditions" facilitate cultural change? One is that *a dramatic crisis occurs*, such as an unexpected financial setback, the loss of a major customer, or a dramatic technological innovation by a competitor. Such a shock can weaken the status quo and make people start thinking about the relevance of the current culture. Another condition may be that *leadership changes hands*. New top leadership can provide an alternative set of key values and may be perceived as more capable of responding to the crisis than the old leaders were. Another is that *the organization is young and small*. The younger the organization, the less entrenched its culture. It's easier for managers to communicate new values in a small organization than in a large one. Finally, the *culture is weak*. Weak cultures are more receptive to change than strong ones.[51]

LEADER making a DIFFERENCE

Source: Stuart Isett/Polaris/Newscom

When the news broke late summer 2013 that Microsoft's CEO (Steve Ballmer) was stepping down, the search for his replacement was on. Analysts said that whoever the replacement was, that individual would face the challenge of "rebooting Microsoft's corporate culture, in which charting the safe but profitable course... too often wins out over innovation...."[49] ***Satya Nadella*** *is that person. Named CEO in February 2014, Nadella is a 22-year veteran of Microsoft. His new "slogan" is innovation, innovation, innovation. When asked what his plans are for the software giant, he answered with that one word, innovation. How does he plan to make innovation part of the culture? By "ruthlessly removing any obstacles that allow us to be innovative; every individual to innovate."[50]* What can you learn from this leader making a difference?

MAKING CHANGES IN CULTURE If conditions are right, how do managers change culture? No single action is likely to have the impact necessary to change something ingrained and highly valued. Managers need a strategy for managing cultural change, as described in Exhibit 6-7. These suggestions focus on specific actions that managers can take. Following them, however, is no guarantee that the cultural change efforts will succeed. Organizational members don't quickly let go of values that they understand and that have worked well for them in the past. Change, if it comes, will be slow. Also, managers must stay alert to protect against any return to old, familiar traditions.

Employee Stress

As a student, you've probably experienced stress—class projects, exams, even juggling a job and school. Then, there's the stress associated with getting a decent job after graduation. But even after you've landed that job, stress isn't likely to stop. For many employees, organizational change creates stress. An uncertain environment

Exhibit 6-7
Changing Culture

- ***Set the tone through management behavior;*** top managers, particularly, need to be positive role models.
- Create ***new stories, symbols, and rituals*** to replace those currently in use.
- Select, promote, and support employees who ***adopt*** the new values.
- ***Redesign socialization processes*** to align with the new values.
- To encourage acceptance of the new values, ***change the reward system.***
- Replace unwritten norms with ***clearly specified expectations.***
- ***Shake up current subcultures*** through job transfers, job rotation, and/or terminations.
- Work to get consensus through ***employee participation*** and creating a ***climate with a high level of trust.***

characterized by time pressures, increasing workloads, mergers, and restructuring has created a large number of employees who are overworked and stressed.[52] In fact, depending on which survey you look at, the number of employees experiencing job stress in the United States ranges anywhere from 40 percent to 80 percent.[53] However, workplace stress isn't just an American problem. Global studies indicate that some 50 percent of workers surveyed in 16 European countries reported that stress and job responsibility have risen significantly over a five-year period; 35 percent of Canadian workers surveyed said they are under high job stress; in Australia, cases of occupational stress jumped 21 percent in a one-year period; more than 57 percent of Japanese employees suffer from work-related stress; some 83 percent of call-center workers in India suffer from sleeping disorders; and a study of stress in China showed that managers are experiencing more stress.[54] Another interesting study found that stress was the leading cause of people quitting their jobs. Surprisingly, however, employers were clueless. They said that stress wasn't even among the top five reasons why people leave and instead wrongly believed that insufficient pay was the main reason.[55]

stress
The adverse reaction people have to excessive pressure placed on them from extraordinary demands, constraints, or opportunities

WHAT IS STRESS? **Stress** is the adverse reaction people have to excessive pressure placed on them from extraordinary demands, constraints, or opportunities.[56] Stress isn't always bad. Although it's often discussed in a negative context, stress can be positive, especially when it offers a potential gain. For instance, functional stress allows an athlete, stage performer, or employee to perform at his or her highest level at crucial times.

However, stress is more often associated with constraints and demands. A constraint prevents you from doing what you desire; demands refer to the loss of something desired. When you take a test at school or have your annual performance review at work, you feel stress because you confront opportunity, constraints, and demands. A good performance review may lead to a promotion, greater responsibilities, and a higher salary. But a poor review may keep you from getting the promotion. An extremely poor review might lead to your being fired.

- A recent study revealed that workplace stress is roughly as hazardous to one's health as secondhand smoke.[57]

stressors
Factors that cause stress

WHAT CAUSES STRESS? Stress can be caused by personal factors and by job-related factors called **stressors**. Clearly, change of any kind—personal or job-related—has the potential to cause stress because it can involve demands, constraints, or opportunities. Organizations have no shortage of factors that can cause stress. Pressures to avoid errors or complete tasks in a limited time period, changes in the way reports are filed, a demanding supervisor, and unpleasant coworkers are a few examples. Let's look at five categories of organizational stressors: task demands, role demands, interpersonal demands, organization structure, and organizational leadership.

Task demands are factors related to an employee's job. They include the design of a person's job (autonomy, task variety, degree of automation), working conditions, and the physical work layout. Work quotas can put pressure on employees when their "outcomes" are perceived as excessive.[58] The more interdependence between an employee's tasks and the tasks of others, the greater the potential for stress. *Autonomy*, on the other hand, tends to lessen stress. Jobs in which temperatures, noise, or other working conditions are dangerous or undesirable can increase anxiety. So, too, can working in an overcrowded room or in a visible location where interruptions are constant.

role conflicts
Work expectations that are hard to satisfy

role overload
Having more work to accomplish than time permits

role ambiguity
When role expectations are not clearly understood

Role demands relate to pressures placed on an employee as a function of the particular role he or she plays in the organization. **Role conflicts** create expectations that may be hard to reconcile or satisfy. **Role overload** is experienced when the employee is expected to do more than time permits. **Role ambiguity** is created when role expectations are not clearly understood and the employee is not sure what he or she is to do. Sandi Peterson, group worldwide chairman of Johnson & Johnson, states the importance of goal setting to help employees understand their roles, particularly during organizational change: "Defining a clear set of goals for your team demonstrates that there is an end in sight. However, it's crucial during this time to move through the transition in phases."[59]

Interpersonal demands are pressures created by other employees. Lack of social support from colleagues and poor interpersonal relationships can cause considerable stress, especially among employees with a high social need.

Organization structure can increase stress. Excessive rules and an employee's lack of opportunity to participate in decisions that affect him or her are examples of structural variables that might be potential sources of stress.

Organizational leadership represents the supervisory style of the organization's managers. Some managers create a culture characterized by tension, fear, and anxiety. They establish unrealistic pressures to perform in the short run, impose excessively tight controls, and routinely fire employees who don't measure up. This style of leadership filters down through the organization and affects all employees.

Personal factors that can create stress include family issues, personal economic problems, and inherent personality characteristics. Because employees bring their personal problems to work with them, a full understanding of employee stress requires a manager to be understanding of these personal factors.[60] Evidence also indicates that employees' personalities have an effect on how susceptible they are to stress. The most commonly used labels for these personality traits are Type A and Type B.

Type A personality is characterized by chronic feelings of a sense of time urgency, an excessive competitive drive, and difficulty accepting and enjoying leisure time. The opposite of Type A is **Type B personality**. Type Bs don't suffer from time urgency or impatience. Until quite recently, it was believed that Type As were more likely to experience stress on and off the job. A closer analysis of the evidence, however, has produced new conclusions. Studies show that only the hostility and anger associated with Type A behavior are actually associated with the negative effects of stress. And Type Bs are just as susceptible to the same anxiety-producing elements. For managers, it is important to recognize that Type A employees are more likely to show symptoms of stress, even if organizational and personal stressors are low.

Type A personality
People who have a chronic sense of urgency and an excessive competitive drive

Type B personality
People who are relaxed and easygoing and accept change easily

WHAT ARE THE SYMPTOMS OF STRESS? We see stress in a number of ways. For instance, an employee who is experiencing high stress may become depressed, accident prone, or argumentative; may have difficulty making routine decisions; may be easily distracted, and so on. Employees in companies where downsizing is occurring tend to get ill at twice the rate of employees whose jobs are secure.[61] As Exhibit 6-8 shows, stress symptoms can be grouped under three general categories: physical, psychological, and behavioral. All of these can significantly affect an employee's work.

In Japan, there's a stress phenomenon called *karoshi*, which is translated literally as "death from overwork," and *karojisatsu*, which refers to suicide related to overwork.[62] During the late 1980s, "several high-ranking Japanese executives still in their prime years suddenly died without any previous sign of illness."[63] As Japanese multinational companies expand operations to China, Korea, and Taiwan, it's feared that the karoshi culture may follow. Recently, Yumi Nakata, a Japanese blogger, commented on one

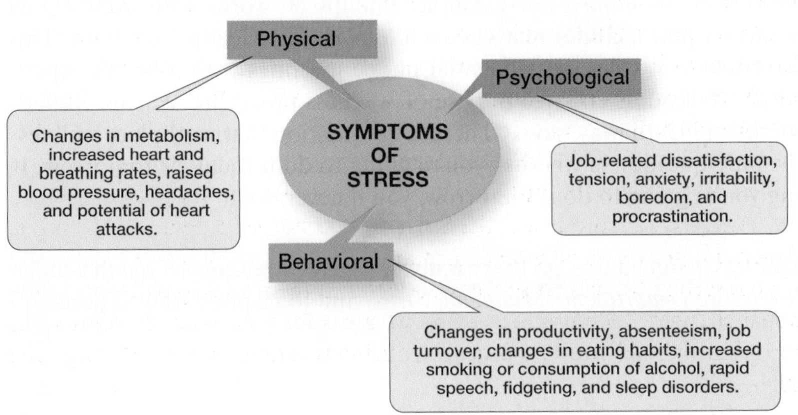

Exhibit 6-8
Symptoms of Stress

reason for karojisatsu: "Japan can be a very stressful society to live in as the employment system is very rigid, and it is not easy for those who have been laid off to find another job."[64]

Similar intense pressures are evident in China where *guolaosi* refers to "death by overwork." Approximately 600,000 Chinese workers die from work-related stress each year.[65] According to Yang Heqing, dean of the School of Labor Economics at the Capital University of Economics and Business in Beijing, "in China there is still the belief that you do things for the development of the good of the nation, for the development of the economy, to forget yourself."[66]

HOW CAN STRESS BE REDUCED? As mentioned earlier, not all stress is dysfunctional. Because stress can never be totally eliminated from a person's life, managers want to reduce the stress that leads to dysfunctional work behavior. How? Through controlling certain organizational factors to reduce job-related stress, and to a more limited extent, offering help for personal stress.

Things managers can do in terms of job-related factors begin with employee selection. Managers need to make sure an employee's abilities match the job requirements. When employees are in over their heads, their stress levels are typically high. A realistic job preview during the selection process can minimize stress by reducing ambiguity over job expectations. Improved organizational communications will keep ambiguity-induced stress to a minimum. Similarly, a performance planning program such as MBO (management by objectives) will clarify job responsibilities, provide clear performance goals, and reduce ambiguity through feedback. Job redesign is also a way to reduce stress. If stress can be traced to boredom or to work overload, jobs should be redesigned to increase challenge or to reduce the workload. Redesigns that increase opportunities for employees to participate in decisions and to gain social support also have been found to reduce stress.[67] For instance, at U.K. pharmaceutical maker GlaxoSmithKline, a team-resilience program in which employees can shift assignments, depending on people's workload and deadlines, has helped reduce work-related stress by 60 percent.[68] And Royal Dutch Shell found that its resilience training program has been successful. Data show positive effects of training for up to four years.[69]

Stress from an employee's personal life raises two problems. First, it's difficult for the manager to control directly. Second, ethical considerations include whether the manager has the right to intrude—even in the most subtle ways—in an employee's personal life. If a manager believes it's ethical and the employee is receptive, the manager might consider several approaches. Employee *counseling* can provide stress relief. Employees often want to talk to someone about their problems, and the organization—through its managers, in-house human resource counselors, or free or low-cost outside professional help—can meet that need. Companies such as Marathon Petroleum, Target, and PepsiCo provide extensive counseling services for their employees. A *time management program* can help employees whose personal lives suffer from a lack of planning to sort out their priorities.[70] (See Chapter 1 opener on pages 38–39 for suggestions on efficiently managing your time.) Still another approach is organizationally sponsored *wellness programs.* For example, Phillips 66 works with WebMD as their wellness partner and includes services such as WebMD Health Coaching. This service enables employees to have confidential phone meetings with a health expert. Oftentimes, corporate leaders endorse the use of wellness programs. Warren Buffett, chairman of Berkshire Hathaway, says, "There is no question that workplace wellness is worth it. The only question is whether you're going to do it today or tomorrow. If you keep saying you're going to do it tomorrow, you'll never do it."[71]

★ Watch It 1!

If your professor has assigned this, go to **www.mymanagementlab.com** to watch a video titled: *East Haven Fire Department: Managing Stress* and to respond to questions.

WORKPLACE **CONFIDENTIAL** Coping with Job Stress

We asked several dozen recent college graduates whether they had experienced job stress and, if so, what was the source. Almost all said they had. Here are a few of their responses: "I've got ridiculous deadlines to meet;" "They let several people in my department go, and two of us had to absorb their work;" "Business is slow and there are rumors of layoffs;" and "I hoped to take my two-week vacation next month but I can't. Too much work to do."

These recent graduates don't appear to be unusual. Numerous studies indicate that *job stress* is far and away the major source of stress for American adults. For instance, a recent survey found that 83 percent of American workers said they were stressed at work. And what was stressing them out? Their answers included unreasonable workloads, poor compensation, frustration with coworkers, commuting, working in a job that was not their first choice, poor work-life balance, lack of opportunity for advancement, and fear of being fired or laid off. Interestingly, those aged 18 to 29 indicated the highest stress levels due largely, they said, to work and job stability concerns.

So if you're among those stressing out at work, what can you do to help reduce that stress? Here's what the experts suggest:

Time management. Start with time management. As noted in Chapter 1, effective time management can allow you to be more efficient, get more things done, and help to reduce workload-based stress. We know that many people manage their time poorly. If you're well-organized, you can often accomplish twice as much as the person who is poorly organized. So an understanding and utilization of basic time-management principles can help you better cope with tensions created by job demands.

Work breaks. A growing body of research shows that simply taking breaks from work at routine intervals can facilitate psychological recovery and significantly reduce stress. If you work at a desk or a fixed workstation, for both reducing stress and your general health, get up at least every half-hour and walk around for a few minutes.

Deep-relaxation techniques. You can teach yourself to reduce tension through deep-relaxation techniques such as deep breathing. The objective is to reach a state of deep physical relaxation, in which you focus all your energy on release of muscle tension.

Deep breathing is one of the simplest techniques for addressing stress. The technique requires you to avoid shallow breaths and to learn to breathe from the abdomen. This technique works on neuromuscular functioning and leads to relaxing the neuromuscular system.

An extension of deep breathing is progressive muscle relaxation. With this technique, you assume a comfortable position and begin to breathe deeply. Then you relax groups of muscles one at a time, beginning with the feet and working up.

Deep relaxation for 15 to 20 minutes a day releases strain and provides a pronounced sense of peacefulness, as well as significant changes in heart rate, blood pressure, and other physiological factors.

Meditation. While meditation is another form of relaxation, we separate it out because of its wide popularity and long history as a stress-reducing practice. Meditation has been done for thousands of years and continues to be a well-recognized approach to stress reduction. It's a group of self-regulated techniques you use to refocus your attention through concentration to attain a subjective, even "blissful," state that proponents describe as calmness, clarity, and concentration. Although meditation is done in many forms, a popular Western variety has individuals blank out their mind and stop conscious thinking. This is often combined with a mantra or focusing on an object. Advocates of meditation report that it increases calmness and physical relaxation, improves psychological balance, and enhances overall health and well-being.

Yoga. The American Yoga Association suggests that a few yoga exercises practiced daily help to regulate breathing and relax the body. Exercises, such as the sun salutation sequence of poses, have been shown to be particularly helpful because they encourage you to breathe deeply and rhythmically.

Imagery. When life and work seem to overwhelm you, try putting your mind in a more peaceful place. Think of the most peaceful and serene location that you can envision—such as a quiet Caribbean beach, a peaceful setting in a forest, or a sailboat on a calm lake. Then close your eyes and imagine yourself there. So, using the beach example, imagine the waves gently coming ashore, the rhythmic sounds of the waves, the smell of salt air, and the warm sun on your skin. Then apply some of the relaxation techniques described previously.

Physical exercise. Physicians have recommended noncompetitive physical exercise—such as aerobics, Pilates, walking, jogging, swimming, and riding a bicycle—as a way to deal with excessive stress levels. These activities increase lung capacity, lower the resting heart rate, and provide a mental diversion from work pressures, effectively reducing work-related levels of stress.

Social support network. Finally, friends, family, or work colleagues can provide an outlet when stress levels become excessive. Expanding your social support network provides someone to hear your problems and offer a perspective on a stressful situation more objective than your own.

Source: C. J. Hobson and L. DeLunes, "Efficacy of Different Techniques for Reducing Stress: A Study Among Business Students in the United States," *International Journal of Management*, August 2009, pp. 186–196; M. Clayton, *Brilliant Stress Management: How to Manage Stress in Any Situation* (New York: FT Press, 2012); "Work Stress on the Rise: 8 in 10 Americans Are Stressed About Their Jobs, Survey Finds," *HuffingtonPost Healthy Living*, April 10, 2013; H. Hanna, *Stressaholic: 5 Steps to Transform Your Relationship with Stress* (Hoboken, NJ: Wiley, 2014); and H. Anisman, *Stress and Your Health: From Vulnerability to Resilence* (Hoboken, NJ: Wiley-Blackwell, 2015).

Innovation was the foundation of Thomas Edison's highly successful business enterprise. To stimulate innovation, Edison established an industrial research and development facility for creating new products and adapting them to the needs of users. His invention of a long-lasting electric light bulb and a power grid system to generate and deliver electricity brought power and light to individual homes and offices through the United States.
Source: Mondadori Portfolio/Getty Images

STIMULATING **Innovation**

LO6.6 Thomas A. Edison once said: "I find out what the world needs. Then I go ahead and try to invent it."[72] Today, innovation is the foundation of highly successful organizations. In fact, Ajay Banga, CEO of MasterCard, maintains that "innovation is the key to continued success."[73] In the dynamic, chaotic world of global competition, organizations must create new products and services and adopt state-of-the-art technology if they're going to compete successfully.[74]

What companies come to mind when you think of successful innovators? Maybe it's Apple with its iPad, iPhone, iPod, Apple Pay, and its wide array of computers. Maybe it's Google with its continually evolving Web platform. And Google is a good example of the new, faster pace of innovation. The company runs 50 to 200 online search experiments with users at any given time. In one instance, Google asked selected users how many search results they'd like to see on a single screen. The reply from the users was more, many more. So Google ran an experiment that tripled the number of search results per screen to 30. The result: traffic declined because "it took about a third of a second longer for search results to appear—a seemingly insignificant delay that nonetheless upset many of the users."[76] Google tried something new and quickly found out it wasn't something they wanted to pursue. Even Procter & Gamble, the global household and personal products giant, is doing the "vast majority of our concept testing online, which has created truly substantial savings in money and time," according to the company's global consumer and market knowledge officer.[77] What's the secret to the success of these and other innovator champions? What can other managers do to make their organizations more innovative? In the following sections, we'll try to answer those questions as we discuss the factors behind innovation.

- Only 28 percent of organizations consider themselves innovative.[75]

Creativity Versus Innovation

The definition of innovation varies widely, depending on who you ask. For instance, the Merriam-Webster dictionary defines innovation as "the introduction of something new" and "a new idea, method, or device; novelty." The CEO of the company that makes Bubble Wrap says, "It means inventing a product that has never existed." To the CEO of Ocean Spray Cranberries, it means "turning an overlooked commodity, such as leftover cranberry skins into a consumer snack like Craisins."[78] We're going to define it by first looking at the concept of creativity. **Creativity** refers to the ability to combine ideas in a unique way or to make unusual associations between ideas.[79] A creative organization develops unique ways of working or novel solutions to problems. But creativity by itself isn't enough. The outcomes of the creative process need to be turned into useful products or work methods, which is defined as **innovation**. Thus, the innovative organization is characterized by its ability to generate new ideas that are implemented into new products, processes, and procedures designed to be useful—that is, to channel creativity into useful outcomes. When managers talk about changing an organization to make it more creative, they usually mean they want to stimulate and nurture innovation.

creativity
The ability to combine ideas in a unique way or to make unusual associations between ideas

innovation
Taking creative ideas and turning them into useful products or work methods

Stimulating and Nurturing Innovation

The systems model (see Management History Module, p. 75) can help us understand how organizations become more innovative.[80] Getting the desired outputs (innovative products and work methods) involves transforming inputs. These inputs include creative people and groups within the organization. But having creative people isn't enough. It takes the right environment to help transform those inputs into innovative products or work methods. This "right" environment—that is, an environment that stimulates innovation—includes three variables: the organization's structure, culture, and human resource practices. (See Exhibit 6-9.)

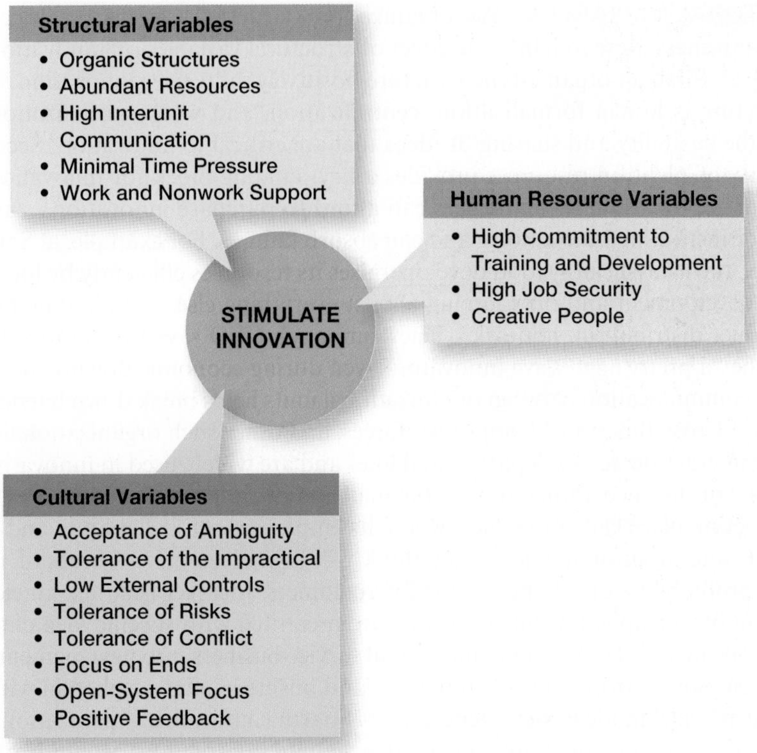

Exhibit 6-9
Innovation Variables

Structural Variables
- Organic Structures
- Abundant Resources
- High Interunit Communication
- Minimal Time Pressure
- Work and Nonwork Support

Human Resource Variables
- High Commitment to Training and Development
- High Job Security
- Creative People

STIMULATE INNOVATION

Cultural Variables
- Acceptance of Ambiguity
- Tolerance of the Impractical
- Low External Controls
- Tolerance of Risks
- Tolerance of Conflict
- Focus on Ends
- Open-System Focus
- Positive Feedback

FUTURE VISION The Internet of Things

The "Internet of Things" (IoT) allows everyday "things" to generate and store data about their own performance and share that information across the Internet.[81] From industrial machines to kitchen appliances, the world of the IoT is growing quickly. With an estimated 21 billion IoT devices in our lives by the year 2020, the IoT is an innovation that businesses need to figure out how to embrace and benefit from. It is challenging to imagine how innovations resulting from the IoT could impact our daily lives.

We already have wearable technology that tracks how many steps we take and gives us advice on how to change to more healthy behaviors. But what if your refrigerator could take inventory of its own contents and restock itself by ordering food online to be delivered to your home? Or if your car knows you are on the way to a meeting and detects an upcoming traffic jam, so it sends a message to the meeting organizers to let them know you'll be late? The possibilities that the IoT provides are endless.

The IoT will not only provide us more products and services, but it also has potential to disrupt the supply chain in every industry. It can improve efficiency of manufacturing, customer service, and distribution. Manufactured products can diagnose their own problems and contact the manufacturer for solutions. These smart, connected products will challenge companies to rethink almost everything. Companies may need to change manufacturing processes, IT processes, logistics, marketing, and sales. Furthermore, these changes will require more intense coordination across these areas. So while the IoT is full of opportunities for businesses, the changes ahead will also create many challenges.

If your professor has chosen to assign this, go to ***www.mymanagementlab.com*** *to discuss the following questions.*

TALK ABOUT IT 1: Can you imagine some future innovations that the Internet of Things could create?

TALK ABOUT IT 2: How can organizations prepare for the changes in processes that the Internet of Things will require?

- 65 percent of companies innovate by integrating both the past and the future.[82]

STRUCTURAL VARIABLES An organization's structure can have a huge impact on innovativeness. Research into the effect of structural variables on innovation shows five things.[83] First, an organic-type structure positively influences innovation. Because this structure is low in formalization, centralization, and work specialization, it facilitates the flexibility and sharing of ideas that are critical to innovation. Second, the availability of plentiful resources provides a key building block for innovation. With an abundance of resources, managers can afford to purchase innovations, can afford the cost of instituting innovations, and can absorb failures. For example, at Smart Balance, Inc., the heart-healthy food developer uses its resources efficiently by focusing on product development and outsourcing almost everything else, including manufacturing, product distribution, and sales. The company's CEO says this approach allows them to be "a pretty aggressive innovator" even during economic downturns.[84] Third, frequent communication between organizational units helps break down barriers to innovation.[85] Cross-functional teams, task forces, and other such organizational designs facilitate interaction across departmental lines and are widely used in innovative organizations. For instance, Pitney Bowes, the mail and documents company, uses an electronic meeting place called IdeaNet, where its employees can collaborate and provide comments and input on any idea they think will help create new sources of revenue, improve profitability, or add new value for customers. IdeaNet isn't just an electronic suggestion box or open forum; employees are presented with specific idea challenges. A recent one involved how to expand its mail service business into new segments. Hundreds of employees from multiple functions and business units weighed in with ideas, and eight promising ideas were generated.[86] Fourth, innovative organizations try to minimize extreme time pressures on creative activities despite the demands of white-water rapids environments. Although time pressures may spur people to work harder and may make them feel more creative, studies show that it actually causes them to be less creative.[87] Companies such as Google, 3M, and Hewlett-Packard actually urge staff researchers to spend a chunk of their workweek on self-initiated projects, even if those projects are outside the individual's work area of expertise.[88] Finally, studies have shown that an employee's creative performance was enhanced when an organization's structure explicitly supported creativity. Beneficial kinds of support included things like encouragement, open communication, readiness to listen, and useful feedback.[89]

★ **Watch It 2!**

If your professor has assigned this, go to **www.mymanagementlab.com** to watch a video titled: *iRobot: Creativity and Innovation* and to respond to questions.

CULTURAL VARIABLES "Throw the bunny" is part of the lingo used by a product development team at toy company Mattel. It refers to a juggling lesson where team members learn to juggle two balls and a stuffed bunny. Most people easily learn to juggle two balls but can't let go of that third object. Creativity, like juggling, is learning to let go—that is, to "throw the bunny." And for Mattel, having a culture where people are encouraged to "throw the bunny" is important to its continued product innovations.[90]

Innovative organizations tend to have similar cultures.[91] They encourage experimentation, set creativity goals, reward both successes and failures, and celebrate mistakes. An innovative organization is likely to have the following characteristics.

- *Accept ambiguity*. Too much emphasis on objectivity and specificity constrains creativity.
- *Tolerate the impractical*. Individuals who offer impractical, even foolish, answers to what-if questions are not stifled. What at first seems impractical might lead to innovative solutions. Encourage entrepreneurial thinking.[92]
- *Keep external controls minimal*. Rules, regulations, policies, and similar organizational controls are kept to a minimum.

These Google Inc. employees working at the company's offices in Berlin, Germany, are encouraged to accept the inevitability of failure as part of the way to be innovative and successful. Google nurtures a culture of innovation that tolerates risks, encourages experimentation, and views mistakes as learning opportunities.
Source: Krisztian Bocsi/Bloomberg/Getty Images

- *Tolerate risk*. Employees are encouraged to experiment without fear of consequences should they fail.[93] "Failure, and how companies deal with failure, is a very big part of innovation."[94] Treat mistakes as learning opportunities. You don't want your employees to fear putting forth new ideas. In an uncertain economic environment, it's especially important that employees don't feel they have to avoid innovation and initiative because it's unsafe for them to do so. A recent study found that one fear employees have is that their coworkers will think negatively of them if they try to come up with better ways of doing things. Another fear is that they'll "provoke anger among others who are comfortable with the status quo."[95] In an innovative culture, such fears are not an issue.
- *Tolerate conflict*. Diversity of opinions is encouraged. Harmony and agreement between individuals or units are *not* assumed to be evidence of high performance.
- *Focus on ends rather than means*. Goals are made clear, and individuals are encouraged to consider alternative routes toward meeting the goals. Focusing on ends suggests that several right answers might be possible for any given problem.[96]
- *Provide positive feedback*. Managers provide positive feedback, encouragement, and support so employees feel that their creative ideas receive attention.
- *Exhibit empowering leadership*. Be a leader who lets organizational members know that the work they do is significant. Provide organizational members the opportunity to participate in decision making. Show them you're confident they can achieve high performance levels and outcomes. Being this type of leader will have a positive influence on creativity.[97]

let's get REAL

The Scenario:

The challenge to find new candidates is at the top of Katie Franklin's priority list. As a branch manager for a national temporary employee agency, Katie must lead her team to keep their database full of high-quality candidates to make sure the agency can quickly provide temporary employees to their clients on short notice. At the last staff meeting, Katie's team had a lot of creative ideas on how to recruit new candidates. However, a few weeks later none of the ideas have been developed and implemented. Creative ideas are great, but without implementation, they can't help the business.

How can Katie help her employees turn their creative ideas into innovative new practices?

Sounds like too many ideas with too little accountability. Bring the team back together and narrow the list of creative ideas down to a more manageable list, engaging the entire team in the dialogue. With only a few ideas to work through, delegate a leader and discuss the next best step for each one, jotting down a brief outline of action items, resources needed and due dates. Regularly check in with the team, removing roadblocks and discussing challenges. With employee time and resources at stake, if the idea is not producing results, you will want to know early on and put those resources toward the more successful ideas.

Christina Moser
Strategic Account Manager

Source: Christina Moser

idea champion
Individual who actively and enthusiastically supports new ideas, builds support, overcomes resistance, and ensures that innovations are implemented

HUMAN RESOURCE VARIABLES In this category, we find that innovative organizations actively promote the training and development of their members so their knowledge remains current; offer their employees high job security to reduce the fear of getting fired for making mistakes; and encourage individuals to become **idea champions**, actively and enthusiastically supporting new ideas, building support, overcoming resistance, and ensuring that innovations are implemented. Research finds that idea champions have common personality characteristics: extremely high self-confidence, persistence, energy, and a tendency toward risk taking. They also display characteristics associated with dynamic leadership. They inspire and energize others with their vision of the potential of an innovation and through their strong personal conviction in their mission. Denise Morrison, president and CEO of the Campbell Soup Company, is a good example of an idea champion. "There is power in helping people get excited about what they do, and inspiring and motivating them to unleash their full potential."[98] They're also good at gaining the commitment of others to support their mission. Ivanka Trump, EVP of development and acquisitions at Trump Organization, explains that "leadership is the ability to articulate a vision and unite a team of passionate people to bring that goal to life."[99] In addition, idea champions have jobs that provide considerable decision-making discretion. This autonomy helps them introduce and implement innovations in organizations.[100]

Innovation and Design Thinking

We introduced you to the concept of design thinking in Chapter 2 on decision making. Undoubtedly, a strong connection exists between design thinking and innovation. "Design thinking can do for innovation what TQM did for quality."[101] Just as TQM provides a process for improving quality throughout an organization, design thinking can provide a process for coming up with things that don't exist. When a business approaches innovation with a design-thinking mentality, the emphasis is on getting a deeper understanding of what customers need and want. The toy company LEGO, creator and manufacturer of LEGO building blocks since 1958, is an excellent example of an innovative company that employs design thinking. The company literally listens to what consumers prefer as well as what they don't prefer. Ricco Rejnholdt Krog, a design director at LEGO, states: "We're really listening [to the children], we're paying attention to what they say."[102] He gave the example that LEGO made changes to a police station box set "after a Chinese child complained there weren't enough getaway possibilities to make for exciting 'cops and robbers' play."[103] Moreover, LEGO leadership recognizes that children use digital technology—video games, iPads and smartphones—as part of their play activities.[104] The company has since created a line of programmable robots, including the popular R3PTAR.

A design-thinking mentality also entails knowing customers as real people with real problems—not just as sales targets or demographic statistics. But it also entails being able to convert those customer insights into real and usable products. For instance, at Intuit, the company behind TurboTax software, founder Scott Cook felt "the company wasn't innovating fast enough,"[105] so he decided to apply design thinking. He called the initiative "Design for Delight," and it involved customer field research to understand their "pain points"—that is, what most frustrated them as they worked in the office and at home. Then, Intuit staffers brainstormed (they nicknamed it "painstorm") a "variety of solutions to address the problems and experiment with customers to find the best ones." For example, one pain point uncovered by an Intuit team was how customers could take pictures of tax forms to reduce typing errors. Some younger customers, used to taking photos with their smartphones, were frustrated that they couldn't just complete their taxes on their mobiles. To address this, Intuit developed a mobile app called SnapTax, which the company says has been downloaded more than a million times since it was introduced in 2010. That's how design thinking works in innovation.

DISRUPTIVE **Innovation**

LO6.7 Twenty-five years ago, every Main Street and shopping mall in the United States had a bookstore. Chains like Borders and Barnes & Noble had hundreds of locations. In addition, there were literally thousands of small bookstores scattered across America. Then along came Amazon.com. Amazon offered book buyers a million-plus titles at super-low prices, all accessible without leaving the comfort of home. Amazon single-handedly disrupted the brick-and-mortar bookstore.

Definition

Disruptive innovation describes innovations in products, services or processes that radically change an industry's rules of the game.[106] Oftentimes, a smaller company with fewer resources successfully challenges established companies.[107] Those smaller companies prove themselves to be disruptive by serving overlooked segments of possible consumers with products or services at relatively low prices. Although the term "disruptive innovation" is relatively new, the concept isn't. For instance, economist Joseph Shumpeter used the term "creative destruction" more than 70 years ago to describe how capitalism builds on processes that destroy old technologies but replaces them with new and better ones.[108] That, in essence, is disruptive innovation.

disruptive innovation
Innovations in products, services or processes that radically change an industry's rules of the game

In practice, disruptive innovation has been around for centuries. Vanderbilt's railroads disrupted the sailing-ship business. Alexander Bell's telephone rang the death-knell for Western Union's telegraphy. Ford and other automobile builders destroyed horse-drawn-buggy manufacturers. As Exhibit 6-10 illustrates, there is no shortage of businesses that have suffered at the expense of disruptive innovation.

It's helpful to distinguish disruptive innovation from sustaining innovation. When most of us think of innovations, we tend to think of things like the introduction of the high-definition television, back-up cameras on cars, fingerprint technology on

Exhibit 6-10
Examples of Past Disruptive Innovators

Established Business	Disruptor
Compact disc	Apple iTunes
Carbon paper	Xerox copy machine
Canvas tennis shoes	Nike athletic shoes
Portable radio	Sony Walkman
Sony Walkman	Apple iPod
Typewriters	IBM PC
Weekly news magazines	CNN
TV networks	Cable and Netflix
Local travel agencies	Expedia
Stockbrokers	eTrade
Traveler's checks	ATMs and Visa
Encyclopedias	Wikipedia
Newspaper classified ads	Craig's List
AM/FM radio stations	Sirius XM
Tax preparation services	Intuit's Turbo Tax
Yellow Pages	Google
Paper maps	Garmin's GPS
Paperback books	Kindle
Lawyers	Legal Zoom
Taxis	Uber

sustaining innovation
Small and incremental changes in established products rather than dramatic breakthroughs

smartphones, or Double Stuf Oreos. These are examples of **sustaining innovation** because they sustain the status quo. They represent small and incremental changes in established products rather than dramatic breakthroughs. While the original television set disrupted the radio industry, high-def TV just improved the quality of the TV picture.

Why Disruptive Innovation Is Important

It's often said that "success breeds success." But success can also breed failure. How? Companies that are successful tend to grow. With growth comes expanded size. And as we'll describe, large size frequently makes successful companies vulnerable to disruptive competitors.

Large organizations create rules and regulations to standardize operations. They create multiple departments with defined areas of responsibility. And they create socialization processes—like new-employee orientations and corporate handbooks—that convey to employees "the way we do things around here." The result is that these successful organizations establish entrenched cultures and values that, on one hand, guide employees, but, on the other hand, also act as constraints on change. Companies like Kodak, Polaroid, and Woolworths were iconic companies in their day that became hostage to their previous successes—and it led to their eventual decline.

New ideas for products or services that differ significantly from the status quo are a threat to the established power structure within large companies. And as we'll elaborate later, entrenched cultures tend to be threatened by disruptive ideas. For instance, when Ross Perot worked for IBM and suggested that the company move into the computer services' business, he was told that IBM sold computer hardware, not services. Perot resigned, created EDS Corp. to provide computer support, and became a billionaire. Similarly, when Xerox engineers invented the computer mouse and the graphical user interface, which would ultimately become the standard for personal computers, Xerox executives dismissed these products with "we're in the copying business," and then literally gave the inventions to Steve Jobs and Apple. Jobs then featured these innovations on Apple's Mac computer.

The fact is that disruptive innovations are a threat to many established businesses, and responding with sustaining innovations isn't enough. Making incremental improvements to the BlackBerry smartphone, for instance, couldn't help its manufacturer compete against the far superior iOS and Android devices from Apple and Samsung. Of course, all "disruptive" innovations don't succeed. The radical nature of the changes they initiate implies a high level of risk. The Segway "personal transporter" was introduced with much fanfare. It was hyped as a replacement to the automobile for short trips. It didn't happen. Similarly, the Google Glass wearable computer was promoted as a hands-free disruptive replacement for a smartphone, but it failed in the marketplace.

Who's Vulnerable?

So which businesses are most vulnerable to disruptive innovations? The answer, as alluded to previously, is large, established, and highly profitable organizations. Why? Because they have the most to lose and are most vested in their current markets and technologies.

Successful organizations focus on what they do best. They repeat what has succeeded in the past, and they put their resources into the ventures that have the highest probability of generating maximum profits. Small markets, which typically describe those applicable to early disruptive innovations, don't fit with the growth needs of large organizations. Importantly, large organizations have distinct cultures and values that define their capabilities and limit their ability to move into new products or markets. Sears' management, for instance, might have seen a need for discount department stores in the 1970s, but it didn't have the personnel, buying channels, structure, or low-cost locations to move into this market. Upstart Walmart didn't have those limitations and was able to radically disrupt the market. Similarly, Tesla was able to conceive, design, and produce an electric car in a time frame and at a quality level that could never have been done by a General Motors.

Disruptive innovations, especially at the beginning, typically apply to emerging or small markets and project lower profits than a firm's mainline products. And their novelty has little or no appeal to the organization's most profitable customers. Ken Olson, founder of Digital Equipment Corporation, said in 1977, "there is no reason anyone would want a computer in their home." What he was acknowledging was that he couldn't see investing DEC resources into microcomputers when his company was making huge profits from selling much larger systems. And his customers were perfectly happy with DEC's larger systems. So large and successful companies are motivated to repeat what has succeeded in the past and invest in ideas that offer the highest probability of generating maximum profits—and those aren't disruptive innovations. This is why, for instance, VW, Honda, and Toyota were able to disrupt the U.S. auto market by introducing compact cars. GM, Ford, and Chrysler were initially reluctant to pursue this market segment because they made their money making big cars.

Which businesses or occupations are currently in the throes of disruptive innovation? Here's a few: bank tellers (to ATMs), camera manufacturers (smartphones), financial services (to online providers), and travel agents (to online travel services). Which others may be vulnerable in the near future? General Motors (the Google car), actuaries (computer algorithms), maintenance personnel (robotics), truck drivers (self-driving vehicles), model builders (3-D printers), and pipeline workers and oil drillers (renewable energy) are vulnerable.

Implications

Disruptive innovation has the potential to upend entrepreneurs, corporate managers, and even your career plans. Let's take a specific look at what the future might hold for each.

FOR ENTREPRENEURS. Think opportunity! Entrepreneurs thrive on change and innovation. Major disruptions open the door for new products and services to replace established and mature businesses. If you're looking to create a new business with a large potential upside, look for established businesses that can be disrupted with a cheaper, simpler, smaller, or more convenient substitute.

"Despite their endowments in technology, brand names, manufacturing prowess, management experience, distribution muscle, and just plain cash, successful companies populated by good managers have a genuinely hard time doing what does not fit their model for how to make money."[109] So lack of resources, which create high barriers of entry into established markets, isn't a critical liability for entrepreneurs. The small size of new entrepreneurial firms typically comes with low overhead and a minimal cost structure, which can translate into a huge competitive advantage. Large companies come with big overhead; bureaucratic rules, regulations, and hierarchies that limit flexibility and speed of response; and entrenched cultures that are highly effective at killing ideas that don't fit neatly into their current business models.

FOR CORPORATE MANAGERS. For managers in large, successful businesses, the challenge to disruptive innovation is to create an appropriate response. Contrary to popular belief, management in these organizations is not powerless. They can become disruptive innovators themselves. But the evidence is overwhelming that their disruptive response must be carried out by a separate group that is physically and structurally disconnected from the businesses' main operations. "With few exceptions, the only instances in which mainstream firms have successfully established a timely position in a disruptive technology were those in which the firms' managers set up an autonomous organization charged with building a new and independent business around the disruptive technology."[110] This can be achieved by either creating a new business from scratch or acquiring a small company and keeping it separate.

These separate groups are frequently referred to as **skunk works**—defined as a small group within a large organization, given a high degree of autonomy and

skunk works
A small group within a large organization, given a high degree of autonomy and unhampered by corporate bureaucracy, whose mission is to develop a project primarily for the sake of radical innovation

unhampered by corporate bureaucracy, whose mission is to develop a project primarily for the sake of radical innovation. These skunk works, in effect, are entrepreneurial operations running inside a large company. Their small size allows employees to be enthusiastic about their mission and to see the impact of their efforts. To be successful, however, they can't carry the cultural values or cost structure of the main organization. They need enough autonomy so that they don't have to compete with projects in the primary organization for resources.

IBM succeeded in developing a personal computer by creating a product team and locating it in Florida—some 1,200 miles from IBM's headquarters in Armonk, New York. Steve Jobs created a separate and autonomous unit at Apple to develop the Macintosh computer. And in 2010, Google created the X Lab, a semisecret facility located a half mile from the company's corporate headquarters, whose 50-member team was assigned the challenge of developing a self-driving car. In contrast, Johnson & Johnson has aggressively bought numerous small companies, kept them independent, and provided them with a large degree of autonomy.

FOR CAREER PLANNING. What career advice can we offer you in a disruptive world? Here are some suggestions:

Never get comfortable with a single employer. You can't build your hopes on working in one organization for your entire career. There are no longer any secure jobs, and the days of an organization providing employees with lifetime employment are mostly gone. So, your first loyalty should be to yourself and making yourself marketable.

Keep your skills current. Disruptive technologies will continue to make established jobs and professions obsolete. To keep yourself marketable, you need to keep your skills current. Learning no longer ends when you finish school. You need to make a continual commitment to learning new things.

You are responsible for your future. Don't assume your employer is going to be looking out for your long-term interests. Your personal skill development, career progression, and retirement plans are all decisions that you need to make. Don't delegate your future to someone else. You need to actively manage your career.

Take risks while you're young. Few people have achieved great results without taking a risk. They quit a secure job, or went back to school, or moved to a new city, or started a business. While risks don't always pay off, setbacks or failures are much easier to recover from when you're 25 than when you are 55.

Chapter 6 PREPARING FOR: Exams/Quizzes

CHAPTER SUMMARY by Learning Objectives

LO6.1 DESCRIBE making the case for change.

Organizational change is any alteration of people, structure, or technology. A change agent acts as a catalyst and assumes responsibility for the change process. External forces that create the need for change include changing consumer needs and wants, new governmental laws, changing technology, and economic changes. Internal forces that create a need for change include a new organizational strategy, a change in the composition of the workforce, new equipment, and changing employee attitudes.

LO6.2 COMPARE and contrast views on the change process.

The calm waters metaphor suggests that change is an occasional disruption in the normal flow of events and can be planned and managed as it happens. Lewin's three-step model says change can be managed by unfreezing the status quo (old behaviors), changing to a new state, and refreezing the new behaviors. In the white-water rapids metaphor, change is ongoing and managing it is a continual process. Organizations can take a reactive or a proactive change process approach.

LO6.3 CLASSIFY areas of organizational change.

Organizational change can focus on strategy, structure, technology, or people. Changing strategy signifies a change in how managers ensure the success of the company. Changing structure involves any changes in structural components or structural design. Changing technology involves introducing new equipment, tools, or methods; automation; or computerization. Changing people involves changing attitudes, expectations, perceptions, and behaviors. Organizational development is the term used to describe change methods that focus on people and the nature and quality of interpersonal relationships.

LO6.4 EXPLAIN how to manage change.

People resist change because of uncertainty, habit, concern over personal loss, and the belief that the change is not in the organization's best interest.

The techniques for reducing resistance to change include education and communication (educating employees about and communicating to them the need for the change), participation (allowing employees to participate in the change process), facilitation and support (giving employees the support they need to implement the change), negotiation (exchanging something of value to reduce resistance), manipulation and co-optation (using negative actions to influence), and coercion (using direct threats or force).

LO 6.5 DISCUSS contemporary issues in managing change.

Managers at all levels of the organization must lead the change process through making the organization change capable, understanding their own role in the process, and giving individual employees a role in the change process. An organization's culture is made up of relatively stable and permanent characteristics, which makes it difficult to change. Managers can create a culture of change through understanding the situational factors that facilitate change. Managers must have a strategy for managing cultural change, which includes being positive role models; creating new stories, symbols, and rituals; selecting, promoting, and supporting employees who adopt the new values; redesigning socialization processes; changing the reward system; clearly specifying expectations; shaking up current subcultures; and getting employees to participate in change.

Organizational change can cause employees to experience stress. Stress is the adverse reaction people have to excessive pressure placed on them from extraordinary demands, constraints, or opportunities. To help employees deal with stress, managers can address job-related factors by making sure an employee's abilities match the job requirements, improve organizational communications, use a performance planning program, or redesign jobs. Addressing personal stress factors is trickier, but managers could offer employee counseling, time management programs, and wellness programs.

LO6.6 DESCRIBE **techniques for stimulating innovation.**

Creativity is the ability to combine ideas in a unique way or to make unusual associations between ideas. Innovation is turning the outcomes of the creative process into useful products or work methods. Important structural variables that impact innovation include an organic-type structure, abundant resources, frequent communication between organizational units, minimal time pressure, and support. Important cultural variables include accepting ambiguity, tolerating the impractical, keeping external controls minimal, tolerating risk, tolerating conflict, focusing on ends not means, using an open-system focus, providing positive feedback, and being an empowering leader. Important human resource variables include high commitment to training and development, high job security, and encouraging individuals to be idea champions.

A close and strong connection exists between design thinking and innovation. It involves knowing customers as real people with real problems and converting those insights into usable and real products.

LO6.7 EXPLAIN **why managing disruptive innovation is important.**

Disruptive innovation exists when a smaller company with fewer resources is able to successfully challenge established incumbent businesses. Disruptive innovation presents an asset to organizations that recognize the market potential of the technology. Companies can become a victim of disruptive innovation when they choose to conduct business as usual.

Pearson **MyLab** Management

Go to **mymanagementlab.com** to complete the problems marked with this icon .

REVIEW AND DISCUSSION QUESTIONS

6-1. Identify and discuss the four key internal forces of change.

6-2. With an example, explain the term organizational development.

6-3. What are the three ways to address people's resistance to change?

6-4. Distinguish between role overload and role ambiguity with the help of examples.

6-5. What are the common techniques that can be used to minimize resistance to change?

6-6. Why do people resist change, even though they may carry the potential for a better tomorrow? Discuss.

6-7. Job stress is a major problem for employees working in many organizations today. What causes job stress and what can a manager do to reduce job-related stress for employees? Discuss.

6-8. Is it possible for managers to spot the warning signs of stress among their employees? Discuss.

Pearson **MyLab** Management

If your professor has assigned these, go to **mymanagementlab.com** for the following Assisted-graded writing questions:

6-9. Explain how you would handle employees fearful and anxious about change.

6-10. Describe the structural, cultural, and human resources variables that are necessary for innovation.

PREPARING FOR: My Career

✪ PERSONAL INVENTORY ASSESSMENTS

Are You a Type A Personality?

Do you think you're a Type A personality? Take this PIA and find out so you can better control the negative aspects of being a Type A!

✪ ETHICS DILEMMA

Change usually involves some kind of modification in the way a business does things. Invariably it means alterations in products or services, and processes. Research seems to suggest that organizations undergo some form of change every three years. Within that three-year cycle there are constant minor changes taking place. The fact is that change often means restructuring, redundancies, and alterations in working practices. Change can alter almost everything and challenges people's perceptions.[111]

6-11. Why is it absolutely necessary to ensure that change is managed in an ethical way?

6-12. What is the role of a change agent and how does it ensure that change is achieved ethically?

SKILLS EXERCISE Developing Your Change Management Skill

About the Skill

Managers play an important role in organizational change. That is, they often serve as a catalyst for the change—a change agent. However, managers may find that change is resisted by employees. After all, change represents ambiguity and uncertainty, or it threatens the status quo. How can this resistance to change be effectively managed? Here are some suggestions.[112]

Steps in Practicing the Skill

- ***Assess the climate for change.*** One major factor in why some changes succeed while others fail is the readiness for change. Assessing the climate for change involves asking several questions. The more affirmative answers you get, the more likely it is that change efforts will succeed. Here are some guiding questions:
  a. Is the sponsor of the change high enough in the organization to have power to effectively deal with resistance?
  b. Is senior management supportive of the change and committed to it?
  c. Do senior managers convey the need for change, and is this feeling shared by others in the organization?
  d. Do managers have a clear vision of how the future will look after the change?
  e. Are objective measures in place to evaluate the change effort, and have reward systems been explicitly designed to reinforce them?
  f. Is the specific change effort consistent with other changes going on in the organization?
  g. Are managers willing to sacrifice their personal self-interests for the good of the organization as a whole?
  h. Do managers pride themselves on closely monitoring changes and actions by competitors?
  i. Are managers and employees rewarded for taking risks, being innovative, and looking for new and better solutions?
  j. Is the organizational structure flexible?
  k. Does communication flow both down and up in the organization?
  l. Has the organization successfully implemented changes in the past?
  m. Are employees satisfied with, and do they trust, management?
  n. Is a high degree of interaction and cooperation typical between organizational work units?
  o. Are decisions made quickly, and do they take into account a wide variety of suggestions?
- ***Choose an appropriate approach for managing the resistance to change.*** In this chapter, six strategies have been suggested for dealing with resistance to change—education and communication, participation, facilitation and support, negotiation, manipulation and co-optation, and coercion. Review Exhibit 6-5 (p. 224) for the advantages and disadvantages and when it is best to use each approach.

- ***During the time the change is implemented and after the change is completed, communicate with employees regarding what support you may be able to provide.*** Your employees need to know you are there to support them during change efforts. Be prepared to offer the assistance that may be necessary to help them enact the change.

Practicing the Skill

Read through the following scenario. Write down some notes about how you would handle the situation described. Be sure to refer to the suggestions for managing resistance to change.

You're the nursing supervisor at a community hospital employing both emergency room and floor nurses. Each of these teams of nurses tends to work almost exclusively with others doing the same job. In your professional reading, you've come across the concept of cross-training nursing teams and giving them more varied responsibilities, which in turn has been shown to improve patient care while lowering costs. You call the two team leaders, Sue and Scott, into your office to discuss your plan to have the nursing teams move to this approach. To your surprise, they're both opposed to the idea. Sue says she and the other emergency room nurses feel they're needed in the ER, where they fill the most vital role in the hospital. They work special hours when needed, do whatever tasks are required, and often work in difficult and stressful circumstances. They think the floor nurses have relatively easy jobs for the pay they receive. Scott, leader of the floor nurses team, tells you that his group believes the ER nurses lack the special training and extra experience that the floor nurses bring to the hospital. The floor nurses claim they have the heaviest responsibilities and do the most exacting work. Because they have ongoing contact with the patients and their families, they believe they shouldn't be pulled away from vital floor duties to help ER nurses complete their tasks. Now—what would you do?

WORKING TOGETHER Team Exercise

Let's see how creative you can be! Form teams of 3–4 people. From the list below, choose one activity to complete (or your professor may assign you one).

- How could you recycle old keys? Come up with as many suggestions as you can. (The more the better!)
- Think about different uses for a golf tee. Be as creative as possible as you list your suggestions.
- List different ways that a brick can be used. See how many ideas you can come up with. Think beyond the obvious.

MY TURN TO BE A MANAGER

- Choose two organizations you're familiar with and assess whether these organizations face a calm waters or white-water rapids environment. Write a short report describing these organizations and your assessment of the change environment each faces. Be sure to explain your choice of change environment.
- Reflect on a significant change you've experienced in your life (for example, moving to a new school, going to college, or a family problem such as a divorce). Did you resist the change? Why? Did you use any strategies to adjust to the change? What could you have done differently? Write your reflection and make note of how you could effectively manage future changes in your life.
- Choose an organization with which you're familiar (employer, student organization, family business, etc.). Describe its culture (shared values and beliefs). Select two of those values/beliefs and describe how you would go about changing them. Put this information in a report.
- When you find yourself experiencing dysfunctional stress, write down what's causing the stress, what stress symptoms you're exhibiting, and how you're dealing with the stress. Keep this information in a journal and evaluate how well your stress reducers are working and how you could handle stress better. Your goal is to get to a point where you recognize that you're stressed and can take positive actions to deal with the stress.
- Visit www.testmycreativity.com to take an assessment to measure your creativity. What is your level of creativity in comparison with others? What are your strengths? Your weaknesses? Do you agree with the assessment?
- Research information on how to be a more creative person. Write down suggestions in a bulleted-list format and be prepared to present your information in class.
- Is innovation more about (1) stopping something old or (2) starting something new? Prepare arguments supporting or challenging each view.

CASE APPLICATION 1 A. S. Watson Group

Founded in 1828, the A. S. Watson Group began as a small dispensary in southern China's Guangdong Province. In 1841, the dispensary was relocated to Hong Kong, and the company officially traded under the name A. S. Watson & Company since the 1870s. In 1981, it was acquired by Hutchinson Whampoa—a Hong Kong conglomerate controlled by business magnate Sir Ka-Shing Li. Benefiting from Hutchinson Whampoa's solid economic strength, A. S. Watson launched a number of mergers and acquisitions in Asia and Europe in the late 1990s. For example, in 2000, it entered the United Kingdom by acquiring Savers Health & Beauty. In 2002, the company expanded its European business by acquiring Dutch Kruidvat Group. In 2014, Singapore's Temasek, a state-owned investment company, paid $5.7 billion to acquire a 25 percent stake in Ka-shing's Watson. Today, A. S. Watson Group is one of the largest health and beauty retail groups with more than 12,000 stores operating in more than 30 countries. Its business spans from health and beauty products and luxury perfumeries and cosmetics to food, beverages (fine wine, bottled water, fruit juice, and tea drinks), and electronic products.[113]

Despite the successes, managers at A. S. Watson Group find it difficult to integrate newly acquired businesses with existing ones. How to transfer a local pharmacy into a global health and beauty retail group is a huge challenge for the company's senior managers. Effective procurement, efficient logistics, and distribution systems can help to achieve positive financial returns in the retail industry. Indeed, many retailers endeavour to maintain efficient distribution systems, lower labor costs, and firm-level economies that give them bargaining powers over their suppliers in order to cut costs. Compared to many other big players in this field who rely on price wars and low costs to gain sales revenue and expand market share, A. S. Watson is gaining competitive advantage by providing unique shopping experiences to its customers.

In recent years, A. S. Watson Group highlighted its uniqueness with the proposition to help customers to "Look Good, Feel Great, and Have Fun." A. S. Watson Group adopts a set of employee training modes to not only improve staff's product knowledge, sales, and service skills but also to promote the group's business philosophy to each employee. The top management team believes that appropriate training will facilitate employees to understand the company's strategy and, hence, smooth its change from a regional company to a global retailer.

Following these managerial techniques, A. S. Watson Group has expanded its business in a creative way. The company introduced a "personal care store" concept in more than 15 Asian countries and regions, offering food, drugs, and health and beauty products. Compared to traditional "one-stop" supermarkets (e.g., Walmart, Tesco, and Carrefour) and local cosmetics boutiques, an A. S. Watson Group personal care store emphasizes excellent customer services and sells its own brand products. Although its own brands account for an average of 15 percent of all sales in the retail sector in developed countries, this branding strategy was at the introduction stage in Asian countries in the 1990s. This new business model caters to local emerging middle-class tastes and thus sets up the new industrial standard in many Asian countries. So what have made A. S. Watson Group and its personal care stores successful in Asia? The economic strength from its parent company? Its international mergers and acquisition strategy? Or managerial capabilities that enable A. S. Watson Group to identify market niches in Asian economies and then creatively implement a "personal care store" concept to fill the niche? It seems like there is no single answer to this question. A. S. Watson Group was the first retailer to realize the importance of the emerging middle-class customers and develop a business model to meet their needs. However, such first-movers advantage will not be sustainable as competitors can easily imitate its business model. Into its 175th year of operation, the firm's continued success depends on its competency to provide innovative products and services in response to individual market preferences.

DISCUSSION QUESTIONS

6-13. What kind of change processes did A. S. Watson Group experience since the late 1990s? Discuss the activities that were conducted to smooth the change.

6-14. What's your interpretation of the company's philosophy "Look Good, Feel Great, and Have Fun"? How does such philosophy make A. S. Watson Group's personal care store differ from its competitors?

6-15. What could other companies learn from A. S. Watson Group's "new business model"?

6-16. What underpins A. S. Watson Group's success?

CASE APPLICATION 2 The iPhone: A Technology Disruptor

In early 2007, after 30 years as a computer company, Apple Computers, Inc. became Apple, Inc., dropping "Computer" from the company name.[114] Apple would still make computers, but with the introduction of the iPhone, Apple became more than just a computer company. The iPhone, which further developed the iPod by merging it with a cell phone, was about to disrupt the entire personal computing industry. The introduction of the iPhone clearly threatened the smartphones on the market at the time; however, the iPhone's impact ultimately was broader than anyone could have predicted. Essentially, the iPhone was a game changer, creating a new mobile computing market.

The iPhone initially competed with smartphones such as the BlackBerry and it was immediately successful because it was a better product. However, the iPhone moved on to create competition in the laptop computer market due to a key feature, a new way to access the Internet. Far easier and more convenient than the laptop, the iPhone connected users to the Internet on the go with easy, touchscreen technology. Ultimately the iPhone was the catalyst for a new mobile computing market as the product merged cellphone and Internet services into a single device.

Within a year of the launch of the iPhone, there were 5.4 million users, and developers created more than 17,000 "web applications" now known as "apps." This new app market changed the way we look at software. Instead of software created by a small number of large software development companies, the evolution of the app created a new mini-economy of software developers. This new market led to a new group of entrepreneurs creating businesses around mobile applications. Before the iPhone, companies such as Twitter and Snapchat could not have existed.

The introduction of apps allowed consumers to create a customized product with their iPhone as users could download apps based on their own needs and preferences. The demand for customization and easy access led technology companies to respond, essentially shifting the direction of the personal computing industry. The iPhone led to the development of the iPad and the entire tablet market. The laptop market also responded by integrating the features that consumers prefer, including the ability to install apps and touchscreen access.

The iPhone created a disruption in the technology world through its innovative business model that created a new market for access to the Internet. App developers and phone users were connected and the impact shifted not only the cellphone industry, but also challenged the laptop market. Apple isn't finished yet. With the company's innovations, the mobile computing market continues to evolve, most recently with the introduction of the Apple Watch. What's next?

DISCUSSION QUESTIONS

6-17. Are you surprised about the impact that the iPhone has had on the technology marketplace? Why or why not?

6-18. Why is the iPhone considered a disruptive innovation?

6-19. Apple is known as an innovative company. Why do you think Apple has been able to stimulate innovation successfully?

ENDNOTES

1. J. Goudreau, "12 Ways to Eliminate Stress at Work," *Forbes*, www.forbes.com, March 20, 2013.
2. R. Lawrence, "Many Fish in a Global Development Pond," *Chief Learning Officer*, November 2011, pp. 26–31; K. Roose, "Outsiders' Ideas Help Bank of America Cut Jobs and Costs," *New York Times* online, www./nytimes.com, September 12, 2011; and "How HR Made A Difference," *PeopleManagement.co.uk*, February 2011, p. 31.
3. J. Muller, "Ford Embraces Car-Sharing and Electric Bikes on a Crowded Planet, *The Wall Street Journal* online, www.wsj.com, June 24, 2015.
4. "Clear Direction in a Complex World: How Top Companies Create Clarity, Confidence and Community to Build Sustainable Performance," Towers Watson, www.towerswatson.com, 2011–2012; R. Soparnot, "The Concept of Organizational Change Capacity," *Journal of Organizational Change*, vol. 24, no. 1, 2011, pp. 640–661; A. H. Van de Ven and K. Sun, "Breakdowns in Implementing Models of Organization Change," *Academy of Management Perspectives*, August 2011, pp. 58–74; L. Dragoni, P. E. Tesluk, J. E. A. Russell, and I. S. Oh, "Understanding Managerial Development: Integrating Developmental Assignments, Learning Orientation, and Access to Developmental Opportunities in Predicting Managerial Competencies," *Academy of Management Journal*, August 2009, pp. 731–743; G. Nadler and W. J. Chandon, "Making Changes: The FIST Approach," *Journal of Management Inquiry*, September 2004, pp. 239–246; and C. R. Leana and B. Barry, "Stability and Change as Simultaneous Experiences in Organizational Life," *Academy of Management Review*, October 2000, pp. 753–759.
5. J. Jargon, "Burger King Returns to Its Roots," *The Wall Street Journal* online, www.wsj.com, March 9, 2016.
6. Jeevan Vasagar, "In Singapore, Service Comes with Robotic Smile," *Financial Times*, September 18, 2016, https://www.ft.com/content/04fbcae2-7d51-11e6-bc52-0c7211ef3198 (accessed December 16, 2016); Chun Han Wong, "China's Slowing Growth Forces Rethink on Worker Protections," *Wall Street Journal*, November 29, 2016, http://www.wsj.com/articles/china-looks-to-loosen-job-security-law-in-face-of-slowing-economic-growth-1480415405.
7. "18th Annual Global CEO Survey," *PwC*, www.pwc.com, January 2015.
8. J. Karsten and D. M. West, "Five Emerging Battery Technologies for Electric Vehicles," The Brookings Institute, www.brookings.edu, September 15, 2015.
9. U.S. Bureau of Labor Statistics, "The Recession of 2007–2009," *Spotlight on Statistics*, www.bls.gov, February 2012.
10. C. H. Wong, "China May Rein in Wage Increases to Boost Economy," *The Wall Street Journal* online, www.wsj.com, March 10, 2016.
11. M. Ponsford and N. Glass, "The Night I Invented 3D Printing," *CNN.com*, February 14, 2014.
12. C. Mims, "3-D Printing Promises to Change Manufacturing," *The Wall Street Journal* online, February 29, 2016; R. O. Bagley, "How 3D Printing Can Transform Your Business," *Forbes* online, www.forbes.com, May 3, 2014.
13. K. Chaudhary, R. Luss, and U. Shriram, "The Human Factor: How Employee Attitudes Toward Change Affect Change Management," Towers Watson, www.towerswatson.com, June 23, 2015.
14. The idea for these metaphors came from J. E. Dutton, S. J. Ashford, R. M. O'Neill, and K. A. Lawrence, "Moves That Matter: Issue Selling and Organizational Change," *Academy of Management Journal*, August 2001, pp. 716–736; B. H. Kemelgor, S. D. Johnson, and S. Srinivasan, "Forces Driving Organizational Change: A Business School Perspective," *Journal of Education for Business*, January/February 2000, pp. 133–137; G. Colvin, "When It Comes to Turbulence, CEOs Could Learn a Lot from Sailors," *Fortune*, March 29, 1999, pp. 194–196; and P. B. Vaill, *Managing as a Performing Art: New Ideas for a World of Chaotic Change* (San Francisco: Jossey-Bass, 1989).
15. K. Lewin, *Field Theory in Social Science* (New York: Harper & Row, 1951).
16. R. Safian, "Generation Flux," *FastCompany.com*, February 2012, p. 62.
17. "Who's Next," *FastCompany.com*, December 2010/January 2011, p. 39.
18. D. Lieberman, "Nielsen Media Has Cool Head at the Top," *USA Today*, March 27, 2006, p. 3B.
19. S. A. Mohrman and E. E. Lawler III, "Generating Knowledge That Drives Change," *Academy of Management Perspectives*, February 2012, pp. 41–51; S. Ante, "Change Is Good—So Get Used to It," *BusinessWeek*, June 22, 2009, pp. 69–70; L. S. Lüscher and M. W. Lewis, "Organizational Change and Managerial Sensemaking: Working Through Paradox," *Academy of Management Journal*, April 2008, pp. 221–240; F. Buckley and K. Monks, "Responding to Managers' Learning Needs in an Edge-of-Chaos Environment: Insights from Ireland," *Journal of Management*, April 2008, pp. 146–163; and G. Hamel, "Take It Higher," *Fortune*, February 5, 2001, pp. 169–170.
20. "Electrolux Cops Top Design Honors," *This Week in Consumer Electronics*, June 4, 2012, p. 48; A. Wolf, "Electrolux Q1 Profits Up 23%," *This Week in Consumer Electronics*, May 7, 2012, p. 30; M. Boyle, "Persuading Brits to Give Up Their Dishrags,"

Bloomberg BusinessWeek, March 26, 2012, pp. 20–21; "Electrolux Earnings Down in 2011, Hopeful for 2012," *Appliance Design*, www.appliancedesign.com, March 2012, pp. 7–8; "Electrolux Breaks Ground on Memphis Factory," *Kitchen & Bath Design News*, December 2011, p. 15; J. R. Hagerty and B. Tita, "Appliance Sales Tumble," *Wall Street Journal*, October 29, 2011, p. B1; and A. Sains and S. Reed, "Electrolux Cleans Up," *BusinessWeek*, February 27, 2006, pp. 42–43.

21. J. Wattles, "Dunkin' Donuts' Top Executive Says a $15 Minimum Wage for Fast Food Workers Is 'Absolutely Outrageous,'" *CNN Money* online, www.money.cnn.com, July 23, 2015.
22. C. Dulaney, "Dunkin's Brands Sales Growth Slows," *The Wall Street Journal* online, www.wsj.com, February 5, 2015.
23. J. R. Hagerty, "3M Begins Untangling Its Hairballs," *Wall Street Journal*, May 17, 2012, pp. B1+.
24. R. Wall, "Ryanair's New Strategy: Being Nice," *The Wall Street Journal* online, www.wsj.com, March 13, 2016.
25. J. Zhiguo, "How I Did It: Tsingtao's Chairman on Jump-Starting a Sluggish Company," *Harvard Business Review*, April 2012, pp. 41–44.
26. B. Hollingsworth, "U.S. Postal Service Lost $5.1B in FY 2015," *CBS News* online, www.cbsnews.com, November 18, 2015.
27. M. Martinez, "New Smartphone App Improves Ford Vehicle Quality Checks," *Detroit News* online, www.Detroitnews.com, February 10, 2016.
28. J. Jesitus, "Change Management: Energy to the People," *Industry Week*, September 1, 1997, pp. 37, 40.
29. D. Lavin, "European Business Rushes to Automate," *Wall Street Journal*, July 23, 1997, p. A14.
30. See, for example, B. B. Bunker, B. T. Alban, and R. J. Lewicki, "Ideas in Currency and OD Practice," *The Journal of Applied Behavioral Science*, December 2004, pp. 403–422; L. E. Greiner and T. G. Cummings, "Wanted: OD More Alive Than Dead!," *Journal of Applied Behavioral Science*, December 2004, pp. 374–391; S. Hicks, "What Is Organization Development?," *Training & Development*, August 2000, p. 65; W. Nicolay, "Response to Farias and Johnson's Commentary," *Journal of Applied Behavioral Science*, September 2000, pp. 380–381; and G. Farias, "Organizational Development and Change Management," *Journal of Applied Behavioral Science*, September 2000, pp. 376–379.
31. T. White, "Supporting Change: How Communicators at Scotiabank Turned Ideas into Action," *Communication World*, April 2002, pp. 22–24.
32. M. Javidan, P. W. Dorfman, M. S. deLuque, and R. J. House, "In the Eye of the Beholder: Cross-Cultural Lessons in Leadership from Project GLOBE," *Academy of Management Perspective*, February 2006, pp. 67–90; and E. Fagenson-Eland, E. A. Ensher, and W. W. Burke, "Organization Development and Change Interventions: A Seven-Nation Comparison," *The Journal of Applied Behavioral Science*, December 2004, pp. 432–464.
33. E. Fagenson-Eland, E. A. Ensher, and W. W. Burke, "Organization Development and Change Interventions: A Seven-Nation Comparison," p. 461.
34. S. Shinn, "Stairway to Reinvention," *BizEd*, January/February 2010, p. 6; M. Scott, "A Stairway to Marketing Heaven," *BusinessWeek*, November 2, 2009, p. 17; and The Fun Theory, http://thefuntheory.com, November 10, 2009.
35. See, for example, J. D. Ford, L. W. Ford, and A. D'Amelio, "Resistance to Change: The Rest of the Story," *Academy of Management Review*, April 2008, pp. 362–377; A. Deutschman, "Making Change: Why Is It So Hard to Change Our Ways?," *Fast Company*, May 2005, pp. 52–62; S. B. Silverman, C. E. Pogson, and A. B. Cober, "When Employees at Work Don't Get It: A Model for Enhancing Individual Employee Change in Response to Performance Feedback," *Academy of Management Executive*, May 2005, pp. 135–147; C. E. Cunningham, C. A. Woodward, H. S. Shannon, J. MacIntosh, B. Lendrum, D. Rosenbloom, and J. Brown, "Readiness for Organizational Change: A Longitudinal Study of Workplace, Psychological and Behavioral Correlates," *Journal of Occupational and Organizational Psychology*, December 2002, pp. 377–392; M. A. Korsgaard, H. J. Sapienza, and D. M. Schweiger, "Beaten Before Begun: The Role of Procedural Justice in Planning Change," *Journal of Management*, 2002, vol. 28, no. 4, pp. 497–516; R. Kegan and L. L. Lahey, "The Real Reason People Won't Change," *Harvard Business Review*, November 2001, pp. 85–92; S. K. Piderit, "Rethinking Resistance and Recognizing Ambivalence: A Multidimensional View of Attitudes Toward an Organizational Change," *Academy of Management Review*, October 2000, pp. 783–794; C. R. Wanberg and J. T. Banas, "Predictors and Outcomes of Openness to Changes in a Reorganizing Workplace," *Journal of Applied Psychology*, February 2000, pp. 132–142; A. A. Armenakis and A. G. Bedeian, "Organizational Change: A Review of Theory and Research in the 1990s," *Journal of Management*, vol. 25, no. 3, 1999, pp. 293–315; and B. M. Staw, "Counterforces to Change," in *Change in Organizations, ed.* P. S. Goodman and Associates (San Francisco: Jossey-Bass, 1982), pp. 87–121.
36. A. Reichers, J. P. Wanous, and J. T. Austin, "Understanding and Managing Cynicism About Organizational Change," *Academy of Management Executive*, February 1997, pp. 48–57; P. Strebel, "Why Do Employees Resist Change?," *Harvard Business Review*, May–June 1996, pp. 86–92; and J. P. Kotter and L. A. Schlesinger, "Choosing Strategies for Change," *Harvard Business Review*, March–April 1979, pp. 107–109.
37. "Why Hot Desking Isn't Always the Answer," *Australian Financial Review*, December 5, 2016, http://www.afr.com/leadership/company-culture/why-hot-desking-isnt-always-the-answer-20161202-gt2nyu (accessed December 16, 2016); Brad Howarth, "Activity-based Working: Welcome to the Office of the Future," *CRN Magazine*, May 2016, http://www.crn.com.au/feature/activity-based-working-welcome-to-the-office-of-the-future-419478 (accessed December 16, 2016).
38. S. Clayton, "Change Management Meets Social Media," *Harvard Business Review* online, www.hbr.org, November 10, 2015.
39. C. Null, "Does Gaming at Work Improve Productivity," *PCWorld* online, www.pcmag.com, accessed March 9, 2016.
40. P. A. McLagan, "Change Leadership Today," *T&D*, November 2002, pp. 27–31.
41. D. Meinert, "Wings of Change," *HR Magazine*, November 2012, p. 32.
42. P. A. McLagan, "Change Leadership Today," *T&D*, November 2002, p. 29.
43. K. Kingsbury, "Road to Recovery," *Time*, March 18, 2010, Global pp. 14–16; and C. Haddad, "UPS: Can It Keep Delivering?," *BusinessWeek Online Extra*, www.businessweek.com, Spring 2003.

44. W. Pietersen, "The Mark Twain Dilemma: The Theory and Practice for Change Leadership," *Journal of Business Strategy*, September/October 2002, p. 35.
45. P. A. McLagan, "The Change-Capable Organization," *T&D*, January 2003, pp. 50–58.
46. R. Yu, "Korean Air Upgrades Service, Image," *USA Today*, August 24, 2009, pp. 1B+.
47. See P. Anthony, *Managing Culture* (Philadelphia: Open University Press, 1994); P. Bate, *Strategies for Cultural Change* (Boston: Butterworth-Heinemann, 1994); C. G. Smith and R. P. Vecchio, "Organizational Culture and Strategic Management: Issues in the Strategic Management of Change," *Journal of Managerial Issues*, Spring 1993, pp. 53–70; P. F. Drucker, "Don't Change Corporate Culture—Use It!," *Wall Street Journal*, March 28, 1991, p. A14; and T. H. Fitzgerald, "Can Change in Organizational Culture Really Be Managed?" *Organizational Dynamics*, Autumn 1988, pp. 5–15.
48. K. Maney, "Famously Gruff Gerstner Leaves IBM a Changed Man," *USA Today*, November 11, 2002, pp. 1B+; and Louis V. Gerstner, *Who Says Elephants Can't Dance: Inside IBM's Historic Turnaround* (New York: Harper Business, 2002).
49. S. Ovide, "Next CEO's Job: Fix Microsoft Culture," *Wall Street Journal*, August 26, 2013, pp. B1+.
50. N. Bilton, "With New Chief, Microsoft's New Mantra Is 'Innovation' Over and Over," *New York Times* online, www.nytimes.com, February 4, 2014.
51. See, for example, D. C. Hambrick and S. Finkelstein, "Managerial Discretion: A Bridge Between Polar Views of Organizational Outcomes," in *Research in Organizational Behavior*, vol. 9, ed. L. L. Cummings and B. M. Staw (Greenwich, CT: JAI Press, 1987), p. 384; and R. H. Kilmann, M. J. Saxton, and R. Serpa, eds., *Gaining Control of the Corporate Culture* (San Francisco: Jossey-Bass, 1985).
52. S. Ilgenfritz, "Are We Too Stressed to Reduce Our Stress?," *Wall Street Journal*, November 10, 2009, p. D2; C. Daniels, "The Last Taboo," *Fortune*, October 28, 2002, pp. 137–144; J. Laabs, "Time-Starved Workers Rebel," *Workforce*, October 2000, pp. 26–28; M. A. Verespej, "Stressed Out," *Industry Week*, February 21, 2000, pp. 30–34; and M. A. Cavanaugh, W. R. Boswell, M. V. Roehling, and J. W. Boudreau, "An Empirical Examination of Self-Reported Work Stress Among U.S. Managers," *Journal of Applied Psychology*, February 2000, pp. 65–74.
53. A report on job stress compiled by the American Institute of Stress, www.stress.org/job, 2002–2003.
54. "Chinese Workers Chill, While Japanese Workers Stress," www.cnbc.com, June 17, 2015; M. Conlin, "Go-Go-Going to Pieces in China," *Business Week*, April 23, 2007, p. 88; V. P. Sudhashree, K. Rohith, and K. Shrinivas, "Issues and Concerns of Health Among Call Center Employees," *Indian Journal of Occupational Environmental Medicine,"* vol. 9, no. 3, 2005, pp. 129–132; E. Muehlchen, "An Ounce of Prevention Goes a Long Way," Wilson Banwell, www.wilsonbanwell.com, January 2004; UnionSafe, "Stressed Employees Worked to Death," unionsafe.labor.net.au/news, August 23, 2003; O. Siu, "Occupational Stressors and Well-Being Among Chinese Employees: The Role of Organizational Commitment," *Applied Psychology: An International Review*, October 2002, pp. 527–544; O. Siu, P. E. Spector, C. L. Cooper, L. Lu, and S. Yu, "Managerial Stress in Greater China: The Direct and Moderator Effects of Coping Strategies and Work Locus of Control," *Applied Psychology: An International Review*, October 2002, pp. 608–632; A. Oswald, "New Research Reveals Dramatic Rise in Stress Levels in Europe's Workplaces," University of Warwick, www.warwick.ac.uk/news/pr, 1999; and Y. Shimizu, S. Makino, and T. Takata, "Employee Stress Status During the Past Decade [1982–1992] Based on a Nation-Wide Survey Conducted by the Ministry of Labour in Japan," Japan Industrial Safety and Health Association, July 1997, pp. 441–450.
55. G. Kranz, "Job Stress Viewed Differently by Workers, Employers," *Workforce Management*, www.workforce.com, January 15, 2008.
56. Adapted from the UK National Work-Stress Network, website, www.workstress.net.
57. T. Tritch, "How Stressful Work Environments Hurt Workers' Health," *The New York Times* online, www.nytimes.com, August 25, 2015.
58. J. B. Rodell and T. A. Judge, "Can 'Good' Stressors Spark 'Bad' Behaviors? The Mediating Role of Emotions in Links of Challenge and Hindrance Stressors with Citizenship and Counterproductive Behaviors," *Journal of Applied Psychology*, November 2009, pp. 1438–1451; and see, for example, "Stressed Out: Extreme Job Stress: Survivors' Tales," *Wall Street Journal*, January 17, 2001, p. B1.
59. S. Peterson, "A Good Boss Never Leaves Their Employees in the Dark," *Fortune* online, www.fortune.com, June 24, 2015.
60. See, for instance, S. Bates, "Expert: Don't Overlook Employee Burnout," *HR Magazine*, August 2003, p. 14.
61. G. B. White, "Job-Related Stress Can Have Fatal Consequences," *The Atlantic* online, www.theatlantic.com, February 5, 2015.
62. "How Are Different Countries Addressing Worker Burnout?" *Huffington Post* online, www.huffingtonpost.com, August 1, 2013.
63. "Chinese Workers Chill, While Japanese Workers Stress," www.cnbc.com, June 17, 2015; "The Japanese Are Dying to Get to Work," www.tofugu.com, January 26, 2012; A. Kanai, "Karoshi (Work to Death) in Japan," *Journal of Business Ethics*, January 2009, Supplement 2, pp. 209–216; "Jobs for Life," *The Economist*, www.economist.com, December 19, 2007; and B. L. de Mente, "Karoshi: Death from Overwork," Asia Pacific Management Forum, www.apmforum.com, May 2002.
64. Y. Nakata, "Dealing with Japan's High Suicide Rate," blog.gaijinpot.com, January 13, 2015.
65. S. Pant, "No More Fake Smiles: Can a Chinese Company Reduce Stress with Masks?," *The Christian Science Monitor* online, www.csmonitor.com, July 15, 2015.
66. Ibid.
67. H. Benson, "Are You Working Too Hard?" *Harvard Business Review*, November 2005, pp. 53–58; B. Cryer, R. McCraty, and D. Childre, "Pull the Plug on Stress," *Harvard Business Review*, July 2003, pp. 102–107; C. Daniels, "The Last Taboo;" C. L. Cooper and S. Cartwright, "Healthy Mind, Healthy Organization—A Proactive Approach to Occupational Stress," *Human Relations*, April 1994, pp. 455–471; C. A. Heaney et al., "Industrial Relations, Worksite Stress Reduction and Employee Well-Being: A Participatory Action Research Investigation," *Journal of Organizational Behavior*, September 1993, pp. 495–510; C. D. Fisher, "Boredom at Work: A Neglected Concept," *Human Relations*, March 1993, pp. 395–417; and S. E. Jackson,

"Participation in Decision Making as a Strategy for Reducing Job-Related Strain," *Journal of Applied Psychology*, February 1983, pp. 3–19.

68. C. Mamberto, "Companies Aim to Combat Job-Related Stress," *Wall Street Journal*, August 13, 2007, p. B6.
69. L. Landro, "Why Resilience Is Good for Your Health and Career," *The Wall Street Journal* online, www.wsj.com, February 15, 2016.
70. J. Goudreau, "Dispatches from the War on Stress," *BusinessWeek*, August 6, 2007, pp. 74–75.
71. Health Fitness Revolution, "The Fortune 100 and Their Fitness and Wellness Programs," www.healthfitness.com, August 15, 2015.
72. T. A. Edison, "Famous Quotations from Thomas Edison," Thomas A. Edison Innovation Foundation, www.thomasedison.org, accessed March 10, 2016.
73. A. Saha-Bubna and M. Jarzemsky, "MasterCard President Is Named CEO," *Wall Street Journal*, April 13, 2010, p. C3; and S. Vandebook, "Quotable," *IndustryWeek*, April 2010, p. 18.
74. R. M. Kanter, "Think Outside the Building," *Harvard Business Review*, March 2010, p. 34; T. Brown, "Change by Design," *BusinessWeek*, October 5, 2009, pp. 54–56; J. E. Perry-Smith and C. E. Shalley, "The Social Side of Creativity: A Static and Dynamic Social Network Perspective," *Academy of Management Review*, January 2003, pp. 89–106; and P. K. Jagersma, "Innovate or Die: It's Not Easy, But It Is Possible to Enhance Your Organization's Ability to Innovate," *Journal of Business Strategy*, January–February 2003, pp. 25–28.
75. S. Castellano, "Guidelines to Innovation," *T&D*, September 2013, p. 20.
76. E. Brynjolfsson and M. Schrage, "The New Faster Face of Innovation," *Wall Street Journal*, August 17, 2009, p. R3.
77. Ibid.
78. L. Kwoh, "You Call That Innovation?" *Wall Street Journal*, May 23, 2012, pp. B1+.
79. These definitions are based on E. Miron-Spektor, M. Erez, and E. Naveh, "The Effect of Conformist and Attentive-to-Detail Members on Team Innovation: Reconciling the Innovation Paradox," *Academy of Management Journal*, August 2011, pp. 740–760; and T. M. Amabile, *Creativity in Context* (Boulder, CO: Westview Press, 1996).
80. U. R. Hülsheger, N. Anderson, and J. F. Salgado, "Team-Level Predictors of Innovation at Work: A Comprehensive Meta-Analysis Spanning Three Decades of Research," *Journal of Applied Psychology*, September 2009, pp. 1128–1145; R. W. Woodman, J. E. Sawyer, and R. W. Griffin, "Toward a Theory of Organizational Creativity," *Academy of Management Review*, April 1993, pp. 293–321.
81. Future Vision box based on A. VanderMey, "The 12 Disruptive Tech Trends You Need to Know," *Fortune* online, www.fortune.com, July 22, 2015; P. Nunes & L. Downes, "Big Bang Disruption: The 'Internet Of Things' Takes Off, Gradually and Then Suddenly," *Forbes* online, www.forbes.com, December 16, 2016; M. Porter & J. Heppelmann, "How Smart, Connected Products Are Transforming Companies," *Harvard Business Review*, October, 2015, vol. 93, no. 10, pp. 96-114; B. Morgan, "5 Easy to Understand Examples of the Internet of Things," *Forbes* online, www.forbes.com, January 27, 2016; J. Morgan, "A Simple Explanation of the Internet of Things," *Forbes* online, www.forbes.com, May 13, 2014.
82. "SmartPulse," smartbrief.com, June 19, 2013.
83. G. Hirst, D. Van Knippenberg, C. H. Chen, and C. A. Sacramento, "How Does Bureaucracy Impact Individual Creativity? A Cross-Level Investigation of Team Contextual Influences on Goal Orientation-Creativity Relationships," *Academy of Management Journal*, June 2011, pp. 624–641; L. Sagiv, S. Arieli, J. Goldenberg, and A. Goldschmidt, "Structure and Freedom in Creativity: The Interplay Between Externally Imposed Structure and Personal Cognitive Style," *Journal of Organizational Behavior*, November 2010, pp. 1086–1100; J. van denEnde and G. Kijkuit, "Nurturing Good Ideas," *Harvard Business Review*, April 2009, p. 24; T. M. Egan, "Factors Influencing Individual Creativity in the Workplace: An Examination of Quantitative Empirical Research," *Advances in Developing Human Resources*, May 2005, pp. 160–181; N. Madjar, G. R. Oldham, and M. G. Pratt, "There's No Place Like Home? The Contributions of Work and Nonwork Creativity Support to Employees' Creative Performance," *Academy of Management Journal*, August 2002, pp. 757–767; T. M. Amabile, C. N. Hadley, and S. J. Kramer, "Creativity Under the Gun," *Harvard Business Review*, August 2002, pp. 52–61; J. B. Sorensen and T. E. Stuart, "Aging, Obsolescence, and Organizational Innovation," *Administrative Science Quarterly*, March 2000, pp. 81–112; G. R. Oldham and A. Cummings, "Employee Creativity: Personal and Contextual Factors at Work," *Academy of Management Journal*, June 1996, pp. 607–634; and F. Damanpour, "Organizational Innovation: A Meta-Analysis of Effects of Determinants and Moderators," *Academy of Management Journal*, September 1991, pp. 555–590.
84. J. S. Lublin, "Smart Balance Keeps Tight Focus on Creativity," *Wall Street Journal*, June 8, 2009, p. B4.
85. P. R. Monge, M. D. Cozzens, and N. S. Contractor, "Communication and Motivational Predictors of the Dynamics of Organizational Innovations," *Organization Science*, May 1992, pp. 250–274.
86. D. Dobson, "Integrated Innovation at Pitney Bowes," *Strategy+Business* [www.strategy-business.com], October 26, 2009.
87. T. M. Amabile, C. N. Hadley, and S. J. Kramer, "Creativity Under the Gun."
88. T. Jana, "Dusting Off a Big Idea in Hard Times," *BusinessWeek*, June 22, 2009, pp. 44–46.
89. N. Madjar, G. R. Oldham, and M. G. Pratt, "There's No Place Like Home?"
90. C. Salter, "Mattel Learns to 'Throw the Bunny,'" *Fast Company*, November 2002, p. 22.
91. See, for instance, K. E. M. De Stobbeleir, S. J. Ashford, and D. Buyens, "Self-Regulation of Creativity at Work: The Role of Feedback-Seeking Behavior in Creative Performance," *Academy of Management Journal*, August 2011, pp. 811–831; J. Cable, "Building an Innovation Culture," *Industry Week*, March 2010, pp. 32–37; M. Hawkins, "Create a Climate of Creativity," *Training*, January 2010, p. 12; D. C. Wyld, "Keys to Innovation: The Right Measures and the Right Culture?," *Academy of Management Perspective*, May 2009, pp. 96–98; J. E. Perry-Smith, "Social Yet Creative: The Role of Social Relationships in Facilitating Individual Creativity," *Academy of Management Journal*, February 2006, pp. 85–101; C. E. Shalley, J. Zhou, and G. R. Oldham, "The Effects of Personal and Contextual Characteristics on Creativity: Where Should

We Go from Here?," *Journal of Management*, vol. 30, no. 6, 2004, pp. 933–958; J. E. Perry-Smith and C. E. Shalley, "The Social Side of Creativity: A Static and Dynamic Social Network Perspective"; J. M. George and J. Zhou, "When Openness to Experience and Conscientiousness Are Related to Creative Behavior: An Interactional Approach," *Journal of Applied Psychology*, June 2001, pp. 513–524; J. Zhou, "Feedback Valence, Feedback Style, Task Autonomy, and Achievement Orientation: Interactive Effects on Creative Behavior," *Journal of Applied Psychology*, 1998, vol. 83, pp. 261–276; T. M. Amabile, R. Conti, H. Coon, J. Lazenby, and M. Herron, "Assessing the Work Environment for Creativity," *Academy of Management Journal*, October 1996, pp. 1154–1184; S. G. Scott and R. A. Bruce, "Determinants of Innovative People: A Path Model of Individual Innovation in the Workplace," *Academy of Management Journal*, June 1994, pp. 580–607; R. Moss Kanter, "When a Thousand Flowers Bloom: Structural, Collective, and Social Conditions for Innovation in Organization," in *Research in Organizational Behavior*, vol. 10, ed. B. M. Staw and L. L. Cummings (Greenwich, CT: JAI Press, 1988), pp. 169–211; and Amabile, *Creativity in Context*.

92. L. A. Schlesinger, C. F. Kiefer, and P. B. Brown, "New Project? Don't Analyze—Act," *Harvard Business Review*, March 2012, pp. 154–158.
93. T. L. Stanley, "Creating a No-Blame Culture," *Supervision*, October 2011, pp. 3–6; S. Shellenbarger, "Better Ideas Through Failure," *Wall Street Journal*, October 27, 2011, pp. D1+; and R. W. Goldfarb, "When Fear Stifles Initiative," *New York Times* online, www.nytimes.com, May 14, 2011.
94. S. Shellenbarger, "Better Ideas Through Failure."
95. F. Yuan and R. W. Woodman, "Innovative Behavior in the Workplace: The Role of Performance and Image Outcome Expectations," *Academy of Management Journal*, April 2010, pp. 323–342.
96. K. E. M. De Stobbeleir, S. J. Ashford, and D. Buyens, "Self-Regulation of Creativity at Work: The Role of Feedback-Seeking Behavior in Creative Performance."
97. X. Zhang and K. M. Bartol, "Linking Empowering Leadership and Employee Creativity: The Influence of Psychological Empowerment, Intrinsic Motivation, and Creative Process Engagement," *Academy of Management Journal*, February 2010, pp. 107–128.
98. M. Sena, "9 of the Most Inspiring Acts of Leadership," *Fortune* online, www.fortune.com, March 26, 2015.
99. Ibid.
100. J. H. Dyer, H. B. Gregersen, and C. M. Christensen, "The Innovator's DNA," *Harvard Business Review*, December 2009, pp. 60–67; J. Gong, J-C Huang, and J-L. Farh, "Employee Learning Orientation, Transformational Leadership, and Employee Creativity: The Mediating Role of Employee Creative Self-Efficacy," *Academy of Management Journal*, August 2009, pp. 765–778; B. Buxton, "Innovation Calls for I-Shaped People," *BusinessWeek Online*, www.businessweek.com, July 13, 2009; J. Ramos, "Producing Change That Lasts," *Across the Board*, March 1994, pp. 29–33; T. Stjernberg and A. Philips, "Organizational Innovations in a Long-Term Perspective: Legitimacy and Souls-of-Fire as Critical Factors of Change and Viability," *Human Relations*, October 1993, pp. 1193–2023; and J. M. Howell and C. A. Higgins, "Champions of Change," *Business Quarterly*, Spring 1990, pp. 31–32.
101. J. Liedtka and T. Ogilvie, *Designing for Growth: A Design Thinking Tool Kit for Managers*, (New York: Columbia Business School Press, 2011).
102. Reuters, "Lego Sticks to Bricks, Despite Apps, Games and Flicks," *The New York Times*, online, www.nytimes.com, March 9, 2016.
103. Ibid.
104. D. Basulto, "Why LEGO Is the Most Innovative Toy Company in the World," *The Washington Post* online, www.washingtonpost.com, February 13, 2014.
105. R. E. Silverman, "Companies Change Their Way of Thinking," *Wall Street Journal*, June 7, 2012, p. B8; and R. L. Martin, "The Innovation Catalysts," *Harvard Business Review*, June 2011, pp. 82–87.
106. See C. M. Christensen, *The Innovator's Dilemma: When New Technologies Cause Great Firms to Fail* (Boston: Harvard Business Review Press, 1997); and "What Disruptive Innovation Means: The Economist Explains," *The Economist* online, www.economist.com, January 25, 2015.
107. C. M. Christensen, M. Raynor, and R. McDonald, "What is Disruptive Innovation?," *Harvard Business Review*, December 2015, pp. 44–53.
108. J. Schumpeter, *Capitalism, Socialism and Democracy* (New York: Harper & Row, 1942).
109. C. M. Christensen, *The Innovator's Dilemma*, p. 228.
110. Ibid.
111. Ethics Dilemma based on information collated by acas.org.uk, "How to manage change," March 2014, www.acas.org.ukmedia/pdf/k/m/Acas-How-to-manage-change-advisory-booklet.pdf.
112. Developing Your Skill box based on J. P. Kotter and L. A. Schlesinger, "Choosing Strategies for Change," *Harvard Business Review*, March–April 1979, pp. 106–114; and T. A. Stewart, "Rate Your Readiness to Change," *Fortune*, February 7, 1994, pp. 106–110.
113. A. S. Watson Group Web site, http://www.aswatson.com, accessed February 2017; Global Sources Web site, http://www.ceconlinebbs.com, accessed January 03, 2017; Ray Chan, "Li Ka-shing Sells Nearly 25pc of as Watson to Singapore Investment Giant Temasek," *South China Morning Post*, March 22, 2014; and Denny Thomas and Donny Kwok, "Temasek Agrees to Buy Stake in Beauty Retailer A. S. Watson for $5.7 Billion," *Reuters*, March 21, 2014.
114. "What's in a Name Change? Look at Apple," *Forbes* online, www.forbes.com, January 27, 2007; C. Christensen, M. Raynor, & R. McDonald, "What Is Disruptive Innovation?," *Harvard Business Review* online, www.hbr.org, December 2015; M. Wilson, "The Apple Effect: Nine Ways the Apple Changed the World with the iPhone," *Fast Company*, Dec 2015/Jan 2016, no. 201, p62–63; H. Kelly, "5 Ways the iPhone Changed the World," *CNN*, www.cnn.com, June 30, 2012; K. Martin & B. Pon, "Structuring the Smartphone Industry: Is the Mobile Internet OS Platform the Key?," *Journal of Industry, Competition, and Trade*, Sept. 2011, 11 no. 3, p239–261; J. Scanlon, "Moving to the Mobile Web," *Bloomberg Business* online, www.bloomberg.com, June 23, 2008.

Chapter 7 Constraints on Managers

It's Your Career

Source: Robuart/Shutterstock.

Reading an Organization's Culture: Find One Where You'll Be Happy

Wouldn't it be nice to one day find a job you enjoy in an organization you're excited to go to every day (or at least most days!)? Although other factors influence job choice, an organization's culture can be an important indicator of "fit." Organizational cultures differ and so do individuals. Being able to "read" an organization's culture should help you find one that's right for you. By matching your personal preferences to an organization's culture, you are more likely to find satisfaction in your work, are less likely to leave, and have a greater probability of getting positive performance evaluations. Here's a list of things you can do to "read" culture:

A key to success in management and in your career is knowing how to "read" an organization's culture so you can find one in which you'll be happy.

*1. **Do background work.** Check out the company's website. What impression do you get from it? Are corporate values listed? Mission statement? Look for current news items about the company, especially for evidence of high turnover or recent management shake-ups. Look for clues in stories told in annual reports and other organizational literature. Get the names of former employees if you can and talk with them. You might also talk with members of professional trade associations to which the organization's employees belong.*

*2. **Observe the physical surroundings and corporate symbols.** Pay attention to logos, signs, posters, pictures, photos, style of dress, length of hair, degree of openness between offices, and office furnishings and arrangements. Where do employees park? What does the physical condition of the building and offices look like? What does the office layout look like? What activities are encouraged or discouraged by the physical layout? What do these things say about what the organization values? Could you see yourself working there—and enjoying it?*

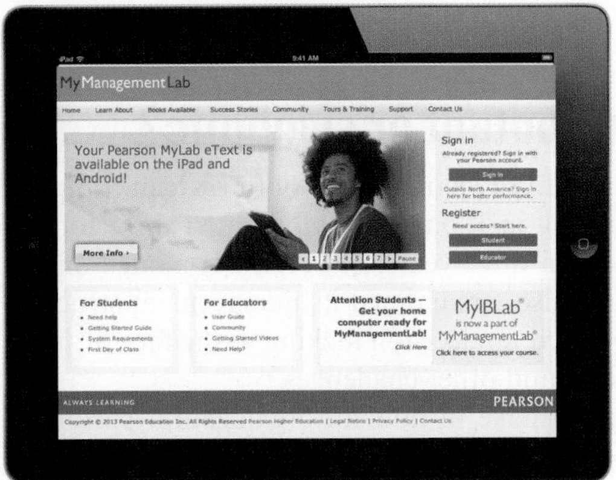

Pearson MyLab Management®

Improve Your Grade!

When you see this icon, visit **www.mymanagementlab.com** for activities that are applied, personalized, and offer immediate feedback.

Learning Objectives

• SKILL OUTCOMES

7.1 ***Contrast*** *the actions of managers according to the omnipotent and symbolic views.*

7.2 ***Describe*** *the constraints and challenges facing managers in today's external environment.*

- **Develop your skill** at scanning the environment so you can anticipate and interpret changes taking place.

7.3 ***Discuss*** *the characteristics and importance of organizational culture.*

- **Know how** to read and assess an organization's culture.

7.4 ***Describe*** *current issues in organizational culture.*

3. ***How would you characterize the people you meet?*** *Are they formal? Casual? Serious? Jovial? Open? Restrained in providing information? What stories are repeated? Are jokes/anecdotes used in conversation? How are employees addressed? What do job titles say about the organization? Does the organization's hierarchy appear to be strict or loose? What do these things say about what the organization values?*

4. ***Look at the organization's HR manual (if you can).*** *Are there formal rules and regulations? How detailed are they? What do they cover? Could you see yourself working within these parameters?*

5. ***Ask questions of the people you meet.*** *For instance: What's the background of current senior managers? Were they promoted from within or hired from the outside? What does the organization do to get new employees up and running? How is job success defined/determined? What rituals are important, and what events get commemorated? Why? Can you describe a decision that didn't work out well, and what the consequences were for that decision maker? Could you describe a crisis or critical event that occurred recently in the organization and how top management responded? What do these things say about what the organization values?*

When you apply for a job, much about the organization's culture is right there for you to see. Know the clues to look for and decide if it's for you!

In this chapter, we're going to look at culture and other important aspects of management's context. We'll examine the challenges in the external environment and discuss the characteristics of organizational culture. But before we address these topics, we first need to look at two perspectives on how much impact managers actually have on an organization's success or failure.

THE MANAGER: omnipotent or symbolic?

LO7.1 Is one CEO better than three? LG Electronics, a South Korean company with 77,000 employees working in 125 nations, appointed three top executives as co-CEOs in 2014. After less than three years, however, LG named one of the three as sole company CEO. The firm also streamlined its management structure in India and other regions. The goal: to speed up decision making in the face of fierce competition, difficult economic conditions, and other challenges.[1]

How much difference *does* a manager make in how an organization performs? The dominant view in management theory and society in general is that managers are directly responsible for an organization's success or failure. We call this perspective the **omnipotent view of management**. In contrast, others have argued that much of an organization's success or failure is due to external forces outside managers' control. This perspective is called the **symbolic view of management**. Let's look at each perspective to try and clarify just how much credit or blame managers should get for their organization's performance.

omnipotent view of management
The view that managers are directly responsible for an organization's success or failure

symbolic view of management
The view that much of an organization's success or failure is due to external forces outside managers' control

The Omnipotent View

In Chapter 1, we stressed how important managers were to organizations. Differences in an organization's performance are assumed to be due to the decisions and actions of its managers. Good managers anticipate change, exploit opportunities, correct poor performance, and lead their organizations. When profits are up, managers take the credit and are rewarded with bonuses, stock options, and the like. When profits are down, top managers are often fired in the belief that "new blood" will bring improved results. For instance, Twitter Chief Executive Jack Dorsey fired the head of engineering, summoning "bold rethinking" as the company's growth has slowed.[2] In the omnipotent view, someone has to be held accountable when organizations perform poorly regardless of the reasons, and that "someone" is the manager. Of course, when things go well, managers also get the credit—even if they had little to do with achieving the positive outcomes.

This view of managers as omnipotent is consistent with the stereotypical picture of the take-charge business executive who overcomes any obstacle in seeing that the organization achieves its goals. And this view isn't limited to business organizations. It also explains turnover among college and professional sports coaches, who are considered the "managers" of their teams. Coaches who lose more games than they win are usually fired and replaced by new coaches who are expected to correct the poor performance.

The Symbolic View

In the 2000s, online auction site eBay was the picture of success. Growing rapidly, the company's stock value rose at a healthy pace, satisfying shareholders. However, interest in online auctions has declined more recently, which poses a threat to eBay's long-term viability. In a short period, eBay's stock price declined more than 80 percent in value. The company diversified its business portfolio by acquiring PayPal and creating web design services for companies. Still, eBay has been struggling to remain competitive, particularly as competition from firms such as Amazon.com intensified. Was declining performance due to the managers' decisions and actions, or was it due to external circumstances beyond their control? The symbolic view would suggest the latter.

The symbolic view says that a manager's ability to affect performance outcomes is influenced and constrained by external factors.[3] According to this view, it's unreasonable to expect managers to significantly affect an organization's performance. Instead, performance is influenced by factors over which managers have little control, such as the economy, customers, governmental policies, competitors' actions, industry conditions, and decisions made by previous managers.

This view is labeled "symbolic" because it's based on the belief that managers symbolize control and influence.[4] How? By developing plans, making decisions, and

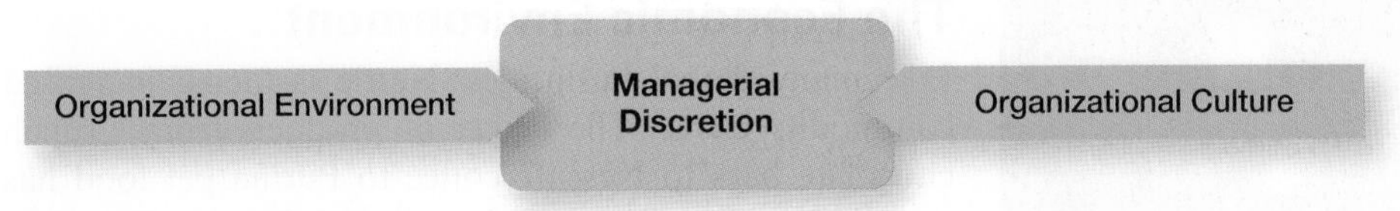

Exhibit 7-1
Constraints on Managerial Discretion

engaging in other managerial activities to make sense out of random, confusing, and ambiguous situations. However, the actual part that managers play in organizational success or failure is limited according to this view.

In reality, managers are neither all-powerful nor helpless. But their decisions and actions are constrained. As you can see in Exhibit 7-1, external constraints come from the organization's environment and internal constraints come from the organization's culture.

THE EXTERNAL ENVIRONMENT: constraints and challenges

LO7.2 Digital technology has disrupted all types of industries—from financial services and retail to entertainment and automotive. Choosing to embrace these changes, BMW borrowed a page from Apple's playbook and decided to replace its old way of doing things at dealerships.[5] Rather than the standard rows of cars, banners, and showroom cubicles, BMW has brought in "BMW Geniuses" to help shoppers better understand and to demonstrate the complex technology now in cars. Other car manufacturers are doing similar things. For instance, General Motors has worked with its dealerships to install "connection centers" in showrooms. Anyone who doubts the impact the external environment has on managing just needs to look at what's happened in the automotive industry and many other industries during the last few years.

The term **external environment** refers to factors and forces outside the organization that affect its performance. As shown in Exhibit 7-2, it includes several different components. The economic component encompasses factors such as interest rates, inflation, changes in disposable income, stock market fluctuations, and business cycle stages. The demographic component is concerned with trends in population characteristics such as age, race, gender, education level, geographic location, income, and family composition. The political/legal component looks at federal, state, and local laws as well as global laws and laws of other countries. It also includes a country's political conditions and stability. The sociocultural component is concerned with societal and cultural factors such as values, attitudes, trends, traditions, lifestyles, beliefs, tastes, and patterns of behavior. The technological component is concerned with scientific or industrial innovations. The global component encompasses those issues associated with globalization and a world economy. Although all these components pose potential constraints on managers' decisions and actions, we're going to take a closer look at two of them—the economic and demographic—by looking at how changes taking place in those components constrain managers and organizations. Then, we'll wrap up this section by examining environmental uncertainty and stakeholder relationships.

external environment
Those factors and forces outside the organization that affect its performance

Exhibit 7-2
Components of External Environment

Kiyoshi Kimura, the owner of a Japanese sushi restaurant chain, poses with a 441-pound bluefin tuna he bought at a Tokyo fish market for $117,306. The rising costs of bluefin tuna and other fish as ingredients of sushi are a volatile economic factor faced by sushi restaurateurs due in part to the growing popularity of sushi throughout the world and the overfishing of some sushi fish.
Source: Tomohiro Ohsumi/Getty Images

The Economic Environment

Like many global businesses, Nestlé is facing increased commodity costs.[6] The maker of products from Crunch chocolate bars to Nescafé coffee to Purina pet food has seen the price of chocolate, for instance, increase by nearly 30 percent in five years. Overall, Nestlé spends more than $30 billion a year on raw materials. To get a better feel for what that number reflects, think about this: annually, the company purchases about 10 percent of the world's coffee crop, 12 million metric tons of milk, and more than 300,000 tons of cocoa. Rising costs are also affecting the cost of sushi. Higher global demand for fish and the Japanese and U.S. currency exchange rates are influencing prices.[7]

Commodity (raw materials) costs are just one of the many volatile economic factors facing organizations. Managers need to be aware of the economic context so they can make the best decisions for their organizations.

THE GLOBAL ECONOMY AND THE ECONOMIC CONTEXT The lingering global economic challenges—once described as the "Great Recession" by some analysts—began with turmoil in home mortgage markets in the United States, as many homeowners found themselves unable to make their mortgage payments.[8] The problems soon affected businesses as credit markets collapsed. All of a sudden, credit was no longer readily available to fund business activities. And due to our globally connected world, it didn't take long for economic troubles in the United States to spread to other countries. The slow, fragile recovery of global economies has continued to be a constraint on organizational decisions and actions. Christine Lagarde, the Managing Director of the International Monetary Fund, said that while the global economy appears to be strengthening, global growth is still sluggish.[9] In addition, the World Economic Forum identified two significant risks facing business leaders and policy makers over the next decade: severe income disparity and chronic fiscal imbalances.[10] Let's take a quick look at the first of these risks, economic inequality, since it reflects that it's not just the economic numbers, but also societal attitudes that can constrain managers.

ECONOMIC INEQUALITY AND THE ECONOMIC CONTEXT Seven in 10 people in the world live on $10 or less per day.[11] A Pew Research Center poll found that majorities in each of 44 countries surveyed believe that the gap between rich and poor is a "big problem," and in 28 of the nations, majorities believe that the gap is a "very big problem."[12] Why has this issue become so sensitive? After all, those who worked hard and were rewarded because of their hard work or innovativeness have long been admired. And yes, an income gap has always existed. In the United States, that gap between the rich and the rest has been one of the highest among developed countries. For the past 40 years, income for the top 1 percent of earners increased 200 percent while income for the bottom fifth increased only 48 percent.[13] However, our acceptance of an ever-increasing income gap may be diminishing.[14] As economic growth has languished and sputtered, and as people's belief that anyone could grab hold of an opportunity and have a decent shot at prosperity has wavered, social discontent over growing income gaps has increased. The bottom line is that business leaders need to recognize how societal attitudes in the economic context also may create constraints as they make decisions and manage their businesses.[15]

The Demographic Environment

Demography is destiny. Have you ever heard this phrase? What it means is that the size and characteristics of a country's population can have a significant effect on what it's able to achieve and on virtually every aspect of life including politics, economics, and culture. This should make it obvious why it's important to examine demographics. Age is a particularly important demographic since the workplace often has different age groups all working together.

Baby Boomers. Gen Y. Post-Millennials. Maybe you've heard or seen these terms before. Population researchers use these terms to refer to three of the more well-known age groups found in the U.S. population. Baby Boomers are those individuals born between 1946 and 1964. So much is written and reported about "boomers" because there are so many of them. The sheer number of people in that cohort means they've significantly affected every aspect of the external environment (from the educational system to entertainment/lifestyle choices to the Social Security system and so forth) as they've cycled through the various life stages.

Gen Y (or the "Millennials") is typically considered to encompass those individuals born between 1978 and 1994. As the children of the Baby Boomers, this age group is also large in number and making its imprint on external environmental conditions as well. From technology to clothing styles to work attitudes, Gen Y is making its imprint on workplaces.

Gen Y is an important demographic at Facebook, where most employees are under 40. The company values the passion and pioneering spirit of its young employees who embrace the challenges of building groundbreaking technology and of working in a fast-paced environment with considerable change and ambiguity.
Source: Paul Sakuma/AP Images

Then, we have the Post-Millennials—the youngest identified age group—basically teens and middle-schoolers.[16] This group has also been called the iGeneration, primarily because they've grown up with technology that customizes everything to the individual.[17] Population experts say it's too early to tell whether elementary school–aged children and younger are part of this demographic group or whether the world they live in will be so different that they'll comprise a different demographic cohort.[18] Although this youngest group has not officially been "named," some are referring to them as "Gen Z" or the "touch-screen generation."[19]

Demographic age cohorts are important to our study of management because, as we said earlier, large numbers of people at certain stages in the life cycle can constrain decisions and actions taken by businesses, governments, educational institutions, and other organizations. Demographics not only looks at current statistics, but also looks to the future. For instance, recent analysis of birth rates shows that the vast majority of babies born worldwide are from Africa and Asia.[20] And here's an interesting fact: India has one of the world's youngest populations, with more males under the age of 5 than the entire population of France. And by 2050, it's predicted that China will have more people age 65 and older than

FUTURE VISION Tomorrow's Workplace: Sustainability and You

One external factor that has the capacity to affect all the components of the external environment as shown in Exhibit 7-2 is the *natural* environment. (Note: It's easy to confuse the term "external environment" with the term "natural environment" because people often talk about environmental problems and environmental damage, words which are typically used to describe the natural environment. As you've read, however, we use the term "external environment" specifically to refer to those factors and forces outside the organization that affect its performance.)

So why are we bringing up and discussing the natural environment? Because tomorrow's workplace is likely to be influenced by and focused on sustainability programs and strategies as many global businesses pursue solutions to current and potential environmental problems. Sustainability, and particularly natural environment sustainability, has become a mainstream issues for organizations.

As managers look for ways to pursue sustainability, there are many workplace elements that would affect their efforts. From property decisions (facility design, workspace design, energy usage, office locations, etc.) to technology decisions (data storage, networking capabilities, computing devices, etc.) to people decisions (where and how employees will do their work), sustainability implications must be taken into consideration. As these decisions are made with sustainability as the goal, there's likely to arise fascinating new ways of working.

As you can see, being a truly sustainable organization encompasses many factors that would need to be planned, organized, and implemented in order to find the best sustainability solutions that could be integrated into its very culture and workplace. (For more information about sustainability, see Chapter 5.)

*If your professor has chosen to assign this, go to **www.mymanagementlab.com** to discuss the following questions.*

TALK ABOUT IT 1: How might employees benefit from a workplace that's sustainability-focused?

TALK ABOUT IT 2: What challenges might employees face in a workplace that's sustainability-focused?

the rest of the world combined and the highest life expectancy (88.1 years) in the world.[21] Consider the impact of such population trends on future organizations and managers.

How the External Environment Affects Managers

Knowing *what* the various components of the external environment are and examining certain aspects of that environment are important to managers. However, understanding *how* the environment affects managers is equally as important. We're going to look at three ways the environment constrains and challenges managers—first, through its impact on jobs and employment; next, through the environmental uncertainty that is present; and finally, through the various stakeholder relationships that exist between an organization and its external constituencies.

JOBS AND EMPLOYMENT As any or all external environmental conditions (economic, demographic, technological, globalization, etc.) change, one of the most powerful constraints managers face is the impact of such changes on jobs and employment—both in poor conditions and in good conditions. The power of this constraint was painfully obvious during the last global recession as millions of jobs were eliminated and unemployment rates rose to levels not seen in many years. Businesses have been slow to reinstate jobs, creating continued hardships for those individuals looking for work.[22] Years later, there is also evidence that companies are again cutting spending and instituting large layoffs. For example, Yahoo Inc. and a few other large companies announced layoffs totaling about 14,000 workers.[23] Many college grads have struggled to find jobs or ended up taking jobs that don't require a college degree.[24] Other countries face the same issues. Although such readjustments aren't bad in and of themselves, they do create challenges for managers who must balance work demands and having enough of the right types of people with the right skills to do the organization's work.

Not only do changes in external conditions affect the types of jobs that are available, they affect how those jobs are created and managed. For instance, many employers use

let's get REAL

Source: Kelly Nelson

Kelly Nelson
Organizational Development and Training Manager

The Scenario:

As the administrative manager at a small consulting firm, David Garcia continues to face staffing challenges. He must recruit and hire the right number of consultants to be prepared for upcoming projects. The economy seems to be heading in the right direction, and the firm's client base is growing. David wants to ensure that the firm is able to continue to maintain appropriate staffing to meet future business needs.

How can David stay informed about the impact the external environment will have on his business?

Understanding and anticipating changes in the external environment is a key factor that impacts a business leader's ability to influence the company's success and to strategically plan workforce levels. Having a diverse network can help a business leader stay abreast of upcoming challenges or opportunities. Connecting with customers, competitors, and other industry professionals through industry functions or community events is one way to develop a diverse network. Additionally, more formal methods, such as market research or scenario planning, are proactive actions so that when external shifts occur in the environment, the business is prepared to adjust quickly.

flexible work arrangements to meet work output demand.[25] For instance, work tasks may be done by freelancers hired to work on an as-needed basis, or by temporary workers who work full-time but are not permanent employees, or by individuals who share jobs. Keep in mind that such responses have come about because of the constraints from the external environment. As a manager, you'll need to recognize how these work arrangements affect the way you plan, organize, lead, and control. This whole issue of flexible work arrangements has become so prevalent and part of how work is done in organizations that we'll address it in other chapters as well.

ASSESSING ENVIRONMENTAL UNCERTAINTY Another constraint posed by external environments is the amount of uncertainty found in that environment, which can affect organizational outcomes. **Environmental uncertainty** refers to the degree of change and complexity in an organization's environment. The matrix in Exhibit 7-3 shows these two aspects.

environmental uncertainty
The degree of change and complexity in an organization's environment

The first dimension of uncertainty is the degree of change. If the components in an organization's environment change frequently, it's a *dynamic* environment. If change is minimal, it's a *stable* one. A stable environment might be one with no new competitors, few technological breakthroughs by current competitors, little activity by pressure groups to influence the organization, and so forth. For instance, Almarai, based in Saudi Arabia, faces a relatively stable environment for its food products. One external concern is ongoing competition from local and regional competitors. Another concern is changes in government policies that are leading to higher costs for electricity and water. Almarai is therefore focusing on improving efficiencies to boost profitability and arranging long-term supply sources through its international subsidiaries.[26] Another concern is the use of e-cigarettes, which rely on lithium batteries rather than fire. In contrast, the recorded music industry faces a dynamic (highly uncertain and unpredictable) environment. Digital formats and music-downloading sites turned the industry upside down and brought high levels of uncertainty. And now, music streaming services such as Spotify and Pandora have added doubt to the equation.

If change is predictable, is that considered dynamic? No. Think of department stores that typically make one-quarter to one-third of their sales in November and December. The drop-off from December to January is significant. But because the change is predictable, the environment isn't considered dynamic. When we talk about degree of change, we mean change that's unpredictable. If change can be accurately anticipated, it's not an uncertainty for managers.

The other dimension of uncertainty describes the degree of **environmental complexity**, which looks at the number of components in an organization's environment and the extent of the knowledge that the organization has about those

environmental complexity
The number of components in an organization's environment and the extent of the organization's knowledge about those components

Exhibit 7-3
Environmental Uncertainty Matrix

Degree of Complexity	Degree of Change: Stable	Degree of Change: Dynamic
Simple	**Cell 1** Stable and predictable environment Few components in environment Components are somewhat similar and remain basically the same Minimal need for sophisticated knowledge of components	**Cell 2** Dynamic and unpredictable environment Few components in environment Components are somewhat similar but are continually changing Minimal need for sophisticated knowledge of components
Complex	**Cell 3** Stable and predictable environment Many components in environment Components are not similar to one another and remain basically the same High need for sophisticated knowledge of components	**Cell 4** Dynamic and unpredictable environment Many components in environment Components are not similar to one another and are continually changing High need for sophisticated knowledge of components

components. An organization with fewer competitors, customers, suppliers, government agencies, and so forth faces a less complex and uncertain environment. Organizations deal with environmental complexity in various ways. For example, Hasbro Toy Company simplified its environment by acquiring many of its competitors.

Complexity is also measured in terms of the knowledge an organization needs about its environment. For instance, managers at Pinterest must know a great deal about their Internet service provider's operations if they want to ensure their website is available, reliable, and secure for their customers. On the other hand, managers of college bookstores have a minimal need for sophisticated knowledge about their suppliers.

How does the concept of environmental uncertainty influence managers? Looking again at Exhibit 7-3, each of the four cells represents different combinations of degree of complexity and degree of change. Cell 1 (stable and simple environment) represents the lowest level of environmental uncertainty and cell 4 (dynamic and complex environment) the highest. Not surprisingly, managers have the greatest influence on organizational outcomes in cell 1 and the least in cell 4. Because uncertainty poses a threat to an organization's effectiveness, managers try to minimize it. Given a choice, managers would prefer to operate in the least uncertain environments. However, they rarely control that choice. In addition, the nature of the external environment today is that most industries are facing more dynamic change, making their environments more uncertain.

LEADER making a DIFFERENCE

Source: Newscom

*PepsiCo has experienced continual growth during the nine years **Indra Nooyi** has held the reins as CEO, reporting a 4 percent increase in organic revenue in just the last year.[27] Under Nooyi's leadership, PepsiCo is focusing on the shift in the external environment that includes a more health-conscious customer population. When Nooyi stepped in as CEO, PepsiCo's core products were soda and chips, the ultimate junk food. Nooyi insisted on taking a long-term view for the company and created three categories of products to allow the company to hold onto their historic focus while providing healthier options. Now the company's "fun for you" product line includes their traditional soda and chip fare. The "better for you" products include healthier versions of those products, and the "good for you" products are healthy options such as oatmeal and orange juice. Nooyi's leadership was key in shifting to these new product offerings. For example, she hired a chief design officer to use design thinking to explore the user experience with PepsiCo's products and support new product development. Nooyi believes in flawless execution and often focuses on small details. She asks a lot of questions and visits a market every week to look at the company's products on the shelf and also the competitor's products. Furthermore, she looks at them not only as a CEO, but also as a mom keeping the customer's perspective in view. She takes note of small details such as improperly shelved products and expects problems to be corrected quickly. A demanding leader, Nooyi is also characterized as sophisticated, witty, warm, and loyal. Her ability to take the long view and shift the company's strategy in response to the changing external environment, coupled with her effective management style, has secured her eighth year on* Fortune's *list of Most Powerful Women, landing in the number two spot in 2015.* What can you learn from this leader making a difference?

MANAGING STAKEHOLDER RELATIONSHIPS What makes YouTube an increasingly popular media outlet? On YouTube there are millions of videos available for entertainment and education as well as an outlet for social commentary. Anybody can make a video and post it to the YouTube website for others to enjoy. One factor in its success is in building relationships with its various stakeholders: viewers, celebrities and reality stars, public service groups, and others. The nature of stakeholder relationships is another way in which the environment influences managers. The more obvious and secure these relationships, the more influence managers will have over organizational outcomes.

stakeholders
Any constituencies in the organization's environment that are affected by an organization's decisions and actions

Stakeholders are any constituencies in the organization's environment affected by an organization's decisions and actions. These groups have a stake in or are significantly influenced by what the organization does. In turn, these groups can influence the organization. For example, think of the groups that might be affected by the decisions and actions of Starbucks—coffee bean farmers, employees, specialty coffee competitors, local communities, and so forth. Some of these stakeholders also, in turn, may influence decisions and actions of Starbucks' managers. The idea that organizations have stakeholders is now widely accepted by both management academics and practicing managers.[28]

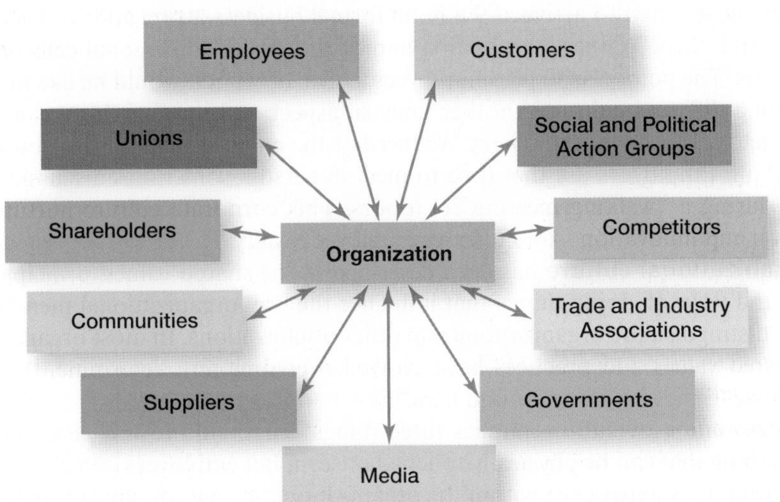

Exhibit 7-4
Organizational Stakeholders

Exhibit 7-4 identifies some of an organization's most common stakeholders. Note that these stakeholders include internal and external groups. Why? Because both can affect what an organization does and how it operates. For instance, the Dodd-Frank Act requires that many U.S. companies report their executives' compensation in publicly available sources and in a manner that can be easily comprehended by the public at large. How would this information affect stakeholders?

Why should managers even care about managing stakeholder relationships?[29] For one thing, it can lead to desirable organizational outcomes such as improved predictability of environmental changes, more successful innovations, greater degree of trust among stakeholders, and greater organizational flexibility to reduce the impact of change. But does it affect organizational performance? The answer is yes! Management researchers who have looked at this issue are finding that managers of high-performing companies tend to consider the interests of all major stakeholder groups as they make decisions.[30]

Another reason for managing external stakeholder relationships is that it's the "right" thing to do. Because an organization depends on these external groups as sources of inputs (resources) and as outlets for outputs (goods and services), managers need to consider their interests as they make decisions. We'll address this issue in more detail in the chapter on corporate social responsibility.

- 84 percent of managers believe culture is critical to business success.
- 35 percent think their company's culture is effectively managed.[31]

ORGANIZATIONAL CULTURE: **constraints and challenges**

LO7.3 Each of us has a unique personality—traits and characteristics that influence the way we act and interact with others. When we describe someone as warm, open, relaxed, shy, or aggressive, we're describing personality traits. An organization, too, has a personality, which we call its *culture.* And that culture influences the way employees act and interact with others. An organization's culture can make employees feel included, empowered, and supported, or it can have the opposite effect. Because culture can be powerful, it's important for managers to pay attention to it.

What Is Organizational Culture?

Virgin Group, headquartered in London, owns a variety of businesses, from workout facilities and financial services to travel and telecommunications. The corporate culture reflects the influence of founder Sir Richard Branson, known for his entrepreneurial spirit and sense of adventure. Branson sets the tone for a positive workplace where individual initiative is valued and employees are encouraged to balance their professional and personal lives. He once staged a "corporate day," during which Virgin

Group employees had to arrive at 9 a.m. in formal business attire, address each other as "Mr." and "Mrs." rather than by first names, and make no personal calls or social media posts. The point was to give employees a taste of what it would be like in a company with a different culture. Another unusual aspect of Virgin's culture is a weekly "digital detox." For two hours every Wednesday, the email system in some businesses is turned off. Employees use that time to meet in person, sometimes discussing work matters during a "walking meeting" outdoors. This corporate culture nurtures collaboration and innovation—and inspires employee loyalty.[32]

organizational culture
The shared values, principles, traditions, and ways of doing things that influence the way organizational members act and that distinguish the organization from other organizations

Organizational culture has been described as the shared values, principles, traditions, and ways of doing things that influence the way organizational members act and that distinguish the organization from other organizations. In most organizations, these shared values and practices have evolved over time and determine, to a large extent, how "things are done around here."[33]

Our definition of culture implies three things. First, culture is a *perception.* It's not something that can be physically touched or seen, but employees perceive it on the basis of what they experience within the organization. Second, organizational culture is *descriptive.* It's concerned with how members perceive the culture and describe it, not with whether they like it. Finally, even though individuals may have different backgrounds or work at different organizational levels, they tend to describe the organization's culture in similar terms. That's the *shared* aspect of culture.

Research suggests seven dimensions that seem to capture the essence of an organization's culture.[34] These dimensions (shown in Exhibit 7-5) range from low to high, meaning it's not very typical of the culture (low) or is very typical of the culture (high). Describing an organization using these seven dimensions gives a composite picture of the organization's culture. In many organizations, one cultural dimension often is emphasized more than the others and essentially shapes the organization's personality and the way organizational members work. For instance, at Tesla Motors, the focus is product innovation (innovation and risk taking). Its innovation has led to the creation of batteries that enable its automobiles to travel greater distances on one charge than those of most other automobile manufacturers. In contrast, Southwest Airlines has made its employees a central part of its culture (people orientation). Exhibit 7-6 describes how the dimensions can create significantly different cultures.

Exhibit 7-5
Dimensions of Organizational Culture

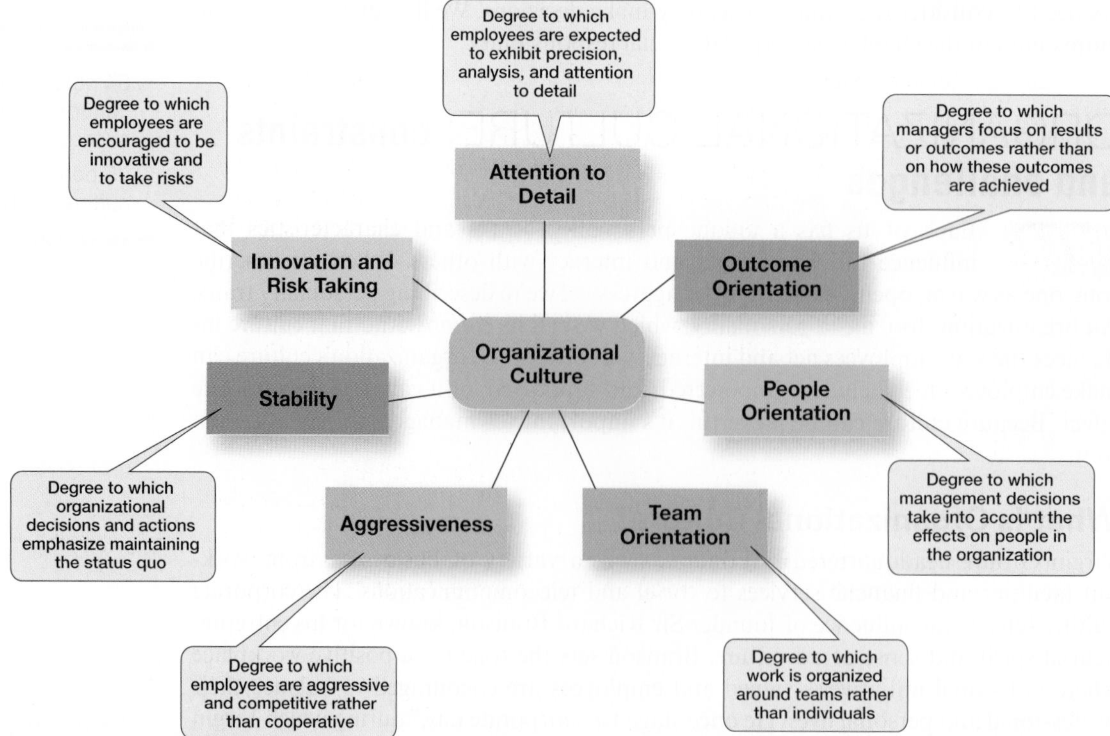

Exhibit 7-6

Contrasting Organizational Cultures

Organization A

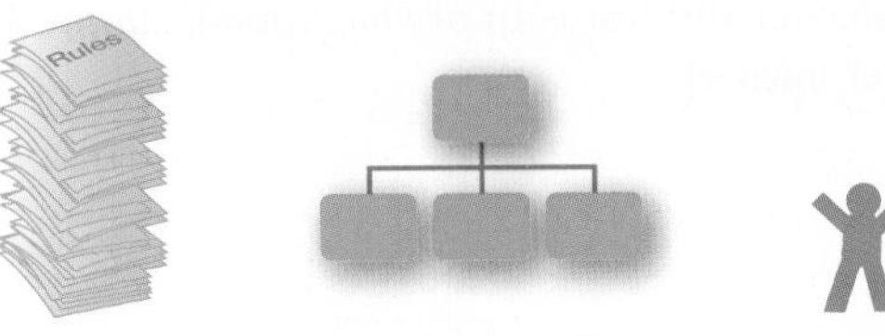

This organization is a manufacturing firm. Managers are expected to fully document all decisions, and "good managers" are those who can provide detailed data to support their recommendations. Creative decisions that incur significant change or risk are not encouraged. Because managers of failed projects are openly criticized and penalized, managers try not to implement ideas that deviate much from the status quo. One lower-level manager quoted an often-used phrase in the company: "If it ain't broke, don't fix it."

Employees are required to follow extensive rules and regulations in this firm. Managers supervise employees closely to ensure there are no deviations. Management is concerned with high productivity, regardless of the impact on employee morale or turnover.

Work activities are designed around individuals. There are distinct departments and lines of authority, and employees are expected to minimize formal contact with other employees outside their functional area or line of command. Performance evaluations and rewards emphasize individual effort, although seniority tends to be the primary factor in the determination of pay raises and promotions.

Organization B

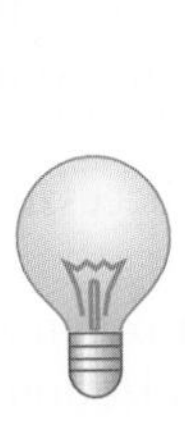

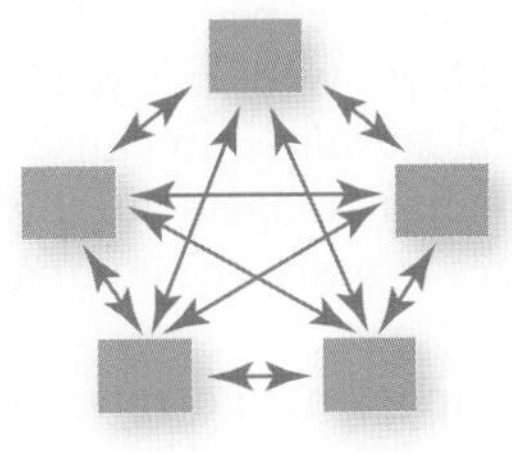

This organization is also a manufacturing firm. Here, however, management encourages and rewards risk taking and change. Decisions based on intuition are valued as much as those that are well rationalized. Management prides itself on its history of experimenting with new technologies and its success in regularly introducing innovative products. Managers or employees who have a good idea are encouraged to "run with it," and failures are treated as "learning experiences." The company prides itself on being market driven and rapidly responsive to the changing needs of its customers.

There are few rules and regulations for employees to follow, and supervision is loose because management believes its employees are hardworking and trustworthy. Management is concerned with high productivity but believes this comes through treating its people right. The company is proud of its reputation as a good place to work.

Job activities are designed around work teams, and team members are encouraged to interact with people across functions and authority levels. Employees talk positively about the competition between teams. Individuals and teams have goals, and bonuses are based on achievement of outcomes. Employees are given considerable autonomy in choosing the means by which the goals are attained.

Organizational Culture—If your instructor is using Pearson MyLab Management, log onto **mymanagementlab.com** and test your *organizational culture knowledge.* **Be sure to refer back to the chapter opener!**

Strong Cultures

strong cultures
Organizational cultures in which the key values are intensely held and widely shared

All organizations have cultures, but not all cultures equally influence employees' behaviors and actions. **Strong cultures**—those in which the key values are deeply held and widely shared—have a greater influence on employees than weaker cultures. (Exhibit 7-7 contrasts strong and weak cultures.) The more employees accept the organization's key values and the greater their commitment to those values, the stronger the culture. Most organizations have moderate to strong cultures; that is, there is relatively high agreement on what's important, what defines "good" employee behavior, what it takes to get ahead, and so forth. The stronger a culture becomes, the more it affects the way managers plan, organize, lead, and control.[35] Recreational Equipment, Inc. (REI) is an example of a company with a strong culture. The company designs and sells outdoor gear and clothing. Management has established a strong culture based on the idea that its employees give "life to their purpose" and attributes success to their employees.[36] The company's commitment to outdoor adventure attracts outdoor-oriented employees who can relate to customers. Management gives employees the opportunity to submit a "challenge grant" proposal to support a challenging personal outdoor adventure (for example, a hiking expedition). Employees even receive two paid "Yay Days" twice per year to enjoy an outdoor activity or contribute to an environmental stewardship cause. Also, the company holds regular town hall meetings, which help management stay abreast of issues within the workplace, empowering employees to assist the company in successfully meeting business objectives.[37]

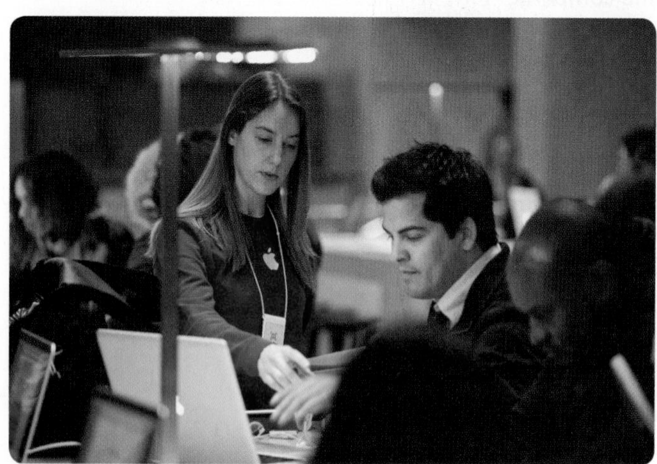

Apple's strong culture of product innovation and customer-responsive service reflects the core values of its visionary cofounder Steve Jobs. Jobs instilled these core values in all employees, from top executives to sales associates, such as the Genius Bar employee shown here training a customer at the Apple Store in Manhattan.
Source: Melanie Stetson Freeman/The Christian Science Monitor/AP Images

Why is having a strong culture important? For one thing, in organizations with strong cultures, employees are more loyal than employees in organizations with weak cultures.[38] Wehuns Tan, CEO of Wishabi, a Canadian technology company, states: "Culture is infectious—it's viral and it's central to accelerating your business."[39] Research also suggests that strong cultures are associated with high organizational

Exhibit 7-7
Strong Versus Weak Cultures

Strong Cultures	Weak Cultures
Values widely shared	Values limited to a few people—usually top management
Culture conveys consistent messages about what's important	Culture sends contradictory messages about what's important
Most employees can tell stories about company history or heroes	Employees have little knowledge of company history or heroes
Employees strongly identify with culture	Employees have little identification with culture
Strong connection between shared values and behaviors	Little connection between shared values and behaviors

performance.[40] And it's easy to understand why. After all, if values are clear and widely accepted, employees know what they're supposed to do and what's expected of them, so they can act quickly to take care of problems.[41] However, the drawback is that a strong culture also might prevent employees from trying new approaches, especially when conditions change rapidly.[42]

Where Culture Comes From and How It Continues

Exhibit 7-8 illustrates how an organization's culture is established and maintained. The original source of the culture usually reflects the vision of the founders. For instance, as we described earlier, W. L. Gore's culture reflects the values of founder Bill Gore. Company founders are not constrained by previous customs or approaches and can establish the early culture by articulating a vision of what they want the organization to be. Also, the small size of most new organizations makes it easier to instill that vision with all organizational members.

Once the culture is in place, however, certain organizational practices help maintain it. For instance, during the employee selection process, managers typically judge job candidates not only on the job requirements, but also on how well they might fit into the organization.[43] At the same time, job candidates find out information about the organization and determine whether they are comfortable with what they see.

The actions of top managers also have a major impact on the organization's culture. For instance, at CarMax, CEO Tom Folliard was a key member of the team that developed and launched CarMax. As one of the original developers of the company's unique and strong culture, Folliard is very focused on listening. He visits numerous stores every year, connecting with associates and answering questions and soliciting feedback. Does it work? You bet! CarMax has grown to be the nation's largest retailer of used vehicles by keeping associates happy, leading to happy customers.[44] The company has been on *Fortune*'s "100 Best Companies to Work For" list since 2006. Through what they say and how they behave, top managers establish norms that filter down through the organization and can have a positive effect on employees' behaviors. For instance, IKEA's leaders have set ambitious goals for protecting the planet. When employees see managers recycling leftover packaging or watch their workplace switch to solar panels, they understand that IKEA's managers are truly committed to sustainability. Consumers are getting the message, too, and their purchases are helping IKEA continue to expand profitably despite expensive sustainability projects.[45] However, as we've seen in numerous corporate ethics scandals, the actions of top managers also can lead to undesirable outcomes. Just look at Volkswagen. In 2015, evidence surfaced that revealed the company had created a device to intentionally lower harmful by-products from its diesel engines during emissions testing.

Exhibit 7-8
Establishing and Maintaining Culture

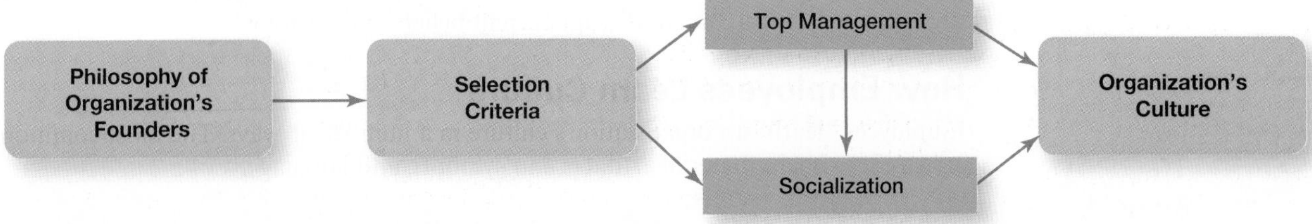

let's get REAL

The Scenario:

Source: Alfonso Marrese

Alfonso Marrese
Retail Executive

Paulo, the manager of a Web communications agency, is discovering that hiring employees can be frustrating. His last three hires are having trouble fitting in with the other 12 employees. For instance, one of the individuals—who's actually been there for six months now—doesn't want to jump in and help out the other team members when a deadline is fast approaching. And this same person doesn't say anything in team meetings and lets everyone else make decisions. And then there's the way they dress. "I don't expect them to 'suit up' or wear ties, but ripped cargo shorts and tattered flip-flops are a little too casual. Why don't these people 'get it'?"

What advice about organizational culture would you give Paulo?

During the interview process, Human Resources needs to explain the company's brand values and how the company works as a team to meet goals. Depending on what level or position the candidate is being hired for, maybe a second interview with a senior manager would help to see if the candidate will fit in with the group. During the interview process, dress code, policies and procedures should be explained to the candidate. During the first week or two on the job, the manager should be giving the new hire feedback on how he/she is doing. If there are any issues, they need to be addressed.

If your professor has assigned this, go to **www.mymanagementlab.com** to watch a video titled *Rudi's Bakery: Organizational Culture* and to respond to questions.

socialization
The process that helps employees adapt to the organization's culture

Finally, organizations help employees adapt to the culture through **socialization**, a process that helps new employees learn the organization's way of doing things. For instance, new employees at Starbucks stores go through 24 hours of intensive training that helps turn them into brewing consultants (baristas). They learn company philosophy, company jargon, and even how to assist customers with decisions about beans, grind, and espresso machines. One benefit of socialization is that employees understand the culture and are enthusiastic and knowledgeable with customers.[46] Another benefit is that it minimizes the chance that new employees who are unfamiliar with the organization's culture might disrupt current beliefs and customs.

How Employees Learn Culture

Employees "learn" an organization's culture in a number of ways. The most common are stories, rituals, material artifacts and symbols, and language.

STORIES Organizational "stories" typically contain a narrative of significant events or people, including such things as the organization's founders, rule breaking, reactions to past mistakes, and so forth.[47] Many Disney employees have heard the story that Walt Disney once said to an employee: "My brother won't give me money to make movies. Can you help get more money out of the park (Disneyland)?"[48] This question prompted Disney managers to come up with ideas to generate more revenue. When such ideas translated into higher revenue, Walt Disney provided those individuals with lavish rewards (Ferraris and substantial cash). Those rewards prompted managers to come up with additional ideas, which led to more additional revenue and more lavish rewards. Such stories help convey what's important and provide examples that people can learn from. Every LEGO employee knows that the company's name derives from the Danish phrase *leg godt*, meaning "play well." They also know the story of how the firm nearly went broke early this century, hurt by competition from electronic toys and expensive product experiments. A new CEO got LEGO back on track by focusing employees on "play experiences," meaning how children actually play with brick sets. Soon LEGO was launching one hit product after another, including the hugely popular LEGO Friends for girls. Now, when employees work on product innovations, they bring bins of bricks, talk about "play experiences," and sing the theme from *The LEGO Movie* as a team-building exercise.[49] To help employees learn the culture, organizational stories anchor the present in the past, provide explanations and legitimacy for current practices, exemplify what is important to the organization, and provide compelling pictures of an organization's goals.[50]

RITUALS In the early days of Facebook, founder Mark Zuckerberg had an artist paint a mural at company headquarters showing children taking over the world with laptops. Also, he would end employee meetings by pumping his fist in the air and leading employees in a chant of "domination." Although the cheering ritual was intended to be something simply fun, other company executives suggested he drop it because it made him seem silly, and they feared that competitors might cite it as evidence of monopolistic goals.[51] Some rituals are rites of passage for new employees. Boston-based Gentle Giant Moving Company has new recruits run the steps at Harvard Stadium as a test of fitness and determination.[52] Other rituals are outwardly focused on supporting charitable causes. For instance, Convergint Technologies sponsors an annual "Social Responsibility Day," during which time the business closes for employees to engage in a day of community service.[53] That's the power that rituals can have in shaping what employees believe is important. Corporate rituals are repetitive sequences of activities that express and reinforce the important values and goals of the organization. One corporate ritual practiced throughout the hotel company Marriott International is a 15-minute meeting at the start of every shift. For a global business that employs hundreds of thousands of people, this meeting is an opportunity to build teamwork at the local level and have fun at the same time. Depending on the hotel, these brief meetings usually include a few announcements, followed by stretching or music for a positive start to the workday. Marriott's corporate culture focuses on satisfying employees and managers at all levels and providing opportunities for professional growth so everyone in the organization will have the skills and motivation to satisfy hotel guests. Another hallmark of the corporate culture is a high degree of empowerment, enabling Marriott to grow quickly in competitive markets like India because of the ability to attract and retain talented managers. Marriott has won employer excellence awards in India, Indonesia, Japan, Malaysia, Australia, and many other regions. Its multifaceted Take Care wellness program, adapted to each culture, helps employees stay physically and mentally fit, with local "Wellness Champions" offering support and guidance. Once a year, the company holds its highest-visibility ritual: the Marriott Awards of Excellence, honoring top-performing individuals and teams from around the world. These rituals, local and international, are embedded in the corporate culture to "keep our employees engaged and happy to come to work," says the Chief Human Resources Officer.[54] But rituals don't have to be this elaborate. For instance, at Minneapolis-based Salo LLC, employees ring an office gong when a deal is signed.[55]

German carmaker BMW helps employees learn about its culture by telling the "story of 1959"—the year when BMW almost went bankrupt. To keep the company afloat, managers asked employees to help them implement a turnaround plan. The employees shown here signing a new car model they produced signifies the powerful role they continue to play in BMW's success.
Source: Andreas Gebert/EPA/Newscom

MATERIAL ARTIFACTS AND SYMBOLS When you walk into different businesses, do you get a "feel" for what type of work environment it is—formal, casual, fun, serious, and so forth? These reactions demonstrate the power of material symbols or artifacts in creating an organization's personality.[56] The layout of an organization's facilities, how employees dress, the types of automobiles provided to top executives, and the availability of corporate aircraft are examples of material symbols. Others include the size of offices, the elegance of furnishings, executive "perks" (extra benefits provided to managers such as health club memberships, use of company-owned facilities, and so forth), employee fitness centers or on-site dining facilities, and reserved parking spaces for certain employees. At WorldNow, a business that helps local media companies develop new online distribution channels and revenue streams, an important material symbol is an old dented drill that the founders purchased for $2 at a thrift store. The drill symbolizes the company's culture of "drilling down to solve problems." When an employee is presented with the drill in recognition of outstanding work, he or she is expected to personalize the drill in some way and devise a new rule for caring for it. One employee installed a Bart Simpson trigger; another made the drill wireless by adding an antenna. The company's "icon" carries on the culture even as the organization evolves and changes.[57]

Material symbols convey to employees who is important and the kinds of behavior (for example, risk taking, conservative, authoritarian, participative, individualistic, and so forth) that are expected and appropriate.

★ Watch It 2!

If your professor has assigned this, go to **www.mymanagementlab.com** to watch a video titled *Inside Google's Culture and Leadership: New Book Tells 'How Google Works'* and to respond to questions.

LANGUAGE Many organizations and units within organizations use language as a way to identify and unite members of a culture. By learning this language, members attest to their acceptance of the culture and their willingness to help preserve it. For instance, when managers and employees at OCBC Bank in Singapore talk about a culture of "life-long learning," they are referring to how the organization values personal and professional development for everyone. OCBC Bank has a catalog of more than 100 courses for employees, covering on-the-job skills like customer service and personal-growth interests like financial planning. It also invites employees over 50 years old to continue life-long learning through courses on digital literacy, physical fitness, and nutrition.[58]

Over time, organizations often develop unique terms to describe equipment, key personnel, suppliers, customers, processes, or products related to its business. New employees are frequently overwhelmed with acronyms and jargon that, after a short period of time, become a natural part of their language. Once learned, this language acts as a common denominator that bonds members.

How Culture Affects Managers

Houston-based Apache Corp. has become one of the best performers in the independent oil-drilling business because it has fashioned a culture that values risk taking and quick decision making. Potential hires are judged on how much initiative they've

WORKPLACE CONFIDENTIAL Adjusting to a New Job or Work Team

Almost all of us have made transitions in our lives. Maybe your parents moved and you had to make new friends and adjust to a new school. Or you joined a new church, social club, or sports team. As a result, you'd think that most of us would be pretty confident and successful in making the transition into a new job. This is often not the case, especially for younger employees.

For our discussion, we'll focus on the outsider-to-insider transition and both external (between organizations) and internal (between horizontal departments or vertical promotions) adjustments.

The importance of this issue is underlined by research that tells us that the typical individual changes jobs 10.2 times over 20 years—so you need to be prepared to do a lot of adjusting to new work situations.

One of your goals in any new job situation should be to make the adjustment successful. What does that entail? You've made a successful transition if, after six months in your new position, you can say that you feel comfortable, confident, and accepted by your peers. And the evidence tells us that this is most likely to occur where you know what is required to function in your job, you have confidence that you have the knowledge and skills to perform it, and you know what the job demands are in terms of relationships with others. Moreover, successful adjustment should result in satisfaction with your job and a minimal degree of anxiety and stress.

Successful adjustment should begin by assessing the new situation. Assuming you have concluded that the job is a good fit for you, you need to determine the following: What's the history of the organization or work unit? Which individuals are held in high esteem and what factors—age, experience, specific skills, personality, contacts in high places—have led to their influence? And what does the culture value? Learning to read the organization's culture—as addressed at the opening of this chapter—can provide you with answers to many of these questions.

Organizations have a variety of socialization options that they use to shape employees and help them adjust to the organization. Let's briefly review some options and consider their impact on you:

Formal vs. Informal. Specific orientation and training programs are examples of formal socialization. The informal variety puts new employees directly into the job.

Individual vs. Collective. When you're grouped with others and processed through an identical set of experiences, it's collective. Most small organizations socialize new members individually.

Fixed vs. Variable. A fixed schedule establishes standardized time targets for transition—such as a six-month probationary period or a rotational training program. Variable schedules have no advance notice of transitions—for instance, you'll be promoted when you're "ready."

Serial vs. Random. In serial socialization, you'll have a role model who will train and encourage you. Apprenticeship and mentoring programs are examples. In random socialization, you're left on your own to figure things out.

Investiture vs. Divestiture. When the organization wants to affirm and support your qualities and qualifications, they basically leave you alone. But in divestiture, the organization will attempt to strip away certain characteristics. For instance, fraternities and sororities use divestiture rites when they put "pledges" through rituals to shape new members into the proper role.

As you move into your new job, be aware that the socialization programs, or lack of such programs, you'll be exposed to will have a significant influence on your adjustment. For instance, if you see yourself as a conformist and want a job that fits you, choose a job that relies on institutional socialization—one that is formal, collective, fixed, serial, and shapes you through divestiture rites. In contrast, if you see yourself as a "wave-maker" who likes to develop your own approaches to problems, choose a job that focuses on individualized socialization—one that is informal, individual, variable, random, and affirms your uniqueness through investiture.

The evidence indicates most people end up more satisfied with, and committed to, their job when they go through institutional socialization. This is largely because its structured learning helps reduce the uncertainty inherent in a new situation and smooths transition into the new job.

An additional insight on new-job adjustment is the value of organizational insiders as a valuable resource for information. Colleagues, supervisors, and mentors are more useful as sources for accurate information about your job and the organization than formal orientation programs or organizational literature. People give you a better and more accurate reading of "the ropes to skip and the ropes to know."

Finally, don't forget the power of first impressions. A positive first impression on your boss and new colleagues can both speed up and smooth your transition. Think about the image you want to convey and make sure your dress, posture, attitude, and speech fit that image.

So what are the specific implications of all this? How can you use this information to increase the probability that you'll have a successful adjustment in a new job? The answer is to focus on those things you can control. First, to summarize, choose a job where the socialization process matches up well with your personality. And based on the evidence, choosing a job with institutionalized socialization will reduce uncertainty, lessen stress, and facilitate adjustment. Second, use insiders to provide background information and to reduce surprises. Lastly, start off on the right foot by making a good first impression. If colleagues like and respect you, they are more likely to share with you key insights into the organization's values and culture.

Based on B. Ashforth, "Socialization and Newcomer Adjustment: The Role of Organizational Context," *Human Relations*, July 1998, pp. 897–926; H. D. Cooper-Thomas and N. Anderson, "Organizational Socialization: A New Theoretical Model and Recommendations for Future Research and HRM Practices in Organizations," *Journal of Managerial Psychology*, vol. 21, no. 5, 2006, pp. 492–516; and T. N. Bauer et al., "Newcomer Adjustment During Organizational Socialization: A Meta-Analytic Review of Antecedents, Outcomes, and Methods," *Journal of Applied Psychology*, May 2007, pp. 707–721.

shown in getting projects done at other companies. And company employees are handsomely rewarded if they meet profit and production goals.[59] Because an organization's culture constrains what they can and cannot do and how they manage, it's particularly relevant to managers. Such constraints are rarely explicit. They're not written down. It's unlikely they'll even be spoken. But they're there, and all managers quickly learn what to do and not do in their organization. For instance, you won't find the following values written down, but each comes from a real organization.

- Look busy, even if you're not.
- If you take risks and fail around here, you'll pay dearly for it.
- Before you make a decision, run it by your boss so that he or she is never surprised.
- We make our product only as good as the competition forces us to.
- What made us successful in the past will make us successful in the future.
- If you want to get to the top here, you have to be a team player.

The link between values such as these and managerial behavior is fairly straightforward. Take, for example, a so-called "ready-aim-fire" culture. In such an organization, managers will study and analyze proposed projects endlessly before committing to them. However, in a "ready-*fire*-aim" culture, managers take action and then analyze what has been done. Or, say an organization's culture supports the belief that profits can be increased by cost cutting and that the company's best interests are served by achieving slow but steady increases in quarterly earnings. Managers are unlikely to pursue programs that are innovative, risky, long term, or expansionary. In an organization whose culture conveys a basic distrust of employees, managers are more likely to use an authoritarian leadership style than a democratic one. Why? The culture establishes for managers appropriate and expected behavior. For example, Banco Santander, whose headquarters are located 20 kilometers from downtown Madrid, has been described as a "risk-control freak." The company's managers adhered to "banking's stodgiest virtues—conservatism and patience." However, it's those values that triggered the company's growth from the sixth largest bank in Spain to the leading bank in the euro zone.[60]

As shown in Exhibit 7-9, a manager's decisions are influenced by the culture in which he or she operates. An organization's culture, especially a strong one, influences and constrains the way managers plan, organize, lead, and control.

Exhibit 7-9
Types of Managerial Decisions Affected by Culture

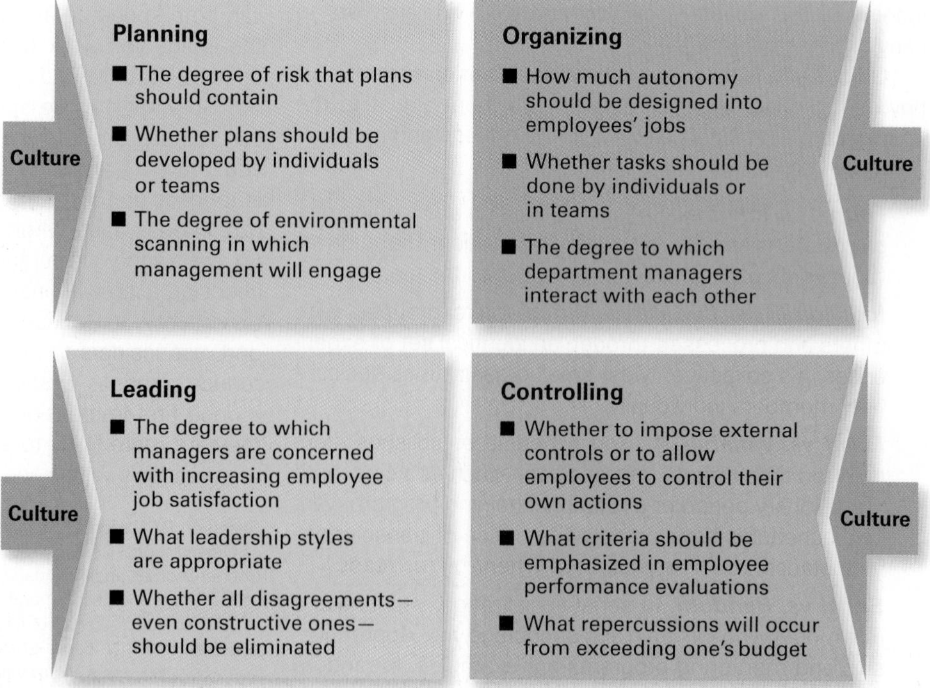

Culture
Planning
■ The degree of risk that plans should contain
■ Whether plans should be developed by individuals or teams
■ The degree of environmental scanning in which management will engage
Organizing
■ How much autonomy should be designed into employees' jobs
■ Whether tasks should be done by individuals or in teams
■ The degree to which department managers interact with each other
Culture
Culture
Leading
■ The degree to which managers are concerned with increasing employee job satisfaction
■ What leadership styles are appropriate
■ Whether all disagreements—even constructive ones—should be eliminated
Controlling
■ Whether to impose external controls or to allow employees to control their own actions
■ What criteria should be emphasized in employee performance evaluations
■ What repercussions will occur from exceeding one's budget
Culture

CURRENT issues in organizational culture

LO7.4 Nordstrom, the specialty retail chain, is renowned for its attention to customers. Nike's innovations in athletic shoe and apparel technology are legendary. Tom's of Maine is known for its commitment to doing things ethically and spiritually. How have these organizations achieved such reputations? Their organizational cultures have played a crucial role. Let's look at three current cultural issues: creating an innovative culture, creating a customer-responsive culture, and creating a sustainability culture.

Creating an Innovative Culture

You may not recognize IDEO's name, but you've probably used a number of its products. As a product design firm, it takes the ideas that corporations bring it and turns those ideas into reality. Some of its creations range from the first commercial mouse (for Apple) to the first stand-up toothpaste tube (for Procter & Gamble), to Michelob beer packaging (for Anheuser-Busch), to kitchen design concepts (for IKEA). It's critical that IDEO's culture support creativity and innovation.[61] And you might actually own and use products from another well-known innovative organization—Apple.[62] From its founding in 1976 to today, Apple has been on the forefront of product design and development. They've brought us Mac, iPod, iTunes, iPhone, and the iPad, which have changed the way you read and interact with materials such as this text. Although both these companies are in industries where innovation is critical to success, the fact is that any successful organization needs a culture that supports innovation. How important is culture to innovation? In a survey of senior executives, over half said that the most important driver of innovation for companies was a supportive corporate culture.[63] But not every company has established an adequate culture to foster innovation. In a survey of employees, about half expressed that a culture of management support is very important to the generation of innovative ideas, but only 20 percent believe that management actually provides such support.[64]

What does an innovative culture look like? According to Swedish researcher Goran Ekvall, it would be characterized by the following:

- **Challenge and involvement**—Are employees involved in, motivated by, and committed to the long-term goals and success of the organization?
- **Freedom**—Can employees independently define their work, exercise discretion, and take initiative in their day-to-day activities?
- **Trust and openness**—Are employees supportive and respectful of each other?
- **Idea time**—Do individuals have time to elaborate on new ideas before taking action?
- **Playfulness/humor**—Is the workplace spontaneous and fun?
- **Conflict resolution**—Do individuals make decisions and resolve issues based on the good of the organization versus personal interest?
- **Debates**—Are employees allowed to express opinions and put forth ideas for consideration and review?
- **Risk taking**—Do managers tolerate uncertainty and ambiguity, and are employees rewarded for taking risks?[65]

A supportive corporate culture at BuzzFeed is an important driver of innovation. The digital media firm's co-founder and CEO Jonah Peretti (left) created a culture of autonomy, collaboration, learning, open communication, and intelligent risk taking that allows employees to adapt quickly to constant changes in the business environment.
Source: Francesco Guidicini/Newscom

Creating a Customer-Responsive Culture

Internet retailer Amazon.com is fanatical about customer service—and for good reason. The company's self-proclaimed "customer obsession" contributes to a high level of customer satisfaction. Nearly 60 percent of customers surveyed reported excellent

Exhibit 7-10
Creating a Customer-Responsive Culture

Characteristics of Customer-Responsive Culture	Suggestions for Managers
Type of employee	Hire people with personalities and attitudes consistent with customer service: friendly, attentive, enthusiastic, patient, good listening skills
Type of job environment	Design jobs so employees have as much control as possible to satisfy customers, without rigid rules and procedures
Empowerment	Give service-contact employees the discretion to make day-to-day decisions on job-related activities
Role clarity	Reduce uncertainty about what service-contact employees can and cannot do by continual training on product knowledge, listening, and other behavioral skills
Consistent desire to satisfy and delight customers	Clarify organization's commitment to doing whatever it takes, even if it's outside an employee's normal job requirements

customer service, while fewer than 2 percent reported poor customer service.[66] Amazon.com has a reputation of putting customer satisfaction before profits; yet, its stock price has increased through the years, and it experienced a 25 percent increase in sales in 2014. When customer service translates into these types of results, of course managers would want to create a customer-responsive culture![67]

What does a customer-responsive culture look like?[68] Exhibit 7-10 describes five characteristics of customer-responsive cultures and offers suggestions as to what managers can do to create that type of culture.

If your professor has assigned this, go to **www.mymanagementlab.com** to complete the *Simulation: Organizational Culture* and see how well you can apply the ideas of organizational culture.

Creating a Sustainability Culture

In Chapter 1, we described as a company's ability to achieve its business goals and increase long-term shareholder value by integrating economic, environmental, and social opportunities into its business strategies. For many companies, sustainability is developed into the organization's overall culture. Tish Lascelle, Johnson & Johnson's Senior Director of Environment, said, "Sustainability is embedded in our culture. It's been a part of who we are for more than 65 years, long before the notion of sustainability became trendy."[69]

Companies can create rituals to create and maintain sustainability cultures. Earlier in this chapter, we referred to Convergint Technologies' "Social Responsibility Day." Alternatively, managers may use rewards. For instance, global polystyrene leader, Styron LLC, has more than 2,000 employees at 20 plants worldwide with annual sales of $5 billion. Management begins each corporate meeting with the topic of sustainability. Employees' bonuses are tied to meeting sustainability goals. Management's efforts seem to be working: Recently, Styron introduced a recycled-content grade of polycarbonate at the Chinaplas trade show in Guangzhou, China.[70]

Chapter 7 PREPARING FOR: Exams/Quizzes

CHAPTER SUMMARY by Learning Objectives

LO7.1 CONTRAST the actions of managers according to the omnipotent and symbolic views.

According to the omnipotent view, managers are directly responsible for an organization's success or failure. The symbolic view argues that much of an organization's success or failure is due to external forces outside managers' control. The two constraints on managers' discretion are the organization's culture (internal) and the environment (external). Managers aren't totally constrained by these two factors since they can and do influence their culture and environment.

LO7.2 DESCRIBE the constraints and challenges facing managers in today's external environment.

The external environment includes those factors and forces outside the organization that affect its performance. The main components include economic, demographic, political/legal, sociocultural, technological, and global. Managers face constraints and challenges from these components because of the impact they have on jobs and employment, environmental uncertainty, and stakeholder relationships.

LO7.3 DISCUSS the characteristics and importance of organizational culture.

The seven dimensions of culture are attention to detail, outcome orientation, people orientation, team orientation, aggressiveness, stability, and innovation and risk taking. In organizations with strong cultures, employees are more loyal and performance tends to be higher. The stronger a culture becomes, the more it affects the way managers plan, organize, lead, and control. The original source of a culture reflects the vision of organizational founders. A culture is maintained by employee selection practices, the actions of top managers, and socialization processes. Also, culture is transmitted to employees through stories, rituals, material symbols, and language. These elements help employees "learn" what values and behaviors are important as well as who exemplifies those values. The culture affects how managers plan, organize, lead, and control.

LO7.4 DESCRIBE current issues in organizational culture.

The characteristics of an innovative culture are challenge and involvement, freedom, trust and openness, idea time, playfulness/humor, conflict resolution, debates, and risk taking. A customer-responsive culture has five characteristics: outgoing and friendly employees; jobs with few rigid rules, procedures, and regulations; empowerment; clear roles and expectations; and employees who are conscientious in their desire to please the customer. Companies that achieve business goals and increase long-term shareholder value by integrating economic, environmental, and social opportunities into business strategies may develop sustainability into the organization's overall culture.

Pearson **MyLab** Management

Go to **mymanagementlab.com** to complete the problems marked with this icon .

REVIEW AND DISCUSSION QUESTIONS

7-1. Is there a real difference between an omnipotent manager and a "good" manager? Explain.

7-2. What does the term external environment mean? Which external environmental factor is more important for a manager to pay attention to?

7-3. Would a manager's job be fundamentally different if the same person were to work in different companies in the same industry?

7-4. How is a shareholder different from a stakeholder? If a stakeholder can hold no shares or any ownership in the organization, why then would the managers care about stakeholder relationships?

7-5. Distinguish between people and team orientation as dimensions of organizational culture.

7-6. Why is strong culture likely to have a greater influence on employees compared to weak culture?

7-7. What are the four common ways an organization communicates its culture to employees?

7-8. How can an innovative culture be characterized according to Goran Ekvall?

Pearson **MyLab** Management

If your professor has assigned these, go to **mymanagementlab.com** for the following Assisted-graded writing questions:

7-9. Why is it important for managers to understand the external environmental components?

7-10. Identify and describe an example of a typical organization with a) an attention to detail culture; and b) an outcome orientated culture.

PREPARING FOR: My Career

PERSONAL INVENTORY ASSESSMENTS

PERSONAL INVENTORY ASSESSMENT

What's My Comfort with Change?

As you saw in this chapter, change is a big part of the external environment and an organization's culture. This PIA will assess how comfortable you are with change.

ETHICS DILEMMA

Technological or process developments de-skill the global workforce. Take factory-built, flat-pack furniture—there seems to be no future for the role of an experienced carpenter. Similarly in the automobile industry, some vehicles have on-board computers that simply run a program to diagnose a problem. What will skilled mechanics employed in such industries do in the future? Many technologically advanced products, such as mobile phones, simply cannot be repaired, they are disposable. The qualified technicians' days may be numbered. In almost every industry this trend continues to accelerate.

7-11. Is it ethical that skilled workers are being replaced in industries?

7-12. Is deskilling inevitable? Machinery has been replacing humans for some generations now. Suggest types of activities where machines do a better job.

7-13. Would you consider it a priority to save people's jobs or would you follow this trend and automate the entire production?

SKILLS EXERCISE Developing Your Environmental Scanning Skill

About the Skill

Anticipating and interpreting changes that take place in the environment is an important skill managers need. Information that comes from scanning the environment can be used in making decisions and taking actions. And managers at all levels of an organization need to know how to scan the environment for important information and trends.

Steps in Practicing the Skill

You can be more effective at scanning the environment if you use the following suggestions:[71]

- *Decide which type of environmental information is important to your work.* Perhaps you need to know changes in customers' needs and desires, or perhaps you need to know what your competitors are doing. Once you know the type of information you'd like to have, you can look at the best ways to get that information.
- *Regularly read and monitor pertinent information.* There is no scarcity of information to scan, but what you need to do is read pertinent information sources. How do you know information sources are pertinent? They're pertinent if they provide you with the information you identified as important.
- *Incorporate the information you get from your environmental scanning into your decisions and actions.* Unless you use the information you're getting, you're wasting your time getting it. Also, the more you use information from your environmental scanning, the more likely it is that you'll want to continue to invest time and other resources into gathering it. You'll see that this information is important to your ability to manage effectively and efficiently.
- *Regularly review your environmental scanning activities.* If you're spending too much time getting information you can't use, or if you're not using the pertinent information you've gathered, you need to make some adjustments.
- *Encourage your subordinates to be alert to information that is important.* Your employees can be your "eyes and ears" as well. Emphasize to them the importance of gathering and sharing information that may affect your work unit's performance.

Practicing the Skill

Whether you are currently a manager or not one quite yet, you can practice environmental scanning to learn about relevant considerations in the external environment. Identify several different sources of business information and start practicing regularly collecting information from those sources. Subscribe to a news feed or follow a news organization on Twitter. Incorporate checking the external environment somewhere in your daily routine.

WORKING TOGETHER Team Exercise

Managers take steps to help new employees learn a company's culture. However, as you learned at the beginning of this chapter, it is a good idea to learn about a culture before you accept a job at a new company. It is important to find a work culture that aligns with your values and work style. In groups of three or four students, discuss the different types of organizational cultures. If you have work experience, share what the culture was like at your company. After you have discussed a variety of elements of culture, consider how you could learn about culture in the interview process. Create a list of questions that you could ask an employer in order to understand the culture at the company. Be prepared to share some of your questions with the class.

MY TURN TO BE A MANAGER

- Find two current examples in any popular business periodicals of the omnipotent and symbolic views of management. Write a paper describing what you found and how the two examples you found represent these views of management.
- Consider a business that you frequent (for example, a restaurant or coffee shop) and review the six aspects of the external environment discussed in the text. Create a list of factors in the external environment that could affect the management of the business you selected.
- Choose an organization with which you're familiar or one you would like to know more about. Create a table identifying potential stakeholders of this organization. Then indicate what particular interests or concerns these stakeholders might have.
- If you belong to a student organization, evaluate its culture by answering the following: How would you describe the culture? How do new members learn the culture? How is the culture maintained? If you don't belong to a student organization, talk to another student who does and evaluate it using the same questions.

CASE APPLICATION 1 Tesco: Time to Refocus

Founded in 1919, Tesco has been a business success story. With its core business focusing on food retail, in just under a century, Tesco has grown from a market-stall in the East End of London into the largest supermarket in the United Kingdom, and the third largest globally. In 2012–13, Tesco boasted group sales of £72.4 billion, with £2 billion profit before tax.

At the end 2014, Dave Lewis, who had been Tesco's CEO for only three weeks till then, sent an email to the company's staff members saying that the organization's culture had to change. He said that Tesco needed to focus on its customers and work hard on being open, honest, and transparent. Most people in his position would have probably waited more than three weeks before recommending such sweeping changes, especially for something as significant as the organizational culture. So what caused Mr. Lewis to make such a dramatic public announcement? Put simply, a financial scandal.

With significant issues, related to the drive for growth and positive market results, being brought to light by a whistle-blower, at the end of September 2014, Tesco had to make an embarrassing announcement—they had overstated their mid-year profits by £250 million, later revising this to £263 million.

The issues faced were twofold. In order to improve its own financial position, Tesco delayed its payments to some of its suppliers and it had also been including payments from suppliers as profit. It appeared that these payments were made against suppliers getting more favorable positioning for their products and more shelf space. Tesco's announcement resulted in an 8 percent fall in the share price, wiping £1.5 billion off the company's market value. A total of £3 billion was wiped off the share price in the three weeks following the announcement. On top of this, both the Grocery Code Adjudicator (an independent body set up to oversee the relationship between suppliers and supermarkets) and the Serious Fraud Office (SFO), the section of U.K. law enforcement focusing on serious or complex fraud and corruption, announced that they would be carrying out an investigation into the matter.

When you look at company documents from this period, this type of activity would seem out of step with the culture of the organization. In 2013, the then-CEO, Philip Clarke, stated that the company should do all it could to earn stakeholder loyalty and trust. In fact, the 2013 annual report identified poor relations with suppliers as a reputational risk and reaffirmed the company's aim to comply with the Groceries Supply Code of Practice. However, the satisfaction of customers and other stakeholders was replaced by a drive to meet financial targets and maintain share value.

In January 2016, Christine Tacon, the Grocery Code Adjudicator, released her report. It didn't make for a pleasant reading for Tesco management. She found evidence of internal emails that suggested staff members should not make payments to suppliers before a certain date, in order to temporarily improve margins and ensure that the company was not seen to be underperforming against targets. A list explaining how the staff could help Tesco reach mid-year targets was uncovered, which included an instruction not to pay money owed. Some payments were delayed by nearly two years and in some cases the supplier simply gave up asking!

Following the overstatement in 2014, 125 institutional funds filed a joint lawsuit for £100 million, and Tesco is still under investigation by the SFO. It may be some time before a new culture of trust and transparency will be allowed to flourish; however, Tesco seems to have seen the error of its ways. The company has improved its communication channels with suppliers, a majority of whom now say they have a more positive relationship with Tesco than they did previously.[72]

DISCUSSION QUESTIONS

7-14. Which stakeholder groups are affected by the financial scandal discussed in the case?

7-15. How could the omnipotent and symbolic management perspectives explain Tesco's financial scandal?

7-16. How is the email sent to staff members linked to Dave Lewis' view that the organization's culture needs to change?

7-17. Imagine you are looking to join Tesco. How would the organizational story of this scandal affect your decision? Consider both the scandal and how it was managed.

CASE APPLICATION 2 The Sky is the Limit

Between November 2015 and 2016, the United Kingdom saw online sales increase by 24.9 percent. So why was December 7, 2016, a special delivery day for the country? For the answer, you need to look to the skies. One Amazon customer had to wait for only 13 minutes to receive his Amazon streaming media player and a bag of popcorn, the first products delivered in the United Kingdom by a drone.

Five months earlier, Amazon announced it would be working with the British government to test drone delivery. Though in its latent stage, Amazon Prime Air has big plans for the future. Apart from developing the system in the United Kingdom, it is also looking into the feasibility of drone delivery other countries.

However, there are still many issues to overcome. For example, the United Kingdom has specific rules regarding the use of drones—drones must fly at a height of 400 feet (122 m) or less, and must avoid flying within 150 metres of congested areas and 50 metres of a person or structure. Even with these rules in place, there have been a number of worrying incidents. In April 2016, a British Airways flight reported hitting a drone while approach the Heathrow Airport, and the U.K. Airprox Board (an organization tasked with monitoring U.K. air safety) investigated 23 near-miss incidents between April and October 2015, 12 of which were in serious risk of collision.

Drone testing is certainly not exclusive to Amazon nor restricted just to the United Kingdom. In the United States, the first delivery approved by the Federal Aviation Administration (FAA) took place in 2015. An Australian-built drone made three short trips to successfully deliver 4.5 kg of medical equipment. Walmart estimated that 70 percent of the U.S. population is within 5 miles of one of their stores and, in October 2015, it applied to the authorities for permission to test drone home deliveries. From September 2016, hungry diners at Virginia Tech have been able to have their Chipotle burrito delivered by a Google drone. While Google appears to be grounding its drone venture with partner Starbucks, it is still looking at possibilities in Ireland, where the rules governing drone use are less stringent.

Though government legislations are a concern, they are not the only external challenges. Who will be the main users of this new delivery system? This may in part be a generational issue and organizations are trying to figure out whether the more tech-savvy Post-Millenials are the most likely to accept delivery by air. With some countries predicting significant increases in life expectancy and an aging, less mobile population, the demand for home delivery from this age group may also increase. These, and many other external factors, present managers with some tricky decisions to make in planning, capital spend, marketing, and recruitment.

The U.K. Amazon tests are limited to the delivery of items of 2.7 kg or less. While this limit may appear quite restrictive, it is believed to account for around 90 percent of Amazon sales. But what if you wanted to send something bigger? Or perhaps even someone? In January 2016, Chinese firm Ehang unveiled the *Ehang 184* passenger drone. The company claims that this eight-propeller electric drone can carry a passenger for up to 23 minutes. The machine, given clearance for testing in Nevada, United States, is capable of a vertical lift-off of up to 3.5 km (11,500 feet) and speed of up to 100 kmph (63 mph). However, it is unclear whether there will be a market for a personal drone-delivery system. Even the economics are questionable—a drone delivers one parcel at a time while a delivery truck can deliver several hundred parcels across 120 destinations.

However, the development of drone technology offers an innovative alternative to delivery problems. With consumers increasingly looking for convenience and speed, it is likely that more businesses will be considering drone delivery in the future.[73]

DISCUSSION QUESTIONS

7-18. What immediate and long-term issues can managers face in organizations that embrace this new drone technology?

7-19. In the case, many of the organizations operate in different countries. Will the external forces vary between countries?

7-20. When considering the employment of drone technology, are there any demographic environmental forces to consider? Consider the differences between the baby boomers and the iGeneration.

7-21. Which stakeholder groups do Amazon need to consider for this new venture? Who do you think has the greatest influence over them?

ENDNOTES

1. Yoon Sung-won, "Jo Seong-jin to Lead LG Electronics as Sole CEO," *Korea Times*, December 1, 2016, http://www.koreatimes.co.kr/www/news/tech/2016/12/133_219329.html (accessed December 12, 2016); Writankar Mukherjee, "LG India Rejigs Rules in Senior Management to Streamline Operations," *Economic Times of India*, December 25, 2015, http://economictimes.indiatimes.com/industry/cons-products/durables/lg-india-rejigs-roles-in-senior-management-to-streamline-operations/articleshow/50318268.cms (accessed December 12, 2016).
2. Reuters, "Top Twitter Executives to Leave Company, CEO Dorsey Tweets," *The New York Times* online, www.nytimes.com, January 25, 2016.
3. For insights into the symbolic view, see "Why CEO Churn Is Healthy," *BusinessWeek*, November 13, 2000, p. 230; S. M. Puffer and J. B. Weintrop, "Corporate Performance and CEO Turnover: The Role of Performance Expectations," *Administrative Science Quarterly*, March 1991, pp. 1–19; C. R. Schwenk, "Illusions of Management Control? Effects of Self-Serving Attributions on Resource Commitments and Confidence in Management," *Human Relations*, April 1990, pp. 333–347; J. R. Meindl and S. B. Ehrlich, "The Romance of Leadership and the Evaluation of Organizational Performance," *Academy of Management Journal*, March 1987, pp. 91–109; J. A. Byrne, "The Limits of Power," *BusinessWeek*, October 23, 1987, pp. 33–35; D. C. Hambrick and S. Finkelstein, "Managerial Discretion: A Bridge Between Polar Views of Organizational Outcomes," in *Research in Organizational Behavior*, vol. 9, ed. L. L. Cummings and B. M. Staw (Greenwich, CT: JAI Press, 1987), pp. 369–406; and J. Pfeffer, "Management as Symbolic Action: The Creation and Maintenance of Organizational Paradigms," in *Research in Organizational Behavior*, vol. 3, ed. L. L. Cummings and B. M. Staw (Greenwich, CT: JAI Press, 1981), pp. 1–52.
4. T. M. Hout, "Are Managers Obsolete?" *Harvard Business Review*, March–April 1999, pp. 161–168; and Pfeffer, "Management as Symbolic Action."
5. C. Rogers and J. B. White, "BMW Tosses Salesmen for 'Geniuses,'" *Wall Street Journal*, February 20, 2014, p. B1+; M. Campbell, "BMW Advancing 'Product Geniuses' Plans as Apple's Retail Model Extends into Automotive," appleinsider.com, February 19, 2014; "BMW Geniuses to Help Shoppers Understand Technology," www.autotrader.com, February 19, 2014; and K. Kerwin, "BMW Asks, Does It Take a Genius to Sell a Car?" www.forbes.com, January 13, 2014.
6. E. Terazono, "Rising Cocoa Prices Eat into Chocolate Bars," *Financial Times* online, June 30, 2015; R. Roberson, "Are High Commodity Prices Here to Stay?," *Southeast Farm Press*, October 5, 2011, pp. 18–20; A. Hanacek, "Deli Processing: Cost Crunch," *National Provisioner*, October 2011, pp. 111–114; and T. Mulier, "Nestlé's Recipe for Juggling Volatile Commodity Costs," *Bloomberg BusinessWeek*, March 21–27, 2011, pp. 29–30.
7. T. Lovgreen, *CBC News* online, www.cbc.ca, May 27, 2015.
8. A. R. Sorkin, "What Might Have Been, and the Fall of Lehman," *New York Times* online, www.nytimes.com, September 9, 2013; and D. H. Henderson, "When the Rain Came Down: A Masterful Account of How the Housing Crisis and Credit Crunch Nearly Brought Down the Economy," *Wall Street Journal*, January 19–20, 2013, p. C5.
9. P. Davidson, "Global Growth Appears Stunted, IMF Chief Says," *USA Today*, April 3, 2014, p. 2B.
10. G. Wearden, "Davos 2016: Eight Key Themes for the World Economic Forum," *The Guardian* online, www.theguardian.com, January 19, 2016; E. Pfanner, "Economic Troubles Cited as the Top Risks in 2012," *New York Times* online, www.nytimes.com, January 11, 2012; and E. Pfanner, "Divining the Business and Political Risks of 2012," *New York Times* online, January 11, 2012.
11. R. Kochhar, "Seven-in-Ten People Globally Live on $10 or Less per Day," *PewResearchCenter* online, www.pewresearch.org, September 23, 2015.
12. Pew Research Center, "Emerging and Developing Economies Much More Optimistic than Rich Countries About the Future," www.pewresearch.org, October 9, 2014.
13. E. E. Deprez, "Income Inequality," *Bloomberg Quick Take* online, www.bloombergview.com, December 11, 2015.

14. F. Newport, "Americans Continue to Say U.S. Wealth Distribution is Unfair," *Gallup*, www.gallup.com, May 4, 2015.
15. D. M. Owens, "Why Care About Income Disparity: An Interview with Timothy Noah," *HRMagazine*, March 2013, p. 53; J. Cox, "Occupy Wall Street: They're Back, But Does Anyone Care?," CNBC.com, April 30, 2012; L. Visconti, "Ask the White Guy: Why Are Disparities in Income Distribution Increasing?," DiversityInc.com, April 10, 2012; P. Meyer, "Income Inequality *Does* Matter," *USA Today*, March 28, 2012, p. 9A; E. Porter, "Inequality Undermines Democracy," *New York Times* online, www.nytimes.com, March 20, 2012; T. Cowen, "Whatever Happened to Discipline and Hard Work?," *New York Times* online, www.nytimes.com, November 12, 2011; and A. Davidson, "It's Not Just About the Millionaires," *New York Times* online, www.nytimes.com, November 9, 2011.
16. S. Jayson, "iGeneration Has No Off Switch," *USA Today*, February 10, 2010, pp. 1D+; and L. Rosen, *Rewired: Understanding the iGeneration and the Way They Learn* (New York: Palgrave-McMillan, 2010).
17. C. Gibson, "Gen Z, iGen, Founders: What Should We Call the Post-Millennials?," *The Washington Post* online, www.washingtonpost.com, December 3, 2015.
18. B. Horovitz, "Generation Whatchamacallit," *USA Today*, May 4, 2012, p. 1B+.
19. C. Gibson, "Gen Z, iGen, Founders"; H. Rosin, "The Touch-Screen Generation," *The Atlantic*, April 2013, pp. 56–65.
20. *CIA World Factbook*, www.cia.gov/library/publications/the-world-factbook/, 2015.
21. Department of Economic and Social Affairs, "World Population Prospects: The 2015 Revision," United Nations, p. 44; Y. Hori, J-P. Lehmann, T. Ma Kam Wah, and V. Wang, "Facing Up to the Demographic Dilemma," *Strategy & Business Online*, Spring 2010; and E. E. Gordon, "Job Meltdown or Talent Crunch?," *Training*, January 2010, p. 10.
22. S. Jayson, "Recession Has Broad Effects for Ages 18–34," *USA Today*, February 9, 2012, p. 4D; and M. Rich, "For Jobless, Little Hope of Restoring Better Days," *New York Times* online, www.nytimes.com, December 1, 2011.
23. T. Francis, "Big Companies Pull Back After Rough Quarter," *The Wall Street Journal* online, www.wsj.com, February 7, 2016.
24. R. Singh, "Generation U: Too Many Underemployed College Grads," www.ere.net, July 19, 2013.
25. S. G. Hauser, "Independent Contractors Helping to Shape the New World of Work," Workforce.com, February 3, 2012; H. G. Jackson, "Flexible Workplaces: A Business Imperative," *HRMagazine*, October 2011, p. 10; I. Speitzer, "Contingent Staffing," Workforce.com, October 4, 2011; M. Steen, "More Employers Take on Temps, but Planning Is Paramount," Workforce.com, May 2011; P. Davidson, "More Temp Workers Are Getting Hired," *USA Today*, March 8, 2010, p. 1B; S. Reddy, "Wary Companies Rely on Temporary Workers," *Wall Street Journal*, March 6/7, 2010, p. A4; P. Davidson, "Cuts in Hours Versus Cuts in Jobs," *USA Today*, February 25, 2010, p. 1B; and S. A. Hewlett, L. Sherbin, and K. Sumberg, "How Gen Y and Boomers Will Reshape Your Agenda," *Harvard Business Review*, July–August, 2009, pp. 71–76.
26. Eliot Beer, "Almarai Profits Up 14%, But Costs Set to Soar," *Food Navigator.com,* January 28, 2016, http://www.foodnavigator.com/Regions/Middle-East/Almarai-profits-up-14-but-costs-set-to-soar (accessed December 12, 2016); Dean Best, "Almarai Reports Bakery Boost as Poultry Sales Nosedive," *Just Food,* October 10, 2016, http://www.just-food.com/news/almarai-reports-bakery-boost-as-poultry-sales-nosedive_id134636.aspx (accessed December 12, 2016).
27. Leader Making a Difference box based on A. Ignatius, "How Indra Nooyi Turned Design Thinking Into Strategy," *Harvard Business Review,* September 2015, p. 81–85; "Fortune's Most Powerful Women List," *Fortune* online, www.fortune.com, September 15, 2015; J. Reingold, "Indra Nooyi was Right. Now What?," *Fortune,* June 15, 2015, p. 246–253.
28. J. P. Walsh, "Book Review Essay: Taking Stock of Stakeholder Management," *Academy of Management Review*, April 2005, pp. 426–438; R. E. Freeman, A. C. Wicks, and B. Parmar, "Stakeholder Theory and 'The Corporate Objective Revisited,'" *Organization Science*, June 2004, pp. 364–369; T. Donaldson and L. E. Preston, "The Stakeholder Theory of the Corporation: Concepts, Evidence, and Implications," *Academy of Management Review*, January 1995, pp. 65–91; and R. E. Freeman, *Strategic Management: A Stakeholder Approach* (Boston: Pitman/Ballinger, 1984).
29. J. S. Harrison and C. H. St. John, "Managing and Partnering With External Stakeholders," *Academy of Management Executive*, May 1996, pp. 46–60.
30. S. L. Berman, R. A. Phillips, and A. C. Wicks, "Resource Dependence, Managerial Discretion, and Stakeholder Performance," *Academy of Management Proceedings* Best Conference Paper, August 2005; A. J. Hillman and G. D. Keim, "Shareholder Value, Stakeholder Management, and Social Issues: What's the Bottom Line?," *Strategic Management Journal*, March 2001, pp. 125–139; J. S. Harrison and R. E. Freeman, "Stakeholders, Social Responsibility, and Performance: Empirical Evidence and Theoretical Perspectives," *Academy of Management Journal*, July 1999, pp. 479–487; and J. Kotter and J. Heskett, *Corporate Culture and Performance* (New York: The Free Press, 1992).
31. Booz & Company, "Culture and Change: Why Culture Matters and How It Makes Change Stick," www.strategy-business.com, January 9, 2014.
32. Jo Faragher, "Personnel Today Awards 2016: Virgin Money Takes Award for Talent Management," *Personnel Today,* November 22, 2016, http://www.personneltoday.com/hr/personnel-today-awards-2016-award-talent-management/ (accessed December 12, 2016); Rebecca Burn-Callander, "Is Flexible Working Really a Good Thing?" *Raconteur,* December 7, 2016, http://raconteur.net/business/is-flexible-working-really-a-good-thing (accessed December 12, 2016); Gianluca Mezzofiore, "This Company's Employees Are Turning Off Email for a Weekly 'Digital Detox,'" *Mashable,* September 29, 2016, http://mashable.com/2016/09/29/virgin-digital-detox/#RrX1ztScEOqV (accessed December 12, 2016).
33. K. Shadur and M. A. Kienzle, "The Relationship Between Organizational Climate and Employee Perceptions of Involvement," *Group & Organization Management*, December 1999, pp. 479–503; M. J. Hatch, "The Dynamics of Organizational Culture," *Academy of Management Review*, October 1993, pp. 657–693; D. R. Denison, "What Is the Difference Between Organizational Culture and Organizational Climate? A Native's Point of View on a Decade of Paradigm Wars," paper presented at Academy of Management Annual Meeting, 1993, Atlanta, GA; and L. Smircich, "Concepts of Culture and Organizational Analysis," *Administrative Science Quarterly*, September 1983, p. 339.
34. J. A. Chatman and K. A. Jehn, "Assessing the Relationship Between Industry Characteristics and Organizational Culture: How Different Can You Be?" *Academy of Management Journal*, June 1994, pp. 522–553; and C. A. O'Reilly III, J. Chatman, and D. F. Caldwell, "People and Organizational Culture: A Profile Comparison Approach to Assessing Person-Organization Fit," *Academy of Management Journal*, September 1991, pp. 487–516.
35. Y. Berson, S. Oreg, and T. Dvir, "CEO Values, Organizational Culture, and Firm Outcomes," *Journal of Organizational Behavior*, July 2008, pp. 615–633; and E. H. Schien, *Organizational Culture and Leadership* (San Francisco: Jossey-Bass, 1985), pp. 314–315.
36. Recreational Equipment, Inc., "Pay and Benefits," available online, www.rei.com, accessed February 10, 2016.

37. S. Patel, "10 Examples of Companies with Fantastic Cultures," www.entrepreneur.com, August 6, 2015.
38. A. E. M. Va Vianen, "Person-Organization Fit: The Match Between Newcomers' and Recruiters' Preferences for Organizational Cultures," *Personnel Psychology*, Spring 2000, pp. 113–149; K. Shadur and M. A. Kienzle, *Group & Organization Management*; P. Lok and J. Crawford, "The Relationship Between Commitment and Organizational Culture, Subculture, and Leadership Style," *Leadership & Organization Development Journal*, vol. 20, no. 6/7, 1999, pp. 365–374; C. Vandenberghe, "Organizational Culture, Person-Culture Fit, and Turnover: A Replication in the Health Care Industry," *Journal of Organizational Behavior*, March 1999, pp. 175–184; and C. Orphen, "The Effect of Organizational Cultural Norms on the Relationships Between Personnel Practices and Employee Commitment," *Journal of Psychology*, September 1993, pp. 577–579.
39. S. Olenski, "How One Brand Uses Corporate Culture to Maximize Productivity," *Forbes* online, www.forbes.com, August 27, 2014.
40. See, for example, J. B. Sorensen, "The Strength of Corporate Culture and the Reliability of Firm Performance," *Administrative Science Quarterly*, 2002, vol. 47, no. 1, pp. 70–91; R. Goffee and G. Jones, "What Holds the Modern Company Together?," *Harvard Business Review*, November–December 1996, pp. 133–148; J. C. Collins and J. I. Porras, "Building Your Company's Vision," *Harvard Business Review*, September–October 1996, pp. 65–77; J. C. Collins and J. I. Porras, *Built to Last* (New York: HarperBusiness, 1994); G. G. Gordon and N. DiTomaso, "Predicting Corporate Performance from Organizational Culture," *Journal of Management Studies*, November 1992, pp. 793–798; J. P. Kotter and J. L. Heskett, *Corporate Culture and Performance* (New York: Free Press, 1992), pp. 15–27; and D. R. Denison, *Corporate Culture and Organizational Effectiveness* (New York: Wiley, 1990).
41. S. Olenski, "How One Brand Uses Corporate Culture to Maximize Productivity," *Forbes* online, www.forbes.com, August 27, 2014.
42. J. A. Chatman, D. F. Caldwell, C. A. O'Reilly, and B. Doerr, "Parsing Organizational Culture: How the Norm for Adaptability Influences the Relationship Between Culture Consensus and Financial Performance in High-Technology Firms," *Journal of Organizational Behavior*, vol. 35, 2014, pp. 785–808; Sorensen, "The Strength of Corporate Culture and the Reliability of Firm Performance," pp. 70–91; and L. B. Rosenfeld, J. M. Richman, and S. K. May, "Information Adequacy, Job Satisfaction, and Organizational Culture in a Dispersed-Network Organization," *Journal of Applied Communication Research*, vol. 32, 2004, pp. 28–54.
43. K. Bouton, "Recruiting for Cultural Fit," *Harvard Business Review* online, www.hbr.org, July 17, 2015.
44. "What They Do, What Makes CarMax Great, What Employees Say, Great Perks," us.greatrated.com/carmax, February 2014; and "Great Workplaces: How CarMax Cares," *Fortune*, April 8, 2013, p. 21.
45. Yoni Van Looveren, "IKEA Achieves Strong Growth Despite Investing in Sustainability," *Retail Dive,* July 12, 2016, https://www.retaildetail.eu/en/news/wonen/ikea-achieves-strong-growth-despite-investing-sustainability (accessed December 12, 2016); Emma Howard, "IKEA Vows to Be Net Exporter of Renewable Energy by 2020," *The Guardian (UK),* May 27, 2016, https://www.theguardian.com/sustainable-business/2016/may/27/ikea-net-exporter-renewable-energy-2020-cop21 (accessed December 12, 2016); Beth Kowitt, "Can IKEA Turn Its Blonde World Green?" *Fortune,* March 10, 2015, http://fortune.com/2015/03/10/can-ikea-turn-green/.
46. C. C. Miller, "Now at Starbucks: A Rebound," *New York Times* online, www.nytimes.com, January 21, 2010; J. Jargon, "Latest Starbucks Buzzword: 'Lean' Japanese Techniques," *Wall Street Journal*, August 4, 2009, pp. A1+; P. Kafka, "Bean Counter," *Forbes*, February 28, 2005, pp. 78–80; A. Overholt, "Listening to Starbucks," *Fast Company*, July 2004, pp. 50–56; and B. Filipczak, "Trained by Starbucks," *Training*, June 1995, pp. 73–79.
47. P. Guber, "The Four Truths of the Storyteller," *Harvard Business Review*, December 2007, pp. 53–59; S. Denning, "Telling Tales," *Harvard Business Review*, May 2004, pp. 122–129; T. Terez, "The Business of Storytelling," *Workforce*, May 2002, pp. 22–24; J. Forman, "When Stories Create an Organization's Future," *Strategy & Business*, Second Quarter 1999, pp. 6–9; C. H. Deutsch, "The Parables of Corporate Culture," *New York Times*, October 13, 1991, p. F25; and D. M. Boje, "The Storytelling Organization: A Study of Story Performance in an Office-Supply Firm," *Administrative Science Quarterly*, March 1991, pp. 106–126.
48. G. Bradt, "Disney's Best Ever Example of Motivating Employees," *Forbes* online, www.forbes.com, May 20, 2015.
49. Debra Killalea, "LEGO: How Toy Company's Failures Led to Its Success," *News.com Australia,* September 9, 2016, http://www.news.com.au/finance/business/other-industries/lego-how-toy-companys-failures-led-to-its-success/news-story/2cb6a43167a624858b2c311f74b3bd0c (accessed December 12, 2016); Dominic Basulto, "Why LEGO Is the Most Innovative Toy Company in the World," *Washington Post,* February 13, 2014, https://www.washingtonpost.com/news/innovations/wp/2014/02/13/why-lego-is-the-most-innovative-toy-company-in-the-world/?utm_term=.eccab762b221 (accessed December 12, 2016); Jonathan Ringen, "How LEGO Became the Apple of Toys," *Fast Company,* January 8, 2015, https://www.fastcompany.com/3040223/when-it-clicks-it-clicks.
50. Denning, "Telling Tales," 2004; and A. M. Pettigrew, "On Studying Organizational Cultures," *Administrative Science Quarterly*, December 1979, p. 576.
51. J. E. Vascellaro, "Facebook CEO in No Rush to 'Friend' Wall Street," *Wall Street Journal*, March 4, 2010, p. A1+.
52. "About Gentle Giant Moving Company," www.gentlegiant.com, accessed February 10, 2016.
53. "Convergint Culture," www.convergint.com, accessed February 10, 2016.
54. Rica Bhattacharyya, "India's Best Workplaces of 2016: Hierarchies, a Strict No-No at Marriott Hotels," *The Economic Times (India),* July 4, 2016, http://economictimes.indiatimes.com/news/company/corporate-trends/indias-best-workplaces-of-2016-hierarchies-a-strict-no-no-at-marriott-hotels/articleshow/52987908.cms (accessed December 13, 2016); Ali Ahmed, "Employee Well-Being at Marriott —David Rodriguez," *Wharton Work/Life Integration Project,* October 23, 2015, http://worklife.wharton.upenn.edu/2015/10/employee-well-marriott-david-rodriguez/ (accessed December 13, 2016); "Marriott Names Aon Best Employer in Asia Pacific, Capping a Momentous Year," *AsiaOne*, December 8, 2016, http://business.asiaone.com/corporate-news-media-outreach/marriott-named-aon-best-employer-asia-pacific-capping-momentous-year (accessed December 13, 2016); Leigh Gallagher, "Why Employees Love Staying at Marriott," *Fortune,* March 5, 2015, http://fortune.com/2015/03/05/employees-loyalty-marriott/ (accessed December 13, 2016).
55. S. Shellenbarger, "Believers in the 'Project Beard' and Other Office Rituals," *Wall Street Journal*, June 26, 2013, pp. D1+.
56. E. H. Schein, "Organizational Culture," *American Psychologist*, February 1990, pp. 109–119.
57. M. Zagorski, "Here's the Drill," *Fast Company*, February 2001, p. 58.

58. "An Age-inclusive Workplace," *Straits Times (Singapore)*, November 4, 2016, http://www.straitstimes.com/business/an-age-inclusive-workplace (accessed December 13, 2016); Sham Majid, "A Premiere of Epic Proportions at OCBC Bank," *HRM Asia*, August 3, 2016, http://www.hrmasia.com/content/premiere-epic-proportions-ocbc-bank (accessed December 13, 2016).
59. C. Palmeri, "The Fastest Drill in the West," *BusinessWeek*, October 24, 2005, pp. 86–88.
60. J. Levine, "Dare to Be Boring," *Time*, February 1, 2010, pp. Global Business 1–2.
61. J. Guthrie, "David Kelley of IDEO Raises Level of Design," SFGate.com, October 23, 2011; C. T. Greer, "Innovation 101," WSJ.com, October 17, 2011; "The World's 50 Most Innovative Companies," *Fast Company*, March 2010, p. 90; L. Tischler, "A Designer Takes On His Biggest Challenge," *Fast Company*, February 2009, pp. 78+; T. Kelley and J. Littman, *The Ten Faces of Innovation: IDEO's Strategies for Defeating the Devil's Advocate and Driving Creativity Throughout Your Organization* (New York: Currency, 2005); C. Fredman, "The IDEO Difference," *Hemispheres*, August 2002, pp. 52–57; and T. Kelley and J. Littman, *The Art of Innovation* (New York: Currency, 2001).
62. D. Lyons, "Think Really Different," *Newsweek*, April 5, 2010, pp. 46–51; and R. Brands, "Innovation Made Incarnate," *Bloomberg BusinessWeek Online*, January 11, 2010.
63. J. Yang and R. W. Ahrens, "Culture Spurs Innovation," *USA Today*, February 25, 2008, p. 1B.
64. Accenture, "Corporate Innovation Is Within Reach: Nurturing and Enabling an Entrepreneurial Culture," www.accenture.com, 2013.
65. J. Cable, "Building an Innovative Culture," *Industry Week*, March 2010, pp. 32–37; M. Hawkins, "Create a Climate of Creativity," *Training*, January 2010, p. 12; and L. Simpson, "Fostering Creativity," *Training*, December 2001, p. 56.
66. M. B. Sauter, T. C. Frohlich, and S. Stubbins, "2015's Customer Service Hall of Fame," *USA Today* online, www.usatoday.com, August 2, 2015.
67. M. Millstein, "Customer Relationships Make Playing the Odds Easy," *Chain Store Age*, December 2007, p. 22A; and L. Gary, "Simplify and Execute: Words to Live by in Times of Turbulence," *Harvard Management Update*, January 2003, p. 12.
68. Based on J. McGregor, "Customer Service Champs," *BusinessWeek*, March 3, 2008, pp. 37–57; B. Schneider, M. G. Ehrhart, D. M. Mayer, J. L. Saltz, and K. Niles-Jolly, "Understanding Organization-Customer Links in Service Settings," *Academy of Management Journal*, December 2006, pp. 1017–1032; B. A. Gutek, M. Groth, and B. Cherry, "Achieving Service Success Through Relationships and Enhanced Encounters," *Academy of Management Executive*, November 2002, pp. 132–144; K. A. Eddleston, D. L. Kidder, and B. E. Litzky, "Who's the Boss? Contending with Competing Expectations From Customers and Management," *Academy of Management Executive*, November 2002, pp. 85–95; S. D. Pugh, J. Dietz, J. W. Wiley, and S. M. Brooks, "Driving Service Effectiveness Through Employee-Customer Linkages," *Academy of Management Executive*, November 2002, pp. 73–84; L. A. Bettencourt, K. P. Gwinner, and M. L. Mueter, "A Comparison of Attitude, Personality, and Knowledge Predictors of Service-Oriented Organizational Citizenship Behaviors," *Journal of Applied Psychology*, February 2001, pp. 29–41; M. D. Hartline, J. G. Maxham III, and D. O. McKee, "Corridors of Influence in the Dissemination of Customer-Oriented Strategy to Customer Contact Service Employees," *Journal of Marketing*, April 2000, pp. 35–50; L. Lengnick-Hall and C. A. Lengnick-Hall, "Expanding Customer Orientation in the HR Function," *Human Resource Management*, Fall 1999, pp. 201–214; M. D. Hartline and O. C. Ferrell, "The Management of Customer-Contact Service Employees: An Empirical Investigation," *Journal of Marketing*, October 1996, pp. 52–70; and M. J. Bitner, B. H. Booms, and L. A. Mohr, "Critical Service Encounters: The Employee's Viewpoint," *Journal of Marketing*, October 1994, pp. 95–106.
69. M. Laff, "Triple Bottom Line," *T+D*, Vol 63, February 2009, pp. 34–39.
70. F. Esposito, "Styron's Sustainability Goals, Progress Detailed in Report," *Plastics News* 23 July 18, 2011, p. 4.
71. Based on C. K. Prahalad, "Best Practices Get You Only So Far," *Harvard Business Review*, April 2010, p. 32; J. R. Oreja-Rodriguez and V. Yanes-Estévez, "Environmental Scanning: Dynamism with Rack and Stack Rasch Model," *Management Decision*, vol. 48, no. 2, 2010, pp. 260–276; C. Heavey, Z. Simsek, F. Roche, and A. Kelly, "Decision Comprehensiveness and Corporate Entrepreneurship: The Moderating Role of Managerial Uncertainty Preferences and Environmental Dynamism," *Journal of Management Studies*, December 2009, pp. 1289–1314; R. Subramanian, N. Fernandes, and E. Harper, "Environmental Scanning in U.S. Companies: Their Nature and Their Relationship to Performance," *Management International Review*, July 1993, pp. 271–286; E. H. Burack and N. J. Mathys, "Environmental Scanning Improves Strategic Planning," *Personnel Administrator*, 1989, pp. 82–87; and L. M. Fuld, *Monitoring the Competition* (New York: Wiley, 1988).
72. "Working to Make What Matters Better, Together," Tesco PLC Annual Report and Financial Statements 2013, https://www.tescoplc.com; "Groceries Supply Code of Practice," *Department for Business, Energy & Industrial Strategy,* published August 4, 2009, accessed January 3, 2017, https://www.gov.uk/government/publications/groceries-supply-code-of-practice/groceries-supply-code-of-practice; Groceries Code Adjudicator, *https://www.gov.uk/government/organisations/groceries-code-adjudicator,* accessed January 7, 2017; Seán Meehan, Charlie Dawson, and Karine Avagyan, "The Hidden Threat of Customer-led Growth," *Wiley Online Library,* http://onlinelibrary.wiley.com, published March, 2016; Kedar Grandhi, "Tesco: Serious Fraud Office will not Charge Ex-CEO Philip Clarke over Accounting Scandal, says Lawyer," *IBT online,* https://amp.ibtimes.co.uk, November 29, 2016; Seam Farrell, "Tesco Suspends Senior Staff and Starts Investigation into Overstated Profits," *The Guardian* online, www.theguardian.com, September 22, 2014; Graham Ruddick, "Tesco Boss Pledges to Change Culture," *The Telegraph* online, http://www.telegraph.co.uk, September 26, 2014; Kedar Grandhi, "Tesco Faces £100m Civil Lawsuit in Relation to its Overstatement of Earnings Two Year Ago," http://www.ibtimes.co.uk, November 1, 2016.
73. "Retail sales in Great Britain," *Office for National Statistics (ONS),* November 2016, https://www.ons.gov.uk/businessindustryandtrade/retailindustry/bulletins/retailsales/nov2016#main-points; "Amazon Makes First Drone Delivery," *BBC News*, December 14, 2016; Nicky Woolf and Samuel Gibbs, "Amazon to Test Drone Delivery in Partnership with UK Government," *The Guardian,* July 26, 2016; Amazon Prime Air Web site, https://www.amazon.com/b?tag=skim1x164751-20&node=8037720011; Sophie Curtis, "Drone Laws in the UK—What are the Rules?" *The Telegraph,* April 18, 2016; Samuel Gibbs, "First Successful Drone Delivery Made in the US," *The Guardian,* July 20, 2015; Nathan Layne, "Wal-Mart Seeks to Test Drones for Home Delivery, Pickup," *Reuters,* October 26, 2015; Samuel Gibbs, "World's First Passenger Drone Cleared for Testing in Nevada," *The Guardian,* June 8, 2016; and Dan Wang, "The Economics of Drone Delivery," *IEEE Spectrum,* http://spectrum.ieee.org/automaton/robotics/drones/the-economics-of-drone-delivery, January 5, 2016.

PART 2 Management Practice

A Manager's Dilemma

One of the biggest fears of a food service company manager has to be the hepatitis A virus, a highly contagious virus transmitted by sharing food, utensils, cigarettes, or drug paraphernalia with an infected person. Food service workers aren't any more susceptible to the illness than anyone else, but an infected employee can easily spread the virus by handling food, especially cold foods. The virus, which is rarely fatal, can cause flulike illness for several weeks. There is no cure for hepatitis A, but a vaccine can prevent it. Jim Brady, manager of a restaurant, is facing a serious dilemma. He recently learned one of his cooks could have exposed as many as 350 people to hepatitis A during a five-day period when he was at work. The cook was thought to have contracted the virus through an infant living in his apartment complex. Because children usually show no symptoms of the disease, they can easily pass it on to adults. Jim has a decision to make. Should he go public with the information, or should he only report it to the local health department as required by law?

Using what you learned in Part 2, and especially in Chapter 5, what would you do in this situation?

Global Sense

A vice president for engineering at a major chip manufacturer who found one of his projects running more than a month late felt that perhaps the company's Indian engineers "didn't understand the sense of urgency" in getting the project completed. In the Scottish highlands, the general manager of O'Bryant's Kitchens is quite satisfied with his non-Scottish employees—cooks who are German, Swedish, and Slovak, and waitresses who are mostly Polish. Other highland hotels and restaurants also have a large number of Eastern European staff. Despite the obvious language barriers, these Scottish employers are finding ways to help their foreign employees adapt and be successful. When the manager of a telecommunications company's developer forum gave a presentation to a Finnish audience and asked for feedback, he was told, "That was good." Based on his interpretation of that phrase, he assumed it must have been just an okay presentation—nothing spectacular. However, since Finns tend to be generally much quieter and more reserved than Americans, that response actually meant, "That was great, off the scale." And the owner of a Chicago-based manufacturing company, who now has two factories in Suzhou, China, is dealing with the challenges that many companies moving to China face: understanding the way their Chinese employees view work and nurturing Chinese managerial talent.

It's not easy being a successful global manager, especially when it comes to dealing with cultural differences. Those cultural differences have been described as an "iceberg," of which we only see the top 15 percent, mainly food, appearance, and language. Although these elements can be complicated, it's the other 85 percent of the "iceberg" that's not apparent initially that managers need to be especially concerned about. What does that include? Workplace issues such as communication styles, priorities, role expectations, work tempo, negotiation styles, nonverbal communication, attitudes toward planning, and so forth. Understanding these issues requires developing a global mindset and skill set. Many organizations are relying on cultural awareness training to help them do just that.

Discuss the following questions in light of what you learned in Part 2:

- *What global attitude do you think would most encourage, support, and promote cultural awareness? Explain.*
- *Would legal-political and economic differences play a role as companies design appropriate cultural awareness training for employees? Explain.*
- *Is diversity management related to cultural awareness? Discuss.*
- *Pick one of the countries mentioned above and do some cultural research on it. What did you find out about the culture of that country? How might this information affect the way a manager in that country plans, organizes, leads, and controls?*
- *What advice might you give to a manager who has little experience globally?*

Sources: P. Korkki, "More Courses Get You Ready to Face the World," New York Times online, *February 29, 2012; N. Bloom, C. Genakos, R. Sadun, and J. Van Reenen, "Management Practices Across Firms and Countries,"* Academy of Management Perspectives, *February 2012, pp. 12–33; E. Spitznagel, "Impress Your Chinese Boss,"* Bloomberg BusinessWeek, *January 9–15, 2012, pp. 80–81; R. S. Vassolo, J. O. De Castro, and L. R. Gomez-Mejia, "Managing in Latin America: Common Issues and A Research Agenda,"* Academy of Management Perspectives, *November 2011, pp. 22–37; P. Thorby, "Great Expectations: Mastering Cultural Sensitivity in Business and HR,"* www.workforce.com, *August 17, 2011; K. Tyler, "Global Ease,"* HR Magazine, *May 2011, pp. 41–48; J. S. Lublin, "Cultural Flexibility In Demand,"* Wall Street Journal, *April 11, 2011, pp. B1+; and S. Russwurm, L. Hernandez, S. Chambers, and K. Chung, "Developing Your Global Know-How,"* Harvard Business Review, *March 2011, pp. 70–75.*

Continuing Case

Starbucks—Basics of Managing in Today's Workplace

As managers manage in today's workplace, they must be aware of some specific integrative issues that can affect the way they plan, organize, lead, and control. The characteristics and nature of these integrative issues will

These customers are enjoying "the Starbucks experience" at a coffee shop in Guangzhou, China. Starbucks sees an enormous potential for growth in China, where 140 cities have a population exceeding one million people. While expanding in China and other global markets, Starbucks managers must take into account the cultural, economic, legal, and political aspects of different markets as they plan, organize, lead, and control.

Source: Imaginechina/Associated Press

influence what managers and other employees do and how they do it. And more importantly, it will affect how efficiently and effectively managers do their job of coordinating and overseeing the work of other people so that goals—organizational and work-level or work-unit—can be accomplished. What are these integrative managerial issues, and how does Starbucks accommodate and respond to them as they manage in today's workplace? In this part of the Continuing Case, we're going to look at Starbucks' external environment/organizational culture, global business, diversity, and social responsibility/ethical challenges.

Starbucks—Defining the Terrain: Culture and Environment

As managers manage, they must be aware of the terrain or broad environment within which they plan, organize, lead, and control. The characteristics and nature of this "terrain" will influence what managers and other employees do and how they do it. And more importantly, it will affect how efficiently and effectively managers do their job of coordinating and overseeing the work of other people so that goals—organizational and work-level or work-unit—can be accomplished. What does Starbucks' terrain look like, and how is the company adapting to that terrain?

An organization's culture is a mix of written and unwritten values, beliefs, and codes of behavior that influence the way work gets done and the way people behave in organizations. And the distinct flavor of Starbucks' culture can be traced to the original founders' philosophies and Howard Schultz's unique beliefs about how a company should be run. The three friends (Jerry Baldwin, Gordon Bowker, and Zev Siegl) who founded Starbucks in 1971 as a store in Seattle's historic Pike Place Market district did so for one reason: They loved coffee and tea and wanted Seattle to have access to the best. They had no intention of building a business empire. Their business philosophy, although never written down, was simple: "Every company must stand for something; don't just give customers what they ask for or what they think they want; and assume that your customers are intelligent and seekers of knowledge." The original Starbucks was a company passionately committed to world-class coffee and dedicated to educating its customers, one-on-one, about what great coffee can be. It was these qualities that ignited Howard Schultz's passion for the coffee business and inspired him to envision what Starbucks could become. Schultz continues to have that passion for his business—he is the visionary and soul behind Starbucks. He visits at least 30 to 40 stores a week, talking to partners (employees) and to customers. His ideas for running a business have been called "unconventional," but Schultz doesn't care. He says, "We can be extremely profitable and competitive, with a highly regarded brand, and also be respected for treating our people well." One member of the company's board of directors says about him, "Howard is consumed with his vision of Starbucks. That means showing the good that a corporation can do for its workers, shareholders, and customers."

The company's mission and guiding principles (which you can find at www.starbucks.com) are meant to guide the decisions and actions of company partners from top to bottom. They also have significantly influenced the organization's culture. Starbucks' culture emphasizes keeping employees motivated and content. One thing that's been important to Howard Schultz from day one is the relationship he has with his employees. He treasures those relationships and feels they're critically important to the way the company develops its relationships with its customers and the way it is viewed by the public. He says, "We know that our people are the heart and soul of our success." Starbucks' 235,000-plus employees worldwide serve millions of customers each week. That's a lot of opportunities to either satisfy or disappoint the customer. The experiences customers have in the stores ultimately affect the company's relationships with its customers. That's why Starbucks has created a unique relationship with its employees. Starbucks provides a set of generous employee benefits, referred to as "Your Special Blend," to all employees who work more than 20 hours a week: health care benefits and a compensation plan that includes stock options. Schultz says, "The most important thing I ever did was give our partners (employees) bean stock (options to buy the company's stock). That's what sets us apart and gives us a higher-quality employee, an employee that cares more." In 2015, the company announced that it would pay for most employees (currently, about 140,000 out of 235,000-plus) to earn a bachelor's degree from Arizona State University's online course offerings. The program is called the College Achievement Program. CEO Howard Schultz believes that "by giving our partners access to four years of full tuition reimbursement, we will provide them a critical tool for lifelong opportunity." Also, he believes the company's educational benefits will enable more educated workers to participate in the labor force.

It's clear that Starbucks cares about its employees. For instance, when three Starbucks employees were murdered in a botched robbery attempt in Washington, D.C., Schultz immediately flew there to handle the situation. In addition, he decided that all future profits from that store would go to organizations working for victims' rights and violence prevention. Another example of the company's concern: Starbucks recently announced that it was committed to hiring 10,000 veterans and military spouses over the next five years.

As a global company with revenues of $19.2 billion, Starbucks' executives recognize they must be aware of the impact the environment has on their decisions and actions. Starbucks began lobbying legislators in Washington, D.C., on issues including lowering trade barriers, health care costs, and tax breaks. It's something that Schultz didn't really want to do, but he recognized that such efforts could be important to the company's future.

Global Challenges

You could say that Starbucks has been a global business from day one. While on a business trip in 1983 to Milan, Howard Schultz (who worked in marketing for Starbucks' original founders and is now the company's CEO) experienced firsthand Italy's coffee culture and had an epiphany about how such an approach might work back home in the United States. Now, almost 40 years later, Starbucks stores are found in 68 countries, including stores from China and Australia to the Netherlands and Switzerland. Doing business globally, as Chapter 3 points out, can be challenging. Since much of the company's future growth prospects are global, the company has targeted some markets for additional global expansion, including China, Brazil, and Vietnam. Schultz is clear about the fact that his company sees China as the number one growth opportunity for Starbucks. During a visit in late 2011, a government official informed him that 140 cities in China now have a population exceeding one million people. That's a lot of potential coffee drinkers buying cups of Starbucks coffee and other Starbucks products! But in China and all of its global markets, Starbucks must be cognizant of the economic, legal–political, and cultural aspects that characterize those markets. For instance, in Europe—the "birthplace of café and coffeehouse culture"—Starbucks is struggling, even after a decade of doing business there. Take France, where Starbucks has been since 2004 and has 76 stores. It has never made a profit. Of course, part of that could be attributed to the debt crisis and sluggish economy. And rents and labor costs are notoriously high. Yet the biggest challenge for Starbucks may be trying to appeal to the vast array of European tastes. The company's chief of Starbucks operations for Europe, the Middle East, and Africa decided to take an "anthropological tour" to get a better feel for the varying wants and needs of coffee lovers in Europe. Although it was initially thought that the well-established coffeehouse culture in places like Paris or Vienna might be what customers wanted, what was discovered instead was that customers wanted the "Starbucks experience." But even that means different things in different markets. For instance, the British drink take-away (to-go) coffee, so Starbucks is planning for hundreds of drive-through locations there. In the rest of Europe, Starbucks plans to put many new sites in airports and railway stations on the continent.

In 2016, Starbucks announced that it would open stores in Italy even though some are skeptical about whether it will be successful. Orlando Chiari, owner of a century-old coffee shop, expressed his skepticism: "We worship coffee in Italy, while Americans drink coffee on the go in large cups." Mr. Chiari elaborated. "It's two extremely different cultures." Although the growth potential seems real, cultural challenges still remain, not only in Europe but in Starbucks' other markets as well. The company is recognizing that not every customer wants a standardized experience. So, as Starbucks continues its global expansion, it's attempting to be respectful of the cultural differences.

Managing Diversity and Inclusion

Not only does Starbucks attempt to be respectful of global cultural differences, it is committed to being an organization that embraces and values diversity in how it does business. The company-wide diversity strategy encompasses four areas: customers, suppliers, partners (employees), and communities. Starbucks attempts to make the Starbucks experience accessible to all customers and to respond to each customer's unique preferences and needs. Starbucks' supplier diversity program works to provide opportunities for developing a business relationship to women- and minority-owned suppliers. As far as its partners, the company is committed to a workplace that values and respects people from diverse backgrounds. The most current company diversity statistics available show that 33 percent of employees are minorities and 64 percent are women. And Starbucks aims to enable its partners to do their best work and to be successful in the Starbucks environment. The company does support partner networks (what we call employee resource groups in Chapter 4). Some of the current ones include Starbucks Access Alliance, a forum for partners with disabilities; Starbucks Armed Forces Support Network, which supports veterans and those currently in the armed forces and their families; and the Starbucks Black Partner Network, which strengthens relationships and connections among partners of African descent. Finally, Starbucks supports diversity in its local neighborhoods and global communities through programs and investments that deepen its ties in those areas. Although Starbucks is committed to practicing and valuing diversity, by no means is it perfect. For instance, an Americans with Disabilities Act case was filed against a specific Starbucks store by a job applicant who had short height because of the condition of dwarfism. The store management refused to hire her for a barista job even though she claimed she could do the job using a step stool. And they did not even offer to try this accommodation. Starbucks quickly settled the case and agreed to provide training to managers on proper ADA procedures. The company's response earned praise from the Equal Employment Opportunity Commission for its prompt resolution of the issue.

Starbucks has often extended its reach to embrace diversity in local communities. With good intentions, the CEO launched the "Race Together" campaign to encourage discussion and understanding of longstanding societal racial and ethnic divides. Following Schultz's instructions, Starbucks' workers wrote "race together" on beverage cups. Widespread negative sentiment flooded social media. Some posts expressed that it wasn't Starbucks' place to foster this complex and deeply emotion-laden discussion. Shortly thereafter, Starbucks terminated this campaign.

Social Responsibility and Ethics

Doing good coffee is important to Starbucks, but so is doing good. Starbucks takes its social responsibility and ethical commitments seriously. In 2001, the company began issuing an annual corporate social responsibility report, which addresses the company's decisions and actions in relation to its products, society, the environment, and the workplace. These reports aren't simply a way for Starbucks to brag about its socially responsible actions, but are intended to stress the importance of doing business in a responsible way and to hold employees and managers accountable for their actions.

Starbucks focuses its corporate responsibility efforts on three main areas: ethical sourcing (buying), environmental stewardship, and community involvement. Starbucks approaches ethical sourcing from the perspective of helping the farmers and suppliers who grow and produce their products use responsible growing methods and helping them be successful, thus promoting long-term sustainability of the supply of quality coffee. It's a win-win situation. The farmers have a better (and more secure) future and Starbucks is helping create a long-term supply of a commodity they depend on. Environmental stewardship has been one of the more challenging undertakings for Starbucks, especially when you think about the number of disposable containers generated by the more than three billion customers served annually. And front-of-the-store waste is only half the battle. Behind-the-counter waste is also generated in the form of cardboard boxes, milk jugs, syrup bottles, and, not surprisingly, coffee grounds. Even with recycling bins provided, one wrong item in a recycle bin can make the whole thing unrecyclable to a hauler. Despite this, the company has made significant strides in recycling. In a 2010 test program, 100,000 paper coffee cups were made into new ones. The company's goal by 2015 was to recycle all four-billion-plus cups sold annually. An ambitious goal, for sure. It wasn't able to meet that goal, as customer recycling is available at only 39 percent of its company-operated stores. However, the company has made progress possible only through a cooperative effort with other companies in the materials value chain (even competitors) to find recycling solutions that work. Starbucks is totally committed to being a good environmental steward. Finally, Starbucks has always strived to be a good neighbor by providing a place for people to come together and by committing to supporting financially and in other ways the communities where its stores are located. Partners (and customers, for that matter) are encouraged to get involved in volunteering in their communities. In addition, the Starbucks Foundation, which started in 1997 with funding for literacy programs in the United States and Canada, now makes grants to a wide variety of community projects and service programs.

Starbucks is also very serious about doing business ethically. In fact, it was named to the 2016 list of World's Most Ethical Companies, as it has been for the last 10 years. From the executive level to the store level, individuals are expected and empowered to protect Starbucks' reputation through how they conduct business and how they treat others. And individuals are guided by the *Standards of Business Conduct,* a resource created for employees in doing business ethically, with integrity and honesty. These business conduct standards cover the workplace environment, business practices, intellectual property and proprietary information, and community involvement. A flow-chart model included in the standards document is used to illustrate an ethical decision-making framework for partners. Despite the thorough information in the standards, if partners face a situation where they're unsure how to respond or where they want to voice concerns, they're encouraged to seek out guidance from their manager, their partner resources representative, or even the corporate office of business ethics and compliance. The company also strongly states that it does not tolerate any retaliation against or victimization of any partner who raises concerns or questions.

Innovation, Innovation

Starbucks has always thought "outside the box." From the beginning, it took the concept of the corner coffee shop and totally revamped the coffee experience. And the company has always had the ability to roll out new products relatively quickly. Starbucks invests heavily in R&D (research and development). It received the 2014 Outstanding Corporate Innovator (OCI) Award; honorees were chosen for corporate commitment to innovation as a strategy to grow their businesses. Starbucks' System to Accelerate Results (STAR) process has enabled the company to test and measure new products and measure customer interest. In 2015, Starbucks was recognized by *Forbes* magazine as one of the 100 most innovative companies in the world.

A glimpse of Starbucks' innovation process can be seen in how it approaches the all-important Christmas season, since "Starbucks has Christmas down to a science." It takes many months of meetings and tastings before rolling out the flavors and aromas. For the 2011 season, the process started in October 2010, when customers had the opportunity to fill out in-store and online surveys used to gauge their "mindset." In mid-December 2010, Schultz—who has final approval on all new products and themes—reviewed the 2011 theme. And things better be "Christmas-perfect." In March 2011, the 2011 theme (Let's Merry) was approved. By mid-March, the "core holiday team" started to meet weekly. On June 1, production cranked up on the company's seasonal red cups (which were introduced in 1997 and remain very popular). By the end of June, the holiday team had assembled a mock-up of a Starbucks café for Schultz to review and approve. By mid-August, all of the in-store signs, menu boards, and window decals were on their way to the printer. All of these pieces came together for the full holiday rollout on November 15, 2011. It's important to get everything right for this season. Want proof? The company had revenues of almost $3 billion during the holiday quarter. That's a lot of Christmas cheer!

The company's product innovation process must be doing something right, as many of its Christmas products have been popular for years. For instance, the company's Christmas Blend debuted in 1985. The Gingerbread Latte was a Christmas 2000 innovation. The Caramel Brulée Latte came out during the 2009 holiday season. During the Christmas 2011 season, customers got their first taste of the Skinny Peppermint Mocha—a nod to the trend of healthier, but still tasty, products—and the line of petite desserts, which were introduced to commemorate the company's 40th birthday. But obviously, given Starbucks' outcomes, it's not only the Christmas products that have been successful. One of Starbucks' creations was a line of light-roasted coffee beans and brews. And the popularity of energy drinks led the company to create a line of "natural" energy drinks called Refreshers. The new fruity, carbonated drink that's high in antioxidants will get its energy boost from unroasted green coffee extract. Schultz told shareholders that the company is continuing to create lots of Starbucks products that "live outside of our stores." Starbucks Refreshers are sold at 160,000 grocery stores and made-to-order versions are sold in Starbucks stores.

Discussion Questions

P2-1. Do you think Howard Schultz views his role more from the omnipotent or from the symbolic perspective? Explain.

P2-2. What has made Starbucks' culture what it is? How is that culture maintained?

P2-3. Does Starbucks encourage a customer responsive culture? An ethical culture? Explain.

P2-4. Describe some of the specific and general environmental components that are likely to impact Starbucks.

P2-5. How would you classify the uncertainty of the environment in which Starbucks operates? Explain.

P2-6. What stakeholders do you think Starbucks might be most concerned with? Why? What issue(s) might each of these stakeholders want Starbucks to address?

P2-7. Why do you think Howard Schultz is uncomfortable with the idea of legislative lobbying? Do you think his discomfort is appropriate? Why or why not?

P2-8. What types of global economic and legal–political issues might Starbucks face as it does business globally?

P2-9. You're responsible for developing a global cultural awareness program for Starbucks' executives who are leading the company's international expansion efforts. Describe what you think will be important for these executives to know.

P2-10. Using information from the case and information you pull from Starbucks' website, what global attitude do you think Starbucks exhibits? Defend your choice.

P2-11. Pick one of the countries mentioned as an important target for Starbucks. Make a bulleted list of economic, political-legal, and cultural characteristics of this country.

P2-12. What workforce challenges might Starbucks face in global markets in regard to its partners?

P2-13. How does Starbucks manage diversity? What is Starbucks doing to manage diversity in each of the four areas: customers, suppliers, partners, and communities?

P2-14. With more than 235,000 partners worldwide, what challenges would Starbucks face in making sure its diversity values are practiced and adhered to?

P2-15. Starbucks defines diversity on its website in the form of an equation:

Diversity = Inclusion + Equity + Accessibility.

Explain what you think this means. What do you think of this definition of diversity?

P2-16. What other workplace diversity initiatives discussed in Chapter 3 (besides employee resource groups) might be appropriate for an organization like Starbucks?

P2-17. Go to the company's website, www.starbucks.com, and find the latest corporate social responsibility report. Choose one of the key areas in the report (or your professor may assign one of these areas). Describe and evaluate what the company has done in this key area.

P2-18. What do you think of Starbucks' goal to recycle all four billion cups sold annually by 2015? What challenges did it face in meeting that goal?

P2-19. Why is the concept of "empowering" employees important in doing business ethically?

P2-20. Again, go to the company's website. Find the *Standards of Business Conduct* document. First, what's your impression of this document? Then, choose one topic from one of the main areas covered. Describe what advice is provided to partners.

P2-21. What do you think the company's use of the term *partners* instead of employees implies? What's your reaction to this? Do you think it matters what companies call their employees? (For instance, Walmart calls its employees *associates*.) Why or why not?

P2-22. Howard Schultz is adamant about providing the best "Starbucks experience" to each and every customer. As a store manager, how would you keep your employees from experiencing high levels of stress when lines are out the door and customers want their Starbucks now?

P2-23. Would you classify Starbucks' environment as more calm waters or white-water rapids? Explain. How does the company manage change in this type of environment?

P2-24. Using Exhibit 6-9, describe Starbucks' innovation environment.

P2-25. Review the company's mission and guiding principles (at www.starbucks.com). Explain how these might affect the following: managing its external environment and its organizational culture, global efforts, diversity efforts, social responsibility and ethics issues, and change and innovation issues.

Notes for the Part 2 Continuing Case

Information from Starbucks Corporation Fiscal Year 2015 Annual Report, www.investor.starbucks.com, March 23, 2016; "2016 World's Most Ethical Companies," http://worldsmostethicalcompanies.ethisphere.com/honorees/, March 2016; B. Rooney, "Starbucks to Give Workers a Full Ride for College," *CNN Money* online, www.money.cnn.com, April 6, 2015; J. Yardley, "With Humility, Starbucks Will Enter Italian Market," *New York Times* online, www.nytimes.com, February 28, 2016; N. Tadena, "Starbucks' Race Campaign Gets Social Media Talking—It's Just Not Positive," *The Wall Street Journal* online, www.wsj.com, March 20, 2015; J. Dean and I. Brat, "Starbucks Ends Key Phase in 'Race Together' Campaign," *The Wall Street Journal* online, www.wsj.com, March 22, 2015; "The World's Most Innovative Companies," *Forbes* online, www.forbes.com, March 2016; A. Minter, "Why Starbucks Won't Recycle Your Cup," www.bloombergview.com, April 7, 2014; "Starbucks Corporation Business Ethics and Compliance: Standards of Business Conduct," www.assets.starbucks.com, August 6, 2012; Starbucks News Release, "Starbucks Reports Record Third Quarter Results," www.investor.starbucks.com, July 26, 2012; L. Alderman, "In Europe, Starbucks Adjusts to a Café Culture," *New York Times* online, www.nytimes.com, March 30, 2012; V. Varma and B. Packard, "Starbucks Global Responsibility Report Year in Review: Fiscal 2011," www.starbucks.com, March 16, 2012; B. Gregg, "Is Professor's 'Hi, Sweetie' Comment Sexual Harassment?" www.diversityinc.com, March 12, 2012; S. Faris, "Grounds Zero," *Bloomberg BusinessWeek* online, www.bloomberg.com/businessweek, February 9, 2012; "Howard Schultz, on Getting a Second Shot," *Inc.*, April 2011, pp. 52–54; "A Shout Out to Starbucks," Wholeliving.com, April 2011, p. 111; and "Starbucks Quest for Healthy Growth: An Interview with Howard Schultz," *McKinsey Quarterly*, no. 2, 2011, pp. 34–43.

Chapter 8 Planning and Goal-Setting

It's Your Career

Source: Davooda/Shutterstock

A key to success in management and in your career is knowing how to set goals, professionally and personally.

You Gotta Have Goals

It's been said that if you don't know where you're going, any road will get you there. It has also been said that the shortest distance between two points is a straight line. These two sayings emphasize the importance of goals. Organizations want people who can get things done. And goal-setting is an essential component of long-term career success. Successful athletes, businesspeople, and achievers in all fields use goals (a) to focus their efforts, (b) as short-term motivation, and (c) to build self-confidence as goals are successfully completed. You need to do the same thing. So how can you be better at setting goals? Here are some suggestions:

*1. **Identify what you'd like to do or achieve in important life areas** such as career, financial, education, family, physical, public service/community involvement, and so forth. Focus on your most important broad goals. Try to identify where or what you'd like to be in 5 years, 10 years, 20 years. What is your dream? Your vision? If you're having trouble doing that, try thinking about what you don't want (I don't want to be working for someone else), and then turn that around to find your goal (I'd like to start my own business).*

*2. **Make your goals actionable.** Although having broad, visionary goals is important, you need to set smaller goals with more specific, achievable actions. You can do this by:*

- *WRITING YOUR GOALS DOWN. Something about writing the goals makes them more real and gives them more force. Plus, having a visual reminder can be very motivating!*
- *USING THE S.M.A.R.T. APPROACH. This means you write goals that are Specific, Measurable, Attainable, Relevant (or Realistic), and Time-trackable. Using this approach forces you to set goals that aren't just daydreams or that are unrealistic.*

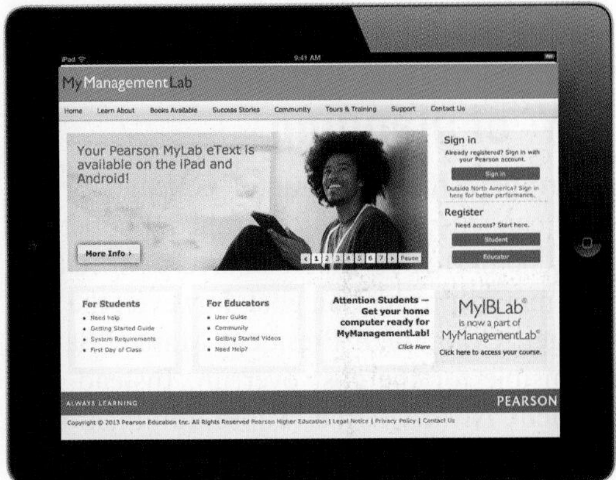

Pearson MyLab Management®

Improve Your Grade!

When you see this icon, visit **www.mymanagementlab.com** for activities that are applied, personalized, and offer immediate feedback.

Learning Objectives

• SKILL OUTCOMES

***8.1 Define** the nature and purposes of planning.*

***8.2 Classify** the types of goals organizations might have and the plans they use.*

***8.3 Compare** and contrast approaches to goal-setting and planning.*

- **Know how** to set goals personally and create a useful, functional to-do list.
- **Develop your skill** at helping your employees set goals.

***8.4 Discuss** contemporary issues in planning.*

- *AVOIDING GOALS THAT ARE ambiguous, overly ambitious or unrealistic, undocumented, and planless (without a plan).*

*3. **Make your plans for reaching those goals.** Setting goals is important, but so is deciding how you're going to achieve them. Your plans, just like your goals, need to be short term and long term. Having and using to-do lists can be productive. (Be sure to check out what this skill involves at the end of the chapter on pages 306-307.)*

*4. **Determine how you'll measure progress toward your goal.** You need to think about how you will know you've achieved a goal. It's easy for some goals; for instance, getting your MBA degree. You measure progress by whether you're completing all necessary coursework and other requirements that will eventually lead to being awarded that degree. Other goals may not be quite that easy to measure for progress. However, having some way to assess progress is important to staying on track. It's also important that when you do achieve a goal (or goals), you enjoy the satisfaction of having done so. Reward yourself appropriately!*

*5. **Review your goals periodically.** Are the goals that you set still appropriate? Do they reflect your changing priorities or experiences? As your life and career circumstances change, change your goals to reflect that.*

You may think "planning" is relevant to large companies, but not something that's relevant to you right now. But when you figure out your class schedule for the next term or when you decide what you need to do to finish a class project on time, you're planning. And planning is something that all managers need to do. Although what they plan and how they plan may differ, it's still important that they do plan. In this chapter, we present the basics: what planning is, why managers plan, and how they plan.

THE WHAT AND WHY of planning

LO8.1 In 2006, the Colombian government hired contractor Chicago Bridge and Iron NV to increase the capacity of state-controlled Ecopetrol's Cartagena oil refinery daily output from 80,000 barrels to 165,000 barrels. More than 10 years later, the company has successfully met its production goal; however, the cost to get there was double the $4 billion budget. Colombian President Manuel Santos expressed outrage, but says he's not responsible for the cost overrun. Instead, he's placed blame on former Colombian President Álvaro Uribe, whose administration started the project, and the contractor. Mr. Uribe announced on social media that the Santos's government "now wants to wash its hands."[1] Could the contractors and Colombian government have planned better?

What Is Planning?

planning
Management function that involves setting goals, establishing strategies for achieving those goals, and developing plans to integrate and coordinate work activities

As we stated in Chapter 1, **planning** involves defining the organization's goals, establishing strategies for achieving those goals, and developing plans to integrate and coordinate work activities. It's concerned with both ends (what) and means (how).

When we use the term "planning," we mean formal planning. In formal planning, specific goals covering a specific time period are defined. These goals are written and shared with organizational members to reduce ambiguity and create a common understanding about what needs to be done. Finally, specific plans exist for achieving these goals.

Why Do Managers Plan?

Planning seems to take a lot of effort. So why should managers plan? We can give you at least four reasons:

1. *Planning provides direction* to managers and nonmanagers alike. When employees know what their organization or work unit is trying to accomplish and what they must contribute to reach goals, they can coordinate their activities, cooperate with each other, and do what it takes to accomplish those goals. Without planning, departments and individuals might work at cross-purposes and prevent the organization from efficiently achieving its goals.
2. *Planning reduces uncertainty* by forcing managers to look ahead, anticipate change, consider the impact of change, and develop appropriate responses. Although planning won't eliminate uncertainty, managers plan so they can respond effectively.
3. *Planning minimizes waste and redundancy.* When work activities are coordinated around plans, inefficiencies become obvious and can be corrected or eliminated.
4. *Planning establishes the goals or standards* used in controlling. When managers plan, they develop goals and plans. When they control, they see whether the plans have been carried out and the goals met. Without planning, there would be no goals against which to measure work effort.

Planning contributes to the profitable performance of Recreational Equipment, Inc. Formal expansion plans have helped REI grow from one store in 1944 to become a major retailer of outdoor gear with more than 130 stores, 10,000 employees, and annual sales of $2 billion. Shown here are employees at an REI store opening in New York City's SoHo shopping district.
Source: Matt Peyton/AP Images

Planning and Performance

Is planning worthwhile? Numerous studies have looked at the relationship between planning and performance.[2] Although most have shown generally positive relationships, we can't say that organizations that formally plan always outperform those that don't plan. But *what* can we conclude?

First, generally speaking, formal planning is associated with positive financial results—higher profits, higher return on assets, and so forth. Second, it seems that doing a good job planning and implementing those plans play a bigger part in high performance than how much planning is done. Next, in those studies where formal planning didn't lead to higher performance, the external environment often was the culprit. When external forces—think governmental regulations or powerful labor unions—constrain managers' options, it reduces the impact planning has on an organization's performance. Finally, the planning-performance relationship seems to be influenced by the planning time frame. It seems that at least four years of formal planning is required before it begins to affect performance.

- 38 percent of leaders say planning for next year is a challenge.[3]

GOALS **and plans**

LO8.2 Planning is often called the primary management function because it establishes the basis for all the other things managers do as they organize, lead, and control. It involves two important aspects: goals and plans.

Goals (objectives) are desired outcomes or targets.[4] They guide management decisions and form the criteria against which work results are measured. That's why they're often described as the essential elements of planning. You have to know the desired target or outcome before you can establish plans for reaching it. **Plans** are documents that outline how goals are going to be met. They usually include resource allocations, schedules, and other necessary actions to accomplish the goals. As managers plan, they develop both goals and plans.

goals (objectives)
Desired outcomes or targets

plans
Documents that outline how goals are going to be met

Types of Goals

It might seem that organizations have a single goal. Businesses want to make a profit and not-for-profit organizations want to meet the needs of some constituent group(s). However, a single goal can't adequately define an organization's success. And if managers emphasize only one goal, other goals essential for long-term success are ignored. Also, as we discussed in Chapter 5, using a single goal such as profit may result in unethical behaviors because managers and employees will ignore other aspects of their jobs in order to look good on that one measure.[5] In reality, all organizations have multiple goals. For instance, businesses may want to increase market share, keep employees enthused about working for the organization, and work toward more environmentally sustainable practices. And a church provides a place for religious practices, but also assists economically disadvantaged individuals in its community and acts as a social gathering place for church members.

We can classify most company's goals as either strategic or financial. Financial goals are related to the financial performance of the organization, while strategic goals are related to all other areas of an organization's performance. For instance, discount retailer Dollar General announced its plan to demonstrate sales growth of 7 percent to 10 percent in 2016, with earnings per share (profit divided by the total number of company stock shares) to increase by 10 percent to 15 percent.[6] And here's an example of a strategic goal from the United Nations World Food Programs: to ensure that no child goes to bed hungry.[7]

The goals just described are **stated goals**—official statements of what an organization says, and what it wants its stakeholders to believe, its goals are. However, stated goals—which can be found in an organization's charter, annual report, public relations announcements, or in public statements made by managers—are often conflicting and influenced by what various stakeholders think organizations should do. For instance, Nike's goal is "delivering inspiration and innovation to every athlete." Canadian company EnCana's vision is to "be the world's high performance benchmark independent oil and gas company." The Chipotle restaurant chain states that one of its goals is to serve "food with integrity."[8] Such statements are vague and probably better represent management's public relations skills than being meaningful guides to what the organization is actually trying to accomplish. It shouldn't be surprising then to find that an organization's stated goals are often irrelevant to what actually goes on.[9]

stated goals
Official statements of what an organization says, and what it wants its various stakeholders to believe, its goals are

If you want to know an organization's **real goals**—those goals an organization actually pursues—observe what organizational members are doing. Actions define

real goals
Goals that an organization actually pursues, as defined by the actions of its members

let's get REAL

The Scenario:

Tommy and Kate Larkin recently started a restaurant and specialty food store in northern California. The store also sells wine and locally made crafts. Although the business does well during the summer tourist months, things get pretty lean from October to April when visitor numbers dwindle. The Larkins felt that the potential opportunities in this location were good.

What types of plans do the Larkins need to survive the off-season?

The slow season is a wonderful time for a business owner. This is the perfect opportunity for brand and business development. If a new website needs to be designed, this is the time to do it. If new recipes need to be tested, this would be the perfect time to run trials. Research and development during these months could make the busy season even more profitable. The "business development" season also presents a great opportunity to deepen ties in the community, and it is the prime time to diversify business offerings. Perhaps the restaurant could focus on hosting events on site or catering off-site meals, making themselves more valuable to the local community rather than depending so heavily on tourism. Finally, it is a great time for the owners to rest, recover, and rejuvenate themselves from the last season and gear up for the next.

Prudence Rufus
Business Owner/Photographer

Source: Prudence Rufus

priorities. For example, universities may say their goal is limiting class sizes, facilitating close student-faculty relations, and actively involving students in the learning process, but then they put students into 300+ student lecture classes! Knowing that real and stated goals may differ is important for recognizing what you might otherwise think are management inconsistencies.

Types of Plans

The most popular ways to describe organizational plans are breadth (strategic versus operational), time frame (short-term versus long-term), specificity (directional versus specific), and frequency of use (single use versus standing). As Exhibit 8-1 shows, these types of plans aren't independent. That is, strategic plans are usually long-term, directional, and single use, whereas operational plans are usually short-term, specific, and standing. What does each include?

strategic plans
Plans that apply to the entire organization and establish the organization's overall goals

Strategic plans are plans that apply to the entire organization and establish the organization's overall goals. For example, the strategic plan of Egyptian Transport and Commercial Services Company (Egytrans) is to "make integrated transport easy, safe, and cost-effective," by providing its business customers with world-class transport and logistics services. This multi-year plan identifies new markets with significant profit opportunity and sets goals for increasing revenue, improving cost efficiencies, and service innovations for future growth.[10] Plans that encompass a particular operational area of the organization are called **operational plans**. The operational plans of Egytrans guide decisions about new products and business units to support the strategic plan.[11] These two types of plans differ because strategic plans are broad while operational plans are narrow.

operational plans
Plans that encompass a particular operational area of the organization

The number of years used to define short-term and long-term plans has declined considerably because of environmental uncertainty. Long term used to mean anything over seven years. Try to imagine what you're likely to be doing in seven years, and you

Exhibit 8-1
Types of Plans

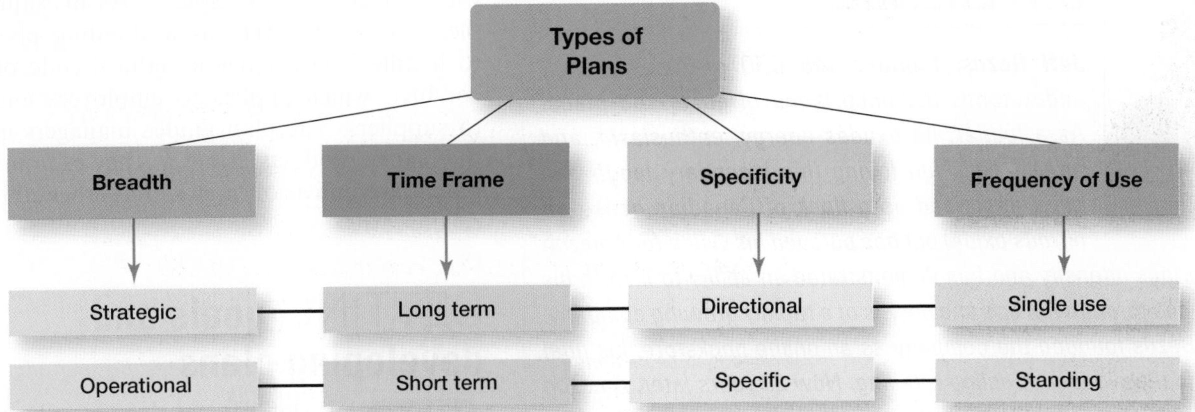

can begin to appreciate how difficult it would be for managers to establish plans that far in the future. We define **long-term plans** as those with a time frame beyond three years.[12] The U.S. National Aeronautical Space Administration's long-term goal is to answer some basic questions. What's out there in space? How do we get there? What will we find?[13] **Short-term plans** cover one year or less. Any time period in between would be an intermediate plan. Although these time classifications are fairly common, an organization can use any planning time frame it wants. For instance, Dollar General stated a short-term plan to increase store sales and profitability in 2016.

long-term plans
Plans with a time frame beyond three years

short-term plans
Plans covering one year or less

Intuitively, it would seem that specific plans would be preferable to directional, or loosely guided, plans. **Specific plans** are clearly defined and leave no room for interpretation. A specific plan states its objectives in a way that eliminates ambiguity and problems with misunderstanding. A manager who seeks to increase his or her unit's work output by 8 percent over a given 12-month period might establish specific procedures, budget allocations, and schedules of activities to reach that goal. For example, Rolls-Royce's marine equipment business announced a specific plan to save costs by eliminating 800 jobs in several countries, which amounts to 17 percent of its total workforce.[14]

specific plans
Plans that are clearly defined and leave no room for interpretation

However, when uncertainty is high and managers must be flexible in order to respond to unexpected changes, directional plans are preferable. **Directional plans** are flexible plans that set out general guidelines. They provide focus but don't lock managers into specific goals or courses of action. For example, at the Morning Star Company, professional employees self-manage their relationships with colleagues, customers, and suppliers without specific directions from company executives. These employees are simply expected to hold themselves accountable to achieve the company's mission, which is "to produce tomato products and services which consistently achieve the quality and service expectations of our customers in a cost effective, environmentally responsible manner."[15] Keep in mind, however, that the flexibility of directional plans must be weighed against the lack of clarity of specific plans.

directional plans
Plans that are flexible and set out general guidelines

If your professor has assigned this, go to **www.mymanagementlab.com** to watch a video titled: *Planning* and to respond to questions.

Some plans that managers develop are ongoing while others are used only once. A **single-use plan** is a one-time plan specifically designed to meet the needs of a unique situation. For instance, when Walmart wanted to expand the number of its stores in China, top-level executives formulated a single-use plan as a guide. In contrast, **standing plans** are ongoing plans that provide guidance for activities

single-use plan
A one-time plan specifically designed to meet the needs of a unique situation

standing plans
Ongoing plans that provide guidance for activities performed repeatedly

LEADER making a DIFFERENCE

Source: Kim White/Reuters

Jeff Bezos, *founder and CEO of Amazon.com, understands the importance of goals and plans. As a leader, he exudes energy, enthusiasm, and drive.*[17] *He's fun loving (his legendary laugh has been described as a flock of Canadian geese on nitrous oxide) but has pursued his vision for Amazon with serious intensity and has demonstrated an ability to inspire his employees through the ups and downs of a rapidly growing company. When Bezos founded the company as an online bookstore, his goal was to be the leader in online retailing. Now 20 years later, Amazon has become the world's general store, selling not only books, CDs, and DVDs, but LEGOs, power drills, and Jackalope Buck taxidermy mounts, to name a few of the millions of products you can buy.* What can you learn from this leader making a difference?

performed repeatedly. Standing plans include policies, rules, and procedures, which we defined in Chapter 2. As an example, France's LVMH has a standing plan to handle issues under its ethical code of conduct, which applies to employees and to suppliers. The plan guides managers at the luxury products group as they examine potential conflicts of interest and other ethical concerns.[16]

SETTING goals and developing plans

LO8.3 Taylor Haines has just been elected president of her business school's honor society. She wants the organization to be more actively involved in the business school than it has been. Francisco Garza graduated from Tecnologico de Monterrey with a degree in marketing and computers three years ago and went to work for a regional consulting services firm. He recently was promoted to manager of an eight-person social media development team and hopes to strengthen the team's financial contributions to the firm. What should Taylor and Francisco do now? Their first step should be to set goals.

Approaches to Setting Goals

As we stated earlier, goals provide the direction for all management decisions and actions and form the criteria against which actual accomplishments are measured. Everything organizational members do should be oriented toward achieving goals. These goals can be set either through a traditional process or by using management by objectives.

traditional goal-setting
An approach to setting goals in which top managers set goals that then flow down through the organization and become subgoals for each organizational area

In **traditional goal-setting**, goals set by top managers flow down through the organization and become subgoals for each organizational area. This traditional perspective assumes that top managers know what's best because they see the "big picture." And the goals passed down to each succeeding level guide individual employees as they work to achieve those assigned goals. If Taylor were to use this approach, she would see what goals the dean or director of the school of business had set and develop goals for her group that would contribute to achieving those goals. Or take a manufacturing business, for example. The president tells the vice president of production what he expects manufacturing costs to be for the coming year and tells the marketing vice president what level he expects sales to reach for the year. These goals are passed to the next organizational level and written to reflect the responsibilities of that level, passed to the next level, and so forth. Then, at some later time, performance is evaluated to determine whether the assigned goals have been achieved. Although the process is supposed to happen in this way, in reality it doesn't always do so. Turning broad strategic goals into departmental, team, and individual goals can be a difficult and frustrating process.

Another problem with traditional goal-setting is that when top managers define the organization's goals in broad terms—such as achieving "sufficient" profits or increasing "market leadership"—these ambiguous goals have to be made more specific as they flow down through the organization. Managers at each level define the goals and apply their own interpretations and biases as they make them more

WORKPLACE CONFIDENTIAL When You Face a Lack of Clear Directions

Today's workplace is often described as exhibiting rapid change. New competitors pop out of nowhere. Innovative ideas disrupt established businesses. Products and services find their life cycles increasingly shortened. And employees are finding themselves having to cope with change and the ambiguity that comes with it.

While some people thrive on ambiguity, most of us find it frustrating and stressful. This is particularly true at work. What does my boss want me to do? What's a priority and what can wait? When problems arise, whom should I see for help? How far can I go without overstepping my job responsibilities?

There are essentially two solutions to a lack of clear directions. One is a boss who offers explicit and precise guidelines. He or she tells you, in unambiguous terms, what your job entails. In your boss's leadership role, the lines of where your job responsibilities start and end are made perfectly clear to you. The other solution is a formal position description.

Reducing ambiguity can be largely facilitated by having a written position description. This is a statement of the essential components of your job—what work is to be performed, your primary duties and responsibilities, and the criteria that will be used to evaluate your performance. Most large organizations will have position descriptions available.

Ideally, your employer has a position description for your job. One might exist but you may have never received it when you took your job. If so, ask your boss or human resource department for a copy.

There is strong evidence indicating that position descriptions provide role clarity and that employees who have role clarity are much more likely to be engaged with the work they're doing. Of course, these position descriptions need to be updated regularly to reflect the changing nature of work and specific jobs. You might suggest to your boss that, following your annual performance evaluation, the two of you sit down, assess the changes that have taken place in the past year, and then update your position description to reflect if, or how, these changes have reshaped your job responsibilities.

But let's assume a position description for your job doesn't exist and your boss doesn't excel at providing you with clear directives. What then? Consider creating a position description in partnership with your boss. Explain to your boss how a detailed position description can help you do your job better and reduce your dependence on him or her. Importantly, if this document is truly to be effective, it needs to contain shared expectations. That is, it has to be created in cooperation with your boss so he or she "owns" the final document with you.

Realistically, even with a great boss who provides clear directions or a detailed position description, there will still be times when you'll feel a lack of clear directions. Here are three suggestions that can help you through these times:

Suppress your urge to control things. No matter how much we want to control those things around us, we have to accept that there are elements of our life that we can't control. This is certainly true in relation to work. In terms of our concern here, we rarely get to choose our boss. And you may find that it's not realistic to impose structure—in the terms of a position description—in a culture where they have never existed. Add in the fact that, in many organizations, changes are occurring so rapidly that the valid life span of a position description may be only a few months or even weeks. End result: You need to learn to accept the reality that you can't control everything related to your job.

Learn to act without the complete picture. Rational decision making assumes that problems are clear and unambiguous, and that you know all possible alternatives and consequences. That's not the real world of work; hence, you will rarely, if ever, have all the information you need when making a decision. You need to accept that you will regularly face ambiguous situations and you will have to take actions without clear directions either from your boss, colleagues, or a procedure manual.

You can make decisions based on the information you have, even if the information isn't complete. Don't be afraid to make a mistake. Often, a wrong decision is better than no decision. Don't be gun shy, or as one executive once described a colleague: "It was always, 'ready, aim, aim, aim, aim.' He was afraid to pull the trigger!" You don't want to become characterized as someone who's afraid to do anything without your boss's direction or without first getting his or her approval. If you're going to move ahead in the organization and be seen as a leader, you will have to take assertive action under conditions of ambiguity. And that means your decisions are not always going to be proven correct. Live with it! Baseball players who fail 60 percent of the time end up in the Hall of Fame.

Source: Based on J. A. Breaugh and J. P. Colihan, "Measuring Facets of Job Ambiguity: Construct Validity Evidence," *Journal of Applied Psychology*, March 1994, pp. 191–202; "Position Description Essential for Role Clarity and Engagement," hrdaily online, July 16, 2012; and C. Shaw, "Dealing with Ambiguity: The New Business Imperative," LinkedIn online, August 29, 2013.

Exhibit 8-2
The Downside of Traditional Goal-Setting

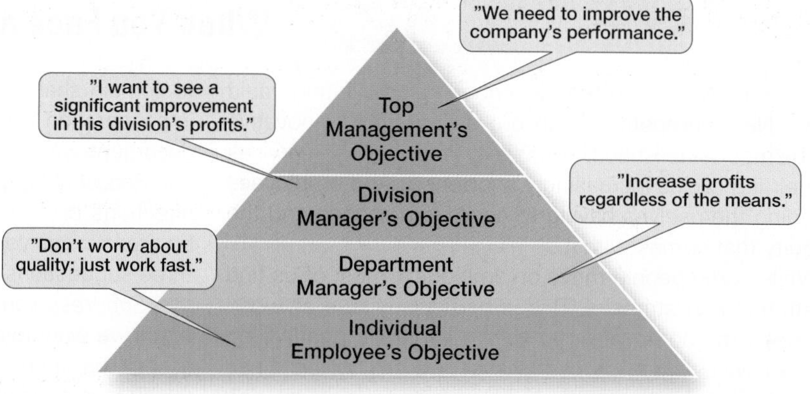

specific. However, what often happens is that clarity is lost as the goals make their way down from the top of the organization to lower levels. Exhibit 8-2 illustrates what can happen. But it doesn't have to be that way. For example, top managers at Swisscom, a leading telecommunications provider in Switzerland, understand the importance of focusing all 21,000 employees on the firm's main goals and strategies. Knowing that technology is advancing rapidly, they also expect the workforce to react quickly to changing market conditions, with the strategic goals in mind. So Swisscom's managers create operational plans for short-term projects and set deadlines measured in terms of days or weeks, rather than over many months or years. Every other week, employee teams meet to assess success and determine next steps to ensure that innovations are implemented with speed and quality. By giving employees the information and ability to make decisions and innovate within the framework of the goals and strategy, Swisscom is maintaining its competitiveness and meeting the needs of its customers.[18]

means-ends chain
An integrated network of goals in which the accomplishment of goals at one level serves as the means for achieving the goals, or ends, at the next level

When the hierarchy of organizational goals is clearly defined, as it is at Carrier-Carlyle Compressor, it forms an integrated network of goals, or a **means-ends chain**. Higher-level goals (or ends) are linked to lower-level goals, which serve as the means for their accomplishment. In other words, the goals achieved at lower levels become the means to reach the goals (ends) at the next level. And the accomplishment of goals at that level becomes the means to achieve the goals (ends) at the next level and on up through the different organizational levels. That's how traditional goal-setting is supposed to work.

management by objectives (MBO)
A process of setting mutually agreed-upon goals and using those goals to evaluate employee performance

Instead of using traditional goal-setting, many organizations use **management by objectives (MBO)**, a process of setting mutually agreed-upon goals and using those goals to evaluate employee performance. If Francisco were to use this approach, he would sit down with each member of his team and set goals and periodically review whether progress was being made toward achieving those goals. Companies such as Adobe, GE, and Microsoft have replaced traditional performance ratings with MBO programs. Adobe refers to its MBO program as Check In. Each year, employees and managers meet to establish goals. Then, at least every two months, employees check in with their managers to discuss their progress. At the end of the year, managers meet for a "rewards check-in" session where they discuss how well employees attained their goals, and pay increases and bonuses are awarded based on goal attainment. According to Donna Morris, Adobe's global senior vice president of people and places, "Managers are empowered to make those decisions," says Morris. "HR isn't involved."[19]

MBO programs have four elements: goal specificity, participative decision making, an explicit time period, and performance feedback.[20] Instead of using goals to make sure employees are doing what they're supposed to be doing, MBO uses goals to motivate them as well. The appeal is that it focuses on employees working to accomplish goals they've had a hand in setting. Exhibit 8-3 lists the steps in a typical MBO program.

Exhibit 8-3
Steps in MBO

Step 1: The organization's ***overall objectives*** and ***strategies*** are formulated.

Step 2: Major objectives are allocated among ***divisional and departmental units.***

Step 3: Unit managers ***collaboratively set specific objectives*** for their units with their managers.

Step 4: Specific objectives are collaboratively set with ***all department members.***

Step 5: ***Action plans,*** defining how objectives are to be achieved, are specified and agreed upon by managers and employees.

Step 6: The action plans are ***implemented.***

Step 7: Progress toward objectives is ***periodically reviewed,*** and ***feedback is provided.***

Step 8: Successful achievement of objectives is reinforced by ***performance-based rewards.***

Does MBO work? Studies have shown that it can increase employee performance and organizational productivity. For example, one review of MBO programs found productivity gains in almost all of them.[21] But is MBO relevant for today's organizations? If it's viewed as a way of setting goals, then yes, because research shows that goal-setting can be an effective approach to motivating employees.[22]

CHARACTERISTICS OF WELL-WRITTEN GOALS Goals aren't all written the same way. Some are better than others at making the desired outcomes clear. For instance, in 2009 Samsung Electronics announced specific lofty goals in its written plan titled "Vision 2020." By 2020, it plans to achieve $400 billion in sales, becoming first in the global IT industry, and growing into a top 10 global company.[23] These

let's get REAL

Source: Christina Moser

Christina Moser
Strategic Account Manager

The Scenario:

Jerry Kennedy is sitting down with his new manager to discuss his recent promotion to a line supervisor at a manufacturing plant. The plant is expecting a lot of growth in the next year, and Jerry will have many challenges in his new role. Jerry's manager starts the meeting by asking Jerry to work on writing some specific goals for the upcoming year. Jerry is hesitant to work on writing goals as he feels he has a lot to learn and a lot of work to do. Writing goals seems like a waste of time.

What would you tell Jerry about the value of setting goals for his new role?

Setting goals improves focus and is a catalyst for success, which makes it even more valuable for someone who feels overwhelmed in a new role. Knowing that the plant is expecting growth in the next year, Jerry will need to produce results quickly. Once Jerry writes out his goals, he can begin to detail the steps and milestones to achieve them. He should also make them SMART—specific, measurable, achievable, realistic and time-bound. For example, one of his goals might be to learn the new payroll system for employee timekeeping in the next 30 days.

Exhibit 8-4
Well-Written Goals

- Written in terms of outcomes rather than actions
- Measurable and quantifiable
- Clear as to a time frame
- Challenging yet attainable
- Written down
- Communicated to all necessary organizational members

A survey of managers revealed:
- 51 percent said they could secure resources to pursue attractive opportunities outside their strategic objectives, and
- only 11 percent said all their company's strategic priorities have the resources they need for success.[25]

are ambitious but specific goals. Managers should be able to write well-written work goals. What makes a "well-written" work goal?[24] Exhibit 8-4 lists the characteristics.

STEPS IN GOAL-SETTING Managers should follow five steps when setting goals.

1. *Review the organization's mission, or purpose.* A **mission** is a broad statement of an organization's purpose that provides an overall guide to what organizational members think is important. Managers should review the mission before writing goals because goals should reflect that mission. For instance, the Coca-Cola Company's mission entails the following: To refresh the world, to inspire moments of optimism and happiness, and to create value and make a difference.[26]
2. *Evaluate available resources.* You don't want to set goals that are impossible to achieve given your available resources. Even though goals should be challenging, they should be realistic. After all, if the resources you have to work with won't allow you to achieve a goal no matter how hard you try or how much effort is exerted, you shouldn't set that goal. That would be like the person with a $50,000 annual income and no other financial resources setting a goal of building an investment portfolio worth $1 million in three years. No matter how hard he or she works at it, it's not going to happen.
3. *Determine the goals individually or with input from others.* The goals reflect desired outcomes and should be congruent with the organizational mission and goals in other organizational areas. These goals should be measurable, specific, and include a time frame for accomplishment.
4. *Write down the goals and communicate them to all who need to know.* Writing down and communicating goals forces people to think them through. The written goals also become visible evidence of the importance of working toward something.
5. *Review results and whether goals are being met.* If goals aren't being met, change them as needed.

mission
The purpose of an organization

Once the goals have been established, written down, and communicated, a manager is ready to develop plans for pursuing the goals.

Goal-Setting—If your instructor is using **Pearson MyLab Management**, log onto *mymanagementlab.com* and test your *goal-setting knowledge.* **Be sure to refer back to the chapter opener!**

Developing Plans

The process of developing plans is influenced by three contingency factors and by the planning approach followed.

CONTINGENCY FACTORS IN PLANNING Three contingency factors affect the choice of plans: organizational level, degree of environmental uncertainty, and length of future commitments.[27]

Exhibit 8-5

Planning and Organizational Level

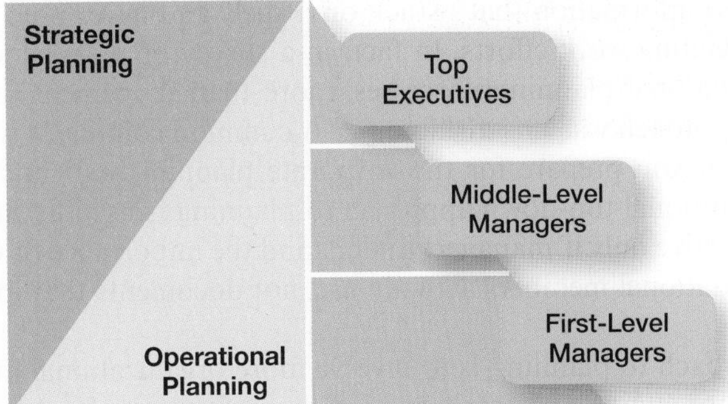

Exhibit 8-5 shows the relationship between a manager's level in the organization and the type of planning done. For the most part, lower-level managers do operational planning while upper-level managers do strategic planning.

The second contingency factor is environmental uncertainty. When uncertainty is high, plans should be specific, but flexible. Managers must be prepared to change or amend plans as they're implemented. At times, they may even have to abandon the plans.[28] For example, office supply chain Staples, Inc. recently engaged in a takeover bid of its competitor Office Depot, Inc. Its goal is to gain greater market share; however, the U.S. government filed a lawsuit to prevent the acquisition. Staples is considering an alternative plan if they lose the lawsuit, and the company's CEO Ron Sargent says: "We've been working on Plan B for several months at this point."[29]

The last contingency factor also is related to the time frame of plans. The **commitment concept** says that plans should extend far enough to meet those commitments made when the plans were developed. Planning for too long or too short a time period is inefficient and ineffective. For instance, Walmart, like many businesses during the 2008–2009 recession cut staff. Yet, it continued to add stores that need to be stocked and restocked with merchandise. With fewer employees, however, merchandise is piling up in stockrooms, shelves are going unstocked, checkout lines are longer, and fewer employees are in the store itself to help customers.[30] How does this illustrate the commitment concept? By deciding to cut staff, Walmart "committed" to the consequences of that decision—good and bad.

IBM replaced its traditional annual top-down planning process with an ongoing planning approach that involves employees from line managers to senior executives. The new approach enables IBM to explore and identify customer needs, new markets, technologies, and competitors from around the world and to create new ventures such as the IBM Watson Group for developing and commercializing cognitive computing innovations.
Source: Jon Simon/Newscom

commitment concept
Plans should extend far enough to meet those commitments made when the plans were developed

Approaches to Planning

Swisscom works closely with key suppliers, including Huawei, to jointly plan new technology for improving telecommunications services. At the U.K. retailer John Lewis, which is employee-owned, top managers discuss major plans and policies with the 15-member Partnership Board of employees. Executives at Inditex, the Spanish parent company of Zara and other thriving retail chains, seek input from small groups of employees and listen closely to store managers during the planning process, especially when preparing for the design and introduction of new products. In each of these situations, planning is done a little differently.[31]

In the traditional approach, planning is done entirely by top-level managers who often are assisted by a **formal planning department**, a group of planning specialists whose sole responsibility is to help write the various organizational plans. Under this approach, plans developed by top-level managers flow down through other organizational levels, much like the traditional approach to goal-setting. As they flow down through the organization, the plans are tailored to the particular needs of each level. Although this approach makes managerial planning thorough, systematic, and coordinated, all too often the focus is on developing "the plan"—a thick binder (or binders)

formal planning department
A group of planning specialists whose sole responsibility is helping to write organizational plans

full of meaningless information that's stuck on a shelf and never used by anyone for guiding or coordinating work efforts. In fact, in a survey of managers about formal top-down organizational planning processes, more than 75 percent said their company's planning approach was unsatisfactory.[32] A common complaint was that "plans are documents that you prepare for the corporate planning staff and later forget." Although this traditional top-down approach to planning is used by many organizations, it can be effective only if managers understand the importance of creating documents that organizational members actually use, not documents that look impressive but are ignored.

Another approach to planning is to involve more organizational members in the process. In this approach, plans aren't handed down from one level to the next, but instead are developed by organizational members at the various levels and in the various work units to meet their specific needs. For instance, at Dell, employees from production, supply management, and channel management meet weekly to make plans based on current product demand and supply. In addition, work teams set their own daily schedules and track their progress against those schedules. If a team falls behind, team members develop "recovery" plans to try to get back on schedule.[33] When organizational members are more actively involved in planning, they see that the plans are more than just something written down on paper. They can actually see that the plans are used in directing and coordinating work.

CONTEMPORARY issues in planning

LO8.4 The second floor of the 21-story Hyundai Motor headquarters buzzes with data 24 hours a day. That's where you'd find the company's Global Command and Control Center (GCCC), which is modeled after the CNN newsroom with numerous "computer screens relaying video and data keeping watch on Hyundai operations around the world." Managers get information on parts shipments from suppliers to factories. Cameras watch assembly lines and closely monitor the company's massive Ulsan, Korea, factory looking for competitors' spies and any hints of labor unrest. The GCCC also keeps tabs on the company's R&D activities in Europe, Japan, and North America. Hyundai can identify problems in an instant and react quickly. The company is all about aggressiveness and speed and is representative of how a successful twenty-first-century company approaches planning.[34]

We conclude this chapter by addressing three contemporary issues in planning. Specifically, we're going to look at how managers can plan effectively in dynamic environments; how managers can use environmental scanning, especially competitive intelligence; and how digital tools can be used to assist in planning activities.

If your professor has assigned this, go to **www.mymanagementlab.com** to complete the Simulation: *Planning* and get a better understanding of the challenges of planning in organizations.

- About half of all new businesses survive 5 years or more and one-third survive 10 years or more.[35]

How Can Managers Plan Effectively in Dynamic Environments?

As we saw in Chapter 7, the external environment is continually changing. For instance, cloud computing storage is revolutionizing all kinds of industries from financial services to health care to engineering.[36] Social networking sites are used by companies to connect with customers, employees, and potential employees. Amounts spent on eating out instead of cooking at home are predicted to start rising after years of decline during the economic downturn. And experts believe that China and India are transforming the twenty-first-century global economy.

How can managers effectively plan when the external environment is continually changing? We already discussed uncertain environments as one of the contingency factors that affect the types of plans managers develop. Because dynamic environments are more the norm than the exception, let's look at how managers can effectively plan in such environments.

In an uncertain environment, managers should develop plans that are specific, but flexible. Although this may seem contradictory, it's not. To be useful, plans need some specificity, but the plans should not be set in stone. Managers need to recognize that planning is an ongoing process. The plans serve as a road map, although the destination may change due to dynamic market conditions. They should be ready to change directions if environmental conditions warrant. This flexibility is particularly important as plans are implemented. Managers need to stay alert to environmental changes that may impact implementation and respond as needed. Keep in mind, also, that even when the environment is highly uncertain, it's important to continue formal planning in order to see any effect on organizational performance. It's the persistence in planning that contributes to significant performance improvement. Why? It seems that, as with most activities, managers "learn to plan," and the quality of their planning improves when they continue to do it.[37] Finally, make the organizational hierarchy flatter to effectively plan in dynamic environments. This means allowing lower organizational levels to set goals and develop plans because there's little time for goals and plans to flow down from the top. Managers should teach their employees how to set goals and to plan and then trust them to do it. And you need look no further than California's Silicon Valley to find a company that effectively understands this. In 2003, professional networking website LinkedIn was launched. The company initially struggled to enlist subscribers, sometimes adding only 20 per day, but it has since grown to more than 400 million subscribers in approximately 200 countries.[38] LinkedIn achieved success quickly, becoming profitable after three years in business, and, in its fifth year, unveiled versions of its website in Spanish and French. Today, LinkedIn specializes in "Online Professional Network, Jobs, People Search, Company Search, Address Book, Advertising, Professional Identity, and Group Collaboration."[39] The company empowers employees to take responsibility for managing projects that will enhance the LinkedIn's products and service delivery through the LinkedIn INCubator program. "It's a little bit like a venture capital thing," says Kevin Scott, LinkedIn's senior vice president for engineering. "When we find something we really like, we want to make it successful. . . . To have [cofounder and executive chairman] Reid Hoffman sit down with you one-on-one to help you make your hack successful is great."[40] If Hoffman approves the project, the employee gets matched up with an executive mentor. Then, the employee builds a team and directs the project. According to Florina Grosskurth, who runs the company's engineering programs, "LinkedIn sees [in]cubator projects as small investments that have the potential to become big wins for the company."[41]

If your professor has assigned this, go to **www.mymanagementlab.com** to watch a video titled: *CH2MHill: Planning* and to respond to questions.

How Can Managers Use Environmental Scanning?

Crammed into a small Shanghai apartment that houses four generations of a Chinese family, Indra Nooyi, chairman and CEO of PepsiCo, Inc., asked the inhabitants several questions about "China's rapid development, their shopping habits, and how they feel about Western brands." This visit was part of an "immersion" tour of China for Ms. Nooyi, who hoped to strengthen PepsiCo's business in emerging markets. She said, "I wanted to look at how people live, how they eat, what the growth possibilities are."[42] The information gleaned from her research—a prime example of environmental scanning up close and personal—will help in establishing PepsiCo's future goals and plans.

A manager's analysis of the external environment may be improved by **environmental scanning**, which involves screening information to detect emerging trends. One of the fastest-growing forms of environmental scanning is

environmental scanning
Screening information to detect emerging trends

Operating in a dynamic global environment, the Swedish music-streaming service Spotify gathers information about competitors such as Google's YouTube and Apple's Beats in the United States, Deezer in France, and SoundCloud in Germany. Competitive intelligence helps Spotify managers and employees develop plans for new business ventures such as its video-streaming service. *Source: Melanie Stetson Freeman/The Christian Science Monitor/AP Images*

competitor intelligence, gathering information about competitors that allows managers to anticipate competitors' actions rather than merely react to them.[43] It seeks basic information about competitors: Who are they? What are they doing? How will what they're doing affect us?

competitor intelligence
Gathering information about competitors that allows managers to anticipate competitors' actions rather than merely react to them

Many who study competitive intelligence suggest that much of the competitor-related information managers need to make crucial strategic decisions is available and accessible to the public.[44] In other words, competitive intelligence isn't corporate espionage. Advertisements, promotional materials, press releases, reports filed with government agencies, annual reports, want ads, newspaper reports, information on the Internet, and industry studies are readily accessible sources of information. Specific information on an industry and associated organizations is increasingly available through electronic databases. Managers can literally tap into this wealth of competitive information by purchasing access to databases. Attending trade shows and debriefing your own sales staff also can be good sources of information on competitors. In addition, many organizations even regularly buy competitors' products and ask their own employees to evaluate them to learn about new technical innovations.[45]

In a changing global business environment, environmental scanning and obtaining competitive intelligence can be quite complex, especially since information must be gathered from around the world. However, one thing managers could do is subscribe to news services that review newspapers and magazines from around the globe and provide summaries to client companies.

Managers do need to be careful about the way information, especially competitive intelligence, is gathered to prevent any concerns about whether it's legal or ethical.[46] For instance, Agilent Technologies is suing former employee Emily Leproust and her new employer Twist Bioscience for stealing trade secrets, which enables the company to manufacture genes quicker and more economically. Agilent's lead attorney Daniel Petrocelli said: "This was a highly orchestrated scheme to misappropriate Agilent's intellectual property and violate its valuable rights. We will vigorously protect the company's interests."[47]

Competitive intelligence becomes illegal corporate spying when it involves the theft of proprietary materials or trade secrets by any means. The Economic Espionage Act makes it a crime in the United States to engage in economic espionage or to steal a trade secret. Difficult decisions about competitive intelligence arise because often there's a fine line between what's considered legal and ethical and what's considered legal but unethical. Although the top manager at one competitive intelligence firm contends that 99.9 percent of intelligence gathering is legal, there's no question that some people or companies will go to any lengths—some unethical—to get information about competitors.[48]

Digital Tools

Increasingly, we're finding that companies are making strategic changes based on data, as distinct from day-to-day decisions. These leaders understand the importance of business intelligence in their planning process. **Business intelligence** refers to a variety of data that managers can use to make more effective strategic decisions. Sources of business intelligence are company records, industry trends, and competitors' financial (for example, profits) or market (for example, market penetration) data.

business intelligence
data that managers can use to make more effective strategic decisions

How do managers make sense of vast amounts of data? Managers can use digital tools to make sense of business intelligence data. **Digital tools** refer to technology, systems, or software that allow the user to collect, visualize, understand, or analyze data. Specific examples of digital tools include software such as Microsoft Excel, online services such as Google Analytics, or networks that connect computers and people, such as social media.

digital tools
technology, systems, or software that allow the user to collect, visualize, understand, or analyze data

FUTURE VISION | Using Social Media for Environmental Scanning

While most companies have a strategy to use social media for marketing, many companies have expanded their use of social media to support organizational planning.[49] A growing number of social media sites are providing businesses with real-time information to support environmental scanning efforts.

Social media is particularly valuable in collecting competitor intelligence. Businesses can identify emerging trends by monitoring online conversations and other information transmitted via social media. For example, through LinkedIn you might learn that a competitor is expanding a certain division as more people update their profiles indicating they are joining an organization. Or you could identify a competitor's strategic promotions or hires that might reflect a shift in their business.

It may seem like a daunting task to monitor social media; however, businesses can use new software tools and analytic techniques to learn about competitors, suppliers, and customers. For example, software can be used to calculate "buzz volume," which isolates relevant messages about a specific company's brand online. Small businesses in particular could benefit from social media as local happenings are often shared on Twitter or other sites, even if they don't make it to traditional news sources.

To effectively gather business intelligence from social media, organizations should take a strategic approach, otherwise it is easy to get buried in the overwhelming amount of information that exists. This unprecedented access to immediate and endless information could shift how businesses conduct organizational planning. Business managers must be able to shift plans quickly in response to trends or other intelligence identified via social media scanning efforts.

*If your professor has chosen to assign this, go to **www.mymanagementlab.com** to discuss the following questions:*

TALK ABOUT IT 1: With so much information available through social media, how can businesses focus their efforts to scan for relevant information?

TALK ABOUT IT 2: How can a business determine if information gathered from social media is reliable?

Increasingly, digital tools enable managers to make decisions based on a variety of *quantitative information*, much of which we refer to as big data. In Chapter 2, we defined big data as the vast amount of quantifiable information that can be analyzed by highly sophisticated data processing. It's important to reiterate that managers make plans using their understanding of *qualitative information*, including internal factors such as how organizational culture influences employee motivation, and external factors, such as why competitors have adopted new technology to advance their organizational objectives. Digital tools, while increasingly important, should complement current planning approaches rather than replace them. Let's briefly review three of the more prevalent digital tools available today.

DATA VISUALIZATION TOOLS What do pie charts, bar charts, and trend lines have in common? They're methods to organize and summarize data for visual display. For example, managers can use bar charts to display profits for several industries across multiple years. Tableau is an example of a company that provides software tools and interactive dashboards that allow users to generate useful business insights through the analysis and visualization of data. The company is on the cutting edge of data imaging solutions for end-users, creating products such as Elastic which allows users to create graphics from spreadsheets.

CLOUD COMPUTING **Cloud computing** refers to storing and accessing data on the Internet rather than on a computer's hard drive or a company's network. The cloud is just a metaphor for the Internet.[50] Salesforce.com is an example of a company that provides cloud services to businesses. The company offers Customer Success Platform, which helps clients collect, analyze, and distribute customer information. This service permits integration of multiple data sources into a single location, enabling companies to make timely decisions.

cloud computing
Refers to storing and accessing data on the Internet rather than on a computer's hard drive or a company's network.

Internet of things
Allows everyday "things" to generate and store and share data across the Internet

INTERNET OF THINGS In the *Future Vision* feature in Chapter 6, we described the **Internet of Things (IoT)**, which allows everyday "things" to generate and store data about their own performance and share that information across the Internet. For instance, tire manufacturer Michelin created the EFFIFUEL service. EFFIFUEL relies on experts and digital tools to help companies reduce fuel costs. Sensors placed in vehicles collect data on fuel consumption, tire pressure, temperature, speed, and location. These data are sent to a cloud service and fuel experts then analyze the data and make recommendations to fleet managers regarding how to use less fuel when driving. The EFFIFUEL service has been able to help fleet managers save about 2 liters of fuel for every 100 kilometers driven.[51]

In sum, business intelligence has become an increasingly important asset for strategic planning. Digital tools enable managers to make sense of the data. However, while these tools are increasingly important, they should complement current planning approaches rather than replace them.

Chapter 8 PREPARING FOR: Exams/Quizzes

CHAPTER SUMMARY by Learning Objectives

LO8.1 DEFINE the nature and purposes of planning.

Planning involves defining the organization's goals, establishing an overall strategy for achieving those goals, and developing plans for organizational work activities. The four purposes of planning include providing direction, reducing uncertainty, minimizing waste and redundancy, and establishing the goals or standards used in controlling. Studies of the planning-performance relationship have concluded that formal planning is associated with positive financial performance, for the most part; it's more important to do a good job of planning and implementing the plans than doing more extensive planning; the external environment is usually the reason why companies that plan don't achieve high levels of performance; and the planning-performance relationship seems to be influenced by the planning time frame.

LO8.2 CLASSIFY the types of goals organizations might have and the plans they use.

Goals are desired outcomes. Plans are documents that outline how goals are going to be met. Goals might be strategic or financial, and they might be stated or real. Strategic plans apply to the entire organization, while operational plans encompass a particular functional area. Long-term plans are those with a time frame beyond three years. Short-term plans cover one year or less. Specific plans are clearly defined and leave no room for interpretation. Directional plans are flexible and set out general guidelines. A single-use plan is a one-time plan designed to meet the needs of a unique situation. Standing plans are ongoing plans that provide guidance for activities performed repeatedly.

LO8.3 COMPARE and contrast approaches to goal-setting and planning.

In traditional goal-setting, goals are set at the top of the organization and then become subgoals for each organizational area. MBO (management by objectives) is a process of setting mutually agreed-upon goals and using those goals to evaluate employee performance. Well-written goals have six characteristics: They are (1) written in terms of outcomes, (2) measurable and quantifiable, (3) clear as to time frame, (4) challenging but attainable, (5) written down, and (6) communicated to all organizational members who need to know them. Goal-setting involves these steps: review the organization's mission; evaluate available resources; determine the goals individually or with input from others; write down the goals and communicate them to all who need to know them; and review results and change goals as needed. The contingency factors that affect planning include the manager's level in the organization, the degree of environmental uncertainty, and the length of future commitments. The two main approaches to planning include the traditional approach, which has plans developed by top managers that flow down through other organizational levels and which may use a formal planning department. The other approach is to involve more organizational members in the planning process.

LO8.4 DISCUSS contemporary issues in planning.

One contemporary planning issue is planning in dynamic environments, which usually means developing plans that are specific but flexible. Also, it's important to continue planning, even when the environment is highly uncertain. Finally, because there's little time in a dynamic environment for goals and plans to flow down from the top, lower organizational levels should be allowed to set goals and develop plans. Another contemporary planning issue involves using environmental scanning to help do a better analysis of the external environment. One form of environmental scanning, competitive intelligence, can be especially helpful in finding out what competitors are doing. Organizations can gather business intelligence using a variety of digital tools to collect and analyze quantitative and qualitative data to support decision making.

Pearson **MyLab** Management

Go to **mymanagementlab.com** to complete the problems marked with this icon ✪.

✪ REVIEW AND DISCUSSION QUESTIONS

8-1. Explain what studies have shown about the relationship between planning and performance.

8-2. Planning takes a lot of effort. Why do you think people should engage in it?

8-3. Define the term goal and explain how planning fits into an organization's goal.

8-4. What are organizational goals? How many types are there? How would you discern an organization's actual goals?

8-5. Outline the five steps required for setting goals in an organization. Explain how they work.

8-6. What is the fastest-growing area of environmental scanning? What does it provide to an organization?

8-7. Setting organizational goals is an important step in planning. What are the approaches to setting organizational goals? Which do you consider the best?

8-8. Hyundai's Global Command and Control Center (GCCC) have cameras strategically placed across its centers to monitor assembly lines. This helps identify problems and respond quickly. What drives Hyundai to plan this way?

Pearson **MyLab** Management

If your professor has assigned these, go to **mymanagementlab.com** for the following Assisted-graded writing questions:

8-9. Describe how the owner of an SME could use environmental scanning.

8-10. The late Peter Drucker, an eminent management author, coined the SMART format for setting goals back in 1954: S (specific), M (measurable), A (attainable), R (relevant), and T (time-bound). Are these still relevant today? Discuss.

PREPARING FOR: My Career

PERSONAL INVENTORY ASSESSMENTS

Tolerance of Ambiguity Scale

Managers often have to deal with ambiguous situations, which can make effective planning very challenging. In this PIA, you'll assess your level of tolerance for ambiguity.

ETHICS DILEMMA

While important, rules may sometimes create more problems than they resolve. Websites like TripAdvisor are valuable for tourism, providing businesses with greater exposure. The problem is not all reviews are positive. Recently a hotel in Blackpool, England, fined two guests £100 for leaving scathing comments on TripAdvisor. On enquiry, the hotel had reportedly informed them that this was a policy—to charge guests who leave bad reviews.[52] The couple was later refunded. Another example is a Canadian hotel routinely criticized for its strict rules—guests required to go to sleep by 10 PM and a "no talking" policy in its corridors and public areas. After 11 PM, the hotel's staff would patrol the site, threatening people with the non-return of their deposit. If noise was heard from within any of the rooms, the reception would call. Many reviews suggested that the reception was downright rude. Despite this, the hotel's rooms were regarded as clean and the breakfast reasonable.

8-11. To what extent do you think it's ethical for businesses to impose such strict rules on guests?

8-12. Would it be legal for the hotel to exclude some customers from the restrictions?

8-13. How would you react if a business imposed overly restrictive rules on you?

SKILLS EXERCISE Making a To-Do List That Works and Using It

Do you have lots to do and limited time in which to do it? That sounds familiar, doesn't it! One tool that many successful people use is a to-do list. Lists can be useful because they: help organize and make sense of what needs to be done; keep details of work/life events; track progress; and help overcome procrastination. Making a to-do list that works and then using it is a skill that every manager needs to develop.

Steps in Practicing the Skill

- ***Break project(s) into smaller tasks and prioritize those tasks.*** When you have a major project to complete, spend some time up front identifying as many of the sequential tasks necessary to complete that project. Also, prioritize, prioritize, prioritize. It's the only way to get done what's most important.
- ***Be realistic about your to-do list.*** Whether your to-do list is daily, weekly, or monthly—or all of these—you've got to realize that interruptions will and do happen. Don't overestimate what you can get done. And you will face conflicting priorities. Reprioritize when this happens.
- ***Know and pay attention to your own time and energy.*** Develop your own personal routines. You know when you're the most productive. Those are the times you need to do your most important tasks. Or maybe you need to do the task you like least first. You'll want to get it done faster so you can move on to tasks that you enjoy doing.
- ***Know your biggest time wasters and distractions.*** We all have them, whether they're found online or on the television or elsewhere. (And you probably already know what yours are!) Also, realize you probably can't (nor do you want to) eliminate them. But do be leery of them, especially when you're trying to get something done or need to get something done.
- ***Let technology be a tool, not a distraction.*** Find an app (or written approach) that works FOR YOU. There are many available. And don't constantly try out new ones—that, in itself, wastes precious time. Find one that works for your needs and your personal situation and that you'll USE.
- ***Conquer the e-mail/instant messaging challenge.*** Although coworkers communicate in many ways in organizations, e-mail and instant messaging are popular *and* can be overwhelming to deal with when you're trying to accomplish work tasks. Again, you need to find what works best for you. Some ideas for "conquering" this distraction include:

- Check only at certain times during the day.
- Maybe avoid e-mail first thing in the morning because it's so easy to get sidetracked.
- Come up with a system for responding—if a response can be given in less than three minutes (or whatever time control you choose), respond immediately; if it can't, set the e-mail/message aside for later when you have more time. And a good rule: the faster your response time, the shorter the e-mail.
- Weed out any "subscriptions" that you're not reading/using. You know, those you thought sounded really interesting and you end up deleting immediately anyway. So, don't even get them—unsubscribe.
- Use your e-mail system tools—filters that move e-mails to folders, canned responses, auto-responders, and so forth—to manage your e-mail messages.

Practicing the Skill

The best way to practice this skill is to pick a project (school, work, personal) that you're facing and try to use the above suggestions. To get better at using to-do lists, you've just got to jump in, create them, and most importantly use them to guide what you do and when you do it. Commit to making your to-do list a habit by referring to it on a daily basis for at least a month.

WORKING TOGETHER **Team Exercise**

Effective goal writing requires practice. Think about something you would like to accomplish in the future. It could be something related to your job, school, or an organization you are involved with, or something in your personal life. Next, put your goal in writing. Pair up with another student and share your goal. Give each other feedback on your goals. Refer to Exhibit 8-4—does the goal have the characteristics of well-written goals? Discuss with each other your future plans to accomplish the goal.

MY TURN TO BE A MANAGER

- Practice setting goals for various aspects of your personal life such as academics, career preparation, family, hobbies, and so forth. Set at least two short-term goals and at least two long-term goals for each area.
- For these goals that you have set, write out plans for achieving those goals. Think in terms of what you will have to do to accomplish each. For instance, if one of your academic goals is to improve your grade-point average, what will you have to do to reach it?
- Write a personal mission statement. Although this may sound simple to do, it's not going to be simple or easy. Our hope is that it will be something you'll want to keep, use, and revise when necessary and that it will help you be the person you'd like to be and live the life you'd like to live. Start by doing some research on personal mission statements. There are some wonderful Web resources that can guide you. Good luck!
- Interview three managers about the types of planning they do. Ask them for suggestions on how to be a better planner. Write a report describing and comparing your findings.
- Choose two companies, preferably in different industries. Research the companies' websites and find examples of goals they have stated. (Hint: A company's annual report is often a good place to start.) Evaluate these goals. Are they well-written? Rewrite those that don't exhibit the characteristics of well-written goals so that they do.
- Effective managers are always screening information to look for emerging trends that might affect their industries. Start looking for trends in an industry you are interested in by subscribing to a variety of social media sources that are related to the industry.

CASE APPLICATION 1 Hermès: Delivering change

Hermès is a pan-European courier company with over 40 years' experience in the business. It operates primarily in the United Kingdom, Austria, Germany, Italy, and Russia. In the United Kingdom, Hermès handles more than 245 million parcels a year. It relies on the growing "gig economy" employment trend with over 10,000 self-employed couriers and a network of 4,500 Parcel Shops. Hermès provides door-to-door services for any leading retailers including Next, ASOS, John Lewis, and Tesco.

With a large and disparate workforce, planning and control is the key element in ensuring that the network remains effective and robust. Hermès needed a way to move the day-to-day management of their U.K. courier network to decision makers on the ground. Given the unpredictable demands on th courier network, Hermès needed to be able to reallocate delivery rounds quickly if one courier was overloaded and another in an adjacent area had capacity to take up the extra work.

In the United Kingdom, there are 1.8 million unique postcode addresses. Hermès has allocated the 10,000 couriers to a number of these postcodes. The network is, therefore, extremely granular and subject to enormous changes on a daily basis. While initially employing a centralized system to create and update courier rounds, Hermès realized this was time consuming and that the delivery maps produced became outdated by the time the couriers started their deliveries. Hermès needed a management-planning tool to optimize its network and assess what-if scenarios.

In designing the new tools, Hermès decided to opt for a dynamic online mapping system that allowed them to create, view, organize, and manage the courier rounds. The key elements include the viewing tools (allowing users to visualize the territories and courier rounds), the planning and operations tool (allows field management to change the structure of territories and submit their suggestions for approval), and the scenario planning tool (allows the central operations team to optimize and model territories to identify any possible efficiencies to the structure). The new planning system enables the 200 field managers to make subtle and real-time adjustments to their operative areas on a local and tactical level. It also allows the central management a chance to look at the impact and effectiveness of the changes and then approve the changes in a matter of minutes.

The key benefits of the new planning tools had a direct and positive impact on the goals of the organisation. There were operational savings (expenses and delivery costs were cut) and an improvement in service performance and efficiency. Courier turnover dropped as network members had a more even workload. It provided a holistic view of the network, allowed peak planning, and a continuous review of the network. Field managers can access the system via an iPad and they can make and see their planning changes immediately.

The new planning system is scalable; so as Hermès continues to grow, they recognize the need to make continuous and significant changes to their network structure. The system allows Hermès to visualize and identify existing and potential problems and model solutions for them. The system allows Hermès to pledge that every parcel entering the U.K. Hermès network by December 21, 2016, would have at least one delivery attempt, or Hermès would refund the delivery charge.[53]

DISCUSSION QUESTIONS

8-14. How can a planning and mapping software help Hermès to achieve a 95 percent first-time delivery target?

8-15. How can planning ensure that Hermès continues to meet its delivery targets in the future and at times when there is bad weather or high peak-demand?

8-16. Would it be valuable for Hermès to gather competitive intelligence? Why or why not?

8-17. What other trends in the courier deliveries could affect the industry in the future?

CASE APPLICATION 2 Shifting Direction

As the global leader in satellite navigation equipment, Garmin Ltd. recently hit a milestone number. It has sold more than 100 million of its products to customers—from motorists to runners to geocachers and more—who depend on the company's equipment to "help show them the way." Despite this milestone, the company's core business is in decline due to changing circumstances.[54] In response, managers at Garmin, the biggest maker of personal navigation devices, are shifting direction. Many of you probably have a dashboard-mounted navigation device in your car, and chances are it might be a Garmin. However, a number of cars now have "dashboard command centers which combine smartphone docking stations with navigation systems." Sales of Garmin devices have declined as consumers increasingly use their smartphones for directions and maps. However, have you ever tried to use your smartphone navigation system while holding a phone to look at its display? It's dangerous to hold a phone and steer. Also, GPS apps can "crash" if multiple apps are running. That's why Olathe, the Kansas-based company, is taking explicitly aggressive actions to team up with automakers to embed its GPS systems in car dashboards. Right now, its biggest in-dash contract is with Chrysler, and its Uconnect dashboard system is found in several models of Jeep, Dodge, and Chrysler vehicles. Garmin also is working with Honda and Toyota for dashboard systems in the Asian market.

Despite these new market shifts, customers have gotten used to the GPS devices, and they've become an essential part of their lives. That's why Garmin's executive team still believes there's a market for dedicated navigation systems. It's trying to breathe some life into the product with new features, better designs, and more value for the consumer's money. For instance, some of the new features include faster searching for addresses or points of interest, voice-activated navigation, and highlighting exit services such as gas stations and restaurants.

DISCUSSION QUESTIONS

8-18. What role do you think goals would play in planning the change in direction for the company? List some goals you think might be important. (Make sure these goals have the characteristics of well-written goals.)

8-19. What types of plans would be needed in an industry such as this one? (For instance, long-term plans or short-term plans, or both?) Explain why you think these plans would be important.

8-20. What contingency factors might affect the planning Garmin executives have to do? How might those contingency factors affect the planning?

8-21. What planning challenges do you think Garmin executives face with continuing to be the global market leader? How should they cope with those challenges?

ENDNOTES

1. J. S. Cobb, N. Bocanegra, and C. Vargas, "Colombia to complain to CB&I about multi-billion-dollar refinery overruns," *The Wall Street Journal* online, www.wsj.com, February 10, 2016.
2. See, for example, A. Ghobadian, N. O'Regan, H. Thomas, and J. Liu, "Formal Strategic Planning, Operating Environment, Size, Sector, and Performance," *Journal of General Management,* Winter 2008, pp. 1–19; F. Delmar and S. Shane, "Does Business Planning Facilitate the Development of New Ventures?," *Strategic Management Journal,* December 2003, pp. 1165–1185; R. M. Grant, "Strategic Planning in a Turbulent Environment: Evidence from the Oil Majors," *Strategic Management Journal,* June 2003, pp. 491–517; P. J. Brews and M. R. Hunt, "Learning to Plan and Planning to Learn: Resolving the Planning School/Learning School Debate," *Strategic Management Journal,* December 1999, pp. 889–913; C. C. Miller and L. B. Cardinal, "Strategic Planning and Firm Performance: A Synthesis of More Than Two Decades of Research," *Academy of Management Journal,* March 1994, pp. 1649–1685; N. Capon, J. U. Farley, and J. M. Hulbert, "Strategic Planning and Financial Performance: More Evidence," *Journal of Management Studies,* January 1994, pp. 22–38; D. K. Sinha, "The Contribution of Formal Planning to Decisions," *Strategic Management Journal,* October 1990, pp. 479–492; J. A. Pearce II, E. B. Freeman, and R. B. Robinson Jr., "The Tenuous Link Between Formal Strategic Planning and Financial Performance," *Academy of Management Review,* October 1987, pp. 658–675; L. C. Rhyne, "Contrasting Planning Systems in High, Medium, and Low Performance Companies," *Journal of Management Studies,* July 1987, pp. 363–385; and J. A. Pearce II, K. K. Robbins, and R. B. Robinson, Jr., "The Impact of Grand Strategy and Planning Formality on Financial Performance," *Strategic Management Journal,* March–April 1987, pp. 125–134.
3. "As Q4 Approaches, Which of the Following Is Most Challenging for You As a Leader?," SmartBrief on Leadership, smartbrief.com/leadership, October 15, 2013.
4. R. Molz, "How Leaders Use Goals," *Long Range Planning,* October 1987, p. 91.
5. C. Hymowitz, "When Meeting Targets Becomes the Strategy, CEO Is on Wrong Path," *Wall Street Journal,* March 8, 2005, p. B1.
6. A. Steele, "Dollar General Profit Rises on Higher Sales," *The Wall Street Journal* online, www.wsj.com, March 14, 2016.
7. "About Us," World Food Programs, www.wfp.org, accessed March 19, 2016.
8. Nike, www.nikebiz.com/crreport/; Chipotle, www.chipotle.com/food-with-integrity; and EnCana Corporate Constitution (2010), www.encana.com.
9. See, for instance, J. Pfeffer, *Organizational Design* (Arlington Heights, IL: AHM Publishing, 1978), pp. 5–12; and C. K. Warriner, "The Problem of Organizational Purpose," *Sociological Quarterly,* Spring 1965, pp. 139–146.
10. "Egypt's Transport Firm Unveils New Strategy to Accelerate Growth," *Thomson Reuters Zawya*, December 13, 2016, http://www.zawya.com/mena/en/story/Egypts_transport_firm_unveils_new_strategy_to_accelerate_growth-ZAWYA20161213044432/ (accessed December 22, 2016).
11. Egytrans Website, January 2015, http://egytrans.com/news/press-center/ (accessed December 20, 2016).
12. J. D. Hunger and T. L. Wheelen, *Strategic Management and Business Policy,* 10th ed. (Upper Saddle River, NJ: Prentice Hall, 2006).
13. U.S. National Aeronautical Space Administration, About NASA page, What Does NASA Do? https://www.nasa.gov/about/highlights/what_does_nasa_do.html, accessed March 19, 2016.
14. Christopher Jasper, "Rolls-Royce to Cut Another 800 Jobs at Ailing Marine Business," *Bloomberg*, December 1, 2016, https://www.bloomberg.com/news/articles/2016-12-01/rolls-royce-to-cut-another-800-jobs-at-ailing-marine-business (accessed December 22, 2016).
15. The Morning Star Company's Mission, www.morningstarco.com, accessed March 19, 2016. Copyright (c) 2016 The Morning Star Company.
16. LVMH Governance page and Code of Conduct, https://www.lvmh.com/investors/profile/governance-sri/ (accessed December 22, 2016).
17. Leader Making a Difference box based on R. L. Brandt, "Birth of a Salesman," *Wall Street Journal,* October 15–16, 2012, pp. C1+; D. Lyons, "Jeff Bezos," *Newsweek,* December 28, 2009/January 4, 2010, pp. 85–86; B. Stone, "Can Amazon Be Wal-Mart of the Web?" *New York Times* online, www.nytimes.com, September 20, 2009; and K. Kelleher, "Why Amazon Is Bucking the Trend," CNNMoney.com, March 2, 2009.
18. Nye Longman, "Swisscom: How to Transform a Telco," *Business Review Europe*, December 22, 2016, http://www.businessrevieweurope.eu/Swisscom-Ltd/profiles/227/Swisscom:-how-to-transform-a-telco (accessed December 22, 2016); Swisscom, https://www.swisscom (accessed December 22, 2016).
19. A. Fisher, "How Adobe Keeps Key Employees from Quitting," *Fortune* online, www.fortune.com, June 16, 2015.
20. P. N. Romani, "MBO by Any Other Name Is Still MBO," *Supervision,* December 1997, pp. 6–8; and A. W. Schrader and G. T. Seward, "MBO Makes Dollar Sense," *Personnel Journal,* July 1989, pp. 32–37.
21. R. Rodgers and J. E. Hunter, "Impact of Management by Objectives on Organizational Productivity," *Journal of Applied Psychology,* April 1991, pp. 322–336.
22. E. A. Locke and G. P. Latham, "Has Goal Setting Gone Wild, or Have Its Attackers Abandoned Good Scholarship?" *Academy of Management Perspectives,* February 2009, pp. 17–23; and G. P. Latham, "The Motivational Benefits of Goal-Setting," *Academy of Management Executive,* November 2004, pp. 126–129.
23. Samsung Electronics Corporation, "Samsung's 10-Year Plan Turns Five: The Sustainability Report 2014," www.samsung.com, accessed March 19, 2016.
24. For additional information on goals, see, for instance, P. Drucker, *The Executive in Action* (New York: HarperCollins Books, 1996), pp. 207–214; and E. A. Locke and G. P. Latham, *A Theory of Goal Setting and Task Performance* (Upper Saddle River, NJ: Prentice Hall, 1990).
25. D. Sull, R. Homkes, and C. Sull, "Why Strategy Execution Unravels—and What to Do About It," *Harvard Business Review* online, www.hbr.org, March 2015.
26. The Coca-Cola Company, "Mission, Vision & Values," www.coca-colacompany.com, accessed March 19, 2016.
27. Several of these factors were suggested by R. K. Bresser and R. C. Bishop, "Dysfunctional Effects of Formal Planning: Two Theoretical Explanations," *Academy of Management Review,* October 1983, pp. 588–599; and J. S. Armstrong, "The Value of Formal Planning for Strategic Decisions: Review of Empirical Research," *Strategic Management Journal,* July–September 1982, pp. 197–211.

28. Brews and Hunt, "Learning to Plan and Planning to Learn: Resolving the Planning School/Learning School Debate."
29. D. Fitzgerald and J. Jamerson, "Staples Prepares Plan B as Merger Stalls, Sales Sink," *The Wall Street Journal* online, www.wsj.com, March 4, 2016.
30. R. Dudley, "What Good Are Low Prices If the Shelves Are Empty?," *Bloomberg BusinessWeek,* April 1–7, 2013, pp. 23–24.
31. Nye Longman, "Swisscom: How to Transform a Telco," *Business Review Europe*, December 22, 2016, http://www.businessrevieweurope.eu/Swisscom-Ltd/profiles/227/Swisscom:-how-to-transform-a-telco (accessed December 22, 2016); Michael Skapinker and Andrea Felsted, "John Lewis: Trouble in Store," *Financial Times*, October 16, 2015, https://www.ft.com/content/92c95704-6c6d-11e5-8171-ba1968cf791a (accessed December 22, 2016); "The Management Style of Amancio Ortega," *The Economist*, December 17, 2016, http://www.economist.com/news/business/21711948-founder-inditex-has-become-worlds-second-richest-man-management-style-amancio (accessed December 22, 2016); Patricia Kowsmann, "Fast-Fashion Leader Inditex Charts Own Path," *Wall Street Journal*, December 6, 2016, http://www.wsj.com/articles/fast-fashion-leader-inditex-charts-own-path-1481020202 (accessed December 22, 2016).
32. A. Campbell, "Tailored, Not Benchmarked: A Fresh Look at Corporate Planning," *Harvard Business Review,* March–April 1999, pp. 41–50.
33. J. H. Sheridan, "Focused on Flow," *IW,* October 18, 1999, pp. 46–51.
34. A. Taylor III, "Hyundai Smokes the Competition," *Fortune,* January 18, 2010, pp. 62–71.
35. U.S. Bureau of Labor Statistics, "Entrepreneurship and the U.S. Economy," *Business Employment Dynamics,* www.bls.gov, accessed March 25, 2016.
36. J. Vance, "Ten Cloud Computing Leaders," *IT Management Online,* May 26, 2010; A. Rocadela, "Amazon Looks to Widen Lead in Cloud Computing," *Bloomberg BusinessWeek* online, www.bloomberg.com, April 28, 2010; and S. Lawson, "Cloud Computing Could Be a Boon for Flash Storage," *Bloomberg BusinessWeek* online, www.bloomberg.com, August 24, 2009.
37. Brews and Hunt, "Learning to Plan and Planning to Learn: Resolving the Planning School/Learning School Debate."
38. LinkedIn, https://www.linkedin.com/company/linkedin, accessed March 20, 2016.
39. Ibid.
40. R. Tate, "LinkedIn Gone Wild: '20 Percent Time' to Tinker Spreads Beyond Google," *Wired*, www.wired.com, December 6, 2012.
41. I. Lapouski, "Why Every Company Is Now an Incubator," *Inc.* online, www.inc.com, December 21, 2012.
42. G. Fairclough and V. Bauerlein, "Pepsi CEO Tours China to Get a Feel for Market," *Wall Street Journal,* July 1, 2009, p. B5.
43. See, for example, P. Tarraf and R. Molz, "Competitive Intelligence," *SAM Advanced Management Journal,* Autumn 2006, pp. 24–34; W. M. Fitzpatrick, "Uncovering Trade Secrets: The Legal and Ethical Conundrum of Creative Competitive Intelligence," *SAM Advanced Management Journal,* Summer 2003, pp. 4–12; L. Lavelle, "The Case of the Corporate Spy," *BusinessWeek,* November 26, 2001, pp. 56–58; C. Britton, "Deconstructing Advertising: What Your Competitor's Advertising Can Tell You About Their Strategy," *Competitive Intelligence,* January/February 2002, pp. 15–19; and L. Smith, "Business Intelligence Progress in Jeopardy," *Information Week,* March 4, 2002, p. 74.
44. S. Greenbard, "New Heights in Business Intelligence," *Business Finance,* March 2002, pp. 41–46; K. A. Zimmermann, "The Democratization of Business Intelligence," *KN World,* May 2002, pp. 20–21; and C. Britton, "Deconstructing Advertising: What Your Competitor's Advertising Can Tell You About Their Strategy," *Competitive Intelligence,* January/February 2002, pp. 15–19.
45. L. Weathersby, "Take This Job and ***** It," *Fortune,* January 7, 2002, p. 122.
46. D. Leonard, "The Corporate Side of Snooping," *New York Times* online, www.nytimes.com, March 5, 2010; B. Acohido, "Corporate Espionage Surges in Tough Times," *USA Today,* July 29, 2009, pp. 1B+; and B. Rosner, "HR Should Get a Clue: Corporate Spying is Real," *Workforce,* April 2001, pp. 72–75.
47. B. Gormley and P. Haggin, "Agilent Sues Start-Up Twist Bioscience Over Alleged Trade Secrets Theft," *The Wall Street Journal* online, www.wsj.com, February 4, 2016.
48. S. Bergsman, "Corporate Spying Goes Mainstream," *CFO,* December 1997, p. 24; and K. Western, "Ethical Spying," *Business Ethics,* September–October 1995, pp. 22–23.
49. M. Ojala, "Minding Your Own Business: Social Media Invades Business Research," *Online*, July/August 2012, pp. 51–53; "Competitive Intelligence Becomes Even More Important," *Trends E-Magazine*, March 2015, pp. 1-5; J. Song, S. Shin, L.Jia, C. Cegielski, and R. Rainer, "The Effect of Social Media on Supply Chain Sensing Capability: An Environmental Scanning Perspective," 21st Americas Conference on Information Systems, August 2015, Puerto Rico, pp. 1–13; M. Harrysson, E. Metayer, and H. Sarrazin, "How 'Social Intelligence' Can Guide Decisions," *McKinsey Quarterly*, 2012, no. 4, pp. 81–89.
50. E. Griffith, "What Is Cloud Computing?," *PC Magazine* online, www.pcmag.com, April 17, 2015.
51. P. Daugherty, P. Banerjee, W. Negm, and A. E. Alter, "Driving Unconventional Growth through the Industrial Internet of Things," *Accenture Technologies*, www.accenture.com, 2015.
52. Peter Wilkinson, "Guests Fined for Leaving Review of 'Filthy, Dirty Rotten' Hotel on Tripadvisor," *CNN Travel,* November 19, 2014; "Trip Advisor Bad Review 'Fine' to be Refunded by Blackpool Hotel," *BBC News England,* November 19, 2014.
53. Based on information available at the Hermès Web site, http://www.hermes.com/index_uk.html, accessed February 2017; Robert Booth, "Ministers Order HMRC Crackdown on 'Gig Economy' Firms," *The Guardian* online, October 20, 2016, https://www.theguardian.com; Emma Munbodh, "The last Royal Mail Posting Dates Before Christmas 2016—Including Collect+, DHL, Hermes, TNT and Yodel," Mirror, http://www.mirror.co.uk, December 22, 2016; "Ecommerce logistics companies in Europe," Ecommerce News Europe, accessed February 10, 2017.
54. K. Naughton, "Recalculating Navigation Needs," *Bloomberg BusinessWeek,* July 29, 2013, pp. 35–36; "Garmin Finds Route Higher," Forbes online, www.forbes.com, May 2, 2012; "Come on Baby, Drive My Car," *Tech Talk,* April 2012, pp. 24–28; E. Rhey, "A GPS Maker Shifts Gears," *Fortune,* March 19, 2012, p. 62; "Garmin Arrives at a Milestone: 100 Million Products Sold," Garmin.com, May 2, 2012; and B. Charny, "Garmin's Positioning Comes under Scrutiny," *Wall Street Journal,* April 2, 2008, p. A5.

Chapter 9 Strategic Planning

It's Your Career

Source: Login/Fotolia

Learning Your Strengths and Weaknesses: Accentuate the Positive

Do you know your individual personal strengths and weaknesses? You need to! Why? One important reason is that interviewers commonly ask what you consider your strengths and weaknesses and you want to be prepared to answer those questions and demonstrate your level of self-knowledge and self-awareness. Another reason is that in today's knowledge-work world, you need to find, know, and leverage your workplace strengths so you can be the best employee possible. Finally, by knowing your strengths and weaknesses you can size up where you stand in your career and make good decisions about what you need to do to keep advancing. So here are some suggestions to help you learn your strengths and weaknesses so you can accentuate your positive attributes and minimize or compensate for your weaknesses:

A key to success in management and in your career is knowing how to identify, evaluate, and make the best use of your personal strengths and weaknesses.

*1. **Focus first on identifying your strengths.** Your strengths are your individual personal positive attributes and characteristics. As you look at your strengths, assess the following: skills (what you are good at), interests (what you enjoy doing), educational background (what qualifications you have), your values (what things are important to you), and your personality (what characteristics you have). As you evaluate these, think in terms of what sets you apart. What things do you like to do? What things do you do well? What things do you do better than others? It's also helpful to ask others you trust what they see as your strengths.*

*2. **Take a look at your weaknesses.** Your weaknesses are your individual personal negative attributes and characteristics, and it's never easy to look for those. Nobody likes to admit that they have weaknesses. But it is important to know the areas where you need improvement. What things could you improve about yourself? What are your negative*

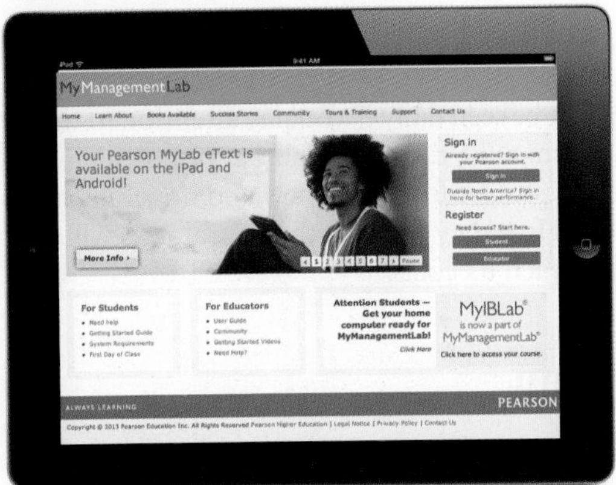

Pearson MyLab Management®

Improve Your Grade!

When you see this icon, visit **www.mymanagementlab.com** for activities that are applied, personalized, and offer immediate feedback.

Learning Objectives

SKILL OUTCOMES

9.1 ***Define*** *strategic management and explain why it's important.*

9.2 ***Explain*** *what managers do during the six steps of the strategic management process.*

- **Know how** to identify your own personal strengths and weaknesses and deal with them.
- **Develop your skill** at strategic planning.

9.3 ***Describe*** *the three types of corporate strategies.*

9.4 ***Describe*** *competitive advantage and the competitive strategies organizations use to get it.*

9.5 ***Discuss*** *current strategic management issues.*

personal/work habits? What things do you not like to do? What professional or career skills/training/education/qualifications are you lacking, the possession of which would make you a more valuable employee? Are you lacking career direction or focus? What things do others do better than you do? Again, it's helpful to ask others you trust what they see as your weaknesses.

3. ***As noted in Chapter 9's "It's Your Career" and "Workplace Confidential," develop a strategy to do something about your strengths and weaknesses.*** *What actions can you take to get the job you want or to best meet the requirements of your current job or a promotion you're seeking? Accentuate your positives! You want to leverage, emphasize, and capitalize on your strengths. This might involve strengthening a specific skill or attribute. Or it could mean following the great advice given in a commencement speech at MIT by Dropbox founder Drew Houston, "The most successful people are obsessed with solving an important problem, something that matters to them. They remind me of a dog chasing a tennis ball."[1] What's your tennis ball? What things grab your attention in a way you can't resist and how can you exploit those passions in your work life and career?*

Minimize or compensate for your weaknesses. Improve upon your weaker skills, attitudes, habits, or qualifications to increase your present and future job opportunities.

4. ***Update your list of strengths and weaknesses periodically.*** *As you gain new experiences and as your life circumstances change, you'll want to revise your list of strengths and weaknesses. Sharpen your self-awareness so you can craft the kind of life—professionally and personally—you want to live.*

The importance of having good strategies can be seen daily if you pay attention to what's happening in the world of business. Managers must recognize market opportunities to exploit, take steps to correct company weaknesses, or formulate new and hopefully more effective strategies to be strong competitors. How they manage those strategies will play an important role in a company's ability to reach its goals.

STRATEGIC **management**

LO9.1

- Online retailer Zalando is considering an alliance with Uber to make it easier for customers to return unwanted merchandise.
- Kroger Company and CVS Health Corporation are planning to replace conventional eggs with cage-free eggs, promising shareholders higher profits.
- Japan's NTT Data Corporation plans to purchase Dell's information technology service, which will expand sales outside Japan.
- Amazon, Google, and Microsoft are waging a price war on cloud services.
- Al Jazeera is closing its American cable channel and laying off 10 percent of its workforce to lower operating costs.[2]

These are just a few of the business news stories from a single week, and each one is about a company's strategies. Strategic management is very much a part of what managers do. In this section, we want to look at what strategic management is and why it's important.

What Is Strategic Management?

The cell phone industry is a good place to see what strategic management is all about. Blackberry successfully sold cellular products in the 1990s that appealed to the business market. In 2007, the introduction of Apple's iPhone posed a significant threat to Blackberry's success. The quality of the iPhone's hardware was vastly superior to Blackberry smartphones, and Apple enabled developers to create a diverse set of apps, making the iPhone more appealing to a broader audience. However, Blackberry stayed the course by focusing on business enterprise and it made little effort to help developers create apps for the Blackberry operating system. It's not surprising that, today, the iPhone accounts for more than 40 percent of the U.S. market while Blackberry's share is less than 1 percent. Why the difference in performance? Because of different strategies and competitive abilities.[3] Apple has excelled by effectively managing strategies while Blackberry has struggled by not effectively managing its strategies.

strategic management
What managers do to develop the organization's strategies

strategies
The plans for how the organization will do what it's in business to do, how it will compete successfully, and how it will attract and satisfy its customers in order to achieve its goals

business model
How a company is going to make money

Strategic management is what managers do to develop the organization's strategies. It's an important task involving all the basic management functions—planning, organizing, leading, and controlling. What are an organization's **strategies**? They're the plans for how the organization will do whatever it's in business to do, how it will compete successfully, and how it will attract and satisfy its customers in order to achieve its goals.[4]

One term often used in strategic management is **business model**, which simply is how a company is going to make money. It focuses on two things: (1) whether customers will value what the company is providing and (2) whether the company can make any money doing that.[5] For instance, Jeff Bezos pioneered a new business model for selling books to consumers directly online instead of selling through bookstores. Did customers "value" that? Absolutely! Did Amazon make money doing it that way? Not at first, but now, absolutely! What began as the world's biggest bookstore is now the world's biggest everything store. As managers think about strategies, they need to think about the economic viability of their company's business model. (Check out the Developing Your Business Planning Skill at the end of the chapter on p. 334.)

Why Is Strategic Management Important?

As the home of Spider-Man, Captain America, and other iconic characters, Marvel Entertainment, LLC, has long been the comic book world's biggest player. But in the mid-1990s the comics market crashed, Marvel went broke, and there was no superpower strong enough to stave off bankruptcy. But fear not! After restructuring, our hero changed its approach, focusing on movies rather than paper and ink. Today, Iron Man, the Avengers, Spider-Man, and X-Men are all billion-dollar franchises, and the company's master plan—to connect many of its characters in a single cinematic universe—has turned it into one of pop culture's most powerful brands. The managers behind Marvel seem to understand the importance of strategic management.

Using strategic management has helped Marvel Entertainment achieve higher levels of organizational performance. When market demand for its comic books declined, the company broadened its focus from print readership to a wider audience of moviegoers by featuring Spider-Man and other comic book characters in films.
Source: COLUMBIA PICTURES/MARVEL ENTERTAINMENT/John Bramley/Album/ Newscom

Why is strategic management so important? There are three reasons. The most significant one is that it can make a difference in how well an organization performs. Why do some businesses succeed and others fail, even when faced with the same environmental conditions? (Remember our Blackberry and Apple example.) Research has found a generally positive relationship between strategic planning and performance.[6] In other words, it appears that organizations that use strategic management do have higher levels of performance. And that fact makes it pretty important for managers!

Another reason it's important has to do with the fact that managers in organizations of all types and sizes face continually changing situations (as we discussed in Chapter 6). They cope with this uncertainty by using the strategic management process to examine relevant factors and decide what actions to take. For instance, as business executives across a wide spectrum of industries coped with the global recession, they focused on making their strategies more flexible. At Office Depot, for example, store managers throughout the company told corporate managers that cash-strapped consumers no longer wanted to buy pens or printer paper in bulk. So the company created special displays promoting single Sharpie pens and introduced five-ream packages of paper, half the size of the normal big box of paper.[7]

Finally, strategic management is important because organizations are complex and diverse. Each part needs to work together toward achieving the organization's goals; strategic management helps do this. For example, with more than 2.1 million employees worldwide working in various departments, functional areas, and stores, Walmart Stores, Inc., uses strategic management to help coordinate and focus employees' efforts on what's important as determined by its goals.

If your professor has assigned this, go to **www.mymanagementlab.com** to watch a video titled: *Rudi's Bakery: Strategic Management* and to respond to questions.

★ Watch It 1!

Today, both business organizations and not-for-profit organizations use strategic management. For instance, the nonprofit Royal Flying Doctors Service (RFDS) in Australia sees ever-increasing urgency for the medical and dental services it has been providing to people in remote locations since 1928.[8] Facing difficult challenges such as economic pressures, competitive programs, and new technology, the RFDS units spread from coast to coast recently came together in a joint venture structure for closer collaboration and unified management. Through strategic management, the nonprofit can more effectively plan to address the needs of the people it serves and leverage all organizational resources for higher efficiency.[9] Just as important, strategic management enables RFDS to prepare for even more productive fundraising efforts. Half of the nonprofit's funding comes from government sources, with the remainder of the money contributed by corporate sponsors and individuals. Clearly, strategic management is vital as RFDS expands beyond 280,000 annual patient contacts, acquires new equipment, and trains new staff to fulfill its mission.[10] Strategic management will continue to be important to its operation. Although strategic management in not-for-profits hasn't been as well researched as it has been for for-profit organizations, we know it's important for them as well.

Exhibit 9-1
Strategic Management Process

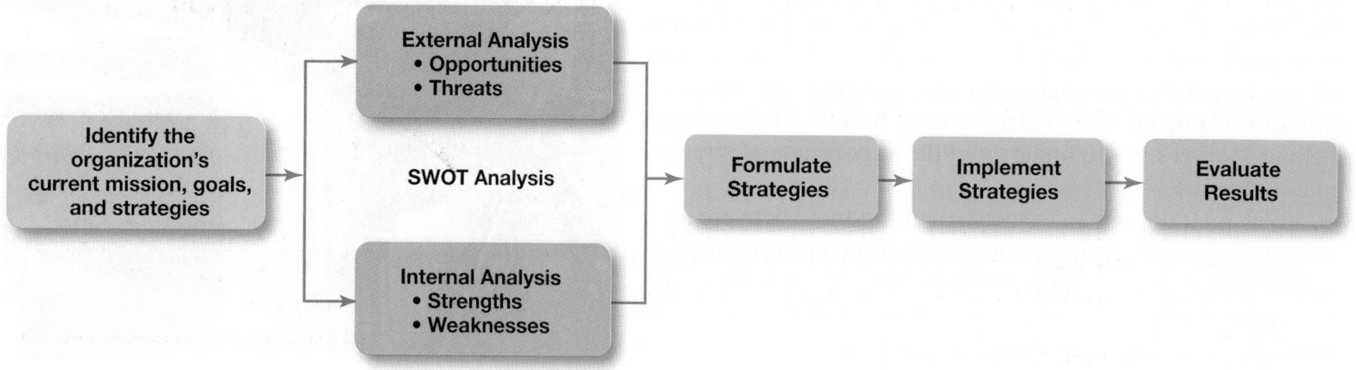

THE STRATEGIC **management process**

strategic management process
A six-step process that encompasses strategic planning, implementation, and evaluation

LO9.2 The **strategic management process** (see Exhibit 9-1) is a six-step process that encompasses strategy planning, implementation, and evaluation. Although the first four steps describe the planning that must take place, implementation and evaluation are just as important! Even the best strategies can fail if management doesn't implement or evaluate them properly.

Step 1: Identifying the Organization's Current Mission, Goals, and Strategies

mission
The purpose of an organization

Every organization needs a **mission**—a statement of its purpose. Defining the mission forces managers to identify what it's in business to do. But sometimes that mission statement can be too limiting. For example, Nike's mission is to "bring inspiration and innovation to every athlete in the world."[11] Not everybody plays one or more sports, which is why Nike wisely defines athlete more broadly. "If you have a body, you are an athlete." Had Nike not expanded its mission statement in this way, it surely would have compromised its overall appeal, sales, and profits. What *should* a mission statement include? Exhibit 9-2 describes some typical components.

Exhibit 9-2
Components of a Mission Statement

Source: Based on R. R. Davic, *Strategic Management*, 13th ed. (Upper Saddle River, NJ: Pearson Education, Inc., 2011.)

Customers:	Who are the firm's customers?
Markets:	Where does the firm compete geographically?
Concern for survival, growth, and profitability:	Is the firm committed to growth and financial stability?
Philosophy:	What are the firm's basic beliefs, values, and ethical priorities?
Concern for public image:	How responsive is the firm to societal and environmental concerns?
Products or services:	What are the firm's major products or services?
Technology:	Is the firm technologically current?
Self-concept:	What are the firm's major competitive advantage and core competencies?
Concern for employees:	Are employees a valuable asset of the firm?

If your professor has assigned this, go to **www.mymanagementlab.com** to complete the Writing Assignment *MGMT 11: Mission Statement.*

Step 2: Doing an External Analysis

What impact might the following trends have for businesses?

- With the passage of the national health care legislation, every big restaurant chain must now post calorie information on their menus and drive-through signs.
- Cell phones are now used by customers more for data transmittal and retrieval than for phone calls and the number of smartphones and tablet computers continues to soar.
- The unemployment rate has been declining.
- More young adults are earning college degrees according to data released from the U.S. Department of Education.[13]

- Only 41 percent of employees know what their company stands for.[12]

We described the external environment in Chapter 7 as an important constraint on a manager's actions. Analyzing that environment is a critical step in the strategic management process. Managers do an external analysis so they know, for instance, what the competition is doing, what pending legislation might affect the organization, or what the labor supply is like in locations where it operates. In an external analysis, managers should examine the economic, demographic, political/legal, sociocultural, technological, and global components to see the trends and changes. For example, Aetna now offers customized health insurance because consumers want more control over the design and cost of their plans. The company's external analysis revealed that Internet websites such as *WebMD* help many people to become more savvy health care consumers, and national health care legislation promises lower insurance costs.[14]

Once they've analyzed the environment, managers need to pinpoint opportunities that the organization can exploit and threats that it must counteract or buffer against. **Opportunities** are positive trends in the external environment; **threats** are negative trends.

opportunities
Positive trends in the external environment

threats
Negative trends in the external environment

Let's take a look at ongoing strategic opportunities and threats in the pharmaceutical industry. Patent protection laws provide U.S. pharmaceutical companies with the opportunity to recoup research and development costs and generate profits from the sale of its products. For up to several years, the U.S. government grants pharmaceutical companies the right to be the exclusive provider of their own patented products. Without exclusivity provisions, pharmaceutical companies such as Wyeth Pharmaceuticals would be placed at a competitive disadvantage because other pharmaceutical companies would manufacture and distribute a therapeutically equivalent product at a lower cost. For example, Wyeth Pharmaceuticals developed Protonix, a product that treats gastroesophageal reflux disease. The company enjoyed exclusivity protection until 2011. The expiration of an exclusivity clause posed a threat for Wyeth Pharmaceuticals; yet, this was an opportunity for more pharmaceutical companies to compete for market share. On the other hand, consider the strategy of GlaxoSmithKline, which is based in the United Kingdom but markets pharmaceutical products worldwide. The company decided not to file for patent protection in countries where incomes are extremely low, because its long-term strategy is to expand access to pharmaceutical treatments to as many people as possible. This is how the company establishes itself in emerging markets, builds goodwill, and prepares for future profits.[15]

Step 3: Doing an Internal Analysis

Now we move to the internal analysis, which provides important information about an organization's specific resources and capabilities. An organization's **resources** are its assets—financial, physical, human, and intangible—that it uses to develop,

resources
An organization's assets that are used to develop, manufacture, and deliver products to its customers

capabilities
An organization's skills and abilities in doing the work activities needed in its business

core competencies
The organization's major value-creating capabilities that determine its competitive weapons

strengths
Any activities the organization does well or its unique resources

weaknesses
Activities the organization does not do well or resources it needs but does not possess

manufacture, and deliver products to its customers. They're "what" the organization has. On the other hand, its **capabilities** are its skills and abilities in doing the work activities needed in its business—"how" it does its work. The major value-creating capabilities of the organization are known as its **core competencies**.[16] Both resources and core competencies determine the organization's competitive weapons. For instance, transportation giant Norfolk Southern's CEO indicates that "we believe we have the right strategic plan to streamline operations, accelerate growth, and enhance value for shareholders."[17] The leadership plans to leverage the company's two core competencies—superior customer service and reliability—to meet the company's strategic goals.

After completing an internal analysis, managers should be able to identify organizational strengths and weaknesses. Any activities the organization does well or any unique resources that it has are called **strengths**. **Weaknesses** are activities the organization doesn't do well or resources it needs but doesn't possess.

Personal Strengths/Weaknesses—If your instructor is using Pearson MyLab Management, log onto **mymanagementlab.com** and test your knowledge about learning your *personal strengths/weaknesses.* **Be sure to refer back to the chapter opener!**

SWOT analysis
An analysis of the organization's strengths, weaknesses, opportunities, and threats

The combined external and internal analyses are called the **SWOT analysis**, an analysis of the organization's *s*trengths, *w*eaknesses, *o*pportunities, and *t*hreats. After completing the SWOT analysis, managers are ready to formulate appropriate strategies—that is, strategies that (1) exploit an organization's strengths and external opportunities, (2) buffer or protect the organization from external threats, or (3) correct critical weaknesses.

let's get REAL

The Scenario:

Emily's Bakery found success quickly. Emily Smith was surprised by how fast the bakery, started just three years ago, became profitable. The growth was mostly due to timing and location. She just happened to open in a busy neighborhood around the same time a competing bakery closed because the owner wanted to relocate to a new city. However, over the last few months sales have slowed a little, and Emily has had some time to think about the future. She needs to figure out her next step and thinks maybe she needs a strategic plan for her business, but she isn't sure where to start.

How should Emily start her strategic planning process?

The strategic plan will be the company's road map that future decisions will be based on, and effectively planning the strategy at the beginning is a critical step. A starting point to begin the process is analyzing the current state of the business. This includes outlining strengths and weaknesses and identifying external factors that could pose threats or opportunities for growth. With this information, the business leader can then begin planning the desired future state by developing short- and long-term goals and aligning these with the company culture, available resources, and realistic time frames to develop an actionable plan.

Kelly Nelson
Organizational Development
and Training Manager

Source: Kelly Nelson

If your professor has assigned this, go to **www.mymanagementlab.com** to complete the Writing Assignment *MKTG 2: SWOT Analysis.*

★ **Write It 2!**

Step 4: Formulating Strategies

As managers formulate strategies, they should consider the realities of the external environment and their available resources and capabilities in order to design strategies that will help an organization achieve its goals. The three main types of strategies managers will formulate include corporate, competitive, and functional. We'll describe each shortly.

Step 5: Implementing Strategies

Once strategies are formulated, they must be implemented. No matter how effectively an organization has planned its strategies, performance will suffer if the strategies aren't implemented properly.

Step 6: Evaluating Results

The final step in the strategic management process is evaluating results. How effective have the strategies been at helping the organization reach its goals? What adjustments are necessary? For example, after assessing the results of previous strategies and determining that changes were needed, Xerox CEO Ursula Burns made strategic adjustments to regain market share and improve her company's bottom line. The company cut jobs, sold assets, and reorganized management.

If your professor has assigned this, go to **www.mymanagementlab.com** to complete the Writing Assignment *MGMT 7: Planning (Business Plan Research).*

★ **Write It 3!**

CORPORATE **strategies**

LO9.3 As we said earlier, organizations use three types of strategies: corporate, competitive, and functional. (See Exhibit 9-3.) Top-level managers typically are responsible for corporate strategies, middle-level managers for competitive strategies, and lower-level managers for the functional strategies. In this section, we'll look at corporate strategies.

Exhibit 9-3
Types of Organizational Strategies

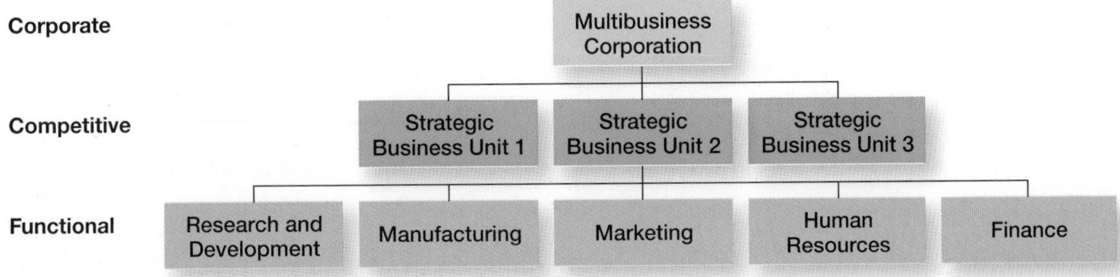

WORKPLACE CONFIDENTIAL Developing a Career Strategy

The concept of strategy is not limited to managers and organizations. You can use it to "think strategically" about your career.

Let's start by acknowledging that, if you're reading this book, you are likely either at an early point in starting to build a career or considering a new career direction. Either way, your career plans are a top priority. Here are some suggestions for helping you develop a career plan.

Start by creating your own SWOT analysis. What are your strengths? What talents have you developed that give you a comparative advantage to others? Are you good with numbers, an excellent writer, a smooth talker, an outstanding debater, uniquely creative? And what qualities can give you an edge-up? Consider your work experience, education, technical knowledge, networking contacts, and personal characteristics, like your work ethic or self-discipline. Think hard about what differentiates you and what might give you an advantage. Next, consider your weaknesses. None of us are without them. Try to be honest with yourself and identify those things that either others do better than you or that you tend to avoid. Examples might include a lack of work experience, a low GPA, lack of specific job knowledge, weak communication skills, or previous legal problems. Now move to consider opportunities and threats that you see in the job market. Where are the growth industries? Examples, for instance, might include health care, solar energy, counterterrorism, or Internet businesses. All appear to have strong growth opportunities. Then focus on organizations within these industries that might benefit from this growth. Finally, look for geographic opportunities. What cities or towns appear to offer above-average job growth? Of course, you also want to look at the other side. Which are the declining industries, downsizing or stagnant organizations, and shrinking job markets? Integrating this analysis should provide you with a blueprint of where you're likely to find the best career opportunities.

Now, let's talk about fit. By this, we mean the match between you and specific jobs and the match between you and specific organizational cultures. The former we call the person-job fit and the latter the person-organization fit. Here's an obvious, but often overlooked, observation: Not everyone is fit for certain jobs or certain organizations. Regardless of the opportunity, one size does not fit all.

In Chapter 15, Holland's personality-job fit theory is discussed. In essence, the theory proposes six personality types and argues that people who are in jobs congruent with their personality are more satisfied with their jobs and less likely to quit. We suggest that you look over these six personalities, see which one best describes you, and use the information to guide you in selecting a job that best fits you.

The person-organization fit essentially argues that people are attracted and selected by organizations that match their values, and they leave organizations that are not compatible with their personalities. So, for instance, if you tend to be high on the extroversion scale, you're likely to fit well with aggressive and team-oriented cultures; if you're high on agreeableness, you match up better with a supportive organizational culture than one focused on aggressiveness; and if you're open to new experiences, you'll fit better into organizations that emphasize innovation rather than standardization.

One final suggestion: Don't delegate your future to someone else. You are responsible for your personal career plan, your career progression, and your eventual retirement. In the 1950s and 1960s, most people either didn't think about shaping their career to maximize their potential or assumed that this was the responsibility of their employer. Even retirement programs were essentially designed by your employer, controlled by your employer, and nontransferable between employers. While they did offer predictability, they also put control of an employee's future in the hands of the employer. In today's disruptive world, your career is in your hands. Never get comfortable with a single employer. Keep your skills current and think long term. Continually ask yourself: How will each job I take help to build a pattern of accomplishment? How will this job and my next one get me to where I eventually want to be?

Sources: Based on W. Arthur Jr., S. T. Bell, A.J. Villado, and D. Doverspike, "The Use of Person-Organization Fit in Employment Decision-Making: An Assessment of Its Criterion-Related Validity," *Journal of Applied Psychology*, July 2006, pp. 786–801; D. A. McKay and D. M. Tokar, "The HEXACO and Five-Factor Models of Personality in Relation to RIASEC Vocational Interests," *Journal of Vocational Behavior*, October 2012, pp. 138–149; L. Quast, "How to Conduct a Personal SWOT Analysis," *Forbes* online, *www.Forbes.com*, April 15, 2013; and M. Martin, "Conducting a Personal SWOT Analysis for Your Career," *Business News Daily*, November 25, 2015.

What Is Corporate Strategy?

A **corporate strategy** is one that determines what businesses a company is in or wants to be in and what it wants to do with those businesses. It's based on the mission and goals of the organization and the roles that each business unit of the organization will play. We can see both of these aspects with PepsiCo, for instance. Its mission: To be the world's premier consumer products company focused on convenient foods and beverages. It pursues that mission with a corporate strategy that has put it in different businesses, including its PepsiCo Americas Beverage (beverage business), PepsiCo Americas Foods (snack and prepared foods businesses including Frito-Lay and Quaker Oats), and then its global businesses—PepsiCo Europe and PepsiCo Asia/Middle East/Africa. The other part of corporate strategy is when top managers decide what to do with those businesses: grow them, keep them the same, or renew them.

corporate strategy
An organizational strategy that determines what businesses a company is in or wants to be in, and what it wants to do with those businesses

What Are the Types of Corporate Strategy?

The three main types of corporate strategies are growth, stability, and renewal. Let's look at each type.

growth strategy
A corporate strategy that's used when an organization wants to expand the number of markets served or products offered, either through its current business(es) or through new business(es)

GROWTH Even though Amazon.com is the world's largest retailer, it continues to grow internationally and in the United States.[18] A **growth strategy** is when an organization expands the number of markets served or products offered, either through its current business(es) or through new business(es). Because of its growth strategy, an organization may increase revenues, number of employees, or market share. Organizations grow by using concentration, vertical integration, horizontal integration, or diversification.

An organization that grows using *concentration* focuses on its primary line of business and increases the number of products offered or markets served in this primary business. For instance, Buick has used concentration as a strategy to work toward becoming a luxury automobile brand. In the United States, the brand's sales have increased nearly 25 percent, outselling Audi and closing the sales gap with BMW.[19] Another example of a company using concentration is Bose Corporation of Framingham, Massachusetts, which focuses on developing innovative audio products. It has become one of the world's leading manufacturers of speakers for home entertainment, automotive, and professional audio markets with annual sales of more than $3 billion.

A company also might choose to grow by *vertical integration*, either backward, forward, or both. In backward vertical integration, the organization becomes its own supplier so it can control its inputs. For instance, Walmart plans to build a dairy-processing plant in Indiana to supply private-label milk to hundreds of its stores at a lower cost than purchasing milk from an outside supplier.[21] In forward vertical integration, the organization becomes its own distributor and is able to control its outputs. For example, Apple has more than 400 retail stores worldwide to distribute its products.

LEADER making a DIFFERENCE

Source: dpa picture alliance/Alamy Stock Photo

***Mary Barra** became the first female CEO of a major automaker in 2014 when she was promoted to the top spot at General Motors (GM), leading a company that generates $150 billion in annual revenue and has over 219,000 employees.[20] The daughter of a GM tool and die maker, Barra is considered a "lifer" at GM, starting her career there more than 30 years ago as a co-op student. She stepped into the CEO role while GM was still recovering from a bankruptcy and government bailout, and soon faced a massive vehicle recall. In just a short time, however, Barra started leading GM in a positive strategic direction. In addition to shifting what she characterized as a dysfunctional corporate culture that allowed an ignition switch problem that led to the recall of 2.6 million vehicles in 2014, she also has laid out a clear strategic direction for the company. Her growth strategy addresses personal mobility in a broad sense instead of focusing on just cars, essentially asking, How will people get from point A to point B in the future? Her plan outlines strategies to address the growing consumer interest in car sharing, emerging alternate transportation options, promises of zero emissions, and autonomous driving. Barra's achievements so far at GM earned her the top spot on* Fortune's *Most Powerful Women list in 2015. She is characterized as energetic yet down-to-earth. She is well-liked within the company, noted for her strong communication skills and emotional intelligence. Barra is also considered a change agent within GM, which is particularly impressive given that she essentially grew up in the company.* What can you learn from this leader making a difference?

In *horizontal integration*, a company grows by combining with competitors. For instance, NMC Healthcare, which is based in the United Arab Emirates, recently acquired Al Zahra Hospital in Sharjah. NMC is continuing its expansion throughout the Gulf region, and the acquisition of this large, private hospital complements the company's existing medical facilities and construction plans. Spain's Banco Santandor has acquired a number of banks in different nations, including Portugal, for global growth and efficiency. But government regulators often scrutinize mergers, with an eye toward preserving competition. When competitors Vodafone and Liberty Global wanted to merge their Netherlands cable and mobile telecommunications businesses, they had to obtain the approval of European Union regulators. The merger was only approved after Vodafone agreed to divest its Netherlands fixed-line telephone business to allay concerns about competition.[22] Other countries may have similar restrictions. For instance, the European Commission, the "watchdog" for the European Union, conducted an in-depth investigation into Unilever's acquisition of the body and laundry care units of Sara Lee.

Finally, an organization can grow through *diversification*, either related or unrelated. Related diversification happens when a company combines with other companies in different, but related, industries. For example, Google has acquired a number of businesses (some 150 total), including YouTube, DoubleClick, Nest, and Motorola Mobility. Although this mix of businesses may seem odd, the company's "strategic fit" is its information search capabilities and efficiencies. Unrelated diversification is when a company combines with firms in different and unrelated industries. For instance, the Tata Group of India has businesses in chemicals, communications and IT, consumer products, energy, engineering, materials, and services. Again, an odd mix. But in this case, there's no strategic fit among the businesses.

stability strategy
A corporate strategy in which an organization continues to do what it is currently doing

renewal strategy
A corporate strategy designed to address declining performance

STABILITY The Boeing Company has many aspirations. One of them illustrates a stability strategy: ". . . to continue building strength-on-strength to deliver on our existing plans and commitments."[23] A **stability strategy** is a corporate strategy in which an organization continues to do what it is currently doing. Examples of this strategy include continuing to serve the same clients by offering the same product or service, maintaining market share, and sustaining the organization's current business operations. The organization doesn't grow, but doesn't fall behind, either.

RENEWAL In 2013, AMR (American Airlines' parent) lost almost $1.8 billion. Hewlett-Packard lost $12 billion, JCPenney lost over $985 million, and many energy and technology services companies faced serious financial issues with huge losses. When an organization is in trouble, something needs to be done. Managers need to develop strategies, called **renewal strategies**, that address declining performance. The two main types of renewal strategies are retrenchment and turnaround strategies. A *retrenchment strategy* is a short-run renewal strategy used for minor performance problems. This strategy helps an organization stabilize operations, revitalize organizational resources and capabilities, and prepare to compete once again. For instance, Biogen reduced its workforce by 11 percent to cut costs.[24] With those savings, the company has increased spending for research and development and for marketing Tecfidera, its potentially highly profitable multiple-sclerosis drug. When an organization's problems are more serious, more drastic action—the *turnaround strategy*—is needed. Managers do two things for both renewal strategies: cut costs and restructure organizational operations. However, in a turnaround strategy, these measures are more extensive than in a retrenchment strategy. For example, the CIT Group's declining profits prompted management to cut costs by $125 million and sell the company's aircraft financing business unit to more effectively focus on commercial lending and leasing.[25]

After nearly collapsing in 2003, the Danish firm Lego named Jorgen Vig Knudstorp as CEO to lead a new team of managers in developing a renewal strategy. Part of Knudstorp's successful turnaround strategy included cutting costs by trimming Lego's product line, restructuring its supply chain, and refocusing on the company's core product of unique plastic bricks.
Source: Edgar Su/Reuters Pictures

How Are Corporate Strategies Managed?

When an organization's corporate strategy encompasses a number of businesses, managers can manage this collection, or portfolio, of businesses using a tool called a corporate portfolio matrix. This matrix provides a framework for understanding diverse businesses and helps managers establish priorities for allocating resources.[26] The first portfolio matrix—the **BCG matrix**—was developed by the Boston Consulting Group and introduced the idea that an organization's various businesses could be evaluated and plotted using a 2 × 2 matrix to identify which ones offered high potential and which were a drain on organizational resources.[27] The horizontal axis represents market share (low or high), and the vertical axis indicates anticipated market growth (low or high). A business unit is evaluated using a SWOT analysis and placed in one of the four categories, which are as follows:

BCG matrix
A strategy tool that guides resource allocation decisions on the basis of market share and growth rate of SBUs

- **Stars:** High market share/High anticipated growth rate
- **Cash Cows:** High market share/Low anticipated growth rate
- **Question Marks:** Low market share/High anticipated growth rate
- **Dogs:** Low market share/Low anticipated growth rate

What are the strategic implications of the BCG matrix? The dogs should be sold off or liquidated as they have low market share in markets with low growth potential. Managers should "milk" cash cows for as much as they can, limit any new investment in them, and use the large amounts of cash generated to invest in stars and question marks with strong potential to improve market share. Heavy investment in stars will help take advantage of the market's growth and help maintain high market share. The stars, of course, will eventually develop into cash cows as their markets mature and sales growth slows. The hardest decision for managers relates to the question marks. After careful analysis, some will be sold off and others strategically nurtured into stars.

COMPETITIVE **strategies**

LO9.4 A **competitive strategy** is a strategy for how an organization will compete in its business(es). For a small organization in only one line of business or a large organization that has not diversified into different products or markets, its competitive strategy describes how it will compete in its primary or main market. For organizations in multiple businesses, however, each business will have its own competitive strategy that defines its competitive advantage, the products or services it will offer, the customers it wants to reach, and the like. For example, GE has different competitive strategies for its businesses, which include GE Aviation (aircraft engines), GE Healthcare (ultrasound equipment), consumer appliances (washers and dryers), and many products in diverse industry sectors. When an organization is in several different businesses, those single businesses that are independent and that have their own competitive strategies are referred to as **strategic business units (SBUs)**.

competitive strategy
An organizational strategy for how an organization will compete in its business(es)

strategic business unit (SBU)
The single independent businesses of an organization that formulate their own competitive strategies

The Role of Competitive Advantage

Michelin has mastered a complex technological process for making superior radial tires. Apple has created the world's best and most powerful brand using innovative design and merchandising capabilities.[28] The Ritz-Carlton hotels have a unique ability to deliver personalized customer service. Each of these companies has created a competitive advantage.

Developing an effective competitive strategy requires an understanding of **competitive advantage**, which is what sets an organization apart—that is, its distinctive edge.[29] That distinctive edge can come from the organization's core competencies by doing something that others cannot do or doing it better than others can do it. For example, Rolls-Royce has a competitive advantage because of its skills at giving customers exactly what they want—a hand-crafted, ultraluxurious automobile, which can be customized to suit unique color, interior, and equipment preferences. Or competitive advantage can come from the company's resources because the organization has something its competitors do not have. For instance, Walmart's state-of-the-art information system allows it to monitor and control inventories and supplier relations more efficiently than its competitors, which Walmart has turned into a cost advantage.

competitive advantage
What sets an organization apart; its distinctive edge

At this Dolce & Gabbana store in Moscow, a saleswoman helps a customer select a leather handbag. Personalized service combined with high-quality products create a competitive advantage for Dolce & Gabbana, which designs and produces distinctive luxury apparel, leather goods, footwear, and accessories that it sells at its elegant retail stores throughout the world.
Source: Andrey Rudakov/Bloomberg/Getty Images

QUALITY AS A COMPETITIVE ADVANTAGE When W. K. Kellogg started manufacturing his cornflake cereal in 1906, his goal was to provide his customers with a high-quality, nutritious product that was enjoyable to eat. That emphasis on quality is still important today. Every employee has a responsibility to maintain the high quality of Kellogg products. If implemented properly, quality can be a way for an organization to create a sustainable competitive advantage.[30] That's why many organizations apply quality management concepts in an attempt to set themselves apart from competitors. If a business is able to continuously improve the quality and reliability of its products, it may have a competitive advantage that can't be taken away.[31]

DESIGN THINKING AS A COMPETITIVE ADVANTAGE In today's world, consumers can find just about anything they want online. And those consumers also expect a greater variety of choices and faster service when ordering online than ever before. One company that recognized the opportunities—and challenges—of this is Kiva Systems.[32] Kiva makes autonomous robots used in flexible automation systems that are critical to companies' strategic e-commerce efforts. By doing this efficiently, the company's robots can gather goods within minutes of an order and deliver them to warehouse pickworkers, who can then ship up to four times more packages in an hour. Kiva (which was recently acquired by Amazon) also has "taught" its robots to move cardboard boxes to the trash compactor and to assist in gift-wrapping.

Here's a company that understands the power of design thinking—defined in Chapter 2 as approaching management problems the way designers approach design problems. Using design thinking means thinking in unusual ways about what the business is and how it's doing what it's in business to do—or as one person said, "solving wicked problems with creative resolutions by thinking outside existing alternatives and creating new alternatives."[33] After all, who would have thought to "teach" robots to help wrap gifts so that e-commerce warehouse fulfillment could be made even more efficient? However, as important as design thinking is to the design of amazing products, it also means recognizing that "design" isn't just for products or processes but for any organizational work problems that can arise. That's why a company's ability to use design thinking in the way its employees and managers strategically manage can be a powerful competitive tool.

FUTURE VISION Big Data as a Strategic Weapon

Big data can be an effective counterpart to the information exchange generated through social media. All the enormous amounts of data collected about customers, partners, employees, markets, and other quantifiables can be used to respond to the needs of these same stakeholders. With big data, managers can measure and know more about their businesses and "translate that knowledge into improved decision making and performance."[34] Case in point: When Walmart began looking at its enormous database, it noticed that when a hurricane was forecasted, not only did sales of flashlights and batteries increase, but so did sales of Pop-Tarts. Now, when a hurricane is threatening, stores stock Pop-Tarts with other emergency storm supplies at the front entrance. This helps them better serve customers and drive sales.[35] By helping a business do what it's in business to do—compete successfully—and attract and satisfy its customers in order to achieve its goals, big data is a critical strategic weapon for organizations in the future.

If your professor has chosen to assign this, go to ***www.mymanagementlab.com*** *to discuss the following questions.*

TALK ABOUT IT 1: What strategic connection(s) do you see between big data and social media?

TALK ABOUT IT 2: What ethical obstacles might big data present? How can managers overcome those obstacles?

SOCIAL MEDIA AS A COMPETITIVE ADVANTAGE Many organizations are making substantial investments in social media because its use can provide a competitive advantage. L'Oréal uses social media for competitive advantage in several ways. First, the French beauty company is forging long-term relationships with "influencers," popular social-media users who have large followings on Instagram, Twitter, and other networks. Not only can L'Oréal tap their insights for product and marketing ideas, it can also reach a wider and more diverse audience through these influencers. Second, the company uses social media to deliver a steady stream of content valued by the audience, such as how-to makeup instructions, product demonstrations, updates on beauty trends, and answers to questions or concerns. With 25 million likes for its main Facebook page, plus tens of thousands of followers on its multiple Twitter, Instagram, YouTube, and Snapchat accounts, L'Oréal knows how to engage its target customers. Clearly, L'Oréal understands that using social media strategically can build competitive advantage worldwide.[36]

Successful social media strategies should (1) help people—inside and outside the organization—connect and (2) reduce costs or increase revenue possibilities or both. As managers look at how to strategically use social media, it's important to have goals and a plan. For instance, at global banking firm Wells Fargo & Co., executives realized that social media tools don't just "exist for their own sake" and that they wanted ". . . to know how we can use them to enhance business strategy."[37] Now Wells Fargo uses blogs, wikis, and other social media tools for a variety of specific needs that align with their business goals.

It's not just for the social connections that organizations are employing social media strategies. Many are finding that social media tools can boost productivity.[38] For example, many physicians are tapping into online postings and sharing technologies as part of their daily routines. Collaborating with colleagues and experts allows them to improve the speed and efficiency of patient care. At Trunk Club, an online men's clothes shopping service that sends out, on request, trunks to clients with new clothing items, the CEO uses a software tool called Chatter to let the company's personal shoppers know about hot new shipments of shoes or clothes. He says that when he "chats" that information out to the team, he immediately sees the personal shoppers putting the items into customers' "trunks."[39] When used strategically, social media can be a powerful competitive weapon!

- 52 percent of managers say social media are important/somewhat important to their business.

SUSTAINING COMPETITIVE ADVANTAGE Every organization has resources (assets) and capabilities (how work gets done). So what makes some organizations more successful than others? Why do some professional baseball teams consistently win championships or draw large crowds? Why do some organizations have consistent and continuous growth in revenues and profits? Why do some colleges, universities, or departments experience continually increasing enrollments? Why do some companies consistently appear at the top of lists ranking the "best," or the "most admired," or the "most profitable"? The answer is that not every organization is able to effectively exploit its resources and to develop the core competencies that can provide it with a competitive advantage. And it's not enough simply to create a competitive advantage. The organization must be able to sustain that advantage; that is, to keep its edge despite competitors' actions or evolutionary changes in the industry. But that's not easy to do! Market instabilities, new technology, and other changes can challenge managers' attempts at creating a long-term, sustainable competitive advantage. However, by using strategic management, managers can better position their organizations to get a sustainable competitive advantage.

Many important ideas in strategic management have come from the work of Michael Porter.[40] One of his major contributions was explaining how managers can create a sustainable competitive advantage. An important part of doing this is an industry analysis, which is done using the five forces model.

FIVE FORCES MODEL In any industry, five competitive forces dictate the rules of competition. Together, these five forces determine industry attractiveness and profitability, which managers assess using these five factors:

1. *Threat of new entrants.* How likely is it that new competitors will come into the industry?
2. *Threat of substitutes.* How likely is it that other industries' products can be substituted for our industry's products?
3. *Bargaining power of buyers.* How much bargaining power do buyers (customers) have?
4. *Bargaining power of suppliers.* How much bargaining power do suppliers have?
5. *Current rivalry.* How intense is the rivalry among current industry competitors?

Choosing a Competitive Strategy

Once managers have assessed the five forces and done a SWOT analysis, they're ready to select an appropriate competitive strategy—that is, one that fits the competitive strengths (resources and capabilities) of the organization and the industry it's in. According to Porter, no firm can be successful by trying to be all things to all people. He proposed that managers select a strategy that will give the organization a competitive advantage, either from having lower costs than all other industry competitors or by being significantly different from competitors.

When an organization competes on the basis of having the lowest costs (costs or expenses, not prices) in its industry, it's following a *cost leadership strategy*. A low-cost leader is highly efficient. Overhead is kept to a minimum, and the firm does everything it can to cut costs. For example, you won't find many frills in Ross Stores. "We believe in "no frills"—no window displays, mannequins, fancy fixtures or decorations in our stores so we can pass more savings on to our customers."[41] Low overhead costs allow Ross to sell quality apparel and home items at 20 to 60 percent less than most department store prices, and the company is profitable.[42]

A company that competes by offering unique products that are widely valued by customers is following a *differentiation strategy*. Product differences might come from exceptionally high quality, extraordinary service, innovative design, technological capability, or an unusually positive brand image. Practically any successful consumer product or service can be identified as an example of the differentiation strategy; for instance, 3M Corporation (product quality and innovative design); Coach (design and brand image); Apple (product design); and L.L.Bean (customer service). L.L.Bean allows customers to return merchandise at any time if not completely satisfied: "We make pieces that last, and if they don't, we want to know about it. So if it's not working or fitting or standing up to its task, we'll take it back. L.L. himself always said that he didn't consider a sale complete 'until goods are worn out and the customer still satisfied.'"[43]

Although these two competitive strategies are aimed at the broad market, the final type of competitive strategy—the *focus strategy*—involves a cost advantage (cost focus) or a differentiation advantage (differentiation focus) in a narrow segment or niche. Segments can be based on product variety, customer type, distribution channel, or geographical location. For example, Denmark's Bang & Olufsen, whose revenues exceed $490 million, focuses on high-end audio equipment sales. Whether a focus strategy is feasible depends on the size of the segment and whether the organization can make money serving that segment.

What happens if an organization can't develop a cost or a differentiation advantage? Porter called that being *stuck in the middle* and warned that's not a good place to be. An organization becomes stuck in the middle when its costs are too high to compete with the low-cost leader or when its products and services aren't differentiated enough to compete with the differentiator. Getting unstuck means choosing which competitive advantage to pursue and then doing so by aligning resources, capabilities, and core competencies.

Although Porter said you had to pursue either the low cost or the differentiation advantage to prevent being stuck in the middle, more recent research has shown that organizations *can* successfully pursue both a low cost and a differentiation advantage and achieve high performance.[44] Needless to say, it's not easy to pull off! You have to keep costs low *and* be truly differentiated. But companies such as Southwest Airlines, Colgate-Palmolive, Inc., and Boeing have been able to do it.

If your professor has assigned this, go to **www.mymanagementlab.com** to complete the Writing Assignment *MGMT 13: Strategic Decision Making (Competitive Marketing Strategy)*.

Before we leave this section, we want to point out the final type of organizational strategy, the **functional strategies**, which are the strategies used by an organization's various functional departments to support the competitive strategy. For example, when R. R. Donnelley & Sons Company, a Chicago-based printer, wanted to become more competitive and invested in high-tech digital printing methods, its marketing department had to develop new sales plans and promotional pieces, the production department had to incorporate the digital equipment in the printing plants, and the human resources department had to update its employee selection and training programs. We don't cover specific functional strategies in this book because you'll cover them in other business courses you take.

functional strategy
A strategy used by an organization's various functional departments to support the competitive strategy

If your professor has assigned this, go to **www.mymanagementlab.com** to complete the Simulation: *Strategic Management* and get a better understanding of the challenges of managing strategy in organizations.

★ Try It!

CURRENT strategic management issues

LO9.5 There's no better example of the strategic challenges faced by managers in today's environment than the recorded music industry. Overall, sales of CDs have plummeted in the last decade. As a *Billboard* magazine article title stated so plainly, "Is 2014 the Year Digital Takes Over?"[45] Not only has this trend impacted music companies, but music retailers as well. Retailers have been forced to look to other products to replace the lost revenue. For instance, Best Buy, the national electronics retailer, experimented with selling musical instruments. Other major music retailers, such as Walmart, have shifted selling space used for CDs to other departments. Survival means finding ways to diversify. Managers are struggling to find strategies that will help their organizations succeed in such an environment. Many have had to shift into whole new areas of business.[46] But it isn't just the music industry that's dealing with strategic challenges. Managers everywhere face increasingly intense global competition and high performance expectations by investors and customers. How have they responded to these new realities? In this section, we look at three current strategic management issues, including the need for strategic leadership, the need for strategic flexibility, and how managers design strategies to emphasize e-business, customer service, and innovation.

The Need for Strategic Leadership

"Amazon is so serious about its next big thing that it hired three women to do nothing but try on size 8 shoes for its Web reviews. Full time." Hmmmm . . . now that sounds like a fun job! What exactly is Amazon's CEO Jeff Bezos thinking? Having conquered the book publishing, electronics, and toy industries (among others), his next target is high-end clothing. And he's doing it as he always does—all out."[47]

An organization's strategies are usually developed and overseen by its top managers. An organization's top manager is typically the CEO (chief executive officer). This individual usually works with a top management team that includes other executive or senior managers such as a COO (chief operating officer), CFO (chief financial officer), CIO (chief information officer), and other individuals who may have various titles. Traditional descriptions of the CEO's role in strategic management include being the "chief" strategist, structural architect, and developer of the organization's information/control systems.[48] Other descriptions of the strategic role of the "chief executive" include key decision maker, visionary leader, political actor, monitor and interpreter of environment changes, and strategy designer.[49]

let's get REAL

The Scenario:

Caroline Fulmer was just promoted to executive director of a municipal art museum in a medium-sized city in the Midwest. Although she's very excited about her new position and what she hopes to accomplish there, she knows the museum's board is adamant about solidifying the organization's strategic future. Although she knows they feel she's capable of doing so since they hired her for the position, she wants to be an effective strategic leader.

Source: Denise Nueva

Denise Nueva
Art Director

What skills do you think Caroline will need to be an effective strategic leader?

To be an effective strategic leader, Caroline must be able to manage day-to-day processes of the museum while keeping in mind the big picture of the organization's mission. With this mission in mind, Caroline must align her team of likewise talented individuals to share her passion and commitment. Lastly, it is important for Caroline to remain an unbiased leader and quickly identify and work through issues that may arise.

No matter how top management's job is described, you can be certain that from their perspective at the organization's upper levels, it's like no other job in the organization. By definition, top managers are ultimately responsible for every decision and action of every organizational employee. One important role that top managers play is that of strategic leader. Organizational researchers study leadership in relation to strategic management because an organization's top managers must provide effective strategic leadership. What is **strategic leadership**? It's the ability to anticipate, envision, maintain flexibility, think strategically, and work with others in the organization to initiate changes that will create a viable and valuable future for the organization.[50] How can top managers provide effective strategic leadership? Eight key dimensions have been identified.[51] (See Exhibit 9-4.) These dimensions include determining the organization's purpose or vision; exploiting and maintaining the organization's core

strategic leadership
The ability to anticipate, envision, maintain flexibility, think strategically, and work with others in the organization to initiate changes that will create a viable and valuable future for the organization

Exhibit 9-4
Effective Strategic Leadership

Sources: Based on J. P. Wallman, "Strategic Transactions and Managing the Future: A Druckerian Perspective," *Management Decision*, vol. 48, no. 4, 2010, pp. 485–499; D. E. Zand, "Drucker's Strategic Thinking Process: Three Key Techniques," *Strategy & Leadership*, vol. 38, no. 3, 2010, pp. 23–28; and R. D. Ireland and M. A. Hitt, "Achieving and Maintaining Strategic Competitiveness in the 21st Century: The Role of Strategic Leadership," *Academy of Management Executive*, February 1999, pp. 43–57.

competencies; developing the organization's human capital; creating and sustaining a strong organizational culture; creating and maintaining organizational relationships; reframing prevailing views by asking penetrating questions and questioning assumptions; emphasizing ethical organizational decisions and practices; and establishing appropriately balanced organizational controls. Each dimension encompasses an important part of the strategic management process.

The Need for Strategic Flexibility

Not surprisingly, the economic recession changed the way that many companies approached strategic planning.[52] For instance, at Spartan Motors, a maker of specialty vehicles, managers used to draft a one-year strategic plan and a three-year financial plan, reviewing each one every financial quarter. However, CEO John Sztykiel felt that type of fixed approach led to a drastic drop in sales and profits. Now, the company uses a three-year strategic plan that the top management team updates every month.[53] And at J. C. Penney Company, an ambitious five-year strategic growth plan rolled out in 2007 was put on hold as the economy floundered.[54] In its place, the CEO crafted a tentative "bridge" plan to guide the company. This plan worked as the company improved its profit margins and did not have to lay off any employees.

Berkshire Hathaway CEO Warren Buffett is known for admitting his mistakes. He said "I will commit more errors; you can count on that."[55] And Amazon's Jeff Bezos told company shareholders that Amazon is the"best place in the world to fail at," while adding that negative outcomes are inevitable in experimentation: "Given a 10 percent chance of a 100 times payoff, you should take that bet every time. But you're still going to be wrong nine times out of ten."[56] You wouldn't think that smart individuals who are paid lots of money to manage organizations would make mistakes when it comes to strategic decisions. But even when managers use the strategic management process, there's no guarantee that the chosen strategies will lead to positive outcomes. Reading any of the current business periodicals would certainly support this assertion! But the key is responding quickly when it's obvious the strategy isn't working. In other words, they need **strategic flexibility**—that is, the ability to recognize major external changes, to quickly commit resources, and to recognize when a strategic decision isn't working. Given the highly uncertain environment that managers face today, strategic flexibility seems absolutely necessary! Exhibit 9-5 provides suggestions for developing such strategic flexibility.

Share of managers who say their companies adapt quickly to changing market conditions:

- Only 30 percent shift funds across units to support strategy.
- Only 20 percent shift people across units to support strategy.
- Only 22 percent exit declining businesses or unsuccessful initiatives.[57]

strategic flexibility
The ability to recognize major external changes, to quickly commit resources, and to recognize when a strategic decision was a mistake

If your professor has assigned this, go to **www.mymanagementlab.com** to watch a video titled: *2010 Joie de Vivre Hospitality: Strategic Management* and to respond to questions.

Exhibit 9-5
Developing Strategic Flexibility

- *Encourage leadership unity* by making sure everyone is on the same page.
- *Keep resources fluid* and move them as circumstances warrant.
- *Have the right mindset* to explore and understand issues and challenges.
- Know what's happening with strategies currently being used by *monitoring and measuring results.*
- Encourage employees to *be open about disclosing and sharing negative information.*
- *Get new ideas and perspectives from outside* the organization.
- Have *multiple alternatives* when making strategic decisions.
- *Learn from mistakes.*

Sources: Based on Y. L. Doz and M. Kosonen, "Embedding Strategic Agility: A Leadership Agenda for Accelerating Business Model Renewal," *Long Range Planning*, April 2010, pp. 370–382; E. Lewis, D. Romanaggi, and A. Chapple, "Successfully Managing Change During Uncertain Times," *Strategic HR Review*, vol. 9, no. 2, 2010, pp. 12–18; and K. Shimizu and M. Hitt, "Strategic Flexibility: Organizational Preparedness to Reverse Ineffective Strategic Decisions," *Academy of Management Executive*, November 2004, pp. 44–59.

Important Organizational Strategies for Today's Environment

ESPN.com gets more than 16 million unique users a month. Sixteen million! That's almost twice the population of New York City. And its popular online business is just one of many of ESPN's businesses. Originally founded as a television channel, ESPN is now into original programming, radio, online, publishing, gaming, X Games, ESPY Awards, ESPN Zones, global, and is looking to move into more local sports coverage.[58] Company president John Skipper "runs one of the most successful and envied franchises in entertainment" and obviously understands how to successfully manage its various strategies in today's environment! We think three strategies are important in today's environment: e-business, customer service, and innovation.

E-BUSINESS STRATEGIES Managers use e-business strategies to develop a sustainable competitive advantage.[59] A cost leader can use e-business to lower costs in a variety of ways. For instance, it might use online bidding and order processing to eliminate the need for sales calls and to decrease sales force expenses; it could use Web-based inventory control systems that reduce storage costs; or it might use online testing and evaluation of job applicants.

A differentiator needs to offer products or services that customers perceive and value as unique. For instance, a business might use Internet-based knowledge systems to shorten customer response times, provide rapid online responses to service requests, or automate purchasing and payment systems so that customers have detailed status reports and purchasing histories.

Finally, because the focuser targets a narrow market segment with customized products, it might provide chat rooms or discussion boards for customers to interact with others who have common interests, design niche websites that target specific groups with specific interests, or use websites to perform standardized office functions such as payroll or budgeting.

Research also has shown that an important e-business strategy might be a clicks-and-bricks strategy. A clicks-and-bricks firm is one that uses both online (clicks) and traditional stand-alone locations (bricks).[60] For example, Walgreens established an online site for ordering prescriptions, but some 90 percent of its customers who placed orders on the Web preferred to pick up their prescriptions at a nearby store rather than have them shipped to their home. So its "clicks-and-bricks" strategy has worked well! Other retailers, such as Walmart, The Container Store, and Home Depot, are transforming their stores into extensions of their online operations by adding Web return centers, pickup locations, free shipping outlets, and payment booths.[61]

CUSTOMER SERVICE STRATEGIES Companies emphasizing excellent customer service need strategies that cultivate that atmosphere from top to bottom. Such strategies involve giving customers what they want, communicating effectively with them, and providing employees with customer service training. Let's look first at the strategy of giving customers what they want.

It shouldn't surprise you that an important customer service strategy is giving customers what they want, which is a major aspect of an organization's overall marketing strategy. For instance, New Balance Athletic Shoes gives customers a truly unique product: shoes in varying widths. No other athletic shoe manufacturer has shoes for narrow or wide feet and in practically any size.[62]

Having an effective customer communication system is an important customer service strategy. Managers should know what's going on with customers. They need to find out what customers liked and didn't like about their purchase encounter—from their interactions with employees to their experience with the actual product or service. It's also important to let customers know if something is going on with the company that might affect future purchase decisions. Finally, an organization's culture is important to providing excellent customer service. This typically requires that employees be trained to provide exceptional customer service. For example, Singapore Airlines is well-known for its customer treatment. "On everything facing the customer, they do not scrimp," says an analyst based in Singapore.[63] Employees are expected to "get service right," leaving employees with no doubt about the expectations as far as how to treat customers.

Dr. Aurelie Juhem is a scientist and research director at Ecrins Therapeutics, a start-up biotechnology firm in France that specializes in the discovery of new bioactive molecules. At Ecrins, basic scientific research and development is the strategic approach to innovation. Juhem's research led to the discovery of a new molecule with anti-cancer properties.
Source: BONY/SIPA/AP Images

INNOVATION STRATEGIES When Procter & Gamble purchased the Iams pet food business, it did what it always does—used its renowned research division to look for ways to transfer technology from its other divisions to make new products.[64] One outcome of this cross-divisional combination: a new tartar-fighting ingredient from toothpaste that's included in all of its dry adult pet foods.

As this example shows, innovation strategies aren't necessarily focused on just the radical, breakthrough products. They can include applying existing technology to new uses. And organizations have successfully used both approaches. What types of innovation strategies do organizations need in today's environment? Those strategies should reflect their innovation philosophy, which is shaped by two strategic decisions: innovation emphasis and innovation timing.

Managers must first decide where the emphasis of their innovation efforts will be. Is the organization going to focus on basic scientific research, product development, or process improvement? Basic scientific research requires the most resource commitment because it involves the nuts-and-bolts work of scientific research. In numerous industries (for instance, genetics engineering, pharmaceuticals, information technology, or cosmetics), an organization's expertise in basic research is the key to a sustainable competitive advantage. However, not every organization requires this extensive commitment to scientific research to achieve high performance levels. Instead, many depend on product development strategies. Although this strategy also requires a significant resource investment, it's not in areas associated with scientific research. Instead, the organization takes existing technology and improves on it or applies it in new ways, just as Procter & Gamble did when it applied tartar-fighting knowledge to pet food products. Both of these first two strategic approaches to innovation (basic scientific research and product development) can help an organization achieve high levels of differentiation, which can be a significant source of competitive advantage.

Finally, the last strategic approach to innovation emphasis is a focus on process development. Using this strategy, an organization looks for ways to improve and enhance its work processes. The organization innovates new and improved ways for employees to do their work in all organizational areas. This innovation strategy can lead to lower costs, which, as we know, also can be a significant source of competitive advantage.

Once managers have determined the focus of their innovation efforts, they must decide their innovation timing strategy. Some organizations want to be the first with innovations, whereas others are content to follow or mimic the innovations. An organization that's first to bring a product innovation to the market or to use a new process innovation is called a **first mover**. Being a first mover has certain strategic advantages and disadvantages, as shown in Exhibit 9-6. Some organizations pursue this route, hoping to develop a sustainable competitive advantage. For example, Yum! Brands was the first major fast-food company to establish itself in China when it opened a KFC restaurant in Beijing's Tiananmen Square. Now it has more than 5,000 KFC restaurants in over 1,100 cities throughout China. Others have successfully developed a sustainable competitive advantage by being the followers in the industry. They let the first movers pioneer the innovations and then mimic their products or processes. For instance, Visicorp pioneered the development and marketing of Visicalc, the first desktop spreadsheet program. Its success ended abruptly after Lotus Development created 1-2-3, a more versatile spreadsheet program offering database and graphical chart functions. Eventually, Microsoft developed a superior product—Excel, for its

first mover
An organization that's first to bring a product innovation to the market or to use a new process innovation

Exhibit 9-6
First Mover Advantages and Disadvantages

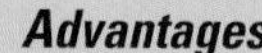

Advantages
- Reputation for being innovative and industry leader
- Cost and learning benefits
- Control over scarce resources and keeping competitors from having access to them
- Opportunity to begin building customer relationships and customer loyalty

Disadvantages
- Uncertainty over exact direction technology and market will go
- Risk of competitors imitating innovations
- Financial and strategic risks
- High development costs

Windows platform—with a graphical interface and more powerful features. Which approach managers choose depends on their organization's innovation philosophy and specific resources and capabilities.

Chapter 9 PREPARING FOR: Exams/Quizzes

CHAPTER SUMMARY by Learning Objectives

LO9.1 DEFINE strategic management and explain why it's important.

Strategic management is what managers do to develop the organization's strategies. Strategies are the plans for how the organization will do whatever it's in business to do, how it will compete successfully, and how it will attract and satisfy its customers in order to achieve its goals. A business model is how a company is going to make money. Strategic management is important for three reasons. First, it makes a difference in how well organizations perform. Second, it's important for helping managers cope with continually changing situations. Finally, strategic management helps coordinate and focus employee efforts on what's important.

LO9.2 EXPLAIN what managers do during the six steps of the strategic management process.

The six steps in the strategic management process encompass strategy planning, implementation, and evaluation. These steps include the following: (1) identify the current mission, goals, and strategies; (2) do an external analysis; (3) do an internal analysis (steps 2 and 3 collectively are known as SWOT analysis); (4) formulate strategies; (5) implement strategies; and (6) evaluate strategies. Strengths are any activities the organization does well or its unique resources. Weaknesses are activities the organization doesn't do well or resources it needs. Opportunities are positive trends in the external environment. Threats are negative trends.

LO9.3 DESCRIBE the three types of corporate strategies.

A growth strategy is when an organization expands the number of markets served or products offered, either through current or new businesses. The types of growth strategies include concentration, vertical integration (backward and forward), horizontal integration, and diversification (related and unrelated). A stability strategy is when an organization makes no significant changes in what it's doing. Both renewal strategies—retrenchment and turnaround—address organizational weaknesses leading to performance declines. The BCG matrix is a way to analyze a company's portfolio of businesses by looking at a business's market share and its industry's anticipated growth rate. The four categories of the BCG matrix are cash cows, stars, question marks, and dogs.

LO9.4 DESCRIBE competitive advantage and the competitive strategies organizations use to get it.

An organization's competitive advantage is what sets it apart, its distinctive edge. A company's competitive advantage becomes the basis for choosing an appropriate competitive strategy. Porter's five forces model assesses the five competitive forces that dictate the rules of competition in an industry: threat of new entrants, threat of substitutes, bargaining power of buyers, bargaining power of suppliers, and current rivalry. Porter's three competitive strategies are as follows: cost leadership (competing on the basis of having the lowest costs in the industry), differentiation (competing on the basis of having unique products that are widely valued by customers), and focus (competing in a narrow segment with either a cost advantage or a differentiation advantage).

LO9.5 DISCUSS current strategic management issues.

Managers face three current strategic management issues: strategic leadership, strategic flexibility, and important types of strategies for today's environment. Strategic leadership is the ability to anticipate, envision, maintain flexibility, think strategically, and work with others in the organization to initiate changes that will create a viable and valuable future for the organization and includes eight key dimensions. Strategic flexibility—that is, the ability to recognize major external environmental changes, to quickly commit resources, and to recognize when a strategic decision isn't working—is important because managers often face highly uncertain environments. Managers can use e-business strategies to reduce costs, to differentiate their firm's products and services, to target (focus on) specific customer groups, or to lower costs by standardizing certain office functions. Another important e-business strategy is the clicks-and-bricks strategy, which combines online and traditional, stand-alone locations. Strategies managers can use to become more customer oriented include giving customers what they want, communicating effectively with them, and having a culture that emphasizes customer service. Strategies managers can use to become more innovative include deciding their organization's innovation emphasis (basic scientific research, product development, or process development) and its innovation timing (first mover or follower).

Pearson **MyLab** Management

Go to **mymanagementlab.com** to complete the problems marked with this icon ✪.

✪ REVIEW AND DISCUSSION QUESTIONS

9-1. Why is strategic management important to managers? Discuss.

9-2. Distinguish between an organization's external opportunities and its threats.

9-3. There are three different types of corporate strategies. Do you think all corporate strategies revolve around growth? Why or why not?

9-4. Explain how managers can use a BCG Matrix to manage strategies by analyzing a corporate portfolio.

9-5. In how many ways can managers create a competitive advantage so that they can compete against their industry rivals?

9-6. Describe the role of competitive advantage. How can Porter's competitive strategies help an organization develop a competitive advantage?

9-7. Creating a competitive advantage over rivals is advantageous, but it's only a matter of time before they catch up, or changes in the industry nullifies the advantage. How does an organization sustain its competitive advantage?

9-8. Describe first-mover advantage and provide examples.

Pearson MyLab Management

If your professor has assigned these, go to **mymanagementlab.com** for the following Assisted-graded writing questions:

9-9. Explain why strategic management is important.

9-10. How does strategic management direct the basic management functions?

PREPARING FOR: My Career

PERSONAL INVENTORY ASSESSMENT

Creative Style Indicator

Good strategic decision makers are creative in formulating and implementing strategies. Take this PIA and get a better feel for your creative style.

ETHICS DILEMMA

The luxury goods market is incredibly lucrative. Most studies on counterfeiting have tended to focus on the supply side. In recent years, however, there has been greater interest in studies pertaining to the demand side of the counterfeit business. There are many different reasons why people are motivated to consume counterfeit products. Clearly the status symbol created by the brand is one motivator. People want to buy into it even if they can't afford to buy the brand itself. The second reason is related to the channel of distribution. Often these brands are simply not available in the local market or are only available in select stores. Perhaps the most important reason is the price. Consumers tend to buy fake goods in order to avoid paying what they perceive to be inflated prices.[65]

9-11. Are customers victims of deception when they buy counterfeit goods or is it something different? Are they in some way complicit?

9-12. Would you knowingly buy counterfeit goods? Explain.

9-13. Consumers will buy counterfeit products purely for its visual attributes and functions, and not the quality. Do you think this would create a problem?

SKILLS EXERCISE Developing Your Business Planning Skill

About the Skill

An important step in starting a business or in determining a new strategic direction is preparing a business plan.[66] Not only does the business plan aid in thinking about what to do and how to do it, but it can be a sound basis from which to obtain funding and resources.

Steps in Practicing the Skill

- ***Describe your company's background and purpose.*** Provide the history of the company. Briefly describe the company's history and what this company does that's unique. Describe what your product or service will be, how you intend to market it, and what you need to bring your product or service to the market.

- ***Identify your short- and long-term goals.*** What is your intended goal for this organization? Clearly, for a new company three broad objectives are relevant: creation, survival, and profitability. Specific objectives can include such things as sales, market share, product quality, employee morale, and social responsibility. Identify how you plan to achieve each objective, how you intend to determine whether you met the objective, and when you intend the objective to be met (e.g., short or long term).
- ***Do a thorough market analysis.*** You need to convince readers that you understand what you are doing, what your market is, and what competitive pressures you'll face. In this analysis, you'll need to describe the overall market trends, the specific market you intend to compete in, and who the competitors are. In essence, in this section you'll perform your SWOT analysis.
- ***Describe your development and production emphasis.*** Explain how you're going to produce your product or service. Include time frames from start to finish. Describe the difficulties you may encounter in this stage as well as how much you believe activities in this stage will cost. Provide an explanation of what decisions (e.g., make or buy?) you will face and what you intend to do.
- ***Describe how you'll market your product or service.*** What is your selling strategy? How do you intend to reach your customers? In this section, describe your product or service in terms of your competitive advantage and demonstrate how you'll exploit your competitors' weaknesses. In addition to the market analysis, provide sales forecasts in terms of the size of the market, how much of the market you can realistically capture, and how you'll price your product or service.
- ***Put together your financial statements.*** What's your bottom line? Investors want to know this information. In the financial section, provide projected profit-and-loss statements (income statements) for approximately three to five years, a cash flow analysis, and the company's projected balance sheets. In the financial section, give thought to how much start-up costs will be and develop a financial strategy—how you intend to use funds received from a financial institution and how you'll control and monitor the financial well-being of the company.
- ***Provide an overview of the organization and its management.*** Identify the key executives, summarizing their education, experience, and any relevant qualifications. Identify their positions in the organization and their job roles. Explain how much salary they intend to earn initially. Identify others who may assist the organization's management (e.g., company lawyer, accountant, board of directors). This section should also include, if relevant, a subsection on how you intend to deal with employees. For example, how will employees be paid, what benefits will be offered, and how will employee performance be assessed?
- ***Describe the legal form of the business.*** Identify the legal form of the business. For example, is it a sole proprietorship, a partnership, a corporation? Depending on the legal form, you may need to provide information regarding equity positions, shares of stock issued, and the like.
- ***Identify the critical risks and contingencies facing the organization.*** In this section, identify what you'll do if problems arise. For instance, if you don't meet sales forecasts, what then? Similar responses to such questions as problems with suppliers, inability to hire qualified employees, poor-quality products, and so on should be addressed. Readers want to see if you've anticipated potential problems and if you have contingency plans. This is the "what if" section.
- ***Put the business plan together.*** Using the information you've gathered from the previous nine steps, it's now time to put the business plan together into a well-organized document. A business plan should contain a cover page that shows the company name, address, contact person, and numbers at which the individual can be reached. The cover page should also contain the date the business was established and, if one exists, the company logo. The next page of the business plan should be a table of contents. Here you'll want to list and identify the location of each major section and subsection in the business plan. Remember to use proper outlining techniques. Next comes the executive summary, the first section the readers will actually read. Thus, it's one of the more critical elements of the business plan, because if the executive summary is poorly done, readers may not read any further. In a two- to three-page summary, highlight information about the company, its management, its market and competition, the funds requested, how the funds will be used, financial history (if available), financial projections, and when investors can expect to get their money back (called the exit). Next come the main sections of your business plan; that is, the material you've researched and written about in steps 1 through 9. Close out the business plan with a section that summarizes the highlights of what you've just presented. Finally, if you have charts, exhibits, photographs, tables, and the like, you might want to include an appendix in the back of the business plan. If you do, remember to cross-reference this material to the relevant section of the report.

Practicing the Skill

You have a great idea for a business and need to create a business plan to present to a bank. Choose one of the following products or services, or choose a product or service of your own. Draft the parts of your plan that describe how you will price and market it (see step 5) and that identify critical risks and contingencies (see step 9).

1. Haircuts at home (you make house calls)
2. Olympic snowboarding computer game for consoles and mobile devices
3. Online apartment rental listing
4. Voice-activated house alarm

WORKING TOGETHER Team Exercise

Organizational mission statements—are they a promise, a commitment, or just a ball of hot air? Form small groups of three to four individuals and find examples of three different organizational mission statements. Your first task is to evaluate the mission statements. How do they compare to the components listed in Exhibit 9-2? Would you describe each as an effective mission statement? Why or why not? How might you rewrite each mission statement to make it better? Your second task is to use the mission statements to describe the types of corporate and competitive strategies each organization might use to fulfill that mission statement. Explain your rationale for choosing each strategy.

MY TURN TO BE A MANAGER

- Using current business periodicals, find two examples of each of the corporate and competitive strategies. Write a description of what these businesses are doing and how it represents that particular strategy.
- Pick five companies from the latest version of *Fortune*'s "Most Admired Companies" list. Research these companies and identify their (a) mission statement, (b) strategic goals, and (c) strategies used.
- Consider several businesses from which you purchase products or services on a regular basis. Identify the business model for each business.
- Customer service, social media, and innovation strategies are particularly important to managers today. We described specific ways companies can pursue these strategies. Your task is to pick customer service, e-business, or innovation and find one example for each of the specific approaches in that category. For instance, if you choose customer service, find an example of (a) giving customers what they want, (b) communicating effectively with them, and (c) providing employees with customer service training. Write a report describing your examples.

CASE APPLICATION 1 Fast Fashion

When Amancio Ortega, a Spanish former bathrobe maker, opened his first Zara clothing store, his business model was simple: sell high-fashion look-alikes to price-conscious Europeans.[67] After succeeding in this, he decided to tackle the outdated clothing industry in which it took six months from a garment's design to consumers being able to purchase it in a store. What Ortega envisioned was "fast fashion"—getting designs to customers quickly. And that's exactly what Zara has done!

The company has been described as having more style than Gap, faster growth than Target, and logistical expertise rivaling Walmart's. Zara, owned by the Spanish fashion retail group Inditex SA, recognizes that success in the fashion world is based on a simple rule—get products to market quickly. Accomplishing this, however, isn't so simple. It involves a clear and focused understanding of fashion, technology, and their market, *and* the ability to adapt quickly to trends.

Inditex, the world's largest fashion retailer by sales worldwide, has seven chains: Zara (including Zara Kids and Zara Home), Pull and Bear, Massimo Dutti, Stradivarius, Bershka, Oysho, and Uterqüe. The company has more than 6,340 stores in 87 countries, although Zara pulls in more than 60 percent of the company's revenues. Despite its global presence, Zara is not yet a household name in the United States, with just 45 stores open, including a flagship store in New York City.

What is Zara's secret to excelling at fast fashion? It takes approximately two weeks to get a new design from drawing board to store floor. And stores are stocked with new designs twice a week as clothes are shipped directly to the stores from the factory. Thus, each aspect of Zara's business contributes to the fast turnaround. Sales managers at "the Cube"—what employees call their futuristic-looking headquarters—sit at a long row of computers and scrutinize sales at every store. They see the hits and the misses almost instantaneously. They ask the in-house designers, who work in teams, sketching out new styles and deciding which fabrics will provide the best combination of style and price, for new designs. Once a design is drawn, it's sent electronically to Zara's factory across the street, where a clothing sample is made. To minimize waste, computer programs arrange and rearrange clothing patterns on the massive fabric rolls before a laser-guided machine does the cutting. Zara produces most of its designs close to home—in Morocco, Portugal, Spain, and Turkey. Finished garments are returned to the factory within a week. Finishing touches (buttons, trim, detailing, etc.) are added, and each garment goes through a quality check. Garments that don't pass are discarded while those that do pass are individually pressed. Then, garment labels (indicating to which country garments will be shipped) and security tags are added. The bundled garments proceed along a moving carousel of hanging rails via a maze of tunnels to the warehouse, a four-story, five-million-square-foot building (about the size of 90 football fields). As the merchandise bundles move along the rails, electronic bar code tags are read by equipment that send them to the right "staging area," where specific merchandise is first sorted by country and then by individual store, ensuring that each store gets exactly the shipment it's supposed to. From there, merchandise for European stores is sent to a loading dock and packed on a truck with other shipments in order of delivery. Deliveries to other locations go by plane. Some 60,000 items each hour—more than 2.6 million items a week—move through this ultrasophisticated distribution center. And this takes place with only a handful of workers, who monitor the entire process. The company's just-in-time production (an idea borrowed from the auto industry) gives it a competitive edge in terms of speed and flexibility.

Despite Zara's success at fast fashion, its competitors are working to be faster. But CEO Pablo Isla isn't standing still. To maintain Zara's leading advantage, he's introducing new methods that enable store managers to order and display merchandise faster and is adding new cargo routes for shipping goods. Also, the company recently announced that it's developing a new logistics hub that will be able to distribute almost half a million garments daily to its stores on five continents. Zara's CEO says that this new facility will lay the groundwork for continued rapid expansion worldwide. And the company has finally made the jump into online retailing. One analyst forecasts that the company could quadruple sales, with a majority of that coming from online sales.

DISCUSSION QUESTIONS

9-14. How is strategic management illustrated by this case story?

9-15. How might SWOT analysis be helpful to Inditex executives? To Zara store managers?

9-16. What competitive advantage do you think Zara is pursuing? How does it exploit that competitive advantage?

9-17. Do you think Zara's success is due to external or internal factors or both? Explain.

9-18. What strategic implications does Zara's move into online retailing have? (Hint: Think in terms of resources and capabilities.)

CASE APPLICATION 2 A Simple Strategy at Costco

Costco launched the warehouse shopping model when it opened its first location in 1976, requiring customers to purchase an annual membership in order to shop at the store.[68] The first location was called Price Club and initially sold only to small businesses. More than 40 years later, Costco is one of the nation's top retailers and the nation's largest membership warehouse chain. They operate more than 700 warehouses located around the world, with more than 80 million members and over $116 billion in annual revenues. In addition to demonstrating steady growth throughout its history, the company consistently performs better than competitors. For example, Costco's sales per square foot are nearly 70 percent higher than their closest competitor, Sam's Club.

So how has Costco achieved this level of success? Experts agree that Costco's simple strategy has allowed the company to persist, even in challenging times. In fact, some say Costco has the best business model in the retail industry. The company's strategies that differentiate it from its competitors are to treat employees well, limit the number of items it sells, and keep markups low.

Costco clearly values its employees. The company pays its employees on average 40 percent higher than competitors and offers health care insurance to all employees who work more than 20 hours per week. The company is also known for promoting from within, with 98 percent of their store managers and many of their company executives having started out as stock clerks or cashiers. These efforts have helped build a loyal and hard-working employee base that actively contributes to building a profitable bottom line. Furthermore, low employee turnover helps save the company in recruiting and training expenses. The company's average annual turnover rate is about 5 percent, compared to the average turnover rate of about 20 percent in the rest of the retail industry.

Costco also has a sales strategy that has contributed to its success. They only sell a limited number of brands and, as a result, they are able to increase sales volume that leads to purchasing discounts. For example, Costco only carries four brands of toothpaste, compared to about 60 brands you'd find on the shelf at Walmart. Thus, the company is able to purchase those four brands in significant volumes, which allows them to negotiate with the product manufacturers for discounts. The company then passes along those savings to their customers through lower prices. Costco prices items at no more than 15 percent above their purchasing price. This markup strategy assures they are offering the lowest price possible, which is what draws customers and creates a loyal customer base.

Sticking with these simple strategies has helped Costco build their retail empire. Can the company continue their growth trajectory and maintain their leadership position in the retail industry? There is some speculation that as consumers build confidence in online shopping, Costco and other brick-and-mortar retailers will face declining sales due to the competition. Costco has responded to this threat by expanding the diversity of their inventory, offering deep discounts on high-ticket items such as jewelry, electronics, and even cars. Such tactics help to encourage membership by making the company the go-to location for purchases that consumers prefer to make in person. And while they are there, they can pick up some toothpaste at a pretty good price.

DISCUSSION QUESTIONS

9-19. How is Costco's business model different from other retailers such as Walmart and Sam's Club? Why do you think Costco's strategy works?

9-20. Beyond lower turnover, how else does Costco benefit from treating its employees well?

9-21. Are you surprised that Costco sells cars? How does offering diverse products help the company attract new members?

9-22. Costco now has a comprehensive website and sells online. Is this a threat to Costco's business model? Is there a downside to selling online?

ENDNOTES

1. W. Berger, "Find Your Passion with These 8 Thought-Provoking Questions," www.fastcodesign.com, April 14, 2014; and G. Anders, "MIT's Inspired Call: Graduation Talk by Dropbox CEO, Age 30," www.forbes.com, June 8, 2013.
2. A. Ricadela, "Zalando Aims for $11 Billion in Sales by Seeking Technology Edge, *Bloomberg* online, www.bloomberg.com, March 18, 2016; J. Morton, "Cage-Free Eggs May Be Golden Goose for Retail Profits," *Bloomberg* online, www.bloomberg.com, March 25, 2016; J. Soble, "Dell to Sell Perot Systems to NTT Data of Japan for About $3.1 Billion," *New York Times* online, www.nytimes.com, March 28, 2016; A. Gupta, "Ajit Gupta: How to Compete on Price without Sacrificing Profits," *The Wall Street Journal* online, www.wsj.com, March 23, 2014; "Al Jazeera to Cut 500 Jobs," *The Wall Street Journal* online, March 27, 2016.
3. J. W. Dean Jr. and M. P. Sharfman, "Does Decision Process Matter? A Study of Strategic Decision-Making Effectiveness," *Academy of Management Journal*, April 1996, pp. 368–396.

4. Based on A. A. Thompson Jr., A. J. Strickland III, and J. E. Gamble, *Crafting and Executing Strategy*, 14th ed. (New York: McGraw-Hill Irwin, 2005).
5. J. Magretta, "Why Business Models Matter," *Harvard Business Review*, May 2002, pp. 86–92.
6. M. Song, S. Im, H. van der Bij, and L. Z. Song, "Does Strategic Planning Enhance or Impede Innovation and Firm Performance?," *Journal of Product Innovation Management*, July 2011, pp. 503–520; M. Reimann, O. Schilke, and J. S. Thomas, "Customer Relationship Management and Firm Performance: The Mediating Role of Business Strategy," *Journal of the Academy of Marketing Science*, Summer 2010, pp. 326–346; J. Aspara, J. Hietanen, and H. Tikkanen, "Business Model Innovation vs. Replication: Financial Performance Implications of Strategic Emphases," *Journal of Strategic Marketing*, February 2010, pp. 39–56; J. C. Short, D. J. Ketchen Jr., T. B. Palmer, and G. T. M. Hult, "Firm, Strategic Group, and Industry Influences on Performance," *Strategic Management Journal*, February 2007, pp. 147–167; H. J. Cho and V. Pucik, "Relationship Between Innovativeness, Quality, Growth, Profitability, and Market Value," *Strategic Management Journal*, June 2005, pp. 555–575; A. Carmeli and A. Tischler, "The Relationships Between Intangible Organizational Elements and Organizational Performance," *Strategic Management Journal*, December 2004, pp. 1257–1278; D. J. Ketchen, C. C. Snow, and V. L. Street, "Improving Firm Performance by Matching Strategic Decision-Making Processes to Competitive Dynamics," *Academy of Management Executive*, November 2004, pp. 29–43; E. H. Bowman and C. E. Helfat, "Does Corporate Strategy Matter?," *Strategic Management Journal*, vol. 22, 2001, pp. 1–23; P. J. Brews and M. R. Hunt, "Learning to Plan and Planning to Learn: Resolving the Planning School-Learning School Debate," *Strategic Management Journal*, vol. 20, 1999, pp. 889–913; D. J. Ketchen Jr., J. B. Thomas, and R. R. McDaniel Jr., "Process, Content and Context: Synergistic Effects on Performance," *Journal of Management*, vol. 22, no. 2, 1996, pp. 231–257; C. C. Miller and L. B. Cardinal, "Strategic Planning and Firm Performance: A Synthesis of More Than Two Decades of Research," *Academy of Management Journal*, December 1994, pp. 1649–1665; and N. Capon, J. U. Farley, and J. M. Hulbert, "Strategic Planning and Financial Performance: More Evidence," *Journal of Management Studies*, January 1994, pp. 105–110.
7. J. S. Lublin and D. Mattioli, "Strategic Plans Lose Favor," *Wall Street Journal*, January 25, 2010, p. B7.
8. Malcolm Sutton, "Royal Flying Doctor Service Gears Up for the 21st Century with New Facilities at Adelaide," *891 ABC News*, October 19, 2016, http://www.abc.net.au/news/2016-10-20/rfds-gearing-up-for-the-21st-century/7949444 (accessed December 22, 2016).
9. Julie Power, "Royal Flying Doctor Service Gets an $18 Million Boost," *Sydney Morning Herald*, April 8, 2016, http://www.smh.com.au/nsw/royal-flying-doctor-gets-an-18-million-funding-boost—20160408-go1jc0.html (accessed December 22, 2016); Nick Lowther, "Australian-first Flight Simulator to be Built in Dubbo for Royal Flying Doctors Service," April 12, 2016, http://www.abc.net.au/news/2016-04-08/flight-sim-for-dubbo-rfds/7311700 (accessed December 20, 2016).
10. Royal Flying Doctor Service site https://www.flyingdoctor.org.au (accessed December 22, 2016).
11. Official NIKE, Inc. website, "Our Mission," www.about.nike.com, accessed March 19, 2016.
12. C. Groscurth, "Why Your Company Must Be Mission-Driven," *Gallup Business Journal*, businessjournal.gallup.com, March 6, 2014.
13. U.S. Bureau of Labor Statistics, "The Employment Situation—March 2016," USDL-16-0662, www.bls.gov, April 1, 2016; U.S. Department of Education, "Enrollment in Degree-Granting Institutions, by Age: Fall 1970 through Fall 2016," *Digest of Education Statistics* online, www.nces.ed.gov, accessed April 3, 2016; "Angry Birds Maker Posted Revenue of $106.3 Million in 2011," *New York Times* online, www.nytimes.com, May 7, 2012; J. Wortham, "Cellphones Now Used More for Data Than for Calls," *New York Times* online, www.nytimes.com, May 13, 2010; and S. Rosenbloom, "Calorie Data to Be Posted at Most Chains," *New York Times* online, www.nytimes.com, March 23, 2010.
14. M. Bertolini, D. Duncan, and A. Waldeck, "Knowing When to Reinvent," *Harvard Business Review* online, www.hbr.org, December 2015.
15. Sy Mukherjee, "How GlaxoSmithKline Is Changing the World," *Fortune*, August 18, 2016, http://fortune.com/2016/08/18/glaxosmithkline-change-world (accessed December 22, 2016).
16. C. K. Prahalad and G. Hamel, "The Core Competence of the Corporation," *Harvard Business Review*, https://hbr.org, May–June 1990, pp. 79–91.
17. Norfolk Southern Corporation's website, "Norfolk Southern Announces Further Details of Its Strategic Plan to Reduce Costs, Drive Profitability, and Accelerate Growth," www.nscorp.com, accessed March 25, 2016.
18. S. Li, "Amazon Overtakes Wal-Mart as Biggest Retailer," *LA Times* online, www.latimes.com, July 24, 2015.
19. K. Stock, "How Boring Old Buick Is Crushing the Luxury Car Market," *Bloomberg* online, www.bloomberg.com, March 22, 2016.
20. Leader Making a Difference box based on K. Bellstrom, B. Kowitt, M. Lev-Ram, L. Rao, J. Reingold, P. Sellers, et al., "Fortune's Most Powerful Women List," *Fortune*, September 15, 2015, vol. 172, no. 4, pp. 90–97; J. Amend, "GM CEO Barra Outlines Future Mobility Strategy," *Ward's Auto World*, October 2015, vol. 51, no. 10, pp. 12–12; R. Foroohar, "Mary Barra's Bumpy Ride," *Time Magazine*, vol. 184, no. 13, 2014, pp. 32–38; M. DeBord, "General Motors CEO Mary Barra: 'We Are Disrupting Ourselves, We're Not Trying to Preserve a Model of Yesterday,'" *Business Insider* online, www.businessinsider.com, November 16, 2015.
21. J. Gress, "Wal-Mart Jumps into Milk Processing, Hits Dean Foods' Stock," *Reuters* online, www.reuters.com, March 22, 2016.
22. "UAE's NMC Health Buys Sharjah Hospital for $560m," *Gulf Business*, December 14, 2016, http://gulfbusiness.com/uaes-nmc-health-buys-sharjah-hospital-560m/ (accessed December 22, 2016); Jim Brunsden, "Vodafone and Liberty Global Win EU Approval for Dutch Merger," *Financial Times*, August 3, 2016, https://www.ft.com/content/72aec658-5997-11e6-8d05-4eaa66292c32 (accessed December 22, 2016); Max Colchester and Jeannette Neumann, "Bank-Merger Drought Puts Europe in Bind," December 22, 2016, http://www.wsj.com/articles/bank-merger-drought-puts-eu-in-a-bind-1482404547 (accessed December 22, 2016).
23. The Boeing Company, "2015 Annual Report," p. 4.
24. K. Kingsbury, "Biogen Retrenches, Despite Strong Quarter," *The Wall Street Journal* online, www.wsj.com, October 21, 2015.
25. J. Jamerson, "CIT Group to Focus on Commercial Businesses in Turnaround Plan," *The Wall Street Journal* online, www.wsj.com, March 23, 2016.
26. H. Quarls, T. Pernsteiner, and K. Rangan, "Love Your Dogs," *Strategy & Business*, Spring 2006, pp. 58–65; and P. Haspeslagh, "Portfolio Planning: Uses and Limits," *Harvard Business Review*, January–February 1982, pp. 58–73.

27. Boston Consulting Group, *Perspective on Experience* (Boston: Boston Consulting Group, 1970).
28. "Global 500 2014: The World's Most Valuable Brands," http://brandirectory.com/league_Tables/table/global-500-2014.
29. J. B. Barney, "Looking Inside for Competitive Advantage," *Academy of Management Executive*, November 1995, pp. 49–61; M. A. Peteraf, "The Cornerstones of Competitive Advantage: A Resource-Based View," *Strategic Management Journal*, March 1993, pp. 179–191; J. Barney, "Firm Resources and Sustained Competitive Advantage," *Journal of Management* vol. 17, no. 1, 1991, pp. 99–120; M. E. Porter, *Competitive Advantage: Creating and Sustaining Superior Performance* (New York: Free Press, 1985); and R. Rumelt, "Towards a Strategic Theory of the Firm," in *Competitive Strategic Management*, ed. R. Lamb (Upper Saddle River, NJ: Prentice Hall, 1984), pp. 556–570.
30. R. D. Spitzer, "TQM: The Only Source of Sustainable Competitive Advantage," *Quality Progress*, June 1993, pp. 59–64; T. C. Powell, "Total Quality Management as Competitive Advantage: A Review and Empirical Study," *Strategic Management Journal*, January 1995, pp. 15–37; and N. A. Shepherd, "Competitive Advantage: Mapping Change and the Role of the Quality Manager of the Future," *Annual Quality Congress*, May 1998, pp. 53–60.
31. See special issue of *Academy of Management Review* devoted to TQM, July 1994, pp. 390–584; B. Voss, "Quality's Second Coming," *Journal of Business Strategy*, March–April 1994, pp. 42–46; R. Krishnan, A. B. Shani, R. M. Grant, and R. Baer, "In Search of Quality Improvement Problems of Design and Implementation," *Academy of Management Executive*, November 1993, pp. 7–20; C. A. Barclay, "Quality Strategy and TQM Policies: Empirical Evidence," *Management International Review*, Special Issue 1993, pp. 87–98; and R. Jacob, "TQM: More Than a Dying Fad?," *Fortune*, October 18, 1993, pp. 66–72; and R. J. Schonenberger, "Is Strategy Strategic? Impact of Total Quality Management on Strategy," *Academy of Management Executive*, August 1992, pp. 80–87.
32. "Executive Insight: An Interview with Peter Blair, Senior Director of Marketing, Kiva Systems," *Apparel Magazine*, June 2012, p. 24; A. Noto, "Amazon's Robotics Play Underscores Industry Trend," *Mergers & Acquisitions: The Dealmaker's Journal*, May 2012, p. 14; "Amazon to Acquire Kiva Systems for $775 Million," *Material Handling & Logistics*, April 2012, p. 7; and C. Chaey, "The World's 50 Most Innovative Companies: Kiva Systems," FastCompany.com, March 2012, p. 110.
33. D. Dunne and R. Martin, "Design Thinking and How It Will Change Management Education: An Interview and Discussion," *Academy of Management Learning & Education*, December 2006, pp. 512–523.
34. A. McAfee and E. Brynjolfsson, "Big Data: The Management Revolution," *Harvard Business Review*, October 2012, p. 62.
35. K. Cukier and V. Mayer-Schönberger, "The Financial Bonanza of Big Data," *Wall Street Journal*, March 8, 2013, p. A15.
36. Natalie Mortimer, "L'Oréal: how influencers are 'challenging' the way it creates products and campaigns," *The Drum (UK)*, September 20, 2016, http://www.thedrum.com/news/2016/09/20/l-or-al-how-influencers-are-challenging-the-way-it-creates-products-and-campaigns (accessed December 22, 2016); Andrew Hutchinson, "Big Brand Theory: L'Oréal Stays Connected to Their Audience via Social, Social Media Today," *Social Media Today*, September 9, 2015, http://www.socialmediatoday.com/special-columns/adhutchinson/2015-09-09/big-brand-theory-loreal-stays-connected-their-audience (accessed December 22, 2016); Lucy Whitehouse, "L'Oréal Leads the Way for Beauty Marketing on Snapchat," *Cosmetics Design-Asia*, June 7, 2016, http://www.cosmeticsdesign-asia.com/Brand-Innovation/L-Oreal-leads-the-way-for-beauty-marketing-on-Snapchat (accessed December 22, 2016).
37. B. Roberts, "Social Media Gets Strategic," *HR Magazine*, October 2012, p. 30.
38. B. Acohido, "Social-Media Tools Boost Productivity," *USA Today*, August 13, 2012, pp. 1B+.
39. Ibid.
40. See, for example, A. Brandenburger, "Porter's Added Value: High Indeed!," *Academy of Management Executive*, May 2002, pp. 58–60; N. Argyres and A. M. McGahan, "An Interview with Michael Porter," *Academy of Management Executive*, May 2002, pp. 43–52; D. F. Jennings and J. R. Lumpkin, "Insights Between Environmental Scanning Activities and Porter's Generic Strategies: An Empirical Analysis," *Strategic Management Journal*, vol. 18, no. 4, 1992, pp. 791–803; I. Bamberger, "Developing Competitive Advantage in Small and Medium-Sized Firms," *Long Range Planning*, October 1989, pp. 80–88; C. W. L. Hill, "Differentiation Versus Low Cost or Differentiation and Low Cost: A Contingency Framework," *Academy of Management Review*, July 1988, pp. 401–412; A. I. Murray, "A Contingency View of Porter's 'Generic Strategies,'" *Academy of Management Review*, July 1988, pp. 390–400; M. E. Porter, "From Competitive Advantage to Corporate Strategy," *Harvard Business Review*, May–June 1987, pp. 43–59; G. G. Dess and P. S. Davis, "Porter's (1980) Generic Strategies and Performance: An Empirical Examination with American Data—Part II: Performance Implications," *Organization Studies*, no. 3, 1986, pp. 255–261; G. G. Dess and P. S. Davis, "Porter's (1980) Generic Strategies and Performance: An Empirical Examination with American Data—Part I: Testing Porter," *Organization Studies*, no. 1, 1986, pp. 37–55; G. G. Dess and P. S. Davis, "Porter's (1980) Generic Strategies as Determinants of Strategic Group Membership and Organizational Performance," *Academy of Management Journal*, September 1984, pp. 467–488; Porter, *Competitive Advantage: Creating and Sustaining Superior Performance*; and M. E. Porter, *Competitive Strategy: Techniques for Analyzing Industries and Competitors* (New York: Free Press, 1980).
41. From the Ross Stores website, "About Us," www.rossstores.com/about-us, accessed March 5, 2016.
42. J. Bennett, "Ross Stores: Rare Winner Amid the Retail Rubble," *Barrons* online, www.barrons.com, March 2, 2016.
43. From the L.L.Bean website, "100% Satisfaction Guarantee," http://www.llbean.com/customerService/aboutLLBean/guarantee.html, accessed February 28, 2016.
44. J. W. Bachmann, "Competitive Strategy: It's O.K. to Be Different," *Academy of Management Executive*, May 2002, pp. 61–65; S. Cappel, P. Wright, M. Kroll, and D. Wyld, "Competitive Strategies and Business Performance: An Empirical Study of Select Service Businesses," *International Journal of Management*, March 1992, pp. 1–11; D. Miller, "The Generic Strategy Trap," *Journal of Business Strategy*, January–February 1991, pp. 37–41; R. E. White, "Organizing to Make Business Unit Strategies Work," in *Handbook of Business Strategy*, 2d ed., ed. H. E. Glass (Boston: Warren Gorham and Lamont, 1991), pp. 1–24; and Hill, "Differentiation Versus Low Cost or Differentiation and Low Cost: A Contingency Framework."
45. K. Caulfield, "CD Album Sales Fall Behind Album Downloads, Is 2014 the Year Digital Takes Over?," www.billboard.com, February 11, 2014.

46. B. Sisario, "Out to Shake Up Music, Often with Sharp Words," *New York Times* online, www.nytimes.com, May 6, 2012; and J. Plambeck, "As CD Sales Wane, Music Retailers Diversify," *New York Times* online, www.nytimes.com, May 30, 2010.
47. J. Greene, "Amazon Woos Fashion Industry as New Studio Opens in N.Y.," *The Seattle Times*, seattletimes.com, October 21, 2013; S. Clifford, "Amazon Leaps into High End of the Fashion Pool," *New York Times* online, www.nytimes.com, May 7, 2012; and "Can Amazon Be A Fashion Player?" *Women's Wear Daily*, May 4, 2012, p. 1.
48. S. Ghoshal and C. A. Bartlett, "Changing the Role of Top Management: Beyond Structure to Process," *Harvard Business Review*, January–February 1995, pp. 86–96.
49. R. Calori, G. Johnson, and P. Sarnin, "CEO's Cognitive Maps and the Scope of the Organization," *Strategic Management Journal*, July 1994, pp. 437–457.
50. R. D. Ireland and M. A. Hitt, "Achieving and Maintaining Strategic Competitiveness in the 21st Century: The Role of Strategic Leadership," *Academy of Management Executive*, February 1999, pp. 43–57.
51. J. P. Wallman, "Strategic Transactions and Managing the Future: A Druckerian Perspective," *Management Decision*, vol. 48, no. 4, 2010, pp. 485–499; D. E. Zand, "Drucker's Strategic Thinking Process: Three Key Techniques," *Strategy & Leadership*, vol. 38, no. 3, 2010, pp. 23–28; and R. D. Ireland and M. A. Hitt, "Achieving and Maintaining Strategic Competitiveness in the 21st -Century: The Role of Strategic Leadership."
52. Lublin and Mattioli, "Strategic Plans Lose Favor."
53. Based on J. S. Lublin and D. Mattioli, "Strategic Plans Lose Favor: Slump Showed Bosses Value of Flexibility, Quick Decisions," *Wall Street Journal*, January 25, 2010, p. B7.
54. Ibid.
55. G. Colvin, "Warren Buffett's Leadership Lessons," *Fortune* online, www.fortune.com, February 29, 2016.
56. R. Mac, "Jeff Bezos Calls Amazon 'Best Place in the World to Fail' in Shareholder Letter," *Forbes* online, www.forbes.com, April 5, 2016.
57. D. Sull, R. Homkes, and C. Sull, "Why Strategy Execution Unravels—and What to Do About It," *Harvard Business Review* online, www.hbr.org, March 2015.
58. B. Barnes, "Across U.S., ESPN Aims to Be the Home Team," *New York Times* online, www.nytimes.com, July 20, 2009; P. Sanders and M. Futterman, "Competition Pushes Up Content Costs for ESPN," *Wall Street Journal*, February 23, 2009, pp. B1+; T. Lowry, "ESPN's Cell-Phone Fumble," *BusinessWeek* online, www.bloomberg.com/news, October 30, 2006; and T. Lowry, "In the Zone," *BusinessWeek*, October 17, 2005, pp. 66–77.
59. E. Kim, D. Nam, and J. L. Stimpert, "The Applicability of Porter's Generic Strategies in the Digital Age: Assumptions, Conjectures, and Suggestions," *Journal of Management*, vol. 30, no. 5, 2004, pp. 569–589; and G. T. Lumpkin, S. B. Droege, and G. G. Dess, "E-Commerce Strategies: Achieving Sustainable Competitive Advantage and Avoiding Pitfalls," *Organizational Dynamics*, Spring 2002, pp. 325–340.
60. Kim, Nam, and Stimpert, "The Applicability of Porter's Generic Strategies in the Digital Age."
61. S. Clifford, "Luring Online Shoppers Offline," *New York Times* online, www.nytimes.com, July 4, 2012.
62. J. Gaffney, "Shoe Fetish," *Business 2.0*, March 2002, pp. 98–99.
63. D. Fickling, "The Singapore Girls Aren't Smiling Anymore," *Bloomberg BusinessWeek*, May 21–27, 2012, pp. 25–26; L. Heracleous and J. Wirtz, "Singapore Airlines' Balancing Act," *Harvard Business Review*, July–August 2010, pp. 145–149; and J. Doebele, "The Engineer," *Forbes*, January 9, 2006, pp. 122–124.
64. "Innovation at Work: Is Anyone in Charge?" *Wall Street Journal*, January 22, 2013, p. B14.
65. Ethics Dilemma case based on Ian Phau, Min Teah, and Agnes Lee's "Targeting Buyers of Counterfeits of Luxury Brands: A Study on Attitudes of Singaporean Consumers," *Palgrave Macmillan*, Journal of Targeting, Measurement and Analysis for Marketing, May 17, 2008, p.17. www.palgrave-journals.com
66. Materials for developing a business plan can be found at Small Business Administration, *The Business Plan Workbook* (Washington, DC: SBA, May 17, 2001); and on the Small Business Administration website (www.sba.gov). In addition, readers may find software such as Business Plan Pro Software, available at www.businessplanpro.com, useful.
67. C. Bjork, "Zara Owner Lays Ground for Rapid Expansion," *Wall Street Journal*, March 20, 2014, p. B9; C. Moon, "The Secret World of Fast Fashion," www.psmag.com, March 17, 2014; V. Walt, "Meet the Third-Richest Man in the World," *Fortune*, January 14, 2013, pp. 74–79; S. Hansen, "How Zara Grew into the World's Largest Fashion Retailer," *New York Times* online, www.nytimes.com, November 9, 2012; D. Roman and W. Kemble-Diaz, "Owner of Fast-Fashion Retailer Zara Keeps Up Emerging-Markets Push," *Wall Street Journal*, June 14, 2012, p. B3; Press Releases, "Inditex Achieves Net Sales of 9,709 Million Euros, an Increase of 10 percent," www.inditex.com, February 22, 2012; C. Bjork, "'Cheap Chic' Apparel Sellers Heat Up U.S. Rivalry on Web," *Wall Street Journal*, September 6, 2011, pp. B1+; A. Kenna, "Zara Plays Catch-up with Online Shoppers," *Bloomberg BusinessWeek*, August 29–September 4, 2011, pp. 24–25; K. Girotra and S. Netessine, "How to Build Risk into Your Business Model," *Harvard Business Review*, May 2011, pp. 100–105; M. Dart and R. Lewis, "Break the Rules the Way Zappos and Amazon Do," *Bloomberg BusinessWeek Online*, http://www.bloomberg.com, April 29, 2011; K. Cappell, "Zara Thrives by Breaking All the Rules," *BusinessWeek*, October 20, 2008, p. 66; and C. Rohwedder and K. Johnson, "Pace-Setting Zara Seeks More Speed to Fight Its Rising Cheap-Chic Rivals," *Wall Street Journal*, February 20, 2008, pp. B1+.
68. A. Lutz, "Costco's Unorthodox Strategy to Survive the Big Box Apocalypse," *Business Insider* online, www.businessinsider.com, March 7, 2013; A. Fisher, "A Blueprint for Creating Better Jobs—and Bigger Profits," *Fortune* online, www.fortune.com, December 13, 2013; K. Taylor, "Costco Is Beating Walmart and Amazon with the 'Best Business Model' in Retail," *Business Insider* online, www.businessinsider.com, February 22, 2016; L. Lorenzetti, "You Won't Believe How Many Cars Costco Sells," *Time Magazine* online, www.time.com, June 4, 2015; www.costco.com.

Chapter 10 Fostering Entrepreneurship

It's Your Career

Source: Alvin555/Shutterstock

A key to success in management and your career is knowing how to take control of your career.

Being Entrepreneurial Even If You Don't Want to Be an Entrepreneur

As a student, you are learning which course topics most interest you and where your future lies. Deciding on a career is an essential first step. To get where you'd like to go, you must develop a plan that will help you to meet your career objectives. We suggest you might want to think "entrepreneurial" in developing your career strategy. What does that mean?

*1. **Take control of your career.** Don't let what your parents or friends say limit your options. And don't put your future wholly into the hands of your employer. Make it your responsibility to plan and execute your career future.*

*2. **Think outside the box.** Look for opportunities that others might have missed. What works for creating a business can also work for creating a career.*

*3. **Assess your strengths and talents.** As noted in Chapter 9's "It's Your Career," we all have specific strengths and weaknesses. Being honest with yourself—and acknowledging that we're all not great at everything—can allow you to avoid pursuing opportunities where you have no competitive advantage. But it can additionally help you to see, and invest in, those areas where you do have the advantage.*

*4. **Don't be afraid to fail.** As we will address in this chapter's "Workplace Confidential," setbacks are not failures. They are failures only if you don't learn from them. Finding your right road often first requires you to run into a few dead-ends.*

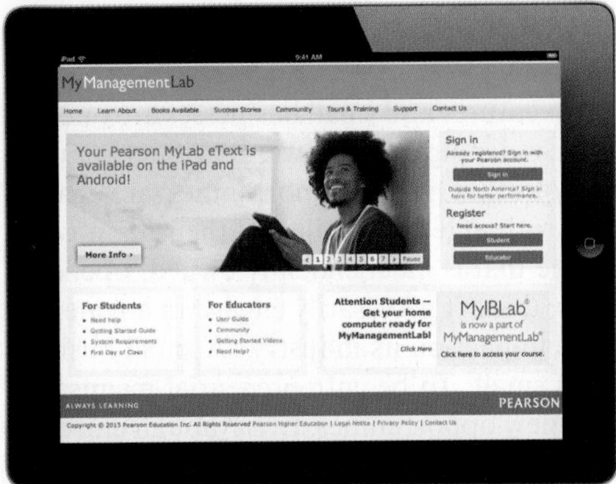

Pearson MyLab Management®

Improve Your Grade!

When you see this icon, visit **www.mymanagementlab.com** for activities that are applied, personalized, and offer immediate feedback.

Learning Objectives

10.1 ***Define*** *entrepreneurship and explain why it's important.*

10.2 ***Explain*** *what entrepreneurs do in the planning process for new ventures.*

- **Know how** to think creatively about solving a common problem.
- **Develop your skill** for writing an executive summary for effectively communicating novel ideas.

10.3 ***Describe*** *the six legal forms of organization and the choice of appropriate organizational structure.*

10.4 ***Describe*** *how entrepreneurs lead organizations.*

10.5 ***Explain*** *how managers control organizations for growth, downturns, and exiting the venture.*

Sarah Tulin is an entrepreneur. She is the cofounder of Oxie Innovations. The company sells a portable air cleaner that is worn under the shirt collar. The product is unique because it uses real-time sensors and an interactive mobile app. Tulin got the idea one day when she found herself in a cloud of bus smoke and decided to find a better alternative to uncomfortable face masks. Her product also effectively reduces asthma sufferers' dependence on expensive medication. *Forbes* has named Tulin as one of its most impressive young entrepreneurs while *Fortune* named her one of the most promising female entrepreneurs of 2015.

THE CONTEXT **of entrepreneurship**

In this chapter, we're going to look at the activities of entrepreneurs like Sarah Tulin. Let's begin by defining *entrepreneurship*.

What Is Entrepreneurship?

Entrepreneurship is the process of starting new businesses, generally in response to opportunities. Entrepreneurs are pursuing opportunities by changing, revolutionizing, transforming, or introducing new products or services. For example, Nanxi Liu, founder of start-up Nanoly Bioscience, recognized the challenges of refrigerating vaccines, which is necessary to maintain potency. Nanoly Bioscience develops and distributes polymers that allow vaccines to be stored without refrigeration. This innovation enables doctors to provide lifesaving vaccinations in developing countries where millions die from preventable diseases.

entrepreneurship
The process of starting new businesses, generally in response to opportunities

Many people think that entrepreneurial ventures and small businesses are one and the same, but they're not. Some key differences distinguish the two. Entrepreneurs create **entrepreneurial ventures**—organizations that pursue opportunities, are characterized by innovative practices, and have growth and profitability as their main goals. On the other hand, a **small business** is one that is independently owned, operated, and financed; has fewer than 100 employees; doesn't necessarily engage in any new or innovative practices; and has relatively little impact on its industry.[1] A small business isn't necessarily entrepreneurial because it's small. To be entrepreneurial means that the business must be innovative, seeking out new opportunities. Even though entrepreneurial ventures may start small, they pursue growth. Some new small firms may grow, but many remain small businesses, by choice or by default.

entrepreneurial ventures
Organizations that pursue opportunities, are characterized by innovative practices, and have growth and profitability as their main goals

small business
An organization that is independently owned, operated, and financed; has fewer than 100 employees; doesn't necessarily engage in any new or innovative practices; and has relatively little impact on its industry

Entrepreneurship Versus Self-Employment?

Many people confuse entrepreneurship with self-employment. Are they the same? The answer is: sometimes. Let's start by defining self-employment.

Self-employment refers to individuals who work for profit or fees in their own business, profession, trade, or farm.[2] This arrangement focuses on established professions such as electricians and insurance agents. For comparison, recall that we described entrepreneurship as the process of capitalizing on opportunities by starting new businesses for the purposes of changing, revolutionizing, transforming, or introducing new products or services. Now let's consider three points of comparison.

self-employment
Individuals who work for profit or fees in their own business, profession, trade, or farm

First, entrepreneurs and self-employed individuals understand market needs. For instance, Mark recognizes demand for house-cleaning services, and he decides to start a business cleaning houses for a fee. There is nothing revolutionary about cleaning houses (though it is a worthy endeavor). Mark is *self-employed*. In contrast, Nanxi Liu is an entrepreneur because she saw an opportunity to make vaccinations available to individuals where refrigeration is not available. Serving market needs provides both Mark and Nanxi the opportunity to provide services or products at a profit.

Second, entrepreneurs may be self-employed or they become employees of the company they have started. As we described earlier, entrepreneur Sarah Tulin turned her portable air purifier idea into Oxie Innovations, where she is the CEO. Self-employed persons always work for themselves. They are not paid employees of another company, and they rely on their own initiative to ensure income generation. Also, self-employed individuals make all the business decisions about how the work gets done. Finally, self-employment does not preclude having one or more employees. For example, Mark's cleaning business took off and he realized he couldn't handle everything himself. So Mark hires two individuals, better enabling him to meet clients' needs.

Third, tax requirements and certain laws require that both entrepreneurs and self-employed individuals create a legally recognized organization. There are several types, which we'll discuss later in the chapter. For instance, Mark may set up a sole proprietorship, while Nanxi's company is registered as a corporation.

Why Is Entrepreneurship Important?

Entrepreneurship is, and continues to be, important to every industry sector in the United States and in most advanced countries.[3] Its importance in the United States can be shown in three areas: innovation, number of new start-ups, and job creation.

INNOVATION Innovating is a process of changing, experimenting, transforming, and revolutionizing, and is a key aspect of entrepreneurial activity. The "creative destruction" process that characterizes innovation leads to technological changes and employment growth. Entrepreneurial firms act as "agents of change" by providing an essential source of new and unique ideas that may otherwise go untapped.[4] Statistics back this up. The National Science Foundation reports that small firms generate nearly three times the number of patents per research and development dollar spent than do large organizations.[5] In addition, small firms produce approximately 30 times more patents per employee than large patenting firms.[6] These statistics are further proof of how important small business is to innovation in America.

NUMBER OF NEW START-UPS Because all businesses—whether they fit the definition of entrepreneurial ventures or not—were new start-ups at one point in time, the most suitable measure we have of the important role of entrepreneurship is to look at the number of new firms over a period of time. Data collected by the U.S. Bureau of Labor Statistics shows that the growth rate of new start-ups has been steady every year since 2005. Estimates for 2014, the latest available data, showed that approximately 200,000 new businesses were created every three months![7]

JOB CREATION We know that job creation is important to the overall long-term economic health of communities, regions, and nations. The latest figures show that small businesses accounted for most of the net new jobs. In fact, over the last 20 years, small businesses have created some 63 percent of the net new jobs.[8] And recent numbers show that 48.9 percent of U.S. workers were employed by small businesses.[9] Small organizations have been creating jobs at a fast pace even as many of the world's largest and well-known global corporations continued to downsize. These numbers reflect the importance of entrepreneurial firms as job creators.

GLOBAL ENTREPRENEURSHIP What about entrepreneurial activity outside the United States? What kind of impact has it had? An annual assessment of global entrepreneurship called the Global Entrepreneurship Monitor (GEM) studies the impact of entrepreneurial activity on economic growth in various countries. The GEM 2015/2016 report covered 60 countries that were divided into three clusters identified by phase of economic development: factor-driven economies, efficiency-driven economies, and innovation-driven economies. What did the researchers find? One of the principal aspects that GEM examines is "total early-stage entrepreneurial activity (TEA)," or the proportion of people who are involved in setting up a business. Generally, as economic development increases, the overall levels of TEA decline. With large variations found in the three different categories, however, it's obvious that countries have unique types of conditions that influence entrepreneurial activity. The GEM report concludes, however, that entrepreneurship is important for economic development.[10]

The Entrepreneurial Process

Entrepreneurs must address four key steps as they start and manage their entrepreneurial ventures.

The first is *exploring the entrepreneurial context.* The context includes the realities of today's economic, political/legal, social, and work environment. It's important to look at each of these aspects of the entrepreneurial context because they determine the "rules" of the game and which decisions and actions are likely to meet with success. Also, it's through exploring the context that entrepreneurs confront the next critically important step in the entrepreneurial process—*identifying opportunities and possible competitive advantages.* We know from our definition of entrepreneurship that the pursuit of opportunities is an important aspect.

Once entrepreneurs have explored the entrepreneurial context and identified opportunities and possible competitive advantages, they must look at the issues involved with actually bringing their entrepreneurial venture to life. Therefore, the next step in the entrepreneurial process is *starting the venture.* Included in this phase are researching the feasibility of the venture, planning the venture, organizing the venture, and launching the venture.

Finally, once the entrepreneurial venture is up and running, the last step in the entrepreneurial process is *managing the venture*, which an entrepreneur does by managing processes, managing people, and managing growth. We can explain these important steps in the entrepreneurial process by looking at what it is that entrepreneurs do.

What Do Entrepreneurs Do?

Describing what entrepreneurs do isn't an easy or simple task! No two entrepreneurs' work activities are exactly alike. In a general sense, entrepreneurs create something new, something different. They search for change, respond to it, and exploit it.

Initially, an entrepreneur is engaged in assessing the potential for the entrepreneurial venture and then dealing with start-up issues. In exploring the entrepreneurial context, entrepreneurs gather information, identify potential opportunities, and pinpoint possible competitive advantage(s). Then, armed with this information, the entrepreneur researches the venture's feasibility—uncovering business ideas, looking at competitors, and exploring financing options.

After looking at the potential of the proposed venture and assessing the likelihood of pursuing it successfully, the entrepreneur proceeds to plan the venture. Planning includes such activities as developing a viable organizational mission, exploring organizational culture issues, and creating a well-thought-out business plan. Once these planning issues have been resolved, the entrepreneur must look at organizing the venture, which involves choosing a legal form of business organization, addressing other legal issues such as patent or copyright searches, and coming up with an appropriate organizational design for structuring how work is going to be done.

A growing number of people consider entrepreneurship an attractive career option:[11]

- 51 percent believe there exist good opportunities for starting a business
- 80 percent who plan to start a business in the next three years are doing something about it (for example, leasing space)

Only after these start-up activities have been completed is the entrepreneur ready to actually launch the venture. Such a launch involves setting goals and strategies, and establishing the technology-operations methods, marketing plans, information systems, financial-accounting systems, and cash flow management systems.

Once the entrepreneurial venture is up and running, the entrepreneur's attention switches to managing it. What's involved with actually managing the entrepreneurial venture? An important activity is managing the various processes that are part of every business: making decisions, establishing action plans, analyzing external and internal environments, measuring and evaluating performance, and making needed changes. Also, the entrepreneur must perform activities associated with managing people, including selecting and hiring, appraising and training, motivating, managing conflict, delegating tasks, and being an effective leader. Finally, the entrepreneur must manage the venture's growth, including such activities as developing and designing growth strategies, dealing with crises, exploring various avenues for financing growth, placing a value on the venture, and perhaps even eventually exiting the venture.

Social Responsibility and Ethics Issues Facing Entrepreneurs

As they launch and manage their ventures, entrepreneurs are faced with the often-difficult issues of social responsibility and ethics. Just how important are these issues to entrepreneurs? An overwhelming majority of respondents (95 percent) in a study of small companies believed that developing a positive reputation and relationship in communities where they do business is important for achieving business goals.[12] However, despite the importance these individuals placed on corporate citizenship, more than half lacked formal programs for connecting with their communities. In fact, some 70 percent of the respondents admitted that they failed to consider community goals in their business plans.

Yet, some entrepreneurs take their social responsibilities seriously. For example, Deane Kirchner, George Wang, and Kiah Williams cofounded SIRUM, which stands for Supporting Initiatives to Redistribute Unused Medicine. The group recognized that unexpired medications worth billions of dollars are discarded while underfunded medical clinics do not have the means to purchase medication for low-income patients. Kirchner and her team use a digital platform for hospitals and clinics to find matches, and SIRUM then ships medication to where it's needed most. "Our goal is to save lives by saving unused medications," says Kirchner. "We thought we could use technology to bridge this gap between surplus and need."[13]

Other entrepreneurs have pursued opportunities with products and services that protect the global environment. For example, PurposeEnergy of Woburn, Massachusetts, developed a technology that removes waste by-products from the beer brewing industry and changes them to renewable natural gas, treated water, and organic fertilizer. Another company, Botl of Toronto, Canada, sells a biodegradable portable water filter. Founder Emily Wilkinson sought to protect the environment by reducing the

WORKPLACE CONFIDENTIAL Dealing with Risks

Former hockey great Wayne Gretzky captured the importance of risk taking when he said, "You miss 100 percent of the shots you never take." His message: You have to risk failure to achieve success.

The easy route in life is to stay the course and not make waves. This typically means making choices that provide predictable outcomes and minimal threats to your known world: staying in the town you grew up in; keeping the same job for your entire career; going to your "regular" vacation spot every year; maintaining constant hobbies and interests; and so on. You might think that by minimizing change, you minimize risk. As you'll see, if you think that's true, there's a good chance you're wrong.

Risk has both positive and negative outcomes. Risk-avoiders tend to emphasize its negative aspects. Risk-seekers focus on the positives. You need to understand when to take risks, when to avoid them, and how to turn risk taking to your advantage.

Let's begin with a brief analysis of risk perception. That is, what shapes your perception of risk? There are four elements you want to consider: uncertainty, gains, losses, and your risk profile. Uncertainty reflects doubt or acknowledging the unknown. As uncertainty increases, decisions become more risky. As such, we try to avoid uncertainty or minimize its influence. We do this by accumulating as much appropriate information as possible. A potential risk outcome is derived by comparing gains and losses. Larger anticipated gains are preferred over smaller gains and smaller potential losses to larger losses. Riskiness increases as possible returns become smaller or potential losses appear larger. You want to take on risks where the potential gains exceed potential losses—and the larger the gain, the better. So you have to answer the question: Is it worth the risk? Finally, you need to take into consideration your risk profile. What's your risk tolerance? People differ in their willingness to take chances. Low-risk-seekers are likely to identify, value, and choose decision options that have low chances for failure. Right or wrong, that often means choosing alternatives that contain minimal change from the status quo. High-risk-takers, on the other hand, are more likely to identify, value, and choose alternatives that are unique and that have a greater chance of failing.

Now let's turn our attention to the positive aspects of risk. There are few truisms in life, but one is, with the exception of those lucky enough to be born into wealth, you can't achieve success in this world without taking risks. Oprah Winfrey, Jeff Bezos, Dustin Hoffman, Bill Clinton, Ray Kroc, Dolly Parton, Steve Jobs, I.M. Pei—they all took risks. They quit a job, they moved to a new city, they started a business, they ran for political office. They did something that made them vulnerable and exposed themselves to rejection and failure. We're not proposing here that risk taking guarantees success. Clearly, it doesn't. What we are saying is that it's hard to become successful without giving up some security and taking a chance.

As we noted, we all don't have the same tolerance for risk. If you see yourself as a risk taker, your concern should be focused on keeping your risk taking under control. You want to take calculated risks and avoid throwing caution to the wind. For those of you who tend to be risk-averse, the following should be relevant.

If you tend to be risk averse, remind yourself that it's easier to take risks while you're young. Setbacks and failures are much easier to recover from when you're 25 than when you're 55. In fact, in comparing risk-taking propensity among people between ages 22 and 58, it was found that both risk taking and the value placed upon risk was negatively related to age. That is, as we get older, we tend to become more conservative toward assuming risk. This is probably because older individuals perceive themselves as having more to lose. So leverage your "youth and inexperience." If you're going to quit a job or start a business, consider doing it sooner rather than later. It's easier to accept a setback when you're young and you're more likely to become risk averse as you get older.

For those who fear failure, you need to be reminded that setbacks are not fatal. The landscape is littered with people who confronted early failure but rebounded to phenomenal success. Walt Disney was fired from the Kansas City Star because his editor felt he "lacked imagination and had no good ideas." Oprah Winfrey was fired from her first television job in Baltimore for getting "too emotionally invested in her stories." Sam Walton failed in his early attempts at retailing but eventually hit it big with Walmart. A film executive made the following assessment at seeing one of Fred Astaire's first screen tests: "can't sing; can't act; slightly balding; can dance a little." Theodor Geisel, aka Dr. Seuss, had his first book rejected by 27 different publishers. And Steven Spielberg was rejected multiple times by the University of Southern California School of Cinematic Arts.

Nothing in our discussion should be interpreted as promoting unrestrained risk taking. Risk taking needs to be undertaken thoughtfully, intelligently, selectively, and with careful consideration of probabilities. Options with minimal chance of success, regardless of payoffs, are gambles and should be avoided. However, you don't want to miss opportunities with good chances of success just because they have potential for failure.

Sources: Based on V. H. Vroom and B. Pahl, "Relationship Between Age and Risk Taking Among Managers," *Journal of Applied Psychology*, October 1971, pp. 399–405; J. G. March and Z. Shapira, "Managerial Perspectives on Risk and Risk-Taking," *Management Science*, November 1987, pp. 1404–1418; and J. F. Yates and E. R. Stone, "The Risk Construct," in *Risk-Taking Behavior*, ed. J. F. Yates (Chichester, UK: Wiley, 1992), pp. 1–25.

amount of plastic waste going into landfills. Rather than using and disposing one plastic container of filtered bottled water after another, consumers can quickly filter tap water by dropping the filter in any container filled with tap water and then shaking it.

Ethical considerations also play a role in decisions and actions of entrepreneurs. Entrepreneurs do need to be aware of the ethical consequences of what they do. The example they set—particularly for other employees—can be profoundly significant in influencing behavior.

If ethics are important, how do entrepreneurs stack up? Unfortunately, not well! In a survey of employees from different sizes of businesses who were asked if they thought their organization was highly ethical, 20 percent of employees at companies with 99 or fewer employees disagreed.[14]

FUTURE VISION The Growth of Social Businesses

Tomorrow's new business is more likely to get its start from a desire to do good in the world than a desire to make big money.[15] We learned about social entrepreneurs in Chapter 5 and know that they start ventures that make the world a better place. We are going to see more of them, and a growing number will seek to be financially sustainable by incorporating a for-profit business model. In the last 10 years we have seen a growth in businesses that are focused on both profit and purpose, and the trend is expected to continue. Rather than separating revenue-generating and philanthropy, many start-ups are integrating them and finding that they can generate greater impact and sustain the business longer.

For example, Blake Mycoskie, founder of TOMS shoes (Case Application 1 in Chapter 5) wanted to help children in Argentina who needed shoes. He could have started a not-for-profit organization to raise money to purchase shoes, but instead, he started a for-profit business that donates a pair of shoes for every pair purchased. The result? A sustainable business model that has donated more than 50 million pairs of shoes in just 10 years, far more than the few hundred pairs of shoes his initial investment in the company would have provided.

In addition to the fact that it works financially, the growth in social businesses is expected because future entrepreneurs—the millennial generation—are not motivated by profit alone. Why do they have interest in making social change? Some suggest that their access to the Internet growing up has led to an increased awareness of global issues and social concerns. They have connected themselves to world problems such as poverty, gender inequity, climate change, and terrorism. Another view is that they were raised to question consumerism and believe they can make change in the world. Pursuing profit while focusing on a social purpose may be the way future entrepreneurs will be able to make that change.

If your professor has chosen to assign this, go to ***www.mymanagementlab.com*** *to discuss the following questions.*

TALK ABOUT IT 1: How can a social entrepreneur decide if they should make their venture a for-profit or not-for-profit business?

TALK ABOUT IT 2: Do you think consumers are skeptical of for-profit businesses that claim to have a social cause as a mission?

START-UP and planning issues

LO10.2 Although pouring a bowl of cereal may seem like a simple task, even the most awake and alert morning person has probably ended up with cereal on the floor. Philippe Meert, a product designer based in Erpe-Mere, Belgium, has come up with a better way. Meert sensed an opportunity to correct the innate design flaw of cereal boxes and developed the Cerealtop, a plastic cover that snaps onto a cereal box and channels the cereal into a bowl.[16]

The first thing that entrepreneurs like Philippe Meert must do is to identify opportunities and possible competitive advantages. Once they've identified the opportunities, they're ready to start the venture by researching its feasibility and then planning for its launch. These start-up and planning issues are what we're going to look at in this section.

Identifying Environmental Opportunities and Competitive Advantage

How important is the ability to identify environmental opportunities? Consider the following: More than 4 million baby boomers turn 50 every year. Almost 8,000 turned 60 each day starting in 2006. More than 57.5 million baby boomers are projected to be alive in 2030, which would put them between the ages of 66 and 84. J. Raymond Elliott, CEO of Zimmer Holdings, is well aware of that demographic trend. Why? His company, which makes orthopedic products, including reconstructive implants for hips, knees, shoulders, and elbows, sees definite marketing opportunities.[18]

In 1994, when Jeff Bezos first saw that Internet usage was increasing by 2,300 percent a month, he knew that something dramatic was happening. "I hadn't seen growth that fast outside of a Petri dish," he said. Bezos was determined to be a part of it. He quit his successful career as a stock market researcher and hedge fund manager on Wall Street and pursued his vision for online retailing, now the Amazon.com website.[19]

What would you have done had you seen that type of number somewhere? Ignored it? Written it off as a fluke? The skyrocketing Internet usage that Bezos observed and the recognition of the Baby Boomer demographic by Elliott's Zimmer Holdings are prime examples of identifying environmental opportunities. Remember the discussion in Chapter 9 that described how opportunities are positive trends in external environmental factors. These trends provide unique and distinct possibilities for innovating and creating value. Entrepreneurs need to be able to pinpoint these pockets of opportunities that a changing context provides. After all, "organizations do not see opportunities, individuals do."[20] And they need to do so quickly, especially in dynamic environments, before those opportunities disappear or are exploited by others.[21]

The late Peter Drucker, a well-known management author, identified seven potential sources of opportunity that entrepreneurs might look for in the external context.[22] These include the unexpected, the incongruous, the process need, industry and market structures, demographics, changes in perception, and new knowledge.

- 43.5 percent of Americans saw an opportunity to start a business last year.
- 55.9 percent of Americans thought they were capable of launching a company.
- 8.9 percent of Americans took material steps to start a business.[17]

1. *The unexpected.* When situations and events are unanticipated, opportunities can be found. The event may be an unexpected success (positive news) or an unexpected failure (bad news). Either way, it may present opportunities for entrepreneurs to pursue. For instance, Sony cofounder Masaru Ibuka wanted to listen to music while on long international flights, but portable music players did not exist at the time.[23] In 1979, he asked engineers to develop a portable device for personal use. Ibuka was impressed with the results, which led him to present the device to Sony Chairman Akio Morita. It's believed that Ibuka said, "Try this. Don't you think a stereo cassette player that you can listen to while walking around is a good idea?"[24] At the time, there were doubts that anyone would want to listen to music while walking. Despite these reservations, the unexpected interest in portable music players proved to be an opportunity giving way to the highly successful Sony Walkman.
2. *The incongruous.* When something is incongruous, it exhibits inconsistencies and incompatibilities in the way it appears. Things "ought to be" a certain way, but aren't. When conventional wisdom about the way things should be no longer holds true, for whatever reason, opportunities are present. Entrepreneurs who are willing to "think outside the box"—that is, to think beyond the traditional and conventional approaches—may find pockets of potential profitability. Herb Kelleher, founder and president of Southwest Airlines, recognized incongruities in the way that commercial airlines catered to the traveling public. Most airlines focused on providing full service, including meals, to business travelers on routes between large business hubs. Ticket prices were high, but business

The unexpected interest in portable music players presented an opportunity that Sony cofounders Akio Morita (shown here) and Masaru Ibuka pursued and developed into the Sony Walkman. By allowing people to listen to music wherever and whenever they wanted, the Walkman became one of the company's most successful brands.
Source: Neal Ulevich/AP Photo

travelers could absorb the cost. Although this approach was profitable, it ignored the opportunity to serve leisure travelers who wanted to travel between smaller cities (not business hubs). Kelleher knew that a better way was possible. His company offered lower fares with no-frill service.[25] Southwest Airlines has been profitable ever since. Another example of how the incongruous can be a potential source of entrepreneurial opportunity is Fred Smith, founder of FedEx, who recognized in the early 1970s the inefficiencies in the delivery of packages and documents. His approach was: Who says that overnight delivery isn't possible? Smith's recognition of the incongruous led to the creation of FedEx, now a multibillion-dollar corporation.

3. *The process need.* What happens when technology doesn't immediately come up with the "big discovery" that's going to fundamentally change the nature of some product or service? What happens is the emergence of pockets of entrepreneurial opportunity in the various stages of the process as researchers and technicians continue to work for the monumental breakthrough. Because the full leap hasn't been possible, opportunities abound in the tiny steps. Take the medical products industry, for example. Although researchers haven't yet discovered a cure for cancer, many successful entrepreneurial biotechnology ventures have been created as knowledge about a possible cure continues to grow. Some process needs are more easily addressed. Decades ago, a variety of inventors developed technology that led to the creation of ATMs in the late 1960s.[26] As customers became more comfortable with self-service banking, ATMs became ubiquitous. Later, the Internet gave way to full-service, online banking.
4. *Industry and market structures.* When changes in technology change the structure of an industry and market, existing firms can become obsolete if they're not attuned to the changes or are unwilling to change. Even changes in social values and consumer tastes can shift the structures of industries and markets. These markets and industries become open targets for nimble and smart entrepreneurs. For instance, while working part-time at an auto body shop while finishing his engineering graduate degree, Joe Born wondered if the industrial paint buffer used to smooth out a car's paint job could be used to smooth out scratches on CDs. He tried it out on his favorite Clint Black CD that had been ruined, and the newly polished CD played flawlessly. After this experience, Born spent almost four years perfecting his disc repair kit invention, the SkipDr.[27] The arena of the Internet provides several good examples of existing industries and markets being challenged by upstart entrepreneurial ventures. For instance, eBay has prospered as an online intermediary between buyers and sellers. eBay's CEO says that the company's job is connecting people, not selling them things. And connect them, they do! The online auction firm has more than 160 million active users.[28]
5. *Demographics.* The characteristics of the world population are changing. These changes influence industries and markets by altering the types and quantities of products and services desired and customers' buying power. Although many of these changes are fairly predictable if you stay alert to demographic trends, others aren't as obvious. Either way, significant entrepreneurial opportunities can be realized by anticipating and meeting the changing needs of the population. For example, WebMD has been successful partly because it anticipated the needs of the aging population. WebMD publishes news and information about human health and well-being for health care providers and consumers. Pharmaceutical companies also recognize the importance of demographic trends, which has led to substantial advertising on WebMD.[29]
6. *Changes in perception.* Perception is one's view of reality. When changes in perception take place, the facts do not vary, but their meanings do. Changes in perception get at the heart of people's psychographic profiles—what they value, what they believe in, and what they care about. Changes in these attitudes and values create potential market opportunities for alert entrepreneurs. For example, think about your perception of healthy foods. Changes in our perception of whether certain food groups are good has brought about product and service opportunities for entrepreneurs to recognize and capture. For instance, John

Mackey started Whole Foods Market in Austin, Texas, as a place for customers to purchase food and other items free of pesticides, preservatives, sweeteners, and cruelty. Now, as the world's number one natural foods chain, Mackey's entrepreneurial venture consists of about 275 stores in the United States, Canada, and the United Kingdom.[30] Airbnb cofounders Brian Chesky, Nathan Blecharczyk, and Joe Gebbia changed the perception that short-term home and apartment rentals to strangers is a bad idea. Brian Chesky said "It's about people and experiences. At the end of the day, what we're trying to do is bring the world together. You're not getting a room, you're getting a sense of belonging."[31] In a few short years, the company began generating billions of dollars in revenue.

7. *New knowledge.* New knowledge is a significant source of entrepreneurial opportunity. Although not all knowledge-based innovations are significant, new knowledge ranks pretty high on the list of sources of entrepreneurial opportunity! It takes more than just having new knowledge, though. Entrepreneurs must be able to do something with that knowledge and to protect important proprietary information from competitors. For example, French scientists are using new knowledge about textiles to develop a wide array of innovative products to keep wearers healthy and smelling good. Neyret, the Parisian lingerie maker, created lingerie products woven with tiny perfume microcapsules that stay in the fabric through about ten washings. Another French company, Francital, developed a fabric treated with chemicals to absorb perspiration and odors.[32]

Being alert to entrepreneurial opportunities is only part of an entrepreneur's initial efforts. He or she must also understand competitive advantage. As we discussed in Chapter 9, when an organization has a competitive advantage, it has something that other competitors don't; does something better than other organizations; or does something that others can't. Competitive advantage is a necessary ingredient for an entrepreneurial venture's long-term success and survival. Getting and keeping a competitive advantage is tough. However, it is something that entrepreneurs must consider as they begin researching the venture's feasibility.

Where entrepreneurs said their idea for a business came from:[34]

- 34.3 percent said sudden insight/chance
- 23.5 percent said following a passion
- 11.8 percent said a suggestion or collaboration
- 11.8 percent said somebody else's product or service
- 10.8 percent said market research
- 7.8 percent said "other"

Researching the Venture's Feasibility—Ideas

On a trip to New York, Miho Inagi got her first taste of the city's delicious bagels. After her palate-expanding experience, she had the idea of bringing bagels to Japan. Five years after her first trip to New York and a subsequent apprenticeship at a New York bagel business, Miho opened Maruichi Bagel in Tokyo. After a struggle to get the store up and running, it now has a loyal following of customers.[33]

It's important for entrepreneurs to research the venture's feasibility by generating and evaluating business ideas. Entrepreneurial ventures thrive on ideas. Generating ideas is an innovative, creative process. It's also one that will take time, not only in the beginning stages of the entrepreneurial venture, but throughout the life of the business. Where do ideas come from?

Dissatisfaction with current mops on the market that were difficult to rinse and ineffective in absorbing messes was the source of Joy Mangano's entrepreneurial venture. To make mopping floors easier and more effective, Mangano developed Miracle Mop, a durable cotton product with an easy-to-use wringing mechanism.
Source: John Lamparski/WireImage/Getty Images

GENERATING IDEAS As this data shows, entrepreneurs cite unique and varied sources for their ideas. Another survey found that "working in the same industry" was the major source of ideas for an entrepreneurial venture (60 percent of respondents).[35] Other sources cited in this survey included personal interests or hobbies, looking at familiar and unfamiliar products and services, and opportunities in external environmental sectors (technological, sociocultural, demographics, economic, or legal-political).

What should entrepreneurs look for as they explore these idea sources? They should look for limitations of what's currently available, new and different approaches, advances and breakthroughs, unfilled niches, or trends and changes. For example, Joy

let's get REAL

The Scenario:

Nick Rossi is excited to start working on his business plan to pursue his dream of opening a music store. He plans to sell mostly guitars, but thinks he should also sell some percussion instruments and a wide variety of accessories. However, he still has some research to do on the feasibility of his ideas. His competition is one area that he needs to explore further.

Whitney Portman
Senior Marketing Communications Manager

What should Nick learn about his competitors?

Learning about your competitive set is a key component to the success of your business plan. First, start with researching direct competitors, then expand to indirect competitors, either in close geographical proximity or online. How long have they been in business? What did they start out selling and how have they expanded? What's been the biggest contributors to their success and failures? You can learn a lot from those that have come before you. Then you should also consider future competitors: Are there any innovations on the horizon that would threaten your business plan? How can you safeguard against them? The goal is to determine where the unmet need is in the marketplace. What are customers looking for that the current competitive landscape does not offer? Once you can answer that question, you've identified your opportunity.

Mangano, creator of the Miracle Mop, wanted to make mopping floors easier. She came up with the idea of a loop construction of the mop head fibers and a twisting wringing mechanism to keep hands out of the dirty water. The Miracle Mop became an instant success, selling more than 18,000 units in less than 30 minutes when introduced on TV shopping network QVC.[36]

EVALUATING IDEAS Evaluating entrepreneurial ideas revolves around personal and marketplace considerations. Each of these assessments will provide an entrepreneur with key information about the idea's potential. Exhibit 10-1 describes some questions that entrepreneurs might ask as they evaluate potential ideas.

Exhibit 10-1
Evaluating Potential Ideas

Personal Considerations	Marketplace Considerations
• Do you have the capabilities to do what you've selected? • Are you ready to be an entrepreneur? • Are you prepared emotionally to deal with the stresses and challenges of being an entrepreneur? • Are you prepared to deal with rejection and failure? • Are you ready to work hard? • Do you have a realistic picture of the venture's potential? • Have you educated yourself about financing issues? • Are you willing and prepared to do continual financial and other types of analyses?	• Who are the potential customers for your idea: who, where, how many? • What similar or unique product features does your proposed idea have compared to what's currently on the market? • How and where will potential customers purchase your product? • Have you considered pricing issues and whether the price you'll be able to charge will allow your venture to survive and prosper? • Have you considered how you will need to promote and advertise your proposed entrepreneurial venture?

Exhibit 10-2
Feasibility Study

A. Introduction, historical background, description of product or service
1. Brief description of proposed entrepreneurial venture
2. Brief history of the industry
3. Information about the economy and important trends
4. Current status of the product or service
5. How you intend to produce the product or service
6. Complete list of goods or services to be provided
7. Strengths and weaknesses of the business
8. Ease of entry into the industry, including competitor analysis

B. Accounting considerations
1. Pro forma balance sheet
2. Pro forma profit and loss statement
3. Projected cash flow analysis

C. Management considerations
1. Personal expertise—strengths and weaknesses
2. Proposed organizational design
3. Potential staffing requirements
4. Inventory management methods
5. Production and operations management issues
6. Equipment needs

D. Marketing considerations
1. Detailed product description
2. Identify target market (who, where, how many)
3. Describe place product will be distributed (location, traffic, size, channels, etc.)
4. Price determination (competition, price lists, etc.)
5. Promotion plans (role of personal selling, advertising, sales promotion, etc.)

E. Financial considerations
1. Start-up costs
2. Working capital requirements
3. Equity requirements
4. Loans—amounts, type, conditions
5. Breakeven analysis
6. Collateral
7. Credit references
8. Equipment and building financing—costs and methods

F. Legal considerations
1. Proposed business structure (type; conditions, terms, liability, responsibility; insurance needs; buyout and succession issues)
2. Contracts, licenses, and other legal documents

G. Tax considerations: sales/property/employee; federal, state, and local

H. Appendix: charts/graphs, diagrams, layouts, résumés, etc.

A more structured evaluation approach that an entrepreneur might want to use is a **feasibility study**—an analysis of the various aspects of a proposed entrepreneurial venture designed to determine its feasibility. Not only is a well-prepared feasibility study an effective evaluation tool to determine whether an entrepreneurial idea is a potentially successful one, it also can serve as a basis for the all-important business plan.

feasibility study
An analysis of the various aspects of a proposed entrepreneurial venture designed to determine its feasibility

A feasibility study should give descriptions of the most important elements of the entrepreneurial venture and the entrepreneur's analysis of the viability of these elements. Exhibit 10-2 provides an outline of a possible approach to a feasibility study. Yes, it covers a lot of territory and takes a significant amount of time, energy, and effort to prepare it. However, an entrepreneur's potential future success is worth that investment.

Researching the Venture's Feasibility—Competitors

Part of researching the venture's feasibility is looking at the competitors. What would entrepreneurs like to know about their potential competitors? Here are some possible questions:

What types of products or services are competitors offering?
What are the major characteristics of these products or services?
What are their products' strengths and weaknesses?
How do they handle marketing, pricing, and distribution?
What do they attempt to do differently from other competitors?
Do they appear to be successful at it? Why or why not?
What are they good at?
What competitive advantage(s) do they appear to have?
What are they not so good at?
What competitive disadvantage(s) do they appear to have?
How large and profitable are these competitors?

For instance, the CEO of The Children's Place carefully examined the competition as he took his chain of children's clothing stores nationwide. Although he faces stiff competition from the likes of GapKids, JCPenney, and Gymboree, he feels that his company's approach to manufacturing and marketing will give it a competitive edge.[37]

Once an entrepreneur has this information, he or she should assess how the proposed entrepreneurial venture is going to "fit" into this competitive arena. Will the entrepreneurial venture be able to compete successfully? This type of competitor analysis becomes an important part of the feasibility study and the business plan. If, after all this analysis, the situation looks promising, the final part of researching the venture's feasibility is to look at the various financing options. This step isn't the final determination of how much funding the venture will need or where this funding will come from but is simply gathering information about various financing alternatives.

Researching the Venture's Feasibility—Financing

Getting financing isn't always easy. For instance, Matthew Griffin, cofounder of Baker's Edge, funded his company with personal savings and a business line of credit. Griffin recalls: "What we experienced is that outside investment takes notice only after you have considerable traction. Ironically, we only had offers after we didn't need the start-up money."[38]

Because funds likely will be needed to start the venture, an entrepreneur must research the various financing options. Possible financing options available to entrepreneurs are shown in Exhibit 10-3.

If your professor has assigned this, go to **www.mymanagementlab.com** to complete the Simulation: *Entrepreneurship*.

Exhibit 10-3
Possible Financing Options

- Entrepreneur's personal resources (personal savings, home equity, personal loans, credit cards, etc.)
- Financial institutions (banks, savings and loan institutions, government-guaranteed loan, credit unions, etc.)
- **Venture capitalists**—external equity financing provided by professionally managed pools of investor money
- **Angel investors**—a private investor (or group of private investors) who offers financial backing to an entrepreneurial venture in return for equity in the venture
- **Initial public offering (IPO)**—the first public registration and sale of a company's stock
- National, state, and local governmental business development programs
- Unusual sources (television shows, judged competitions, crowdfunding, etc.)

venture capitalists
External equity financing provided by professionally managed pools of investor money

angel investors
A private investor (or group of private investors) who offers financial backing to an entrepreneurial venture in return for equity in the venture

initial public offering (IPO)
The first public registration and sale of a company's stock

Developing a Business Plan

Planning is also important to entrepreneurial ventures. Once the venture's feasibility has been thoroughly researched, the entrepreneur then must look at planning the venture. The most important thing that an entrepreneur does in planning the venture is developing a **business plan**—a written document that summarizes a business opportunity and defines and articulates how the identified opportunity is to be seized and exploited.

business plan
A written document that summarizes a business opportunity and defines and articulates how the identified opportunity is to be seized and exploited

For many would-be entrepreneurs, developing and writing a business plan seems like a daunting task. However, a good business plan is valuable. It pulls together all of the elements of the entrepreneur's vision into a single coherent document. The business plan requires careful planning and creative thinking. But if done well, it can be a convincing document that serves many functions. It serves as a blueprint and road map for operating the business. And the business plan is a "living" document, guiding organizational decisions and actions throughout the life of the business, not just in the start-up stage.

If an entrepreneur has completed a feasibility study, much of the information included in it becomes the basis for the business plan. A good business plan covers six major areas: executive summary, analysis of opportunity, analysis of the context, description of the business, financial data and projections, and supporting documentation.

EXECUTIVE SUMMARY The executive summary summarizes the key points that the entrepreneur wants to make about the proposed entrepreneurial venture. These points might include a brief mission statement; primary goals; brief history of the entrepreneurial venture, maybe in the form of a timeline; key people involved in the venture; nature of the business; concise product or service descriptions; brief explanations of market niche, competitors, and competitive advantage; proposed strategies; and selected key financial information.

ANALYSIS OF OPPORTUNITY In this section of the business plan, an entrepreneur presents the details of the perceived opportunity. Essentially, details include (1) sizing up the market by describing the demographics of the target market, (2) describing and evaluating industry trends, and (3) identifying and evaluating competitors.

ANALYSIS OF THE CONTEXT Whereas the opportunity analysis focuses on the opportunity in a specific industry and market, the context analysis takes a much broader perspective. Here, the entrepreneur describes the broad external changes and trends taking place in the economic, political-legal, technological, and global environments.

DESCRIPTION OF THE BUSINESS In this section, an entrepreneur describes how the entrepreneurial venture is going to be organized, launched, and managed. It includes a thorough description of the mission statement; a description of the desired organizational culture; marketing plans including overall marketing strategy, pricing, sales tactics, service-warranty policies, and advertising and promotion tactics; product development plans such as an explanation of development status, tasks, difficulties and risks, and anticipated costs; operational plans including a description of proposed geographic location, facilities and needed improvements, equipment, and work flow; human resource plans including a description of key management persons, composition of board of directors, including their background experience and skills, current and future staffing needs, compensation and benefits, and training needs; and an overall schedule and timetable of events.

FINANCIAL DATA AND PROJECTIONS Every effective business plan contains financial data and projections. Although the calculations and interpretation may be difficult, they are absolutely critical. No business plan is complete without financial information. Financial plans should cover at least three years and contain projected income statements, pro forma cash flow analysis (monthly for the first year and quarterly for the next two), pro forma balance sheets, breakeven analysis, and cost controls. If major equipment or other capital purchases are expected, the items, costs, and available collateral should be listed. All financial projections and analyses should include explanatory notes, especially where the data seem contradictory or questionable.

SUPPORTING DOCUMENTATION For this important component of an effective business plan, the entrepreneur should back up his or her descriptions with charts, graphs, tables, photographs, or other visual tools. In addition, it might be important to include information (personal and work-related) about the key participants in the entrepreneurial venture.

Just as the idea for an entrepreneurial venture takes time to germinate, so does the writing of a good business plan. It's important for the entrepreneur to put serious thought and consideration into the plan. It's not an easy thing to do. However, the resulting document should be valuable to the entrepreneur in current and future planning efforts.

The Sharing Economy

Have you ever wanted the companionship of a dog, but because you don't have the time or money to keep one, you "rent" one every weekend? Have you ever rented someone else's bike? Answering yes to either question probably means that you have participated in the sharing economy.

sharing economy
Business arrangements that are based on people sharing something they own or providing a service for a fee

The **sharing economy** refers to business arrangements that are based on people sharing something they own or providing a service for a fee. Airbnb (described earlier in the chapter), Bark'N'Borrow, TaskRabbit, and Liquidity are examples of businesses that operate in the sharing economy. You can say that many of those businesses are

let's get REAL

Source: Matt O'Rourke

Matt O'Rourke
Supply Chain Engineer

The Scenario:

Isabella Sanchez is excited about her idea for a new business on campus. She wants to start a car-sharing business where students who own cars can connect with students who are willing to pay a fee to borrow the car. She came up with the idea after a friend who just was hired for an internship asked her if she knew anyone with a car that he could borrow to get to his new job. Isabella knows many students who have cars who don't need them every day and could also use a little extra money. Her business idea is to make the matches and make money by charging a small percentage of the "rental" fee. It seems like it would work, but she isn't sure if it can make enough money to make it worth her time.

How can Isabella evaluate the feasibility of her idea?

An important first step would be to gauge her idea through market research. How many students are looking to rent cars, and how often? Are the students with cars willing to rent them out on an as-needed basis? A business won't be successful without a solid group of customers. She could also consider conducting a trial of the new service with a small team of people. This would help her gain valuable insight and feedback to understand the feasibility and potential success of her idea.

entrepreneurial ventures because they offer consumers desirable alternatives to conventional options. For instance, Bark'N'Borrow has an app that enables pet lovers to share their dogs with other animal lovers.[39] Liquidity is a bike-sharing service. While some of these businesses are recent start-ups (Bark'N'Borrow), established businesses (Airbnb) are thriving. In Airbnb's case, many people prefer to rent a room in a stranger's house because it is a less expensive alternative to staying in a hotel.

If your professor has assigned this, go to **www.mymanagementlab.com** to watch a video titled: *Our Labor of Love* and to respond to questions.

★ Watch It 1!

ORGANIZING **issues**

LO10.3 Roy Ng, chief operating officer of Twilio in San Francisco, California, redesigned his organization's structure by transforming it into an employee-empowered company. He wanted to drive authority down through the organization so employees were responsible for their own efforts. One way he did this was by creating employee teams to handle specific projects. He says, "Small teams allow for autonomy, rapid experimentation and innovation. Small teams have enabled Twilio's ability to grow and scale, and at the same time maintain the same level of passion, hunger, resourcefulness and productivity our founding team had on day one."[40]

Once the start-up and planning issues for the entrepreneurial venture have been addressed, the entrepreneur is ready to begin organizing the entrepreneurial venture. Then, the entrepreneur must address five organizing issues: the legal forms of organization, organizational design and structure, human resource management, stimulating and making changes, and the continuing importance of innovation.

Legal Forms of Organization

The first organizing decision that an entrepreneur must make is a critical one. It's the form of legal ownership for the venture. The two primary factors affecting this decision are taxes and legal liability. An entrepreneur wants to minimize the impact of both of these factors. The right choice can protect the entrepreneur from legal liability as well as save tax dollars, in both the short run and the long run.

What alternatives are available? The three basic ways to organize an entrepreneurial venture are sole proprietorship, partnership, and corporation. However, when you include the variations of these basic organizational alternatives, you end up with six possible choices, each with its own tax consequences, liability issues, and pros and cons. These six choices are sole proprietorship, general partnership, limited liability partnership (LLP), C corporation, S corporation, and limited liability company (LLC). Let's briefly look at each one with their advantages and drawbacks. (Exhibit 10-4 summarizes the basic information about each organizational alternative.)

SOLE PROPRIETORSHIP A **sole proprietorship** is a form of legal organization in which the owner maintains sole and complete control over the business and is personally liable for business debts. The legal requirements for establishing a sole proprietorship consist of obtaining the necessary local business licenses and permits. In a sole proprietorship, income and losses "pass through" to the owner and are taxed at the owner's personal income tax rate. The biggest drawback, however, is the unlimited personal liability for any and all debts of the business.

sole proprietorship
A form of legal organization in which the owner maintains sole and complete control over the business and is personally liable for business debts

GENERAL PARTNERSHIP A **general partnership** is a form of legal organization in which two or more business owners share the management and risk of the business. Even though a partnership is possible without a written agreement, the potential and inevitable problems that arise in any partnership make a written partnership agreement drafted by legal counsel a highly recommended thing to do.

general partnership
A form of legal organization in which two or more business owners share the management and risk of the business

Exhibit 10-4

Legal Forms of Business Organization

Structure	Ownership Requirements	Tax Treatment	Liability	Advantages	Drawbacks
Sole proprietorship	One owner	Income and losses "pass through" to owner and are taxed at personal rate	Unlimited personal liability	*Low start-up costs* Freedom from most regulations *Owner has direct control* All profits go to owner *Easy to exit business*	Unlimited personal liability *Personal finances at risk* Miss out on many business tax deductions *Total responsibility* May be more difficult to raise financing
General partnership	Two or more owners	Income and losses "pass through" to partners and are taxed at personal rate; *flexibility in profit-loss allocations to partners*	Unlimited personal liability	*Ease of formation* Pooled talent *Pooled resources* Somewhat easier access to financing *Some tax benefits*	*Unlimited personal liability* Divided authority and decisions *Potential for conflict* Continuity of transfer of ownership
Limited liability partnership (LLP)	Two or more owners	Income and losses "pass through" to partner and are taxed at personal rate; *flexibility in profit-loss allocations to partners*	Limited, although one partner must retain unlimited liability	Good way to acquire capital from limited partners	*Cost and complexity of forming can be high* Limited partners cannot participate in management of business without losing liability protection
C corporation	Unlimited number of shareholders; *no limits on types of stock or voting arrangements*	Dividend income is taxed at corporate and personal shareholder levels; *losses and deductions are corporate*	Limited	*Limited liability* Transferable ownership *Continuous existence* Easier access to resources	*Expensive to set up* Closely regulated *Double taxation* Extensive record keeping *Charter restrictions*
S corporation	Up to 75 shareholders; *no limits on types of stock or voting arrangements*	Income and losses "pass through" to partners and are taxed at personal rate; *flexibility in profit-loss allocation to partners*	Limited	*Easy to set up* Enjoy limited liability protection and tax benefits of partnership *Can have a tax-exempt entity as a shareholder*	Must meet certain requirements *May limit future financing options*
Limited liability company (LLC)	Unlimited number of "members"; *flexible membership arrangements for voting rights and income*	Income and losses "pass through" to partners and are taxed at personal rate; *flexibility in profit-loss allocations to partners*	Limited	Greater flexibility Not constrained by regulations on C and S corporations *Taxed as partnership, not as corporation*	Cost of switching from one form to this can be high *Need legal and financial advice in forming operating agreement*

LIMITED LIABILITY PARTNERSHIP (LLP) The **limited liability partnership (LLP)** is a legal organization formed by general partner(s) and limited partner(s). The general partners actually operate and manage the business. They are the ones who have unlimited liability. At least one general partner is necessary in an LLP, but any number of limited partners are allowed. These partners are usually passive investors, although they can make management suggestions to the general partners. They also have the right to inspect the business and make copies of business records. The limited partners are entitled to a share of the business's profits as agreed to in the partnership agreement, and their risk is limited to the amount of their investment in the LLP.

limited liability partnership (LLP)
A form of legal organization consisting of general partner(s) and limited liability partner(s)

C CORPORATION Of the three basic types of ownership, the corporation (also known as a C corporation) is the most complex to form and operate. A **corporation** is a legal business entity that is separate from its owners and managers. Many entrepreneurial ventures are organized as a **closely held corporation**, which, very simply, is a corporation owned by a limited number of people who do not trade the stock publicly. Whereas the sole proprietorship and partnership forms of organization do not exist separately from the entrepreneur, the corporation does. The corporation functions as a distinct legal entity and, as such, can make contracts, engage in business activities, own property, sue and be sued, and of course, pay taxes. A corporation must operate in accordance with its charter and the laws of the state in which it operates.

corporation
A legal business entity that is separate from its owners and managers

closely held corporation
A corporation owned by a limited number of people who do not trade the stock publicly

S CORPORATION The **S corporation** (also called a subchapter S corporation) is a specialized type of corporation that has the regular characteristics of a corporation but is unique in that the owners are taxed as a partnership as long as certain criteria are met. The S corporation has been the classic organizing approach for getting the limited liability of a corporate structure without incurring corporate tax. However, this form of legal organization must meet strict criteria. If any of these criteria are violated, a venture's S status is automatically terminated.

S corporation
A specialized type of corporation that has the regular characteristics of a C corporation but is unique in that the owners are taxed as a partnership as long as certain criteria are met

LIMITED LIABILITY COMPANY (LLC) The **limited liability company (LLC)** is a relatively new form of business organization that's a hybrid between a partnership and a corporation. The LLC offers the liability protection of a corporation, the tax benefits of a partnership, and fewer restrictions than an S corporation. However, the main drawback of this approach is that it's quite complex and expensive to set up. Legal and financial advice is an absolute necessity in forming the LLC's **operating agreement**, the document that outlines the provisions governing the way the LLC will conduct business.

limited liability company (LLC)
A form of legal organization that's a hybrid between a partnership and a corporation

operating agreement
The document that outlines the provisions governing the way an LLC will conduct business

SUMMARY OF LEGAL FORMS OF ORGANIZATION The organizing decision regarding the legal form of organization is an important one because it can have significant tax and liability consequences. Although the legal form of organization can be changed, it's not an easy thing to do. An entrepreneur needs to think carefully about what's important, especially in the areas of flexibility, taxes, and amount of personal liability in choosing the best form of organization.

Organizational Design and Structure

The choice of an appropriate organizational structure is also an important decision when organizing an entrepreneurial venture. At some point, successful entrepreneurs find that they can't do everything alone. More people are needed. The entrepreneur must then decide on the most appropriate structural arrangement for effectively and efficiently carrying out the organization's activities. Without some suitable type of organizational structure, the entrepreneurial venture may soon find itself in a chaotic situation.

In many small firms, the organizational structure tends to evolve with little intentional or deliberate planning by the entrepreneur. For the most part, the structure may be simple—one person does whatever is needed. As the entrepreneurial venture grows and the entrepreneur finds it increasingly difficult to go it alone, employees are brought on board to perform certain functions or duties that the entrepreneur can't handle. These individuals tend to perform those same functions as the company grows. Then, as the entrepreneurial venture continues to grow, each of these functional areas may require managers and employees.

With the evolution to a more deliberate structure, the entrepreneur faces a whole new set of challenges. All of a sudden, he or she must share decision making and operating responsibilities. This transition is typically one of the most difficult things for an entrepreneur to do—letting go and allowing someone else to make decisions. *After all,* he or she reasons, *how can anyone know this business as well as I do*? Also, what might have been a fairly informal, loose, and flexible atmosphere that worked well when the organization was small may no longer be effective. Many entrepreneurs are greatly concerned about keeping that "small company" atmosphere alive even as the venture grows and evolves into a more structured arrangement. But having a structured organization doesn't necessarily mean giving up flexibility, adaptability, and freedom. In fact, the structural design may be as fluid as the entrepreneur feels comfortable with and yet still have the rigidity it needs to operate efficiently.

Organizational design decisions in entrepreneurial ventures revolve around the six key elements of organizational structure discussed in Chapter 11: work specialization, departmentalization, chain of command, span of control, amount of centralization-decentralization, and amount of formalization. Decisions about these six elements will determine whether an entrepreneur designs a more mechanistic or organic organizational structure (concepts also discussed in Chapter 11). When would each be preferable? A mechanistic structure would be preferable when cost efficiencies are critical to the venture's competitive advantage, when more control over employees' work activities is important, if the venture produces standardized products in a routine fashion, and when the external environment is relatively stable and certain. An organic structure would be most appropriate when innovation is critical to the organization's competitive advantage; for smaller organizations where rigid approaches to dividing and coordinating work aren't necessary; if the organization produces customized products in a flexible setting; and where the external environment is dynamic, complex, and uncertain.

Human Resource Management

As an entrepreneurial venture grows, additional employees will need to be hired to perform the increased workload. As employees are brought on board, the entrepreneur faces certain human resource management (HRM) issues. Two HRM issues of particular importance to entrepreneurs are employee recruitment and employee retention.

EMPLOYEE RECRUITMENT An entrepreneur wants to ensure that the venture has the people to do the required work. Recruiting new employees is one of the biggest challenges that entrepreneurs face. In fact, the ability of small firms to successfully recruit appropriate employees is consistently rated as one of the most important factors influencing organizational success.

Entrepreneurs, particularly, are looking for high-potential people who can perform multiple roles during various stages of venture growth. They look for individuals who "buy into" the venture's entrepreneurial culture—individuals who have a passion for the business. Unlike their corporate counterparts who often focus on filling a job by matching a person to the job requirements, entrepreneurs look to fill in critical skills gaps. They're looking for people who are exceptionally capable and self-motivated, flexible, multiskilled, and who can help grow the entrepreneurial venture.[41] While corporate managers tend to focus on using traditional HRM practices and techniques, entrepreneurs are more concerned with matching characteristics of the person to the values and culture of the organization; that is, they focus on matching the person to the organization.

EMPLOYEE RETENTION Getting competent and qualified people into the venture is just the first step in effectively managing the human resources. An entrepreneur wants to keep the people he or she has hired and trained. Founder and CEO Scott Signore of Matter Communications, a public relations agency based in Newburyport, Massachusetts, understands the importance of having good people on board and keeping them. Signore says: "There's a lot of credit to share amongst our team for embracing a healthy, energetic, fun culture that sets us apart as a PR agency."[42] For instance, one of the benefits is "Summer Fridays," which includes a beer keg on tap in the kitchen and an early closing time. Its fun culture has helped land the company a spot on the *Boston Globe's* Top Places to Work list for three years in a row. Katie Johnston, *Boston Globe* workplace reporter, said: "The winning companies have developed innovative ways to engage and motivate their workers, which often serves as a key factor in innovation and leads to better professional performance."[43] This type of HRM approach helps keep employees loyal and productive.

A unique and important employee retention issue entrepreneurs must deal with is compensation. Whereas traditional organizations are more likely to view compensation from the perspective of monetary rewards (base pay, benefits, and incentives), smaller entrepreneurial firms are more likely to view compensation from a total rewards perspective. For these firms, compensation encompasses psychological rewards, learning opportunities, and recognition in addition to monetary rewards (base pay and incentives).[44]

Initiating Change

We know that the context facing entrepreneurs is one of dynamic change. Both external and internal forces (see Chapter 6) may bring about the need for making changes in the entrepreneurial venture. Entrepreneurs need to be alert to problems and opportunities that may create the need to change. In fact, of the many hats an entrepreneur wears, that of change agent may be one of the most important.[45] If changes are needed in the entrepreneurial venture, often it is the entrepreneur who first recognizes the need for change and acts as the catalyst, coach, cheerleader, and chief change consultant. Change isn't easy in any organization, but it can be particularly challenging for entrepreneurial ventures. Even if a person is comfortable with taking risks—as entrepreneurs usually are—change can be hard. That's why it's important for an entrepreneur to recognize the critical role he or she plays in stimulating and implementing change. For instance, Jayna Cooke, CEO of Chicago-based Eventup, is well aware of the important role she plays in stimulating and implementing changes. As the leading online tool for matching event planners with venues, Cooke had to continually look for ways to keep her company competitive. The company's business model was not working, and it needed to be fixed before the company went out of business. Cooke says being competitive means "being agile, . . . figuring out where we needed to go from there without being rigid and stuck in our old ways, because being rigid leads to problems."[46] One change was simplifying the fee structure.

During any type of organizational change, an entrepreneur also may have to act as chief coach and cheerleader. Because organizational change of any type can be disruptive and scary, the entrepreneur must explain the change to employees and encourage change efforts by supporting employees, getting them excited about the change, building them up, and motivating them to put forth their best efforts.

Finally, the entrepreneur may have to guide the actual change process as changes in strategy, technology, products, structure, or people are implemented. In this role, the entrepreneur answers questions, makes suggestions, gets needed resources, facilitates conflict, and does whatever else is necessary to get the change(s) implemented.

The Importance of Continuing Innovation

In today's dynamically chaotic world of global competition, organizations must continually innovate new products and services if they want to compete successfully. Innovation is a key characteristic of entrepreneurial ventures and, in fact, it's what makes the entrepreneurial venture "entrepreneurial."

What must an entrepreneur do to encourage innovation in the venture? Having an innovation-supportive culture is crucial. What does such a culture look like?[47] It's one in which employees perceive that supervisory support and organizational reward systems are consistent with a commitment to innovation. It's also important in this type of culture that employees not perceive their workload pressures to be excessive or unreasonable. And research has shown that firms with cultures supportive of innovation tend to be smaller, have fewer formalized human resource practices, and have less abundant resources.[48]

LEADING issues

LO10.4 The employees at the software firm ClearCompany have to be flexible. Everyone is expected to contribute ideas. CEO and cofounder Andre Lavoie said: "One way to give employees more [creative] freedom over how they work is to shift the focus from to-do lists and deadlines to goals and objectives—quantity to quality." In return, Lavoie is a supportive leader who gives his employees considerable latitude.[49]

Leading is an important function of entrepreneurs. As an entrepreneurial venture grows and people are brought on board, an entrepreneur takes on a new role—that of a leader. In this section, we want to look at what's involved with the leading function. First, we're going to look at the unique personality characteristics of entrepreneurs. Then we're going to discuss the important role entrepreneurs play in motivating employees through empowerment and leading the venture and employee teams.

Personality Characteristics of Entrepreneurs

Think of someone you know who is an entrepreneur. Maybe it's someone you personally know, or maybe it's someone like Bill Gates of Microsoft. How would you describe this person's personality? One of the most researched areas of entrepreneurship has been the search to determine what—if any—psychological characteristics entrepreneurs have in common, what types of personality traits entrepreneurs have that might distinguish them from nonentrepreneurs, and what traits entrepreneurs have that might predict who will be a successful entrepreneur.

Is there a classic "entrepreneurial personality"? Trying to pinpoint specific personality characteristics that all entrepreneurs share presents the same problem as identifying the trait theories of leadership—that is, being able to identify specific personality traits that *all* entrepreneurs share. This challenge hasn't stopped entrepreneurship researchers from listing common traits, however. For instance, one list of personality characteristics included the following: high level of motivation, abundance of self-confidence, ability to be involved for the long term, high energy level, persistent problem solver, high degree of initiative, ability to set goals, and moderate risk-taker. Another list of characteristics of "successful" entrepreneurs included high energy level, great persistence, resourcefulness, the desire and ability to be self-directed, and relatively high need for autonomy.

Another development in defining entrepreneurial personality characteristics was the proactive personality scale to predict an individual's likelihood of pursuing entrepreneurial ventures. We introduce the proactive personality trait in Chapter 15. A **proactive personality** is a trait of individuals who are more prone to take actions to influence their environment—that is, they're more proactive. Obviously, an entrepreneur is likely to exhibit proactivity as he or she searches for opportunities and acts to take advantage of those opportunities. Various items on the proactive personality scale were found to be good indicators of a person's likelihood of becoming

proactive personality
A personality trait that describes individuals who are more prone to take actions to influence their environments

an entrepreneur, including gender, education, having an entrepreneurial parent, and possessing a proactive personality. In addition, studies have shown that entrepreneurs have greater risk propensity than do managers. However, this propensity is moderated by the entrepreneur's primary goal. Risk propensity is greater for entrepreneurs whose primary goal is growth versus those whose focus is on producing family income.

If your professor has assigned this, go to **www.mymanagementlab.com** to watch a video titled: *Entrepreneurship* and to respond to questions.

★ **Watch It 2!**

Motivating Employees Through Empowerment

At Sapient Corporation (creators of Internet and software systems for e-commerce and automating back-office tasks such as billing and inventory), cofounders Jerry Greenberg and J. Stuart Moore recognized that employee motivation was vitally important to their company's ultimate success.[50] They designed their organization so individual employees are part of an industry-specific team that works on an entire project rather than on one small piece of it. Their rationale was that people often feel frustrated when they're doing a small part of a job and never get to see the whole job from start to finish. They figured people would be more productive if they got the opportunity to participate in all phases of a project.

When you're motivated to do something, don't you find yourself energized and willing to work hard at doing whatever it is you're excited about? Wouldn't it be great if all of a venture's employees were energized, excited, and willing to work hard at their jobs? Having motivated employees is an important goal for any entrepreneur, and employee empowerment is an important motivational tool entrepreneurs can use.

Although it's not easy for entrepreneurs to do, employee empowerment—giving employees the power to make decisions and take actions on their own—is an important motivational approach. Why? Because successful entrepreneurial ventures must be quick and nimble, ready to pursue opportunities and go off in new directions. Empowered employees can provide that flexibility and speed. When employees are empowered, they often display stronger work motivation, better work quality, higher job satisfaction, and lower turnover.

For example, employees at Butler International, Inc., a technology consulting services firm based in Montvale, New Jersey, work at client locations. President and CEO Ed Kopko recognized that employees had to be empowered to do their jobs if they were going to be successful.[51] Another entrepreneurial venture that found employee empowerment to be a strong motivational approach is Stryker Instruments in Kalamazoo, Michigan, a division of Stryker Corporation. Each of the company's production units is responsible for its operating budget, cost reduction goals, customer-service levels, inventory management, training, production planning and forecasting, purchasing, human resource management, safety, and problem solving. In addition, unit members work closely with marketing, sales, and R&D during new product introductions and continuous improvement projects. Says one team supervisor, "Stryker lets me do what I do best and rewards me for that privilege."[52]

Empowerment is a philosophical concept that entrepreneurs have to "buy into." This doesn't come easily. In fact, it's hard for many entrepreneurs to do. Their life is tied up in the business. They've built it from the ground up. But continuing to grow the entrepreneurial venture is eventually going to require handing over more responsibilities to employees. How can entrepreneurs empower employees? For many entrepreneurs, it's a gradual process.

Entrepreneurs can begin by using participative decision making in which employees provide input into decisions. Although getting employees to participate in decisions isn't quite taking the full plunge into employee empowerment, at least it's a way to begin tapping into the collective array of employees' talents, skills, knowledge, and abilities.

Recognized worldwide for its outstanding customer service, the Ritz-Carlton Hotel Company gives employees empowerment training that teaches them how to anticipate guest needs and provide service that ensures complete guest satisfaction. The hotelier involves employees in planning their work and in identifying and resolving problems.
Source: Toshifumi Kitamura/Getty Images

Another way to empower employees is through delegation—the process of assigning certain decisions or specific job duties to employees. By delegating decisions and duties, the entrepreneur is turning over the responsibility for carrying them out.

When an entrepreneur is finally comfortable with the idea of employee empowerment, fully empowering employees means redesigning their jobs so they have discretion over the way they do their work. It's allowing employees to do their work effectively and efficiently by using their creativity, imagination, knowledge, and skills.

If an entrepreneur implements employee empowerment properly—that is, with complete and total commitment to the program and with appropriate employee training—results can be impressive for the entrepreneurial venture and for the empowered employees. The business can enjoy significant productivity gains, quality improvements, more satisfied customers, increased employee motivation, and improved morale. Employees can enjoy the opportunities to do a greater variety of work that is more interesting and challenging.

In addition, employees are encouraged to take the initiative in identifying and solving problems and doing their work. For example, the Ritz-Carlton hotel invests heavily in empowerment training. It starts with teaching employees about the Customer Loyalty Anticipation Satisfaction System, which is designed to fulfill "even the unexpressed wishes and needs of our guests."[53] The Ritz Carton is serious about customer satisfaction. Most employees have the authority to spend up to $2,000 each day per guest to resolve any complaint.

LEADER making a DIFFERENCE

Source: Kristoffer Tripplaar / Alamy

*With over a billion average daily users, Facebook has come a long way from an idea in **Mark Zuckerberg's** college dorm room in 2004.[54] The Facebook founder took the title of CEO at just 19 years old and has grown the company to generate now more than $12 billion in annual revenue and employ more than 12,000 people.*

While Zuckerberg has made some mistakes along the way, he has learned from them and demonstrated a natural leadership ability that has made his company a success. He has a clear mission for the company that keeps employees focused on building systems that connect people. Zuckerberg has created what he calls a "hacker culture" that rewards creative problem solving and rapid decision making. He pays attention to the details, sometimes finding problems on Facebook before anyone else; and he keeps his coding skills sharp, often fixing problems himself. His employees say that he is inquisitive, persistent, and good at effectively deploying resources. Zuckerberg is demanding, but is also passionate about his work. He believes strongly in teamwork, relying on his executive team for support while still encouraging debate. His hard work has been rewarded. The initial public offering (IPO) of Facebook in 2012 made Zuckerberg the world's youngest self-made billionaire. What can you learn from this leader making a difference?

The Entrepreneur as Leader

The last topic we want to discuss in this section is the role of the entrepreneur as a leader. In this role, the entrepreneur has certain leadership responsibilities in leading the venture and in leading employee work teams.

LEADING THE VENTURE Today's successful entrepreneur must be like the leader of a jazz ensemble known for its improvisation, innovation, and creativity. Max DePree, former head of Herman Miller, Inc., a leading office furniture manufacturer known for its innovative leadership approaches, said it best in his book, *Leadership Jazz*. "Jazz band leaders must choose the music, find the right musicians, and perform—in public. But the effect of the performance depends on so many things—the environment, the volunteers playing in the band, the need for everybody to perform as individuals and as a group, the absolute dependence of the leader on the members of the band, the need for the followers to play well. . . . The leader of the jazz band has the beautiful opportunity to draw the best out of the other musicians. We have much to learn from jazz band leaders, for jazz, like leadership, combines the unpredictability of the future with the gifts of individuals."[55]

The way an entrepreneur leads the venture should be much like the jazz leader—drawing the best out of other individuals, even given the unpredictability of the situation. One way an entrepreneur leads is through the vision he or she creates for the organization. In fact, the driving force through the early stages of the entrepreneurial venture is often the visionary leadership of the entrepreneur. The entrepreneur's ability to articulate a coherent, inspiring, and attractive vision of the future is a key test of his or her leadership. But if an entrepreneur can articulate such a vision, the results can be worthwhile. A study contrasting visionary and nonvisionary companies showed that visionary companies outperformed the nonvisionary ones by six times on standard financial criteria, and their stocks outperformed the general market by 15 times.[56]

LEADING EMPLOYEE WORK TEAMS As we will show in Chapter 12, many organizations—entrepreneurial and otherwise—are using employee work teams to perform organizational tasks, create new ideas, and resolve problems.

Employee work teams tend to be popular in entrepreneurial ventures. An *Industry Week* Census of Manufacturers showed that nearly 68 percent of survey respondents used teams to varying degrees.[57] The three most common teams respondents said they used included empowered teams (teams that have the authority to plan and implement process improvements), self-directed teams (teams that are nearly autonomous and responsible for many managerial activities), and cross-functional teams (work teams composed of individuals from various specialties who work together on various tasks).

These entrepreneurs also said that developing and using teams is necessary because technology and market demands are forcing them to make their products faster, cheaper, and better. Tapping into the collective wisdom of the venture's employees and empowering them to make decisions just may be one of the best ways to adapt to change. In addition, a team culture can improve the overall workplace environment and morale.

For team efforts to work, however, entrepreneurs must shift from the traditional command-and-control style to a coach-and-collaboration style (refer to the discussion of team leadership in Chapter 16). Entrepreneurs must recognize that individual employees can understand the business and can innovate just as effectively as they can. For example, at Marque, Inc., of Goshen, Indiana, CEO Scott Jessup recognized that he wasn't the smartest guy in the company as far as production problems were concerned, but he was smart enough to realize that if he wanted his company to expand its market share in manufacturing medical-emergency-squad vehicles, new levels of productivity needed to be reached. He formed a cross-functional team—bringing together people from production, quality assurance, and fabrication—that could spot production bottlenecks and other problems and then gave the team the authority to resolve the constraints.[58]

CONTROL **issues**

LO10.5 Philip McCaleb still gets a kick out of riding the scooters his Chicago-based company, Genuine Scooter Co., makes. However, in building his business, McCaleb has had to acknowledge his own limitations. As a self-described "idea" guy, he knew that he would need someone else to come in and ensure that the end product was *what* it was supposed to be, *where* it was supposed to be, and *when* it was supposed to be there.[59]

Entrepreneurs must look at controlling their venture's operations in order to survive and prosper in both the short run and long run. Those unique control issues that face entrepreneurs include managing growth, managing downturns, and exiting the venture.

Managing Growth

Growth is a natural and desirable outcome for entrepreneurial ventures. Growth is what distinguishes an entrepreneurial venture. Entrepreneurial ventures pursue growth. Growing slowly can be successful, but so can rapid growth.

Growing successfully doesn't occur randomly or by luck. Successfully pursuing growth typically requires an entrepreneur to manage all the challenges associated with growing—in other words, planning, organizing, and controlling for growth.

PLANNING FOR GROWTH Although it may seem we've reverted back to discussing planning issues instead of controlling issues, actually controlling is closely tied to planning, as we will discuss in Chapter 18 (see Exhibit 18-1). And the best growth strategy is a well-planned one.[60] Ideally, the decision to grow doesn't come about spontaneously, but instead is part of the venture's overall business goals and plan. Rapid growth without planning can be disastrous. Entrepreneurs need to address growth strategies as part of their business planning but shouldn't be overly rigid in that planning. The plans should be flexible enough to exploit unexpected opportunities that arise. With plans in place, the successful entrepreneur must then organize for growth.

ORGANIZING FOR GROWTH The key challenges for an entrepreneur in organizing for growth include finding capital, finding people, and strengthening the organizational culture. Norbert Otto is the founder of Sport Otto, an online business based in Germany that sold almost $2 million worth of skates, skis, snowboards, and other sporting goods on eBay. As the company grows, Otto is finding that he has to be more organized.[61]

Having enough capital is a major challenge facing growing entrepreneurial ventures. The money issue never seems to go away, does it? It takes capital to expand. The processes of finding capital to fund growth are much like going through the initial financing of the venture. Hopefully, at this time, the venture has a successful track record to back up the request. If it doesn't, it may be extremely difficult to acquire the necessary capital. That's why we said earlier that the best growth strategy is a planned one.

Part of that planning should be how growth will be financed. For example, the Boston Beer Company, America's largest microbrewer and producer of Samuel Adams beer, grew rapidly by focusing almost exclusively on increasing its top-selling product line. However, the company was so focused on increasing market share that it had few financial controls and an inadequate financial infrastructure. During periods of growth, cash flow difficulties would force company chairman and brewmaster Jim Koch to tap into a pool of unused venture capital funding. However, when a chief financial officer joined the company, he developed a financial structure that enabled the company to manage its growth more efficiently and effectively by setting up a plan for funding growth.[62]

Inadequate financial controls and infrastructure resulted in cash flow problems for Boston Beer Company's popular Samuel Adams beer. Hiring a chief financial officer who developed a financial structure and plan for funding rapid growth helped the brewer manage Samuel Adams' rapid growth more efficiently and effectively.
Source: David Koh/AP Photo

Another important issue that a growing entrepreneurial venture needs to address is finding people. If the venture is growing quickly, this challenge may be intensified because of time constraints. It's important to plan the numbers and types of employees needed as much as possible in order to support the increasing workload of the growing venture. It may also be necessary to provide additional training and support to employees to help them handle the increased pressures associated with the growing organization.

Finally, when a venture is growing, it's important to create a positive, growth-oriented culture that enhances the opportunities to achieve success, both organizationally and individually. Encouraging the culture can sometimes be difficult to do, particularly when changes are rapidly happening. However, the values, attitudes, and beliefs that are established and reinforced during these times are critical to the entrepreneurial venture's continued and future success. Exhibit 10-5 lists some suggestions that entrepreneurs might use to ensure that their venture's culture is one that embraces and supports a climate in which organizational growth is viewed as desirable and important. Keeping employees focused and committed to what the venture is doing is critical to the ultimate success of its growth strategies. If employees

Exhibit 10-5
Achieving a Supportive, Growth-Oriented Culture

- Keep the lines of communication open—inform employees about major issues.
- Establish trust by being honest, open, and forthright about the challenges and rewards of being a growing organization.
- Be a good listener—find out what employees are thinking and facing.
- Be willing to delegate duties.
- Be flexible—be willing to change your plans if necessary.
- Provide consistent and regular feedback by letting employees know the outcomes—good and bad.
- Reinforce the contributions of each person by recognizing employees' efforts.
- Continually train employees to enhance their capabilities and skills.
- Maintain the focus on the venture's mission even as it grows.
- Establish and reinforce a "we" spirit that supports the coordinated efforts of all the employees and helps the growing venture be successful.

don't "buy into" the direction the entrepreneurial venture is headed, it's unlikely the growth strategies will be successful.

CONTROLLING FOR GROWTH Another challenge that growing entrepreneurial ventures face is reinforcing already established organizational controls. Maintaining good financial records and financial controls over cash flow, inventory, customer data, sales orders, receivables, payables, and costs should be a priority of every entrepreneur—whether pursuing growth or not. However, it's particularly important to reinforce these controls when the entrepreneurial venture is expanding. It's all too easy to let things "get away" or to put them off when there's an unrelenting urgency to get things done. Rapid growth—or even slow growth—does not eliminate the need to have effective controls in place. In fact, it's particularly important to have established procedures, protocols, and processes and to use them. Even though mistakes and inefficiencies can never be eliminated entirely, an entrepreneur should at least ensure that every effort is being made to achieve high levels of productivity and organizational effectiveness. For example, at Green Gear Cycling, cofounder Alan Scholz recognized the importance of controlling for growth. How? By following a "Customers for Life" strategy, which meant continually monitoring customer relationships and orienting organizational work decisions around their possible impacts on customers. Through this type of strategy, Green Gear hopes to keep customers for life. That's significant because they figured that, if they could keep a customer for life, the value would range from $10,000 to $25,000 per lifetime customer.[63]

Managing Downturns

Although organizational growth is a desirable and important goal for entrepreneurial ventures, what happens when things don't go as planned—when the growth strategies don't result in the intended outcomes and, in fact, result in a decline in performance? Significant challenges can come in managing the downturns.

Nobody likes to fail, especially entrepreneurs. However, when an entrepreneurial venture faces times of trouble, what can be done? How can downturns be managed successfully? The first step is recognizing that a crisis is brewing.

RECOGNIZING CRISIS SITUATIONS An entrepreneur should be alert to the warning signs of a business in trouble. Some signals of potential performance decline include inadequate or negative cash flow, excess number of employees, unnecessary and cumbersome administrative procedures, fear of conflict and taking risks, tolerance of work incompetence, lack of a clear mission or goals, and ineffective or poor communication within the organization.[64]

Another perspective on recognizing performance declines revolves around what is known as the **"boiled frog" phenomenon**, in which subtly declining situations

"boiled frog" phenomenon
A perspective on recognizing performance declines that suggests watching out for subtly declining situations

are difficult to recognize.[65] The "boiled frog" is a classic psychological response experiment. In one case, a live frog that's dropped into a boiling pan of water reacts instantaneously and jumps out of the pan. But in the second case, a live frog that's dropped into a pan of mild water that is gradually heated to the boiling point fails to react and dies. A small firm may be particularly vulnerable to the boiled frog phenomenon because the entrepreneur may not recognize the "water heating up"—that is, the subtle decline of the situation. When changes in performance are gradual, a serious response may never be triggered or may be initiated too late to intervene effectively in the situation.

So what does the boiled frog phenomenon teach us? It teaches us that entrepreneurs need to be alert to signals that the venture's performance may be worsening. Don't wait until the water has reached the boiling point before you react. Using this metaphor, it actually may be possible to save the frog. Justin Spring, cofounder of Adept Digital Marketing, encourages entrepreneurs to think about something he calls a "reverse frog pot theory": "I think that cooking frogs can also be a powerful metaphor for how *success* happens."[66] He goes on to say: "My success today isn't due to one single event, acquisition, sale or decision. It's due to a combination of all the small wins, minor setbacks and uneventful hard-working hours."

DEALING WITH DOWNTURNS, DECLINES, AND CRISES Although an entrepreneur hopes to never have to deal with organizational downturns, declines, or crises, a time may come when he or she must do just that. After all, nobody likes to think about things going bad or taking a turn for the worse. But that's exactly what the entrepreneur should do—think about it *before* it happens (refer to feedforward control in Chapter 18).[67] It's important to have an up-to-date plan for covering crises. It's like mapping exit routes from your home in case of a fire. An entrepreneur wants to be prepared before an emergency hits. This plan should focus on providing specific details for controlling the most fundamental and critical aspects of running the venture—cash flow, accounts receivable, costs, and debt. Beyond having a plan for controlling the venture's critical inflows and outflows, other actions would involve identifying specific strategies for cutting costs and restructuring the venture.

★ Write It!

If your professor has assigned this, go to **www.mymanagementlab.com** to complete the Writing Assignment *BIZ 17: New Business Management*.

Exiting the Venture

harvesting
Exiting a venture when an entrepreneur hopes to capitalize financially on the investment in the venture

Getting out of an entrepreneurial venture may seem to be a strange thing for entrepreneurs to do. However, the entrepreneur may decide at some point that it's time to move on. That decision may be based on the fact that the entrepreneur hopes to capitalize financially on the investment in the venture—called **harvesting**—or that the entrepreneur is facing serious organizational performance problems and wants to get out, or even on the entrepreneur's desire to focus on other pursuits (personal or business). The issues involved with exiting the venture include choosing a proper business valuation method and knowing what's involved in the process of selling a business.[68]

BUSINESS VALUATION METHODS Valuation techniques generally fall into three categories: (1) asset valuations, (2) earnings valuations, and (3) cash flow valuations.[69] Setting a value on a business can be a little tricky. In many cases, the entrepreneur has sacrificed much for the business and sees it as his or her "baby." Calculating the value of the baby based on objective standards such as cash flow or some multiple of net profits can sometimes be a shock. That's why it's important for an entrepreneur who wishes to exit the venture to get a comprehensive business valuation prepared by professionals.

OTHER IMPORTANT CONSIDERATIONS IN EXITING THE VENTURE Although the hardest part of preparing to exit a venture is valuing it, other factors also should be considered.[70] These factors include being prepared, deciding who will sell the business, considering the tax implications, screening potential buyers, and deciding whether to tell employees before or after the sale. The process of exiting the entrepreneurial venture should be approached as carefully as the process of launching it. If the entrepreneur is selling the venture on a positive note, he or she wants to realize the value built up in the business. If the venture is being exited because of declining performance, the entrepreneur wants to maximize the potential return.

Chapter 10 PREPARING FOR: Exams/Quizzes

CHAPTER SUMMARY by Learning Objectives

LO10.1 DEFINE entrepreneurship and explain why it's important.

Entrepreneurship is the process of starting new businesses, generally in response to opportunities. Entrepreneurial ventures are different from small businesses. Entrepreneurial ventures are characterized by innovative practices and have growth and profitability as their main goals, whereas a small business is one that is independently owned, operated, and financed; has fewer than 100 employees; doesn't engage in any new or innovative practices and has relatively little impact on its industry. Entrepreneurship is also not the same as self-employment. Entrepreneurship is important because it brings forward innovative ideas, creates new start-up firms, and creates jobs. Entrepreneurs must explore the entrepreneurial context, identify opportunities and possible competitive advantages, start the venture, and manage the venture. Entrepreneurs must also manage concerns related to social responsibility and ethics.

LO10.2 EXPLAIN what entrepreneurs do in the planning process for new ventures.

Entrepreneurs must identify environmental opportunities and competitive advantage. They must research a venture's feasibility, first generating and then evaluating ideas. A feasibility study is an analysis of the various aspects of a proposed entrepreneurial venture designed to determine its feasibility. This analysis includes looking at the competitors, determining how to get financing, and developing a business plan. The business plan should include an executive summary, an analysis of the opportunity, an analysis of the context, a description of the business, financial data and projections, and supporting documentation. The sharing economy that is emerging is creating many new entrepreneurial opportunities through people sharing something they own or providing a service for a fee.

LO10.3 DESCRIBE the six legal forms of organization and the choice of appropriate organizational structure.

Two primary factors that affect the decision about how to organize a business are taxes and legal liability. In a sole proprietorship, the owner maintains sole and complete control over the business and is personally liable for business debts. In a general partnership, two or more owners share the management and risk of the business. A limited liability partnership is formed by general partner(s) and limited partner(s). A corporation (C corporation) is a legal business entity that is separate from its owners and managers. It is a closely held corporation when it is owned by a limited number of people who do not trade the stock publically. An S corporation is a corporation that is unique because the owners are taxed as a partnership as long as certain criteria are met. A limited liability company (LLC) is a hybrid between a partnership and a corporation. As an organization grows, the entrepreneur must decide on an appropriate structure for the organization. The entrepreneur must also face human resource management issues such as employee recruitment and employee retention. Entrepreneurs must be open to initiating change and must also continue to innovate.

LO10.4 DESCRIBE how entrepreneurs lead organizations.

While there is no specific personality characteristic that all entrepreneurs have, researchers suggest that there are several personality traits that are more common among entrepreneurs. These include a high level of motivation, an abundance of self-confidence, the ability to be involved for the long term, and a high energy level. Entrepreneurs are often persistent problem solvers; have a high degree of initiative; have the ability to set goals; are moderate risk-takers; possess great persistence, resourcefulness, the desire and ability to be self-directed; and have a relatively high need for autonomy. Entrepreneurs may also have a proactive personality trait, which means they are more prone to take actions to influence their environment. Entrepreneurs motivate employees through empowerment. Entrepreneurs must lead the venture and also lead employee work teams.

LO10.5 EXPLAIN how managers control organizations under different circumstances.

Entrepreneurs must manage growth through planning for growth, organizing for growth, and controlling for growth. Entrepreneurs must manage downturns through recognizing crisis situations and then dealing with downturns, declines, and crisis. At some point an entrepreneur may determine that it is time to exit a venture in order to capitalize financially on the investment (called harvesting) because the entrepreneur is facing serious organizational performance problems or because the entrepreneur wants to pursue other business or personal opportunities. To do so, the entrepreneur must use a method to value the business and consider a variety of other important factors in the process.

Pearson **MyLab** Management

Go to **mymanagementlab.com** to complete the problems marked with this icon ✪.

✪ REVIEW AND DISCUSSION QUESTIONS

10-1. What do you think would be the hardest thing about being an entrepreneur? What do you think would be the most fun?

10-2. How many options are there for a new entrepreneur to start up their business venture?

10-3. Would a good manager be a good entrepreneur? Discuss.

10-4. Why do you think many entrepreneurs find it hard to step aside and let others manage their business?

10-5. Do you think a person can be taught to be an entrepreneur? Why or why not?

Pearson **MyLab** Management

If your professor has assigned these, go to **mymanagementlab.com** for the following Assisted-graded writing questions:

10-6. Researchers have identified a set of characteristics associated with the entrepreneurial profile. Based on your personality and traits, do you fit the profile? Would you make a successful entrepreneur? Explain, citing specific ways you match or diverge from the profile.

10-7. It took four years for Airbnb to build an inventory of 600,000 rooms (World Economic Forum). It took the hotel chain, Hilton, 93 years to achieve the same goal. Outline a workable model for a sharing economy venture.

PREPARING FOR: My Career

PERSONAL INVENTORY ASSESSMENTS

Innovative Attitude Scale

To become an entrepreneur you have to have confidence in your innovative abilities. Take this PIA to understand your attitude toward innovation.

ETHICS DILEMMA

Everyone *can* make mistakes, but sometimes these can have severe consequences. The employees of the insurance company Aviva Investor's asset management division simultaneously received an email from the company's HR department, which stated that they had been dismissed with immediate effect. Unfortunately, the email should have been sent to only one of the 1,300 employees in the division. Instead, the email informed all employees in the asset management division to hand over any company property and to maintain confidentiality after their dismissal. As shocked employees tried to come to terms with the news, they received a second email that retracted the earlier statement and issued an apology for the company's error.[71]

10-9. Do you think it is ethical to dismiss anyone by email?

10-10. What might have happened if the mistake had not been spotted?

SKILLS EXERCISE Developing Grit

Those who succeed as entrepreneurs have at least one thing in common; they possess grit.[72] Having grit means you have the perseverance and passion for long-term goals. When you have grit, you work hard and maintain effort and interest even after facing failure or adversity. Some say having grit means you have mental toughness. It is a trait that brings together other qualities such as optimism, self-discipline, and self-motivation. You must have talent to accomplish your goals, but you must also have focused and sustained use of that talent over time in order to accomplish difficult goals. Grit helps entrepreneurs because they often face challenges and setbacks in the process of launching a venture. An entrepreneur with grit will continue working hard, even in the face of seemingly endless obstacles.

Steps in Practicing the Skill

- ***Practice your resilience:*** Resilience is the ability to bounce back. As you are faced with an obstacle, notice your reaction to the challenge. Are you ready to quit? If so, it is time to build your resilience. Learn from your mistake and make yourself give it another try instead of giving up.
- ***Pursue your passion:*** Figure out what you are passionate about in life and pursue it. Our passions inspire us and give us the internal drive to keep moving forward. Identifying and pursuing your passion can help develop your perseverance.
- ***Practice positive self-talk:*** Grit means you have a strong belief in yourself. By engaging in positive self-talk, you can develop the internal motivation to keep moving forward even as you face obstacles. Remind yourself of your abilities and be your own biggest cheerleader. With every challenge you face, make sure you encourage yourself to keep moving forward with a positive attitude.
- ***Build in practice time:*** Understand that anything significant you are going to accomplish in life is going to take time and effort. When working toward a goal, you must consider how you can practice whatever it is you are trying to accomplish. For example, if you have the dream to open a restaurant, spend some time working in other restaurants in order to really understand the business before jumping in on your own.
- ***Put together a support team:*** Identify some trusted friends and let them know you are working on developing grit. Share with them your future goals and what you want to work toward. Ask them to encourage you and make sure you call them for support when you are feeling like you might want to give up.

Practicing the Skill

Identify a challenging goal you would like to attain. You can start small, but make sure it is something that will test your abilities. For example, have you ever considered running a 5k race? Getting an A in your next statistics course? What is something significant you would like to accomplish? Once you set your goal, use the steps above as you work toward your goal. Once you accomplish your goal, move on to a new one. As you overcome the challenges along the way, you will find yourself developing grit. And then you can accomplish anything!

WORKING TOGETHER Team Exercise

Have you ever considered starting a business? Take a few minutes and brainstorm business ideas that you could start on your campus. What are problems that could be solved? Considering the idea of the sharing economy, what are things that students could share or a service you could provide for a fee? What kinds of products or services would students be willing to purchase? Get together in groups of three or four students and share your business ideas. Pick one idea to explore further. What would be your competitive advantage? Is the idea feasible? Who would be your competitors? Would it require financing to get started? Make a few notes on what you would write as an executive summary for a business plan for your idea. Be prepared to share with the class.

MY TURN TO BE A MANAGER

- To be an entrepreneur, you must first have an idea. Entrepreneurs get their ideas from many sources; however, an idea often hits when the entrepreneur steps out of his or her own comfort zone. Start by exposing yourself to new ideas and information. Subscribe to social media feeds for websites or journals in a wide variety of disciplines such as science, technology, sports, and the arts. Take as many classes outside of your own major that you can. Attend diverse events and network with people from a wide variety of backgrounds. Keep an idea journal with interesting ideas or information that you come across on a daily basis.
- Explore the innovations or business ideas of others. Visit www.springwise.com, a website that discovers and shares innovative ideas from around the world and www.socialbusiness.org, a website that shares ideas and businesses that are creating positive social change. Add your thoughts and reflections on what you learn to your idea journal.
- Interview an entrepreneur. Ask how he or she discovered his or her business idea. What challenges did he or she face in starting the business? What do you think made the business succeed?
- Look online to find local resources or organizations that support entrepreneurs. Make a list of the resources that are available to entrepreneurs in your area.

Rachel Nilsson, founder of Rags to Raches, appeared on the television show *Shark Tank* seeking $200,000 for 10 percent equity to fund her clothing company for kids. She cut a $200,000 deal with Robert Herjavec for 15% of Rags to Raches, and, in less than a month after appearing on *Shark Tank,* her daily sales quintupled. The funding helped Nilsson turn her venture into a million-dollar clothing brand.
Source: Michael Desmond/Getty Images

- One of the biggest challenges start-ups face is obtaining funding. While only a very few businesses are able to obtain funding through the popular television show *Shark Tank,* you can learn a lot by watching how the “sharks” or venture capitalists on the show’s panel make decisions on which ideas to invest in. Go online and watch an episode of the show. Take note of why the sharks decide to invest in a particular business and why they let some contestants leave empty handed.

CASE APPLICATION 1 The Fear of Failure

Aspiring entrepreneurs are told not to fear failure. In fact, they are often told to embrace failure, that it is an important part of the entrepreneurial process. You must fail before you can succeed! But is it true? Do you really have to experience failure before you can find success? And what is it about failing that helps you succeed in the future?

Many successful entrepreneurs throughout history experienced failure first.[73] Before starting Microsoft, Bill Gates and friend Paul Allen launched Traf-O-Data, a company that used a computerized microprocessor to analyze data from traffic counters that were placed on roads. The intent was to support government traffic engineers' efforts to optimize traffic and end road congestion. But the equipment did not work correctly during their big presentation to local county officials, and the company eventually folded. Good thing, as the pair did go on to create the software used so widely around the world.

Worth $20.4 billion, Jack Ma is the wealthiest person in China. He is the founder of Alibaba, the world's largest e-commerce company, which has over 100 million shoppers a day. However, at one point he couldn't even get a job. After failing the college entrance exams three times, his decision to just get a job instead didn't work out either. He was turned down by 30 companies, including a new franchise of KFC that was opening near his home. KFC had 24 applicants for 23 jobs, and Ma was the one who didn't make the cut. Eventually he launched Alibaba, creating not only a job for himself, but also jobs for more than 30,000 other people who now work there.

At some point you've probably read an article from the successful online journal *The Huffington Post*. Founder Arianna Huffington experienced some significant failures prior to launching the journal. After she wrote a successful first book, her second book proposal was rejected 26 times. She also unsuccessfully ran for governor of California in 2003, before eventually starting *The Huffington Post* in 2005. Since then she has been recognized consistently in Forbes' Most Influential Women in Media and in 2015 ranked 61st on Forbes' 100 Most Powerful Women list.

You are familiar with Blogger and Twitter, but you probably haven't heard of Evan Williams' other ventures, Pyra Labs and Odeo. Blogger was a side project that Williams started while trying to build his first company Pyra Labs. Financial challenges led to the closing of Pyra Labs, but Williams was able to keep Blogger going. Odeo was going to be a podcasting company, but the platform wasn't as good as Williams' team hoped, and Apple's timing of opening the podcast section of the iTunes store led to the company's closing. Fortunately Williams and his cofounders had Twitter in the works at the time.

There are, of course, many failures that we don't hear about because that's where the story ends. So why do some entrepreneurs succeed after failure, while others just fail? Some say it depends on the entrepreneur's mindset. Is the entrepreneur's mindset fixed, or growth oriented? A fixed mindset assumes failure means lack of ability. As a result, failure leads to being more risk averse and eventually giving up. In contrast, entrepreneurs with a growth mindset learn from failure. They don't attribute failure to a fixed trait; rather, they are more likely to analyze a failure more deeply and more effectively apply learning to the next problem or challenge. The fact is, most entrepreneurs aren't going to be successful with their first idea or venture. Those who are successful ultimately are those who stand back up, dust themselves off, learn something from the failure, and try again.

DISCUSSION QUESTIONS

10-10. Why do so many entrepreneurs experience failure?

10-11. Do you think someone could be an immediate success when starting a business? Or is a first failure really necessary?

10-12. Is a growth mindset something you are born with? Or, can you develop a growth mindset?

CASE APPLICATION 2 The Right Recipe for Entrepreneurs: Fifteen

In 2002, British restaurateur and television celebrity-chef, James Trevor "Jamie" Oliver opened Fifteen, a nonprofit restaurant and bar in London. This restaurant offers jobs to unemployed teenagers and every year it allows a group to graduate as chefs from the kitchen. All the profits earned from the business are ploughed back into the training and development of the youth.[74]

Oliver is the author of several best-selling cookery books and is the owner of various restaurant chains. In 2017, Richtopia listed him as the third most influential British entrepreneur with a net worth of around $310 million. As a father of five children, Oliver has expressed the importance of healthy eating. He has been involved in a number of controversial schemes to improve the diet of children, to reduce sugar in foods, and to encourage home cooking rather than a reliance on packaged foods.

Having few formal qualifications and being dyslexic, Oliver wanted the purpose of the chain to be a source of inspiration for disadvantaged young people, including those who are unemployed, homeless, and with drug or alcohol dependencies. With one new restaurant launched in Amsterdam, 2004, and Cornwall, 2006, Oliver's Fifteen Foundation aims to open more such restaurants across the world.

However, in January 2017, Oliver announced that he would be closing six of his restaurants by the end of the first quarter. The CEO of Jamie Oliver Restaurant Group, Simon Blagden, blamed the decision on the uncertainty arising out of Brexit and the United Kingdom's decision to leave the European Union (EU). The closures affected around 5 percent of the chain's total workforce. Most of those who were affected found alternative employment in other restaurants under the chain.

Oliver's success is based not only on his talent as a chef, but also on his behaviour. He can be abrupt, but consumers connect with his down-to-Earth approach. He isn't scared of taking risks and has invested millions of dollars into the Fifteen project. He has spent a great deal of his time and money to help successfully convince numerous British children to give up fast food. Where necessary, he has taken government assistance for investments of more than $400 million toward school meals—improvement of facilities, recipes, and training.

Oliver has often admitted that he could have retired many years ago, but instead has decided to invest in social enterprises to promote healthy food and encourage the youth in the cooking industry.

DISCUSSION QUESTIONS

10-13. Entrepreneurs are important because of the impact they have on the world around them. List and explain the different ways that Fifteen benefits its community.

10-14. What characteristics do you think Jamie Oliver has that have helped make his various enterprises a success?

10-15. The decision to close some of the restaurants would have been a difficult one for Oliver to have made. How should an entrepreneur tackle such downturns?

10-16. Many entrepreneurs want to grow their businesses. How can an entrepreneur, like Oliver, develop their ventures in the future?

ENDNOTES

1. J. W. Carland, F. Hoy, W. R. Boulton, and J. C. Carland, "Differentiating Entrepreneurs from Small Business Owners: A Conceptualization," *Academy of Management Review*, vol. 9, no. 2, 1984, pp. 354–359.
2. U.S. Bureau of Labor Statistics, "Glossary," www.bls.gov, accessed March 16, 2016.
3. J. McDowell, "Small Business Continues to Drive U.S. Economy," Office of Advocacy, U.S. Small Business Administration, www.sba.gov/advo/press, October 3, 2005.
4. P. Almeida and B. Kogut, "The Exploration of Technological Diversity and Geographic Localization in Innovation: Start-Up Firms in the Semiconductor Industry," *Small Business Economics*, vol. 9, no. 1, 1997, pp. 21–31.
5. National Science Foundation, "One in Five U.S. Businesses with R&D Applied for a U.S. Patent in 2008," NSF 13-307, February 2013.
6. Ibid.
7. U.S. Bureau of Labor Statistics, "Business Employment Dynamics—Fourth Quarter 2014," USDL-15-1484, July 29, 2015.
8. "Frequently Asked Questions," U.S. Small Business Administration, Office Advocacy http://www.sba.gov/sites/default/files/FAQ_March_2014_0.pdf, March 2014.
9. U.S. Bureau of the Census, "Number of Firms, Establishments, and Annual Pay by Enterprise Employment Size by the United States and States, Totals: 2013," www.census.gov, accessed March 30, 2016.
10. D. Kelley, S. Singer, and M. Herrington, "2015/16 Global Report," Global Entrepreneurship Monitor, www.gemconsortium.org.
11. L. Buchanan, "The U.S. Now Has 27 Million Entrepreneurs," *Inc.* online, www.inc.com, September 2, 2015.
12. W. Royal, "Real Expectations," *Industry Week*, September 4, 2000, pp. 31–34.
13. D. Bornstein, "Recycling Unused Medicines to Save Money and Lives," *New York Times* online, www.nytimes.com, March 20, 2015.
14. C. Sandlund, "Trust Is a Must," *Entrepreneur,* October 2002, pp. 70–75.
15. Future Vision box based on P. Haid, "4 Companies Leading the Next Wave of Profit with Purpose," *Fast Company's Exist* online, www.fastcoexist.com, May 28, 2015; N. Godfrey, "Business Not as Usual: The Millennial Social Entrepreneur," *Forbes* online, www.forbes.com, August 23, 2015; B. Freeman, "5 Great Companies That Make Money and Do Good," *Inc. Magazine* online, www.inc.com, August 16, 2012; E. Chhabra, "The Social Entrepreneur's Quandry: Nonprofit or For-profit?," *New York Times* online, www.nytimes.com, July 10, 2013; www.toms.com.
16. B. I. Koerner, "Cereal in the Bowl, Not on the Floor," *New York Times* online, www.nytimes.com, June 18, 2006.
17. N. Parmar, "You Have a Great Idea. Now What Do You Do?," *Wall Street Journal,* September 30, 2013, p. R1.
18. "Facts for Features," *U.S. Census Bureau Newsroom,* www.census.gov/newsroom, January 3, 2006; and M. Arndt, "Zimmer: Growing Older Gracefully," *BusinessWeek,* June 9, 2003, pp. 82–84.
19. G. B. Knight, "How Wall Street Whiz Found a Niche Selling Books on the Internet," *Wall Street Journal*, May 15, 1996, pp. A1+.
20. N. F. Krueger, Jr., "The Cognitive Infrastructure of Opportunity Emergence," *Entrepreneurship Theory and Practice,* Spring 2000, p. 6.
21. D. P. Forbes, "Managerial Determinants of Decision Speed in New Ventures," *Strategic Management Journal,* April 2005, pp. 355–366.
22. P. Drucker, *Innovation and Entrepreneurship* (New York: Harper & Row, 1985).
23. "July 01, 1979: The First Sony Walkman Goes on Sale," *History*, A&E Television Networks, www.history.com, accessed April 3, 2016.
24. M. Haire, "A Brief History of the Walkman," *Time* online, www.time.com, July 1, 2009.
25. V. Bhaskara, "Southwest Airlines Opens for Business Customers," *Forbes* online, www.forbes.com, April 22, 2014.
26. "Automated Teller Machines," *History* (A+E Networks), www.history.com, accessed April 3, 2016.
27. S. Schubert, "The Ultimate Music Buff," *Business 2.0,* March 2006, p. 64.
28. L. Rao, "On Monday, eBay Will Separate from PayPal, and Will Start a New Chapter as an Independent Company," *Fortune* online, www.fortune.com, July 19, 2015.
29. T. Stynes, "WebMD Says Profit Rises 69%, Gives Upbeat Outlook," *The Wall Street Journal* online, www.wsj.com, February 23, 2016.
30. Information on Whole Foods Market from Hoovers Online, www.hoovers.com, July 13, 2008.
31. B. Helm, "Airbnb Is Inc.'s 2014 Company of the Year," *Inc.* online, www.inc.com, accessed April 3, 2016.
32. A. Eisenberg, "What's Next: New Fabrics Can Keep Wearers Healthy and Smelling Good," *New York Times*, February 3, 2000, pp. D1+.
33. A. Morse, "An Entrepreneur Finds Tokyo Shares Her Passion for Bagels," *Wall Street Journal,* October 18, 2005, pp. B1+.
34. P. Reikofski, "Where 'Aha' Comes From," *Wall Street Journal,* April 29, 2013, p. R2.
35. S. Greco, "The Start-Up Years," *Inc. 500*, October 21, 1997, p. 57.

36. T. Moore, "Joy Mangano," *Biography,* A&E Television Networks, www.history.com, accessed April 3, 2016.
37. E. Neuborne, "Hey, Good-Looking," *BusinessWeek*, May 29, 2000, p. 192.
38. A. Srinivasan, "Successful Entrepreneurs Offer 5 Tips for Finding Elusive Startup Funding," *Entrepreneur* online, www.entrepreneur.com, June 30, 2014.
39. O. B. Waxman, "Finally, an App That Lets You Borrow a Corgi," *Fortune* online, www.fortune.com, March 26, 2016.
40. C. Forrest, "How to Structure Your Startup as the Company Grows," *TechRepublic* online, www.techrepublic.com, September 22, 2015.
41. K. Sundheim, "Entrepreneurial Recruiting: Staying Competitive When Staffing Top Talent," *Forbes* online, www.forbes.com, April 4, 2013.
42. "The *Boston Globe* Names PR Agency Matter Communications a Top Place to Work for 2015," *Businesswire* online, www.businesswire.com, November 16, 2015.
43. Ibid.
44. R. L. Heneman, J. W. Tansky, and S. J. Camp, "Human Resource Management Practices in Small and Medium-Sized Enterprises: Unanswered Questions and Future Research Perspectives," *Entrepreneurship Theory and Practice,* vol. 25, no. 1, pp. 11–26.
45. Based on G. Fuchsberg, "Small Firms Struggle with Latest Management Trends," *Wall Street Journal*, August 26, 1993, p. B2; M. Barrier, "Reengineering Your Company," *Nation's Business*, February 1994, pp. 16–22; J. Weiss, "Reengineering the Small Business," *Small Business Reports*, May 1994, pp. 37–43; and K. D. Godsey, "Back on Track," *Success*, May 1997, pp. 52–54.
46. D. Port, "4 Examples of Risks Leading to Reward," *Entrepreneur* online, www.entrepreneur.com, March 21, 2015.
47. G. N. Chandler, C. Keller, and D. W. Lyon, "Unraveling the Determinants and Consequences of an Innovation-Supportive Organizational Culture," *Entrepreneurship Theory and Practice*, Fall 2000, pp. 59–76.
48. Ibid.
49. A. Lavoie, "The Top Thing Employees Want from Their Bosses, and It's Not a Promotion," *Entrepreneur* online, www.entrepreneur.com, March 31, 2015.
50. Information from company's website, www.sapient.com, July 7, 2003; and S. Herrera, "People Power," *Forbes*, November 2, 1998, p. 212.
51. "Saluting the Global Awards Recipients of Arthur Andersen's Best Practices Awards 2000," *Fortune* online, www.fortune.com, January 16, 2001.
52. T. Purdum, "Winning with Empowerment," *Industry Week*, October 16, 2000, pp. 109–110.
53. M. Solomon, "What Steve Jobs Stole from Ritz-Carlton (and You Should Steal from Apple)," *Inc.* online, www.inc.com, June 16, 2015.
54. Leader Making a Difference box based on T. Taulli, "10 Years Later: Entrepreneurial Lessons from Mark Zuckerberg," *Forbes* online, www.forbes.com, February 2, 2014; H. McCracken, "Inside Mark Zuckerberg's Bold Plan for the Future of Facebook," *Fast Company* online, www.fastcompany.com, November 16, 2015; E. Walter, "How to Lead Like Zuck," *Inc. Magazine* online, www.inc.com, May 14, 2014; N. Carson, "Confessions of a Facebook Employee: What It Is Really Like to Work for Mark Zuckerberg," *Business Insider* online, www.businessinsider.com, January 25, 2012; K. Elkins, "The Age When 17 Self-made Billionaires Made Their First Million," *Inc. Magazine* online, www.inc.com, February 11, 2016; http://newsroom.fb.com.
55. M. Depree, *Leadership Jazz* (New York: Dell, 1993).
56. J. C. Collins and J. I. Porras, *Built to Last: Successful Habits of Visionary Companies* (New York: Harper-Business, 1994).
57. P. Strozniak, "Teams at Work," *Industry Week*, September 18, 2000, pp. 47–50.
58. Ibid.
59. T. Siegel Bernard, "Scooter's Popularity Offers a Chance for Growth," *Wall Street Journal,* September 20, 2005, p. B3.
60. J. Bailey, "Growth Needs a Plan or Only Losses May Build," *Wall Street Journal,* October 29, 2002, p. B9; and L. Beresford, "Growing Up," *Entrepreneur*, July 1995, pp. 124–128.
61. R. D. Hof, "EBay's Rhine Gold," *BusinessWeek,* April 3, 2006, pp. 44–45.
62. J. Summer, "More, Please!," *Business Finance,* July 2000, pp. 57–61.
63. T. Stevens, "Pedal Pushers," *Industry Week*, July 17, 2000, pp. 46–52.
64. P. Lorange and R. T. Nelson, "How to Recognize—and Avoid—Organizational Decline," *Sloan Management Review*, Spring 1987, pp. 41–48.
65. S. D. Chowdhury and J. R. Lange, "Crisis, Decline, and Turnaround: A Test of Competing Hypotheses for Short–Term Performance Improvement in Small Firms," *Journal of Small Business Management*, October 1993, pp. 8–17.
66. J. Spring, "Success and the Reverse Frog Pot Theory," *Forbes* online, www.forbes.com, March 13, 2014.
67. C. Farrell, "How to Survive a Downturn," *BusinessWeek*, April 28, 1997, pp. ENT4–ENT6.
68. R. W. Price, "Why Is an Exit Strategy Important for Entrepreneurs?," Global Entrepreneurship Institute, www.gcase.org, June 19, 2014.
69. R. W. Pricer and A. C. Johnson, "The Accuracy of Valuation Methods in Predicting the Selling Price of Small Firms," *Journal of Small Business Management*, October 1997, pp. 24–35.
70. J. Bailey, "Selling the Firm and Letting Go of the Dream," *Wall Street Journal,* December 10, 2002, p. B6; P. Hernan, "Finding the Exit," *Industry Week,* July 17, 2000, pp. 55–61; D. Rodkin, "For Sale by Owner," *Entrepreneur*, January 1998, pp. 148–53; A. Livingston, "Avoiding Pitfalls When Selling a Business," *Nation's Business*, July 1998, pp. 25–26; and G. Gibbs Marullo, "Selling Your Business: A Preview of the Process," *Nation's Business*, August 1998, pp. 25–26.
71. The Ethics Dilemma is based on Richard, "Mistake at Aviva as 1,300 Employees Dismissed," *Redmans Solicitors*, April 20, 2012.
72. Skills Exercise based on A. Duckworth, C. Peterson, M. Matthews, & D. Kelly, "Grit: Perseverance and Passion for Long-term Goals," *Journal of Personality and Social Psychology*, vol. 92, no. 6, p. 1087–1101, 2007; J. Stillworth, "You Can Train Yourself to Have More Grit," *Inc. Magazine* online, www.inc.com, September 26, 2014; F. Hoque, "How Entrepreneurs Can Develop Grit: The Most Important Trait of Successful People," *Business Insider* online, www.businessinsider.com, October 8, 2014; P. Campbell, "How to Get True Grit," *The Huffington Post* online, www.huffingtonpost.com, February 16, 2013.

73. S. Vozza, "5 Famous Entrepreneurs Who Learned from Their First Spectacular Failures," *Fast Company* online, www.fastcompany.com, February 12, 2014; J. Demers, "6 Stories of Super Successes Who Overcame Failure," *Entrepreneur Magazine* online, www.entrepreneur.com, December 8, 2014; A. Pilon, "21 Entrepreneurs Who Failed Big Before Becoming a Success," *Small Business Trends* online, www.smallbiztrends.com, January 20, 2016; B. Campbell, "What's Behind a 10-year 'Overnight' Success?," *Entrepreneur* online, www.entrepreneur.com, March 17, 2016; C. Howard "The World's Most Powerful Women," *Forbes* online, www.forbes.com, May 26, 2015; J. Goudreau, "The New Feminine Face of the Media Elite," *Forbes* online, www.forbes.com, August 30, 2011; I. Lapowsky, "Arianna Huffington's Rule for Success: Dare to Fail," *Inc. Magazine* online, www.inc.com, January 24, 2013; I. Lapowsky, "Evan Williams' Rule for Success: Do Less," *Inc. Magazine* online, www.inc.com, May 27, 2015; S. Monslave, "The Secret Sauce of Successful Entrepreneurs? It's All in Their Head," *Entrepreneur* online, www.entrepreneur.com, February 25, 2014; A. Lutz, "Alibaba Founder Jack Ma Was Rejected from 30 Jobs, Including KFC, Before Becoming China's Richest Man," *Business Insider* online, www.businessinsider.com, February 17, 2015.
74. Based on information from Jamie Oliver's Fifteen Web site, http://www.fifteen.net/, accessed February 2017; "The 100 Most Influential British Entrepreneurs," *RichTopia*, May 20, 2017; Callan Boys, "Jamie Oliver on Rescuing his Australian Restaurants and the Sugar Tax," GoodFood, http://www.goodfood.com.au, May 16, 2017; "Jamie Oliver's 15 Restaurant Offering Unemployed Teens Jobs Is Looking at Redundancies," *Express* online, January 12, 2016; Belinda Robinson, "Sour Grapes, Jamie? He Blames Brexit for Closure of Six Italian Restaurants . . . But Customers Point to High Prices, Bland Food and Poor Service," *Mail Online*, January 6, 2017, http://www.dailymail.co.uk; and Mark Wingett, "Jamie Oliver Apprenticeship Scheme to Go Nationwide," *Big Hospitality*, March 24, 2016, http://www.bighospitality.co.uk/.

PART 3 Management Practice

A Manager's Dilemma

Habitat for Humanity is a nonprofit, ecumenical Christian housing ministry dedicated to building affordable housing for individuals dealing with poverty or homelessness. Habitat's approach is simple. Families in need of decent housing apply to a local Habitat affiliate. Homeowners are chosen based on their level of need, their willingness to become partners in the program, and their ability to repay the loan. And that's the unique thing about Habitat's approach. It's not a giveaway program. Families chosen to become homeowners have to make a down payment and monthly mortgage payments, and invest hundreds of hours of their own labor into building their Habitat home. And they have to commit to helping build other Habitat houses. Habitat volunteers (maybe you've been involved on a Habitat build) provide labor and donations of money and materials as well.

Social service organizations often struggle financially to provide services that are never enough to meet the overwhelming need. Habitat for Humanity, however, was given an enormous financial commitment—$100 million—from an individual who had worked with Habitat and seen the gift it offers to families in poverty. That amount of money means that Habitat can have a huge impact now and in the future. But the management team wants to use the gift wisely—a definite planning, strategy, and control challenge.

Pretend you're part of that management team. Using what you've learned in the chapters on planning and strategic management in Part 3, what five things would you suggest the team focus on? Think carefully about your suggestions to the team.

Global Sense

Manufacturers have spent years building low-cost global supply chains. However, when those businesses are dependent on a global supply chain, any unplanned disruptions (political, economic, weather, natural disaster, etc.) can wreak havoc on plans, schedules, and budgets. The Icelandic Eyjafjallajokull volcano in 2010 and the Japanese earthquake/tsunami and Thailand flooding in 2011 are still fresh in the minds of logistics, transportation, and operations managers around the globe. Although unexpected problems in the supply chain have always existed, now the far-reaching impact of something happening not in your own facility but thousands of miles away has created additional volatility and risk for managers and organizations. For instance, when the Icelandic volcano erupted, large portions of European airspace were shut down for more than a week, which affected air traffic worldwide. At BMW's plant in Spartanburg, South Carolina, air shipments of car components were delayed and workers' hours had to be scaled back and plans made for a possible shutdown of the entire facility. During the Thailand floods in late 2011, industrial parks that manufactured semiconductors for companies like Apple and Samsung were underwater and crawling with crocodiles. After the 2011 Japanese earthquake and tsunami shut down dozens of contractors and subcontractors that supply many parts to the auto and technology industries, companies like Toyota, Honda, and Hewlett-Packard had to adjust to critical parts shortages.

Discuss the following questions in light of what you learned in Part 3:

- *You see the challenges associated with a global supply chain; what are some of the benefits of it? What can managers do to minimize the impact of such disruptions?*
- *What types of plans would be best in these unplanned events?*
- *As Chapter 9 asks, how can managers plan effectively in dynamic environments?*
- *Could SWOT analysis be useful in these instances? Explain.*
- *How might managers use scenario planning in preparing for such disasters? (Scenario planning is discussed in the Planning and Control Techniques module)*

Sources: R. Teijken, "Local Issues in Global Supply Chains," Logistics & Transport Focus, *April 2012, pp. 41–43; J. Beer, "Sighted: The Ends of the Earth,"* Canadian Business, *Winter 2011/2012, pp. 19–22; B. Powell, "When Supply Chains Break,"* Fortune, *December 26, 2011, pp. 29–32; A. H. Merrill, R. E. Scale, and M. D. Sullivan, "Post-Natural Disaster Appraisal and Valuation: Lessons from the Japan Experience,"* The Secured Lender, *November/December 2011, pp. 30–33; J. Rice, "Alternate Supply,"* Industrial Engineer, *May 2011, p. 10; and "Risk Management: An Increasingly Small World,"* Reactions, *April 2011, p. 252.*

Continuing Case

Starbucks—Planning

All managers plan. The planning they do may be extensive or it may be limited. It might be for the next week or month, or it might be for the next couple of years. It might cover a work group or it might cover an entire division or the entire organization. No matter what type or extent of planning a manager does, the important thing is that planning takes place. Without planning, there would be nothing for managers to organize, lead, or control.

Based on Starbucks' numerous achievements, there's no doubt that managers have done their planning. Let's take a look.

During a presentation at the Starbucks biennial investor conference, CEO Howard Schultz stands before a large photograph of the first Starbucks Reserve Roastery & Tasting Room. With the first store opened in Seattle, the Roastery is an innovative concept that integrates coffee roasting, coffee education, a café, a restaurant, and a retail store that features the Starbucks small-lot Reserve coffee line. Starbucks' expansion plan to open 100 more Roastery stores throughout the world will help the company achieve its financial goal of reaching $30 billion in annual revenue by 2019.

Source: Ted S. Warren/AP Photo

Company Goals

In 2016, Starbucks had over 31,000 stores in more than 70 countries. The company continues to add stores, planning for 30,000 worldwide by 2019. Of the planned expansion, 2,500 new stores will be added in China. Starbucks successfully opened a new type of store in Seattle that combines a roastery along with a café. It is set to open a similar facility in New York City, which will be the company's largest store yet at 20,000 square feet. CEO Howard Schultz said, "In New York, we want to take elements from what we originally created and build something even bigger and bolder, celebrating coffee and craft in a completely unique and differentiated way."[1] Starbucks' financial goals are ambitious, including revenue growth of 10 percent to 13 percent and $30 billion in annual revenue by 2019. In addition to the quantitative/fiscal goals, Starbucks focuses on continuing to develop new coffee/tea/juice/bakery products in multiple forms and staying true to its global social responsibilities. Starbucks' ambition is to rank among the world's most admired brands and enduring companies through its "laser focus on disciplined execution and robust innovation" and to maintain Starbucks' standing as one of the most recognized brands in the world.

Company Strategies

Starbucks has been called the most dynamic retail brand over the last two decades. It has been able to rise above the commodity nature of its product and become a global brand leader by reinventing the coffee experience. Over 60 million times a week, a customer receives a product (hot drink, chilled drink, food, etc.) from a Starbucks partner. It's a reflection of the success that Howard Schultz has had in creating something that never really existed in the United States—café life. And in so doing, he created a cultural phenomenon. Starbucks is changing what we eat and drink. It's shaping how we spend our time and money.

Starbucks has found a way to appeal to practically every customer demographic, as its customers cover a broad base. It's not just the affluent or the urban professionals and it's not just the intellectuals or the creative types who frequent Starbucks. You'll find soccer moms, construction workers, bank tellers, and office assistants at Starbucks. And despite the high price of its products, customers pay it because they think it's worth it. What they get for that price is some of the finest coffee available commercially, custom preparation, and, of course, that Starbucks ambiance—the comfy chairs, the music, the aromas, the hissing steam from the espresso machine—all invoking that warm feeling of community and connection that Schultz experienced on his first business trip to Italy and knew instinctively could work elsewhere.

As the world's number one specialty coffee retailer, Starbucks' portfolio includes goods and services under its flagship Starbucks brand and the Teavana, Tazo Tea, Seattle's Best Coffee, Starbucks VIA, Starbucks Refreshers, Evolution Fresh, La Boulange, and Verismo brands. Recent product introductions include a Cherry Blossom Frappuccino®, a single-origin coffee from Indonesia, and a Chocolate Cookie Dough Cake Pop.

Here's something you might be surprised at. You can expect to get carded at your neighborhood Starbucks soon. What? Starbucks is making a more intentional move into wine and beer sales. The company tested the concept at a single Seattle store in 2010 and now offers alcohol at 26 locations, where store sales have shown a significant increase during the time of day when alcohol is offered. The "Starbucks' Evenings" concept offers selected adult beverages (beer and wine... tailored to regional taste preferences) and an expanded food menu after 4 P.M. So, the plan is to roll out Starbucks' Evenings to thousands of stores over the next several years.

Starbucks' loyalty program continues to distinguish it from competitors, and it is an integral part of the company's growth strategy. Its My Starbucks Rewards™ has almost 12 million active members with more than $4 billion loaded onto the cards. And the company has made a huge investment in mobile payments, accounting for more than four million transactions every week in the United States. Its Starbucks Card apps for Android phones and iPhones have been hugely popular. The company also announced enhancements to its loyalty program by offering a new prepaid Starbucks Card. Cardholders can use the card anywhere Visa cards are accepted, and earn two "stars" for every dollar spent, which they can redeem for beverage or food items at any Starbucks store. In addition to building customer loyalty, the company states that expanding the program "is just the beginning of Starbucks opening up its digital ecosystem as well as extending its payment platform."

Starbucks' primary competition comes from quick-service restaurants and specialty coffee shops. McDonalds, for one, has invested heavily in its McCafé concept, which offers coffee, real fruit smoothies, shakes, and frappés. And there are numerous specialty coffee shops, but most of these tend to be in local markets only.

Discussion Questions

P3-1. Make a list of Starbucks' goals. Describe what type of goal each is. Then, describe how that stated goal might affect how the following employees do their job: (a) a part-time store employee—a barista—in Omaha; (b) a quality assurance technician at the company's roasting plant in Amsterdam; (c) a regional sales manager; (d) the executive vice president of global supply chain operations; and (e) the CEO.

P3-2. Discuss the types of growth strategies that Starbucks has used. Be specific.

P3-3. What competitive advantages do you think Starbucks has? What will it have to do to maintain those advantages?

P3-4. Do you think the Starbucks brand can become too saturated—that is, extended to too many different products? Why or why not?

P3-5. What companies might be good benchmarks for Starbucks? Why? What companies might want to benchmark Starbucks? Why?

P3-6. Describe how the following Starbucks managers might use forecasting, budgeting, and scheduling (be specific): (a) a retail store manager; (b) a regional marketing manager; (c) the manager for global development; and (d) the CEO.

P3-7. Describe Howard Schultz as a strategic leader.

P3-8. Is Starbucks "living" its mission? (You can find the company mission on its website at www.starbucks.com.) Discuss.

P3-9. What ethical and social responsibility issues can you see with Starbucks' decision to sell alcohol after 4 P.M.? Think in terms of the various stakeholders and how those stakeholders might respond to this strategy?

Notes for the Part 3 Continuing Case

Information from Starbucks Corporation 2015 Annual Report, www.investor.starbucks.com, April 2016; J. Jargon, "Starbucks to Expand Customer Rewards Program Beyond Its Coffee Shops," *The Wall Street Journal* online, www.wsj.com, March 23, 2016; A. Medhani, "'Evenings' at Starbucks: Coffee Shop to Sell Wine, Craft Beer, Small Plates," *USA Today* online, www.usatoday.com, August 18, 2015; L. Burkitt, "Starbucks to Add Thousands of Stores in China," *The Wall Street Journal* online, www.wsj.com, January 12, 2016; L. Patton, "Starbucks Plans to Open Biggest Store in Its History in New York," *The Wall Street Journal* online, www.wsj.com, April 6, 2016; R. Dooley, "Will Starbucks Alcohol 'Infect' Other Products?" www.forbes.com, April

9, 2014; V. Wong, "What to Expect from Starbucks' New Booze Menu," www.businessweek.com, March 20, 2014; C. Cain Miller, "Starbucks and Square to Team Up," *New York Times* online, www.nytimes.com, August 8, 2012; R. Ahmed, "Tata Setting Up Starbucks Coffee Roasting Facility," www.online.wsj.com, July 26, 2012; B. Horovitz, "Starbucks Rolling Out Pop with Pep," *USA Today,* March 22, 2012, p. 1B; Starbucks News Release, "Starbucks Spotlights Connection Between Record Performance, Shareholder Value, and Company Values at Annual Meeting of Shareholders," news.starbucks.com, March 21, 2012; D. A. Kaplan, "Strong Coffee," *Fortune,* December 12, 2011, pp. 100–116; J. A. Cooke, Editor, "From Bean to Cup: How Starbucks Transformed Its Supply Chain," www.supplychainquarterly.com, Quarter 4, 2010; R. Ruggless, "Starbucks Exec: Security from Employee Theft Important When Implementing Gift Card Strategies," *Nation's Restaurant News,* December 12, 2005, p. 24; and R. Ruggless, "Transaction Monitoring Boosts Safety, Perks Up Coffee Chain Profits," *Nation's Restaurant News,* November 28, 2005, p. 35.

[1] L. Patton, "Starbucks Plans to Open Biggest Store in Its History in New York," *The Wall Street Journal* online, www.wsj.com, April 6, 2016.

Chapter 11 Organization Design

It's Your Career

Source: RAJ CREATIONZS/Shutterstock

A key to success in management and in your career is knowing how to stay connected and in the organizational loop when you're in a nontraditional working arrangement.

Staying Connected

The odds are good that at some point in your career, you'll be offered the opportunity to telecommute/work at home. (According to a recent survey, 37 percent of workers say their company offers that option.[1]) And working from home can be a good thing. (A recent study showed that an employee's efficiency can improve by 13 percent.[2]) Although you might be efficient, not being physically at the workplace can make it seem like you're totally disconnected from what's going on. (Another recent study showed that telecommuters move up more slowly than their in-office peers.[3]) When working as a remote employee—or even if you, at some point, manage someone in that kind of work arrangement—it's important to find ways to make the work relationship, well . . . . work. And work well! Here are some suggestions for staying in the organizational loop and making yourself a valuable employee:

*1. **Stay focused and productive.** Time management is absolutely critical. Plan ahead using goal setting and to-do lists (see Chapter 8's opener and end-of-chapter skill application). Control—or even better, eliminate—interruptions and distractions. When you have work appointments (online, phone, Skype, etc.), keep them; and make sure you're prepared by having the materials you will need for the conversation. Respect the schedules and time requirements of your colleagues. Finally, build in the kind of accountability you'd have in a traditional work arrangement. Recruit your manager or a colleague to be your accountability partner. Let them know what you intend to accomplish that day (or week) and check in daily (or weekly) to discuss what you've accomplished.*

*2. **Communicate. Communicate. Communicate.** Communication is always important—regardless of where you do your work—but especially so when face-to-face exchanges are minimal or nonexistent. It's critical to think before you communicate. Choose your communication approach carefully. There are times when a more matter-of-fact approach is the*

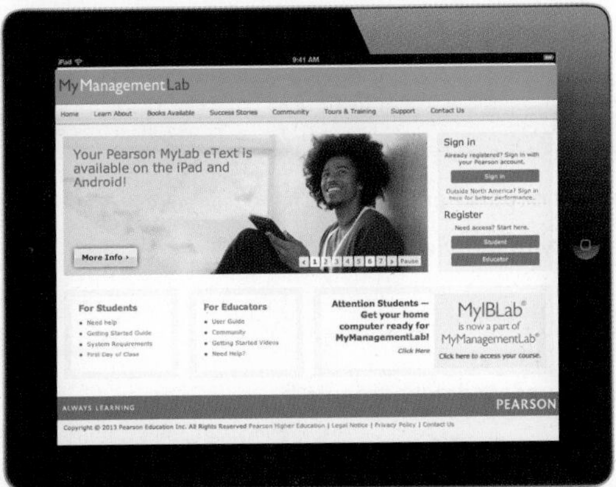

Pearson MyLab Management®

Improve Your Grade!

When you see this icon, visit **www.mymanagementlab.com** for activities that are applied, personalized, and offer immediate feedback.

Learning Objectives

11.1 ***Describe*** *six key elements in organizational design.*

11.2 ***Contrast*** *mechanistic and organic structures.*

11.3 ***Discuss*** *the contingency factors that favor either the mechanistic model or the organic model of organizational design.*

11.4 ***Describe*** *traditional organizational design options.*

11.5 ***Discuss*** *organizing for flexibility in the twenty-first century.*

- **Develop your skill** at acquiring and using power.
- **Know how** to stay connected and "in the loop" when working remotely.

best and times when a more personal touch is appropriate. Watch your "tone" (even in written communications) and be courteous. Hone your listening and "interpretation" skills. Try to understand the meaning behind what someone is saying in writing or when speaking.

*3. **Choose appropriate technology.** Know and choose the tools that are most appropriate for your situation. Will you need to collaborate with others or will your work be mainly solitary? What type of communication will be necessary—e-mail, instant messaging, video messaging, etc.? Choose your tech tools wisely.*

*4. **Be aware of the "people" aspects of remote work arrangements.** When a person is not physically at a workplace, it is hard to build closeness and camaraderie. But those things are still important. Find ways to combat the isolation and loneliness. Get to know your other team members (remote and in the workplace).*

Welcome to the fascinating world of organizational structure and design. In this chapter, we present the basics of organizing. We define the key organizing concepts and their components and how managers use these to create a structured environment in which organizational members can do their work efficiently and effectively. Once the organization's goals, plans, and strategies are in place, managers must develop a structure that will best facilitate the attainment of those goals.

SIX **elements of organizational design**

LO11.1 The Boeing Company is reducing the build time for a 787 model wide-body jetliner from 30 days to 24 days. That may not sound like much, but it is. Boeing Vice President Larry Loftis stated: "All in all, this is considered quite a feat

Exhibit 11-1
Purposes of Organizing

- Divides work to be done into specific jobs and departments.
- Assigns tasks and responsibilities associated with individual jobs.
- Coordinates diverse organizational tasks.
- Clusters jobs into units.
- Establishes relationships among individuals, groups, and departments.
- Establishes formal lines of authority.
- Allocates and deploys organizational resources.

for an aircraft composed of 2.3 million parts."[4] Management must be doing something right. The reliability of 787 aircraft is 99 percent. Getting there requires careful planning and coordination. Loftis indicated: "So the timing is really good for us because it allows us to take the personnel off the temporary surge line, move a number of them over to the main line, get the training in place, get them used to the jobs they're going to be working to really de-risk the ramp up on the main line."[5] Clearly, the work gets done efficiently and effectively here. Work also gets done efficiently and effectively at Cisco Systems, although not in such a structured and formal way. At Cisco, some 70 percent of the employees work from home at least 20 percent of the time.[6] Both of these organizations get needed work done, although each does so using a different structure.

organizing
Management function that involves arranging and structuring work to accomplish the organization's goals

organizational structure
The formal arrangement of jobs within an organization

organizational chart
The visual representation of an organization's structure

organizational design
Creating or changing an organization's structure

work specialization
Dividing work activities into separate job tasks

Few topics in management have undergone as much change in the past few years as that of organizing and organizational structure. Managers are reevaluating traditional approaches to find new structural designs that best support and facilitate employees doing the organization's work—designs that can achieve efficiency but are also flexible.[7]

In Chapter 1, we defined **organizing** as arranging and structuring work to accomplish organizational goals. It's an important process, during which managers design an organization's structure. **Organizational structure** is the formal arrangement of jobs within an organization. This structure, which can be shown visually in an **organizational chart**, also serves many purposes. (See Exhibit 11-1.) When managers create or change the structure, they're engaged in **organizational design**, a process that involves decisions about six key elements: work specialization, departmentalization, chain of command, span of control, centralization and decentralization, and formalization.[8]

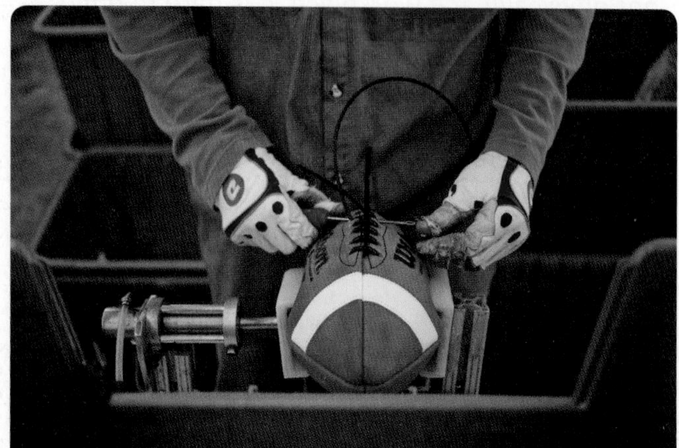

Lacing is one of 13 separate tasks involved in hand-crafting a Wilson Sporting Goods football. The company uses work specialization in dividing job activities as an organizing mechanism that helps employees boost their productivity and makes efficient use of workers' diverse skills.
Source: Bloomberg/Getty Images

Work Specialization

What do Joël Robuchon and Aureole have in common? Both are Las Vegas gourmet restaurants. Also, both restaurants staff their kitchens with culinary experts. For instance, pastry chefs prepare sumptuous desserts. The chef garde managers take responsibility for preparation of all cold food items, and multiple chefs de partie each take responsibility for preparing one type of food, such as fish, roasts, or fried foods. This is an example of **work specialization**, which is dividing work activities into separate job tasks. Individual employees "specialize" in doing part of an activity rather than the entire activity in order to increase work output and quality. It's also known as division of labor, a concept we introduced in the management history module. Back at the gourmet restaurants, skilled executive chefs effectively manage all of the kitchen staff to ensure food quality and the coordinated preparation of the dinner courses from appetizers to desserts.

Work specialization makes efficient use of the diversity of skills that workers have. In most organizations, some tasks require highly developed skills; others can be performed by employees with lower skill levels. If all workers were engaged in all the steps of, say,

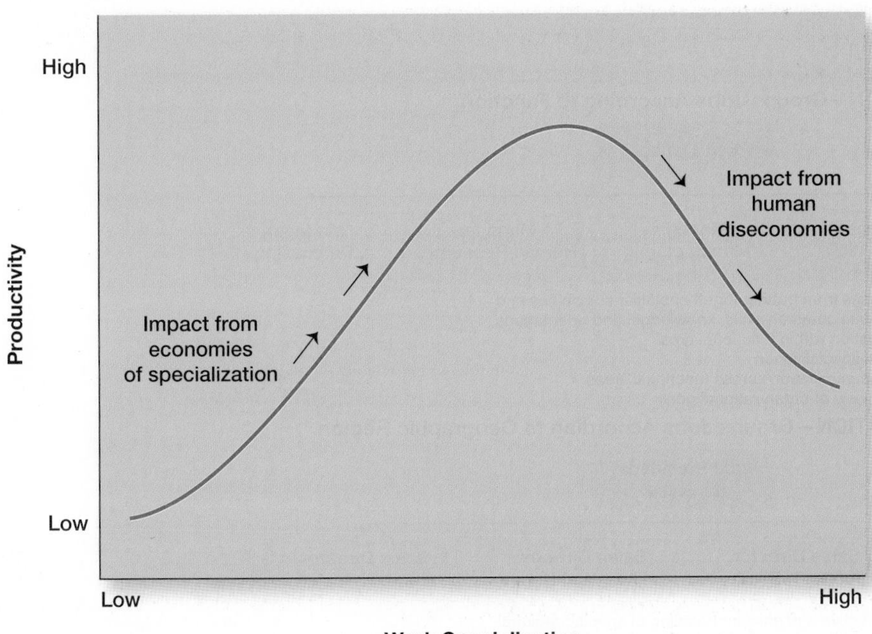

Exhibit 11-2
Economies and Diseconomies of Work Specialization

a manufacturing process, all would need the skills necessary to perform both the most demanding and the least demanding jobs. Thus, except when performing the most highly skilled or highly sophisticated tasks, employees would be working below their skill levels.

Early proponents of work specialization believed it could lead to great increases in productivity. At the beginning of the twentieth century, that generalization was reasonable. Because specialization was not widely practiced, its introduction almost always generated higher productivity. But, as Exhibit 11-2 illustrates, a good thing can be carried too far. At some point, the human diseconomies from division of labor—boredom, fatigue, stress, low productivity, poor quality, increased absenteeism, and high turnover—exceed the economic advantages.[9]

TODAY'S VIEW Most managers today continue to see work specialization as important because it helps employees be more efficient. For example, McDonald's uses high work specialization to get its products made and delivered to customers efficiently and quickly—that's why it's called "fast" food. One person takes orders at the drive-through window, others cook and assemble the hamburgers, another works the fryer, another bags orders, and so forth. Such single-minded focus on maximizing efficiency has contributed to increasing productivity. In fact, at many McDonald's, you'll see a clock that times how long it takes employees to fill the order; look closer and you'll probably see posted somewhere an order fulfillment time goal. At some point, however, work specialization no longer leads to productivity. That's why companies such as Avery Dennison, Ford Australia, Hallmark, and American Express use minimal work specialization and instead give employees a broad range of tasks to do.

Departmentalization

Does your college have a department of student services or financial aid department? Are you taking this course through a management department? After deciding what job tasks will be done by whom, common work activities need to be grouped back together so work gets done in a coordinated and integrated way. How jobs are grouped together is called **departmentalization**. Five common forms of departmentalization are used, although an organization may develop its own unique classification. (For instance, a hotel might have departments such as front desk operations, sales and catering, housekeeping and laundry, and maintenance.) Exhibit 11-3 illustrates each type of departmentalization as well as the advantages and disadvantages of each.

departmentalization
The basis by which jobs are grouped together

Exhibit 11-3
The Five Common Forms of Departmentalization

FUNCTIONAL DEPARTMENTALIZATION—Groups Jobs According to Function

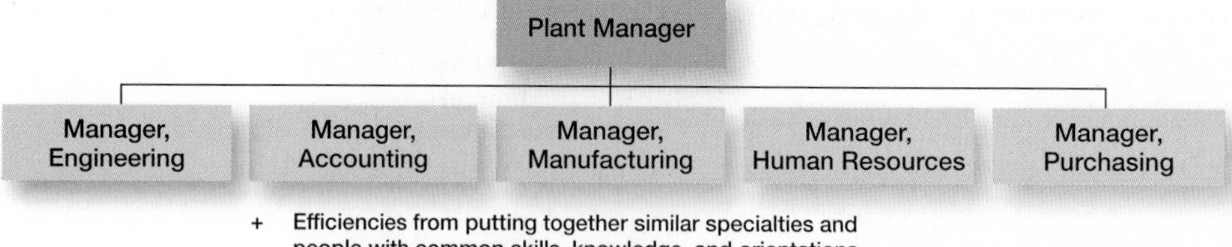

+ Efficiencies from putting together similar specialties and people with common skills, knowledge, and orientations
+ Coordination within functional area
+ In-depth specialization
– Poor communication across functional areas
– Limited view of organizational goals

GEOGRAPHICAL DEPARTMENTALIZATION—Groups Jobs According to Geographic Region

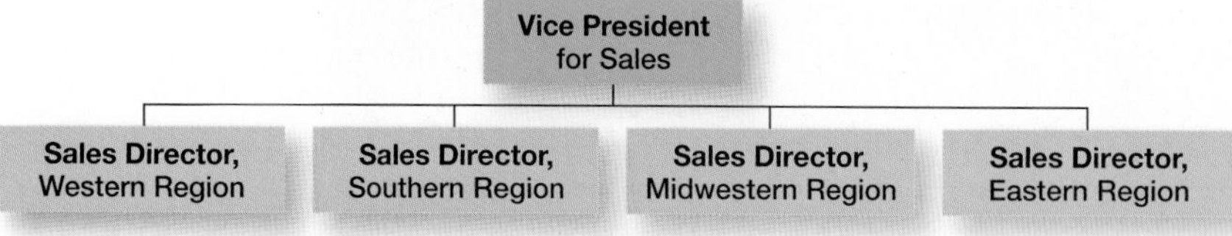

+ More effective and efficient handling of specific regional issues that arise
+ Serve needs of unique geographic markets better
– Duplication of functions
– Can feel isolated from other organizational areas

PRODUCT DEPARTMENTALIZATION—Groups Jobs by Product Line

Source: Bombardier Annual Report.

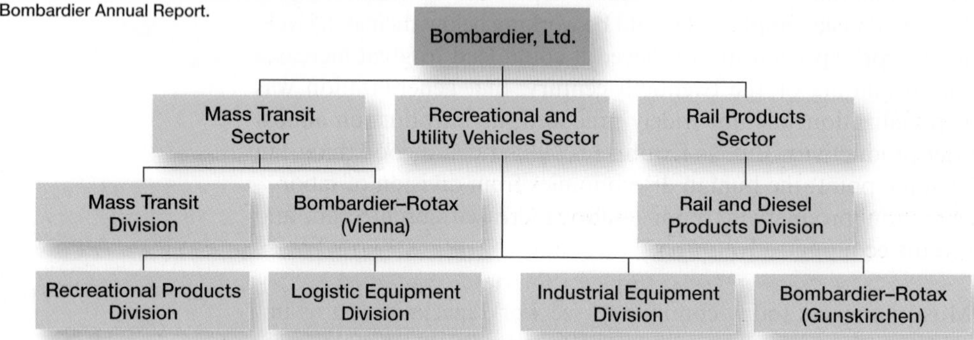

+ Allows specialization in particular products and services
+ Managers can become experts in their industry
+ Closer to customers
– Duplication of functions
– Limited view of organizational goals

PROCESS DEPARTMENTALIZATION—Groups Jobs on the Basis of Product or Customer Flow

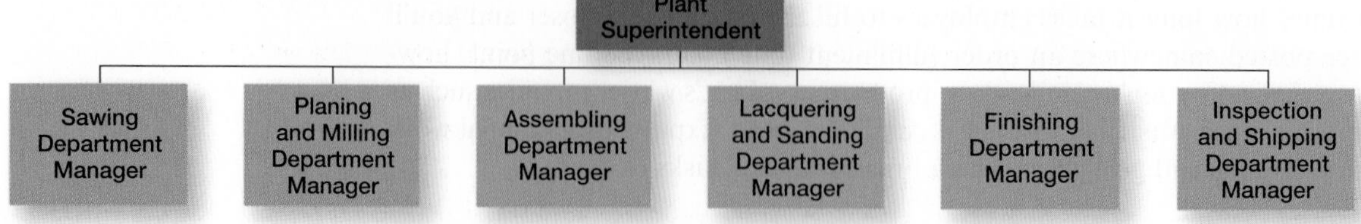

+ More efficient flow of work activities
– Can only be used with certain types of products

CUSTOMER DEPARTMENTALIZATION—Groups Jobs on the Basis of Specific and Unique Customers Who Have Common Needs

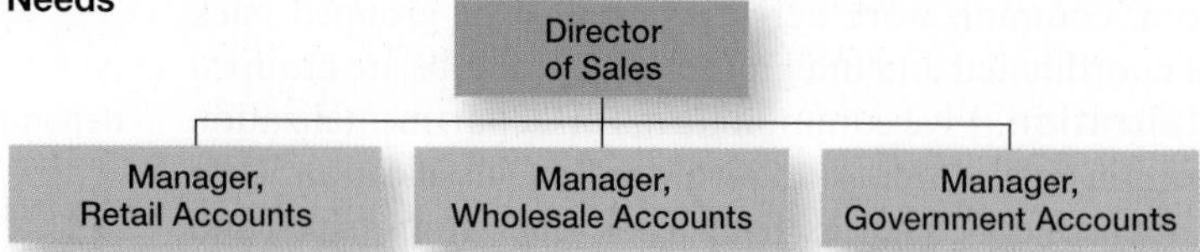

+ Customers' needs and problems can be met by specialists
– Duplication of functions

TODAY'S VIEW Most large organizations continue to use combinations of most or all of these types of departmentalization. For example, General Electric (GE) organizes its corporate staff along functional lines, including public relations, legal, global research, human resources, and finance. Pearson Education, publisher of this textbook, arranges its business by educational market segment (Pre K–12, higher education, and professional) and its customers (students, professors, and workplace educators), and arranges its sales function around customers and geographic regions (for example, the United States, Europe, and Asia). Black & Decker organizes its divisions along functional lines, its manufacturing units around processes, its sales around geographic regions, and its sales regions around customer groupings. We can also find similar structures in the U.S. federal government, which is organized into branches: legislative (makes law), executive (carries out laws), and judicial (evaluates laws).

One popular departmentalization trend is the increasing use of customer departmentalization. Because getting and keeping customers is essential for success, this approach works well because it emphasizes monitoring and responding to changes in customers' needs. Another popular trend is the use of teams, especially as work tasks have become more complex and diverse skills are needed to accomplish those tasks. One specific type of team that more organizations are using is a **cross-functional team**, a work team composed of individuals from various functional specialties. For instance, Harley-Davidson relies on cross-functional teams at all levels of the company to conceptualize and design new products. Former CEO Richard Teerlink instituted a process called "creative friction," which was designed to ensure that multiple, sometimes conflicting perspectives are considered throughout product development.[10] We'll discuss cross-functional teams (and all types of teams) more fully in Chapter 12.

cross-functional team
A work team composed of individuals from various functional specialties

Chain of Command

Suppose you were at work and had a problem with an issue that came up. What would you do? Who would you ask to help you resolve that issue? People need to know who their boss is. That's what the chain of command is all about. The **chain of command** is the line of authority extending from upper organizational levels to lower levels, which clarifies who reports to whom. Managers need to consider it when organizing work because it helps employees with questions such as "Who do I report to?" or "Who do I go to if I have a problem?" To understand the chain of command, you have to understand three other important concepts: authority, responsibility, and unity of command.

chain of command
The line of authority extending from upper organizational levels to the lowest levels, which clarifies who reports to whom

Authority refers to the rights inherent in a managerial position to tell people what to do and to expect them to do it.[11] The early management writers distinguished between two forms of authority: line authority and staff authority. **Line authority** entitles a manager to direct the work of an employee. It is the employer–employee authority relationship that extends from the top of the organization to the lowest echelon, according to the chain of command. As a link in the chain of command, a manager with line authority has the right to direct the work of employees and to make certain decisions without consulting anyone.

authority
The rights inherent in a managerial position to tell people what to do and to expect them to do it

line authority
Authority that entitles a manager to direct the work of an employee

As organizations get larger and more complex, line managers find that they do not have the time, expertise, or resources to get their jobs done effectively. In response, they create **staff authority** functions to support, assist, advise, and generally reduce some of their informational burdens. For instance, a human resource management director who cannot effectively handle managing all the activities the department needs creates a recruitment department, performance management department, and compensation and rewards department, which are staff functions.

staff authority
Positions with some authority that have been created to support, assist, and advise those holding line authority

When managers use their authority to assign work to employees, those employees take on an obligation to perform those assigned duties. This obligation or expectation to perform is known as **responsibility**. And employees should be held accountable

responsibility
The obligation or expectation to perform any assigned duties

let's get REAL

Source: Matt Ramos

Matt Ramos
Director of Marketing

The Scenario:

Reid Lawson is a project manager for a lighting design company in Los Angeles. He's one of 30 project managers in the company, each with a team of 10–15 employees. Although the company's top managers say they want employees to be "innovative" in their work, Reid and the other project managers face tight-fisted control from the top. Reid's already lost two of his most talented designers (who went to work for a competitor) because he couldn't get approval for a project because the executive team kept nit-picking the design these two had been working on.

How can Reid and the other project managers get their bosses to loosen up the control? What would you suggest?

Losing top-notch talent is bad. Losing top-notch talent to a direct competitor is killer, especially when it's avoidable. Reid's first step should be an honest meeting with his boss. The evidence is fairly clear that something needs to change, so it should be a simple conversation to get the ball rolling. If that doesn't produce results, he should turn to HR and recruiting as his biggest advocate. They almost always have the ear of the executive team. With their help, this is a very resolvable situation.

for their performance! Assigning work authority without responsibility and accountability can create opportunities for abuse. Likewise, no one should be held responsible or accountable for work tasks over which he or she has no authority to complete those tasks.

unity of command
The management principle that each person should report to only one manager

Finally, the **unity of command** principle (one of Fayol's 14 management principles—see page 70 in the Management History module) states that a person should report to only one manager. Without unity of command, conflicting demands from multiple bosses can occur.

TODAY'S VIEW Although early management theorists (Fayol, Weber, Taylor, Barnard, and others) believed that chain of command, authority (line and staff), responsibility, and unity of command were essential, times have changed.[12] Those elements are far less important today. Information technology has made such concepts less relevant today. Employees can access information that used to be available only to managers in a matter of a few seconds. It also means that employees can communicate with anyone else in the organization without going through the chain of command. Also, many employees, especially in organizations where work revolves around projects, find themselves reporting to more than one boss, thus violating the unity of command principle.

WORKPLACE CONFIDENTIAL Coping with Multiple Bosses

Sue Lee was complaining about her job at a large property development company. "I work for Ted in our marketing department. But I've been assigned to help promote our new luxury condo project on Park Avenue. The project manager, Xu Xiang, thinks she's my boss. She is constantly giving me things to do, priorities, and deadlines. Meanwhile, I'm getting text massages, e-mails, and phone calls from Ted with conflicting requests. I wish these two would talk to each other. I only have so many hours in my day. I can't do two jobs at once. What do I do? Whose directives get priority? Did I mention that I spend most of my time on Xu's project but Ted does my annual performance review?"

Sue's complaint is not unique. An increasing number of people are finding themselves reporting to more than one boss. In some cases, the problem is a poorly designed organization where the lines of authority aren't clearly defined and the unity-of-command principle is broken. In other cases, especially small or family-run businesses, it can be blurred authority lines with overlapping roles. In still other cases it might be the formation of temporary teams where people report to multiple bosses. But more often, nowadays, the culprit is a matrix organization structure. As noted later in this chapter, organizations are increasingly imposing project structures on top of functional departments to better manage specific businesses, regions, or product lines. In so doing, they create overlapping responsibilities. If you find yourself in one of these situations, you very well may need to deal with bosses that have different management styles or who impose conflicting directives, vague communications, or unrealistic workloads.

Multiple bosses can create multiple headaches but three challenges standout. First is dealing with an excessive workload. Multiple bosses often aren't aware of what others are asking of you. Whether deliberate or not, each may treat you as if you are solely working for him or her and have no other responsibilities. So two bosses might result in your having twice the workload. With three or more bosses, of course, the problem might only increase. Second is the challenge of conflicting messages. Different bosses have different expectations and different leadership styles. What do you do when you have multiple bosses wanting you to meet their deadlines "ASAP"? Finally there is the issue of loyalty. Who do you give first priority to? Reporting to more than one person may require you to negotiate between competing demands for your time, goals, and priorities.

So what can you do if you find yourself having to cope with multiple bosses? Here are some suggestions:

Prioritize your bosses. Like it or not, you need to choose to whom your first loyalty lies. Who is more powerful and who would hurt you the least? Make sure you know who your ultimate boss is and make sure he or she is satisfied with your work. The person who completes your reviews and decides on your compensation is typically the person who should never be ignored. Consistent with our discussion of organizational politics in Chapter 1, you want to support your boss and, when you have more than one, give first priority to the one with the most power.

Be proactive about your workload. It's your responsibility to make sure your multiple bosses are kept up-to-date on your workload. That includes telling each what the others have asked of you. When the load exceeds your capacity, share this information with each boss and ask for their suggestions regarding priorities.

Prioritize your workload and list. Make a list of all your ongoing tasks and projects, prioritize them, and then share this list with your bosses. The list needs to be updated regularly and communicated in weekly check-in meetings. These meetings are your best opportunity to anticipate and reconcile potential conflicts.

Set boundaries. Don't be afraid to set limits. Identify how many hours you can devote to each boss's project and how you've allocated priorities. If your bosses know ahead of time what the boundaries are, you can eliminate a lot of potential conflicts.

Get your bosses to communicate with each other. Get your bosses to talk with each other. Try to avoid becoming the vehicle through whom they communicate. It's not your job to represent each boss's agenda to the other. When there are conflicts that are directly affecting you, bring your bosses together, explain the conflicts, and encourage them to come to a resolution.

Look at the bright side. There is a positive side to multiple bosses. First, the fact that two or more bosses want you working for them says that you have valuable skills and that they trust you. Second, the complexity and ambiguity created by the absence of a single boss can allow you to expand your autonomy and influence. When you set the boundaries and define priorities, you take control over variables typically held by a boss. Finally there is the opportunity to play one boss off against another. "Like a kid playing parents off each other, ask the person who you know will give you the answer you want."

Based on "How to Deal with 'Multiple Boss Madness,'" *share.com*, February 23, 2011; A. Gallo, "Managing Multiple Bosses," *Harvard Business Review* (online), www.hbr.org, August 18, 2011; K. Hall, "Making the Matrix Work," *Training Journal*, July 2013, pp. 45-48; R. I. Sutton, *Good Boss, Bad Boss: How to Be the Best . . . and Learn from the Worst* (New York: Business Plus, 2012); and J. Simmons, "Who's the Boss? Answering to Multiple Bosses," *monster.com*, January 1, 2015.

Exhibit 11-4
Contrasting Spans of Control

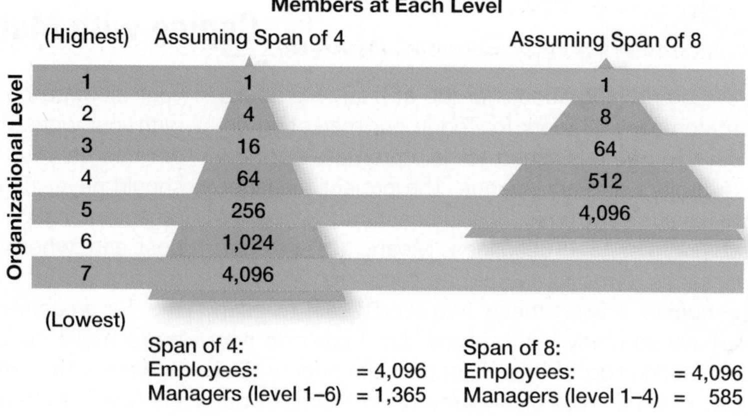

Span of Control

span of control
The number of employees a manager can efficiently and effectively manage

How many employees can a manager efficiently and effectively manage? That's what **span of control** is all about. The traditional view was that managers could not—and should not—directly supervise more than five or six subordinates. Determining the span of control is important because, to a large degree, it determines the number of levels and managers in an organization—an important consideration in how efficient an organization will be. All other things being equal, the wider or larger the span, the more efficient the organization. Here's why.

Assume two organizations both have approximately 4,100 employees. As Exhibit 11-4 shows, if one organization has a span of four and the other a span of eight, the organization with the wider span will have two fewer levels and approximately 800 fewer managers. At an average manager's salary of $62,000 a year, the organization with the wider span would save over $49 million a year! Obviously, wider spans are more efficient in terms of cost. However, at some point, wider spans may reduce effectiveness if employee performance worsens because managers no longer have the time to lead effectively.

- The average span of control is 9.7 employees, rising as high as 11.4 employees.[13]

TODAY'S VIEW The contemporary view of span of control recognizes there is no magic number. Many factors influence the number of employees a manager can efficiently and effectively manage. These factors include the skills and abilities of the manager and the employees and the characteristics of the work being done. For instance, managers with well-trained and experienced employees can function well with a wider span. Apple CEO Tim Cook has 17 direct reports. At first glance, that seems like a lot. But Cook indicates otherwise: "If you have smart people, a strong organizational culture, and a well-defined and articulated strategy that everyone understands, you can [have] numerous direct reports because your job isn't to tell people what to do."[14] Other contingency variables that determine the appropriate span include similarity and complexity of employee tasks; the physical proximity of subordinates; the degree to which standardized procedures are in place; the sophistication of the organization's information system; the strength of the organization's culture, as Cook noted; and the preferred style of the manager.[15]

The trend in recent years has been toward larger spans of control, which is consistent with managers' efforts to speed up decision making, increase flexibility, get closer to customers, empower employees, and reduce costs. Managers are beginning to recognize that they can handle a wider span when employees know their jobs well and when those employees understand organizational processes. Spans also take into account the nature of the work and the needs of employees. For instance, at one Nissan plant, 300 supervisors are responsible for 4,300 employees who produce thousands of vehicles daily. This span allows the supervisors time to coach individual employees on ergonomics and continuous improvement techniques.[16]

Centralization and Decentralization

One of the questions that needs to be answered when organizing is "At what organizational level are decisions made?" **Centralization** is the degree to which decision making takes place at upper levels of the organization. If top managers make key decisions with little input from below, then the organization is more centralized. On the other hand, the more that lower-level employees provide input or actually make decisions, the more **decentralization** there is. Keep in mind that centralization–decentralization is not an either-or concept. The decision is relative, not absolute—that is, an organization is never completely centralized or decentralized.

centralization
The degree to which decision making is concentrated at upper levels of the organization

decentralization
The degree to which lower-level employees provide input or actually make decisions

Early management writers proposed that the degree of centralization in an organization depended on the situation.[17] Their goal was the optimum and efficient use of employees. Traditional organizations were structured in a pyramid, with power and authority concentrated near the top of the organization. Given this structure, historically, centralized decisions were the most prominent, but organizations today have become more complex and responsive to dynamic changes in their environments. As such, many managers believe decisions need to be made by those individuals closest to the problems, regardless of their organizational level. In fact, the trend over the past several decades—at least in U.S. and Canadian organizations—has been a movement toward more decentralization in organizations.[18] Exhibit 11-5 lists some of the factors that affect an organization's use of centralization or decentralization.[19]

- 68 percent of organizations say they've increased centralization in the last five years.[20]

TODAY'S VIEW Today, managers often choose the amount of centralization or decentralization that will allow them to best implement their decisions and achieve organizational goals.[21] What works in one organization, however, won't necessarily work in another, so managers must determine the appropriate amount of decentralization for each organization and work units within it.

As organizations have become more flexible and responsive to environmental trends, there's been a distinct shift toward decentralized decision making.[22] This trend, also known as **employee empowerment**, gives employees more authority (power) to make decisions. (We'll address this concept more thoroughly in our discussion of leadership in Chapter 16.) In large companies especially, lower-level managers are "closer to the action" and typically have more detailed knowledge about problems and how best to solve them than top managers. For instance, decentralized management is the cornerstone of Johnson & Johnson's business model. Alex Gorsky, chairman and CEO, indicates that "our decentralized management approach acknowledges that those closest to patients and customers are in the best position to understand and address their needs."[23] The company's approach has paid off. It has three business divisions with 265 operating companies located across

employee empowerment
Giving employees more authority (power) to make decisions

Exhibit 11-5
Centralization or Decentralization

More Centralization	More Decentralization
• Environment is stable.	• Environment is complex, uncertain.
• Lower-level managers are not as capable or experienced at making decisions as upper-level managers.	• Lower-level managers are capable and experienced at making decisions.
• Lower-level managers do not want a say in decisions.	• Lower-level managers want a voice in decisions.
• Decisions are relatively minor.	• Decisions are significant.
• Organization is facing a crisis or the risk of company failure.	• Corporate culture is open to allowing managers a say in what happens.
• Company is large.	• Company is geographically dispersed.
• Effective implementation of company strategies depends on managers retaining say over what happens.	• Effective implementation of company strategies depends on managers having involvement and flexibility to make decisions.

60 countries, enabling Johnson & Johnson to serve more than one billion people per day.[24] Another example can be seen at Kellogg's plant in Manchester, England, where more than 400 employees work in shifts around the clock to produce one million boxes of breakfast cereal every day. Despite cutbacks, this plant has successfully engaged employees and encouraged creativity to achieve its production targets.[25]

Formalization

formalization
How standardized an organization's jobs are and the extent to which employee behavior is guided by rules and procedures

Formalization refers to how standardized an organization's jobs are and the extent to which employee behavior is guided by rules and procedures. In highly formalized organizations, there are explicit job descriptions, numerous organizational rules, and clearly defined procedures covering work processes. Employees have little discretion over what's done, when it's done, and how it's done. However, where there is less formalization, employees have more discretion in how they do their work.

TODAY'S VIEW Although some formalization is necessary for consistency and control, many organizations today rely less on strict rules and standardization to guide and regulate employee behavior. For instance, consider the following situation: A customer came into a coffee shop to buy a cinnamon roll, but the tray was empty, prompting her to ask whether there were cinnamon rolls in the kitchen. The employee informed her that several were just removed from the tray because the sell-by date had elapsed. She strongly expressed her disappointment and became quite angry. The customer insisted that he sell her a cinnamon roll. Even though policy dictates that he should not, he did so anyway because the company has a policy of ensuring high customer satisfaction. And he reasoned that the pastry should still be good to eat because the rolls were removed just two hours before.

Has this employee done something wrong? He did "break" the rule. But by "breaking" the rule, he actually brought in revenue and provided good customer service.

Considering there are numerous situations where rules may be too restrictive, many organizations have allowed employees some latitude, giving them sufficient autonomy to make those decisions that they feel are best under the circumstances. It doesn't mean throwing out all organizational rules because there *will* be rules that are important for employees to follow—and these rules should be explained so employees understand why it's important to adhere to them. But for other rules, employees may be given some leeway.[26]

MECHANISTIC and organic structures

LO11.2 Basic organizational design revolves around two organizational forms, described in Exhibit 11-6.[27]

mechanistic organization
An organizational design that's rigid and tightly controlled

The **mechanistic organization** (or bureaucracy) was the natural result of combining the six elements of structure. Adhering to the chain-of-command principle ensured the existence of a formal hierarchy of authority, with each person controlled and supervised by one superior. Keeping the span of control small at increasingly higher levels in the organization created tall, impersonal structures. As the distance between the top and the bottom of the organization expanded, top management would increasingly impose rules and regulations. Because top managers couldn't

Exhibit 11-6
Mechanistic Versus Organic Organizations

Mechanistic	Organic
• High specialization	• Cross-functional teams
• Rigid departmentalization	• Cross-hierarchical teams
• Clear chain of command	• Free flow of information
• Narrow spans of control	• Wide spans of control
• Centralization	• Decentralization
• High formalization	• Low formalization

control lower-level activities through direct observation and ensure the use of standard practices, they substituted rules and regulations. The early management writers' belief in a high degree of work specialization created jobs that were simple, routine, and standardized. Further specialization through the use of departmentalization increased impersonality and the need for multiple layers of management to coordinate the specialized departments.[28]

The **organic organization** is a highly adaptive form that is as loose and flexible as the mechanistic organization is rigid and stable. Rather than having standardized jobs and regulations, the organic organization's loose structure allows it to change rapidly, as required.[29] It has division of labor, but the jobs people do are not standardized. Employees tend to be professionals who are technically proficient and trained to handle diverse problems. They need few formal rules and little direct supervision because their training has instilled in them standards of professional conduct. For instance, a petroleum engineer doesn't need to follow specific procedures on how to locate oil sources miles offshore. The engineer can solve most problems alone or after conferring with colleagues. Professional standards guide his or her behavior. The organic organization is low in centralization so that the professional can respond quickly to problems and because top-level managers cannot be expected to possess the expertise to make necessary decisions.

organic organization
An organizational design that's highly adaptive and flexible

If your professor has assigned this, go to **www.mymanagementlab.com** to watch a video titled: *Elm City Market: Organizational Structure* and to respond to questions.

CONTINGENCY factors affecting structural choice

LO11.3 When is a mechanistic structure preferable and when is an organic one more appropriate? Let's look at the main contingency factors that influence the decision.

Strategy and Structure

An organization's structure should facilitate goal achievement. Because goals are an important part of the organization's strategies, it's only logical that strategy and structure are closely linked. Alfred Chandler initially researched this relationship.[30] He studied several large U.S. companies and concluded that changes in corporate strategy led to changes in an organization's structure that support the strategy.

Research has shown that certain structural designs work best with different organizational strategies.[31] For instance, the flexibility and free-flowing information of the organic structure works well when an organization is pursuing meaningful and unique innovations. The mechanistic organization with its efficiency, stability, and tight controls works best for companies wanting to tightly control costs.

LEADER making a DIFFERENCE

Source: Wang Jun/EyePress EPN/Newscom

As chairman and CEO of Haier Group, ***Zhang Ruimin*** *runs a successful enterprise with annual revenues of almost $30 billion, and he has turned Haier into one of China's first global brands.*[32] *Zhang is considered by many to be China's leading corporate executive. When he took over a floundering refrigerator plant in Qingdao, he quickly found out it produced terrible refrigerators. The story goes that he gave the workers sledgehammers and ordered them to destroy every one. His message: Poor quality would no longer be tolerated. Using his business training, Zhang successfully organized Haier for efficient mass production. But here in the twenty-first century, Zhang believes success requires a different competency. So he reorganized the company into self-managed groups, each devoted to a customer or group of similar customers. Zhang gets it! He understands clearly how an organization's design can help it be successful.* What can you learn from this leader making a difference?

3M Company's organic structure helps it to adapt quickly to dynamic environmental forces of global competition and product innovation. With a flexible structure, 3M can satisfy customers' fast-growing demand for touch-screen products such as Ideum's new coffee table PC shown here that incorporates 3M's multitouch technology, an application that is key to expanding the reach of 3M's interactive systems and displays.
Source: Ideum/REX/AP Images

Size and Structure

There's considerable evidence that an organization's size affects its structure.[33] Large organizations—typically considered to be those with more than 2,000 employees—tend to have more specialization, departmentalization, centralization, and rules and regulations than do small organizations. However, once an organization grows past a certain size, size has less influence on structure. Why? Essentially, once there are around 2,000 employees, it's already fairly mechanistic. Adding another 500 employees won't impact the structure much. On the other hand, adding 500 employees to an organization with only 300 employees is likely to make it more mechanistic.

Technology and Structure

Every organization uses some form of technology to convert its inputs into outputs. For instance, CloudDDM uses 3D printers to make prototypes and product parts for corporate customers. This technology has made it possible to conduct the work with few workers. According to Mitch Free, CloudDDM's founder, "we'll have 100 high-tech 3D printers running 24 hours, 7 days a week. And it'll need just three employees: one for each of the eight-hour shifts."[34] Employees at FedEx Office produce custom design and print jobs for individual customers. And employees at Bayer's facility in Karachi, Pakistan, are involved in producing pharmaceuticals on a continuous-flow production line.

The initial research on technology's effect on structure can be traced to Joan Woodward, who studied small manufacturing firms in southern England to determine the extent to which structural design elements were related to organizational success.[35] She couldn't find any consistent pattern until she divided the firms into three distinct technologies that had increasing levels of complexity and sophistication. The first category, **unit production**, described the production of items in units or small batches. The second category, **mass production**, described large-batch manufacturing. Finally, the third and most technically complex group, **process production**, included continuous-process production. A summary of her findings is shown in Exhibit 11-7.

unit production
The production of items in units or small batches

mass production
The production of items in large batches

process production
The production of items in continuous processes

Other studies also have shown that organizations adapt their structures to their technology depending on how routine their technology is for transforming inputs into outputs.[36] In general, the more routine the technology, the more mechanistic the structure can be, and organizations with more nonroutine technology are more likely to have organic structures.[37]

Environmental Uncertainty and Structure

Some organizations face stable and simple environments with little uncertainty; others face dynamic and complex environments with a lot of uncertainty. Managers try to minimize environmental uncertainty by adjusting the organization's structure.[38] In stable and simple environments, mechanistic designs can be more effective. On the other hand, the greater the uncertainty, the more an organization needs the flexibility

Exhibit 11-7
Woodward's Findings on Technology and Structure

	Unit Production	Mass Production	Process Production
Structural characteristics:	Low vertical differentiation	Moderate vertical differentiation	High vertical differentiation
	Low horizontal differentiation	High horizontal differentiation	Low horizontal differentiation
	Low formalization	High formalization	Low formalization
Most effective structure:	Organic	Mechanistic	Organic

of an organic design. For example, the uncertain nature of the commercial air travel industry means that airlines need to be flexible. Several mergers reduced the number of major airlines from nine to four. For instance, United and Continental merged in 2010 and American acquired US Airways in 2015. Combining airlines reduced the number of competitors and pressures to continually lower airfares.[39] The merged companies also were able to streamline corporate structure and operations.

The evidence on the environment–structure relationship helps explain why so many managers today are restructuring their organizations to be lean, fast, and flexible. Worldwide economic downturns, global competition, accelerated product innovation by competitors, and increased demands from customers for high quality and faster deliveries are examples of dynamic environmental forces. Mechanistic organizations are not equipped to respond to rapid environmental change and environmental uncertainty. As a result, we're seeing organizations become more organic.

If your professor has assigned this, go to **www.mymanagementlab.com** to complete the *Simulation: Organizational Structure* and get a better understanding of the challenges of designing appropriate organizational structures.

TRADITIONAL **organizational design options**

LO11.4 They're a big hit with the elementary-school crowd, and millions of them were sold every month. Even after decades in the automotive business, Toyota is still rethinking the way it structures its organization. The company employs more than 340,000 people worldwide and produces vehicles in plants on five continents. In the past, Toyota grouped jobs mainly according to function. Now, to speed up decision making and increase responsiveness to market trends, Toyota groups jobs according to product, such as compact car, mid-size car, commercial vehicle, or Lexus luxury vehicle. Some functions, such as research and development, serve multiple product groups.[40] In making structural decisions, managers have some common designs from which to choose. In this chapter, we're describing the traditional organizational designs and more contemporary types of organizational designs.

When designing a structure, managers may choose one of the traditional organizational designs. These structures tend to be more mechanistic in nature. A summary of the strengths and weaknesses of each can be found in Exhibit 11-8.

Simple Structure

Most companies start as entrepreneurial ventures using a **simple structure**, an organizational design with little departmentalization, wide spans of control, authority centralized in a single person, and little formalization.[41] As employees are added, however, most don't remain as simple structures. The structure tends to become more specialized and formalized. Rules and regulations are introduced, work becomes specialized, departments are created, levels of management are added, and the organization becomes increasingly bureaucratic. At this point, managers might choose a functional structure or a divisional structure.

simple structure
An organizational design with little departmentalization, wide spans of control, centralized authority, and little formalization

Functional Structure

A **functional structure** is an organizational design that groups similar or related occupational specialties together. You can think of this structure as functional departmentalization applied to the entire organization.

functional structure
An organizational design that groups together similar or related occupational specialties

Divisional Structure

The **divisional structure** is an organizational structure made up of separate business units or divisions.[42] In this structure, each division has limited autonomy, with a division manager who has authority over his or her unit and is responsible for performance. In divisional structures, however, the parent corporation typically acts as an

divisional structure
An organizational structure made up of separate, semiautonomous units or divisions

Exhibit 11-8
Traditional Organizational Designs

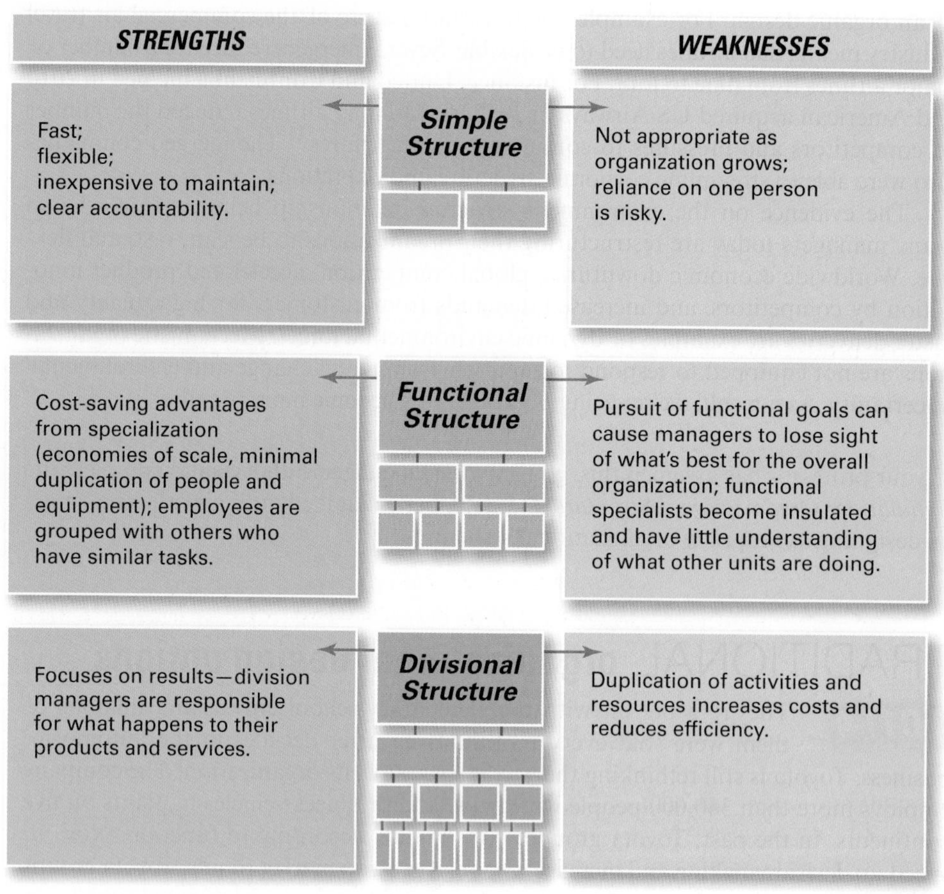

external overseer to coordinate and control the various divisions, and often provides support services such as financial and legal. Walmart, for example, has two divisions: retail (Walmart Stores, International, Sam's Clubs, and others) and support (distribution centers).

As you've seen in this chapter, organizational structure and design (or redesign) are important managerial tasks. Also, we hope that you recognize that organizing decisions aren't only important for upper-level managers. Managers at all levels may have to deal with work specialization or authority or span-of-control decisions. Later in this chapter, we'll continue our discussion of the organizing function by looking at contemporary organizational designs.

ORGANIZING for flexibility in the twenty-first century

LO11.5 Many organizations are finding that traditional organizational designs often aren't appropriate for today's increasingly dynamic and complex environment. Instead, organizations need to be lean, flexible, and innovative; that is, they need to be more organic. So managers are finding creative ways to structure and organize work.

Team Structures

team structure
An organizational structure in which the entire organization is made up of work teams

Larry Page and Sergey Brin, cofounders of Google, created a corporate structure that organized projects around "small, tightly focused teams."[43] A **team structure** is one in which the entire organization is made up of work teams that do the organization's work.[44] In this structure, employee empowerment is crucial because no line of managerial authority flows from top to bottom. Rather, employee teams design and do work in the way they think is best, but the teams are also held responsible for all work performance results in their respective areas. Google found that its best teams share five traits: psychological safety, dependability, structure and clarity, meaningful membership, and purpose.[45]

In large organizations, the team structure complements what is typically a functional or divisional structure and allows the organization to have the efficiency of a bureaucracy *and* the flexibility that teams provide. Companies such as Amazon, Boeing, HP, Louis Vuitton, Motorola, and Xerox, for instance, extensively use employee teams to improve productivity.

Matrix and Project Structures

Other popular contemporary designs are the matrix and project structures. The **matrix structure** assigns specialists from different functional departments to work on projects led by a project manager. (See Exhibit 11-9.) One unique aspect of this design is that it creates a *dual chain of command* because employees in a matrix organization have two managers, their functional area manager and their product or project manager, who share authority. The project manager has authority over the functional members who are part of his or her project team in areas related to the project's goals. However, any decisions about promotions, salary recommendations, and annual reviews typically remain the functional manager's responsibility. The matrix design "violates" the unity-of-command principle, which says that each person should report to only one boss; however, it can—and does—work effectively if both managers communicate regularly, coordinate work demands on employees, and resolve conflicts together.[46] For instance, matrix structures are common in health care settings. Physical therapists could be assigned to different programs. Some may help geriatric patients recover from hip replacement surgery. Others may work with trauma patients who have lost one or more limbs. All of the therapists report to the director of physical rehabilitation and to directors of their specialties.

Many organizations use a **project structure**, in which employees continuously work on projects. Unlike the matrix structure, a project structure has no formal departments where employees return at the completion of a project. Instead, employees take their specific skills, abilities, and experiences to other projects. Also, all work in project structures is performed by teams of employees. For instance, at design firm IDEO, project teams form, disband, and form again as the work requires. Employees "join"

The matrix structure is an appropriate design for the dynamic and complex environment of construction projects. Employees in a matrix design report to two bosses: a project team manager responsible for organizing and completing the project on time and within budget and a functional manager who leads the engineering, marketing, and other functional departments.
Source: Morsa Images/DigitalVision/Getty Images

matrix structure
An organizational structure that assigns specialists from different functional departments to work on one or more projects

project structure
An organizational structure in which employees continuously work on projects

Exhibit 11-9
Example of a Matrix Organization

	R&D	Marketing	Customer Services (CS)	Human Resources (HR)	Finance	Information Systems (IS)
Product 1	R&D Group	Marketing Group	CS Group	HR Group	Finance Group	IS Group
Product 2	R&D Group	Marketing Group	CS Group	HR Group	Finance Group	IS Group
Product 3	R&D Group	Marketing Group	CS Group	HR Group	Finance Group	IS Group

project teams because they bring needed skills and abilities to that project. Once a project is completed, however, they move on to the next one.[47]

Project structures tend to be more flexible organizational designs, without the departmentalization or rigid organizational hierarchy that can slow down making decisions or taking action. In this structure, managers serve as facilitators, mentors, and coaches. They eliminate or minimize organizational obstacles and ensure that teams have the resources they need to effectively and efficiently complete their work.

The Boundaryless Organization

The Large Hadron Collider is a $6 billion particle accelerator lying in a tunnel that's 27 kilometers (17 miles) in circumference and 175 meters (574 feet) below ground near Geneva, Switzerland. "The atom smasher is so large that a brief status report lists 2,900 authors, so complex that scientists in 34 countries have readied 100,000 computers to process its data, and so fragile that a bird dropping a bread crust can short-circuit its power supply."[48] But exploiting the collider's potential to expand the frontiers of knowledge has required that scientists around the world cut across "boundaries of place, organization, and technical specialty to conduct ever more ambitious experiments."

The structural arrangement for getting work done that has developed around the massive collider is an example of another contemporary organizational design called the **boundaryless organization**, an organization whose design is not defined by, or limited to, the horizontal, vertical, or external boundaries imposed by a predefined structure.[49] Former GE chairman Jack Welch coined the term because he wanted to eliminate vertical and horizontal boundaries within GE and break down external barriers between the company and its customers and suppliers. Although the idea of eliminating boundaries may seem odd, many of today's most successful organizations find that they can operate most effectively by remaining flexible and *un*structured: that the ideal structure for them is *not* having a rigid, bounded, and predefined structure.[50]

boundaryless organization
An organization whose design is not defined by, or limited to, the horizontal, vertical, or external boundaries imposed by a predefined structure

VIRTUAL ORGANIZATIONS Is an internship something you've ever thought about doing (or maybe have done)? How about an internship that you could do, not in a workplace cubicle, but from your couch using your computer?[51] Such virtual internships are becoming quite popular, especially with smaller and midsize companies and, of course, with online businesses. The type of work virtual interns do typically involves "researching, sales, marketing, and social media development"—tasks that can be done anywhere with a computer and online access. Some organizations are structured in a way that allows most employees to be virtual employees.

- 64 percent of people said if given a choice, they'd rather work virtually than in an office.[52]

A **virtual organization** typically consists of a small core of full-time employees and outside specialists temporarily hired as needed to work on projects.[53] An example is when Second Life, a company creating a virtual world of colorful online avatars, was building its software. Founder Philip Rosedale hired programmers from around the world and divided up the work into about 1,600 individual tasks, "from setting up databases to fixing bugs." The process worked so well, the company used it for all sorts of work.[54] Another example is Nashville-based Emma Inc., an e-mail marketing firm with 100 employees who work from home or offices in Austin, Denver, New York, and Portland.[55] The biggest challenge they've faced is creating a "virtual" culture, a task made more challenging by the fact that the organization is virtual.

virtual organization
An organization that consists of a small core of full-time employees and outside specialists temporarily hired as needed to work on projects

If your professor has assigned this, go to **www.mymanagementlab.com** to watch a video titled: *Rudi's Bakery: Adaptive Organizational Design* and to respond to questions.

FUTURE VISION Flexible Organizations

By 2025, a considerably smaller proportion of the labor force will hold full-time jobs. Organizations will increasingly rely on contract employees and part-timers to get the work done, giving the organization greater flexibility. Many workers will be doing pieces of what is today a single job. From the employee's standpoint, it will mean greater individual control of the employee's future rather than being dependent on a single employer.

Future workers will be more like outside consultants than full-time employees. Assignments will be temporary. They might last a few weeks or a few years, but the presumption is—on the part of both workers and employers—that the relationship will not become permanent. As such, you will find yourself consistently working on new projects with a different group of coworkers.

Additionally, expect to see fewer large corporate headquarter buildings and centralized corporate centers. Work demands will not require organizations to house large numbers of workers in one place. "Headquarter" cities such as New York, Toronto, or London will find themselves with lots of empty office space. Conversely, job opportunities will be geographically dispersed, and in many cases, not dependent at all on where employees reside. An increasing proportion of the labor force will work from home. And many organizations will create regional satellite centers where employees meet or work. These centers will be less costly to operate than centralized offices and will cut down on commuting distances for workers.

*If your professor has chosen to assign this, go to **www.mymanagementlab.com** to discuss the following questions.*

TALK ABOUT IT 1: What are the challenges of "flexibility" for organizations and managers? For workers?

TALK ABOUT IT 2: What about you? How do you feel about working like this?

TASK FORCES Another structural option organizations might use is a **task force** (also called an **ad hoc committee**), a temporary committee or team formed to tackle a specific short-term problem affecting several departments. The temporary nature of a task force is what differentiates it from a cross-functional team. Task force members usually perform many of their normal work tasks while serving on the task force; however, the members of a task force must collaborate to resolve the issue that's been assigned to them. When the issue or problem is solved, the task force is no longer needed and members return to their regular assignments. Many organizations, from government agencies to universities to businesses, use task forces. For instance, at San Francisco–based accounting firm Eichstaedt & Devereaux, employee task forces have helped develop formal recruiting, mentoring, and training programs. And at Frito-Lay, a subsidiary of PepsiCo, Inc., a task force that included members of the company's Hispanic employees' resource group helped in the development of two products: Lay's Cool Guacamole potato chips and Doritos Guacamole tortilla chips.[56]

task force (or ad hoc committee)
A temporary committee or team formed to tackle a specific short-term problem affecting several departments

The days may be numbered when businesses generate their own product development ideas and develop, manufacture, market, and deliver those products to customers. Today, many companies are trying **open innovation**, opening up the search for new ideas beyond the organization's boundaries and allowing innovations to easily transfer inward and outward. For instance, Under Armour, a sports shoes and sportswear company, created the Idea House, which is an online platform available to employees and the public. Anyone may submit an idea for a new product or product improvement. The Idea House has been a worthwhile investment because it led to important innovations; for example, the Recharge® compression suit that helps muscles recover more quickly after strenuous physical activities.

open innovation
Opening up the search for new ideas beyond the organization's boundaries and allowing innovations to easily transfer inward and outward

As you can see, many of today's successful companies are collaborating directly with customers in the product development process. Others are partnering with suppliers, other outsiders, and even competitors. Exhibit 11-10 describes some of the benefits and drawbacks of open innovation.

Exhibit 11-10
Benefits and Drawbacks of Open Innovation

Sources: Based on S. Lindegaard, "The Side Effects of Open Innovation," *Bloomberg BusinessWeek* online, June 7, 2010; H. W. Chesbrough and A. R. Garman, "How Open Innovation Can Help You Cope in Lean Times," *Harvard Business Review,* December 2009, pp. 68–76; A. Gabor, "The Promise [and Perils] of Open Collaboration," *Strategy & Business* online, Autumn 2009; and J. Winsor, "Crowdsourcing: What It Means for Innovation," *BusinessWeek* online, June 15, 2009.

Benefits

- Gives customers what they want—a voice
- Allows organizations to respond to complex problems
- Nurtures internal and external relationships
- Brings focus back to marketplace
- Provides way to cope with rising costs and uncertainties of product development

Drawbacks

- High demands of managing the process
- Extensive support needed
- Cultural challenges
- Greater need for flexibility
- Crucial changes required in how knowledge is controlled and shared

Xerox Corporation has more than 8,000 employees—11 percent of its workforce—who work from home full-time in a wide variety of jobs including customer care, technical support, quality control, and software development. Xerox believes that telecommuting opportunities result in higher employee productivity and increased morale and job satisfaction.
Source: Bloomberg/Getty Images

telecommuting
A work arrangement in which employees work at home and are linked to the workplace by computer

Telecommuting

Eve Gelb used to endure hour-and-a-half commutes morning and evening on the 405 freeway in Los Angeles to her job as a project manager at SCAN Health Plan.[57] Now, she's turned her garage into an office and works from home as a telecommuter. On the days when she does have to go in to the corporate office, she shares a space with her three subordinates who also work flexibly. Information technology has made telecommuting possible, and external environmental changes have made it necessary for many organizations. **Telecommuting** is a work arrangement in which employees work at home and are linked to the workplace by computer. Needless to say, not every job is a candidate for telecommuting, but many are.

Working from home used to be considered a "cushy perk" for a few lucky employees, and such an arrangement wasn't allowed very often. Now, many businesses view telecommuting as a business necessity. For instance, at Avnet, Inc., the company's chief executive officer said that he favors telecommuting because it can improve employee engagement. Also, SCAN Health Plan's chief financial officer said that getting more employees to telecommute provided the company a way to grow without having to incur any additional fixed costs such as office buildings, equipment, or parking lots. In addition, some companies view the arrangement as a way to combat high gas prices and to attract talented employees who want more freedom and control over their work.

Despite its apparent appeal, many managers are reluctant to have their employees become "laptop hobos."[59] They argue that employees will waste time surfing the Internet or playing online games instead of working, that they'll ignore clients, and that they'll desperately miss the camaraderie and social exchanges of the workplace. In addition, managers wonder how they'll "manage" these employees. How do you interact with an employee and gain his or her trust when they're not physically present? And what if their work performance isn't up to par? How do you make suggestions for improvement? Another significant challenge is making sure that company information is kept safe and secure when employees are working from home.

Employees often express the same concerns about working remotely, especially when it comes to the isolation of not being "at work." At Accenture, where employees are scattered around the world, the chief human resources officer says it isn't easy to maintain that esprit de corps.[60] However, the company has put in place a number of programs and processes to create that sense of belonging for its workforce, including Web-conferencing tools, assigning each employee to a career counselor, and holding quarterly community events at its offices. In addition, the telecommuter employee may find that the line between work and home becomes even more blurred, which can be stressful.[61] Finally, many women believe that taking advantage of flexible work arrangements may stunt career advancement. Managers and organizations must address these important organizing issues as they move toward having employees telecommute. For instance, Moody's Corporation uses its intranet to showcase women who advanced to executive positions. One woman was promoted to senior vice president after telecommuting two days a week for many years.[62]

- 82 percent of employers offer telecommuting work arrangements.[58]

Staying Connected Knowledge—If your instructor is using Pearson MyLab Management, log onto **mymanagementlab.com** and test your *staying connected knowledge*. **Be sure to refer back to the chapter opener!**

★ It's Your Career

let's get REAL

Source: Justin Kidwell

Justin Kidwell
Management Consultant

The Scenario:

Isabella Castillo, vice president of professional services at a consulting company that helps IT organizations deliver better service to their customers, needs help with her professional staff of 16 consultants, who all work from home. Her problem: dealing with the realities of telecommuting—lack of direct interaction, lack of camaraderie, feeling isolated and out-of-the-loop, etc. For their type of business, remote work makes good business sense, but how can she connect and engage her employees?

What advice would you give Isabella?

I would focus on a few things:

1. *Making people development a strategic goal*
2. *Semiannual retreats*
3. *Leveraging technology*

Embedding people development into the performance measurement equation ensures interaction and teaming. The semiannual retreats provide a bonding environment and opportunity to gain buy-in to management priorities. Collaborative tools make phone-only meetings obsolete.

Flexible work arrangements accommodate employees' needs and desires to achieve a balance between their work lives and personal lives. For example, work options such as compressed workweeks, flextime, and job sharing give parents the opportunity to spend time during the day with their children.
Source: Iakov Filimonov/Shutterstock

Compressed Workweeks, Flextime, and Job Sharing

During the global economic crisis in the United Kingdom, accounting firm KPMG needed to reduce costs. It decided to use flexible work options as a way of doing so. The company's program, called Flexible Futures, offered employees four options to choose from: a four-day workweek with a 20 percent salary reduction; a two- to twelve-week sabbatical at 30 percent of pay; both options; or continue with their regular schedule. Some 85 percent of the U.K. employees agreed to the reduced-workweek plan. "Since so many people agreed to the flexible work plans, KPMG was able to cap the salary cut at about 10 percent for the year in most cases." The best thing, though, was that as a result of the plan, KPMG didn't have to do large-scale employee layoffs.[63]

As this example shows, organizations may sometimes find they need to restructure work using forms of flexible work arrangements. One approach is a **compressed workweek**, a workweek where employees work longer hours per day but fewer days per week. The most common arrangement is four 10-hour days (a 4–40 program). For example, in Utah, state employees have a mandated (by law) four-day workweek, with offices closed on Fridays in an effort to reduce energy costs. After a year's time, the state found that its compressed workweek resulted in a 13 percent reduction in energy use and estimated that state employees saved as much as $6 million in gasoline costs.[64] And the accounting/consulting firm, KPMG, permits some U.S. employees to select a compressed workweek option. Barbara Wankoff, KPMG's director of workplace solutions, said: "Their satisfaction goes way up when they have control over their time. And it increases employee morale and productivity and retention."[65] Another alternative is **flextime** (also known as **flexible work hours**), a scheduling system in which employees are required to work a specific number of hours a week but are free to vary those hours within certain limits. A flextime schedule typically designates certain common core hours when all employees are required to be on the job, but allows starting, ending, and lunch-hour times to be flexible. According to a survey of companies by the Families and Work Institute, 81 percent of the respondents now offer flextime benefits.[66] Another survey by Watson Wyatt of mid- and large-sized companies found that a flexible work schedule was the most commonly offered benefit.[67]

compressed workweek
A workweek where employees work longer hours per day but fewer days per week

flextime (or flexible work hours)
A scheduling system in which employees are required to work a specific number of hours a week but are free to vary those hours within certain limits

In Great Britain, McDonald's experimented with an unusual program—dubbed the Family Contract—to reduce absenteeism and turnover at some of its restaurants. Under this Family Contract, employees from the same immediate family can fill in for one another for any work shift without having to clear it first with their manager.[68] This type of job scheduling is called **job sharing**—the practice of having two or more people split a full-time job. Although something like McDonald's Family Contract may be appropriate for a low-skilled job, other organizations might offer job sharing to professionals who want to work but don't want the demands and hassles of a full-time position. For instance, at Ernst & Young and Google, employees in many of the company's locations can choose from a variety of flexible work arrangements, including job sharing. Also, many companies have used job sharing during the economic downturn to avoid employee layoffs.[69]

job sharing
The practice of having two or more people split a full-time job

- 47 percent of employees say that asking for flexible work options would hurt their career advancement.[70]

The Contingent Workforce

Around the world, many organizations are coping with labor shortages and peak work demands by hiring employees on a temporary or part-time basis. Top managers at Toyota, for example, understand the need to have valuable skills and technical know-how available within the organization, even as their workforce ages. Toyota's factories frequently hire contract workers but also retain a number as permanent, full-time employees to enhance the workforce's capabilities—and to keep production going when more experienced employees help out on projects at other Toyota factories.[71] According to the U.S. Bureau of Labor Statistics, **contingent workers** are persons who do not expect their jobs to last or who reported that their jobs are temporary. Also, they do not have an implicit or explicit contract for ongoing employment. Alternative employment arrangements include persons employed as independent contractors, on-call workers, temporary help agency workers, and workers provided by contract firms. Aramark is an example of a contract organization. It provides food service, facilities and uniform services to hospitals, universities, and other businesses. For instance, most food service workers in a hospital's cafeteria are employees of the contract company, not the hospital.

contingent workers
Temporary, freelance, or contract workers whose employment is contingent on demand for their services

"Companies are starting to rethink the way they get work done."[72] As full-time jobs are eliminated through downsizing and other organizational restructurings, managers often rely on a contingent workforce to fill in as needed. A recent survey of top executives revealed that a majority of companies from a variety of industries are engaging contingent workers. For example, 81 percent of organizations in the health care industry use contingent workers.[73] And one of the top-ranking forecasts in a survey that asked HR experts to look ahead to 2018 was that "firms will become adept at sourcing and engaging transient talent around short-term needs, and will focus considerable energy on the long-term retention of smaller core talent groups."[74] The model for the contingent worker structural approach can be seen in the film industry. There, people are essentially "free agents" who move from project to project applying their skills—directing, talent casting, costuming, makeup, set design, and so forth—as needed. They assemble for a movie, then disband once it's finished and move on to the next project. This type of contingent worker is common in project organizations. But contingent workers can also be temporary employees brought in to help with special needs such as seasonal work. Let's look at some of the organizational issues associated with contingent workers.

One of the main issues businesses face with their contingent workers, especially those who are independent contractors or freelancers, is classifying who actually qualifies as one.[75] The decision on who is and who isn't an independent contractor isn't as easy or as unimportant as it may seem. Companies don't have to pay Social Security, Medicare, or unemployment insurance taxes on workers classified as independent contractors. And those individuals also aren't covered by most workplace laws. So it's an important decision. For instance, Uber Technologies, Inc., treats some 450,000 of its drivers as contractors. Their classification of these workers as independent contractors has caused battles in the courts. Uber drivers claim that they should be treated as employees because the company controls their work, sets compensation, and imposes vehicle standards. To the drivers' dismay, a court ruled that Uber drivers in California and Massachusetts are independent contractors. The legal definition of a contract worker depends on how much control a company has over the person; that is, does the company control what the worker does and how the worker does his or her job? When a company has more control, the individual is more likely to be considered an employee, not an independent contractor, but not always, as the recent court ruling conveys. And it isn't just the legal/tax issues that are important in how workers are classified. The structural implications, especially in terms of getting work done and how performance problems are resolved, are important as well. In the Uber case, the court ruled that the company must explain its decisions to terminate drivers and provide warnings first.

If your professor has assigned this, go to **www.mymanagementlab.com** to complete the Writing Assignment *MGMT 2: Organizational Structures.*

Chapter 11 PREPARING FOR: Exams/Quizzes

CHAPTER SUMMARY by Learning Objectives

LO11.1 DESCRIBE six key elements in organizational design.

The key elements in organizational design are work specialization, departmentalization, chain of command, span of control, centralization–decentralization, and formalization. Work specialization is dividing work activities into separate job tasks. Today's view is that work specialization can help employees be more efficient. Departmentalization is how jobs are grouped together. Today most large organizations use combinations of different forms of departmentalization. The chain of command and its companion concepts—authority, responsibility, and unity of command—were viewed as important ways of maintaining control in organizations. The contemporary view is that they are less relevant in today's organizations. The traditional view of span of control was that managers should directly supervise no more than five to six individuals. The contemporary view is that the span of control depends on the skills and abilities of the manager and the employees and on the characteristics of the situation. Centralization–decentralization is a structural decision about who makes decisions—upper-level managers or lower-level employees. Formalization concerns the organization's use of standardization and strict rules to provide consistency and control. Today, organizations rely less on strict rules and standardization to guide and regulate employee behavior.

LO11.2 CONTRAST mechanistic and organic structures.

A mechanistic organization is a rigid and tightly controlled structure. An organic organization is highly adaptive and flexible.

LO11.3 DISCUSS the contingency factors that favor either the mechanistic model or the organic model of organizational design.

An organization's structure should support the strategy. If the strategy changes, the structure also should change. An organization's size can affect its structure up to a certain point. Once an organization reaches a certain size (usually around 2,000 employees), it's fairly mechanistic. An organization's technology can affect its structure. An organic structure is most effective with unit production and process production technology. A mechanistic structure is most effective with mass production technology. The more uncertain an organization's environment, the more it needs the flexibility of an organic design.

LO11.4 DESCRIBE traditional organizational design options.

A simple structure is one with little departmentalization, wide spans of control, authority centralized in a single person, and little formalization. A functional structure groups similar or related occupational specialties together. A divisional structure is made up of separate business units or divisions.

LO11.5 DISCUSS organizing for flexibility in the twenty-first century.

In a team structure, the entire organization is made up of work teams. The matrix structure assigns specialists from different functional departments to work on one or more projects being led by project managers. A project structure is one in which employees continuously work on projects. A boundaryless organization's design is not defined by, or limited by, the horizontal, vertical, or external boundaries imposed by a predefined structure. A virtual organization consists of a small core of full-time employees and outside specialists temporarily hired as needed to work on projects. Another structural option is a task force, which is a temporary committee or team formed to tackle a specific short-term problem affecting several departments.

Telecommuting is a work arrangement in which employees work at home and are linked to the workplace by computer. A compressed workweek is one in which employees work longer hours per day but fewer days per week. Flextime is a scheduling system in which employees are required to work a specific number of hours a week but are free to vary those hours within certain limits. Job sharing is when two or more people split a full-time job.

Contingent workers are temporary, freelance, or contract workers whose employment is contingent on demand for their services. Organizing issues include classifying who actually qualifies as an independent contractor; setting up a process for recruiting, screening, and placing contingent workers; and having a method in place for establishing goals, schedules, and deadlines and for monitoring work performance.

Pearson **MyLab** Management

Go to **mymanagementlab.com** to complete the problems marked with this icon ✪.

✪ REVIEW AND DISCUSSION QUESTIONS

11-1. Any organizational design has traditionally had a chain of command. How does a chain of command work?

11-2. Contrast mechanistic and organic organizations.

11-3. Discuss why you think an organization might be keen to increase its managers' span of control.

11-4. Why is structure important? Why does an organization need a clear structure? Are there any other reasons for organizational structures beyond the formal arrangement of jobs, roles, and responsibilities?

11-5. In terms of organizational designs, what is a simple structure?

11-6. There is evidence that an organization's size will affect its structure. The larger the number of employees, the more mechanistic the organization will tend to become. Can this problem be overcome?

11-7. An organization's structure is dictated by its organizational strategy. Which structural design is best if a manufacturing company's goal is to keep costs low as a competitive advantage?

11-8. What are the main challenges facing organizational designs today?

Pearson **MyLab** Management

If your professor has assigned these, go to **mymanagementlab.com** for the following Assisted-graded writing questions:

11-9. Can an organization's structure be changed quickly? Why or why not? Should it be changed quickly? Explain.

11-10. The gradual move toward more flexible working practices will radically change the way organizations operate. Do you agree or disagree? Explain your answer.

PREPARING FOR: My Career

PERSONAL INVENTORY ASSESSMENTS  PERSONAL INVENTORY ASSESSMENT

Organizational Structure Assessment

As this chapter described, there are many different approaches to designing organizational structure. What type of structure appeals to you? Take this PIA and find out.

ETHICS DILEMMA

Thomas Lopez, a lifeguard in the Miami area, was fired for leaving his assigned area to save a drowning man.[76] His employer, Jeff Ellis and Associates, which has a contract with the Florida city of Hallandale, said that by leaving his assigned patrol area uncovered, Lopez opened the company up to possible legal action. Lopez said he had no choice but to do what he did. He wasn't putting his job rules first over helping someone who desperately needed help. "I'm going to do what I felt was right, and I did." After this story hit the media, the company offered Lopez his job back, but he declined.

11-11. What do you think? What ethical concerns do you see in this situation?

11-12. What lessons can be applied to organizational design from this story?

SKILLS EXERCISE Developing Your Acquiring Power Skill

About the Skill

Power is a natural process in any group or organization, and to perform their jobs effectively, managers need to know how to acquire and use power.[77] Why is having power important? Because power makes you less dependent on others. When a manager has power, he or she is not as dependent on others for critical resources. And if the resources a manager controls are important, scarce, and nonsubstitutable, her power will increase because others will be more dependent on her for those resources. (See Chapter 16 for more information on leader power.)

Steps in Practicing the Skill

You can be more effective at acquiring and using power if you use the following eight behaviors.

- ***Frame arguments in terms of organizational goals.*** To be effective at acquiring power means camouflaging your self-interest. Discussions over who controls what resources should be framed in terms of the benefits that will accrue to the organization; do not point out how you personally will benefit.
- ***Develop the right image.*** If you know your organization's culture, you already understand what the organization wants and values from its employees in terms of dress, associates to cultivate and those to avoid, whether to appear risk taking or risk aversive, the preferred leadership style, the importance placed on getting along well with others, and so forth. With this knowledge, you're equipped to project the appropriate image. Because the assessment of your performance isn't always a fully objective process, you need to pay attention to style as well as substance.
- ***Gain control of organizational resources.*** Controlling organizational resources that are scarce *and* important is a source of power. Knowledge and expertise are particularly effective resources to control. They make you more valuable to the organization and therefore more likely to have job security, chances for advancement, and a receptive audience for your ideas.
- ***Make yourself appear indispensable.*** Because we're dealing with appearances rather than objective facts, you can enhance your power by appearing to be indispensable. You don't really have *to be* indispensable, as long as key people in the organization believe that you are.
- ***Be visible.*** If you have a job that brings your accomplishments to the attention of others, that's great. However, if you don't have such a job, you'll want to find ways to let others in the organization know what you're doing by highlighting successes in routine reports, having satisfied customers relay their appreciation to senior executives, being seen at social functions, being active in your professional associations, and developing powerful allies who speak positively about your accomplishments. Of course, you'll want to be on the lookout for those projects that will increase your visibility.

- ***Develop powerful allies.*** To get power, it helps to have powerful people on your side. Cultivate contacts with potentially influential people above you, at your own level, and at lower organizational levels. These allies often can provide you with information that's otherwise not readily available. In addition, having allies can provide you with a coalition of support—if and when you need it.
- ***Avoid "tainted" members.*** In almost every organization, there are fringe members whose status is questionable. Their performance and/or loyalty may be suspect. Keep your distance from such individuals.
- ***Support your boss.*** Your immediate future is in the hands of your current boss. Because he or she evaluates your performance, you'll typically want to do whatever is necessary to have your boss on your side. You should make every effort to help your boss succeed, make her look good, support her if she is under siege, and spend the time to find out the criteria she will use to assess your effectiveness. Don't undermine your boss. And don't speak negatively of her to others.

Practicing the Skill

The following suggestions are activities you can do to practice the behaviors associated with acquiring power.

1. Keep a one-week journal of your behavior describing incidences when you tried to influence others around you. Assess each incident by asking: Were you successful at these attempts to influence them? Why or why not? What could you have done differently?
2. Review recent issues of a business periodical (such as *Bloomberg BusinessWeek, Fortune, Forbes, Fast Company, Industry Week,* or *The Wall Street Journal*). Look for articles on reorganizations, promotions, or departures from management positions. Find at least two articles where you believe power issues are involved. Relate the content of the articles to the concepts introduced in this skill module.

WORKING TOGETHER Team Exercise

Businesses need to be adaptable and available on a 24-hour basis. Working in groups of three or four, discuss how you would organize a small workforce such that it is able to respond on a 24-hour basis, all year round. The workforce will be centrally located. You need to be able to make accommodations for employees with external commitments. You are required to offer flexible working, job sharing, or compressed working packages. As a group, draft guidelines for the management and other employees. Be prepared to share your group's suggestions with the rest of the class.

MY TURN TO BE A MANAGER

- Find three different examples of an organizational chart. (A company's annual reports are a good place to look.) In a report, describe each of these. Try to decipher the organization's use of organizational design elements, especially departmentalization, chain of command, centralization-decentralization, and formalization.
- Survey at least 10 different managers as to how many employees they supervise. Also ask them whether they feel they could supervise more employees or whether they feel the number they supervise is too many. Graph your survey results and write a report describing what you found. Draw some conclusions about span of control.
- Using current business periodicals, research open innovation efforts by companies. Choose three examples of businesses using this and describe and evaluate what each is doing.
- Visit the When Work Works website at www.whenworkworks.org. This organization works to bring research on workplace flexibility into practice. Visit the "Find Solutions" page of the website and review the guidance provided for employers. What resources are available for managers looking to create more flexible work arrangements?

CASE APPLICATION 1 A New Kind of Structure

Admit it. Sometimes the projects you're working on (school, work, or both) can get pretty boring and monotonous. Wouldn't it be great to have a magic button you could push to get someone else to do that boring, time-consuming stuff? At Pfizer, that "magic button" is a reality for a large number of employees.[78]

As a global pharmaceutical company, Pfizer is continually looking for ways to help employees be more efficient and effective. The company's senior director of organizational effectiveness found that the highly educated MBAs it hired to "develop strategies and innovate were instead Googling and making PowerPoints."[79] Indeed, internal studies conducted to find out just how much time its valuable talent was spending on menial tasks was startling. The average Pfizer employee was spending 20 percent to 40 percent of his or her time on support work (creating documents, typing notes, doing research, manipulating data, scheduling meetings) and only 60 percent to 80 percent on knowledge work (strategy, innovation, networking, collaborating, critical thinking). And the problem wasn't just at lower levels. Even the highest-level employees were affected. Take, for instance, David Cain, an executive director for global engineering. He enjoys his job—assessing environmental real estate risks, managing facilities, and controlling a multimillion-dollar budget. But he didn't so much enjoy having to go through spreadsheets and put together PowerPoints. Now, however, with Pfizer's "magic button," those tasks are passed off to individuals outside the organization.

Just what is this "magic button"? Originally called the Office of the Future (OOF), the renamed PfizerWorks allows employees to shift tedious and time-consuming tasks with the click of a single button on their computer desktop. They describe what they need on an online form, which is then sent to one of two Indian service-outsourcing firms. When a request is received, a team member in India calls the Pfizer employee to clarify what's needed and by when. The team member then e-mails back a cost specification for the requested work. If the Pfizer employee decides to proceed, the costs involved are charged to the employee's department. About this unique arrangement, Cain said that he relishes working with what he prefers to call his "personal consulting organization."

The number 66,500 illustrates just how beneficial PfizerWorks has been for the company. That's the number of work hours estimated to have been saved by employees who've used PfizerWorks. What about David Cain's experiences? When he gave the Indian team a complex project researching strategic actions that worked when consolidating company facilities, the team put the report together in a month, something that would have taken him six months to do alone. "Pfizer pays me not to work tactically, but to work strategically," he says.[80]

DISCUSSION QUESTIONS

11-13. Describe and evaluate what Pfizer is doing with its PfizerWorks.

11-14. What structural implications—good and bad—does this approach have? (Think in terms of the six organizational design elements.)

11-15. Do you think this arrangement would work for other types of organizations? Why or why not? What types of organizations might it also work for?

11-16. What role do you think organizational structure plays in an organization's efficiency and effectiveness? Explain.

CASE APPLICATION 2 Organizational Volunteers

They're individuals you might never have thought of as being part of an organization's structure, but for many organizations, volunteers provide a much-needed source of labor.[81] Maybe you've volunteered at a Habitat for Humanity build, a homeless shelter, or some other nonprofit organization. However, would you consider a volunteer assignment at a for-profit business? Many large corporations and start-up companies are relying on the willingness of enthusiastic product users to voluntarily help other users with questions about products or services via online discussion boards. Some suggest that this movement will transform the field of customer service, using fewer paid employees and more volunteers to respond to technical questions such as how to program a new high-definition television or set up an Internet home network.

Self check-outs. Self check-ins. Self order-placing. Pumping your own gas (although most of you are probably too young to remember having an attendant who pumped your gas, checked your oil, and washed your windshield). Filling out online forms. Businesses have become very good at getting customers to do free work. Now, they're taking the concept even further, especially in customer service settings, by getting "volunteers" to perform specialized work tasks.

The role that these volunteer "enthusiasts" have played, especially in contributing innovations to research and development efforts, has been closely researched in recent years. For example, case studies highlight the product tweaks made by early skateboarders and mountain bikers to their gear. Researchers have also studied the programmers behind open-source software like the Linux operating system. It seems that individuals who do this type of "volunteering" are motivated mainly by a payoff in enjoyment and respect among their peers and to some extent the skills they're able to develop. Now, as the concept of individuals volunteering for work tasks moves to the realm of customer service, can it work and what does it mean for managers?

For instance, at Verizon's high-speed fiber optic Internet, television, and telephone service, "volunteers" are answering customer questions about technical matters on a company-sponsored customer-service website for no pay. Mark Studness, director of Verizon's e-commerce unit, was familiar with sites where users offered tips and answered questions. His challenge? Find a way to use that potential resource for customer service. His solution? "Super," or lead, users—that is, users who provided the best answers and dialogue in Web forums.

The experiment at Verizon seems to be working well and these online "volunteers" can be an important addition to a company's customer service efforts. Studness says that creating an atmosphere that these super users find desirable is a key consideration because without that, you have nothing. A company that worked with Verizon to set up its structure said that these super or lead users are driven by the same online challenges and aspects as fervent gamers are. So they set up the structure with an elaborate rating system for contributors with ranks, badges, and "kudos counts." So far, Studness is happy with how it's gone. He says the company-sponsored customer-service site has been extremely useful and cost efficient in redirecting thousands of questions that would have been answered by staff at a Verizon call center.

DISCUSSION QUESTIONS

11-17. What do you think about using "volunteers" to do work that other people get paid to do?

11-18. If you were in Mark Studness's position, what would you be most concerned about in this arrangement? How would you "manage" that concern?

11-19. How do these "volunteers" fit into an organization's structure? Take each of the six elements of organizational design and discuss how each would affect this structural approach.

11-20. Do you think this approach could work for other types of work being done or in other types of organizations? Explain.

ENDNOTES

1. A. R. Carey and P. Trap, "Fewer Hours at the Office," *USA Today,* October 17, 2013, p. 1A.
2. "The Simple List," *Real Simple,* September 2013, p. 14.
3. Ibid.
4. C. Sloan, "787 Program: Delivery & Dispatch Reliability Catching Up with Demand," *Airways News* online, www.airwaysnews.com, June 29, 2015.
5. G. Polek, "After Record Ramp-Up, Boeing Fine-Tunes 787 Production," *Aviation International News* online, www.ainonline.com, June 11, 2015.
6. D. Hudepohl, "Finesse a Flexible Work Schedule," *Wall Street Journal,* February 19, 2008, p. B8.
7. J. Nickerson, C. J. Yen, and J. T. Mahoney, "Exploring the Problem-Finding and Problem-Solving Approach for Designing Organizations," *Academy of Management Perspectives,* February 2012, pp. 52–72; R. Greenwood and D. Miller, "Tackling Design Anew: Getting Back to the Heart of Organizational Theory," *Academy of Management Perspectives,* November 2010, pp. 78–89.
8. See, for example, R. L. Daft, *Organization Theory and Design,* 10th ed. (Mason, OH: South-Western College Publishing, 2009).
9. C. Dougherty, "Workforce Productivity Falls," *Wall Street Journal,* May 4, 2012, p. A5; and S. E. Humphrey, J. D. Nahrgang, and F. P. Morgeson, "Integrating Motivational, Social, and Contextual Work Design Features: A Meta-Analytic Summary and Theoretical Expansion of the Work Design Literature," *Journal of Applied Psychology,* September 2007, pp. 1332–1356.
10. A. J. Ward, M. J. Lankau, A. C. Amason, J. A. Sonnenfeld, and B. R. Agle, "Improving the Performance of Top Management Teams," *MIT Sloan Management Review* online, www.sloanreview.mit.edu, April 1, 2007.
11. For a discussion of authority, see W. A. Kahn and K. E. Kram, "Authority at Work: Internal Models and Their Organizational Consequences," *Academy of Management Review*, January 1994, pp. 17–50.
12. R. Ashkenas, "Simplicity-Minded Management," *Harvard Business Review,* December 2007, pp. 101–109; and P. Glader, "It's Not Easy Being Lean," *Wall Street Journal,* June 19, 2006, pp. B1+.
13. "Global Human Capital Trends 2016–The New Organization: Different by Design," *Deloitte University* Press, www.deloitte.com, 2016.
14. S. Lebowitz, "Apple CEO Tim Cook Now Has 17 Direct Reports—and That's Probably Too Many," Business Insider online, www.businessinsider.com, July 8, 2015.
15. G. L. Neilson and J. Wulf, "How Many Direct Reports?," *Harvard Business Review,* April 2012, pp. 112–119; and D. Van Fleet, "Span of Management Research and Issues," *Academy of Management Journal*, September 1983, pp. 546–552.
16. Chris Tighe, "Nissan Builds on Loyalty at Sunderland Plant," *Financial Times,* March 7, 2016, https://www.ft.com/content/7487772a-d703-11e5-829b-8564e7528e54 (accessed December 23, 2016).
17. H. Fayol, *General and Industrial Management*, trans. C. Storrs (London: Pitman Publishing, 1949), pp. 19–42.
18. J. Zabojnik, "Centralized and Decentralized Decision Making in Organizations," *Journal of Labor Economics,* January 2002, pp. 1–22.
19. See, for example, H. Mintzberg, *Power In and Around Organizations* (Upper Saddle River, NJ: Prentice Hall, 1983); and J. Child, *Organization: A Guide to Problems and Practices* (London: Kaiser & Row, 1984).
20. M. Weinstein, "It's a Balancing Act," *Training,* May 2009, p. 10.
21. See P. Kenis and D. Knoke, "How Organizational Field Networks Shape Interorganizational Tie-Formation Rates," *Academy of Management Review,* April 2002, pp. 275–293.
22. A. D. Amar, C. Hentrich, and V. Hlupic, "To Be a Better Leader, Give Up Authority," *Harvard Business Review,* December 2009, pp. 22–24.
23. Johnson & Johnson, *Annual Report, 2015*, http://www.jnj.com/about-jnj/publications, accessed April 22, 2016.
24. K. King, "Johnson & Johnson: Company Overview," *Harvard Business School Open Knowledge* online, https://rctom.hbs.org, December 8, 2015.
25. Noli Dinkoviski, "Kellogg's Cutbacks Make the Factory More Efficient," *Food Manufacture UK,* August 11, 2016, http://www.foodmanufacture.co.uk/Manufacturing/Kellogg-s-cutbacks-make-the-factory-more-efficient (accessed December 23, 2016); Matt Atherton, "Kellogg's Factory Features in BBC Documentary," *Food Manufacture UK,* July 25, 2016, http://www.foodmanufacture.co.uk/Manufacturing/BBC-documentary-reveals-Kellogg-s-secrets (accessed December 23, 2016).
26. Ibid.
27. D. A. Morand, "The Role of Behavioral Formality and Informality in the Enactment of Bureaucratic Versus Organic Organizations," *Academy of Management Review*, October 1995, pp. 831–872; and T. Burns and G. M. Stalker, *The Management of Innovation* (London: Tavistock, 1961).
28. C. Feser, "Long Live Bureaucracy!," *Leader to Leader,* Summer 2012, pp. 57–62.
29. "How to Bust Corporate Barriers," *Gallup Management Journal online,* August 18, 2011; and D. Dougherty, "Re-imagining the Differentiation and Integration of Work for Sustained Product Innovation," *Organization Science* (September–October 2001), pp. 612–631.
30. A. D. Chandler, Jr., *Strategy and Structure: Chapters in the History of the Industrial Enterprise* (Cambridge, MA: MIT Press, 1962).

31. See, for instance, W. Chan Kim and R. Mauborgne, "How Strategy Shapes Structure," *Harvard Business Review,* September 2009, pp. 73–80; L. L. Bryan and C. I. Joyce, "Better Strategy Through Organizational Design," *The McKinsey Quarterly,* 2007, no. 2, pp. 21–29; D. Jennings and S. Seaman, "High and Low Levels of Organizational Adaptation: An Empirical Analysis of Strategy, Structure, and Performance," *Strategic Management Journal*, July 1994, pp. 459–475; D. C. Galunic and K. M. Eisenhardt, "Renewing the Strategy-Structure-Performance Paradigm," in *Research in Organizational Behavior*, vol. 16, ed. B. M. Staw and L. L. Cummings (Greenwich, CT: JAI Press, 1994), pp. 215–255; R. Parthasarthy and S. P. Sethi, "Relating Strategy and Structure to Flexible Automation: A Test of Fit and Performance Implications," *Strategic Management Journal*, vol. 14, no. 6 (1993), pp. 529–549; H. A. Simon, "Strategy and Organizational Evolution," *Strategic Management Journal*, January 1993, pp. 131–142; H. L. Boschken, "Strategy and Structure: Re-conceiving the Relationship," *Journal of Management*, March 1990, pp. 135–150; D. Miller, "The Structural and Environmental Correlates of Business Strategy," *Strategic Management Journal*, January–February 1987, pp. 55–76; and R. E. Miles and C. C. Snow, *Organizational Strategy, Structure, and Process* (New York: McGraw-Hill, 1978).
32. Leader Making a Difference box based on M. Schuman, "Zhang Ruimin's Haier Power," time.com, April 4, 2014; "Fortune Names Haier Group Chairman & CEO Zhang Ruimin Among 'The World's 50 Greatest Leaders,'" globenewswire.com, March 21, 2014; P. Day, "Smashing Way to Start a Global Business," www.bbc.news, October 22, 2013; "Haier and Higher," www.economist.com, October 12, 2013; R. Gluckman, "Every Customer Is Always Right," *Forbes,* May 21, 2012, pp. 38–40; G. Colvin, "The Next Management Icon: Would You Believe He's from China?," *Fortune,* July 25, 2011, p. 77; and D. J. Lynch, "CEO Pushes China's Haier as Global Brand," *USA Today,* January 3, 2003, pp. 1B+.
33. See, for instance, R. Z. Gooding and J. A. Wagner III, "A Meta-Analytic Review of the Relationship Between Size and Performance: The Productivity and Efficiency of Organizations and Their Subunits," *Administrative Science Quarterly*, December 1985, pp. 462–481; D. S. Pugh, "The Aston Program of Research: Retrospect and Prospect," in *Perspectives on Organization Design and Behavior, ed.* A. H. Van de Ven and W. F. Joyce (New York: John Wiley, 1981), pp. 135–166; and P. M. Blau and R. A. Schoenherr, *The Structure of Organizations* (New York: Basic Books, 1971).
34. P. Kavilanz, "Louisville's CloudDDM Factory: 100 Printers, 3 Employees," *CNN Money* online, www.money.cnn.com, May 4, 2015.
35. J. Woodward, *Industrial Organization: Theory and Practice* (London: Oxford University Press, 1965).
36. See, for instance, J. Zhang and C. Baden-Fuller, "The Influence of Technological Knowledge Base and Organizational Structure on Technology Collaboration," *Journal of Management Studies,* June 2010, pp. 679–704; C. C. Miller, W. H. Glick, Y. D. Wang, and G. Huber, "Understanding Technology-Structure Relationships: Theory Development and Meta-Analytic Theory Testing," *Academy of Management Journal,* June 1991, pp. 370–399; J. Hage and M. Aiken, "Routine Technology, Social Structure, and Organizational Goals," *Administrative Science Quarterly*, September 1969, pp. 366–377; J. D. Thompson, *Organizations in Action* (New York: McGraw-Hill, 1967); and C. Perrow, "A Framework for the Comparative Analysis of Organizations," *American Sociological Review*, April 1967, pp. 194–208.
37. D. M. Rousseau and R. A. Cooke, "Technology and Structure: The Concrete, Abstract, and Activity Systems of Organizations," *Journal of Management*, Fall–Winter 1984, pp. 345–361; and D. Gerwin, "Relationships Between Structure and Technology," in *Handbook of Organizational Design*, vol. 2, ed. P. C. Nystrom and W. H. Starbuck (New York: Oxford University Press, 1981), pp. 3–38.
38. S. Rausch and J. Birkinshaw, "Organizational Ambidexterity: Antecedents, Outcomes, and Moderators," *Journal of Management,* June 2008, pp. 375–409; M. Yasai-Ardekani, "Structural Adaptations to Environments," *Academy of Management Review*, January 1986, pp. 9–21; P. Lawrence and J. W. Lorsch, *Organization and Environment: Managing Differentiation and Integration* (Boston: Harvard Business School, Division of Research, 1967); and F. E. Emery and E. Trist, "The Causal Texture of Organizational Environments," *Human Relations*, February 1965, pp. 21–32.
39. B. Mutzabaugh, "Era of Airline Merger Mania Comes to a Close with Last US Airways Flight," *USA Today* online, www.usatoday.com, October 16, 2015.
40. "Toyota Shakes Up Corporate Structure to Focus on Product Lines," *Reuters,* March 2, 2016, http://www.reuters.com/article/us-toyota-management-structure-idUSKCN0W41CB (accessed December 23, 2016); Toyota global site http://www.toyota-global.com/company/profile/facilities/ (accessed December 23, 2016).
41. H. Mintzberg, *Structure in Fives: Designing Effective Organizations* (Upper Saddle River, NJ: Prentice Hall, 1983), p. 157.
42. R. J. Williams, J. J. Hoffman, and B. T. Lamont, "The Influence of Top Management Team Characteristics on M-Form Implementation Time," *Journal of Managerial Issues*, Winter 1995, pp. 466–480.
43. Q. Hardy, "Google Thinks Small," *Forbes,* November 14, 2005, pp. 198–202.
44. See, for example, A. C. Edmondson, "Teamwork on the Fly," *Harvard Business Review,* April 2012, pp. 72–80; D. R. Denison, S. L. Hart, and J. A. Kahn, "From Chimneys to Cross-Functional Teams: Developing and Validating a Diagnostic Model," *Academy of Management Journal*, December 1996, pp. 1005–1023; D. Ray and H. Bronstein, *Teaming Up: Making the Transition to a Self-Directed Team-Based Organization* (New York: McGraw Hill, 1995); J. R. Katzenbach and D. K. Smith, *The Wisdom of Teams* (Boston: Harvard Business School Press, 1993); J. A. Byrne, "The Horizontal Corporation," *BusinessWeek,* December 20, 1993, pp. 76–81; B. Dumaine, "Payoff from the New Management," *Fortune,* December 13, 1993, pp. 103–110; and H. Rothman, "The Power of Empowerment," *Nation's Business*, June 1993, pp. 49–52.
45. R. Feloni, "Google Has Found That Its Most Successful Teams Have 5 Traits in Common," *Business Insider* online, www.businessinsider.com, November 18, 2015.
46. E. Krell, "Managing the Matrix," *HR Magazine,* April 2011, pp. 69–71.
47. J. Hyatt, "Engineering Inspiration," *Newsweek,* June 14, 2010, p. 44; T. McKeough, "Blowing Hot and Cold," *Fast Company,*

December 2009–January 2010, p. 66; H. Walters, "Inside the Design Thinking Process," *BusinessWeek* online, December 15, 2009; P. Kaihla, "Best-Kept Secrets of the World's Best Companies," *Business 2.0,* April 2006, p. 83; C. Taylor, "School of Bright Ideas," *Time Inside Business,* April 2005, pp. A8–A12; and B. Nussbaum, "The Power of Design," *BusinessWeek,* May 17, 2004, pp. 86–94.

48. R. L. Hotz, "More Scientists Treat Experiments as a Team Sport," *Wall Street Journal,* November 20, 2009, p. A23.
49. See, for example, G. G. Dess, A. M. A. Rasheed, K. J. McLaughlin, and R. L. Priem, "The New Corporate Architecture," *Academy of Management Executive*, August 1995, pp. 7–20.
50. For additional readings on boundaryless organizations, see Rausch and Birkinshaw, "Organizational Ambidexterity," June 2008; M. F. R. Kets de Vries, "Leadership Group Coaching in Action: The Zen of Creating High-Performance Teams," *Academy of Management Executive,* February 2005, pp. 61–76; J. Child and R. G. McGrath, "Organizations Unfettered: Organizational Form in an Information-Intensive Economy," *Academy of Management Journal,* December 2001, pp. 1135–1148; M. Hammer and S. Stanton, "How Process Enterprises Really Work," *Harvard Business Review*, November–December 1999, pp. 108–118; T. Zenger and W. Hesterly, "The Disaggregation of Corporations: Selective Intervention, High-Powered Incentives, and Modular Units," *Organization Science,* 1997, vol. 8, pp. 209–222; R. Ashkenas, D. Ulrich, T. Jick, and S. Kerr, *The Boundaryless Organization: Breaking the Chains of Organizational Structure* (San Francisco: Jossey-Bass, 1997); R. M. Hodgetts, "A Conversation with Steve Kerr," *Organizational Dynamics*, Spring 1996, pp. 68–79; and J. Gebhardt, "The Boundaryless Organization," *Sloan Management Review*, Winter 1996, pp. 117–119. For another view of boundaryless organizations, see B. Victor, "The Dark Side of the New Organizational Forms: An Editorial Essay," *Organization Science*, November 1994, pp. 479–482.
51. J. Marte, "An Internship from Your Couch," *Wall Street Journal,* September 9, 2009, pp. D1+.
52. J. Yang and A. Gonzalez, "If Given A Choice, I'd Rather Work… " *USA Today,* January 22, 2013, p. 1B.
53. See, for instance, R. J. King, "It's a Virtual World," *Strategy+Business,* www.strategy-business.com, April 21, 2009; Y. Shin, "A Person-Environment Fit Model for Virtual Organizations," *Journal of Management,* December 2004, pp. 725–743; D. Lyons, "Smart and Smarter," *Forbes,* March 18, 2002, pp. 40–41; W. F. Cascio, "Managing a Virtual Workplace," *Academy of Management Executive,* August 2000, pp. 81–90; G. G. Dess, A. M. A. Rasheed, K. J. McLaughlin, and R. L. Priem, "The New Corporate Architecture"; H. Chesbrough and D. Teece, "When Is Virtual Virtuous: Organizing for Innovation," *Harvard Business Review,* January–February 1996, pp. 65–73; and W. H. Davidow and M. S. Malone, *The Virtual Corporation* (New York: Harper Collins, 1992).
54. Q. Hardy, "Bit by Bit, Work Exchange Site Aims to Get Jobs Done," *New York Times* online, November 6, 2011.
55. M. V. Rafter, "Cultivating a Virtual Culture," *Workforce Management Online,* April 5, 2012.
56. C. Kauffman, "Employee Involvement: A New Blueprint for Success," *Journal of Accountancy,* May 2010, pp. 46–49; and R. L. Daft, *Management,* 9th ed. (Mason, OH: South-Western Cengage Learning, 2010), p. 262.
57. M. Conlin, "Home Offices: The New Math," *BusinessWeek,* March 9, 2009, pp. 66–68.
58. C. Wells and J. S. Lublin, "Employees Like Flexible Work Programs, But Few Use Them," *The Wall Street Journal* online, www.wsj.com, September 30, 2015.
59. M. Conlin, "Home Offices: The New Math."
60. J. Marquez, "Connecting a Virtual Workforce."
61. S. Jayson, "Working At Home: Family-Friendly," *USA Today,* April 15, 2010, pp. 1A+; T. D. Hecht and N. J. Allen, "A Longitudinal Examination of the Work-Nonwork Boundary Strength Construct," *Journal of Organizational Behavior,* October 2009, pp. 839–862; and G. E. Kreiner, E. C. Hollensbe, and M. L. Sheep, "Balancing Borders and Bridges: Negotiating the Work-Home Interface via Boundary Work Tactics," *Academy of Management Journal,* August 2009, pp. 704–730.
62. C. Wells and J. S. Lublin, "Employees Like Flexible Work Programs."
63. J. T. Marquez, "The Future of Flex," *Workforce Management Online,* January 27, 2010.
64. B. Walsh, "Thank God It's Thursday," *Time,* September 7, 2009, p. 58.
65. J. Sahadi, "The 4-Day Workweek Is Real for Employees at These Companies," *CNN Money,* www.money.cnn.com, April 27, 2015.
66. K. Matos and E. Galinsky, "2014 National Study of Employers," Family and Work Institute, 2014.
67. J. Sahadi, "Flex-time, Time Off—Who's Getting These Perks?," *CNNMoney.com,* June 25, 2007.
68. M. Arndt, "The Family That Flips Together …" *BusinessWeek,* April 17, 2006, p. 14.
69. S. Greenhouse, "Work-Sharing May Help Companies Avoid Layoffs," *New York Times* online, www.nytimes.com, June 16, 2009.
70. J. Yang and A. Gonzalez, "Would Asking for Flexible Work Options Hurt Your Career Advancement?," *USA Today,* October 2, 2013, p. 1B.
71. "Toyota Group Making 1,000 Temp Workers Full-time," *Nikkei Asian Review,* November 24, 2016, http://asia.nikkei.com/Business/Companies/Toyota-group-making-1-000-temp-workers-full-time (accessed December 23, 2016).
72. I. Speizer, "Special Report on Contingency Staffing—The Future of Contingent Staffing Could Be Like Something Out of a Movie," *Workforce Management Online,* October 19, 2009.
73. SAP, "The Rise of the Contingent Worker," *Forbes* online, www.forbes.com, December 19, 2014.
74. E. Frauenheim, "Special Report on HR Technology: Tracking the Contingents," *Workforce Management Online,* April 2010.
75. S. G. Hauser, "Independent Contractors Helping to Shape the New World of Work," *Workforce Management Online,* February 3, 2012; S. Greenhouse, "U.S. Cracks Down on 'Contractors' as a Tax Dodge," *New York Times* online, www.nytimes.com, February 18, 2010; and M. Orey, "FedEx: They're Employees. No, They're Not," *Bloomberg BusinessWeek,* November 5, 2009, pp. 73–74.
76. C. Hausman, "Lifeguard Fired for Leaving Patrol Zone to Save Drowning Man," *Ethics Newsline online,* July 9, 2012; S. Grossman, "Lifeguard Who Got Fired for Saving Drowning

Swimmer Declines Offer to Return," newsfeed.time.com, July 6, 2012; E. Illades and C. Teproff, "Fired Lifeguard Says 'No Thanks' When He's Re-offered Job," MiamiHerald.com, July 5, 2012; and W. Lee, "Florida Lifeguard Helps Save Life, Gets Fired," *USA Today* online, July 4, 2012.

77. Based on H. Mintzberg, *Power In and Around Organizations* (Upper Saddle River, NJ: Prentice Hall, 1983), p. 24; P. L. Hunsaker, *Training in Management Skills* (Upper Saddle River, NJ: Prentice Hall, 2001), pp. 339–364; G. Ferris, S. Davidson, and P. Perrewé, "Developing Political Skill at Work," *Training,* November 2005, pp. 40–45; B. Uzzi and S. Dunlap, "How to Build Your Network," *Harvard Business Review,* December 2005, pp. 53–60; and B. Brim, "The Best Way to Influence Others," *Gallup Management Journal,* http://gmj.gallup.com, February 9, 2006.
78. S. Silbermann, "How Culture and Regulation Demand New Ways to Sell," *Harvard Business Review,* July/August 2012, pp. 104–105; P. Miller and T. Wedell-Wedellsborg, "How to Make an Offer That Managers Can't Refuse?" *IESE Insight,* 2011 (second quarter), issue 9, pp. 66–67; S. Hernández, "Prove Its Worth," *IESE Insight,* 2011 (second quarter), no. 9, p. 68; T. Koulopoulos, "Know Thyself," *IESE Insight,* 2011 (second quarter), no. 9, p. 69; M. Weinstein, "Retrain and Restructure Your Organization," *Training,* May 2009, p. 36; J. McGregor, "Outsourcing Tasks Instead of Jobs," *Bloomberg BusinessWeek,* March 11, 2009; "Pfizer: Making It 'Leaner, Meaner, More Efficient,'" *BusinessWeek* online, www.bloomberg.com/businessweek, March 2, 2009; and A. Cohen, "Scuttling Scut Work," *Fast Company,* February 1, 2008, pp. 42–43.
79. A. Cohen, "Scuttling Scut Work," *Fast Company,* February 1, 2008, pp. 42–43.
80. J. McGregor, "Outsourcing Tasks Instead of Jobs," *Bloomberg BusinessWeek,* March 11, 2009.
81. J. Graham, "Product Fans Can Become Customer Service Reps," *USA Today,* May 31, 2012, p. 3B; A. Fox, "Pave the Way for Volunteers," *HR Magazine,* June 2010, pp. 70–74; G. Morse, "The Power of Unwitting Workers," *Harvard Business Review,* October 2009, p. 27; S. Lohr, "Customer Service? Ask A Volunteer," *New York Times Online*, April 26, 2009; and B. Xu, D. R. Jones, and B. Shao, "Volunteers' Involvement in Online Community Based Software Development," *Information & Management,* April 2009, pp. 151–158.

Chapter 12 Organizing Around Teams

It's Your Career

Source: Kev Draws/Shutterstock

Developing Your Coaching Skills

Teams—sports teams, volunteer teams, work teams—often have coaches.

If you've ever been on any of these types of teams (or any type of team), you know how important the coach can be to the team's success. The coach plays an important role in encouraging and guiding the team. A coach's job is to get the best out of each team member and to help team members to work together to achieve the team's goal.

As you prepare yourself for your career, you would do well to develop your coaching skills. Let's look at some specific suggestions on how to do that:

A key to success in management and your career is knowing how to coach effectively.

*1. **Know the goal.** One of the characteristics of an effective team, as you'll see in this chapter, is having clear goals. Teams that are able to achieve high levels of performance have a clear understanding of the goals to be achieved. Team members will be committed to the team's goals, know what they're expected to accomplish, and understand how they need to work together to achieve these goals.*

*2. **Know your team.** Just as important as having clear goals and knowing the goals is knowing the skills, abilities, and motivations of each team member. An effective coach knows what each team member brings to the team and where each person might contribute most effectively.*

*3. **Build a relationship of mutual trust.** The foundation of an excellent team-coach relationship is mutual trust. Again, you'll see this discussed in the chapter as one of the characteristics of an effective team. Without mutual trust, a coach won't be able to be honest in guiding the team and in giving feedback and team members won't be open to receiving the feedback and being guided.*

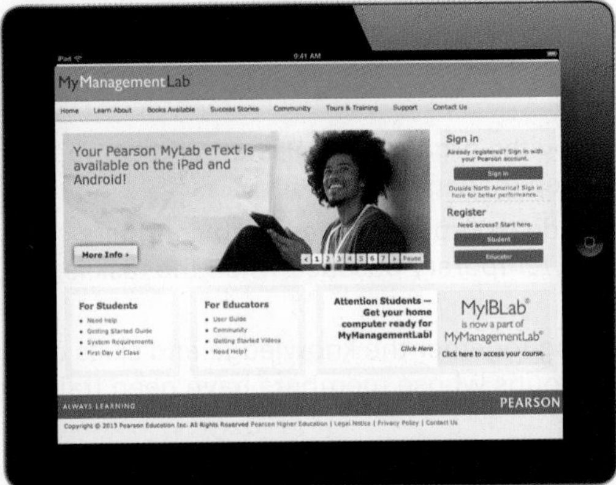

Pearson MyLab Management®

Improve Your Grade!

When you see this icon, visit www.mymanagementlab.com for activities that are applied, personalized, and offer immediate feedback.

Learning Objectives

12.1 ***Define*** *groups and the stages of group development.*

12.2 ***Describe*** *the major components that determine group performance and satisfaction.*

12.3 ***Define*** *teams and best practices influencing team performance.*

- **Know how** to maximize outcomes through effective negotiating.
- **Develop your skill** at coaching team members.

12.4 ***Discuss*** *contemporary issues in managing teams.*

4. ***Provide feedback.*** *Effective coaches recognize and understand the value and importance of giving continual performance feedback—both positive and corrective—to their team. Anyone who has played a sport knows that a good coach constantly gives feedback so that you can get better at it. If you want your team to be effective, team members need to know where they stand and where they need to "step up their game." (See Chapter 18's* It's Your Career *for advice on how to be effective at giving feedback.)*

5. ***Create an atmosphere of accountability.*** *In a team environment where work is done collectively, it's important that team members and the coach are accountable to each other and to the team. What does it mean to be accountable? Be responsible. Follow through on commitments to each other. Don't make excuses. Don't whine. Don't point fingers at each other. That's what it means to be accountable. And it's important!*

You've probably had a lot of experience working in groups—class project teams, maybe an athletic team, a fundraising committee, or even a sales team at work. Work teams are one of the realities—and challenges—of managing in today's dynamic global environment. Many organizations have made the move to restructure work around teams rather than individuals. Why? What do these teams look like? And how can managers build effective teams? We will look at answers to these questions throughout this chapter. Before we can understand teams, however, we first need to understand some basics about groups and group behavior.

Exhibit 12-1
Examples of Formal Work Groups

- *Command groups*—Groups determined by the organizational chart and composed of individuals who report directly to a given manager.
- *Task groups*—Groups composed of individuals brought together to complete a specific job task; their existence is often temporary because when the task is completed, the group disbands.
- *Cross-functional teams*—Groups that bring together the knowledge and skills of individuals from various work areas or groups whose members have been trained to do each others' jobs.
- *Self-managed teams*—Groups that are essentially independent and that, in addition to their own tasks, take on traditional managerial responsibilities such as hiring, planning and scheduling, and evaluating performance.

GROUPS and group development

LO12.1 Each person on the rapid intervention firefighting team partners with another firefighter whose sole responsibility is to search and rescue other firefighters in distress. This group's success at its task is a matter of life or death.

While most groups in organizations do not deal with life or death situations, managers would like their groups to be successful at their tasks. But what do we mean when we use the term "group," and how do groups develop?

What Is a Group?

group
Two or more interacting and interdependent individuals who come together to achieve specific goals

A **group** is defined as two or more interacting and interdependent individuals who come together to achieve specific goals. *Formal groups* are work groups defined by the organization's structure and have designated work assignments and specific tasks directed at accomplishing organizational goals. Exhibit 12-1 provides some examples. *Informal groups* are social groups. These groups occur naturally in the workplace and tend to form around friendships and common interests. For example, five employees from different departments who regularly eat lunch together are an informal group.

Stages of Group Development

Research shows that groups develop through five stages.[1] As shown in Exhibit 12-2, these five stages are *forming, storming, norming, performing,* and *adjourning*.

Exhibit 12-2
Stages of Group Development

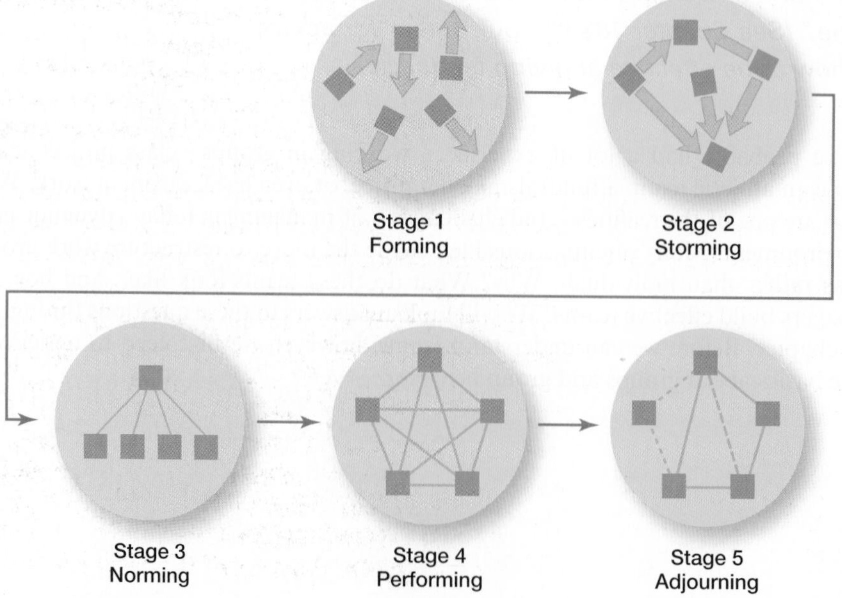

The **forming stage** has two phases. The first occurs as people join the group. In a formal group, people join because of some work assignment. Once they've joined, the second phase begins: defining the group's purpose, structure, and leadership. This phase involves a great deal of uncertainty as members "test the waters" to determine what types of behavior are acceptable. This stage is complete when members begin to think of themselves as part of a group.

forming stage
The first stage of group development in which people join the group and then define the group's purpose, structure, and leadership

The **storming stage** is appropriately named because of the intragroup conflict. There's conflict over who will control the group and what the group needs to be doing. During this stage, a relatively clear hierarchy of leadership and agreement on the group's direction emerge.

storming stage
The second stage of group development, characterized by intragroup conflict

The **norming stage** is one in which close relationships develop and the group becomes cohesive. There's now a strong sense of group identity and camaraderie. This stage is complete when the group structure solidifies and the group has assimilated a common set of expectations (or norms) regarding member behavior.

norming stage
The third stage of group development, characterized by close relationships and cohesiveness

The fourth stage is the **performing stage.** The group structure is in place and accepted by group members. Their energies have moved from getting to know and understand each other to working on the group's task. This is the last stage of development for permanent work groups. However, for temporary groups—project teams, task forces, or similar groups that have a limited task to do—the final stage is **adjourning.** In this stage, the group prepares to disband. The group focuses its attention on wrapping up activities instead of task performance. Group members react in different ways. Some are upbeat and thrilled about the group's accomplishments. Others may be sad over the loss of camaraderie and friendships.

performing stage
The fourth stage of group development when the group is fully functional and works on group task

adjourning
The final stage of group development for temporary groups during which group members are concerned with wrapping up activities rather than task performance

Many of you have probably experienced these stages as you've worked on a group project for a class. Group members are selected or assigned and then meet for the first time. There's a "feeling out" period to assess what the group is going to do and how it's going to be done. What usually follows is a battle for control: Who's going to be in charge? Once this issue is resolved and a "hierarchy" agreed upon, the group identifies specific work that needs to be done, who's going to do each part, and dates by which the assigned work needs to be completed. General expectations are established. These decisions form the foundation for what you hope will be a coordinated group effort culminating in a project that's been done well. Once the project is complete and turned in, the group breaks up. Of course, some groups don't get much beyond the forming or storming stages. These groups may have serious interpersonal conflicts, turn in disappointing work, and get lower grades.

As a permanent work group in the performing stage, chef Andoni Aduriz (right) and his staff prepare a dish in the kitchen of his Mugaritz restaurant in Errenteria, Spain. Aduriz and his team of 35 chefs have a strong sense of group identity and focus their energies on creating elaborate and adventurous dining experiences for their guests.
Source: Vincent West/Thomson Reuters (Markets) LLC

Does a group become more effective as it progresses through the first four stages? Some researchers say yes, but it's not that simple.[2] That assumption may be generally true, but what makes a group effective is a complex issue. Under some conditions, high levels of conflict are conducive to high levels of group performance. In some situations, groups in the storming stage outperform those in the norming or performing stages. Also, groups don't always proceed sequentially from one stage to the next. Sometimes, groups are storming and performing at the same time. Groups even occasionally regress to previous stages; therefore, don't assume that all groups precisely follow this process or that performing is always the most preferable stage. Think of this model as a general framework that underscores the fact that groups are dynamic entities and managers need to know the stage a group is in so they can understand the problems and issues most likely to surface.

If your professor has assigned this, go to **www.mymanagementlab.com** to watch a video titled: *Herman Miller: Motivation, Leadership & Teamwork* and to respond to questions.

Exhibit 12-3
Group Performance/Satisfaction Model

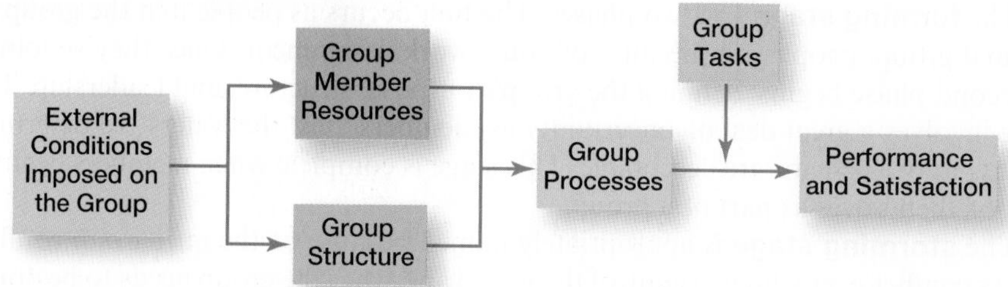

WORK group performance and satisfaction

LO12.2 Many people consider them the most successful "group" of our times. Who? The Beatles. "The Beatles were great artists and entertainers, but in many respects they were four ordinary guys who, as a group, found a way to achieve extraordinary artistic and financial success.[3] Every business team can learn from their story."[4]

Why *are* some groups more successful than others? Why do some groups achieve high levels of performance and high levels of member satisfaction and others do not? The answers are complex, but include variables such as the abilities of the group's members, the size of the group, the level of conflict, and the internal pressures on members to conform to the group's norms. Exhibit 12-3 presents the major factors that determine group performance and satisfaction.[5] Let's look at each.

External Conditions Imposed on the Group

Work groups are affected by the external conditions imposed on it such as the organization's strategy, authority relationships, formal rules and regulations, availability of resources, employee selection criteria, the performance management system and culture, and the general physical layout of the group's work space. For instance, most U.S. organizations create safety teams to ensure compliance with the Occupational Safety and Health Act. Or an organization might be pursuing a strategy of lowering costs or improving quality, which will affect what a group does and how it does it. For example, in Japan, *kaizen* is defined as continuous improvement, and most Japanese companies create temporary teams to improve business processes. As a case in point, Toyota was a pioneer in using kaizen to create efficient manufacturing processes and high-quality vehicles.

Group Member Resources

A group's performance potential depends to a large extent on the resources each individual brings to the group. These resources include knowledge, abilities, skills, and personality traits, and they determine what members can do and how effectively they will perform in a group. Interpersonal skills—especially conflict management and resolution, collaborative problem solving, and communication—consistently emerge as important for high performance by work groups.[6]

Personality traits also affect group performance because they strongly influence how the individual will interact with other group members. Research has shown that traits viewed as positive in our culture (such as sociability, self-reliance, and independence) tend to be positively related to group productivity and morale. In contrast, negative personality characteristics, such as authoritarianism, dominance, and unconventionality, tend to be negatively related to group productivity and morale.[7] Some organizations recognize the importance of having the appropriate mix of personalities on a team. For instance, car review website Edmunds.com uses the results of personality testing as one consideration for assembling its executive team.[8]

Group Structure

Work groups aren't unorganized crowds. They have an internal structure that shapes members' behavior and influences group performance. The structure defines roles, norms, conformity, status systems, group size, group cohesiveness, and leadership.

Let's look at the first six of these aspects of group structure. Leadership is discussed in Chapter 16.

ROLES We introduced the concept of roles in Chapter 1 when we discussed what managers do. (Remember Mintzberg's managerial roles?) Of course, managers aren't the only individuals in an organization who play various roles. The concept of roles applies to all employees and to their lives outside an organization as well. (Think of the various roles you play: student, friend, sibling, employee, spouse or significant other, etc.)

A **role** refers to behavior patterns expected of someone occupying a given position in a social unit. In a group, individuals are expected to do certain things because of their position (role) in the group. These roles are generally oriented toward either getting work done or keeping group members happy.[9] For instance, it takes well-coordinated teams to ensure the safe operations of a cruise ship. The captain as well as the first, second, and third officers lead ship operations. The captain is equivalent to the CEO of a company, the first officer is responsible for navigating the ship, and the second and third officers assist the first officer in ship navigation. Also, think about groups you've been in and the roles you played in those groups. Were you continually trying to keep the group focused on getting its work done? If so, you were performing a task accomplishment role. Or were you more concerned that group members had the opportunity to offer ideas and that they were satisfied with the experience? If so, you were performing a group member satisfaction role. Both roles are important to the group's ability to function effectively and efficiently.

role
Behavior patterns expected of someone occupying a given position in a social unit

A problem arises when individuals play multiple roles and adjust their roles to the group to which they belong at the time. However, the differing expectations of these roles often means that employees face *role conflicts*.

Dark suits, dress shirts, and conservative ties for men and dark suits and tailored blouses for women is the norm for lawyers working at this law firm in New Delhi, India. In the legal industry, the norm of formal dress conveys a polished, professional image that can help lawyers command respect and inspire trust during court appearances and client meetings.
Source: Hemant Chawla/The India Today Group/Getty Images

NORMS All groups have **norms**—standards or expectations that are accepted and shared by a group's members. Norms dictate things such as work output levels, absenteeism, promptness, and the amount of socializing on the job.

For example, norms in Korean culture pressure workers to "pull late nights" because they feel the need to please their superiors. One observer described these workers: "They just sit in their chairs and they just watch their team leaders, and they're thinking, 'What time is he going to leave the office?'"[10] Then, there is an expectation that the boss and employees will go out for drinks, and it is important that employees participate. In Korea, drinking together helps build workplace camaraderie and trust.[11]

Although a group has its own unique set of norms, common organizational norms focus on effort and performance, dress, and loyalty. The most widespread norms are those related to work effort and performance. Work groups typically provide their members with explicit cues on how hard to work, level of output expected, when to look busy, when it's acceptable to goof off, and the like. These norms are powerful influences on an individual employee's performance. They're so powerful that you can't predict someone's performance based solely on his or her ability and personal motivation. Dress norms frequently dictate what's acceptable to wear to work. If the norm is more formal dress, anyone who dresses casually may face subtle pressure to conform. Finally, loyalty norms will influence whether individuals work late, work on weekends, or move to locations they might not prefer to live.

norms
Standards or expectations that are accepted and shared by a group's members

One negative thing about group norms is that being part of a group can increase an individual's antisocial actions. If the norms of the group include tolerating deviant behavior, someone who normally wouldn't engage in such behavior might be more likely to do so. For instance, one study found that those working in a group were more likely to lie, cheat, and steal than individuals working alone.[12] Why? Because groups provide

Exhibit 12-4
Examples of Asch's Cards

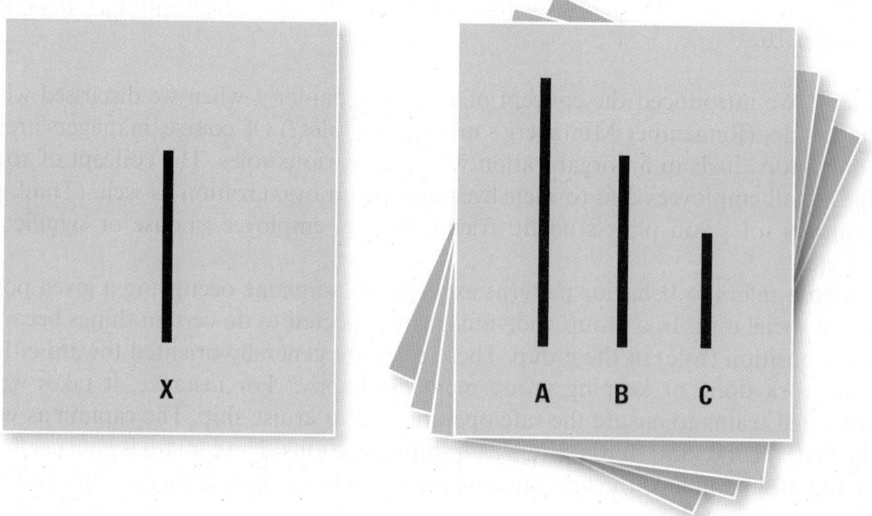

anonymity, thus giving individuals—who might otherwise be afraid of getting caught—a false sense of security. There are, for instance, numerous cases of employee theft rings in retail settings. At a Home Depot store in Connecticut, surveillance video revealed that seven employees stole about $300,000 worth of tools over a 10-month period.[13] All the while, the shift manager admitted to intentionally ignoring the illegal activity.

CONFORMITY Because individuals want to be accepted by groups to which they belong, they're susceptible to pressures to conform. Early experiments done by Solomon Asch demonstrated the impact conformity has on an individual's judgment and attitudes.[14] In these experiments, groups of seven or eight people were asked to compare two cards held up by the experimenter. One card had three lines of different lengths and the other had one line that was equal in length to one of the three lines on the other card (see Exhibit 12-4). Each group member was to announce aloud which of the three lines matched the single line. Asch wanted to see what would happen if members began to give incorrect answers. Would pressures to conform cause individuals to give wrong answers just to be consistent with the others? The experiment was "fixed" so that all but one of the members (the unsuspecting subject) were told ahead of time to start giving obviously incorrect answers after one or two rounds. Over many experiments and trials, the unsuspecting subject conformed over a third of the time.

Are these conclusions still valid? Research suggests that conformity levels have declined since Asch's studies. However, managers can't ignore conformity because it can still be a powerful force in groups.[15] Group members often want to be seen as one of the group and avoid being visibly different. We find it more pleasant to agree than to be disruptive, even if being disruptive may improve the group's effectiveness. So we conform. But conformity can go too far, especially when an individual's opinion differs significantly from that of others in the group. In such a case, the group often exerts intense pressure on the individual to align his or her opinion to conform to others' opinions, a phenomenon known as **groupthink.** Groupthink seems to occur when group members hold a positive group image they want to protect and when the group perceives a collective threat to this positive image.[16] Sometimes, groupthink can lead to catastrophic outcomes. For example, NASA's so-called "go for launch" mentality is believed to have hastened the launch of the space shuttle Challenger in 1986 in spite of concerns that the O-ring seal could malfunction. Unfortunately, the shuttle exploded shortly after takeoff, and investigations into this disaster revealed that the O-ring's malfunction was likely the cause.

groupthink
When a group exerts extensive pressure on an individual to align his or her opinion with others' opinions

STATUS SYSTEMS Status systems are an important factor in understanding groups. **Status** is a prestige grading, position, or rank within a group. As far back as researchers have been able to trace groups, they have found status hierarchies. Status

status
A prestige grading, position, or rank within a group

can be a significant motivator with behavioral consequences, especially when individuals see a disparity between what they perceive their status to be and what others perceive it to be.

Status may be informally conferred by characteristics such as education, age, skill, or experience. Anything can have status value if others in the group evaluate it that way. Of course, just because status is informal doesn't mean it's unimportant or hard to determine who has it or who does not. Group members have no problem placing people into status categories and usually agree about who has high or low status.

Status is also formally conferred, and it's important for employees to believe the organization's formal status system is congruent—that is, the system shows consistency between the perceived ranking of an individual and the status symbols he or she is given by the organization. For instance, status incongruence would occur when a supervisor earns less than his or her subordinates, a desirable office is occupied by a person in a low-ranking position, or paid country club memberships are provided to division managers but not to vice presidents. Employees expect the "things" an individual receives to be congruent with his or her status. When they're not, employees may question the authority of their managers and may not be motivated by job promotion opportunities.

GROUP SIZE What's an appropriate size for a group? At Amazon, work teams have considerable autonomy to innovate and to investigate their ideas. And Jeff Bezos, founder and CEO, uses a "two-pizza" philosophy; that is, a team should be small enough that it can be fed with two pizzas. This "two-pizza" philosophy usually limits groups to five to seven people depending, of course, on team member appetites.[17]

Group size affects performance and satisfaction, but the effect depends on what the group is supposed to accomplish.[18] Research indicates, for instance, that small groups are faster than larger ones at completing tasks. However, for groups engaged in problem solving, large groups consistently get better results than smaller ones. What do these findings mean in terms of specific numbers? Large groups—those with a dozen or more members—are good for getting diverse input. Thus, if the goal of the group is to find facts, a larger group should be more effective. For instance, the Department of Defense recently assembled an investigation team to determine why U.S. military forces bombed a friendly target—a Doctors Without Borders hospital in Afghanistan—killing dozens of innocent people. A Defense official said that the investigation team included "over a dozen subject matter experts from several specialty fields."[19] Within six months, the team identified the causes of the incident, which included human error and faulty equipment. While this example illustrates the effectiveness of large teams, smaller groups—from five to seven members—are better at doing something productive with those facts.

social loafing
The tendency for individuals to expend less effort when working collectively than when working individually

One important research finding related to group size concerns **social loafing,** which is the tendency for an individual to expend less effort when working collectively than when working individually.[20] Social loafing may occur because people believe others in the group aren't doing their fair share. Thus, they reduce their work efforts in an attempt to make the workload more equivalent. Also, the relationship between an individual's input and the group's output is often unclear. Thus, individuals may become "free riders" and coast on the group's efforts because individuals believe their contribution can't be measured.

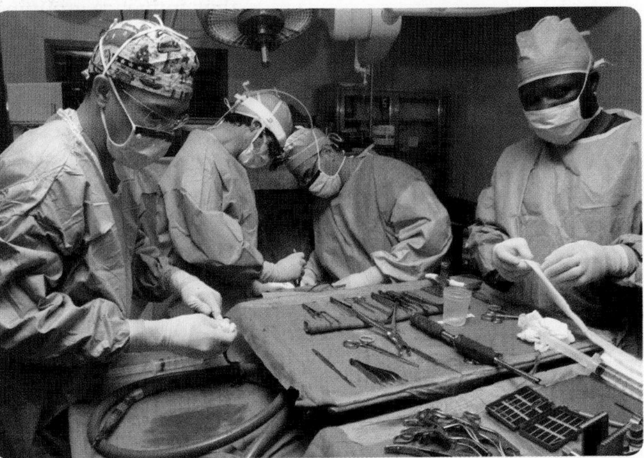

Group cohesiveness is high for this operating room surgical team at a New York hospital as it performs spinal surgery. The success of surgical and operative procedures and patients' pain control and safety requires individual expertise plus high levels of concentration, coordination, cooperation, agreement, and respect for each other among group members.
Source: David Grossman/Alamy

The implications of social loafing are significant. When managers use groups, they must find a way to identify individual efforts. If not, group productivity and individual satisfaction may decline.[21]

GROUP COHESIVENESS Cohesiveness is important because it has been found to be related to a group's productivity. Groups in which there's a lot of internal disagreement and lack of cooperation are less effective in completing their tasks than groups

Exhibit 12-5
Group Cohesiveness and Productivity

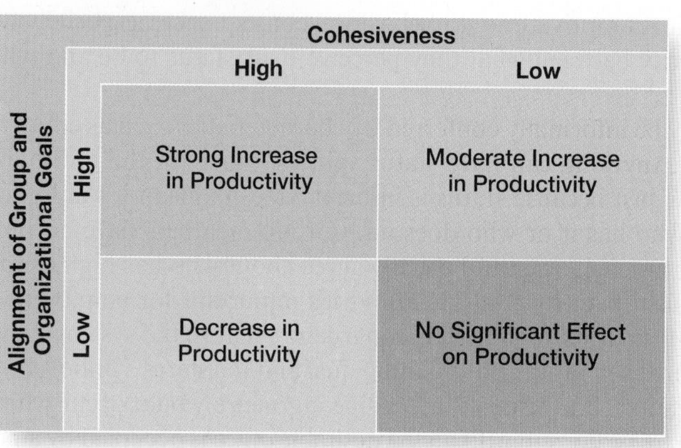

group cohesiveness
The degree to which group members are attracted to one another and share the group's goals

in which members generally agree, cooperate, and like each other. Research in this area has focused on **group cohesiveness,** or the degree to which members are attracted to a group and share the group's goals.[22]

Research has generally shown that highly cohesive groups are more effective than less-cohesive ones.[23] However, the relationship between cohesiveness and effectiveness is complex. A key moderating variable is the degree to which the group's attitude aligns with its goals or with the goals of the organization.[24] (See Exhibit 12-5.) The more cohesive the group, the more its members will follow its goals. If the goals are desirable (for instance, high output, quality work, cooperation with individuals outside the group), a cohesive group is more productive than a less-cohesive group. But if cohesiveness is high and attitudes are unfavorable, productivity decreases. If cohesiveness is low, but goals are supported, productivity increases, but not as much as when both cohesiveness and support are high. When cohesiveness is low and goals are not supported, productivity is not significantly affected.

FYI

- A study by MIT researchers predicted 35 percent of a team's performance by counting the number and quality of face-to-face interactions between team members.[25]

Group Processes

The next factor that determines group performance and satisfaction concerns the processes that go on within a work group such as communication, decision making, conflict management, and the like. These processes are important to understanding work groups because they influence group performance and satisfaction positively or negatively. An example of a positive process factor is the synergy of four people on a marketing research team who are able to generate far more ideas as a group than the members could produce individually. However, the group also may have negative process factors such as social loafing, high levels of conflict, or poor communication, which may hinder group effectiveness. We'll look at two important group processes: group decision making and conflict management.

GROUP DECISION MAKING It's a rare organization that doesn't use committees, task forces, review panels, study teams, or other similar groups to make decisions. Studies show that managers may spend up to 30 hours a week in group meetings.[26] Undoubtedly, a large portion of that time is spent formulating problems, developing solutions, and determining how to implement the solutions. It's possible, in fact, for groups to be assigned any of the eight steps in the decision-making process. (Refer to Chapter 2 to review these steps.)

What advantages do group decisions have over individual decisions? One is that groups generate more complete information and knowledge. They bring a diversity of experience and perspectives to the decision process that an individual cannot. In addition, groups generate more diverse alternatives because they have a greater amount and diversity of information. Next, groups increase acceptance of a solution. Group members are reluctant to fight or undermine a decision they helped develop. Finally, groups increase legitimacy. Decisions made by groups may be perceived as more legitimate than decisions made by one person.

Group decisions also have disadvantages. One is that groups almost always take more time to reach a solution than it would take an individual. Another is that a

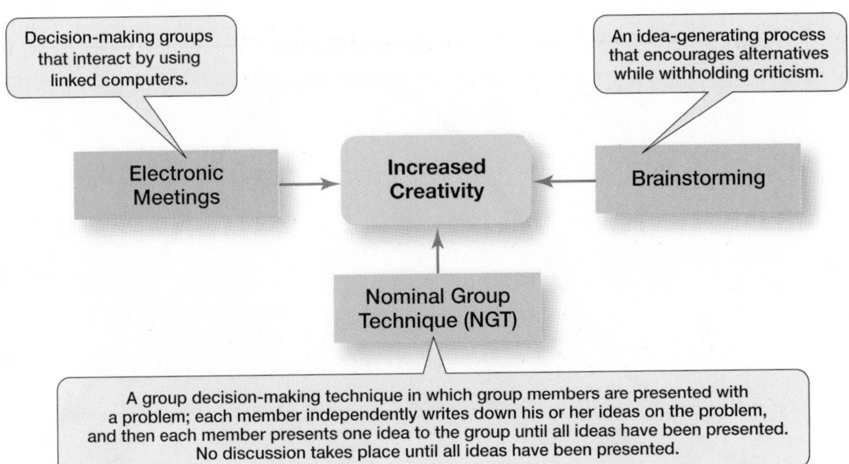

Exhibit 12-6
Creative Group Decision Making

dominant and vocal minority can heavily influence the final decision. In addition, groupthink can undermine critical thinking in the group and harm the quality of the final decision.[27] Finally, in a group, members share responsibility, but the responsibility of any single member is ambiguous.

Determining whether groups are effective at making decisions depends on the criteria used to assess effectiveness.[28] If accuracy, creativity, and degree of acceptance are important, then a group decision may work best. However, if speed and efficiency are important, then an individual decision may be the best. In addition, decision effectiveness is influenced by group size. Although a larger group provides more diverse representation, it also requires more coordination and time for members to contribute their ideas. Evidence indicates that groups of five, and to a lesser extent seven, are the most effective for making decisions.[29] Having an odd number in the group helps avoid decision deadlocks. Also, these groups are large enough for members to shift roles and withdraw from unfavorable positions but still small enough for quieter members to participate actively in discussions.

What techniques can managers use to help groups make more creative decisions? Exhibit 12-6 describes three possibilities.

CONFLICT MANAGEMENT Another important group process is how a group manages conflict. As a group performs its assigned tasks, disagreements inevitably arise. **Conflict** is *perceived* incompatible differences resulting in some form of interference or opposition. Whether the differences are real is irrelevant. If people in a group perceive that differences exist, then there is conflict. Surveys show that managers spend about 25 percent of their time resolving conflicts. [30]

Three different views have evolved regarding conflict.[31] The **traditional view of conflict** argues that conflict must be avoided—that it indicates a problem within the group. Another view, the **human relations view of conflict,** argues that conflict is a natural and inevitable outcome in any group and need not be negative, but it has potential to be a positive force in contributing to a group's performance. The third and most recent view, the **interactionist view of conflict,** proposes that not only can conflict be a positive force in a group but also that some conflict is *absolutely necessary* for a group to perform effectively.

The interactionist view doesn't suggest that all conflicts are good. Some conflicts—**functional conflicts**—are constructive and support the goals of the work group and improve its performance. Other conflicts—**dysfunctional conflicts**—are destructive and prevent a group from achieving its goals. Exhibit 12-7 on the next page illustrates the challenge facing managers.

When is conflict functional and when is it dysfunctional? Research indicates that you need to look at the *type* of conflict.[32] **Task conflict** relates to the content and goals of the work. **Relationship conflict** focuses on interpersonal relationships. **Process conflict**

conflict
Perceived incompatible differences that result in interference or opposition

traditional view of conflict
The view that all conflict is bad and must be avoided

human relations view of conflict
The view that conflict is a natural and inevitable outcome in any group

interactionist view of conflict
The view that some conflict is necessary for a group to perform effectively

functional conflicts
Conflicts that support a group's goals and improve its performance

dysfunctional conflicts
Conflicts that prevent a group from achieving its goals

task conflict
Conflicts over content and goals of the work

relationship conflict
Conflict based on interpersonal relationships

process conflict
Conflict over how work gets done

Exhibit 12-7
Conflict and Group Performance

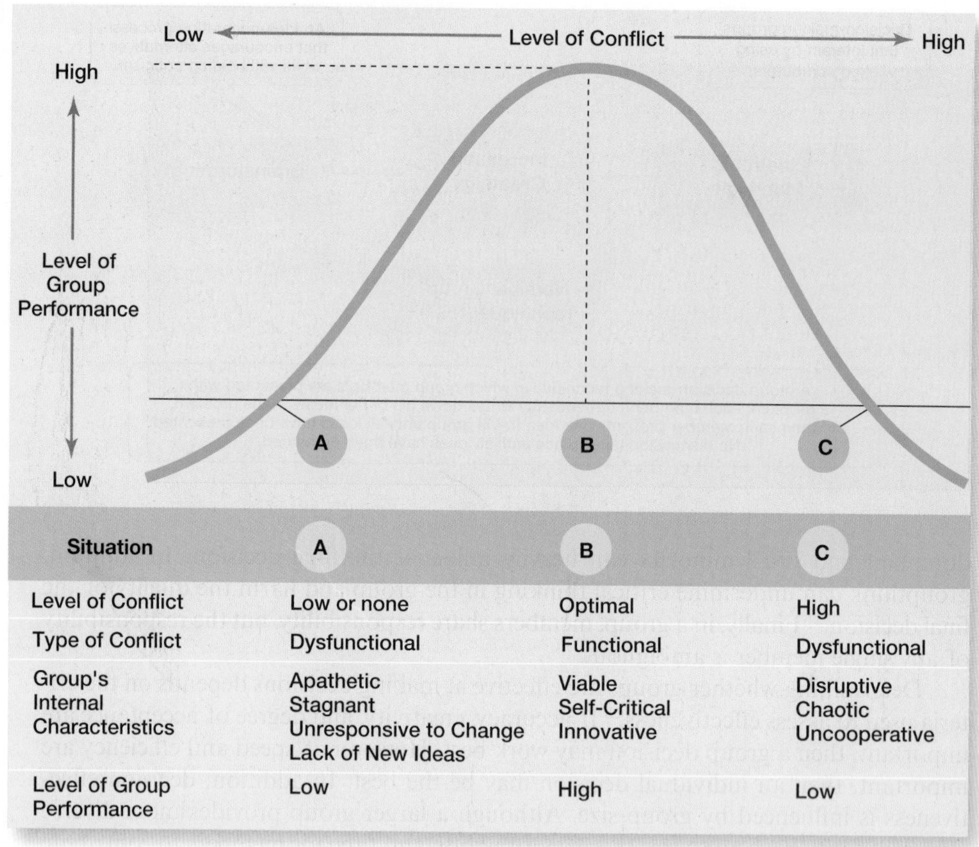

Situation	A	B	C
Level of Conflict	Low or none	Optimal	High
Type of Conflict	Dysfunctional	Functional	Dysfunctional
Group's Internal Characteristics	Apathetic Stagnant Unresponsive to Change Lack of New Ideas	Viable Self-Critical Innovative	Disruptive Chaotic Uncooperative
Level of Group Performance	Low	High	Low

refers to how the work gets done. Research shows that *relationship* conflicts are almost always dysfunctional because the interpersonal hostilities increase personality clashes and decrease mutual understanding, and the tasks don't get done. On the other hand, low levels of process conflict and low-to-moderate levels of task conflict are functional. For *process* conflict to be productive, it must be minimal. Otherwise, intense arguments over who should do what may become dysfunctional and can lead to uncertainty about task assignments, increase the time to complete tasks, and result in members working at cross-purposes. However, a low-to-moderate level of *task* conflict consistently has a positive effect on group performance because it stimulates discussion of ideas that help groups be more innovative.[33] Because we don't yet have a sophisticated measuring instrument for assessing whether conflict levels are optimal, too high, or too low, the manager must try to judge that intelligently.

Have you ever been part of a class group in which all teammates received the same grade, even though some team members didn't fulfill their responsibilities? How did that make you feel? Did it create conflict within the group, and did you feel that the process and outcome were unfair? Recent research also has shown that organizational justice or fairness is an important aspect of managing group conflict.[34] How group members feel about how they're being treated both by each other within the group and by outsiders can affect their work attitudes and behaviors. To promote the sense of fairness, it's important that group leaders build a strong sense of community based on fair and just treatment.

★ Write It 1!

If your professor has assigned this, go to **www.mymanagementlab.com** to complete the Writing Assignment *BCOMM 2: Managing Conflict.*

let's get REAL

Source: Alfonso Marrese

Alfonso Marrese
Retail Executive

The Scenario:

Fran Waller is the manager of a retail store that's part of a large national chain. Many of her employees are going to school and working, but she also has some full-time employees. A conflict over vacation and holiday work schedules has been building for some time now, and it's creating a very tense atmosphere, which isn't good for customer service. She's got to resolve it NOW.

What suggestions would you give Fran for managing this conflict?

In the beginning of the year, when the vacation schedule comes out, the manager should tell all the employees that the vacation schedule is based on tenure. This will help with the arguing of the associates. To handle the issue now, she should talk to the associates who want the same weeks for their vacation, see if any of them would be willing to switch to a different week, and possibly give them a little incentive for switching. Some examples could be giving them an extra weekend off or an extra day of vacation. The same should be done with the holidays; if there are six holidays, have each associate work three. This will help maximize coverage on busy days and provide the best customer service.

Group Tasks

At the Rotterdam Eye Hospital in the Netherlands, skilled teams of medical specialists not only deliver quality health care, they also collaborate with other staff members to improve the experience for patients and their families. The hospital, which fosters teamwork with special training, is always looking for new ways to improve the patient experience. One team researched innovations implemented by other hospitals and presented them internally for informal testing and experimentation at the

FUTURE VISION Conflict 2.0

Successful organizations will come to recognize that functional conflict—in the form of tolerating dissent—makes an organization stronger, not weaker. Tomorrow's organizations will use blogs, social networking sites, and other vehicles to allow employees to question practices, criticize decisions, and offer improvement suggestions.

The historical practice of minimizing conflict and seeking "peace at any price" didn't produce harmony and loyalty. It merely masked employee concerns and frustrations. To maintain competitiveness, organizations will see conflict in a positive light. And the result will be organizations that adapt faster, generate more and better ideas, and have employees who aren't threatened by saying what's on their minds.

If your professor has chosen to assign this, go to ***www.mymanagementlab.com*** *to discuss the following questions.*

TALK ABOUT IT 1: What do you think? Will functional conflict make an organization stronger? Discuss.

TALK ABOUT IT 2: What issues—good and bad—might managers have to deal with if employees can use social media and other digital tools to question practices, criticize decisions, and offer suggestions for improvement? What might managers have to do to deal with these issues?

Rotterdam Eye Hospital. If a team experimented with a particular idea and the result was positive, other teams began asking to adapt it for testing in their areas of expertise. Not every innovation worked out, but improvements that tested well and were implemented throughout the hospital were found to increase patient satisfaction and employee satisfaction.[35]

As the group performance/satisfaction model shows, the impact that group processes have on group performance and member satisfaction is modified by the task the group is doing. More specifically, it's the *complexity* and *interdependence* of tasks that influence a group's effectiveness.[36]

- 50 percent of managers say that their team members collaborate well with other teams.[37]

Tasks are either simple or complex. Simple tasks are routine and standardized. Complex tasks tend to be novel or nonroutine. It appears that the more complex the task, the more a group benefits from group discussion about alternative work methods. For instance, advertising agencies such as BBDO, a well-known agency that is responsible for branding Snickers candy and Post-It Notes, assign teams to create a brand identity for a client's products or services. Group members don't need to discuss such alternatives for a simple task, but can rely on standard operating procedures. Similarly, a high degree of interdependence among the tasks that group members must perform means they'll need to interact more. Thus, effective communication and controlled conflict are most relevant to group performance when tasks are complex and interdependent.

TURNING groups into effective teams

LO12.3 When companies like W. L. Gore, Volvo, and Kraft Foods introduced teams into their production processes in the 1970s, it made news because no one else was doing it. Today, it's just the opposite—the organization that *doesn't* use teams would be newsworthy. It's estimated that some 80 percent of *Fortune* 500 companies have at least half of their employees on teams. And 83 percent of respondents in a Center for Creative Leadership study said teams are a key ingredient to organizational success.[38] Without a doubt, team-based work is a core feature of today's organizations. And teams are likely to continue to be popular. Why? Research suggests that teams typically outperform individuals when the tasks being done require multiple skills, judgment, and experience.[39] Organizations are using team-based structures because they've found that teams are more flexible and responsive to changing events than traditional departments or other permanent work groups. Teams have the ability to quickly assemble, deploy, refocus, and disband. In this section, we'll discuss what a work team is, the different types of teams organizations might use, and how to develop and manage work teams.

★ Write It 2! If your professor has assigned this, go to **www.mymanagementlab.com** to complete the Writing Assignment *MGMT 15: Team-Based Structures.*

The Difference Between Groups and Teams

Most of you are probably familiar with teams, especially if you've watched or participated in organized sports events. Work *teams* differ from work *groups* and have their own unique traits (see Exhibit 12-8). Work groups interact primarily to share information and to make decisions to help each member do his or her job more efficiently and effectively. There's no need or opportunity for work groups to engage in collective work that requires joint effort. On the other hand, **work teams** are groups whose members work intensely on a specific, common goal using their positive synergy, individual and mutual accountability, and complementary skills. For instance, at the Sparta, Tennessee, facility of Philips Professional Luminaires, a work team came up with a startling innovation. One team member was commenting on the efficient way that Subway restaurants make their sandwiches, with workers lining up all their

work teams
Groups whose members work intensely on a specific, common goal using their positive synergy, individual and mutual accountability, and complementary skills

Exhibit 12-8
Groups Versus Teams

Work Teams	Work Groups
Leadership role is shared	One leader clearly in charge
Accountable to self and team	Accountable only to self
Team creates specific purpose	Purpose is same as broader organizational purpose
Work is done collectively	Work is done individually
Meetings characterized by open-ended discussion and collaborative problem-solving	Meetings characterized by efficiency; no collaboration or open-ended discussion
Performance is measured directly by evaluating collective work output	Performance is measured indirectly according to its influence on others
Work is decided upon and done together	Work is decided upon by group leader and delegated to individual group members
Can be quickly assembled, deployed, refocused, and disbanded	

Sources: J. R. Katzenbach and D. K. Smith, "The Wisdom of Teams," *Harvard Business Review*, July–August 2005, p. 161; A. J. Fazzari and J. B. Mosca, "Partners in Perfection: Human Resources Facilitating Creation and Ongoing Implementation of Self-Managed Manufacturing Teams in a Small Medium Enterprise," *Human Resource Development Quarterly*, Fall 2009, pp. 353–376.

ingredients in an easy-to-reach, highly adaptable format. The team decided to apply that same flexible principle to their work of producing lighting fixtures and together figured out a way to make that happen.[40]

Performance Tech Motorsports racing team executes a full-service pit stop with James French stepping out of the driver's seat and Conor Daly stepping in while team members check the car, fix and adjust parts, change tires, and pump gas. Using their positive synergy and complementary skills, team members work quickly and intensely to achieve the common goal of winning the race.
Source: Brian Cleary/Getty Images

Types of Work Teams

Teams can do a variety of things. They can design products, provide services, negotiate deals, coordinate projects, offer advice, and make decisions.[41] For instance, at Rockwell Automation's facility in North Carolina, teams are used in work process optimization projects. At Sylvania, the New Ventures Group creates cool LED-based products. At Arkansas-based Acxiom Corporation, a team of human resource professionals planned and implemented a cultural change. And every summer weekend at any NASCAR race, you can see work teams in action during drivers' pit stops.[42] The four most common types of work teams are problem-solving teams, self-managed work teams, cross-functional teams, and virtual teams.

When work teams first became popular, most were **problem-solving teams,** teams from the same department or functional area involved in efforts to improve work activities or to solve specific problems. Members share ideas or offer suggestions on how work processes and methods can be improved. However, these teams are rarely given the authority to implement any of their suggested actions. For instance, a large Midwest university in the United States assembled a team of faculty members to study how to increase faculty retention. The team completed a variety of activities, including interviews with current and former faculty members. Then, members prepared a report for the university's provost in which they discussed their findings and recommendations. The decision whether to implement any of the recommendations rested with the provost and not the committee.

problem-solving team
A team from the same department or functional area that's involved in efforts to improve work activities or to solve specific problems

Although problem-solving teams were helpful, they didn't go far enough in getting employees involved in work-related decisions and processes. This shortcoming led to another type of team, a **self-managed work team,** a formal group of employees who operate without a manager and are responsible for a complete work process or segment. A self-managed team is responsible for getting the work done *and* for managing themselves, which usually includes planning and scheduling of work, assigning tasks to members, collective control over the pace of work, making operating decisions, and taking action on problems. For instance, teams at Corning have no shift supervisors and work closely with other manufacturing divisions to solve production-line problems and coordinate deadlines and deliveries. The teams have the authority to make and implement decisions, finish projects, and address problems.[43]

self-managed work team
A type of work team that operates without a manager and is responsible for a complete work process or segment

Other organizations such as Xerox, Boeing, PepsiCo, and Hewlett-Packard also use self-managed teams. An estimated 30 percent of U.S. employers now use this form of team; among large firms, the number is probably closer to 50 percent.[44] Most organizations that use self-managed teams find them to be effective.[45]

cross-functional team
A work team composed of individuals from various functional specialties

The third type of team is the **cross-functional team,** which we introduced in Chapters 10 and 11 and defined as a work team composed of individuals from various functional specialties. Many organizations use cross-functional teams. For example, General Motors uses cross-functional teams of sculptors, systems analysts, engineers, and creative designers to come up with innovative car designs. The concept of cross-functional teams is even applied in health care. For example, global pharmaceutical giant Novartis introduces cross-functional teamwork to university students while inspiring its own employees by sponsoring an annual International BioCamp. For three days, 60 students from 18 nations work in teams to solve an assigned problem by pooling their cross-functional expertise in biology, technology, and other specialties. One recent challenge was to develop a digital device that reminds people to take medicine on time. Novartis honors the top teams for their creative accomplishments and also awards prizes for individual leadership.[46]

virtual team
A type of work team that uses technology to link physically dispersed members in order to achieve a common goal

A survey of information workers in 17 countries revealed that:

- 94 percent use e-mail.
- 33 percent participate in videoconferencing (such as Skype).
- 25 percent use room-based videoconferencing.[47]

The final type of team is the **virtual team,** a team that uses technology to link physically dispersed members to achieve a common goal. For instance, a virtual team at Boeing-Rocketdyne played a pivotal role in developing a radically new product.[48] Another company, Automattic, employs 450 individuals distributed throughout 45 countries, and their job is to support more than 25 percent of the websites on the Internet. This is truly a virtual company because there is no physical office space.

How does Automattic get work accomplished? In a virtual team, members collaborate online with tools such as wide-area networks, videoconferencing, fax, e-mail, or websites where the team can hold online conferences.[49] Virtual teams can do all the things that other teams can—share information, make decisions, and complete tasks; however, they lack the normal give-and-take of face-to-face discussions. That's why virtual teams tend to be more task-oriented, especially if the team members have never met in person.

If your professor has assigned this, go to **www.mymanagementlab.com** to complete the Simulation: *Virtual Teams* and get a better understanding of the challenges of managing virtual teams in organizations.

If your professor has assigned this, go to **www.mymanagementlab.com** to watch a video titled: *Witness.org—Managing Groups and Teams* and to respond to questions.

Creating Effective Work Teams

As our chapter opener illustrated, teams are not always effective. They don't always achieve high levels of performance. However, research on teams provides insights into the characteristics typically associated with effective teams.[50] These characteristics are listed in Exhibit 12-9. One element you might notice is missing but think is important to being an effective team is that a team be harmonious and friendly.[51] In fact, friendliness is not a necessary ingredient. Even a grumpy team can be effective if these other team characteristics are present. When a team is productive, has done something good together, and is recognized for its efforts, team members can feel good about their effectiveness.

CLEAR GOALS High-performance teams have a clear understanding of the goal to be achieved. Members are committed to the team's goals, know what they're expected to accomplish, and understand how they will work together to achieve these goals.

Exhibit 12-9
Characteristics of Effective Teams

RELEVANT SKILLS Effective teams are composed of competent individuals who have the necessary technical and interpersonal skills to achieve the desired goals while working well together. This last point is important because not everyone who is technically competent has the interpersonal skills to work well as a team member.

MUTUAL TRUST Effective teams are characterized by high mutual trust among members. That is, members believe in each other's ability, character, and integrity. But as you probably know from personal relationships, trust is fragile. Maintaining this trust requires careful attention by managers.[52]

- 72 percent of employees surveyed say that they strongly/moderately trust their coworkers.[53]

UNIFIED COMMITMENT Unified commitment is characterized by dedication to the team's goals and a willingness to expend extraordinary amounts of energy to achieve them. Members of an effective team exhibit intense loyalty and dedication to the team and are willing to do whatever it takes to help their team succeed.

GOOD COMMUNICATION Not surprisingly, effective teams are characterized by good communication.[54] Members convey messages, verbally and nonverbally, between each other in ways that are readily and clearly understood. Also, feedback helps guide team members and correct misunderstandings. Like a couple who has been together for many years, members of high-performing teams are able to quickly and efficiently share ideas and feelings.

NEGOTIATING SKILLS Effective teams are continually making adjustments to who does what. This flexibility requires team members to possess negotiating skills. Because problems and relationships regularly change within teams, members need to be able to confront and reconcile differences.

Negotiating—If your instructor is using Pearson MyLab Management, log onto **mymanagementlab.com** and test your *negotiating knowledge*. **Be sure to refer back to the chapter opener!**

APPROPRIATE LEADERSHIP Effective leaders are important. They can motivate a team to follow them through the most difficult situations. How? By clarifying goals, demonstrating that change is possible by overcoming inertia, increasing the self-confidence of team members, and helping members to more fully realize their potential. Increasingly, effective team leaders act as coaches and facilitators. They help guide and support the team, but don't control it. Studies have shown that when a team leader's emotional displays—positive *and* negative—are used at appropriate times, the team's functioning and performance can be enhanced.[55]

INTERNAL AND EXTERNAL SUPPORT The final condition necessary for an effective team is a supportive climate. Internally, the team should have a sound infrastructure, which means proper training, a clear and reasonable measurement system that team members can use to evaluate their overall performance, an incentive program that recognizes and rewards team activities, and a supportive human resource system. The right infrastructure should support members and reinforce behaviors that lead to high levels of performance. Externally, managers should provide the team with the resources needed to get the job done.

If your professor has assigned this, go to **www.mymanagementlab.com** to complete the Simulation: *Teams* and get a better understanding of the challenges of managing teams in organizations.

let's get REAL

The Scenario:

What a mess. When Walter Smith agreed to take over managing a team of client service representatives at a financial services company, he didn't realize how poorly the team was working together. He has learned that there have been many disagreements about work responsibilities and that two team members avoid talking to each other entirely. As a result, the team is not performing well. Walter must now take steps to get the team working together again.

What can Walter do to improve the effectiveness of his team?

As a leader, begin with setting the tone for the team. Bring everyone together and explain your vision and expectations for working together. Be empathetic and explain that you want to better understand the current challenges and work together to improve it. After laying out the vision, work with each individual to detail a clear list of individual roles and responsibilities, becoming familiar with their current workload, career goals, and strengths. What might seem minor can lead to major changes, such as celebrating wins and publicly expressing your appreciation.

Be sure to also address the two embittered employees quickly or they could sabotage your efforts. Depending on the severity of their conflict, you may need to involve your HR partners in the discussion.

Christina Moser
Strategic Account Manager

Source: Christina Moser

WORKPLACE CONFIDENTIAL Handling Difficult Coworkers

We've all been around people who, to put it nicely, are difficult to get along with. These people might be chronic complainers, they might be meddlers who think they know everything about everyone else's job and don't hesitate to tell you so, or they might exhibit any number of other unpleasant interpersonal characteristics. They can make your job extremely hard and your workday very stressful if you don't know how to deal with them. Being around difficult people tends to bring out the worst in all of us. What can you do? How do you learn to get along with these difficult people?

We suggest you start by recognizing that it's the behavior of the coworker that is getting to you, not the person himself or herself. Don't make this personal. Understanding the behavior will help you identify the source of the problem and how it might be solved.

Next, ask yourself: To what degree might I be contributing to the problem? The key here is just to remove any controllable factors that you might be bringing to the situation. For instance, do you tend to be moody, and if so, is that a contributing factor? If you're on a team project with the person, are you being too pushy or demanding? Since your behavior is controllable, the difficulty might be eliminated quickly by your making a few changes.

Now consider the source of your coworker's behavior. What is it, specifically, that bothers you? Put yourself in that person's shoes and attempt to see things from his or her perspective.

It's important to assess the source of your coworker's behavior. It makes a big difference whether you're dealing with just a clash of styles or whether you're facing a toxic worker. The latter has something inside—such as anger or distrust—that infects those around them. Conflicts with toxic types are more difficult to resolve.

A clash of styles might include different importance placed on promptness, deadlines, or ways of communicating. Or it might include how the two of you handle change, stressful situations, mistakes, excessive talking, or interruptions. The key here is recognizing that you're not dealing with objective states of right and wrong. Rather, the source of the difficulty is different ways of doing or seeing things.

So how do you handle differences in style? Here are some common types of difficult people you're likely to meet at work and some strategies for dealing with them.

The aggressive types. With these types, you need to stand up for yourself; give them time to run down; don't worry about being polite, jump in if you need to; get their attention carefully; speak from your own point of view; avoid a head-on fight; and be ready to be friendly.

The complainers. With the complainers, you need to listen attentively; acknowledge their concerns; be prepared to interrupt their litany of complaints; don't agree, but do acknowledge what they're saying; state facts without comment or apology; and switch them to problem solving.

The silent or nonresponsive types. With these types, you need to ask open-ended questions; use the friendly, silent stare; don't fill the silent pauses for them in conversations; comment on what's happening and help break the tension by making them feel more at ease.

The know-it-all experts. The keys to dealing with these types are to be on top of things; listen and acknowledge their comments; question firmly, but don't confront; avoid being a counterexpert; and work with them to channel their energy in positive directions.

The toxic coworker provides a tougher challenge. This person is destructive and abusive. While they often have a number of desirable traits, such as charm, leadership, and impression management skills, they also have a dark side. That dark side surfaces in one or more of three traits: psychopathy, Machiavellianism, and narcissism. Psychopathy is a personality disorder. It's characterized by a lack of remorse and empathy. Psychopaths are emotionally cold and disconnected. And unlike those who make newspaper headlines, most live relatively normal lives—including working for a living. Machiavellian types are master manipulators. They're cunning and duplicitous. Not surprisingly, they are often your boss or upper-level manager. This is because these people are very good at exhibiting charm and impressing others. The third component of toxicity is narcissism. Narcissists are highly self-centered people who are egotistical and think the world revolves around them. Studies have found that Machiavellian and narcissistic types use "soft" tactics like compliments and reason to get their way; psychopathic individuals use "hard" tactics such as assertiveness and direct manipulations.

So how do you deal with a toxic coworker? Experts suggest that the best advice is to physically distance yourself from him or her. Keep a safe distance away in order to avoid getting sucked into the toxicity. Toxic behavior is contagious! If physical avoidance isn't an option, try to distance yourself mentally and emotionally. This can best be achieved by setting boundaries. Tell your toxic coworker what you will and won't accept. It may take a lot of repetition but hold to your boundaries. In addition, make clear the consequences if the boundaries are crossed. And be prepared to take your complaints about inappropriate behavior to your superiors. If it gets to this stage, make sure your complaint is succinct and professional. You want to make it clear which workplace rules are being broken and how this action affects yours, and others', work performance.

Based on A. A. Cavaiola and N. J. Lavender, *Toxic Coworkers: How to Deal with Dysfunctional People on the Job* (Oakland, CA: New Harbinger Publications, 2000); M. Solomon, *Working with Difficult People* (Upper Saddle River, NJ: Prentice Hall, 2002); P. K. Jonason, S. Slomski, and J. Partyka, "The Dark Triad at Work: How *Toxic* Employees Get Their Way," *Personality and Individual Differences*, February 2012, pp. 449–453; A. Goforth, "12 of the Most Toxic Employees," *Benefits Selling*, June 8, 2015.

CONTEMPORARY challenges in managing teams

LO12.4 Few trends have influenced how work gets done in organizations as much as the use of work teams. The shift from working alone to working on teams requires employees to cooperate with others, share information, confront differences, and sublimate personal interests for the greater good of the team. Managers can build effective teams by understanding what influences performance and satisfaction. However, managers also face some current challenges in managing teams, primarily those associated with managing global teams, building team skills, and understanding organizational social networks.

Managing Global Teams

Two characteristics of today's organizations are obvious: They're global, and work is increasingly done by teams. These two aspects mean that any manager is likely to have to manage a global team. What do we know about managing global teams? We know there are both drawbacks and benefits in using global teams (see Exhibit 12-10). Using our group model as a framework, we can see some of the issues associated with managing global teams.

GROUP MEMBER RESOURCES IN GLOBAL TEAMS In global organizations, understanding the relationship between group performance and group member resources is more challenging because of the unique cultural characteristics represented by members of a global team. In addition to recognizing team members' abilities, skills, knowledge, and personality, managers need to be familiar with and clearly understand the cultural characteristics of the groups and the group members they manage.[56] For instance, is the global team from a culture in which uncertainty avoidance is high? If so, members will not be comfortable dealing with unpredictable and ambiguous tasks. Also, as managers work with global teams, they need to be aware of the potential for stereotyping, which can lead to problems.

GROUP STRUCTURE Some of the structural areas where we see differences in managing global teams include conformity, status, social loafing, and cohesiveness.

Are conformity findings generalizable across cultures? Research suggests that Asch's findings are culture-bound.[57] For instance, as might be expected, conformity to social norms tends to be higher in collectivistic cultures than in individualistic cultures. Despite this tendency, however, groupthink tends to be less of a problem in global teams because members are less likely to feel pressured to conform to the ideas, conclusions, and decisions of the group.[58]

Also, the importance of status varies between cultures. The French, for example, are extremely status conscious. Also, countries differ on the criteria that confer status. For instance, in Latin America and Asia, status tends to come from family position and formal roles held in organizations. In contrast, while status is important in countries like the United States and Australia, it tends to be less "in your face." And it tends to be given based on accomplishments rather than on titles and family history. Managers must understand who and what holds status when interacting with people from a culture different from their own. An American manager who doesn't understand that office size isn't a mea-

Exhibit 12-10
Global Teams

Drawbacks	Benefits
• Dislike of team members • Mistrust of team members • Stereotyping • Communication problems • Stress and tension	• Greater diversity of ideas • Limited groupthink • Increased attention on understanding others' ideas, perspectives, etc.

Source: Based on N. Adler, *International Dimensions in Organizational Behavior*, 4th ed. (Cincinnati, OH: South-Western Publishing, 2002), pp. 141–147.

sure of a Japanese executive's position or who fails to grasp the importance the British place on family genealogy and social class is likely to unintentionally offend others and lessen his or her interpersonal effectiveness.

Social loafing has a Western bias. It's consistent with individualistic cultures, like the United States and Canada, which are dominated by self-interest. It's not consistent with collectivistic societies, in which individuals are motivated by group goals. For instance, teamwork is an integral element in Japan's corporate culture. The emphasis on group versus individual achievement begins in elementary school, where students in Japan learn to work collaboratively on projects that benefit the class and the school. In Japanese businesses, employees are expected to be active team members, and they get things done by group consensus.[60]

Cohesiveness is another group structural element where managers may face special challenges. In a cohesive group, members are unified and "act as one." These groups exhibit a great deal of camaraderie, and group identity is high. In global teams, however, cohesiveness is often more difficult to achieve because of higher levels of "mistrust, miscommunication, and stress."[61]

LEADER making a DIFFERENCE

Source: WENN Ltd/Alamy

As the CEO of the YWCA USA, Inc., ***Dr. Dara Richardson-Heron*** *must motivate her team to tackle some of society's biggest challenges.[59] The organization is focused on the empowerment and economic advancement of women and girls, as well as on eliminating racism and promoting civil rights. Providing leadership to the 225 associations across the country that are working toward these overall goals and also addressing local concerns requires a talent in motivating a diverse leadership team.*

Richardson-Heron joined the YWCA, one of the world's largest charities, as the CEO in 2012. When she was hired, she knew she needed to put the right people on her leadership team, which is a challenge when taking on the top spot in a new organization as an outsider. Richardson-Heron believes that people are more likely to be successful doing what they like to do so she carefully selected and promoted those who she believed would be her best direct reports and placed others where she thought they would excel. Richardson-Heron also notes it is essential to remain humble. She believes as a leader you must create a culture where the team feels comfortable bringing you bad news, otherwise small problems can quickly turn into big ones. Richardson-Heron developed her leadership skills early in her career as a lead physician over mostly men who were skeptical of her because she was a woman. She learned quickly that the best strategy to earn the respect of others is through demonstrating your abilities. What can you learn from this leader making a difference?

GROUP PROCESSES The processes global teams use to do their work can be particularly challenging for managers. For one thing, communication issues often arise because not all team members may be fluent in the team's working language. This can lead to inaccuracies, misunderstandings, and inefficiencies.[62] However, research also has shown that a multicultural global team is better able to capitalize on the diversity of ideas represented if a wide range of information is used.[63]

Managing conflict in global teams isn't easy, especially when those teams are virtual teams. Conflict can interfere with how information is used by the team. However, research shows that in collectivistic cultures, a collaborative conflict management style can be most effective.[64]

MANAGER'S ROLE Despite the challenges associated with managing global teams, managers can provide the group with an environment in which efficiency and effectiveness are enhanced.[65] First, because communication skills are vital, managers should focus on developing those skills. Also, as we've said earlier, managers must consider cultural differences when deciding what type of global team to use. For instance, evidence suggests that self-managed teams have not fared well in Mexico largely due to that culture's low tolerance of ambiguity and uncertainty and employees' strong respect for hierarchical authority.[66] Finally, it's vital that managers be sensitive to the unique differences of each member of the global team, but it's also important that team members be sensitive to each other.

Building Team Skills

Have you ever participated in a team-building exercise? Such exercises are commonly used to illustrate and develop specific aspects or skills of being on a team. For instance,

Teachers and staff of a middle school participate in a rowing team-building exercise to learn how to work together in achieving the school's missions and goals, boosting faculty morale, and increasing student performance. Many organizations incorporate team-building strategies that help create a positive, enthusiastic, and collaborative workplace environment.
Source: Gregory Shaver/Associated Press

maybe you've completed *Lost on the Moon* or *Stranded at Sea* or some other written exercise in which you rank-order what items are most important to your survival. Then, you do the same thing with a group—rank-order the most important items. The rank-ordered items are compared against some expert ranking to see how many you got "right." The intent of the exercise is to illustrate how much more effective decisions can be when made as a team. Or maybe you've been part of a trust-building exercise in which you fall back and team members catch you, or an exercise in which your team had to figure out how to get all members across an imaginary river or up a rock wall. Such exercises help team members bond or connect and learn to rely on one another. One of the important tasks managers have is building effective teams.[67] These types of team-building exercises can be an important part of that process. And team-building efforts can work. For example, a research project that looked at star performers with poor team skills who went through two cycles of team-building exercises found that those individuals learned how to collaborate better.[68]

With the emphasis on teams in today's organizations, managers need to recognize that people don't automatically know how to be part of a team or to be an effective team member. Like any behavior, sometimes you have to learn about the skill and then keep practicing and reinforcing it. In building team skills, managers must view their role as more of being a coach and developing team members in order to create more committed, collaborative, and inclusive teams.[69] It's important to recognize that not everyone is a team player or can learn to be a team player. If attempts at team building aren't working, then maybe it's better to put those people in positions where their work is done individually.

Understanding Social Networks

social network structure
The patterns of informal connections among individuals within a group

We can't leave this chapter on managing teams without looking at the patterns of informal connections among individuals within groups—that is, at the **social network structure.**[70] What actually happens *within* groups? How *do* group members relate to each other, and how does work get done?

Managers need to understand the social networks and social relationships of work groups. Why? Because a group's informal social relationships can help or hinder its effectiveness. For instance, research on social networks has shown that when people need help getting a job done, they'll choose a friendly colleague over someone who may be more capable.[71] Another recent review of team studies showed that teams with high levels of interpersonal interconnectedness actually attained their goals better and were more committed to staying together.[72] Organizations are recognizing the practical benefits of knowing the social networks within teams. For instance, when Ken Loughridge, an IT manager with MWH Global, was transferred from Cheshire, England, to New Zealand, he had a "map" of the informal relationships and connections among company IT employees. This map had been created a few months before using the results of a survey that asked employees who they "consulted most frequently, who they turned to for expertise, and who either boosted or drained their energy levels." Not only did this map help him identify well-connected technical experts, it helped him minimize potential problems when a key manager in the Asia region left the company because Loughridge knew who this person's closest contacts were. Loughridge said, "It's as if you took the top off an ant hill and could see where there's a hive of activity. It really helped me understand who the players were."[73]

Chapter 12 PREPARING FOR: Exams/Quizzes

CHAPTER SUMMARY by Learning Objectives

LO12.1 DEFINE groups and the stages of group development.

A group is two or more interacting and interdependent individuals who come together to achieve specific goals. Formal groups are work groups defined by the organization's structure and have designated work assignments and specific tasks directed at accomplishing organizational goals. Informal groups are social groups.

The forming stage consists of two phases: joining the group and defining the group's purpose, structure, and leadership. The storming stage is one of intragroup conflict over who will control the group and what the group will be doing. The norming stage is when close relationships and cohesiveness develop as norms are determined. The performing stage is when group members begin to work on the group's task. The adjourning stage is when the group prepares to disband.

LO12.2 DESCRIBE the major components that determine group performance and satisfaction.

The major components that determine group performance and satisfaction include external conditions, group member resources, group structure, group processes, and group tasks.

External conditions, such as availability of resources, organizational goals, and other factors, affect work groups. Group member resources (knowledge, skills, abilities, personality traits) can influence what members can do and how effectively they will perform in a group.

Group roles generally involve getting the work done or keeping group members happy. Group norms are powerful influences on a person's performance and dictate things such as work output levels, absenteeism, and promptness. Pressures to conform can heavily influence a person's judgment and attitudes. If carried to extremes, groupthink can be a problem. Status systems can be a significant motivator with individual behavioral consequences, especially if incongruence is a factor. What size group is most effective and efficient depends on the task the group is supposed to accomplish. Cohesiveness is related to a group's productivity.

Group decision making and conflict management are important group processes that play a role in performance and satisfaction. If accuracy, creativity, and degree of acceptance are important, a group decision may work best. Relationship conflicts are almost always dysfunctional. Low levels of process conflicts and low-to-moderate levels of task conflicts are functional. Effective communication and controlled conflict are most relevant to group performance when tasks are complex and interdependent.

LO12.3 DEFINE teams and best practices influencing team performance.

Characteristics of work groups include a strong, clearly focused leader; individual accountability; purpose that's the same as the broader organizational mission; individual work product; efficient meetings; effectiveness measured by influence on others; and the ability to discuss, decide, and delegate together. Characteristics of teams include shared leadership roles; individual and mutual accountability; specific team purpose; collective work products; meetings with open-ended discussion and active problem solving; performance measured directly on collective work products; and the ability to discuss, decide, and do real work.

A problem-solving team is one that's focused on improving work activities or solving specific problems. A self-managed work team is responsible for a complete work process or segment and manages itself. A cross-functional team is composed of individuals from various specialties. A virtual team uses technology to link physically dispersed members in order to achieve a common goal.

The characteristics of an effective team include clear goals, relevant skills, mutual trust, unified commitment, good communication, negotiating skills, appropriate leadership, and internal and external support.

LO12.4 DISCUSS contemporary issues in managing teams.

The challenges of managing global teams can be seen in the group member resources, especially the diverse cultural characteristics; group structure, especially conformity, status, social loafing, and cohesiveness; group processes, especially with communication and managing conflict; and the manager's role in making it all work.

With the emphasis on teams in today's organizations, managers need to recognize that people don't automatically know how to be part of a team or to be an effective team member. Like any behavior, team members have to learn about the skill and then keep practicing and reinforcing it. In building team skills, managers must view their role as more of being a coach and developing others to create more committed, collaborative, and inclusive teams.

Managers need to understand the patterns of informal connections among individuals within groups because those informal social relationships can help or hinder the group's effectiveness.

Pearson **MyLab** Management

Go to **mymanagementlab.com** to complete the problems marked with this icon ✪.

✪ REVIEW AND DISCUSSION QUESTIONS

12-1. How does knowing the five stages of group development help you as the manager?

12-2. What is an informal group and can informal groups form within an organization?

12-3. Discuss how group structure, group processes, and group tasks influence group performance and satisfaction.

12-4. What are "group norms"?

12-5. Why are virtual teams not suitable for all situations?

12-6. Discuss how having clear goals can make a team more effective.

12-7. List and describe the key benefits of global teams.

Pearson **MyLab** Management

If your professor has assigned these, go to **mymanagementlab.com** for the following Assisted-graded writing questions:

12-8. What challenges do managers face in managing global teams? How should those challenges be handled?

12-9. When is conflict functional and when is it dysfunctional? Explain your answers and give examples of functional and dysfunctional conflict.

PREPARING FOR: My Career

PERSONAL INVENTORY ASSESSMENTS

Diagnosing the Need for Team Building

Creating and managing an effective team requires knowing when the team needs some help. Use this PIA to assess teams you're leading or are part of.

ETHICS DILEMMA

When coworkers work closely on a team project, is there such a thing as becoming too close? Not everyone thinks so. A recent survey revealed that 51 percent of employees said they have had an office romance.[74] And another survey found that workers in their 20s and 30s view workplace romances more positively than older generations do.[75] Sometimes, coworkers feel free to share personal information. For example, at one company, a team that had just finished a major project went out to lunch to celebrate. During lunch, one colleague mentioned that he was training for a 20-mile bike race. In addition to a discussion of his new helmet and Lycra shorts, the person also described shaving his whole body to reduce aerodynamic drag. Later, another team member said, "Why, why, why do we need to go there? This is information about a coworker, not someone I really consider a friend."

12-10. What do you think? Why do many work colleagues become romantically involved? Why do some coworkers choose to share personal information?

12-11. Should employees inform their managers about such relationships? Explain your reasoning.

12-12. What are the ethical implications of coworkers' becoming romantically involved? Sharing too much information?

SKILLS EXERCISE Developing Your Coaching Skills

About the Skill

Effective work team managers are increasingly being described as coaches rather than bosses. Just like coaches, they're expected to provide instruction, guidance, advice, and encouragement to help team members improve their job performance.

Steps in Practicing the Skill

- ***Analyze ways to improve the team's performance and capabilities.*** A coach looks for opportunities for team members to expand their capabilities and improve performance. How? You can use the following behaviors. Observe your team members' behaviors on a day-to-day basis. Ask questions of them: Why do you do a task this way? Can it be improved? What other approaches might be used? Show genuine interest in team members as individuals, not merely as employees. Respect them individually. Listen to each employee.
- ***Create a supportive climate.*** It's the coach's responsibility to reduce barriers to development and to facilitate a climate that encourages personal performance improvement. How? You can use the following behaviors. Create a climate that contributes to a free and open exchange of ideas. Offer help and assistance. Give guidance and advice when asked. Encourage your team. Be positive and upbeat. Don't use threats. Ask, "What did we learn from this that can help us in the future?" Reduce obstacles. Assure team members that you value their contribution to the team's goals. Take personal responsibility for the outcome, but don't rob team members of their full responsibility. Validate team members' efforts when they succeed. Point to what was missing when they fail. Never blame team members for poor results.
- ***Influence team members to change their behavior.*** The ultimate test of coaching effectiveness is whether an employee's performance improves. You must encourage ongoing growth and development. How can you do this? Try the following behaviors. Recognize and reward small improvements and treat coaching as a way of helping employees to continually work toward improvement. Use a collaborative style by allowing team members to participate in identifying and choosing among improvement ideas. Break difficult tasks down into simpler ones. Model the qualities you expect from your team. If you want openness, dedication, commitment, and responsibility from your team members, demonstrate these qualities yourself.

Practicing the Skill
Find a friend or a classmate that you can coach on a project or assignment. Maybe it is a coworker, a new member in an organization you belong to, or a friend taking a challenging course you have already taken. Following the guidance provided above, practice your coaching skills by working with your friend or classmate to improve his or her performance.

WORKING TOGETHER Team Exercise

How easy is it to create effective teams? It is not always easy to come up with the right mix of individuals, and often there are clashes. They need to have complementary skills.[76] For as many teams that exist there are as many theories to suggest how they should be organized, and what they should look like. Create small groups of three to four individuals. Your team's task is to come up with some suggestions for what a truly effective team should look like and what its characteristics should be. Come up with a bullet list of your ideas. You should then share your ideas with the class and try to come up with a definitive list.

MY TURN TO BE A MANAGER

- Think of a group to which you belong (or have belonged). Trace its development through the stages of group development as shown in Exhibit 12-2. How closely did its development parallel the group development model? How might the group development model be used to improve this group's effectiveness?
- Using this same group, write a report describing the following things about this group: types of roles played by whom, group norms, group conformity issues, status system, size of group and how effective/efficient it is, and group cohesiveness.
- Using the same group, describe how decisions are made. Is the process effective? Efficient? Describe what types of conflicts seem to arise most often (relationship, process, or task) and how those conflicts are handled. Add this information to your report on the group's development and structure.
- Select two of the characteristics of effective teams listed in Exhibit 12-9 and develop a team-building exercise for each characteristic that will help a group improve that characteristic. Be creative. Write a report describing your exercises, and be sure to explain how your exercises will help a group improve or develop that characteristic.
- Often new teams that must become productive quickly start off by writing ground rules or a team working agreement. Conduct some research on team working agreements and create a summary of what such an agreement might include. When assigned your next team project, try writing a team working agreement to kick off your project.

CASE APPLICATION 1 Who Needs a Manager?

Can employees really manage themselves? At W.L. Gore and Associates self-managed teams have helped create a thriving business that has operated profitably for more than 50 years.[77] Gore is a manufacturer that develops innovative solutions for demanding environments. Focusing primarily on protective fabrics, Gore products might be found in clothing worn on a hike up Mt. Everest or in medical implants for the human body. You may have encountered their best known product, Gore-Tex fabric, in a pair of gloves that keep your hands warm in even the coldest temperatures.

Self-management is not just a trend at Gore, it is a management structure that has been in place since the company was founded in 1958. The company has no titles, no bosses, and no hierarchy. Employees work in self-managed teams of 8 to 12 employees and they make all of the decisions including hiring and pay. This structure was created by company founders Wilbert "Bill" Lee and Genevieve Gore when they established the company to combat traditional management practices and encourage innovative thinking. There is a CEO and some respected leaders, but otherwise no clear management structure exists. The current CEO Terri Kelly stepped into the role in 2005 after 22 years with the company. While she is in charge, she was selected in a peer-driven process.

Why does it work? In this self-managed environment, employees are committed to make the organization a success and everyone is working in the company's best interest. Employees are all partial owners of the company, which encourages them to focus on the company's success. Each employee has the freedom to decide what they will work on, but then also must make a commitment to deliver. There are leaders in the organization, but they are determined by who is willing to follow them. The test of leadership is, if you call a meeting, does anyone show up?

Self-management could easily turn into chaos, especially with more than 10,000 employees. However, Gore has a culture that reinforces the expectations for performance of the self-managed teams. The company has established norms of behavior and expected guidelines to follow. It often takes more time for decisions to be made because of the need for team buy-in when making the decision. But once decisions are made, actions are completed more quickly because the buy-in already exists. The self-managed teams at Gore aren't built easily. They spend a lot of time coming together building relationships and building trust. This foundation of trust helps the team work better together, as everyone knows everyone else is working toward the same goals.

Could any company duplicate Gore's management practices? Probably not, say many management experts. Self-managed teams aren't effective in just any company. Self-managed teams are most appropriate in organizations where innovation is strategically important. They are also a useful structure in environments that change rapidly. Finally, in order for self-managed teams to be a success, a company must also have strongly shared values that direct work activities.

DISCUSSION QUESTIONS

12-13. Would you want to work at W.L. Gore and Associates? Why or why not?

12-14. Why are self-managed teams effective at Gore?

12-15. What are challenges for organizations that have self-managed teams?

CASE APPLICATION 2 737 Teaming Up for Takeoff

The Boeing 737, a short- to medium-range twin-engine, narrow-body jet, first rolled off the assembly line in 1967.[78] Here, almost half a century later, it's the best-selling jet airliner in the history of aviation. As airlines replace their aging narrow-body jet fleets, the burden is on Boeing to ramp up production to meet demand and to do so efficiently. As Boeing managers state, "How do you produce more aircraft without expanding the building?" Managing production of the multimillion dollar product—a 737-800 is sold for $84.4 million—means "walking an increasingly fine line between generating cash and stoking an airplane glut." And Boeing is relying on its employee innovation teams to meet the challenge.

Boeing has been using employee-generated ideas since the 1990s, when its manufacturing facility in Renton, Washington, began adopting "lean" manufacturing techniques. Today, employee teams are leaving "few stones unturned." For instance, a member of one team thought of a solution to a problem of stray metal fasteners sometimes puncturing the tires as the airplane advanced down the assembly line. The solution? A canvas wheel cover that hugs the four main landing-gear tires. Another team figured out how to rearrange its work space to make four engines at a time instead of three. Another team of workers in the paint process revamped their work routines and cut 10 minutes to 15 minutes per worker off each job. It took five years for another employee team to perfect a process for installing the plane's landing gear hydraulic tubes, but it eventually paid off.

These employee teams are made up of 7 to 10 workers with "varying backgrounds"—from mechanics to assembly workers to engineers—and tend to focus on a specific part of a jet, such as the landing gear or the passenger seats or the galleys. These teams may meet as often as once a week. What's the track record of these teams? Today, it takes about 11 days for the final assembly of a 737 jet. That's down from 22 days about a decade ago. The near-term goal is to eventually shave off two more days.

DISCUSSION QUESTIONS

12-16. What type of team(s) do these employee teams appear to be? Explain.

12-17. As this story illustrated, sometimes it may take a long time for a team to reach its goal. As a manager, how would you motivate a team to keep on trying?

12-18. What role do you think a team leader needs to play in this type of setting? Explain.

12-19. Using Exhibit 12-9, what characteristics of effective teams would these teams need? Explain.

ENDNOTES

1. M. F. Maples, "Group Development: Extending Tuckman's Theory," *Journal for Specialists in Group Work,* Fall 1988, pp. 17–23; and B. W. Tuckman and M. C. Jensen, "Stages of Small-Group Development Revisited," *Group and Organizational Studies,* December 1977, pp. 419–427.
2. D. Coutou, interview with J. R. Hackman, "Why Teams Don't Work," *Harvard Business Review,* May 2009, pp. 99–105; M. Kaeter, "Repotting Mature Work Teams," *Training*, April 1994, pp. 54–56; and L. N. Jewell and H. J. Reitz, *Group Effectiveness in Organizations* (Glenview, IL: Scott Foresman, 1981).
3. K. Caulfield, "Greatest Billboard 200 Albums and Artists of All Time: Adele's '21' and The Beatles Are Tops," *Billboard* online, www.billboard.com, November 12, 2015.
4. A. Sobel, "The Beatles Principles," *Strategy & Business,* Spring 2006, p. 42.
5. This model is based on the work of P. S. Goodman, E. Ravlin, and M. Schminke, "Understanding Groups in Organizations," in *Research in Organizational Behavior*, vol. 9, ed. L. L. Cummings and B. M. Staw (Greenwich, CT: JAI Press, 1987), pp. 124–128; J. R. Hackman, "The Design of Work Teams," in *Handbook of Organizational Behavior, ed.* J. W. Lorsch (Upper Saddle River, NJ: Prentice Hall, 1987), pp. 315–342; G. R. Bushe and A. L. Johnson, "Contextual and Internal Variables Affecting Task Group Outcomes in Organizations," *Group and Organization Studies,* December 1989, pp. 462–482; M. A. Campion, C. J. Medsker, and A. C. Higgs, "Relations Between Work Group Characteristics and Effectiveness: Implications for Designing Effective Work Groups," *Personnel Psychology,* Winter 1993, pp. 823–850; D. E. Hyatt and T. M. Ruddy, "An Examination of the Relationship Between Work Group Characteristics, and Performance: Once More into the Breach," *Personnel Psychology,* Autumn 1997, pp. 553–585; and P. E. Tesluk and J. E. Mathieu, "Overcoming Roadblocks to Effectiveness: Incorporating Management of Performance Barriers into Models of Work Group Effectiveness," *Journal of Applied Psychology,* April 1999, pp. 200–217.
6. G. L. Stewart, "A Meta-Analytic Review of Relationships Between Team Design Features and Team Performance," *Journal of Management,* February 2006, pp. 29–54; T. Butler and J. Waldroop, "Understanding 'People' People," *Harvard Business Review,* June 2004, pp. 78–86; J. S. Bunderson, "Team Member Functional Background and Involvement in Management Teams: Direct Effects and the Moderating Role of Power Centralization," *Academy of Management Journal,* August 2003, pp. 458–474; and M. J. Stevens and M. A. Campion, "The Knowledge, Skill, and Ability Requirements for Teamwork: Implications for Human Resource Management," *Journal of Management,* Summer 1994, pp. 503–530.
7. V. U. Druskat and S. B. Wolff, "The Link between Emotions and Team Effectiveness: How Teams Engage Members and Build Effective Task Processes," *Academy of Management Proceedings*, August 1999; D. C. Kinlaw, *Developing Superior Work Teams: Building Quality and the Competitive Edge* (San Diego, CA: Lexington, 1991); and M. E. Shaw, *Contemporary Topics in Social Psychology* (Morristown, NJ: General Learning Press, 1976), pp. 350–351.
8. T. Chamorro-Premuzic and D. Winsborough, "Personality Tests Can Help Balance a Team," *Harvard Business Review* online, www.hbr.org, March 19, 2015.
9. McMurry, Inc., "The Roles Your People Play," *Managing People at Work,* October 2005, p. 4; G. Prince, "Recognizing Genuine Teamwork," *Supervisory Management*, April 1989, pp. 25–36; R. F. Bales, *SYMOLOG Case Study Kit* (New York: Free Press, 1980); and K. D. Benne and P. Sheats, "Functional Roles of Group Members," *Journal of Social Issues*, vol. 4 (1948), pp. 41–49.
10. K. Novak, "Never Say No! South Korea's Pressure-Cooker Work Culture," *CNN* online, www.cnn.com, July 23, 2015.

11. "South Korea's Hangover," *Al Jazeera* online, www.aljazeera.com, February 5, 2016.
12. A. Erez, H. Elms, and E. Fong, "Lying, Cheating, Stealing: Groups and the Ring of Gyges," paper presented at the Academy of Management annual meeting, Honolulu, HI: August 8, 2005.
13. S. Coulter, "Home Depot Employee Theft Ring Exposed in Trumbull," *Trumbull Times* online, www.trumbulltimes.com, April 11, 2016.
14. S. E. Asch, "Effects of Group Pressure upon the Modification and Distortion of Judgments," in *Groups, Leadership and Men,* ed. H. Guetzkow (Pittsburgh: Carnegie Press, 1951), pp. 177–190; and S. E. Asch, "Studies of Independence and Conformity: A Minority of One Against a Unanimous Majority," *Psychological Monographs: General and Applied,* vol. 70, no. 9, 1956, pp. 1–70.
15. R. Bond and P. B. Smith, "Culture and Conformity: A Meta-Analysis of Studies Using Asch's [1952, 1956] Line Judgment Task," *Psychological Bulletin,* January 1996, pp. 111–137.
16. M. E. Turner and A. R. Pratkanis, "Mitigating Groupthink by Stimulating Constructive Conflict," in *Using Conflict in Organizations,* ed. C. DeDreu and E. Van deVliert (London: Sage, 1997), pp. 53–71.
17. A. Deutschman, "Inside the Mind of Jeff Bezos," *Fast Company,* August 2004, pp. 50–58.
18. See, for instance, E. J. Thomas and C. F. Fink, "Effects of Group Size," *Psychological Bulletin*, July 1963, pp. 371–384; and M. E. Shaw, *Group Dynamics: The Psychology of Small Group Behavior*, 3rd ed. (New York: McGraw-Hill, 1981).
19. P. Sonne, "Military Disciplines 16 for Errors Leading to 2015 Attack on Afghan Hospital," *The Wall Street Journal* online, www.wsj.com, April 29, 2016.
20. A. Jassawalla, H. Sashittal, and A. Malshe, "Students' Perceptions of Social Loafing: Its Antecedents and Consequences in Undergraduate Business Classroom Teams," *Academy of Management Learning & Education,* March 2009, pp. 42–54; R. C. Liden, S. J. Wayne, R. A. Jaworski, and N. Bennett, "Social Loafing: A Field Investigation," *Journal of Management,* April 2004, pp. 285–304; and D. R. Comer, "A Model of Social Loafing in Real Work Groups," *Human Relations,* June 1995, pp. 647–667.
21. S. G. Harkins and K. Szymanski, "Social Loafing and Group Evaluation," *Journal of Personality and Social Psychology,* December 1989, pp. 934–941.
22. C. R. Evans and K. L. Dion, "Group Cohesion and Performance: A Meta-Analysis," *Small Group Research,* May 1991, pp. 175–186; B. Mullen and C. Copper, "The Relation Between Group Cohesiveness and Performance: An Integration," *Psychological Bulletin*, March 1994, pp. 210–227; and P. M. Podsakoff, S. B. MacKenzie, and M. Ahearne, "Moderating Effects of Goal Acceptance on the Relationship Between Group Cohesiveness and Productivity," *Journal of Applied Psychology,* December 1997, pp. 974–983.
23. See, for example, L. Berkowitz, "Group Standards, Cohesiveness, and Productivity," *Human Relations*, November 1954, pp. 509–519; and B. Mullen and C. Copper, "The Relation Between Group Cohesiveness and Performance: An Integration."
24. S. E. Seashore, *Group Cohesiveness in the Industrial Work Group* (Ann Arbor: University of Michigan, Survey Research Center, 1954).
25. Gensler, "2013 U.S. Workplace Survey: Key Findings," http://www.gensler.com/uploads/document/337/file/2013_US_Workplace_Survey_07_15_2013.pdf, accessed April 30, 2016.
26. C. Shaffran, "Mind Your Meeting: How to Become the Catalyst for Culture Change," *Communication World,* February–March 2003, pp. 26–29.
27. I. L. Janis, *Victims of Groupthink* (Boston: Houghton Mifflin, 1972); R. J. Aldag and S. Riggs Fuller, "Beyond Fiasco: A Reappraisal of the Groupthink Phenomenon and a New Model of Group Decision Processes," *Psychological Bulletin*, May 1993, pp. 533–552; and T. Kameda and S. Sugimori, "Psychological Entrapment in Group Decision Making: An Assigned Decision Rule and a Groupthink Phenomenon," *Journal of Personality and Social Psychology*, August 1993, pp. 282–292.
28. See, for example, L. K. Michaelson, W. E. Watson, and R. H. Black, "A Realistic Test of Individual vs. Group Consensus Decision Making," *Journal of Applied Psychology,* vol. 74, no. 5, 1989, pp. 834–839; R. A. Henry, "Group Judgment Accuracy: Reliability and Validity of Postdiscussion Confidence Judgments," *Organizational Behavior and Human Decision Processes*, October 1993, pp. 11–27; P. W. Paese, M. Bieser, and M. E. Tubbs, "Framing Effects and Choice Shifts in Group Decision Making," *Organizational Behavior and Human Decision Processes*, October 1993, pp. 149–165; N. J. Castellan Jr. (ed.), *Individual and Group Decision Making* (Hillsdale, NJ: Lawrence Erlbaum Associates, 1993); and S. G. Straus and J. E. McGrath, "Does the Medium Matter? The Interaction of Task Type and Technology on Group Performance and Member Reactions," *Journal of Applied Psychology*, February 1994, pp. 87–97.
29. E. J. Thomas and C. F. Fink, "Effects of Group Size," *Psychological Bulletin,* July 1963, pp. 371–384; F. A. Shull, A. L. Delbecq, and L. L. Cummings, *Organizational Decision Making* (New York: McGraw-Hill, 1970), p. 151; A. P. Hare, *Handbook of Small Group Research* (New York: Free Press, 1976); M. E. Shaw, *Group Dynamics: The Psychology of Small Group Behavior*, 3rd ed. (New York: McGraw-Hill, 1981); and P. Yetton and P. Bottger, "The Relationships Among Group Size, Member Ability, Social Decision Schemes, and Performance," *Organizational Behavior and Human Performance,* October 1983, pp. 145–159.
30. S. Shellenbarger, "Work & Family Mailbox," *Wall Street Journal,* July 17, 2013, p. D2.
31. This section is adapted from S. P. Robbins, *Managing Organizational Conflict: A Nontraditional Approach* (Upper Saddle River, NJ: Prentice Hall, 1974), pp. 11–14. Also, see D. Wagner-Johnson, "Managing Work Team Conflict: Assessment and Preventative Strategies," Center for the Study of Work Teams, University of North Texas, www.workteams.unt.edu/reports, November 3, 2000; and M. Kennedy, "Managing Conflict in Work Teams," Center for the Study of Work Teams, University of North Texas, www.workteams.unt.edu/reports, November 3, 2000.
32. See K. J. Behfar, E. A. Mannix, R. S. Peterson, and W. M. Trochim, "Conflict in Small Groups: The Meaning and Consequences of Process Conflict," *Small Group Research,* April 2011, pp. 127–176; M. A. Korsgaard et al., "A Multilevel View of Intragroup Conflict," *Journal of Management,* December 2008, pp. 1222–1252; C. K. W. DeDreu, "The Virtue and Vice of Workplace Conflict: Food for (Pessimistic) Thought," *Journal of Organizational Behavior,* January 2008, pp. 5–18; K. A. Jehn, "A Multimethod Examination of the Benefits and Detriments of Intragroup Conflict," *Administrative Science Quarterly*, June 1995, pp. 256–282; K. A. Jehn, "A Qualitative Analysis of Conflict Type and Dimensions in Organizational Groups," *Administrative Science Quarterly*, September 1997, pp. 530–557; K. A. Jehn,

"Affective and Cognitive Conflict in Work Groups: Increasing Performance Through Value-Based Intragroup Conflict," in *Using Conflict in Organizations,* ed. C. DeDreu and E. Van deVliert (London: Sage Publications, 1997), pp. 87–100; K. A. Jehn and E. A. Mannix, "The Dynamic Nature of Conflict: A Longitudinal Study of Intragroup Conflict and Group Performance," *Academy of Management Journal,* April 2001, pp. 238–251; C. K. W. DeDreu and A. E. M. Van Vianen, "Managing Relationship Conflict and the Effectiveness of Organizational Teams," *Journal of Organizational Behavior,* May 2001, pp. 309–328; and J. Weiss and J. Hughes, "Want Collaboration? Accept—and Actively Manage—Conflict," *Harvard Business Review,* March 2005, pp. 92–101.

33. C. K. W. DeDreu, "When Too Little or Too Much Hurts: Evidence for a Curvilinear Relationship Between Task Conflict and Innovation in Teams," *Journal of Management,* February 2006, pp. 83–107.
34. A. Li and R. Cropanzano, "Fairness at the Group Level: Justice Climate and Intraunit Justice Climate," *Journal of Management,* June 2009, pp. 564–599.
35. Dirk Deichmann and Roel van der Heijde, "How Design Thinking Turned One Hospital into a Bright and Comforting Place," *Harvard Business Review,* December 2, 2016, https://hbr.org/2016/12/how-design-thinking-turned-one-hospital-into-a-bright-and-comforting-place (accessed December 23, 2016).
36. See, for example, J. R. Hackman and C. G. Morris, "Group Tasks, Group Interaction Process, and Group Performance Effectiveness: A Review and Proposed Integration," in *Advances in Experimental Social Psychology,* ed. L. Berkowitz (New York: Academic Press, 1975), pp. 45–99; R. Saavedra, P. C. Earley, and L. Van Dyne, "Complex Interdependence in Task-Performing Groups," *Journal of Applied Psychology,* February 1993, pp. 61–72; M. J. Waller, "Multiple-Task Performance in Groups," *Academy of Management Proceedings* on Disk, 1996; and K. A. Jehn, G. B. Northcraft, and M. A. Neale, "Why Differences Make a Difference: A Field Study of Diversity, Conflict, and Performance in Workgroups," *Administrative Science Quarterly,* December 1999, pp. 741–763.`
37. "Smart Pulse," www.smartbrief.com/leadership, November 19, 2013.
38. B. J. West, J. L. Patera, and M. K. Carsten, "Team Level Positivity: Investigating Positive Psychological Capacities and Team Level Outcomes," *Journal of Organizational Behavior,* February 2009, pp. 249–267; T. Purdum, "Teaming, Take 2," *Industry Week,* May 2005, p. 43; and C. Joinson, "Teams at Work," *HRMagazine,* May 1999, p. 30.
39. See, for example, S. A. Mohrman, S. G. Cohen, and A. M. Mohrman, Jr., *Designing Team-Based Organizations* (San Francisco: Jossey-Bass, 1995); P. MacMillan, *The Performance Factor: Unlocking the Secrets of Teamwork* (Nashville, TN: Broadman & Holman, 2001); and E. Salas, C. A. Bowers, and E. Eden (eds.), *Improving Teamwork in Organizations: Applications of Resource Management Training* (Mahwah, NJ: Lawrence Erlbaum, 2002).
40. P. Alpern, "Spreading the Light," *Industry Week,* January 2010, p. 35.
41. See, for instance, J. R. Hollenbeck, B. Beersma, and M. E. Schouten, "Beyond Team Types and Taxonomies: A Dimensional Scaling Conceptualization for Team Description," *Academy of Management Review,* January 2012, p. 85; and E. Sundstrom, K. P. DeMeuse, and D. Futrell, "Work Teams: Applications and Effectiveness," *American Psychologist,* February 1990, pp. 120–133.
42. M. Fitzgerald, "Shine a Light," *Fast Company,* April 2009, pp. 46–48; J. S. McClenahen, "Bearing Necessities," *Industry Week,* October 2004, pp. 63–65; P. J. Kiger, "Acxiom Rebuilds from Scratch," *Workforce,* December 2002, pp. 52–55; and T. Boles, "Viewpoint—Leadership Lessons from NASCAR," *Industry Week,* www.industryweek.com, May 21, 2002.
43. M. Cianni and D. Wanuck, "Individual Growth and Team Enhancement: Moving Toward a New Model of Career Development," *Academy of Management Executive,* February 1997, pp. 105–115.
44. "Teams," *Training,* October 1996, p. 69; and C. Joinson, "Teams at Work," p. 30.
45. G. M. Spreitzer, S. G. Cohen, and G. E. Ledford, Jr., "Developing Effective Self-Managing Work Teams in Service Organizations," *Group & Organization Management*, September 1999, pp. 340–366.
46. "Theresa Maier Wins Global Novartis International BioCamp," *University of Cambridge, Department of Chemical Engineering and Biotechnology,* September 8, 2016, http://www.ceb.cam.ac.uk/news/news-list/theresa-maier-novartis-sept16 (accessed December 23, 2016); "Students Take on the Challenges of Digital Medicine," *Novartis,* August 26, 2016, www.novartis.com (accessed December 23, 2016).
47. T. Neeley, "Global Teams That Work," *Harvard Business Review* online, www.hbr.org, October 2015.
48. A. Malhotra, A. Majchrzak, R. Carman, and V. Lott, "Radical Innovation Without Collocation: A Case Study at Boeing-Rocketdyne," *MIS Quarterly,* June 2001, pp. 229–249.
49. F. Siebdrat, M. Hoegl, and H. Ernst, "How to Manage a Virtual Team," *MIT Sloan Management Review,* Summer 2009, pp. 63–68; A. Malhotra, A. Majchrzak, and B. Rosen, "Leading Virtual Teams," *Academy of Management Perspectives,* February 2007, pp. 60–70; B. L. Kirkman and J. E. Mathieu, "The Dimensions and Antecedents of Team Virtuality," *Journal of Management,* October 2005, pp. 700–718; J. Gordon, "Do Your Virtual Teams Deliver Only Virtual Performance?" *Training,* June 2005, pp. 20–25; L. L. Martins, L. L. Gilson, and M. T. Maynard, "Virtual Teams: What Do We Know and Where Do We Go from Here?," *Journal of Management,* December 2004, pp. 805–835; S. A. Furst, M. Reeves, B. Rosen, and R. S. Blackburn, "Managing the Life Cycle of Virtual Teams," *Academy of Management Executive,* May 2004, pp. 6–20; B. L. Kirkman, B. Rosen, P. E. Tesluk, and C. B. Gibson, "The Impact of Team Empowerment on Virtual Team Performance: The Moderating Role of Face-to-Face Interaction," *Academy of Management Journal,* April 2004, pp. 175–192; F. Keenan and S. E. Ante, "The New Teamwork," *Business Week e.biz,* February 18, 2002, pp. EB12–EB16; and G. Imperato, "Real Tools for Virtual Teams?," *Fast Company*, July 2000, pp. 378–387.
50. B. L. Kirkman, C. B. Gibson, and D. L. Shapiro, "Exporting Teams: Enhancing the Implementation and Effectiveness of Work Teams in Global Affiliates," *Organizational Dynamics,* Summer 2001, pp. 12–29; C. G. Andrews, "Factors That Impact Multi-Cultural Team Performance," Center for the Study of Work Teams, University of North Texas, www.workteams.unt.edu/reports/, November 3, 2000; P. Christopher Earley and E. Mosakowski, "Creating Hybrid Team Cultures: An Empirical Test of Transnational Team Functioning," *Academy of Management Journal*, February 2000, pp. 26–49; J. Tata, "The

Cultural Context of Teams: An Integrative Model of National Culture, Work Team Characteristics, and Team Effectiveness," *Academy of Management Proceedings*, 1999; D. I. Jung, K. B. Baik, and J. J. Sosik, "A Longitudinal Investigation of Group Characteristics and Work Group Performance: A Cross-Cultural Comparison," *Academy of Management Proceedings*, 1999; and C. B. Gibson, "They Do What They Believe They Can? Group—Efficacy Beliefs and Group Performance Across Tasks and Cultures," *Academy of Management Proceedings*, 1996.

51. D. Coutou, interview with J. R. Hackman, "Why Teams Don't Work."
52. A. C. Costa and N. Anderson, "Measuring Trust in Teams: Development and Validation of a Multifaceted Measure of Formative and Reflective Indicators of Team Trust," *European Journal of Work and Organizational Psychology,* vol. 20, no. 1, 2011, pp. 119–154.
53. "Fast Fact: The Good News About Workplace Trust," *T&D,* October 2012, p. 21.
54. A. Pentland, "The New Science of Building Great Teams," *Harvard Business Review,* April 2012, pp. 60–70.
55. J. C. Santora and M. Esposito, "Do Happy Leaders Make for Better Team Performance," *Academy of Management Perspective,* November 2011, pp. 88–90; G. A. Van Kleef et al., "Searing Sentiment or Cold Calculation? The Effects of Leader Emotional Displays on Team Performance Depend on Follower Epistemic Motivation," *Academy of Management Journal,* June 2009, pp. 562–580.
56. R. Bond and P. B. Smith, "Culture and Conformity: A Meta-Analysis of Studies Using Asch's [1952, 1956] Line Judgment Task."
57. I. L. Janis, *Groupthink,* 2nd ed. (New York: Houghton Mifflin Company, 1982), p. 175.
58. See P. C. Earley, "Social Loafing and Collectivism: A Comparison of the United States and the People's Republic of China," *Administrative Science Quarterly,* December 1989, pp. 565–581; and P. C. Earley, "East Meets West Meets Mideast: Further Explorations of Collectivistic and Individualistic Work Groups," *Academy of Management Journal,* April 1993, pp. 319–348.
59. Leader Making a Difference box based on A. Bryant, "Dara Richardson-Heron of the Y.W.C.A., on Persistence," *The New York Times* online, www.nytimes.com, December 7, 2013; K. Caprina, "How YWCA USA Is Evolving to Better Support Women and People of Color," *Forbes* online, www.forbes.com, January 30, 2016; see also www.ywca.org.
60. Teru Clavel, "From Classroom to Boardroom: A Lesson in Business Practices from Japan's Elementary Schools," *Japan Today,* January 10, 2016, https://www.japantoday.com/category/lifestyle/view/from-classroom-to-boardroom-a-lesson-in-business-practices-from-japans-elementary-schools (accessed December 23, 2016); Erin Meyer, "Managing Multi-cultural Teams," *HR Magazine (UK),* November 27, 2014, http://www.hrmagazine.co.uk/article-details/managing-multi-cultural-teams (accessed December 23, 2016).
61. Ibid., p. 144.
62. K. B. Dahlin, L. R. Weingart, and P. J. Hinds, "Team Diversity and Information Use," *Academy of Management Journal,* December 2005, pp. 1107–1123.
63. Adler, *International Dimensions of Organizational Behavior,* p. 142.
64. P. S. Hempel, Z-X. Zhang, and D. Tjosvold, "Conflict Management Between and Within Teams for Trusting Relationships and Performance in China," *Journal of Organizational Behavior,* January 2009, pp. 41–65; and S. Paul, I. M. Samarah, P. Seetharaman, and P. P. Mykytyn, "An Empirical Investigation of Collaborative Conflict Management Style in Group Support System-Based Global Virtual Teams," *Journal of Management Information Systems,* Winter 2005, pp. 185–222.
65. S. Chang and P. Tharenou, "Competencies Needed for Managing a Multicultural Workgroup," *Asia Pacific Journal of Human Resources,* vol. 42, no. 1, 2004, pp. 57–74; and Adler, *International Dimensions of Organizational Behavior,* p. 153.
66. C. E. Nicholls, H. W. Lane, and M. Brehm Brechu, "Taking Self-Managed Teams to Mexico," *Academy of Management Executive,* August 1999, pp. 15–27.
67. M. O'Neil, "Leading the Team," *Supervision,* April 2011, pp. 8–10; and A. Gilley, J. W. Gilley, C. W. McConnell, and A. Veliquette, "The Competencies Used by Effective Managers to Build Teams: An Empirical Study," *Advances in Developing Human Resources,* February 2010, pp. 29–45.
68. B. V. Krishnamurthy, "Use Downtime to Enhance Skills," *Harvard Business Review,* December 2008, pp. 29–30.
69. "Women Leaders: The Hard Truth About Soft Skills," *BusinessWeek Online,* February 17, 2010, p. 8.
70. J. Reingold and J. L. Yang, "The Hidden Workplace: What's Your OQ?," *Fortune,* July 23, 2007, pp. 98–106; and P. Balkundi and D. A. Harrison, "Ties, Leaders, and Time in Teams: Strong Inference About Network Structures' Effects on Team Viability and Performance," *Academy of Management Journal,* February 2006, pp. 49–68.
71. T. Casciaro and M. S. Lobo, "Competent Jerks, Lovable Fools, and the Formation of Social Networks," *Harvard Business Review,* June 2005, pp. 92–99.
72. Balkundi and Harrison, "Ties, Leaders, and Time in Teams: Strong Inference About Network Structures' Effects on Team Viability and Performance."
73. P. Dvorak, "Engineering Firm Charts Ties," *Wall Street Journal,* January 26, 2009, p. B7; and J. McGregor, "The Office Chart That Really Counts," *Business Week*, February 27, 2006, pp. 48–49.
74. Vault Careers, "Finding Love at Work Is More Acceptable Than Ever," www.vault.com, February 11, 2015.
75. J. Yang and V. Salazar, "Would You Date a Co-Worker?," *USA Today,* February 14, 2008, p. 1B.
76. Douglas Murray McGregor, "The Human Side of Enterprise," 1960; and Jon R. Katzenbach and Douglas K. Smith, "The Wisdom of Teams," McKinsey & Company Inc.
77. D. Roberts, "At W.L. Gore, 57 Years of Authentic Culture," *Fortune Magazine* online, www.fortune.com, March 5, 2015; T. Castille, "Hierarchy Is Overrated," *Harvard Business Review* online, www.hbr.org, November 20, 2013; G. Hamel, "W.L. Gore: Lessons from a Management Revolutionary," *The Wall Street Journal* online, www.wsj.com, March 18, 2010; C. Blakeman, "Why Self-Managed Teams Are the Future of Business," *Inc. Magazine* online, www.inc.com, November 24, 2014; www.gore.com.
78. D. Michaels and J. Ostrower, "Airbus, Boeing Walk a Fine Line on Jetliner Production," *Wall Street Journal,* July 16, 2012, p. B3; D. Kesmodel, "Boeing Teams Speed Up 737 Output," *Wall Street Journal,* February 7, 2012, p. B10; and A. Cohen, "Boeing Sees Demand for Existing, Re-engined 737s," blog on *Seattle Post-Intelligencer Online,* October 26, 2011.

Chapter 13 Human Resource Management

It's Your Career

Source: Myvector/Shutterstock

Negotiating Your Salary

Congratulations! You just received your first job offer, which contains a lot of important information. For instance, you will be informed of your pay and benefits such as vacation time. Understandably, you are excited and are tempted to accept the job on the spot. But don't do it just yet. Take the opportunity to think about questions that have come up since receiving your offer. Also, think about whether your salary represents your worth. After doing some homework on the subject, you may decide to negotiate for a higher salary. Here are some suggestions for your preparation:

A key to success in management and in your career is knowing how to negotiate pay.

*1. **Do you want the job?** This is perhaps the most important question you must answer. Set pay considerations aside and weigh the pros and cons of the job. The following questions are the ones you should think about: Will this job help me embark on a rewarding career path? Do I fit well with the culture? Am I happy with the location? If you do want the job, then it's time to think about your salary offer.*

*2. **Research what similar companies pay new hires.** It's important to consider a variety of sources to ensure that you understand the pay norm for your job offer. Start with your school's career services counselors. They have worked with many students in your situation and the companies that hire them. Also, check out online resources that provide information about pay. There are many you can choose from. For example, the U.S. Bureau of Labor Statistics publishes the Occupational Outlook Handbook, which lists pay information for a variety of jobs and occupations. Consider websites such as Glassdoor (www.glassdoor.com), where you may find employee self-reports of pay for similar jobs, and, perhaps even for your prospective employer. There are many others, including jobstar.org, salary.com, and payscale.com.*

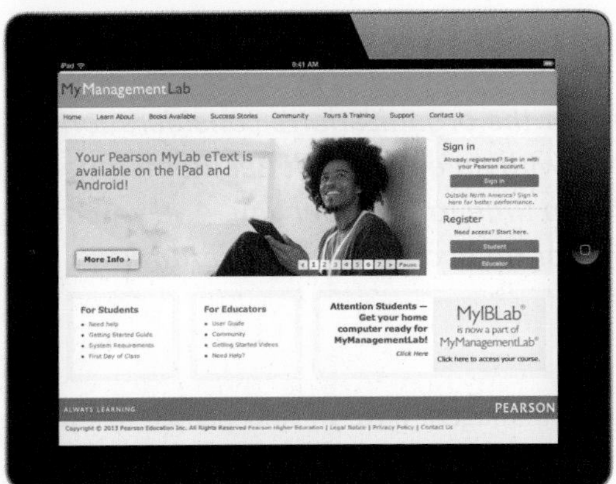

Pearson **MyLab** Management®

Improve Your Grade!

When you see this icon, visit **www.mymanagementlab.com** for activities that are applied, personalized, and offer immediate feedback.

Learning Objectives

13.1 ***Explain*** *the importance of human resource management and the human resource management process.*

13.2 ***Describe*** *the external influences that affect the human resource management process.*

13.3 ***Discuss*** *the tasks associated with identifying and selecting competent employees.*

- **Know how** to write effective job descriptions.
- **Develop your skill** at being a good interviewer.

13.4 ***Explain*** *how companies provide employees with skills and knowledge.*

13.5 ***Describe*** *strategies for retaining competent, high-performing employees.*

13.6 ***Discuss*** *contemporary issues in managing human resources.*

---

3. ***Make sense of the data.*** *Look at whether companies in different industries pay similarly. For example, companies in manufacturing industries generally pay more than companies in service industries. Also, watch for whether pay differs based on location. It will cost you a lot more to rent an apartment in San Francisco than in Fargo, North Dakota.*

4. ***Prepare for the pay discussion.***[1] *Think about your reservation pay rate; that is, the lowest amount you are willing to accept. Come up with a range of pay rather than a single amount. It is important to show flexibility and signal that you are willing to be a team player. Prepare the rationale for making your request. Always make reference to the data. Companies will give consideration to objective data. Never base your request on statements such as "I'm worth it." Job offers are based on future potential. Remember that you have yet to prove yourself.*

5. ***Have the discussion.*** *Thank the organization's representative for making the job offer and express your excitement about the opportunity. Briefly summarize how you will become a productive member of the team. Before discussing pay, ask your other questions. Then, make your case for higher pay. Listen carefully to the representative's response. For example, you may hear that every new hire makes the same rate. Or the organization's policy is to start new hires with lower pay and award bonuses based on performance. Possible responses include denying your request, accepting your request, or offering a lower additional amount than requested. In any event, be sure to thank the company representative for their consideration.*

6. Communicate your decision. *If you plan to accept the offer, tell the representative that you will do so promptly after receiving written confirmation. If you choose not to accept the offer, express your appreciation for the organization's consideration and follow up with an e-mail or letter. Remember, they have taken time to consider you. And you may want to work for that company in the future.*

With the organization's structure in place, managers have to find people to fill the jobs that have been created or to remove people from jobs if business circumstances require. That's where human resource management (HRM) comes in. It's an important task that involves having the right number of the right people in the right place at the right time. In this chapter, we'll look at the process managers use to do just that. In addition, we'll look at some contemporary HRM issues facing managers.

A major HRM challenge for managers is ensuring that their company has a high-quality workforce. Getting and keeping competent and talented employees is critical to the success of every organization, whether an organization is just starting or has been in business for years. If an organization doesn't take its HRM responsibilities seriously, performance may suffer. Therefore, part of every manager's job when organizing is human resource management. Research has shown that when line managers are responsible for recruiting, performance management, and retention, their companies are 29 percent more successful.[2] That's a good reason for all managers to engage in some HRM activities, such as interviewing job candidates, orienting new employees, and evaluating their employees' work performance, even if there is a separate HRM department.

WHY **human resource management is important and the human resource management process**

LO13.1 HRM is important for three reasons. First, as various studies have concluded, it can be a significant source of competitive advantage.[3] And that's true for organizations around the world, not just U.S. firms. The Human Capital Index, a comprehensive study of more than 2,000 global firms, concluded that people-oriented HR gives an organization an edge by creating superior shareholder value.[4] Another study found that 71 percent of CEOs say that their "human capital" is the key source of sustained economic value.[5]

Second, HRM is an important part of organizational strategies. Michelle Ho, managing director for UPS Singapore, sees her company's human resources professionals "as strategic partners that manage human capital, the main performance driver of any business." Netherlands-based ING, a multinational financial services firm, completely reinvented itself through the strategy of managing its human resources as "people with purpose, mastery, and talent," in the words of one top official. ING reorganized thousands of employees into cross-functional teams empowered to resolve problems in meeting the needs of 34 million customers worldwide. Whether the solution is inside or outside their assigned roles, ING's employees have the training, skills, and initiative to tackle problems and keep the bank strategically "a step ahead" in today's challenging and competitive business environment.[6]

Finally, the way organizations treat their people has been found to significantly impact organizational performance.[7] For instance, one study reported that improving work practices could increase market value by as much as 30 percent.[8] Another study that tracked average annual shareholder returns of companies on *Fortune's* list of 100 Best Companies to Work For found that these companies significantly beat the S&P 500 over 10-year, 5-year, 3-year, and 1-year periods.[9] Another study found a positive relationship between companies' high-performance work practices and the ability of the organization to efficiently adapt to changing and challenging markets.[10] Work practices that lead to both high individual and high organizational performance are known as **high-performance work practices**. (See some examples in Exhibit 13-1.) The common thread among these practices seems to be a commitment to involving

high-performance work practices
Work practices that lead to both high individual and high organizational performance

Exhibit 13-1
High-Performance Work Practices

- Self-managed teams
- Decentralized decision making
- Training programs to develop knowledge, skills, and abilities
- Flexible job assignments
- Open communication
- Performance-based compensation
- Staffing based on person-job and person-organization fit
- Extensive employee involvement
- Giving employees more control over decision making
- Increasing employee access to information

Sources: C. H. Chuang and H. Liao, "Strategic Human Resource Management in Service Context: Taking Care of Business by Taking Care of Employees and Customers," *Personnel Psychology,* Spring 2010, pp. 153–196; M. Subramony, "A Meta-Analytic Investigation of the Relationship Between HRM Bundles and Firm Performance," *Human Resource Management,* September–October 2009, pp. 745–768; M. M. Butts et al., "Individual Reactions to High Involvement Work Practices: Investigating the Role of Empowerment and Perceived Organizational Support," *Journal of Occupational Health Psychology,* April 2009, pp. 122–136; and W. R. Evans and W. D. Davis, "High-Performance Work Systems and Organizational Performance: The Mediating Role of Internal Social Structure," *Journal of Management,* October 2005, p. 760.

employees; improving the knowledge, skills, and abilities of an organization's employees; increasing their motivation; reducing loafing on the job; and enhancing the retention of quality employees while encouraging low performers to leave.

Even if an organization doesn't use high-performance work practices, other specific HRM activities must be completed in order to ensure that the organization has qualified people to perform the work that needs to be done—activities that compose the HRM process. Exhibit 13-2 shows the eight activities in this process. The first three activities ensure that competent employees are identified and selected; the next two involve providing employees with up-to-date knowledge and skills; and the final three ensure that the organization retains competent and high-performing employees. Before we discuss those specific activities, we need to look at external factors that affect the HRM process.

Exhibit 13-2
HRM Process

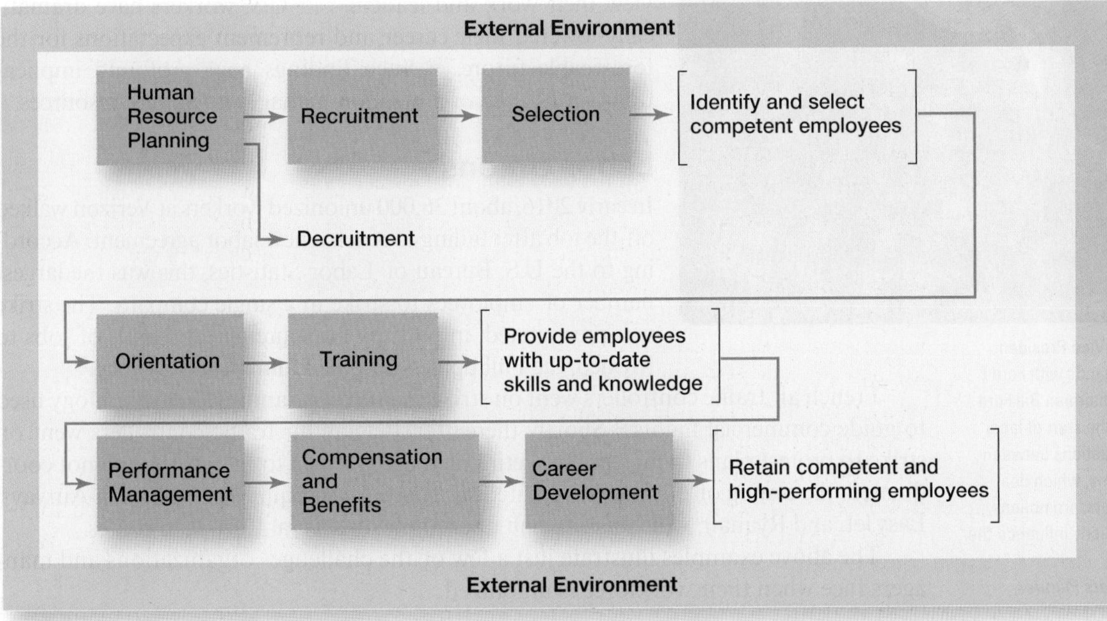

EXTERNAL factors that affect the human resource management process

LO13.2 An administrative assistant job opening paying $13 an hour at a Burns Harbor, Indiana, truck driver training school for C. R. England, a nationwide trucking company, was posted on a Friday afternoon.[11] By the time the company's head of corporate recruiting arrived at work on Monday morning, there were about 300 applications in the company's e-mail inbox. And an inch-and-a-half stack of résumés was piled up by the now out-of-paper fax machine. Out of those 500-plus applicants, one person, who had lost her job four months earlier, impressed the hiring manager so much that the job was hers, leaving the remaining 499-plus people—including a former IBM analyst with 18 years of experience, a former director of human resources, and someone with a master's degree and 12 years of experience at accounting firm Deloitte & Touche—still searching for a job. During the economic slowdown, filling job openings was an almost mind-boggling exercise.

As you can see, the entire HRM process is influenced by the external environment. Those factors most directly influencing it include the economy, employee labor unions, governmental laws and regulations, and demographic trends.

The Economy

The Great Recession left what many experts believe to be an enduring mark on HRM practices worldwide. For instance, in Japan, workers used to count on two things: a job for life and a decent pension. Now, lifetime employment is long gone and corporate pension plans are crumbling.[12] And a lower-tier labor class has emerged based on lower-paid part-time employment in less desirable jobs.[13] In the European Union, the early 2016 jobless rate was 10.3 percent, with Greece and Spain being hit hardest with an unemployment rate of 25.8 percent and 22.5 percent respectively.[14] And in China, the Labor Ministry has urged companies to reduce wage growth.[15] In the United States, labor economists say that jobs are coming back slowly but aren't the same ones employees were used to. Many of these jobs are temporary or part-time positions, rather than full-time jobs with benefits.[16] Most of the employment gains have occurred in health care, retail, and food service industries,[17] where pay tends to be less than in industries such as manufacturing.[18] All of these changes have affected employers and workers. A Global Workforce Study survey by global professional services company Towers Watson confirmed that the recession has "fundamentally altered the way U.S. employees view their work and leaders. . . . U.S. workers have dramatically lowered their career and retirement expectations for the foreseeable future."[19] Such findings have profound implications for how an organization manages its human resources.

United Auto Workers (UAW) Vice President Jimmy Settles (left) shakes hands with Ford Motor Company Executive Chairman Bill Ford during a ceremony marking the start of labor contract negotiations. Negotiations between labor unions and organizations, which deal with employee wages, benefits, promotions, layoffs, and other issues, directly influence the HRM process.
Source: Rebecca Cook/Reuters Pictures

Labor Unions

In early 2016, about 36,000 unionized workers at Verizon walked off the job after failing to reach a new labor agreement. According to the U.S. Bureau of Labor Statistics, this was the largest number of employees to strike in a single company. The strike was precipitated, in part, by outsourcing thousands of jobs to Mexico, the Philippines, and the Dominican Republic.[20]

French air traffic controllers went on strike in protest of antiquated technology used to guide commercial flights.[21] Shortly thereafter, Belgian air traffic controllers went on strike to protest plans to increase the retirement age from 55 to 58.[22] Although not coordinated, the timing of both strikes created substantial consequences for British Airways, EasyJet, and Ryanair, which had to halt operations on several European routes.

The above examples illustrate just a few of the challenges organizations and managers face when their workforce is unionized.

A **labor union** is an organization that represents workers and seeks to protect their interests through collective bargaining. In unionized organizations, many HRM decisions are dictated by collective bargaining agreements, which usually define things such as recruitment sources; criteria for hiring, promotions, and layoffs; training eligibility; and disciplinary practices. Due to information availability, it's difficult to pin down how unionized global workforces are. Current estimates are that about 11.1 percent of the U.S. workforce is unionized.[23] But the percentage of unionized workers tends to be higher in other countries, except in Turkey, where some 6 percent of workers are unionized. For instance, in Japan, some 18 percent of the labor force belongs to a union; in Germany, 18 percent; in Denmark, 66.8 percent; in Australia, 15.5 percent; in Canada, 26.4 percent; Mexico, 13.5 percent; and in Iceland, 86.4 percent.[24] One union membership trend we're seeing, especially in the more industrialized countries, is that the rate in private enterprise is declining while that in the public sector (which includes teachers, police officers, firefighters, and government workers) is climbing. Although labor unions can affect an organization's HRM practices, the most significant environmental constraint is governmental laws, especially in North America.

labor union
An organization that represents workers and seeks to protect their interests through collective bargaining

Laws and Rulings

Not following the laws governing HRM practices can be costly for organizations of all sizes. The Swindon Town Football club was fined more than £20,000 for failing to enroll eligible employees into a pension scheme, as required by U.K. law. Hundreds of other U.K. organizations, including a football club, have been fined for not following minimum wage laws governing employee compensation.[25] As this example shows, an organization's HRM practices are governed by a country's laws and not following those laws can be costly. (See Exhibit 13-3 for some of the important U.S. laws that affect the HRM process.) For example, decisions regarding who will be hired or which employees will be chosen for a training program or what an employee's compensation will be must be made without regard to race, sex, religion, age, color, national origin, pregnancy, or disability. Exceptions can occur only in special circumstances. For instance, a community fire department can deny employment to a firefighter applicant who is confined to a wheelchair; but if that same individual is applying for a desk job, such as a dispatcher, the disability cannot be used as a reason to deny employment. The issues, however, are rarely that clear-cut. For example, employment laws protect most employees whose religious beliefs require a specific style of dress—robes, long shirts, long hair, and the like. However, if the specific style of dress may be hazardous or unsafe in the work setting (such as when operating machinery), a company could refuse to hire a person who won't adopt a safer dress code.

As you can see, a number of important laws and regulations affect what you can and cannot do legally as a manager. Because workplace lawsuits are increasingly targeting supervisors, as well as their organizations, managers must know what they can and cannot do by law.[26] Trying to balance the "shoulds" and "should nots" of many laws often falls within the realm of **affirmative action**. Many U.S. organizations have affirmative action programs to ensure that decisions and practices enhance the employment, upgrading, and retention of members from protected groups such as minorities and females. And efforts are now underway to ensure affirmative action for qualified individuals with disabilities. That is, an organization refrains from discrimination and actively seeks to enhance the status of members from protected groups. However, U.S. managers are not completely free to choose whom they hire, promote, or fire, or free to treat employees any way they want. Although laws have helped reduce employment discrimination and unfair work practices, they have, at the same time, reduced managers' discretion over HRM decisions.

affirmative action
Organizational programs that enhance the status of members of protected groups

We do want to mention some U.S. laws that will and some that are likely to affect future HRM practices. The first of these, the Patient Protection and Affordable Care Act (PPACA and commonly called the Affordable Care Act), was signed into law in March 2010 and upheld by the Supreme Court of the United States twice—once in 2012 and again in 2015.[27] This law challenges managers to provide cost-effective health insurance plans that satisfy the law's requirements. Other proposed legislation that is likely to affect HRM practices includes immigration reform, which is aimed at providing a way for undocumented individuals to become legal citizens. And, recent changes to the Fair Labor Standards Act make more employees eligible to receive overtime pay.

Exhibit 13-3
Major HRM Laws

LAW OR RULING	YEAR	DESCRIPTION
Equal Employment Opportunity and Discrimination		
■ **Equal Pay Act**	1963	Prohibits pay differences for equal work based on gender
■ **Civil Rights Act, Title VII**	1964 (amended in 1972)	Prohibits discrimination based on race, color, religion, national origin, or gender
■ **Age Discrimination in Employment Act**	1967 (amended in 1978)	Prohibits discrimination against employees 40 years and older
■ **Vocational Rehabilitation Act**	1973	Prohibits discrimination on the basis of physical or mental disabilities
■ **Americans with Disabilities Act**	1990	Prohibits discrimination against individuals who have disabilities or chronic illnesses; also requires reasonable accommodations for these individuals
Compensation/Benefits		
■ **Worker Adjustment and Retraining Notification Act**	1990	Requires employers with more than 100 employees to provide 60 days' notice before a mass layoff or facility closing
■ **Family and Medical Leave Act**	1993	Gives employees in organizations with 50 or more employees up to 12 weeks of unpaid leave each year for family or medical reasons
■ **Health Insurance Portability and Accountability Act**	1996	Permits portability of employees' insurance from one employer to another
■ **Lilly Ledbetter Fair Pay Act**	2009	Changes the statute of limitations on pay discrimination to 180 days from each paycheck
■ **Patient Protection and Affordable Care Act**	2010	Health care legislation that puts in place comprehensive health insurance reforms
Health/Safety		
■ **Occupational Safety and Health Act (OSHA)**	1970	Establishes mandatory safety and health standards in organizations
■ **Privacy Act**	1974	Gives employees the legal right to examine personnel files and letters of reference
■ **Consolidated Omnibus Reconciliation Act (COBRA)**	1985	Requires continued health coverage following termination (paid by employee)

Sources: U.S. Equal Employment Opportunity Commission, www.eeoc.gov; U.S. Department of Labor, www.dol.gov; U.S. Occupational Safety and Health Administration, www.osha.gov.

The best source of advice about these and other important legal issues will be your company's HR department.

What about HRM laws globally? It's important that managers in other countries be familiar with the specific laws that apply there. Further, managers of multinationals must understand the variety of federal laws that apply to employees in every country where their firms operate. Ireland-based Ryanair, for instance, generally hires pilots and cabin crew under Irish labor contracts, regardless of where they live and work for the airline. As a result, Ryanair's managers must navigate a complex set of obligations across national borders. In 2014, the airline lost a court appeal and paid a hefty fine to France over government-mandated social security and pension payments for workers based in France who had Irish labor contracts. Ryanair made all social payments as required in Ireland, but it became caught up in the legal battle because those amounts are lower than the social payments required under French law.

Not only do Federal laws differ widely, these laws are updated or changed from time to time. In Sweden, the amount of paid parental leave for fathers has been increased over the years to encourage men to use this benefit. Today, new parents receive 480 days of paid leave that can be divided between the parents as they choose. Another recent change increases protections for whistle-blowing employees who report serious violations, so firms are not allowed to retaliate against these employees. In addition, employers must now establish internal systems to enable employees to report violations internally. Managers of businesses that operate in Sweden need to be aware of these changes so they can take immediate steps to comply.

In Singapore, the Ministry of Manpower oversees regulation of HRM practices governed by laws such as the Employment Act and the Retirement and Re-employment Act. These laws determine minimum age for workers, terms of employment, detailed pay itemization, parental leave, retirement age, and pay for older workers. Laws have been changed in Singapore to increase the age of mandatory retirement, reflecting the ability and interest of employees to continue working as they age—and a corresponding need for employers to tap the knowledge, experience, and skills of these workers.

Australia's labor and industrial relations laws were overhauled two decades ago to increase productivity and reduce union power. The Workplace Relations Bill gives employers greater flexibility to negotiate directly with employees on pay, hours, and benefits. It also simplifies federal regulation of labor-management relations. And, in 2015, the Fair Work Amendment Act extended family leave protection. The act provides that a request for extended unpaid parental leave cannot be refused unless the employer has given the employee a reasonable opportunity to discuss the request.[28]

LEADER making a DIFFERENCE

Source: Google, Inc.

*He's in charge of the people/HR function at the company that's number one on the World's Most Attractive Employer list and the number one company on the list of the 100 Best Companies to Work For.[29] As senior vice president of people operations at Google Inc., **Laszlo Bock** knows and understands people and work. You shouldn't be surprised that the comprehensive (and complicated) analysis that goes into Google search efforts also characterizes its approach to managing its human resources. Bock's current pursuit is a long-term study of work (patterned after the long-running Framingham Heart Study that transformed what we know about heart disease). Bock says, "I believe that the experience of work can be—should be—so much better."[30] He and his team hope to learn more about work-life balance, improving employee well-being, cultivating better leaders, doing a better job of engaging Googlers (the name for Google employees) long term, and how happiness and work impact each other. Undoubtedly, there will be some interesting insights that result! (P.S. If you'd like to work at Google and want to know more about getting hired, check out the references cited above! There are good tips in there!)* What can you learn from this leader making a difference?

Our final example, Germany, is similar to most Western European countries when it comes to HRM practices. Legislation requires companies to practice representative participation, in which the goal is to redistribute power within the organization, putting labor on a more equal footing with the interests of management and stockholders. The two most common forms of representative participation are work councils and board representatives. **Work councils** link employees with management. They are groups of nominated or elected employees who must be consulted when management makes decisions involving personnel. **Board representatives** are employees who sit on a company's board of directors and represent the interests of the firm's employees.

work councils
Groups of nominated or elected employees who must be consulted when management makes decisions involving personnel

board representatives
Employees who sit on a company's board of directors and represent the interests of the firm's employees

Demography

A few years back, the head of BMW's 2,500-employee power train plant in Dingolfing, Lower Bavaria, was worried about the potential inevitable future decline in productivity due to an aging workforce.[31] That's when company executives decided to redesign its factory for older workers. With input from employees, they implemented physical changes to the workplace—for instance, new wooden floors to reduce joint strain and special chairs for sitting down or relaxing for short periods—that would reduce wear and tear on workers' bodies. Other organizations worldwide are preparing for a shift as Baby Boomers retire. Many older workers delayed their retirement during the recession, reducing the threat of mass turnover for a few years. "But now it's sneaking up on companies." Companies are responding by creating succession plans, bringing retirees on as consultants, and increasing cross-training efforts to prepare younger workers to fill the void. Unfortunately, solutions have been elusive in other countries. Take China as an example. Demographic shifts have been a cause for concern. A shortage of skilled workers is partly due to the aging Chinese population created by 30 years of its one-child policy. Economic growth has created the need for new jobs; however, the policy vastly reduced the number of young workforce entrants. As these examples show, demographic trends impact HRM practices worldwide.

Much of the change in the U.S. workforce over the last 50 years can be attributed to federal legislation enacted in the 1960s that prohibited employment discrimination. With these laws, avenues opened up for minority and female job applicants. These two groups dramatically changed the workplace in the latter half of the twentieth century. Women, in particular, have changed the composition of the workforce as they now hold some 46.8 percent of jobs.[32] And because women tend to be employed in education and health care industries, their jobs are less sensitive to economic ups and downs.[33] If this trend continues, women may, at some point, become the majority group in the workforce.

Workforce trends in the early twenty-first century will be notable for three reasons: (1) changes in racial and ethnic composition, (2) an aging baby boom generation, and (3) an expanding cohort of Gen Y workers. By 2024, Hispanics will grow from today's 13 percent of the workforce to 19.8 percent, blacks will remain steady at about 13 percent, and Asians will increase slightly from 5.6 percent to 6.6 percent. Meanwhile, the labor force is aging. The 55-and-older age group, which currently makes up 16.3 percent of the workforce, will increase to 24.8 percent by 2024.[34] Another group that's having a significant impact on today's workforce is Gen Y, a population group that includes individuals born from about 1978 to 1994. Gen Y has been the fastest-growing segment of the workforce—increasing from 14 percent to more than 24 percent. With Gen Y now in the workforce, analysts point to the four generations that are working side-by-side in the workplace:[35]

- The oldest, most experienced workers (those born before 1946) make up 6 percent of the workforce.
- The Baby Boomers (those born between 1946 and 1964) make up 41.5 percent of the workforce.
- Gen Xers (those born 1965 to 1977) make up almost 29 percent of the workforce.
- Gen Yers (those born 1978 to 1994) make up almost 24 percent of the workforce.

These and other demographic trends are important because of the impact they're having on current and future HRM practices.

Hertz is always on the lookout for talent who can ensure the highest level of customer service and smooth operations. Hertz's recruiting staff seeks potential job candidates by participating in career fairs that attract college students and others who bring a wealth of work experience.
Source: Damon Higgins/The Palm Beach Post/ZUMA Press/Newscom

IDENTIFYING **and selecting competent employees**

LO13.3 Executives at Texas-based global engineering giant Fluor are expected to recognize and mentor high-performing employees. The company's senior vice president of human resources and administration says such efforts are necessary because "you can't create a senior mechanical engineer overnight. It takes years." Here's a company that understands the importance of tracking talent on a global scale.[36] Is a job in the insurance industry on your list of jobs you'll apply for after graduation? Unfortunately for the insurance industry, it's not for many college graduates. Like many other nonglamorous industries, including transportation, utilities, and manufacturing, the insurance industry is not "particularly attractive to the so-called 'millennials'—people who turned 21 in 2000 or later." In all these industries, the number of skilled jobs is already starting to overtake the number of qualified people available to fill them.[37]

Every organization needs people to do whatever work is necessary for doing what the organization is in business to do. How do they get those people? And more importantly, what can they do to ensure they get competent, talented people? This first phase of the HRM process involves three tasks: human resource planning, recruitment and decruitment, and selection.

Human Resource Planning

Human resource planning is the process by which managers ensure that they have the right number and kinds of capable people in the right places and at the right times. Through planning, organizations avoid sudden people shortages and surpluses.[38] HR planning entails two steps: (1) assessing current human resources and (2) meeting future HR needs.

human resource planning
Ensuring that the organization has the right number and kinds of capable people in the right places and at the right times

CURRENT ASSESSMENT Managers begin HR planning by inventorying current employees. This inventory usually includes information on employees such as name, education, training, prior employment, languages spoken, special capabilities, and specialized skills. Sophisticated databases make getting and keeping this information quite easy. For example, the international dairy cooperative FrieslandCampina, headquartered in the Netherlands, doesn't just examine functional knowledge and skills in assessing its work force of 22,000 employees. It also analyzes the depth of employee talent in each geographic region and employees capable of being promoted into more responsible positions. In this way, FrieslandCampina identifies future leaders who will receive mentoring, additional training, and feedback as their careers progress.[39] As another example, Santander UK regularly assesses its bank employees' skills as it plans to develop their leadership qualities, with structured training and professional growth opportunities. The goal is to transfer skills and knowledge in the workplace and support the leaders of tomorrow.[40] That's what good HR planning should do—help managers identify the people they need.

An important part of a current assessment is **job analysis**, an assessment that defines a job and the behaviors necessary to perform it. For instance, what are the duties of a level 3 accountant who works for General Motors? What minimal knowledge, skills, and abilities are necessary to adequately perform this job? How do these requirements compare with those for a level 2 accountant or for an accounting manager? Information for a job analysis is gathered by directly observing individuals on the job, interviewing employees individually or in a group, having employees complete a questionnaire or record daily activities in a diary, or having job "experts" (usually managers) identify a job's specific characteristics.

job analysis
An assessment that defines jobs and the behaviors necessary to perform them

Using this information from the job analysis, managers develop or revise job descriptions and job specifications. A **job description** (or **position description**) is a written statement describing a job—typically job content, environment, and conditions of employment. A **job specification** states the minimum qualifications that a person must possess to successfully perform a given job. It identifies the knowledge, skills, and attitudes needed to do the job effectively. Both the job description and job specification are important documents when managers begin recruiting and selecting. Unfortunately, not every organization chooses to follow good practice. For instance, the New York Department of Education permitted a candidate for the Director of Communication job to rewrite her job description because she did not have the required five years of journalism or public relations experience.[41]

job description (position description)
A written statement that describes a job

job specification
A written statement of the minimum qualifications a person must possess to perform a given job successfully

MEETING FUTURE HR NEEDS Future HR needs are determined by the organization's mission, goals, and strategies. Demand for employees results from demand for the organization's products or services. After assessing both current capabilities and future needs, managers can estimate areas in which the organization will be understaffed or overstaffed. Then they're ready to proceed to the next step in the HRM process.

INCREASED SCRUTINY IN THE SELECTION PROCESS A driver at Fresh Direct, an online grocer that delivers food to masses of apartment-dwelling New Yorkers, was charged with, and later pled guilty to, stalking and harassing female customers.[42] San Francisco and Los Angeles prosecutors have accused ride-hailing service Uber of misleading the public about the rigor of driver background checks and claim of "safety you can trust."[43] The prosecutors maintain that Uber's selection process led to the employment of individuals using false names and convicted of sex offenses, murder, and kidnapping.

What do these outcomes suggest? Both companies have used selection processes that do not consistently screen out unsuitable applicants. Companies that do not carefully scrutinize the qualifications or backgrounds of employees surely pose risks of increased liability, poor reputation, and lower performance.

What can companies do to avoid disastrous outcomes? As we discuss shortly, they should make investments in developing reliable and valid selection procedures to help make appropriate hiring choices.

Recruitment and Decruitment

Competition for talent by India's two largest technology outsourcing companies has led to an all-out recruiting war. In the United States, the tech sector is also in a hiring push, pitting start-up companies against giants such as Google and Intel in the hunt for employees.[44] At CH2MHill, a global engineering firm based in Colorado, it's a real struggle to recruit foreign employees. To be successful at global talent acquisition, its company's talent acquisition director has a plan for dealing with different recruiting cultures in different parts of the world.[45]

If your professor has assigned this, go to **www.mymanagementlab.com** to watch a video titled: *CH2MHill: Human Resource Management* and to respond to questions.

recruitment
Locating, identifying, and attracting capable applicants

decruitment
Reducing an organization's workforce

If employee vacancies exist, managers should use the information gathered through job analysis to guide them in **recruitment**—that is, locating, identifying, and attracting capable applicants.[46] On the other hand, if HR planning shows a surplus of employees, managers may want to reduce the organization's workforce through **decruitment**.[47]

RECRUITMENT Some organizations have interesting approaches to finding employees. For instance, McDonald's, the world's largest hamburger chain, held a National Hiring Day hoping to hire 50,000 people. The chain and its franchisees actually hired 62,000 workers.[48] Ikea launched a cost-effective recruitment campaign in Australia. The company advertised job opportunities to its customers with a "Careers Instructions" sheet packed inside product boxes. Customers were *instructed* to apply for a job. The campaign was highly successful for generating nearly 4,300 quality applicants that yielded 280 new hires.[49] Accounting firm Deloitte & Touche created its Deloitte Film Festival to get employee team-produced films about "life" at Deloitte to use in college recruiting.[50] Even the U.S. Army is getting social by seeking recruits using social media.[51] A survey of what organizations are using to recruit potential job applicants reported that 92 percent of organizations were using social networking sites.[52] Exhibit 13-4 explains different recruitment sources managers can use to find potential job candidates.[53]

Exhibit 13-4
Recruiting Sources

Source	Advantages	Disadvantages
Internet	Reaches large numbers of people; can get immediate feedback	Generates many unqualified candidates
Employee referrals	Knowledge about the organization provided by current employee; can generate strong candidates because a good referral reflects on the recommender	May not increase the diversity and mix of employees
Company website	Wide distribution; can be targeted to specific groups	Generates many unqualified candidates
College recruiting	Large centralized body of candidates	Limited to entry-level positions
Professional recruiting organizations	Good knowledge of industry challenges and requirements	Little commitment to specific organization

WORKPLACE CONFIDENTIAL Job Search

Finding the right job is a complex task. But selecting the appropriate search channel can significantly increase your chances for success. We'll take a quick look at some of your search options. After that, we'll discuss the importance of choosing the right organization.

Your grandfather probably found jobs by looking at classified ads in the newspaper, going to an employment agency, or following up on a referral from a friend or relative. But newspaper ads have gone the way of the dinosaur, replaced by online websites; and employment agencies have been largely replaced by search firms that focus on executive and high-level professional positions. Job referrals, however, continue to be an excellent source of job openings.

Referrals from a current employee of an organization tends to provide accurate and realistic information, the kind of information you're not likely to get from a company recruiter. As a result, referrals tend to reduce unrealistic expectations. If, what a motel chain ad once said is true—"the best surprise is no surprise"—you should place a high value on information provided by a current employee.

If you're nearing the completion of your college degree or are a recent graduate, consider using your college's placement service. For college graduates, college placement services have been shown to be excellent channels for securing jobs.

Where you find jobs depends on the channels employers choose. So what do employers favor? Research on employment channels has shown that employers generally favor informal sources—such as contacts and networks—for most workers; but more formal channels for professionals, managers, and college graduates. Let's take a look at some of these formal channels.

Job fairs offer organizations a good opportunity to build their employment brand. Companies like to use them to contact prospective employees and collect information and résumés. For instance, the Cleveland Clinic recently conducted three job fairs in northeast Ohio in their search to fill 500 nursing positions. Note that it's not uncommon for a job fair to include multiple employers. Typically staffed by company employees, such job fairs give you a chance to meet face-to-face with some company employees and interview with multiple employers at one site.

Many *professional organizations* operate placement services for the benefit of their members. Professional organizations serving such varied occupations as human resource management, industrial engineering, psychology, accounting, and law publish rosters of job vacancies and distribute these lists to members. It's also common practice to provide placement facilities at regional and national meetings where individuals looking for employment and organizations looking for employees can find each other.

Today, much of the job search process is done *online*. Most organizations, large and small, now use the Internet to recruit new employees by adding a "careers" section to their website. One recent survey indicated that 60 percent of employers report hiring new employees from online sources. In addition to an employer's website, you'll want to check out job boards, social media, and job search apps. Job boards allow searches by location, key words, industry, level of education, salary, and any combination of these criteria. Popular job boards include CareerBuilder.com and Monster.com. Social media sites such as Facebook and LinkedIn include "career" sections. And two apps you might want to investigate are Switch and Jobmaster. Switch is to job searches what Tinder is to dating. It provides job seekers with anonymity as they scan job postings, swiping right for positions of interest. If the user's qualifications match the employer's needs, the parties can initiate an in-app chat. Jobmaster aggregates job listings from some 1,000 job boards around the world. It has national job boards as well as boards devoted to particular professions.

Now we turn to our other concern regarding a job search: making sure that a job vacancy is right for you. Specifically, even if the job looks great and an employer extends an offer, is the organization a good match for you?

We've discussed organizational culture in several previous Workplace Confidential boxes (see Chapters 7 and 9). Consistent with those discussions, no job search can be called successful if you end up with a great job but in an organization where you don't fit. So how do you find out what an organization is really like before you actually start working there? During your interviews, read between the lines. Listen to the stories people tell about how management handled setbacks, rule-breakers, nonconformists, or creative types. Does the company, for instance, reward risk taking or punish it? Listen and observe rituals that indicate what employees believe are important. And look for artifacts and symbols that can give you clues as to the kind of employee behaviors that are considered appropriate. As Yogi Berra said, "you can observe a lot just by watching." After you've sized up the organization, ask yourself: Do my personality and beliefs fit with what this organization values? In job searches, too often we focus on the title, position, and salary. They're obviously important, but finding a culture that is the right fit will significantly increase the chances that you'll be happy and successful in your job.

Sources: Based on H. B. Sagen, J. W. Dallam, and J. R. Laverty, "Job Search Techniques as Employment Channels: Differential Effects on the Initial Employment Success of College Graduates," *The Career Development Quarterly*, September 1999, pp. 74–85; L. McKelvey, marketing manager at CareerBuilder.com, Chicago, Illinois, presentation July 15, 2011; and A. Grant, "Which Company Is Right for You?," *The New York Times*, December 20, 2015, p. SR-7.

Exhibit 13-5
Decruitment Options

Option	Description
Firing	Permanent involuntary termination
Layoffs	Temporary involuntary termination; may last only a few days or extend to years
Attrition	Not filling openings created by voluntary resignations or normal retirements
Transfers	Moving employees either laterally or downward; usually does not reduce costs but can reduce intraorganizational supply–demand imbalances
Reduced workweeks	Having employees work fewer hours per week, share jobs, or perform their jobs on a part-time basis
Early retirements	Providing incentives to older and more senior employees for retiring before their normal retirement date
Job sharing	Having employees share one full-time position

Although online recruiting is popular and allows organizations to identify applicants cheaply and quickly, applicant quality may not be as good as other sources. Research has found that employee referrals generally produce the best candidates.[54] Why? Because current employees know both the job and the person being recommended, they tend to refer applicants who are well qualified. Also, current employees often feel their reputation is at stake and refer others only when they're confident that the person will not make them look bad.

DECRUITMENT The other approach to controlling labor supply is decruitment, which is not a pleasant task for any manager. Decruitment options are shown in Exhibit 13-5. Although employees can be fired, other choices may be better. However, no matter how you do it, it's never easy to reduce an organization's workforce.

Selection

selection
Screening job applicants to ensure that the most appropriate candidates are hired

Once you have a pool of candidates, the next step in the HRM process is **selection**, screening job applicants to determine who is best qualified for the job. Managers need to "select" carefully since hiring errors can have significant implications. For instance, at T-Mobile, lousy customer service led to its last-place ranking in the J.D. Power's customer-satisfaction survey. The first step in a total overhaul of the customer service area was revamping the company's hiring practices to increase the odds of hiring employees who would be good at customer service.[55]

A survey of chief financial officers revealed the following concerns with bad hiring decisions:

- 39 percent of respondents were most concerned about degraded morale.
- 34 percent of respondents were most concerned with a drop in productivity.
- 25 percent of respondents were most concerned about the financial consequences.[56]

WHAT IS SELECTION? At Boston's Seaport Hotel & World Trade Center, the HR team decided to integrate an online application with a 20-minute behavioral assessment. After implementing this approach, the company's two-digit turnover rate fell to a single-digit rate.[57] That's the kind of result organizations—and managers—like to see from their hiring process. Selection involves predicting which applicants will be successful if hired. For example, in hiring for a sales position, the selection process should predict which applicants will generate a high volume of sales. As shown in Exhibit 13-6, any selection decision can result in four possible outcomes—two correct and two errors.

A decision is correct when the applicant was predicted to be successful and proved to be successful on the job, or when the applicant was predicted to be unsuccessful and was not hired. In the first instance, we have successfully accepted; in the second, we have successfully rejected.

Exhibit 13-6
Selection Decision Outcomes

Later Job Performance	Selection Decision: Accept	Selection Decision: Reject
Successful	Correct Decision	Reject Error
Unsuccessful	Accept Error	Correct Decision

Problems arise when errors are made in rejecting candidates who would have performed successfully on the job (reject errors) or accepting those who ultimately perform poorly (accept errors). These problems can be significant. Given today's HR laws and regulations, reject errors can cost more than the additional screening needed to find acceptable candidates. Why? Because they can expose the organization to discrimination charges, especially if applicants from protected groups are disproportionately rejected. For instance, employment assessments used by Target Corporation were found to have disproportionately screened out black, Asian, and female applicants for exempt-level professional positions.[58] The Equal Employment Opportunity Commission said that Target violated Title VII of the Civil Rights Act because the tests were not sufficiently job-related and consistent with business necessity. On the other hand, the costs of accept errors include the cost of training the employee, the profits lost because of the employee's incompetence, the cost of severance, and the subsequent costs of further recruiting and screening. The major emphasis of any selection activity should be reducing the probability of reject errors or accept errors while increasing the probability of making correct decisions. Managers do this by using selection procedures that are both valid and reliable.

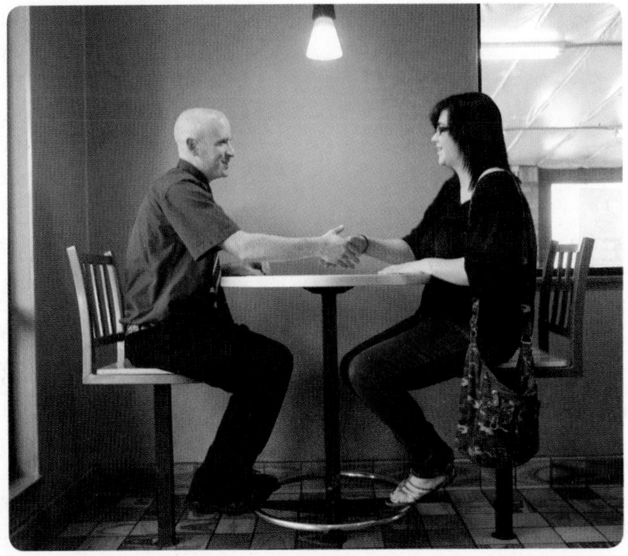

The job interview is a selection tool McDonald's uses for job candidates in both entry-level and professional positions at its 34,000 locations worldwide. During personal interviews, the store manager shown here looks for applicants who possess good communication skills, would qualify in meeting McDonald's customer service standards, and work well as a team member.
Source: Joe Jaszewski/Associated Press

VALIDITY AND RELIABILITY A valid selection device is characterized by a proven relationship between the selection device and some relevant criterion. Federal employment laws prohibit managers from using a test score to select employees unless clear evidence shows that, once on the job, individuals with high scores on this test outperform individuals with low test scores. The burden is on managers to support that any selection device they use to differentiate applicants is validly related to job performance.

A reliable selection device indicates that it measures the same thing consistently. On a test that's reliable, any single individual's score should remain fairly consistent over time, assuming that the characteristics being measured are also stable. No selection device can be effective if it's not reliable. Using such a device would be like weighing yourself every day on an erratic scale. If the scale is unreliable—randomly fluctuating, say, 5 to 10 pounds every time you step on it—the results don't mean much.

A growing number of companies are adopting a new measure of recruitment effectiveness called "quality of fill."[59] This measure looks at the contributions of good hires versus those of hires who have failed to live up to their potential. Five key factors are considered in defining this quality measure: employee retention, performance evaluations, number of first-year hires who make it into high-potential training programs, number of employees who are promoted, and what surveys of new hires indicate. Such measures help an organization assess whether its selection process is working well.

★ It's Your Career

Interviewing—If your instructor is using Pearson MyLab Management, log onto **mymanagementlab.com** and test your *interviewing knowledge*. **Be sure to refer back to the chapter opener!**

TYPES OF SELECTION TOOLS The best-known selection tools include application forms, written and performance-simulation tests, interviews, background investigations, and in some cases, physical exams. Exhibit 13-7 lists the strengths and weaknesses of each.[60] Because many selection tools have limited value for making selection decisions, managers should use those that effectively predict performance for a given job.

REALISTIC JOB PREVIEWS At the Hilton Baltimore BWI Airport, housekeeping job prospects are taken to a guest room and asked to make a bed with the precision that the interviewer demonstrated. By introducing applicants to what's involved in doing the job they're seeking, the hotel is hoping to eliminate misconceptions or surprises.[61] One thing managers need to carefully watch is how they portray the organization and the work an applicant will be doing. If they tell applicants only the good aspects, they're likely to have a workforce that's dissatisfied and prone to high

Exhibit 13-7
Selection Tools

Application Forms

- Almost universally used
- Most useful for gathering information
- Can predict job performance but not easy to create one that does

Written Tests

- Must be job-related
- Include intelligence, aptitude, ability, personality, and interest tests
- Are popular (e.g., personality tests; aptitude tests)
- Relatively good predictor for supervisory positions

Performance-Simulation Tests

- Use actual job behaviors
- Work sampling—test applicants on tasks associated with that job; appropriate for routine or standardized work
- Assessment center—simulate jobs; appropriate for evaluating managerial potential

Interviews

- Almost universally used
- Must know what can and cannot be asked
- Can be useful for managerial positions

Background Investigations

- Used for verifying application data—valuable source of information
- Used for verifying reference checks—not a valuable source of information

Physical Examinations

- Are for jobs that have certain physical requirements
- Mostly used for insurance purposes

let's get REAL

The Scenario:

José Salinas is the HR director at a large food processor. Within the last couple of years, he has seen more frequent parental involvement in their adult child's job hunt. In fact, one candidate's parents actually contacted the company after their child got a job offer wanting to discuss their daughter's salary, relocation package, and educational reimbursement opportunities. He's not sure how to handle these occurrences.

Source: Zakiyyah Rogers

Zakiyyah Rogers
Department Manager,
Human Resources

What advice would you give José?

You may understand a parent's concern but we cannot discuss company information with them. Our relationship is with the potential employee. Let the parent know you are willing to speak directly to their child and answer any questions they may have.

turnover.[62] Negative things can happen when the information an applicant receives is excessively inflated. First, mismatched applicants probably won't withdraw from the selection process. Second, inflated information builds unrealistic expectations, so new employees may quickly become dissatisfied and leave the organization. Third, new hires become disillusioned and less committed to the organization when they face the unexpected harsh realities of the job. In addition, these individuals may feel they were misled during the hiring process and then become problem employees.

To increase employee job satisfaction and reduce turnover, managers should consider a **realistic job preview (RJP)**, one that includes both positive and negative information about the job and the company. For instance, in addition to the positive comments typically expressed during an interview, the job applicant might be told there are limited opportunities to talk to coworkers during work hours, that promotional advancement is unlikely, or that work hours are erratic and they may have to work weekends. Research indicates that applicants who receive an RJP have more realistic expectations about the jobs they'll be performing and are better able to cope with the frustrating elements than applicants who receive only inflated information.

realistic job preview (RJP)
A preview of a job that provides both positive and negative information about the job and the company

PROVIDING employees with needed skills and knowledge

LO13.4 As one of the nation's busiest airports, Miami International Airport serves more than 40 million passengers. But Miami International is doing something that no other airport has done. It has asked different groups of employees to "think and act as ambassadors for regional tourism." These airport workers are discovering how important it is to help travelers find solutions to the frustrating issues they face as they travel into and out of Miami. Accomplishing that means that all employees who work on airport grounds are required to thoroughly learn and understand customer service through a series of tourism training efforts. The required training is tied to renewal of airport ID badges, providing a critical incentive for employees to participate.[63]

If recruiting and selecting are done properly, we should have hired competent individuals who can perform successfully on the job. But successful performance requires more than possessing certain skills. New hires must be acclimated to the organization's culture and be trained and given the knowledge to do the job in a manner consistent with the organization's goals. Current employees, like those at Miami International Airport, may have to complete training programs to improve or update their skills. For these acclimation and skill improvement tasks, HRM uses orientation and training.

Orientation

orientation
Introducing a new employee to his or her job and the organization

Did you participate in some type of organized "introduction to college life" when you started school? If so, you may have been told about your school's rules and the procedures for activities such as applying for financial aid, cashing a check, or registering for classes, and you were probably introduced to some of the college administrators. A person starting a new job needs the same type of introduction to his or her job and the organization. This introduction is called **orientation**.

There are two types of orientation. *Work unit orientation* familiarizes the employee with the goals of the work unit, clarifies how his or her job contributes to the unit's goals, and includes an introduction to his or her new coworkers. *Organization orientation* informs the new employee about the company's goals, history, philosophy, procedures, and rules. It should also include relevant HR policies and maybe even a tour of the facilities.

Many organizations have formal orientation programs, while others use a more informal approach in which the manager assigns the new employee to a senior member of the work group who introduces the new hire to immediate coworkers and shows him or her where important things are located. And then there are intense orientation programs like that at IBM. The company's Succeeding@IBM is a two-year program that provides new hires with information covering corporate values, strategy, tools, and the resources necessary to be successful. IBM distinguishes its orientation program from others by incorporating customized learning plans. Managers have an obligation to effectively and efficiently integrate any new employee into the organization. They should openly discuss mutual obligations of the organization and the employee.[64] It's in the best interests of both the organization and the new employee to get the person up and running in the job as soon as possible. Successful orientation results in an outsider-insider transition that makes the new employee feel comfortable and fairly well adjusted, lowers the likelihood of poor work performance, and reduces the probability of a premature resignation. One study revealed that 22 percent of staff turnover occurs in the first 45 days of employment, and the cost of losing an employee in the first year amounts to about three times annual salary.[65]

Employee Training

On the whole, planes don't cause airline accidents, people do. Most collisions, crashes, and other airline mishaps—nearly three-quarters of them—result from errors by the pilot or air traffic controller, or from inadequate maintenance.[66] For instance, a United Airlines pilot could have avoided a catastrophic accident while attempting to land had he listened to the copilot's warning that fuel levels were rapidly dropping. The airline recognized that this accident could have been avoided if teamwork principles were emphasized in training.[67] We cite this example and these statistics to illustrate the importance of training in the airline industry. Such maintenance and human errors could be prevented or significantly reduced by better employee training, as shown by the amazing "landing" of US Airways Flight 1549 in the Hudson River in January 2009 with no loss of life. Pilot Captain Chesley Sullenberger attributed the positive outcome to the extensive and intensive training that US Air pilots and flight crews undergo.[68] Everything that employees at Ruth's Chris Steak House restaurants need to know can be found on sets of 4 × 8½-inch cards. Whether it's a recipe for caramelized banana cream pie or how to acknowledge customers, it's on the cards. And since the cards for all jobs are readily available, employees know the behaviors and skills it takes to get promoted. It's a unique approach to employee training, but it seems to work.

TYPE	INCLUDES
General	Communication skills, computer systems application and programming, customer service, executive development, management skills and development, personal growth, sales, supervisory skills, and technological skills and knowledge
Specific	Basic life–work skills, creativity, customer education, diversity/cultural awareness, remedial writing, managing change, leadership, product knowledge, public speaking/presentation skills, safety, ethics, sexual harassment, team building, wellness, and others

Exhibit 13-8
Types of Training

Source: Based on "2005 Industry Report—Types of Training," *Training*, December 2005, p. 22.

Since the card system was implemented, employee turnover has decreased, something that's not easy to accomplish in the restaurant industry.[69] Training is just as important at other restaurants, with servers trained to "read" diners and make the service more personal.[70]

Employee training is an important HRM activity. As job demands change, employee skills have to change. In 2015, U.S. business firms spent more than $70.6 billion on formal employee training.[71] Managers, of course, are responsible for deciding what type of training employees need, when they need it, and what form that training should take.

On average, U.S. companies spent $702 per employee for training. The amount varies by company size:

- $1,105 in small-size companies (100–999 employees).
- $544 in medium-size companies (1,000 to 9,999 employees).
- $1,105 in large-size companies (10,000 or more employees).[72]

TYPES OF TRAINING Exhibit 13-8 describes the major types of training that organizations provide. Some of the most popular types include profession/industry-specific training, management/supervisory skills, mandatory/compliance information (such as sexual harassment, safety, etc.), and customer service training. For many organizations, employee interpersonal skills training—communication, conflict resolution, team building, customer service, and so forth—is a high priority. For example, until recently, medical schools did not teach students how to communicate with patients. Many hospitals have now taken on this responsibility as patient satisfaction becomes more important. For instance, the University of Rochester Medical Center provides one-on-one coaching to help doctors improve communication with patients.[73] For Canon, Inc., it's the repair personnel's technical skills that are important.[74] As part of their training, repair people play a video game based on the familiar kids' board game Operation in which "lights flashed and buzzers sounded if copier parts were dragged and dropped poorly." The company found that comprehension levels were 5 to 8 percent higher than when traditional training manuals were used.

Learning the skill of rappelling is an important part of the search and rescue training for U.S. citizen-soldiers serving in the U.S. Army National Guard. Training teaches soldiers the skills, policies, and procedures they need in responding to domestic emergencies such as natural disasters and riots as well as international crises.
Source: Xinhua/Alamy

TRAINING METHODS Although employee training can be done in traditional ways, many organizations are relying more on technology-based training methods because of their accessibility, cost, and ability to deliver information. Exhibit 13-9 provides a description of the various traditional and technology-based training methods that managers might use. Of all these training methods, experts believe that organizations will increasingly rely on e-learning and mobile applications to deliver important information and to develop employees' skills.

If your professor has assigned this, go to **www.mymanagementlab.com** to complete the *Simulation: Human Resource Management* and get a better understanding of the challenges of training in organizations.

Exhibit 13-9
Traditional Training Methods

On-the-job—Employees learn how to do tasks simply by performing them, usually after an initial introduction to the task.

Job rotation—Employees work at different jobs in a particular area, getting exposure to a variety of tasks.

Mentoring and coaching—Employees work with an experienced worker who provides information, support, and encouragement; also called apprenticeships in certain industries.

Experiential exercises—Employees participate in role-playing, simulations, or other face-to-face types of training.

Workbooks/manuals—Employees refer to training workbooks and manuals for information.

Classroom lectures—Employees attend lectures designed to convey specific information.

Technology-Based Training Methods

CD-ROM/DVD/videotapes/audiotapes/podcasts—Employees listen to or watch selected media that convey information or demonstrate certain techniques.

Videoconferencing/teleconferencing/satellite TV—Employees listen to or participate as information is conveyed or techniques demonstrated.

E-learning—Internet-based learning where employees participate in multimedia simulations or other interactive modules.

Mobile learning—Learning delivered via mobile devices.

RETAINING **competent, high-performing employees**

LO13.5 At Procter & Gamble, mid-year employee evaluations were used to adjust work goals to reflect more accurately what could be achieved in such a challenging economic environment. The company has directed managers to focus on employees' achievements rather than just to point out areas that need improvement. P&G's director of human resources said, "Particularly in this economy, people are living in the survival zone. Setting attainable targets was important to keeping up morale."[75]

Once an organization has invested significant dollars in recruiting, selecting, orienting, and training employees, it wants to keep them, especially the competent, high-performing ones! Two HRM activities that play a role in this area are managing employee performance and developing an appropriate compensation and benefits program.

Employee Performance Management

A survey found that two-thirds of surveyed organizations felt they had inefficient performance management processes in place.[76] That's scary because managers need to know whether their employees are performing their jobs efficiently and effectively. That's what a **performance management system** does—establishes performance standards used to evaluate employee performance. How do managers evaluate employees' performance? That's where the different performance appraisal methods come in.

performance management system
Establishes performance standards used to evaluate employee performance

PERFORMANCE APPRAISAL METHODS More than 70 percent of managers admit they have trouble giving a critical performance review to an underachieving employee.[77] It's particularly challenging when managers and employees alike sense they're not beneficial.[78] And some companies—about 6 percent of Fortune 500 companies—

are eliminating the formal performance review entirely.[79] One concern is that performance reviews are typically given annually, allowing for infrequent feedback. For instance, consulting firm Accenture now gives employees timely feedback following the completion of every assignment. General Electric (GE) is also providing more frequent feedback through an app called PD@GE.[80] Although appraising someone's performance is never easy, especially with employees who aren't doing their jobs well, managers can be better at it by using any of the seven different performance appraisal methods, along with providing frequent feedback.[81] A description of each of these methods, including advantages and disadvantages, is shown in Exhibit 13-10.

Compensation and Benefits

Executives at Discovery Communications, Inc., had an employee morale problem on their hands. Many of the company's top performers were making the same salaries

Exhibit 13-10
Performance Appraisal Methods

Written Essay
Evaluator writes a description of employee's strengths and weaknesses, past performance, and potential; provides suggestions for improvement.

+ Simple to use
– May be better measure of evaluator's writing ability than of employee's actual performance

Critical Incident
Evaluator focuses on critical behaviors that separate effective and ineffective performance.

+ Rich examples, behaviorally based
– Time-consuming, lacks quantification

Graphic Rating Scale
Popular method that lists a set of performance factors and an incremental scale; evaluator goes down the list and rates employee on each factor.

+ Provides quantitative data; not time-consuming
– Doesn't provide in-depth information on job behavior

BARS (Behaviorally Anchored Rating Scale)
Popular approach that combines elements from critical incident and graphic rating scale; evaluator uses a rating scale, but items are examples of actual job behaviors.

+ Focuses on specific and measurable job behaviors
– Time-consuming; difficult to develop

Multiperson Comparison
Employees are rated in comparison to others in work group.

+ Compares employees with one another
– Difficult with large number of employees; legal concerns

MBO
Employees are evaluated on how well they accomplish specific goals.

+ Focuses on goals; results oriented
– Time-consuming

360-Degree Appraisal
Utilizes feedback from supervisors, employees, and coworkers.

+ Thorough
– Time-consuming

Department store manager and staff members of British retailer John Lewis Partnership cheer as they celebrate receiving a bonus of 11 percent of their salary based on the company's profits. A bonus is one example of a variable pay system that compensates employees on the basis of some performance measure.
Source: John Stillwell/PA/AP Images

as the poorer performers, and the company's compensation program didn't allow for giving raises to people who stayed in the same position. The only way for managers to reward the top performers was to give them a bonus or promote them to another position. Executives were discovering that not only was that unfair, it was counterproductive. So they overhauled the program.[82]

Just in case you think that compensation and benefits decisions aren't important, a survey showed that 71 percent of workers surveyed said their benefits package would influence their decision to leave their job.[83] Most of us expect to receive appropriate compensation from our employer. Developing an effective and appropriate compensation system is an important part of the HRM process.[84] It can help attract and retain competent and talented individuals who help the organization accomplish its mission and goals. In addition, an organization's compensation system has been shown to have an impact on its strategic performance.[85]

Managers must develop a compensation system that reflects the changing nature of work and the workplace in order to keep people motivated. Organizational compensation can include many different types of rewards and benefits such as base wages and salaries, wage and salary add-ons, incentive payments, and other benefits and services.[86] Employee benefits commonly include offerings such as retirement benefits, health care insurance, and paid time off. Many organizations are addressing the needs of their diverse workforces through offering flexible work options and family-friendly benefits to accommodate employees' needs for work-family life balance.

let's get REAL

The Scenario:

As the human resources manager at Extreme Software Solutions, Kim Yoshida has helped develop the policies and practices to manage the growing staff. As a start-up company 10 years ago, the company hired mostly recent college graduates eager to work any number of hours to help get the company up and running. Now that Extreme Software Solutions is an established company, Kim has noted that many employees are starting families and she has received some requests for reduced or more flexible work schedules. At this point Kim thinks the company should consider offering family-friendly benefits.

What kind of family-friendly benefits should Kim consider?

In order to retain and maintain engagement with employees who started with the company, Kim should consider flexible work programs, benefits that enhance work-life balance, and policies that make it easier for parents to transition back into the workforce after starting a family. Some examples of these include job sharing for employees who are interested in reduced hours, working from home or remotely, an in-house daycare or subsidized daycare programs, and paid leave of absence after the birth or adoption of a child. The benefits put in place should not only enhance an employee's ability to get the job done based on his or her work and personal schedule, but also allow the company to continue to achieve its business goals.

Leya Gaynor
HR Business Partner

Source: Leya Gaynor

Some organizations offer employees some unusual, but popular, benefits. For instance, Campbell's Soup and Mercedes-Benz offer concierge services. Employees can ask a concierge to pick up dry cleaning or make dinner reservations. Employees at accounting firm Barfield, Murphy, Shank, and Smith enjoy on-site massages during tax preparation season. At Bank of America, employees receive $3,000 when they purchase a hybrid or electric car. And here's a benefit that college graduates will appreciate: student loan repayment assistance! Natixis Global Asset Management and ChowNow, an online food ordering platform, offer repayment assistance in hopes of recruiting and retaining top talent.[87]

If your professor has assigned this, go to **www.mymanagementlab.com** to watch a video titled: *Elm City Market: Designing and Administering Benefits* and to respond to questions.

★ **Watch It 2!**

How do managers determine who gets paid what? Several factors influence the compensation and benefit packages that different employees receive. Exhibit 13-11 summarizes these factors, which are job-based and business- or industry-based. Many organizations, however, are using alternative approaches to determining compensation: skill-based pay and variable pay.

Skill-based pay systems reward employees for the job skills and competencies they can demonstrate. Under this type of pay system, an employee's job title doesn't define his or her pay category; skills do.[88] A wide variety of employers have established skill-focused pay programs.[89] Many of the companies known to be using this kind of pay operate in manufacturing, and the average age of the companies is approximately 10 years.[90] How well do these programs work? One study found that a skill-based pay plan in a manufacturing setting increased plant productivity by 58 percent, lowered labor cost per part by 16 percent, and generated favorable quality outcomes.[91] On the other hand, many organizations use **variable pay** systems, in which an individual's compensation is contingent on performance—nearly 90 percent of U.S. organizations use some type of variable pay plans, and about 50 percent of Asian and Latin American organizations do.[92] In Chapter 17, we'll discuss variable pay systems further as they relate to employee motivation.

skill-based pay
A pay system that rewards employees for the job skills they can demonstrate

variable pay
A pay system in which an individual's compensation is contingent on performance

Although many factors influence the design of an organization's compensation system, flexibility is a key consideration. The traditional approach to paying people

Exhibit 13-11
What Determines Pay and Benefits

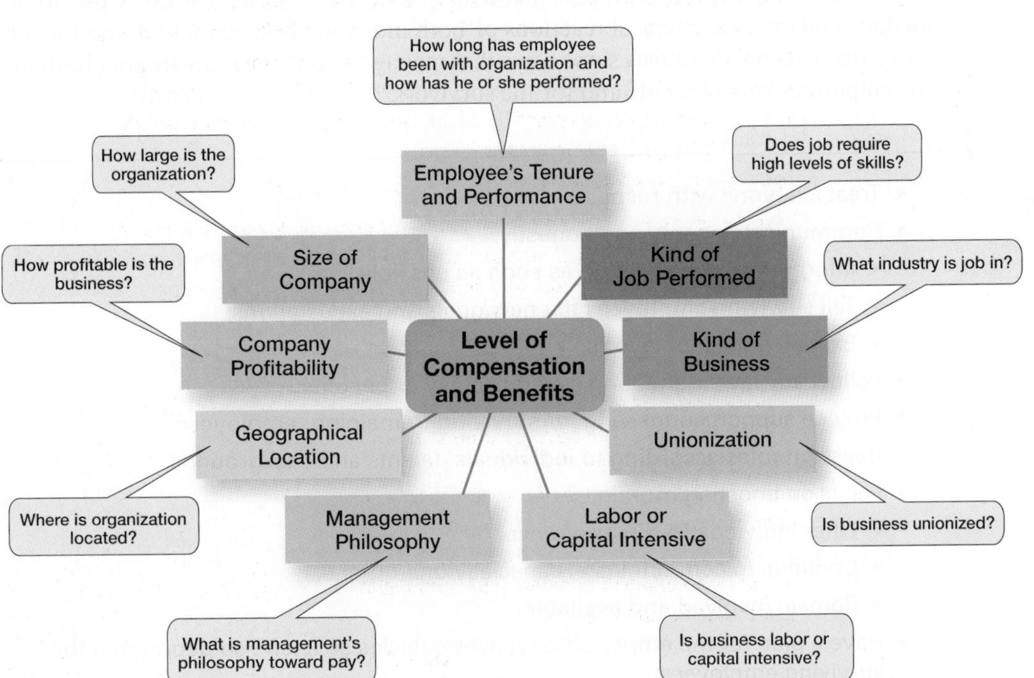

reflected a more stable time when an employee's pay was largely determined by seniority and job level. Given the dynamic environments that many organizations face, the trend is to make pay systems more flexible and to reduce the number of pay levels. However, whatever approach managers use, they must establish a fair, equitable, and motivating compensation system that allows the organization to recruit and keep a talented and productive workforce.

★ Write It!

If your professor has assigned this, go to **www.mymanagementlab.com** to complete the Writing Assignment *MGMT 9: Management & Human Resources (HR Decision Making)*.

CONTEMPORARY issues in managing human resources

LO13.6 We'll conclude this chapter by looking at some contemporary HR issues facing today's managers. These concerns include managing downsizing, sexual harassment, and controlling HR costs.

Managing Downsizing

"Before 1981, the word 'layoff' in the sense of permanent separation from a job with no prospects for recall, was so uncommon that the U.S. Bureau of Labor Statistics didn't even keep track of such cuts."[93] How things have changed!

downsizing
The planned elimination of jobs in an organization

Downsizing (or layoffs) is the planned elimination of jobs in an organization. When an organization has too many employees—which can happen when it's faced with an economic recession, declining market share, overly aggressive growth, or poorly managed operations—one option for improving profits is to eliminate some of those excess workers. During the most recent economic recession, many well-known companies downsized—including, among others, Boeing, Nokia, Procter & Gamble, Hewlett-Packard, Volkswagen, Dell, General Motors, Unisys, Siemens, Merck, Honeywell, and eBay. Years since the recession ended, layoffs continue, although not as frequently. Some HR experts suggest that a "cost" associated with mass layoffs is the damage they can cause to long-term growth prospects.[94]

How can managers best manage a downsized workplace? Disruptions in the workplace and in employees' personal lives should be expected. Stress, frustration, anxiety, and anger are typical reactions of both individuals being laid off and the job survivors. Exhibit 13-12 lists some ways that managers can lessen the trauma both for the employees being laid off and for the survivors.[95]

Exhibit 13-12
Tips for Managing Downsizing

- Treat everyone with respect.
- Communicate openly and honestly:
  - Inform those being let go as soon as possible.
  - Tell surviving employees the new goals and expectations.
  - Explain impact of layoffs.
- Follow any laws regulating severance pay or benefits.
- Provide support/counseling for surviving (remaining) employees.
- Reassign roles according to individuals' talents and backgrounds.
- Focus on boosting morale:
  - Offer individualized reassurance.
  - Continue to communicate, especially one-on-one.
  - Remain involved and available.
- Have a plan for the empty office spaces/cubicles so it isn't so depressing for surviving employees.

Managing Sexual Harassment

Sexual harassment is defined as any unwanted action or activity of a sexual nature that explicitly or implicitly affects an individual's employment, performance, or work environment. In practice, it can occur between members of the opposite sex or the same sex, even though the laws in some countries apply more narrowly. For example, in India, the Sexual Harassment of Women at Workplace (Prevention, Prohibition, and Redressal) Act applies only to sexual harassment of women. Here, harassment is defined as "physical contact, advances; or demand for sexual favors; or making sexually colored remarks; or other unwelcome physical, verbal or nonverbal conduct of sexual nature."[96] In Japan, the Equal Employment Opportunity Law regards as sexual harassment any language or actions that are sexual in nature and directed toward or between employees. This law was recently amended to cover LGBT employees with the addition of language saying that harassment in the workplace was outlawed, regardless of sexual orientation and identity.[97] The Labour Relations Act of South Africa includes in its definition of sexual harassment not just physical and verbal conduct but also harassment actions that take place online or via cellphone messages and images.[98]

sexual harassment
Any unwanted action or activity of a sexual nature that explicitly or implicitly affects an individual's employment, performance, or work environment

Sexual harassment is a serious issue in many job situations and in many countries. According to one survey of U.K. women, 52 percent had experienced unwanted groping, sexual advances, or other types of sexual harassment at work. Among U.K. women aged 16 to 24 who took part in this research, 63 percent had experienced workplace sexual harassment.[99] In Japan, research shows that 29 percent of women have experienced some form of sexual harassment at work.[100] A survey in Australia revealed that 25 percent of women and 16 percent of men have experienced sexual harassment in the workplace.[101] And in China, research suggests that as many as 80 percent of women have been subjected to sexual harassment at some time during their careers.[102]

Although discussions of sexual harassment cases often focus on the legal aspects, there are other important concerns for managers and employers. Sexual harassment creates an unpleasant, even hostile work environment and undermines workers' ability to perform to the best of their abilities. So what can an organization do to prevent sexual harassment and protect itself against claims that harassment has occurred? Experts advise having a clearly written, detailed policy with specifics about what is not allowed and how to report any incidents. Be sure the policy is widely publicized within the organization, provide training to help employees and managers understand and deal with the issue, and demonstrate that sexual harassment, as well as retaliation against anyone who reports it, will not be tolerated.[103]

Even with strict policies in place, employees may hesitate to complain due to embarrassment, fear, or lack of confidence that their reports will be properly investigated and action taken. In India, for instance, nearly 70 percent of women who said they had experienced sexual harassment on the job did not file a complaint because of such concerns. In addition, these women told researchers that their employers were not following the anti-harassment procedures required by law.[104] As you can see, employers need to address this issue aggressively and be consistent in their approach to maintaining a productive and positive working environment for employees at every level.

- 85 percent of workers feel that sexually harassing a coworker is grounds for termination.[105]

Controlling HR Costs

It's estimated that worker obesity costs U.S. companies as much as $153 billion annually.[107] HR costs are skyrocketing, especially employee health care and employee pensions. Organizations are looking for ways to control these costs.

EMPLOYEE HEALTH CARE COSTS At biotech company Amgen, Inc., employees can buy an Apple Watch for only $25. In exchange for this deeply discounted price, they are required to meet fitness goals over a two-year period or pay the full price of

FUTURE VISION Gamification of HR

Could a game help improve a company's human resources (HR) practices? The answer is "yes" according to many organizations that are exploring gamification as a strategy to engage potential job applicants as well as employees.[106]

Gamification is the application of the elements of a game in a non-game context. HR is exploring gamification by presenting some kind of real-life scenario in the form of a game, usually via technology. An organization might use a game during the hiring process, to orient new employees, to provide training, to support career development, or even to help support team-building efforts. Gamification applications are growing as many options exist that can be accessed via a computer or, for those on the go, via tablets and smartphones.

Consider these examples:

- A software firm holding a contest, such as a coding challenge, to test coding skills of job applicants.
- A consulting firm engaging potential job applicants on the company career website by asking them to play a problem-solving game.
- Delivery of a new hire orientation using an app that includes games to learn about the company history, benefits offered, and company culture.
- Tracking a company-wide sales contest on an internal website that features a leaderboard and other game components where employees earn points for a variety of activities they complete and badges as they move up to new levels.
- A manufacturer using an app to provide safety training through short games that help employees learn the safety basics during breaks in their workflow.

Gamification works because it taps into the natural human instinct for competition and recognition, and more importantly, because games are fun! Games offer the opportunity to engage both current and potential employees much more than through the use of traditional practices. Furthermore, a gamified HR practice could also be more effective. For example, a game could potentially better assess problem-solving skills than could a traditional interview question. Or trainees might learn more in a training program when engaged in an online game than when they are sitting all day in a conference room passively listening to a presentation. Don't you agree that playing some games might be a good way to kick off a new job?

If your professor has chosen to assign this, go to ***www.mymanagementlab.com*** *to discuss the following questions.*

TALK ABOUT IT 1: What would you think of a company that used a gaming application as part of its hiring process?

TALK ABOUT IT 2: What are some cautions for human resources practitioners in using gamification?

the watch.[108] At AOL, almost 1,000 employees enrolled in an 11-week activity challenge to take as many steps as possible. By the end of the challenge, those employees had taken more than 530 million total steps—equivalent to walking around the globe more than 10 times. CVS Health recently announced an employee smoking cessation program named "700 Good Reasons." Participants can earn up to $700 when they test tobacco free at 6 and 12 months.[109]

All these examples illustrate how companies are trying to control skyrocketing employee health care costs. Since 2006, employer health care costs have risen steadily each year and are expected to double by the year 2020 from the $2.1 trillion spent in 2006.[110] And smokers cost companies even more—about 25 percent more for health care than nonsmokers.[111] However, the biggest health care cost for companies—estimated at $73 billion a year—is obesity and its related costs arising from medical expenditures and absenteeism.[112] A study of manufacturing organizations found that presenteeism, defined as employees not performing at full capacity, was 1.8 percent higher for workers with moderate to severe obesity than for all other employees.[113] The reason for the lost productivity is likely the result of reduced mobility because of body size or pain problems such as arthritis. Is it any wonder that organizations are looking for ways to control their health care costs? How? First, many organizations are providing opportunities for employees to lead healthy lifestyles. From financial incentives to company-sponsored health and wellness programs, the goal is to limit rising health care costs. About 41 percent of companies use some type of positive incentives aimed at encouraging healthy behavior, up from 34 percent in 1996.[114] Another study indicated that nearly 90 percent of companies surveyed planned to aggressively promote healthy lifestyles to their employees during the next three to five years.[115] Many are starting sooner: Google, Yamaha Corporation of America, Caterpillar, and others are putting health food in company break rooms, cafeterias, and vending machines; providing deliveries of fresh organic fruit; and putting "calorie taxes" on fatty foods.[116] In the case of smokers, however, some companies have taken a more aggressive stance by increasing the amount smokers pay for health insurance or by firing them if they refuse to stop smoking.

EMPLOYEE PENSION PLAN COSTS The other area where organizations are looking to control costs is employee pension plans.

Corporate pensions have been around since the nineteenth century.[117] But the days when companies could afford to give employees a broad-based pension that provided them a guaranteed retirement income are gone. Pension commitments have become such an enormous burden that companies can no longer afford them. In fact, the corporate pension system has been described as "fundamentally broken."[118] Many companies no longer provide pensions. AIG, which closed its pension plan to new hires in 2016, has told its employees that their pension benefits would be frozen.[119] Jeff Hurd, executive vice president of human resources at AIG, stated that the company made this decision because it has been spending substantially more than "most of our peers and that our programs are not in line with where the marketplace is headed."[120] According to the Bureau of Labor Statistics, 49 percent of workers participate in defined contribution plans while only 15 percent participate in a traditional pension plan.[121] Of those with traditional pension plans, 40 percent were closed to new hires.[122]

Obviously, the pension issue is one that directly affects HR decisions. On the one hand, organizations want to attract talented, capable employees by offering them desirable benefits such as pensions. But on the other hand, organizations have to balance offering benefits with the costs of providing such benefits.

Chapter 13 PREPARING FOR: Exams/Quizzes

CHAPTER SUMMARY by Learning Objectives

LO13.1 EXPLAIN the importance of human resource management and the Human Resource Management process.

HRM is important for three reasons. First, it can be a significant source of competitive advantage. Second, it's an important part of organizational strategies. Finally, the way organizations treat their people has been found to significantly impact organizational performance. To meet these objectives, managers rely on eight activities (Exhibit 13-2) that comprise the HRM process.

LO13.2 DESCRIBE the external influences that affect the human resource management process.

The external factors that most directly affect the HRM process are the economy, labor unions, legal environment, and demographic trends. The economy affects how employees view their work and has implications for how an organization manages its human resources. A labor union is an organization that represents workers and seeks to protect their interests through collective bargaining. In unionized organizations, HRM practices are dictated by collective bargaining agreements. HRM practices are governed by a country's laws and not following those laws can be costly. Demographic trends such as changes in the racial and ethnic composition of the workforce, retiring Baby Boomers, and an expanding cohort of Gen Y workers will also have implications for HRM practices.

LO13.3 DISCUSS the tasks associated with identifying and selecting competent employees.

Human resource planning is the process by which managers ensure they have the right number and kinds of capable people in the right places at the right times. A job analysis is part of the assessment process that defines a job and the behaviors necessary to perform it. A job description is a written statement describing a job and typically includes job content, environment, and conditions of employment. A job specification is a written statement that specifies the minimum qualifications a person must possess to successfully perform a given job.

Employers must cautiously screen potential job applicants. Recruitment is the process of locating, identifying, and attracting capable applicants. Decruitment is an approach to controlling the labor supply when there is a surplus.

Selection involves predicting which applicants will be successful if hired. A valid selection device is characterized by a proven relationship between the selection device and some relevant criterion. A reliable selection device indicates that it measures the same thing consistently. The different selection devices include application forms, written and performance-simulation tests, interviews, background investigations, and in some cases physical exams.

A realistic job preview is important because it gives an applicant more realistic expectations about the job, which in turn should increase employee job satisfaction and reduce turnover.

LO13.4 EXPLAIN how companies provide employees with skills and knowledge.

Orientation is important because it results in an outsider-insider transition that makes the new employee feel comfortable and fairly well adjusted, lowers the likelihood of poor work performance, and reduces the probability of an early surprise resignation.

The most popular types of training include profession/industry-specific training, management/supervisory skills, mandatory/compliance information, and customer service training. This training can be provided using traditional training methods (on the job, job rotation, mentoring and coaching, experiential exercises, workbooks/manuals, and classroom lectures) or by technology-based methods (CD/DVD/videotapes/audiotapes, videoconferencing or teleconferencing, or e-learning).

LO13.5 DESCRIBE strategies for retaining competent, high-performing employees.

A performance management system establishes performance standards used to evaluate employee performance. The different performance appraisal methods are written essays, critical incidents, graphic rating scales, BARS, multiperson comparisons, MBO, and 360-degree appraisals.

The factors that influence employee compensation and benefits include the employee's tenure and performance, kind of job performed, kind of business/industry, unionization, whether it is labor or capital intensive, management philosophy, geographical location, company profitability, and size of company.

Skill-based pay systems reward employees for the job skills and competencies they can demonstrate. In a variable pay system, an employee's compensation is contingent on performance.

LO13.6 DISCUSS contemporary issues in managing human resources.

Managers can manage downsizing by communicating openly and honestly, following appropriate laws regarding severance pay or benefits, providing support/counseling for surviving employees, reassigning roles according to individuals' talents and backgrounds, focusing on boosting morale, and having a plan for empty office spaces.

Sexual harassment is any unwanted action or activity of a sexual nature that explicitly or implicitly affects an individual's employment, performance, or work environment. Managers need to be aware of what constitutes an offensive or hostile work environment, educate employees on sexual harassment, and ensure that no retaliatory actions are taken against any person who files harassment charges.

Organizations are controlling HR costs by controlling employee health care costs through employee health initiatives (encouraging healthy behavior and penalizing unhealthy behaviors) and controlling employee pension plans by eliminating or severely limiting them.

Pearson **MyLab** Management

Go to **mymanagementlab.com** to complete the problems marked with this icon ✪.

✪ REVIEW AND DISCUSSION QUESTIONS

13-1. Can labor unions help prevent employees from being unfairly terminated?

13-2. In Malaysia, certain job sectors, like IT and customer services, are increasingly dependent on specialist human resource providers as a common source of trained manpower. Companies like ManpowerGroup provide professional HRM services to clients. Can such companies make HR departments redundant? Discuss.

13-3. Organizations use many methods to assess potential new employees. Are these methods fair?

13-4. With organizational cost-cutting the world over, orientation for new staff has been cut short to just several days. How will this affect retention?

13-5. Describe the two main types of training. How do you think these tend to be delivered?

13-6. Distinguish between MBO and BARS as appraisal methods.

13-7. How do you think downsizing should be handled?

13-8. What do you understand by the term family-friendly benefits? Give some examples of these benefits in action.

Pearson **MyLab** Management

If your professor has assigned these, go to **mymanagementlab.com** for the following Assisted-graded writing questions:

13-9. How does HRM affect all managers?

13-10. Explain how demography can not only determine the HRM process, both in recruitment and at latter stages.

PREPARING FOR: My Career

✪ PERSONAL INVENTORY ASSESSMENTS

Work Performance Assessment

As this chapter indicated, performance assessment is an important HR function. Use this PIA to assess work performance.

ETHICS DILEMMA

Though it might be a challenge, employing individuals with autism could pay off. Britain's National Autistic Society reported only 15 percent of adults with autism are in full-time employment, while 9 percent work part-time; this despite 79 percent actually wanting to work. It's not that people with autism don't have the necessary skills or drive but that employers don't understand the empirical benefits of employing them—benefits that go beyond corporate social responsibility or charity. While the attitude of employers toward the young workforce with autism is changing, there is still a considerable amount of ground to be covered. The British government set up a working group that brought together employees and charities. Collectively they were asked to look at the best ways to harness this pool of untapped talent. One of the things that they discovered was a need for an autism-friendly environment. A few minor adjustments, such as ensuring that the workplace is not too bright or too loud, could make a quite a difference.[123]

13-11. Research and describe the steps being made in your country with regard to autistic employees or those with other challenges.

13-12. Should ethical and diverse recruitment be considered when profit is an organization's primary goal?

SKILLS EXERCISE Developing Your Interviewing Skills

About the Skill

One human resource practice that most managers must master is interviewing candidates in the hiring process. As a manager, you need to develop your interviewing skills. The following discussion highlights the key behaviors associated with this skill.

Steps in Practicing the Skill

- ***Review the job description and job specification.*** Reviewing pertinent information about the job provides valuable information about how to assess the candidate. Furthermore, relevant job requirements help to eliminate interview bias.
- ***Prepare a structured set of questions to ask all applicants for the job.*** By having a set of prepared questions, you ensure that the information you wish to elicit is attainable. Furthermore, if you ask all applicants similar questions, you're better able to compare their answers against a common base.
- ***Before meeting an applicant, review his or her application form and résumé.*** Doing so helps you to create a complete picture of the applicant in terms of what is represented on the résumé or application and what the job requires. You will also begin to identify areas to explore in the interview. That is, areas not clearly defined on the résumé or application but essential for the job will become a focal point of your discussion with the applicant.
- ***Open the interview by putting the applicant at ease and by providing a brief preview of the topics to be discussed.*** Interviews are stressful for job applicants. By opening with small talk (e.g., the weather), you give the person time to adjust to the interview setting. By providing a preview of topics to come, you're giving the applicant an agenda that helps the individual begin framing what he or she will say in response to your questions.
- ***Ask your questions and listen carefully to the applicant's answers.*** Select follow-up questions that naturally flow from the answers given. Focus on the responses as they relate to information you need to ensure that the applicant meets your job requirements. Any uncertainty you may still have requires a follow-up question to probe further for the information.
- ***Close the interview by telling the applicant what's going to happen next.*** Applicants are anxious about the status of your hiring decision. Be honest with the applicant regarding others who will be interviewed and the remaining steps in the hiring process. If you plan to make a decision in two weeks or so, let the individual know what you intend to do. In addition, tell the applicant how you will let him or her know about your decision.
- ***Write your evaluation of the applicant while the interview is still fresh in your mind.*** Don't wait until the end of your day, after interviewing several applicants, to write your analysis of each one. Memory can fail you. The sooner you complete your write-up after an interview, the better chance you have of accurately recording what occurred in the interview.

Practicing the Skill

The most challenging part of interviewing job applicants is preparing for the interview. Practice interview preparation by writing an interview guide that includes a structured set of questions. Look up a sample job description online. Create a list of skills and qualifications that you need to assess in the interview for this job. Next, write a list of questions to assess those qualifications. Make sure you have opening questions to put the applicant at ease, a body of questions that target the skills and qualifications you noted, and closing questions.

WORKING TOGETHER **Team Exercise**

New hire orientation is an important human resource management practice. Take a few minutes and consider the orientation that you received at your last job. Write down some notes about the orientation process. Was the orientation formal or informal? Did you learn about the organization or just your work unit? What was helpful to you? What else would have been helpful to learn or do during the orientation? If you have not held a job, think about a job you might be qualified to apply for now. Make some notes about what you think you would need to learn during the orientation for that job. Get together in groups of three or four students and share your orientation experiences. Next, create a list of your recommended orientation program "dos and don'ts" for companies. Be prepared to share your list with the class.

MY TURN TO BE A MANAGER

- Studies show that women's salaries still lag behind men's, and even with equal opportunity laws and regulations, women are paid about 82 percent of what men are paid.[124] Do some research on designing a compensation system that would address this issue. Write up your findings in a bulleted list format.
- The American Federation of Labor and Congress of Industrial Organizations is a national trade union center and the largest federation of unions in the United States. Visit the organization's website at www.aflcio.org. Explore the website and identify issues that are of current concern for today's labor unions.
- Go to the Society for Human Resource Management website (www.shrm.org) and look for the HR News. Pick one of the news stories to read. (Note: Some of these may be available only to SHRM members, but others should be generally available.) Write a summary of the information. At the end of your summary, discuss the implications of the topic for managers.
- Find *Fortune*'s "Best Companies to Work For" list online. Read the profiles of the top companies. Identify the types of benefits and other company characteristics that are common among these companies. Collect this information in a formal report you can present to your class.
- Visit an online job board and learn about how a company posts a job. Pick any online job board such as www.monster.com, www.careerboard.com, or a local job board in your area. Click on "Employers" tab and read about the process to post a job.
- Work on your résumé. If you don't have one, research what a good résumé should include. If you have one already, make sure it provides specific information that explicitly describes your work skills and experience rather than meaningless phrases such as "results-oriented."
- Set up a profile on LinkedIn. Make sure you use a professional photo and provide a complete profile. Click on the "Business Services" link to learn how companies can use LinkedIn in the hiring process.
- Search online for a sample sexual harassment training program. How could an organization use this training program to help prevent harassment in the workplace?

CASE APPLICATION 1 Maersk and HR Management Challenges in China

Although one of the world's biggest shipping line leaders, Danish company Maersk is increasingly worried about the future of the Chinese market. In a recent interview with the *Wall Street Journal,* Søren Skou, the head of the company's container-shipping division in mainland China, expressed his concern. One issue mentioned is the fact that some of the traditional advantages China was representing, its abundant pool of cheap labor, are rapidly shrinking, and personnel costs are going up. According to Chinese government data, wage income for urban households rose 13 percent year to year in the first half, and average monthly income for migrant workers rose 14.9 percent. This comes on top of other common problems related to human resource management in China, which all Western companies have experienced in one way or another. These issues have been known for a long time, at least since the beginning of Deng's Open Door Policy, which in 1979 opened China to foreign direct investment. One problem is the availability of a qualified manager to lead operations. China has experienced such a high-speed growth that the pool of local talents has dried up quite quickly, and importing managers from overseas is not as simple as it may appear.

Expat managers, the usual choice for the top management and often for the middle management too, present other challenges, including cultural fluency and language skills in the complicated Chinese business environment. Even organizing a banquet can be a daunting experience for someone not acquainted with the local culture. In addition, expats who have a solid experience of the country and speak Mandarin are in such high demand that they are normally very expensive. An alternative is to hire local talents and to train them to function in Western companies. While this seems a reasonable choice, it may be very expensive and the process painfully slow, especially if the hiring is done privately bypassing the expensive, government-owned labor center, FESCO. Furthermore, once the manager is hired, a series of efforts needs to be made to retain the employee.

One of the solutions Maersk and other international corporations have found is to move part of their business further west, in the center of mainland China, where labor costs are lower than on the coast, and to hire better educated, English-speaking younger staff. For instance, the Maersk branch in Chengdu, Sichuan Province, employs more than 2,000 people, with the average age of its employees no higher than 25.[125]

DISCUSSION QUESTIONS

13-13. Why does human resource management represent one of the major challenges faced by foreign companies entering the Chinese market?

13-14. What are the main issues expat managers generally face?

13-15. Why don't foreign companies simply hire local staff instead of reaching out for foreign managers?

13-16. What advice would you give companies such as Maersk on their human resource management policies?

CASE APPLICATION 2 Measuring Output, Not Hours Worked

Despite being a world-renowned business, BAE Systems Naval Ships has hardly changed its working arrangement at its Glasgow sites on the River Clyde, explains Chris Westcott, who is the Head of Employee Relations. Employees are expected to work fixed hours, and paid overtime for extra hours worked. However, when faced with real affordability challenges, BAE Systems did something fundamentally different that tapped into knowledge, expertise, and discretionary effort of the work force. Four and a half years on from that realization—and after hours of hard work from the HR team, the entire professional and executive staff and almost half the employees in the manufacturing division moved to "smart working." In essence, what mattered was output, not attendance with the staff being empowered and trusted to determine their own working schedules, and take time off if their work is completed for the week.

Employees, irrespective of their status, could work flexibly, deciding when they start and finish work. The concept seemed tough to get to grips with initially, but it really boiled down to trust. For BAE Systems, this marked the advent of schedule based working (SBW). A sizeable percentage of production employees in Glasgow could take time off if they complete their weekly targets. In essence, Friday is free time if all the work for the week is completed by Thursday. Westcott, however, emphasized that targets and quality standards must be achieved. But workers were willing to put in all their effort to get it as they valued the new arrangement and the challenge.

The biggest challenge of the whole project was convincing the work force and the influential trade unions. Therefore, this minimized the risk of the project for all involved, particularly the two trade unions, NMB and Unite, which were of the view that something had to be done to secure the long-term success of the business. The organization has been careful to maintain open lines of communication throughout, with teams taken offsite for a day to explore the SBW concept prior to its launch in each area.

Introducing SBW has been a significant achievement for BAE Systems. According to Westcott when the pilot was set up and they realized they had achieved target on Thursday afternoon and could go home, it was a revolutionary vision that has come to stay. And soon after, employees came up with ideas for improvement, such as rotating staff that had to stay late to finish a job—as well as suggesting process improvements, and requesting new tools and training to help them stay on schedule. While the program has so far taken several years, and significant investment, there has been a fundamental cultural change—attracting accountability for output, ownership of work and trust, and discretionary effort is on the rise.

For BAE Systems, the project is viewed as the single best thing to have ever been done. It has not only reshaped the role of HR in the business, but has allowed an understanding of the business that HR would not have achieved if it had focused only on the traditional HR issues.[126]

DISCUSSION QUESTIONS

13-17. Why do you think an organization like BAE would want to adopt schedule-based work (SBW) pattern?

13-18. What possible difficulties can you identify as a result of the proposed changes?

13-19. Analyze the role of HR in embedding the new vision into the culture of the organization.

ENDNOTES

1. J. Smith, "The 7 Worst Body Language Mistakes Job Seekers Make," www.businessinsider.com, April 28, 2014.
2. P. Cappelli, "HR for Neophytes," *Harvard Business Review,* October 2013, pp. 25–27.
3. A. Carmeli and J. Shaubroeck, "How Leveraging Human Resource Capital with Its Competitive Distinctiveness Enhances the Performance of Commercial and Public Organizations," *Human Resource Management,* Winter 2005, pp. 391–412; L. Bassi and D. McMurrer, "How's Your Return on People?" *Harvard Business Review,* March 2004, p. 18; C. J. Collins and K. D. Clark, "Strategic Human Resource Practices, Top Management Team Social Networks, and Firm Performance: The Role of Human Resource Practices in Creating Organizational Competitive Advantage," *Academy of Management Journal,* December 2003, pp. 740–751; J. Pfeffer, *The Human Equation* (Boston: Harvard Business School Press, 1998); J. Pfeffer, *Competitive Advantage Through People* (Boston: Harvard Business School Press, 1994); A. A. Lado and M. C. Wilson, "Human Resource Systems and Sustained Competitive Advantage," *Academy of Management Review,* October 1994, pp. 699–727; and P. M. Wright and G. C. McMahan, "Theoretical Perspectives for Strategic Human Resource Management," *Journal of Management*, vol. 18, no. 1, 1992, pp. 295–320.
4. "Maximizing the Return on Your Human Capital Investment: The 2005 Watson Wyatt Human Capital Index® Report," "WorkAsia 2004/2005: A Study of Employee Attitudes in Asia," and "European Human Capital Index 2002," Watson Wyatt Worldwide (Washington, DC).
5. "Leading Through Connections: Highlights of the Global Chief Executive Officer Study," ibm.com/ceostudy 2012, 2012.
6. Jerene Ang, "Suite Talk: Michelle Ho, managing director of UPS Singapore," *Human Resources Online,* November 14, 2016, http://www.humanresourcesonline.net/suite-talk-michelle-ho-managing-director-ups-singapore/ (accessed January 11, 2017); Bill Goodwin, "Dutch Bank ING to Spend Millions 'Disrupting' Its Own Business," *Computer Weekly,* November 17, 2016, http://www.computerweekly.com/news/450403105/Dutch-bank-ING-to-spend-millions-disrupting-its-own-business (accessed January 11, 2017).
7. See, for example, C. H. Chuang and H. Liao, "Strategic Human Resource Management in Service Context: Taking Care of Business by Taking Care of Employees and Customers," *Personnel Psychology,* Spring 2010, pp. 153–196; M. Subramony, "A Meta-Analytic Investigation of the Relationship Between HRM Bundles and Firm Performance," *Human Resource Management,* September–October 2009, pp. 745–768; M. M. Butts et al., "Individual Reactions to High Involvement Work Practices: Investigating the Role of Empowerment and Perceived Organizational Support," *Journal of Occupational Health Psychology,* April 2009, pp. 122–136; L. Sun, S. Aryee, and K. S. Law, "High-Performance Human Resource Practices, Citizenship Behavior, and Organizational Performance: A Relational Perspective," *Academy of Management Journal,* June 2007, pp. 558–577; A. Carmeli and J. Shaubroeck, "How Leveraging Human Resource Capital with Its Competitive Distinctiveness Enhances the Performance of Commercial and Public Organizations," 2005; Y. Y. Kor and H. Leblebici, "How Do Interdependencies Among Human-Capital Deployment, Development, and Diversification Strategies Affect Firms' Financial Performance?," *Strategic Management Journal,* October 2005, pp. 967–985; D. E. Bowen and C. Ostroff, "Understanding HRM–Firm Performance Linkages: The Role of the 'Strength' of the HRM System," *Academy of Management Review,* April 2004, pp. 203–221; A. S. Tsui, J. L. Pearce, L. W. Porter, and A. M. Tripoli, "Alternative Approaches to the Employee-Organization Relationship: Does Investment in Employees Pay Off?," *Academy of Management Journal*, October 1997, pp. 1089–1121; M. A. Huselid, S. E. Jackson, and R. S. Schuler, "Technical and Strategic Human Resource Management Effectiveness as Determinants of Firm Performance," *Academy of Management Journal*, January 1997, pp. 171–188; J. T. Delaney and M. A. Huselid, "The Impact of Human Resource Management Practices on Perceptions of Organizational Performance," *Academy of Management Journal*, August 1996, pp. 949–969; B. Becker and B. Gerhart, "The Impact of Human Resource Management on Organizational Performance: Progress and Prospects," *Academy of Management Journal*, August 1996, pp. 779–801; M. J. Koch and R. G. McGrath, "Improving Labor Productivity: Human Resource Management Policies Do Matter," *Strategic Management Journal*, May 1996, pp. 335–354; and M. A. Huselid, "The Impact of Human Resource Management Practices on Turnover, Productivity, and Corporate Financial Performance," *Academy of Management Journal*, June 1995, pp. 635–672.
8. "Human Capital a Key to Higher Market Value," *Business Finance*, December 1999, p. 15.
9. M. Boyle, "Happy People, Happy Returns," *Fortune,* January 11, 2006, p. 100.
10. P. C. Patel, J. G. Messersmith, and D. P. Lepak, "Walking the Tightrope: An Assessment of the Relationship Between High-Performance Work Systems and Organizational Ambidexterity," *Academy of Management Journal,* October 2013, pp. 1420–1442.
11. M. Luo, "$13 an Hour? 500 Sign Up, 1 Wins a Job," *New York Times* online, www.nytimes.com, October 22, 2009.
12. J. Clenfield, "A Tear in Japan's Safety Net," *Bloomberg BusinessWeek,* April 12, 2010, pp. 60–61.
13. H. Hoenig and M. Obe, "Why Japan's Economy is Laboring," *The Wall Street Journal* online, www.wsj.com, April 8, 2016.
14. Eurostat "Statistics Explained: Unemployment Statistics," http://ec.europa.eu/eurostat/statistics-explained/, April 16, 2016; "Country Comparison: Unemployment Rate," *The CIA World Factbook,* www.cia.gov/library/publications/the-world-factbook/rankorder/2129rank.html, accessed April 16, 2016.
15. C. H. Wong, "China May Rein in Wage Increases to Boost Economy," *The Wall Street Journal* online, www.wsj.com, March 10, 2016.
16. U.S. Bureau of Labor Statistics, "The Employment Situation—March 2016," USDL-16-0662, April 1, 2016.

17. P. Davidson, "Employers Add Better-Than-Expected 242,000 Jobs in February," *USA Today* online, www.usatoday.com, March 4, 2016.
18. U.S. Bureau of Labor Statistics, "Employer Costs for Employee Compensation—December 2015," USDL-16-0463," March 10, 2016.
19. F. Hansen, "Jobless Recovery Is Leaving a Trail of Recession-Weary Employees in Its Wake," *Compensation & Benefits Review,* May/June 2010, pp. 135–136; J. Hollon, "Worker 'Deal' Is Off," *Workforce Management,* April 2010, p. 42; and "The New Employment Deal: How Far, How Fast, and How Enduring? The 2010 Global Workforce Study," *Towers Watson*, www.towerswatson.com, April 2010.
20. D. Goldman and A. Smith, "36,000 Verizon Workers Have Walked Off the Job Wednesday After Failing to Reach a New Labor Agreement," *CNBC*, www.money.cnn.com, April 13, 2016.
21. C. Morrison, "Hundreds of Flights Cancelled Due to Strikes in France," *City A.M.* online, www.cityam.com, March 20, 2016.
22. R. Wall and G. Steinhauser, "Brussels Airport Closed to Flights in Labor Dispute," *The Wall Street Journal* online, www.wsj.com, April 12, 2016.
23. A. Smith, "Union Membership Inches Up," www.shrm.org, January 27, 2012.
24. "Trade Union Density," OECD. Stat Extracts, http://stats.oecd.org/Index.aspx?DataSetCode=UN_DEN, May 9, 2014.
25. Mark Leftly, "Nearly 700 Firms Fined Total of £1.4m For Not Paying Minimum Wage," *The Guardian (UK),* January 6, 2017, https://www.theguardian.com/society/2017/jan/06/firms-fined-minimum-wage-football-clubs-restaurants (accessed January 11, 2017); Tara Evans, "Swindon Town Football Club Fined for Failing to Give Players Pensions," *The Telegraph (UK),* April 21, 2016, http://www.telegraph.co.uk/pensions-retirement/news/football-club-fined-for-failing-to-give-players-pensions/ (accessed January 11, 2017).
26. E. Arvedlund, "When Workers Complain: Discrimination Lawsuits Accuse Vanguard of Targeting Workers," *The Inquirer Daily News* online, www.philly.com, January 18, 2016; S. Armour, "Lawsuits Pin Target on Managers," *USA Today* online, www.usatoday.com, October 1, 2002.
27. R. Barnes, "Affordable Care Act Survives Supreme Court Challenge," *The Washington Post* online, www.washingtonpost.com, June 25, 2015; G. B. Kushner, "Special Report: What HR Professionals Should Do Now," www.shrm.org, June 28, 2012; and S. G. Stolberg and R. Pear, "Obama Signs Health Care Overhaul Bill, with a Flourish," *New York Times* online, March 23, 2010.
28. Chris Cook, "Global Employers: Can an Employer Choose Which Country's Laws Apply to Its Employment Contracts?" *Personnel Today,* December 4, 2014, http://www.personneltoday.com/hr/global-employers-can-employer-choose-countrys-laws-apply-employment-contracts/ (accessed January 11, 2017); Carol Matlack, "Ryanair Clashes With Denmark Over Labor Laws," *Bloomberg*, June 22, 2015, https://www.bloomberg.com (accessed January 11, 2017); Marcus Hoy, "Sweden: New Law Strengthens Hand of Whistleblowers," *Bloomberg BNA,* July 22, 2016, https://www.bna.com/sweden-new-law-n73014445180?programid=2054&artikel=6507934 (accessed January 11, 2017); Maddy Savage, "The Truth about Sweden's Short Working Hours," BBC News, November 2, 2015, http://www.bbc.com (accessed January 11, 2017); "Swedish Fathers to Get Third Month of Paid Paternity Leave," *The Guardian (UK),* May 28, 2015, https://www.theguardian.com; and Felicity Alexander, "Singapore Employment Law: What Changes Are Coming in 2017?" *Personnel Today* (accessed January 11, 2017).
29. Leader Making a Difference box based on T. L. Friedman, "How to Get a Job at Google, Part 2," *New York Times* online, April 19, 2014; L. Bock, "Google's Scientific Approach to Work-Life Balance (and Much More)," blogs.hbr.org, March 27, 2014; T. L. Friedman, "How to Get a Job at Google," *New York Times* online, February 22, 2014; M. Moskowitz, R. Levering, C. Bessette, C. Dunn, C. Fairchild, and B. Southward, "The 100 Best Companies to Work For," *Fortune,* February 3, 2014, pp. 108+; M. Niesen, "The 50 Companies Young People Want to Work For the Most," www.businessinsider.com, September 20, 2013; M. Niesen, "Google HR Boss Explains Why GPA and Most Interviews Are Useless," www.businessinsider.com, June 19, 2013; and L. Bock, "Passion, Not Perks," www.thinkwithgoogle.com/articles/, September 2011.
30. L. Bock, "Google's Scientific Approach to Work-Life Balance (and Much More)."
31. C. H. Loch, F. J. Sting, N. Bauer, and J. Mauermann, "How BMW Is Defusing the Demographic Time Bomb," *Harvard Business Review,* March 2010, pp. 99–102.
32. U.S. Bureau of Labor Statistics, "Labor Force Projects to 2024: The Labor Force Is Growing, but Slowly," *Monthly Labor Review*, www.bls.gov, December 2015.
33. C. Rampell, "As Layoffs Surge, Women May Pass Men in Job Force," *New York Times* online, February 6, 2009.
34. U.S. Bureau of Labor Statistics, "Labor Force Projects to 2024: The Labor Force Is Growing, but Slowly,"
35. B. Tulgan, "Generation Y Defined: The New Young Workforce," *HR Tools* online, www.hrtools.com/insights/bruce_tulgan, February 25, 2009.
36. S. F. Gale, "From Texas to Timbuktu—How Fluor Tracks Talent on a Global Scale," *Workforce Management* online, www.workforce.com, March 7, 2012.
37. M. A. Costonis and R. Salkowitz, "The Tough Match of Young Workers and Insurance," *New York Times* online, www.nytimes.com, June 11, 2010.
38. E. Seubert, "What Are Your Organization's Critical Positions," *Workforce Management* online, www.workforce.com, December 2009; F. Hansen, "Strategic Workforce Planning in an Uncertain World," *Workforce Management* online, www.workforce.com, July 2009; and J. Sullivan, "Workforce Planning: Why to Start Now," *Workforce,* September 2002, pp. 46–50.
39. Aditi Sharma Kalra, "Q&A with Geraldine Fraser, HR Director, FrieslandCampina Asia," *Human Resources Online,* January 4, 2017, http://www.humanresourcesonline.net/features/qa-geraldine-fraser-hr-director-frieslandcampina-asia/ (accessed January 12, 2017).
40. Laura Kimpton, "Personnel Today Awards 2016," *Personnel Today,* November 22, 2016, http://www.personneltoday.com/hr/personnel-today-awards-2016-excellence-learning-development/ (accessed January 12, 2017).
41. Y. Gonan, "Office in Charge of Fixing Schools 'Bent Rules' to Hire 'Unqualified' Pals," *New York Post*, www.nypost.com, February 11, 2016.

42. J. McGregor, "Background Checks That Never End," *BusinessWeek*, March 20, 2006, p. 40.
43. E. Huet, "Uber's Background Checks Failed to Catch a Murderer and Other Felons, Prosecutors Say," *Forbes* online, www.forbes.com, August 19, 2015.
44. J. Swartz, "Tech Firms Go On A Hiring Binge Again," *USA Today,* April 21, 2011, pp. 1B+; B. Einhorn and K. Gokhale, "Bangalore's Paying Again to Keep the Talent," *Bloomberg BusinessWeek,* May 24–30, 2010, pp. 14–16; D. A. Thoppil, "Pay War Breaks Out as India's Tech Firms Vie for Talent," *Wall Street Journal,* April 27, 2010, p. B8; and C. Tuna, J. E. Vascellaro, and P-W. Tam, "Tech Sector in Hiring Drive," *Wall Street Journal,* April 16, 2010, pp. A1+.
45. S. F. Gale, "Companies Struggle to Recruit Internationally," www.workforce.com, March 4, 2013.
46. A. S. Bargerstock and G. Swanson, "Four Ways to Build Cooperative Recruitment Alliances," *HRMagazine*, March 1991, p. 49; and T. J. Bergmann and M. S. Taylor, "College Recruitment: What Attracts Students to Organizations?" *Personnel*, May–June 1984, pp. 34–46.
47. J. R. Gordon, *Human Resource Management: A Practical Approach* (Boston: Allyn and Bacon, 1986), p. 170.
48. C. Reynolds, "McDonald's Hiring Day Draws Crowds, High Hopes," AP Business Writer, *Springfield, Missouri News-Leader,* April 20, 2011, p. 6A; and A. Gasparro, "Fast-Food Chain Aims to Alter 'McJob' Image," *Wall Street Journal,* April 5, 2011, p. B9.
49. Y. Bahgat, "The Top 10 Most Innovative Recruitment Campaigns," Zoomforth Blog, www.blog.zoomforth.com, May 18, 2015.
50. K. Plourd, "Lights, Camera, Audits!" *CFO,* November 2007, p. 18.
51. S. Elliott, "Army Seeks Recruits in Social Media," *New York Times* online, May 24, 2011.
52. K. Morrison, "Survey: 92% of Recruiters Use Social Media to Find High-Quality Candidates," *Adweek* online, www.adweek.com, September 22, 2015.
53. S. Burton and D. Warner, "The Future of Hiring—Top 5 Sources for Recruitment Today," *Workforce Vendor Directory 2002,* p. 75.
54. See, for example, S. V. Burks, B. Cowgill, M. Hoffman, and M. Housman, "The Value of Hiring Through Employee Referrals," *The Review of Economic Studies,* vol. 83, no. 2, 2016, pp. 514–546; L. G. Klaff, "New Internal Hiring Systems Reduce Cost and Boost Morale," *Workforce Management,* March 2004, pp. 76–79; M. N. Martinez, "The Headhunter Within," *HR Magazine,* August 2001, pp. 48–55; R. W. Griffeth, P. W. Hom, L. S. Fink, and D. J. Cohen, "Comparative Tests of Multivariate Models of Recruiting Sources Effects," *Journal of Management*, vol. 23, no. 1, 1997, pp. 19–36; and J. P. Kirnan, J. E. Farley, and K. F. Geisinger, "The Relationship Between Recruiting Source, Applicant Quality, and Hire Performance: An Analysis by Sex, Ethnicity, and Age," *Personnel Psychology*, Summer 1989, pp. 293–308.
55. A. Fisher, "For Happier Customers, Call HR," *Fortune,* November 28, 2005, p. 272.
56. R. Maurer, "Morale, Productivity Suffer From Bad Hires," *Society for Human Resource Management* online, www.shrm.org, February 2, 2015.
57. B. Roberts, "Most Likely to Succeed," *HR Magazine,* April 2014, pp. 69–71.
58. C. Zillman, "Target to Pay $2.8 Million for Hiring Discrimination Charges," *Fortune* online, www.fortune.com, August 24, 2015.
59. A. Douzet, "Quality of Fill an Emerging Recruitment Metric," *Workforce Management* online, www.workforce.com, June 24, 2010; and "Quality of Hire Metrics Help Staffing Unit Show Its Contribution to Bottom Line," *Society for Human Resource Management* online, https://www.shrm.org, January 25, 2009.
60. A. Shadday, "Assessments 101: An Introduction to Candidate Testing," *Workforce Management* online, www.workforce.com, January 2010; A. M. Ryan and R. E. Ployhart, "Applicants' Perceptions of Selection Procedures and Decisions: A Critical Review and Agenda for the Future," *Journal of Management*, vol. 26, no. 3, 2000, pp. 565–606; C. Fernandez-Araoz, "Hiring Without Firing," *Harvard Business Review*, July–August 1999, pp. 108–120; A. K. Korman, "The Prediction of Managerial Performance: A Review," *Personnel Psychology*, Summer 1986, pp. 295–322; G. C. Thornton, *Assessment Centers in Human Resource Management* (Reading, MA: Addison-Wesley, 1992); I. T. Robertson and R. S. Kandola, "Work Sample Tests: Validity, Adverse Impact, and Applicant Reaction," *Journal of Occupational Psychology*, vol. 55, no. 3, 1982, pp. 171–183; E. E. Ghiselli, "The Validity of Aptitude Tests in Personnel Selection," *Personnel Psychology*, Winter 1973, p. 475; G. Grimsley and H. F. Jarrett, "The Relation of Managerial Achievement to Test Measures Obtained in the Employment Situation: Methodology and Results," *Personnel Psychology*, Spring 1973, pp. 31–48; J. J. Asher, "The Biographical Item: Can It Be Improved?" *Personnel Psychology*, Summer 1972, p. 266; and G. W. England, *Development and Use of Weighted Application Blanks*, rev. ed. (Minneapolis: Industrial Relations Center, University of Minnesota, 1971).
61. M. A. Tucker, "Show and Tell," *HR Magazine,* January 2012, pp. 51–53.
62. See, for example, P. Sweeney, "Sometimes, the Boss Is the One Lying in the Job Interview," qz.com, March 10, 2014; G. Kranz, "New Employees: 'We Were Jobbed About This Job,'" www.workforce.com, February 1, 2013; Y. Ganzach, A. Pazy, Y. Ohayun, and E. Brainin, "Social Exchange and Organizational Commitment: Decision-Making Training for Job Choice as an Alternative to the Realistic Job Preview," *Personnel Psychology,* Autumn 2002, pp. 613–637; B. M. Meglino, E. C. Ravlin, and A. S. DeNisi, "A Meta-Analytic Examination of Realistic Job Preview Effectiveness: A Test of Three Counterintuitive Propositions," *Human Resource Management Review,* vol. 10, no. 4, 2000, pp. 407–434; J. A. Breaugh and M. Starke, "Research on Employee Recruitment: So Many Studies, So Many Remaining Questions," *Journal of Management*, vol. 26, no. 3, 2000, pp. 405–434; and S. L. Premack and J. P. Wanous, "A Meta-Analysis of Realistic Job Preview Experiments," *Journal of Applied Psychology*, November 1985, pp. 706–720.
63. G. Kranz, "Tourism Training Takes Flight in Miami," *Workforce Management* online, www.workforce.com, May 2010.

64. M. Jokisaari and J-E. Nurmi, "Change in Newcomers' Supervisor Support and Socialization Outcomes After Organizational Entry," *Academy of Management Journal,* June 2009, pp. 527–544; D. G. Allen, "Do Organizational Socialization Tactics Influence Newcomer Embeddedness and Turnover?" *Journal of Management,* April 2006, pp. 237–256; C. L. Cooper, "The Changing Psychological Contract at Work: Revisiting the Job Demands-Control Model," *Occupational and Environmental Medicine,* June 2002, p. 355; D. M. Rousseau and S. A. Tijoriwala, "Assessing Psychological Contracts: Issues, Alternatives and Measures," *Journal of Organizational Behavior,* vol. 19, 1998, pp. 679–695; S. L. Robinson, M. S. Kraatz, and D. M. Rousseau, "Changing Obligations and the Psychological Contract: A Longitudinal Study," *Academy of Management Journal,* February 1994, pp. 137–152.
65. S. Patel, "Building Loyalty from the Beginning," *The Wall Street Journal* online, www.wsj.com, December 24, 2014.
66. See, for instance, E. G. Tripp, "Aging Aircraft and Coming Regulations: Political and Media Pressures Have Encouraged the FAA to Expand Its Pursuit of Real and Perceived Problems of Older Aircraft and Their Systems. Operators Will Pay," *Business and Commercial Aviation,* March 2001, pp. 68–75.
67. A. Pasztor, "New United Air Pilot Training Could Raise Safety Bar for Industry," *The Wall Street Journal* online, www.wsj.com, January 31, 2016.
68. "A&S Interview: Sully's Tale," *Air & Space Magazine*, www.airspacemag.com, February 18, 2009; A. Altman, "Chesley B. Sullenberger III," *Time*, www.time.com, January 16, 2009; and K. Burke, Pete Donohue, and C. Siemaszko, "US Airways Airplane Crashes in Hudson River—Hero Pilot Chesley Sullenberger III Saves All Aboard," *New York Daily News*, www.nydailynews.com, January 16, 2009.
69. T. Raphael, "It's All in the Cards," *Workforce,* September 2002, p. 18.
70. S. Nassauer, "How Waiters Read Your Table," *Wall Street Journal,* February 22, 2012, pp. D1+.
71. "2015 Training Industry Report," *Training,* November/December 2015, pp. 20–33.
72. Ibid.
73. S. Luthra, "Will Doctors Be More Empathetic in the Future? How to Improve Doctors' Bedside Manner," *CNN* online, www.cnn.com, September 18, 2015.
74. D. Heath and C. Heath, "The Power of Razzle-Dazzle," *Fast Company,* December 2009–January 2010, pp. 69–70.
75. J. McGregor, "The Midyear Review's Sudden Impact," *BusinessWeek,* July 6, 2009, pp. 50–52.
76. A. Pace, "The Performance Management Dilemma," *T&D,* July 2011, p. 22.
77. K. Sulkowicz, "Straight Talk at Review Time," *BusinessWeek,* September 10, 2007, p. 16.
78. D. Wilke, "Is the Annual Performance Review Dead?," *Society for Human Resource Management* online, www.shrm.org, August 19, 2015; J. Pfeffer, "Low Grades for Performance Appraisals," *BusinessWeek,* August 3, 2009, p. 68.
79. B. Kropp, "Want to Do Away with Performance Reviews? Think Again," *CEB Blogs*, www.cebglobal.com, August 11, 2015.
80. M. Addady, "Here's Why GE is Replacing Performance Reviews with an App," *Fortune* online, www.fortune.com, August 13, 2015.
81. Ibid.
82. J. D. Glater, "Seasoning Compensation Stew," *New York Times,* March 7, 2001, pp. C1+.
83. M. Korn, "Benefits Matter," *Wall Street Journal,* April 4, 2012, p. B8.
84. This section based on R. I. Henderson, *Compensation Management in a Knowledge-Based World,* 10th ed. (Upper Saddle River, NJ: Prentice Hall, 2006).
85. M. P. Brown, M. C. Sturman, and M. J. Simmering, "Compensation Policy and Organizational Performance: The Efficiency, Operational and Financial Implications of Pay Levels and Pay Structure," *Academy of Management Journal,* December 2003, pp. 752–762; J. D. Shaw, N. P. Gupta, and J. E. Delery, "Pay Dispersion and Workforce Performance: Moderating Effects of Incentives and Interdependence," *Strategic Management Journal,* June 2002, pp. 491–512; E. Montemayor, "Congruence Between Pay Policy and Competitive Strategy in High-Performing Firms," *Journal of Management,* vol. 22, no. 6, 1996, pp. 889–908; and L. R. Gomez-Mejia, "Structure and Process of Diversification, Compensation Strategy, and Firm Performance," *Strategic Management Journal,* no. 13, 1992, pp. 381–397.
86. J. J. Martocchio, *Strategic Compensation: A Human Resource Management Approach*, 9th ed. (Hoboken, New Jersey: Pearson Education, Inc.).
87. J. Berman, "More Companies Help Employees Pay Off Student Loans," *The Wall Street Journal* online, www.wsj.com, March 27, 2016.
88. J. D. Shaw, N. Gupta, A. Mitra, and G. E. Ledford, Jr., "Success and Survival of Skill-Based Pay Plans," *Journal of Management,* February 2005, pp. 28–49; C. Lee, K. S. Law, and P. Bobko, "The Importance of Justice Perceptions on Pay Effectiveness: A Two-Year Study of a Skill-Based Pay Plan," *Journal of Management*, vol. 26, no. 6, 1999, pp. 851–873; G. E. Ledford, "Paying for the Skills, Knowledge and Competencies of Knowledge Workers," *Compensation and Benefits Review*, July–August 1995, pp. 55–62; and E. E. Lawler III, G. E. Ledford, Jr., and L. Chang, "Who Uses Skill-Based Pay and Why," *Compensation and Benefits Review*, March–April 1993, p. 22.
89. G. D. Jenkins, Jr., G. E. Ledford, N. Gupta, and D. H. Doty, *Skill-Based Pay: Practices, Payoffs, Pitfalls, and Prescriptions* (Scottsdale, AZ: American Compensation Association).
90. A. Mitra, N. Gupta, and J. D. Shaw, "A Comparative Examination of Traditional and Skill-Based Pay Plans," *Journal of Managerial Psychology*, vol. 4, 2011, pp. 278–296.
91. B. Murray and B. Gerhart, "An Empirical Analysis of a Skill-Based Pay Program and Plant Performance Outcomes," *Academy of Management Journal*, vol. 41, 1998, pp. 68–78.
92. WorldatWork, "Compensation Programs and Practices," www.worldatwork.org, January 2015.
93. T. J. Erickson, "The Leaders We Need Now," *Harvard Business Review,* May 2010, pp. 63–66.
94. S. Thurm, "Recalculating the Cost of Big Layoffs," *Wall Street Journal,* May 5, 2010, pp. B1+; and J. Pfeffer, "Lay Off the Layoffs," *Newsweek,* February 15, 2010, pp. 32–37.
95. W. F. Cascio, "Use and Management of Downsizing as a Corporate Strategy," *HR Magazine,* June 2010, special

insert; D. K. Datta, J. P. Guthrie, D. Basuil, and A. Pandey, "Causes and Effects of Employee Downsizing: A Review and Synthesis," *Journal of Management,* January 2010, pp. 281–348; B. Conaty, "Cutbacks: Don't Neglect the Survivors," *Bloomberg BusinessWeek,* January 11, 2010, p. 68; and P. Korkki, "Accentuating the Positive After a Layoff," *New York Times* online, www.nytimes.com, August 16, 2009.

96. Soumya Pillai and Sweta Goswami, "At the Workplace, a Woman Is Alone after Filing a Sexual Harassment Complaint," *Hindustan Times,* December 21, 2016, http://www.hindustantimes.com (accessed January 12, 2017).
97. "Japan to Define Workplace LGBT Discrimination as Sexual Harassment," *Japan Times,* June 28, 2016, http://www.japantimes.co.jp (accessed January 12, 2017).
98. Kay Vittee, "Sexual Harassment in the Workplace: Know your rights," *City Press (South Africa),* November 12, 2016, http://city-press.news24.com/Careers/sexual-harassment-in-the-workplace-know-your-rights-20161112 (accessed January 12, 2017).
99. Alice Ross, "Half of Women in UK Have Been Sexually Harassed at Work, Study Finds," *The Guardian (UK),* August 10, 2016, https://www.theguardian.com (accessed January 12, 2017).
100. "A Third of Working Women in Japan Were Sexually Harassed on the Job," *South China Morning Post,* March 1, 2016, http://www.scmp.com/news/asia/east-asia/article/1919494/third-working-women-japan-were-sexually-harassed-job (accessed January 12, 2017).
101. David Lee and Laura Sowden, "Australia: Workplace Update July 2016: Sexual Harassment," *Mondaq,* July 27, 2016, http://www.mondaq.com/australia/x/514026/employment+litigation+tribunals/Workplace+Update+July+2016+Sexual+Harassment (accessed January 12, 2017).
102. Jane Li, "Young Chinese Women Dare to Say No to Workplace Sexual Harassment, Says Expert," *South China Morning Post,* December 14, 2016, http://www.scmp.com (accessed January 12, 2017).
103. Keely Rushmore, "An Employer's Guide to Tackling Bullying and Harassment at Work," *The Guardian (UK),* August 11, 2016, https://www.theguardian.com (accessed January 12, 2017).
104. Rashmi Rajput, "38 per cent Women Say They Faced Sexual Harassment at Workplace: Survey," *The Indian Express,* January 5, 2017, http://indianexpress.com, accessed January 12, 2017.
105. J. Yang and A. Gonzalez, "Top Actions Workers Feel Are Grounds for Termination," *USA Today,* May 7, 2012, p. 1B.
106. Future Vision box based on J. Meister, "Future of Work: Using Gamification for Human Resources," *Forbes* online, www.forbes.com, March 30, 2015; B. Roberts, "Gamification, Win, Lose or Draw for HR?," *HR Magazine* online, www.shrm.org, May 1, 2014; P. Shergill, "Winning the Talent Game: How Gamification Is Impacting Business and HR," *Wired* online, www.wired.com, January, 2014.
107. R. Ceniceros, "Workforce Obesity," *Workforce Management* online, www.workforce.com, October 19, 2011; and J. Walsh, "Special Report: Creating a Culture of Wellness Helps Companies Tighten Their Belt," *Workforce Management* online, www.workforce.com, April 2011.
108. R. E. Silverman, "Employees Get Apple Watch for $25 (But There's a Catch)," *The Wall Street Journal*, www.wsj.com, March 3, 2016.
109. R. Redman, "CVS Plans Incentive-Based Smoking Cessation Program," *Chain Drug Review* online, www.chaindrugreview.com, May 14, 2015.
110. Office of the Actuary, Centers for Medicare & Medicaid Services, "National Health Expenditures and Selected Economic Indicators, Levels and Annual Percent Change: Calendar Years 2006-2022," Centers for Medicare & Medicaid Services, www.cms.gov, accessed April 12, 2016.
111. B. Pyenson and K. Fitch, "Smoking May Be Hazardous to Your Bottom Line," *Workforce Management* online, www.workforce.com, December 2007; and L. Cornwell, The Associated Press, "Companies Tack on Fees on Insurance for Smokers," *Springfield, Missouri News-Leader,* February 17, 2006, p. 5B.
112. B. Y. Lee, "Obesity Is Everyone's Business," *Forbes* online, www.forbes.com, September 1, 2015.
113. "Obesity Weighs Down Production," *Industry Week,* March 2008, pp. 22–23.
114. J. Appleby, "Companies Step Up Wellness Efforts," *USA Today,* August 1, 2005, pp. 1A+.
115. G. Kranz, "Prognosis Positive: Companies Aim to Get Workers Healthy," *Workforce Management* online, www.workforce.com, April 15, 2008.
116. M. Conlin, "Hide the Doritos! Here Comes HR," *BusinessWeek,* April 28, 2008, pp. 94–96.
117. J. Fox, "Good Riddance to Pensions," *CNN Money,* January 12, 2006.
118. M. Adams, "Broken Pension System in Crying Need of a Fix," *USA Today,* November 15, 2005, p. 1B+.
119. J. Appleby, "Traditional Pensions Are Almost Gone. Is Employer-Provided Health Insurance Next?," *USA Today,* November 13, 2007, pp. 1A+; S. Kelly, "FedEx, Goodyear Make Big Pension Plan Changes," *Workforce Management* online, www.workforce.com, March 1, 2007; G. Colvin, "The End of a Dream," *Fortune*, www.cnnmoney.com, June 22, 2006; E. Porter and M. Williams Nash, "Benefits Go the Way of Pensions," *NY Times* online, February 9, 2006; and J. Fox, "Good Riddance to Pensions."
120. L. Scism and T. W. Martin, "AIG to Freeze Traditional Pension Plan," *The Wall Street Journal* online, www.wsj.com, September 3, 2015.
121. U.S. Department of Labor, "Employee Benefits in the United States," March 2015 (USDL 15-1432), July 24, 2015.
122. Ibid.
123. Based on Britain's National Autistic Society's Working with People with autism "Employment Services," February 21, 2014, www.autism.org.uk; Kate Kelland, "Thinking Differently: Autism finds space in the workplace," *Reuters,* June 4, 2013; Amelia Hill, "Autism doesn't hold me back. I'm moving up the career ladder," *The Guardian,* March 8, 2013; and Susan Ladika, "Companies find fruitful results when hiring autistic workers," *Workforce,* July 16, 2012.

124. P. Coy and E. Dwoskin, "Shortchanged: Why Women Get Paid Less Than Men," *Bloomberg BusinessWeek* online, www.bloomberg.com/businessweek, June 21, 2012.
125. Maersk Web site, [www.maersk.com/Pages/default.aspx]; C. Murphy & J. T. Areddy, "Shipper Sees China Challenges," August 29, 2012, *Wall Street Journal Online,* http://online.wsj.com; A. Gross, 1998, "Recruiting and Human Resources in China," www.pacificbridge.com/publications/recruiting-and-humanresources-in-china/; Yanrong, Z. and Yu, L., "Navigating Business Success," *China Daily,* November 10, 2012, http://usa.chinadaily.com.cn/weekly/2012-11/09/content_15899057.htm.
126. Modified and Based on BAE Systems, "Measuring output, not hours worked, has revolutionised the warship manufacturer's culture and productivity," *People Management,* October 2016, pp. 22–23.

PART 4 Management Practice

A Manager's Dilemma

Management theory suggests that compared to an individual, a diverse group of people will be more creative because team members will bring a variety of ideas, perspectives, and approaches to the group. For an organization like Google, innovation is critical to its success, and teams are a way of life. If management theory about teams is on target, then Google's research and development center in India should excel at innovation. Why? Because there you'll find broad diversity, even though all employees are from India. These Googlers include Indians, Sikhs, Hindus, Muslims, Buddhists, Christians, and Jains. And they speak English, Hindi, Tamil, Bengali, and more of India's 22 officially recognized languages. One skill Google looks for in potential hires is the ability to work as a team member. As Google continues to grow at a rapid pace, new Googlers are continually added to teams.

Suppose you're a manager at Google's Hyderabad facility. How would you gauge a potential hire's ability to work as a team member, and how would you maintain your team's innovation when new engineers and designers join the group?

Global Sense

Workforce productivity. It's a performance measure that's important to managers and policy makers around the globe. Governments want their labor forces to be productive. Managers want their employees to be productive. Being productive encompasses both efficiency and effectiveness. Think back to our discussion of efficiency and effectiveness in Chapter 1. Efficiency is getting the most output from the least amount of inputs or resources. Or said another way, doing things the right way. Effectiveness was doing those work activities that would result in achieving goals, or doing the right things that would lead to goal achievement. So how does workforce productivity stack up around the world? Here are some of the most recent data on five-year productivity growth rates from the Organization for Economic Cooperation and Development (OECD): Australia, 1.48 percent; Belgium, –0.12 percent; Canada, 0.73 percent; Estonia, 1.49 percent; Greece, –1.04 percent; Ireland, 1.48 percent; Korea, 3.77 percent; Poland, 3.08 percent; Turkey, 0.59 percent; United Kingdom, –0.17 percent; and United States, 1.25 percent. One factor that has a significant effect on workforce productivity rates is the state of the global economy, which is still recovering from the global economic recession. Productivity seems to have spiked through the early part of the downturn, but as the slowdown dragged on, productivity rates for many countries, including the United States, fell. Labor economists suggest that perhaps companies are approaching the limits of how much they can squeeze from the workforce. One way to address this problem is by hiring additional workers to meet demand.

Discuss the following questions in light of what you learned in Part 4:

- *How might workforce productivity be affected by organizational design? Look at the six key elements of organizational design.*
- *What types of adaptive organizational design might be conducive to increasing worker productivity? Which might be detrimental to worker productivity?*
- *How might an organization's human resource management approach affect worker productivity? How could managers use their HR processes to improve worker productivity?*
- *This question is designed to make you think! Are teams more productive than individuals? Discuss and explain.*
- *What's your reaction to the statement by experts that perhaps companies are approaching the limits of how much they can squeeze from the workforce? What are the implications for managers as they make organizing decisions?*

Sources: H. Torry, "U.S. Productivity Shrinks Again in First Quarter," The Wall Street Journal *online, www.wsj.com, May 4, 2016; Organization for Economic Cooperation and Development,* OECD Compendium of Productivity Indicators 2015, *(Paris: OECD Publishing). DOI: http://dx.doi.org/10.1787/pdtvy-2015-en.*

Continuing Case

Starbucks—Organizing

Organizing is an important task of managers. Once the organization's goals and plans are in place, the organizing function sets in motion the process of seeing that those goals and plans are pursued. When managers organize, they're defining what work needs to get done and creating a structure that enables work activities to be completed efficiently and effectively by organizational members hired to do that work. As Starbucks continues its global expansion and pursues innovative strategic initiatives, managers must deal with the realities of continually organizing and reorganizing its work efforts.

Structuring Starbucks

Like many start-up businesses, Starbucks' original founders organized their company around a simple structure based on each person's unique strengths: Zev Siegl became the retail expert; Jerry Baldwin took over the administrative functions; and Gordon Bowker was the dreamer who called himself "the magic, mystery, and romance man" and recognized from the start that a visit to Starbucks could "evoke a brief escape to a distant world." As Starbucks grew to the point where Jerry recognized that he needed to hire professional and experienced managers, Howard Schultz (now Starbucks' chairman, CEO, and president) joined the company, bringing his skills in sales, marketing, and merchandising. When the original owners eventually sold the company to Schultz, he was able to take the company on the path to becoming what it is today and what it hopes to be in the future.

As Starbucks has expanded, its organizational structure has changed to accommodate that growth. Starbucks' success is credited, in part, to its adaptive organizational structure, and the company prides itself on its "lean" corporate structure. Howard Schultz is at the top of the structure and has focused on hiring a team of executives from companies like Nestlé, Procter & Gamble, Corbis, Microsoft, and PepsiCo. Schultz realized how important it was to have an executive team in place that had experience in running divisions or functions of larger companies, and that's what he focused on bringing in to Starbucks. These senior corporate officers include the following: six "C" (chief) officers, seven executive vice presidents, three group presidents, two managing directors, and several "partners." For instance, because technology is an important factor in Starbucks' growth strategy, Schultz created a chief technology officer position. A full description of the team of Starbucks executives and what each is responsible for can be found on the company's website.

Although the executive team provides the all-important strategic direction, the "real" work of Starbucks gets done at the company's support center, zone offices, retail stores, and roasting plants. The support center provides support to and assists all other aspects of corporate operations in the areas of accounting, finance, information technology, and sales and supply chain management.

The zone offices oversee the regional operations of the retail stores and provide support in human resource management, facilities management, account management, financial management, and sales management. The essential link between the zone offices and each retail store is the district manager, each of whom oversees 8 to 10 stores, down from the dozen or so stores they used to oversee. Since district managers need to be out working with the stores, most use mobile technology that allows them to spend more time in the stores and still remain connected to their own office. These district managers have been called "the most important in the company" because it's out in the stores that the Starbucks vision and goals are being carried out. Thus, keeping those district managers connected is vital.

In the retail stores, hourly employees (baristas) service customers under the direction of shift supervisors, assistant store managers, and store managers. These managers are responsible for the day-to-day operations of each Starbucks location. One of the organizational challenges for many store managers has been the company's decision to add more drive-through windows to retail stores, which appears to be a smart, strategic move since the average annual volume at a store with a drive-through window is about 30 percent higher than a store without one. However, a drive-through window often takes up to four people to operate: one to take orders, one to operate the cash register, one to work the espresso machine, and a "floater" who can fill in where needed. And these people have to work rapidly and carefully to get the cars in and out in a timely manner, since the drive-through lane can get congested quickly. Other organizing challenges arise any time the company introduces new products and new, more efficient work approaches.

Finally, without coffee and other beverages and products to sell, there would be no Starbucks. The coffee beans are processed at the company's domestic roasting plants in Washington, Pennsylvania, Nevada, South Carolina, Georgia, and internationally in Amsterdam. There's also a manufacturing plant for Tazo Tea in Oregon, and the company set up a coffee roasting facility with Tata Global Beverages in India. At each manufacturing facility, the production team produces the coffee and other products and the distribution team manages the inventory and distribution of products and equipment to company stores. Because product quality is so essential to Starbucks' success, each person in the manufacturing facilities must be focused on maintaining quality control at every step in the process. The roasting plant in Sandy Run, South Carolina, is a state-of-the-art facility that's also an example of the company's commitment to green design. The plant has been awarded LEED® Silver certification for new construction. And the newest plant in Augusta, Georgia, will also be built to LEED® standards. Starbucks also has warehouse/distribution facilities in Georgia, Tennessee, and Washington.

In joining Starbucks' senior leadership team as executive vice president and chief technology officer, Gerri Martin-Flickinger leads the strategic planning of the company's global information technology function. She brings deep management and technical expertise to Starbucks, including experience in cloud, big data analytics, mobile, and security—areas that are important technology elements in the company's growth strategy.
Source: Ted S. Warren/AP Images

People Management at Starbucks

Starbucks recognizes that what it's been able to accomplish is due to the people it hires. When you have talented and committed people offering their ideas and expertise, success will follow.

Since the beginning, Starbucks has strived to be an employer that nurtured employees and gave them opportunities to grow and be challenged. The company says it is "pro-partner" and has always been committed to providing a flexible and progressive work environment and treating one another with respect and dignity.

As Starbucks continues its expansion both in the United States and internationally, it needs to make sure it has the right number of the right people in the right place at the right time. What kinds of people are "right" for Starbucks? They state they want "people who are adaptable, self-motivated, passionate, creative team players." Starbucks uses a variety of methods to attract potential partners. The company has an interactive and easy-to-use online career center. Job seekers—who must be at least 16—can search and apply online for jobs in the home office (Seattle) support center and in the zone offices, roasting plants, store management, and store hourly (barista) positions in any geographic location. Starbucks also has recruiting events in various locations in the United States throughout the year, which allow job seekers to talk to recruiters and partners face-to-face about working at Starbucks. In addition, job seekers for part-time and full-time hourly positions can also submit an application at any Starbucks store location. The company also has a limited number of internship opportunities for students during the summer. But the company's efforts don't stop there.

The company's commitment to helping people in communities has led to various special hiring initiatives that focus on particular groups. For instance, Starbucks committed to hire at least 10,000 veterans and their spouses by 2018. More recently, the company has partnered with several companies, including CVS Health Corporation, Walmart, and Microsoft to hire at least 100,000 low-income individuals.

Starbucks' workplace policies provide for equal employment opportunities and strictly prohibit discrimination. Diversity and inclusion are very important to Starbucks as the following statistics from its U.S. workforce illustrate: 64 percent of its total workforce are women and 33 percent of its total workforce are people of color. That commitment to diversity starts at the top. At one point, senior executives participated in a 360-degree diversity assessment to identify their strengths and needed areas of improvement. Also, an executive diversity learning series, including a full-day diversity immersion exercise, was developed for individuals at the vice-president level and above to build their diversity competencies.

Although diversity training is important to Starbucks, it isn't the only training provided. The company continually invests in training programs and career development initiatives: baristas, who get a "green apron book" that exhorts them to be genuine and considerate, receive 23 hours of initial training; an additional 29 hours of training as shift supervisor; 112 hours as assistant store manager; and 320 hours as store manager. District manager trainees receive 200 hours of training. And every partner takes a class on coffee education, which focuses on Starbucks' passion for coffee and understanding the core product. In addition, the Starbucks corporate support center offers a variety of classes ranging from basic computer skills to conflict resolution to management training. Starbucks' partners aren't "stuck" in their jobs. The company's rapid growth creates tremendous opportunities for promotion and advancement for all store partners. If they desire, they can utilize career counseling, executive coaching, job rotation, mentoring, and leadership development to help them create a career path that meets their needs. One example of the company's training efforts: When oxygen levels in coffee bags were too high in one of the company's roasting plants (which affected product freshness), partners were retrained on procedures and given additional coaching. After the training, the number of bags of coffee placed on "quality hold" declined by 99 percent. Then, on one day in February 2008, Starbucks did something quite unusual—it closed all its U.S. stores for three-and-a-half hours to train and retrain baristas on espresso. A company spokesperson said, "We felt this training was an investment in our baristas and in the Starbucks' experience." The training, dubbed Perfecting the Art of Espresso, was about focusing on the core product, espresso, as well as on the customer experience. Feedback was quite positive. Customers said they appreciated the company taking the time to do the training and felt it had resulted in a better customer experience. The company also embarked on a series of training for partners to find ways to do work more efficiently. A 10-person "lean team" went from region to region encouraging managers and partners to find ways to be more efficient.

One human resource issue that has haunted Starbucks is its position on labor unions. The company takes the position that the fair and respectful "direct employment relationship" it has with its partners—not a third party that acts on behalf of the partners—is the best way to help ensure a great work environment. Starbucks prides itself on how it treats its employees. However, the company did settle a complaint issued by the National Labor Relations Board that contained more than two dozen unfair labor practice allegations brought against the company by the union Industrial Workers of the World. This settlement arose from disputes at three stores in New York City. In 2011, a strike by partners in Chile—which is the only country where the company has a sizable union presence—over low wages led baristas in other countries to call for a "global week of solidarity" in support of the strikers. The Chilean workers eventually abandoned that strike without reaching an agreement with the company. As Starbucks continues to expand globally, it will face challenges in new markets where local labor groups and government requirements honor collective bargaining. And Starbucks realizes it needs to be cautious so that its "we care" image isn't diminished by labor woes.

Discussion Questions

P4-1. What types of departmentalization are being used? Explain your choices. (Hint: In addition to information in the case, you might want to look at the complete list and description of corporate executives on the company's website.)

P4-2. Do you think it's a good idea to have a president for the U.S. division and for the other international divisions? What are the advantages of such an arrangement? Disadvantages?

P4-3. What examples of the six organizational structural elements do you see discussed in the case? Describe.

P4-4. Considering the expense associated with having more managers, what are some reasons why you think Starbucks decided to decrease the number of stores each district manager was responsible for, thus increasing the number of managers needed? Other than the expense, can you think of any disadvantages to this decision?

P4-5. Why do you think it was important for Starbucks to keep its mobile workforce "connected?" In addition to the technology used to do this, what other things might the company do to make its adaptive organizational design efficient and effective?

P4-6. Starbucks has said its goal is to open nearly 10,000 new stores globally by 2019. In addition, the company has set a financial goal of attaining total net revenue growth of 10 to 13 percent and $30 billion in annual revenue by 2019. How will the organizing function contribute to the accomplishment of these goals?

P4-7. Starbucks has said that it wants people who are "adaptable, self-motivated, passionate, and creative team players." How does the company ensure that its hiring and selection process identifies those kinds of people?

P4-8. Select one of the job openings posted on the company's website. Do you think the job description and job specification for this job are adequate? Why or why not? What changes might you suggest?

P4-9. Evaluate Starbucks' training efforts. What types of training are available? What other type(s) of training might be necessary? Explain your choices.

P4-10. Pretend that you're a local Starbucks' store manager. You have three new hourly partners (baristas) joining your team. Describe the orientation you would provide these new hires.

P4-11. Which of the company's principles affect the organizing function of management? Explain how the one(s) you chose would affect how Starbucks' managers deal with (a) structural issues; (b) HRM issues; and (c) issues in managing teams. (Hint: The principles can be found on the company's website.)

Notes for the Part 4 Continuing Case

Information from Starbucks Corporation 2015 Annual Report, www.investor.starbucks.com, April 2016; company website, www.starbucks.com; P. Meyer, "Starbucks Coffee Company's Organizational Structure," Panmore Institute, www.panmore.com, September 13, 2015; J. Jargon, "Starbucks Hires First Chief Technology Officer," *The Wall Street Journal* online, www.wsj.com, October 6, 2015; J. Jargon, "Starbucks Leads Multi-Company Initiative to Hire 100,000 Young, Minority Workers," *The Wall Street Journal* online, www.wsj.com, July 13, 2015; based on H. Schultz and J. Gordon, *Onward: How Starbucks Fought for Its Life Without Losing Its Soul*, © Howard Schultz (New York: Rodale Publishing, 2011); Reuters, M. Moskowitz, R. Levering, O. Akhtar, E. Fry, C. Leahey, and A. VanderMey, "The 100 Best Companies to Work For," *Fortune,* February 4, 2013, pp. 85+; "Chile Fines, Blacklists Starbucks, Wal-Mart Over Labor Practices," www.reuters.com, August 9, 2012; R. Ahmed, "Tata Setting Up Starbucks Coffee Roasting Facility," online.wsj.com, July 26, 2012; News release, "Starbucks Spotlights Connection Between Record Performance, Shareholder Value and Company Values at Annual Meeting of Shareholders," news.starbucks.com, March 21, 2012; M. Moskowitz and R. E. Levering, "The 100 Best Companies to Work For," *Fortune,* February 6, 2012, pp. 117+; J. Jargon, "Baristas Put Pressure on Starbucks," *Wall Street Journal,* July 26, 2011, p. B3; "Starbucks Finds Ways to Speed Up," *Training Online,* August 11, 2009; M. Herbst, "Starbucks' Karma Problem," *BusinessWeek,* January 12, 2009, p. 26; "Fresh Cup of Training," *Training Online,* May 1, 2008; "Training 135,000 Employees in One Day—Starbucks Closes Store to Do It," www.thecareerrevolution.com, February 27, 2008; K. Maher and J. Adamy," Do Hot Coffee and 'Wobblies' Go Together?," *Wall Street Journal,* March 21, 2006, pp. B1+; A. Serwer, "Interview with Howard Schultz," *Fortune (Europe),* March 20, 2006, pp. 35–36; S. Gray, "Fill 'er Up—with Latte," *Wall Street Journal,* January 6, 2006, pp. A9+; W. Meyers, "Conscience in a Cup of Coffee," *US News & World Report,* October 31, 2005, pp. 48–50; J. M. Cohn, R. Khurana, and L. Reeves, "Growing Talent as If Your Business Depended on It," *Harvard Business Review,* October 2005, pp. 62–70; P. B. Nussbaum, R. Berner, and D. Brady, "Get Creative," *BusinessWeek,* August 1, 2005, pp. 60–68; S. Holmes, "A Bitter Aroma at Starbucks," *BusinessWeek,* June 6, 2005, p. 13; J. Cummings, "Legislative Grind," *Wall Street Journal,* April 12, 2005, pp. A1+; "Starbucks: The Next Generation," *Fortune,* April 4, 2005, p. 20; P. Kafka, "Bean Counter," *Forbes,* February 28, 2005, pp. 78–80; A. Lustgarten, "A Hot, Steaming Cup of Customer Awareness," *Fortune,* November 15, 2004, p. 192; and A. Serwer and K. Bonamici, "Hot Starbucks to Go," *Fortune,* January 26, 2004, pp. 60–74.

Chapter 14 Interpersonal and Organizational Communication

It's Your Career

Source: TheModernCanvas/Shutterstock

A key to success in management and in your career is knowing how to be an active listener.

I'm Listening!

How well do you listen to others? Active listening requires you to concentrate on what is being said. It's more than just hearing the words. It involves a concerted effort to understand and interpret the speaker's message. Here are some insights that you'll want to remember and integrate into your efforts to be a better listener:

1. ***Make eye contact.*** *Making eye contact with the speaker focuses your attention, reduces the likelihood that you will become distracted, and encourages the speaker.*

2. ***Exhibit affirmative nods and appropriate facial expressions.*** *Affirmative nods and appropriate facial expressions, when added to good eye contact, convey to the speaker that you're listening.*

3. ***Pay attention to nonverbal cues.*** *Sometimes, what the speaker vocalizes and how they feel do not match. For instance, the speaker may begin by stating "It isn't a big deal ..." when in fact, their body language shows that what they are saying is a big deal. It isn't difficult to tell when someone is anxious, angry, happy, or sad based on facial expressions.*

4. ***Ask questions and paraphrase what's been said.*** *The critical listener analyzes what he or she hears and asks questions. This behavior provides clarification, ensures understanding, and assures the speaker that you're listening. And the effective listener uses phrases such as "What I hear you saying is..." or "Do you mean...?" Paraphrasing is an excellent control device to check on whether you're listening carefully and to verify that what you heard is accurate.*

5. ***Make smooth transitions between the roles of speaker and listener.*** *The effective listener makes transitions smoothly from speaker to listener and back to speaker. From a listening perspective, this means concentrating on what a speaker has to say and practicing not thinking about what you're going to say as soon as you get your chance.*

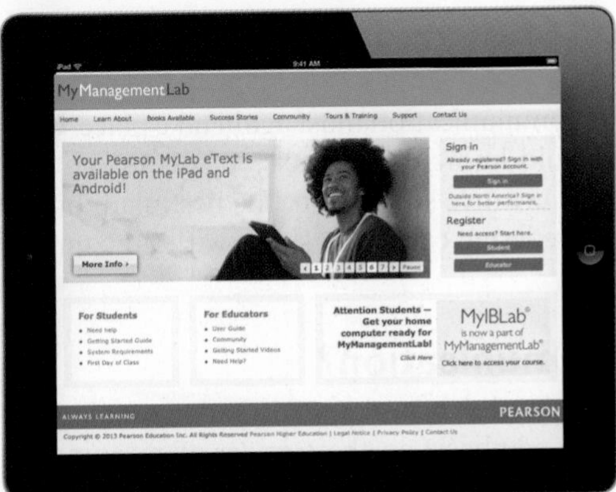

Pearson MyLab Management®

Improve Your Grade!

When you see this icon, visit **www.mymanagementlab.com** for activities that are applied, personalized, and offer immediate feedback.

Learning Objectives

14.1 ***Define*** *the nature and function of communication.*

14.2 ***Describe*** *methods and challenges of interpersonal communication.*

- **Develop your skill** at listening effectively.
- **Know how** to overcome barriers to communication.

14.3 ***Explain*** *how communication can flow most effectively in organizations.*

14.4 ***Describe*** *how the Internet and social media affect managerial communication and organizations.*

14.5 ***Summarize*** *communication issues in today's organizations.*

14.6 ***Discuss*** *how to become a better communicator.*

Ahhhh … welcome to the world of communication! In this "world," managers must understand both the importance and the drawbacks of communication—all forms of communication. Communication between managers and employees is important because it provides the information necessary to get work done in organizations. Thus, there's no doubt that communication is fundamentally linked to managerial performance.[1]

THE nature and function of communication

LO14.1 Volkswagen has had some challenging times since the revelation that its diesel vehicles had been rigged to give false results on government emissions testing. Executives found themselves in the midst of a large-scale communication crisis as they recalled millions of cars and struggled to find answers to questions from regulators, car dealers, car buyers, reporters, and the general public. The CEO stepped down and VW created a special group to respond to inquiries, in a process that a top communications manager called "a step-by-step thing, learning by doing." This example shows the vital nature of communication in a crisis, as well as for everyday operations.[2]

The ability to communicate effectively is a skill that must be mastered by any person who wants to be an effective manager. The importance of effective communication for managers can't be overemphasized for one specific reason: Everything a manager does involves communicating. Not *some* things, but everything! A manager can't make a decision without information. That information has to be communicated. Once a

Communication with new employees at Columbus Company, Ltd., a shoe care firm in Tokyo, serves the functions of information, motivation, and socialization. During their initiation, new hires learn about the company's products and how to use them and interact socially with each other and senior staff members.
Source: Everett Kennedy Brown/Newscom

decision is made, communication must again take place. Otherwise, no one would know that a decision was made. The best idea, the most creative suggestion, the best plan, or the most effective job redesign can't take shape without communication.

What Is Communication?

communication
The transfer and understanding of meaning

interpersonal communication
Communication between two or more people

organizational communication
All the patterns, networks, and systems of communication within an organization

Communication is the transfer and understanding of meaning. Note the emphasis on the *transfer* of meaning: If information or ideas have not been conveyed, communication hasn't taken place. The speaker who isn't heard or the writer whose materials aren't read hasn't communicated. More importantly, however, communication involves the *understanding* of meaning. For communication to be successful, the meaning must be imparted and understood. A letter written in Spanish addressed to a person who doesn't read Spanish can't be considered communication until it's translated into a language the person does read and understand. Perfect communication, if such a thing existed, would be when a transmitted thought or idea was received and understood by the receiver exactly as it was envisioned by the sender.

Another point to keep in mind is that *good* communication is often erroneously defined by the communicator as *agreement* with the message instead of clear understanding of the message.[3] If someone disagrees with us, we assume that the person just didn't fully understand our position. In other words, many of us define good communication as having someone accept our views. But I can clearly understand what you mean and just *not* agree with what you say.

The final point we want to make about communication is that it encompasses both **interpersonal communication**—communication between two or more people—and **organizational communication**, which is all the patterns, networks, and systems of communication within an organization. Both types are important to managers.

Functions of Communication

Irene Lewis, CEO of SAIT Polytechnic, a Calgary, Alberta, Canada-based technical institute, was awarded an Excellence in Communication Leadership (EXCEL) Award by the International Association of Business Communicators. This award recognizes leaders who foster excellence in communication and contribute to the development and support of organizational communication. The selection committee noted Lewis's leadership and commitment to communication and her impact on SAIT's reputation and growth. "She is involved in a wide variety of issues and uses communications wisely to engage relevant stakeholders."[4]

Throughout SAIT Polytechnic and many other organizations, communication serves four major functions: control, motivation, emotional expression, and information.[5] Each function is equally important.

Communication acts to *control* employee behavior in several ways. As we know from Chapter 10, organizations have authority hierarchies and formal guidelines that employees are expected to follow. For instance, when employees are required to communicate any job-related grievance to their immediate manager, to follow their job description, or to comply with company policies, communication is being used to control. Informal communication also controls behavior. When a work group teases a member who's ignoring the norms by working too hard, they're informally controlling the member's behavior.

Next, communication acts to *motivate* by clarifying to employees what is to be done, how well they're doing, and what can be done to improve performance if it's not up to par. As employees set specific goals, work toward those goals, and receive feedback on progress toward goals, communication is required.

For many employees, their work group is a primary source of social interaction. The communication that takes place within the group is a fundamental mechanism by which members share frustrations and feelings of satisfaction. Communication, therefore, provides a release for *emotional expression* of feelings and for fulfillment of social needs.

Finally, individuals and groups need information to get things done in organizations. Communication provides that *information.* Unfortunately, there can sometimes be a breakdown in information sharing, leading to confusion. For instance, low-budget airline Ryanair publicly announced that it would offer inexpensive trans-Atlantic flights between Europe and the United States when, in fact, that wasn't the case. Ryanair's CEO Michael O'Leary stated "It was a miscommunication," and he blamed the media department for this error.[6] Rather than communicating the inaccuracy to the public right away, the company chose to wait a few days, creating confusion among prospective customers. This example not only illustrates poor information sharing, but also the consequences of not making timely corrections.

If your professor has assigned this, go to **www.mymanagementlab.com** to complete the Writing Assignment *BCOMM3: Importance of Communication.*

METHODS and challenges of interpersonal communication

LO14.2 Before communication can take place, a purpose, expressed as a **message** to be conveyed, must exist. It passes between a source (the sender) and a receiver. The message is converted to symbolic form (called **encoding**) and passed by way of some medium (**channel**) to the receiver, who retranslates the sender's message (called **decoding**). The result is the transfer of meaning from one person to another.[7]

message
A purpose to be conveyed

encoding
Converting a message into symbols

channel
The medium a message travels along

decoding
Retranslating a sender's message

communication process
The seven elements involved in transferring meaning from one person to another

noise
Any disturbances that interfere with the transmission, receipt, or feedback of a message

Methods

Exhibit 14-1 illustrates the elements of the **communication process**. Note that the entire process is susceptible to **noise**—disturbances that interfere with the transmission, receipt, or feedback of a message. Typical examples of noise include illegible print, phone static, inattention by the receiver, or background sounds of machinery or coworkers. However, anything that interferes with understanding can be noise, and noise can create distortion at any point in the communication process.

A personal written letter from a U.S. Army commander in Afghanistan to his troops assured them that they were "contributing to the overall success of the mission" there. Colonel David Haight, of the 10th Mountain Division's 3rd Brigade Combat Team, sent the letter to each of the 3,500 men and women after two of their fellow soldiers were killed in combat and his chaplains reported that many were disillusioned about the war. In that letter, Haight said it's important for a leader to explain why certain tasks are important to the accomplishment of the overall mission. Communicating in that way ensures that the mission is not only accomplished, but is accomplished in an exemplary way.[8] Here's a manager who understands the role of communication and how best to communicate to his subordinates.

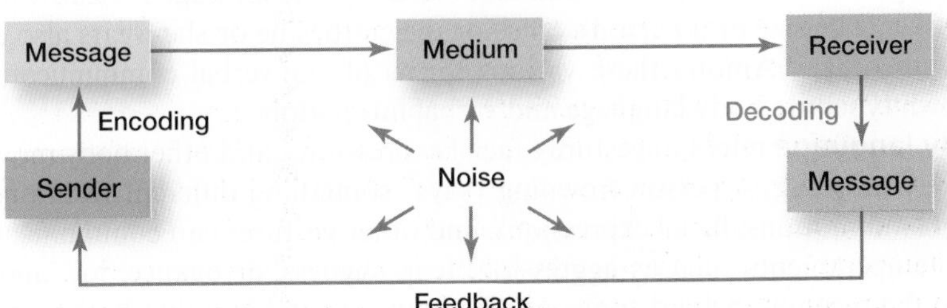

Exhibit 14-1
The Interpersonal Communication Process

You need to communicate to your employees the organization's new policy on sexual harassment; you want to compliment one of your workers on the extra hours she's put in to help your team complete a customer's order; you must tell one of your employees about changes to his job; or you would like to get employees' feedback on your proposed budget for next year. In each of these instances, how would you communicate? Managers have a wide variety of communication methods from which to choose and can use 12 questions to help them evaluate these methods.[9]

1. *Feedback:* How quickly can the receiver respond to the message?
2. *Complexity capacity:* Can the method effectively process complex messages?
3. *Breadth potential:* How many different messages can be transmitted using this method?
4. *Confidentiality:* Can communicators be reasonably sure their messages are received only by those intended?
5. *Encoding ease:* Can sender easily and quickly use this channel?
6. *Decoding ease:* Can receiver easily and quickly decode messages?
7. *Time-space constraint:* Do senders and receivers need to communicate at the same time and in the same space?
8. *Cost:* How much does it cost to use this method?
9. *Interpersonal warmth:* How well does this method convey interpersonal warmth?
10. *Formality:* Does this method have the needed amount of formality?
11. *Scanability:* Does this method allow the message to be easily browsed or scanned for relevant information?
12. *Time of consumption:* Does the sender or receiver exercise the most control over when the message is dealt with?

Warren Buffett, CEO of Berkshire Hathaway, is well known for his ability to communicate complex information to the company's shareholders.[10] He prepares a letter to shareholders every year in which he explains complicated concepts in a simple way. Buffett does this by using metaphors and a mix of formal and conversational language. For instance, he said about two highly accomplished employees' technical expertise: "Each is the da Vinci of his craft."[11]

Exhibit 14-2 provides a comparison of various communication methods. Which method a manager ultimately chooses should reflect the needs of the sender, the attributes of the message, the attributes of the channel, and the needs of the receiver. For instance, if you need to communicate to an employee about the changes being made in her job, face-to-face communication would be a better choice than a memo because you want to be able to address immediately any questions and concerns she might have.

If your professor has assigned this, go to **www.mymanagementlab.com** to watch a video titled: *CH2MHill: Communication* and to respond to questions.

nonverbal communication
Communication transmitted without words

An important part of interpersonal communication is **nonverbal communication**—that is, communication transmitted without words. Some of the most meaningful communications are neither spoken nor written. When a college instructor is teaching a class, she doesn't need words to tell her that students are tuned out when they begin to read a newspaper in the middle of class. Similarly, when students start putting their book, papers, and notebooks away, the message is clear: Class time is about over. The size of a person's office or the clothes he or she wears also conveys messages to others. Among these various forms of nonverbal communication, the best-known types are body language and verbal intonation.

body language
Gestures, facial configurations, and other body movements that convey meaning

Body language refers to gestures, facial expressions, and other body movements that convey meaning. A person frowning "says" something different from one who's smiling. Hand motions, facial expressions, and other gestures can communicate emotions or temperaments such as aggression, fear, shyness, arrogance, joy, and anger. Knowing the meaning behind someone's body moves and learning how to put forth

Exhibit 14-2
Comparison of Communication Methods

Source: Based on P. G. Clampitt, *Communicating for Managerial Effectiveness* (Newbury Park, CA: Sage Publications, 1991), p. 136.

High	Low
High Feedback Potential	***Low Feedback Potential***
Face-to-face Telephone Computer conference	Publications
High Complexity Capacity	***Low Complexity Capacity***
Face-to-face	Bulletin boards
High Breadth Potential	***Low Breadth Potential***
Face-to-face Bulletin boards E-mail	Postal mail Audio-videotapes
High Confidentiality	***Low Confidentiality***
Face-to-face Voice mail	Publications Bulletin boards Audio-videotapes Teleconference
High Encoding Ease	***Low Encoding Ease***
Face-to-face Telephone	Publications
High Time-Decoding Ease	***Low Time-Decoding Ease***
Face-to-face Telephone Hotlines Voice mail	Memos Postal mail Fax Publications
High Space Constraint	***Low Space Constraint***
Face-to-face Group meetings Formal presentations	Memos Postal mail Fax Publications Voice mail
High Cost	***Low Cost***
Group meetings Formal presentations Videoconference	Bulletin boards
High Personal Warmth	***Low Personal Warmth***
Face-to-face	Memos Bulletin boards
High Formality	***Low Formality***
Postal mail Publications	Face-to-face Telephone Voice mail
High Scanability	***Low Scanability***
Memos Postal mail Fax Publications Bulletin boards	Formal presentations Face-to-face Telephone Group meetings Audio-videotapes Hotlines E-mail Computer conference Voice mail Teleconference Videoconference

LEADER making a DIFFERENCE

Source: Tony Avelar/AP Images

*As senior vice president of retail and online stores for Apple, **Angela Ahrendts** holds one of the top positions at Apple.[15] She surprised many in 2015 when she gave up her post as CEO of London-based Burberry, where she revived the failing fashion line, to make the move to Apple. Known to excite passion in her employees, Ahrendts was hired for her leadership ability. She believes that the key to Apple's future is not just creating innovative products; it is engaging and energizing the company's nearly 100,000 employees. Ahrendt believes that communication is essential for a leader, especially in today's technology-focused workplace. When she joined Apple, she engaged in a "listening tour" of Apple's retail stores. She visited about 100 stores and just listened to concerns. She learned that management turnover had created low morale and determined that better communication could help move the retail stores in the right direction. To improve communication with the stores, Ahrendts creates a weekly video sent to all retail employees that includes three key thoughts for the week to share objectives and boost morale. She also launched "Share Your Ideas," which is an internal app employees can use to share suggestions or concerns. Ahrendts reads every comment sent via the app and makes sure she replies within 48 hours. So far, employee satisfaction and retention suggests Ahrendts's strategies to improve communication and build employee morale are working.* What can you learn from this leader making a difference?

your best body language can help you personally and professionally.[12] For instance, research has shown that keeping your arms by your sides rather than crossing them is more likely to encourage information sharing.[13]

Verbal intonation refers to the emphasis someone gives to words or phrases in order to convey meaning. To illustrate how intonations can change the meaning of a message, consider the student who asks the instructor a question. The instructor replies, "What do you mean by that?" The student's reaction will vary, depending on the tone of the instructor's response. A soft, smooth vocal tone conveys interest and creates a different meaning from one that is abrasive and puts a strong emphasis on saying the last word. Most of us would view the first intonation as coming from someone sincerely interested in clarifying the student's concern, whereas the second suggests that the person resents the question. And did you know that verbal intonation can impact career success? For instance, studies have found that male CEOs with lower-pitched voices compared to higher-pitched voices tend to work for larger companies, make substantially more money, and remain in their positions longer.[14] Should you be concerned? Probably not. Some speech experts believe that voice intonation can be learned.

Managers need to remember that as they communicate, the nonverbal component usually carries the greatest impact. It's not *what* you say, but *how* you say it.

verbal intonation
An emphasis given to words or phrases that conveys meaning

Barriers

A company with 100 employees can expect to lose approximately $450,000 a year, or more, because of e-mail blunders, inefficiencies, and misunderstandings.[16] The chief executive of a marketing firm in New York was in a meeting with a potential client. For the entire hour-and-a-half meeting, the client was fiddling with his iPhone. Doing what? Playing a racing game, although he did glance up occasionally and ask questions.[17]

Somewhere, somehow, communication isn't being as effective as it needs to be. One reason is that managers face barriers that can distort the interpersonal communication process. Let's look at these barriers to effective communication.

COGNITIVE Managers should be familiar with two cognitive barriers to communication: information overload and filtering.

information overload
When information exceeds our processing capacity

Information overload occurs when information exceeds our processing capacity. For instance, a marketing manager goes on a week-long sales trip to Spain where he doesn't have access to his e-mail and faces 1,000 messages on his return. Today's employees frequently complain of information overload. Statistics show that 87 percent of employees use e-mail and that the average business e-mail user devotes 107 minutes a day to it—about 25 percent of the workday. Other statistics show that the number of daily business-related e-mails sent and received is rising rapidly from 121 and will number at least 140 by 2019.[18] This translates to 12 incoming and 5 outgoing e-mails in the same period. As you know, there is also the barrage of personal e-mails, not to mention those pesky spam messages. Altogether, the number of worldwide e-mail messages sent daily is a staggering 215 billion.[19] The demands of keeping up with e-mail, text messages, phone calls, faxes, meetings, and professional reading create an onslaught of data. What happens when individuals have more information than they can process? They tend to ignore, pass over, forget, or selectively choose information. Or they may stop communicating. The challenges don't stop there. The full extent of information may not be accurately conveyed, as a result of intentional filtering.

Filtering is the deliberate manipulation of information to make it appear more favorable to the receiver. For example, when a person tells his or her manager what the manager wants to hear, information is being filtered. Or if information being communicated up through organizational levels is condensed by senders, that's filtering.

filtering
The deliberate manipulation of information to make it appear more favorable to the receiver

How much filtering takes place tends to be a function of the number of vertical levels in the organization and the organizational culture. The more vertical levels in an organization, the more opportunities there are for filtering. As organizations use more collaborative, cooperative work arrangements, information filtering may become less of a problem. In addition, e-mail reduces filtering because communication is more direct. Finally, the organizational culture encourages or discourages filtering by the type of behavior it rewards. The more that organizational rewards emphasize style and appearance, the more managers may be motivated to filter communications in their favor. In sum, either barrier—information overload or filtering—can be problematic. The result is lost information and ineffective communication.

EMOTIONS How a receiver feels influences how he or she interprets it. Extreme emotions are most likely to hinder effective communication. In such instances, we often disregard our rational and objective thinking processes and substitute emotional judgments.

When people feel they're being threatened, they tend to react in ways that hinder effective communication and reduce their ability to achieve mutual understanding. They become defensive—verbally attacking others, making sarcastic remarks, being overly judgmental, or questioning others' motives.[20]

SOCIOCULTURAL Conservative author/journalist Ann Coulter and rapper Nelly both speak English, but the language each uses is vastly different. Words mean different things to different people. Age, education, and cultural background are three of the more obvious variables that influence the language a person uses and the definitions he or she gives to words.

In an organization, employees come from diverse backgrounds and have different patterns of speech. Even employees who work for the same organization but in different departments often have different **jargon**—specialized terminology or technical language that members of a group use to communicate among themselves. For instance, human resource managers discuss bona fide occupational qualifications (BFOQs) as a defense against illegal discrimination; and accounting managers use the term FIFO—meaning first-in, first-out—as a reference to an inventory-valuing method.

jargon
Specialized terminology or technical language that members of a group use to communicate among themselves

NATIONAL CULTURE For technological and cultural reasons, the Chinese people dislike voice mail.[21] This general tendency illustrates how communication differences can arise from national culture as well as different languages. For example, let's compare countries that value individualism (such as the United States) with countries that emphasize collectivism (such as Japan).[22]

In an individualistic country like the United States, communication is more formal and is clearly spelled out. Managers rely heavily on reports, memos, and other formal forms of communication. In a collectivist country like Japan, more interpersonal contact takes place, and face-to-face communication is encouraged. A Japanese manager extensively consults with subordinates over an issue first and draws up a formal document later to outline the agreement that was made.

If your professor has assigned this, go to **www.mymanagementlab.com** to complete the Writing Assignment *BCOMM4: Multicultural Communication.*

Overcoming the Barriers

On average, an individual must hear new information seven times before he or she truly understands it.[23] In light of this fact and the communication barriers just described, what can managers do to be more effective communicators?

The frequency of feedback influences employees' satisfaction at work:

- 80 percent of employees are still satisfied within 1 month of receiving feedback.
- 71 percent of employees are still satisfied between 3 and 5 months after receiving feedback.
- 69 percent of employees are still satisfied between 6 and 12 months after receiving feedback.
- 51 percent of employees are still satisfied between 1 and 2 years after receiving feedback.
- 42 percent of employees are still satisfied more than 2 years after receiving feedback.[24]

USE FEEDBACK Many communication problems are directly attributed to misunderstanding and inaccuracies. These problems are less likely to occur if the manager gets feedback, both verbal and nonverbal.

A manager can ask questions about a message to determine whether it was received and understood as intended. Or the manager can ask the receiver to restate the message in his or her own words. If the manager hears what was intended, understanding and accuracy should improve. Feedback can also be more subtle, and general comments can give a manager a sense of the receiver's reaction to a message.

Feedback also doesn't have to be verbal. If a sales manager e-mails information about a new monthly sales report that all sales representatives will need to complete and some of them don't turn it in, the sales manager has received feedback. This feedback suggests that the sales manager needs to clarify the initial communication. Similarly, managers can look for nonverbal cues to tell whether someone's getting the message.

SIMPLIFY LANGUAGE Because language can be a barrier, managers should consider the audience to whom the message is directed and tailor the language to them.[25] Remember, effective communication is achieved when a message is both *received* and *understood*. For example, a hospital administrator should always try to communicate in clear, easily understood terms and to use language tailored to different employee groups. Messages to the surgical staff should be purposefully different from those used with office employees. Jargon can facilitate understanding if it's used within a group that knows what it means, but can cause problems when used outside that group.

LISTEN ACTIVELY We addressed active listening at the beginning of this chapter. We discuss it again here because it's an important method for improving communication.

When someone talks, we hear, but too often we don't listen. Listening is an active search for meaning, whereas hearing is passive. In listening, the receiver is also putting effort into the communication.

active listening
Listening for full meaning without making premature judgments or interpretations

Many of us are poor listeners. Why? Because it's difficult, and most of us would rather do the talking. Listening, in fact, is often more tiring than talking. Unlike hearing, **active listening**, which is listening for full meaning without making premature judgments or interpretations, demands total concentration. The average person normally speaks at a rate of about 125 to 200 words per minute. However, the average listener can comprehend up to 400 words per minute.[26] The difference leaves lots of idle brain time and opportunities for the mind to wander.

Active listening is enhanced by developing empathy with the sender—that is, by putting yourself in the sender's position. Because senders differ in attitudes, interests, needs, and expectations, empathy makes it easier to understand the actual content of a message. An empathetic listener reserves judgment on the message's content and carefully listens to what is being said. The goal is to improve one's ability to get the full meaning of a communication without distorting it by premature judgments or interpretations. Other specific behaviors that active listeners demonstrate are listed in Exhibit 14-3. As you can see, active listening takes effort, but it can help make communication much more effective.

CONSTRAIN EMOTIONS It would be naïve to assume that managers always communicate in a rational manner. We know that emotions can cloud and distort communication. A manager who's upset over an issue is more likely to misconstrue incoming messages and fail to communicate his or her outgoing messages clearly and accurately. What to do? The simplest answer is to calm down and get emotions under control before communicating.

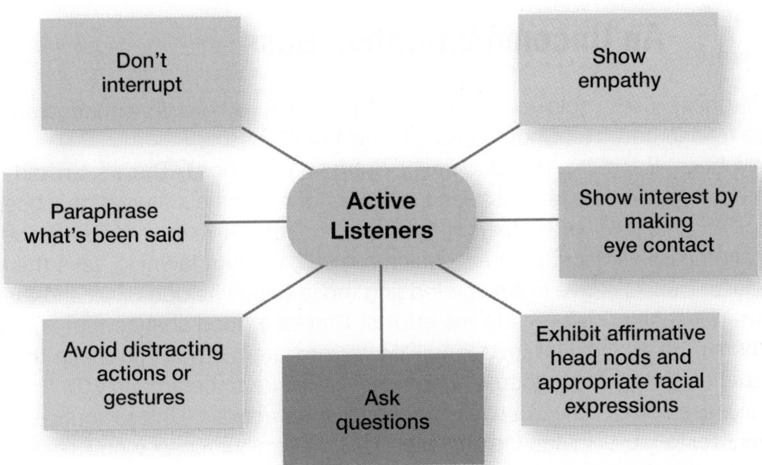

Exhibit 14-3
Active Listening Behaviors

Sources: Based on J. V. Thill and C. L. Bovee, *Excellence in Business Communication,* 9th ed. (Upper Saddle River, NJ: Prentice Hall, 2011), pp. 48–49; and S. P. Robbins and P. L. Hunsaker, *Training in Interpersonal Skills,* 5th ed. (Upper Saddle River, NJ: Prentice Hall, 2009), pp. 90–92.

let's get REAL

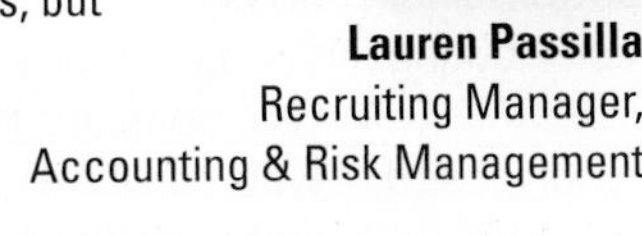

Source: Lauren Passilla

Lauren Passilla
Recruiting Manager,
Accounting & Risk Management

The Scenario:

Tod Stewart can't believe one of his loan processors has made yet another error. Tod is the manager of the loan-processing department of a regional bank, and his department has had a lot of errors in the last six months. He knows the bank has changed loan-processing guidelines, but he clearly explained the new guidelines at the last department meeting. Everyone seemed to be paying attention at the meeting, but the loan processors keep making errors.

How can Tod make sure that his employees understand the directions he provides?

Implementing change as a manager is difficult, but it is important that Tod stays positive for his team. One way to ensure the new directions are being effectively communicated is to utilize a "train the trainer" model. Tod can encourage a couple of his employees who are struggling to spend additional time with him to further understand the changes, then teach what they learn back to the team. The individuals will be empowered, the team engaged, and everyone will better retain the information.

Gender Communication—If your instructor is using Pearson MyLab Management, log onto **mymanagementlab.com** and test your *gender communication knowledge*. **Be sure to refer back to the chapter opener!**

★ It's Your Career

WATCH NONVERBAL CUES If actions speak louder than words, then it's important to make sure your actions align with and reinforce the words that go along with them. An effective communicator watches his or her nonverbal cues to ensure that they convey the desired message.

WORKPLACE **CONFIDENTIAL** An Uncommunicative Boss

Many of us fantasize about having a job where our boss just leaves us alone. Out of sight, out of mind. We're free to get our work done, with an absence of bother from a boss. But be careful what you wish for! It can be very frustrating to work for someone who is uncommunicative.

We use the term "uncommunicative" to encompass a long list of behaviors you might face in the workplace. There's the absentee boss, who is never around. You have questions or concerns but no one with whom to discuss them. There's the shy or introverted boss who avoids interacting. There's the boss who hates conflicts or confrontations and who hides from the tough issues. There's also the boss who always seems too busy to talk with you. And then there's the boss who doesn't respond to tweets, e-mails or phone messages. You know they're being received, but it's as if they vanish into thin air. As you can see, there are lots of ways to be uncommunicative!

The following suggestions can help you deal with, and work around, an uncommunicative boss.

Ask yourself: Am I being singled out? Start by assessing whether your boss is uncommunicative with everyone or whether you've been singled out. It's possible that your boss is purposely distancing herself from you. Have you done anything to upset her? Is she purposely avoiding you? If you're annoyed or irritated with your boss, she might be picking this up and distancing herself from you in order to avoid a conflict. On the other hand, if your boss treats all her employees similarly, assume you're not being singled out. Bottom line: Start by determining whether or not you may be contributing to the problem.

Does your organization's culture encourage your boss's behavior? Take a good look at your organization's culture. Does your organization encourage managers to be "hands off?" In some cases, organizations promote this behavior by the criteria they use to evaluate managers and by what they reward. For instance, a laissez-faire leadership style might be encouraged as a way to develop future managers. It may well be that, in such a culture, your boss is giving you the freedom to take on tasks and show initiative with a view toward preparing you for increased responsibilities. If most managers in your organization seem to be showing a similar, uncommunicative style, don't expect significant changes in your boss.

Are there good reasons for your boss to be uncommunicative? Look at your boss objectively. There may be good reasons for his hands-off approach. One common explanation is that he's spending his time "managing up," that is, working to get increased resources or support from those above. Other possibilities include your boss having too much to do or too many employees to supervise. These explanations can help you better empathize with your boss's situation and better understand why he's not available.

Be proactive: Support your boss. There's an old saw: "The boss isn't always right, but he's always the boss." If you're feeling underappreciated, give your boss the benefit of the doubt. Reach out and, without fawning, take the initiative in acknowledging those things he does well and that you appreciate his efforts. There's a good chance that your positive outreach will be reciprocated. When you make the boss feel good, it increases his desire to be around you.

Share your needs with your boss. Unless you say something, there's a good chance your boss won't realize that there's a problem. Meet with your boss and frame your conversation about your needs. Be prepared to express exactly the kind of support you're seeking. Do you want to have weekly meetings with her? Do you seek quicker e-mail responses? Don't be aggressive or pushy. Show that you're empathetic to her situation and the demands on her time; then be clear and concise about your needs.

Act, but keep your boss informed. If your efforts to improve communications fall on deaf ears, move forward on your own. Take the initiative but, very importantly, keep your boss in the loop. Even though you might not be getting any feedback, continue to give your boss brief, written status reports. If problems arise in the future, you will have at least created a paper trail to support that you were keeping your boss informed.

Look for a boss-substitute. If your boss isn't there for you, consider looking around your organization for someone who can fill the void. Find another person who can mentor and support you.

Protect yourself: Get to know your boss's boss. It rarely hurts to develop a relationship with your boss's superior. It can be as simple as just exchanging pleasantries or sharing a coffee in the lunchroom. From a political perspective, it makes sense to protect yourself and build alliances with those in power.

Turn this situation to your favor. Finally, look at the positive side. This is an opportunity for you to step up, show your initiative, and impress others in the organization. Those in non-managerial positions often don't get opportunities to demonstrate leadership. But if the opportunity is opened to you, don't let it get away. You can fill the void in leadership, grow your reach in the organization, make a positive impression on upper management, and possibly open the door to a promotion.

Sources: Based on R. Bhattacharyya, "5 Ways to Deal with an Absentee Boss," *The Economic Times* online, January 16, 2015; and S. Stibitz, "Get What You Need From Your Hands-off Boss," *hbr.org,* June 12, 2015.

EFFECTIVE organizational communication

LO14.3 A recent European economic downturn had employees everywhere on edge. So when all 1,300 workers at Aviva Investors, the asset management division of a United Kingdom insurance company, opened their e-mail one morning, they found out they'd been fired. Except—it was a mistake. Only one unfortunate employee was supposed to get the message. Can you imagine the stunned silence in that office? A spokesman for the company said an apology was quickly issued for the mistaken e-mail message, but had damage already been done?[27]

Maybe you've had the experience of sitting in an employee meeting with managers when they ask if anyone has any questions—only to be met with deafening silence.[28] Communication can be an interesting thing, especially in organizations. As we've seen, managerial communication is important, but it is a two-way street. An understanding of managerial communication isn't possible without looking at organizational communication. In this section, we look at several important aspects of organizational communication, including formal versus informal communication, the flow patterns of communication, formal and informal communication networks, and workplace design.

A survey of 400 companies revealed:

- Effective communication strategies yield 47 percent returns to shareholders.
- Financial loss due to employee misunderstanding or poor communication is estimated to be $37 billion.[29]

Formal Versus Informal

Communication within an organization is described as formal or informal. **Formal communication** refers to communication that takes place within prescribed organizational work arrangements. For example, when a manager asks an employee to complete a task, that's formal communication. Another example of formal communication occurs when an employee communicates a problem to his or her manager.

formal communication
Communication that takes place within prescribed organizational work arrangements

Informal communication is organizational communication not defined by the organization's structural hierarchy. When employees talk with each other in the lunch room, as they pass in hallways, or as they're working out at the company wellness facility, they engage in informal communication. Employees form friendships and communicate with each other. The informal communication system fulfills two purposes in organizations: (1) It permits employees to satisfy their need for social interaction, and (2) it can improve an organization's performance by creating alternative, and frequently faster and more efficient, channels of communication.

informal communication
Communication that is not defined by the organization's structural hierarchy

Direction of Flow

Let's look at the ways that organizational communication can flow: downward, upward, laterally, or diagonally.

DOWNWARD Every morning and often several times a day, managers at UPS package delivery facilities gather workers for mandatory meetings that last precisely three minutes. During those 180 seconds, managers relay company announcements and go over local information like traffic conditions or customer complaints. Then, each meeting ends with a safety tip. The three-minute meetings have proved so successful that many of the company's office workers are using the idea.[30] CEOs use town hall meetings to communicate with employees. These **town hall meetings** are informal public meetings where top executives relay information, discuss issues, or bring employees together to celebrate accomplishments. For example, India's Flipkart regularly holds town hall meetings with employees to discuss the online retailer's financial results and proposed internal policies. A spokesman says these town hall meetings are part of its "culture of openness."[31] These are examples of **downward communication**, which is communication that flows from a manager to employees. It's used to inform, direct, coordinate, and evaluate employees. When managers assign goals to their employees, they're using downward communication. They're also using downward communication when providing employees with job

Volkswagen CEO Matthias Müller demonstrates the concept of downward communication when speaking to 20,000 employees at the carmaker's headquarters production plant in Germany. During his address, Müller informed employees about new developments in the ongoing investigation of the company's alleged manipulation of emission tests for its diesel cars.
Source: ODD ANDERSEN/AFP/Getty Images

descriptions, informing them of organizational policies and procedures, pointing out problems that need attention, or evaluating their performance. Downward communication can take place through any of the communication methods we described earlier.

town hall meeting Informal public meetings where information can be relayed, issues can be discussed, or employees can be brought together to celebrate accomplishments

downward communication Communication that flows downward from a manager to employees

upward communication Communication that flows upward from employees to managers

UPWARD COMMUNICATION Managers rely on their employees for information. For instance, reports are given to managers to inform them of progress toward goals or to report any problems. **Upward communication** is communication that flows from employees to managers. It keeps managers aware of how employees feel about their jobs, their coworkers, and the organization in general. Managers also rely on upward communication for ideas on how things can be improved. Some examples of upward communication include performance reports prepared by employees, suggestion boxes, employee attitude surveys, grievance procedures, manager-employee discussions, and informal group sessions in which employees have the opportunity to discuss problems with their manager or representatives of top-level management.

How much upward communication is used depends on the organizational culture. If managers have created a climate of trust and respect and use participative decision making or empowerment, considerable upward communication will occur as employees provide input to decisions. In a more highly structured and authoritarian environment, upward communication still takes place, but is limited.

lateral communication Communication that takes place among any employees on the same organizational level

LATERAL COMMUNICATION Communication that takes place among employees on the same organizational level is called **lateral communication**. In today's dynamic environment, horizontal communications are frequently needed to save time and facilitate coordination. Cross-functional teams, for instance, rely heavily on this form of communication interaction. However, conflicts can arise if employees don't keep their managers informed about decisions they've made or actions they've taken.

diagonal communication Communication that cuts across work areas and organizational levels

DIAGONAL COMMUNICATION **Diagonal communication** is communication that crosses both work areas *and* organizational levels. A credit analyst who communicates directly with a regional marketing manager about a customer's problem—note the different department and different organizational level—uses diagonal communication. Because of its efficiency and speed, diagonal communication can be beneficial. Increased e-mail use facilitates diagonal communication. In many organizations, any employee can communicate by e-mail with any other employee, regardless of organizational work area or level, even with upper-level managers. In many organizations, CEOs have adopted an "open inbox" e-mail policy. For example, William H. Swanson, head of defense contractor Raytheon Company, figures he has received and answered more than 150,000 employee e-mails. And Henry McKinnell Jr., former CEO of Pfizer, says the approximately 75 internal e-mails he received every day were "an avenue of communication I didn't otherwise have."[32] However, diagonal communication also has the potential to create problems if employees don't keep their managers informed.

Networks

communication networks The variety of patterns of vertical and horizontal flows of organizational communication

The vertical and horizontal flows of organizational communication can be combined into a variety of patterns called **communication networks**. Exhibit 14-4 illustrates three common communication networks.

TYPES OF COMMUNICATION NETWORKS In the *chain* network, communication flows according to the formal chain of command, both downward and upward. The *wheel* network represents communication flowing between a clearly identifiable and strong leader and others in a work group or team. The leader serves as the hub through whom all communication passes. Finally, in the *all-channel* network, communication flows freely among all members of a work team.

The form of network you should use depends on your goal. Exhibit 14-4 also summarizes each network's effectiveness according to four criteria: speed, accuracy, the probability that a leader will emerge, and the importance of member satisfaction. One observation is immediately apparent: No single network is best for all situations.

Exhibit 14-4
Organizational Communication Networks

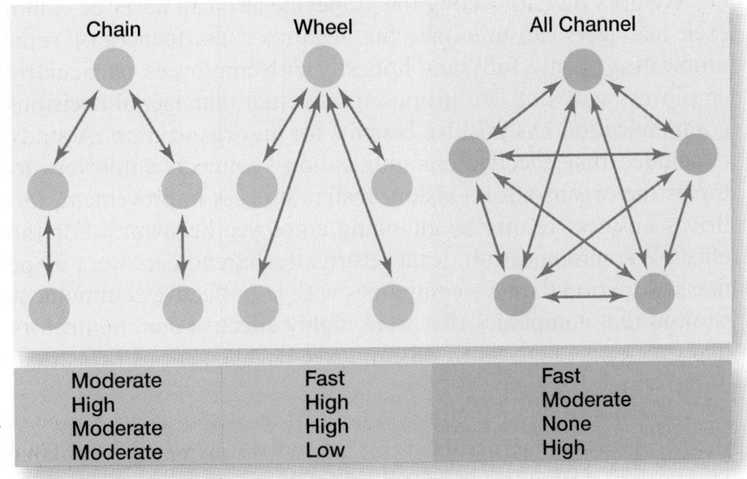

CRITERIA	Chain	Wheel	All Channel
Speed	Moderate	Fast	Fast
Accuracy	High	High	Moderate
Emergence of leader	Moderate	High	None
Member satisfaction	Moderate	Low	High

THE GRAPEVINE We can't leave our discussion of communication networks without discussing the **grapevine**—the informal organizational communication network. The grapevine is active in almost every organization. Is it an important source of information? You bet! One survey reported that 63 percent of employees say they hear about important matters first through rumors or gossip on the grapevine.[33]

grapevine
The informal organizational communication network

Certainly, the grapevine is an important part of any communication network and well worth understanding.[34] Acting as both a filter and a feedback mechanism, it pinpoints those bewildering issues that employees consider important. More importantly, from a managerial point of view, it *is* possible to analyze what is happening on the grapevine—what information is being passed, how information seems to flow, and what individuals seem to be key information conduits. By staying aware of the grapevine's flow and patterns, managers can identify issues that concern employees and in turn use the grapevine to disseminate important information. Because the grapevine can't be eliminated, managers should "manage" it as an important information network.

let's get REAL

The Scenario:

Alexandra Pavlou has a delicate, potentially touchy issue she needs to discuss with her team of real estate appraisers. How can she approach this discussion with care and yet address the issue frankly?

What advice would you give Alexandra?

First consider if it's an issue best addressed in several one-on-one meetings or in a group setting. Do your best to anticipate the reactions and think through how you will respond/react in turn. Be honest at the onset with your team that the forthcoming discussion(s) may make some people uncomfortable but explain why the topic is important to address.

Maribel Lara
Director, Account Management

Source: Maribel Lara

Rumors that flow along the grapevine also can never be eliminated entirely. However, managers can minimize the negative consequences of rumors. How? By communicating openly, fully, and honestly with employees, particularly in situations where employees may not like proposed or actual managerial decisions. Open and honest communication has positive benefits for an organization. A study by Towers Watson concluded that effective communication "connects employees to the business, reinforces the organization's vision, fosters process improvement, facilitates change, and drives business results by changing employee behavior." For those companies with effective communication, total returns to shareholders were 91 percent higher over a five-year period than for companies with less effective communication. This study also showed that companies that were highly effective communicators were four times as likely to report high levels of employee engagement as firms that communicated less effectively.[35]

★ Try It!

If your professor has assigned this, go to **www.mymanagementlab.com** to complete the Simulation: *Communication* and get a better understanding of the challenges of managing communication in organizations.

An open workplace design supports Skype's business goal of breaking down the barriers to communication by developing technology that is inventive, dependable, and easy to use. Skype offices throughout the world provide employees with an informal environment where they can easily communicate, collaborate, and socialize with each other.
Source: Amruth/Caro Fotos/SIPA/Newscom

Workplace Design and Communication

In addition to the direction of communication flow and organizational communication networks, another factor that influences organizational communication is workplace design. Despite all the information technology and associated employee mobility (which we'll discuss in the next section), much of an organization's communication still occurs in the workplace. In fact, some 74 percent of an employee's average workweek is spent in an office.[36] How that office workspace is designed and configured can affect the communication that occurs as well as influence an organization's overall performance. In fact, in a survey of American workers, 90 percent believed that better workplace design and layout result in better overall employee performance.[37]

Research shows that a workplace design should successfully support four types of employee work: focused work, collaboration, learning, and socialization.[38] Focused work is when an employee needs to concentrate on completing a task. In collaboration, employees need to work together to complete a task. Learning is when employees are engaged in training or doing something new and could involve both focused work and collaboration. And socialization happens when employees informally gather to chat or to exchange ideas. A survey found that when workers had these types of "oases" or informal meeting places nearby, they had 102 percent more face-to-face communication than people who had only minimal access to such spots.[39] Because communication can and does take place in each of these settings, the workplace design needs to accommodate these organizational and interpersonal communications—all directions and all types—in order to be most effective.

open workplaces
Workplaces with few physical barriers and enclosures

- Body odor and idea-stealing rank number one as the most common workplace pet peeves.[40]

As managers design the physical work environment, two common design elements have the greatest impact on communication.[41] First, the enclosures and barriers used in the workspace. Many organizational workplaces today—some 70 percent—are **open workplaces**; that is, they include few physical barriers and enclosures.[42] Research has shown both the merits and the drawbacks of an open workplace.[43] One of the things we know for sure about this type of arrangement and its effect on communication is *visibility*. People in open cubicles placed along main routes of circulation or adjacent to atria reported almost 60 percent more face-to-face communication with team members than did those in lower-visibility locations. Another thing is *density*. More people populating an immediate work area meant that more face-to-face interactions took place. Workspaces with a high density yielded 84 percent more team-member communication than did workspace arrangements with a low density. If it's important that employees communicate and collaborate, managers need to consider visibility and density in workplace design. Some companies are taking this concept to the executive suite. For example, Citigroup, Inc., recently renovated office space so that the CEO will not have a door to his workspace.[44] Another consideration in any open workplace is making sure to have some area where sensitive discussions can take place when needed. For instance, when private personnel matters need to be addressed, those shouldn't take place where interruptions or eavesdropping can occur. Apart from privacy, managers should provide separate space where few distractions are likely to occur, particularly when pressing deadlines are approaching. A review of 100 studies on open work spaces revealed that the frequency of interruptions and distractions is greater in some open work spaces compared to traditional work spaces.[45]

Another workplace design element is the availability of adjustable work arrangements, equipment, and furnishings. As organizations have moved toward nontraditional work arrangements, the adjustability and customizability of employee workspace have become essential and influence organizational communication. For instance, one study found that adjustable partitions were associated with both greater perceived privacy and better communication.

As companies shrink workspaces to save money, managers need to ensure that the smaller and generally more open workspaces are useful and contribute to efficient and effective work.[46] By providing workspaces where employees can have some privacy and still have opportunities for collaborative efforts, both interpersonal and organizational communication can flourish and contribute to the organization's overall performance. Still, managers need to consider all of the pros and cons in deciding whether to create open spaces.

If your professor has assigned this, go to **www.mymanagementlab.com** to watch a video titled: *Rudi's Bakery: Communication* and to respond to questions.

★ Watch It 2!

COMMUNICATION **in the Internet and social media age**

LO14.4 Technology is changing the way we live and work. Need proof? An average knowledge worker spends 28 percent of his or her week writing, reading, or answering e-mail.[47] Also, consider the following five examples: Chefs are using digital approaches to solve a kitchen crisis—recipe clutter. Japanese employees, managers, housewives, and teens use wireless interactive Web phones to send e-mail, surf the Web, swap photos, and play computer games. At DreamWorks Animation, a sophisticated videoconferencing system allows animators in three different locations to collaboratively edit films. Several thousand employees at Ford use cell phones exclusively at work. A survey of employees showed that 93 percent of those polled use the Internet at work. Employees at Lockheed Martin Corporation can access an internal social media site called Unity, which includes tools such as blogs, wikis, file-sharing, discussion forums, and social bookmarking.[48]

Lockheed Martin's Unity intranet has helped the corporation become more efficient and innovative. The aircraft and missile builder credits its companywide social media site for raising productivity and leading to improved collaboration and knowledge exchange among its 125,000 employees worldwide.
Source: Erik S. Lesser/EPA/Newscom

The world of communication isn't what it used to be! Although changing technology has been a significant source of the environmental uncertainty facing organizations, these same technological changes have enabled managers to coordinate employees' work efforts in more efficient and effective ways. Information technology (IT) now touches every aspect of almost every company's business. The implications for how, where, and when managers communicate are profound.

The 24/7 Work Environment

There was a time not so long ago when most employees rarely communicated after traditional work hours. That's because it was not convenient to do so. IT has made it possible to stay connected around the clock, seven days per week. And IT has radically changed the way organizational members communicate. For example, IT has significantly improved a manager's ability to monitor individual and team performance, has allowed employees to have more complete information to make faster decisions, and has provided employees more opportunities to collaborate and share information. In addition, IT has made it possible for people in organizations to be fully accessible, at any time, regardless of where they are. Employees don't have to be at their desk with their computers running to communicate with others in the organization.

Working from Anywhere

At Seattle-based Starbucks, district managers use mobile technology that allows them more time to visit company stores. A company executive says, "These [district managers] are the most important people in the company. Each has between eight [and] ten stores that he or she services. And while their primary job is outside of the office—and in those stores—they still need to be connected."[49] As this example shows, wireless communication technology has the ability to improve work for managers and employees. Internet access is increasingly available through Wi-Fi and wireless access hotspots. And the number of these hotspot locations continues to grow.

Because Volkswagen (VW) has 600,000 employees worldwide, it has designated English as its official language to facilitate internal communication. In the United Kingdom, as in some other areas, VW operates an online information "hub" for employees to access from anywhere, at any time, using any digital device.[50] Employees don't have to be at their desks to communicate with others in the organization. As wireless technology continues to improve, we'll see more organizational members using it as a way to collaborate and share information.

Social Media

An executive vice president of sales tells his team of 100 district sales managers that they need to read the results of a survey regarding trends in consumer preferences. He posts the report on the company's HipChat channel created for information exchange about this subject. This allows the entire team to read the report and exchange their experiences. His employees can now read, comment, and exchange related articles on this same channel, much as they would with a group chat on Facebook. This approach provides two important benefits. First, most employees send and receive dozens of business e-mails every day, and sometimes important e-mails get lost in crowded inboxes. Devoting a channel for information exchange about a specific topic can help compartmentalize the conversation. Second, the sales manager in this example is not only conveying important information, but he also is starting a useful conversation in which employees can share their experiences and make suggestions for creating competitive advantage.

While YouTube has become a popular social media tool, Monsanto is using a YouTube type of approach to raise the visibility of some projects and make a stronger argument for bioengineered crops. The company sent camera crews to the Philippines, Australia, and other countries to film testimonials from farmers using Monsanto products to grow bioengineered crops. The clips were posted on a company website, which now attracts more than 15,000 visitors a month. The PR manager in charge of the project said, "When the people involved relate how their life has changed and you actually see it, it's more compelling."[51] That's the power of IT at work. Employees—working in teams or as individuals—need information to make decisions and to do their work. It's clear that technology *can* significantly affect the way that organizational members communicate, share information, and do their work.

Balancing the Pluses and Minuses

Communication and the exchange of information among organizational members are no longer constrained by geography or time. Collaborative work efforts among widely dispersed individuals and teams, sharing of information, and integration of decisions and work throughout an entire organization have the potential to increase organizational efficiency and effectiveness. However, companies need to guard against relying exclusively on IT for collaborative work. For example, constantly staying connected has its downsides, such as impeding creativity. Communication expert Maura Thomas said: "Creativity, inspiration, and motivation are your competitive advantage, but they are also depletable resources that need to be recharged."[52] Some companies recognize the importance of downtime. For instance, Vynamic, a health care consulting firm, keeps after-hours e-mails down to a minimum by using software that automatically holds e-mails until the beginning of work hours. And while the economic benefits of IT are obvious, managers must not forget the psychological drawbacks.[53] For example, what is the psychological cost of an employee always being accessible? Will it lead to increased pressure for employees to "check in" even during their off hours? How important is it for employees to separate their work and personal lives? These questions don't come with easy answers, and managers will have to face these and similar issues.

Choosing the Right Media

We've reviewed a variety of communication media in this chapter. Now it becomes important for managers to understand the situations in which one or more media facilitates effective communication. Electronic media—social media, e-mail, and instant messaging—are all effective and efficient methods for communicating relatively straightforward information to one or more individuals. For instance, electronic communication is appropriate for announcing meeting times, locations, and an overview

FUTURE VISION | No Longer Lost in Translation

Globalization creates many communication challenges for organizations. While many international companies have adopted English as their official business language, such a move often creates complications for organizations and negatively impacts employee productivity.[54] While Google Translate made some progress in international communication, at least eliminating the need for pocket dictionaries, the future of translation machines has arrived and might just change the way business people communicate when they travel.

Imagine simply speaking into a device that translates your message instantly and accurately, almost as if you have a native language speaker traveling with you. The first such machine is already on the market. Technology company Logbar launched Ili, a device that is worn around your neck and is voice activated. It does not require an Internet connection, one of the limitations of Google Translate and other online translation services, making translation available at anytime, anywhere. The device provides more precise, grammatically correct translations allowing easy communication in any setting. Such technology will open the door to international business for non-English speakers. The future now holds exciting opportunities for businesses to expand globally more easily, in particular into markets that are now considered too difficult to navigate because of the language barrier.

If your professor has chosen to assign this, go to ***www.mymanagementlab.com*** *to discuss the following questions.*

TALK ABOUT IT 1: Why is communication across different languages important for the global marketplace?

TALK ABOUT IT 2: Would you feel comfortable traveling to a country where you do not speak the language if you had a mobile translator?

of the agenda. However, exchanging confidential information about an employee's performance or a company's competitive secrets should be left for face-to-face meetings or telephone conversations. This should also be the case for complex issues such as communicating revisions to project schedules. The electronic form of face-to-face meetings, videoconferencing, can bring geographically dispersed colleagues together to share multiple perspectives of key stakeholders. For instance, making strategy for a new marketing campaign requires the participation of the client and marketing department employees for creative input and finance department employees for budgetary advice. In sum, we considered some of the situations in which particular communication methods are better or more appropriate than others. Now, it's important to look at some of the important communication issues that managers are facing in organizations.

For Nestlé, the world's largest consumer goods company, with more than 2,000 brands, being an effective communicator means being connected with employees and customers. Nestlé has created a Digital Acceleration Team (DAT) that serves as a digital leadership training program for employees to monitor social networks and as a test lab for developing innovative digital marketing projects.
Source: Denis Balibouse/Reuters Pictures

COMMUNICATION **issues in today's organizations**

LO14.5 "Pulse lunches." That's what managers at Citibank's offices throughout Malaysia used to address pressing problems of declining customer loyalty and staff morale and increased employee turnover. By connecting with employees and listening to their concerns—that is, taking their "pulse"—during informal lunch settings, managers were able to make changes that boosted both customer loyalty and employee morale by more than 50 percent and reduced employee turnover to nearly zero.[55]

Being an effective communicator in today's organizations means being connected—not only to employees and customers, but to all of the organization's stakeholders. In this section, we examine five communication issues of particular significance to today's managers: managing communication in a digitally connected world, managing the organization's knowledge resources, communicating with customers, getting employee input, and communicating ethically.

Managing Communication in a Digitally Connected World

Number one—that's where e-mail ranks in terms of problems of the modern workplace.[56] Lars Dalgaard, founder and chief executive of SuccessFactors, a human resource management software company, recently sent an e-mail to his employees banning in-house e-mail for a week. His goal? Getting employees to "authentically address issues amongst each other."[57] And he's not alone. Other companies have tried the same thing. As we discussed earlier, e-mail can consume employees, but it's not always easy for them to let go of it, even when they know it can be "intexticating." But e-mail is only one communication challenge in this Internet world. One survey found that 20 percent of employees at large companies say they contribute regularly to blogs, social networks, wikis, and other Web services.[58] Managers are learning, the hard way sometimes, that all this new technology has created special communication challenges. The two main ones are (1) legal and security issues and (2) lack of personal interaction.

LEGAL AND SECURITY ISSUES Chevron paid $2.2 million to settle a sexual-harassment lawsuit stemming from inappropriate jokes being sent by employees over company e-mail. U.K. firm Norwich Union had to pay £450,000 in an out-of-court settlement after an employee sent an e-mail stating that their competitor Western Provident Association was experiencing financial difficulties. Whole Foods Market was investigated by federal regulators and its board after CEO John P. Mackey used a pseudonym to post comments on a blog attacking the company's rival Wild Oats Markets.[59]

Although e-mail, blogs, tweets, and other forms of online communication are quick and easy ways to communicate, managers need to be aware of potential legal problems from inappropriate usage. Electronic information is potentially admissible in court. For instance, during the Enron trial, prosecutors entered into evidence e-mails and other documents they say showed that the defendants defrauded investors. Says one expert, "Today, e-mail and instant messaging are the electronic equivalent of DNA evidence."[60] But legal problems aren't the only issue—security concerns are as well.

For instance, Sony Pictures Entertainment was the target of hackers who successfully obtained sensitive information about employee pay, financial information, and confidential communications about particular movie stars.[61] In another example, hackers penetrated the federal government's human resources database from which they obtained information about security clearances and health care records.[62] These security breaches are a reminder that computer networks are not impenetrable. Corporate computer and e-mail systems should be protected against hackers and spam mail. These serious issues must be addressed if the benefits of communication technology are to be realized.

PERSONAL INTERACTION It may be called social media, but another communication challenge posed by the Internet age we live and work in is the lack of personal interaction.[63] Even when two people are communicating face-to-face, understanding is not always achieved. However, it can be especially challenging to achieve understanding and collaborate on getting work done when communication takes place in a virtual environment. In response, some companies have banned e-mail on certain days, as we saw earlier. Others have simply encouraged employees to collaborate more in person. Yet, in some situations and at certain times, personal interaction isn't physically possible—your colleagues work across the continent or even across the globe. In those instances, real-time collaboration software (such as private workplace wikis, blogs, instant messengers, and other types of groupware) may be a better communication choice than sending an e-mail and waiting for a response.[64] Instead of fighting it, other companies are encouraging employees to utilize the power of social networks to collaborate on work and to build strong connections. This form of interaction is especially appealing to younger workers who are comfortable with this communication medium. Some companies have gone as far as creating their own in-house social networks. For instance, employees at Starcom MediaVest Group tap into SMG Connected to find colleague profiles that outline their jobs, list the brands they admire, and describe their values. A company vice president says, "Giving our employees a way to connect over the Internet around the world made sense because they were doing it anyway."[65]

Managing the Organization's Knowledge Resources

Kara Johnson is a materials expert at product design firm IDEO. To make finding the right materials easier, she's building a master library of samples linked to a database that explains their properties and manufacturing processes.[66] What Johnson is doing is managing knowledge and making it easier for others at IDEO to learn and benefit from her knowledge. That's what today's managers need to do with the organization's knowledge resources—make it easy for employees to communicate and share their knowledge so they can learn from each other ways to do their jobs more effectively and efficiently. One way organizations can do this is to build online information databases that employees can access. For example, William Wrigley Jr. Co. launched an interactive website that allows sales agents to access marketing data and other product information. The sales agents can question company experts about products or search an online knowledge bank. In its first year, Wrigley estimates that the site cut research time of the sales force by 15,000 hours, making them more efficient and effective.[67]

The Role of Communication in Customer Service

You've been a customer many times; in fact, you probably find yourself in a customer service encounter several times a day. So what does this have to do with communication? As it turns out, a lot! *What* communication takes place and *how* it takes place can have a significant impact on a customer's satisfaction with the service and the likelihood of being a repeat customer. Managers in service organizations need to make sure that employees who interact with customers are communicating appropriately and effectively with those customers. How? By first recognizing the three components in any service delivery process: the customer, the service organization, and the individual service provider.[68] Each plays a role in whether communication is working. Obviously, managers don't have a lot of control over what or how the customer communicates, but they can influence the other two.

An organization with a strong service culture already values taking care of customers—finding out what their needs are, meeting those needs, and following up to make sure that their needs were met satisfactorily. Each of these activities involves communication, whether face-to-face, by phone or e-mail, or through other channels. In addition, communication is part of the specific customer service strategies the organization pursues. One strategy that many service organizations use is personalization. For instance, at Ritz-Carlton Hotels, customers are provided with more than a clean bed and room. Customers who have stayed at a location previously and indicated that certain items are important to them—such as extra pillows, hot chocolate, or a certain brand of shampoo—will find those items waiting in their room at arrival. The hotel's database allows service to be personalized to customers' expectations. In addition, all employees are asked to communicate information related to service provision. For instance, if a room attendant overhears guests talking about celebrating an anniversary, he or she is supposed to relay the information so something special can be done.[69] Communication plays an important role in the hotel's customer personalization strategy.

Communication also is important to the individual service provider or contact employee. The quality of the interpersonal interaction between the customer and that contact employee does influence customer satisfaction, especially when the service encounter isn't up to expectations.[70] People on the front line involved with those "critical service encounters" are often the first to hear about or notice service failures or breakdowns. They must decide *how* and *what* to communicate during these instances. Their ability to listen actively and communicate appropriately with the customer goes a long way in determining whether the situation is resolved to the customer's satisfaction or spirals out of control. At a small chain of boutique hotels, all employees are being trained on body language so that they can "read" guests' needs.[71] Another important communication concern for the individual service provider is making sure that he or she has the information needed to deal with customers efficiently and effectively. If the service provider doesn't personally have the information, some way needs to be devised to get the information easily and promptly.[72]

Sisters Jenny Briones (left) and Lisa De Bono (right), owner-operators of several McDonald's restaurants, value the opinions and ideas of employees. Shown here seeking feedback from a manager, they believe that communication plays a big part in the growth and success of their business as it engenders trust and respect among managers, employees, and customers.
Source: H. Lorren Au Jr.,/ZUMApress/Newscom

Getting Employee Input

Nokia set up an intranet soapbox known as Blog-Hub, opening it up to employee bloggers around the world. There, employees have griped about their employer, but rather than shutting it down, Nokia managers want them to "fire away." They feel that Nokia's growth and success can be attributed to allowing employees to speak up about what's bothering them, trusting that innovative "ideas will result."[73]

In today's challenging environment, companies need to get input from their employees. Have you ever worked somewhere that had an employee suggestion box? When an employee had an idea about a new way of doing something—such as reducing costs, improving delivery time, and so forth—it went into the suggestion box, where it usually sat until someone decided to empty the box. Businesspeople frequently joked about the suggestion box, and cartoonists lambasted the futility of putting ideas in the employee suggestion box. And unfortunately, this attitude about suggestion boxes still

Exhibit 14-5

How to Let Employees Know Their Input Matters

- ***Hold town hall meetings*** where information is shared and input solicited.
- ***Provide information*** about what's going on, good and bad.
- ***Invest in training*** so that employees see how they impact the customer experience.
- ***Analyze problems together***—managers and employees.
- ***Make it easy*** for employees to give input by setting up different ways for them to do so (online, suggestion box, preprinted cards, and so forth).

persists in many organizations, and it shouldn't. Managers do business in a world today where you can't afford to ignore such potentially valuable information. Exhibit 14-5 lists some suggestions for letting employees know that their opinions matter.

Letting employees know that their opinions matter is an essential first step in building effective suggestions systems. But what happens afterward is also critically important. Managers should explain how suggestions are reviewed, and feedback about the feasibility of suggestions should be shared, not just *whether* the ideas are feasible, but also *why* suggestions are feasible or not.[74] For feasible ideas, the next steps leading toward possible implementation should be communicated. Approaching suggestions systems in this manner will go a long way toward encouraging employees to think about how they can improve the way work gets done, providing better customer service, and possibly contributing to positive financial outcomes.

Communicating Ethically

It's particularly important today that a company's communication efforts be ethical. **Ethical communication** "includes all relevant information, is true in every sense, and is not deceptive in any way."[75] On the other hand, unethical communication often distorts the truth or manipulates audiences. What are some ways that companies communicate unethically? It could be by omitting essential information. For instance, not telling employees that an impending merger is going to mean some of them will lose their jobs is unethical. It's unethical to plagiarize, which is "presenting someone else's words or other creative product as your own."[76] It would also be unethical communication to selectively misquote, misrepresent numbers, distort visuals, and fail to respect privacy or information security needs. For instance, although British Petroleum attempted to communicate openly and truthfully about the Gulf Coast oil spill in the summer of 2010, the public still felt that much of the company's communication contained some unethical elements.

ethical communication
Communication that includess all relevant information, is true in every sense, and is not deceptive in any way

So how can managers encourage ethical communications? One way is to establish clear guidelines for ethical behavior, including ethical business communication.[77] In a global survey by the International Association of Business Communicators, 70 percent of communication professionals said their companies clearly define what is considered ethical and unethical behavior.[78] If no clear guidelines exist, it's important to answer the following questions:

- Has the situation been defined fairly and accurately?
- Why is the message being communicated?
- How will the people who may be affected by the message or who receive the message be impacted?
- Does the message help achieve the greatest possible good while minimizing possible harm?
- Will this decision that appears to be ethical now seem so in the future?
- How comfortable are you with your communication effort? What would a person you admire think of it?[79]

Remember that as a manager, you have a responsibility to think through your communication choices and the consequences of those choices. If you always operate with these two things in mind, you're likely to have ethical communication.

BECOMING a better communicator

LO14.6 Most managers will tell you that becoming an effective communicator is one ingredient of a successful career. They're right. You should always take the opportunity to improve your communication skills. In addition to listening skills, which we discussed in our chapter opening, other important communication skills include persuasion, speaking, writing, and reading. Let's briefly look at each of these. The *Skills Exercise* (page 512) gives you an opportunity to develop some of these important communication skills.

Sharpening Your Persuasion Skills

persuasion skills
Skills that enable a person to influence others to change their minds or behavior

Successful managers demonstrate good persuasion skills. **Persuasion skills** enable a person to influence others to change their minds or behavior. Consider the following. Richard Branson, founder of conglomerate Virgin (including Virgin Mobile and Virgin Megastore), learned the value of persuasion at an early age. While attending boarding school, Branson launched his first business venture, creating *Student* magazine. But he recognized that he could not do so without the backing of investors. Branson successfully learned how to make five-minute pitches over the telephone and was quite successful at it: The magazine has been in business since 1968. What made his pitches successful? Branson said: "Any fool can make something complicated. It's hard to make something simple."[80]

Apart from brevity, there are other elements to effective persuasion. For instance, communication expert Mark Rodgers indicates that effective persuasion starts with stating the importance of following a course of action and the likely benefits.[81] Another characteristic of persuasive messages is to use descriptive language such as metaphors, humor, and analogies.

Sharpening Your Speaking Skills

By now, you have probably made many class presentations. An advantage of giving class presentations is the chance to develop speaking skills. **Speaking skills** refer to the ability to communicate information and ideas by talking so others will understand. One survey revealed that 70 percent of employees who make presentations say that good presentation skills are important to career success.[82] Yet, discomfort with public speaking holds some employees back. About 20 percent of survey respondents revealed that they would avoid making presentations even if it meant "losing respect."[83] Fortunately, there are resources to help you overcome discomfort with public speaking, such as local Toastmasters clubs, which provide opportunities to make formal and impromptu speeches in a supportive environment.

speaking skills
Skills that refer to the ability to communicate information and ideas in talking so others will understand

Once you develop greater confidence to speak before others, it is necessary to understand the characteristics of effective speaking. Attending successful business professionals' presentations or watching them online is a good starting point. You will likely notice the following speaker's characteristics in effective speakers: authenticity, humility, brevity, and a clear understanding of the audience.[84]

Sharpening Your Writing Skills

writing skills
Skills that entail communicating effectively in text as appropriate for the needs of the audience

Writing skills entail communicating effectively in text that is most appropriate for its audience. As a starting point, here is what not to do:

> "AFIK, the meating will take place at 2 2morow. HTH! I look 4 u so that u and me can sit 2gether."

There are many problems with this message. It contains abbreviations with which others may not be familiar, and there are multiple spelling and grammatical errors. Writing in this manner will surely undermine your credibility and raise questions about your creativity, organization skills, trustworthiness, consideration of others, and intelligence.[85] It also demonstrates a degree of laziness because spell and grammar check features are available in most e-mail and word processing programs. And a note to millennials: Abbreviations and jargon that are standard in texting among friends and family are not always appreciated in a business setting.

Some additional points: First, don't be in a rush to press the send button or drop the memo in the mail. Oftentimes, poorly constructed e-mail messages or written memos are the result of rushing. The same applies to sending communiques when you're emotionally upset. Set your message aside; then, review it with fresh eyes. You might also ask a colleague to review it. Second, express information and ideas logically and don't switch back and forth between topics. Third, check the accuracy of the content. For instance, the meeting is scheduled for 3 pm, but 2 pm was written in error. Finally, read the message carefully to ensure that an inaccurate word for the context doesn't slip in. Spell-check programs can fix misspellings but not the wrong word choice. For example, you mistakenly typed *manger* when you meant to type *manager* or *polices* when you meant to type *policies*.

Sharpening Your Reading Skills

As discussed earlier, employees receive an average of 121 work e-mails daily, and that number is expected to rise. They also receive many written memos, reports, and policy statements. The sheer volume alone requires good reading skills. What are they? **Reading skills** entail an understanding of written sentences and paragraphs in work-related documents. If your reading skills aren't up to par—either in comprehension or speed—don't be afraid to sign up for a reading-improvement class.

reading skills
Skills that entail an understanding of written sentences and paragraphs in work-related documents.

Chapter 14 PREPARING FOR: Exams/Quizzes

CHAPTER SUMMARY by Learning Objectives

LO14.1 DEFINE the nature and function of communication.

Communication is the transfer and understanding of meaning. Interpersonal communication is communication between two or more people. Organizational communication includes all the patterns, networks, and systems of communication within an organization.

The functions of communication include controlling employee behavior, motivating employees, providing a release for emotional expression of feelings and fulfillment of social needs, and providing information.

LO14.2 DESCRIBE methods and challenges of interpersonal communication.

The communication process contains seven elements. First, a *sender* has a message. A *message* is a purpose to be conveyed. *Encoding* converts a message into symbols. A *channel* is the medium a message travels along. *Decoding* happens when the *receiver* retranslates a sender's message. Finally, *feedback* occurs.

Managers can evaluate the various communication methods according to their feedback, complexity capacity, breadth potential, confidentiality, encoding ease, decoding ease, time-space constraint, cost, interpersonal warmth, formality, scanability, and time of consumption. Nonverbal communication is transmitted without words and includes body language and verbal intonation.

Cognitive barriers to effective communication include information overload and filtering. Emotions, sociocultural differences, and national culture also create barriers.

Feedback, simplified language, active listening, constraining emotions, and watching nonverbal cues can help overcome barriers.

LO14.3 EXPLAIN how communication can flow most effectively in organizations.

Formal communication is communication that takes place within prescribed organizational work arrangements. Informal communication is not defined by the organization's structural hierarchy. Communication in an organization can flow downward, upward, laterally, and diagonally.

The three communication networks include the chain, in which communication flows according to the formal chain of command; the wheel, in which communication flows between a clearly identifiable and strong leader and others in a work team; and the all-channel, in which communication flows freely among all members of a work team. The grapevine is the informal organizational communication network.

Workplace design also influences organizational communication. That design should support four types of employee work: focused work, collaboration, learning, and socialization. In each of these circumstances, communication must be considered.

LO14.4 DESCRIBE how the Internet and social media affect managerial communication and organizations.

Technology has changed the way we live and work. It has created a 24/7 work environment as it is possible to stay connected around the clock and work from anywhere. Social media allows managers to communicate through one channel and encourages sharing experiences. While IT allows collaborative work, managers must be cautious that they do not overuse technology and impede creativity. Managers must also choose the right media for the message they are sending.

LO14.5 SUMMARIZE communication issues in today's organizations.

The main challenges of communicating in a digitally connected world are legal and security issues and the lack of personal interaction.

Organizations can manage knowledge by making it easy for employees to communicate and share their knowledge, which can help them learn from each other ways to do their jobs more effectively and efficiently. One way is through online information databases.

Communicating with customers is an important managerial issue since *what* communication takes place and *how* it takes place can significantly affect a customer's satisfaction with the service and the likelihood of being a repeat customer.

It's important for organizations to get input from their employees. Such potentially valuable information should not be ignored. Managers should explain how suggestions are reviewed and feedback about the feasibility of suggestions should be shared.

Finally, a company's communication efforts need to be ethical. Ethical communication can be encouraged through clear guidelines and through answering questions that force a communicator to think through the communication choices made and the consequences of those choices.

LO14.6 DISCUSS how to become a better communicator.

You can become a better communicator through sharpening your active listening, persuasion, speaking, writing, and reading skills.

Pearson **MyLab** Management

Go to **mymanagementlab.com** to complete the problems marked with this icon ✪.

REVIEW AND DISCUSSION QUESTIONS

14-1. What is communication and how can a manager ensure proper communication exists in the organization?

14-2. Do men and women communicate differently? Discuss.

14-3. "Thanks a lot." What does this phrase mean?

14-4. What are barriers to communication? What can managers do to reduce the chances of barriers to communication from occurring?

14-5. What does "active listening" mean?

14-6. How can changes in the physical work environment have a direct impact on communication systems?

14-7. Discuss the role of communication in customer service.

14-8. "Ethical communication includes all information, is true in every sense, and is not deceptive in any way." Discuss.

Pearson **MyLab** Management

If your professor has assigned these, go to **mymanagementlab.com** for the following Assisted-graded writing questions:

14-9. What are the barriers to effective communication? How can those barriers be overcome?

14-10. Explain how IT can be positive and negative in managerial communication terms.

PREPARING FOR: My Career

PERSONAL INVENTORY ASSESSMENT

COMMUNICATION STYLES

What type of communication style(s) do you use? Take this PIA and learn more about communication styles.

ETHICS DILEMMA

Forty-nine percent of workers would prefer not to connect with coworkers on Facebook.[86]

Social networking websites can be fun. Staying in touch with old friends or even family is one of the pleasures of joining. However, what happens when colleagues or even your boss want to "friend" you? Experts say that you should proceed with caution.[87]

14-11. What do you think? Is it okay to provide people you know in a professional sense a "window into your personal life?"

14-12. What ethical issues might arise in such a situation?

SKILLS EXERCISE Developing Your Presentation Skills

About the Skill

Managers make presentations for a variety of reasons. Whether you are sharing information about a new product or process, proposing a solution to a problem, training new employees, or selling a product to a customer; your ability to effectively deliver a presentation is an essential communication skill. Your effectiveness as a speaker will often impact whether or not your presentation achieves the desired outcome. The good news is that with some planning and practice, you can become an engaging presenter.[88]

Steps in Practicing the Skill

- ***Know your audience.*** Consider your audience for the presentation. What do they already know about your presentation topic? What do they need to learn from the presentation? Are they interested in your topic? Understanding your audience and their needs can help you tailor your message and content.
- ***Organize your content.*** Start with an opening that allows you to connect with the audience. Include a story or scenario that engages the audience or use some data or other information to help them understand the problem at hand. For the body of the presentation, try to stick to three or four main points that you organize your information around. Have a clear closing to your presentation that leaves the audience with something to consider or remember.
- ***Prepare compelling visuals.*** Only use presentation slides to complement your presentation; don't make your visuals a distraction. Keep it simple, don't include too many words on your slides or your audience will be reading instead of listening to you. Consider using graphics or photos that help illustrate your points.
- ***Practice, practice, practice!*** While it is fine to have note cards, you should not read the presentation. Rehearse so that you are comfortable with the content, but don't sound like you've just memorized it. Consider video recording yourself when you are rehearsing so you can identify where you need improvement.
- ***Calm your nerves.*** Everyone gets nervous before a presentation. Make sure you take some deep breaths and stand tall and confident. Preparation is the best antidote to nervousness.
- ***Focus on your delivery.*** Use a confident tone and watch out for the use of "nonwords" (ah, um, or like). Make eye contact and ask questions to engage the audience.

Practicing the Skill

Look for opportunities to deliver presentations. Volunteer to take the lead in class presentations, make presentations for organizations you are involved with, or ask your boss for an opportunity to present. Use the above guidelines to prepare and deliver your presentation. Your confidence will grow as you gain experience in giving presentations.

WORKING TOGETHER Team Exercise

Increasingly, businesses need to ensure that they are not only connected with the employees and customers, but also that their employees are connected with one another.[89] Form groups of three or four individuals. Discuss why connection is essential and draw up a list of points. Discuss and list the advantages and disadvantages of constant connectivity. Then share your points with the rest of the class.

MY TURN TO BE A MANAGER

- For one day, keep track of the types of communication you use (see Exhibit 14-2 for a list of various types). Which do you use most? Least? Were your choices of communication methods effective? Why or why not? Could they have been improved? How?
- For one day, track nonverbal communication that you notice in others. What types did you observe? Was the nonverbal communication always consistent with the verbal communication taking place? Describe.
- Survey five different managers for their advice on being a good communicator. Put this information in a bulleted list format and be prepared to present it in class.
- Improve your oral speaking skills by joining a Toastmasters Club (www.toastmasters.org). Toastmasters

is a nonprofit organization that teaches public speaking through a network of clubs where you can practice giving speeches to an audience that provides feedback to help you improve your skills.

- Identify at least one company that effectively uses social media to communicate with customers and/or employees. What social media applications does the company use? Subscribe to the company's social media feeds and take notes regarding their social media communications for at least one week. What patterns do you see? What are social media messages that are effective based on the number of "likes" or "shares"?
- Given that e-mail is still a primary method of communication within most organizations, it is important to practice using it effectively. Research e-mail etiquette and create a list of "do's" and "don'ts" for using e-mail.
- There are many software applications on the market to help organizations manage their knowledge resources. Research knowledge management software and create a list of different software applications available and the key features of each product.

CASE APPLICATION 1 Is Anytime Feedback Too Much?

Founded by Jeff Bezos in 1994 (see Chapter 8, Leader Making a Difference), Amazon is the world's biggest retailer based on market value.[90] Many credit the organization's work environment and culture for motivating employees to create innovations such as the Kindle and drone delivery. Like others in the technology sector, Amazon is known for an unconventional workplace. However, unlike the "perk"-heavy, country-club style workplace that characterizes many tech companies, Amazon's workplace culture emphasizes hard work and competition.

Managers at Amazon are data-driven and focused on productivity. Some say that the environment can be harsh because employees who don't make the grade are eliminated through the annual performance review process. Competition is encouraged, and workplace conflict occurs often. Amazon's culture is reinforced by 14 principles that guide employee behavior. Number 13, "disagree and commit," reflects Bezos's belief that harmony in the workplace is overvalued and it can stifle honest critique. Feedback on performance is encouraged, and many Amazon employees claim the competitive work environment helps them thrive as it pushes them past their limits.

Not everyone at Amazon agrees with the way the feedback is delivered. Some Amazonians report that feedback is sometimes very blunt and interpreted as confrontational or even painful. Furthermore, sometimes managers deliver feedback to employees on performance that they did not observe first-hand. Managers often receive reviews of their employees' performance via a controversial online feedback tool. The Anytime Feedback Tool is a widget in the company directory that allows employees to easily send feedback about coworkers to management. The bosses know who sends the feedback, but in practice they keep feedback anonymous when shared back to employees. Amazon claims this is just another tool to send feedback to managers, similar to e-mail. However, some claim that the anonymous use of this tool, coupled with its ease of use, creates problems. Given the competitive nature of the organization, some Amazonians claim that the tool is often used to sabotage others. Employees can send false or misleading feedback via the tool, and those getting the feedback are unable to defend themselves from the anonymous feedback.

Jeff Bezos claims that while the organization is competitive, reports of such callous behavior do not reflect the Amazon he knows. He noted in a letter to shareholders that organizational culture evolves over time, and people self-select into an organization. While Amazon does see a high level of employee turnover, in the more than two decades since the company was founded, they have collected a significant number of employees who thrive in their feedback-rich environment.

DISCUSSION QUESTIONS

14-13. Can a manager provide honest feedback to employees without being confrontational?

14-14. Do you think the Anytime Feedback Tool is a useful communication tool for an organization? Why or why not?

14-15. How could Amazon eliminate concerns with employees using the tool to sabotage other employees?

14-16. Would you like to work in a competitive organization like Amazon? Why or why not?

CASE APPLICATION 2 Neutralizing the Concordia Effect!

Communication has become crucial in Costa Cruises (the Italian cruise company owned by Carnival Corporation). In recent events, the *Costa Concordia* keeled over off the Italian coast near the island of Giglio in Tuscany, Italy, in January 2012 and the *Costa Allegra* was hit by fire and drifts in the Indian Ocean a few weeks later. Captain Schettino's preliminary abandoning of the *Costa Concordia* as well as his denial to return onboard the sinking ship brought into question the competence of the company crew as well as the effectiveness of recruitment procedures. After a few days of the company stressing that the complete responsibilities of the accident were attributed to the captain, Costa Cruises decided to suspend all social media activities as a sign of respect for the victims and as an attempt to prevent inappropriate comments.

However, the lack of disclosure and the distorted information coming from other media aroused contrasting reactions by customers, some of whom expressed solidarity and closeness to the victims as well as to the company, and others who were upset and frustrated by the company's silence. Later, in collaboration with the communication agency Burson-Marsteller, Costa Cruises decided to launch an exceptional communication campaign to defend the company's reputation and market share in the highly competitive and global cruise market. This time, the strategy was based on a complete disclosure of all rescue operations on social networks. Here are some examples of the actions undertaken: 1) continuous updates via social media on the rescue, recovery, and safety operations as well as on the assistance provided to the guests and their families in order to document the status of relief efforts; 2) information on the strategy for the removal of the wreck; 3) the reduction of the environmental impact of the accident; and 4) diligent communication of the protection of the island's eco-system (seriously threatened by heavy fuel oil).

The news of a friendly and successful negotiation for settling the initial compensation package for passengers of the shipwreck was promptly communicated with official press releases. The announcement of new safety measures was given during a ceremony celebrating the delivery of the company's new $665 million flagship *Costa Fascinosa*. Indeed, the number of bookings reserved four months later, showing an increase of 25 percent from what they were at the same time the year before was a big sigh of relief for Costa Cruises' executives.[91]

DISCUSSION QUESTIONS

14-17. Beyond possible human error and tragedy responsibilities, what do you think of this situation from the perspective of managing communications?

14-18. Why do you think the company's executives decided to silence communication on social media? Was this an appropriate strategy?

14-19. In the first weeks, how could the communication have been better managed by the management?

14-20. The increase in the number of bookings seems to corroborate the success of the latter communication strategy of a complete disclosure on social media. Discuss the communication management implications.

ENDNOTES

1. P. G. Clampitt, *Communicating for Managerial Effectiveness*, 5th ed. (Thousand Oaks, CA: Sage Publications, 2009); T. Dixon, *Communication, Organization, and Performance* (Norwood, NJ: Ablex Publishing Corporation, 1996), p. 281; and L. E. Penley, E. R. Alexander, I. Edward Jernigan, and C. I. Henwood, "Communication Abilities of Managers: The Relationship to Performance," *Journal of Management*, March 1991, pp. 57–76.
2. Jim Brunsden, "Volkswagen Set to Accelerate Diesel Recalls in Europe," *Financial Times*, September 25, 2016, https://www.ft.com, accessed December 27, 2016; Danny Hakim, "VW's Crisis Strategy: Forward, Reverse, U-Turn," *New York Times*, February 26, 2016, http://www.nytimes.com, accessed December 27, 2016.
3. C. O. Kursh, "The Benefits of Poor Communication," *Psychoanalytic Review*, Summer–Fall 1971, pp. 189–208.
4. "Irene Lewis, CEO of SAIT Polytechnic, to Receive IABC's 2012 EXCEL Award," www.iabc.com/awards, July 29, 2012.
5. W. G. Scott and T. R. Mitchell, *Organization Theory: A Structural and Behavioral Analysis* (Homewood, IL: Richard D. Irwin, 1976).
6. N. Clark, "After Backtracking on Trans-Atlantic Flights, Ryanair Learns Its Lessons," *The New York Times* online, www.nytimes.com, March 20, 2015.
7. D. K. Berlo, *The Process of Communication* (New York: Holt, Rinehart & Winston, 1960), pp. 30–32.
8. G. Zoroya, "Commander's Letter Tackles Morale," *USA Today*, October 16, 2009, p. 1A+.
9. Clampitt, *Communicating for Managerial Effectiveness*.
10. S. Parr, "Read These Books Instead of Getting an MBA," *Fortune* online, www.fortune.com, February 23, 2016.
11. W. Buffett, "Annual Letter to Shareholders 2015," http://berkshirehathaway.com/letters/2015ltr.pdf, accessed May 5, 2016.
12. A. Semnani-Azad and W. L. Adair, "Reading the Body Language in International Negotiations," *Strategy+Business* online, September 16, 2011; S. Smith, "But What Are You *Really* Saying?," Realsimple.com, December 2010, pp. 195+; J. Cloud, "Strike a Pose," *Time*, November 29, 2010, p. 61; L. Talley, "Body Language: Read It or Weep," *HR Magazine*, July 2010, pp. 64–65; Interview with A. Pentland, "The Impact of Unconscious Communication," *Gallup Management Journal* online, September 3, 2009; D. Tannen, "Every Move You Make," *O Magazine*, August 2006, pp. 175–176; A. Warfield, "Do You Speak Body Language?," *Training & Development*, April 2001, pp. 60–61; D. Zielinski, "Body Language Myths," *Presentations*, April 2001, pp. 36–42; and "Visual Cues Speak Loudly in Workplace," *Springfield, Missouri, News-Leader*, January 21, 2001, p. 8B.
13. J. R. Detert and E. R. Burris, "Nonverbal Cues Get Employees to Open Up—or Shut Down," *Harvard Business Review* online, www.hbr.org, December 11, 2015.
14. R. Lee Hotz, "How to Train Your Voice to be More Charismatic," *The Wall Street Journal* online, www.wsj.com, December 1, 2014.
15. Leader Making a Difference box based on J. Reingold, "What the Heck is Angela Ahrendts Doing at Apple?," *Fortune* online, www.fortune.com, September 10, 2015; V. Manning-Schaffel, " Introducing the 50 Most Powerful Moms of 2016," *Working Mother Magazine* online, www.workingmother.com, April 28, 2016; M. Stone, "Angela Ahrendts: How Last Year's Highest-Paid Female Exec Spends Her Millions," *Business Insider* online, www.businessinsider.com, May 12, 2015; A. Ahrendts, "The Power of Human Energy," TedxTalk, www.tedxtalks.com, May 1, 2013.
16. "Employee E-Mail Blunders," *Training*, September 2009, p. 8.
17. A. Williams, "At Meetings, It's Mind Your BlackBerry or Mind Your Manners," *New York Times* online, June 22, 2009.
18. C. Jenkin, "Emails Expected to Rise to 140 a Day in 2018," *News Corp Australia* online, www.news.com.au, May 4, 2014.
19. "Email Statistics Report, 2015–2019," *The Radicati Group, Inc.*, http://www.radicati.com/wp/wp-content/uploads/2015/02/Email-Statistics-Report-2015-2019-Executive-Summary.pdf, 2015, accessed May 5, 2016.
20. Berlo, *The Process of Communication*, p. 103.
21. R. Buckman, "Why the Chinese Hate to Use Voice Mail," *Wall Street Journal*, December 1, 2005, p. B1+.
22. A. Mehrabian, "Communication Without Words," *Psychology Today*, September 1968, pp. 53–55.
23. L. Haggerman, "Strong, Efficient Leadership Minimizes Employee Problems," *Springfield, Missouri, Business Journal*, December 9–15, 2002, p. 23.
24. D. Sturt, "The Easiest Thing You Can Do to Be a Great Boss," *Harvard Business Review* online, www.hbr.org, November 9, 2015.
25. N. Bendapudi and V. Bendapudi, "How to Use Language That Employees Get," *Harvard Business Review*, September 2009, p. 24.
26. See, for instance, S. P. Robbins and P. L. Hunsaker, *Training in Interpersonal Skills*, 5th ed. (Upper Saddle River, NJ: Prentice Hall, 2009); M. Young and J. E. Post, "Managing to Communicate, Communicating to Manage: How Leading Companies Communicate with Employees," *Organizational Dynamics*, Summer 1993, pp. 31–43; J. A. DeVito, *The Interpersonal Communication Book*, 6th ed. (New York: HarperCollins, 1992); and A. G. Athos and J. J. Gabarro, *Interpersonal Behavior* (Upper Saddle River, NJ: Prentice Hall, 1978).
27. D. Beucke, "Aviva Fires Everyone: Great Moments in Employee Motivation," www.businessweek.com, April 26, 2012.
28. K. O'Sullivan, "Escaping the Executive Bubble," *CFO*, January–February 2010, pp. 27–30.

29. M. Newlands, "5 Proven Ways to Improve Your Company's Communication," *Forbes* online, www.forbes.com, January 26, 2016.
30. O. Thomas, "Best-Kept Secrets of the World's Best Companies: The Three Minute Huddle," *Business 2.0,* April 2006, p. 94.
31. "Flipkart Does Soul-searching at Town Hall in Tech Hub," *India Today*, August 23, 2016, http://indiatoday.intoday.in, accessed December 27, 2016.
32. J. S. Lublin, "The 'Open Inbox,'" *Wall Street Journal,* October 10, 2005, pp. B1+.
33. Cited in "Shut Up and Listen," *Money*, November 2005, p. 27.
34. See, for instance, J. Smerd, "Gossip's Toll on the Workplace," *Workforce Management* online, March 2010; D. L. Wheeler, "Going After Gossip," *Workforce Management* online, July 2009; D. Sagario and L. Ballard, "Workplace Gossip Can Threaten Your Office," *Springfield News-Leader,* September 26, 2005, p. 5B; A. Bruzzese, "What to Do About Toxic Gossip," *USA Today*, www.usatoday.com, March 14, 2001; N. B. Kurland and L. H. Pelled, "Passing the Word: Toward a Model of Gossip and Power in the Workplace," *Academy of Management Review,* April 2000, pp. 428–438; N. DiFonzo, P. Bordia, and R. L. Rosnow, "Reining in Rumors," *Organizational Dynamics*, Summer 1994, pp. 47–62; M. Noon and R. Delbridge, "News from Behind My Hand: Gossip in Organizations," *Organization Studies*, vol. 14, no. 1, 1993, pp. 23–26; and J. G. March and G. Sevon, "Gossip, Information and Decision Making," in *Decisions and Organizations*, ed. J. G. March (Oxford: Blackwell, 1988), pp. 429–442.
35. "Secrets of Top Performers: How Companies with Highly Effective Employee Communication Differentiate Themselves, 2007/2008 Communication ROI Study™," Towers Watson, Washington, DC.
36. Gensler, "The U.S. Workplace Survey, 2008," www.gensler.com, July 11, 2010.
37. Ibid., p. 11.
38. C. C. Sullivan and B. Horwitz-Bennett, "High-Performance Workplaces," *Building Design + Construction,* January 2010, pp. 22–26.
39. J. B. Stryker, "In Open Workplaces, Traffic and Head Count Matter," *Harvard Business Review,* December 2009, p. 24.
40. SHRM Online Staff, "When Work Stinks," *HR Magazine,* June 2012, p. 26.
41. K. D. Elsbach and M. G. Pratt, "The Physical Environment in Organizations," in *The Academy of Management Annals,* vol. 1, 2007, ed. J. P. Walsh and A. P. Brief, pp. 181–114.
42. R. Feintzeig, "Study: Open Offices Are Making Us All Sick," blgs.wsj.com, February 25, 2014.
43. H. Stuart, "Companies Are Rethinking the Open Office, and It's About Time," *The Huffington Post* online, www.huffingtonpost.com, February 12, 2015.
44. C. Rexrode, "Citigroup's New Office Plan: No Offices," *The Wall Street Journal* online, www.wsj.com, December 26, 2015.
45. H. Stuart, "Companies Are Rethinking the Open Office, and It's About Time," *The Huffington Post* online, www.huffingtonpost.com, February 12, 2015.
46. S. E. Needleman, "Office Personal Space Is Crowded Out," *Wall Street Journal,* December 7, 2009, p. B7.
47. K. Komando, "Sending Less E-mail Could Allow More Work to Be Completed," *Springfield, Missouri, News-Leader,* September 11, 2012, p. 4B.
48. These examples taken from A. Dizik, "Chefs Solve a Modern Kitchen Crisis: Recipe Clutter," *Wall Street Journal,* June 30, 2011, p. D1+; T. Henneman, "At Lockheed Martin, Social Networking Fills Key Workforce Needs While Improving Efficiency and Lowering Costs," *Workforce Management* online, March 2010; S. Kirsner, "Being There," *Fast Company,* January–February 2006, pp. 90–91; R. Breeden, "More Employees Are Using the Web at Work," *Wall Street Journal,* May 10, 2005, p. B4; C. Woodward, "Some Offices Opt for Cellphones Only," *USA Today,* January 25, 2005, p. 1B; and J. Rohwer, "Today, Tokyo. Tomorrow, the World," *Fortune*, September 18, 2000, pp. 140–152.
49. J. Karaian, "Where Wireless Works," *CFO,* May 2003, pp. 81–83.
50. Dave Brown, "New Hub Will 'Future-proof' VW's Internal Communications," *Car Dealer Magazine*, October 19, 2016, http://cardealermagazine.co.uk/publish/new-hub-will-future-proof-internal-communications-volkswagen/123682 (accessed December 27, 2016); Christiaan Hetzner, "VW's Switch to English as Its Company Language Is a Key Reform," *Automotive News*, December 15, 2016, http://www.autonews.com/article/20161215/BLOG06/312159512/vws-switch-to-english-as-its-company-language-is-a-key-reform (accessed December 27, 2016).
51. B. White, "Firms Take a Cue from YouTube," *Wall Street Journal,* January 2, 2007, p. B3.
52. M. Thomas, "Your Late-Night Emails Are Hurting Your Team," *Harvard Business Review* online, www.hbr.org, March 16, 2015.
53. K. Hafner, "For the Well Connected, All the World's an Office," *New York Times,* March 30, 2000, pp. D1+.
54. Future Vision box based on T. Neeley, "Global Business Speaks English," *Harvard Business Review* online, www.hbr.org, May 2012; A. Ross, "The Language Barrier Is About to Fall," *The Wall Street Journal* online, www.wsj.com, January 29, 2016; T. Wells Lynch, "New Wearable Translator Aims to Smash Language Barriers, *USA Today* online, www.usatoday.com, January 7, 2016.
55. S. Luh, "Pulse Lunches at Asian Citibanks Feed Workers' Morale, Lower Job Turnover," *Wall Street Journal,* May 22, 2001, p. B11.
56. J. Rosenstein, "Fix This Workplace," *Bloomberg BusinessWeek,* December 18, 2013, pp. 84–85.
57. S. Shellenbager, "Backlash Against E-Mail Builds," *Wall Street Journal,* April 29, 2010, p. D6.
58. H. Green, "The Water Cooler Is Now on the Web," *BusinessWeek,* October 1, 2007, pp. 78–79.
59. The Associated Press, "Whole Foods Chief Apologizes for Posts," *New York Times* online, www.nytimes.com, July 18, 2007; E. White, J. S. Lublin, and D. Kesmodel, "Executives Get the Blogging Bug," *Wall Street Journal,* July 13, 2007, pp. B1+; C. Alldred, "U.K. Libel Case Slows E-Mail Delivery," *Business Insurance,* August 4, 1997, pp. 51–53; and T. Lewin, "Chevron Settles Sexual Harassment Charges," *New York Times* online, www.nytimes.com, February 22, 1995.
60. J. Eckberg, "E-Mail: Messages Are Evidence," *Cincinnati Enquirer*, www.enquirer.com, July 27, 2004.
61. C. Kang, C. Timberg, and E. Nakashima, "Sony's Hacked E-Mails Expose Spats, Director Calling Angelina Jolie a 'Brat,'" *The Washington Post* online, www.washingtonpost.com, December 11, 2014.

62. J. Sciutto, "OPM Government Data Breach Impacted 21.5 Million," *CNN* online, www.cnn.com, July 10, 2015.
63. K. Byron, "Carrying Too Heavy a Load? The Communication and Miscommunication of Emotion by E-Mail," *Academy of Management Review,* April 2008, pp. 309–327.
64. J. Marquez, "Virtual Work Spaces Ease Collaboration, Debate Among Scattered Employees," *Workforce Management,* May 22, 2006, p. 38; and M. Conlin, "E-Mail Is So Five Minutes Ago," *BusinessWeek,* November 28, 2005, pp. 111–112.
65. H. Green, "The Water Cooler Is Now on the Web," *BusinessWeek,* October 1, 2007, pp. 78–79; E. Frauenheim, "Starbucks Employees Carve Out Own 'Space,'" *Workforce Management,* October 22, 2007, p. 32; and S. H. Wildstrom, "Harnessing Social Networks," *BusinessWeek,* April 23, 2007, p. 20.
66. J. Scanlon, "Woman of Substance," *Wired,* July 2002, p. 27.
67. H. Dolezalek, "Collaborating in Cyberspace," *Training,* April 2003, p. 33.
68. B. A. Gutek, M. Groth, and B. Cherry, "Achieving Service Success Through Relationship and Enhanced Encounters," *Academy of Management Executive,* November 2002, pp. 132–144.
69. R. C. Ford and C. P. Heaton, "Lessons from Hospitality That Can Serve Anyone," *Organizational Dynamics,* Summer 2001, pp. 30–47.
70. M. J. Bitner, B. H. Booms, and L. A. Mohr, "Critical Service Encounters: The Employee's Viewpoint," *Journal of Marketing,* October 1994, pp. 95–106.
71. C. Jones, "Hotel Staff 'Reads' Guests' Needs," *USA Today,* October 25, 2011, p. 1A.
72. S. D. Pugh, J. Dietz, J. W. Wiley, and S. M. Brooks, "Driving Service Effectiveness Through Employee-Customer Linkages," *Academy of Management Executive,* November 2002, pp. 73–84.
73. J. Ewing, "Nokia: Bring on the Employee Rants," *BusinessWeek,* June 22, 2009, p. 50.
74. E. R. Burris, "Employee Suggestion Schemes Don't Have to Be Exercises in Futility," *Harvard Business Review* online, www.hbr.org, January 26, 2016.
75. J. V. Thill and C. L. Bovee, *Excellence in Business Communication,* 9th ed. (Upper Saddle River, NJ: Prentice Hall, 2011), pp. 24–25.
76. Ibid.
77. Ibid.
78. Ibid.
79. Ibid.
80. C. Gallo, "Branson, Buffett Agree: This Skill Is Your Ticket To Career Success," *Forbes* online, www.forbes.com, February 18, 2016.
81. M. Rodgers, *The Benefits of Persuasion.* New York: American Management Association, 2015.
82. C. Gallo, "New Survey: 70% Say Presentation Skills Are Critical for Career Success," *Forbes* online, www.forbes.com, September 25, 2014.
83. Ibid.
84. R. Bradley, "Why Public Speaking Is Linked to Being Successful," *Huffington Post* online, www.huffingtonpost.com, October 12, 2015.
85. B. A. Garner, "Quiz Yourself: Is Your Grammar Holding You Back?," *Harvard Business Review* online, www.hbr.org, August 27, 2015.
86. "To Friend or Not to Friend?" *T&D,* November 2013, p. 14.
87. A. R. McIlvaine, "When Bosses Want to Be 'Friends,'" www.hreonline.com, July 17, 2013; and M. Villano, "The Online Divide Between Work and Play," *New York Times* online, www.nytimes.com, April 26, 2009.
88. C. Anderson, "How to Give a Killer Presentation," *Harvard Business Review* online, www.hbr.org, June, 2013; S. Kessler, "How to Improve Your Presentation Skills," *Inc. Magazine* online, www.inc.com, February 22, 2010.
89. Steve Evans, "Wired VS Wireless in the Enterprise," *Computer Weekly.com,* www.computerweekly.com/feature/Wired-vs-wireless-in-the-enterprise.
90. S. Pettypiece, "Amazon Passes Wal-Mart as Biggest Retailer by Market Value," *Bloomberg* online, www.bloomberg.com, July 23, 2015; C. Myers, "Don't Try This At Home: Why Amazon's Culture Isn't Right for Your Business," *Forbes* online, www.forbes.com, August 16, 2015; J. Kantor and D. Streitfeld, "Inside Amazon: Wrestling Big Ideas in a Bruising Workplace," *The New York Times* online, www.nytimes.com, August 15, 2015; J. McGregor, "Amazon CEO Jeff Bezos Shares Thoughts on Corporate Culture, Decision-making and Failure," *Los Angeles Times* online, www.latimes.com, April 10, 2016.
91. This case is written by Marcello Russo, Assistant Professor, Rouen Business School, France. "Italy: Consumer Groups Win Compensation for Passengers of Shipwrecked Costa Concordia," Consumers International, January 31, 2012, [www.consumersinternational.org/ourmembers/member-activity/2012/01/italy-consumer-groups-wincompensation-for-passengers-of-shipwrecked-costa-concordia].

Chapter 15 Organizational Behavior

It's Your Career

Source: Mooltfilm/Fotolia

Self-Awareness: You Need to Know Yourself Before You Can Know Others

Do you know your real self? Many of us don't. We work hard to protect, maintain, and enhance our self-concept and the images others have of us. But if you want to maximize your potential, you need to know your weaknesses as well as your strengths. Knowledge of your strengths and weaknesses can help you gain insights into areas you want to change and improve. And it can help you better understand how others see you.

The following identifies five key elements of your personality. Understanding how you rate on these elements is critical to your self-awareness:

A key to success in management and in your career is knowing who you are and how you interact with others.

Introversion versus Extraversion*. Are you quiet and reserved? Are you shy in new situations? At work, do you prefer quiet for concentration, take care with details, think a lot before you act, and work contentedly alone? If so, you are probably best described as an introvert. In contrast, are you outgoing, sociable, and assertive? At work, do you prefer variety and action; dislike complicated procedures; and are you impatient with long, slow tasks? This characterizes extraverts.*

Thinking versus Feeling*. In making decisions, do you put the emphasis on reason and logic? If so, your preference is for thinking. If you make decisions by emphasizing human values, emotions, and your personal beliefs, then your focus is on feelings.*

Internal Control versus External Control*. Do you believe that you're the master of your own fate? Do you believe you control what happens to you? If so, you have an internal locus of control. If you believe that what happens to you is controlled by outside forces such as luck or chance, you have an external locus of control.*

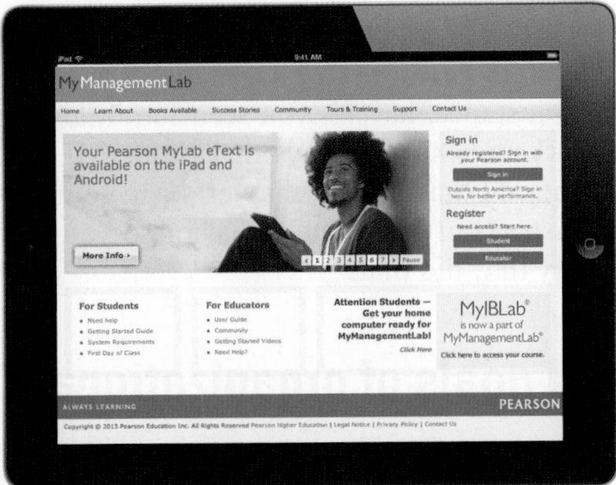

Pearson MyLab Management®

Improve Your Grade!

When you see this icon, visit **www.mymanagementlab.com** for activities that are applied, personalized, and offer immediate feedback.

Learning Objectives

15.1 ***Identify*** *the focus and goals of individual behavior within organizations.*

15.2 ***Explain*** *the role that attitudes play in job performance.*

15.3 ***Describe*** *different personality theories.*

- **Know how** to be more self-aware.

15.4 ***Describe*** *perception and factors that influence it.*

15.5 ***Discuss*** *learning theories and their relevance in shaping behavior.*

- **Develop your skill** at shaping behavior.

Organized versus Disorganized*. Are you conscientious, responsible, dependable, and consistent? If so, then you'd be organized. Are you easily distracted, unreliable, and have difficulty meeting deadlines and commitments? If so, then you'd be classified as disorganized.*

Open to Change versus Comfortable with the Familiar*. Finally, do you tend to be creative, curious, and enjoy new experiences? You'd be open to change. If you're better described as someone who is conventional and uncomfortable with change, you'd be described as comfortable with the familiar.*

There is no right personality. Each side of each dimension has both strengths and weaknesses. The importance is knowing who you are and where you best fit.

Many of us don't have a good read on who we are. If that's you, here are three suggestions on what you can do to increase your self-awareness:

1. ***Seek feedback.*** *Find individuals you trust and seek their honest feedback.*
2. ***Reflect.*** *Review your experiences, situations, and actions to better understand and learn from them.*
3. ***Keep a journal.*** *Keep a written, ongoing account that includes comments about personal events and interactions you have with others. Include descriptions of good and bad ways that you handled situations.*

Most managers are concerned with the attitudes of their employees and want to attract and retain employees with the right attitudes and personalities. They want people who show up and work hard, get along with coworkers and customers, have good attitudes, and exhibit good work behaviors in other ways. But as you're probably already aware, people don't always behave like that "ideal" employee. They job hop at the first opportunity or they may post critical comments in blogs. People differ in their behaviors, and even the same person can behave one way one day and a completely different

As the feel-good manager of Jimdo, a Web-hosting service in Hamburg, Germany, Magdalena Bethge (raised arms) is charged with creating a positive work environment that will increase employee satisfaction and productivity. She helps employees achieve a work-life balance and organizes ongoing employee feedback sessions, mentoring for new employees, and office get-togethers.
Source: Georg Wendt/Newscom

way another day. For instance, haven't you seen family members, friends, or coworkers behave in ways that prompted you to wonder: Why did they do that? In this chapter, we're going to explore the different aspects of individual behavior so you can better understand "why they did that!"

FOCUS and goals of organizational behavior

LO15.1 Managers need good people skills. The material in this and the next three chapters draws heavily on the field of study that's known as *organizational behavior (OB)*. Although it's concerned with the subject of **behavior**—that is, the actions of people—**organizational behavior** is the study of the actions of people at work.

behavior
The actions of people

organizational behavior (OB)
The study of the actions of people at work

One of the challenges in understanding organizational behavior is that it addresses issues that aren't obvious. Like an iceberg, OB has a small visible dimension and a much larger hidden portion. (See Exhibit 15-1.) What we see when we look at an organization is its visible aspects: strategies, goals, policies and procedures, structure, technology, formal authority relationships, and chain of command. But under the surface are other elements that managers need to understand—elements that also influence how employees behave at work. As we'll show, OB provides managers with considerable insights into these important, but hidden, aspects of the organization. For instance, thousands of managers and employees objected not long ago, when U.K.-based HSBC Bank suddenly announced it would freeze salaries and not fill job openings. Although the CEO cited a challenging economic climate and the urgent need to cut costs as reasons for this decision, outraged staff members complained through internal channels and union channels. Less than two weeks later, the CEO sent another email to 250,000 employees, saying: "We have listened to feedback and as a result decided to change the way these cost savings are to be achieved." Based on the organization's negative response, HSBC switched course and implemented pay increases that had already been approved, maintaining the hiring freeze for some cost-cutting.[2]

Focus of Organizational Behavior

Based predominantly on contributions from psychologists, this area includes such topics as attitudes, personality, perception, learning, and motivation. Second, OB is concerned with *group behavior*, which includes norms, roles, team building, leadership, and conflict. Our knowledge about groups comes basically from the work of

Exhibit 15-1
Organization as Iceberg

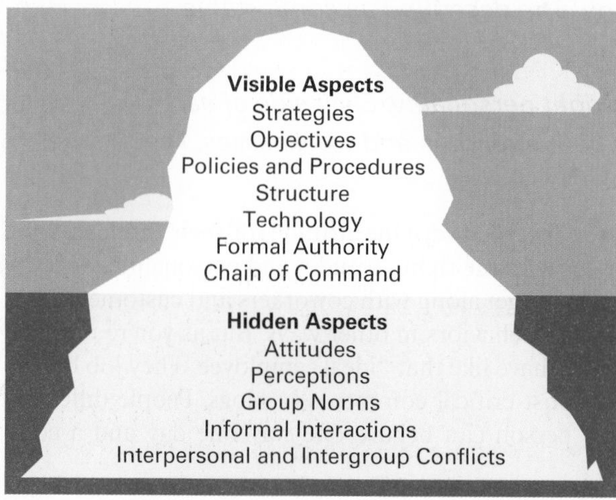

sociologists and social psychologists. Finally, OB also looks at *organizational* aspects including structure, culture, and human resource policies and practices. We've addressed group and organizational aspects in previous chapters. In this chapter, we'll look at individual behavior.

Goals of Organizational Behavior

The goals of OB are to *explain, predict,* and *influence* behavior. Managers need to be able to *explain* why employees engage in some behaviors rather than others, *predict* how employees will respond to various actions and decisions, and *influence* how employees behave.

What employee behaviors are we specifically concerned with explaining, predicting, and influencing? Six important ones have been identified: employee productivity, absenteeism, turnover, organizational citizenship behavior (OCB), job satisfaction, and counterproductive workplace behavior. **Employee productivity** is a performance measure of both efficiency and effectiveness. Managers want to know what factors will influence the efficiency and effectiveness of employees. **Absenteeism** is the failure to show up for work. It's difficult for work to get done if employees don't show up. Studies have shown that unscheduled absences cost companies around $84 billion each year.[3] Although absenteeism can't be totally eliminated, excessive levels have a direct and immediate impact on the organization's functioning. **Turnover** is the voluntary and involuntary permanent withdrawal from an organization. It can be a problem because of increased recruiting, selection, and training costs and work disruptions. And it's costly to companies—ranging from 16 percent of an unskilled worker's pay to 213 percent of a highly trained employee.[4] Just like absenteeism, managers can never eliminate turnover, but it is something they want to minimize, especially among high-performing employees. **Organizational citizenship behavior (OCB)** is discretionary behavior that's not part of an employee's formal job requirements but promotes the effective functioning of the organization.[5] Examples of good OCBs include helping others on one's work team, volunteering for extended job activities, avoiding unnecessary conflicts, and making constructive statements about one's work group and the organization. Organizations need individuals who will do more than their usual job duties, and the evidence indicates that organizations that have such employees outperform those that don't.[6] However, drawbacks of OCB occur when employees experience work overload, stress, and work–family life conflicts.[7] **Job satisfaction** refers to an employee's general attitude toward his or her job. Although job satisfaction is an attitude rather than a behavior, it's an outcome that concerns many managers because satisfied employees are more likely to show up for work, have higher levels of performance, and stay with an organization. **Counterproductive workplace behavior** is any intentional employee behavior that is potentially harmful to the organization or individuals within the organization. Counterproductive workplace behavior shows up in organizations in four ways: deviance, aggression, antisocial behavior, and violence.[8] Such behaviors can range from playing loud music just to irritate coworkers to verbal aggression to sabotaging work, all of which can create havoc in any organization. In the following sections, we'll address how an understanding of four psychological factors—employee attitudes, personality, perception, and learning—can help us predict and explain these employee behaviors.

employee productivity
A performance measure of both efficiency and effectiveness

absenteeism
The failure to show up for work

turnover
The voluntary and involuntary permanent withdrawal from an organization

organizational citizenship behavior (OCB)
Discretionary behavior that is not part of an employee's formal job requirements, but which promotes the effective functioning of the organization

job satisfaction
An employee's general attitude toward his or her job

counterproductive workplace behavior
Any intentional employee behavior that is potentially damaging to the organization or to individuals within the organization

ATTITUDES and job performance

LO15.2 **Attitudes** are evaluative statements—favorable or unfavorable—concerning objects, people, or events. They reflect how an individual feels about something. When a person says, "I like my job," he or she is expressing an attitude about work.

An attitude is made up of three components: cognition, affect, and behavior.[9] The **cognitive component** of an attitude refers to the beliefs, opinions, knowledge, or information held by a person (for instance, the belief that "discrimination is wrong").

attitudes
Evaluative statements, either favorable or unfavorable, concerning objects, people, or events

cognitive component
That part of an attitude that's made up of the beliefs, opinions, knowledge, or information held by a person

affective component
That part of an attitude that's the emotional or feeling part

behavioral component
That part of an attitude that refers to an intention to behave in a certain way toward someone or something

The **affective component** of an attitude is the emotional or feeling part of an attitude. Using our example, this component would be reflected by the statement, "I don't like Pat because he discriminates against minorities." Finally, affect can lead to behavioral outcomes. The **behavioral component** of an attitude refers to an intention to behave in a certain way toward someone or something. To continue our example, I might choose to avoid Pat because of my feelings about him. Understanding that attitudes are made up of three components helps show their complexity. But keep in mind that the term *attitude* usually refers only to the affective component.

Naturally, managers aren't interested in every attitude an employee has. They're especially interested in job-related attitudes. The three most widely known are job satisfaction, job involvement, and organizational commitment. Another concept that's generating widespread interest is employee engagement.[10]

Job Satisfaction

As we know from our earlier definition, job satisfaction refers to a person's general attitude toward his or her job. A person with a high level of job satisfaction has a positive attitude toward his or her job. A person who is dissatisfied has a negative attitude. When people speak of employee attitudes, they usually are referring to job satisfaction.

HOW SATISFIED ARE EMPLOYEES? Studies of U.S. workers over the past 30 years generally indicated that the majority of workers were satisfied with their jobs. A Conference Board study in 1995 found that some 60 percent of Americans were satisfied with their jobs.[11] However, since then the number has been declining. By 2010, that percentage was down to its lowest level, 42.6 percent, but rose slightly in 2014 to 48.3 percent.[12] Although job satisfaction tends to increase as income increases, only 41.2 percent of individuals earning between $35,000 and $50,000 are satisfied with their jobs, and 61.6 percent of individuals earning more than $125,000 are satisfied. For individuals earning less than $15,000, about 41.8 percent of workers say they are satisfied with their jobs.[13] Even though it's possible that higher pay translates into higher job satisfaction, an alternative explanation for the difference in satisfaction levels is that higher pay reflects different types of jobs. Higher-paying jobs generally require more advanced skills, give jobholders greater responsibilities, are more stimulating and provide more challenges, and allow workers more control. It's more likely that the reports of higher satisfaction among higher-income levels reflect those factors rather than the pay itself. What about job satisfaction levels in other countries? A survey by Kelly Services, a staffing agency, found that 48 percent of global employees were unhappy in their current jobs.[14]

The global recession likely had an impact on global job satisfaction rates. For instance, a study by a British consulting group found that 67 percent of workers surveyed were putting in unpaid overtime. Also, 63 percent said their employers did not appreciate their extra effort, and 57 percent felt that employees were treated like dispensable commodities.[15]

- 72 percent of employees are completely satisfied with their coworkers.
- 54 percent of employees are completely satisfied with their boss or immediate supervisors.[16]

SATISFACTION AND PRODUCTIVITY After the Hawthorne Studies (discussed in the Management History Module), managers believed that happy workers were productive workers. Because it's not been easy to determine whether job satisfaction caused job productivity or vice versa, some management researchers felt that belief was generally wrong. However, we can say with some certainty that the correlation between satisfaction and productivity is fairly strong.[17] Also, organizations with more satisfied employees tend to be more effective than organizations with fewer satisfied employees.[18]

SATISFACTION AND ABSENTEEISM Although research shows that satisfied employees have lower levels of absenteeism than dissatisfied employees, the correlation isn't strong.[19] It certainly makes sense that dissatisfied employees are more likely to miss work, but other factors affect the relationship. For instance, organizations that provide liberal sick leave benefits are encouraging all their employees—including those who are highly satisfied—to take "sick" days. Assuming your job has some variety in it, you can find work satisfying and yet still take a "sick" day to enjoy a three-day weekend or to golf on a warm spring day if taking such days results in no penalties.

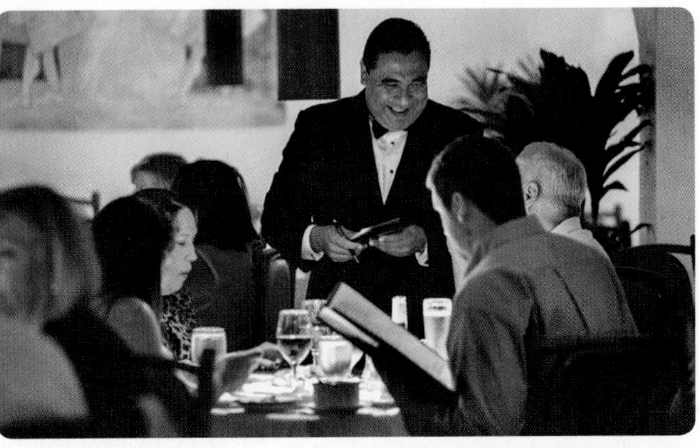

Customers of Donatello Italian Restaurant in Tampa value the exceptional service they receive from waiter Gilson Fernandez, a 29-year employee. Diners appreciate the warm and friendly service of the restaurant's experienced, long-term wait staff. Donatello hires positive people and then trains them to deliver the polished, attentive, and efficient service that results in satisfied customers.
Source: Cherie Diez/ZUMA Press/Newscom

SATISFACTION AND TURNOVER Research on the relationship between satisfaction and turnover is much stronger. Satisfied employees have lower levels of turnover, while dissatisfied employees have higher levels of turnover.[20] Yet, things such as labor-market conditions, expectations about alternative job opportunities, and length of employment with the organization also affect an employee's decision to leave.[21] Research suggests that the level of satisfaction is less important in predicting turnover for superior performers because the organization typically does everything it can to keep them—pay raises, praise, increased promotion opportunities, and so forth.[22] What can managers do to promote job satisfaction? They could start by identifying incentives that are valued by employees. For instance, Dabo & Company runs exercises weekly classes in its Dubai offices and allows employees to either arrive an hour late or leave an hour early two days a week, as a way to help the staff members better balance their personal and professional obligations.[23]

JOB SATISFACTION AND CUSTOMER SATISFACTION Is job satisfaction related to positive customer outcomes? For frontline employees who have regular contact with customers, the answer is "yes." Satisfied employees increase customer satisfaction and loyalty.[24] Why? In service organizations, customer retention and defection are highly dependent on how frontline employees deal with customers. Satisfied employees are more likely to be friendly, upbeat, and responsive, which customers appreciate. And because satisfied employees are less likely to leave their jobs, customers are more likely to encounter familiar faces and receive experienced service. These qualities help build customer satisfaction and loyalty. However, the relationship also seems to work in reverse. Dissatisfied customers can increase an employee's job dissatisfaction. Employees who have regular contact with customers report that rude, thoughtless, or unreasonably demanding customers adversely affect their job satisfaction.[25]

A number of companies appear to understand this connection. Service-oriented businesses, such as L.L.Bean, Costco, and Starbucks, obsess about pleasing their customers. They also focus on building employee satisfaction—recognizing that satisfied employees will go a long way toward contributing to their goal of having happy customers. These firms seek to hire upbeat and friendly employees, they train employees in customer service, they reward customer service, they provide positive work climates, and they regularly track employee satisfaction through attitude surveys. For instance, at shoe retailer Zappos (now part of Amazon.com), employees are encouraged to "create fun and a little weirdness" and have been given high levels of discretion to make customers satisfied. Zappos even offers a bribe of up to $5,000 to employees to quit the company after training if they're not happy working there.[26] According to Jeff Bezos, "In the long run, an employee staying somewhere they don't want to be isn't healthy for the employee or the company."[27]

JOB SATISFACTION AND OCB It seems logical to assume that job satisfaction should be a major determinant of an employee's OCB.[28] Satisfied employees would seem more likely to talk positively about the organization, help others, and go above and beyond normal job expectations. Research suggests a modest overall relationship between job satisfaction and OCB.[29] But that relationship is tempered by perceptions of fairness.[30] Basically, if you don't feel as though your supervisor, organizational procedures, or pay policies are fair, your job satisfaction is likely to suffer significantly. This has been the case for workers employed in U.S. federal government agencies where pay satisfaction has declined 10 points from 56 percent over a recent five-year period.[31] However, when you perceive that these things are fair, you have more trust in your employer and are more willing to voluntarily engage in behaviors that go beyond your formal job requirements. Another factor that influences individual OCB is the type of citizenship behavior a person's work group exhibits. In a work group with low group-level OCB, any individual in that group who engaged in OCB had higher job performance ratings. One possible explanation may be that the person was trying to find some way to "stand out" from the crowd.[32] No matter why it happens, the point is that OCB can have positive benefits for organizations.

JOB SATISFACTION AND COUNTERPRODUCTIVE BEHAVIOR When employees are dissatisfied with their jobs, they are likely to engage in counterproductive behaviors.[33] The problem comes from the difficulty in predicting *how* they'll respond. One person might quit. Another might respond by using work time to play computer games. And another might verbally abuse a coworker. If managers want to control the undesirable consequences of job dissatisfaction, they'd be better off attacking the problem—job dissatisfaction—than trying to control the different employee responses. A good start is understanding the source of dissatisfaction. For instance, does the employee feel that she was treated unfairly by her supervisor, or is she upset because a new company policy requires that employees pay for their uniforms? Or, does the employee feel slighted by the coworker who doesn't pull his weight? Three other job-related attitudes we need to look at include job involvement, organizational commitment, and employee engagement.

★ Watch It 1!

If your professor has assigned this, go to **www.mymanagementlab.com** to watch a video titled: *Rudi's Bakery: Job Satisfaction* and to respond to questions.

Employee engagement is high at St. Jude Children's Research Hospital, where employees share a deep commitment to the hospital's mission of "finding cures, saving children." Shown here delivering Halloween treats to patients, employees feel their contributions at work are meaningful and make a difference in the lives of young children.
Source: St. Jude Children's Research Hospital/ Associated Press

Job Involvement and Organizational Commitment

Job involvement is the degree to which an employee identifies with his or her job, actively participates in it, and considers his or her job performance to be important to his or her self-worth.[34] Employees with a high level of job involvement strongly identify with and really care about the kind of work they do. Their positive attitude leads them to contribute in positive ways to their work. High levels of job involvement have been found to be related to fewer absences, lower resignation rates, and higher employee engagement with their work.[35]

Organizational commitment is the degree to which an employee identifies with a particular organization and its goals and wishes to maintain membership in that organization.[36] Whereas job involvement is identifying with your job, organizational commitment is identifying with your employing organization. Research suggests that organizational commitment also leads to lower levels of both absenteeism and turnover and, in fact, is a better indicator of turnover than job satisfaction.[37] Why? Probably because it's a more global and enduring response to the organization than satisfaction with a particular job.[38] However, organizational commitment is less important as a work-related attitude than it once was. Employees don't generally stay with a single organization for most of their career, and the relationship they have with their employer has changed considerably.[39] Although the commitment of *an employee to an organization* may not be as important as it once was, research about **perceived organizational support**—employees' general belief that their organization values their contribution and cares about their well-being—shows that the commitment of *the organization to the employee* can be beneficial. High levels of perceived organizational support lead to increased job satisfaction and lower turnover.[40]

job involvement
The degree to which an employee identifies with his or her job, actively participates in it, and considers his or her job performance to be important to self-worth

Employee Engagement

A low-level trader employed by Société Générale, a giant French bank, loses billions of dollars through dishonest trades and no one reports suspicious behavior. An internal investigation uncovered evidence that many back-office employees failed to alert their supervisors about the suspicious trades.[41] Employee indifference can have serious consequences.

Managers want their employees to be connected to, satisfied with, and enthusiastic about their jobs. This concept is known as **employee engagement**.[42] Highly engaged employees are passionate about and deeply connected to their work, and disengaged employees have essentially "checked out" and don't care.[43] They show up for work, but have no energy or passion for it. A global study of more than 12,000 employees found the following factors as contributing to employee engagement: respect, type of work, work-life balance, providing good service to customers, base pay, people you work with, benefits, long-term career potential, learning and development opportunities, flexible work, promotion opportunities, and variable pay/bonuses.[44]

A number of benefits come from having highly engaged employees. First, highly engaged employees are two-and-a-half times more likely to be top performers than their less-engaged coworkers. In addition, companies with highly engaged employees have higher retention rates, which help keep recruiting and training costs low. And both of these outcomes—higher performance and lower costs—contribute to superior financial performance.[45] Managers have a lot of work to do to reap these benefits. Worldwide, only 13 percent of employees describe themselves as engaged.[46] The news is only somewhat better in the United States where 32 percent of employees are engaged.

organizational commitment
The degree to which an employee identifies with a particular organization and its goals and wishes to maintain membership in that organization

perceived organizational support
Employees' general belief that their organization values their contribution and cares about their well-being

employee engagement
When employees are connected to, satisfied with, and enthusiastic about their jobs

Attitudes and Consistency

Have you ever noticed that people change what they say so it doesn't contradict what they do? Perhaps a friend of yours has repeatedly said that she thinks joining a sorority is an important part of college life. But then she goes through rush and doesn't get accepted. All of a sudden, she's saying that sorority life isn't all that great.

Research has generally concluded that people seek consistency among their attitudes *and* between their attitudes and behavior.[47] This tendency means that individuals try to reconcile differing attitudes and align their attitudes and behavior so they appear rational and consistent. When they encounter an inconsistency, individuals will do something to make it consistent by altering the attitudes, altering the behavior, or rationalizing the inconsistency.

For example, a campus recruiter for Enterprise Rent-a-Car who visits college campuses and sells students on the advantages of Enterprise as a good place to work would experience inconsistency if he personally believed that Enterprise had poor working conditions and few opportunities for promotion. This recruiter could, over time, find his attitudes toward Enterprise becoming more positive. He might actually convince himself by continually articulating the merits of working for the company. Another alternative is that the recruiter could become openly negative about Enterprise and the opportunities within the company for prospective applicants. The original enthusiasm the recruiter might have had would dwindle and might be replaced by outright cynicism toward the company. Finally, the recruiter might acknowledge that Enterprise is an undesirable place to work but, as a professional, realize that his obligation is to present the positive aspects of working for the company. He might further rationalize that no workplace is perfect and that his job is to present a favorable picture of the company, not to present both sides.

- 64 percent of employed adults feel their organization treats them fairly.
- 25 percent of employed adults feel their employer is open and upfront with them.[48]

Cognitive Dissonance Theory

Can we assume from this consistency principle that an individual's behavior can always be predicted if we know his or her attitude on a subject? The answer isn't a simple "yes" or "no." Why? *Cognitive dissonance theory*.

Cognitive dissonance theory sought to explain the relationship between attitudes and behavior.[49] **Cognitive dissonance** is any incompatibility or inconsistency

cognitive dissonance
Any incompatibility or inconsistency between attitudes or between behavior and attitudes

between attitudes or between behavior and attitudes. The theory argued that inconsistency is uncomfortable and that individuals will try to reduce the discomfort and, thus, the dissonance.

Of course, no one can avoid dissonance. You know you should floss your teeth every day but don't do it. There's an inconsistency between attitude and behavior. How do people cope with cognitive dissonance? The theory proposes that how hard we'll try to reduce dissonance is determined by three things: (1) the *importance* of the factors creating the dissonance, (2) the degree of *influence* the individual believes he or she has over those factors, and (3) the *rewards* that may be involved in dissonance.

If the factors creating the dissonance are relatively unimportant, the pressure to correct the inconsistency will be low. However, if those factors are important, individuals may change their behavior, conclude that the dissonant behavior isn't so important, change their attitude, or identify compatible factors that outweigh the dissonant ones.

How much influence individuals believe they have over the factors also affects their reaction to the dissonance. If they perceive the dissonance is something about which they have no choice, they won't be receptive to attitude change or feel a need to be. If, for example, the dissonance-producing behavior was required as a result of a manager's order, the pressure to reduce dissonance would be less than if the behavior had been performed voluntarily. Although dissonance exists, it can be rationalized and justified by the need to follow the manager's orders—that is, the person had no choice or control.

Finally, rewards also influence the degree to which individuals are motivated to reduce dissonance. Coupling high dissonance with high rewards tends to reduce the discomfort by motivating the individual to believe that consistency exists.

Attitude Surveys

attitude surveys
Surveys that elicit responses from employees through questions about how they feel about their jobs, work groups, supervisors, or the organization

Many organizations regularly survey their employees about their attitudes.[50] Exhibit 15-2 shows an example of an actual attitude survey. Typically, **attitude surveys** present the employee with a set of statements or questions eliciting how they feel about their jobs, work groups, supervisors, or the organization. Ideally, the items will be designed to obtain the specific information that managers desire. An attitude score is achieved by summing up responses to individual questionnaire items. These scores can then be averaged for work groups, departments, divisions, or the organization as a whole. For instance, Ford Motor Company came up with an "Employee Satisfaction Index" to measure employee attitudes. Each year, the company measures employee satisfaction with company-offered training and their satisfaction with the recognition they receive for doing a good job. Managers use the results to develop action plans for improvement and for evaluating the success of previously implemented plans.[51]

Regularly surveying employee attitudes provides managers with valuable feedback on how employees perceive their working conditions. Policies and practices that managers view as objective and fair may not be seen that way by employees. The use of

Exhibit 15-2
Sample Employee Attitude Survey

Here are some sample statements from an employee attitude survey:

- I have ample opportunities to use my skills/abilities in my job.
- My manager has a good relationship with my work group.
- My organization provides me professional development opportunities.
- I am told if I'm doing good work or not.
- I feel safe in my work environment.
- My organization is a great place to work.

regular attitude surveys can alert managers to potential problems and employees' intentions early so that action can be taken to prevent repercussions.[52]

Implications for Managers

Managers should be interested in their employees' attitudes because they influence behavior. Satisfied and committed employees, for instance, have lower rates of turnover and absenteeism. If managers want to keep resignations and absences down—especially among their more productive employees—they'll want to do things that generate positive job attitudes.

Satisfied employees also perform better on the job. So managers should focus on those factors that have been shown to be conducive to high levels of employee job satisfaction: making work challenging and interesting, providing equitable rewards, creating supportive working conditions, and encouraging supportive colleagues.[54] These factors are likely to help employees be more productive.

Managers should also survey employees about their attitudes. As one study put it, "A sound measurement of overall job attitude is one of the most useful pieces of information an organization can have about its employees."[55]

Finally, managers should know that employees will try to reduce dissonance. If employees are required to do things that appear inconsistent to them or that are at odds with their attitudes, managers should remember that pressure to reduce the dissonance is not as strong when the employee perceives that the dissonance is externally imposed and uncontrollable. It's also decreased if rewards are significant enough to offset the dissonance. So the manager might point to external forces such as competitors, customers, or other factors when explaining the need to perform some work that the individual may have some dissonance about. Or the manager can provide rewards that an individual desires.

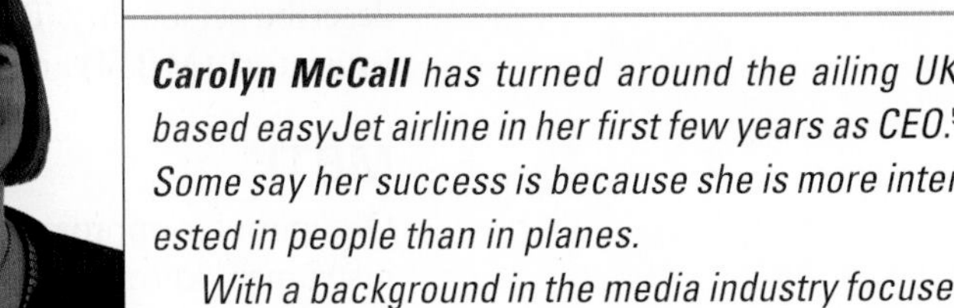

LEADER making a DIFFERENCE

Source: BERND SETTNIK/Alamy

***Carolyn McCall** has turned around the ailing UK-based easyJet airline in her first few years as CEO.*[53] *Some say her success is because she is more interested in people than in planes.*

With a background in the media industry focused on marketing, many were skeptical of McCall's potential as the CEO of the low-cost airline. When McCall came to easyJet, there was a distrust of management, so one of her first priorities was to restore employee morale. She started by canceling a cost-saving initiative that was going to cut the portions on in-flight meals for the crew, insisting that while the airline needed to be efficient, employees should still be treated well. That one decision helped build loyalty from the crew.

McCall notes an important skill that has helped her succeed as a leader is emotional intelligence, suggesting that it helps you relate to other people, which is essential to developing relationships. Those who know her say she really does understand people and is full of fun and energy. Voted the Most Admired Leader in Britain in 2015 by Management Today *magazine, McCall says leadership is about getting people to come with you toward your vision.* What can you learn from this leader making a difference?

PERSONALITY

LO15.3 "Let's face it, dating is a drag. There was a time when we thought the computer was going to make it all better.... But most of us learned the hard way that finding someone who shares our love of film noir and obscure garage bands does not a perfect match make."[56] Using in-depth personality assessment and profiling, Chemistry.com has tried to do something about making the whole dating process better.

Personality. We all have one. Some of us are quiet and passive; others are loud and aggressive. When we describe people using terms such as *quiet, passive, loud, aggressive, ambitious, extraverted, loyal, tense,* or *sociable*, we're describing their personalities. An individual's **personality** is a unique combination of emotional, thought, and behavioral patterns that affect how a person reacts to situations and interacts with others. It's our natural way of doing things and relating to others. Personality is most often described in terms of measurable traits a person exhibits. We're interested in looking

personality
The unique combination of emotional, thought, and behavioral patterns that affect how a person reacts to situations and interacts with others

at personality because, just like attitudes, it, too, affects how and why people behave the way they do.

Over the years, researchers have attempted to identify those traits that best describe personality. The two most well-known approaches are the Myers-Briggs Type Indicator® (MBTI) and the Big Five Model.

MBTI®

One popular approach to classifying personality traits is the personality-assessment instrument known as the MBTI®. This 100-question assessment asks people how they usually act or feel in different situations.[57] On the basis of their answers, individuals are classified as exhibiting a preference in four categories: extraversion or introversion (E or I), sensing or intuition (S or N), thinking or feeling (T or F), and judging or perceiving (J or P). These terms are defined as follows:

- *Extraversion (E) Versus Introversion (I).* Individuals showing a preference for extraversion are outgoing, social, and assertive. They need a work environment that's varied and action oriented, that lets them be with others, and that gives them a variety of experiences. Individuals showing a preference for introversion are quiet and shy. They focus on understanding and prefer a work environment that is quiet and concentrated, that lets them be alone, and that gives them a chance to explore in depth a limited set of experiences.
- *Sensing (S) Versus Intuition (N).* Sensing types are practical and prefer routine and order. They dislike new problems unless there are standard ways to solve them, have a high need for closure, show patience with routine details, and tend to be good at precise work. On the other hand, intuition types rely on unconscious processes and look at the "big picture." They're individuals who like solving new problems, dislike doing the same thing over and over again, jump to conclusions, are impatient with routine details, and dislike taking time for precision.
- *Thinking (T) Versus Feeling (F).* Thinking types use reason and logic to handle problems. They're unemotional and uninterested in people's feelings, like analysis and putting things into logical order, are able to reprimand people and fire them when necessary, may seem hard-hearted, and tend to relate well only to other thinking types. Feeling types rely on their personal values and emotions. They're aware of other people and their feelings, like harmony, need occasional praise, dislike telling people unpleasant things, tend to be sympathetic, and relate well to most people.
- *Judging (J) Versus Perceiving (P).* Judging types want control and prefer their world to be ordered and structured. They're good planners, decisive, purposeful, and exacting. They focus on completing a task, make decisions quickly, and want only the information necessary to get a task done. Perceiving types are flexible and spontaneous. They're curious, adaptable, and tolerant. They focus on starting a task, postpone decisions, and want to find out all about the task before starting it.

Combining these preferences provides descriptions of 16 personality types, with every person identified with one of the items in each of the four pairs. Exhibit 15-3 summarizes two of them. As you can see from these descriptions, each personality type would approach work and relationships differently—neither one better than the other, just different.

More than 3.5 million people a year take the MBTI®. Some organizations that have used the MBTI® include Apple, AT&T, GE, 3M, hospitals, educational institutions, and even the U.S. Armed Forces. No hard evidence shows that the MBTI® is a valid measure of personality, but that doesn't seem to deter its widespread use. More than 80 percent of the *Fortune* 100 companies use personality tests like the MBTI® to help build effective work teams.[58] For instance, a spokesperson for General Motors said

Exhibit 15-3

Examples of MBTI® Personality Types

Type	Description
I–S–F–P (introversion, sensing, feeling, perceiving)	Sensitive, kind, modest, shy, and quietly friendly. Such people strongly dislike disagreements and will avoid them. They are loyal followers and quite often are relaxed about getting things done.
E–N–T–J (extraversion, intuition, thinking, judging)	Warm, friendly, candid, and decisive; also skilled in anything that requires reasoning and intelligent talk, but may sometimes overestimate what they are capable of doing.

Source: Based on I. Briggs-Myers, *Introduction to Type* (Palo Alto, CA: Consulting Psychologists Press, 1980), pp. 7–8.

that the company has been using Myers-Briggs for 30 years. And a spokesperson for Procter & Gamble said that thousands of its staff "have benefited, and are still benefiting" from taking the test.[59]

How could the MBTI® help managers? Proponents believe it's important to know these personality types because they influence the way people interact and solve problems. For instance, if your boss is an intuition type and you're a sensing type, you'll gather information in different ways. An intuitive type prefers gut reactions, whereas a sensor prefers facts. To work well with your boss, you would have to present more than just facts about a situation and bring out how you feel about it. Also, the MBTI® has been used to help managers better match employees to certain types of jobs.

let's get REAL

Source: Lauren Passilla

Lauren Passilla
Recruiting Manager,
Accounting & Risk Management

Jennifer King is excited that her company has decided to use the Myers-Briggs Type Indicator (MBTI) to help her manage her employees. She manages a team of creative professionals at an advertising agency. The team must work together on a variety of projects creating advertising campaigns for their clients. Her entire staff has taken the MBTI, and she has learned a lot about her employees. However, now she is not sure what to do with this information.

How can Jennifer use the MBTI results to improve the performance of her staff?

Since Jennifer's employees are frequently required to work as a team, one of the best ways to utilize the MBTI results is to compile the individual profiles to create a team MBTI. From that type, she can not only identify and capitalize on the strengths of the team, but also the potential gaps. By understanding the gaps, Jennifer can encourage individuals with the preferences that are not dominant on the team to suggest alternative solutions and viewpoints. The result will be a more productive and well-rounded team.

Sara Blakely, founder and owner of Spanx, scores high on all of the personality dimensions of the Big Five Model. She is sociable, agreeable, conscientious, emotionally stable, and open to experiences. These traits have contributed to Blakely's success in launching her shapewear firm and in leading its rapid growth as a global brand with estimated annual sales of $400 million.
Source: Paul Morigi/Getty Images for FORTUNE

The Big Five Model

In recent years, research has shown that five basic personality dimensions underlie all others and encompass most of the significant variation in human personality.[60] The five personality traits in the **Big Five Model** are:

Big Five Model
Personality trait model that includes extraversion, agreeableness, conscientiousness, emotional stability, and openness to experience

1. *Extraversion:* The degree to which someone is sociable, talkative, assertive, and comfortable in relationships with others.
2. *Agreeableness:* The degree to which someone is good-natured, cooperative, and trusting.
3. *Conscientiousness:* The degree to which someone is reliable, responsible, dependable, persistent, and achievement oriented.
4. *Emotional stability:* The degree to which someone is calm, enthusiastic, and secure (positive) or tense, nervous, depressed, and insecure (negative).
5. *Openness to experience:* The degree to which someone has a wide range of interests and is imaginative, fascinated with novelty, artistically sensitive, and intellectual.

The Big Five Model provides more than just a personality framework. Research has shown that important relationships exist between these personality dimensions and job performance. For example, one study examined five categories of occupations: *professionals* (such as engineers, architects, and attorneys), *police, managers, salespeople,* and *semiskilled and skilled employees.*[61] The results showed that conscientiousness predicted job performance for all five occupational groups. Predictions for the other personality dimensions depended on the situation and on the occupational group. For example, extraversion predicted performance in managerial and sales positions—occupations in which high social interaction is necessary. Openness to experience was found to be important in predicting training competency. Ironically, emotional security wasn't positively related to job performance in any of the occupations. Another study that looked at whether the five-factor model could predict managerial performance found it could if 360-degree performance ratings (that is, performance ratings from supervisors, peers, and subordinates) were used.[62] Other studies have shown that employees who score higher in conscientiousness develop higher levels of job knowledge, probably because highly conscientious people learn more. In fact, a review of 138 studies revealed that conscientiousness was rather strongly related to GPA.[63]

Additional Personality Insights

Although the traits in the Big Five are highly relevant to understanding behavior, they aren't the only personality traits that can describe someone's personality. Five other personality traits are powerful predictors of behavior in organizations.

locus of control
A personality attribute that measures the degree to which people believe they control their own fate

1. *Locus of Control.* Some people believe they control their own fate. Others see themselves as pawns, believing that what happens to them in their lives is due to luck or chance. The **locus of control** in the first case is *internal*; these people believe they control their own destiny. The locus of control in the second case is *external*; these people believe their lives are controlled by outside forces.[64] Research indicates that employees who are externals are less satisfied with their jobs, more alienated from the work setting, and less involved in their jobs than those who rate high on internality.[65] A manager might also expect externals to blame a poor performance evaluation on their boss's prejudice, their coworkers, or other events outside their control; internals would explain the same evaluation in terms of their own actions.

Machiavellianism
A measure of the degree to which people are pragmatic, maintain emotional distance, and believe that ends justify means

2. *Machiavellianism.* The second characteristic is called **Machiavellianism** (Mach), named after Niccolo Machiavelli, who wrote in the sixteenth century on how to gain and manipulate power. An individual high in Machiavellianism

is pragmatic, maintains emotional distance, and believes that ends can justify means.[66] "If it works, use it" is consistent with a high Mach perspective. Do high Machs make good employees? That depends on the type of job and whether you consider ethical factors in evaluating performance. In jobs that require bargaining skills (such as a purchasing manager) or that have substantial rewards for excelling (such as a salesperson working on commission), high Machs are productive.

3. *Self-Esteem.* People differ in the degree to which they like or dislike themselves, a trait called **self-esteem**.[67] Research on self-esteem (SE) offers some interesting behavioral insights. For example, self-esteem is directly related to expectations for success. Those high in SE believe they possess the ability they need to succeed at work. Individuals with high SEs will take more risks in job selection and are more likely to choose unconventional jobs than people with low SE.

   The most common finding on self-esteem is that low SEs are more susceptible to external influence than high SEs. Low SEs are dependent on receiving positive evaluations from others. As a result, they're more likely to seek approval from others and are more prone to conform to the beliefs and behaviors of those they respect than high SEs. In managerial positions, low SEs will tend to be concerned with pleasing others and, therefore, will be less likely to take unpopular stands than high SEs. Finally, self-esteem has also been found to be related to job satisfaction. A number of studies confirm that high SEs are more satisfied with their jobs than low SEs.

self-esteem
An individual's degree of like or dislike for himself or herself

4. *Self-Monitoring.* Have you ever had the experience of meeting someone new and feeling a natural connection and hitting it off right away? At some time or another, we've all had that experience. That natural ability to "click" with other people may play a significant role in determining career success[68] and is another personality trait called **self-monitoring**, which refers to the ability to adjust behavior to external, situational factors.[69] Individuals high in self-monitoring show considerable adaptability in adjusting their behavior. They're highly sensitive to external cues and can behave differently in different situations. High self-monitors are capable of presenting striking contradictions between their public persona and their private selves. Low self-monitors can't adjust their behavior. They tend to display their true dispositions and attitudes in every situation, and there's high behavioral consistency between who they are and what they do.

   Research on self-monitoring suggests that high self-monitors pay closer attention to the behavior of others and are more flexible than low self-monitors.[70] In addition, high self-monitoring managers tend to be more mobile in their careers, receive more promotions (both internal and cross-organizational), and are more likely to occupy central positions in an organization.[71] The high self-monitor is capable of putting on different "faces" for different audiences, an important trait for managers who must play multiple, or even contradicting, roles.

self-monitoring
A personality trait that measures the ability to adjust behavior to external situational factors

5. *Risk-Taking.* People differ in their willingness to take chances. Differences in the propensity to assume or to avoid risk have been shown to affect how long it takes managers to make a decision and how much information they require before making their choice. For instance, in one study where managers worked on simulated exercises that required them to make hiring decisions, high risk-taking managers took less time to make decisions and used less information in making their choices than low risk-taking managers.[72] Interestingly, the decision accuracy was the same for the two groups. To maximize organizational effectiveness, managers should try to align employee risk-taking propensity with specific job demands.

Self-Awareness—If your instructor is using Pearson MyLab Management, log onto **mymanagementlab.com** and test your *self-awareness knowledge*. **Be sure to refer back to the chapter opener!**

OTHER PERSONALITY TRAITS A couple of other personality traits deserve mention. In Chapter 6, we introduced the Type A personality, which describes someone who is continually and aggressively struggling to achieve more and more in less and less time.[73] In the North American culture, the Type A personality is highly valued. Type A individuals subject themselves to continual time pressure and deadlines and have moderate to high levels of stress. They emphasize quantity over quality and managers should be aware that self-imposed pressure could manifest in hostility.[74] On the other hand, a Type B person isn't harried by the desire to achieve more and more. Type Bs don't suffer from a sense of time urgency and are able to relax without guilt. Not surprisingly, Type B individuals tend to be less punctual.[75]

proactive personality
A personality trait that describes individuals who are more prone to take actions to influence their environments

Another interesting trait that's been studied extensively is the **proactive personality**, which describes people who identify opportunities, show initiative, take action, and persevere until meaningful change occurs. Not surprisingly, research has shown that proactives have many desirable behaviors that organizations want.[76] For instance, they are more likely to be seen as leaders and more likely to act as change agents in organizations; they're more likely to challenge the status quo; they have entrepreneurial abilities; and they're more likely to achieve career success.

resilience
An individual's ability to overcome challenges and turn them into opportunities

Finally, the economic recession prompted a reexamination of **resilience**, an individual's ability to overcome challenges and turn them into opportunities.[77] A study by a global consulting firm showed that it is a key factor in keeping a job: A resilient person is likely to be more adaptable, flexible, and goal-focused, which translates into higher productivity and lower absenteeism.[78] OB researchers also have looked at resilience and other individual characteristics, including efficacy, hope, and optimism in a concept called positive psychological capital.[79] These characteristics have been found to be related to higher feelings of well-being and less work stress, which ultimately affect how and why people behave the way they do at work. There is more good news: While some people are naturally resilient, research indicates "that resilience can be developed, and you can give people the resources to build within them the power to bounce back from adversity."[80]

Personality Types in Different Cultures

Do personality frameworks, like the Big Five Model, transfer across cultures? Are dimensions like locus of control relevant in all cultures? Let's try to answer these questions.

The five personality factors studied in the Big Five Model appear in almost all cross-cultural studies.[81] These studies include a wide variety of diverse cultures such as China, Israel, Germany, Japan, Spain, Nigeria, Norway, Pakistan, and the United States. Differences are found in the emphasis on dimensions. The Chinese, for example, use the category of conscientiousness more often and use the category of agreeableness less often than do Americans. But a surprisingly high amount of agreement is found, especially among individuals from developed countries. As a case in point, a comprehensive review of studies covering people from the European Community found that conscientiousness was a valid predictor of performance across jobs and occupational groups.[82] Studies in the United States found the same thing.

Sisters Lucky, Dicky, and Nicky Chhetri exhibited the personality dimension of conscientiousness in starting 3 Sisters Adventure Trekking Company in Nepal. Persistence and a high achievement drive helped them not only to break into a male-dominated industry but also to grow their business by training other women to become guides. Today they run a booming business, with 150 female guides leading some 1,000 trekkers a year.
Source: Niranjan Shrestha/AP Images

We know that no personality type is common for a given country. You can, for instance, find high risk takers and low risk takers in almost any culture. Yet a country's culture influences the *dominant* personality characteristics of its people. We can see this effect of national culture by looking at one of the personality traits we just discussed: locus of control.

National cultures differ in terms of the degree to which people believe they control their environment. For instance, North Americans believe they can dominate their environment; other societies, such as those in Middle Eastern countries, believe life is essentially predetermined. Notice how closely this distinction parallels the concept of

let's get REAL

Source: Theodore Peterson

The Scenario:

"Why can't we all just get along?" wondered Bonnie, as she sat in her office. Today, she had already dealt with an employee who came in nearly every day with a complaint about something another coworker had said or done. Then, on top of that, Bonnie had to soothe over the hurt feelings of another employee who had overheard a conversation in the break room. She thought to herself, "I love being a manager, but there are days when the emotional tension in this place is too much."

Theodore Peterson
Lead Mentor/Behavioral Assistant

What would you tell Bonnie about emotions in the workplace and how to deal with them?

I would tell Bonnie that emotions in the workplace are always going to be present and are beyond her control. People will be people. However, don't let the emotions in the workplace affect your mood. Unfortunately as a manager, sometimes you have to smile even when you don't feel like doing so. I would recommend Bonnie find a self-care activity that she can do outside of work, or that she take a few minutes during the workday to close the door in her office to take a few deep breaths; or to take a vacation if she has any time available. We all can feel overwhelmed but it's all in how one deals with it that really matters.

internal and external locus of control. On the basis of this particular cultural characteristic, we should expect a larger proportion of internals in the U.S. and Canadian workforces than in the workforces of Saudi Arabia or Iran.

As we have seen throughout this section, personality traits influence employees' behavior. For global managers, understanding how personality traits differ takes on added significance when looking at it from the perspective of national culture.

Emotions and Emotional Intelligence

"Trying to sell wedding gowns to anxious brides-to-be" can be quite a stressful experience for the salesperson, needless to say. To help its employees stay "cheery," David's Bridal, a chain of more than 270 stores, relied on research into joyful emotions. Now, when "faced with an indecisive bride," salespeople have been taught emotional coping techniques and know how to focus on "things that bring them joy."[83]

We can't leave the topic of personality without looking at the important behavioral aspect of emotions. Employees rarely check their feelings at the door to the workplace, nor are they unaffected by things that happen throughout the workday.[84] How we respond emotionally and how we deal with our emotions are typically functions of our personality. **Emotions** are intense feelings directed at someone or something. They're object specific; that is, emotions are reactions to an object.[85] For instance, when a work colleague criticizes you for the way you spoke to a client, you might become angry at him. That is, you show emotion (anger) toward a specific object (your colleague). Sometimes negative feelings can be a good thing. Having bad feelings can make people think that something is wrong and motivate them to "look for external information to support your argument, to be much more rigorous about questioning your own presumptions and other people's perspectives, [and have] much more reliance on objective data."[86] Because employees bring an emotional component with them to work every day, managers need to understand the role that emotions play in employee behavior.[87]

emotions
Intense feelings that are directed at someone or something

WORKPLACE CONFIDENTIAL An Abusive Boss

No one *wants* an abusive boss but sometimes we end up with one. Studies estimate that about 13 percent of U.S. workers suffer from such a boss. And this behavior appears to be most prevalent in fields such as the military and health care. A possible explanation is that these organizations tend to be characterized by high work demands, pressure, risk, and high costs associated with failure—all factors that can stress bosses out.

It is hoped that you'll never face an abusive boss. But if you do, you'll want to have a strategy for dealing with him or her.

Let's first clarify what we mean by an *abusive boss*. We define it as your perception that your supervisor is engaging in sustained displays of hostile verbal or nonverbal behaviors. What specific behaviors does this encompass? Here are some examples: bullying, belittling, threats, intimidation, vindictiveness, public ridiculing, and angry outbursts. Note two things about our definition. First, it's a perception. Regardless of whether your boss is actually abusive or not, if you think he is, he is. Second, our analysis isn't concerned with the occasional rant or mistreatment. The action we're concerned with is a regular feature of your boss's behavior.

Here's an interesting insight that might help you better cope. Abusive bosses are strategic. They pick and choose their targets. Studies find that they particularly like to go after those they view as weak or vulnerable. You're rarely going to see a boss throwing abuse at a powerful or well-connected member of her department. The message here is obvious: Regardless of your actual confidence level, don't give the appearance that you're weak or unsure of yourself.

If you're on the receiving end of abuse at work, what can you do? Here are some options.

- ***Confrontation:*** Directly talk to your abusive boss to discuss the problem.
- ***Passive-aggressiveness:*** Indirectly express your hostility through actions such as procrastination, stubbornness, moodiness, or deliberately making half-hearted efforts to accomplish required tasks.
- ***Ingratiation:*** Try to win over your boss, and get him or her to "lighten up" on you, by actions such as doing favors or using flattery.
- ***Seeking Support from Others:*** Assuming that there is power in numbers, this approach has others acknowledge your problem and has them act in your behalf.
- ***Avoidance:*** Keep away from your boss and limit his or her opportunities to harass you.
- ***Reframing:*** Since abuse is a perception, try to mentally restructure your boss's actions in a way so that it no longer seems to be abusive.
- ***Complain to Higher-ups:*** Take your complaint to higher-ups in your organization to gain their support and "encourage" your boss to change his or her behavior.

Which of the above strategies do the experts suggest? Taking your complaint to upper levels in the organization is not likely to work where the culture tolerates or even supports abusive behavior. Hostile work climates *do* exist! And they encourage those with abusive tendencies to act out. So before you consider complaining to higher-ups, make sure your culture frowns on, and acts against, managers who abuse their employees.

Studies have found that the most common employee response to abuse is to avoid contact with the boss and seek social support. Not surprisingly, confrontation was the least used strategy. But were these the most effective ways for dealing with abuse? Apparently not. Avoidance and seeking support resulted in employees experiencing negative emotions. Their stress levels were increased because this approach only increased feelings of weakness and perpetuated fear of the boss. Somewhat counterintuitively, research indicates that standing up to your boss was most related to positive emotions. It reinforces the desire to stick up for yourself, outwardly conveys that you're aware of your boss's behavior, and demonstrates that you do not find this behavior acceptable. Another counterintuitive finding was that passive-aggressiveness paid off. So it appears that bosses are less likely to go after employees if they are assertive, speak up, or perform acts of upward hostility. The evidence indicates that standing up for yourself or retaliating are less likely to make you feel like a victim. If you're firm and outspoken, you're less likely to see yourself as a victim, and it sends a message to your boss that you have a backbone and don't want to be messed with.

Keep in mind that trying to avoid your boss or reframe his or her abusive behavior does nothing toward actually resolving the problem. It merely covers it up and is likely to leave you still feeling like a victim. If you're planning on leaving your organization shortly or expect to get a new boss soon, avoidance can be effective. Otherwise, the use of avoidance or reframing doesn't change anything.

Sources: Based on B. J. Tepper, "Abusive Supervision in Work Organizations: Review, Synthesis, and Research Agenda," *Journal of Management*, June 2007, pp. 261–289; D. Yagil, H. Ben-Zur, and I. Tamir, "Do Employees Cope Effectively with Abusive Supervision at Work? An Exploratory Study," *International Journal of Stress Management*, January 31, 2011, pp. 5–23; and B. J. Tepper, et al., "On the Exchange of Hostility with Supervisors: An Examination of Self-Enhancing and Self-Defeating Perspectives," *Personnel Psychology*, Winter 2015, pp. 723–758.

FUTURE VISION Increased Reliance on Emotional Intelligence

Whether it goes by the name of emotional intelligence, social intelligence, or something else, the ability to understand yourself and others will be a skill that organizations will seek when hiring employees. In fact, in a survey of critical skills for the workforce in 2020, social intelligence ranked second on a list of the most critical skills.[88] (FYI: The number one skill was sense-making; that is, being able to determine the deeper meaning or significance of what's being expressed.) The ability to get along with others—coworkers, colleagues, team members, bosses, and customers—will be critical to success in most jobs. While more employees are likely to work off-site, there will still be ongoing contact with others. Those employees who have strong technical skills but are weak on emotional intelligence will find it increasingly difficult to find and hold a job.

If your professor has chosen to assign this, go to **www.mymanagementlab.com** *to discuss the following questions.*

TALK ABOUT IT 1: Why do you think the ability to get along with others is so critical?

TALK ABOUT IT 2: How can you develop this ability?

How many emotions are there? Although you could probably name several dozen, research has identified six universal emotions: anger, fear, sadness, happiness, disgust, and surprise.[89] Do these emotions surface in the workplace? Absolutely! I get *angry* after receiving a poor performance appraisal. I *fear* that I could be laid off as a result of a company cutback. I'm *sad* about one of my coworkers leaving to take a new job in another city. I'm *happy* after being selected as employee of the month. I'm *disgusted* with the way my supervisor treats women on our team. And I'm *surprised* to find out that management plans a complete restructuring of the company's retirement program.

People respond differently to identical emotion-provoking stimuli. In some cases, differences can be attributed to a person's personality and because people vary in their ability to express emotions. For instance, you undoubtedly know people who almost never show their feelings. They rarely get angry or show rage. In contrast, you probably also know people who seem to be on an emotional roller coaster. When they're happy, they're ecstatic. When they're sad, they're deeply depressed. And two people can be in the exact same situation—one showing excitement and joy, the other remaining calm.

However, at other times how people respond emotionally is a result of job requirements. Jobs make different demands in terms of what types and how much emotion needs to be displayed. For instance, air traffic controllers, ER nurses, and trial judges are expected to be calm and controlled, even in stressful situations. On the other hand, public-address announcers at sporting events and lawyers in a courtroom must be able to alter their emotional intensity as the need arises.

If your professor has assigned this, go to **www.mymanagementlab.com** to watch a video titled: *East Haven Fire Department: Emotions and Moods* and to respond to questions.

One area of emotions research with interesting insights into personality is **emotional intelligence (EI)**, the ability to notice and to manage emotional cues and information.[90] It's composed of five dimensions:

emotional intelligence (EI)
The ability to notice and to manage emotional cues and information

Self-awareness: The ability to be aware of what you're feeling.
Self-management: The ability to manage one's own emotions and impulses.
Self-motivation: The ability to persist in the face of setbacks and failures.
Empathy: The ability to sense how others are feeling.
Social skills: The ability to handle the emotions of others.

EI has been shown to be positively related to job performance at all levels. For instance, one study looked at the characteristics of Lucent Technologies' (now Alcatel-Lucent) engineers who were rated as stars by their peers. The researchers concluded that stars were better at relating to others. That is, it was EI, not academic intelligence that characterized high performers. A study of Air Force recruiters generated similar findings. Top-performing recruiters exhibited high levels of EI. Despite these findings, EI has been a controversial topic in OB.[91] Supporters say EI has intuitive appeal and predicts important behavior.[92] Critics say that EI is vague, can't be measured, and has questionable validity.[93] One thing we can conclude is that EI appears to be relevant to success in jobs that demand a high degree of social interaction.

Implications for Managers

About 80 percent of U.S. private companies are using personality tests when recruiting and hiring.[94] Perhaps the major value in understanding personality differences lies in this area. Managers are likely to have higher-performing and more satisfied employees if consideration is given to matching personalities with jobs. The best-documented personality-job fit theory was developed by psychologist John Holland, who identified six basic personality types.[95] His theory states that an employee's satisfaction with his or her job, as well as his or her likelihood of leaving that job, depends on the degree to which the individual's personality matches the job environment. Exhibit 15-4 describes the six types, their personality characteristics, and examples of suitable occupations for each.

Holland's theory proposes that satisfaction is highest and turnover lowest when personality and occupation are compatible. Social individuals should be in "people" type jobs, and so forth. The key points of this theory are that (1) intrinsic differences in personality are apparent among individuals; (2) the types of jobs vary; and (3) people in job environments compatible with their personality types should be more satisfied and less likely to resign voluntarily than people in incongruent jobs.

Exhibit 15-4
Holland's Personality–Job Fit

Source: Based on J. L. Holland, *Making Vocational Choices: A Theory of Vocational Personalities and Work Environments* (Odessa, FL: Psychological Assessment Resources, 1997).

TYPE	PERSONALITY CHARACTERISTICS	SAMPLE OCCUPATIONS
Realistic. Prefers physical activities that require skill, strength, and coordination	Shy, genuine, persistent, stable, conforming, practical	Mechanic, drill press operator, assembly-line worker, farmer
Investigative. Prefers activities involving thinking, organizing, and understanding	Analytical, original, curious, independent	Biologist, economist, mathematician, news reporter
Social. Prefers activities that involve helping and developing others	Sociable, friendly, cooperative, understanding	Social worker, teacher, counselor, clinical psychologist
Conventional. Prefers rule-regulated, orderly, and unambiguous activities	Conforming, efficient, practical, unimaginative, inflexible	Accountant, corporate manager, bank teller, file clerk
Enterprising. Prefers verbal activities that offer opportunities to influence others and attain power	Self-confident, ambitious, energetic, domineering	Lawyer, real estate agent, public relations specialist, small business manager
Artistic. Prefers ambiguous and unsystematic activities that allow creative expression	Imaginative, disorderly, idealistic, emotional, impractical	Painter, musician, writer, interior decorator

In addition, other benefits arise from understanding personality. By recognizing that people approach problem solving, decision making, and job interactions differently, a manager can better understand why an employee is uncomfortable with making quick decisions or why another employee insists on gathering as much information as possible before addressing a problem. Or, for instance, managers can expect that individuals with an external locus of control may be less satisfied with their jobs than internals and may be less willing to accept responsibility for their actions.

Finally, being a successful manager and accomplishing goals means working well together with others both inside and outside the organization. In order to work effectively together, you need to understand each other. This understanding comes, at least in part, from an appreciation of personality traits and emotions. Also, one of the skills you have to develop as a manager is learning to fine-tune your emotional reactions according to the situation. In other words, you have to learn to recognize when "you have to smile and when you have to bark."[96]

PERCEPTION

LO15.4 Maybe you've seen this in a Facebook post or on some other online source: AOCRNDICG TO RSCHEEARCH AT CMABRIGDE UINERVTISY, IT DSENO'T MTAETR WAHT OERDR THE LTTERES IN A WROD ARE, THE OLNY IPROAMTNT TIHNG IS TAHT THE FRSIT AND LSAT LTTEER BE IN THE RGHIT PCLAE. TIHS IS BCUSEAE THE HUAMN MNID DEOS NOT RAED ERVEY LTETER BY ISTLEF, BUT THE WROD AS A WLOHE. IF YOU CAN RAED...TIHS, PSOT IT TO YUOR WLAL. OLNY 55% OF PLEPOE CAN.[97] How'd you do in trying to read this? If you were able to make sense out of this jumbled message, that's the perceptual process at work. **Perception** is a process by which we give meaning to our environment by organizing and interpreting sensory impressions. Research on perception consistently demonstrates that individuals may look at the same thing yet perceive it differently. One manager, for instance, can interpret the fact that her assistant regularly takes several days to make important decisions as evidence that the assistant is slow, disorganized, and afraid to make decisions. Another manager with the same assistant might interpret the same tendency as evidence that the assistant is thoughtful, thorough, and deliberate. The first manager would probably evaluate her assistant negatively; the second manager would probably evaluate the person positively. The point is that none of us sees reality. We interpret what we see and call it reality. And, of course, as the example shows, we behave according to our perceptions.

perception
A process by which we give meaning to our environment by organizing and interpreting sensory impressions

Factors That Influence Perception

How do we explain the fact that people can perceive the same thing differently? A number of factors act to shape and sometimes distort perception. These factors are in the *perceiver*, in the *target* being perceived, or in the *situation* in which the perception occurs.

When a person looks at a target and attempts to interpret what he or she sees, the individual's personal characteristics will heavily influence the interpretation. These personal characteristics include attitudes, personality, motives, interests, experiences, or expectations. For instance, the perception of employees sporting tattoos differs based on age. Older workers tend to perceive tattoos in the office as inappropriate or objectionable, while younger workers don't.[98] Differences in these perceptions may be due, in part, to more young people having tattoos or knowing others who do.

The characteristics of the target being observed can also affect what's perceived. Loud people are more likely than quiet people to be noticed in a group, as are extremely attractive or unattractive individuals. The relationship of a target to its background also influences perception, as does our tendency to group close things and similar things together. You can experience these tendencies by looking at the visual perception examples shown in Exhibit 15-5. Notice how what you see changes as you look differently at each one.

Exhibit 15-5
What Do You See?

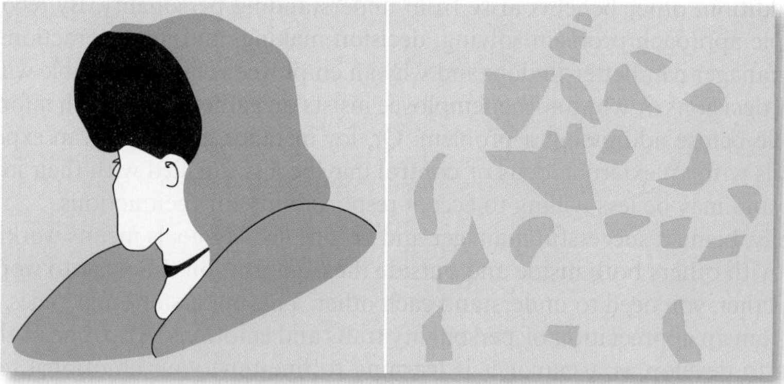

Old woman or young woman? A knight on a horse?

Finally, the context in which we see objects or events is also important. The time at which an object or event is seen can influence perception, as can location, light, heat, color, and any number of other situational factors.

- 22 percent of employees say they've planned to come in to work late or leave work early when they knew their boss was going to be out.[99]

attribution theory
A theory used to explain how we judge people differently depending on what meaning we attribute to a given behavior

Attribution Theory

Much of the research on perception is directed at inanimate objects. Managers, however, are concerned with people. Our perceptions of people differ from our perception of inanimate objects because we make inferences about the behaviors of people that we don't make about objects. Objects don't have beliefs, motives, or intentions; people do. The result is that when we observe an individual's behavior, we try to develop explanations of why they behave in certain ways. Our perception and judgment of a person's actions are significantly influenced by the assumptions we make about the person.

Attribution theory was developed to explain how we judge people differently depending on what meaning we attribute to a given behavior.[100] Basically, the theory suggests that when we observe an individual's behavior, we attempt to determine whether it was internally or externally caused. Internally caused behaviors are those believed to be under the personal control of the individual. Externally caused behavior results from outside factors; that is, the person is forced into the behavior by the situation. That determination, however, depends on three factors: distinctiveness, consensus, and consistency.

Distinctiveness refers to whether an individual displays different behaviors in different situations. Is the employee who arrived late today the same person who some employees complain of as being a "goof-off"? What we want to know is whether this behavior is unusual. If it's unusual, the observer is likely to attribute the behavior to external forces, something beyond the control of the person. However, if the behavior isn't unusual, it will probably be judged as internal.

If everyone who's faced with a similar situation responds in the same way, we can say the behavior shows *consensus.* A tardy employee's behavior would meet this criterion if all employees who took the same route to work were also late. From an attribution perspective, if consensus is high, you're likely to give an external attribution to the employee's tardiness; that is, some outside factor—maybe road construction or a traffic accident—caused the behavior. However, if other employees who come the same way to work made it on time, you would conclude that the cause of the late behavior was internal.

Finally, an observer looks for *consistency* in a person's actions. Does the person engage in the behaviors regularly and consistently? Does the person respond the same way over time? Coming in 10 minutes late for work isn't perceived in the same way if, for one employee, it represents an unusual case (she hasn't been late in months), while for another employee, it's part of a routine pattern (she's late two or three times every week). The more consistent the behavior, the more the observer is inclined to attribute it to internal causes. Exhibit 15-6 summarizes the key elements of attribution theory.

Exhibit 15-6
Attribution Theory

OBSERVATION	INTERPRETATION	ATTRIBUTION OF CAUSE
Does person behave this way in other situations?	*YES:* Low distinctiveness *NO:* High distinctiveness	Internal attribution External attribution
Do other people behave the same way in similar situations?	*YES:* High consensus *NO:* Low consensus	External attribution Internal attribution
Does person behave this way consistently?	*YES:* High consistency *NO:* Low consistency	Internal attribution External attribution

One interesting finding from attribution theory is that errors or biases distort our attributions. For instance, substantial evidence supports the fact that when we make judgments about the behavior of other people, we have a tendency to *under*estimate the influence of external factors and to *over*estimate the influence of internal or personal factors.[101] This tendency is called the **fundamental attribution error** and can explain why a sales manager may attribute the poor performance of her sales representative to laziness rather than to the innovative product line introduced by a competitor. Another tendency is to attribute our own successes to internal factors, such as ability or effort, while putting the blame for personal failure on external factors, such as luck. This tendency is called the **self-serving bias** and suggests that feedback provided to employees in performance reviews will be distorted by them depending on whether it's positive or negative. In some cases, these distortions can be serious. A recent survey found that employees with self-serving tendencies were 25 percent more likely to rate their bosses as abusive.[102] Obviously, these perceptions can damage reputations of nonabusive managers.

fundamental attribution error
The tendency to underestimate the influence of external factors and overestimate the influence of internal factors when making judgments about the behavior of others

self-serving bias
The tendency for individuals to attribute their own successes to internal factors while putting the blame for failures on external factors

Are these errors or biases that distort attributions universal across different cultures? We can't say for sure, but preliminary evidence indicates cultural differences.[103] For instance, a study of Korean managers found that, contrary to the self-serving bias, they tended to accept responsibility for group failure "because I was not a capable leader" instead of attributing it to group members.[104] Attribution theory was developed largely based on experiments with Americans and Western Europeans. But the Korean study suggests caution in making attribution theory predictions in non-Western societies, especially in countries with strong collectivist traditions.

Air Force General Lori Robinson salutes during the ceremony installing her as the new commander of the North American Aerospace Defense Command and U.S. Northern Command. Robinson's successful 34-year Air Force career challenges the gender stereotyping in the military that women are too emotionally fragile to lead men in combat effectively and is an inspiration to women pursuing military jobs.
Source: Brennan Linsley/Associated Press

Shortcuts Used in Judging Others

Perceiving and interpreting people's behavior is a lot of work, so we use shortcuts to make the task more manageable. These techniques can be valuable when they let us make accurate interpretations quickly and provide valid data for making predictions. However, they aren't perfect. They can and do get us into trouble.

It's easy to judge others if we assume they're similar to us. In **assumed similarity**, or the "like me" effect, the observer's perception of others is influenced more by the observer's own characteristics than by those of the person observed. For example, if you want challenges and responsibility in your job, you'll assume that others want the same. People who assume that others are like them can, of course, be right, but not always.

assumed similarity
The assumption that others are like oneself

stereotyping
Judging a person based on a perception of a group to which that person belongs

halo effect
A general impression of an individual based on a single characteristic

When we judge someone on the basis of our perception of a group he or she is part of, we're using the shortcut called **stereotyping**. For instance, "Married people are more stable employees than single persons" is an example of stereotyping. To the degree that a stereotype is based on fact, it may produce accurate judgments. However, many stereotypes aren't factual and distort our judgment.[105]

When we form a general impression about a person on the basis of a single characteristic, such as intelligence, sociability, or appearance, we're influenced by the **halo effect**. This effect frequently occurs when students evaluate their classroom instructor. Students may isolate a single trait such as enthusiasm and allow their entire evaluation to be slanted by the perception of this one trait. An instructor may be quiet, assured, knowledgeable, and highly qualified, but if his classroom teaching style lacks enthusiasm, he might be rated lower on a number of other characteristics.

Implications for Managers

Managers need to recognize that their employees react to perceptions, not to reality. So whether a manager's appraisal of an employee's performance is actually objective and unbiased or whether the organization's wage levels are among the highest in the community is less relevant than what employees perceive them to be. If individuals perceive appraisals to be biased or wage levels as low, they'll behave as if those conditions actually exist. Employees organize and interpret what they see, so the potential for perceptual distortion is always present. The message is clear: Pay close attention to how employees perceive both their jobs and management actions.

LEARNING

LO15.5 The German chemical company BASF employs tens of thousands all over the world. To ease the transition after a corporate acquisition or hiring new employees, some divisions have implemented formal mentoring programs. "Mentees" complete a form describing what they want from a mentor, such as advice about an overseas assignment or feedback about leadership style. Then BASF uses software to match each person with one or more potential mentors, for a series of monthly meetings that continue over the next six months. BASF even has mentoring champions who answer employees' questions about the program.[106]

Mentoring is a good example of the last individual behavior concept we're going to look at—learning. Learning is included in our discussion of individual behavior for the obvious reason that almost all behavior is learned. If we want to explain, predict, and influence behavior, we need to understand how people learn.

learning
Any relatively permanent change in behavior that occurs as a result of experience

The psychologists' definition of learning is considerably broader than the average person's view that "it's what we do in school." Learning occurs all the time as we continuously learn from our experiences. A workable definition of **learning** is any relatively permanent change in behavior that occurs as a result of experience. Two learning theories help us understand how and why individual behavior occurs.

operant conditioning
A theory of learning that says behavior is a function of its consequences

Operant Conditioning

Operant conditioning argues that behavior is a function of its consequences. People learn to behave to get something they want or to avoid something they don't want. Operant behavior is voluntary or learned behavior, not reflexive or unlearned behavior. The tendency to repeat learned behavior is influenced by reinforcement or lack of reinforcement that happens as a result of the behavior. Reinforcement strengthens a behavior and increases the likelihood that it will be repeated. Lack of reinforcement weakens a behavior and lessens the likelihood that it will be repeated.

B. F. Skinner's research widely expanded our knowledge of operant conditioning.[107] Behavior is assumed to be determined from without—that is, *learned*—rather than from within—reflexive or unlearned. Skinner argued that people will most likely engage in desired behaviors if they are positively reinforced for doing so, and rewards are most effective if they immediately follow the desired response. In addition, behavior that isn't rewarded or is punished is less likely to be repeated.

You see examples of operant conditioning everywhere. Any situation in which it's either explicitly stated or implicitly suggested that reinforcement (rewards) is contingent on some action on your part is an example of operant conditioning. Your instructor says that if you want a high grade in this course, you must perform well on tests by giving correct answers. A salesperson working on commission knows that earning a sizeable income is contingent on generating high sales in his or her territory. And, in some companies, employees with perfect attendance receive bonuses. Of course, the linkage between behavior and reinforcement can also work to teach the individual to behave in ways that work against the best interests of the organization. Assume your boss tells you that if you'll work overtime during the next three-week busy season, you'll be compensated for it at the next performance appraisal. Then, when performance appraisal time comes, you are given no positive reinforcements (such as being praised for pitching in and helping out when needed). What will you do the next time your boss asks you to work overtime? You'll probably refuse. Your behavior can be explained by operant conditioning: If a behavior isn't positively reinforced, the probability that the behavior will be repeated declines.

Social Learning

Some 60 percent of the Radio City Rockettes have danced in prior seasons. The veterans help newcomers with "Rockette style"—where to place their hands, how to hold their hands, how to keep up stamina, and so forth.[108]

As the Rockettes are well aware, individuals can also learn by observing what happens to other people and just by being told about something as well as by direct experiences. Much of what we have learned comes from watching others (models)—parents, teachers, peers, television and movie actors, managers, and so forth. This view that we can learn both through observation and direct experience is called **social learning theory**.

social learning theory
A theory of learning that says people can learn through observation and direct experience

The influence of others is central to the social learning viewpoint. The amount of influence these models have on an individual is determined by four processes:

1. *Attentional processes.* People learn from a model when they recognize and pay attention to its critical features. We're most influenced by models who are attractive, repeatedly available, thought to be important, or seen as similar to us.
2. *Retention processes.* A model's influence will depend on how well the individual remembers the model's action, even after the model is no longer readily available.
3. *Motor reproduction processes.* After a person has seen a new behavior by observing the model, the watching must become doing. This process then demonstrates that the individual can actually do the modeled activities.
4. *Reinforcement processes.* Individuals will be motivated to exhibit the modeled behavior if positive incentives or rewards are provided. Behaviors that are reinforced will be given more attention, learned better, and performed more often.

Shaping: A Managerial Tool

Because learning takes place on the job as well as prior to it, managers are concerned with how they can teach employees to behave in ways that most benefit the organization. Thus, managers will often attempt to "mold" individuals by guiding their learning in graduated steps, through a method called **shaping behavior**.

shaping behavior
The process of guiding learning in graduated steps using reinforcement or lack of reinforcement

Consider the situation in which an employee's behavior is significantly different from that sought by a manager. If the manager reinforced the individual only when he or she showed desirable responses, the opportunity for reinforcement might occur too infrequently. Shaping offers a logical approach toward achieving the desired behavior. We shape behavior by systematically reinforcing each successive step that moves the individual closer to the desired behavior. If an employee who has chronically been a half-hour late for work comes in only 20 minutes late, we can reinforce the improvement. Reinforcement would increase as an employee gets closer to the desired behavior.

Four ways to shape behavior include positive reinforcement, negative reinforcement, punishment, and extinction. When a behavior is followed by something pleasant, such as praising an employee for a job well done, it's called *positive reinforcement.* Positive reinforcement increases the likelihood that the desired behavior will be repeated. Rewarding a response by eliminating or withdrawing something unpleasant is *negative reinforcement.* A manager who says, "I won't dock your pay if you start getting to work on time" is using negative reinforcement. The desired behavior (getting to work on time) is being encouraged by the withdrawal of something unpleasant (the employee's pay being docked). On the other hand, *punishment* penalizes undesirable behavior and will eliminate it. Suspending an employee for two days without pay for habitually coming to work late is an example of punishment. Finally, eliminating any reinforcement that's maintaining a behavior is called *extinction.* When a behavior isn't reinforced, it gradually disappears. In meetings, managers who wish to discourage employees from continually asking irrelevant or distracting questions can eliminate this behavior by ignoring those employees when they raise their hands to speak. Soon this behavior should disappear.

Both positive and negative reinforcement result in learning. They strengthen a desired behavior and increase the probability that the desired behavior will be repeated. Both punishment and extinction also result in learning, but do so by weakening an undesired behavior and decreasing its frequency.

Implications for Managers

Employees are going to learn on the job. The only issue is whether managers are going to manage their learning through the rewards they allocate and the examples they set, or allow it to occur haphazardly. If marginal employees are rewarded with pay raises and promotions, they will have little reason to change their behavior. In fact, productive employees who see marginal performance rewarded might change their behavior. If managers want behavior A, but reward behavior B, they shouldn't be surprised to find employees learning to engage in behavior B. Similarly, managers should expect that employees will look to them as models. Managers who are consistently late to work, or take two hours for lunch, or help themselves to company office supplies for personal use should expect employees to read the message they are sending and model their behavior accordingly.

Chapter 15 PREPARING FOR: Exams/Quizzes

CHAPTER SUMMARY by Learning Objectives

LO15.1 IDENTIFY the focus and goals of individual behavior within organizations.

Just like an iceberg, it's the hidden organizational elements (attitudes, perceptions, norms, etc.) that make understanding individual behavior so challenging.

Organizational behavior (OB) focuses on three areas: individual behavior, group behavior, and organizational aspects. The goals of OB are to explain, predict, and influence behavior.

Employee productivity is a performance measure of both efficiency and effectiveness. Absenteeism is the failure to report to work. Turnover is the voluntary and involuntary permanent withdrawal from an organization. Organizational citizenship behavior (OCB) is discretionary behavior that's not part of an employee's formal job requirements, but it promotes the effective functioning of an organization. Job satisfaction is an individual's general attitude toward his or her job. Counterproductive workplace behavior is any intentional employee behavior that is potentially harmful to the organization or individuals within the organization.

LO15.2 EXPLAIN the role that attitudes play in job performance.

The cognitive component refers to the beliefs, opinions, knowledge, or information held by a person. The affective component is the emotional or feeling part of an attitude. The behavioral component refers to an intention to behave in a certain way toward someone or something.

Job satisfaction refers to a person's general attitude toward his or her job. Job involvement is the degree to which an employee identifies with his or her job, actively participates in it, and considers his or her job performance to be important to his or her self-worth. Organizational commitment is the degree to which an employee identifies with a particular organization and its goals and wishes to maintain membership in that organization. Employee engagement is when employees are connected to, satisfied with, and enthusiastic about their jobs.

Job satisfaction positively influences productivity, lowers absenteeism levels, lowers turnover rates, promotes positive customer satisfaction, moderately promotes OCB, and helps minimize counterproductive workplace behavior.

Individuals try to reconcile attitude and behavior inconsistencies by altering their attitudes, altering their behavior, or rationalizing the inconsistency. Many organizations regularly survey their employees about their attitudes.

LO15.3 DESCRIBE different personality theories.

The MBTI measures four dimensions: social interaction, preference for gathering data, preference for decision making, and style of making decisions. The Big Five Model consists of five personality traits: extraversion, agreeableness, conscientiousness, emotional stability, and openness to experience.

The five personality traits that help explain individual behavior in organizations are locus of control, Machiavellianism, self-esteem, self-monitoring, and risk-taking. Other personality traits include Type A/Type B personalities, proactive personality, and resilience.

How people respond emotionally and how they deal with their emotions is a function of personality. A person who is emotionally intelligent has the ability to notice and to manage emotional cues and information.

LO15.4 DESCRIBE perception and factors that influence it.

Perception is how we give meaning to our environment by organizing and interpreting sensory impressions. Because people behave according to their perceptions, managers need to understand it.

Attribution theory depends on three factors. Distinctiveness is whether an individual displays different behaviors in different situations (that is, is the behavior unusual). Consensus is whether others facing a similar situation respond in the same way. Consistency is when a person engages in behaviors regularly and consistently. Whether these three factors are high or low helps managers determine whether employee behavior is attributed to external or internal causes.

The fundamental attribution error is the tendency to underestimate the influence of external factors and overestimate the influence of internal factors. The self-serving bias is the tendency to attribute our own successes to internal factors and to put the blame for personal failure on external factors.

Three shortcuts used in judging others are assumed similarity, stereotyping, and the halo effect.

LO15.5 DISCUSS learning theories and their relevance in shaping behavior.

Operant conditioning argues that behavior is a function of its consequences. Managers can use it to explain, predict, and influence behavior.

Social learning theory says that individuals learn by observing what happens to other people and by directly experiencing something.

Managers can shape behavior by using positive reinforcement (reinforcing a desired behavior by giving something pleasant), negative reinforcement (reinforcing a desired response by withdrawing something unpleasant), punishment (eliminating undesirable behavior by applying penalties), or extinction (not reinforcing a behavior to eliminate it).

Pearson **MyLab** Management

Go to **mymanagementlab.com** to complete the problems marked with this icon ✪.

✪ REVIEW AND DISCUSSION QUESTIONS

15-1. All of us have different personalities. How does an organization bring together a diverse group of individuals and expect them to work together harmoniously and productively? Discuss.

15-2. Which employee behaviors are more critical for a manager to influence? Discuss.

15-3. What are the goals of organizational behaviour?

15-4. Satisfied and happy employees make for better productivity, lower absenteeism, and turnover rate. Discuss.

15-5. How does the cognitive dissonance theory seek to explain the relationships between attitudes and behavior? How is this useful?

15-6. People differ in the degree to which they like or dislike themselves. Explain this statement. How is it applied?

15-7. On what basis does the attribution theory attempt to explain how we judge people differently?

15-8. How might a manager be tempted to use shaping behavior?

Pearson **MyLab** Management

If your professor has assigned these, go to **mymanagementlab.com** for the following Assisted-graded writing questions:

15-9. Describe the focus and goals of OB.

15-10. How can a manager effectively use a combination of punishment and extinction to shape behavior?

PREPARING FOR: My Career

✪ PERSONAL INVENTORY ASSESSMENTS

PERSONAL INVENTORY ASSESSMENT

Emotional Intelligence Assessment

How emotionally intelligent are you? This PIA will help you assess your level of emotional intelligence.

✪ ETHICS DILEMMA

Department manager Bill Ashworth reviewed dozens of résumés because he needed to fill an open assistant department manager position. Based on his review, Bill decided to interview three candidates in the following order: Sarah Bidwell, Marcus Green, and Robert Smith. After interviewing Sarah and Marcus, Bill knew that the hiring decision would be difficult because both Sarah and Marcus performed extremely well. During Robert's interview, Bill recognized him from their children's soccer games and recalled that Bill volunteered to help out the team. After Robert left the office, Bill felt that Robert's performance was merely adequate. Later that day, Bill offered the job to Robert.

15-11. What ethical issues might arise for Bill in hiring Robert?

15-12. How could Bill have approached the hiring decision?

SKILLS EXERCISE Developing Your Shaping Behavior Skill

About the Skill

In today's dynamic work environments, learning is continual. But this learning shouldn't be done in isolation or without any guidance. Most employees need to be shown what's expected of them on the job. As a manager, you must teach your employees the behaviors most critical to their and the organization's success.

Steps in Practicing the Skill

- ***Identify the critical behaviors that have a significant impact on an employee's performance.*** Not everything employees do on the job is equally important in terms of performance outcomes. A few critical behaviors may, in fact, account for the majority of one's results. These high-impact behaviors need to be identified.
- ***Establish a baseline of performance.*** A baseline is obtained by determining the number of times the identified behaviors occur under the employee's present job conditions.
- ***Analyze the contributing factors to performance and their consequences.*** A number of factors, such as the norms of a group, may be contributing to the baseline performance. Identify these factors and their effect on performance.
- ***Develop a shaping strategy.*** The change that may occur will entail changing some element of performance—structure, processes, technology, groups, or the task. The purpose of the strategy is to strengthen the desirable behaviors and weaken the undesirable ones.
- ***Apply the appropriate strategy.*** Once the strategy has been developed, it needs to be implemented. In this step, an intervention occurs.
- ***Measure the change that has occurred.*** An intervention should produce the desired results in performance behaviors. Evaluate the number of times the identified behaviors now occur. Compare these with the baseline evaluation in step 2.
- ***Reinforce desired behaviors.*** If an intervention has been successful and the new behaviors are producing the desired results, maintain these behaviors through reinforcement mechanisms.

Practicing the Skill

a. Imagine that your assistant is ideal in all respects but one—he or she is hopeless at taking phone messages for you when you're not in the office. You're often in training sessions and the calls are sales leads you want to follow up, so you have identified taking accurate messages as a high-impact behavior for your assistant.

b. Focus on steps 3 and 4, and devise a way to shape your assistant's behavior. Identify some factors that might contribute to his or her failure to take messages—these could range from a heavy workload to a poor understanding of the task's importance (you can rule out insubordination). Then develop a shaping strategy by determining what you can change—the available technology, the task itself, the structure of the job, or some other element of performance.

c. Now plan your intervention and take a brief meeting with your assistant in which you explain the change you expect. Recruit a friend to help you role-play your intervention. Do you think you would succeed in a real situation?

WORKING TOGETHER Team Exercise

As time passes, businesses have to adapt not only to new products and services, markets, trends in the external environment, and a host of other factors, but also to their employees. In small groups of three or four, take the role of a management team of a large multinational organization. The bulk of your employees are under 25, yet your HR policies have barely changed over the last decade. What might need to be done in order to address the needs of attaining work-life balance? Can it be changed? Your team's task is to come up with a specific plan for changing the HR policy. Once you've done this, share your thoughts with the rest of the class.[109]

MY TURN TO BE A MANAGER

- Write down three attitudes you have. Identify the cognitive, affective, and behavioral components of those attitudes.
- Survey 15 employees (at your place of work or at some campus office). Be sure to obtain permission before doing this anonymous survey. Ask them what rude or negative behaviors they've seen at work. Compile your findings in a report and be prepared to discuss this in class. If you were the manager in this workplace, how would you handle this behavior?
- If you've never taken a personality or career compatibility test, contact your school's testing center to see if you can take one. Once you get your results, evaluate what they mean for your career choice. Have you chosen a career that "fits" your personality? What are the implications?

- Have you ever heard of the "waiter rule"? A lot of business people think that how you treat service workers says a lot about your character and attitudes. What do you think this means? Do you agree with this idea? Why or why not? How would you be evaluated on the "waiter rule"?
- Like it or not, each of us is continually shaping the behavior of those around us. For one week, keep track of how many times you use positive reinforcement, negative reinforcement, punishment, or extinction to shape behaviors. At the end of the week, which one did you tend to use most? What were you trying to do; that is, what behaviors were you trying to shape? Were your attempts successful? Evaluate. What could you have done differently if you were trying to change someone's behavior?
- Find two companies that have been recognized for their employee engagement efforts. Compare the different strategies each company uses to build and engage their workforce. Are any the same? Different? Why do you think each company has been successful with employee engagement?
- What is your level of emotional intelligence? Visit www.mindtools.com, search for "emotional intelligence" and select "How Emotionally Intelligent Are You?" to take a brief self-assessment.

CASE APPLICATION 1 A Great Place to Work

In line with Apple and Google, Tencent Holdings Limited, China's leading internet service portal, has become the world's tenth most valuable public companies and is one of the largest gaming companies in the world. Founded in 1998, the company is based in Shenzhen, China. What began as just mobile-messaging service quickly turned into a platform for gaming, bills payment, and money-market funds services. Its ubiquitous WeChat has more than 800 million users. To continue increasing the Internet company's business, founder, Ma Huateng, understands that staffing is the key and that the employees must have a vested interest in its success.

Huateng strives to provide open and comfortable atmosphere in the workplace, an ease of communication with management, and recognition of individual accomplishments. At Tencent's monthly meetings, staff members ranging from senior management to trainee managers discuss their latest projects. The decision-making process is not as formal as in other big conglomerates. Extolled by Goldman Sachs and General Electric, the founder viewed that internal competition between coworkers is a necessary driver of innovation. He wants the teams to run in parallel, as no one knows which team will come out with a better product.

While moral satisfaction is important, to boost employee enthusiasm Tencent won't underestimate the importance of linking remuneration to performance. Employees receive cash prizes as rewards for valuable results, such as redesigning an interface to new and significant innovations. One manager remarked that an employee is gratified when they win something, no matter how small and big the reward. Cash rewards have become part of the ingrained Tencent culture. Along with it, an annual bonus, often paid prior to the Lunar New Year holiday, can be higher than an employee's yearly salary at Tencent.

By becoming the company's shareholders alongside the company's founders, profit or equity sharing is one of the most effective incentives. In 2016, Tencent gave its 31,557 employees 300 shares each as part of the company's anniversary celebrations. This means that each Tencent employee received U.S. $8,000 worth of shares.[110]

DISCUSSION QUESTIONS

15-13. Do you think the work culture at Tencent is effective? Would it work in other organizations? Why or why not?

15-14. How would an understanding of organization behavior help Ma Huateng? What do you think will be Tencent's biggest challenge in the future?

15-15. Using what you've learned from the various behavior theories, what does Tencent's situation tell you about employee behavior?

15-16. Looking at the incentives system offered by Tencent, what does that tell you about the importance of understanding individual behavior?

CASE APPLICATION 2 Employees First

"Employees first." That's the most important cultural value that former HCL Technologies' CEO, Vineet Nayar, believed it would take the company into the future. Although most managers think that customers should come first, Nayar's philosophy is that employee satisfaction needs to be the top priority.

As one of the largest companies in India, HCL sells various information technology products and services, such as laptops, custom software development, and technology consulting. Luring and retaining talent is one of the challenges HCL faces. And, given its size, it doesn't have the atmosphere of a fun and quirky start-up.

Part of that "employee first" philosophy is a no-layoff policy, which was difficult to uphold during the pressures of the economic downturn. Like its competitors, HCL had excess employees and had suspended raises. However, HCL kept its promise and didn't lay off any HCLite (Nayar's name for HCL employees). As business has picked up, however, employees begin looking at competitors' job offers. During the first quarter alone of 2010, HCL lost 22 percent of its workforce. Maybe it was time to monitor and track employee satisfaction.

HCL Technologies is headquartered in the world's largest democracy, so it's quite fitting that the New Delhi–based company attempted a radical experiment in workplace democracy. Nayar was committed to creating a company where the job of company leaders is to enable people to find their own destiny by gravitating to their strengths. During his tenure, Nayar had pioneered a culture in which employees were first. What had he done to put employees first? Part of the cultural initiative dealt with the organization's structure. HCL inverted its organizational structure and placed more power in the hands of frontline employees, especially those in direct contact with customers and clients. It increased its investment in employee development and improved communication through greater transparency. Employees were encouraged to communicate directly with Nayar. Through a forum called U&I (You and I), Nayar fielded more than a hundred questions from employees every week. "I threw open the door and invited criticism," he said. However, the signature piece of the company's cultural mission was what HCL called "trust pay." In contrast to the industry standard, in which the average employee's pay is 30 percent variable, HCL decided to pay higher fixed salaries and reduce the variable component.

Did the unique "employees first" culture at HCL Technologies attract unique employees? Rajeev Sawhney, HCL's former European president, would say it did. He used *Slumdog Millionaire*, a movie that won the 2009 Academy Award for Best Picture, as a parallel. "It (the movie) is a reflection of the Indian race. It shows the adversity that creates the desire in people to reach out and create. . . . With each adversity they face, there is a greater desire to reach out and do something more." Sawhney said that entrepreneurialism is a key value of the HCL culture.[111]

DISCUSSION QUESTIONS

15-17. What is your impression of the "employees first" culture? Would this culture be effective in other organizations? Why or why not? What would it take to make it work?

15-18. How would an understanding of organizational behavior have helped Vineet Nayar lead his company? How about first-line company supervisors? Explain.

15-19. What aspects of personality do you see in this story about HCL? How have the personality traits of HCL employees contributed to make HCL what it is?

15-20. Design an employee attitude survey for the employees at HCL.

ENDNOTES

1. "Thousands of Employees Rally Behind Ousted Market Basket CEO," *Free Enterprise* online, www.freeenterprise.com, October 16, 2014.
2. Emma Dunkley, "HSBC Drops Pay Freeze Plan in U-Turn After Staff Protest," *Financial Times*, February 11, 2016, https://www.ft.com/content/8645ee10-d0b9-11e5-92a1-c5e23ef99c77 (accessed December 27, 2016); Jill Treanor, "HSBC Axes 2016 Pay Freeze After Staff Protests," *The Guardian (UK)*, February 11, 2016, https://www.theguardian.com/business/2016/feb/11/hsbc-axes-2016-pay-freeze-after-staff-protests (accessed December 27, 2016).
3. W. Hamilton, "Absenteeism Costs U.S. Business $84 Billion a Year, Report Says," *The Los Angeles Times* online, www.latimes.com, May 8, 2013.
4. J. Kantor, "High Turnover Costs Way More Than You Think," *Huffington Post* online, www.huffingtonpost.com, February 11, 2016.
5. K. H. Dekas, T. N. Bauer, B. Welle, J. Kurkoski, and S. Sullivan, "Organizational Citizenship Behavior, Version 2.0: A Review and Qualitative Investigation of OCBs for Knowledge Workers at Google and Beyond," *Academy of Management Perspective,* August 2013, pp. 219–237; D. W. Organ, *Organizational Citizenship Behavior: The Good Soldier Syndrome* (Lexington, MA: Lexington Books, 1988), p. 4. See also J. L. Lavell, D. E. Rupp, and J. Brockner, "Taking a Multifoci Approach to the Study of Justice, Social Exchange, and Citizenship Behavior: The Target Similarity Model," *Journal of Management,* December 2007, pp. 841–866; and J. A. LePine, A. Erez, and D. E. Johnson, "The Nature and Dimensionality of Organizational Citizenship Behavior: A Critical Review and Meta-Analysis," *Journal of Applied Psychology,* February 2002, pp. 52–65.
6. R. Ilies, B. A. Scott, and T. A. Judge, "The Interactive Effects of Personal Traits and Experienced States on Intraindividual Patterns of Citizenship Behavior," *Academy of Management Journal,* June 2006, pp. 561–575; P. Cardona, B. S. Lawrence, and P. M. Bentler, "The Influence of Social and Work Exchange Relationships on Organizational Citizenship Behavior," *Group & Organization Management,* April 2004, pp. 219–247; M. C. Bolino and W. H. Turnley, "Going the Extra Mile: Cultivating and Managing Employee Citizenship Behavior," *Academy of Management Executive,* August 2003, pp. 60–73; M. C. Bolino, W. H. Turnley, and J. J. Bloodgood, "Citizenship Behavior and the Creation of Social Capital in Organizations," *Academy of Management Review,* October 2002, pp. 505–522; and P. M. Podsakoff, S. B. MacKenzie, J. B. Paine, and D. G. Bachrach, "Organizational Citizenship Behaviors: A Critical Review of the Theoretical and Empirical Literature and Suggestions for Future Research," *Journal of Management,* vol. 26, no. 3, 2000, pp. 543–548.
7. M. C. Bolino and W. H. Turnley, "The Personal Costs of Citizenship Behavior: The Relationship Between Individual Initiative and Role Overload, Job Stress, and Work-Family Conflict," *Journal of Applied Psychology,* July 2005, pp. 740–748.
8. This definition adapted from R. W. Griffin and Y. P. Lopez, "Bad Behavior in Organizations: A Review and Typology for Future Research," *Journal of Management,* December 2005, pp. 988–1005.
9. S. J. Breckler, "Empirical Validation of Affect, Behavior, and Cognition as Distinct Components of Attitude," *Journal of Personality and Social Psychology,* May 1984, pp. 1191–1205; and S. L. Crites Jr., L. R. Fabrigar, and R. E. Petty, "Measuring the Affective and Cognitive Properties of Attitudes: Conceptual and Methodological Issues," *Personality and Social Psychology Bulletin,* December 1994, pp. 619–634.
10. D. R. May, R. L. Gilson, and L. M. Harter, "The Psychological Conditions of Meaningfulness, Safety and Availability and the Engagement of the Human Spirit at Work," *Journal of Occupational and Organizational Psychology,* March 2004, pp. 11–37; R. T. Keller, "Job Involvement and Organizational Commitment as Longitudinal Predictors of Job Performance: A Study of Scientists and Engineers," *Journal of Applied Psychology,* August 1997, pp. 539–545; W. Kahn, "Psychological Conditions of Personal Engagement and Disengagement at Work," *Academy of Management Journal,* December 1990, pp. 692–794; and P. P. Brooke Jr., D. W. Russell, and J. L. Price, "Discriminant Validation of Measures of Job Satisfaction, Job Involvement, and Organizational Commitment," *Journal of Applied Psychology,* May 1988, pp. 139–145.
11. P. Korkki, "With Jobs Few, Most Workers Aren't Satisfied," *New York Times* online, www.nytimes.com, January 10, 2010.
12. B. Cheng, M. Kan, G. Levanon, and R. L. Ray, "Job Satisfaction: 2015 Edition: A Lot More Jobs—A Little More Satisfaction," www.conference-board.org, September 2015; L. Weber, "U.S. Workers Can't Get No (Job) Satisfaction," *The Wall Street Journal* online, www.wsj.com, June 18, 2014.
13. B. Cheng, M. Kan, G. Levanon, and R. L. Ray, "Job Satisfaction: 2015 Edition: A Lot More Jobs—A Little More Satisfaction."
14. A. Harjani, "Nearly Half of Global Employees Unhappy in Jobs: Survey," cnbc.com, September 17, 2013.
15. "Overstretched," *The Economist,* www.economist.com, May 20, 2010.
16. J. McCarthy, "Americans' Satisfaction with Job Aspects Up from 2005," *Gallup* online, www.gallup.com, August 28, 2015.
17. T. A. Judge, C. J. Thoresen, J. E. Bono, and G. K. Patton, "The Job Satisfaction-Job Performance Relationship: A Qualitative and Quantitative Review," *Psychological Bulletin,* May 2001, pp. 376–407.
18. J. K. Harter, F. L. Schmidt, and T. L. Hayes, "Business-Unit Level Relationship Between Employee Satisfaction, Employee Engagement, and Business Outcomes: A Meta-Analysis," *Journal of Applied Psychology,* April 2002, pp. 268–279; A. M. Ryan, M. J. Schmit, and R. Johnson, "Attitudes and Effectiveness: Examining Relations at an Organizational Level," *Personnel Psychology,* Winter 1996, pp. 853–882; and C. Ostroff, "The Relationship Between Satisfaction, Attitudes, and Performance: An Organizational Level Analysis," *Journal of Applied Psychology,* December 1992, pp. 963–974.
19. E. A. Locke, "The Nature and Causes of Job Satisfaction," in *Handbook of Industrial and Organizational Psychology,* ed. M. D. Dunnette (Chicago: Rand McNally, 1976), p. 1331; S. L. McShane, "Job Satisfaction and Absenteeism: A Meta-Analytic Re-Examination," *Canadian Journal of Administrative Science,* June 1984, pp. 61–77; R. D. Hackett and R. M. Guion, "A Reevaluation of the Absenteeism-Job Satisfaction Relationship," *Organizational Behavior and Human Decision Processes,* June 1985, pp. 340–381; K. D. Scott and G. S. Taylor, "An Examination of Conflicting Findings on the Relationship Between Job Satisfaction and Absenteeism: A Meta-Analysis," *Academy of Management Journal,* September 1985, pp. 599–612; R. D. Hackett, "Work Attitudes and Employee Absenteeism: A Synthesis of the Literature," paper presented at the 1988 National Academy of Management Meeting, August 1988, Anaheim, CA; and R. Steel and J. R. Rentsch, "Influence of Cumulation Strategies on the Long-Range Prediction of Absenteeism," *Academy of Management Journal,* December 1995, pp. 1616–1634.

20. P. W. Hom and R. W. Griffeth, *Employee Turnover* (Cincinnati, OH: Southwestern, 1995); R. W. Griffith, P. W. Hom, and S. Gaertner, "A Meta-Analysis of Antecedents and Correlates of Employee Turnover: Update, Moderator Tests, and Research Implications for the Next Millennium," *Journal of Management,* vol. 26, no. 3, 2000, p. 479; and P. W. Hom and A. J. Kinicki, "Toward a Greater Understanding of How Dissatisfaction Drives Employee Turnover," *Academy of Management Journal,* October 2001, pp. 975–987.
21. See, for example, J. M. Carsten and P. E. Spector, "Unemployment, Job Satisfaction, and Employee Turnover: A Meta-Analytic Test of the Muchinsky Model," *Journal of Applied Psychology,* August 1987, pp. 374–381; and C. L. Hulin, M. Roznowski, and D. Hachiya, "Alternative Opportunities and Withdrawal Decisions: Empirical and Theoretical Discrepancies and an Integration," *Psychological Bulletin,* July 1985, pp. 233–250.
22. T. A. Wright and D. G. Bonett, "Job Satisfaction and Psychological Well-Being as Nonadditive Predictors of Workplace Turnover," *Journal of Management,* April 2007, pp. 141–160; and D. G. Spencer and R. M. Steers, "Performance as a Moderator of the Job Satisfaction-Turnover Relationship," *Journal of Applied Psychology,* August 1981, pp. 511–514.
23. Jennifer Bell, "Work Incentives: Staff Perks Generate Gains for Companies," *The National (UAE)*, June 25, 2016, http://www.thenational.ae/uae/work-incentives-staff-perks-generate-gains-for-companies (accessed December 27, 2016).
24. See, for instance, M. Schulte, C. Ostroff, S. Shmulyian, and A. Kinicki, "Organizational Climate Configurations: Relationships to Collective Attitudes, Customer Satisfaction, and Financial Performance," *Journal of Applied Psychology,* May 2009, pp. 618–634; S. P. Brown and S. K. Lam, "A Meta-analysis of Relationships Linking Employee Satisfaction to Customer Responses," *Journal of Retailing,* vol. 84, 2008, pp. 243–255; X. Luo and C. Homburg, "Neglected Outcomes of Customer Satisfaction," *Journal of Marketing,* April 2007, pp. 133–149; P. B. Barger and A. A. Grandey, "Service with a Smile and Encounter Satisfaction: Emotional Contagion and Appraisal Mechanisms," *Academy of Management Journal,* December 2006, pp. 1229–1238; C. Homburg and R. M. Stock, "The Link Between Salespeople's Job Satisfaction and Customer Satisfaction in a Business-to-Business Context: A Dyadic Analysis," *Journal of the Academy of Marketing Science,* Spring 2004, pp. 144–158; J. K. Harter, F. L. Schmidt, and T. L. Hayes, "Business-Unit-Level Relationship Between Employee Satisfaction, Employee Engagement, and Business Outcomes: A Meta-Analysis," *Journal of Applied Psychology,* April 2002, pp. 268–279; J. Griffeth "Do Satisfied Employees Satisfy Customers? Support-Services Staff Morale and Satisfaction Among Public School Administrators, Students, and Parents," *Journal of Applied Social Psychology,* August 2001, pp. 1627–1658; D. J. Koys, "The Effects of Employee Satisfaction, Organizational Citizenship Behavior, and Turnover on Organizational Effectiveness: A Unit-Level, Longitudinal Study," *Personnel Psychology,* Spring 2001, pp. 101–114; E. Naumann and D. W. Jackson Jr., "One More Time: How Do You Satisfy Customers?," *Business Horizons,* May–June 1999, pp. 71–76; W. W. Tornow and J. W. Wiley, "Service Quality and Management Practices: A Look at Employee Attitudes, Customer Satisfaction, and Bottom-Line Consequences," *Human Resource Planning,* vol. 4, no. 2, 1991, pp. 105–116; and B. Schneider and D. E. Bowen, "Employee and Customer Perceptions of Service in Banks: Replication and Extension," *Journal of Applied Psychology,* August 1985, pp. 423–433.
25. M. J. Bitner, B. H. Blooms, and L. A. Mohr, "Critical Service Encounters: The Employees' Viewpoint," *Journal of Marketing,* October 1994, pp. 95–106.
26. R. E. Silverman, "At Zappos, Some Employees Find Offer to Leave Too Good to Refuse," *The Wall Street Journal* online, www.wsj.com, May 7, 2015; M. O'Brien, "Zappos Knows How to Kick It," *Fortune,* February 2, 2009, pp. 55–60.
27. R. E. Silverman, "At Zappos, Some Employees Find Offer to Leave Too Good to Refuse."
28. See T. M. Glomb, D. P. Bhave, A. G. Miner, and M. Wall, "Doing Good, Feeling Good: Examining the Role of Organizational Citizenship Behaviors in Changing Mood," *Personnel Psychology,* Spring 2011, pp. 191–223; L. M. Little, D. L. Nelson, J. C. Wallace, and P. D. Johnson, "Integrating Attachment Style, Vigor at Work, and Extra-Role Performance," *Journal of Organizational Behavior,* April 2011, pp. 464–484; N. P. Podsakoff, P. J. Podsakoff, S. W. Whiting, and P. Hisra, "Effects of Organizational Citizenship Behavior on Selection Decisions in Employment Interviews," *Journal of Applied Psychology,* March 2011, pp. 310–326; J. A. LePine, A. Erez, and D. E. Johnson, "The Nature and Dimensionality of Organizational Citizenship Behavior: A Critical Review and Meta-Analysis"; P. Podsakoff, S. B. Mackenzie, J. B. Paine, and D. G. Bachrach, "Organizational Citizenship Behaviors: A Critical Review of the Theoretical and Empirical Literature and Suggestions for Future Research," *Journal of Management,* May 2000, pp. 513–563; T. S. Bateman and D. W. Organ, "Job Satisfaction and the Good Soldier: The Relationship Between Affect and Employee 'Citizenship,'" *Academy of Management Journal,* December 1983, pp. 587–595.
29. B. J. Hoffman, C. A. Blair, J. P. Maeriac, and D. J. Woehr, "Expanding the Criterion Domain? A Quantitative Review of the OCB Literature," *Journal of Applied Psychology,* vol. 92, no. 2, 2007, pp. 555–566; J. A. LePine, A. Erez, and D. E. Johnson, "The Nature and Dimensionality of Organizational Citizenship Behavior: A Critical Review and Meta-Analysis"; and D. W. Organ and K. Ryan, "A Meta-Analytic Review of Attitudinal and Dispositional Predictors of Organizational Citizenship Behavior," *Personnel Psychology,* Winter 1995, pp. 775–802.
30. N. A. Fassina, D. A. Jones, and K. L. Uggerslev, "Relationship Clean-Up Time: Using Meta-Analysis and Path Analysis to Clarify Relationships Among Job Satisfaction, Perceived Fairness, and Citizenship Behaviors," *Journal of Management,* April 2008, pp. 161–188; M. A. Konovsky and D. W. Organ, "Dispositional and Contextual Determinants of Organizational Citizenship Behavior," *Journal of Organizational Behavior,* May 1996, pp. 253–266; R. H. Moorman, "Relationship Between Organization Justice and Organizational Citizenship Behaviors: Do Fairness Perceptions Influence Employee Citizenship?" *Journal of Applied Psychology,* December 1991, pp. 845–855; and J. Fahr, P. M. Podsakoff, and D. W. Organ, "Accounting for Organizational Citizenship Behavior: Leader Fairness and Task Scope Versus Satisfaction," *Journal of Management,* December 1990, pp. 705–722.
31. M. Trottman, "Federal Workers' Job Satisfaction Slips," *The Wall Street Journal* online, www.wsj.com, October 24, 2014.
32. W. H. Bommer, E. C. Dierdorff, and R. S. Rubin, "Does Prevalence Mitigate Relevance? The Moderating Effect of Group-Level OCB on Employee Performance," *Academy of Management Journal,* December 2007, pp. 1481–1494.
33. M. Mount, R. Ilies, and E. Johnson, "Relationship of Personality Traits and Counterproductive Work Behaviors: The Mediating Effects of Job Satisfaction," *Personnel Psychology*, vol. 59, 2006, pp. 359–622.

34. See, for example, S. Rabinowitz and D. T. Hall, "Organizational Research in Job Involvement," *Psychological Bulletin,* March 1977, pp. 265–288; G. J. Blau, "A Multiple Study Investigation of the Dimensionality of Job Involvement," *Journal of Vocational Behavior,* August 1985, pp. 19–36; and N. A. Jans, "Organizational Factors and Work Involvement," *Organizational Behavior and Human Decision Processes,* June 1985, pp. 382–396.
35. D. A. Harrison, D. A. Newman, and P. L. Roth, "How Important Are Job Attitudes?: Meta-Analytic Comparisons of Integrative Behavioral Outcomes and Time Sequences," *Academy of Management Journal,* April 2006, pp. 305–325; G. J. Blau, "Job Involvement and Organizational Commitment as Interactive Predictors of Tardiness and Absenteeism," *Journal of Management,* Winter 1986, pp. 577–584; and K. Boal and R. Cidambi, "Attitudinal Correlates of Turnover and Absenteeism: A Meta-Analysis," paper presented at the meeting of the American Psychological Association, 1984, Toronto, Canada.
36. G. J. Blau and K. Boal, "Conceptualizing How Job Involvement and Organizational Commitment Affect Turnover and Absenteeism," *Academy of Management Review,* April 1987, p. 290.
37. See, for instance, P. W. Hom, R. Katerberg, and C. L. Hulin, "Comparative Examination of Three Approaches to the Prediction of Turnover," *Journal of Applied Psychology,* June 1979, pp. 280–290; R. T. Mowday, L. W. Porter, and R. M. Steers, *Employee Organization Linkages: The Psychology of Commitment, Absenteeism, and Turnover* (New York: Academic Press, 1982); H. Angle and J. Perry, "Organizational Commitment: Individual and Organizational Influence," *Work and Occupations,* May 1983, pp. 123–145; and J. L. Pierce and R. B. Dunham, "Organizational Commitment: Pre-Employment Propensity and Initial Work Experiences," *Journal of Management,* Spring 1987, pp. 163–178.
38. L. W. Porter, R. M. Steers, R. T. Mowday, and V. Boulian, "Organizational Commitment, Job Satisfaction, and Turnover Among Psychiatric Technicians," *Journal of Applied Psychology,* October 1974, pp. 603–609.
39. D. M. Rousseau, "Organizational Behavior in the New Organizational Era," in *Annual Review of Psychology,* vol. 48, ed. J. T. Spence, J. M. Darley, and D. J. Foss (Palo Alto, CA: Annual Reviews, 1997), p. 523.
40. P. Eder and R. Eisenberger, "Perceived Organizational Support: Reducing the Negative Influence of Coworker Withdrawal Behavior," *Journal of Management,* February 2008, pp. 55–68; R. Eisenberger, F. Stinglhamber, C. Vandenberghe, I. L. Sucharski, and L. Rhoades, "Perceived Supervisor Support: Contributions to Perceived Organizational Support and Employee Retention," *Journal of Applied Psychology,* June 2002, pp. 565–573; L. Rhoades and R. Eisenberger, "Perceived Organizational Support: A Review of the Literature," *Journal of Applied Psychology,* August 2002, pp. 698–714; J. L. Kraimer and S. J. Wayne, "An Examination of Perceived Organizational Support as a Multidimensional Construct in the Context of an Expatriate Assignment," *Journal of Management,* vol. 30, no. 2, 2004, pp. 209–237; J. W. Bishop, K. D. Scott, J. G. Goldsby, and R. Cropanzano, "A Construct Validity Study of Commitment and Perceived Support Variables," *Group & Organization Management,* April 2005, pp. 153–180; and J. A-M. Coyle-Shapiro and N. Conway, "Exchange Relationships: Examining Psychological Contracts and Perceived Organizational Support," *Journal of Applied Psychology,* July 2005, pp. 774–781.
41. J. Marquez, "Disengaged Employees Can Spell Trouble at Any Company," *Workforce Management,* www.workforce.com, May 13, 2008.
42. J. Smythe, "Engaging Employees to Drive Performance," *Communication World,* May–June 2008, pp. 20–22; A. B. Bakker and W. B. Schaufeli, "Positive Organizational Behavior: Engaged Employees in Flourishing Organizations," *Journal of Organizational Behavior,* February 2008, pp. 147–154; U. Aggarwal, S. Datta, and S. Bhargava, "The Relationship Between Human Resource Practices, Psychological Contract, and Employee Engagement—Implications for Managing Talent," *IIMB Management Review,* September 2007, pp. 313–325; M. C. Christian and J. E. Slaughter, "Work Engagement: A Meta-Analytic Review and Directions for Research in an Emerging Area," *AOM Proceedings,* August 2007, pp. 1–6; C. H. Thomas, "A New Measurement Scale for Employee Engagement: Scale Development, Pilot Test, and Replication," *AOM Proceedings,* August 2007, pp. 1–6; A. M. Saks, "Antecedents and Consequences of Employee Engagement," *Journal of Managerial Psychology,* vol. 21, no. 7, 2006, pp. 600–619; and A. Parsley, "Road Map for Employee Engagement," *Management Services,* Spring 2006, pp. 10–11.
43. A. Adkins, "Employee Engagement in U.S. Stagnant in 2015," *Gallup* online, www.gallup.com, January 13, 2016.
44. J. Katz, "The Engagement Dance," *Industry Week,* April 2008, p. 24.
45. "Driving Employee Engagement in a Global Workforce," *Watson Wyatt Worldwide,* 2007–2008, p. 2.
46. A. Mann and J. Harter, "The Worldwide Employee Engagement Crisis," *Gallup* online, www.gallup.com, January 7, 2016.
47. A. J. Elliott and P. G. Devine, "On the Motivational Nature of Cognitive Dissonance: Dissonance as Psychological Discomfort," *Journal of Personality and Social Psychology*, September 1994, pp. 382–394.
48. "Employee Distrust Is Pervasive in U.S. Workforce," American Psychological Association, www.apa.org, April 23, 2014.
49. L. Festinger, *A Theory of Cognitive Dissonance* (Stanford, CA: Stanford University Press, 1957); and C. Crossen, "Cognitive Dissonance Became a Milestone in 1950s Psychology," *Wall Street Journal,* December 4, 2006, p. B1.
50. See, for example, S. V. Falletta, "Organizational Intelligence Surveys," *T&D,* June 2008, pp. 52–58; R. Fralicx, P. Foley, H. Friedman, P. Gilberg, D. P. McCauley, and L. F. Parra, "Point of View: Using Employee Surveys to Drive Business Decisions," Mercer Human Resource Consulting, July 1, 2004; L. Simpson, "What's Going on in Your Company? If You Don't Ask, You'll Never Know," *Training,* June 2002, pp. 30–34; and B. Fishel, "A New Perspective: How to Get the Real Story from Attitude Surveys," *Training,* February 1998, pp. 91–94.
51. "Sustainability Report 2014/15," Ford Motor Company, www.corporate.ford.com, 2015.
52. See J. Welch and S. Welch, "Employee Polls: A Vote in Favor," *BusinessWeek,* January 28, 2008, p. 90; E. White, "How Surveying Workers Can Pay Off," *Wall Street Journal,* June 18, 2007, p. B3; A. Kover, "And the Survey Says...," R. Fralicx, P. Foley, H. Friedman, P. Gilberg, D. P. McCauley, and L. F. Parra, "Point of View: Using Employee Surveys to Drive Business Decisions"; and S. Shellenbarger, "Companies Are Finding It Really Pays to Be Nice to Employees," *Wall Street Journal,* July 22, 1998, p. B1.
53. P. Hollinger, "Carolyn McCall: Flying High at EasyJet," *The Financial Times* online, www.ft.com, November 21, 2014; L. Roderick, "EasyJet CEO Carolyn McCall on How Marketers Can Soar," *Marketing Week* online, www.marketingweek.com, March 9, 2016; M. Gwyther, "Why Heathrow got the Backing of Gatwick's Biggest Customer," *Management Today* online,

www.managementtoday.co.uk, July 1, 2015; R. Burn-Callander, "EasyJet's Carolyn McCall 'Most Admired Leader' in Britain," *The Telegraph* online, www.telgraph.co.uk, December 2, 2015.

54. L. Saari and T. A. Judge, "Employee Attitudes and Job Satisfaction," *Human Resource Management,* Winter 2004, pp. 395–407; and T. A. Judge and A. H. Church, "Job Satisfaction: Research and Practice," in *Industrial and Organizational Psychology: Linking Theory with Practice,* ed. C. L. Cooper and E. A. Locke (Oxford, UK: Blackwell, 2000).
55. Harrison, Newman, and Roth, "How Important Are Job Attitudes?" pp. 320–321.
56. A. Tugend, "Blinded by Science in the Online Dating Game," *New York Times* online, www.nytimes.com, July 18, 2009; and Catherine Arnst, "Better Loving Through Chemistry?" *Bloomberg BusinessWeek,* October 23, 2010.
57. I. Briggs-Myers, *Introduction to Type* (Palo Alto, CA: Consulting Psychologists Press, 1980); W. L. Gardner and M. J. Martinko, "Using the Myers-Briggs Type Indicator to Study Managers: A Literature Review and Research Agenda," *Journal of Management*, vol. 22, no. 1, 1996, pp. 45–83; and N. L. Quenk, *Essentials of Myers-Briggs Type Indicator Assessment* (New York: Wiley, 2000).
58. E. Bajic, "How the MBTI Can Help You Build a Stronger Company," *Forbes* online, www.forbes.com, September 28, 2015.
59. M. Ahmed, "Is Myers-Briggs Up to the Job?," *Financial Times* online, www.ft.com, February 11, 2016.
60. R. D. Meyer, R. S. Dalal, and S. Bonaccio, "A Meta-Analytic Investigation into the Moderating Effects of Situational Strength on the Conscientiousness–Performance Relationship," *Journal of Organizational Behavior,* November 2009, pp. 1077–1102; C. G. DeYoung, L. C. Quilty, and J. B. Peterson, "Between Facets and Domains: 10 Aspects of the Big Five," *Journal of Personality and Social Psychology,* November 2007, pp. 880–896; T. A. Judge, D. Heller, and M. K. Mount, "Five-Factor Model of Personality and Job Satisfaction: A Meta-Analysis," *Journal of Applied Psychology,* June 2002, pp. 530–541; G. M. Hurtz and J. J. Donovan, "Personality and Job Performance: The Big Five Revisited," *Journal of Applied Psychology,* December 2000, pp. 869–879; M. K. Mount, M. R. Barrick, and J. P. Strauss, "Validity of Observer Ratings of the Big Five Personality Factors," *Journal of Applied Psychology*, April 1996, pp. 272–280; O. P. John, "The Big Five Factor Taxonomy: Dimensions of Personality in the Natural Language and in Questionnaires," in *Handbook of Personality Theory and Research,* ed. L. A. Pervin (New York: Guilford Press, 1990), pp. 66–100; and J. M. Digman, "Personality Structure: Emergence of the Five-Factor Model," in *Annual Review of Psychology*, vol. 41, ed. M. R. Rosenweig and L. W. Porter (Palo Alto, CA: Annual Review, 1990), pp. 417–440.
61. M. R. Barrick and M. K. Mount, "The Big Five Personality Dimensions and Job Performance: A Meta-Analysis," *Personnel Psychology,* vol. 44, 1991, pp. 1–26; A. J. Vinchur, J. S. Schippmann, F. S. Switzer III, and P. L. Roth, "A Meta-Analytic Review of Predictors of Job Performance for Salespeople," *Journal of Applied Psychology,* August 1998, pp. 586–597; G. M. Hurtz and J. J. Donovan, "Personality and Job Performance Revisited," *Journal of Applied Psychology,* December 2000, pp. 869–879; T. A. Judge and J. E. Bono, "Relationship of Core Self-Evaluations Traits—Self Esteem, Generalized Self-Efficacy, Locus of Control, and Emotional Stability—with Job Satisfaction and Job Performance: A Meta-Analysis," *Journal of Applied Psychology,* February 2001, pp. 80–92; T. A. Judge, D. Heller, and M. K. Mount, "Five-Factor Model of Personality and Job Satisfaction: A Meta-Analysis"; and D. M. Higgins, J. B. Peterson, R. O. Pihl, and A. G. M. Lee, "Prefrontal Cognitive Ability, Intelligence, Big Five Personality, and the Prediction of Advanced Academic and Workplace Performance," *Journal of Personality and Social Psychology,* August 2007, pp. 298–319.
62. I-S. Oh and C. M. Berry, "The Five-Factor Model of Personality and Managerial Performance: Validity Gains Through the Use of 360 Degree Performance Ratings," *Journal of Applied Psychology,* November 2009, pp. 1498–1513.
63. A. E. Poropat, "A Meta-Analysis of the Five-Factor Model of Personality and Academic Performance," *Psychological Bulletin,* vol. 135, no. 2, 2009, pp. 322–338.
64. J. B. Rotter, "Generalized Expectancies for Internal Versus External Control of Reinforcement," *Psychological Monographs* 80, no. 609, 1966.
65. See, for instance, D. W. Organ and C. N. Greene, "Role Ambiguity, Locus of Control, and Work Satisfaction," *Journal of Applied Psychology*, February 1974, pp. 101–102; and T. R. Mitchell, C. M. Smyser, and S. E. Weed, "Locus of Control: Supervision and Work Satisfaction," *Academy of Management Journal*, September 1975, pp. 623–631.
66. S. Weinberg, "Poor, Misunderstood Little Machiavelli," *USA Today,* June 13, 2011, p. 2B; S. R. Kessler, P. E. Spector, W. C. Borman, C. E. Nelson, A. C. Bandelli, and L. J. Penney, "Re-Examining Machiavelli: A Three-Dimensional Model of Machiavellianism in the Workplace," *Journal of Applied Social Psychology,* August 2010, pp. 1868–1896; W. Amelia, "Anatomy of a Classic: Machiavelli's Daring Gift," *Wall Street Journal,* August 30–31, 2008, p. W10; R. G. Vleeming, "Machiavellianism: A Preliminary Review," *Psychological Reports*, February 1979, pp. 295–310; and S. A. Snook, "Love and Fear and the Modern Boss," *Harvard Business Review,* January 2008, pp. 16–17.
67. See J. Brockner, *Self-Esteem at Work: Research, Theory, and Practice* (Lexington, MA: Lexington Books, 1988), chapters 1–4; and N. Branden, *Self-Esteem at Work* (San Francisco: Jossey-Bass, 1998).
68. "Social Studies," *Bloomberg BusinessWeek,* June 14–20, 2010, pp. 72–73.
69. See M. Snyder, *Public Appearances/Private Realities: The Psychology of Self-Monitoring* (New York: W. H. Freeman, 1987); and D. V. Day, D. J. Schleicher, A. L. Unckless, and N. J. Hiller, "Self-Monitoring Personality at Work: A Meta-Analytic Investigation of Construct Validity," *Journal of Applied Psychology,* April 2002, pp. 390–401.
70. Snyder, *Public Appearances/Private Realities*; and J. M. Jenkins, "Self-Monitoring and Turnover: The Impact of Personality on Intent to Leave," *Journal of Organizational Behavior*, January 1993, pp. 83–90.
71. M. Kilduff and D. V. Day, "Do Chameleons Get Ahead? The Effects of Self-Monitoring on Managerial Careers," *Academy of Management Journal,* August 1994, pp. 1047–1060; and A. Mehra, M. Kilduff, and D. J. Brass, "The Social Networks of High and Low Self-Monitors: Implications for Workplace Performance," *Administrative Science Quarterly,* March 2001, pp. 121–146.
72. N. Kogan and M. A. Wallach, "Group Risk Taking as a Function of Members' Anxiety and Defensiveness," *Journal of Personality*, March 1967, pp. 50–63; and J. M. Howell and C. A. Higgins, "Champions of Technological Innovation," *Administrative Science Quarterly*, June 1990, pp. 317–341.
73. M. Friedman and R. H. Rosenman, *Type A Behavior and Your Heart* (New York: Alfred A. Knopf, 1974).

74. S. Reddy, "We Know Why You're Always Late," *The Wall Street Journal* online, www.wsj.com, February 3, 2015.
75. Ibid.
76. S. K. Parker and C. G. Collins, "Taking Stock: Integrating and Differentiating Multiple Proactive Behaviors," *Journal of Management,* May 2010, pp. 633–662; J. D. Kammeyer-Mueller and C. R. Wanberg, "Unwrapping the Organizational Entry Process: Disentangling Multiple Antecedents and Their Pathways to Adjustment," *Journal of Applied Psychology,* October 2003, pp. 779–794; S. E. Seibert, M. L. Kraimer, and J. M. Crant, "What Do Proactive People Do? A Longitudinal Model Linking Proactive Personality and Career Success," *Personnel Psychology,* Winter 2001, pp. 845–874; J. M. Crant, "Proactive Behavior in Organizations," *Journal of Management,* vol. 26, no. 3, 2000, pp. 435–462; J. M. Crant and T. S. Bateman, "Charismatic Leadership Viewed from Above: The Impact of Proactive Personality," *Journal of Organizational Behavior,* February 2000, pp. 63–75; S. E. Seibert, J. M. Crant, and M. L. Kraimer, "Proactive Personality and Career Success," *Journal of Applied Psychology,* June 1999, pp. 416–427; R. C. Becherer and J. G. Maurer, "The Proactive Personality Disposition and Entrepreneurial Behavior Among Small Company Presidents," *Journal of Small Business Management,* January 1999, pp. 28–36; and T. S. Bateman and J. M. Crant, "The Proactive Component of Organizational Behavior: A Measure and Correlates," *Journal of Organizational Behavior,* March 1993, pp. 103–118.
77. "Resilience Key to Keeping Your Job, Accenture Research Finds," Accenture.com, March 5, 2010; J. D. Margolis and P. G. Stoltz, "How to Bounce Back from Adversity," *Harvard Business Review,* January–February, 2010, pp. 86–92; and A. Ollier-Malaterre, "Contributions of Work-Life Resilience Initiatives to the Individual/-Organization Relationship," *Human Relations,* January 2010, pp. 41–62.
78. L. Landro, "Why Resilience Is Good for Your Health and Career," *The Wall Street Journal* online, www.wsj.com, February 15, 2016.
79. J. B. Avey, F. Luthans, R. M. Smith, and N. F. Palmer, "Impact of Positive Psychological Capital on Employee Well-Being Over Time," *Journal of Occupational Health Psychology,* January 2010, pp. 17–28; and J. B. Avey, F. Luthans, and S. M. Jensen, "Psychological Capital: A Positive Resource for Combating Employee Stress and Turnover," *Human Resource Management,* September–October 2009, pp. 677–693.
80. L. Landro, "Why Resilience Is Good for Your Health and Career."
81. See, for instance, G. W. M. Ip and M. H. Bond, "Culture, Values, and the Spontaneous Self-Concept," *Asian Journal of Psychology,* vol. 1, 1995, pp. 30–36; J. E. Williams, J. L. Saiz, D. L. FormyDuval, M. L. Munick, E. E. Fogle, A. Adom, A. Haque, F. Neto, and J. Yu, "Cross-Cultural Variation in the Importance of Psychological Characteristics: A Seven-Year Country Study," *International Journal of Psychology,* October 1995, pp. 529–550; V. Benet and N. G. Walker, "The Big Seven Factor Model of Personality Description: Evidence for Its Cross-Cultural Generalizability in a Spanish Sample," *Journal of Personality and Social Psychology,* October 1995, pp. 701–718; R. R. McCrae and P. T. Costa Jr., "Personality Trait Structure as a Human Universal," *American Psychologist,* 1997, pp. 509–516; and M. J. Schmit, J. A. Kihm, and C. Robie, "Development of a Global Measure of Personality," *Personnel Psychology,* Spring 2000, pp. 153–193.
82. J. F. Salgado, "The Five Factor Model of Personality and Job Performance in the European Community," *Journal of Applied Psychology,* February 1997, pp. 30–43. Note: This study covered the original 15-nation European community and did not include the countries that have joined since.
83. J. Zaslow, "Happiness Inc.," *Wall Street Journal,* March 18–19, 2006, p. P1+.
84. N. P. Rothbard and S. L. Wilk, "Waking Up on the Right or Wrong Side of the Bed: Start-of-Workday Mood, Work Events, Employee Affect, and Performance," *Academy of Management Journal,* October 2011, pp. 959–980.
85. N. H. Frijda, "Moods, Emotion Episodes, and Emotions," in M. Lewis and J. M. Havilland (eds.), *Handbook of Emotions* (New York: Guilford Press, 1993), pp. 381–403.
86. A. North, "The Power of Bad Feelings," *The New York Times* online, www.nytimes.com, October 21, 2014.
87. T-Y. Kim, D. M. Cable, S-P. Kim, and J. Wang, "Emotional Competence and Work Performance: The Mediating Effect of Proactivity and the Moderating Effect of Job Autonomy," *Journal of Organizational Behavior,* October 2009, pp. 983–1000; J. M. Diefendorff and G. J. Greguras, "Contextualizing Emotional Display Rules: Examining the Roles of Targets and Discrete Emotions in Shaping Display Rule Perceptions," *Journal of Management,* August 2009, pp. 880–898; J. Gooty, M. Gavin, and N. M. Ashkanasy, "Emotions Research in OB: The Challenges That Lie Ahead," *Journal of Organizational Behavior,* August 2009, pp. 833–838; N. M. Ashkanasy and C. S. Daus, "Emotion in the Workplace: The New Challenge for Managers," *Academy of Management Executive,* February 2002, pp. 76–86; and N. M. Ashkanasy, C. E. J. Härtel, and C. S. Daus, "Diversity and Emotions: The New Frontiers in Organizational Behavior Research," *Journal of Management,* vol. 28, no. 3, 2002, pp. 307–338.
88. "Critical Skills for Workforce 2020," *T&D,* September 2011, p. 19.
89. H. M. Weiss and R. Cropanzano, "Affective Events Theory," in *Research in Organizational Behavior,* vol. 18, B. M. Staw and L. L. Cummings (Greenwich, CT: JAI Press, 1996), pp. 20–22.
90. This section is based on D. Goleman, *Emotional Intelligence* (New York: Bantam, 1995); M. Davies, L. Stankov, and R. D. Roberts, "Emotional Intelligence: In Search of an Elusive Construct," *Journal of Personality and Social Psychology*, October 1998, pp. 989–1015; D. Goleman, *Working with Emotional Intelligence* (New York: Bantam, 1999); R. Bar-On and J. D. A. Parker, eds. *The Handbook of Emotional Intelligence: Theory, Development, Assessment, and Application at Home, School, and in the Workplace* (San Francisco: Jossey-Bass, 2000); and P. J. Jordan, N. M. Ashkanasy, and C. E. J. Härtel, "Emotional Intelligence as a Moderator of Emotional and Behavioral Reactions to Job Insecurity," *Academy of Management Review,* July 2002, pp. 361–372.
91. F. Walter, M. S. Cole, and R. H. Humphrey, "Emotional Intelligence? Sine Qua Non of Leadership or Folderol?," *Academy of Management Perspective,* February 2011, pp. 45–59.
92. E. J. O'Boyle Jr., R. H. Humphrey, J. M. Pollack, T. H. Hawver, and P. A. Story, "The Relation Between Emotional Intelligence and Job Performance: A Meta-Analysis," *Journal of Organizational Behavior online,* June 2010; R. D. Shaffer and M. A. Shaffer, "Emotional Intelligence Abilities, Personality, and Workplace Performance," *Academy of Management Best Conference Paper—HR,* August 2005; K. S. Law, C. Wong, and L. J. Song, "The Construct and Criterion Validity of Emotional Intelligence and Its Potential Utility for Management Studies," *Journal of Applied Psychology,* August 2004, pp. 483–496; D. L.

Van Rooy and C. Viswesvaran, "Emotional Intelligence: A Meta-Analytic Investigation of Predictive Validity and Nomological Net," *Journal of Vocational Behavior,* August 2004, pp. 71–95; P. J. Jordan, N. M. Ashkanasy, and C. E. J. Härtel, "The Case for Emotional Intelligence in Organizational Research," *Academy of Management Review,* April 2003, pp. 195–197; H. A. Elfenbein and N. Ambady, "Predicting Workplace Outcomes from the Ability to Eavesdrop on Feelings," *Journal of Applied Psychology,* October 2002, pp. 963–971; and C. Cherniss, "The Business Case for Emotional Intelligence," Consortium for Research on Emotional Intelligence in Organizations, www.eiconsortium.org, 1999.

93. F. J. Landy, "Some Historical and Scientific Issues Related to Research on Emotional Intelligence," *Journal of Organizational Behavior,* June 2005, pp. 411–424; E. A. Locke, "Why Emotional Intelligence Is an Invalid Concept," *Journal of Organizational Behavior,* June 2005, pp. 425–431; J. M. Conte, "A Review and Critique of Emotional Intelligence Measures," *Journal of Organizational Behavior,* June 2005, pp. 433–440; T. Becker, "Is Emotional Intelligence a Viable Concept?" *Academy of Management Review,* April 2003, pp. 192–195; and M. Davies, L. Stankov, and R. D. Roberts, "Emotional Intelligence: In Search of an Elusive Construct," *Journal of Personality and Social Psychology,* October 1998, pp. 989–1015.
94. L. Weber, "Today's Personality Tests Raise the Bar for Job Seekers," *The Wall Street Journal* online, www.wsj.com, April 14, 2015.
95. J. L. Holland, *Making Vocational Choices: A Theory of Vocational Personalities and Work Environments* (Odessa, FL: Psychological Assessment Resources, 1997).
96. A. O'Connell, "Smile, Don't Bark in Tough Times," *Harvard Business Review,* November 2009, p. 27; and G. A. Van Kleef et al., "Searing Sentiment or Cold Calculation? The Effects of Leader Emotional Displays on Team Performance Depend on Follower Epistemic Motivation," *Academy of Management Journal,* June 2009, pp. 562–580.
97. Copyright © 2012 by Matt Davis, Cambridge University. Reprinted with permission.
98. T. Priestley, "How Technology Is Changing the Perception of Tattoos in the Workplace," *Forbes* online, www.wsj.com, December 10, 2015.
99. J. Yang and S. Ward, "Planned Absenteeism," *USA Today,* April 23, 2014, p. 1B.
100. See, for instance, M. J. Martinko (ed.), *Attribution Theory: An Organizational Perspective* (Delray Beach, FL: St. Lucie Press, 1995); and H. H. Kelley, "Attribution in Social Interaction," in E. Jones et al. (eds.), *Attribution: Perceiving the Causes of Behavior* (Morristown, NJ: General Learning Press, 1972).
101. See A. G. Miller and T. Lawson, "The Effect of an Informational Option on the Fundamental Attribution Error," *Personality and Social Psychology Bulletin*, June 1989, pp. 194–204.
102. P. Harvey, "Entitled & Self-Serving Employees Are More Likely to Accuse Bosses of Abuse," *Forbes* online, www.forbes.com, December 9, 2015.
103. See, for instance, G. R. Semin, "A Gloss on Attribution Theory," *British Journal of Social and Clinical Psychology,* November 1980, pp. 291–330; and M. W. Morris and K. Peng, "Culture and Cause: American and Chinese Attributions for Social and Physical Events," *Journal of Personality and Social Psychology,* December 1994, pp. 949–971.
104. S. Nam, "Cultural and Managerial Attributions for Group Performance," unpublished doctoral dissertation; University of Oregon. Cited in R. M. Steers, S. J. Bischoff, and L. H. Higgins, "Cross-Cultural Management Research," *Journal of Management Inquiry,* December 1992, pp. 325–326.
105. See, for example, S. T. Fiske, "Social Cognition and Social Perception," *Annual Review of Psychology*, 1993, pp. 155–194; G. N. Powell and Y. Kido, "Managerial Stereotypes in a Global Economy: A Comparative Study of Japanese and American Business Students' Perspectives," *Psychological Reports*, February 1994, pp. 219–226; and J. L. Hilton and W. von Hippel, "Stereotypes," in *Annual Review of Psychology,* vol. 47, ed. J. T. Spence, J. M. Darley, and D. J. Foss (Palo Alto, CA: Annual Reviews Inc., 1996), pp. 237–271.
106. Steve Minter, "Mentoring at BASF Offers Employees 'Deeper Connection,'" *Industry Week*, December 2, 2015, www.industryweek.com/leadership/mentoring-basf-offers-employees-deeper-commnection (accessed December 27, 2016).
107. B. F. Skinner, *Contingencies of Reinforcement* (East Norwalk, CT: Appleton-Century-Crofts, 1971).
108. A. Applebaum, "Linear Thinking," *Fast Company,* December 2004, p. 35.
109. "Winning the generation game," *The Economist*, September 28, 2013, www.economist.com/news/business/21586831-businesses-are-worrying-about-how-manage-different-age-groups-widely-different.
110. Thomas Hout and David Michael, "A Chinese Approach to Management," *Harvard Business Review*, September 2014, https://hbr.org; Zhi-Xue Zhang and Jianjun Zhang, "Understanding Chinese Firms from Multiple Perspectives," Copyright Holder *Peking University Press* and *Springer-Verlag Berlin Heidelberg*, 2014; Cathy Zhang, "Tencent Edges Out China Mobile to Become Asia's Most Valuable Company," South China Morning Post, September 6, 2016, http://www.cnbc.com; Alice Woodhouse, He Huifeng, and Jack Liu, "Tencent Executive Earned More Than Hk$274 Million in Annual Salary, Filings Reveal–Leaving Even Canning Fok in the Shade," *South China Morning Post*, April 26, 2016, http://www.scmp.com; Lulu Yilun Chen, "Inside the cannibalistic culture of China's most valuable company," *The Sydney Morning Herald*, September 19, 2016, http://www.smh.com.au; and Lulu Yilun Chen, "How Tencent, China's Most-Valuable Company, Pushes Employees for Growth," *Financial Review*, September 19, 2016, http://www.afr.com/.
111. R. Mobbs, "The Employee Is Always Right," *In the Black*, April 2011, pp. 12–15; V. Nayar, "Employee Happiness: Zappos vs. HCL," *Bloomberg BusinessWeek*, January 5, 2011; G. Hamel, "Extreme Makeover," *Leadership Excellence*, January 2011, pp. 3–4; V. Nayar, "The World in 2036: Vineet Nayar Envisages Bottom-Up Leadership," *Economist*, November 27, 2010, p. 114; V. Nayar, "Employees First, Customers Second," *Chief Learning Officer*, October 2010, pp. 20–23; V. Nayar, "Back to Front," *People Management*, August 12, 2010, pp. 26–29; V. Nayar, "A Maverick CEO Explains How He Persuaded His Team to Leap into the Future," *Harvard Business Review*, June 2010, pp. 110–113; B. Einhorn and K. Gokhale, "Bangalore's Paying Again to Keep the Talent," *Bloomberg BusinessWeek*, May 24, 2010, pp. 14–16; M. Srivastava and S. Hamm, "Using the Slump to Get Bigger in Bangalore," *BusinessWeek*, September 3, 2009, pp. 50–51; and S. Lauchlan, "HCL Embraces Slumdog Effect," *Computer Weekly*, June 23, 2009, p. 8.

Chapter 16 Leadership

It's Your Career

Source: Aleksandr Bryliaev/Shutterstock

A key to success in management and in your career is knowing how to become more charismatic.

Being a More Charismatic Leader

Charisma. Can you think of someone you would describe as having charisma? How would you describe that person? Enthusiastic? Self-confident? Engaging? Inspiring? Likable? Able to relate to anyone? Maybe even magical? So are you born with charisma or can you learn to be a charismatic leader? The answer is yes and yes. Individuals are born with traits that make them charismatic. But that isn't the only way to develop charisma. The good news is that charisma is a skill you can cultivate. Why is that good news? Because being viewed as charismatic can be a valuable asset in your career. So let's look at some suggestions on how you can develop your charisma:

*1. **Focus on others, not yourself.** Take a sincere interest in whoever you're interacting with. Look them in the eye and emotionally connect with them. Be sensitive to others' needs. Empathy is a powerful tool. Charismatic individuals have the ability to read others' emotions and make an emotional connection with them. Make others feel as if they're the most important person in the room. Show by word and deed that you do indeed understand and care about them and their concerns.*

*2. **Be more extroverted.** Yes, you have to put yourself "out there." Actively seek out and engage others in different situations and environments. Although this may be harder for an individual who is more inclined to be an introvert, it just means you may have to try a little harder to connect with other people. Remember, you're trying to develop your skill set and position yourself to be successful.*

*3. **Work on your communication skills.** Charismatic individuals are skilled at expressive verbal communication. How can you get better at this? Use passion as a catalyst for generating enthusiasm and communicate with your whole body, not just with words. Use an animated*

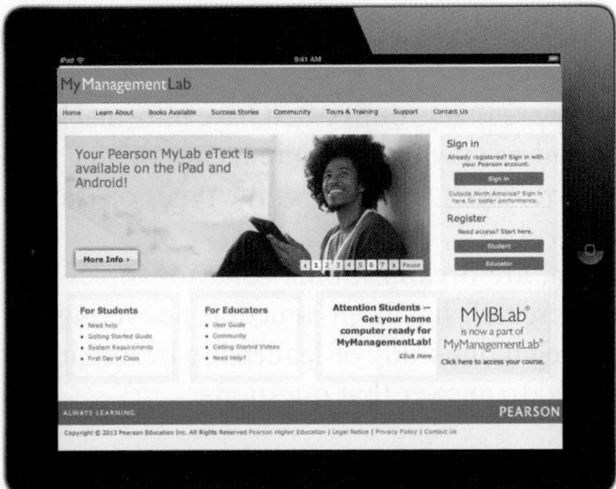

Pearson MyLab Management®

Improve Your Grade!

When you see this icon, visit **www.mymanagementlab.com** for activities that are applied, personalized, and offer immediate feedback.

Learning Objectives

16.1 Define *leader and leadership.*

16.2 Compare *and contrast early theories of leadership.*

16.3 Describe *the three major contingency theories of leadership.*

- **Develop your skill** at choosing an effective leadership style.

16.4 Describe *contemporary views of leadership.*

- **Know how** to prepare for an effective transition to a leadership position.

16.5 Discuss *twenty-first century issues affecting leadership.*

voice and reinforce your message with eye contact and facial expressions. Use gestures for emphasis. Work at becoming a skilled and entertaining conversationalist. But you have to be sincere in your communication—whether it's one-on-one or with a group of people.

*4. **Control your emotions.** A charismatic leader has the ability to control and regulate his or her emotions. For instance, know when, where, and how to use certain emotions to make a point. . . . whether that's being outraged at some situation or by turning on the charm in another.*

*5. **Exhibit self-confidence.** As you develop your work skills, be confident in your interactions with others. Become someone that others like, trust, and admire.*

If someone asked you to name a great leader, who would you name? Many individuals point to the late Steve Jobs of Apple as a great leader. And he does provide a fascinating example of the "whats" and "hows" of leadership. His leadership approach and style is not what you'd read about in most books on leadership. And how he led Apple probably wouldn't work in all situations, if any others. But leadership *is* needed in *all* organizations. Why? Because it's the leaders in organizations who make things happen.

WHO are leaders and what is leadership?

LO16.1 Let's begin by clarifying who leaders are and what leadership is. Our definition of a **leader** is someone who can influence others and who has managerial authority. **Leadership** is a process of leading a group and influencing that group to achieve its goals. It's what leaders do.

leader
Someone who can influence others and who has managerial authority

leadership
A process of influencing a group to achieve goals

Are all managers leaders? Because leading is one of the four management functions, yes, ideally, all managers *should* be leaders. Thus, we're going to study leaders and leadership from a managerial perspective.[1] However, even though we're looking at these from a managerial perspective, we're aware that groups often have informal leaders who emerge. Although these informal leaders may be able to influence others, they have not been the focus of most leadership research and are not the types of leaders we're studying in this chapter.

Leaders and leadership, like motivation, are organizational behavior topics that have been researched a lot. Most of that research has been aimed at answering the question: *What is an effective leader*? We'll begin our study of leadership by looking at some early leadership theories that attempted to answer that question.

EARLY **leadership theories**

LO16.2 People have been interested in leadership since they started coming together in groups to accomplish goals. However, it wasn't until the early part of the twentieth century that researchers actually began to study leadership. These early leadership theories focused on the *leader* (leadership trait theories) and how the *leader interacted* with his or her group members (leadership behavior theories).

Leadership Traits

Researchers at the Universities of Florida and North Carolina reported that taller men, compared to shorter men, tended to possess higher levels of social esteem, become successful leaders, earn more money, and have greater career success.[2] What does a study of height have to do with trait theories of leadership? Well, that's also what leadership trait theories have attempted to do—identify certain traits that all leaders have.

Leadership research in the 1920s and 1930s focused on isolating leader traits—that is, characteristics—that would differentiate leaders from nonleaders. Some of the traits studied included physical stature, appearance, social class, emotional stability, fluency of speech, and sociability. Despite the best efforts of researchers, it proved impossible to identify a set of traits that would *always* differentiate a leader (the person) from a nonleader. Maybe it was a bit optimistic to think that a set of consistent and unique traits would apply universally to all effective leaders, no matter whether they were in charge of Mary Kay Cosmetics, the Moscow Ballet, the country of France, a local collegiate chapter of Alpha Chi Omega, Ted's Malibu Surf Shop, or Oxford University. However, later attempts to identify traits consistently associated with *leadership* (the process of leading, not the person) were more successful. The eight traits shown to be associated with effective leadership are described briefly in Exhibit 16-1.[3]

Researchers eventually recognized that traits alone were not sufficient for identifying effective leaders since explanations based solely on traits ignored the interactions of leaders and their group members as well as situational factors. Possessing the appropriate traits only made it more likely that an individual would be an effective leader. Therefore, leadership research from the late 1940s to the mid-1960s concentrated on the preferred behavioral styles that leaders demonstrated. Researchers wondered whether something unique in what effective leaders *did*—in other words, in their *behavior*—was the key.

- 79 percent of senior executives say that showing confidence and "grace under fire" contribute to a woman's executive presence.
- 76 percent of senior executives say these characteristics contribute to a man's executive presence.[4]

Leadership Behaviors

Carter Murray, CEO of advertising agency FCB, once told a colleague, "Look, I think you're amazing, incredibly talented and you can do even more than you think in your wildest dreams. And I am not going to manage you to do that. You will determine that yourself."[5] In contrast, Martha Stewart, founder of Martha Stewart Living Omnimedia, was known for her demanding leadership approach. It was reported that she micromanaged employees and treated them as a commodity.[6] (We say more about dealing with micromanaging bosses in the *Workplace Confidential* feature on page 570.) These two leaders, as you can see, behaved in two very different ways. What do we know about leader behavior and how can it help us in our understanding of what an effective leader is?

Exhibit 16-1

Eight Traits Associated with Leadership

1. ***Drive.*** Leaders exhibit a high effort level. They have a relatively high desire for achievement, they are ambitious, they have a lot of energy, they are tirelessly persistent in their activities, and they show initiative.
2. ***Desire to lead.*** Leaders have a strong desire to influence and lead others. They demonstrate the willingness to take responsibility.
3. ***Honesty and integrity.*** Leaders build trusting relationships with followers by being truthful or nondeceitful and by showing high consistency between word and deed.
4. ***Self-confidence.*** Followers look to leaders for an absence of self-doubt. Leaders, therefore, need to show self-confidence in order to convince followers of the rightness of their goals and decisions.
5. ***Intelligence.*** Leaders need to be intelligent enough to gather, synthesize, and interpret large amounts of information, and they need to be able to create visions, solve problems, and make correct decisions.
6. ***Job-relevant knowledge.*** Effective leaders have a high degree of knowledge about the company, industry, and technical matters. In-depth knowledge allows leaders to make well-informed decisions and to understand the implications of those decisions.
7. ***Extraversion.*** Leaders are energetic, lively people. They are sociable, assertive, and rarely silent or withdrawn.
8. ***Proneness to guilt.*** Guilt proneness is positively related to leadership effectiveness because it produces a strong sense of responsibility for others.

Sources: Based on S. A. Kirkpatrick and E. A. Locke, "Leadership: Do Traits Really Matter?" *Academy of Management Executive,* May 1991, pp. 48–60; T. A. Judge, J. E. Bono, R. Ilies, and M. W. Gerhardt, "Personality and Leadership: A Qualitative and Quantitative Review," *Journal of Applied Psychology,* August 2002, pp. 765–780; and R. L. Schaumberg and F. J. Flynn, "Uneasy Lies the Head That Wears the Crown: The Link Between Guilt Proneness and Leadership," *Journal of Personality and Social Psychology,* August 2012, pp. 327–342.

Researchers hoped that the **behavioral theories** approach would provide more definitive answers about the nature of leadership than did the trait theories.[7] The four main leader behavior studies are summarized in Exhibit 16-2.

behavioral theories
Leadership theories that identify behaviors that differentiate effective leaders from ineffective leaders

UNIVERSITY OF IOWA STUDIES The University of Iowa studies explored three leadership styles to find which was the most effective.[8] The **autocratic style** described a leader who dictated work methods, made unilateral decisions, and limited employee participation. The **democratic style** described a leader who involved employees in decision making, delegated authority, and used feedback as an opportunity for coaching employees. Finally, the **laissez-faire style** leader let the group make decisions and complete the work in whatever way it saw fit. The researchers' results seemed to indicate that the democratic style contributed to both good quantity and quality of work. Had the answer to the question of the most effective leadership style been found? Unfortunately, it wasn't that simple. Later studies of the autocratic and democratic styles showed mixed results. For instance, the democratic style sometimes produced higher performance levels than the autocratic style, but at other times, it didn't. However, more consistent results were found when a measure of employee satisfaction was used. Group members were more satisfied under a democratic leader than under an autocratic one.[9]

autocratic style
A leader who dictates work methods, makes unilateral decisions, and limits employee participation

democratic style
A leader who involves employees in decision making, delegates authority, and uses feedback as an opportunity for coaching employees

laissez-faire style
A leader who lets the group make decisions and complete the work in whatever way it sees fit

Now leaders had a dilemma! Should they focus on achieving higher performance or on achieving higher member satisfaction? This recognition of the dual nature of a leader's behavior—that is, focus on the task and focus on the people—was also a key characteristic of the other behavioral studies.

THE OHIO STATE STUDIES The Ohio State studies identified two important dimensions of leader behavior.[10] Beginning with a list of more than 1,000 behavioral dimensions, the researchers eventually narrowed it down to just two that accounted for most of the leadership behavior described by group members. The first was called **initiating structure**, which referred to the extent to which a leader defined his or her role and the roles of group members in attaining goals. It included behaviors that involved attempts to organize work, work relationships, and goals. For instance, the typical medical and health services manager job exemplifies initiating structure behaviors. According to the U.S. Bureau of Labor Statistics, medical and health services managers "plan, implement and administer programs and services in a health care or medical facility, including personnel administration, training, and coordination of

initiating structure
The extent to which a leader defines his or her role and the roles of group members in attaining goals

Exhibit 16-2
Behavioral Theories of Leadership

	Behavioral Dimension	Conclusion
University of Iowa	*Democratic style:* involving subordinates, delegating authority, and encouraging participation	Democratic style of leadership was most effective, although later studies showed mixed results.
	Autocratic style: dictating work methods, centralizing decision making, and limiting participation	
	Laissez-faire style: giving group freedom to make decisions and complete work	
Ohio State	*Consideration:* being considerate of followers' ideas and feelings	High–high leader (high in consideration and high in initiating structure) achieved high subordinate performance and satisfaction, but not in all situations.
	Initiating structure: structuring work and work relationships to meet job goals	
University of Michigan	*Employee oriented:* emphasized interpersonal relationships and taking care of employees' needs	Employee-oriented leaders were associated with high group productivity and higher job satisfaction.
	Production oriented: emphasized technical or task aspects of job	
Managerial Grid	*Concern for people:* measured leader's concern for subordinates on a scale of 1 to 9 (low to high)	Leaders performed best with a 9,9 style (high concern for production and high concern for people).
	Concern for production: measured leader's concern for getting job done on a scale of 1 to 9 (low to high)	

consideration
The extent to which a leader has work relationships characterized by mutual trust and respect for group members' ideas and feelings

high–high leader
A leader high in both initiating structure and consideration behaviors

medical, nursing and physical plant staff."[11] The second was called **consideration**, which was defined as the extent to which a leader had work relationships characterized by mutual trust and respect for group members' ideas and feelings. A leader who was high in consideration helped group members with personal problems, was friendly and approachable, and treated all group members as equals. He or she showed concern for (was considerate of) his or her followers' comfort, well-being, status, and satisfaction. One researcher described leader consideration this way: "The daily practice of putting the well-being of others first has a compounding and reciprocal effect in relationships, in friendships, in the way we treat our clients and our colleagues."[12] Research found that a leader who was high in both initiating structure and consideration (a **high–high leader**) sometimes achieved high group task performance and high group member satisfaction, but not always.

UNIVERSITY OF MICHIGAN STUDIES Leadership studies conducted at the University of Michigan at about the same time as those done at Ohio State also hoped to identify behavioral characteristics of leaders that were related to performance effectiveness. The Michigan group also came up with two dimensions of leadership behavior, which they labeled employee oriented and production oriented.[13] Leaders who were *employee oriented* were described as emphasizing interpersonal relationships. The *production-oriented* leaders, in contrast, tended to emphasize the task aspects of the job. Unlike the other studies, the Michigan researchers concluded that leaders who were employee oriented were able to get high group productivity and high group member satisfaction.

Oprah Winfrey, founder of Oprah Winfrey Network, is an employee-oriented leader. Her compassionate and nurturing behavior towards subordinates helps them realize their full potential, inspires them to succeed, and results in their loyalty and job satisfaction. Caring for her employees has contributed to Oprah's success as an entrepreneur and business leader.
Source: Greg Allen/AP Images

THE MANAGERIAL GRID The behavioral dimensions from these early leadership studies provided the basis for the development of a two-dimensional grid for appraising leadership styles. This **managerial grid** used the behavioral dimensions "concern for people" (the vertical part of the grid) and "concern for production" (the horizontal part of the grid) and evaluated a leader's use of these behaviors, ranking them on a scale from 1 (low) to 9 (high).[14] Although the grid had 81 potential categories into which a leader's behavioral style might fall, only five styles were named: impoverished management (1,1, or low concern for production, low concern for people), task management (9,1, or high concern for production, low concern for people), middle-of-the-road management (5,5, or medium concern for production, medium concern for people), country club management (1,9, or low concern for production, high concern for people), and team management (9,9, or high concern for production, high concern for people). Of these five styles, the researchers concluded that managers performed best when using a 9,9 style. Unfortunately, the grid offered no answers to the question of what made a manager an effective leader; it only provided a framework for conceptualizing leadership style. In fact, little substantive evidence supports the conclusion that a 9,9 style is most effective in all situations.[15]

managerial grid
A two-dimensional grid for appraising leadership styles

Leadership researchers were discovering that predicting leadership success involved something more complex than isolating a few leader traits or preferable behaviors. They began looking at situational influences; specifically, which leadership styles might be suitable in different situations and what these different situations might be.

If your professor has assigned this, go to **www.mymanagementlab.com** to watch a video titled: *Leading* and to respond to questions.

CONTINGENCY theories of leadership

LO16.3 "The corporate world is filled with stories of leaders who failed to achieve greatness because they failed to understand the context they were working in."[16] In this section, we examine three contingency theories—Fiedler, Hersey-Blanchard, and path-goal. Each looks at defining leadership style and the situation and attempts to answer the *if-then* contingencies (that is, *if* this is the context or situation, *then* this is the best leadership style to use).

The Fiedler Model

The first comprehensive contingency model for leadership was developed by Fred Fiedler.[17] The **Fiedler contingency model** proposed that effective group performance depended on properly matching the leader's style and the amount of control and influence in the situation. The model was based on the premise that a certain leadership style would be most effective in different types of situations. The keys were to (1) define those leadership styles and the different types of situations and then (2) identify the appropriate combinations of style and situation.

Fiedler contingency model
A leadership theory proposing that effective group performance depends on the proper match between a leader's style and the degree to which the situation allows the leader to control and influence

Fiedler proposed that a key factor in leadership success was an individual's basic leadership style, either task oriented or relationship oriented. To measure a leader's

least-preferred coworker (LPC) questionnaire
A questionnaire that measures whether a leader is task or relationship oriented

style, Fiedler developed the **least-preferred coworker (LPC) questionnaire**. This questionnaire contained 18 pairs of contrasting adjectives—for example, pleasant–unpleasant, cold–warm, boring–interesting, or friendly–unfriendly. Respondents were asked to think of all the coworkers they had ever had and to describe that one person they *least enjoyed* working with by rating him or her on a scale of 1 to 8 for each of the 18 sets of adjectives (the 8 always described the positive adjective out of the pair and the 1 always described the negative adjective out of the pair).

If the leader described the least-preferred coworker in relatively positive terms (in other words, a "high" LPC score—a score of 64 or above), then the respondent was primarily interested in good personal relations with coworkers and the style would be described as *relationship oriented.* In contrast, if you saw the least-preferred coworker in relatively unfavorable terms (a low LPC score—a score of 57 or below), you were primarily interested in productivity and getting the job done; thus, your style would be labeled as *task oriented.* Fiedler did acknowledge that a small number of people might fall between these two extremes and not have a cut-and-dried leadership style. One other important point is that Fiedler assumed a person's leadership style was fixed regardless of the situation. In other words, if you were a relationship-oriented leader, you'd always be one, and the same would be true for being task oriented.

After an individual's leadership style had been assessed through the LPC, it was time to evaluate the situation in order to match the leader with the situation. Fiedler's research uncovered three contingency dimensions that defined the key situational factors in leader effectiveness.

leader–member relations
One of Fiedler's situational contingencies that describes the degree of confidence, trust, and respect employees have for their leader

task structure
One of Fiedler's situational contingencies that describes the degree to which job assignments are formalized and structured

position power
One of Fiedler's situational contingencies that describes the degree of influence a leader has over activities such as hiring, firing, discipline, promotions, and salary increases

- **Leader–member relations:** the degree of confidence, trust, and respect employees have for their leader; rated as either good or poor.
- **Task structure:** the degree to which job assignments are formalized and structured; rated as either high or low.
- **Position power:** the degree of influence a leader has over activities such as hiring, firing, discipline, promotions, and salary increases; rated as either strong or weak.

Each leadership situation was evaluated in terms of these three contingency variables, which, when combined, produced eight possible situations that were either favorable or unfavorable for the leader. (See the bottom of the chart in Exhibit 16-3.) Situations I, II, and III were classified as highly favorable for the leader. Situations IV, V, and VI were moderately favorable for the leader. And situations VII and VIII were described as highly unfavorable for the leader.

Once Fiedler had described the leader variables and the situational variables, he had everything he needed to define the specific contingencies for leadership effectiveness. To do so, he studied 1,200 groups where he compared relationship-oriented versus task-oriented leadership styles in each of the eight situational categories. He concluded that task-oriented leaders performed better in very favorable situations and in very unfavorable situations. (See the top of Exhibit 16-3, where performance is shown on the vertical axis and situation favorableness is shown on the horizontal axis.) On the other hand, relationship-oriented leaders performed better in moderately favorable situations.

Because Fiedler treated an individual's leadership style as fixed, only two ways could improve leader effectiveness. First, you could bring in a new leader whose style better fit the situation. For instance, if the group situation was highly unfavorable but was led by a relationship-oriented leader, the group's performance could be improved by replacing that person with a task-oriented leader. The second alternative was to change the situation to fit the leader. This could be done by restructuring tasks; by increasing or decreasing the power that the leader had over factors such as salary increases, promotions, and disciplinary actions; or by improving the leader–member relations.

Research testing the overall validity of Fiedler's model has shown considerable evidence to support the model.[18] However, his theory wasn't without critics. The major criticism is that it's probably unrealistic to assume that a person can't change his or her leadership style to fit the situation. Effective leaders can, and do, change their styles.

Exhibit 16-3
The Fiedler Model

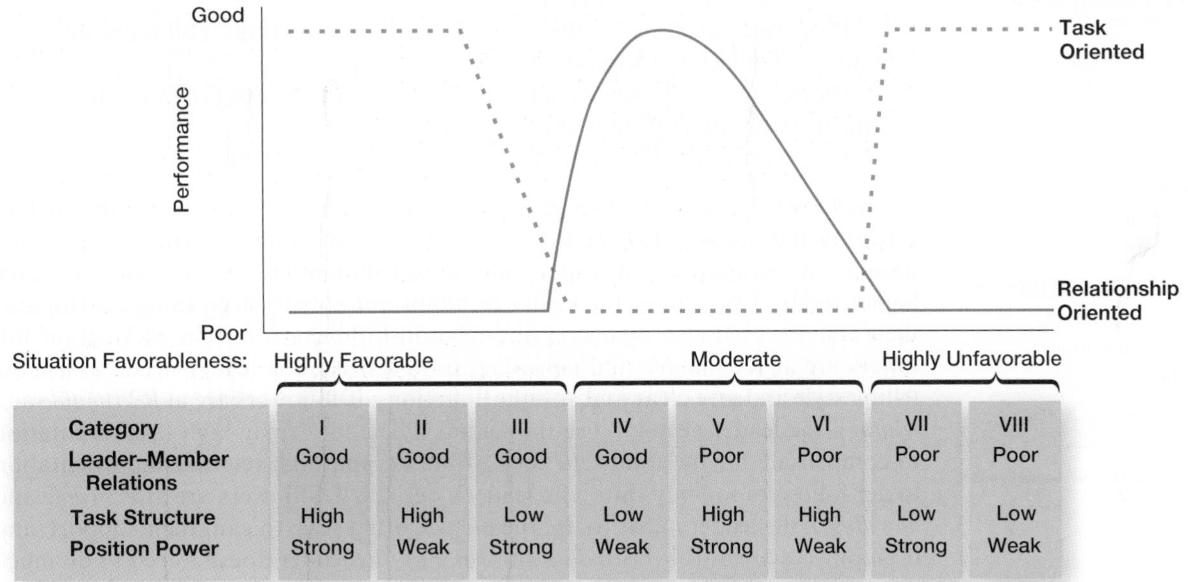

Category	I	II	III	IV	V	VI	VII	VIII
Leader–Member Relations	Good	Good	Good	Good	Poor	Poor	Poor	Poor
Task Structure	High	High	Low	Low	High	High	Low	Low
Position Power	Strong	Weak	Strong	Weak	Strong	Weak	Strong	Weak

Another is that the LPC wasn't very practical. Finally, the situation variables were difficult to assess.[19] Despite its shortcomings, the Fiedler model showed that effective leadership style needed to reflect situational factors.

With a high level of follower readiness, these designers are working on new bag ideas at Timbuk2 Design, a firm that creates and makes bags with company logos for new employees and salespeople at Twitter, Google, and other technology firms. Creative and responsible, they are willing and able to complete their tasks under leadership that gives them freedom to make and implement decisions, a relationship consistent with Hersey and Blanchard's situational theory.
Source: David Paul Morris/Getty Images

Hersey and Blanchard's Situational Leadership Theory

Paul Hersey and Ken Blanchard developed a leadership theory that has gained a strong following among management development specialists.[20] This model, called **situational leadership theory (SLT)**, is a contingency theory that focuses on followers' readiness. Before we proceed, two points need clarification: why a leadership theory focuses on the followers and what is meant by the term *readiness*.

The emphasis on the followers in leadership effectiveness reflects the reality that it *is* the followers who accept or reject the leader. Regardless of what the leader does, the group's effectiveness depends on the actions of the followers. This important dimension has been overlooked or underemphasized in most leadership theories. And **readiness**, as defined by Hersey and Blanchard, refers to the extent to which people have the ability and willingness to accomplish a specific task.

SLT uses the same two leadership dimensions that Fiedler identified: task and relationship behaviors. However, Hersey and Blanchard go a step further by considering each as either high or low and then combining them into four specific leadership styles described as follows:

- *Telling* (high task–low relationship): The leader defines roles and tells people what, how, when, and where to do various tasks.
- *Selling* (high task–high relationship): The leader provides both directive and supportive behavior.
- *Participating* (low task–high relationship): The leader and followers share in decision making; the main role of the leader is facilitating and communicating.
- *Delegating* (low task–low relationship): The leader provides little direction or support.

situational leadership theory (SLT)
A leadership contingency theory that focuses on followers' readiness

readiness
The extent to which people have the ability and willingness to accomplish a specific task

The percentage of leaders who consider themselves to be highly effective differs by skill sets:

- 74 percent in communicating and interacting with others.
- 67 percent in building consensus and commitment.
- 56 percent in fostering employee creativity and innovation.
- 39 percent in intercultural communication.
- 34 percent in leading across countries and cultures.[22]

path-goal theory
A leadership theory that says the leader's job is to assist followers in attaining their goals and to provide direction or support needed to ensure that their goals are compatible with the goals of the group or organization

The final component in the model is the four stages of follower readiness:

- *R1:* People are both *unable and unwilling* to take responsibility for doing something. Followers aren't competent or confident.
- *R2:* People are *unable but willing* to do the necessary job tasks. Followers are motivated but lack the appropriate skills.
- *R3:* People are *able but unwilling* to do what the leader wants. Followers are competent, but don't want to do something.
- *R4:* People are both *able and willing* to do what is asked of them.

SLT essentially views the leader–follower relationship as being like that of a parent and a child. Just as a parent needs to relinquish control when a child becomes more mature and responsible, so too should leaders. As followers reach higher levels of readiness, the leader responds not only by decreasing control over their activities but also by decreasing relationship behaviors. The SLT says if followers are at R1 (*unable* and *unwilling* to do a task), the leader needs to use the telling style and give clear and specific directions; if followers are at R2 (*unable* and *willing*), the leader needs to use the selling style and display high task orientation to compensate for the followers' lack of ability and high relationship orientation to get followers to "buy into" the leader's desires; if followers are at R3 (*able* and *unwilling*), the leader needs to use the participating style to gain their support; and if employees are at R4 (both *able* and *willing*), the leader doesn't need to do much and should use the delegating style.

SLT has intuitive appeal. It acknowledges the importance of followers and builds on the logic that leaders can compensate for ability and motivational limitations in their followers. However, research efforts to test and support the theory generally have been disappointing.[21] Possible explanations include internal inconsistencies in the model as well as problems with research methodology. Despite its appeal and wide popularity, we have to be cautious about any enthusiastic endorsement of SLT.

Bono (waving), U2's leader, lead singer, and lyricist, uses the supportive and participative approaches of the path-goal theory. He includes band members in decision making, believing that their input is necessary to achieve excellence. And he supports them by expressing his appreciation for their talents in contributing to U2's success and in achieving the band's goal of improving the world through its music and influence.
Source: Gregg DeGuire/WireImage/Getty Images

Path-Goal Model

Another approach to understanding leadership is **path-goal theory**, which states that the leader's job is to assist followers in attaining their goals and to provide direction or support needed to ensure that their goals are compatible with the goals of the group or organization. Developed by Robert House, path-goal theory takes key elements from the expectancy theory of motivation.[23] The term *path-goal* is derived from the belief that effective leaders remove the roadblocks and pitfalls so that followers have a clearer path to help them get from where they are to the achievement of their work goals.

House identified four leadership behaviors:

- *Directive leader:* Lets subordinates know what's expected of them, schedules work to be done, and gives specific guidance on how to accomplish tasks.
- *Supportive leader:* Shows concern for the needs of followers and is friendly.
- *Participative leader:* Consults with group members and uses their suggestions before making a decision.
- *Achievement-oriented leader:* Sets challenging goals and expects followers to perform at their highest level.

In contrast to Fiedler's view that a leader couldn't change his or her behavior, House assumed that leaders are flexible and can display any or all of these leadership styles depending on the situation.

As Exhibit 16-4 illustrates, path-goal theory proposes two situational or contingency variables that moderate the leadership behavior–outcome relationship: those in the *envi-*

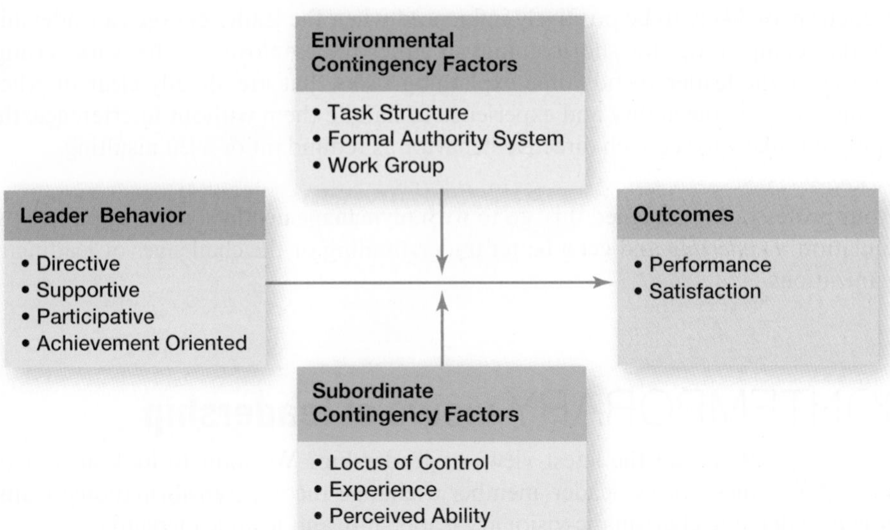

Exhibit 16-4
Path-Goal Model

ronment that are outside the control of the follower (factors including task structure, formal authority system, and the work group) and those that are part of the personal characteristics of the *follower* (including locus of control, experience, and perceived ability). Environmental factors determine the type of leader behavior required if subordinate outcomes are to be maximized; personal characteristics of the follower determine how the environment and leader behavior are interpreted. The theory proposes that a leader's behavior won't be effective if it's redundant with what the environmental structure is providing or is incongruent with follower characteristics. For example, some predictions from path-goal theory are:

- Directive leadership leads to greater satisfaction when tasks are ambiguous or stressful than when they are highly structured and well laid out. The followers aren't sure what to do, so the leader needs to give them some direction.
- Supportive leadership results in high employee performance and satisfaction when subordinates are performing structured tasks. In this situation, the leader only needs to support followers, not tell them what to do.
- Directive leadership is likely to be perceived as redundant among subordinates with high perceived ability or with considerable experience. These followers are quite capable, so they don't need a leader to tell them what to do.
- The clearer and more bureaucratic the formal authority relationships, the more leaders should exhibit supportive behavior and deemphasize directive behavior. The organizational situation has provided the structure as far as what is expected of followers, so the leader's role is simply to support.
- Directive leadership will lead to higher employee satisfaction when there is substantive conflict within a work group. In this situation, the followers need a leader who will take charge.
- Subordinates with an internal locus of control will be more satisfied with a participative style. Because these followers believe they control what happens to them, they prefer to participate in decisions.
- Subordinates with an external locus of control will be more satisfied with a directive style. These followers believe that what happens to them is a result of the external environment, so they would prefer a leader who tells them what to do.
- Achievement-oriented leadership will increase subordinates' expectancies that effort will lead to high performance when tasks are ambiguously structured. By setting challenging goals, followers know what the expectations are.

Testing path-goal theory has not been easy. A review of the research suggests mixed support.[24] To summarize the model, however, an employee's performance and satisfaction are likely to be positively influenced when the leader chooses a leadership style that compensates for shortcomings in either the employee or the work setting. However, if the leader spends time explaining tasks that are already clear or when the employee has the ability and experience to handle them without interference, the employee is likely to see such directive behavior as redundant or even insulting.

If your professor has assigned this, go to **www.mymanagementlab.com** to complete the Simulation: *Leadership* and get a better understanding of the challenges of leading in organizations.

CONTEMPORARY **views of leadership**

LO16.4 What are the latest views of leadership? We want to look at four of these views: leader–member exchange theory, transformational-transactional leadership, charismatic-visionary leadership, and team leadership.

leader–member exchange theory (LMX)
The leadership theory that says leaders create in-groups and out-groups and those in the in-group will have higher performance ratings, less turnover, and greater job satisfaction

Leader–Member Exchange (LMX) Theory

Have you ever been in a group in which the leader had "favorites" who made up his or her in-group? If so, that's the premise behind leader–member exchange (LMX) theory.[25] **Leader–member exchange theory (LMX)** says leaders create in-groups and out-groups, and those in the in-group will have higher performance ratings, less turnover, and greater job satisfaction.

- 92 percent of executives see favoritism in who gets job promotions.[26]

LMX theory suggests that early on in the relationship between a leader and a given follower, a leader will implicitly categorize a follower as an "in" or as an "out." That relationship tends to remain fairly stable over time. Leaders also encourage LMX by rewarding those employees with whom they want a closer linkage and punishing those with whom they do not.[27] For the LMX relationship to remain intact, however, both the leader and the follower must "invest" in the relationship.

It's not exactly clear how a leader chooses who falls into each category, but evidence shows that in-group members have demographic, attitude, personality, and even gender similarities with the leader or they have a higher level of competence than out-group members.[28] The leader does the choosing, but the follower's characteristics drive the decision.

Research on LMX has been generally supportive. It appears that leaders do differentiate among followers; that these disparities are not random; and followers with in-group status will have higher performance ratings, engage in more helping or "citizenship" behaviors at work, and report greater satisfaction with their boss.[29] A recent LMX study found that leaders who establish a supportive relationship with key subordinates by providing emotional and other kinds of support generate organizational commitment on the part of these employees, which leads to increases in employee performance.[30] This probably shouldn't be surprising since leaders invest their time and other resources in those whom they expect to perform best.

transactional leaders
Leaders who lead primarily by using social exchanges (or transactions)

transformational leaders
Leaders who stimulate and inspire (transform) followers to achieve extraordinary outcomes

Transformational-Transactional Leadership

Many early leadership theories viewed leaders as **transactional leaders**; that is, leaders who lead primarily by using social exchanges (or transactions). Transactional leaders guide or motivate followers to work toward established goals by exchanging rewards for their productivity.[31] But another type of leader—a **transformational leader**—stimulates and inspires (transforms) followers to achieve extraordinary outcomes. Examples include Jim Goodnight of SAS Institute and Denise Morrison of Campbell Soup Company. They pay attention to the concerns and developmental needs of individual followers; they change followers' awareness of issues by helping those followers look at old problems in new ways; and they are able to excite, arouse, and inspire followers to exert extra effort to achieve group goals.

Transactional and transformational leadership shouldn't be viewed as opposing approaches to getting things done.[33] Transformational leadership develops from transactional leadership. Transformational leadership produces levels of employee effort and performance that go beyond what would occur with a transactional approach alone. Moreover, transformational leadership is more than charisma because the transformational leader attempts to instill in followers the ability to question not only established views but also those views held by the leader.[34]

The evidence supporting the superiority of transformational leadership over transactional leadership is overwhelmingly impressive. For instance, studies that looked at managers in different settings, including the military and business, found that transformational leaders were evaluated as more effective, higher performers, more promotable than their transactional counterparts, and more interpersonally sensitive.[35] In addition, evidence indicates that transformational leadership is strongly correlated with lower turnover rates and higher levels of productivity, employee satisfaction, creativity, goal attainment, follower well-being, and corporate entrepreneurship, especially in start-up firms.[36]

LEADER making a DIFFERENCE

Source: Roadell Hickman/Zuma Press/Newscom

*Over the past several years, the Cleveland Clinic has experienced tremendous growth under the leadership of **Dr. Delos "Toby" Cosgrove**.[32] The nonprofit health care organization now has nearly 50,000 employees and locations around the world including Ohio, Florida, Nevada, Ontario, and Abu Dhabi. Since Cosgrove stepped up as CEO, the organization has almost doubled in size, experienced increased patient satisfaction, and improved overall clinical outcomes.*

Cosgrove joined the Cleveland Clinic as a surgeon in 1975 and became CEO in 2004. Earning a Bronze Star as a surgeon in the Vietnam War, Cosgrove clearly is at the top of his profession, having performed 22,000 surgeries over his career and published more than 450 articles. He acknowledges, however, that while technical knowledge and expertise are important, effective leaders must possess other characteristics such as honesty, humility, listening skills, and respect for others.

Cosgrove believes leaders should create workplaces that encourage continual learning. He sets the example for lifelong learning by continuing to grow personally as a leader. While talking to some medical students shortly after taking on the CEO role, he realized he needed to be more empathetic toward patients and their experience. As a result, he initiated Patients First, a system-wide effort to view care from the patient's viewpoint, prioritizing not only taking care of a patient's physical body, but also the patient's mind and spirit. What can you learn from this leader making a difference?

Charismatic-Visionary Leadership

Jeff Bezos, founder and CEO of Amazon.com, is a person who exudes energy, enthusiasm, and drive.[37] He's fun loving (his legendary laugh has been described as a flock of Canada geese on nitrous oxide), but he has pursued his vision for Amazon with serious intensity and has demonstrated an ability to inspire his employees through the ups and downs of a rapidly growing company. Bezos is what we call a **charismatic leader**—that is, an enthusiastic, self-confident leader whose personality and actions influence people to behave in certain ways.

charismatic leader
An enthusiastic, self-confident leader whose personality and actions influence people to behave in certain ways

Several authors have attempted to identify personal characteristics of the charismatic leader.[38] The most comprehensive analysis identified five such characteristics: they have a vision, the ability to articulate that vision, a willingness to take risks to achieve that vision, a sensitivity to both environmental constraints and follower needs, and behaviors that are out of the ordinary.[39] For example, Kat Cole, group president of FOCUS Brands, is an example of a charismatic leader. When asked about her leadership, Cole said that "Leadership is believing in the future, yourself, others, and in a higher purpose. It's about building culture, courage, and confidence through your actions and words and building teams that work to achieve common goals."[40]

An increasing body of evidence shows impressive correlations between charismatic leadership and high performance and satisfaction among followers.[41] Although one study found that charismatic CEOs had no impact on subsequent organizational performance, charisma is still believed to be a desirable leadership quality.[42]

If charisma is desirable, can people learn to be charismatic leaders? Or are charismatic leaders born with their qualities? Although a small number of experts still think that charisma can't be learned, most believe that individuals can be trained to exhibit charismatic behaviors.[43] For example, researchers have succeeded in teaching undergraduate students to "be" charismatic. How? They were taught to articulate a far-reaching goal, communicate high performance expectations, exhibit confidence in the ability of subordinates to meet those expectations, and empathize with the needs of their subordinates; they learned to project a powerful, confident, and dynamic presence; and they practiced using a captivating and engaging voice tone. The researchers also trained the student leaders to use charismatic nonverbal behaviors, including leaning toward the follower when communicating, maintaining direct eye contact, and having a relaxed posture and animated facial expressions. In groups with these "trained" charismatic leaders, members had higher task performance, higher task adjustment, and better adjustment to the leader and to the group than did group members who worked in groups led by noncharismatic leaders.

- A 60 percent increase in leadership ratings is what executives saw after they had been trained in charismatic tactics.[44]

One last thing we should say about charismatic leadership is that it may not always be necessary to achieve high levels of employee performance. It may be most appropriate when the follower's task has an ideological purpose or when the environment involves a high degree of stress and uncertainty.[45] This distinction may explain why, when charismatic leaders surface, it's more likely to be in politics, religion, or wartime, or when a business firm is starting up or facing a survival crisis. For example, Martin Luther King Jr. used his charisma to bring about social equality through nonviolent means, and Steve Jobs achieved unwavering loyalty and commitment from Apple's technical staff in the early 1980s by articulating a vision of personal computers that would dramatically change the way people lived.

visionary leadership
The ability to create and articulate a realistic, credible, and attractive vision of the future that improves upon the present situation

Although the term *vision* is often linked with charismatic leadership, **visionary leadership** is different; it's the ability to create and articulate a realistic, credible, and attractive vision of the future that improves on the present situation.[46] This vision, if properly selected and implemented, is so energizing that it "in effect jump-starts the future by calling forth the skills, talents, and resources to make it happen."[47]

An organization's vision should offer clear and compelling imagery that taps into people's emotions and inspires enthusiasm to pursue the organization's goals. It should be able to generate possibilities that are inspirational and unique and offer new ways of doing things that are clearly better for the organization and its members. Visions that are clearly articulated and have powerful imagery are easily grasped and accepted. For instance, Jack Ma cofounded Alibaba with the vision of helping small and large Chinese firms do business anywhere in the world. Alibaba has become the world's largest e-commerce company under Ma's visionary leadership. LEGO's founder, Ole Kirk Kristiansen, wanted to invent innovative toys that would stimulate children's creativity. His leadership set the tone for LEGO to become one of today's most successful toy businesses.[48]

Authentic Leadership

Anand Mahindra, CEO of the Indian multinational Mahindra Group, cites his father as a role model in the importance of empathy for leaders. In Mahindra's words, "true empathy is rooted in humility and the understanding that there are many people with as much to contribute in life as you." He believes that leaders must instill empathy and act in accordance with their values to influence the behavior of others. As head of a conglomerate operating in 100 countries, Mahindra demonstrates transparency in his management style and champions the innovative ideas of talented young employees who can make a difference.[49]

authentic leadership
Leaders who know who they are, know what they believe in, and act on those values and beliefs openly and candidly

Authentic leadership focuses on the moral aspects of being a leader. **Authentic leaders** know who they are, know what they believe in, and act on those values and beliefs openly and candidly.[50] For instance, Raymond Davis, CEO of Umpqua Bank, said, "I always tell our people that they're entitled to get answers to every question they have. . . . That doesn't mean they're going to like the answers. . . ."[51]

Ethical Leadership

Shortly after becoming CEO of General Motors, Mary Barra faced a character-defining choice: Should she take responsibility for the company's installation of faulty ignition switches in millions of vehicles even though she was not CEO at the time? Barra chose to take the high road: "I want to start by saying how sorry personally and how sorry General Motors is for what has happened."[52] She then appointed Jeff Boyer as the vice president of global safety. Barra said that "If there are any obstacles in his way, Jeff has the authority to clear them. If he needs any additional resources, he will get them."[53] Mary Barra is an example of an ethical leader because she is placing public safety ahead of profits. She is holding culpable employees accountable, and she stands behind her employees by creating a culture in which they feel that they could and should do a better job.

Team Leadership

Because leadership is increasingly taking place within a team context and more organizations are using work teams, the role of the leader in guiding team members has become increasingly important. The role of team leader *is* different from the traditional leadership role, as J. D. Bryant, a supervisor at Texas Instruments' Forest Lane plant in Dallas, discovered. One day he was contentedly overseeing a staff of 15 circuit board assemblers. The next day, he was told that the company was going to use employee teams and he was to become a "facilitator." He said, "I'm supposed to teach the teams everything I know and then let them make their own decisions." Confused about his new role, he admitted, "There was no clear plan on what I was supposed to do."[54] What *is* involved in being a team leader?

Janay Everett (left) is a marketing field team leader for Whole Foods Market, a company that is organized around employee teams. Her job requires the skills of building and maintaining good relationships with store leaders, department team leaders, and team members at several different locations. She collaborates and communicates with store leadership in developing marketing plans that achieve store-specific sales and growth goals.
Source: Zuma Press Inc./Alamy

Many leaders are not equipped to handle the change to employee teams. As one consultant noted, "Even the most capable managers have trouble making the transition because all the command-and-control type things they were encouraged to do before are no longer appropriate. There's no reason to have any skill or sense of this."[55] This same consultant estimated that "probably 15 percent of managers are natural team leaders; another 15 percent could never lead a team because it runs counter to their personality—that is, they're unable to sublimate their dominating style for the good of the team. Then there's that huge group in the middle: Team leadership doesn't come naturally to them, but they can learn it."[56]

The challenge for many managers is learning how to become an effective team leader. They have to learn skills such as patiently sharing information, and being able to trust others and to give up authority. For example, Raphaël Gorgé, chairman and CEO of Groupe Gorgé, a French high-tech company, embraces these practices: "It is important to have self-confidence as a manager. I surround myself with high-quality people who are far better than myself in their respective roles. I believe in putting together the best team possible and creating an ecosystem where individuals can strive."[57] And effective team leaders have mastered the difficult balancing act of knowing when to leave their teams alone and when to get involved. For instance, Jane Rosenthal, founder of the Tribeca Film Festival, described her leadership style in the following way: "I'm hands-off until there's a big problem, and then I'm completely hands-on. As long as I trust that everybody is doing what they're supposed to do, it's great."[58] Do these leadership styles produce different results? Not always. For example, new team leaders may try to retain too much control at a time when team members need more autonomy, or they may abandon their teams at times when the teams need support and help.[59]

One study looking at organizations that reorganized themselves around employee teams found certain common responsibilities of all leaders. These leader

Exhibit 16-5
Team Leadership Roles

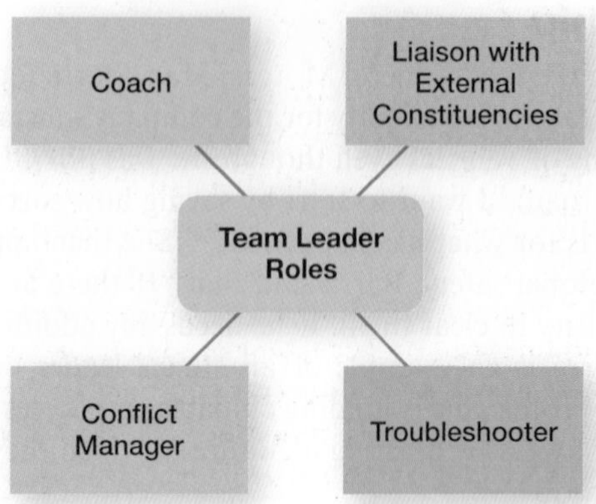

responsibilities included coaching, facilitating, handling disciplinary problems, reviewing team and individual performance, training, and communication.[60] However, a more meaningful way to describe the team leader's job is to focus on two priorities: (1) managing the team's external boundary and (2) facilitating the team process.[61] These priorities entail four specific leadership roles, which are identified in Exhibit 16-5.

If your professor has assigned this, go to **www.mymanagementlab.com** to watch a video titled: *Herman Miller: Motivation, Leadership & Teamwork* and to respond to questions.

let's get REAL

Source: Kevin Krossber

Kevin Krossber
Director of Operations

The Scenario:

Brianna Porter is struggling with her role as a team leader at a nonprofit organization that provides support programs for at-risk youth in her community. She recently was promoted to lead a team of fundraisers that reach out to local businesses and wealthy individuals to secure the funding that keeps the organization running. She initially took a "hands-off" approach and encouraged her staff to make their own decisions on who to target for donations. But now donations are declining and she knows she needs to intervene.

What advice can you give Brianna on how to be supportive of her team?

Knowing what you want accomplished may seem clear to you but it is even more important that your team shares that same vision. You won't all be working toward the same goal if your team does not understand how to accomplish the goal. Make the effort to be involved, meet with your staff, and provide clear direction on how to be successful so your team can be confident with their ability to do what is expected of them. If you expect your team to work hard to produce quality results, you must lead by example to show them it can be done.

LEADERSHIP **issues in the twenty-first century**

LO16.5 It's not easy being a chief information officer (CIO) today. The person responsible for managing a company's information technology activities will find that the task comes with a lot of external and internal pressures. Technology continues to change rapidly—almost daily, it sometimes seems. Business costs continue to rise. Mazen Chilet, CIO of Abu Dhabi University, leads the team enhancing the student experience through on-demand digital access to university resources and a mobile app for downloading forms and checking grades. Chilet is an effective leader in this fast-changing environment, working cooperatively with colleagues, listening carefully to students, and communicating clearly about plans for new technology.[62]

Leading effectively in today's environment is likely to involve such challenging circumstances for many leaders. In addition, twenty-first-century leaders do face some important leadership issues. In this section, we look at these issues, which include managing power, developing trust, empowering employees, leading across cultures, and becoming an effective leader.

Managing Power

Where do leaders get their power—that is, their right and capacity to influence work actions or decisions? Five sources of leader power have been identified: legitimate, coercive, reward, expert, and referent.[63]

Legitimate power and authority are the same. Legitimate power represents the power a leader has as a result of his or her position in the organization. Although people in positions of authority are also likely to have reward and coercive power, legitimate power is broader than the power to coerce and reward.

legitimate power
The power a leader has as a result of his or her position in the organization

Coercive power is the power a leader has to punish or control. Followers react to this power out of fear of the negative results that might occur if they don't comply. Managers typically have some coercive power, such as being able to suspend or demote employees or to assign them work they find unpleasant or undesirable.

coercive power
The power a leader has to punish or control

Reward power is the power to give positive rewards. A reward can be anything a person values, such as money, favorable performance appraisals, promotions, interesting work assignments, friendly colleagues, and preferred work shifts or sales territories.

reward power
The power a leader has to give positive rewards

Expert power is power based on expertise, special skills, or knowledge. If an employee has skills, knowledge, or expertise that's critical to a work group, that person's expert power is enhanced.

expert power
Power that's based on expertise, special skills, or knowledge

Finally, **referent power** is the power that arises because of a person's desirable resources or personal traits. If I admire you and want to be associated with you, you can exercise power over me because I want to please you. Referent power develops out of admiration of another and a desire to be like that person.

referent power
Power that arises because of a person's desirable resources or personal traits

Most effective leaders rely on several different forms of power to affect the behavior and performance of their followers. For example, the commanding officer of one of Australia's state-of-the-art submarines, the HMAS *Sheean*, employs different types of power in managing his crew and equipment. He gives orders to the crew (legitimate), praises them (reward), and disciplines those who commit infractions (coercive). As an effective leader, he also strives to have expert power (based on his expertise and knowledge) and referent power (based on his being admired) to influence his crew.

WORKPLACE CONFIDENTIAL A Micromanaging Boss

Micromanaging has been described as "probably the most common complaint about a boss." What exactly is *micromanaging*, and what can you do if you find yourself working for a micromanager?

A micromanaging boss is someone who wants to control every particular, down to the smallest detail, of your work. For you, it can be very frustrating, stressful, and demoralizing. What are some signs that your boss may be micromanaging you? He checks on your progress multiple times a day; asks for frequent updates; tells you how to complete tasks; is obsessed with meaningless details; or becomes irritated if you make a decision without consulting him first. But just because your boss monitors your work doesn't mean he's a micromanager. Every manager has a responsibility for controlling activities for which he or she is responsible. And good managers are detail oriented. The difference is that micromanagers obsess on details, lose sight of priorities, and behave as if they don't trust you. Good managers, on the other hand, understand the value of delegation. Unfortunately, you might not always have one of these.

There's a long list of reasons why your boss might be micromanaging you. That list would include insecurity, lack of trust in others, risk aversion, or lack of confidence in your ability. Additionally, other reasons might be having too little to do, thinking he or she is being helpful, or just being a control freak.

Self-assessment. If you feel that your boss is micromanaging you, the place to start is with self-assessment. Ask yourself: "Is it *me*?" Is there any reason your boss might feel the need to micromanage? For instance, have you shown up late to work? Have you missed some deadlines? Have you been distracted at work lately? Have you made mistakes that have reflected negatively on your boss? Start your assessment by making sure that your boss's behavior isn't rational and reasonable.

New to the job. The next question to ask is are either you or your boss new on the job? If you're new, your boss may just be temporarily monitoring your work until he or she is confident of your ability and you prove yourself. If your boss is new, either to her current position or in her first managerial position, you will want to give her some slack as she adjusts. Micromanaging is not uncommon among new managers who, with little experience, are fearful of delegation and being held accountable for results. And experienced managers, in a new position, may be overly controlling until they're confident of your abilities. So if either you or your boss is new, you might want to give it some time.

Changing conditions. A final step before you take any action should be to assess whether conditions have changed. If your boss's micromanaging behavior is a change from her past behavior, consider whether it might be justified by changing conditions. Is your organization going through layoffs? Is there a major reorganization going on? Has your boss been given additional projects with pressing deadlines? Has your boss got a new boss? Any of these types of conditions can increase stress and lead your boss to micromanaging. If the conditions creating stress are temporary, her strong oversight behavior may be just short term.

Talk to your boss. If you've come to the conclusion that your boss's behavior isn't temporary and it's creating difficulties for you to do your job properly, you and your boss need to talk.

It's very possible your boss is unaware that there's a problem. In a nonconfrontational voice, specifically explain how his oversight is impacting your work, creating stress, and making it harder for you to perform at your full capabilities. You want to show him that you've got things under control and that you know what his expectations are.

Keep your boss updated. In addition to talking to your boss, you want to alleviate any concerns she might have that work isn't being done correctly or that she might be unable to answer questions about your work progress. This is best achieved by regularly updating her on your work's status. No boss likes surprises, especially ones that might reflect negatively on her management skills. This can best be achieved by proactively providing your boss with updates before they're requested.

Reinforce your boss's positive behaviors. When your boss leaves you alone, let her know you appreciate her hands-off approach. Thank her for trusting you. By positively reinforcing her trust, you increase the probability that she'll demonstrate more of that behavior. Over time, when combined with your regular updates and your solid performance, you're very likely to see a decline in the micromanaging behavior.

Sources: Based on R.D. White, "The Micromanagement Disease: Symptoms, Diagnosis, and Cure," *Public Personnel Management*, Spring 2010, pp. 71-76; G. Campbell, "Confronting Micromanaging Bosses," *Nursing Management*, September 2010, p. 56; Amy Gallo, "Stop Being Micromanaged," hbr.org, September 2011; and P. Ganeshan-Singh, "7 Ways to Survive Working for a Micromanaging Boss," payscale.com, October 29, 2014.

Developing Trust

If you looked back at each chapter's Leader Making a Difference box, you'd see an amazing group of leaders who not only excel at leading their organizations but also have a strong trusting relationship with their employees. In today's uncertain environment, an important consideration for leaders is building trust and credibility, both of which can be extremely fragile. Before we can discuss ways leaders can build trust and credibility, we have to know what trust and credibility are and why they're so important.

The main component of credibility is honesty. Surveys show that honesty is consistently singled out as the number one characteristic of admired leaders. "Honesty is absolutely essential to leadership. If people are going to follow someone willingly, whether it be into battle or into the boardroom, they first want to assure themselves that the person is worthy of their trust."[65] In addition to being honest, credible leaders are competent and inspiring. They are personally able to effectively communicate their confidence and enthusiasm. Thus, followers judge a leader's **credibility** in terms of his or her honesty, competence, and ability to inspire.

FYI

- 60 percent of people trust a stranger more than their boss.[64]

credibility
The degree to which followers perceive someone as honest, competent, and able to inspire

Trust is closely entwined with the concept of credibility, and, in fact, the terms are often used interchangeably. **Trust** is defined as the belief in the integrity, character, and ability of a leader. Followers who trust a leader are willing to be vulnerable to the leader's actions because they are confident that their rights and interests will not be abused.[66] Research has identified five dimensions that make up the concept of trust:[67]

trust
The belief in the integrity, character, and ability of a leader

- *Integrity:* honesty and truthfulness
- *Competence:* technical and interpersonal knowledge and skills
- *Consistency:* reliability, predictability, and good judgment in handling situations
- *Loyalty:* willingness to protect a person, physically and emotionally
- *Openness:* willingness to share ideas and information freely

Of these five dimensions, integrity seems to be the most critical when someone assesses another's trustworthiness.[68] Both integrity and competence were seen in our earlier discussion of leadership traits found to be consistently associated with leadership. Workplace changes have reinforced why such leadership qualities are important.

let's get REAL

The Scenario:

Source: Matt Ramos

Matt Ramos
Director of Marketing

Adhita Chopra is stumped. Three months ago, he was assigned to lead a team of phone app designers, and although no one has come out and said anything directly, he feels like his team doesn't trust him. They have been withholding information and communicating only selectively when asked questions. And they have persistently questioned the team's goals and strategies and even Adhita's actions and decisions. How can he build trust with his team?

What advice would you give Adhita?

Trust in the workplace is always a tricky subject. I've seen a similar situation unfold once before. If Adhita feels this, but hasn't heard it directly, he's probably right. Earning trust at work comes down to three things: being good at what you do, being passionate about your work and the people around you, and having the ability to listen and follow through. Adhita should make sure he's producing top-notch work and set up weekly one-on-one meetings with the team. Hard work and careful listening will see Adhita through this.

Exhibit 16-6
Building Trust

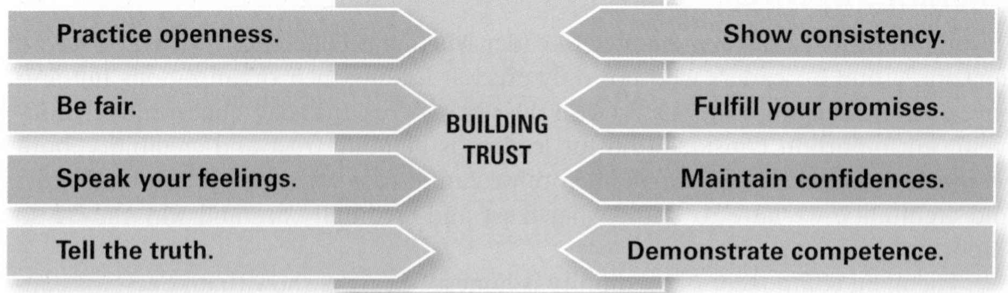

For instance, the trends toward empowerment and self-managed work teams have reduced many of the traditional control mechanisms used to monitor employees. If a work team is free to schedule its own work, evaluate its own performance, and even make its own hiring decisions, trust becomes critical. Employees have to trust managers to treat them fairly, and managers have to trust employees to conscientiously fulfill their responsibilities.

Also, leaders have to increasingly lead others who may not be in their immediate work group or may even be physically separated—members of cross-functional or virtual teams, individuals who work for suppliers or customers, and perhaps even people who represent other organizations through strategic alliances. These situations don't allow leaders the luxury of falling back on their formal positions for influence. Many of these relationships, in fact, are fluid and fleeting, so the ability to quickly develop trust and sustain that trust is crucial to the success of the relationship.

Why is it important that followers trust their leaders? Research has shown that trust in leadership is significantly related to positive job outcomes including job performance, organizational citizenship behavior, job satisfaction, and organizational commitment.[69] Given the importance of trust to effective leadership, how can leaders build trust? Exhibit 16-6 lists some suggestions. (Also, see the Building Your Skill exercise in Chapter 5.)[70]

Now, more than ever, managerial and leadership effectiveness depends on the ability to gain the trust of followers.[71] Downsizing, financial challenges, and the increased use of temporary employees have undermined employees' trust in their leaders and shaken the confidence of investors, suppliers, and customers. Today's leaders are faced with the challenge of rebuilding and restoring trust with employees and with other important organizational stakeholders.

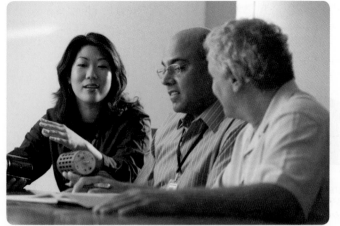

Employee empowerment is part of the people-oriented culture at W. L. Gore & Associates. The company encourages individuals and work teams to take ownership in their jobs by using their talents and abilities in finding the best ways to get things done and to achieve company goals. Empowered employees feel they are trusted, respected, and valued contributors to their company's success.
Source: W. L. Gore/AP Images

Empowering Employees

Employees at DuPont's facility in Uberaba, Brazil, planted trees to commemorate the site's 10th anniversary. Although they had several things to celebrate, one of the most important was the fact that since production began, the facility has had zero environmental incidents and no recordable safety violations. The primary reason for this achievement was the company's implementation of STOP (Safety Training Observation Program)—a program in which empowered employees were responsible for observing one another, correcting improper procedures, and encouraging safe procedures.[72]

As we've described in different places throughout the text, managers are increasingly leading by empowering their employees. As we've said before, empowerment involves increasing the decision-making discretion of workers. Millions of individual employees and employee teams are making the key operating decisions that directly affect their work. They're developing budgets, scheduling workloads, controlling inventories, solving quality problems, and engaging in similar activities that until very recently were viewed exclusively as part of the manager's job.[73] For instance, at The Container Store, any employee who gets a customer request has permission to take care of it. Garret Boone, chairman emeritus, says, "Everybody we hire, we hire as a leader. Anybody in our store can take an action that you might think of typically being a manager's action."[74]

One reason more companies are empowering employees is the need for quick decisions by those people who are most knowledgeable about the issues—often those at lower organizational levels. If organizations want to successfully compete in a dynamic global economy, employees have to be able to make decisions and implement changes quickly. Another reason is that organizational downsizings left many managers with larger spans of control. In order to cope with the increased work demands, managers had to empower their people. Although empowerment is not a universal answer, it can be beneficial when employees have the knowledge, skills, and experience to do their jobs competently.

Leading Across Cultures

"In the United States, leaders are expected to look great, sound great, and be inspiring. In other countries—not so much."[75] In this global economy, how can managers account for cross-cultural differences as they lead?

One general conclusion that surfaces from leadership research is that effective leaders do not use a single style. They adjust their style to the situation. Although not mentioned explicitly, national culture is certainly an important situational variable in determining which leadership style will be most effective. What works in the United States, for instance, isn't likely to be effective in Denmark. Lars Sørensen, CEO of pharmaceutical company Novo Nordisk, knows from experience that effective leadership is contextual. In Denmark, he leads by consensus on all decisions. When he leads his U.S. team, he takes on an aggressive top-down approach.[76]

National culture affects leadership style because it influences how followers will respond. Leaders can't (and shouldn't) just choose their styles randomly. They're constrained by the cultural conditions their followers have come to expect. Exhibit 16-7 provides some findings from selected examples of cross-cultural leadership studies.

Exhibit 16-7
Cross-Cultural Leadership

- Korean leaders are expected to be paternalistic toward employees.
- Arab leaders who show kindness or generosity without being asked to do so are seen by other Arabs as weak.
- Chinese leaders are expected to stay positive when facing attacks.
- European leaders are expected to be more action oriented.
- Japanese leaders are expected to be humble and speak frequently.
- Latin American leaders should not feel rejected when others behave formally.
- Scandinavian and Dutch leaders who single out individuals with public praise are likely to embarrass, not energize, those individuals.
- Effective leaders in Malaysia are expected to show compassion while using more of an autocratic than a participative style.
- Effective German leaders are characterized by high performance orientation, low compassion, low self-protection, low team orientation, high autonomy, and high participation.
- Effective leaders in Sub-Saharan Africa build deep relationships and close teamwork.

Sources: Based on "Leadership Across Cultures," *Harvard Business Review*, www.hbr.org, May 2015; J. C. Kennedy, "Leadership in Malaysia: Traditional Values, International Outlook," *Academy of Management Executive*, August 2002, pp. 15–17; F. C. Brodbeck, M. Frese, and M. Javidan, "Leadership Made in Germany: Low on Compassion, High on Performance," *Academy of Management Executives*, February 2002, pp. 16–29; M. F. Peterson and J. G. Hunt, "International Perspectives on International Leadership," *Leadership Quarterly*, Fall 1997, pp. 203–231; R. J. House and R. N. Aditya, "The Social Scientific Study of Leadership: Quo Vadis?" *Journal of Management*, vol. 23, no. 3, 1997, p. 463; and R. J. House, "Leadership in the Twenty-First Century," in *The Changing Nature of Work*, ed. A Howard (San Francisco: Jossey-Bass, 1995), p. 442.

FUTURE VISION Flexible Leadership

As organizations become flatter (that is, fewer hierarchical levels) and more globally and technologically interconnected, old leadership models will become outdated. Although the three elements of leadership—the leader, the followers, and the situation—will still be part of the whole leadership equation, how these three elements interact to successfully accomplish a team's mission and goals is changing. Successful leaders in tomorrow's workplaces will need to be more like chameleons, adapting to complex and dynamic environments. Under these circumstances, leaders can do three things: (1) share responsibility and accountability by empowering employees; recognize that "leading" can come from anywhere and everywhere and that sometimes the best approach may be to step out of the way and let someone else take charge; (2) keep calm and stay focused in the midst of the fast pace and the uncertainty; when faced with such conditions, focus on the most important tasks at hand and present a confident demeanor when others may be panicking or at a loss as to what to do; and (3) be a leader who listens, encourages participation, recognizes that others' needs are as important as your own, encourages and supports collaboration in achieving common goals—that is, a leader who puts people first. After all, without people, leaders are nothing.

*If your professor has chosen to assign this, go to **www.mymanagementlab.com** to discuss the following questions.*

TALK ABOUT IT 1: Why are old leadership models becoming outdated?

TALK ABOUT IT 2: Without people, leaders are nothing. What does this mean?

Because most leadership theories were developed in the United States, they have an American bias. They emphasize follower responsibilities rather than rights; assume self-gratification rather than commitment to duty or altruistic motivation; assume centrality of work and democratic value orientation; and stress rationality rather than spirituality, religion, or superstition.[77] However, the GLOBE research program, which we first introduced in Chapter 3, is the most extensive and comprehensive cross-cultural study of leadership ever undertaken. The GLOBE study found that leadership has some universal aspects. Specifically, a number of elements of transformational leadership appear to be associated with effective leadership regardless of what country the leader is in.[78] These elements include vision, foresight, providing encouragement, trustworthiness, dynamism, positiveness, and proactiveness. The results led two members of the GLOBE team to conclude that "effective business leaders in any country are expected by their subordinates to provide a powerful and proactive vision to guide the company into the future, strong motivational skills to stimulate all employees to fulfill the vision, and excellent planning skills to assist in implementing the vision."[79] Some people suggest that the universal appeal of these transformational leader characteristics is due to the pressures toward common technologies and management practices as a result of global competitiveness and multinational influences.

Leadership Transition—If your instructor is using Pearson MyLab Management, log onto **mymanagementlab.com** and test your *leadership transition knowledge.* **Be sure to refer back to the chapter opener!**

Becoming an Effective Leader

Organizations need effective leaders. Two issues pertinent to becoming an effective leader are leader training and recognizing that sometimes being an effective leader means *not* leading. Let's take a look at these issues.

Global executive leadership programs at Ford Motor Company develop effective leaders such as Mark Fields, a 25-year Ford employee who leads the company as CEO and president. Ford offers a wide range of leadership development programs for employees at all levels that focus on fostering functional and technical excellence, risk taking, decision making, managing change, and entrepreneurial thinking.
Source: Paul Warner, Contributor/Getty Images Entertainment/Getty Images

LEADER TRAINING Organizations around the globe spend billions of dollars, yen, and euros on leadership training and development. In the United States alone, it has been estimated that companies spend $70.6 billion a year on formal training and development.[80] These efforts take many forms—from $50,000 leadership programs offered by universities such as Harvard and organizations such as GE to sailing experiences at the Outward Bound School. Although much of the money spent on leader training may provide doubtful benefits, our review suggests that managers can do some things to get the maximum effect from such training.[81] Still, there is some consensus about characteristics of effective leadership training. One is contextualization (ensuring that learning is set in the strategy and culture of the organization), and another is personalization (enabling participants to seek out learning related to their aspirations).[82]

First, let's recognize the obvious. Some people don't have what it takes to be a leader. Period. For instance, evidence indicates that leadership training is more likely to be successful with individuals who are high self-monitors rather than with low self-monitors. Such individuals have the flexibility to change their behavior as different situations may require. In addition, organizations may find that individuals with higher levels of a trait called motivation to lead are more receptive to leadership development opportunities.[84]

What kinds of things can individuals learn that might be related to being a more effective leader? It may be a bit optimistic to think that "vision-creation" can be taught, but implementation skills can be taught. People can be trained to develop "an understanding about content themes critical to effective visions."[85] We can also teach skills such as trust-building and mentoring. And leaders can be taught situational analysis skills. They can learn how to evaluate situations, how to modify situations to make them fit better with their style, and how to assess which leader behaviors might be most effective in given situations.

The percentage of women in leadership positions varies by country:

- 45 percent in Russia.
- 39 percent in the Philippines and Lithuania.
- 37 percent in Estonia.
- 16 percent in India.
- 15 percent in Germany.
- 7 percent in Japan.[83]

SUBSTITUTES FOR LEADERSHIP Despite the belief that some leadership style will always be effective regardless of the situation, leadership may not always be important! Research indicates that, in some situations, any behaviors a leader exhibits are irrelevant. In other words, certain individual, job, and organizational variables can act as "substitutes for leadership," negating the influence of the leader.[86]

For instance, follower characteristics such as experience, training, professional orientation, or need for independence can neutralize the effect of leadership. These characteristics can replace the employee's need for a leader's support or ability to create structure and reduce task ambiguity. Similarly, jobs that are inherently unambiguous and routine or intrinsically satisfying may place fewer demands on leaders. Finally, such organizational characteristics as explicit formalized goals, rigid rules and procedures, or cohesive work groups can substitute for formal leadership.

Chapter 16 PREPARING FOR: Exams/Quizzes

CHAPTER SUMMARY by Learning Objectives

LO16.1 DEFINE leader and leadership.

A leader is someone who can influence others and who has managerial authority. Leadership is a process of leading a group and influencing that group to achieve its goals. Managers should be leaders because leading is one of the four management functions.

LO16.2 COMPARE and contrast early theories of leadership.

Early attempts to define leader traits were unsuccessful, although later attempts found eight traits associated with leadership.

The University of Iowa studies explored three leadership styles. The only conclusion was that group members were more satisfied under a democratic leader than under an autocratic one. The Ohio State studies identified two dimensions of leader behavior—initiating structure and consideration. A leader high in both those dimensions at times achieved high group task performance and high group member satisfaction, but not always. The University of Michigan studies looked at employee-oriented leaders and production-oriented leaders. They concluded that leaders who were employee oriented could get high group productivity and high group member satisfaction. The managerial grid looked at leaders' concern for production and concern for people and identified five leader styles. Although it suggested that a leader who was high in concern for production and high in concern for people was the best, there was no substantive evidence for that conclusion.

As the behavioral studies showed, a leader's behavior has a dual nature: a focus on the task and a focus on the people.

LO16.3 DESCRIBE the three major contingency theories of leadership.

Fiedler's model attempted to define the best style to use in particular situations. He measured leader style—relationship oriented or task oriented—using the least-preferred coworker questionnaire. Fiedler also assumed a leader's style was fixed. He measured three contingency dimensions: leader–member relations, task structure, and position power. The model suggests that task-oriented leaders performed best in very favorable and very unfavorable situations, and relationship-oriented leaders performed best in moderately favorable situations.

Hersey and Blanchard's situational leadership theory focused on followers' readiness. They identified four leadership styles: telling (high task–low relationship), selling (high task–high relationship), participating (low task–high relationship), and delegating (low task–low relationship). They also identified four stages of readiness: unable and unwilling (use telling style), unable but willing (use selling style), able but unwilling (use participative style), and able and willing (use delegating style).

The path-goal model developed by Robert House identified four leadership behaviors: directive, supportive, participative, and achievement oriented. He assumed that a leader can and should be able to use any of these styles. The two situational contingency variables were found in the environment and in the follower. Essentially, the path-goal model says that a leader should provide direction and support as needed; that is, structure the path so the followers can achieve goals.

LO16.4 DESCRIBE contemporary views of leadership.

Leader–member exchange theory (LMX) says that leaders create in-groups and out-groups and those in the in-group will have higher performance ratings, less turnover, and greater job satisfaction.

A transactional leader exchanges rewards for productivity where a transformational leader stimulates and inspires followers to achieve goals.

A charismatic leader is an enthusiastic and self-confident leader whose personality and actions influence people to behave in certain ways. People can learn to be charismatic. A visionary leader is able to create and articulate a realistic, credible, and attractive vision of the future.

Authentic leadership focuses on the moral aspects of being a leader. Ethical leaders create a culture in which employees feel that they could and should do a better job. A team leader has two priorities: manage the team's external boundary and facilitate the team process. Four leader roles are involved: liaison with external constituencies, troubleshooter, conflict manager, and coach.

LO16.5 DISCUSS twenty-first century issues affecting leadership.

The five sources of a leader's power are legitimate (authority or position), coercive (punish or control), reward (give positive rewards), expert (special expertise, skills, or knowledge), and referent (desirable resources or traits).

Today's leaders face the issues of managing power, developing trust, empowering employees, leading across cultures, and becoming an effective leader.

Pearson **MyLab** Management

Go to **mymanagementlab.com** to complete the problems marked with this icon ✪.

✪ REVIEW AND DISCUSSION QUESTIONS

16-1. What are the eight key traits associated with leadership that summarize the four main theories?

16-2. Briefly explain what a managerial grid is.

16-3. Explain Hersey and Blanchard's situational leadership styles and the two key behaviors associated with it.

16-4. What is the purpose of a charismatic leader's enthusiasm and self-confidence?

16-5. You are a team leader. What are your daily priorities for your team?

16-6. Can a leader get power from multiple sources? Discuss.

16-7. Do you think most managers in real life use a contingency approach to increase their leadership effectiveness? Explain.

16-8. Do the followers make a difference in whether a leader is effective? Discuss.

Pearson **MyLab** Management

If your professor has assigned these, go to **mymanagementlab.com** for the following Assisted-graded writing questions:

16-9. Define leader and leadership and explain why managers should be leaders.

16-10. Which source of leader's power is most effective and why?

PREPARING FOR: My Career

PERSONAL INVENTORY ASSESSMENTS  PERSONAL INVENTORY ASSESSMENT

Leadership Style Inventory

What's your leadership style? Take this PIA and find out!

ETHICS DILEMMA

Have you ever watched the show *Undercover Boss?* It features a company's "boss" working undercover in his or her own company to find out how the organization really works. Typically, the executive works undercover for a week, and then the employees the leader has worked with are summoned to company headquarters and either rewarded or punished for their actions. Bosses from organizations ranging from Waste Management and White Castle to NASCAR and Family Dollar have participated.

16-11. What do you think? Is it ethical for a leader to go undercover in his or her organization? Why or why not?

16-12. What ethical issues could arise? How could managers deal with those issues?

SKILLS EXERCISE Developing Your Choosing an Effective Leadership Style Skill

About the Skill

Effective leaders are skillful at helping the groups they lead be successful as the group goes through various stages of development. No leadership style is consistently effective. Situational factors, including follower characteristics, must be taken into consideration in the selection of an effective leadership style. The key situational factors that determine leadership effectiveness include stage of group development, task structure, position power, leader–member relations, the work group, employee characteristics, organizational culture, and national culture.

Steps in Practicing the Skill

You can choose an effective leadership style if you use the following six suggestions.

- ***Determine the stage in which your group or team is operating: forming, storming, norming, or performing.*** Because each team stage involves specific and different issues and behaviors, it's important to know in which stage your team is. *Forming* is the first stage of group development, during which people join a group and then help define the group's purpose, structure, and leadership. *Storming* is the second stage, characterized by intragroup conflict. *Norming* is the third stage, characterized by close relationships and cohesiveness. *Performing* is the fourth stage, when the group is fully functional.
- ***If your team is in the forming stage, you want to exhibit certain leader behaviors.*** These include making certain that all team members are introduced to one another, answering member questions, working to establish a foundation of trust and openness, modeling the behaviors you expect from the team members, and clarifying the team's goals, procedures, and expectations.
- ***If your team is in the storming stage, you want to exhibit certain leader behaviors.*** These behaviors include identifying sources of conflict and adopting a mediator role, encouraging a win-win philosophy, restating the team's vision and its core values and goals, encouraging open discussion, encouraging an analysis of team processes in order to identify ways to improve, enhancing team cohesion and commitment, and providing recognition to individual team members as well as the team.
- ***If your team is in the norming stage, you want to exhibit certain leader behaviors.*** These behaviors include clarifying the team's goals and expectations, providing performance feedback to individual team members and the team, encouraging the team to articulate a vision for the future, and finding ways to publicly and openly communicate the team's vision.
- ***If your team is in the performing stage, you want to exhibit certain leader behaviors.*** These behaviors include providing regular and ongoing performance feedback, fostering innovation and innovative behavior, encouraging the team to capitalize on its strengths, celebrating achievements (large and small), and providing the team whatever support it needs to continue doing its work.

- ***Monitor the group for changes in behavior and adjust your leadership style accordingly.*** Because a group is not a static entity, it will go through up periods and down periods. You should adjust your leadership style to the needs of the situation. If the group appears to need more direction from you, provide it. If it appears to be functioning at a high level on its own, provide whatever support is necessary to keep it functioning at that level.

Practicing the Skill

The following suggestions are activities you can do to practice the behaviors in choosing an effective leadership style.

1. Think of a group or team to which you currently belong or of which you have been a part. What type of leadership style did the leader of this group appear to exhibit? Give some specific examples of the types of leadership behaviors he or she used. Evaluate the leadership style. Was it appropriate for the group? Why or why not? What would you have done differently? Why?
2. Observe a sports team (either college or professional) that you consider extremely successful and one that you would consider not successful. What leadership styles appear to be used in these team situations? Give some specific examples of the types of leadership behaviors you observe. How would you evaluate the leadership style? Was it appropriate for the team? Why or why not? To what degree do you think leadership style influenced the team's outcomes?

WORKING TOGETHER Team Exercise

So what really makes a good leader? Is it giving people the time and space to grow as individuals? Giving people that vital opportunity to make their own decisions? Or have individual responsibilities perhaps? Think of a leader you have encountered so far and recall what was good about them. Write down as many positives about your relationship with that leader. Share your thoughts with a small group of three or four members. Try to collate the ideal characteristics discussed. Once you've done this, share your ideas with the rest of the class.

MY TURN TO BE A MANAGER

- Think of the different organizations to which you belong. Note the different styles of leadership used by the leaders in these organizations. Write a paper describing these individual's style of leading (no names, please) and evaluate the styles being used.
- Write down three people you consider effective leaders. Make a bulleted list of the characteristics these individuals exhibit that you think make them effective leaders.
- Think about the times you have had to lead. Describe your own personal leadership style. What could you do to improve your leadership style? Come up with an action plan of steps you can take. Put all this information into a brief paper.
- Managers say that increasingly they must use influence to get things done. Do some research on the art of persuasion. Make a bulleted list of suggestions you find on how to improve your skills at influencing others.
- Here's a list of leadership skills. Choose two and develop a training exercise that will help develop or improve that skill: building employee communities; building teams; coaching and motivating others; communicating with impact, confidence, and energy; leading by example; leading change; making decisions; providing direction and focus; and valuing diversity.
- Select one of the topics in the section on leadership issues in the twenty-first century. Do some additional research on the topic, and put your findings in a bulleted list that you are prepared to share in class. Be sure to cite your sources.
- Interview three managers about what they think it takes to be a good leader. Write up your findings in a report and be prepared to present it in class.
- Try out your leadership skills! Volunteer for a leadership position with an organization you are involved in.

CASE APPLICATION 1 Indra Nooyi: An Inspiring Leader

PepsiCo, Inc. is regarded as the second largest food and beverage business in the world, and a large part of the success of this multinational corporation can be attributed to its leader. Indra Nooyi, the Chairperson and CEO, is an inspiring and visionary leader for several reasons. First, she has been one of the first women outside America to become CEO of such a large multinational. Second, for over a decade, she has featured on Forbes magazine's list of the 100 most influential women in the world. Third, Nooyi has been known to be an employee-oriented and a customer-oriented leader, with her innovative strategies inspiring and forging the way for women worldwide.

Being particularly attentive to PepsiCo's customers' needs and preferences, Nooyi uses every occasion to better understand and improve the rapidly changing beverage patterns. In a recent business trip to China, she toured different cities in the region for ten days, closely studying the strategic market for PepsiCo. In an interview with David Rubenstein at Bloomberg, she shared a funny anecdote that confirms her attention to customers' preferences—every time she is invited by a friend, she tries to find a way to go into the kitchen and look at what products they use every day (also hoping to find some products of the PepsiCo group).

Nooyi is visionary in many of her decisions. In 2012, she decided to create a design team, headed by the Italian designer Mauro Porcini (former Head of Global Design at 3M), and assigned him the task of refreshing the company's brand, rethink the shape of the bottles, and redesigning the vending machines. That was a pioneering decision in the food and drink industry at that time (now such decision has been imitated by competitors) and even people inside PepsiCo were unsure about the this decision at the beginning. However, this audacious choice revealed to be successful as the company could improve the top land bottom line and become more appealing among customers and restaurants. For example, the new fountain machine designed by the Design & Innovation Center, which enables customers to select their flavor coke from more than 1,000 combinations, has been a great success and one of the reason for which the restaurant chain Buffalo Wild Wings decided to switch from Coke to Pepsi in 2013.

Nooyi is a supportive leader who makes of women's innate caring attitude a big strength of her leadership style. For example, she conveys a deep sense of gratitude to all her employees for the effort and energy they put in the company. To express this feeling, she sometimes writes gratitude letters to the executive's parents to let them know how well their sons or daughters are doing for PepsiCo and to give them credit for such amazing achievements.

Notably, not forgetting her privileged condition of being a woman who has been able to break the highest glass ceiling in the company, Nooyi is fully committed to promote diversity and inclusion at all organizational levels. In 2010, the company launched a survey with women manager, who were good represented in middle-level management positions but very low represented in top-level positions to understand the reasons of such under-representation. Women confessed to lack self-confidence and to believe that men were more capable to make themselves noticeable in the company and cultivate high influential networks, something they were less good in doing. In response to this, PepsiCo created a leadership development program for women, called "Strategies for Success," aimed at helping women boosting their self-confidence and guiding them in rising up through the organization. In just two years, women's representation in senior positions in the operation team raised from 0 to 33 percent.

When asked about her secret, Indra has no doubts: the family. She attributes most of her strength to her family and to teachings and example received by her parents. She recalls that in India, at the time she was an adolescent, the preoccupation of most parents was to find a husband for their daughters. Her parents were different in many things, for instance supporting Nooyi's decision to leave India for studying in the United States. Moreover, since her childhood, they sought to make her (and the sister) more confident and aware of their unique talents. A game that the mother was used to play with them during the dinners consisted of pretending that they became a President or a very important ministry of India and, every evening, they had to write a list of things that they would have done in such an important position. Albeit it was only a game, Nooyi confessed that it helped her a lot to boost her self-confidence and inform her leadership style and, probably, without that evening ritual she would have not been capable of achieving what she got today in her life- and being the so-highly loved leader she is.[87]

DISCUSSION QUESTIONS

16-13. What leadership models/theories/issues do you see in this case? List and describe.

16-14. What do you think about Indra Nooyi's decision to create a design unit at PepsiCo? Is it appropriate for the food and drink industry? Why or why not?

16-15. How do you think leadership is changing in contemporary society? What behaviors exhibited by Indra Nooyi indicate such change?

16-16. What did the case teach you about leadership?

CASE APPLICATION 2 Leadership Development at L'Oréal

Jean Paul Agon, the president and CEO of L'Oréal, joined the company right after his university graduation in 1978 and has continued to grow as a leader over his almost 40 years with the company.[88] Headquartered in France with more than 80,000 employees around the globe, L'Oréal is the world's largest cosmetics company. Today, L'Oréal management still believes leadership development starts at the beginning of your career and continues throughout it.

Each year almost 650 recent university graduates join one of L'Oréal's management training programs. The format of each program varies based on geographic location, with trainees spending between 6 and 18 months taking on different missions throughout the organization to learn the business. Each trainee has a personal development plan that includes learning about the organization, understanding the business models utilized by the different brands, and developing relationships throughout the organization. The program immerses the trainee into the organizational culture and the trainee learns about what it takes to succeed in the work environment. Most trainees are also connected with a mentor to answer questions and provide guidance.

A significant contributor to L'Oréal's overall success is the cross-cultural awareness of managers who often lead diverse teams developing customized products for different regions of the world. While some of these leaders are recruited externally, many are developed through a specific international management training program that includes a 12-month rotation through Paris, New York, Singapore, and Rio. This program seeks out graduates who are curious and able to adapt to other cultures from international business schools, knowing this skill set is important to help tailor international brands to local markets.

Doing business globally also requires ethical leadership, which is an important component of the firm's leadership development. L'Oréal has been recognized for their efforts on the ethics front. In 2016, the Ethics & Compliance Initiative recognized

L'Oréal's innovation in ethical leadership. The company was also named as one of the World's Most Ethical Companies by Ethisphere.

L'Oréal's leadership development efforts do not stop with recent graduates. In fact, managers at all levels of the organization have the opportunity to further develop their leadership ability through a variety of programs. These programs are primarily based on coaching leaders and are offered with the belief that an investment in leaders goes farther as those leaders then develop their own teams. Managers throughout the organization are held accountable for the development of their employees. Those that fail at developing their own teams, even if they meet business outcomes, lose out on performance rewards. All this emphasizes this important point: Leadership matters at L'Oréal.

DISCUSSION QUESTIONS

16-17. Why do you think L'Oréal invests so much in leadership development?

16-18. What role does a mentor play in leadership development?

16-19. Why is cross-cultural awareness important for leaders at a company such as L'Oréal?

16-20. Do you think a management training program would be a good way to start a career with a company? Why or why not?

ENDNOTES

1. Most leadership research has focused on the actions and responsibilities of managers and extrapolated the results to leaders and leadership in general.
2. J. Pinsker, "The Financial Perks of Being Tall," *The Atlantic* online, www.theatlantic.com, May 18, 2015; T. A. Judge and D. M. Cable, "The Effect of Physical Height on Workplace Success and Income: Preliminary Test of a Theoretical Model," *Journal of Applied Psychology*, vol. 89, no. 3, 2004, pp. 428–441.
3. See R. L. Schaumberg and F. J. Flynn, "Uneasy Lies the Head That Wears the Crown: The Link Between Guilt Proneness and Leadership," *Journal of Personality and Social Psychology*, August 2012, pp. 327–342; D. S. DeRue, J. D. Nahrgang, N. Wellman, and S. E. Humphrey, "Trait and Behavioral Theories of Leadership: An Integration and Meta-Analytic Test of Their Relative Validity," *Personnel Psychology*, Spring 2011, pp. 7–52; T. A. Judge, J. E. Bono, R. Ilies, and M. W. Gerhardt, "Personality and Leadership: A Qualitative and Quantitative Review," *Journal of Applied Psychology*, August 2002, pp. 765–780; and S. A. Kirkpatrick and E. A. Locke, "Leadership: Do Traits Matter?" *Academy of Management Executive*, May 1991, pp. 48–60.
4. R. Working, "Executive Qualities Differ by Gender, Study Finds," www.hrcommunication.com, March 8, 2013.
5. A. Bryant, "Carter Murray Giving Talented People Room to Bloom," *The New York Times* online, www.nytimes.com, May 13, 2016.
6. N. Nayab, "A Review of Companies with Autocratic Leadership," Bright Hub Project Management, online, www.brighthubpm.com, July 29, 2015.
7. D. S. DeRue, J. D. Nahrgang, N. Wellman, and S. E. Humphrey, "Trait and Behavioral Theories of Leadership: An Integration and Meta-Analytic Test of Their Relative Validity."
8. K. Lewin and R. Lippitt, "An Experimental Approach to the Study of Autocracy and Democracy: A Preliminary Note," *Sociometry*, vol. 1, 1938, pp. 292–300; K. Lewin, "Field Theory and Experiment in Social Psychology: Concepts and Methods," *American Journal of Sociology*, vol. 44, 1939, pp. 868–896; K. Lewin, L. Lippitt, and R. K. White, "Patterns of Aggressive Behavior in Experimentally Created Social Climates," *Journal of Social Psychology*, vol. 10, 1939, pp. 271–301; and L. Lippitt, "An Experimental Study of the Effect of Democratic and Authoritarian Group Atmospheres," *University of Iowa Studies in Child Welfare*, vol. 16, 1940, pp. 43–95.
9. B. M. Bass, *Stogdill's Handbook of Leadership* (New York: Free Press, 1981), pp. 289–299.
10. R. M. Stogdill and A. E. Coons, eds., *Leader Behavior: Its Description and Measurement*, Research Monograph no. 88 (Columbus: Ohio State University, Bureau of Business Research, 1951). For an updated literature review of Ohio State research, see S. Kerr, C. A. Schriesheim, C. J. Murphy, and R. M. Stogdill, "Toward a Contingency Theory of Leadership Based upon the Consideration and Initiating Structure Literature," *Organizational Behavior and Human Performance*, August 1974, pp. 62–82; and B. M. Fisher, "Consideration and Initiating Structure and Their Relationships with Leader Effectiveness: A Meta-Analysis," in F. Hoy (ed.), *Proceedings of the 48th Annual Academy of Management Conference*, Anaheim, California, 1988, pp. 201–205.
11. U.S. Bureau of Labor Statistics, "Medical and Health Services Managers," *Occupational Outlook Handbook, 2016-17 Ed.*
12. "Why the Empathetic Leader Is the Best Leader," www.success.com, April 21, 2014.
13. R. Kahn and D. Katz, "Leadership Practices in Relation to Productivity and Morale," in *Group Dynamics: Research and*

Theory, 2d ed., ed. D. Cartwright and A. Zander (Elmsford, NY: Row, Paterson, 1960).

14. R. R. Blake and J. S. Mouton, *The Managerial Grid III* (Houston: Gulf Publishing, 1984).
15. L. L. Larson, J. G. Hunt, and R. N. Osborn, "The Great Hi-Hi Leader Behavior Myth: A Lesson from Occam's Razor," *Academy of Management Journal*, December 1976, pp. 628–641; and P. C. Nystrom, "Managers and the Hi-Hi Leader Myth," *Academy of Management Journal*, June 1978, pp. 325–331.
16. W. G. Bennis, "The Seven Ages of the Leader," *Harvard Business Review*, January 2004, p. 52.
17. F. E. Fiedler, *A Theory of Leadership Effectiveness* (New York: McGraw-Hill, 1967).
18. R. Ayman, M. M. Chemers, and F. Fiedler, "The Contingency Model of Leadership Effectiveness: Its Levels of Analysis," *Leadership Quarterly*, Summer 1995, pp. 147–167; C. A. Schriesheim, B. J. Tepper, and L. A. Tetrault, "Least Preferred Coworker Score, Situational Control, and Leadership Effectiveness: A Meta-Analysis of Contingency Model Performance Predictions," *Journal of Applied Psychology*, August 1994, pp. 561–573; and L. H. Peters, D. D. Hartke, and J. T. Pholmann, "Fiedler's Contingency Theory of Leadership: An Application of the Meta-Analysis Procedures of Schmidt and Hunter," *Psychological Bulletin*, March 1985, pp. 274–285.
19. See E. H. Schein, *Organizational Psychology*, 3rd ed. (Upper Saddle River, NJ: Prentice Hall, 1980), pp. 116–117; and B. Kabanoff, "A Critique of Leader Match and Its Implications for Leadership Research," *Personnel Psychology*, Winter 1981, pp. 749–764.
20. P. Hersey and K. Blanchard, "So You Want to Know Your Leadership Style?," *Training and Development Journal*, February 1974, pp. 1–15; and P. Hersey and K. H. Blanchard, *Management of Organizational Behavior: Leading Human Resources*, 8th ed. (Englewood Cliffs, NJ: Prentice Hall, 2001).
21. See, for instance, E. G. Ralph, "Developing Managers' Effectiveness: A Model with Potential," *Journal of Management Inquiry*, June 2004, pp. 152–163; C. L. Graeff, "Evolution of Situational Leadership Theory: A Critical Review," *Leadership Quarterly*, vol. 8, no. 2, 1997, pp. 153–170; and C. F. Fernandez and R. P. Vecchio, "Situational Leadership Theory Revisited: A Test of an Across-Jobs Perspective," *Leadership Quarterly*, vol. 8, no. 1, 1997, pp. 67–84.
22. Ready-Now Leaders: 25 Findings to Meet Tomorrow's Business Challenges," The Conference Board and Development Dimensions International, www.ddiworld.org, 2014.
23. R. J. House, "A Path-Goal Theory of Leader Effectiveness," *Administrative Science Quarterly*, September 1971, pp. 321–338; R. J. House and T. R. Mitchell, "Path-Goal Theory of Leadership," *Journal of Contemporary Business*, Autumn 1974, p. 86; and R. J. House, "Path-Goal Theory of Leadership: Lessons, Legacy, and a Reformulated Theory," *Leadership Quarterly*, Fall 1996, pp. 323–352.
24. M. L. Dixon and L. K. Hart, "The Impact of Path-Goal Leadership Styles on Work Group Effectiveness and Turnover Intention," *Journal of Managerial Issues*, Spring 2010, pp. 52–69; J. C. Wofford and L. Z. Liska, "Path-Goal Theories of Leadership: A Meta-Analysis," *Journal of Management*, Winter 1993, pp. 857–876; and A. Sagie and M. Koslowsky, "Organizational Attitudes and Behaviors as a Function of Participation in Strategic and Tactical Change Decisions: An Application of Path-Goal Theory," *Journal of Organizational Behavior*, January 1994, pp. 37–47.
25. R. M. Dienesch and R. C. Liden, "Leader–Member Exchange Model of Leadership: A Critique and Further Development," *Academy of Management Review*, July 1986, pp. 618–634; G. B. Graen and M. Uhl-Bien, "Relationship-Based Approach to Leadership: Development of Leader–Member Exchange (LMX) Theory of Leadership over 25 Years: Applying a Multi-Domain Perspective," *Leadership Quarterly*, Summer 1995, pp. 219–247; R. C. Liden, R. T. Sparrowe, and S. J. Wayne, "Leader–Member Exchange Theory: The Past and Potential for the Future," in *Research in Personnel and Human Resource Management*, vol. 15, ed. G. R. Ferris (Greenwich, CT: JAI Press, 1997), pp. 47–119; and C. P. Schriesheim, S. L. Castro, X. Zhou, and F. J. Yammarino, "The Folly of Theorizing 'A' but Testing 'B': A Selective Level-of-Analysis Review of the Field and a Detailed Leader–Member Exchange Illustration," *Leadership Quarterly*, Winter 2001, pp. 515–551.
26. P. Drexler, "The Upside of Favoritism," *Wall Street Journal*, June 8–9, 2013, p. C3.
27. R. C. Liden and G. Graen, "Generalizability of the Vertical Dyad Linkage Model of Leadership," *Academy of Management Journal*, September 1980, pp. 451–465; R. C. Liden, S. J. Wayne, and D. Stilwell, "A Longitudinal Study of the Early Development of Leader–Member Exchanges," *Journal of Applied Psychology*, August 1993, pp. 662–674; S. J. Wayne, L. J. Shore, W. H. Bommer, and L. E. Tetrick, "The Role of Fair Treatment and Rewards in Perceptions of Organizational Support and Leader–Member Exchange," *Journal of Applied Psychology*, June 2002, pp. 590–598; and S. S. Masterson, K. Lewis, and B. M. Goldman, "Integrating Justice and Social Exchange: The Differing Effects of Fair Procedures and Treatment on Work Relationships," *Academy of Management Journal*, August 2000, pp. 738–748.
28. D. Duchon, S. G. Green, and T. D. Taber, "Vertical Dyad Linkage: A Longitudinal Assessment of Antecedents, Measures, and Consequences," *Journal of Applied Psychology*, February 1986, pp. 56–60; R. C. Liden, S. J. Wayne, and D. Stilwell, "A Longitudinal Study of the Early Development of Leader–Member Exchanges"; M. Uhl-Bien, "Relationship Development as a Key Ingredient for Leadership Development," in *Future of Leadership Development*, ed. S. E. Murphy and R. E. Riggio (Mahwah, NJ: Lawrence Erlbaum, 2003), pp. 129–147; R. Vecchio and D. M. Brazil, "Leadership and Sex-Similarity: A Comparison in a Military Setting," *Personnel Psychology*, vol. 60, 2007, pp. 303–335; and V. L. Goodwin, W. M. Bowler, and J. L. Whittington, "A Social Network Perspective on LMX Relationships: Accounting for the Instrumental Value of Leader and Follower Networks," *Journal of Management*, August 2009, pp. 954–980.
29. See, for instance, C. R. Gerstner and D. V. Day, "Meta-Analytic Review of Leader–Member Exchange Theory: Correlates and Construct Issues," *Journal of Applied Psychology*, December 1997, pp. 827–844; R. Ilies, J. D. Nahrgang, and F. P. Morgeson, "Leader–Member Exchange

and Citizenship Behaviors: A Meta-analysis," *Journal of Applied Psychology*, January 2007, pp. 269–277; Z. Chen, W. Lam, and J. A. Zhong, "Leader–Member Exchange and Member Performance: A New Look at Individual-Level Negative Feedback-Seeking Behavior and Team-Level Empowerment Culture," *Journal of Applied Psychology*, January 2007, pp. 202–212; and Z. Zhang, M. Wang, and J. Shi, "Leader-Follower Congruence in Proactive Personality and Work Outcomes: The Mediating Role of Leader-Member Exchange," *Academy of Management Journal*, February 2012, pp. 111–130.

30. R. Eisenberger, G. Karagonlar, F. Stinglhamber, P. Neves, T. Becker, M. Gonzalez-Morales, and M. Steiger-Mueller, "Leader-Member Exchange and Affective Organizational Commitment: The Contribution of Supervisor's Organizational Embodiment," *Journal of Applied Psychology*, vol. 95, 2010, pp. 1085–1103.
31. B. M. Bass and R. E. Riggio, *Transformational Leadership*, 2d ed. (Mahwah, NJ: Lawrence Erlbaum Associates, Inc., 2006), p. 3.
32. Leader Making a Difference box based on M. Crowley, "How A World-Class Heart Surgeon Found the One Leadership Trait Many Businesses Are Missing," *Fast Company Magazine* online, www.fastcompany.com, August 14, 2014; Z. Budryk, "Cleveland Clinic's Toby Cosgrove on Critical Skills and Traits for Healthcare Leaders," *Fierce Healthcare* online, www.fiercehealthcare.com, March 23, 2016; A. Boissy and T. Gilligan, *Communication the Cleveland Clinic Way*," McGraw Hill, New York, 2016. www.clevelandclinic.org.
33. B. M. Bass, "Leadership: Good, Better, Best," *Organizational Dynamics*, Winter 1985, pp. 26–40; and J. Seltzer and B. M. Bass, "Transformational Leadership: Beyond Initiation and Consideration," *Journal of Management*, December 1990, pp. 693–703.
34. B. J. Avolio and B. M. Bass, "Transformational Leadership, Charisma, and Beyond." Working paper, School of Management, State University of New York, Binghamton, 1985, p. 14.
35. B. J. Hoffman, B. H. Bynum, R. F. Piccolo, and A. W. Sutton, "Person-Organization Value Congruence: How Transformational Leaders Influence Work Group Effectiveness," *Academy of Management Journal*, August 2011, pp. 779–796; G. Wang, In-Sue Oh, S. H. Courtright, and A. E. Colbert, "Transformational Leadership and Performance Across Criteria and Levels: A Meta-Analytic Review of 25 Years of Research," *Group & Organization Management*, 36, no. 2, 2011, pp. 223–270; M. Tims, A. B. Bakker, and D. Xanthopoulou, "Do Transformational Leaders Enhance Their Followers' Daily Work Engagement?," *The Leadership Quarterly*, February 2011, pp. 121–131; S. J. Peterson and F. O. Walumbwa, "CEO Positive Psychological Traits, Transformational Leadership, and Firm Performance in High-Technology Start-up and Established Firms," *Journal of Management*, April 2009, pp. 348–368; R. S. Rubin, D. C. Munz, and W. H. Bommer, "Leading from Within: The Effects of Emotion Recognition and Personality on Transformational Leadership Behavior," *Academy of Management Journal*, October 2005, pp. 845–858; T. A. Judge and J. E. Bono, "Five-Factor Model of Personality and Transformational Leadership," *Journal of Applied Psychology*, October 2000, pp. 751–765; B. M. Bass and B. J. Avolio, "Developing Transformational Leadership: 1992 and Beyond," *Journal of European Industrial Training*, January 1990, p. 23; and J. J. Hater and B. M. Bass, "Supervisors' Evaluation and Subordinates' Perceptions of Transformational and Transactional Leadership," *Journal of Applied Psychology*, November 1988, pp. 695–702.
36. Y. Ling, Z. Simsek, M. H. Lubatkin, and J. F. Veiga, "Transformational Leadership's Role in Promoting Corporate Entrepreneurship: Examining the CEO-TMT Interface," *Academy of Management Journal*, June 2008, pp. 557–576; A. E. Colbert, A. L. Kristof-Brown, B. H. Bradley, and M. R. Barrick, "CEO Transformational Leadership: The Role of Goal Importance Congruence in Top Management Teams," *Academy of Management Journal*, February 2008, pp. 81–96; R. F. Piccolo and J. A. Colquitt, "Transformational Leadership and Job Behaviors: The Mediating Role of Core Job Characteristics," *Academy of Management Journal*, April 2006, pp. 327–340; O. Epitropaki and R. Martin, "From Ideal to Real: A Longitudinal Study of the Role of Implicit Leadership Theories on Leader–Member Exchanges and Employee Outcomes," *Journal of Applied Psychology*, July 2005, pp. 659–676; J. E. Bono and T. A. Judge, "Self-Concordance at Work: Toward Understanding the Motivational Effects of Transformational Leaders," *Academy of Management Journal*, October 2003, pp. 554–571; T. Dvir, D. Eden, B. J. Avolio, and B. Shamir, "Impact of Transformational Leadership on Follower Development and Performance: A Field Experiment," *Academy of Management Journal*, August 2002, pp. 735–744; N. Sivasubramaniam, W. D. Murry, B. J. Avolio, and D. I. Jung, "A Longitudinal Model of the Effects of Team Leadership and Group Potency on Group Performance," *Group and Organization Management*, March 2002, pp. 66–96; J. M. Howell and B. J. Avolio, "Transformational Leadership, Transactional Leadership, Locus of Control, and Support for Innovation: Key Predictors of Consolidated-Business-Unit Performance," *Journal of Applied Psychology*, December 1993, pp. 891–911; R. T. Keller, "Transformational Leadership and the Performance of Research and Development Project Groups," *Journal of Management*, September 1992, pp. 489–501; and Bass and Avolio, "Developing Transformational Leadership."
37. F. Vogelstein, "Mighty Amazon," *Fortune*, May 26, 2003, pp. 60–74.
38. F. Walter and H. Bruch, "An Affective Events Model of Charismatic Leadership Behavior: A Review, Theoretical Integration, and Research Agenda," *Journal of Management*, December 2009, pp. 1428–1452; A. Pentland, "We Can Measure the Power of Charisma," *Harvard Business Review*, January–February 2010, pp. 34–35; J. M. Crant and T. S. Bateman, "Charismatic Leadership Viewed from Above: The Impact of Proactive Personality," *Journal of Organizational Behavior*, February 2000, pp. 63–75; G. Yukl and J. M. Howell, "Organizational and Contextual Influences on the Emergence and Effectiveness of Charismatic Leadership," *Leadership Quarterly*, Summer 1999, pp. 257–283; and J. A. Conger and R. N. Kanungo, "Behavioral Dimensions of Charismatic Leadership," in J. A. Conger, R. N. Kanungo et al., *Charismatic Leadership* (San Francisco: Jossey-Bass, 1988), pp. 78–97.

39. J. A. Conger and R. N. Kanungo, *Charismatic Leadership in Organizations* (Thousand Oaks, CA: Sage, 1998).
40. M. Sena, "9 of the Most Inspiring Acts of Leadership," *Fortune* online, www.fortune.com, March 26, 2015.
41. F. Walter and H. Bruch, "An Affective Events Model of Charismatic Leadership Behavior: A Review, Theoretical Investigation, and Research Agenda," *Journal of Management*, December 2009, pp. 1428–1452; K. S. Groves, "Linking Leader Skills, Follower Attitudes, and Contextual Variables via an Integrated Model of Charismatic Leadership," *Journal of Management*, April 2005, pp. 255–277; J. J. Sosik, "The Role of Personal Values in the Charismatic Leadership of Corporate Managers: A Model and Preliminary Field Study," *Leadership Quarterly*, April 2005, pp. 221–244; A. H. B. deHoogh, D. N. den Hartog, P. L. Koopman, H. Thierry, P. T. van den Berg, J. G. van der Weide, and C. P. M. Wilderom, "Leader Motives, Charismatic Leadership, and Subordinates' Work Attitudes in the Profit and Voluntary Sector," *Leadership Quarterly*, February 2005, pp. 17–38; J. M. Howell and B. Shamir, "The Role of Followers in the Charismatic Leadership Process: Relationships and Their Consequences," *Academy of Management Review*, January 2005, pp. 96–112; J. Paul, D. L. Costley, J. P. Howell, P. W. Dorfman, and D. Trafimow, "The Effects of Charismatic Leadership on Followers' Self-Concept Accessibility," *Journal of Applied Social Psychology*, September 2001, pp. 1821–1844; J. A. Conger, R. N. Kanungo, and S. T. Menon, "Charismatic Leadership and Follower Effects," *Journal of Organizational Behavior*, vol. 21, 2000, pp. 747–767; R. W. Rowden, "The Relationship Between Charismatic Leadership Behaviors and Organizational Commitment," *Leadership & Organization Development Journal*, January 2000, pp. 30–35; G. P. Shea and C. M. Howell, "Charismatic Leadership and Task Feedback: A Laboratory Study of Their Effects on Self-Efficacy," *Leadership Quarterly*, Fall 1999, pp. 375–396; S. A. Kirkpatrick and E. A. Locke, "Direct and Indirect Effects of Three Core Charismatic Leadership Components on Performance and Attitudes," *Journal of Applied Psychology*, February 1996, pp. 36–51; D. A. Waldman, B. M. Bass, and F. J. Yammarino, "Adding to Contingent-Reward Behavior: The Augmenting Effect of Charismatic Leadership," *Group & Organization Studies*, December 1990, pp. 381–394; and R. J. House, J. Woycke, and E. M. Fodor, "Charismatic and Noncharismatic Leaders: Differences in Behavior and Effectiveness," in Conger and Kanungo, *Charismatic Leadership*, pp. 103–104.
42. B. R. Agle, N. J. Nagarajan, J. A. Sonnenfeld, and D. Srinivasan, "Does CEO Charisma Matter? An Empirical Analysis of the Relationships Among Organizational Performance, Environmental Uncertainty, and Top Management Team Perceptions of CEO Charisma," *Academy of Management Journal*, February 2006, pp. 161–174.
43. J. Antonakis, M. Fenley, and S. Liechti, "Learning Charisma," *Harvard Business Review*, June 2012, pp. 127–130; J. Antonakis, M. Fenley, and S. Liechti, "Can Charisma Be Taught? Tests of Two Interventions," *Academy of Management Learning & Education*, September 2011, pp. 374–396; R. Birchfield, "Creating Charismatic Leaders," *Management*, June 2000, pp. 30–31; S. Caudron, "Growing Charisma," *Industry Week*, May 4, 1998, pp. 54–55; and J. A. Conger and R. N. Kanungo, "Training Charismatic Leadership: A Risky and Critical Task," in Conger and Kanungo, *Charismatic Leadership*, pp. 309–323.
44. J. Antonakis et al., "Learning Charisma."
45. J. G. Hunt, K. B. Boal, and G. E. Dodge, "The Effects of Visionary and Crisis-Responsive Charisma on Followers: An Experimental Examination," *Leadership Quarterly*, Fall 1999, pp. 423–448; R. J. House and R. N. Aditya, "The Social Scientific Study of Leadership: Quo Vadis?," *Journal of Management*, vol. 23, no. 3, 1997, pp. 316–323; and R. J. House, "A 1976 Theory of Charismatic Leadership." In J. G. Hunt & L. L. Larson (Eds.), Leadership: The cutting edge (pp. 189–207). Carbondale, IL: Southern Illinois University, 1977.
46. This definition is based on M. Sashkin, "The Visionary Leader," in Conger and Kanungo et al., *Charismatic Leadership*, pp. 124–125; B. Nanus, *Visionary Leadership* (San Francisco: Jossey-Bass, 1992), p. 8; N. H. Snyder and M. Graves, "Leadership and Vision," *Business Horizons*, January–February 1994, p. 1; and J. R. Lucas, "Anatomy of a Vision Statement," *Management Review*, February 1998, pp. 22–26.
47. B. Nanus, *Visionary Leadership* (San Francisco: Jossey-Bass, 1992), p. 8.
48. Chris Chang, "Alibaba's 'Dream-driven' Vision for Taking Over the World," *News.com Australia*, November 1, 2016, http://www.news.com.au/finance/business/retail/alibabas-dreamdriven-vision-for-taking-over-the-world/news-story/69473a9c2404811bef65b69eba4ed5df (accessed January 10, 2017); Jonathen Ringen, "How LEGO Became the Apple of Toys," *Fast Company*, January 8, 2015, https://www.fastcompany.com/3040223/when-it-clicks-it-clicks (accessed January 10, 2017).
49. Ashwin Naik, "Empathy, Not Bureaucracy, Makes Organizations Great; Leadership Lessons from Anand Mahindra," *Forbes*, July 6, 2016, http://www.forbes.com/sites/chrismyers/2017/01/01/this-entrepreneurs-3-new-years-resolutions-for-2017/#557ff4b9140c (accessed January 6, 2017); Reshma Kapadia, "Anand Mahindra: Mahindra & Mahindra, Managing Director Since 1997," *Barron's*, March 19, 2016, http://www.barrons.com/articles/profiles-of-the-worlds-best-ceos-1458364872 (accessed January 6, 2017).
50. S. P. Robbins and T. A. Judge, *Organizational Behavior*, 17th ed. (Boston: Pearson Education, Inc., 2017)
51. P. Economy, "Top 10 Skills Every Great Leader Needs to Succeed," *Inc* online, www.inc.com, December 29, 2014.
52. G. Loftus, "Mary Barra's Leadership Legacy," *Forbes* online, www.fortune.com, March 19, 2014.
53. Ibid.
54. S. Caminiti, "What Team Leaders Need to Know," *Fortune*, February 20, 1995, pp. 93–100.
55. Ibid. p. 93.
56. Ibid. p. 100.
57. N. Lankarani, "Bold Decisions Require Cool Analysis," *The New York Times* online, www.nytimes.com, April 24, 2016.
58. A. Bryant, "Jane Rosenthal: Keep Coaxing Out the Spark in Others," *The New York Times* online, www.nytimees.com, May 20, 2016.

59. S. B. Sitkin and J. R. Hackman, "Developing Team Leadership: An Interview with Coach Mike Krzyzewski," *Academy of Management Learning and Education*, September 2011, pp. 494–501; and N. Steckler and N. Fondas, "Building Team Leader Effectiveness: A Diagnostic Tool," *Organizational Dynamics*, Winter 1995, p. 20.
60. R. S. Wellins, W. C. Byham, and G. R. Dixon, *Inside Teams* (San Francisco: Jossey-Bass, 1994), p. 318.
61. Steckler and Fondas, "Building Team Leader Effectiveness," p. 21.
62. Annie Bricker, "Man of the People," *Computer News Middle East*, January 18, 2016, http://www.cnmeonline.com/cio-spotlight/man-of-the-people/ (accessed January 6, 2017).
63. See J. R. P. French Jr. and B. Raven, "The Bases of Social Power," in *Group Dynamics: Research and Theory*, ed. D. Cartwright and A. F. Zander (New York: Harper & Row, 1960), pp. 607–623; P. M. Podsakoff and C. A. Schriesheim, "Field Studies of French and Raven's Bases of Power: Critique, Reanalysis, and Suggestions for Future Research," *Psychological Bulletin*, May 1985, pp. 387–411; R. K. Shukla, "Influence of Power Bases in Organizational Decision Making: A Contingency Model," *Decision Sciences*, July 1982, pp. 450–470; D. E. Frost and A. J. Stahelski, "The Systematic Measurement of French and Raven's Bases of Social Power in Workgroups," *Journal of Applied Social Psychology*, April 1988, pp. 375–389; and T. R. Hinkin and C. A. Schriesheim, "Development and Application of New Scales to Measure the French and Raven (1959) Bases of Social Power," *Journal of Applied Psychology*, August 1989, pp. 561–567.
64. D. Sturt and T. Nordstrom, "5 Traits of the Worst Leaders and How to Avoid Them," *Forbes* online, www.forbes.com, April 28, 2016.
65. J. M. Kouzes and B. Z. Posner, *Credibility: How Leaders Gain and Lose It, and Why People Demand It* (San Francisco: Jossey-Bass, 1993), p. 14.
66. Based on F. D. Schoorman, R. C. Mayer, and J. H. Davis, "An Integrative Model of Organizational Trust: Past, Present, and Future," *Academy of Management Review*, April 2007, pp. 344–354; G. M. Spreitzer and A. K. Mishra, "Giving up Control Without Losing Control," *Group & Organization Management*, June 1999, pp. 155–187; R. C. Mayer, J. H. Davis, and F. D. Schoorman, "An Integrative Model of Organizational Trust," *Academy of Management Review*, July 1995, p. 712; and L. T. Hosmer, "Trust: The Connecting Link Between Organizational Theory and Philosophical Ethics," *Academy of Management Review*, April 1995, p. 393.
67. P. L. Schindler and C. C. Thomas, "The Structure of Interpersonal Trust in the Workplace," *Psychological Reports*, October 1993, pp. 563–573.
68. H. H. Tan and C. S. F. Tan, "Toward the Differentiation of Trust in Supervisor and Trust in Organization," *Genetic, Social, and General Psychology Monographs*, May 2000, pp. 241–260.
69. H. H. Brower, S. W. Lester, M. A. Korsgaard, and B. R. Dineen, "A Closer Look at Trust Between Managers and Subordinates: Understanding the Effects of Both Trusting and Being Trusted on Subordinate Outcomes," *Journal of Management*, April 2009, pp. 327–347; R. C. Mayer and M. B. Gavin, "Trust in Management and Performance: Who Minds the Shop While the Employees Watch the Boss?" *Academy of Management Journal*, October 2005, pp. 874–888; and K. T. Dirks and D. L. Ferrin, "Trust in Leadership: Meta-Analytic Findings and Implications for Research and Practice," *Journal of Applied Psychology*, August 2002, pp. 611–628.
70. See, for example, Dirks and Ferrin, "Trust in Leadership: Meta-Analytic Findings and Implications for Research and Practice"; J. K. Butler Jr., "Toward Understanding and Measuring Conditions of Trust: Evolution of a Conditions of Trust Inventory," *Journal of Management*, September 1991, pp. 643–663; and F. Bartolome, "Nobody Trusts the Boss Completely—Now What?" *Harvard Business Review*, March–April 1989, pp. 135–142.
71. P. H. Kim, K. T. Dirks, and C. D. Cooper, "The Repair of Trust: A Dynamic Bilateral Perspective and Multilevel Conceptualization," *Academy of Management Review*, July 2009, pp. 401–422; R. Zemke, "The Confidence Crisis," *Training*, June 2004, pp. 22–30; J. A. Byrne, "Restoring Trust in Corporate America," *BusinessWeek*, June 24, 2002, pp. 30–35; S. Armour, "Employees' New Motto: Trust No One," *USA Today*, February 5, 2002, p. 1B; J. Scott, "Once Bitten, Twice Shy: A World of Eroding Trust," *New York Times*, April 21, 2002, p. WK5; J. Brockner, P. A. Siegel, J. P. Daly, T. Tyler, and C. Martin, "When Trust Matters: The Moderating Effect of Outcome Favorability," *Administrative Science Quarterly*, September 1997, p. 558; and J. Brockner, P. A. Siegel, J. P. Daly, T. Tyler, and C. Martin, "When Trust Matters: The Moderating Effect of Outcome Favorability," *Administrative Science Quarterly*, September 1997, p. 558.
72. T. Vinas, "DuPont: Safety Starts at the Top," *Industry Week*, July 2002, p. 55.
73. A. Srivastava, K. M. Bartol, and E. A. Locke, "Empowering Leadership in Management Teams: Effects on Knowledge Sharing, Efficacy, and Performance," *Academy of Management Journal*, December 2006, pp. 1239–1251; P. K. Mills and G. R. Ungson, "Reassessing the Limits of Structural Empowerment: Organizational Constitution and Trust as Controls," *Academy of Management Review*, January 2003, pp. 143–153; W. A. Rudolph and M. Sashkin, "Can Organizational Empowerment Work in Multinational Settings?," *Academy of Management Executive*, February 2002, pp. 102–115; C. Gomez and B. Rosen, "The Leader–Member Link Between Managerial Trust and Employee Empowerment," *Group & Organization Management*, March 2001, pp. 53–69; C. Robert and T. M. Probst, "Empowerment and Continuous Improvement in the United States, Mexico, Poland, and India," *Journal of Applied Psychology*, October 2000, pp. 643–658; R. C. Herrenkohl, G. T. Judson, and J. A. Heffner, "Defining and Measuring Employee Empowerment," *Journal of Applied Behavioral Science*, September 1999, p. 373; R. C. Ford and M. D. Fottler, "Empowerment: A Matter of Degree," *Academy of Management Executive*, August 1995, pp. 21–31; and W. A. Rudolph, "Navigating the Journey to Empowerment," *Organizational Dynamics*, Spring 1995, pp. 19–32.
74. T. A. Stewart, "Just Think: No Permission Needed," *Fortune*, January 8, 2001, pp. 190–192.
75. M. Elliott, "Who Needs Charisma?" *Time*, July 20, 2009, pp. 35–38.

76. A. Ignatius and D. McGinn, "Novo Nordisk CEO Lars Sørensen on What Propelled Him to the Top," *Harvard Business Review*, November 2015.
77. House, "Leadership in the Twenty-First Century," p. 443; M. F. Peterson and J. G. Hunt, "International Perspectives on International Leadership," *Leadership Quarterly*, Fall 1997, pp. 203–231; and J. R. Schermerhorn and M. H. Bond, "Cross-Cultural Leadership in Collectivism and High Power Distance Settings," *Leadership & Organization Development Journal*, vol. 18, no. 4/5, 1997, pp. 187–193.
78. R. J. House, P. J. Hanges, S. A. Ruiz-Quintanilla, P. W. Dorfman et al., "Culture Specific and Cross-Culturally Generalizable Implicit Leadership Theories: Are the Attributes of Charismatic/Transformational Leadership Universally Endorsed?," *Leadership Quarterly*, Summer 1999, pp. 219–256; and D. E. Carl and M. Javidan, "Universality of Charismatic Leadership: A Multi-Nation Study," paper presented at the National Academy of Management Conference, Washington, DC, August 2001.
79. D. E. Carl and M. Javidan, "Universality of Charismatic Leadership: A Multi-Nation Study," paper presented at the National Academy of Management Conference, Washington, DC, August 2001.
80. 2015 Training Industry Report, *Training*, November/December 2015, pp. 20–33.
81. See, for example, D. S. DeRue and N. Wellman, "Developing Leaders via Experience: The Role of Developmental Challenge, Learning Organization, and Feedback Availability," *Journal of Applied Psychology*, July 2009, pp. 859–875; A. A. Vicere, "Executive Education: The Leading Edge," *Organizational Dynamics*, Autumn 1996, pp. 67–81; J. Barling, T. Weber, and E. K. Kelloway, "Effects of Transformational Leadership Training on Attitudinal and Financial Outcomes: A Field Experiment," *Journal of Applied Psychology*, December 1996, pp. 827–832; and D. V. Day, "Leadership Development: A Review in Context," *Leadership Quarterly*, Winter 2000, pp. 581–613.
82. G. Petriglieri, "How to Really Customize Leadership Development," *Harvard Business Review* online, www.hbr.org, February 18, 2016.
83. D. Medland, "Today's Gender Reality in Statistics, or Making Leadership Attractive to Women," *Forbes* online, www.forbes.com, March 7, 2016.
84. K. Y. Chan and F. Drasgow, "Toward a Theory of Individual Differences and Leadership: Understanding the Motivation to Lead," *Journal of Applied Psychology*, June 2001, pp. 481–498.
85. M. Sashkin, "The Visionary Leader," in *Charismatic Leadership, ed.* J. A. Conger, R. N. Kanungo et al. (San Francisco: Jossey-Bass, 1988), p. 150.
86. S. Kerr and J. M. Jermier, "Substitutes for Leadership: Their Meaning and Measurement," *Organizational Behavior and Human Performance*, December 1978, pp. 375–403; J. P. Howell, P. W. Dorfman, and S. Kerr, "Leadership and Substitutes for Leadership," *Journal of Applied Behavioral Science* 22, no. 1, 1986, pp. 29–46; J. P. Howell, D. E. Bowen, P. W. Dorfman, S. Kerr, and P. M. Podsakoff, "Substitutes for Leadership: Effective Alternatives to Ineffective Leadership," *Organizational Dynamics*, Summer 1990, pp. 21–38; and P. M. Podsakoff, B. P. Niehoff, S. B. MacKenzie, and M. L. Williams, "Do Substitutes for Leadership Really Substitute for Leadership? An Empirical Examination of Kerr and Jermier's Situational Leadership Model," *Organizational Behavior and Human Decision Processes*, February 1993, pp. 1–44.
87. "The David Rubenstein Show: Indra Nooyi," *Bloomberg*, November 23, 2016, https://www.bloomberg.com; Jennifer Reingold, "PepsiCo's CEO was Right. Now what?," *Fortune*, June 5, 2015, http://fortune.com; Marcus Fairs, ""Design is improving the top line and the bottom line," says PepsiCo CEO," Dezeen, May 4, 2016, https://www.dezeen.com; and Jane Burkit, "Why Quotas are Out and Openness is in at PepsiCo", *The Guardian*, April 17, 2013 https://www.theguardian.com.
88. J. Faragher, "Get the Leader You Deserve," *People Management*, October, 2014, pp. 22–26; T. Team, "The Secret Sauce for Success in The Aggressive Beauty Business," *Forbes* online, www.forbes.com, April 13, 2015; H. Hong and Y. Doz, "L'Oreal Masters Multiculturalism," *Harvard Business Review* online, www.hbr.org, June, 2013; "ECI Honors L'Oréal's Top Ethics Officer for Leadership in Corporate Ethics," *ECI Connector* online, http://connects.ethics.org, January 21, 2016; www.ethisphere.com, www.loreal.com.

Chapter 17 Motivation

It's Your Career

Source: Artplay711/iStock/Getty

What Motivates You?

What's important to you or excites you in a job? Some say "money." Others might say "challenging work" or "fun coworkers." If you have a solid grounding in and understanding of what motivates you, it can help you make smart career and job choices.

The following is a list of 12 factors that might enter into your decision in selecting a job. Read over the list. Then rank order the items in terms of importance, with 1 being highest in importance and 12 being lowest in importance.

A key to success in management and in your career is knowing what motivates YOU.

________*High pay*
________*Good working conditions*
________*Friendly and supportive colleagues*
________*Flexible working hours*
________*Opportunities for growth and new challenges*
________*Considerate boss*
________*Inclusion in decisions that affect you*
________*Fair and equitable treatment*
________*Job security*
________*Promotion potential*
________*Excellent benefits (vacation time, retirement contributions, etc.)*
________*Freedom and independence*

Now, compare your list with others in your class. How similar were your preferences? It's rare for lists to be exactly the same. This tells us that people differ in terms of what they value. Second, use these results to better understand what you're looking for in a job.

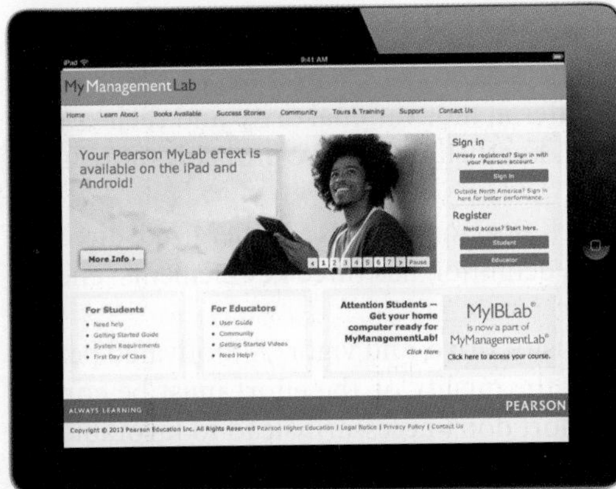

Learning Objectives

17.1 ***Define*** *motivation.*

17.2 ***Compare*** *and contrast early theories of motivation.*

17.3 ***Compare*** *and contrast contemporary theories of motivation.*

- **Develop your skill** at motivating employees.

17.4 ***Discuss*** *current issues in motivation.*

- **Know how** to identify what motivates you.

Successful managers need to understand that what motivates them personally may have little or no effect on others. Just because *you're* motivated by being part of a cohesive work team, don't assume everyone is. Or just because *you're* motivated by your job doesn't mean that everyone is. Effective managers who get employees to put forth maximum effort know how and why those employees are motivated and tailor motivational practices to satisfy their needs and wants.

WHAT is motivation?

LO17.1 Jetstar Asia, a low-fare carrier based in Singapore, encourages its cabin crew to share compliments with the entire workforce via internal social media. When passengers say good things about crew members, everyone in the organization hears the news and is proud of their peers and their employer. Similarly, when employees take part in corporate social responsibility activities, they share their experiences with colleagues. Jetstar Asia also operates Bravo, a social media system where employees can compliment colleagues for actions that embody the airline's values. The airline holds quarterly and yearly award ceremonies for Bravo winners. One recent winner was honored for expediting the return of a passenger's wallet inadvertently left behind in a hotel miles away. An airline with personality, Jetstar Asia encourages cabin crew to celebrate special days like Singapore's National Day with fun events during flights. The airline has a mentoring program for younger employees and a "Career Progression" plan for older employees that want to transition to specialized or non-flight positions as their circumstances change. No wonder Jetstar Asia's employees of all ages and at all levels are engaged and motivated.[1]

Have you *ever even thought about* how to motivate someone? It's an important topic in management, and researchers have long been interested in it.[2] All managers need to be able to motivate their employees, which first requires understanding what motivation is. Let's begin by pointing out what motivation is not. Why? Because many people incorrectly view motivation as a personal trait; that is, they think some people are motivated and others aren't. Our knowledge of motivation tells us that we can't label people that way because individuals differ in motivational drive and their overall motivation varies from situation to situation. For instance, you're probably more motivated in some classes than in others.

motivation
The process by which a person's efforts are energized, directed, and sustained toward attaining a goal

Motivation refers to the process by which a person's efforts are energized, directed, and sustained toward attaining a goal.[3] This definition has three key elements: energy, direction, and persistence.[4]

The *energy* element is a measure of intensity, drive, and vigor. A motivated person puts forth effort and works hard. However, the quality of the effort must be considered as well as its intensity. High levels of effort don't necessarily lead to favorable job performance unless the effort is channeled in a *direction* that benefits the organization. Effort directed toward and consistent with organizational goals is the kind of effort we want from employees. Finally, motivation includes a *persistence* dimension. We want employees to persist in putting forth effort to achieve those goals.

Motivating high levels of employee performance is an important organizational concern, and managers keep looking for answers. For instance, a Gallup Poll found a large majority of U.S. employees—some 68 percent—are disengaged.[5] As the researchers stated, "These employees have essentially 'checked out.' They're sleepwalking through their workday, putting time, but not energy or passion, into their work."[6] The number globally is even more disturbing—some 87 percent are not excited about their work.[7] It's no wonder then that both managers and academics want to understand and explain employee motivation.

Motivators for employees of Procter & Gamble's factory in Urlati, Romania, include satisfying their lower-order needs of a salary, a safe job, benefits, and job security. According to Maslow's hierarchy of needs theory, after these needs are met, managers can motivate them by forming work groups and giving them opportunities for socializing to satisfy their needs of friendship and belongingness.
Source: Aga Luczakowska/Bloomberg/Getty Images

EARLY theories of motivation

LO17.2 We begin by looking at four early motivation theories: *Maslow's hierarchy of needs*, *McGregor's Theories X and Y*, *Herzberg's two-factor theory*, and *McClelland's three-needs theory*. Although more valid explanations of motivation have been developed, these early theories are important because they represent the foundation from which contemporary motivation theories were developed and because many practicing managers still use them.

Maslow's Hierarchy of Needs Theory

Having a car to get to work is a necessity for many workers. When two crucial employees of Vurv Technology in Jacksonville, Florida, had trouble getting to work, owner Derek Mercer decided to buy two inexpensive used cars for the employees. One of the employees who got one of the cars said it wasn't the nicest or prettiest car, but it gave him such a sense of relief to know that he had a reliable way to get to work. So when the company needed him to work hard, he was willing to do so.[8] Derek Mercer understands employee needs and their impact on motivation. The first motivation theory we're going to look at addresses employee needs.

hierarchy of needs theory
Maslow's theory that human needs—physiological, safety, social, esteem, and self-actualization—form a sort of hierarchy

physiological needs
A person's needs for food, drink, shelter, sexual satisfaction, and other physical needs

safety needs
A person's needs for security and protection from physical and emotional harm

The best-known theory of motivation is probably Abraham Maslow's **hierarchy of needs theory**.[9] Maslow was a psychologist who proposed that within every person is a hierarchy of five needs:

1. **Physiological needs**: A person's needs for food, drink, shelter, sex, and other physical requirements.
2. **Safety needs**: A person's needs for security and protection from physical and emotional harm as well as assurance that physical needs will continue to be met.
3. **Social needs**: A person's needs for affection, belongingness, acceptance, and friendship.
4. **Esteem needs**: A person's needs for internal esteem factors such as self-respect, autonomy, and achievement and external esteem factors such as status, recognition, and attention.

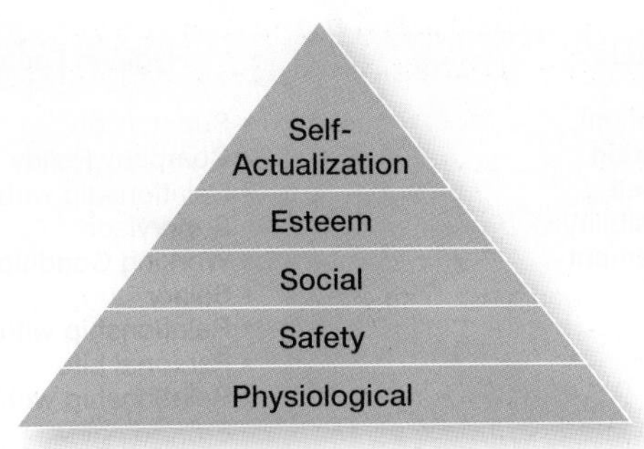

Exhibit 17-1
Maslow's Hierarchy of Needs

Source: A. H. Maslow, R. D. Frager, and J. Fadiman, *Motivation and Personality*, 3rd Edition, © 1987. Reprinted and electronically reproduced by permission of Pearson Education, Inc., Upper Saddle River, NJ.

5. **Self-actualization needs**: A person's needs for growth, achieving one's potential, and self-fulfillment; the drive to become what one is capable of becoming.

social needs
A person's needs for affection, belongingness, acceptance, and friendship

esteem needs
A person's needs for internal factors such as self-respect, autonomy, and achievement, and external factors such as status, recognition, and attention

self-actualization needs
A person's need to become what he or she is capable of becoming

Maslow argued that each level in the needs hierarchy must be substantially satisfied before the next need becomes dominant. An individual moves up the needs hierarchy from one level to the next. (See Exhibit 17-1.) In addition, Maslow separated the five needs into higher and lower levels. Physiological and safety needs were considered *lower-order needs*; social, esteem, and self-actualization needs were considered *higher-order needs.* Lower-order needs are predominantly satisfied externally while higher-order needs are satisfied internally.

How does Maslow's theory explain motivation? Managers using Maslow's hierarchy to motivate employees do things to satisfy employees' needs. But the theory also says that once a need is substantially satisfied, an individual is no longer motivated to satisfy that need. Therefore, to motivate someone, you need to understand at what need level that person is on in the hierarchy and focus on satisfying needs at or above that level.

Maslow's needs theory was widely recognized during the 1960s and 1970s, especially among practicing managers, probably because it was intuitively logical and easy to understand. But Maslow provided no empirical support for his theory, and several studies that sought to validate it could not.[10]

McGregor's Theory X and Theory Y

Andy Grove, cofounder of Intel Corporation and now a senior advisor to the company, was known for being open with his employees. However, he was also known for his tendency to yell. Intel's current CEO, Paul Otellini, said, "When Andy was yelling at you, it wasn't because he didn't care about you. He was yelling at you because he wanted you to do better."[11] Although managers like Andy Grove want their employees to do better, that approach might not have been the best way to motivate employees, as McGregor's Theory X and Theory Y suggest.

Douglas McGregor is best known for proposing two assumptions about human nature: Theory X and Theory Y.[12] Very simply, **Theory X** is a negative view of people that assumes workers have little ambition, dislike work, want to avoid responsibility, and need to be closely controlled to work effectively. **Theory Y** is a positive view that assumes employees enjoy work, seek out and accept responsibility, and exercise self-direction. McGregor believed that Theory Y assumptions should guide management practice and proposed that participation in decision making, responsible and challenging jobs, and good group relations would maximize employee motivation. For example, Walmart gives workers a significant role in decision making. Store associates can provide input into what is sold locally. The company relies on associates' judgment because they interact with customers. Walmart's U.S. CEO stated: "There is nothing I like better than hearing about your [associates'] jobs, your ideas, your hopes and dreams, and frustrations, and listening to how we can make your lives easier."[13] Clearly, this is an example of Walmart putting the philosophy of Theory Y management into practice.

Theory X
The assumption that employees dislike work, are lazy, avoid responsibility, and must be coerced to perform

Theory Y
The assumption that employees are creative, enjoy work, seek responsibility, and can exercise self-direction

Exhibit 17-2
Herzberg's Two-Factor Theory

Source: Based on F. Herzberg, B. Mausner, and B. B. Snyderman, *The Motivation to Work* (New York: John Wiley, 1959).

Motivators		Hygiene Factors
• Achievement • Recognition • Work Itself • Responsibility • Advancement • Growth		• Supervision • Company Policy • Relationship with Supervisor • Working Conditions • Salary • Relationship with Peers • Personal Life • Relationship with Subordinates • Status • Security
Extremely Satisfied	Neutral	Extremely Dissatisfied

- What motivates employees? A survey showed the following in order of importance:[15]

96 percent	Salary
95 percent	Job security
92 percent	My supervisor/manager
91 percent	Training
91 percent	Performance feedback
89 percent	Leadership
87 percent	Vacation/paid time off
85 percent	Career advancement
81 percent	Involved in decisions
75 percent	Corporate culture

Unfortunately, no evidence confirms that either set of assumptions is valid or that being a Theory Y manager is the only way to motivate employees. For instance, Jen-Hsun Huang, founder of Nvidia Corporation, an innovative and successful microchip manufacturer, has been known to use both reassuring hugs and tough love in motivating employees. He also has little tolerance for screw-ups. In one meeting, he supposedly screamed at a project team for its tendency to repeat mistakes. "Do you suck?" he asked the stunned employees. "Because if you suck, just get up and say you suck."[14] His message, delivered in classic Theory X style, was that if you need help, ask for it. It's a harsh approach, but in this case, it worked as employees knew they had to own up to their mistakes and find ways to address them.

Herzberg's Two-Factor Theory

Frederick Herzberg's **two-factor theory** (also called **motivation–hygiene theory**) proposes that intrinsic factors are related to job satisfaction, while extrinsic factors are associated with job dissatisfaction.[16] Herzberg wanted to know when people felt exceptionally good (satisfied) or bad (dissatisfied) about their jobs. (These findings are shown in Exhibit 17-2.) He concluded that the replies people gave when they felt good about their jobs were significantly different from the replies they gave when they felt bad. Certain characteristics were consistently related to job satisfaction (factors on the left side of the exhibit), and others to job dissatisfaction (factors on the right side). When people felt good about their work, they tended to cite intrinsic factors arising from the job itself such as achievement, recognition, and responsibility. On the other hand, when they were dissatisfied, they tended to cite extrinsic factors arising from the job context such as company policy and administration, supervision, interpersonal relationships, and working conditions.

In addition, Herzberg believed the data suggested that the opposite of satisfaction was not dissatisfaction, as traditionally had been believed. Removing dissatisfying characteristics from a job would not necessarily make that job more satisfying (or motivating). As shown in Exhibit 17-3, Herzberg proposed that a dual continuum existed: The opposite of "satisfaction" is "no satisfaction," and the opposite of "dissatisfaction" is "no dissatisfaction."

two-factor theory (motivation–hygiene theory)
The motivation theory that intrinsic factors are related to job satisfaction and motivation, whereas extrinsic factors are associated with job dissatisfaction

Again, Herzberg believed the factors that led to job satisfaction were separate and distinct from those that led to job dissatisfaction. Therefore, managers who sought to eliminate factors that created job dissatisfaction could keep people from being dissatisfied but not necessarily motivate them. The extrinsic factors that create job dissatisfaction were called **hygiene factors**. When these factors are adequate, people won't be dissatisfied, but they won't be satisfied (or motivated) either. To motivate people, Herzberg suggested emphasizing **motivators**, the intrinsic factors having to do with the job itself.

hygiene factors
Factors that eliminate job dissatisfaction, but don't motivate

motivators
Factors that increase job satisfaction and motivation

Herzberg's theory enjoyed wide popularity from the mid-1960s to the early 1980s, despite criticisms of his procedures and methodology. Although some critics said his theory was too simplistic, it has influenced how we currently design jobs, especially when it comes to job enrichment, which we'll discuss at a later point in this chapter.

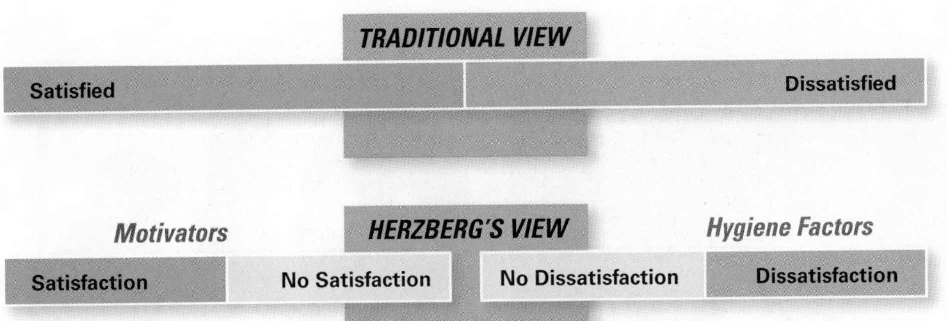

Exhibit 17-3
Contrasting Views of Satisfaction–Dissatisfaction

If your professor has assigned this, go to **www.mymanagementlab.com** to watch a video titled: *Rudi's Bakery: Motivation* and to respond to questions.

Three-Needs Theory

David McClelland and his associates proposed the **three-needs theory**, which says three acquired (not innate) needs are major motives in work.[17] These three are the **need for achievement (nAch)**, the drive to succeed and excel in relation to a set of standards; the **need for power (nPow)**, the need to make others behave in a way they would not have behaved otherwise; and the **need for affiliation (nAff)**, the desire for friendly and close interpersonal relationships. Of these three needs, the need for achievement has been researched the most.

three-needs theory
The motivation theory that says three acquired (not innate) needs—achievement, power, and affiliation—are major motives in work

need for achievement (nAch)
The drive to succeed and excel in relation to a set of standards

need for power (nPow)
The need to make others behave in a way that they would not have behaved otherwise

need for affiliation (nAff)
The desire for friendly and close interpersonal relationships

People with a high need for achievement are striving for personal achievement rather than for the trappings and rewards of success. They have a desire to do something better or more efficiently than it's been done before.[18] They prefer jobs in which they can take personal responsibility for finding solutions to problems, in which they can receive rapid and unambiguous feedback on their performance in order to tell whether they're improving, and in which they can set moderately challenging goals. High achievers avoid what they perceive to be very easy or very difficult tasks. Also, a high need to achieve doesn't necessarily lead to being a good manager, especially in large organizations. That's because high achievers focus on their *own* accomplishments, while good managers emphasize helping *others* accomplish their goals.[19] McClelland showed that employees can be trained to stimulate their achievement need by being in situations where they have personal responsibility, feedback, and moderate risks.[20] Indeed, good managers make a difference. One survey indicated that 67 percent of employees whose managers helped them to grow and develop were highly engaged.[21]

The other two needs in this theory haven't been researched as extensively as the need for achievement. However, we do know that the best managers tend to be high in the need for power and low in the need for affiliation.[22]

All three of these needs can be measured by using a projective test (known as the Thematic Apperception Test or TAT), in which respondents react to a set of pictures. Each picture is briefly shown to a person who writes a story based on the picture. (See Exhibit 17-4 for some examples.) Trained interpreters then determine the individual's levels of nAch, nPow, and nAff from the stories written.

If your professor has assigned this, go to **www.mymanagementlab.com** to complete the Writing Assignment MGMT 14: Theories of Motivation.

Exhibit 17-4
TAT Pictures

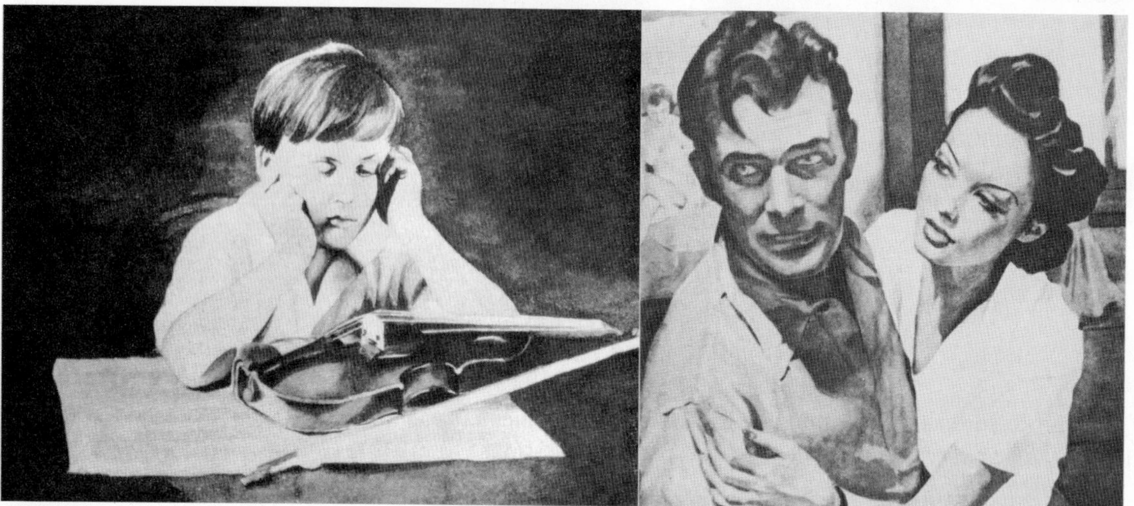

nAch: Indicated by someone in the story wanting to perform or do something better.
nAff: Indicated by someone in the story wanting to be with someone else and enjoy mutual friendship.
nPow: Indicated by someone in the story desiring to have an impact or make an impression on others in the story.

Photo Source: Bill Aron/PhotoEdit

CONTEMPORARY **theories of motivation**

LO17.3 The theories we look at in this section represent current explanations of employee motivation. Although these theories may not be as well known as those we just discussed, they are supported by research.[23] These contemporary motivation approaches include goal-setting theory, reinforcement theory, job design theory, equity theory, expectancy theory, and high-involvement work practices.

Goal-Setting Theory

At Wyeth's research division, scientists were given challenging new product quotas in an attempt to bring more efficiency to the innovation process, and their bonuses were contingent on meeting those goals.[24] Before a big assignment or major class project presentation, has a teacher ever encouraged you to "Just do your best"? What does that vague statement mean? Would your performance on a class project have been higher had that teacher said you needed to score a 93 percent to keep your A in the class? Research on goal-setting theory addresses these issues, and the findings, as you'll see, are impressive in terms of the effect that goal specificity, challenge, and feedback have on performance.[25]

goal-setting theory
The proposition that specific goals increase performance and that difficult goals, when accepted, result in higher performance than do easy goals

Research provides substantial support for **goal-setting theory**, which says that specific goals increase performance and that difficult goals, when accepted, result in higher performance than do easy goals. What does goal-setting theory tell us?

First, working toward a goal is a major source of job motivation. Studies on goal setting have demonstrated that specific and challenging goals are superior motivating forces.[26] Such goals produce a higher output than the generalized goal of "do your best." The specificity of the goal itself acts as an internal stimulus. For instance, when a sales rep commits to making eight sales calls daily, this intention gives him a specific goal to try to attain.

It's not a contradiction that goal-setting theory says that motivation is maximized by *difficult* goals, whereas achievement motivation (from three-needs theory) is stimulated by *moderately challenging* goals.[27] First, goal-setting theory deals with people in general, whereas the conclusions on achievement motivation are based on people who have a high nAch. Given that no more than 10 to 20 percent of North Americans are high achievers (a proportion that's likely lower in underdeveloped countries), difficult goals are still recommended for the majority of employees. Second, the conclusions of goal-setting theory apply to those who accept and are committed to the goals. Difficult goals will lead to higher performance *only* if they are accepted.

Next, will employees try harder if they have the opportunity to participate in the setting of goals? Not always. In some cases, participants who actively set goals elicit superior performance; in other cases, individuals performed best when their manager assigned goals. However, participation is probably preferable to assigning goals when employees might resist accepting difficult challenges.[29]

Finally, we know people will do better if they get feedback on how well they're progressing toward their goals because feedback helps identify discrepancies between what they have done and what they want to do. But all feedback isn't equally effective. Self-generated feedback—where an employee monitors his or her own progress—has been shown to be a more powerful motivator than feedback coming from someone else.[30]

Three other contingencies besides feedback influence the goal-performance relationship: goal commitment, adequate self-efficacy, and national culture.

LEADER making a DIFFERENCE

Source: WENN Ltd/Alamy

What if the group of people you needed to lead and motivate didn't actually work for your company? That's been the challenge faced by ***Susan Wojcicki****, CEO of Google-owned YouTube since 2014.*[28]

No stranger to the tech world before taking the lead at YouTube, Wojcicki was actually the 16th employee hired at Google (in fact, the first few months of Google operations were out of her garage). Her role at YouTube is unique as she needs to motivate both employees and those that provide the content on YouTube, known as "creators." Wojcicki calls the creators the "lifeblood of YouTube," understanding that they are the talent of the company. Many creators depend on making their living through YouTube, generating income from the ads that run before their videos.

Before Wojcicki, the creators had a turbulent relationship with management, describing them as arrogant and closed off from the creators. Wojcicki made the creators her priority, spending time during her first month on the job meeting with them to just listen and take notes. She made an effort to engage the creators by working to understand their needs and goals. In response, she has implemented strategies that help motivate the creators to post their content on YouTube. For example, the company now offers YouTube Spaces which are free production and educational spaces located in six major cities. Creators stay with YouTube because Wojnicki listens and has helped create opportunities for them to pursue their passions. What can you learn from this leader making a difference?

First, goal-setting theory assumes an individual is committed to the goal. Commitment is most likely when goals are made public, when the individual has an internal locus of control, and when the goals are self-set rather than assigned.[31]

Next, **self-efficacy** refers to an individual's belief that he or she is capable of performing a task.[32] The higher your self-efficacy, the more confidence you have in your ability to succeed in a task. So, in difficult situations, we find that people with low self-efficacy are likely to reduce their effort or give up altogether, whereas those with high self-efficacy will try harder to master the challenge.[33] In addition, individuals with high self-efficacy seem to respond to negative feedback with increased effort and motivation, whereas those with low self-efficacy are likely to reduce their effort when given negative feedback.[34]

self-efficacy
An individual's belief that he or she is capable of performing a task

Finally, the value of goal-setting theory depends on national culture. It's well adapted to North American countries because its main ideas align reasonably well with those cultures. It assumes that subordinates will be reasonably independent (not a high score on power distance), that people will seek challenging goals (low in uncertainty avoidance), and that performance is considered important by both managers and subordinates (high in assertiveness). Don't expect goal setting to lead to higher employee performance in countries where the cultural characteristics aren't like this.

Exhibit 17-5 summarizes the relationships among goals, motivation, and performance. Our overall conclusion is that the intention to work toward hard and specific goals is a powerful motivating force. Under the proper conditions, it can lead to higher performance. However, no evidence indicates that such goals are associated with increased job satisfaction.[35]

Exhibit 17-5
Goal-Setting Theory

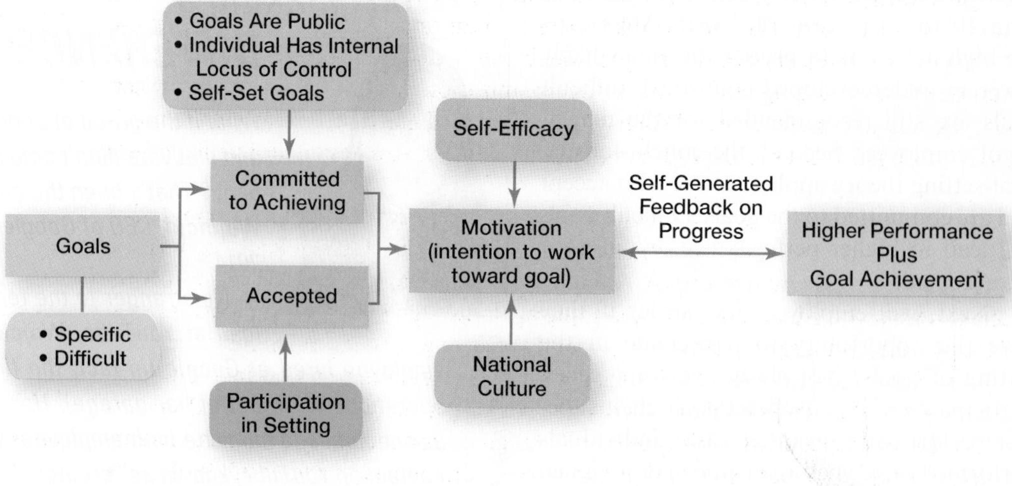

Reinforcement Theory

reinforcement theory
The theory that behavior is a function of its consequences

reinforcers
Consequences immediately following a behavior, which increase the probability that the behavior will be repeated

Reinforcement theory says that behavior is a function of its consequences. Those consequences that immediately follow a behavior and increase the probability that the behavior will be repeated are called **reinforcers**.

Reinforcement theory ignores factors such as goals, expectations, and needs. Instead, it focuses solely on what happens to a person when he or she does something. For instance, Walmart improved its bonus program for hourly employees. Employees who provide outstanding customer service get a cash bonus. And all Walmart hourly full- and part-time store employees are eligible for annual "My$hare" bonuses, which are allocated on store performance and distributed quarterly so that workers are rewarded more frequently.[36] The company's intent: keep the workforce motivated to meet goals by rewarding them when they do, thus reinforcing the behaviors.

In Chapter 15 we showed how managers use reinforcers to shape behavior, but the concept is also widely believed to explain motivation. According to B. F. Skinner, people will most likely engage in desired behaviors if they are rewarded for doing so. These rewards are most effective if they immediately follow a desired behavior; and behavior that isn't rewarded, or is punished, is less likely to be repeated.[37]

Using reinforcement theory, managers can influence employees' behavior by using positive reinforcers for actions that help the organization achieve its goals. And managers should ignore, not punish, undesirable behavior. Although punishment eliminates undesired behavior faster than nonreinforcement, its effect is often temporary and may have unpleasant side effects, including dysfunctional behavior such as workplace conflicts, absenteeism, and turnover. Although reinforcement is an important influence on work behavior, it isn't the only explanation for differences in employee motivation.[38]

- 52 percent of employees say their manager is not interested in their professional development.[39]

Designing Motivating Jobs

Jobs designed with a shorter work day in mind are particularly motivating for employees of some Swedish businesses. Employees of the tech firm Brath aren't expected to work more than six hours a day because, says CEO Maria Brath, "we are very creative—we couldn't keep it up for eight hours." Filimundus, a Swedish app design firm, also has a six-hour work day because "it is a strong motivational factor to be able to go home two hours earlier," notes the CEO. "You still want to do a good job and be productive during six hours, so I think you focus more and are more efficient."[40]

Because managers want to motivate individuals on the job, we need to look at ways to design motivating jobs. If you look closely at what an organization is and how it works, you'll find that it's composed of thousands of tasks. These tasks are, in turn, aggregated into jobs. We use the term **job design** to refer to the way tasks are combined to form complete jobs. The jobs people perform in an organization should not evolve by chance. Managers should design jobs deliberately and thoughtfully to reflect the demands of the changing environment; the organization's technology; and employees' skills, abilities, and preferences.[41] When jobs are designed like that, employees are motivated to work hard. Let's look at some ways that managers can design motivating jobs.[42]

job design
The way tasks are combined to form complete jobs

JOB ENLARGEMENT As we saw in the Management History Module, job design historically has been to make jobs smaller and more specialized. It's difficult to motivate employees when jobs are like this. An early effort at overcoming the drawbacks of job specialization involved horizontally expanding a job through increasing **job scope**—the number of different tasks required in a job and the frequency with which these tasks are repeated. For instance, a dental hygienist's job could be enlarged so that in addition to cleaning teeth, he or she is pulling patients' files, refiling them when finished, and sanitizing and storing instruments. This type of job design option is called **job enlargement**.

job scope
The number of different tasks required in a job and the frequency with which those tasks are repeated

job enlargement
The horizontal expansion of a job by increasing job scope

Most job enlargement efforts that focus solely on increasing the number of tasks don't seem to work. As one employee who experienced such a job redesign said, "Before, I had one lousy job. Now, thanks to job enlargement, I have three lousy jobs!" However, research has shown that *knowledge* enlargement activities (expanding the scope of knowledge used in a job) lead to more job satisfaction, enhanced customer service, and fewer errors.[43]

JOB ENRICHMENT Another approach to job design is the vertical expansion of a job by adding planning and evaluating responsibilities—**job enrichment**. Job enrichment increases **job depth**, which is the degree of control employees have over their work. In other words, employees are empowered to assume some of the tasks typically done by their managers. Thus, an enriched job allows workers to do an entire activity with increased freedom, independence, and responsibility. In addition, workers get feedback so they can assess and correct their own performance. For instance, if our dental hygienist had an enriched job, he or she could, in addition to cleaning teeth, schedule appointments (planning) and follow up with clients (evaluating). Although job enrichment may improve the quality of work, employee motivation, and satisfaction, research evidence has been inconclusive as to its usefulness.[44]

job enrichment
The vertical expansion of a job by adding planning and evaluating responsibilities

job depth
The degree of control employees have over their work

JOB CHARACTERISTICS MODEL Even though many organizations implemented job enlargement and job enrichment programs and experienced mixed results, neither approach provided an effective framework for managers to design motivating jobs. But the **job characteristics model (JCM)** does.[45] It identifies five core job dimensions, their interrelationships, and their impact on employee productivity, motivation, and satisfaction. These five core job dimensions are:

1. **Skill variety**, the degree to which a job requires a variety of activities so that an employee can use a number of different skills and talents.
2. **Task identity**, the degree to which a job requires completion of a whole and identifiable piece of work.
3. **Task significance**, the degree to which a job has a substantial impact on the lives or work of other people.
4. **Autonomy**, the degree to which a job provides substantial freedom, independence, and discretion to the individual in scheduling the work and determining the procedures to be used in carrying it out.
5. **Feedback**, the degree to which doing work activities required by a job results in an individual obtaining direct and clear information about the effectiveness of his or her performance.

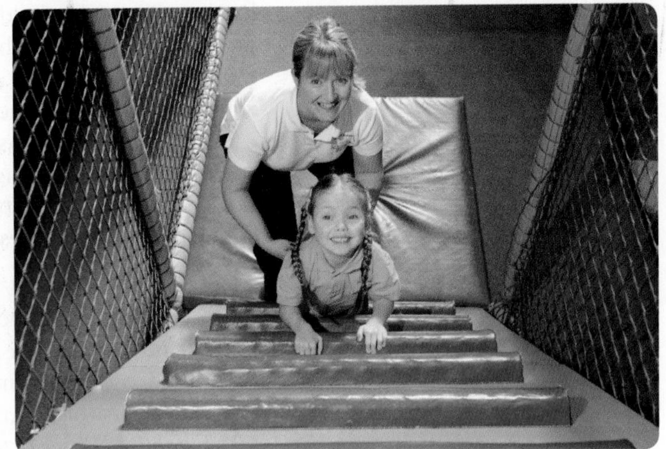

Meaningful work that helps people recover from physical problems caused by illness, injury, or aging gives physiotherapist Diane Leng great motivation and job satisfaction. Shown here working with a young patient, Leng has a job that scores high in skill and task variety plus task significance. She applies her knowledge and skills in identifying patients' needs, organizing and conducting therapy sessions, writing reports, consulting with doctors and nurses, and educating patients about exercise and movement.
Source: Jonathan Hordle / AP Images

Exhibit 17-6
Job Characteristics Model

Source: "Job Characteristics Model," from *Work Redesign*, by J. R. Hackman & G. R. Oldham. Copyright © 1980 by Addison-Wesley (a division of Pearson). Reprinted with permission.

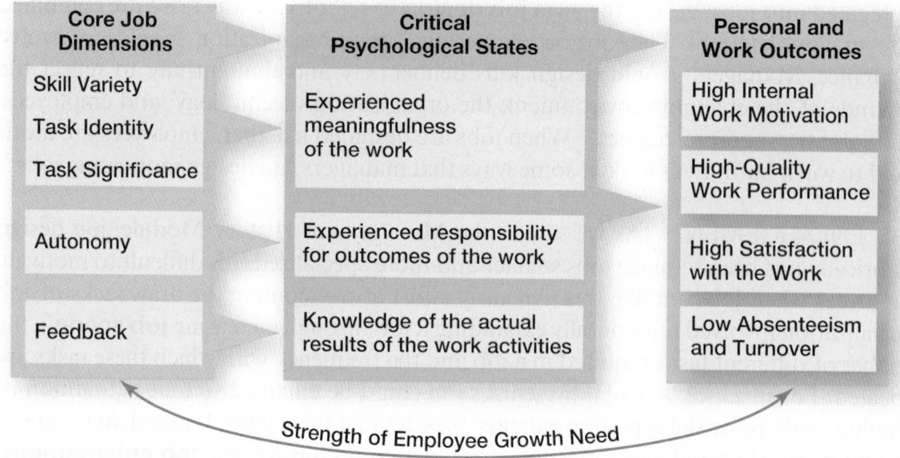

job characteristics model (JCM)
A framework for analyzing and designing jobs that identifies five primary core job dimensions, their interrelationships, and their impact on outcomes

skill variety
The degree to which a job requires a variety of activities so that an employee can use a number of different skills and talents

task identity
The degree to which a job requires completion of a whole and identifiable piece of work

task significance
The degree to which a job has a substantial impact on the lives or work of other people

autonomy
The degree to which a job provides substantial freedom, independence, and discretion to the individual in scheduling work and determining the procedures to be used in carrying it out

feedback
The degree to which carrying out work activities required by a job results in the individual's obtaining direct and clear information about his or her performance effectiveness

The JCM is shown in Exhibit 17-6. Notice how the first three dimensions—skill variety, task identity, and task significance—combine to create meaningful work. In other words, if these three characteristics exist in a job, we can predict that the person will view his or her job as being important, valuable, and worthwhile. Notice, too, that jobs that possess autonomy give the jobholder a feeling of personal responsibility for the results and that if a job provides feedback, the employee will know how effectively he or she is performing.

The JCM suggests that employees are likely to be motivated when they *learn* (knowledge of results through feedback) that they *personally* (experienced responsibility through autonomy of work) performed well on tasks that they *care about* (experienced meaningfulness through skill variety, task identity, or task significance).[46] The more a job is designed around these three elements, the greater the employee's motivation, performance, and satisfaction and the lower his or her absenteeism and likelihood of resigning. As the model shows, the links between the job dimensions and the outcomes are moderated by the strength of the individual's growth need (the person's desire for self-esteem and self-actualization). Individuals with a high-growth need are more likely than low-growth need individuals to experience the critical psychological states and respond positively when their jobs include the core dimensions. This distinction may explain the mixed results with job enrichment: Individuals with low-growth need aren't likely to achieve high performance or satisfaction by having their jobs enriched.

The JCM provides specific guidance to managers for job design. These suggestions specify the types of changes most likely to lead to improvement in the five core job dimensions. You'll notice that two suggestions incorporate job enlargement and job enrichment, although the other suggestions involve more than vertical and horizontal expansion of jobs.

1. *Combine tasks.* Put fragmented tasks back together to form a new, larger work module (job enlargement) to increase skill variety and task identity.
2. *Create natural work units.* Design tasks that form an identifiable and meaningful whole to increase employee "ownership" of the work. Encourage employees to view their work as meaningful and important rather than as irrelevant and boring.
3. *Establish client (external or internal) relationships.* Whenever possible, establish direct relationships between workers and their clients to increase skill variety, autonomy, and feedback.
4. *Expand jobs vertically.* Vertical expansion gives employees responsibilities and controls that were formerly reserved for managers, which can increase employee autonomy.
5. *Open feedback channels.* Direct feedback lets employees know how well they're performing their jobs and whether their performance is improving or not.

The research into the JCM has provided a rich knowledge base for understanding how job design influences employee motivation; however, the research does not directly specify motivating jobs. What are some of the jobs people consider to be more or less meaningful?

A survey of workers employed in more than 450 jobs provides some insights. Approximately 374,000 workers were asked the question: "Does your job make the world a better place?"[47] More than 95 percent of clergy members, surgeons, and education administrators (such as principals) feel that they make the world a better place. In contrast, fewer than 25 percent of gaming supervisors and parking lot attendants feel that they make the world a better place.

Research into the JCM continues. For instance, one recent study looked at using job redesign efforts to change job characteristics and improve employee well-being.[48] Another study examined psychological ownership—that is, a personal feeling of "mine-ness" or "our-ness"—and its role in the JCM.[49]

REDESIGNING JOB DESIGN APPROACHES[50] Although the JCM has proven to be useful, it may not be totally appropriate for today's jobs that are more service and knowledge oriented. The nature of these jobs has also changed the tasks that employees do in those jobs. Two emerging viewpoints on job design are causing a rethinking of the JCM and other standard approaches. Let's take a look at each perspective.

The first perspective, the **relational perspective of work design**, focuses on how people's tasks and jobs are increasingly based on social relationships. In jobs today, employees have more interactions and interdependence with coworkers and others both inside and outside the organization. In doing their job, employees rely more and more on those around them for information, advice, and assistance. So what does this mean for designing motivating jobs? It means that managers need to look at important components of those employee relationships such as access to and level of social support in an organization, types of interactions outside an organization, amount of task interdependence, and interpersonal feedback.

relational perspective of work design
An approach to job design that focuses on how people's tasks and jobs are increasingly based on social relationships

Let's look at an example of the relational perspective of work design. Have you ever called a software company's help line? Isn't your expectation that the product expert will provide straightforward answers and step-by-step instructions for addressing the problem? Of course, we all do! Microsoft understands customers' expectations. Managers help improve the customer service experience by connecting software developers with customers. In this example, the manager's goal is to have developers write software that meets technical specifications and is user friendly.

The second perspective, the **proactive perspective of work design**, says that employees are taking the initiative to change how their work is performed. They're much more involved in decisions and actions that affect their work. Important job design factors according to this perspective include autonomy (which *is* part of the JCM), amount of ambiguity and accountability, job complexity, level of stressors, and social or relationship context. Each of these has been shown to influence employee proactive behavior. For instance, researchers observed cleaners at a hospital took the initiative to craft their own jobs. According to one of the researchers, "the cleaners had tons of rooms they had to clean in a very short period of time so they had very little discretion over the number of tasks they had to get done. . . . [T]o make it more meaningful for themselves, they would do all types of little things to help the patients and their patients' families."[51] One stream of research that's relevant to proactive work design is **high-involvement work practices**, which are designed to elicit greater input or involvement from workers.[52] The level of employee proactivity is believed to increase as employees become more involved in decisions that affect their work. Another term for this approach, which we discussed earlier in Chapter 10, is employee empowerment. (You'll find more information on employee empowerment in Chapter 16.)

proactive perspective of work design
An approach to job design in which employees take the initiative to change how their work is performed

high-involvement work practices
Work practices designed to elicit greater input or involvement from workers

Equity Theory

Do you ever wonder what kind of grade the person sitting next to you in class makes on a test or on a major class assignment? Most of us do! Being human, we tend to compare ourselves with others. If someone offered you $60,000 a year on your first job after graduating from college, you'd probably jump at the offer and report to work enthusiastic, ready to tackle whatever needed to be done, and certainly be satisfied with your pay. How would you react, though, if you found out a month into the job that a coworker—another recent

Exhibit 17-7
Equity Theory

Perceived Ratio Comparison	Employee's Assessment
Outcomes A / Inputs A < Outcomes B / Inputs B	Inequity (underrewarded)
Outcomes A / Inputs A = Outcomes B / Inputs B	Equity
Outcomes A / Inputs A > Outcomes B / Inputs B	Inequity (overrewarded)

graduate, your age, with comparable grades from a comparable school, and with comparable work experience—was getting $65,000 a year? You'd probably be upset! Even though in absolute terms, $60,000 is a lot of money for a new graduate to make (and you know it!), that suddenly isn't the issue. Now you see the issue as what you believe is *fair*—what is *equitable.* The term *equity* is related to the concept of fairness and equitable treatment compared with others who behave in similar ways. Evidence indicates that employees compare themselves to others and that inequities influence how much effort employees exert.[53]

equity theory
The theory that an employee compares his or her job's input-outcomes ratio with that of relevant others and then corrects any inequity

Equity theory, developed by J. Stacey Adams, proposes that employees compare what they get from a job (outcomes) in relation to what they put into it (inputs), and then they compare their inputs-outcomes ratio with the inputs-outcomes ratios of relevant others (Exhibit 17-7). If an employee perceives her ratio to be equitable in comparison to those of relevant others, there's no problem. However, if the ratio is inequitable, she views herself as underrewarded or overrewarded. When inequities occur, employees attempt to do something about it.[54] The result might be lower or higher productivity, improved or reduced quality of output, increased absenteeism, or voluntary resignation. In some cases, employees reveal pay inequities to the public rather than lowering their inputs. For instance, actor Robin Wright who stars in the Netflix series *House of Cards* did just this. After realizing that her pay was significantly less than her male costar's for an equally influential role, Wright demanded higher pay: "You better pay me or I'm going to go public."[55] Her efforts paid off (no pun intended!).

referents
The persons, systems, or selves against which individuals compare themselves to assess equity

distributive justice
Perceived fairness of the amount and allocation of rewards among individuals

procedural justice
Perceived fairness of the process used to determine the distribution of rewards

The **referent**—the other persons, systems, or selves individuals compare themselves against in order to assess equity—is an important variable in equity theory.[56] Each of the three referent categories is important. The "persons" category includes other individuals with similar jobs in the same organization but also includes friends, neighbors, or professional associates. Based on what they hear at work or read about in newspapers or trade journals, employees compare their pay with that of others. The "system" category includes organizational pay policies, procedures, and allocation. The "self" category refers to inputs-outcomes ratios that are unique to the individual. It reflects past personal experiences and contacts and is influenced by criteria such as past jobs or family commitments.

Originally, equity theory focused on **distributive justice**, the perceived fairness of the amount and allocation of rewards among individuals. More recent research has focused on looking at issues of **procedural justice**, the perceived fairness of the process used to determine the distribution of rewards. This research shows that distributive justice has a greater influence on employee satisfaction than procedural justice, while procedural justice tends to affect an employee's organizational commitment, trust in his or her boss, and intention to quit.[57] What are the implications for managers? They should consider openly sharing information on how allocation decisions are made, follow consistent and unbiased procedures, and engage in similar practices to increase the perception of procedural justice. By increasing the perception of procedural justice, employees are likely to view their bosses and the organization as positive even if they're dissatisfied with pay, promotions, and other personal outcomes.

- A woman will earn $430,480 less than her male counterpart over the course of a 40-year career.[58]

WORKPLACE CONFIDENTIAL Feelings of Unfair Pay

For many employees, nothing is likely to act as a demotivator as much as learning that someone in their organization is getting paid more than they are for the same or similar job. Depending on your equity sensitivity, someday you might find yourself angry and frustrated because you believe you're not being fairly compensated.

Let's start with the fact that we're not all equally equity sensitive. Equity sensitivity (ES) is a term that developed out of equity theory. ES acknowledges that not all individuals are equivalently sensitive to equity. ES, therefore, is a personality trait based on an individual's preferred input-to-outcome ratios. For our purposes, we will focus on individuals who believe that they are being underrewarded relative to others. If you're not equity sensitive and you think you're underpaid, you might just want to let it go. As we'll point out, there are risks when you try to correct what you perceive as unfair pay. Sometimes the best strategy is to do nothing. Be sure that you really want to pursue the issue before you act.

If you do feel that you're being paid unfairly, you need to start by asking yourself: What's my evidence? A few organizations make employee salaries public. But that's not the norm. Especially for white-collar jobs, organizations typically don't want employees to know what others are making. In fact, in some organizations, it's a stated policy that employees are *not* to share salary information with each other. Why do organizations do this? The obvious answer is that they don't want employees making comparisons and expecting management to justify every perceived unfairness.

The above suggests that you need to do research before you want to proclaim that you're underpaid. While historically it was difficult to get accurate data for comparing salaries, the Internet has changed that. Salary websites such as Glassdoor and PayScale.com provide comparative data for many jobs and in different markets.

Two questions to consider: What's your basis for concluding you're underpaid, and is there a logical explanation why you might be paid less than someone else in the same or similar job? Keep in mind that there are a lot of reasons to justify salary differences—education, skills, length of time with the organization, relevant experience, different performance ratings, location, and cost of living. There's a reason, for instance, that two insurance adjusters working for Liberty Mutual might be paid differently if one works out of New York City and the other out of Birmingham, Alabama. In the United States, gender is not a justification for paying a woman less than a man for doing the same job. The Equal Pay Act specifically prohibits wage disparities based on sex. Also, remember that most organizations have salary ranges for specific jobs and people have different skills in negotiating. Some differences in pay may be attributable to initial starting salaries that were negotiated at different times and under different conditions.

If you're convinced your pay is unfair and have the evidence to support your claim, ask yourself how much risk you're willing to take. Is it worth pursuing this, and if so, how hard do you want to push? In some organizations, the culture discourages people from comparing salaries or challenging the pay structure. And be prepared to find that your concern falls on deaf ears. Many managers fear that increasing one individual's pay because he or she complained will open up a flood of requests for pay reevaluations.

If you decide to pursue the issue, you'll need a strategy. Start by deciding to whom you are going to make your case. Don't assume your boss has solo discretion to adjust your pay. Pay structures, especially in large organizations, are carefully designed and monitored. While your boss may have some say in recommending pay increases, the final decision usually lies with the human resources department. So you should consider whether you want to present your case to your immediate boss, the human resources manager, or both.

Timing counts! That is, there are times that are better for making your case. The natural time is with your performance evaluation. A strong evaluation strengthens your hand in asking for an adjustment, especially if it is backed up with evidence suggesting that you're underpaid. And what kind of evidence makes your case and helps your boss to get approvals from his or her superiors? If you have objective data that indicates that others in your organization or community are getting paid more than you are for the same or similar job, present the facts. Additionally, elaborate on your contributions. Specifically reference your past accomplishments and what you expect to contribute in the future. Ideally, you'll have concrete evidence to make your case, such as how much you brought the organization in sales or how much you saved through increased productivity. If your job doesn't lend itself to such facts, support your case with positive comments on your accomplishments from customers, suppliers, or work colleagues.

We conclude with some things you should *not* do. (1) Don't go over your boss's head—for instance, talking with your human resources manager—without first getting your boss's approval. No manager wants to feel that you are undermining his or her authority. (2) Don't discuss your compensation with coworkers. Pay is a sensitive subject. It's best not to share salary information. Use other sources, besides coworkers, to get comparative data. (3) Don't make comparisons to a specific person in your department or organization. This is not likely to win you support from your boss or colleagues. (4) Don't go negative. Complaining or making threats rarely results in positive outcomes. And saying that you haven't had a raise in years or that you're doing twice as much work as everyone else is also likely to prove unproductive.

Sources: Based on E. W. Miles, J. D. Hatfield, and R. C. Husman, "The Equity Sensitive Construct: Potential Implications for Worker Performance," *Journal of Management*, December 1989, pp. 581–588; R. Rueff, "Tips on How to Approach Suspected Pay Inequity," *Glassdoor blog,* March 11, 2009; A. Doyle, "What Can You Do When Your Co-Workers Are Paid More Money?," *Career Tool Belt*, June 15, 2015; and "How to Ask for a Raise," Forbes.com, November 5, 2015.

Exhibit 17-8
Expectancy Model

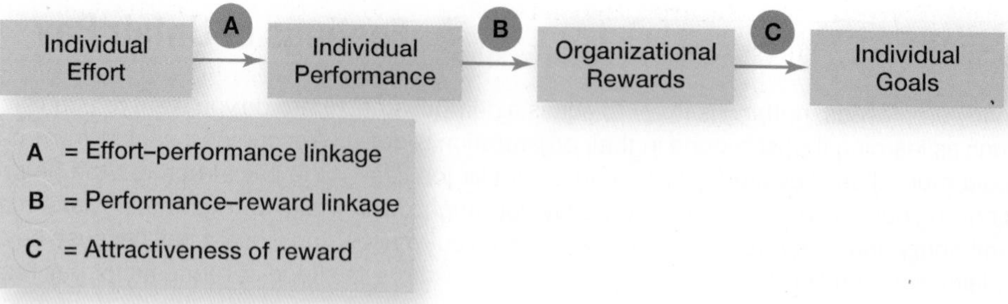

Just Born candy company—makers of Peeps and Mike and Ike brands—uses expectancy theory in motivating employees to achieve annual sales goals. Sales team members shown here expected their efforts would result in winning an all-expenses-paid trip to Hawaii. But they failed to meet their goal and instead earned jackets and bomber hats and a trip to Fargo, North Dakota.
Source: AP Photo/Ann Arbor Miller

Expectancy Theory

The most comprehensive explanation of how employees are motivated is Victor Vroom's **expectancy theory**.[59] Although the theory has its critics,[60] most research evidence supports it.[61]

Expectancy theory states that an individual tends to act in a certain way based on the expectation that the act will be followed by a given outcome and on the attractiveness of that outcome to the individual. It includes three variables or relationships (see Exhibit 17-8):

1. *Expectancy* or *effort-performance linkage* is the probability perceived by the individual that exerting a given amount of effort will lead to a certain level of performance.
2. *Instrumentality* or *performance-reward linkage* is the degree to which the individual believes that performing at a particular level is instrumental in attaining the desired outcome.
3. *Valence* or *attractiveness of reward* is the importance an individual places on the potential outcome or reward that can be achieved on the job. Valence considers both the goals and needs of the individual.

This explanation of motivation might sound complicated, but it really isn't. It can be summed up in the questions: How hard do I have to work to achieve a certain level of performance, and can I actually achieve that level? What reward will performing at that level of performance get me? How attractive is the reward to me, and does it help me achieve my own personal goals? Whether you are motivated to put forth effort (that is, to work hard) at any given time depends on your goals and your perception of whether a certain level of performance is necessary to attain those goals. Let's look at an example. Your second author had a student many years ago who went to work for IBM as a sales rep. Her favorite work "reward" was having an IBM corporate jet fly into Springfield, Missouri, to pick up her best customers and her and take them for a weekend of golfing at some fun location. But to get that particular "reward," she had to achieve at a certain level of performance, which involved exceeding her sales goals by a specified percentage. How hard she was willing to work (that is, how motivated she was to put forth effort) was dependent on the level of performance that had to be met and the likelihood that if she achieved at that level of performance she would receive that reward. Because she valued that reward, she always worked hard to exceed her sales goals. And the performance-reward linkage was clear because her hard work and performance achievements were always rewarded by the company with the reward she valued (access to the corporate jet).

The key to expectancy theory is understanding an individual's goal and the linkage between effort and performance, between performance and rewards, and finally, between rewards and individual goal satisfaction. It emphasizes payoffs, or rewards. As a result, we have to believe that the rewards an organization is offering align with what the individual wants. Expectancy theory recognizes that no universal principle explains what motivates individuals and thus stresses that managers understand why employees view certain outcomes as attractive or unattractive. After all, we want to reward individuals with those things they value positively. Also, expectancy theory emphasizes expected behaviors. Do employees know what is expected of them and how they'll be evaluated? Finally, the theory is concerned with perceptions. Reality is irrelevant. An individual's own perceptions of performance, reward, and goal outcomes—not the outcomes themselves—will determine his or her motivation (level of effort).

expectancy theory
The theory that an individual tends to act in a certain way based on the expectation that the act will be followed by a given outcome and on the attractiveness of that outcome to the individual

Integrating Contemporary Theories of Motivation

Many of the ideas underlying the contemporary motivation theories are complementary, and you'll understand better how to motivate people if you see how the theories fit together.[62] Exhibit 17-9 presents a model that integrates much of what we know about motivation. Its basic foundation is the expectancy model. Let's work through the model, starting on the left.

The individual effort box has an arrow leading into it. This arrow flows from the individual's goals. Consistent with goal-setting theory, this goals-effort link is meant

Exhibit 17-9
Integrating Contemporary Theories of Motivation

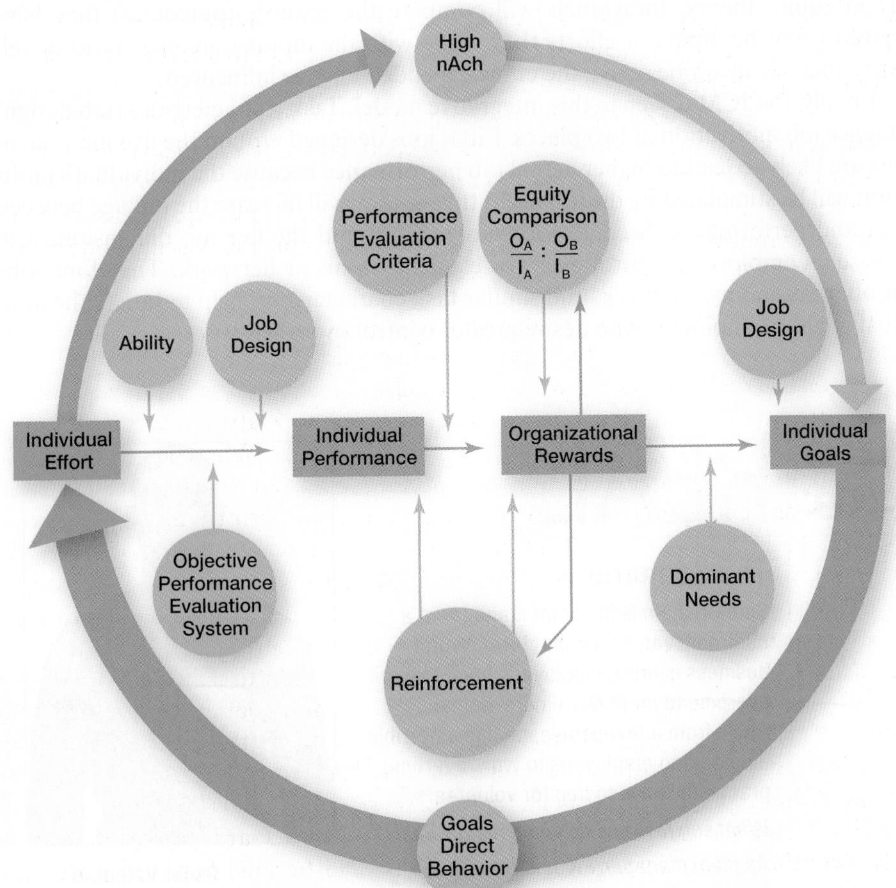

to illustrate that goals direct behavior. Expectancy theory predicts that an employee will exert a high level of effort if he or she perceives a strong relationship between effort and performance, performance and rewards, and rewards and satisfaction of personal goals. Each of these relationships is in turn influenced by certain factors. You can see from the model that the level of individual performance is determined not only by the level of individual effort but also by the individual's ability to perform and by whether the organization has a fair and objective performance evaluation system. The performance-reward relationship will be strong if the individual perceives that performance (rather than seniority, personal favorites, or some other criterion) is what is rewarded. The final link in expectancy theory is the rewards-goal relationship. The traditional need theories come into play at this point. Motivation would be high to the degree that the rewards an individual received for his or her high performance satisfied the dominant needs consistent with his or her individual goals.

A closer look at the model also shows that it considers the achievement-need, reinforcement, equity, and JCM theories. The high achiever isn't motivated by the organization's assessment of his or her performance or organizational rewards; hence the jump from effort to individual goals for those with a high nAch. Remember that high achievers are internally driven as long as the jobs they're doing provide them with personal responsibility, feedback, and moderate risks. They're not concerned with the effort-performance, performance-reward, or rewards-goals linkages.

Reinforcement theory is seen in the model by recognizing that the organization's rewards reinforce the individual's performance. If managers have designed a reward system that is seen by employees as "paying off" for good performance, the rewards will reinforce and encourage continued good performance. Rewards also play a key part in equity theory. Individuals will compare the rewards (outcomes) they have received from the inputs or efforts they made with the inputs-outcomes ratio of relevant others. If inequities exist, the effort expended may be influenced.

Finally, the JCM is seen in this integrative model. Task characteristics (job design) influence job motivation at two places. First, jobs designed around the five job dimensions are likely to lead to higher actual job performance because the individual's motivation will be stimulated by the job itself; that is, they will increase the linkage between effort and performance. Second, jobs designed around the five job dimensions also increase an employee's control over key elements in his or her work. Therefore, jobs that offer autonomy, feedback, and similar task characteristics help to satisfy the individual goals of employees who desire greater control over their work.

let's get REAL

The Scenario:

Sam Grisham is the plant manager at a bathroom vanity manufacturer. When business is brisk, employees have to work overtime to meet customers' demands. Aside from a few people, he has a horrible time getting employees to work overtime. "I practically have to beg for volunteers."

Source: Oscar Valencia

Oscar Valencia
Manufacturing Manager

What suggestions do you have for Sam?

As plant manager, I would rotate the overtime for all employees. During busy times, everyone must chip in. I would also suggest implementing mandatory overtime for employees according to seniority in order to keep it fair.

If your professor has assigned this, go to **www.mymanagementlab.com** to complete the Simulation: *Motivation* and get a better understanding of the challenges of knowing how to motivate employees.

★ Try It!

CURRENT issues in motivation

LO17.4 For its 150th anniversary, the German chemical giant BASF created a year-long employee motivational program called "Connected to Care," combining social responsibility with teamwork and a bit of friendly competition. Each employee had the opportunity to form a volunteer team with coworkers and jointly propose a social responsibility project focusing on one of BASF's key areas of focus: food, urban living, or smart energy. More than 35,000 employees participated in teams, submitting hundreds of ideas for projects to improve BASF communities worldwide. After an organization-wide vote, BASF donated money to implement the 150 projects that received the most votes—adding to the motivation of the winning teams.[63]

Understanding and predicting employee motivation is one of the most popular areas in management research. We've introduced you to several motivation theories. However, even the contemporary theories of employee motivation are influenced by some significant workplace issues—managing cross-cultural challenges, motivating unique groups of workers, and designing appropriate rewards programs.

Managing Cross-Cultural Motivational Challenges

Scores of employees at Denmark's largest brewer, Carlsberg A/S, walked off their jobs in protest after the company tightened rules on workplace drinking and removed beer coolers from work sites.[64] Now that's a motivational challenge you don't often see in U.S. workplaces!

The motivation of these employees working at the research and development facility at the Daihatsu Motor plant near Jakarta, Indonesia, is influenced by their national culture. Indonesia has a strong collectivist culture, where employees are motivated less by receiving individual praise because their culture places a greater emphasis on harmony, belonging, and consensus.
Source: Kyodo/Newscom

In today's global business environment, managers can't automatically assume motivational programs that work in one geographic location are going to work in others. Most current motivation theories were developed in the United States by Americans and about Americans.[65] Maybe the most blatant pro-American characteristic in these theories is the strong emphasis on individualism and achievement. For instance, both goal-setting and expectancy theories emphasize goal accomplishment as well as rational and individual thought. Let's look at the motivation theories to see their level of cross-cultural transferability.

Maslow's needs hierarchy argues that people start at the physiological level and then move progressively up the hierarchy in order. This hierarchy, if it has any application at all, aligns with American culture. In countries like Japan, Greece, and Mexico, where uncertainty avoidance characteristics are strong, security needs would be the foundational layer of the needs hierarchy. Countries that score high on nurturing characteristics—Denmark, Sweden, Norway, the Netherlands, and Finland—would have social needs as their foundational level.[66] We would predict, for instance, that group work will be more motivating when the country's culture scores high on the nurturing criterion.

Another motivation concept that clearly has an American bias is the achievement need. The view that a high achievement need acts as an internal motivator presupposes two cultural characteristics—a willingness to accept a moderate degree of risk (which excludes countries with strong uncertainty avoidance characteristics) and a concern with performance (which applies almost singularly to countries with strong achievement characteristics). This combination is found in countries such as the United States, Canada, and Great Britain.[67] On the other hand, these characteristics are relatively absent in countries such as Chile and Portugal.

Equity theory has a relatively strong following in the United States, which is not surprising given that U.S.-style reward systems are based on the assumption that workers are highly sensitive to equity in reward allocations. In the United States, equity is meant to closely link pay to performance. However, recent evidence suggests that in collectivist cultures, especially in the former socialist countries of Central and Eastern Europe, employees expect rewards to reflect their individual needs as well as their performance.[68] Moreover, consistent with a legacy of communism and centrally planned economies, employees exhibited a greater "entitlement" attitude—that is, they expected outcomes to be greater than their inputs.[69] These findings suggest that U.S.-style pay practices may need to be modified in some countries in order to be perceived as fair by employees.

Another research study of more than 50,000 employees around the world examined two cultural characteristics from the GLOBE framework—individualism and masculinity—(see Chapter 3 for a discussion of these characteristics) in relation to motivation.[70] The researchers found that in individualistic cultures such as the United States and Canada, individual initiative, individual freedom, and individual achievement are highly valued. In more collective cultures such as Iran, Peru, and China, however, employees may be less interested in receiving individual praise but place a greater emphasis on harmony, belonging, and consensus. They also found that in masculine (achievement/assertive) cultures such as Japan and Slovakia, the focus is on material success. Those work environments are designed to push employees hard and then reward top performers with high earnings. However, in more feminine (nurturing) cultures such as Sweden and the Netherlands, smaller wage gaps among employees are common, and employees are likely to have extensive quality-of-life benefits.

Despite these cross-cultural differences in motivation, some cross-cultural consistencies are evident. In a recent study of employees in 13 countries, the top motivators included (ranked from number one on down) being treated with respect, work-life balance, the type of work done, the quality of people worked with and the quality of the organization's leadership (tied), base pay, working in an environment where good service can be provided to others, long-term career potential, flexible working arrangements, learning and development opportunities and benefits (tied), promotion opportunities, and incentive pay or bonus.[71] And other studies have shown that the desire for interesting work seems important to almost all workers, regardless of their national culture. For instance, employees in Belgium, Britain, Israel, and the United States ranked "interesting work" number one among 11 work goals. It was ranked either second or third in Japan, the Netherlands, and Germany.[72] Similarly, in a study comparing job-preference outcomes among graduate students in the United States, Canada, Australia, and Singapore, growth, achievement, and responsibility were rated the top three and had identical rankings.[73] Both studies suggest some universality to the importance of intrinsic factors identified by Herzberg in his two-factor theory. Another recent study examining workplace motivation trends in Japan also seems to indicate that Herzberg's model is applicable to Japanese employees.[74]

Motivating Unique Groups of Workers

At Deloitte, employees are allowed to "dial up" or "dial down" their job responsibilities to fit their personal and professional goals.[75] The company's program called Mass Career Customization has been a huge hit with its employees! In the first 12 months after it was rolled out, employee satisfaction with "overall career/life fit" rose by 25 percent. Also, the number of high-performing employees staying with Deloitte increased.

Motivating employees has never been easy! Employees come into organizations with different needs, personalities, skills, abilities, interests, and aptitudes. They have different expectations of their employers and different views of what they think their employer has a right to expect of them. And they vary widely in what they want from their jobs. For instance, some employees get more satisfaction out of their personal interests and pursuits and only want a weekly paycheck—nothing more. They're not interested in making their work more challenging or interesting or in "winning" performance contests. Others derive a great deal of satisfaction in their jobs and are motivated to exert high levels of effort. Given these differences, how can managers do an effective job of motivating the unique groups of employees found in today's workforce? One thing is to understand the motivational requirements of these groups, including diverse employees, professionals, contingent workers, and low-skilled minimum-wage employees.

MOTIVATING A DIVERSE WORKFORCE To maximize motivation among today's workforce, managers need to think in terms of *flexibility*. For instance, studies tell us that men place more importance on having autonomy in their jobs than women. In contrast, the opportunity to learn, convenient and flexible work hours, and good interpersonal relations are more important to women.[76] Having the opportunity to be independent and to be exposed to different experiences is important to Gen Y employees, whereas older workers may be more interested in highly structured work opportunities.[77] Managers need to recognize that what motivates a single mother with two dependent children who's working full time to support her family may be very different from the needs of a single part-time employee or an older employee who is working only to supplement his or her retirement income. A diverse array of rewards is needed to motivate employees with such diverse needs. For instance, many organizations have developed flexible work arrangements—such as compressed workweeks, flextime, and job sharing, which we discussed in Chapter 11—that recognize different needs. Another job alternative we also discussed earlier is telecommuting. However, keep in mind that not all employees embrace the idea of telecommuting. Some workers relish the informal interactions at work that satisfy their social needs and are a source of new ideas.

Do flexible work arrangements motivate employees? Although such arrangements might seem highly motivational, both positive and negative relationships have been found. For instance, a recent study that looked at the impact of telecommuting on job satisfaction found that job satisfaction initially increased as the extent of telecommuting increased, but as the number of hours spent telecommuting increased, job satisfaction started to level off, decreased slightly, and then stabilized.[78]

Self-Motivation—If your instructor is using Pearson MyLab Management, log onto **mymanagementlab.com** and test your *self-motivation knowledge*. **Be sure to refer back to the chapter opener!**

FUTURE VISION Individualized Rewards

Organizations have historically assumed that "one size fits all" when it comes to allocating rewards. Managers typically assumed that everyone wants more money and more vacation time. But as organizations become less bureaucratic and more capable of differentiating rewards, managers will be encouraged to differentiate rewards among employees as well as for individual employees over time.

Organizations control a vast number of potential rewards that employees might find appealing. A partial list would include increased base pay, bonuses, shortened workweeks, extended vacations, paid sabbaticals, flexible work hours, part-time employment, guaranteed job security, increased pension contributions, college tuition reimbursement, personal days off, help in purchasing a home, recognition awards, paid club memberships, and work-from-home options. In the future, most organizations will structure individual reward packages in ways that will maximize employee motivation.

*If your professor has chosen to assign this, go to **www.mymanagementlab.com** to discuss the following questions.*

TALK ABOUT IT 1: What are the positive aspects of having individualized rewards? (Think in terms of employees and managers.)

TALK ABOUT IT 2: What are the negative aspects of having individualized rewards? (Again, think in terms of employees and managers.)

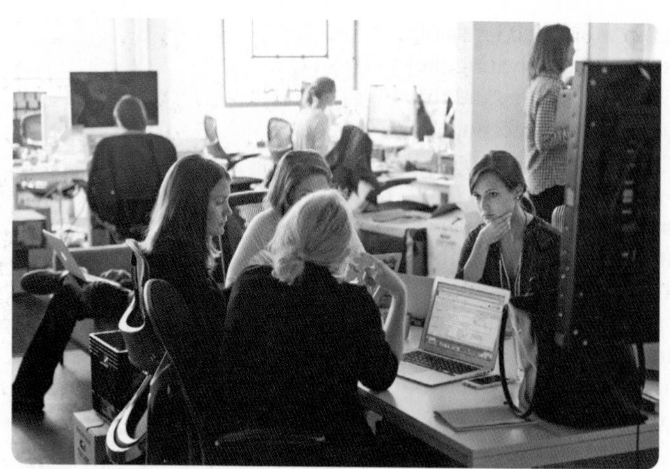

Managers of home rental website Airbnb motivate the firm's young employees at its San Francisco headquarters with an open and collaborative work environment that promotes teamwork and a sense of community and stimulates innovation. Employees have the freedom to work where they want and enjoy amenities such as a cafeteria, nap room, library, yoga classes, organic lunches, and $2,000 each year for personal travel.
Source: Airbnb, San Francisco. USA. Inte/ZUMA Press/Newscom

MOTIVATING PROFESSIONALS In contrast to a generation ago, the typical employee today is more likely to be a professional with a college degree than a blue-collar factory worker. What special concerns should managers be aware of when trying to motivate a team of engineers at Intel's India Development Center, software designers at SAS Institute in North Carolina, or a group of consultants at Accenture in Singapore?

Professionals are different from nonprofessionals.[79] They have a strong and long-term commitment to their field of expertise. To keep current in their field, they need to regularly update their knowledge, and because of their commitment to their profession, they rarely define their workweek as 8 A.M. to 5 P.M., five days a week.

What motivates professionals? Money and promotions typically are low on their priority list. Why? They tend to be well paid and enjoy what they do. In contrast, job challenge tends to be ranked high. They like to tackle problems and find solutions. Their chief reward is the work itself. Professionals also value support. They want others to think that what they are working on is important. That may be true for all employees, but professionals tend to be focused on their work as their central life interest, whereas nonprofessionals typically have other interests outside of work that can compensate for needs not met on the job.

MOTIVATING CONTINGENT WORKERS We discussed in Chapter 11 the increased number of contingent workers employed by organizations. There's no simple solution for motivating these employees. For that small set of individuals who prefer the freedom of their temporary status, the lack of stability may not be an issue. In addition, temporariness might be preferred by highly compensated physicians, engineers, accountants, or financial planners who don't want the demands of a full-time job. But these individuals are the exceptions. For the most part, temporary employees are not temporary by choice.

What will motivate involuntarily temporary employees? An obvious answer is the opportunity to become a permanent employee. In cases in which permanent employees are selected from a pool of temps, the temps will often work hard in hopes of becoming permanent. A less obvious answer is the opportunity for training. The ability of a temporary employee to find a new job is largely dependent on his or her skills. If an employee sees that the job he or she is doing can help develop marketable skills, then motivation is increased. From an equity standpoint, when temps work alongside permanent employees who earn more and get benefits too for doing the same job, the performance of temps is likely to suffer. Separating such employees or perhaps minimizing interdependence between them might help managers counteract potential problems.[80]

How do these issues influence contingent workers' job satisfaction? Research shows that differences in job satisfaction between contingent and permanent workers is not significant until we consider the particular contingent work arrangements—temporary employee versus independent contractor.[81] Temporary workers are less satisfied than permanent workers. This difference may be explained by the fact that most temporary employees do not receive benefits such as paid vacation and are paid lower wages than earned by comparably skilled permanent workers. In contrast, independent contractors are about as equally satisfied as permanent workers. This may be the case because organizations are more likely to recognize the importance of independent contractors' contributions because they're mostly highly skilled individuals. For instance, management consultants are well educated and have a proven track record of success.

MOTIVATING LOW-SKILLED, MINIMUM-WAGE EMPLOYEES Suppose in your first managerial position after graduating, you're responsible for managing a work group of low-skilled, minimum-wage employees. Offering more pay to these employees for high levels of performance is out of the question: Your company just can't afford it. In addition, these employees have limited education and skills. What are your motivational options at this point?

One trap we often fall into is thinking that people are motivated only by money. Although money is important as a motivator, it's not the only reward that people seek and that managers can use. In motivating minimum-wage employees, managers might look at employee recognition programs. Many managers also recognize the power of praise, although these "pats on the back" must be sincere and given for the right reasons. Inventive managers can come up with creative awards that match employees' interests. For instance, one trucking company awarded cases of beer to truck loaders who demonstrated good performance.[82]

Designing Appropriate Rewards Programs

As the Group Company approached its tenth anniversary of success in the travel business, founder Helen Bilton wanted to reward her workforce for outstanding performance. Rather than plan a huge party, she arranged for all 32 employees to visit Barbados on a luxurious, all-expenses-paid three-day holiday. Rewards like this play a powerful role in motivating employee behavior.[83]

OPEN-BOOK MANAGEMENT Within 24 hours after managers of the Heavy Duty Division of Springfield Remanufacturing Company (SRC) gather to discuss a multipage financial document, every plant employee will have seen the same information. If the employees can meet shipment goals, they'll all share in a large year-end bonus.[84] Many organizations of various sizes involve their employees in workplace decisions by opening up the financial statements (the "books"). They share that information so employees will be motivated to make better decisions about their work and better able to understand the implications of what they do, how they do it, and the ultimate impact on the bottom line. In many cases, employees begin to think like owners rather than hired hands.[85] This approach is called **open-book management**, and a number of organizations are using it.[86] For instance, at A Yard & a Half Landscaping, founder Eileen Michaels holds monthly meetings to share the firm's profit and loss statement line by line with her employees. Employees then use this information to assess how to cut expenses and get work done more efficiently.[87]

open-book management
A motivational approach in which an organization's financial statements (the "books") are shared with all employees

The goal of open-book management is to get employees to think like an owner by seeing the impact their decisions have on financial results. Since many employees don't have the knowledge or background to understand the financials, they have to be taught how to read and understand the organization's financial statements. Once employees have this knowledge, however, managers need to regularly share the numbers with them. By sharing this information, employees begin to see the link between their efforts, level of performance, and operational results.

EMPLOYEE RECOGNITION PROGRAMS **Employee recognition programs** consist of personal attention and expressing interest, approval, and appreciation for a job well done.[88] They can take numerous forms. For instance, Kelly Services introduced a new version of its points-based incentive system to better promote productivity and retention among its employees. The program, called Kelly Kudos, gives employees more choices of awards and allows them to accumulate points over a longer time period. It's working. Participants generate three times more revenue and hours than employees not receiving points.[89] Nichols Foods, a British manufacturer, has a comprehensive recognition program. The main hallway in the production department is hung with "bragging boards" on which the accomplishments of employee teams are noted. Monthly awards are presented to people who have been nominated by peers for extraordinary effort on the job. And monthly award winners are eligible for further recognition at an off-site meeting for all employees.[90] At Wayfair.com, a seller of home furnishings, a recognition wall provides space where anyone in the company can write about anyone else in the company and give that person rewards dollars. It's used to recognize people for something they did for a customer or some other accomplishment.[91] Most managers, however, use a far more informal approach. For example, Marks & Spencer encourages spontaneous posts recognizing the extra efforts of employees and peers on the U.K. department

employee recognition programs
Personal attention and expressing interest, approval, and appreciation for a job well done

store's internal social network. Every month, the store posts an award for employee of the month, chosen from peer nominations. In Singapore, managers at the e-commerce firm ShopBack sometimes open a bottle of Champagne during informal celebrations of employee accomplishments such as clearing all outstanding customer service inquiries. At other times, managers surprise high-performing employee teams with free zoo tickets. ShopBack's human resources manager explains the reasoning behind this approach: "Cash rewards connote a transactional relationship, while non-cash rewards are powerful in building team relationships." The restaurant chain PizzaExpress Singapore has a "golden ticket" reward system, with tickets representing travel or shopping vouchers. When senior managers make unscheduled visits to the restaurants, they give away golden tickets to employees who have performed exceptionally well. "Our employees are what make the brand so successful, and we want to give back in more personal ways," says the general manager. Employee recognition is very important, but so is a tangible follow-up reward, he states: "More often than not, an actual gift means more than words."[92]

Companies that have at least one recognition program do the following:

- 87 percent of companies recognize length of service.
- 76 percent of companies recognize above-and-beyond performance.
- 51 percent of companies recognize specific behavior.
- 48 percent of companies use peer-to-peer recognition.
- 34 percent of companies recognize retirement.[96]

A recent survey of organizations found that 89 percent had some type of program to recognize worker achievements.[93] Another survey found that 12 percent of employees say they receive frequent appreciation for a job well done; 7 percent of employees say their company is excellent at showing appreciation for great work.[94] And do employees think these programs are important? You bet! In a survey conducted a few years ago, a wide range of employees was asked what they considered the most powerful workplace motivator. Their response? Recognition, recognition, and more recognition![95]

Consistent with reinforcement theory, rewarding a behavior with recognition immediately following that behavior is likely to encourage its repetition. And recognition can take many forms. You can personally congratulate an employee in private for a good job. You can send a handwritten note or e-mail message acknowledging something positive that the employee has done. For employees with a strong need for social acceptance, you can publicly recognize accomplishments. To enhance group cohesiveness and motivation, you can celebrate team successes. For instance, you can do something as simple as throw a pizza party to celebrate a team's accomplishments. During the economic recession, managers got quite creative in how they showed employees they were appreciated.[97] For instance, employees at one company got to take home fresh vegetables from the company vegetable garden. In others, managers treated employees who really put forth efforts on a project to a special meal or movie tickets. Also, managers can show employees that no matter their role, their contributions matter. Some of these things may seem simple, but they can go a long way in showing employees they're valued.

★ Watch It 2!

If your professor has assigned this, go to **www.mymanagementlab.com** to watch a video titled: *Joie de Vivre Hospitality: Employee Motivation* and to respond to questions.

pay-for-performance programs
Variable compensation plans that pay employees on the basis of some performance measure

PAY-FOR-PERFORMANCE Here's a survey statistic that may surprise you: 40 percent of employees see no clear link between performance and pay.[98] So what are the companies where these employees work paying for? They're obviously not clearly communicating performance expectations.[99] **Pay-for-performance programs** are variable compensation plans that pay employees on the basis of some performance measure.[100] Piece-rate pay plans, wage incentive plans, profit-sharing, and lump-sum bonuses are examples. What differentiates these forms of pay from more traditional compensation plans is that instead of paying a person for time on the job, pay is adjusted to reflect some performance measure. These performance measures might include such things as individual productivity, team or work group productivity, departmental productivity, or the overall organization's profit performance.

Pay-for-performance is probably most compatible with expectancy theory. Individuals should perceive a strong relationship between their performance and the rewards they receive for motivation to be maximized. If rewards are allocated only on nonperformance factors—such as seniority, job title, or across-the-board pay raises—then employees are likely to reduce their efforts. From a motivation perspective, making some or

let's get REAL

The Scenario:

The associates at Footwear Unlimited are paid minimum wage, but can increase their pay with commissions on sales that they ring up. As a result, the associates work hard to greet customers and help them find the right shoe sizes. However, Christy Jefferson, the store manager, is concerned that the current commission plan discourages employees from working as a team. She has noticed that some associates won't help others since only one associate will receive the commission for a sale. Further, associates seem to be ignoring some duties around the store such as straightening displays.

Source: Matt O'Rourke

Matt O'Rourke
Supply Chain Engineer

Should Christy consider a different approach to pay-for-performance?

Don't accept an environment that discourages teamwork; strong teams are a key factor in achieving business results. Rather than reward individual sales, Christy should consider modifying the pay-for-performance plan to incorporate team goals. A bonus could be paid to the team for achieving critical results such as total number of sales for a period of time or a non-monetary reward for straightening up the store. A strong team and company culture is worth the change in approach.

all of an employee's pay conditional on some performance measure focuses his or her attention and effort toward that measure, then reinforces the continuation of the effort with a reward. If the employee's team's or organization's performance declines, so does the reward. Thus, there's an incentive to keep efforts and motivation strong.

Pay-for-performance programs are popular. Some 94 percent of employers have some form of variable pay plan.[101] Common pay-for-performance plans reward employees for project completion or company profits. These types of pay plans have also been tried in other countries, such as Canada and Japan. About 30 percent of Canadian companies and 22 percent of Japanese companies have company-wide pay-for-performance plans.[102] In Japan, most companies reward employees based on age, but many companies are rethinking this practice. For instance, Toyota is considering replacing its seniority-based wage system with a performance-based system. The traditional approach has resulted in pay gaps between younger and older employees, making it difficult to attract younger talent.[103] Performance-based pay also fits with Toyota's mission of efficiency and constant improvement of the quality of its automobiles. Other Japanese companies including Hitachi, Panasonic, and Sony are following suit.[104]

Do pay-for-performance programs work? The jury is still out. For the most part, studies seem to indicate that they do. For instance, one study found companies that used pay-for-performance programs performed better financially than those that did not.[105] Another study showed pay-for-performance programs with outcome-based incentives had a positive impact on sales, customer satisfaction, and profits.[106] In organizations that use work teams, managers should consider group-based performance incentives that will reinforce team effort and commitment. However, others say that linking pay to performance doesn't work.[107] So if a business decides it wants to use pay-for-performance programs, managers need to ensure they're specific about the relationship between an individual's pay and his or her expected level of appropriate performance. Employees must clearly understand exactly how performance—theirs and the organization's—translates into dollars on their paychecks.[108]

Chapter 17 PREPARING FOR: Exams/Quizzes

CHAPTER SUMMARY by Learning Objectives

LO17.1 DEFINE motivation.

Motivation is the process by which a person's efforts are energized, directed, and sustained toward attaining a goal.

The *energy* element is a measure of intensity, drive, or vigor. The high level of effort needs to be *directed* in ways that help the organization achieve its goals. Employees must *persist* in putting forth effort to achieve those goals.

LO17.2 COMPARE and contrast early theories of motivation.

In Maslow's hierarchy, individuals move up the hierarchy of five needs (physiological, safety, social, esteem, and self-actualization) as needs are substantially satisfied. A need that's substantially satisfied no longer motivates.

A Theory X manager believes people don't like to work or won't seek out responsibility so they have to be threatened and coerced to work. A Theory Y manager assumes people like to work and seek out responsibility, so they will exercise self-motivation and self-direction.

Herzberg's theory proposed that intrinsic factors associated with job satisfaction were what motivated people. Extrinsic factors associated with job dissatisfaction simply kept people from being dissatisfied.

Three-needs theory proposed three acquired needs that are major motives in work: need for achievement, need for affiliation, and need for power.

LO17.3 COMPARE and contrast contemporary theories of motivation.

Goal-setting theory says that specific goals increase performance, and difficult goals, when accepted, result in higher performance than easy goals. Important points in goal-setting theory include intention to work toward a goal as a major source of job motivation; specific hard goals that produce higher levels of output than generalized goals; participation in setting goals as preferable to assigning goals, but not always; feedback that guides and motivates behavior, especially self-generated feedback; and contingencies that affect goal setting—goal commitment, self-efficacy, and national culture. Reinforcement theory says that behavior is a function of its consequences. To motivate, use positive reinforcers to reinforce desirable behaviors. Ignore undesirable behavior rather than punishing it.

Job enlargement involves horizontally expanding job scope by adding more tasks or increasing how many times the tasks are done. Job enrichment vertically expands job depth by giving employees more control over their work. The job characteristics model says five core job dimensions (skill variety, task identity, task significance, autonomy, and feedback) are used to design motivating jobs. Another job design approach proposed looking at relational aspects and proactive aspects of jobs.

Equity theory focuses on how employees compare their inputs-outcomes ratios to relevant others' ratios. A perception of inequity will cause an employee to do something about it. Procedural justice has a greater influence on employee satisfaction than distributive justice.

Expectancy theory says an individual tends to act in a certain way based on the expectation that the act will be followed by a desired outcome. Expectancy is the effort-performance linkage (how much effort do I need to exert to achieve a certain level of performance?); instrumentality is the performance-reward linkage (achieving at a certain level of performance will get me a specific reward); and valence is the attractiveness of the reward (is it the reward that I want?).

DISCUSS current issues in motivation.

Managers must cope with three current motivation issues: managing cross-cultural challenges, motivating unique groups of workers, and designing appropriate rewards programs.

Most motivational theories were developed in the United States and have a North American bias. Some theories (Maslow's needs hierarchy, achievement need, and equity theory) don't work well for other cultures. However, the desire for interesting work seems important to all workers, and Herzberg's motivator (intrinsic) factors may be universal.

Managers face challenges in motivating unique groups of workers. A diverse workforce is looking for flexibility. Professionals want job challenge and support and are motivated by the work itself. Contingent workers want the opportunity to become permanent or to receive skills training. Recognition programs and sincere appreciation for work done can be used to motivate low-skilled, minimum-wage workers.

Open-book management is when financial statements (the books) are shared with employees who have been taught what they mean. Employee recognition programs consist of personal attention, approval, and appreciation for a job well done. Pay-for-performance programs are variable compensation plans that pay employees on the basis of some performance measure.

> Pearson **MyLab** Management
>
> Go to **mymanagementlab.com** to complete the problems marked with this icon ✪.

✪ REVIEW AND DISCUSSION QUESTIONS

17-1. What is motivation? Explain the three key elements of motivation.

17-2. Describe each of the four early theories of motivation.

17-3. How do goal-setting, reinforcement, and equity theories explain employee motivation?

17-4. What are the different job design approaches to motivation?

17-5. Briefly explain equity theory and what happens if there are iniquities at work.

17-6. What do you understand by the term open-book management? Is it effective?

17-7. Identify examples of pay-for-performance programs used by some organizations.

17-8. Can an individual be too motivated? Discuss.

> Pearson **MyLab** Management
>
> If your professor has assigned these, go to **mymanagementlab.com** for the following Assisted-graded writing questions:
>
> **17-9.** What economic and cross-cultural challenges do managers face when motivating employees?
>
> **17-10.** Explain, in the context of a diverse and flexible workforce, why managers need to use a range of different motivational approaches. Identify some distinct groups and how they can be motivated.

PREPARING FOR: My Career

PERSONAL INVENTORY ASSESSMENTS

Work Motivation Indicator

How motivated are you? Use this PIA to assess your own level of work motivation.

ETHICS DILEMMA

Advocates of open-book management point to the advantages of getting employees to think like owners and to be motivated to make better decisions about how they do their work once they see how their decisions impact financial results. However, is there such a thing as "too much openness?" At some companies, employees not only have access to company financial details but also to staff performance reviews and individual pay information.[109]

17-11. What do you think? What are the pros and cons of such an approach?

17-12. What potential ethical issues do you see here? How might managers address these ethical issues?

SKILLS EXERCISE Developing Your Motivating Employees Skill

About the Skill

Because a simple, all-encompassing set of motivational guidelines is not available, the following suggestions draw on the essence of what we know about motivating employees.

Steps in Practicing the Skill

- ***Recognize individual differences.*** Almost every contemporary motivation theory recognizes that employees are not homogeneous. They have different needs. They also differ in terms of attitudes, personality, and other important individual variables.
- ***Match people to jobs.*** A great deal of evidence shows the motivational benefits of carefully matching people to jobs. People who lack the necessary skills to perform successfully will be at a disadvantage.
- ***Use goals.*** You should ensure that employees have hard, specific goals and feedback on how well they're doing in pursuit of those goals. In many cases, these goals should be participatively set.
- ***Ensure goals are perceived as attainable.*** Regardless of whether goals are actually attainable, employees who see goals as unattainable will reduce their effort. Be sure, therefore, that employees feel confident that increased efforts can lead to achieving performance goals.
- ***Individualize rewards.*** Because employees have different needs, what acts as a reinforcer for one may not do so for another. Use your knowledge of employee differences to individualize the rewards over which you have control. Some of the more obvious rewards that you can allocate include pay, promotions, autonomy, and the opportunity to participate in goal setting and decision making.
- ***Link rewards to performance.*** You need to make rewards contingent on performance. Rewarding factors other than performance will only reinforce the importance of those other factors. Key rewards such as pay increases and promotions should be given for the attainment of employees' specific goals.
- ***Check the system for equity.*** Employees should perceive that rewards or outcomes are equal to the inputs given. On a simplistic level, experience, ability, effort, and other obvious inputs should explain differences in pay, responsibility, and other obvious outcomes.
- ***Don't ignore money.*** It's easy to get so caught up in setting goals, creating interesting jobs, and providing opportunities for participation that you forget that money is a major reason why most people work. Thus, the allocation of performance-based wage increases, piece-work bonuses, employee stock ownership plans, and other pay incentives are important in determining employee motivation.

Practicing the Skill

Create a motivational plan for each of the groups of employees listed below. Include ideas on what kinds of rewards or incentives would be appropriate for each group.

a. Fast-food workers
b. Software development engineers
c. High school teachers
d. Construction site workers

WORKING TOGETHER Team Exercise

How can you motivate low income workers? In groups of three or four, consider how you might motivate professionals. Identify some common themes of effective motivators and create a list. Be prepared to share your ideas with the class. Have you all come up with the same suggestions?

MY TURN TO BE A MANAGER

- A good habit to get into if you don't already do it is goal-setting. Set goals for yourself using the suggestions from goal-setting theory. Write these down and keep them in a notebook. Track your progress toward achieving these goals.
- Describe a task you've done recently for which you exerted a high level of effort. Explain your behavior, using any three of the motivation approaches described in this chapter.
- Pay attention to times when you're highly motivated and times when you're not as motivated. Write down a description of these. What accounts for the difference in your level of motivation?
- Interview three managers about how they motivate their employees. What have they found that works the best? Write up your findings in a report and be prepared to present it in class.
- Using the job characteristics model, redesign the following jobs to be more motivating: retail store sales associate, utility company meter reader, and checkout cashier at a discount store. In a written report, describe for each job at least two specific actions you would take for each of the five core job dimensions.
- Do some serious thinking about what you want from your job after graduation. Using the chapter-opening *It's Your Career,* make a list of what's important to you. Think about how you will discover whether a particular job will help you get those things.
- Find three different examples of employee recognition programs from organizations with which you're familiar or from articles that you find. Write a report describing your examples and evaluating what you think about the various approaches.
- Have you ever participated in a pay-for-performance program? If not, ask your friends and find someone who has participated in such a program. Consider your or your friend's program. Was it effective in motivating employees? Why or why not? How could the program be improved?

CASE APPLICATION 1 Hong Kong Disneyland: HR Programs to Motivate Employees

Providing a magical experience for every guest (customer), Disney, with all its hotels and parks, is a global leader in the theme-park and service industry. The company's performance depends on a motivated workforce. The HR Training plays a pivotal role in keeping cast (staff) members motivated.

In 2005, Hong Kong Disneyland (HKDL) opened its doors to the public. Since then, the theme park has served 46 million guests from around the world. In 2013, it saw a 10 percent increase in visitors, with a record-high attendance of 7.4 million visitors. Representing about 30 different nationalities, the resort employs workforce of more than 8,000 full-time and part-time employees at the theme park and its two hotels during the most popular summer period. Most of the resort's staff are under 25 years old. The magic begins with the recruitment of employees who are friendly, innovative, responsible, and are passionate about Disney stories. Disney management understands what is important to cast members or what excites them in HKDL. Therefore, HKDL address the value proposition of young talents through comprehensive training programs, transparent career paths and opportunities, recognition and engagement, and by providing a fun environment.

Cast members learn Disney culture in a number of ways such as training and socialization. HKDL provides 380,000 hours of professional and technical training to the entire workforce during the year. They help employees to become knowledgeable cast members, fostering open communication and having fun with their guests. This involves organizing a number of internal and external programs to encourage its cast members to support initiatives for education, health, social, and other outreach services.

The resort also conducts employee surveys to better understand its staff. The results show that cast members in HKDL take pride in their roles and they are motivated and empowered to excel in their roles. As a result, HKDL has received outstanding guest-satisfaction ratings and a range of awards from the hospitality and entertainment sectors including the recipient of the 2014 Randstad Award for Best Workplace Culture.

While the appeal of Disney's characters is enduring, the decade-old HKDL is in the red again. The theme park cited a drop in mainland visitors as the main reason in explaining its disappointing performance. Additional competition with the "one country, two theme parks" situation is imminent as the Shanghai Disney Resort opened in June this year. With regional demand being adequate enough to be shared between the parks, the management at HKDL remain hopeful about the future. In the meantime, they are also working to provide each park with a fresh feel and competitive business environment by providing new investments on theme attractions and promotional offers. Furthermore, the management at HKDL must continue to use HR programs to motivate cast members.[110]

DISCUSSION QUESTIONS

17-13. What would it be like to work at Hong Kong Disneyland (HKDL)?

17-14. Using what you've learned from studying the various motivation theories, what does HKDL's situation tell you about employee motivation?

17-15. What is HKDL's biggest challenge in keeping employees motivated?

17-16. As a manager at HKDL, how would you keep the theme-park employees motivated?

CASE APPLICATION 2 Balancing Success and Happiness

The John Lewis Partnership (JLP) is different; any number of news items or academic journal articles will confirm this. JLP operates 48 John Lewis stores across the United Kingdom, 34 of which are department stores selling everything from lingerie to electrical goods. The partnership also includes 351 Waitrose supermarkets (a company purchased by JLP in 1937). However, it isn't the number of stores, nor the retail offering that make this organization different, it is the 88,900 permanent staff who are the partners of JLP. With profits flowing to the partners and not the external shareholders, JLP is very different to most capitalist enterprises.

In 1864, John Spedan Lewis started trading on Oxford Street in London; however, it was not until 1929 that the John Lewis Partnership was established. John believed that business success should be balanced with the happiness of employees and that by making them partners he was allowing employees to share the responsibility of ownership as well as the rewards in the form of a share of the profits. These rewards have not been insubstantial, averaging 17 percent of average pay, since 1970, when cash bonuses started being paid.

The role of the partners is not limited to simply receiving a share of the partnership profits. The Partnership Council, a democratically elected body, looks after the partners' interests. The Council has a say in how profits are spent, can influence matters such as pay and pensions, and directly elects five members of the Partnership Board. There are mechanisms in place to ensure that this structure allows all partners across the business to have a voice. At a local level, elected partners work alongside managers to influence the running of the individual store. JLP also distributes a weekly in-house newspaper called the Gazette, which actively encourages partners to ask questions, with each question receiving a personal response from management.

So what is it like to work at JLP? In 2010, an article for *The Guardian* newspaper interviewed a number of JLP employees, both present and past. There was a real sense of connection and belonging, even amongst those who had retired. When asked why people stayed with the company twice as long as the industry average, one partner simply replied that if people weren't happy, they had the responsibility and support to do something about it. Other partners referred to a willingness to make extra effort, specifically noting that motivation felt different. Perhaps the greatest praise for this system came from a partner who confirmed she would only begrudgingly move to another company if it offered her twice the salary!

While employee ownership is rare, JLP is not alone. They are members of the Employee Ownership Association (EOA), which represents U.K. organizations that are currently employee-owned or currently moving to this new form of ownership. According to EOA figures, the number of employee owned businesses in the United Kingdom is increasing by 10 percent per annum. In 2009, an independent report by the Demos think tank estimated that the employee-owned sector was worth £25 billion to the U.K. economy and further development should be supported. In 2012, this growing belief in employee-ownership was further supported when the U.K. Deputy Prime Minister called for more companies to follow the JLP model, arguing that firms where staff had more of a stake were more innovative and had higher levels of productivity.

It is unlikely that the JLP model will totally replace the typical capitalist enterprise any time soon. However, the continued success of JLP and the general feeling that a business should be measured against more than share price could see employee-owned organizations becoming far more common in the future.[111]

DISCUSSION QUESTIONS

17-17. Is there a link between the approach at the John Lewis partnership and the earlier theories of motivation?

17-18. Considering the Goal-setting theory, how do you think this partnership structure will affect the setting and achievement of challenging individual goals?

17-19. "Money is not a motivator." Discuss this statement in light of the JLP case.

17-20. Do you think that this partnership approach will solve any of the problems associated with the Equity theory? Why or why not?

17-21. What could be the potential drawbacks of this type of organizational ownership?

ENDNOTES

1. Kelvin Ong, "Elevated by Enjoyment," *HRM Asia*, November 4, 2016, www.hrmasia.com/content/elevated-enjoyment (accessed December 27, 2016).
2. A. Carmeli, B. Ben-Hador, D. A. Waldman, and D. E. Rupp, "How Leaders Cultivate Social Capital and Nurture Employee Vigor: Implications for Job Performance," *Journal of Applied Psychology,* November 2009, pp. 1533–1561.
3. R. M. Steers, R. T. Mowday, and D. L. Shapiro, "The Future of Work Motivation Theory," *Academy of Management Review,* July 2004, pp. 379–387.
4. C. Fritz, C. Fu Lam, and G. M. Spreitzer, "It's the Little Things That Matter: An Examination of Knowledge Workers' Energy Management," *Academy of Management Perspectives,* August 2011, pp. 28–39; A. Carmeli, B. Ben-Hador, D. A. Waldman, and D. E. Rupp, "How Leaders Cultivate Social Capital and Nurture Employee Vigor: Implications for Job Performance," *Journal of Applied Psychology,* November 2009, pp. 1553–1561; and N. Ellemers, D. De Gilder, and S. A. Haslam, "Motivating Individuals and Groups at Work: A Social Identity Perspective on Leadership and Group Performance," *Academy of Management Review,* July 2004, pp. 459–478.
5. A. Mann and J. Harter, "The Worldwide Employee Engagement Crisis," *Gallup* online, www.gallup.com, January 7, 2016.
6. J. Krueger and E. Killham, "At Work, Feeling Good Matters," *Gallup Management Journal,* http://gmj.gallup.com, December 8, 2005.
7. A. Mann and J. Harter, "The Worldwide Employee Engagement Crisis."
8. M. Meece, "Using the Human Touch to Solve Workplace Problems," *New York Times* online, April 3, 2008.
9. A. Maslow, *Motivation and Personality* (New York: McGraw-Hill, 1954); A. Maslow, D. C. Stephens, and G. Heil, *Maslow on Management* (New York: John Wiley & Sons, 1998); M. L. Ambrose and C. T. Kulik, "Old Friends, New Faces: Motivation Research in the 1990s," *Journal of Management*, vol. 25, no. 3, 1999, pp. 231–292; and "Dialogue," *Academy of Management Review*, October 2000, pp. 696–701.
10. See, for example, S. Fowler, "What Maslow's Hierarchy Won't Tell You About Motivation," *Harvard Business Review*, www.hbr.org, November 26, 2014; D. T. Hall and K. E. Nongaim, "An Examination of Maslow's Need Hierarchy in an Organizational Setting," *Organizational Behavior and Human Performance*, February 1968, pp. 12–35; E. E. Lawler III and J. L. Suttle, "A Causal Correlational Test of the Need Hierarchy Concept," *Organizational Behavior and Human Performance*, April 1972, pp. 265–287; R. M. Creech, "Employee Motivation," *Management Quarterly*, Summer 1995, pp. 33–39; J. Rowan, "Maslow Amended," *Journal of Humanistic Psychology*, Winter 1998, pp. 81–92; J. Rowan, "Ascent and Descent in Maslow's Theory," *Journal of Humanistic Psychology*, Summer 1999, pp. 125–133; and M. L. Ambrose and C. T. Kulik, "Old Friends, New Faces: Motivation Research in the 1990s."
11. E. McGirt, "Intel Risks It All… Again," *Fast Company,* November 2009, pp. 88+.
12. D. McGregor, *The Human Side of Enterprise* (New York: McGraw-Hill, 1960). For an updated description of Theories X and Y, see an annotated edition with commentary of *The Human Side of Enterprise* (McGraw-Hill, 2006); and G. Heil, W. Bennis, and D. C. Stephens, *Douglas McGregor, Revisited: Managing the Human Side of Enterprise* (New York: Wiley, 2000).
13. P. Wahba, "One Way Walmart Is Motivating Workers: Less Celine Dion on the PA System," *Fortune* online, www.fortune.com, June 3, 2015.
14. J. M. O'Brien, "The Next Intel," *Wired,* July 2002, pp. 100–107.
15. "What Motivates Employees?" *T&D,* October 2013, p. 16.
16. F. Herzberg, B. Mausner, and B. Snyderman, *The Motivation to Work* (New York: John Wiley, 1959); F. Herzberg, *The Managerial Choice: To Be Effective or to Be Human*, rev. ed. (Salt Lake City: Olympus, 1982); R. M. Creech, "Employee Motivation"; and M. L. Ambrose and C. T. Kulik, "Old Friends, New Faces: Motivation Research in the 1990s."
17. D. C. McClelland, *The Achieving Society* (New York: Van Nostrand Reinhold, 1961); J. W. Atkinson and J. O. Raynor, *Motivation and Achievement* (Washington, DC: Winston, 1974); D. C. McClelland, *Power: The Inner Experience* (New York: Irvington, 1975); and M. J. Stahl, *Managerial and Technical Motivation: Assessing Needs for Achievement, Power, and Affiliation* (New York: Praeger, 1986).
18. McClelland, *The Achieving Society.*

19. McClelland, *Power*; D. C. McClelland and D. H. Burnham, "Power Is the Great Motivator," *Harvard Business Review*, March–April 1976, pp. 100–110.
20. D. Miron and D. C. McClelland, "The Impact of Achievement Motivation Training on Small Businesses," *California Management Review*, Summer 1979, pp. 13–28.
21. J. Harter and A. Adkins, "What Great Managers Do to Engage Employees," *Harvard Business Review* online, www.hbr.org, April 2, 2015.
22. "McClelland: An Advocate of Power," *International Management*, July 1975, pp. 27–29.
23. R. M. Steers, R. T. Mowday, and D. L. Shapiro, "The Future of Work Motivation Theory"; E. A. Locke and G. P. Latham, "What Should We Do About Motivation Theory? Six Recommendations for the Twenty-First Century," *Academy of Management Review,* July 2004, pp. 388–403; and M. L. Ambrose and C. T. Kulik, "Old Friends, New Faces: Motivation Research in the 1990s."
24. A. Barrett, "Cracking the Whip at Wyeth," *BusinessWeek,* February 6, 2006, pp. 70–71.
25. G. P. Latham and E. A. Locke, "Science and Ethics: What Should Count as Evidence Against the Use of Goal Setting?," *Academy of Management Perspective,* August 2009, pp. 88–91; M. L. Ambrose and C. T. Kulik, "Old Friends, New Faces: Motivation Research in the 1990s."
26. J. C. Naylor and D. R. Ilgen, "Goal Setting: A Theoretical Analysis of a Motivational Technique," in *Research in Organizational Behavior*, vol. 6, ed. B. M. Staw and L. L. Cummings (Greenwich, CT: JAI Press, 1984), pp. 95–140; A. R. Pell, "Energize Your People," *Managers Magazine*, December 1992, pp. 28–29; E. A. Locke, "Facts and Fallacies About Goal Theory: Reply to Deci," *Psychological Science*, January 1993, pp. 63–64; M. E. Tubbs, "Commitment as a Moderator of the Goal-Performance Relation: A Case for Clearer Construct Definition," *Journal of Applied Psychology*, February 1993, pp. 86–97; M. P. Collingwood, "Why Don't You Use the Research?" *Management Decision*, May 1993, pp. 48–54; M. E. Tubbs, D. M. Boehne, and J. S. Dahl, "Expectancy, Valence, and Motivational Force Functions in Goal-Setting Research: An Empirical Test," *Journal of Applied Psychology*, June 1993, pp. 361–373; E. A. Locke, "Motivation Through Conscious Goal Setting," *Applied and Preventive Psychology,* vol. 5, 1996, pp. 117–124; M. L. Ambrose and C. T. Kulik, "Old Friends, New Faces: Motivation Research in the 1990s"; E. A. Locke and G. P. Latham, "Building a Practically Useful Theory of Goal Setting and Task Motivation: A 35-Year Odyssey," *American Psychologist,* September 2002, pp. 705–717; Y. Fried and L. H. Slowik, "Enriching Goal-Setting Theory with Time: An Integrated Approach," *Academy of Management Review,* July 2004, pp. 404–422; and G. P. Latham, "The Motivational Benefits of Goal-Setting," *Academy of Management Executive,* November 2004, pp. 126–129.
27. J. B. Miner, *Theories of Organizational Behavior* (Hinsdale, IL: Dryden Press, 1980), p. 65.
28. Leader Making a Difference box based on M. Tabaka, "12 Surprising Facts About YouTube CEO Susan Wojcicki," *Inc. Magazine* online, www.inc.com, September 14, 2015; N. LaPorte, "Rebooting YouTube," *Fast Company* Magazine, www.fastcompany.com, August 4, 2014; G. Weiss, "YouTube CEO Unveils Redesigned App, Additional Creator Spaces," *Entrepreneur Magazine* online, www.entrepreneur.com, July 24, 2015; L. Kroll, "America's Richest Self-made Women," *Forbes* online, www.forbes.com, May 27, 2015.
29. J. A. Wagner III, "Participation's Effects on Performance and Satisfaction: A Reconsideration of Research and Evidence," *Academy of Management Review*, April 1994, pp. 312–330; J. George-Falvey, "Effects of Task Complexity and Learning Stage on the Relationship Between Participation in Goal Setting and Task Performance," *Academy of Management Proceedings* on Disk, 1996; T. D. Ludwig and E. S. Geller, "Assigned Versus Participative Goal Setting and Response Generalization: Managing Injury Control Among Professional Pizza Deliverers," *Journal of Applied Psychology,* April 1997, pp. 253–261; and S. G. Harkins and M. D. Lowe, "The Effects of Self-Set Goals on Task Performance," *Journal of Applied Social Psychology,* January 2000, pp. 1–40.
30. J. M. Ivancevich and J. T. McMahon, "The Effects of Goal Setting, External Feedback, and Self-Generated Feedback on Outcome Variables: A Field Experiment," *Academy of Management Journal*, June 1982, pp. 359–372; and E. A. Locke, "Motivation Through Conscious Goal Setting."
31. J. R. Hollenbeck, C. R. Williams, and H. J. Klein, "An Empirical Examination of the Antecedents of Commitment to Difficult Goals," *Journal of Applied Psychology*, February 1989, pp. 18–23; see also J. C. Wofford, V. L. Goodwin, and S. Premack, "Meta-Analysis of the Antecedents of Personal Goal Level and of the Antecedents and Consequences of Goal Commitment," *Journal of Management*, September 1992, pp. 595–615; Tubbs, "Commitment as a Moderator of the Goal-Performance Relation"; J. W. Smither, M. London, and R. R. Reilly, "Does Performance Improve Following Multisource Feedback? A Theoretical Model, Meta-Analysis, and Review of Empirical Findings," *Personnel Psychology,* Spring 2005, pp. 171–203.
32. Y. Gong, J-C. Huang, and J-L. Farh, "Employee Learning Orientation, Transformational Leadership, and Employee Creativity: The Mediating Role of Employee Self-Efficacy," *Academy of Management Journal,* August 2009, pp. 765–778; M. E. Gist, "Self-Efficacy: Implications for Organizational Behavior and Human Resource Management," *Academy of Management Review*, July 1987, pp. 472–485; and A. Bandura, *Self-Efficacy: The Exercise of Control* (New York: Freeman, 1997).
33. E. A. Locke, E. Frederick, C. Lee, and P. Bobko, "Effect of Self-Efficacy, Goals, and Task Strategies on Task Performance," *Journal of Applied Psychology*, May 1984, pp. 241–251; M. E. Gist and T. R. Mitchell, "Self-Efficacy: A Theoretical Analysis of Its Determinants and Malleability," *Academy of Management Review*, April 1992, pp. 183–211; A. D. Stajkovic and F. Luthans, "Self-Efficacy and Work-Related Performance: A Meta-Analysis," *Psychological Bulletin,* September 1998, pp. 240–261; and A. Bandura, "Cultivate Self-Efficacy for Personal and Organizational Effectiveness," in *Handbook of Principles of Organizational Behavior,* ed. E. Locke (Malden, MA: Blackwell, 2004), pp. 120–136.
34. A. Bandura and D. Cervone, "Differential Engagement in Self-Reactive Influences in Cognitively-Based Motivation," *Organizational Behavior and Human Decision Processes*, August 1986, pp. 92–113; and R. Ilies and T. A. Judge, "Goal Regulation Across Time: The Effects of Feedback and

Affect," *Journal of Applied Psychology,* May 2005, pp. 453–467.

35. See J. C. Anderson and C. A. O'Reilly, "Effects of an Organizational Control System on Managerial Satisfaction and Performance," *Human Relations*, June 1981, pp. 491–501; and J. P. Meyer, B. Schacht-Cole, and I. R. Gellatly, "An Examination of the Cognitive Mechanisms by Which Assigned Goals Affect Task Performance and Reactions to Performance," *Journal of Applied Social Psychology,* vol. 18, no. 5, 1988, pp. 390–408.
36. K. Maher and K. Hudson, "Wal-Mart to Sweeten Bonus Plans for Staff," *Wall Street Journal,* March 22, 2007, p. A11; and Reuters, "Wal-Mart Workers to Get New Bonus Plan," CNNMoney.com, March 22, 2007.
37. B. F. Skinner, *Science and Human Behavior* (New York: Free Press, 1953); and Skinner, *Beyond Freedom and Dignity* (New York: Knopf, 1972).
38. The same data, for instance, can be interpreted in either goal-setting or reinforcement terms, as shown in E. A. Locke, "Latham vs. Komaki: A Tale of Two Paradigms," *Journal of Applied Psychology*, February 1980, pp. 16–23. Also, see M. O. Ambrose and C. T. Kulik, "Old Friends, New Faces: Motivation Research in the 1990s."
39. "Few Managers Get Kudos for Helping Develop Employees," *T&D,* August 2012, p. 22.
40. David Crouch, "Efficiency Up, Turnover Down: Sweden Experiments with Six-Hour Working Day," *The Guardian (UK)*, September 17, 2015, https://www.theguardian.com/world/2015/sep/17/efficiency-up-turnover-down-sweden-experiments-with-six-hour-working-day (accessed December 27, 2016).
41. See, for example, A. M. Grant and S. K. Parker, "Redesigning Work Design Theories: The Rise of Relational and Proactive Perspectives," in *The Academy of Management Annals,* ed. J. P. Walsh and A. P. Brief (Hillsdale, NJ: Psychology Press, 2009), pp. 317–375; R. W. Griffin, "Toward an Integrated Theory of Task Design," in *Research in Organizational Behavior*, vol. 9, ed. L. L. Cummings and B. M. Staw (Greenwich, CT: JAI Press, 1987), pp. 79–120; and M. Campion, "Interdisciplinary Approaches to Job Design: A Constructive Replication with Extensions," *Journal of Applied Psychology*, August 1988, pp. 467–481.
42. N. Tasler, "Help Your Best People Do a Better Job," *BusinessWeek* online, www.bloomberg.com/businessweek, March 26, 2010; S. Caudron, "The De-Jobbing of America," *Industry Week*, September 5, 1994, pp. 31–36; W. Bridges, "The End of the Job," *Fortune*, September 19, 1994, pp. 62–74; and K. H. Hammonds, K. Kelly, and K. Thurston, "Rethinking Work," *BusinessWeek*, October 12, 1994, pp. 75–87.
43. M. A. Campion and C. L. McClelland, "Follow-Up and Extension of the Interdisciplinary Costs and Benefits of Enlarged Jobs," *Journal of Applied Psychology*, June 1993, pp. 339–351; and M. L. Ambrose and C. T. Kulik, "Old Friends, New Faces: Motivation Research in the 1990s."
44. See, for example, J. R. Hackman and G. R. Oldham, *Work Redesign* (Reading, MA: Addison-Wesley, 1980); Miner, *Theories of Organizational Behavior*, pp. 231–266; R. W. Griffin, "Effects of Work Redesign on Employee Perceptions, Attitudes, and Behaviors: A Long-Term Investigation," *Academy of Management Journal,* June 1991, pp. 425–435; J. L. Cotton, *Employee Involvement* (Newbury Park, CA: Sage, 1993), pp. 141–172; and M. L. Ambrose and C. T. Kulik, "Old Friends, New Faces: Motivation Research in the 1990s."
45. J. R. Hackman and G. R. Oldham, "Development of the Job Diagnostic Survey," *Journal of Applied Psychology*, April 1975, pp. 159–170; and J. R. Hackman and G. R. Oldham, "Motivation Through the Design of Work: Test of a Theory," *Organizational Behavior and Human Performance,* August 1976, pp. 250–279.
46. J. R. Hackman, "Work Design," in *Improving Life at Work*, ed. R. Hackman and J. L. Suttle (Glenview, IL: Scott, Foresman, 1977), p. 129; and M. L. Ambrose and C. T. Kulik, "Old Friends, New Faces: Motivation Research in the 1990s."
47. J. Smith, "18 Meaningful Jobs That Pay Very Well," *Business Insider* online, www.businessinsider.com, April 1, 2016; "Most and Least Meaningful Jobs Full List—PayScale," www.payscale.com, accessed May 26, 2016.
48. D. J. Holman, C. M. Axtell, C. A. Sprigg, P. Totterdell, and T. D. Wall, "The Mediating Role of Job Characteristics in Job Redesign Interventions: A Serendipitous Quasi-Experiment," *Journal of Organizational Behavior,* January 2010, pp. 84–105.
49. J. L. Pierce, I. Jussila, and A. Cummings, "Psychological Ownership Within the Job Design Context: Revision of the Job Characteristics Model," *Journal of Organizational Behavior,* May 2009, pp. 477–496.
50. A. M. Grant and S. K. Parker, "Redesigning Work Design Theories: The Rise of Relational and Proactive Perspectives."
51. V. Giang, "Why Innovative Companies Like Google Are Letting Employees Craft Their Own Jobs," *Fast Company* online, www.fastcompany.com, April 29, 2016.
52. J. Camps and R. Luna-Arocas, "High Involvement Work Practices and Firm Performance," *The International Journal of Human Resource Management,* May 2009, pp. 1056–1077; M. M. Butts, R. J. Vandenberg, D. M. DeJoy, B. S. Schaffer, and M. G. Wilson, "Individual Reactions to High Involvement Work Practices: Investigating the Role of Empowerment and Perceived Organizational Support," *Journal of Occupational Health Psychology,* April 2009, pp. 122–136; P. Boxall and K. Macky, "Research and Theory on High-Performance Work Systems: Progressing the High-Involvement Stream," *Human Resource Management Journal,* vol. 19, no. 1, 2009, pp. 3–23; R. D. Mohr and C. Zoghi, "High-Involvement Work Design and Job Satisfaction," *Industrial and Labor Relations Review,* April 2008, pp. 275–296; and C. D. Zatzick and R. D. Iverson, "High-Involvement Management and Workforce Reduction: Competitive Advantage or Disadvantage?," *Academy of Management Journal,* October 2006, pp. 999–1015.
53. J. S. Adams, "Inequity in Social Exchanges," in *Advances in Experimental Social Psychology*, vol. 2, ed. L. Berkowitz (New York: Academic Press, 1965), pp. 267–300; M. L. Ambrose and C. T. Kulik, "Old Friends, New Faces: Motivation Research in the 1990s"; and T. Menon and L. Thompson, "Envy at Work," *Harvard Business Review,* April 2010, pp. 74–79.
54. See, for example, P. S. Goodman and A. Friedman, "An Examination of Adams' Theory of Inequity," *Administrative Science Quarterly*, September 1971, pp. 271–288; M. R. Carrell, "A Longitudinal Field Assessment of Employee Perceptions of Equitable Treatment," *Organizational Behavior and Human Performance*, February 1978, pp. 108–118; E. Walster, G. W. Walster, and W. G. Scott, *Equity: Theory and*

Research (Boston: Allyn & Bacon, 1978); R. G. Lord and J. A. Hohenfeld, "Longitudinal Field Assessment of Equity Effects on the Performance of Major League Baseball Players," *Journal of Applied Psychology*, February 1979, pp. 19–26; J. E. Dittrich and M. R. Carrell, "Organizational Equity Perceptions, Employee Job Satisfaction, and Departmental Absence and Turnover Rates," *Organizational Behavior and Human Performance*, August 1979, pp. 29–40; and J. Greenberg, "Cognitive Reevaluation of Outcomes in Response to Underpayment Inequity," *Academy of Management Journal,* March 1989, pp. 174–184.

55. R. Tulshyan, "Robin Wright's Demand for Equal Pay Should Be a Wake-Up Call for Business Leaders Everywhere," *Forbes* online, www.forbes.com, May 18, 2016.
56. P. S. Goodman, "An Examination of Referents Used in the Evaluation of Pay," *Organizational Behavior and Human Performance*, October 1974, pp. 170–195; S. Ronen, "Equity Perception in Multiple Comparisons: A Field Study," *Human Relations*, April 1986, pp. 333–346; R. W. Scholl, E. A. Cooper, and J. F. McKenna, "Referent Selection in Determining Equity Perception: Differential Effects on Behavioral and Attitudinal Outcomes," *Personnel Psychology*, Spring 1987, pp. 113–127; and C. T. Kulik and M. L. Ambrose, "Personal and Situational Determinants of Referent Choice," *Academy of Management Review*, April 1992, pp. 212–237.
57. See, for example, R. C. Dailey and D. J. Kirk, "Distributive and Procedural Justice as Antecedents of Job Dissatisfaction and Intent to Turnover," *Human Relations,* March 1992, pp. 305–316; D. B. McFarlin and P. D. Sweeney, "Distributive and Procedural Justice as Predictors of Satisfaction with Personal and Organizational Outcomes," *Academy of Management Journal,* August 1992, pp. 626–637; M. A. Konovsky, "Understanding Procedural Justice and Its Impact on Business Organizations," *Journal of Management,* vol. 26, no. 3, 2000, pp. 489–511; J. A. Colquitt, "Does the Justice of One Interact with the Justice of Many? Reactions to Procedural Justice in Teams," *Journal of Applied Psychology,* August 2004, pp. 633–646; J. Brockner, "Why It's So Hard to Be Fair," *Harvard Business Review,* March 2006, pp. 122–129; and B. M. Wiesenfeld, W. B. Swann Jr., J. Brockner, and C. A. Bartel, "Is More Fairness Always Preferred: Self-Esteem Moderates Reactions to Procedural Justice," *Academy of Management Journal,* October 2007, pp. 1235–1253.
58. M. McGrath, "Why Being a Women Can Cost You More Than $400,000," *Forbes* online, www.forbes.com, April 5, 2016.
59. V. H. Vroom, *Work and Motivation* (New York: John Wiley, 1964).
60. See, for example, H. G. Heneman III and D. P. Schwab, "Evaluation of Research on Expectancy Theory Prediction of Employee Performance," *Psychological Bulletin*, July 1972, pp. 1–9; and L. Reinharth and M. Wahba, "Expectancy Theory as a Predictor of Work Motivation, Effort Expenditure, and Job Performance," *Academy of Management Journal*, September 1975, pp. 502–537.
61. See, for example, V. H. Vroom, "Organizational Choice: A Study of Pre- and Postdecision Processes," *Organizational Behavior and Human Performance*, April 1966, pp. 212–225; L. W. Porter and E. E. Lawler III, *Managerial Attitudes and Performance* (Homewood, IL: Richard D. Irwin, 1968); W. Van Eerde and H. Thierry, "Vroom's Expectancy Models and Work-Related Criteria: A Meta-Analysis," *Journal of Applied Psychology,* October 1996, pp. 575–586; and M. L. Ambrose and C. T. Kulik, "Old Friends, New Faces: Motivation Research in the 1990s."
62. See, for instance, M. Siegall, "The Simplistic Five: An Integrative Framework for Teaching Motivation," *The Organizational Behavior Teaching Review*, vol. 12, no. 4, 1987–1988, pp. 141–43.
63. C. B. Bhattacharya, "How Companies Can Tap Sustainability to Motivate Staff," *Knowledge @ Wharton*, September 29, 2016, http://knowledge.wharton.upenn.edu/article/how-companies-tap-sustainability-to-motivate-staff/ (accessed December 27, 2016).
64. J. W. Miller and D. Kesmodel, "Drinking on the Job Comes to a Head at Carlsberg," *Wall Street Journal,* April 10–11, 2010, pp. A1+; and Associated Press, "Carlsberg Workers Balk at Loss of On-the-Job Beer," *Wall Street Journal,* April 9, 2010, p. B2.
65. N. J. Adler with A. Gundersen, *International Dimensions of Organizational Behavior*, 5th ed. (Cincinnati, OH: South-Western College Publishing, 2008).
66. G. Hofstede, "Motivation, Leadership and Organization: Do American Theories Apply Abroad?" *Organizational Dynamics,* Summer 1980, p. 55.
67. Ibid.
68. J. K. Giacobbe-Miller, D. J. Miller, and V. I. Victorov, "A Comparison of Russian and U.S. Pay Allocation Decisions, Distributive Justice Judgments and Productivity Under Different Payment Conditions," *Personnel Psychology,* Spring 1998, pp. 137–163.
69. S. L. Mueller and L. D. Clarke, "Political-Economic Context and Sensitivity to Equity: Differences Between the United States and the Transition Economies of Central and Eastern Europe," *Academy of Management Journal,* June 1998, pp. 319–329.
70. S. D. Sidle, "Building a Committed Global Workforce: Does What Employees Want Depend on Culture?," *Academy of Management Perspective,* February 2009, pp. 79–80; and G. A. Gelade, P. Dobson, and K. Auer, "Individualism, Masculinity, and the Sources of Organizational Commitment," *Journal of Cross-Cultural Psychology,* vol. 39, no. 5, 2008, pp. 599–617.
71. P. Brotherton, "Employee Loyalty Slipping Worldwide; Respect, Work-Life Balance Are Top Engagers," *T&D,* February 2012, p. 24.
72. I. Harpaz, "The Importance of Work Goals: An International Perspective," *Journal of International Business Studies,* First Quarter 1990, pp. 75–93.
73. G. E. Popp, H. J. Davis, and T. T. Herbert, "An International Study of Intrinsic Motivation Composition," *Management International Review,* January 1986, pp. 28–35.
74. R. W. Brislin, B. MacNab, R. Worthley, F. Kabigting Jr., and B. Zukis, "Evolving Perceptions of Japanese Workplace Motivation: An Employee-Manager Comparison," *International Journal of Cross-Cultural Management,* April 2005, pp. 87–104.
75. J. T. Marquez, "Tailor-Made Careers," *Workforce Management Online,* January 2010.
76. J. R. Billings and D. L. Sharpe, "Factors Influencing Flextime Usage Among Employed Married Women," *Consumer*

Interests Annual, 1999, pp. 89–94; and I. Harpaz, "The Importance of Work Goals: An International Perspective," *Journal of International Business Studies*, First Quarter 1990, pp. 75–93.

77. N. Ramachandran, "New Paths at Work," *US News & World Report,* March 20, 2006, p. 47; S. Armour, "Generation Y: They've Arrived at Work with a New Attitude," *USA Today,* November 6, 2005, pp. B1+; and R. Kanfer and P. L. Ackerman, "Aging, Adult Development, and Work Motivation," *Academy of Management Review,* July 2004, pp. 440–458.
78. T. D. Golden and J. F. Veiga, "The Impact of Extent of Telecommuting on Job Satisfaction: Resolving Inconsistent Findings," *Journal of Management,* April 2005, pp. 301–318.
79. See, for instance, M. Alpert, "The Care and Feeding of Engineers," *Fortune*, September 21, 1992, pp. 86–95; G. Poole, "How to Manage Your Nerds," *Forbes ASAP*, December 1994, pp. 132–136; T. J. Allen and R. Katz, "Managing Technical Professionals and Organizations: Improving and Sustaining the Performance of Organizations, Project Teams, and Individual Contributors," *Sloan Management Review,* Summer 2002, pp. S4–S5; and S. R. Barley and G. Kunda, "Contracting: A New Form of Professional Practice," *Academy of Management Perspectives,* February 2006, pp. 45–66.
80. J. P. Broschak and A. Davis-Blake, "Mixing Standard Work and Nonstandard Deals: The Consequences of Heterogeneity in Employment Arrangements," *Academy of Management Journal,* April 2006, pp. 371–393; M. L. Kraimer, S. J. Wayne, R. C. Liden, and R. T. Sparrowe, "The Role of Job Security in Understanding the Relationship Between Employees' Perceptions of Temporary Workers and Employees' Performance," *Journal of Applied Psychology,* March 2005, pp. 389–398; and C. E. Connelly and D. G. Gallagher, "Emerging Trends in Contingent Work Research," *Journal of Management,* November 2004, pp. 959–983.
81. C. L. Wilkin, "I Can't Get No Job Satisfaction: Meta-analysis Comparing Permanent and Contingent Workers," *Journal of Organizational Behavior*, vol. 34, 2013, pp. 47–64.
82. V. Lipman, "The Best Managers," *Forbes* online, www.forbes.com, February 13, 2016.
83. Marianne Calnan, "The Group Company Rewards Staff with Trip to Barbados," *Employee Benefits (UK)*, January 28, 2016, www.employeebenefits.co.uk/issues/january-online-2016/the-group-company-rewards-staff-with-trip-to-barbados (accessed December 27, 2016).
84. K. E. Culp, "Playing Field Widens for Stack's Great Game," *Springfield, Missouri, News-Leader,* January 9, 2005, pp. 1A+.
85. B. Fotsch and J. Case, "Introducing a Blog About Companies That Engage Their Employees by Opening the Books," *Forbes* online, www.forbes.com, July 20, 2015.
86. D. Meinert, "An Open Book," *HR Magazine,* April 2013, pp. 43–46; K. Berman and J. Knight, "What Your Employees Don't Know Will Hurt You," *Wall Street Journal,* February 27, 2012, p. R4; J. Case, "The Open-Book Revolution," *Inc.*, June 1995, pp. 26–50; J. P. Schuster, J. Carpenter, and M. P. Kane, *The Power of Open-Book Management* (New York: John Wiley, 1996); J. Case, "Opening the Books," *Harvard Business Review*, March–April 1997, pp. 118–127; and D. Drickhamer, "Open Books to Elevate Performance," *Industry Week,* November 2002, p. 16.
87. D. Fenn, "Show Me the Money: How Four Companies Profit from Open Book Management," *CBS News* online, www.cbsnews.com, September 22, 2010.
88. P. Lencioni, "The No-Cost Way to Motivate," *BusinessWeek,* October 5, 2009, p. 84; and F. Luthans and A. D. Stajkovic, "Provide Recognition for Performance Improvement," in *Principles of Organizational Behavior*, ed. E. A. Locke (Oxford, England: Blackwell, 2000), pp. 166–180.
89. C. Huff, "Recognition That Resonates," *Workforce Management Online,* April 1, 2008.
90. D. Drickhamer, "Best Plant Winners: Nichols Foods Ltd.," *Industry Week,* October 1, 2001, pp. 17–19.
91. A. Bryant, "A Wall of Honor That's Built by Your Colleagues," *New York Times* online, June 30, 2012.
92. Kelvin Ong, "Small Gestures, Big Impacts," *HRM Asia*, November 3, 2016, www.hrmasia.com/content/small-gestures-big-impacts (accessed December 27, 2016); Marianne Calnan, "Marks and Spencer Takes a Mixed Approach to Staff Motivation," *Employee Benefits (UK)*, May 15, 2015, www.employeebenefits.co.uk/issues/may-2015/marks-and-spencer-takes-a-mixed-approach-to-staff-motivation (accessed December 27, 2016).
93. "Trends in Employee Recognition," *Workspan*, July 2015.
94. K. Piombino, "Infographic: Only 12% of Workers Get Frequent Appreciation," www.hrcommunication.com, January 4, 2013.
95. Cited in S. Caudron, "The Top 20 Ways to Motivate Employees," *Industry Week,* April 3, 1995, pp. 15–16. See also B. Nelson, "Try Praise," *Inc.*, September 1996, p. 115; and J. Wiscombe, "Rewards Get Results," *Workforce,* April 2002, pp. 42–48.
96. "Trends in Employee Recognition," A Report by WorldatWork, May 2015.
97. R. Flandez, "Vegetable Gardens Help Morale Grow," *Wall Street Journal* online, www.wsj.com, August 18, 2009; "Pay Raise Alternatives = Motivated Employees," *Training,* July/August 2009, p. 11; D. Koeppel, "Strange Brew: Beer and Office Democracy," CNNMoney.com, June 9, 2009; and B. Brim and T. Simon, "Strengths on the Factory Floor," *The Gallup Management Journal* online, http://gmj.gallup.com, March 10, 2009.
98. V. M. Barret, "Fight the Jerks," *Forbes,* July 2, 2007, pp. 52–54.
99. E. White, "The Best vs. the Rest," *Wall Street Journal,* January 30, 2006, pp. B1+.
100. R. K. Abbott, "Performance-Based Flex: A Tool for Managing Total Compensation Costs," *Compensation and Benefits Review*, March–April 1993, pp. 18–21; J. R. Schuster and P. K. Zingheim, "The New Variable Pay: Key Design Issues," *Compensation and Benefits Review*, March–April 1993, pp. 27–34; C. R. Williams and L. P. Livingstone, "Another Look at the Relationship Between Performance and Voluntary Turnover," *Academy of Management Journal*, April 1994, pp. 269–298; A. M. Dickinson and K. L. Gillette, "A Comparison of the Effects of Two Individual Monetary Incentive Systems on Productivity: Piece Rate Pay Versus Base Pay Plus Incentives," *Journal of Organizational Behavior Management*, Spring 1994, pp. 3–82; and C. B. Cadsby, F. Song, and F. Tapon, "Sorting and Incentive Effects of Pay for Performance: An Experimental Investigation," *Academy of Management Journal,* April 2007, pp. 387–405.
101. "Incentive Pay Practices: Privately Held Companies," WorldatWork, February 2016.

102. "More Than 20 Percent of Japanese Firms Use Pay Systems Based on Performance," *Manpower Argus*, May 1998, p. 7; and E. Beauchesne, "Pay Bonuses Improve Productivity, Study Shows," *Vancouver Sun*, September 13, 2002, p. D5.
103. C. Trudell and Y. Hagiwara, "Toyota Plans Overhaul to Seniority-Based Pay," *Bloomberg Business* online, www .bloomberg.com, January 26, 2015.
104. K. Inagaki, "Japan Inc Shuns Seniority Pay in Favour of Merit-based Pay," *The Financial Times* online, www.ft.com, January 27, 2015.
105. H. Rheem, "Performance Management Programs," *Harvard Business Review*, September–October 1996, pp. 8–9; G. Sprinkle, "The Effect of Incentive Contracts on Learning and Performance," *Accounting Review*, July 2000, pp. 299–326; and "Do Incentive Awards Work?," *HRFocus*, October 2000, pp. 1–3.
106. R. D. Banker, S. Y. Lee, G. Potter, and D. Srinivasan, "Contextual Analysis of Performance Impacts on Outcome-Based Incentive Compensation," *Academy of Management Journal*, August 1996, pp. 920–948.
107. B. S. Frey and M. Osterloh, "Stop Typing Pay to Performance," *Harvard Business Review*, January–February 2012, pp. 51–52.
108. T. Reason, "Why Bonus Plans Fail," *CFO*, January 2003, p. 53; and "Has Pay For Performance Had Its Day?," *The McKinsey Quarterly*, no. 4, 2002, accessed on Forbes website, www.forbes.com.
109. L. Weber and R. E. Silverman, "Workers Share Their Salary Secrets," *Wall Street Journal*, April 17, 2013, pp. B1+; R. E. Silverman, "Psst…This Is What Your Co-Worker Is Paid," *Wall Street Journal*, January 30, 2013, p. B6; and R. E. Silverman, "My Colleague, My Paymaster," *Wall Street Journal*, April 4, 2012, pp. B1+.
110. "Disneyfication and Localisation: The Cultural Globalisation Process of Hong Kong Disneyland," Vol. 49 issue: 2, pp. 383–397. Article first published online May 3, 2011, Issue published on February 1, 2012; Du, J. (2016). "Opportunities and Challenges for Shanghai Disneyland–A Stakeholder Analysis," *Handbook Event Market China*, 229; SyChangco, J. A., and Singh, R. (2008, November). Hk Disneyland Vs. Ocean Park. In Conference Proceedings, Vol. 9, pp. 188–196; "How Can HK Disneyland Keep Employees Motivated?," Disney monash college, 2013, https://disneymonashcollege .wordpress.com/2013/05/10/how-can-hk-disneyland-keep-employees-motivated-5/; cpjobs.com, Darius Musni, "Disney Training Aims for Stars," September 10, 2013, http://www.cpjobs.com/hk/article/disney-training-aims-stars; Albert Cheng, "Hong Kong Disneyland Has Only Itself to Blame for 2015 Losses," *South China Morning Post*, February 25, 2015, http://www.scmp.com; "Is the fairytale over for Hong Kong Disneyland? Analysts see tough times ahead for 10-year-old theme park amid tourism slump," *South China Morning Post*, 2015, http://www.scmp.com; Mandy Zuo, Daniel Ren, and Nikki Sun,"One Country, Two Disneys: Can Shanghai and Hong Kong Theme Parks Share the Spoils in Battle for the Tourism Dollar?" *South China Morning Post*, January 30, 2016, http://www.scmp. com; Melissa Stevens, "Why Hong Kong Disneyland Loses its Magic in the Rain," *South China Morning Post*, April 13, 2016, http://www.scmp.com; Nikki Sun, "Hong Kong Disneyland Drops Bombshell as It Announces Sudden Resignation of Managing Director for 'Personal Reasons,'" *South China Morning Post*, March 7, 2016, http://www.scmp .com; and Nikki Sun, "It's a Slow Year after All: Hong Kong Disneyland Reports First Annual Business Loss Since 2011," *South China Morning Post*, February 15, 2016, http://www .scmp.com.
111. The John Lewis Partnership Web site, http://www .johnlewispartnership.co.uk/about/our-heritage/our-history/our-history-text-version.html, accessed December, 2016; Keith Bradley and Saul Estrin, "Profit Sharing in the British Retail Trade Sector: The Relative Performance of the John Lewis Partnership," *The Journal of Industrial Economics* Vol. 40, September, 1992, pp. 291–304; "Partnership Council," John Lewis Partnership Web site, http://www .johnlewispartnership.co.uk; Jon Henley, "Is John Lewis the Best Company in Britain to Work for?" *The Guardian*, https://www.theguardian.com, March 16, 2010; William Davies, "Reinventing the Firm," *Mixed Sources*, accessed on December, 2016; and Paranque and Willmott, "Critical Studies on Corporate Responsibility, Governance and Sustainability," Vol. 10, Coops, An Alternative to Capitalism.

PART 5 Management Practice

A Manager's Dilemma

How would you feel as a new employee if your boss asked you to do something and you had to admit that you didn't know how to do it? Most of us would probably feel pretty inadequate and incompetent. Now imagine how strange and uncomfortable it would be if, after experiencing such an incident, you went home with the boss because you were roommates and have been friends since fourth grade. That's the situation faced by John, Glen, and Kurt. John and Kurt are employees at a software company that their friend Glen and four others started. The business now has 39 employees, and the "friends" are finding out that mixing work and friendships can be tricky! At home, they're equals. They share a three-bedroom condo and divide up housework and other chores. However, at work, equality is out the door. Glen is John's boss and Kurt's boss is another company manager. Recently, the company moved into a new workspace. As part of the four-person management team, Glen has a corner office with windows. However, John was assigned a cubicle and is annoyed at Glen for not standing up for him when offices were assigned. But John didn't complain because he didn't want to get an office only because of his friendship with Glen. Another problem brewing is that the roommates compete to outlast one another at working late. Kurt's boss is afraid that he's going to burn out. Other awkward moments arise whenever the company's performance is discussed. When Glen wants to get something off his chest about work matters, he has to stop himself. And then there's the "elephant in the room." If the software company is ever bought out by a larger company, Glen (and his three partners) stand to profit dramatically, thereby creating some interesting emotional issues for the roommates. Although it might seem easy to say the solution is to move, real estate is too expensive and, besides that, these guys are good friends.

Put yourself in Glen's shoes. Using what you've learned in Part 5 about individual behavior, communication, employee motivation, and leadership, how would you handle this situation?

Global Sense

As you discovered in this part of the text, employee engagement is an important focus for managers. Managers want their employees to be connected to, satisfied with, and enthusiastic about their jobs; that is, to be engaged. Why is employee engagement so important? The level of employee engagement serves as an indicator of organizational health and ultimately business results—success or failure. The latest available data (2013) on global employee engagement levels showed that only 13 percent of employees (surveyed from 142 countries) were engaged in their jobs; 63 percent were not engaged, and 24 percent were actively disengaged. That is, only 13 percent of employees worldwide say they're passionate about and deeply connected to their work. The region of East Asia showed the lowest proportion of engaged employees at 6 percent. The global regions of Australia and New Zealand and the United States and Canada showed the highest levels of employee engagement at around 24 percent. And the highest level of active disengagement of employees is in the MENA region—Middle East and North Africa.

So what can managers do to get and keep employees engaged? Some important efforts include providing opportunities for career advancement, offering recognition, and having a good organization reputation.

Discuss the following questions in light of what you learned in Part 5.

- *What role do you think external factors such as the global economic downturn or a country's culture play in levels of employee engagement? Discuss.*
- *What role does an organization's motivational programs play in whether an employee is engaged or not? Discuss.*
- *How might a manager's leadership style affect an employee's level of engagement? Discuss.*
- *Look at what we discussed about managerial communication in this part. What could a manager do in the way he or she communicates to affect an employee's level of engagement?*
- *You're a manager of a workplace that has different "generations." How will you approach engaging your employees? Do you think Gen Y employees are going to be more difficult to "engage"? Discuss.*

Sources: The State of the Global Workplace: Employee Engagement Insights for Business Leaders Worldwide, Gallup Organization, http://www.gallup.com/strategic-consulting/164735/state-global-workplace.aspx, accessed August 15, 2014; M. Wilson, "Study: Employee Engagement Ticking Up, But It's Not All Good News," www.hrcommunication.com, June 18, 2012; "2012 Trends in Global Employee Engagement," www.aon.com, June 17, 2012; K. Gurchiek, "Engagement Erosion Plagues Employers Worldwide," HR Magazine, *June 2012, p. 17; and T. Maylett and J. Nielsen, "There Is No Cookie-Cutter Approach to Engagement,"* T&D, *April 2012, pp. 54–59.*

Continuing Case

Starbucks—Leading

Once people are hired or brought into organizations, managers must oversee and coordinate their work so that organizational goals can be pursued and achieved. This is the leading function of management. And it's an important one! However, it also can be quite challenging. Managing people successfully means understanding their attitudes, behaviors, personalities, individual and team work efforts, motivation, conflicts, and so forth. That's not an easy thing to do. In fact, understanding how people behave and why they do the things they do is downright difficult at times. Starbucks has worked hard to create a workplace environment in which employees (partners) are *encouraged to* and *want to* put forth their best efforts. Howard Schultz says he believes that people everywhere have the same desire—to be respected, valued, and appreciated.

Starbucks—Focus on Individuals

Even with some 235,000 full- and part-time partners around the world, one thing that's been important to Howard Schultz from day one is the relationship he has with employees. Schultz is an ardent proponent of a people-first approach and recognizes that the success of Starbucks is due to its partners (employees). And one way Starbucks demonstrates the concern it has for the relationship with its partners is through an attitude survey that gives partners an opportunity to voice their opinions about their experiences. It also measures overall satisfaction and engagement—the degree to which partners are connected to the company. It's been an effective way for Starbucks to show that it cares about what its employees think.

For example, a partner view survey was conducted in early 2010 with partners in the United States and Canada and in the international regional support centers in Europe/Middle East/Africa, Asia Pacific and Latin America, at Starbucks Coffee Trading Company in Switzerland, at Starbucks Coffee Agronomy Company in Costa Rica, and at the coffee roasting facility in Amsterdam. At the end of the survey, Howard Schultz thanked partners for taking the survey. He also acknowledged that the previous year and a half had been difficult (it was the time of Schultz transitioning back into the CEO position) and that partners had been asked to do a lot during that time. The tough and emotional decisions to be made and the company's financial crisis weren't easy for any of them—from the top to the bottom of the organization. But Schultz also reiterated that his number-one commitment was to the company's partners and reinventing the partner experience at Starbucks. Although results aren't publicly available, it's likely that managers heard the good and the bad stuff that partners experienced and were feeling. It was a good barometer for gauging employee attitudes after a difficult time of transition and transformation for the company. Earlier partner surveys have provided relevant and important clues to employee attitudes. For instance, in a survey from 2005, well over half (64 percent) of partners responded to the survey—much higher than the number of respondents to the previous survey in 2003, in which the partner response rate was only 46 percent. Responses to questions about partner satisfaction and partner engagement were extremely positive: 87 percent of partners said they were satisfied or very satisfied, and 73 percent said they were engaged with the company. (The numbers in 2003 were 82 percent satisfied and 73 percent engaged.) In addition, partners specifically said they "Know what is expected of them at work; believe someone at work cares about them; and work for managers who promote work/life balance." In a 2015 survey, partners ranked themselves as most happy compared to workers in other U.S. retail firms. It shouldn't be a surprise that partners tend to stay with the company. Some reports estimate that Starbucks' turnover rate is 120 percent less than the industry average. But partners also identified some areas where they felt improvements were needed. These included "Celebrate successes more; provide more effective coaching and feedback; and improve communication with partners." And Starbucks' managers try to address any concerns raised in these surveys or concerns expressed in other ways. In another review published by Glassdoor.com, Starbucks employees gave the company 3.8 stars out of 5 and 91 percent approved of CEO Howard Schultz.

Every organization needs employees who will be able to do their jobs efficiently and effectively. Starbucks states that it wants employees who are "adaptable, self-motivated, passionate, creative team players." As you can see, this "ideal" Starbucks partner should have individual strengths and should be able to work as part of a team. In the retail store setting, especially, individuals must work together as a team to provide the experience that customers expect when they

Knowing that its people are the heart and soul of its success, Starbucks values its employees and has created an environment that motivates them to work efficiently and effectively, rewards their accomplishments, and gives them training opportunities and generous benefits. The baristas shown here handing out gift bags to shareholders at an annual meeting represent Starbucks' "ideal" employee who is adaptable, self-motivated, passionate, and a creative team player.
Source: Elaine Thompson/Associated Press

walk into a Starbucks. If that doesn't happen, the company's ability to pursue its mission and goals is likely to be affected.

Communication at Starbucks

Keeping organizational communication flowing in all directions is important to Starbucks. And that commitment starts at the top. Howard Schultz tries to visit at least 30 to 40 stores a week. Not only does this give him an upfront view of what's happening out in the field, it gives partners a chance to talk with the top guy in the company. The CEO also likes to "get out in the field" by visiting the stores and roasting facilities. For instance, Starbucks China established the Partner Family Forum to recognize the special role families play and highlighted Starbucks' commitment to its partners. During one meeting Schultz stated, "I am so incredibly proud of what you (company partners) have accomplished. And I promise you (the parents of Starbucks partners) we will grow this company the right way. I am a true believer in the future of China because of the humanity and the heart and the conscience of the Chinese people." Despite these efforts by the top executives, partners have indicated on past employee surveys that communication needed improvement. Managers listened and made some changes.

An initial endeavor was the creation of an internal video newsletter that conveyed information to partners about company news and announcements. Another change was the implementation of an internal communication audit that asks randomly selected partners for feedback on how to make company communication more effective. In addition, partners can voice concerns about actions or decisions where they believe the company is not operating in a manner consistent with the guiding principles to the Mission Review team, a group formed in 1991 and consisting of company managers and partners. The concept worked so well in North America that many of Starbucks' international units have provided similar communication forums to their partners.

Starbucks—Motivating Employees

A story from Howard Schultz's childhood provides some clues into what has shaped his philosophy about how to treat people. Schultz's father worked hard at various blue-collar jobs. However, when he didn't work, he didn't get paid. When his father broke his ankle when Howard was seven years old, the family "had no income, no health insurance, no worker's compensation, nothing to fall back on." The image of his father with his leg in a cast unable to work left a lasting impression on the young Schultz. Many years later, when his father died of lung cancer, "he had no savings, no pension, and more important, he had never attained fulfillment and dignity from work he found meaningful." The sad realities of the types of work environments his father endured had a powerful effect on Howard, and he vowed that if he were "ever in a position where I could make a difference, I wouldn't leave people behind." And those personal experiences have shaped the way that Starbucks cares for its partners—the relationships and commitments the company has with each and every employee. In fact, during the recent economic recession, Schultz was contacted by an institutional shareholder about trimming the health insurance for part-time employees. Schultz's reply? There's no way that benefit at Starbucks is being cut.

One of the best reflections of how Starbucks treats its eligible part- and full-time partners is its Total Pay package, which includes competitive base pay, bonuses, a comprehensive health plan, paid time-off plans, stock grants, a generous retirement savings program, and partner perks (which includes a pound of coffee each week). In 2015, Starbucks launched the College Achievement Program that will pay for most employees to earn an online bachelor's degree from Arizona State University. Although specific benefits differ between regions and countries, all Starbucks international partners share the "Total Pay" philosophy. For instance, in Malaysia and Thailand, partners are provided extensive training opportunities to further their careers in addition to health insurance, paid vacation, sick leave, and other benefits. In Turkey, the "Total Pay" package for Starbucks' partners includes transportation subsidies and access to a company doctor who provides free treatment. And, in China, partners receive a monthly housing allowance to help them overcome the financial challenges of starting their careers.

Partner (employee) recognition is important to Starbucks. The company has several formal recognition programs in place that partners can use as tools to encourage, reward, and inspire one another. These programs range from formal company awards to informal special acknowledgments given by coworkers. One tool—developed in response to suggestions on the partner survey—is an on-the-spot recognition card that celebrates partner and team successes.

To assist partners who are facing particularly difficult circumstances (such as natural disaster, fire, illness), the company has a CUP (Caring Unites Partners) fund that provides financial support. After Hurricanes Katrina and Rita in 2005, more than 300 partners from the Gulf Coast region received more than $225,000 in assistance from the CUP fund. In China, Starbucks has set aside RMB1 million (about $152,000 in today's currency exchange) for the Starbucks China CUP fund to be used to provide financial assistance to partners in times of significant or immediate needs. This is the type of caring and compassion that Howard Schultz vowed to provide after seeing his father not able to work and have an income because of a broken ankle.

In 2015, Starbucks was named one of the top 10 "Best Workplaces in Canada" for the fifth consecutive year. In 2013, Starbucks again was named one of *Fortune* magazine's 100 Best Companies to Work For (in the United States)—the fifteenth time since 1998 that Starbucks has received this recognition. Although being recognized as a great company to work for is commendable, Starbucks has seen its ranking drop. In 2008, it was ranked number 7; in 2009, number 24; in 2010, number 93; and in 2011, number 98. However, in 2012 its ranking rose to number 73, but it fell to number 94 in 2013 and did not make the list in 2014, 2015, or 2016. Like many companies, Starbucks had to make some tough strategic decisions during one of the toughest economic periods faced recently. Despite the challenges, it's a testament to Starbucks' treatment of its partners that it made the top 100 list for 15 years straight. However, there may be some underlying employee issues to address after failing to be cited as one of the 100 Best Companies to Work For in the most recent survey.

Starbucks—Fostering Leadership

Not surprisingly, Howard Schultz has some definite views about leading and leadership. He says being a great leader involves finding a balance between celebrating what's made a company successful in the past and knowing when to not continue following the status quo. He also said being a great leader means identifying a path your organization needs to follow and then creating enough confidence in your people so they follow that path and don't "veer off course because it's an easier route to go." He also said leaders, particularly of growing companies, need to stay true to those values and principles that have guided how their business is done and not let those values be compromised by ambitions of growth.

Since 1982, Howard Schultz has led Starbucks in a way that has allowed the company to successfully grow and meet and exceed its goals *and* to do so ethically and responsibly. From the creation of the company's Guiding Principles to the various innovative strategic initiatives, Schultz has never veered from his belief about what Starbucks, the company, could be and should be. In 2011, *Fortune* named Howard Schultz the Businessperson of the Year.

Unlike many companies, Starbucks and Howard Schultz have taken their leadership succession responsibilities seriously. In 2000 when Schultz was still CEO, he decided to move into the chairman's position. His replacement, Orin Smith (president and chief operating officer of Starbucks Coffee U.S.), had been "groomed" to take over the CEO position. Smith made it a top priority to plan his own succession. First, he established an exit date—in 2005 at age 62. Then he monitored the leadership skills development of his top executives. Two years into the job, Smith recognized that the internal candidates most likely to replace him would still be too "unseasoned" to assume the CEO position by his stated exit date. At that point, the decision was made to look externally for a promising successor. That's when Jim Donald was hired from Pathmark, a regional grocery chain, where he was chairman, president, and CEO. For three years, Donald was immersed in Starbucks' business as president of the largest division, the North American unit, before assuming the CEO position in 2005, as planned. As described in earlier parts, in early 2008, Jim Donald stepped down from the CEO position, and Howard Schultz once again assumed the position. At that time, Schultz realized his job was to step up as a leader to transform and revitalize Starbucks.

Starbucks also recognizes the importance of having individuals with excellent leadership skills throughout the company. In addition to the leadership development training for upper-level managers, Starbucks offers a program called Learning to Lead for hourly employees (baristas) to develop leadership skills. This training program also covers store operations and effective management practices. In addition, Starbucks offers to managers at all organizational levels additional training courses on coaching and providing feedback to help managers improve their people skills.

Discussion Questions

P5-1. Do the overwhelmingly positive results from the 2005 partner survey surprise you? Why or why not? Do you think giving employees an opportunity to express their opinions in something like an attitude survey is beneficial? Why or why not?

P5-2. How might the results of the partner survey affect the way a local store manager does his or her job? How about a district manager? How about the president of global development? Do you think there are differences in the impact of employee surveys on how managers at different organizational levels lead? Why or why not?

P5-3. As Starbucks continues to expand globally, what factors might affect partner responses on a partner view survey? What are the implications for managers?

P5-4. Look at the description of the types of people Starbucks seeks. What individual behavior issues might arise in managing these types of people? (Think in terms of attitudes, personality, etc.) What work team issues might arise? (Think in terms of what makes teams successful. Hint: Can a person be self-motivated and passionate *and* be a good team player?)

P5-5. Discuss the "ideal" Starbucks employee in terms of the various personality trait theories.

P5-6. Describe in your own words the workplace environment Starbucks has tried to create. What impact might such an environment have on motivating employees?

P5-7. Using the Job Characteristics Model in Exhibit 16–6, redesign a part-time hourly worker's job to be more motivating. Do the same with a store manager's job.

P5-8. Does Starbucks "care" too much for its partners? Can a company ever treat its employees too well? Why or why not?

P5-9. Howard Schultz says, "We all want the same thing as people—to be respected and valued as employees and appreciated as customers." Does the company respect and value its partners (employees)? Explain. What do you think this implies for its employee relationships?

P5-10. Former CEO Jim Donald once said, "Spending money to put people first is smart money." Do you agree or disagree? Why?

P5-11. If you were an executive, would you be concerned about the drastic drop in ranking on the list of best companies to work for and not being ranked in the most current list? Why or why not? What actions might you take?

P5-12. Give some examples of the types of communication taking place at Starbucks.

P5-13. Suppose you're a Starbucks store manager in Birmingham, Alabama. How do you find out what's going on in the company? How might you communicate your concerns or issues?

P5-14. Describe Howard Schultz's leadership style. Would his approach be appropriate in other types of organizations? Why or why not?

P5-15. Do you agree that leadership succession planning is important? Why or why not?

P5-16. What is Starbucks doing "right" with respect to the leading function? Are they doing anything "wrong?" Explain.

P5-17. Which of the company's principles (see website) influence the leading function of management? Explain how the one(s) you chose would affect how Starbucks' managers deal with (a) individual behavior issues, (b) communication issues, (c) motivational techniques, and (d) leadership styles or approaches.

Notes for the Part 5 Continuing Case

Information from Starbucks Corporation 2015 Annual Report, www.investor.starbucks.com, June 2016; news release, "Starbucks Strengthens Commitment in China, www.news.starbucks.com, January 12, 2016; H. Schultz and J. Gordon, *Onward: How Starbucks Fought For Its Life Without Losing Its Soul*, © Howard Schultz (New York: Rodale Publishing, 2011). T. C. Frohlick, M. B. Sauter, S. Stebbins, and A. Kent, "America's 25 Best Companies to Work For," *24/7 Wall Street* online, www.247wallst.com, August 10, 2015; K. Dill, "The 10 Happiest Retailers to Work for This Year," *Forbes* online, www.forbes.com, November 17, 2015; J. Mooney, "Is Starbucks Really a Great Place to Work?" *Society for Human Resource Management* online, www.shrm.org, August 25, 2015; B. Rooney, "Starbucks to Give Workers a Full Ride for College," *CNN Money* online, www.money.cnn.com, April 6, 2015; News release, "Starbucks Named One of the Top 10 Places to Work in Canada," news.starbucks.com, April 10, 2015; "Happy Work & Work Happy," *5hue* online, www.5hue.com/reflections/happywork-work-happy, February 6, 2014; company website, www.starbucks.com; Glassdoor Company Review, "Starbucks," https://www.glassdoor.com/Reviews/Starbucks-Reviews-E2202.htm, June 6, 2016; Corporate Social Responsibility, Starbucks Fiscal 2005 Annual Report, "Beyond the Cup," p. 65; News release, "Starbucks Strengthens Commitment to Being the Employer of Choice in China," news.starbucks.com, April 18, 2012; J. Certner, "Starbucks: For Infusing a Steady Stream of New Ideas to Revive Its Business," *Fast Company,* March 2012, pp. 112+; D. A. Kaplan, "Strong Coffee," *Fortune,* December 12, 2011, pp. 100+; "Howard Schultz, On Getting a Second Shot," *Inc.*, April 2011, pp. 52–54; C. Cain Miller, "A Changed Starbucks. A Changed CEO," *New York Times* online, www.nytimes.com, March 12, 2011; "Howard Schultz Promises Partners a Better Starbucks Experience in the Future," StarbucksMelody.com, www.starbucksmelody.com/2010/03/06/howard-schultz-promises-partners-a-better-starbucks-experience-in-the-future/, March 6, 2010; M. Moskowitz, R. Levering, and C. Tkaczyk, "The List: 100 Best Companies to Work For," *Fortune,* February 8, 2010, pp. 75+; Starbucks Ad, *USA Today,* May 19, 2009, p. 9A; Interview with Jim Donald, *Smart Money,* May 2006, pp. 31–32; A. Serwer, "Interview with Howard Schultz," *Fortune (Europe)*, March 20, 2006, pp. 35–36; W. Meyers, "Conscience in a Cup of Coffee," *US News & World Report,* October 31, 2005, pp. 48–50; J. M. Cohn, R. Khurana, and L. Reeves, "Growing Talent as If Your Business Depended on It," *Harvard Business Review,* October 2005, pp. 62–70; and interview with Jim Donald, *Fortune,* April 4, 2005, p. 30.

Chapter 18

Controlling Activities and Operations

It's Your Career

Source: iQoncept/Shutterstock

A key to success in management and in your career is knowing how to be effective at giving feedback.

How to Be a Pro at Giving Feedback

Everyone needs feedback! If you want people to do their best, they need to know what they're doing well and what they can do better. That's why providing feedback is such an important skill to have. But being effective at giving feedback is tricky! That's why we often see managers either (a) not wanting to give feedback or (b) giving feedback in such a way that it doesn't result in anything positive.

You can feel more comfortable with and be more effective at providing feedback if you use the following specific suggestions:[1]

*1. **Be straightforward by focusing on specific behaviors.** Feedback should be specific rather than general. Avoid such statements as "You have a bad attitude" or "I'm really impressed with the good job you did." They're vague and although they provide information, they don't tell the recipient enough to correct the "bad attitude" or on what basis you concluded that a "good job" had been done so the person knows what behaviors to repeat or to avoid.*

*2. **Be realistic.** Focus your feedback on what can be changed. When people get comments on things over which they have no control, it can be frustrating.*

*3. **Keep feedback impersonal.** Feedback, particularly the negative kind, should be descriptive rather than judgmental or evaluative. No matter how upset you are, keep the feedback focused on job-related behaviors and never criticize someone personally because of an inappropriate action.*

Keep feedback goal oriented. Feedback should not be given primarily to "blow off steam" or "unload" on another person. If you have to say something negative, make sure it's directed toward the recipient's goals. Ask yourself whom the feedback is supposed to help. If the answer is you, bite

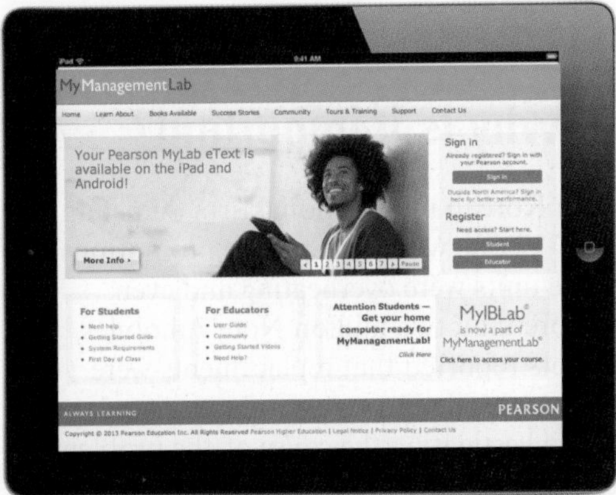

Pearson MyLab Management®

Improve Your Grade!

When you see this icon, visit **www.mymanagementlab.com** for activities that are applied, personalized, and offer immediate feedback.

Learning Objectives

18.1 ***Explain*** *the nature and importance of control.*

18.2 **Describe** the three steps in the control process.

18.3 ***Explain*** *how organizational and employee performance are measured.*

- **Know how** to be effective at giving feedback.

18.4 ***Describe*** *tools used to measure organizational performance.*

18.5 ***Discuss*** *contemporary issues in control.*

- **Develop your skill** at dealing with difficult people.

your tongue and hold the comment. Such feedback undermines your credibility and lessens the meaning and influence of future feedback.

4. Know when to give feedback—make it well timed. *Feedback is most meaningful to a recipient when there's a very short interval between his or her behavior and the receipt of feedback about that behavior. Moreover, if you're particularly concerned with changing behavior, delays in providing feedback on the undesirable actions lessen the likelihood that the feedback will be effective in bringing about the desired change. Of course, making feedback prompt merely for the sake of promptness can backfire if you have insufficient information, if you're angry, or if you're otherwise emotionally upset. In such instances, "well timed" could mean "somewhat delayed."*

5. Ensure understanding. *Make sure your feedback is concise and complete so that the recipient clearly and fully understands the communication. It may help to have the recipient rephrase the content of your feedback to find out whether it fully captured the meaning you intended.*

6. Watch your body language, tone of voice, and facial expressions. *Your body language and tone of voice can speak louder than words. Think about what you want to communicate and make sure your body language supports that message.*

Things don't always go as planned. That's why controlling is so important! Controlling is the final step in the management process. Managers must monitor whether goals that were established as part of the planning process are being accomplished efficiently and effectively as planned. That's what they do when they control. Appropriate controls can help managers look for specific performance gaps and areas for improvement. And that's what we're going to look at in this chapter—the control process, the types of controls that managers can use, and contemporary issues in control.

WHAT is controlling and why is it important?

LO18.1

- Only weeks after the South Korean multinational firm Samsung introduced the Galaxy Note 7 phone with high-profile promotions and publicity, it received reports that some units were overheating and even bursting into flames. Samsung recalled more than two million Note 7 mobiles, but as the recall progressed, some customers reported that replacements were also smoking or catching fire. Samsung then decided to stop production and discontinue the Note 7 while it continued investigating the cause of the problem. Weeks later, when the company reported significantly lower quarterly profits, it blamed the Note 7 for its poor financial results.[2]
- Hundreds of customers were found to have overpaid or underpaid for gas for years because of a mixup when U.K. energy firms replaced old metering equipment but didn't adjust usage measurements to current standards. The old equipment measured gas consumption based on the previous standard of cubic feet, whereas the new equipment measured gas consumption based on the current standard of cubic meters.[3]
- Royal Diamonds Pty Ltd, an Australian jewelry business, tried to back out of selling a two-carat diamond ring after it was mistakenly priced online at A$1,100, rather than the actual price of A$34,000. But after the buyer insisted on making the purchase, a government agency ordered the jeweler to complete the transaction. "We are going to make the ring and close the company," the owner said after the government ruling.[4]
- A developer in Singapore deposited a large check into his account at DBS Bank, only to be informed 82 days later that the entire amount was being removed from his account. Why? Because the bank later learned that the person who wrote the check had insufficient funds to cover it. "The isolated incident was due to an inadvertent human error," explained a DBS spokesperson, adding that the bank was tightening its processes.[5]

Yikes! Can you see why controlling is such an important managerial function?

controlling
Management function that involves monitoring, comparing, and correcting work performance

What is **controlling**? It's the process of monitoring, comparing, and correcting work performance. All managers should control even if their units are performing as planned because they can't really know that unless they've evaluated what activities have been done and compared actual performance against the desired standard.[6] Effective controls ensure that activities are completed in ways that lead to the attainment of goals. Whether controls are effective, then, is determined by how well they help employees and managers achieve their goals.[7]

In David Lee Roth's autobiography (yes, *that* David Lee Roth, the former front man for Van Halen), he tells the story of how he had a clause (article 126) in his touring contract asking for a bowl of M&Ms backstage, but no brown ones.[8] Now, you might think that is just typical demanding rock star behavior, but instead it was a well-planned effort by Roth to see whether the venue management had paid attention. With the technical complexity of his show, he figured if they couldn't get the M&Ms right, he needed to demand a line check of the entire production to ensure that no technical errors would occur during a performance. Now that's how managers should use control!

Why is control so important? Planning can be done, an organizational structure created to facilitate efficient achievement of goals, and employees motivated through effective leadership. But there's no assurance that activities are going as planned and that the goals employees and managers are working toward are, in fact, being attained. Control is important, therefore, because it's the only way that managers know whether organizational goals are being met and, if not, the reasons why. The value of the control function can be seen in three specific areas: planning, empowering employees, and protecting the workplace.

In Chapter 8, we described goals, which provide specific direction to employees and managers, as the foundation of planning. However, just stating goals or having

Exhibit 18-1
Planning-Controlling Link

employees accept goals doesn't guarantee that the necessary actions to accomplish those goals have been taken. As the old saying goes, "The best-laid plans often go awry." The effective manager follows up to ensure that what employees are supposed to do is, in fact, being done and goals are being achieved. Controlling provides a critical link back to planning. (See Exhibit 18-1.) If managers didn't control, they'd have no way of knowing whether their goals and plans were being achieved and what future actions to take.

The second reason controlling is important is because of employee empowerment. Many managers are reluctant to empower their employees because they fear something will go wrong for which they would be held responsible. But an effective control system can provide information and feedback on employee performance and minimize the chance of potential problems.

The final reason why managers control is to protect the organization and its assets.[9] Today's environment brings heightened threats from natural disasters, financial scandals, workplace violence, global supply chain disruptions, security breaches, and even possible terrorist attacks. Managers must protect organizational assets in the event that any of these things should happen. Comprehensive controls and back-up plans will help assure minimal work disruptions.

THE **control process**

LO18.2 Ensuring that expensive products don't go astray during their journey from factory to store shelf is only one reason why Milan-based Moncler embeds a tiny tracking device in each piece of clothing. Thanks to the devices, Moncler is able to track items as they leave the factory, are loaded into trucks, arrive at stores, are put on display, and get purchased. If an item isn't where it should be, Moncler can take immediate action to find it. Customers also benefit, because they can use a special mobile app to check whether a Moncler-branded item they're buying is actually genuine.[10] What a great use of the control process to improve internal efficiency and protect the brand from illegal counterfeiting.

The **control process** is a three-step process of measuring actual performance, comparing actual performance against a standard, and taking managerial action to correct deviations or to address inadequate standards. (See Exhibit 18-2.) The control process assumes that performance standards already exist, and they do. They're the specific goals created during the planning process.

control process
A three-step process of measuring actual performance, comparing actual performance against a standard, and taking managerial action to correct deviations or inadequate standards

Exhibit 18-2
The Control Process

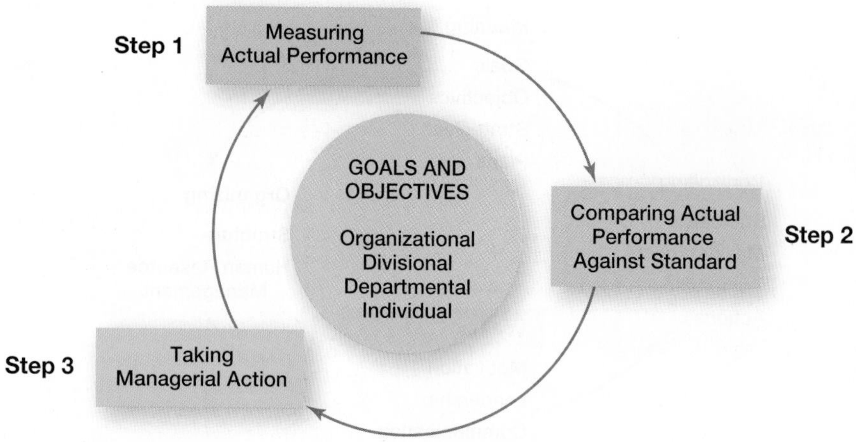

Step 1: Measuring Actual Performance

To determine what actual performance is, a manager must first get information about it. Thus, the first step in control is measuring.

HOW WE MEASURE Four approaches used by managers to measure and report actual performance are personal observations, statistical reports, oral reports, and written reports. Exhibit 18-3 summarizes the advantages and drawbacks of each approach. Most managers use a combination of these approaches.

WHAT WE MEASURE At GEICO, customer service representatives' job performance is measured by metrics—such as selling more expensive insurance policies to customers. Measuring the number of new policies and added revenue makes sense to boost company profits. However, selling more expensive policies isn't always in the best interests of the company. For instance, a customer called a GEICO representative to request a tow truck after becoming stranded. The representative dispatched the tow truck and proceeded to convince the customer that he needed a more expensive insurance policy.[11] Shouldn't the GEICO representative have focused on the customer's well-being during a stressful time? And shouldn't GEICO include customer care as a relevant job performance metric? Yes, what is measured is probably more critical to the control process than how it's measured. Why? Because selecting the wrong criteria can create serious problems. Besides, *what* is measured often determines what employees will do.[12] What control criteria might managers use?

Some control criteria can be used for any management situation. For instance, all managers deal with people, so criteria such as employee satisfaction or turnover and

Exhibit 18-3
Sources of Information for Measuring Performance

	Benefits	Drawbacks
Personal Observations	• Get firsthand knowledge • Information isn't filtered • Intensive coverage of work activities	• Subject to personal biases • Time-consuming • Obtrusive
Statistical Reports	• Easy to visualize • Effective for showing relationships	• Provide limited information • Ignore subjective factors
Oral Reports	• Fast way to get information • Allow for verbal and nonverbal feedback	• Information is filtered • Information can't be documented
Written Reports	• Comprehensive • Formal • Easy to file and retrieve	• Take more time to prepare

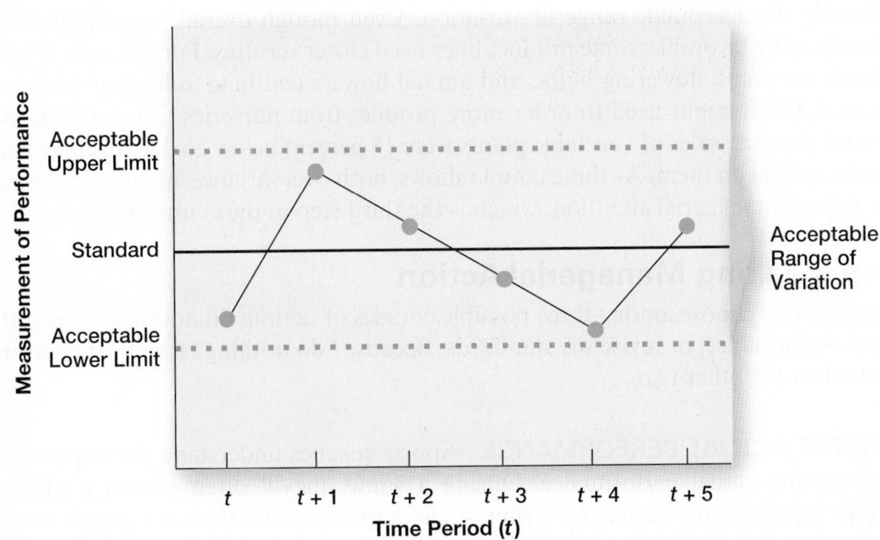

Exhibit 18-4
Acceptable Range of Variation

absenteeism rates can be measured. Keeping costs within budget is also a fairly common control measure. Other control criteria should recognize the different activities that managers supervise. For instance, a manager at a pizza delivery location might use measures such as number of pizzas delivered per day, average delivery time for phone orders versus online orders, or number of coupons redeemed. A manager in a governmental agency might use applications typed per day, client requests completed per hour, or average time to process paperwork.

Most work activities can be expressed in quantifiable terms. However, managers should use subjective measures when necessary. Although such measures may have limitations, they're better than having no standards at all and doing no controlling.

Step 2: Comparing Actual Performance Against the Standard

The comparing step determines the variation between actual performance and the standard. Although some variation in performance can be expected in all activities, it's critical to determine an acceptable **range of variation** (see Exhibit 18-4). Deviations outside this range need attention. Let's work through an example.

range of variation
The acceptable parameters of variance between actual performance and the standard

Chris Tanner is a sales manager for Green Earth Gardening Supply, a distributor of specialty plants and seeds in the Pacific Northwest. Chris prepares a report during the first week of each month that describes sales for the previous month, classified by product line. Exhibit 18-5 displays both the sales goals (standard) and actual sales figures for the month of June. After looking at the numbers, should Chris be concerned? Sales were a bit higher than originally targeted, but does that mean there were no significant deviations? That depends on what Chris thinks is *significant*; that

Exhibit 18-5
Green Earth Gardening Supply—*June Sales*

Product	Standard	Actual	Over (Under)
Vegetable plants	1,075	913	(162)
Perennial flowers	630	634	4
Annual flowers	800	912	112
Herbs	160	140	(20)
Flowering bulbs	170	286	116
Flowering bushes	225	220	(5)
Heirloom seeds	540	672	132
Total	3,600	3,777	177

is, outside the acceptable range of variation. Even though overall performance was generally quite favorable, some product lines need closer scrutiny. For instance, if sales of heirloom seeds, flowering bulbs, and annual flowers continue to be over what was expected, Chris might need to order more product from nurseries to meet customer demand. Because sales of vegetable plants were 15 percent below goal, Chris may need to run a special on them. As this example shows, both overvariance and undervariance may require managerial attention, which is the third step in the control process.

Step 3: Taking Managerial Action

Managers can choose among three possible courses of action: do nothing, correct the actual performance, or revise the standards. Because "do nothing" is self-explanatory, let's look at the other two.

CORRECT ACTUAL PERFORMANCE Sports coaches understand the importance of correcting actual performance. During a game, they'll often correct a player's actions. But if the problem is recurring or encompasses more than one player, they'll devote time during practice before the next game to correcting the actions.[13] That's what managers need to do as well.

Depending on what the problem is, a manager could take different corrective actions. For instance, if unsatisfactory work is the reason for performance variations, the manager could correct it by things such as training programs, disciplinary action, changes in compensation practices, and so forth. One decision a manager must make is whether to take **immediate corrective action**, which corrects problems at once to get performance back on track, or to use **basic corrective action**, which looks at how and why performance deviated before correcting the source of deviation. It's not unusual for managers to rationalize that they don't have time to find the source of a problem (basic corrective action) and continue to perpetually "put out fires" with immediate corrective action. Effective managers analyze deviations and, if the benefits justify it, take the time to pinpoint and correct the causes of variance.

immediate corrective action
Corrective action that corrects problems at once to get performance back on track

basic corrective action
Corrective action that looks at how and why performance deviated before correcting the source of deviation

REVISE THE STANDARD It's possible that the variance was a result of an unrealistic standard—too low or too high a goal. In that situation, the standard needs the corrective action, not the performance. If performance consistently exceeds the goal, then a manager should look at whether the goal is too easy and needs to be raised. On the other hand, managers must be cautious about revising a standard downward. It's natural to blame the goal when an employee or a team falls short. For instance, students who get a low score on a test often attack the grade cut-off standards as too high. Rather than accept the fact that their performance was inadequate, they will argue that the standards are unreasonable. Likewise, salespeople who don't meet their monthly quota often want to blame what they think is an unrealistic quota. The point is that when performance isn't up to par, don't immediately blame the goal or standard. If you believe the standard is realistic, fair, and achievable, tell employees that you expect future work to improve, and then take the necessary corrective action to help make that happen.

Managerial Decisions in Controlling

Exhibit 18-6 summarizes the decisions a manager makes in controlling. The standards are goals developed during the planning process. These goals provide the basis for the control process, which involves measuring actual performance and comparing it against the standard. Depending on the results, a manager's decision is to do nothing, correct the performance, or revise the standard.

If your professor has assigned this, go to **www.mymanagementlab.com** to watch a video titled: *CH2MHill: Foundations of Control* and to respond to questions.

Exhibit 18-6
Managerial Decisions in the Control Process

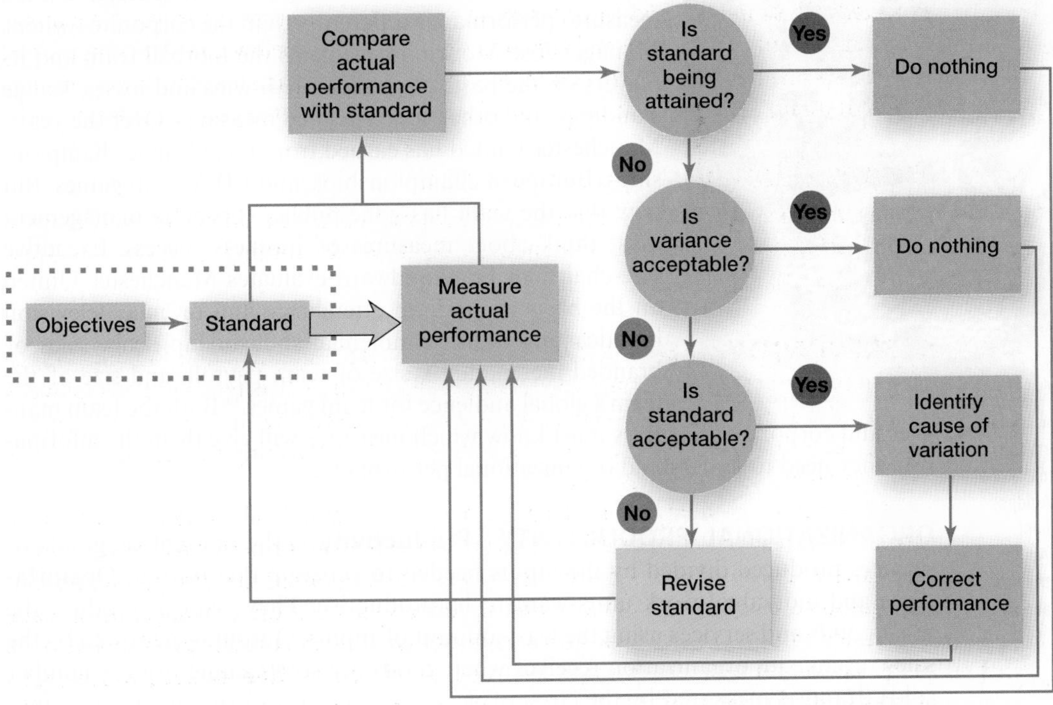

CONTROLLING **for organizational and employee performance**

LO18.3 Cost efficiency. The length of time customers are kept on hold. Customer satisfaction with service provided. These are just a few of the important performance indicators that executives in the intensely competitive call-center service industry measure. To make good decisions, managers in this industry want and need this type of information so they can manage organizational and employee performance. Managers in all types of businesses are responsible for managing organizational and employee performance.

What Is Organizational Performance?

When you hear the word *performance,* what do you think of? A summer evening concert by a local community orchestra? An Olympic athlete striving for the finish line in a close race? A Southwest Airlines ramp agent in Ft. Myers, Florida, loading passengers as efficiently as possible in order to meet the company's 20-minute gate turnaround goal? **Performance** is all of these things. It's the end result of an activity. And whether that activity is hours of intense practice before a concert or race or whether it's carrying out job responsibilities as efficiently and effectively as possible, performance is what results from that activity.

performance
The end result of an activity

Managers are concerned with **organizational performance**—the accumulated results of all the organization's work activities. It's a multifaceted concept, but managers need to understand the factors that contribute to organizational performance. After all, it's unlikely that they want (or intend) to manage their way to mediocre performance. They *want* their organizations, work units, or work groups to achieve high levels of performance.

organizational performance
The accumulated results of all the organization's work activities

Peter Hong, merchandise manager for Adidas, display's the firm's Battle Pack soccer boots and Brazuca soccer ball. According to a global survey of 200,000 business students, Adidas ranks in the top 50 list of the world's most attractive employers. This ranking of Adidas as an ideal employer is one way that the firm's managers can measure their organization's performance.
Source: Anne Peterson/AP Images

Measures of Organizational Performance

How does a professional sports team measure organizational performance? The team manager of Manchester United measures performance differently than the corporate owners. Manager Jose Mourinho evaluates the football team and its players on the basis of goals scored, wins and losses, league standings, and other sports-related measures. Over the years, Manchester United has earned trophies at league championships, European championships, and FIFA Club games. But now that the team has gone public, corporate management must think about measures of business success. Executive vice-chairman Ed Woodward evaluates Manchester United on the basis of stadium attendance and revenue, television broadcasting deals, commercial sponsorship deals, sales of branded merchandise, size of team payroll, and size of the team's global audience for team games.[14] Both the team manager and corporate executives must know which measures will give them the information they need to understand organizational performance.

productivity
The amount of goods or services produced divided by the inputs needed to generate that output

ORGANIZATIONAL PRODUCTIVITY **Productivity** is the amount of goods or services produced divided by the inputs needed to generate that output. Organizations and individual work units want to be productive. They want to produce the most goods and services using the least amount of inputs. Output is measured by the sales revenue an organization receives when goods are sold (selling price × number sold). Input is measured by the costs of acquiring and transforming resources into outputs.

It's management's job to increase this ratio. Of course, the easiest way to do this is to raise prices of the outputs. But in today's competitive environment, that may not be an option. For instance, it is difficult for Walmart to meet its objective of "Everyday Low Prices" because it has increased pay for 1.2 million workers and is facing intense competition from retailers such as Costco.[15] The only other option, then, is to decrease the inputs side. How? By being more efficient in performing work and thus decreasing the organization's expenses. Walmart has been pressuring product suppliers to lower their prices in an effort to reduce expenses and maintain competitive store pricing.[16]

organizational effectiveness
A measure of how appropriate organizational goals are and how well those goals are being met

ORGANIZATIONAL EFFECTIVENESS **Organizational effectiveness** is a measure of how appropriate organizational goals are and how well those goals are met. That's the bottom line for managers, and it's what guides managerial decisions in designing strategies and work activities and in coordinating the work of employees.

INDUSTRY AND COMPANY RANKINGS Industry and company rankings are a popular way for managers to measure their organization's performance. And there's not a shortage of these rankings, as Exhibit 18-7 shows. Rankings are determined by specific performance measures, which are different for each list. For instance, *Fortune's* Best Companies to Work For are chosen by answers given by thousands of randomly selected employees on a questionnaire called "The Great Place to Work® Trust Index®" and on materials filled out by thousands of company managers, including a corporate culture audit created by the Great Place to Work Institute. These rankings give managers (and others) an indicator of how well their company performs in comparison to others. Wegmans Food Markets is an example of a great place to work. It has been on the *Fortune* list every year since 1998. One employee shared the following sentiment: "Management cares about its employees and always asks how we are doing when we come into work or are just shopping."[17] It is not surprising that 97 percent of Wegmans' employees said that they have great bosses and great rewards, and 98 percent indicated that the work atmosphere is great.

Fortune (www.fortune.com)	*IndustryWeek* (www.industryweek.com)
Fortune 500	*IndustryWeek* 1000
Global 500	*IndustryWeek* U.S. 500
World's Most Admired Companies	50 Best Manufacturers
100 Best Companies to Work For	*IndustryWeek* Best Plants
100 Fastest-Growing Companies	
Forbes **(www.forbes.com)**	**Customer Satisfaction Indexes**
World's Biggest Public Companies	American Customer Satisfaction Index—University of Michigan Business School
	Customer Satisfaction Measurement Association

Exhibit 18-7
Popular Industry and Company Rankings

Controlling for Employee Performance

Since managers manage employees, they also have to be concerned about controlling for employee performance; that is, making sure employees' work efforts are of the quantity and quality needed to accomplish organizational goals. How do managers do that? By following the control process: measure actual performance; compare that performance to standard (or expectations); and take action, if needed. It's particularly important for managers to deliver effective performance feedback and to be prepared, if needed, to use **disciplinary actions**—actions taken by a manager to enforce the organization's work standards and regulations.[18] Let's look first at effective performance feedback.

disciplinary actions
Actions taken by a manager to enforce the organization's work standards and regulations

DELIVERING EFFECTIVE PERFORMANCE FEEDBACK Throughout the semester, do you keep track of all your scores on homework, exams, and papers? If you do, why do you like to know that information? For most of us, it's because we like to know where we stand in terms of where we'd like to be and what we'd like to accomplish in our work. We like to know how we're doing. Managers need to provide their employees with feedback so that the employees know where they stand in terms of their work. When giving performance feedback, both parties need to feel heard, understood, and respected. And if done that way, positive outcomes can result. "In a productive performance discussion, organizations have the opportunity to reinforce company values, strengthen workplace culture, and achieve strategic goals."[20] Sometimes, however, performance feedback doesn't work. An employee's performance may continue to be an issue. Under those circumstances, disciplinary actions may be necessary to address the problems.

- 73 percent of managers say they deliver difficult feedback well although they struggle with it sometimes and it doesn't always go perfectly.[19]

Providing Good Feedback—If your instructor is using Pearson MyLab Management, log onto **mymanagementlab.com** and test your *providing good feedback knowledge.* **Be sure to refer back to the chapter opener!**

★ It's Your Career

USING DISCIPLINARY ACTIONS Fortunately, most employees do their jobs well and never need formal correction. Yet, sometimes it is needed. Exhibit 18-8 lists some common types of work discipline problems and examples of each. In those circumstances, it's important for a manager to know what the organization's policies are on discipline. Is there a process for dealing with unsatisfactory job performance? Do warnings need to be given when performance is inadequate? What happens if, after the warnings, performance or the troublesome behavior doesn't improve? Progressive disciplinary action policies help managers to answer these questions. **Progressive disciplinary action** is intended to ensure that the minimum penalty appropriate to the offense is imposed.[21] The typical progression begins with a verbal

progressive disciplinary action
An approach to ensure that the minimum penalty appropriate to the offense is imposed

Exhibit 18-8
Types of Discipline Problems and Examples of Each

PROBLEM TYPE	EXAMPLES OF EACH
Attendance	Absenteeism, tardiness, abuse of sick leave
On-the-Job Behaviors	Insubordination, failure to use safety devices, alcohol or drug abuse
Dishonesty	Theft, lying to supervisors, falsifying information on employment application or on other organizational forms
Outside Activities	Criminal activities, unauthorized strike activities, working for a competing organization (if no-compete clause is part of employment)

warning and proceeds through a written warning, suspension, and, only in the most serious cases, dismissal. Still, disciplinary actions are never easy or pleasant; however, discipline can be used to both control and correct employee performance, and managers must know how to discipline. Don Crosby, vice president of international and corporate HR at McDonald's, said, "It's the hardest thing a manager has to do. It's also rocky terrain for many executives, who simply do not know when or how to hold the stick, swinging it haphazardly and inconsistently, striking too hard, too soft, or not at all."[22]

let's get REAL

Source: Kevin Krossber

Kevin Krossber
Director of Operations

The Scenario:

Malik Green knows today is going to be challenging. As the manager of the pool at the local community center, safety is his top priority. Today he must give a disciplinary action to a part-time lifeguard who failed to follow safety procedures during a shift change at the pool. While he knows he needs to give the employee a warning, he is nervous about the disciplinary meeting. He wants to make sure he provides a clear warning and also encourages the lifeguard to use proper safety procedures moving forward.

What advice can you give Malik about giving the disciplinary action?

Prepare yourself for the conversation by having your talking points clearly defined to explain the logic behind your coaching of the policy. It is important to explain the reasoning behind the safety procedures being enforced. By doing so the manager earns credibility that the culture he or she desires to create is built from commitment rather than compliance. Give the employee an opportunity to ask questions, define your expectations and be sure the policy being enforced is clearly understood.

WORKPLACE **CONFIDENTIAL** Responding to an Unfair Performance Review

A recent survey of 1000 full-time employees, all born after 1980, found a great deal of frustration with their performance reviews. Sixty-two percent, for instance, felt "blindsided" by their reviews; 74 percent frequently felt unsure as to what their managers thought of their performance; 22 percent called in sick because they were anxious about their reviews; and 28 percent reacted to their reviews by looking for another job. Our conclusion: It's very possible that sometime in your career you'll experience frustration as a result of your performance review.

It might surprise you to learn that most bosses actually dislike performance reviews. Why? First, managers are often uncomfortable discussing performance weaknesses directly with employees because they fear a confrontation when presenting negative feedback. Second, many employees become defensive when their weaknesses are pointed out. It's not uncommon for employees to challenge the evaluation by criticizing the manager or redirecting blame to someone else. Finally, employees tend to have an inflated assessment of their own performance. Statistically speaking, half of all employees must be below-average performers. But the evidence indicates that the average employee's estimate of his or her performance level generally falls around the 75th percentile. So even when managers are providing good news, employees are likely to perceive it as not good enough!

The above offers some clues on how best to handle a performance evaluation that you feel isn't fair:

Listen closely to what your boss is saying. The place to begin is to listen carefully to the specifics in your review. What exactly is your boss saying? Don't interrupt your boss as she goes over your review. You specifically want to have clarity on the negative comments. Let your boss complete her review and make sure you understand her concerns before you initiate a response.

Be prepared to accept that there might be truth in some or all of the negative comments. As we noted above, we have a tendency to overestimate our own performance level. Your boss's assessment may be more accurate than your self-evaluation.

Stay calm and cool, and avoid being defensive. Control your emotions and your tongue. Don't get angry and say something you'll regret. Don't react by diverting blame, giving excuses, or getting into a debate with your boss. As you seek clarity, pay attention to your tone so it doesn't appear that you're challenging the truthfulness of her feedback. At this point, just treat her negative comments as constructive criticism.

Ask what you can do to improve. Asking for suggestions on what you might do to improve can work for you in two ways. First, it shows your acceptance of the criticism. Second, it indicates your willingness to change.

Request more feedback between reviews. Once you understand the content of your performance review and what you need to improve, you should talk to your boss about the possibility of getting more feedback between formal reviews. The goal should be to eliminate surprises in your annual review. You want to know if you're underperforming as soon as your boss is concerned so you can correct the problem quickly. The idea is to discourage your boss from accumulating performance problems, then unloading them in the annual review.

Do you want to push back? What if you take issue with your boss's assessment? If you're convinced your boss's evaluation if unfair, you have a serious decision to make. Do you let the evaluation go or do you challenge it? Both have risks. Ignoring a negative review may begin your boss's effort to terminate your employment. On the other hand, challenging your boss's assessment could escalate a conflict that has long-term career implications.

If you truly feel your review is unfair, there is always a possibility to change the decision in your favor. However, before you protest your boss's decision, consider your organization's culture and talk to your colleagues to assess how those who have challenged a bad performance review in the past were treated.

Challenging your performance appraisal. If you decide to challenge your performance appraisal, here are a few suggestions: (1) Request a copy of your appraisal so you can better process the information. (2) Determine what exact aspects of the appraisal that you disagree with. (3) Schedule a meeting with your boss to provide your evidence in support of your position. (4) If the meeting with your boss fails to achieve the ends you desire, present your case to your Human Resources department—but let your boss know ahead of time of your intention.

Writing a rebuttal. If you decide to challenge your review, you will want to write up a formal rebuttal. It should be short and to the point. Don't attack your boss or the organization. Stay positive and respectful, and control your anger or other negative emotions. Finally, address only the specific issues within the review that you feel were unfair.

The worst-case scenario. If you see that your performance review is really just a precursor to being let go, don't despair. This may be an opportunity in disguise. It might just be the impetus you need to find your true calling. As we noted in Chapter 10, there is no shortage of people who turned being "fired" into a success story. Thomas Edison was dismissed from his night-shift telegraph operator job at Western Union. Robert Redford was sacked from a manual labor job at Standard Oil. Madonna was let go after only one day as a counter clerk at Dunkin' Donuts. And early in his career, billionaire Mark Cuban was fired from his job as a computer-store salesman.

Sources: Based on S.P. Robbins, *The Truth About Managing People*, 3rd ed. (Upper Saddle River, NJ: Pearson Education, 2013), pp. 199–201; "How to Handle an Unfair or Negative Performance Review at Work," hubpages.com, November 5, 2014; "Survey: Performance Reviews Drive One in Four Millennials to Search for a New Job or Call in Sick," newstex finance & accounting blogs, October 28, 2015; and "How to Write a Rebuttal to Unfair Performance Review," arkadylaw.com, November 16, 2015.

TOOLS for measuring organizational performance

LO18.4

- Missoni-loving fashionistas scrambling to buy the high-end Italian designer's clothes at Target crashed the company's website. Target executives admitted being unprepared for online shoppers' demand for the items.
- When someone typed the word "bailout" into a Domino's promo code window and found it was good for a free medium pizza, the news spread like wildfire across the Web. Domino's ended up having to give away thousands of free pizzas.
- A simple mistyped Web address by a Google employee caused all search results worldwide during a 55-minute period to warn, "This site may be harmful to your computer," even though it wasn't.[23]

What kinds of tools could managers at these companies have used for monitoring and measuring performance?

All managers need appropriate tools for monitoring and measuring organizational performance. Before describing some specific types of control tools, let's look at the concept of feedforward, concurrent, and feedback control.

Feedforward/Concurrent/Feedback Controls

Managers can implement controls *before* an activity begins, *during* the time the activity is going on, and *after* the activity has been completed. The first type is called feedforward control; the second, concurrent control; and the last, feedback control (see Exhibit 18-9).

feedforward control
Control that takes place before a work activity is done

FEEDFORWARD CONTROL The most desirable type of control—**feedforward control**—prevents problems because it takes place before the actual activity.[24] For instance, hospital emergency rooms are looking to prevent mistakes such as an 18-year-old with fever and chills being sent home from the emergency room with Tylenol and later dying of sepsis, a blood infection; or a 42-year-old woman with chest pains being discharged, only to suffer a heart attack two hours later. Medical experts know that a serious ailment can look a lot like something else in the hubbub and chaos of the ER. So that's why many are setting protocols and oversights in place to prevent these kinds of mistakes.[25] When McDonald's opened its first restaurant in Moscow, it sent company quality control experts to help Russian farmers learn techniques for growing high-quality potatoes and to help bakers learn processes for baking high-quality breads. Why? McDonald's demands consistent product quality no matter the geographical location. They want a cheeseburger in Moscow to taste like one in Omaha. Still another example of feedforward control is the scheduled preventive maintenance programs on nuclear power plants done by energy companies. These programs are designed to detect and hopefully to prevent malfunctions that might lead to an accident.

The key to feedforward controls is taking managerial action *before* a problem occurs. That way, problems can be prevented rather than having to correct them after any damage (poor-quality products, lost customers, lost revenue, etc.) has already been done. However, these controls require timely and accurate information that isn't always easy to get. Thus, managers frequently end up using the other two types of control.

Exhibit 18-9
Types of Control

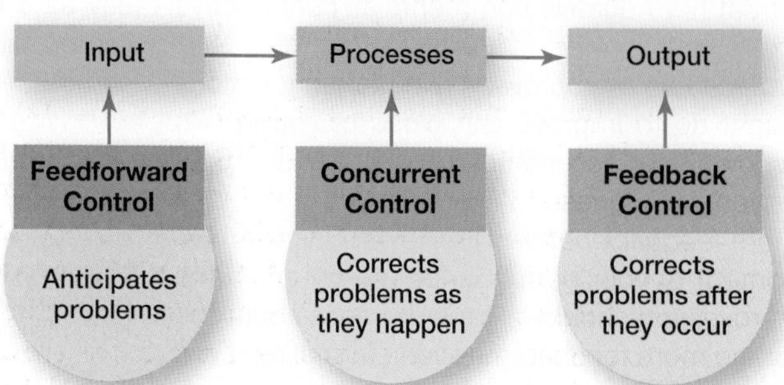

CONCURRENT CONTROL **Concurrent control**, as its name implies, takes place while a work activity is in progress. For instance, Nicholas Fox is director of business product management at Google. He and his team keep a watchful eye on one of Google's most profitable businesses—online ads. They watch "the number of searches and clicks, the rate at which users click on ads, the revenue this generates—everything is tracked hour by hour, compared with the data from a week earlier and charted."[26] If they see something that's not working particularly well, they fine-tune it. There are many examples of concurrent control taking place in manufacturing settings. For example, upholsterers for Rolls-Royce vehicles remove blemishes on leather hides before fitting them to the seat frames. The ongoing monitoring of material quality and proper assembly at every stage virtually eliminates producing a substandard product.

concurrent control
Control that takes place while a work activity is in progress

The best-known form of concurrent control is direct supervision. Another term for it is **management by walking around**, which is when a manager is in the work area interacting directly with employees. For example, Michael Bowman, former CEO of Valley Forge Casino Resort, worked alongside housekeepers to clean guest rooms.[27] He observed that it was taking too long to travel from one room to the next. By observing and listening to the housekeepers, Bowman learned that lengthy wait times for elevators were slowing them down. One housekeeper offered a solution: "Just block this elevator off from 7:00 in the morning until 9:00, so we just have it for the top floors."[28] Implementing this suggestion led to more rooms being cleaned on a timely basis. Bowman could have easily assumed that the housekeepers were just slacking off had he not been on the scene. Even GE's CEO, Jeff Immelt, spends a large portion of his workweek on the road talking to employees and visiting the company's numerous locations.[29] All managers can benefit from using concurrent control, but especially first-line managers, because they can correct problems before they become too costly.

management by walking around
A term used to describe when a manager is out in the work area interacting directly with employees

FEEDBACK CONTROL The most popular type of control relies on feedback. In **feedback control**, the control takes place *after* the activity is done. For instance, the Denver Mint discovered the flawed Wisconsin quarters using feedback control. The damage had already occurred, even though the organization corrected the problem once it was discovered. And that's the major problem with this type of control. By the time a manager has the information, the problems have already occurred, leading to waste or damage. However, in many work areas (for example, financial), feedback is the only viable type of control.

feedback control
Control that takes place after a work activity is done

Feedback controls have two advantages.[30] First, feedback gives managers meaningful information on how effective their planning efforts were. Feedback that shows little variance between standard and actual performance indicates that the planning was generally on target. If the deviation is significant, a manager can use that information to formulate new plans. Second, feedback can enhance motivation. People want to know how well they're doing and feedback provides that information. Now, let's look at some specific control tools that managers can use.

Financial Controls

Every business wants to earn a profit. To achieve this goal, managers need financial controls. For instance, they might analyze quarterly income statements for excessive expenses. They might also calculate financial ratios to ensure that sufficient cash is available to pay ongoing expenses, that debt levels haven't become too high, or that assets are used productively.

Managers might use traditional financial measures such as ratio analysis and budget analysis. Exhibit 18-10 summarizes some of the most popular financial ratios. Liquidity ratios measure an organization's ability to meet its current debt obligations. Leverage ratios examine the organization's use of debt to finance its assets and whether it's able to meet the interest payments on the debt. Activity ratios assess how efficiently a company uses its assets. Finally, profitability ratios measure how efficiently and effectively the company uses its assets to generate profits. These ratios are calculated using selected information from the organization's two primary financial statements (the

Exhibit 18-10
Popular Financial Ratios

Objective	Ratio	Calculation	Meaning
Liquidity	Current ratio	Current assets / Current liabilities	Tests the organization's ability to meet short-term obligations
	Acid test	Current assets less inventories / Current liabilities	Tests liquidity more accurately when inventories turn over slowly or are difficult to sell
Leverage	Debt to assets	Total debt / Total assets	The higher the ratio, the more leveraged the organization
	Times interest earned	Profits before interest and taxes / Total interest charges	Measures how many times the organization is able to meet its interest expenses
Activity	Inventory turnover	Sales / Inventory	The higher the ratio, the more efficiently inventory assets are used
	Total asset turnover	Sales / Total assets	The fewer assets used to achieve a given level of sales, the more efficiently management uses the organization's total assets
Profitability	Profit margin on sales	Net profit after taxes / Total sales	Identifies the profits that are generated
	Return on investment	Net profit after taxes / Total assets	Measures the efficiency of assets to generate profits

balance sheet and the income statement), which are then expressed as a percentage or ratio. Because you've probably studied these ratios in other accounting or finance courses, or will in the near future, we aren't going to elaborate on how they're calculated. We mention them here to remind you that managers use such ratios as internal control tools.

let's get REAL

The Scenario:

Lily Wong manages a product testing lab. Although her team works normal hours (8 to 5), there are times when the product testers need to work after hours or even on the weekend. She doesn't have a supervisor there when these associates are working but is wondering whether she needs to.

Source: Alfonso Marrese

Alfonso Marrese
Retail Executive

What would you suggest to Lily?

Lily needs to start training a few of her key associates to become lead associates. When the supervisor or manager is not around, the lead associate can oversee the project. By doing this, she can have a group of associates work on the weekend with the lead to get more of the projects done. You always need a supervisor around. While the associates are working, the lead will keep them focused and will keep the project going.

Budgets are planning and control tools. (See the Planning and Control Techniques module for more information on budgeting.) When a budget is formulated, it's a planning tool because it indicates which work activities are important and what and how much resources should be allocated to those activities. But budgets are also used for controlling, because they provide managers with quantitative standards against which to measure and compare resource consumption. If deviations are significant enough to require action, the manager examines what has happened and tries to uncover why. With this information, necessary action can be taken. For example, if you use a personal budget for monitoring and controlling your monthly expenses, you might find that one month your miscellaneous expenses were higher than you had budgeted for. At that point, you might cut back spending in another area or work extra hours to get more income.

Information Controls

During the most critical—and worst possible—time period for retailers, Target Corporation found that cybercriminals caused an enormous data breach in late 2013. Six months after the attack, Target executives were still trying to fix the mess. Cyberattackers from China targeted Google and 34 other companies in an attempt to steal information. A large criminal theft of credit card data—account information belonging to millions of people—happened to Heartland Payment Systems, a payments processor. American Express found its Web site under attack, one of several powerful attacks on American financial institutions. An ex-worker at Goldman Sachs stole "black box" computer programs that Goldman uses to make lucrative, rapid-fire trades in the financial markets. Even the U.S. government is getting serious about controlling information. For instance, former Secretary of State Hillary Clinton was under investigation for using a personal e-mail server to send official communications. Financial market sensitive data (think Consumer Price Index, housing starts, inflation numbers, gas prices, corn yields, etc.) will be guarded as a precaution against anyone who might want to take advantage of an accidental or covert leak to get an insider's edge in the financial markets.[31] Talk about the need for information controls! Managers deal with information controls in two ways: (1) as a tool to help them control other organizational activities and (2) as an organizational area they need to control.

management information system (MIS)
A system used to provide management with needed information on a regular basis

HOW IS INFORMATION USED IN CONTROLLING?

Managers need the right information at the right time and in the right amount to monitor and measure organizational activities and performance.

In measuring actual performance, managers need information about what is happening within their area of responsibility and about the standards in order to be able to compare actual performance with the standards. They also rely on information to help them determine if deviations are acceptable. Finally, they rely on information to help them develop appropriate courses of action. Information *is* important! Most of the information tools managers use come from the organization's management information system.

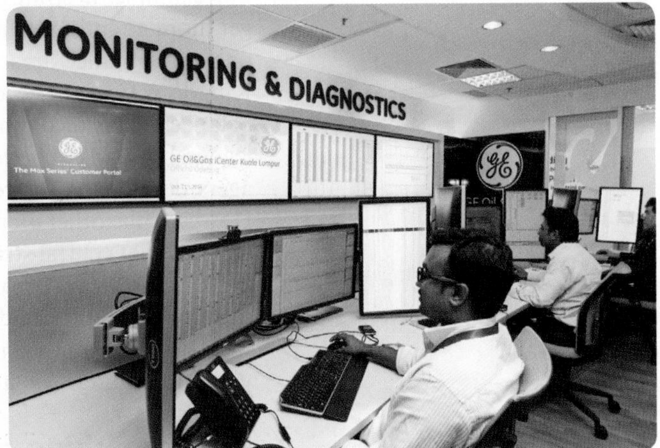

Software engineers at General Electric Company's Diagnostic and Monitoring iCenter in Kuala Lumpur, Malaysia, remotely monitor the performance of customers' oil and gas equipment to acquire and analyze data such as temperature and pressure. The purpose of monitoring the equipment is to provide customers with valuable information that helps them operate it at the highest levels of safety, efficiency, and reliability.
Source: Goh Seng Chong/Bloomberg/Getty Images

A **management information system (MIS)** is a system used to provide managers with needed information on a regular basis. In theory, this system can be manual or computer based, although most organizations have moved to computer-supported applications. The term *system* in MIS implies order, arrangement, and purpose. Further, an MIS focuses specifically on providing managers with *information* (processed and analyzed data), not merely *data* (raw, unanalyzed facts). A library provides a good analogy. Although it can contain millions of volumes, a library doesn't do you any good if you can't find what you want quickly. That's why librarians spend a great deal of time cataloging a library's collections and ensuring that materials are returned to their proper locations. Organizations today are like well-stocked libraries. The issue is not a lack of data; instead, the issue is whether an organization has the ability to process that data so that the right information is available to the right person when he or she needs it. An MIS collects data and turns them into relevant information for managers to use.

CONTROLLING INFORMATION Using pictures of a cute kitty attached to e-mails or as a link, companies are using "ethical hackers" to demonstrate how easily employees can put company data at risk by clicking on them.[32] Although these cute kitties are simulated attacks, it seems that every week, there's another news story about actual information security breaches. A survey shows that 60 percent of companies had a network security breach in the past year.[33] Because information is critically important to everything an organization does, managers must have comprehensive and secure controls in place to protect that information. Such controls can range from data encryption to system firewalls to data back-ups, and other techniques as well.[34] Problems can lurk in places that an organization might not have considered, like blogs, search engines, and Twitter accounts. Sensitive, defamatory, confidential, or embarrassing organizational information has found its way into search engine results. For instance, after Sony Pictures Entertainment's e-mail servers were hacked, unflattering comments about numerous actors, directors, and producers showed up in Web searches.[35] Equipment such as tablet and laptop computers, smartphones, and even RFID tags are vulnerable to viruses and hacking. Needless to say, information controls should be monitored regularly to ensure that all possible precautions are in place to protect important information.

Balanced Scorecard

balanced scorecard
A performance measurement tool that looks at more than just the financial perspective

The **balanced scorecard** approach is a way to evaluate organizational performance from more than just the financial perspective.[36] A balanced scorecard typically looks at four areas that contribute to a company's performance: financial, customer, internal processes, and people/innovation/growth assets. According to this approach, managers should develop goals in each of the four areas and then measure whether the goals are being met.

Although a balanced scorecard makes sense, managers will tend to focus on areas that drive their organization's success and use scorecards that reflect those strategies.[37] For example, if strategies are customer-centered, then the customer area is likely to get more attention than the other three areas. Yet, you can't focus on measuring only one performance area because others are affected as well. For instance, the United Kingdom treasury recommends that financial firms link executive teams to gender balance.[38] This recommendation is based on several studies that showed more diverse leadership leads to better financial returns. At IBM Global Services in Houston, managers developed a scorecard around an overriding strategy of customer satisfaction. However, the other areas (financial, internal processes, and people/innovation/growth) support that central strategy. The division manager described it as follows, "The internal processes part of our business is directly related to responding to our customers in a timely manner, and the learning and innovation aspect is critical for us since what we're selling our customers above all is our expertise. Of course, how successful we are with those things will affect our financial component."[39]

Benchmarking of Best Practices

The Cleveland Clinic is world renowned for delivering high-quality health care, with a top-ranked heart program that attracts patients from around the world. But what you may not realize is that it's also a model of cost-effective health care.[40] It could serve as a model for other health care organizations looking to be more effective and efficient.

Managers in such diverse industries as health care, education, and financial services are discovering what manufacturers have long recognized—the benefits of **benchmarking**, which is the search for the best practices among competitors or noncompetitors that lead to their superior performance. Benchmarking should identify various **benchmarks**, the standards of excellence against which to measure and compare. For instance, chef Claude Bosi sees a Michelin Guide star rating as a key performance benchmark for the high quality of his French restaurant in London.[41] Australian dairy farmers benchmark performance on sustainability targets using the nationwide industry benchmark of reducing greenhouse gas emissions by 30 percent by 2020.[42] Following its motto, "the best or nothing," the German automaker Mercedes-Benz benchmarks improvements against the best of what competing luxury carmakers offer.[43] Many airlines benchmark against the service quality of Hong Kong's Cathay Pacific Airlines, which has been named the world's best carrier four times.[44] Irish supermarkets, pharmacies, and other retail businesses strive to meet the benchmarks for service and customer engagement achieved by winners of the annual Retail Excellence Awards.[45] At its most basic, benchmarking means learning from others. As a tool for monitoring and measuring organizational performance, benchmarking can be used to identify specific performance gaps and potential areas of improvement. But best practices aren't just found externally.

LEADER making a DIFFERENCE

Source: Stewart Cook/Rex Features/AP Images

*Walt Disney Company is one of the world's largest entertainment and media companies and has had a long record of success.[46] When **Bob Iger** was named CEO in 2005, analysts believed that the Disney brand had become outdated. The perception was that there were too many Disney products in the marketplace lacking the quality people expected. Iger decided to address that perception with what he called the Disney Difference. What is the Disney Difference? It's taking the content created company-wide and spreading it out over many different markets and in many different forms. The company's new, obsessive focus on product quality led it to a number-seven ranking in* Fortune's *Most Admired list for 2014.* What can you learn from this leader making a difference?

benchmarking
The search for the best practices among competitors or noncompetitors that lead to their superior performance

benchmark
The standard of excellence against which to measure and compare

Sometimes those best practices can be found inside the organization and just need to be shared. One fertile area for finding good performance improvement ideas is an employee suggestion box, which was discussed in Chapter 14. Research shows that best practices frequently already exist within an organization but usually go unidentified and unnoticed.[47] In today's environment, organizations seeking high performance levels can't afford to ignore such potentially valuable information. For example, Ameren Corporation's power plant managers used internal benchmarking to help identify performance gaps and opportunities.[48] Beer producer SABMiller initiated an ambitious cost-cutting plan that is based on centralizing manufacturing, finance, and strategy. These efforts are expected to double annual cost savings to at least $1.05 billion by 2020.[49] Exhibit 18-11 provides some suggestions for internal benchmarking.

If your professor has assigned this, go to **www.mymanagementlab.com** to complete the Simulation: *Controlling* and get a better understanding of the challenges of monitoring and controlling in organizations.

CONTEMPORARY issues in control

LO18.5 The employees of Integrated Information Systems, Inc. didn't think twice about exchanging digital music over a dedicated office server they had set up. Like office betting on college and pro sports, it was technically illegal, but harmless, or so they thought. But after the company had to pay a $1 million settlement to the Recording Industry Association of America, managers wished they had controlled the situation better.[50] Control is an important managerial function. We're going to look at six control issues that managers face today: cross-cultural differences, workplace privacy, employee theft, workplace violence, customer interactions, and corporate governance.

Exhibit 18-11
Suggestions for Internal Benchmarking

1. *Connect best practices to strategies and goals.* The organization's strategies and goals should dictate what types of best practices might be most valuable to others in the organization.
2. *Identify best practices throughout the organization.* Organizations must have a way to find out what practices have been successful in different work areas and units.
3. *Develop best practices reward and recognition systems.* Individuals must be given an incentive to share their knowledge. The reward system should be built into the organization's culture.
4. *Communicate best practices throughout the organization.* Once best practices have been identified, that information needs to be shared with others in the organization.
5. *Create a best practices knowledge-sharing system.* There needs to be a formal mechanism for organizational members to continue sharing their ideas and best practices.
6. *Nurture best practices on an ongoing basis.* Create an organizational culture that reinforces a "we can learn from everyone" attitude and emphasizes sharing information.

Source: Based on "Extracting Diamonds in the Rough," by Tad Leahy, from *Business Finance*, August 2000.

Adjusting Controls for Cross-Cultural Differences and Global Turmoil

The concepts of control that we've been discussing are appropriate for an organization whose work units are not geographically separated or culturally distinct. But control techniques can be quite different for different countries. The differences are primarily in the measurement and corrective action steps of the control process. In a global corporation, managers of foreign operations tend to be less controlled by the home office, if for no other reason than the distance keeping managers from being able to observe work directly. Because distance creates a tendency to formalize controls, such organizations often rely on extensive formal reports for control, most of which are communicated electronically.

Technology's impact on control is also seen when comparing technologically advanced nations with less technologically advanced countries. Managers in countries where technology is more advanced often use indirect control devices such as computer-generated reports and analyses in addition to standardized rules and direct supervision to ensure that work activities are going as planned. In less technologically advanced countries, however, managers tend to use more direct supervision and highly centralized decision making for control.

Managers in foreign countries also need to be aware of constraints on investigating complaints and corrective actions they can take. Some countries' laws prohibit closing facilities, laying off employees, taking money out of the country, or bringing in a new management team from outside the country.

Another challenge for global managers in collecting data for measurement and comparison is comparability. For instance, a company that manufactures apparel in Cambodia might produce the same products at a facility in Scotland. However, the Cambodian facility might be more labor intensive than its Scottish counterpart to take advantage of lower labor costs in Cambodia. This difference makes it hard to compare, for instance, labor costs per unit.

Finally, global organizations need to have controls in place for protecting their workers and other assets during times of global turmoil and disasters. For instance, when the earthquake/tsunami hit Japan in March 2011, companies scrambled to activate their disaster management plans. In the volatile Middle East, many companies have had to evacuate workers during times of crisis. The best time to be prepared is before an emergency occurs, and many organizations are doing just that, so that if a crisis occurs, employees and other organizational assets are protected as best as possible.

Workplace Privacy

If you work, do you think you have a right to privacy at your job? What can your employer find out about you and your work? You might be surprised at the answers! Employers can (and do), among other things, read your e-mail (even those marked "personal" or "confidential"), tap your telephone, monitor your work by computer, store and review computer files, monitor you in an employee bathroom or dressing room, and track your whereabouts in a company vehicle. And these actions aren't that uncommon.

One survey indicates that 66 percent of U.S. companies monitor Internet use, 45 percent log keystrokes, and 43 percent track e-mails.[51] There are consequences for employees who inappropriately surf the Web or use e-mail. And some companies do not limit monitoring computer use to just the office. For instance, UPS tracks the location of delivery drivers, driving speed, and the number of daily deliveries. Their efforts have paid off. Tracking has allowed the company to deliver 1.4 million more packages per day with 1,000 fewer drivers.[52]

Some 26 percent of companies have fired an employee for e-mail misuse; 26 percent have fired workers for misusing the Internet; 6 percent have fired employees for inappropriate cell phone use; 4 percent have fired someone for instant messaging misuse; and 3 percent have fired someone for inappropriate text messaging.[53]

Why do managers feel they need to monitor what employees are doing? A big reason is that employees are hired to work, not to surf the Web checking stock prices, watching online videos, playing fantasy baseball, or shopping for presents for family or friends. Recreational on-the-job Web surfing is thought to cost billions of dollars in lost work productivity annually. In fact, a survey of U.S. employers said that 87 percent of employees look at non-work-related Web sites while at work and more than half engage in personal Web site surfing every day.[54] Watching online videos has become an increasingly serious problem not only because of the time being wasted by employees but also because it clogs already-strained corporate computer networks.[55] All this nonwork adds up to significant costs to businesses.

Another reason why managers monitor employee e-mail and computer usage is that they don't want to risk being sued for creating a hostile workplace environment because of offensive messages or an inappropriate image displayed on a coworker's computer screen. Concerns about racial or sexual harassment are one reason companies might want to monitor or keep back-up copies of all e-mail. Electronic records can help establish what actually happened so managers can react quickly.[56]

Finally, managers want to ensure that company secrets aren't being leaked.[57] In addition to typical e-mail and computer usage, companies are monitoring instant messaging and banning camera phones in the office. Managers need to be certain that employees are not, even inadvertently, passing information on to others who could use that information to harm the company.

Because of the potentially serious costs and given the fact that many jobs now entail computers, many companies have workplace monitoring policies. Such policies should control employee behavior in a nondemeaning way, and employees should be informed about those policies.[58]

If your professor has assigned this, go to **www.mymanagementlab.com** to complete the Writing Assignment *MGMT 3: Technology*.

FUTURE VISION Real-time Feedback

Keeping track of feedback on employee performance is challenging for managers. While face-to-face feedback is usually best, managers must provide it in a timely manner and also make sure to document it as well, especially if corrective action is needed. Could a mobile app solve this problem?

Some companies are abandoning formal annual reviews of performance in favor of immediate, real-time feedback delivered via a mobile device or an app.[59] Real-time feedback can be delivered to employees by managers or coworkers quickly and efficiently via this technology. Experts claim that instant feedback apps can boost productivity by letting employees know what they are doing well on the job and what they need to improve. Today's younger workforce, raised on instant communication via technology, particularly appreciates the fast feedback from colleagues. A real-time feedback app also allows management to track and document patterns of performance by keeping a timeline of the feedback. The use of such an app can help eliminate the bias that can sometimes arise in the traditional employee review process because the app captures feedback from peers, subordinates, and managers, giving a more complete view of an employee's performance.

*If your professor has chosen to assign this, go to **www.mymanagementlab.com** to discuss the following questions.*

TALK ABOUT IT 1: Would you like getting feedback through an app? Could the use of such an app create any problems?

TALK ABOUT IT 2: Should real-time feedback be delivered anonymously? Why or why not?

Most organizational theft is committed by employees such as Bill Davis, former CEO of Community Action of Minneapolis, a nonprofit organization that provides job search assistance and home heating aid to low-income people. Davis pleaded guilty to 16 counts of theft and fraud for stealing more than $800,000 of taxpayer money on trips, cars, golf, and other personal expenses.
Source: Leila Navidi /AP Photo/The Star Tribune

Employee Theft

At the Saks flagship store in Manhattan, a 23-year-old sales clerk was caught ringing up $130,000 in false merchandise returns and putting the money onto a gift card.[60] And such practices have occurred at other retailers as well.

Would you be surprised to find that up to 85 percent of all organizational theft and fraud is committed by employees, not outsiders?[61] And it's a costly problem—estimated to be around $4,500 per worker per year.[62] In retail settings alone, employee theft accounts for a staggering 43 percent of lost revenue.[63]

employee theft
Any unauthorized taking of company property by employees for their personal use

Employee theft is defined as any unauthorized taking of company property by employees for their personal use.[64] It can range from embezzlement to fraudulent filing of expense reports to removing equipment, parts, software, or office supplies from company premises. Although retail businesses have long faced serious potential losses from employee theft, loose financial controls at start-ups and small companies and the ready availability of information technology have made employee stealing an escalating problem in all kinds and sizes of organizations. Managers need to educate themselves about this control issue and be prepared to deal with it.[65]

Why do employees steal? The answer depends on whom you ask.[66] Experts in various fields—industrial security, criminology, clinical psychology—have different perspectives. The industrial security people propose that people steal because the opportunity presents itself through lax controls and favorable circumstances. Criminologists say it's because people have financial-based pressures (such as personal financial problems) or vice-based pressures (such as gambling debts). And the clinical psychologists suggest that people steal because they can rationalize whatever they're doing as being correct and appropriate behavior ("everyone does it," "they had it coming," "this company makes enough money and they'll never miss anything this small," "I deserve this for all that I put up with," and so forth).[67] Although each approach provides compelling insights into employee theft and has been instrumental in attempts to deter it, unfortunately, employees continue to steal. What can managers do?

FEEDFORWARD	CONCURRENT	FEEDBACK
Use careful prehiring screening.	Treat employees with respect and dignity.	Make sure employees know when theft or fraud has occurred—not naming names but letting people know this is not acceptable.
Establish specific policies defining theft and fraud and discipline procedures.	Openly communicate the costs of stealing.	Use the services of professional investigators.
Involve employees in writing policies.	Let employees know on a regular basis about their successes in preventing theft and fraud.	Redesign control measures.
Educate and train employees about the policies.	Use video surveillance equipment if conditions warrant.	Evaluate your organization's culture and the relationships of managers and employees.
Have a professional review of your internal security controls.	Install "lock-out" options on computers, telephones, and e-mail. Use corporate hotlines for reporting incidences. Set a good example.	

Exhibit 18-12
Controlling Employee Theft

Sources: Based on A. H. Bell and D. M. Smith, "Protecting the Company Against Theft and Fraud," *Workforce Management Online,* December 3, 2000; J. D. Hansen, "To Catch a Thief," *Journal of Accountancy,* March 2000, pp. 43–46; and J. Greenberg, "The Cognitive Geometry of Employee Theft," in *Dysfunctional Behavior in Organizations: Nonviolent and Deviant Behavior,* ed. S. B. Bacharach, A. O'Leary-Kelly, J. M. Collins, and R. W. Griffin (Stamford, CT: JAI Press, 1998), pp. 147–193.

The following statistics describe theft in small businesses:

- 40 percent of thefts were cash.
- $20,000 is the average amount stolen over time.
- 64 percent of businesses experienced employee theft.
- 16 percent of firms reported theft.[68]

The concept of feedforward, concurrent, and feedback control is useful for identifying measures to deter or reduce employee theft.[69] Exhibit 18-12 summarizes several possible managerial actions.

If your professor has assigned this, go to **www.mymanagementlab.com** to watch a video titled: *Sticky Fingers in the Workplace* and to respond to questions.

★ Watch It 2!

Workplace Violence

In Sagamihara, Japan, a man killed 19 residents and wounded 25 others in a knife attack at a care center for disabled people, where he had previously worked. In Scotland, a chef died after being punched multiple times by the restaurant manager during an argument about a customer's order. In a wood processing factory near Lucerne, Switzerland, a former employee brought a firearm to the company cafeteria and opened fire, killing three workers and injuring seven. In India, nurses at SSKM Hospital staged a protest after a nurse and a trainee were attacked by the agitated relatives of a patient.[70]

The above are just some of the violent workplace attacks in recent years. But is workplace violence really an issue for managers? Yes. Despite these examples, thankfully the number of workplace shootings has decreased.[71] However, the U.S. National Institute for Occupational Safety and Health still says that each year, some 2 million American workers are victims of some form of workplace violence. In an average week, one employee is killed and at least 25 are seriously injured in violent assaults by current or former coworkers. And according to a Department of Labor survey, 58 percent of firms reported that managers received verbal threats from workers.[72] Anger, rage, and violence in the workplace are intimidating to coworkers and adversely affect their productivity. The annual cost to U.S. businesses is estimated to be $121 billion.[73] And office rage isn't a uniquely American problem. A survey of aggressive behavior in Britain's workplaces found that 18 percent of managers say they have personally experienced harassment or verbal bullying, and 9 percent claim to have experienced physical attacks.[74]

What factors are believed to contribute to workplace violence? Undoubtedly, employee stress caused by an uncertain economic environment, job uncertainties, declining value of retirement accounts, long hours, information overload, other daily interruptions, unrealistic deadlines, and uncaring managers play a role. Even office layout designs with small cubicles where employees work amid the noise and commotion from those around them have been cited as contributing to the problem.[75] Other experts have described dangerously dysfunctional work environments characterized by the following as primary contributors to the problem:[76]

- Employee work driven by TNC (time, numbers, and crises).
- Rapid and unpredictable change where instability and uncertainty plague employees.
- Destructive communication style where managers communicate in an excessively aggressive, condescending, explosive, or passive-aggressive style; excessive workplace teasing or scapegoating.
- Authoritarian leadership with a rigid, militaristic mindset of managers versus employees; employees aren't allowed to challenge ideas, participate in decision making, or engage in team-building efforts.
- Defensive attitude where little or no performance feedback is given; only numbers count; and yelling, intimidation, or avoidance is the preferred way of handling conflict.
- Double standards in terms of policies, procedures, and training opportunities for managers and employees.
- Unresolved grievances because the organization provides no mechanisms or only adversarial ones for resolving them; dysfunctional individuals may be protected or ignored because of long-standing rules, union contract provisions, or reluctance to take care of problems.
- Emotionally troubled employees and no attempt by managers to get help for these people.
- Repetitive, boring work with no chance for doing something else or for new people coming in.
- Faulty or unsafe equipment or deficient training, which keeps employees from being able to work efficiently or effectively.
- Hazardous work environment in terms of temperature, air quality, repetitive motions, overcrowded spaces, noise levels, excessive overtime, and so forth. To minimize costs, no additional employees are hired when workload becomes excessive, leading to potentially dangerous work expectations and conditions.
- Culture of violence that has a history of individual violence or abuse; violent or explosive role models; or tolerance of on-the-job alcohol or drug abuse.

Reading through this list, you surely hope that workplaces where you'll spend your professional life won't be like this. However, the competitive demands of succeeding in a 24/7 global economy put pressure on organizations and employees in many ways.

What can managers do to deter or reduce possible workplace violence? Once again, the concept of feedforward, concurrent, and feedback control can help identify actions that managers can take.[77] Exhibit 18-13 summarizes several suggestions.

Controlling Customer Interactions

Every month, every local branch of Enterprise Rent-a-Car conducts telephone surveys with customers.[78] Each branch earns a ranking based on the percentage of its customers who say they were "completely satisfied" with their last Enterprise experience—a level of satisfaction referred to as "top box." Top box performance is important to Enterprise because completely satisfied customers are far more likely to be repeat customers. By using this service quality index measure, employees' careers and financial aspirations are linked with the organizational goal of providing consistently superior service to each and every customer. Managers at Enterprise Rent-a-Car understand the connection between employees and customers and the importance of controlling these customer interactions.

Exhibit 18-13
Controlling Workplace Violence

Sources: Based on M. Gorkin, "Five Strategies and Structures for Reducing Workplace Violence," *Workforce Management Online*, December 3, 2000; "Investigating Workplace Violence: Where Do You Start? *Workforce Management Online*, December 3, 2000; "Ten Tips on Recognizing and Minimizing Violence," *Workforce Management Online*, December 3, 2000; and "Points to Cover in a Workplace Violence Policy," *Workforce Management Online*, December 3, 2000.

Feedforward	Concurrent	Feedback
Use MBWA (managing by walking around) to identify potential problems; observe how employees treat and interact with each other.	Ensure management commitment to functional, not dysfunctional, work environments.	Communicate openly about incidences and what's being done.
Provide employee assistance programs (EAPs) to help employees with behavioral problems.	Allow employees or work groups to "grieve" during periods of major organizational change.	Investigate incidents and take appropriate action.
Enforce organizational policy that any workplace rage, aggression, or violence will not be tolerated.	Be a good role model in how you treat others.	Review company policies and change, if necessary.
Use careful prehiring screening.	Use corporate hotlines or some other mechanism for reporting and investigating incidents.	
Never ignore threats.	Use quick and decisive intervention.	
Train employees about how to avoid danger if situation arises.	Get expert professional assistance if violence erupts.	
Clearly communicate policies to employees.	Provide necessary equipment or procedures for dealing with violent situations (cell phones, alarm system, code names or phrases, and so forth).	

There's probably no better area to see the link between planning and controlling than in customer service. If a company proclaims customer service as one of its goals, it quickly and clearly becomes apparent whether that goal is being achieved by seeing how satisfied customers are with their service! How can managers control the interactions between the goal and the outcome when it comes to customers? The concept of a service profit chain can help.[79]

A **service profit chain** is the service sequence from employees to customers to profit. According to this concept, the company's strategy and service delivery system influence how employees deal with customers; that is, how productive they are in providing service and the quality of that service. The level of employee service productivity and service quality influences customer perceptions of service value. When service value is high, it has a positive impact on customer satisfaction, which leads to customer loyalty. And customer loyalty improves organizational revenue growth and profitability.

service profit chain
The service sequence from employees to customers to profit

What does this concept mean for managers? Managers who want to control customer interactions should work to create long-term and mutually beneficial relationships among the company, employees, and customers. How? By creating a work environment that enables employees to deliver high levels of quality service and which makes them feel they're capable of delivering top-quality service. In such a service climate, employees are motivated to deliver superior service. Employee efforts to satisfy customers, coupled with the service value provided by the organization, improve customer satisfaction. And when customers receive high service value, they're loyal and return, which ultimately improves the company's growth and profitability. One study showed that the payoffs can be substantial. Customers who had the best past service experiences spent 140 percent more than those who had the poorest experiences.[80]

There's no better example of this concept in action than Southwest Airlines, which is the most consistently profitable U.S. airline (the year 2015 marked 43 straight years of profitability). Its customers are fiercely loyal because the company's operating strategy (hiring, training, rewards and recognition, teamwork, and so forth) is built around customer service. Employees consistently deliver outstanding service value to customers. And Southwest's customers reward the company by coming back. It's through efficiently and effectively controlling these customer interactions that companies like Southwest and Enterprise have succeeded.

Portland International Jetport employee Ryan Tenny serves doughnuts to customers in celebration of the company being named the best small airport for customer service by Airports Council International. Courteous, cheerful, knowledgeable, and helpful employees are important to Jetport's service profit chain as they provide the high-quality service that leads to high customer satisfaction and loyalty and results in revenue growth and profitability.
Source: Derek Davis/Portland Press Herald/Getty Images

Corporate Governance

Although Andrew Fastow—Enron's former chief financial officer who pled guilty to wire and securities fraud—had an engaging and persuasive personality, that still didn't explain why Enron's board of directors failed to raise even minimal concerns about management's questionable accounting practices. The board even allowed Fastow to set up off-balance-sheet partnerships for his own profit at the expense of Enron's shareholders.

corporate governance
The system used to govern a corporation so that the interests of corporate owners are protected

Corporate governance, the system used to govern a corporation so that the interests of corporate owners are protected, failed abysmally at Enron, as it has at many companies caught in financial scandals. In the aftermath of these scandals, corporate governance has been reformed. Two areas where reform has taken place are the role of boards of directors and financial reporting. Such reforms aren't limited to U.S. corporations; corporate governance problems are global.[81] Some 75 percent of senior executives at U.S. and Western European corporations expect their boards of directors to take a more active role.[82]

A survey of corporate directors revealed the following about their understanding of company issues:

- 47 percent have a complete understanding of the company's financial position.
- 34 percent have a complete understanding of current strategy.
- 22 percent have a complete understanding of value creation.
- 16 percent have a complete understanding of industry dynamics.
- 15 percent have a complete understanding of the risks the company faces.[83]

THE ROLE OF BOARDS OF DIRECTORS The original purpose of a board of directors was to have a group, independent from management, looking out for the interests of shareholders who were not involved in the day-to-day management of the organization. However, it didn't always work that way. Board members often enjoyed a cozy relationship with managers in which each took care of the other.

This type of "quid pro quo" arrangement has changed. The Sarbanes-Oxley Act puts greater demands on board members of publicly traded companies in the United States to do what they were empowered and expected to do.[84] To help boards do this better, the Business Roundtable developed a document outlining principles of corporate governance. (See http://businessroundtable.org/, section Principles of Corporate Governance 2012, for a list and discussion of these principles.)

FINANCIAL REPORTING AND THE AUDIT COMMITTEE In addition to expanding the role of boards of directors, the Sarbanes-Oxley Act of 2002 also called for more disclosure and transparency of corporate financial information. In fact, senior managers in the United States are now required to certify their companies' financial results. Such changes have led to better information—that is, information that is more accurate and reflective of a company's financial condition.

Chapter 18 PREPARING FOR: Exams/Quizzes

CHAPTER SUMMARY by Learning Objectives

LO18.1 EXPLAIN the nature and importance of control.

Controlling is the process of monitoring, comparing, and correcting work performance. As the final step in the management process, controlling provides the link back to planning. If managers didn't control, they'd have no way of knowing whether goals were being met.

Control is important because (1) it's the only way to know if goals are being met, and if not, why; (2) it provides information and feedback so managers feel comfortable empowering employees; and (3) it helps protect an organization and its assets.

LO18.2 DESCRIBE the three steps in the control process.

The three steps in the control process are measuring, comparing, and taking action. Measuring involves deciding how to measure actual performance and what to measure. Comparing involves looking at the variation between actual performance and the standard (goal). Deviations outside an acceptable range of variation need attention.

Taking action can involve doing nothing, correcting the actual performance, or revising the standards. Doing nothing is self-explanatory. Correcting the actual performance can involve different corrective actions, which can either be immediate or basic. Standards can be revised by either raising or lowering them.

LO18.3 EXPLAIN how organizational and employee performance are measured.

Organizational performance is the accumulated results of all the organization's work activities. Three frequently used organizational performance measures include (1) productivity, the output of goods or services produced divided by the inputs needed to generate that output; (2) effectiveness, a measure of how appropriate organizational goals are and how well those goals are being met; and (3) industry and company rankings compiled by various business publications.

Employee performance is controlled through effective performance feedback and through disciplinary actions, when needed.

LO18.4 DESCRIBE tools used to measure organizational performance.

Feedforward controls take place before a work activity is done. Concurrent controls take place while a work activity is being done. Feedback controls take place after a work activity is done.

Financial controls that managers can use include financial ratios (liquidity, leverage, activity, and profitability) and budgets. One information control managers can use is an MIS, which provides managers with needed information on a regular basis. Others include comprehensive and secure controls such as data encryption, system firewalls, data back-ups, and so forth that protect the organization's information.

Managers approach information controls in two ways. Information control can be used as a tool to help them control other organizational activities and as an organizational area they need to control.

Balanced scorecards provide a way to evaluate an organization's performance in four different areas rather than just from the financial perspective. Benchmarking provides control by finding the best practices among competitors or noncompetitors and from inside the organization itself.

LO18.5 DISCUSS contemporary issues in control.

Six management control issues are cross-cultural differences, workplace privacy, employee theft, workplace violence, customer interactions, and corporate governance. For each of these issues, managers need to have policies in place to control inappropriate actions and ensure that work is getting done efficiently and effectively.

Adjusting controls for cross-cultural differences may be needed primarily in the areas of measuring and taking corrective actions. Organizations should clearly communicate to managers and employees how to approach and respond to routine and nonroutine situations within and outside the home country.

Employees who use the Internet and social media for personal use are not entitled to privacy. Organizations need to establish clear policies that outline the differences between proper and improper use and the consequences for using technology inappropriately.

Employee theft is costly to organizations. Procedures for monitoring theft and the consequences for committing a theft should be clearly explained to employees.

Workplace violence is a prevalent problem. Organizations need to develop emergency plans for responding to incidents of violence that include protecting the safety of employees and customers.

Control is important to customer interactions because employee service productivity and service quality influences customer perceptions of service value. Organizations want long-term and mutually beneficial relationships among their employees and customers.

Corporate governance is the system used to govern a corporation so that the interests of corporate owners are protected. A board of directors looks out for the interests of shareholders. The Sarbanes-Oxley Act called for more disclosure and transparency of corporate financial information.

Pearson MyLab Management

Go to **mymanagementlab.com** to complete the problems marked with this icon ✪.

✪ REVIEW AND DISCUSSION QUESTIONS

18-1. Why is control an essential managerial function in all types of organizations?

18-2. State the information sources for measuring performance.

18-3. Discuss the four main workplace discipline problems.

18-4. What do the two liquidity ratios—current and acid—actually measure and reveal?

18-5. Explain the balanced scorecard approach to evaluating organizational performance.

18-6. Why is control important to customer interactions?

18-7. In Chapter 6 we discussed the white-water rapids view of change, which refers to situations in which unpredictable change is normal and expected, and managing it is a continual process. Do you think it's possible to establish and maintain effective standards and controls in this type of environment? Discuss.

18-8. "Every individual employee in an organization plays a role in controlling work activities." Do you agree with this statement, or do you think control is something that only managers are responsible for? Explain.

Pearson MyLab Management

If your professor has assigned these, go to **mymanagementlab.com** for the following Assisted-graded writing questions:

18-9. Why is control important to customer interactions?

18-10. What are some work activities in which the acceptable range of variation might be higher than average? What about lower than average? (Hint: Think in terms of the output from the work activities, whom it might affect, and how it might affect them.)

PREPARING FOR: My Career

✪ PERSONAL INVENTORY ASSESSMENTS

Workplace Discipline Indicator

Disciplining. It's usually not a manager's favorite thing to do. But it is important. Take this PIA and discover how you prefer to discipline employees.

✪ ETHICS DILEMMA

Cyber Monday falls on the first Monday following the Thanksgiving holiday. During Cyber Monday, employers find that a significant number of employees are surfing the Web for holiday deals. A recent survey revealed that among 24 percent of the employees who admitted to being caught shopping online during work hours, only 15 percent were reprimanded.[85] And 31 percent said that being caught resulted in a discussion of shopping tips with the boss.

18-11. Other than the obvious, what problems do you see here, especially as it relates to control?

18-12. How would you handle this? How could organizations make sure they're addressing work controls ethically?

SKILLS EXERCISE Managing Challenging Employees

About the Skill

In Chapter 12, we provided some advice on handling difficult coworkers. Difficult people can be even more challenging to manage. In this section, we expand on the ideas provided in Chapter 12 to provide further guidance in honing your skill as a manager in working with difficult people.

Almost all managers will, at one time or another, have to manage employees who are difficult. There is no shortage of characteristics that can make someone difficult to work with. Some examples include people being short-tempered, demanding, abusive, angry, defensive, complaining, intimidating, aggressive, narcissistic, arrogant, and rigid. Successful managers have learned how to manage difficult people and minimize their negative impact on fellow employees.

Steps in Practicing the Skill

No single approach is always effective in dealing with difficult people.[86] However, we can offer several suggestions that are likely to lessen the angst caused by a difficult employee and may have some influence in reducing their difficult behavior.

- ***Don't let your emotions rule.*** Our first response to a difficult person is often emotional. We get angry. We show frustration. We want to lash out at them or "get even" when we think they've insulted or demeaned us. This response is not likely to reduce your angst and may escalate the other person's negative behavior. So fight your natural tendencies and keep your cool. Stay rational and thoughtful. At worst, while this approach may not improve the situation, it is also unlikely to encourage and escalate the undesirable behavior.
- ***Attempt to limit contact.*** If possible, try to limit your day-to-day interactions with the difficult employee. When appropriate, use communication channels—like e-mail and text messaging—that minimize face-to-face contact and verbal intonations.
- ***Try polite confrontation.*** As a manager it is your responsibility to address the behavior. Let them know that you're aware of their behavior, that you find it unacceptable, and that you won't tolerate it. For people who are unaware of the effect their actions have on you, confrontation might awaken them to altering their behavior. For those who are acting purposefully, taking a clear stand might make them think twice about the consequences of their actions.
- ***Practice positive reinforcement.*** We know that positive reinforcement is a powerful tool for changing behavior. Rather than criticizing undesirable behavior, try reinforcing desirable behaviors with compliments or other positive comments. This focus will tend to weaken and reduce the exhibiting of the undesirable behaviors.

Sources: Based on N. Pelusi, "Dealing with Difficult People," *Psychology Today*, September–October 2006, pp. 68–69; and R. I. Sutton, *The No Asshole Rule: Building a Civilized Workplace and Surviving One That Isn't* (New York: Business Plus, 2007).

Practicing the Skill

Consider a difficult person you have had to deal with in the past. Someone you've worked with? Another student? Write down the person's behaviors that you found challenging or difficult. Consider the strategies that you used to deal with this person. What worked? What didn't work? Using the steps above, what could you do differently to work more effectively with this person? Now, think about what you would do if you are a manager and this person is your direct report. Write down the steps you could take to effectively manage this person and also limit the negative impact of this person's behavior on other employees.

WORKING TOGETHER Team Exercise

According to research, workplace violence is all too common across the globe.[87] Employees do not just face violence from outsiders but also from one another. Create small groups of three to four students. Research the occurrences of workplace violence in your own country. Suggest some ideas of how the government and other organizations could prevent this. Share your findings with the rest of the class.

MY TURN TO BE A MANAGER

- You have a major class project due in a month. Identify some performance measures you could use to help determine whether the project is going as planned and will be completed efficiently (on time) and effectively (with high quality).
- How could you use the concept of control in your personal life? Be specific. (Think in terms of feedforward, concurrent, and feedback controls as well as specific controls for the different aspects of your life—school, work, family relationships, friends, hobbies, etc.)
- Survey 30 people as to whether they have experienced office rage. Ask them specifically whether they have experienced any of the following: yelling or other verbal abuse from a coworker, yelling at coworkers themselves, crying over work-related issues, seeing someone purposely damaging machines or furniture, seeing physical violence in the workplace, or striking a coworker. Compile your findings in a table. Are you surprised at the results? Be prepared to present these in class.
- Pretend you're the manager of a customer call center for timeshare vacations. What types of control measures would you use to see how efficient and effective an employee is? How about measures for evaluating the entire call center?
- Disciplining employees is one of the least favorite tasks of managers, but it is something that all managers have to do. Survey three managers about their experiences with employee discipline. What types of employee actions have caused the need for disciplinary action? What disciplinary actions have they used? What do they think is the most difficult thing to do when disciplining employees? What suggestions do they have for disciplining employees?
- Figure 18-7 lists several industry and company ranking lists. Find the Web site for each list and identify the performance measures that are used to determine the rankings on each. Are there any similar measures? Any unique measures? Summarize your findings in a brief report.

CASE APPLICATION 1 The Challenge of "Healthy" Fast-Food

Non-GMO, organic, locally sourced . . . these terms are now a common part of our food vocabulary, although not typically associated with the fast-food industry. Chipotle entered the fast-food scene in the early 1990s with a seemingly impossible goal of creating a healthy fast-food alternative.[88] Chipotle's promise of "food with integrity" includes fresh, locally sourced ingredients and naturally raised meats. They effectively met this promise for many years, but as the popular fast-food chain has grown to more than 1,500 locations, the restaurant's ability to promise such quality while meeting food safety standards has become a challenge. Attempting to deliver on this promise on a national scale has created a complex and risky supply chain challenge for the company.

Chipotle's food contamination problems started with an *E. coli* outbreak in July of 2015 in Seattle. Next was a norovirus outbreak in California, followed by salmonella in Minnesota. Other foodborne illnesses emerged among Chipotle customers in nine more states. Over the course of a few months, more than 500 customers were sick from contaminated food in Chipotle stores across the country. Sales dropped 30 percent during the outbreak, and several stores closed for an extended period of time. The company's stock value dropped, and the company faced several lawsuits from customers who were sickened at one of the stores.

Most national fast-food restaurant chains control food quality by using a central source for ingredients, exposing the supply chain to fewer outside elements. Simply put, the more basic the food chain, the easier it is to control. To keep their fresh food promise, Chipotle sought to prepare as many foods as possible at the local stores. They also sourced ingredients locally wherever possible, creating relationships with hundreds of vendors. The complexity of their food sourcing, coupled with in-store food preparation, is most likely what caused the food contamination problem. There were no known specific negligent acts on the part of Chipotle; the problems occurred because offering fresh food on such a large scale creates a situation where quality control is difficult.

In most cases Chipotle did not know which foods were contaminated, making the fix even more challenging. In response to the crisis, they have implemented new controls to test for meat contamination and also changed some food-handling and preparation procedures. They've shifted much of their food preparation to centralized kitchens and started sourcing ingredients from fewer vendors, much like their fast-food competitors have done for years. To kick off their new standards, Chipotle closed all of their stores for an afternoon to train employees consistently on the new food-handling standards. While it seems the company is moving in the right direction, critics suggest that a company that claims to focus so much on food quality should have done a better job focusing on food safety.

DISCUSSION QUESTIONS

18-13. Why is it important for Chipotle to revise the company's food-handling standards?

18-14. Which controls would be more important to Chipotle: feedforward, concurrent, or feedback? Explain.

18-15. How can Chipotle make sure that employees are following the new food-handling standards?

18-16. What are some measures of organizational performance that Chipotle management should use?

CASE APPLICATION 2 Bring Your Own Device

When Saman Rajaee resigned from his sales position at Design Tech Homes in Texas, he wasn't prepared for the next move the company made.[89] He used his personal iPhone to conduct business on behalf of the company, and as part of the standard separation process, the company's IT department remotely wiped his phone and restored it to factory settings. He lost all of his contacts, data stored, and also irreplaceable family photos. He then sued the company under Texas privacy laws. The courts ultimately ruled in the employer's favor, but the story creates a cautionary tale for employers.

Complicating the typical privacy and security concerns created by technology in the workplace is the "Bring Your Own Device" (BYOD) trend emerging in many companies. BYOD programs allow employees to use their own personal mobile devices such as smartphones, tablets, or laptops in the workplace. While companies often reimburse employees for expenses related to BYOD programs, the company ultimately saves money by not purchasing the technology. The practice is also appealing to those employees who prefer to use their own devices. Given that the boundaries between work and personal lives are becoming increasingly blurred, many employees want to have access to both on one piece of technology.

From a privacy perspective, some employees fear BYOD programs give the company too much access to their own personal business. A BYOD program typically has guidelines that state that the employer has the right to access the device. When you consider control and security issues, employers should want to access any device that contains work-related information and data. Management must be extra cautious to assure that the technology is secure and does not make company secrets vulnerable. Also if employees are using their device to log in to company systems, the log-in information is typically stored on the device, putting the company at risk if it is lost or stolen.

Many companies have established BYOD policies or asked employees to sign agreements that make the security concerns clear and provide the company permission to access the device. Policies or agreements help establish privacy expectations as well. When it comes to wiping phones, it is best for companies to take more of a "surgical" approach and remove only work-related information from an employee's phone. A more cautious approach can help keep company information secure, while reducing the risk of employees losing precious pictures of Grandma.

DISCUSSION QUESTIONS

18-17. Would you want to use your personal device for work purposes?

18-18. Can you think of any other privacy or security concerns for companies that have a BYOD program?

18-19. Given the privacy and security concerns, are BYOD programs really a good idea for companies?

18-20. Are there any productivity concerns with allowing employees to use their personal devices at work?

ENDNOTES

1. Based on A. Tugend, "You've Been Doing a Fantastic Job. Just One Thing. . .," *New York Times* online, www.nytimes.com, April 5, 2013; C. R. Mill, "Feedback: The Art of Giving and Receiving Help," in *The Reading Book for Human Relations Training*, ed. L. Porter and C. R. Mill (Bethel, ME: NTL Institute for Applied Behavioral Science, 1976), pp. 18–19; and S. Bishop, *The Complete Feedback Skills Training Book* (Aldershot, UK: Gower Publishing, 2000).
2. Matt Burgess, "Samsung Blames Drop in Profits on Galaxy Note 7 Problems," *Wired*, October 27, 2016, http://www.wired.co.uk/article/samsung-profits-drop-note-7 (accessed January 6, 2017); Jonathan Chang and John D. McKinnon, "The Fatal Mistake That Doomed Samsung's Galaxy Note," *Wall Street Journal*, October 23, 2016, http://www.wsj.com/articles/the-fatal-mistake-that-doomed-samsungs-galaxy-note-1477248978 (accessed January 6, 2017).
3. Kiran Stacey, "Energy Suppliers Overcharge UK Gas Consumers after Meter Gaffe," *Financial Times*, August 15, 2016, https://www.ft.com/content/12109e88-620d-11e6-8310-ecf0bddad227 (accessed January 6, 2017).
4. "Australian Man Wins Fight over Bargain Engagement Ring," *BBC News*, November 10, 2016, http://www.bbc.com/news/world-australia-37933251 (accessed January 6, 2017).
5. K.C. Vijayan, "DBS Clears $600,000 Cheque 'By Mistake,'" *Straits Times*, August 9, 2016, http://www.straitstimes.com/singapore/dbs-clears-600000-cheque-by-mistake (accessed January 6, 2017).
6. K. A. Merchant, "The Control Function of Management," *Sloan Management Review*, Summer 1982, pp. 43–55.
7. E. Flamholtz, "Organizational Control Systems Managerial Tool," *California Management Review*, Winter 1979, p. 55.
8. S. D. Levitt and S. J. Dubner, "Traponomics," *Wall Street Journal*, May 10–11, 2014; and D. Heath and C. Heath, "The Telltale Brown M&M," *Fast Company*, March 2010, pp. 36–38.
9. T. Vinas and J. Jusko, "5 Threats That Could Sink Your Company," *Industry Week*, September 2004, pp. 52–61; "Workplace Security: How Vulnerable Are You?" Special section in *Wall Street Journal*, September 29, 2003, pp. R1–R8; P. Magnusson, "Your Jitters Are Their Lifeblood," *BusinessWeek*, April 14, 2003, p. 41; and T. Purdum, "Preparing for the Worst," *Industry Week*, January 2003, pp. 53–55.
10. Evan Schuman, "Apparel Maker Meshes RFID, NFC, and QR together, and Makes It All Work," *Computerworld*, April 8, 2016, http://www.computerworld.com/article/3053547/retail-it/apparel-maker-meshes-rfid-nfc-and-qr-together-and-makes-it-all-work.html (accessed January 9, 2017); Robert

Hackett, "This Luxury Jacket-Maker Is Using Computer Chips to Fight Counterfeiting," *Fortune*, April 5, 2016, http://fortune.com/2016/04/05/moncler-chip-counterfeit/ (accessed January 9, 2017).

11. L. Markidan, "The 6 Customer Service Mistakes That Annoy Customers Most," https://www.groovehq.com/support/customer-service-mistakes-that-annoy-customers, July 14, 2015.
12. S. Kerr, "On the Folly of Rewarding A, While Hoping for B," *Academy of Management Journal,* December 1975, pp. 769–783.
13. D. Heath and C. Heath, "Watch the Game Film," *Fast Company,* June 2010, pp. 52–54.
14. David Conn, "Premier League Finances: The Full Club-by-Club Breakdown and Verdict," *The Guardian (UK)*, May 25, 2016, https://www.theguardian.com/football/2016/may/25/premier-league-finances-club-by-club-breakdown-david-conn (accessed January 9, 2017); Tony Connelly, "Manchester United Break £500m Revenue Barrier in Annual Financial Results," *The Drum (UK)*, September 12, 2016, http://www.thedrum.com/news/2016/09/12/manchester-united-break-500m-revenue-barrier-annual-financial-results (accessed January 9, 2017); Manchester United website, www.manutd.com (accessed January 9, 2017).
15. C. Isidore, "1 Million Walmart Workers Get a Raise on Saturday," *Money CNN* online, www.money.cnn.com, February 18, 2016; P. Ziobro and S. Ng, "Wal-Mart Ratchets Up Pressure on Suppliers to Cut Prices," *The Wall Street Journal* online, www.wsj.com, March 31, 2015.
16. P. Ziobro and S. Ng, "Wal-Mart Ratchets Up Pressure on Suppliers to Cut Prices."
17. "Fortune's 100 Best Companies to Work For, 2016," www.fortune.com, accessed June 5, 2016.
18. A. H. Jordan and P. G. Audia, "Self-Enhancement and Learning from Performance Feedback," *Academy of Management Review,* April 2012, pp. 211–231; D. Busser, "Delivering Effective Performance Feedback," *T&D,* April 2012, pp. 32–34; and "U.S. Employees Desire More Sources of Feedback for Performance Reviews," *T&D,* February 2012, p. 18.
19. "How Well Do You Deliver Difficult Feedback?" smartbrief.com/leadership, October 22, 2013.
20. D. Busser, "Delivering Effective Performance Feedback."
21. R. W. Mondy and J. J. Martocchio, *Human Resource Management*, 14th ed. (New York: Pearson Education, Inc., 2015)
22. V. Liberman, "The Perfect Punishment," *Conference Board Review* 46, January/February 2009, pp. 32–39.
23. S. Clifford, "Demand at Target for Fashion Line Crashes Web Site," *New York Times* online, www.nytimes.com, September 13, 2011; "Domino's Delivered Free Pizzas," *Springfield, Missouri, News-Leader,* April 3, 2009, p. 3B; and L. Robbins, "Goggle Error Sends Warning Worldwide," *New York Times* online, www.nytimes.com, February 1, 2009.
24. H. Koontz and R. W. Bradspies, "Managing Through Feedforward Control," *Business Horizons,* June 1972, pp. 25–36.
25. L. Landro, "Hospitals Overhaul ERs to Reduce Mistakes," *Wall Street Journal,* May 10, 2011, p. D3.
26. M. Helft, "The Human Hands Behind the Google Money Machine," *New York Times* online, www.nytimes.com, June 2, 2008.
27. J. M. Von Bergen, "CEO Lesson: Walking in the Workers' Shoes," *The Philadelphia Inquirer* online, www.philly.com, September 21, 2015.
28. Ibid.
29. T. Laseter and L. Laseter, "See for Yourself," *Strategy+Business*, www.strategy-business.com, November 29, 2007.
30. W. H. Newman, *Constructive Control: Design and Use of Control Systems* (Upper Saddle River, NJ: Prentice Hall, 1975), p. 33.
31. E. A. Harris, "After Data Breach, Target Plans to Issue More Secure Chip-and-Pin Cards," *New York Times* online, www.nytimes.com, April 29, 2014; N. Perlroth and D. E. Sanger, "Cyberattacks Seem Meant to Destroy, Not Just Disrupt," *New York Times* online, www.nytimes.com, March 28, 2013; J. H. Cushman Jr., "U.S. Tightens Security for Economic Data," *New York Times* online, www.nytimes.com, July 16, 2012; B. Worthen, "Private Sector Keeps Mum on Cyber Attacks," *Wall Street Journal,* January 19, 2010, p. B4; G. Bowley, "Ex-Worker Said to Steal Goldman Code," *New York Times* online, www.nytimes.com, July 7, 2009; and R. King, "Lessons from the Data Breach at Heartland," *BusinessWeek* online, July 6, 2009.
32. G. A. Fowler, "You Won't Believe How Adorable This Kitty Is! Click for More!," *Wall Street Journal,* March 27, 2013, pp. A1+.
33. B. Acohido, "To Be a Hacker, You'd Better Be Sneaky," *USA Today,* February 28, 2013, p. 2B.
34. B. Grow, K. Epstein, and C-C. Tschang, "The New E-Spionage Threat," *BusinessWeek,* April 21, 2008, pp. 32–41; S. Leibs, "Firewall of Silence," *CFO,* April 2008, pp. 31–35; J. Pereira, "How Credit-Card Data Went out Wireless Door," *Wall Street Journal,* May 4, 2007, pp. A1+; B. Stone, "Firms Fret as Office E-Mail Jumps Security Walls," *New York Times* online, www.nytimes.com, January 11, 2007.
35. M. Boardman, "Angelina Jolie Blasted as 'Minimally Talented Spoiled Brat' by Producer Scott Rudin in Leaked Sony Emails," *US Magazine* online, www.usmagazine.com, December 10, 2014.
36. K. Hendricks, M. Hora, L. Menor, and C. Wiedman, "Adoption of the Balance Scorecard: A Contingency Variables Analysis," *Canadian Journal of Administrative Sciences,* June 2012, pp. 124–138; E. R. Iselin, J. Sands, and L. Mia, "Multi-Perspective Performance Reporting Systems, Continuous Improvement Systems, and Organizational Performance," *Journal of General Management,* Spring 2011, pp. 19–36; T. L. Albright, C. M. Burgess, A. R. Hibbets, and M. L. Roberts, "Four Steps to Simplify Multimeasure Performance Evaluations Using the Balanced Scorecard," *Journal of Corporate Accounting & Finance,* July–August 2010, pp. 63–68; H. Sundin, M. Granlund, and D. A. Brown, "Balancing Multiple Competing Objectives with a Balanced Scorecard," *European Accounting Review,* vol. 19, no. 2, 2010, pp. 203–246; R. S. Kaplan and D. P. Norton, "How to Implement a New Strategy Without Disrupting Your Organization," *Harvard Business Review,* March 2006, pp. 100–109; L. Bassi and D. McMurrer, "Developing Measurement Systems for Managers in the Knowledge Era," *Organizational Dynamics,* May 2005, pp. 185–196; G. M. J. DeKoning, "Making the Balanced Scorecard Work (Part 2)," *Gallup Brain,* brain.gallup.com, August 12, 2004; G. J. J. DeKoning, "Making the Balanced Scorecard Work (Part 1)," *Gallup Brain,* brain.gallup.com, July 8, 2004;

K. Graham, "Balanced Scorecard," *New Zealand Management,* March 2003, pp. 32–34; K. Ellis, "A Ticket to Ride: Balanced Scorecard," *Training,* April 2001, p. 50; and T. Leahy, "Tailoring the Balanced Scorecard," *Business Finance,* August 2000, pp. 53–56.

37. T. Leahy, "Tailoring the Balanced Scorecard."
38. M. Lemos Stein, "The Morning Risk Report: U.K. Report Highlights Gender Issues," *The Wall Street Journal* online, www.wsj.com, March 24, 2016.
39. Ibid.
40. V. Fuhrmans, "Replicating Cleveland Clinic's Success Poses Major Challenges," *Wall Street Journal,* July 23, 2009, p. A4.
41. Richard Vines, "How Bibendum Finally Plans to Win a Michelin Star," *Bloomberg*, October 5, 2016, https://www.bloomberg.com/news/articles/2016-10-05/french-chef-bosi-wants-to-bring-stars-to-famous-michelin-building-in-london (accessed January 9, 2017).
42. Rosslyn Beeby, "Greener Pastures: The Dairy Farmers Committed to Sustainability," *The Guardian (UK)*, September 22, 2016, https://www.theguardian.com/sustainable-business/2016/sep/23/greener-pastures-the-dairy-farmers-committed-to-sustainability (accessed January 9, 2017).
43. "Mercedes-Benz Overtakes BMW to Become Largest Premium Carmaker," *Channel News Asia*, January 10, 2017, http://www.channelnewsasia.com/news/business/mercedes-benz-overtakes-bmw-to-become-largest-premium-carmaker/3425862.html (accessed January 10, 2017).
44. Natalie Meehan, "Interview: How Cathay Pacific Remains the World's Best Airline on Social," *BrandWatch*, April 11, 2016, https://www.brandwatch.com/blog/interview-cathay-pacific-remain-worlds-best-airline-social/ (accessed January 10, 2017).
45. Andrew Carey, "Limerick Retailers Top Excellence Awards 2017," *Limerick Post*, November 8, 2016, http://www.limerickpost.ie/2016/11/08/limerick-retailers-top-excellence-awards-2017/ (accessed January 10, 2017).
46. Leader Making a Difference box based on S. M. Mehta and C. Fairchild, "The World's Most Admired Companies," *Fortune,* March 17, 2014, pp. 123+; J. Reingold and M. Adamo, "The Fun King," *Fortune,* May 21, 2012, pp. 166–174; P. Sanders, "Disney Angles for Cash, Loyalty," *Wall Street Journal*, March 11, 2009, p. B4; and R. Siklos, "Bob Iger Rocks Disney," *CNN* online, www.cnnmoney.com, January 5, 2009.
47. S. Minter, "How Good Is Your Benchmarking?" *Industry Week,* October 2009, pp. 24–26; and T. Leahy, "Extracting Diamonds in the Rough," *Business Finance,* August 2000, pp. 33–37.
48. B. Bruzina, B. Jessop, R. Plourde, B. Whitlock, and L. Rubin, "Ameren Embraces Benchmarking as a Core Business Strategy," *Power Engineering,* November 2002, pp. 121–124.
49. S. Chaudhuri and T. Mickle, "SABMiller Raises Cost-Savings Target," *The Wall Street Journal* online, www.wsj.com, October 9, 2015.
50. J. Yaukey and C. L. Romero, "Arizona Firm Pays Big for Workers' Digital Downloads," Associated Press, *Springfield, Missouri, News-Leader,* May 6, 2002, p. 6B.
51. "The Rise of Workplace Spying," *The Week* online, www.theweek.com, July 5, 2015.
52. "The Rise of Workplace Spying."
53. L. Petrecca, "Feel Like Someone's Watching? You're Right," *USA Today,* March 17, 2010, pp. 1B+.
54. S. Armour, "Companies Keep an Eye on Workers' Internet Use," *USA Today,* February 21, 2006, p. 2B.
55. B. White, "The New Workplace Rules: No Video-Watching," *Wall Street Journal,* March 4, 2008, pp. B1+.
56. P-W. Tam, E. White, N. Wingfield, and K. Maher, "Snooping E-Mail by Software Is Now a Workplace Norm," *Wall Street Journal,* March 9, 2005, pp. B1+; D. Hawkins, "Lawsuits Spur Rise in Employee Monitoring," *U.S. News & World Report,* August 13, 2001, p. 53; and L. Guernsey, "You've Got Inappropriate Mail," *New York Times,* April 5, 2000, pp. C1+.
57. S. Armour, "More Companies Keep Track of Workers' E-Mail," *USA Today,* June 13, 2005, p. 4B; and E. Bott, "Are You Safe? Privacy Special Report," *PC Computing,* March 2000, pp. 87–88.
58. B. Acohido, "An Invitation to Crime," *USA Today,* March 4, 2010, pp. A1+; W. P. Smith and F. Tabak, "Monitoring Employee -E-mails: Is There Any Room for Privacy?," *Academy of Management Perspectives,* November 2009, pp. 33–38; and S. Boehle, "They're Watching You," *Training,* September 2008, pp. 23–29.
59. J. Bersin, "Employee Feedback is The Killer App: A New Market and Management Model Emerges," *Forbes* online, www.forbes.com, August 26, 2015; D. Wilkie, "If the Annual Performance Review Is on Its Way Out, What Can Replace It?" *The Society for Human Resource Management*, www.shrm.org, December 7, 2015; G. Wright, "Employee Feedback Apps on the Rise," *The Society for Human Resource Management*, www.shrm.org, September 14, 2015.
60. S. Greenhouse, "Shoplifters? Studies Say Keep an Eye on Workers," *New York Times* online, www.nytimes.com, December 30, 2009.
61. A. M. Bell and D. M. Smith, "Theft and Fraud May Be an Inside Job," *Workforce* online www.workforce.com, December 3, 2000.
62. C. C. Verschoor, "New Evidence of Benefits from Effective Ethics Systems," *Strategic Finance,* May 2003, pp. 20–21; and E. Krell, "Will Forensic Accounting Go Mainstream?," *Business Finance,* October 2002, pp. 30–34.
63. A. Fisher, "U.S. Retail Workers Are No. 1 . . . in Employee Theft," *Fortune* online, www.fortune.com, January 26, 2015.
64. J. Greenberg, "The STEAL Motive: Managing the Social Determinants of Employee Theft," in *Antisocial Behavior in Organizations*, ed. R. Giacalone and J. Greenberg (Newbury Park, CA: Sage, 1997), pp. 85–108.
65. B. E. Litzky, K. A. Eddleston, and D. L. Kidder, "The Good, the Bad, and the Misguided: How Managers Inadvertently Encourage Deviant Behaviors," *Academy of Management Perspective,* February 2006, pp. 91–103; "Crime Spree," *BusinessWeek,* September 9, 2002, p. 8; B. P. Niehoff and R. J. Paul, "Causes of Employee Theft and Strategies That HR Managers Can Use for Prevention," *Human Resource Management,* Spring 2000, pp. 51–64; and G. Winter, "Taking at the Office Reaches New Heights: Employee Larceny Is Bigger and Bolder," *New York Times,* July 12, 2000, pp. C1+.
66. This section is based on J. Greenberg, *Behavior in Organizations: Understanding and Managing the Human Side of Work,* 8th ed. (Upper Saddle River, NJ: Prentice Hall, 2003), pp. 329–330.
67. A. H. Bell and D. M. Smith, "Why Some Employees Bite the Hand That Feeds Them," *Workforce Management Online,* December 3, 2000.

68. A. Dizik, "Employee Theft Often Leads Small Firms to Make Bad Choices," *The Wall Street Journal* online, www.wsj.com, January 26, 2015.
69. B. E. Litzky et al., "The Good, the Bad, and the Misguided"; A. H. Bell and D. M. Smith, "Protecting the Company Against Theft and Fraud," *Workforce Management Online*, December 3, 2000; J. D. Hansen, "To Catch a Thief," *Journal of Accountancy,* March 2000, pp. 43–46; and J. Greenberg, "The Cognitive Geometry of Employee Theft," in *Dysfunctional Behavior in Organizations: Nonviolent and Deviant Behavior* (Stamford, CT: JAI Press, 1998), pp. 147–193.
70. "Japan Knife Attack: 19 Killed at Care Centre in Sagamihara," *BBC News*, July 26, 2016, http://www.bbc.com/news/world-asia-36890655 (accessed January 10, 2017); Maryse Goddard, "Deadly Curry Clash," *The Sun (UK)*, December 1, 2016, https://www.thesun.co.uk/news/2306608/indian-restaurant-manager-punched-a-chef-to-death-in-row-over-how-to-cook-tandoori-chicken/ (accessed January 10, 2017); and Sumati Yengkhom, "SSKM Hospital Nurses' Sit-in Protest Seeking Workplace Safety," *The Times of India*, September 2, 2016, http://timesofindia.indiatimes.com/city/kolkata/SSKM-Hospital-nurses-sit-in-protest-seeking-workplace-safety/articleshow/53985931.cms (accessed January 10, 2017).
71. Ibid.
72. J. McCafferty, "Verbal Chills," *CFO,* June 2005, p. 17; S. Armour, "Managers Not Prepared for Workplace Violence," July 15, 2004, pp. 1B+; and "Workplace Violence," OSHA Fact Sheet, https://www.osha.gov/OshDoc/data_General_Facts/factsheet-workplace-violence.pdf, U.S. Department of Labor, Occupational Safety and Health Administration, 2002.
73. "New Violence in the Workplace Fact Sheet Emphasizes that Prevention Outweighs Reaction in the Struggle to Eliminate Workplace Violence," *PRWEB* online, www.prweb.com, November 20, 2012.
74. "Bullying Bosses Cause Work Rage Rise," *Management Issues News*, www.management-issues.com, January 28, 2003.
75. R. McNatt, "Desk Rage," *BusinessWeek,* November 27, 2000, p. 12.
76. M. Gorkin, "Key Components of a Dangerously Dysfunctional Work Environment," *Workforce Management Online,* December 3, 2000.
77. "Ten Tips on Recognizing and Minimizing Violence"; M. Gorkin, "Five Strategies and Structures for Reducing Workplace Violence"; "Investigating Workplace Violence: Where Do You Start?"; and "Points to Cover in a Workplace Violence Policy," all articles from *Workforce Management Online*, December 3, 2000.
78. A. Taylor, "Enterprise Asks What Customer's Thinking and Acts," *USA Today,* May 22, 2006, p. 6B; and A. Taylor, "Driving Customer Satisfaction," *Harvard Business Review,* July 2002, pp. 24–25.
79. S. D. Pugh, J. Dietz, J. W. Wiley, and S. M. Brooks, "Driving Service Effectiveness Through Employee–Customer Linkages," *Academy of Management Executive,* November 2002, pp. 73–84; J. L. Heskett, W. E. Sasser, and L. A. Schlesinger, *The Service Profit Chain* (New York: Free Press, 1997); and J. L. Heskett, T. O. Jones, G. W. Loveman, W. E. Sasser Jr., and L. A. Schlesinger, "Putting the Service Profit Chain to Work," *Harvard Business Review,* March–April 1994, pp. 164–170.
80. P. Kriss, "The Value of Customer Experience, Quantified," *Harvard Business Review* online, www.hbr.org, August 1, 2014.
81. T. Buck and A. Shahrim, "The Translation of Corporate Governance Changes Across National Cultures: The Case of Germany," *Journal of International Business Studies,* January 2005, pp. 42–61; and "A Revolution Where Everyone Wins: Worldwide Movement to Improve Corporate-Governance Standards," *BusinessWeek,* May 19, 2003, p. 72.
82. J. S. McClenahen, "Executives Expect More Board Input," *Industry Week,* October 2002, p. 12.
83. "Improving Board Governance," McKinsey Global Survey Results," *McKinsey & Company*, www.mckinsey.com, August 2013.
84. D. Salierno, "Boards Face Increased Responsibility," *Internal Auditor,* June 2003, pp. 14–15.
85. A. Elejade-Ruiz, "Cyber Monday: Your Boss Is Watching You Shop and Is Probably OK with It," *Chicago Tribune* online, www.chicagotribune.com, November 30, 2015.
86. N. Pelusi, "Dealing with Difficult People," *Psychology Today*, September–October 2006, pp. 68–69; and R. I. Sutton, *The No Asshole Rule: Building a Civilized Workplace and Surviving One That Isn't* (New York: Business Plus, 2007).
87. "Management Has Key Role in Dispelling Threats of Workplace Violence," *International Business Times*, June 4, 2010.
88. E. Dockterman, "Chipotle Will Briefly Close All Its Restaurants to Address Food Safety Issue," *Time Magazine* online, www.time.com, January 15, 2016; D. Alba, "Chipotle's Health crisis Shows Fresh Food Comes at a Price," *Wired Magazine* online, www.wired.com, January 15, 2016; and S. Berfield, "Inside Chipotle's Contamination Crisis," *Bloomberg* online, www.bloomberg.com, December 22, 2015; www.chipotle.com.
89. R. Bellis, "The Privacy Issues You Should (and Shouldn't) Worry About with BYOD," *Fast Company* online, www.fastcompany.com, January 27, 2016; L. Weber, "BYOD? Leaving a Job Can Mean Losing Pictures of Grandma," *The Wall Street Journal* online, www.wsj.com, January 21, 2014; T. Kaneshige," BYOD Lawsuits Loom as Work Gets Personal," CIO online, www.cio.com, April 22, 2013; J. Sahadi, "Can Your Employer See Everything You Do on your Company Phone?," *CNN Money*, www.cnn.com, August 27, 2015; E. Weise, "Bring Your Own Dilemmas: Dealing with BYOD and Security, *USA Today* online, www.usatoday.com, August 26, 2014; K. Seeburn, "BYOD: Security, Privacy and Legal Concerns," *LinkedIn*, www.linkedin.com, July 21, 2015.

Planning and Control Techniques *Module*

Managers at the Disney World Magic Kingdom and Disneyland theme parks decided to charge higher ticket prices during peak visiting times and lower prices during less busy times. The higher prices minimized excessive crowds and provided a better customer experience. By lowering prices at other times, management sought to attract price-sensitive consumers to the parks. Disney spokesperson Jacquee Wahler said, "We continue to evolve the way we think about managing demand—particularly during our busiest seasons—in order to deliver a world-class experience for our guests."[1] This approach by Disney is an example of demand pricing. If it works, Disney expects to increase revenue and improve customer satisfaction.

As this example shows, managers use planning tools and techniques to help their organizations be more efficient and effective. In this module, we discuss three categories of basic planning tools and techniques: techniques for assessing the environment, techniques for allocating resources, and contemporary planning techniques.

TECHNIQUES **for assessing the environment**

Leigh Knopf, former senior manager for strategic planning at the AICPA, says that many larger accounting firms have set up external analysis departments to "study the wider environment in which they, and their clients, operate." These organizations have recognized that "What happens in India in today's environment may have an impact on an American accounting firm in North Dakota."[2] In our description of the planning and strategic management processes in Chapters 8 and 9, we discussed the importance of assessing the organization's environment. Three techniques help managers do that: environmental scanning, forecasting, and benchmarking.

Environmental Scanning

How important is environmental scanning? While looking around on competitor Google's company website, Bill Gates found a help-wanted page with descriptions of all the open jobs. What piqued his interest, however, was that many of these posted job qualifications were identical to Microsoft's job requirements. He began to wonder why Google—a Web search company—would be posting job openings for software engineers with backgrounds that "had nothing to do with Web searches and everything to do with Microsoft's core business of operating-system design, compiler optimization, and distributed-systems architecture." Gates e-mailed an urgent message to some of his top executives saying that Microsoft had better be on its toes because it sure looked like Google was preparing to move into being more of a software company.[3]

How can managers become aware of significant environmental changes, such as a new law in Germany permitting shopping for "tourist items" on Sunday; the increased trend of counterfeit consumer products in South Africa; the precipitous decline in the working-age populations in Japan, Germany, Italy, and Russia; or the decrease in family size in Mexico? Managers in both small and large organizations use environmental scanning. As we discussed in Chapter 8, environmental scanning is an important element of the strategic planning process. The goal is to detect emerging trends, the screening of large amounts of information to anticipate and interpret changes in the environment. Research has shown that companies that use environmental scanning have higher performance.[4] Organizations that don't keep on top of environmental changes are likely to experience the opposite!

There are two fast-growing areas of environmental scanning: competitor intelligence and global scanning.[5] As we discussed in Chapter 8, competitor intelligence is a process by which organizations gather information about their competitors and get answers to questions such as: Who are they? What are they doing? How will what they're doing affect us? Let's look at an example of how one organization used competitor intelligence in its planning. Dun & Bradstreet (D&B), a leading provider of business information, has an active business intelligence division. The division manager received a call from an assistant vice president for sales in one of the company's geographic territories. This person had been on a sales call with a major customer and the customer happened to mention in passing that another company had visited and made a major presentation about its services. It was interesting because, although D&B had plenty of competitors, this particular company wasn't one of them. The manager gathered together a team that sifted through dozens of sources (research services, Internet, personal contacts, and other external sources) and quickly became convinced that there was something to this; that this company was "aiming its guns right at us." Managers at D&B jumped into action to develop plans to counteract this competitive attack.[6] However, jumping into action is not always a prudent choice. Competitive intelligence may also suggest that disengagement from a course of action is most appropriate. For instance, in a survey of managers, one respondent stated that competitive intelligence "identified only a single competitor, while determining others did not have the business case to continue a pursuit."[7]

Competitor intelligence experts suggest that 80 percent of what managers need to know about competitors can be found out from their own employees, suppliers, customers, and online searches.[8] Competitor intelligence doesn't have to involve spying. Advertisements, promotional materials, press releases, reports filed with government agencies, annual reports, want ads, newspaper reports, and industry studies are examples of readily accessible sources of information. Attending trade shows and debriefing the company's sales force can be other good sources of competitor information. Many firms regularly buy competitors' products and have their own engineers study them (through a process called *reverse engineering*) to learn about new technical innovations. In addition, the Internet has opened up vast sources of competitor intelligence as many corporate Web pages include new product information and other press releases.[9]

Managers need to be careful about the way competitor information is gathered to prevent any concerns about whether it's legal or ethical. For instance, at Procter & Gamble, executives hired competitive intelligence firms to spy on its competitors in the hair-care business. At least one of these firms misrepresented themselves to competitor Unilever's employees, trespassed at Unilever's hair-care headquarters in Chicago, and went through trash dumpsters to gain information. When P&G's CEO found out, he immediately fired the individuals responsible and apologized to Unilever.[10] Competitor intelligence becomes illegal corporate spying when it involves the theft of proprietary materials or trade secrets by any means. The Economic Espionage Act makes it a crime in the United States to engage in economic espionage or to steal a trade secret.[11] Espionage is a global problem. For example, U.S. Steel claims that Chinese government hackers broke into its servers and stole proprietary plans for developing new steel technology.[12] The difficult decisions about competitive intelligence arise because often there's a fine line between what's considered *legal and ethical* and what's considered *legal but unethical*. Although the top manager at one competitive intelligence firm contends that 99.9 percent of intelligence gathering is legal, there's no question that some people or companies will go to any lengths—some unethical—to get information about competitors.[13] Certainly, hacking into a competitor's computer system is an unethical act.

Global scanning is another type of environmental scanning that's particularly important. Because world markets are complex and dynamic, managers have expanded the scope of their scanning efforts to gain vital information on global forces that might affect their organizations.[14] The value of global scanning to managers, of course, largely depends on the extent of the organization's global activities. For a company with significant global interests, global scanning can be quite valuable. For instance, Carnival Cruise Lines actively strives to expand the number of itineraries to more regions of the world. Their efforts have paid off. A Carnival cruise ship sailed from the United States to Cuba, making it the first passenger excursion by a U.S.-based cruise operator in more than 50 years.[15] All the while, other U.S. cruise lines were still negotiating access with the Cuban government.[16]

Because the sources that managers use for scanning the domestic environment are too limited for global scanning, managers must globalize their perspectives. For instance, they can subscribe to information-clipping services that review world newspapers and business periodicals and provide summaries of desired information. Also, numerous electronic services will provide topic searches and automatic updates in global areas of special interest to managers.

Forecasting

The second technique managers can use to assess the environment is forecasting. Forecasting is an important part of planning, and managers need forecasts that will allow them to predict future events effectively and in a timely manner. Environmental scanning establishes the basis for **forecasts**, which are predictions of outcomes. Virtually any component in an organization's environment can be forecasted. Let's look at how managers forecast and the effectiveness of those forecasts.

forecasts
Predictions of outcome

FORECASTING TECHNIQUES Forecasting techniques fall into two categories: quantitative and qualitative. **Quantitative forecasting** applies a set of mathematical rules to a series of past data to predict outcomes. These techniques are preferred when managers have sufficient hard data that can be used. **Qualitative forecasting**, in contrast, uses the judgment and opinions of knowledgeable individuals to predict outcomes. Qualitative techniques typically are used when precise data are limited or hard to obtain. Exhibit PC-1 describes some popular forecasting techniques.

quantitative forecasting
Forecasting that applies a set of mathematical rules to a series of past data to predict outcomes

qualitative forecasting
Forecasting that uses the judgment and opinions of knowledgeable individuals to predict outcomes

Today, many organizations collaborate on forecasts using an approach known as CPFR, which stands for collaborative planning, forecasting, and replenishment.[17] CPFR provides a framework for the flow of information, goods, and services between retailers and manufacturers. Each organization relies on its own data to calculate a demand forecast for a particular product. If their respective forecasts differ by a certain amount (say 10 percent), the retailer and manufacturer exchange data and written comments until they arrive at a more accurate forecast. Such collaborative forecasting helps both organizations do a better job of planning.

FORECASTING EFFECTIVENESS The goal of forecasting is to provide managers with information that will facilitate decision-making. Despite its importance to planning, managers have had mixed success with it.[18] For instance, prior to a holiday weekend at the Procter & Gamble factory in Lima, Ohio, managers were preparing to shut down the facility early so as not to have to pay employees for just sitting around and to give them some extra time off. The move seemed to make sense since an analysis of purchase orders and historical sales trends indicated that the factory had already

Exhibit PC-1
Forecasting Techniques

Technique	Description	Application
Quantitative		
Time series analysis	Fits a trend line to a mathematical equation and projects into the future by means of this equation	Predicting next quarter's sales on the basis of four years of previous sales data
Regression models	Predicts one variable on the basis of known or assumed other variables	Seeking factors that will predict a certain level of sales (e.g., price, advertising expenditures)
Econometric models	Uses a set of regression equations to simulate segments of the economy	Predicting change in car sales as a result of changes in tax laws
Economic indicators	Uses one or more economic indicators to predict a future state of the economy	Using change in GNP to predict discretionary income
Substitution effect	Uses a mathematical formula to predict how, when, and under what circumstances a new product or technology will replace an existing one	Predicting the effect of streaming video services on the sale of Blu-ray players
Qualitative		
Jury of opinion	Combines and averages the opinions of experts	Polling the company's human resource managers to predict next year's college recruitment needs
Sales force composition	Combines estimates from field sales personnel of customers' expected purchases	Predicting next year's sales of industrial lasers
Customer evaluation	Combines estimates from established customers' purchases	Surveying major car dealers by a car manufacturer to determine types and quantities of products desired

produced enough cases of Liquid Tide detergent to meet laundry demand over the holiday. However, managers got a real surprise. One of the company's largest retail customers placed a sizable—and unforeseen—order. They had to reopen the plant, pay the workers overtime, and schedule emergency shipments to meet the retailer's request.[19] As this example shows, managers' forecasts aren't always accurate. In a survey of inventory managers of multinational corporations, 70 percent of the respondents said their understanding of inventory management strategies was good; forecasting accuracy ranged between 56 and 75. However, efforts to improve accuracy did not always pay off.[20] Forty percent of the respondents reported improvements to the accuracy of forecasting after adopting inventory management software. Results of a survey on financial forecasting accuracy showed that 39 percent of financial executives said they could reliably forecast revenues only one quarter out. Even more disturbing is that 16 percent of those executives said they were "in the dark" about revenue forecasts.[21] But it is important to try to make forecasting as effective as possible because research shows that a company's forecasting ability can be a distinctive competence.[22] Here are some suggestions for making forecasting more effective.[23]

First, it's important to understand that forecasting techniques are most accurate when the environment is not rapidly changing. The more dynamic the environment, the more likely managers are to forecast ineffectively. Also, forecasting is relatively ineffective in predicting nonseasonal events such as recessions, unusual occurrences, discontinued operations, and the actions or reactions of competitors. Next, use simple forecasting methods. They tend to do as well as, and often better than, complex methods that may mistakenly confuse random data for meaningful information. For instance, at St. Louis–based Emerson Electric, chairman emeritus Chuck Knight found that forecasts developed as part of the company's planning process indicated that the competition wasn't just domestic anymore, but global. He didn't use any complex mathematical techniques to come to this conclusion but instead relied on the information already collected as part of his company's planning process. Next, look at involving more people in the process. At Fortune 100 companies, it's not unusual to have 1,000 to 5,000 managers providing forecasting input. These businesses are finding that as more people are involved in the process, the more the reliability of the outcomes improves.[24] Next, compare every forecast with "no change." A no change forecast is accurate approximately half the time. Next, use *rolling* forecasts that look 12 to 18 months ahead, instead of using a single, static forecast. These types of forecasts can help managers spot trends better and help their organizations be more adaptive in changing environments.[25] It's also important to not rely on a single forecasting method. Make forecasts with several models and average them, especially when making longer-range forecasts. Next, don't assume you can accurately identify turning points in a trend. What is typically perceived as a significant turning point often turns out to be simply a random event. And, finally, remember that forecasting *is* a managerial skill and as such can be practiced and improved. Forecasting software has made the task somewhat less mathematically challenging, although the "number crunching" is only a small part of the activity. Interpreting the forecast and incorporating that information into planning decisions is the challenge facing managers.

Benchmarking

Suppose you're a talented pianist or gymnast. To make yourself better, you want to learn from the best, so you watch outstanding musicians or athletes for motions and techniques they use as they perform. That same approach is involved in the final technique for assessing the environment we're going to discuss—**benchmarking**, the search for the best practices among competitors or noncompetitors that lead to their superior performance.[26]

benchmarking
The search for the best practices among competitors or noncompetitors that lead to their superior performance

Organizations rely on benchmarking for a number of purposes, including recruitment and retaining top talent. For instance, compensation managers benchmark pay rates against companies that compete for the same talent.[27] Most large law firms pay top law school graduates an entry-level salary of $160,000. But in 2016, New York law firm Cravath, Swaine & Moore LLP raised the starting pay for new lawyers from $160,000 to $180,000. Shortly after the announcement, other law firms announced that they would do the same. John Quinn, cofounder of firm Quinn, Emanuel, Urquhart & Sullivan LLP, stated, "No doubt we will be raising as will other firms."[28]

Does benchmarking work? It is too soon to tell whether raising pay will make a difference in recruitment and retention. However, overall studies have shown that benchmarking helped companies achieve 69 percent faster growth and 45 percent greater productivity.[29]

The basic idea behind benchmarking is that managers can improve performance by analyzing and then copying the methods of the leaders in various fields. Organizations such as Nissan, Payless Shoe Source, the U.S. military, General Mills, United Airlines, and Volvo Construction Equipment have used benchmarking as a tool in improving performance. In fact, some companies have chosen some pretty unusual benchmarking partners! IBM studied Las Vegas casinos for ways to discourage employee theft. Many hospitals have benchmarked their admissions processes against Marriott Hotels. And Giordano Holdings Ltd., a Hong Kong–based manufacturer

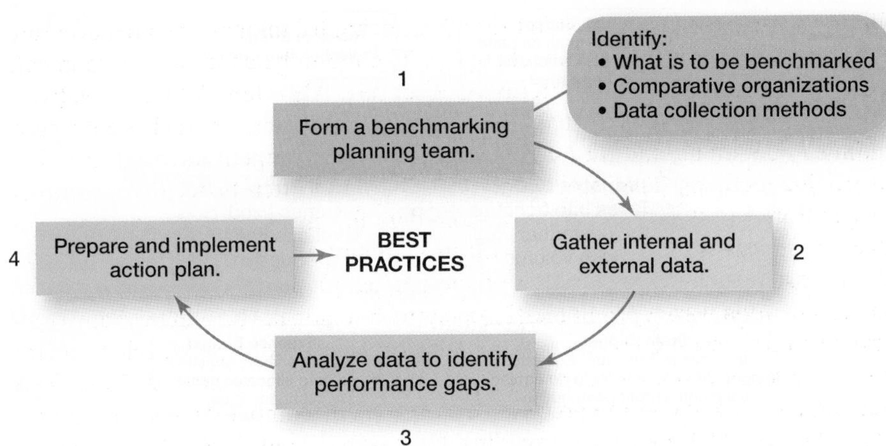

Exhibit PC-2
Steps in Benchmarking

Source: Based on "Aiming High: Competitive Benchmarking for Superior Performance," by Y. K. Shetty, from *Long Range Planning*, vol. 26, no. 1, 1993, pp. 39–44.

and retailer of mass-market casual wear, borrowed its "good quality, good value" concept from Marks & Spencer, used Limited Brands to benchmark its point-of-sales computerized information system, and modeled its simplified product offerings on McDonald's menu.[30]

What does benchmarking involve? Exhibit PC-2 illustrates the four steps typically used in benchmarking.

TECHNIQUES **for allocating resources**

Once an organization's goals have been established, it's important to determine how those goals are going to be accomplished. Before managers can organize and lead as goals are implemented, they must have **resources**, the assets of the organization (financial, physical, human, and intangible). How can managers allocate these resources effectively and efficiently so that organizational goals are met? Although managers can choose from a number of techniques for allocating resources (many of which are covered in courses on accounting, finance, and operations management), we'll discuss four techniques here: budgeting, scheduling, breakeven analysis, and linear programming.

resources
An organization's assets—including financial, physical, human, intangible, and structural/cultural—that are used to develop, manufacture, and deliver products to its customers

Budgeting

Most of us have had some experience, as limited as it might be, with budgets. We probably learned at an early age that unless we allocated our "revenues" carefully, our weekly allowance was spent on "expenses" before the week was half over.

A **budget** is a numerical plan for allocating resources to specific activities. Managers typically prepare budgets for revenues, expenses, and large capital expenditures such as equipment. It's not unusual, though, for budgets to be used for improving time, space, and use of material resources. These types of budgets substitute nondollar numbers for dollar amounts. Such items as person-hours, capacity utilization, or units of production can be budgeted for daily, weekly, or monthly activities. Exhibit PC-3 describes the different types of budgets that managers might use.

budget
A numerical plan for allocating resources to specific activities

Why are budgets so popular? Probably because they're applicable to a wide variety of organizations and work activities within organizations. We live in a world in which almost everything is expressed in monetary units. Dollars, rupees, pesos, euros, yuan, yen, and the like are used as a common measuring unit within a country. That's why monetary budgets are a useful tool for allocating resources and guiding work in such diverse departments as manufacturing and information systems or at various levels in an organization. Budgets are one planning technique that most managers use—regardless of organizational level. It's an important managerial activity because it forces financial discipline and structure throughout the organization. However, many managers don't like preparing budgets because they feel the process is time-

Exhibit PC-3
Types of Budgets

Source: Based on *Production and Operations Management,* by R. S. Russell and B. W. Taylor III. Upper Saddle River, NJ: Prentice-Hall, Inc., 1966.

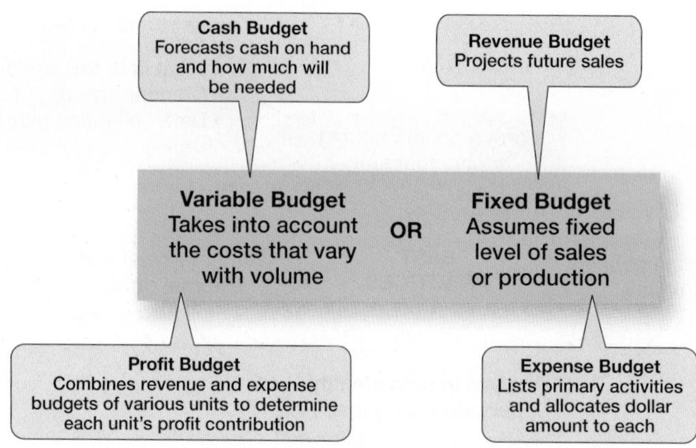

consuming, inflexible, inefficient, and ineffective.[31] How can the budgeting process be improved? Exhibit PC-4 provides some suggestions. Organizations such as Texas Instruments, IKEA, Volvo, and Svenska Handelsbanken have incorporated several of these suggestions as they revamped their budgeting processes. Now that we understand the importance and types of budgets, how do organizations set them?

budgeting
The process of allocating resources to pay for designated future costs

Budgeting is the process of allocating resources to pay for designated future costs. There are two common approaches to setting budgets: incremental budgeting and zero-base budgeting.

incremental budgeting
Process starting with the current budget from which managers decide whether they need additional resources and the justification for requesting it

Incremental budgeting starts with the current budget from which managers decide whether additional resources are needed and the justification for requesting them. This approach is appropriate for adjusting budgets that contain all of the necessary expenditures. For example, manufacturing managers may have underestimated the cost of ongoing equipment maintenance. Based on previous experience and expected higher future costs, managers justify requests for additional money. A possible drawback of incremental budgeting is wasteful spending. If managers do not spend the allotted money, they will probably receive less in the future. Most managers find ways to avoid this situation. For instance, an office manager may decide to purchase an excess of printer toner cartridges before the end of the budget period. The decision to purchase too many cartridges ultimately may not be cost effective. As printers are replaced, newer models will use different cartridges, rendering the supply of cartridges a wasteful expense.

zero-base budgeting (ZBB)
Process starting with an established point of zero rather than using the current budget as the basis for adding, modifying, or subtracting resources

An alternative approach is zero-base budgeting that helps minimize wasteful spending. **Zero-base budgeting (ZBB)** starts with an established point of zero rather than using the current budget as the basis for adding, modifying, or subtracting resources. Anecdotal information suggests that zero-base budgeting has become more popular after the economic recession of 2007–2009. According to one financial expert, "The attraction of ZBB, for many, is that the 'zero' in ZBB sends a powerful message to all stakeholders that the line will be held on spending and that nothing will be taken for granted."[32] When set in a culture of cost management, ZBB helps managers more carefully scrutinize the value of different practices.[33] For instance, do office renovations increase productivity? Do expenditures for advertising products in traditional outlets such as newspapers increase sales? Do onboarding activities promote employee

Exhibit PC-4
How to Improve Budgeting

- Collaborate and communicate.
- Be flexible.
- Goals should drive budgets—budgets should not determine goals.
- Coordinate budgeting throughout the organization.
- Use budgeting/planning software when appropriate.
- Remember that budgets are tools.
- Remember that profits result from smart management, not because you budgeted for them.

retention? ZBB creates a platform for considering the value of alternative expenditures and helps managers redirect resources to areas that will raise productivity and profits.

Scheduling

Jackie is a manager at a Chico's store in San Francisco. Every week, she determines employees' work hours and the store area where each employee will be working. If you observed any group of supervisors or department managers for a few days, you would see them doing much the same—allocating resources by detailing what activities have to be done, the order in which they are to be completed, who is to do each, and when they are to be completed. These managers are **scheduling**. In this section, we'll review some useful scheduling devices, including Gantt charts, load charts, and PERT network analysis.

scheduling
Detailing what activities have to be done, the order in which they are to be completed, who is to do each, and when they are to be completed

GANTT CHARTS The **Gantt chart** was developed during the early 1900s by Henry Gantt, an associate of Frederick Taylor, the scientific management expert. The idea behind a Gantt chart is simple. It's essentially a bar graph with time on the horizontal axis and the activities to be scheduled on the vertical axis. The bars show output, both planned and actual, over a period of time. The Gantt chart visually shows when tasks are supposed to be done and compares those projections with the actual progress on each task. It's a simple but important device that lets managers detail easily what has yet to be done to complete a job or project and to assess whether an activity is ahead of, behind, or on schedule.

Gantt chart
A scheduling chart developed by Henry Gantt that shows actual and planned output over a period of time

Exhibit PC-5 depicts a simplified Gantt chart for book production developed by a manager in a publishing company. Time is expressed in months across the top of the chart. The major work activities are listed down the left side. Planning involves deciding what activities need to be done to get the book finished, the order in which those activities need to be completed, and the time that should be allocated to each activity. Where a box sits within a time frame reflects its planned sequence. The shading represents actual progress. The chart also serves as a control tool because the manager can see deviations from the plan. In this example, both the design of the cover and the review of first pages are running behind schedule. Cover design is about three weeks behind (note that there has been no actual progress—shown by blue color line—as of the reporting date), and first pages review is about two weeks behind schedule (note that as of the report date, actual progress—shown by blue color line—is about six weeks, out of a goal of completing in two months). Given this information, the manager might need to take some action to either make up for the two lost weeks or to ensure that no further delays will occur. At this point, the manager can expect that the book will be published at least two weeks later than planned if no action is taken.

LOAD CHARTS A **load chart** is a modified Gantt chart. Instead of listing activities on the vertical axis, load charts list either entire departments or specific resources. This arrangement allows managers to plan and control capacity utilization. In other words, load charts schedule capacity by work areas.

load chart
A modified Gantt chart that schedules capacity by entire departments or specific resources

Activity
Month
1 2 3 4
Copyedit manuscript
Design sample pages
Draw artwork
Review first pages
Print final pages
Design cover
Actual progress
Goals
Reporting Date

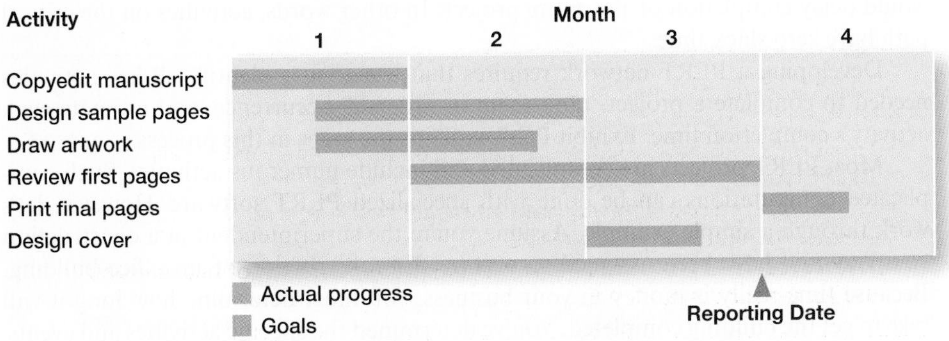

Exhibit PC-5
A Gantt Chart

Exhibit PC-6
A Load Chart

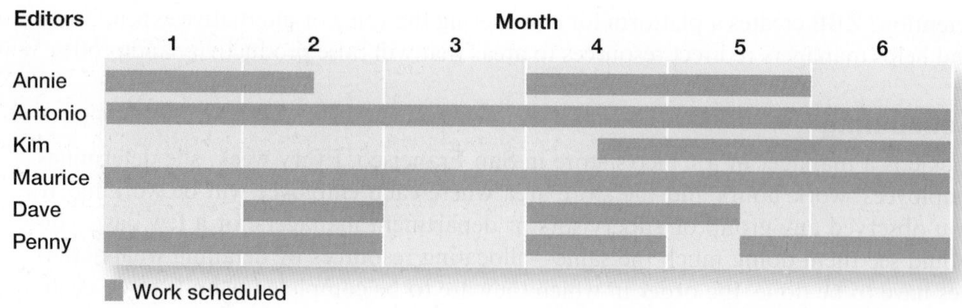

For example, Exhibit PC-6 shows a load chart for six production editors at the same publishing company. Each editor supervises the production and design of several books. By reviewing a load chart, the executive editor, who supervises the six production editors, can see who is free to take on a new book. If everyone is fully scheduled, the executive editor might decide not to accept any new projects, to accept new projects and delay others, to make the editors work overtime, or to employ more production editors. As this exhibit shows, only Antonio and Maurice are completely scheduled for the next six months. The other editors have some unassigned time and might be able to accept new projects or be available to help other editors who get behind.

PERT NETWORK ANALYSIS Gantt and load charts are useful as long as the activities scheduled are few in number and independent of each other. But what if a manager had to plan a large project such as a departmental reorganization, the implementation of a cost-reduction program, or the development of a new product that required coordinating inputs from marketing, manufacturing, and product design? Such projects require coordinating hundreds and even thousands of activities, some of which must be done simultaneously and some of which can't begin until preceding activities have been completed. If you're constructing a building, you obviously can't start putting up the walls until the foundation is laid. How can managers schedule such a complex project? The program evaluation and review technique (PERT) is highly appropriate for such projects.

PERT network
A flowchart diagram showing the sequence of activities needed to complete a project and the time or cost associated with each

A **PERT network** is a flowchart diagram that depicts the sequence of activities needed to complete a project and the time or costs associated with each activity. With a PERT network, a manager must think through what has to be done, determine which events depend on one another, and identify potential trouble spots. PERT also makes it easy to compare the effects alternative actions might have on scheduling and costs. Thus, PERT allows managers to monitor a project's progress, identify possible bottlenecks, and shift resources as necessary to keep the project on schedule.

events
End points that represent the completion of major activities in a PERT network

activities
The time or resources needed to progress from one event to another in a PERT network

slack time
The amount of time an individual activity can be delayed without delaying the whole project

critical path
The longest sequence of activities in a PERT network

To understand how to construct a PERT network, you need to know four terms. **Events** are end points that represent the completion of major activities. **Activities** represent the time or resources required to progress from one event to another. **Slack time** is the amount of time an individual activity can be delayed without delaying the whole project. The **critical path** is the longest or most time-consuming sequence of events and activities in a PERT network. Any delay in completing events on this path would delay completion of the entire project. In other words, activities on the critical path have zero slack time.

Developing a PERT network requires that a manager identify all key activities needed to complete a project, rank them in order of occurrence, and estimate each activity's completion time. Exhibit PC-7 explains the steps in this process.

Most PERT projects are complicated and include numerous activities. Such complicated computations can be done with specialized PERT software. However, let's work through a simple example. Assume you're the superintendent at a construction company and have been assigned to oversee the construction of an office building. Because time really is money in your business, you must determine how long it will take to get the building completed. You've determined the specific activities and events.

Exhibit PC-7

Steps in Developing a PERT Network

1. *Identify every significant activity that must be achieved for a project to be completed.* The accomplishment of each activity results in a set of events or outcomes.
2. *Determine the order in which these events must be completed.*
3. *Diagram the flow of activities from start to finish, identifying each activity and its relationship to all other activities.* Use circles to indicate events and arrows to represent activities. This results in a flowchart diagram called a PERT network.
4. *Compute a time estimate for completing each activity.* This is done with a weighted average that uses an *optimistic* time estimate (t_o) of how long the activity would take under ideal conditions, a *most likely* estimate (t_m) of the time the activity normally should take, and a *pessimistic* estimate (t_p) that represents the time that an activity should take under the worst possible conditions. The formula for calculating the expected time (t_e) is then

$$t_e = \frac{t_o + 4t_m + t_p}{6}$$

5. *Using the network diagram that contains time estimates for each activity, determine a schedule for the start and finish dates of each activity and for the entire project.* Any delays that occur along the critical path require the most attention because they can delay the whole project.

Exhibit PC-8 outlines the major events in the construction project and your estimate of the expected time to complete each. Exhibit PC-9 shows the actual PERT network based on the data in Exhibit PC-8. You've also calculated the length of time that each path of activities will take:

A-B-C-D-I-J-K (44 weeks)
A-B-C-D-G-H-J-K (50 weeks)
A-B-C-E-G-H-J-K (47 weeks)
A-B-C-F-G-H-J-K (47 weeks)

Your PERT network shows that if everything goes as planned, the total project completion time will be 50 weeks. This is calculated by tracing the project's critical path (the

Exhibit PC-8

Events and Activities in Constructing an Office Building

Event	Description	Expected Time (in weeks)	Preceding Event
A	Approve design and get permits	10	None
B	Dig subterranean garage	6	A
C	Erect frame and siding	14	B
D	Construct floor	6	C
E	Install windows	3	C
F	Put on roof	3	C
G	Install internal wiring	5	D, E, F
H	Install elevator	5	G
I	Put in floor covering and paneling	4	D
J	Put in doors and interior decorative trim	3	I, H
K	Turn over to building management group	1	J

Exhibit PC-9
PERT Network for Constructing an Office Building

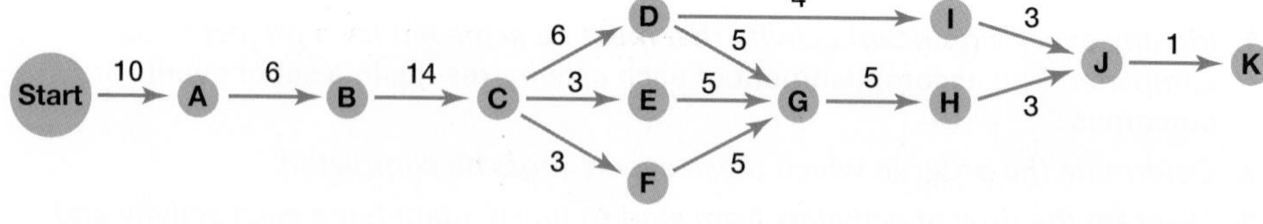

longest sequence of activities), A-B-C-D-G-H-J-K, and adding up the times. You know that any delay in completing the events on this path would delay the completion of the entire project. Taking six weeks instead of four to put in the floor covering and paneling (Event I) would have no effect on the final completion date. Why? Because that event isn't on the critical path. However, taking seven weeks instead of six to dig the subterranean garage (Event B) would likely delay the total project. A manager who needed to get back on schedule or to cut the 50-week completion time would want to concentrate on those activities along the critical path that could be completed faster. How might the manager do this? He or she could look to see if any of the other activities *not* on the critical path had slack time in which resources could be transferred to activities that *were* on the critical path.

Breakeven Analysis

breakeven analysis
A technique for identifying the point at which total revenue is just sufficient to cover total costs

Managers at Glory Foods want to know how many units of their new sensibly seasoned canned vegetables must be sold in order to break even—that is, the point at which total revenue is just sufficient to cover total costs. **Breakeven analysis** is a widely used resource allocation technique to help managers determine breakeven point.[34]

Breakeven analysis is a simple calculation, yet it's valuable to managers because it points out the relationship between revenues, costs, and profits. To compute breakeven point (BE), a manager needs to know the unit price of the product being sold (P), the variable cost per unit (VC), and total fixed costs (TFC). An organization breaks even when its total revenue is just enough to equal its total costs. But total cost has two parts: fixed and variable. *Fixed costs* are expenses that do not change regardless of volume. Examples include insurance premiums, rent, and property taxes. *Variable costs* change in proportion to output and include raw materials, labor costs, and energy costs.

Breakeven point can be computed graphically or by using the following formula:

$$BE = \frac{TFC}{P - VC}$$

This formula tells us that (1) total revenue will equal total cost when we sell enough units at a price that covers all variable unit costs, and (2) the difference between price and variable costs, when multiplied by the number of units sold, equals the fixed costs. Let's work through an example.

Assume that Randy's Photocopying Service charges $0.10 per photocopy. If fixed costs are $27,000 a year and variable costs are $0.04 per copy, Randy can compute his breakeven point as follows: $27,000 ÷ ($0.10−$0.04) = 450,000 copies, or when annual revenues are $45,000 (450,000 copies × $0.10). This same relationship is shown graphically in Exhibit PC-10.

As a planning tool, breakeven analysis could help Randy set his sales goal. For example, he could determine his profit goal and then calculate what sales level is needed to reach that goal. Breakeven analysis could also tell Randy how much volume has to increase to break even if he's currently operating at a loss or how much volume he can afford to lose and still break even.

Linear Programming

linear programming
A mathematical technique that solves resource allocation problems

Maria Sanchez manages a manufacturing plant that produces two kinds of cinnamon-scented home fragrance products: wax candles and a woodchip potpourri sold in bags. Business is good, and she can sell all of the products she can produce. Her dilemma: Given that the bags of potpourri and the wax candles are manufactured in the same facility, how many of each product should she produce to maximize profits? Maria can use **linear programming** to solve her resource allocation problem.

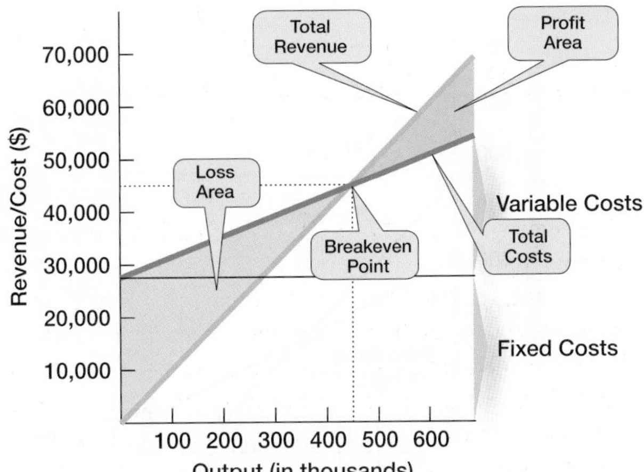

Exhibit PC-10
Breakeven Analysis

Although linear programming can be used here, it can't be applied to all resource allocation problems because it requires that resources be limited, that the goal be outcome optimization, that resources can be combined in alternative ways to produce a number of output mixes, and that a linear relationship exist between variables (a change in one variable must be accompanied by an exactly proportional change in the other).[35] For Maria's business, that last condition would be met if it took exactly twice the amount of raw materials and hours of labor to produce two of a given home fragrance product as it took to produce one.

What kinds of problems can be solved with linear programming? Some applications include selecting transportation routes that minimize shipping costs, allocating a limited advertising budget among various product brands, making the optimal assignment of people among projects, and determining how much of each product to make with a limited number of resources. Let's return to Maria's problem and see how linear programming could help her solve it. Fortunately, her problem is relatively simple, so we can solve it rather quickly. For complex linear programming problems, managers can use computer software programs designed specifically to help develop optimizing solutions.

First, we need to establish some facts about Maria's business. She has computed the profit margins on her home fragrance products at $10 for a bag of potpourri and $18 for a scented candle. These numbers establish the basis for Maria to be able to express her *objective function* as maximum profit $= 10P + \$18S$, where P is the number of bags of potpourri produced and S is the number of scented candles produced. The objective function is simply a mathematical equation that can predict the outcome of all proposed alternatives. In addition, Maria knows how much time each fragrance product must spend in production and the monthly production capacity (1,200 hours in manufacturing and 900 hours in assembly) for manufacturing and assembly. (See Exhibit PC-11.) The production capacity numbers act as *constraints* on her overall capacity. Now Maria can establish her constraint equations:

$$2P + 4S \leq 1{,}200$$
$$2P + 2S \leq 900$$

Of course, Maria can also state that $P \geq 0$ and $S \geq 0$ because neither fragrance product can be produced in a volume less than zero.

	Number of Hours Required (per unit)		
Department	**Potpourri Bags**	**Scented Candles**	**Monthly Production Capacity (in hours)**
Manufacturing	2	4	1,200
Assembly	2	2	900
Profit per unit	$10	$18	

Exhibit PC-11
Production Data for Cinnamon-Scented Products

Exhibit PC-12
Graphical Solution to Linear Programming Problem

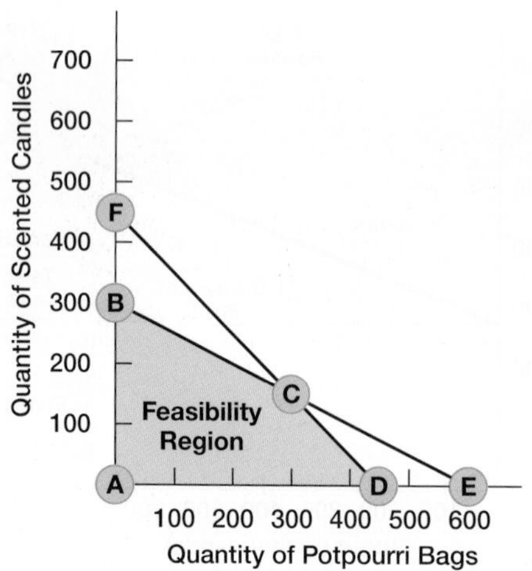

Maria has graphed her solution in Exhibit PC-12. The shaded area represents the options that don't exceed the capacity of either department. What does this mean? Well, let's look first at the manufacturing constraint line BE. We know that total manufacturing capacity is 1,200 hours, so if Maria decides to produce all potpourri bags, the maximum she can produce is 600 (1,200 hours ÷ 2 hours required to produce a bag of potpourri). If she decides to produce all scented candles, the maximum she can produce is 300 (1,200 hours ÷ 4 hours required to produce a scented candle). The other constraint Maria faces is that of assembly, shown by line DF. If Maria decides to produce all potpourri bags, the maximum she can assemble is 450 (900 hours production capacity ÷ 2 hours required to assemble). Likewise, if Maria decides to produce all scented candles, the maximum she can assemble is also 450 because the scented candles also take 2 hours to assemble. The constraints imposed by these capacity limits establish Maria's *feasibility region*. Her optimal resource allocation will be defined at one of the corners within this feasibility region. Point C provides the maximum profits within the constraints stated. How do we know? At point A, profits would be 0 (no production of either potpourri bags or scented candles). At point B, profits would be \$5,400 (300 scented candles × \$18 profit and 0 potpourri bags produced = \$5,400). At point D, profits would be \$4,500 (450 potpourri bags produced × \$10 profit and 0 scented candles produced = \$4,500). At point C, however, profits would be \$5,700 (150 scented candles produced × \$18 profit and 300 potpourri bags produced × \$10 profit = \$5,700).

CONTEMPORARY planning and control techniques

Lowest home mortgage rates since 1950s. MERS and other fast-moving viruses. Global warming. Chemical/biological attacks. Recession/inflation/deflation worries. Category 4 or 5 hurricanes. Changing competition. Today's managers face the challenges of planning in an environment that's both dynamic and complex. Two planning techniques appropriate for this type of environment are project management and scenarios. Both techniques emphasize *flexibility*, something that's important to making planning more effective and efficient in this type of organizational environment.

Project Management

project
A one-time-only set of activities that has a definite beginning and ending point in time

project management
The task of getting a project's activities done on time, within budget, and according to specifications

Different types of organizations, from manufacturers such as Coleman and Boeing to software design firms such as SAS and Microsoft, use projects. A **project** is a one-time-only set of activities that has a definite beginning and ending point in time.[36] Projects vary in size and scope—from Boston's "big dig" downtown traffic tunnel to a sorority's holiday formal. **Project management** is the task of getting a project's activities done on time, within budget, and according to specifications.[37]

Exhibit PC-13

Project Planning Process

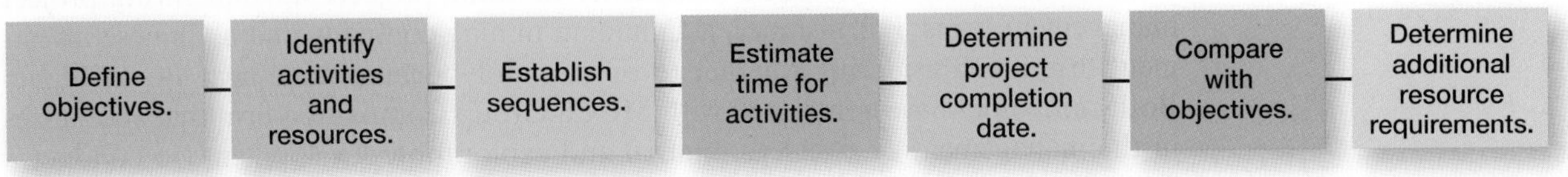
Define objectives.
Identify activities and resources.
Establish sequences.
Estimate time for activities.
Determine project completion date.
Compare with objectives.
Determine additional resource requirements.

Source: Based on *Production and Operations Management,* by R. S. Russell and B. W. Taylor III. Upper Saddle River, NJ: Prentice-Hall, 1996.

More and more organizations are using project management because the approach fits well with the need for flexibility and rapid response to perceived market opportunities. For instance, India's Tata Motors relied on project management to develop and manufacture a subcompact car to be competitive with similar models from Hyundai and Toyota. Girish Wagh, senior vice president for program planning and project management for passenger vehicles, said that Tata's Tiago (new car model) is "one of the important launches from Tata Motors' passenger car business and the first step towards our transformation."[38]

When organizations undertake projects that are unique, have specific deadlines, contain complex interrelated tasks requiring specialized skills, and are temporary in nature, these projects often do not fit into the standardized planning procedures that guide an organization's other routine work activities. Instead, managers use project management techniques to effectively and efficiently accomplish the project's goals. What does the project management process involve?

PROJECT MANAGEMENT PROCESS In the typical project, work is done by a project team whose members are assigned from their respective work areas to the project and who report to a project manager. The project manager coordinates the project's activities with other departments. When the project team accomplishes its goals, it disbands, and members move on to other projects or back to their permanent work area.

The essential features of the project planning process are shown in Exhibit PC-13. The process begins by clearly defining the project's goals. This step is necessary because the manager and the team members need to know what's expected. All activities in the project and the resources needed to do them must then be identified. What materials and labor are needed to complete the project? This step may be time-consuming and complex, particularly if the project is unique and the managers have no history or experience with similar projects. Once the activities have been identified, the sequence of completion needs to be determined. What activities must be completed before others can begin? Which can be done simultaneously? This step often uses flowchart diagrams such as a Gantt chart, a load chart, or a PERT network. Next, the project activities need to be scheduled. Time estimates for each activity are done, and these estimates are used to develop an overall project schedule and completion date. Then the project schedule is compared to the goals, and any necessary adjustments are made. If the project completion time is too long, the manager might assign more resources to critical activities so they can be completed faster.

Today, the project management process can take place online, as a number of Web-based software packages are available. These packages cover aspects from project accounting and estimating to project scheduling and bug and defect tracking.[39]

THE ROLE OF THE PROJECT MANAGER The temporary nature of projects makes managing them different from, say, overseeing a production line or preparing a weekly tally of costs on an ongoing basis. The one-shot nature of the work makes project managers the organizational equivalent of a hired gunman. There's a job to be done. It has to be defined—in detail. And the project manager is responsible for how it's done. At J.B. Hunt Transport Services, the head of project management trains project managers on both technical and interpersonal skills so that they know how to "... run a project effectively."[40] The complexity of some projects warrant hiring project management firms. For instance, a Canadian mining company and a Chinese investment firm are considering whether to open a molybdenum mine near Boise, Idaho. Both companies have contracted with MCC8 Group Company, a firm that specializes in the management of overseas mineral and exploration development, to conduct a feasibility study.[41] MCC8 will undoubtedly assign several project managers to oversee this feasibility study including geologists and environmental impact experts.

Even with the availability of sophisticated computerized and online scheduling programs and other project management tools, the role of project manager remains difficult because he or she is managing people who typically are still assigned to their permanent work areas. The only real influence project managers have is their communication skills and their power of persuasion. To make matters worse, team members seldom work on just one project. They're usually assigned to two or three at any given time. So project managers end up competing with each other to focus a worker's attention on his or her particular project.

Scenario Planning

During the 1990s, business was so good at Colgate-Palmolive that then-chairman Reuben Mark worried about what "might go wrong." He installed an "early warning system to flag problems before they blew up into company-wrecking crises." For instance, a red-flag report alerted Mark "that officials in Baddi, India, had questions about how a plant treated wastewater." Mark's response was to quickly assign an engineering team to check it out and prevent potential problems.[42]

We already know how important it is that today's managers do what Reuben Mark was doing—monitor and assess the external environment for trends and changes. As they assess the environment, issues and concerns that could affect their organization's current or planned operations are likely to be revealed. All of these issues won't be equally important, so it's usually necessary to focus on a limited set that are most important and to develop scenarios based on each.

scenario
A consistent view of what the future is likely to be

A **scenario** is a consistent view of what the future is likely to be. Developing scenarios also can be described as *contingency planning*; that is, if this event happens, then we need to take these actions. If, for instance, environmental scanning reveals increasing interest by U.S. Congress for raising the national minimum wage, managers at Subway could create multiple scenarios to assess the possible consequences of such an action. What would be the implications for its labor costs if the minimum wage was raised to $12 an hour? How about $14 an hour? What effect would these changes have on the chain's bottom line? How might competitors respond? Different assumptions lead to different outcomes. The intent of scenario planning is not to try to predict the future but to reduce uncertainty by playing out potential situations under different specified conditions.[43] Subway could, for example, develop a set of scenarios ranging from optimistic to pessimistic in terms of the minimum wage issue. It would then be prepared to implement new strategies to get and keep a competitive advantage. An expert in scenario planning said, "Just the process of doing scenarios causes executives to rethink and clarify the essence of the business environment in ways they almost certainly have never done before."[44]

Although scenario planning is useful in anticipating events that *can be* anticipated, it's difficult to forecast random events—the major surprises and aberrations that can't be foreseen. For instance, an outbreak of deadly and devastating tornadoes in Kansas and Oklahoma in May 2016 was a scenario that could not be anticipated. The disaster recovery planning that took place after the storms was effective because this type of scenario had been experienced before. A response had already been planned and people knew what to do. But the planning challenge comes from those totally unexpected events. For instance, the shooting of a doctor by a patient's family member in a Boston hospital was unexpected and a total shock to many organizations already concerned about workplace safety. Scenario planning was of little use because no one could have envisioned this scenario. As difficult as it may be for managers to anticipate and deal with these random events, they're not totally vulnerable to the consequences. One suggestion identified by risk experts as particularly important is to have an early warning system in place. (A similar idea is the tsunami warning systems in the Pacific and in Alaska, which alert officials to potentially dangerous tsunamis and give them time to take action.) Early warning indicators for organizations can give managers advance notice of potential risks and changes so they can take action. Then, managers need to have appropriate responses (plans) in place if these unexpected events occur. For instance, five large banks, including Bank of America and Capital One, own Early Warning Services (EWS).[45] EWS enables banks to easily exchange information about a customer's potential risk in an effort to fight fraud.

Planning tools and techniques can help managers prepare confidently for the future. But they should remember that all the tools we've described in this module are just that—tools. They will never replace the manager's skills and capabilities in using the information gained to develop effective and efficient plans.

Pearson **MyLab** Management

Go to **mymanagementlab.com** to complete the problems marked with this icon ✪.

✪ REVIEW AND DISCUSSION QUESTIONS

PC-1. Describe the different approaches to assessing the environment.

PC-2. Describe the four techniques for allocating resources.

PC-3. How does PERT network analysis work?

PC-4. Why is flexibility so important to today's planning techniques?

PC-5. What is project management, and what are the steps managers use in planning projects?

PC-6. "It's a waste of time and other resources to develop a set of sophisticated scenarios for situations that may never occur." Do you agree or disagree? Support your position.

PC-7. Do intuition and creativity have any relevance in quantitative planning tools and techniques? Explain.

PC-8. The *Wall Street Journal* and other business periodicals often carry reports of companies that have not met their sales or profit forecasts. What are some reasons a company might not meet its forecast? What suggestions could you make for improving the effectiveness of forecasting?

PC-9. In what ways is managing a project different from managing a department or other structured work area? In what ways are they the same?

PC-10. What might be some early warning signs of (a) a new competitor coming into your market, (b) an employee work stoppage, or (c) a new technology that could change demand for your product?

ENDNOTES

1. K. Burke, "Your Ticket to Disney May Cost More—or Less—depending on when you go," *Market Watch* online, www.marketwatch.com, February 29, 2016.
2. J. Trotsky, "The Futurists," *US News & World Report,* April 19, 2004, pp. EE4–EE6.
3. F. Vogelstein, "Search and Destroy," *Fortune,* May 2, 2005, pp. 73–82.
4. S. C. Jain, "Environmental Scanning in U.S. Corporations," *Long Range Planning*, April 1984, pp. 117–128; see also L. M. Fuld, *Monitoring the Competition* (New York: John Wiley & Sons, 1988); E. H. Burack and N. J. Mathys, "Environmental Scanning Improves Strategic Planning," *Personnel Administrator*, April 1989, pp. 82–87; R. Subramanian, N. Fernandes, and E. Harper, "Environmental Scanning in U.S. Companies: Their Nature and Their Relationship to Performance," *Management International Review*, July 1993, pp. 271–286; B. K. Boyd and J. Fulk, "Executive Scanning and Perceived Uncertainty: A Multidimensional Model," *Journal of Management*, vol. 22, no. 1, 1996, pp. 1–21; D. S. Elkenov, "Strategic Uncertainty and Environmental Scanning: The Case for Institutional Influences on Scanning Behavior," *Strategic Management Journal*, vol. 18, 1997, pp. 287–302; K. Kumar, R. Subramanian, and K. Strandholm, "Competitive Strategy, Environmental Scanning and Performance: A Context Specific Analysis of Their Relationship," *International Journal of Commerce and Management,* Spring 2001, pp. 1–18; C. G. Wagner, "Top 10 Reasons to Watch Trends," *The Futurist,* March–April 2002, pp. 68–69; and V. K. Garg, B. A. Walters, and R. L. Priem, "Chief Executive Scanning Emphases, Environmental Dynamism, and Manufacturing Firm Performance," *Strategic Management Journal,* August 2003, pp. 725–744.
5. B. Gilad, "The Role of Organized Competitive Intelligence in Corporate Strategy," *Columbia Journal of World Business,* Winter 1989, pp. 29–35; L. Fuld, "A Recipe for Business Intelligence," *Journal of Business Strategy*, January–February 1991, pp. 12–17; J. P. Herring, "The Role of Intelligence in Formulating Strategy," *Journal of Business Strategy*, September–-October 1992, pp. 54–60; K. Western, "Ethical Spying," *Business Ethics*, September–October 1995, pp. 22–23; D. Kinard, "Raising Your Competitive IQ: The Payoff of Paying Attention to Potential Competitors," *Association Management,* February 2003, pp. 40–44; K. Girard, "Snooping on a Shoestring," *Business 2.0,* May 2003, pp. 64–66; and "Know Your Enemy," *Business 2.0,* June 2004, p. 89.
6. C. Davis, "Get Smart," *Executive Edge,* October–November 1999, pp. 46–50.
7. B. Gilad and L. M. Fuld, "Only Half of Companies Actually Use the Competitive Intelligence They Collect," *Harvard Business Review* online, www.hbr.org, January 26, 2016.
8. B. Ettore, "Managing Competitive Intelligence," *Management Review*, October 1995, pp. 15–19.
9. D. DeCarolis, "Why Knowing Your Enemies Is Good for Business," *Forbes* online, www.forbes.com, April 15, 2016.
10. A. Serwer, "P&G's Covert Operation," *Fortune,* September 17, 2001, pp. 42–44.
11. B. Rosner, "HR Should Get a Clue: Corporate Spying Is Real," *Workforce,* April 2001, pp. 72–75.
12. J. W. Miller, "U.S. Steel Accuses China of Hacking," *The Wall Street Journal* online, www.wsj.com, April 28, 2016.
13. Western, "Ethical Spying."
14. W. H. Davidson, "The Role of Global Scanning in Business Planning," *Organizational Dynamics,* Winter 1991, pp. 5–16.
15. Associated Press, "First U.S. Cruise in Decades Arrives in Cuba," *The Wall Street Journal* online, www.wsj.com, May 2, 2016.
16. Ibid.
17. "Is Supply Chain Collaboration Really Happening?" *ERI Journal,* www.eri.com, January–February 2006; L. Denend and H. Lee, "West Marine: Driving Growth Through Shipshape Supply Chain Management, A Case Study," *Stanford Graduate School of Business,* www.vics.org, April 7, 2005; N. Nix, A. G. Zacharia, R. F. Lusch, W. R. Bridges, and A. Thomas, "Keys to Effective Supply Chain Collaboration: A Special Report from the Collaborative Practices Research Program," *Neeley School of Business, Texas Christian University,* www.vics.org, November 15, 2004; Collaborative, Planning, Forecasting, and Replenishment Committee website, www.cpfr.org, May 20, 2003; and J. W. Verity, "Clearing the Cobwebs from the Stockroom," *BusinessWeek*, October 21, 1996, p. 140.
18. See A. B. Fisher, "Is Long-Range Planning Worth It?" *Fortune*, April 23, 1990, pp. 281–284; J. A. Fraser, "On Target," *Inc.*, April 1991, pp. 113–114; P. Schwartz, *The Art of the Long View* (New York: Doubleday/-Currency, 1991); G. Hamel and C. K. Prahalad, "Competing for the Future," *Harvard Business Review*, July–August 1994, pp. 122–128; F. Elikai and W. Hall, Jr., "Managing and Improving the Forecasting Process," *Journal of Business Forecasting Methods & Systems*, Spring 1999, pp. 15–19; L. Lapide, "New Developments in Business Forecasting," *Journal of Business Forecasting Methods & Systems*, Summer 1999, pp. 13–14; and T. Leahy, "Building Better Forecasts," *Business Finance*, December 1999, pp. 10–12.
19. J. Goff, "Start with Demand," *CFO,* January 2005, pp. 53–57.
20. L. Cecere, "What Drives Inventory Effectiveness in a Market-Driven World?" SupplyChainInsights, http://supplychaininsights.com/what-drives-inventory-effectiveness-in-a-market-driven-world/, October 27, 2015.
21. V. Ryan, "Future Tense," *CFO,* December 2008, pp. 37–42.
22. R. Durand, "Predicting a Firm's Forecasting Ability: The Roles of Organizational Illusion of Control and Organizational Attention," *Strategic Management Journal,* September 2003, pp. 821–838.
23. J. Katz, "Forecasts Demand Change," *Industry Week,* May 2010, pp. 26–29; A. Stuart, "Imperfect Futures," *CFO,* July–August 2009, pp. 48–53; C. L. Jain and M. Covas, "Thinking About Tomorrow," *Wall Street Journal,* July 7, 2008, p. R10+; T. Leahy, "Turning Managers into Forecasters," *Business Finance,* August 2002, pp. 37–40; M. A. Giullian, M. D. Odom, and M. W. Totaro, "Developing Essential Skills for Success in the Business World: A Look at Forecasting," *Journal of Applied Business Research*, Summer 2000, pp. 51–65; F. Elikai and W. Hall, Jr., "Managing and Improving the Forecasting Process;" and N. Pant and W. H. Starbuck, "Innocents in the Forest: Forecasting and Research Methods," *Journal of Management*, June 1990, pp. 433–460.
24. T. Leahy, "Turning Managers into Forecasters."
25. J. Hope, "Use a Rolling Forecast to Spot Trends," *Harvard Business School Working Knowledge,* hbswk.hbs.edu, March 13, 2006.

26. This section is based on Y. K. Shetty, "Benchmarking for Superior Performance," *Long Range Planning,* vol. 1, April 1993, pp. 39–44; G. H. Watson, "How Process Benchmarking Supports Corporate Strategy," *Planning Review*, January–February 1993, pp. 12–15; S. Greengard, "Discover Best Practices," *Personnel Journal*, November 1995, pp. 62–73; J. Martin, "Are You as Good as You Think You Are?," *Fortune*, September 30, 1996, pp. 142–152; R. L. Ackoff, "The Trouble with Benchmarking," *Across the Board*, January 2000, p. 13; V. Prabhu, D. Yarrow, and G. Gordon-Hart, "Best Practice and Performance Within Northeast Manufacturing," *Total Quality Management*, January 2000, pp. 113–121; "E-Benchmarking: The Latest E-Trend," *CFO*, March 2000, p. 7; E. Krell, "Now Read This," *Business Finance*, May 2000, pp. 97–103; and H. Johnson, "All in Favor Say Benchmark!," *Training,* August 2004, pp. 30–34.
27. J. J. Martocchio, *Strategic Compensation: A Human Resource Management Approach*, 9th ed. (New York: Pearson Education, 2017).
28. S. Randazzo, "Law Firm Cravath Raising Starting Salaries to $180,000," *The Wall Street Journal* online, www.wsj.com, June 6, 2016.
29. "Newswatch," *CFO,* July 2002, p. 26.
30. Benchmarking examples from the following: S. Carey, "Racing to Improve," *Wall Street Journal,* March 24, 2006, pp. B1+; D. Waller, "NASCAR: The Army's Unlikely Adviser," *Time,* July 4, 2005, p. 19; A. Taylor, III, "Double Duty," *Fortune,* March 7, 2005, p. 108; P. Gogoi, "Thinking Outside the Cereal Box," *BusinessWeek,* July 28, 2003, pp. 74–75; "Benchmarkers Make Strange Bedfellows," *Industry Week*, November 15, 1993, p. 8; G. Fuchsberg, "Here's Help in Finding Corporate Role Models," *Wall Street Journal*, June 1, 1993, p. B1; and A. Tanzer, "Studying at the Feet of the Masters," *Forbes*, May 10, 1993, pp. 43–44.
31. E. Krell, "The Case Against Budgeting," *Business Finance,* July 2003, pp. 20–25; J. Hope and R. Fraser, "Who Needs Budgets?" *Harvard Business Review,* February 2003, pp. 108–115; T. Leahy, "The Top 10 Traps of Budgeting," *Business Finance,* November 2001, pp. 20–26; T. Leahy, "Necessary Evil," *Business Finance*, November 1999, pp. 41–45; J. Fanning, "Businesses Languishing in a Budget Comfort Zone?" *Management Accounting*, July/August 1999, p. 8; "Budgeting Processes: Inefficiency or Inadequate?" *Management Accounting*, February 1999, p. 5; A. Kennedy and D. Dugdale, "Getting the Most from Budgeting," *Management Accounting*, February 1999, pp. 22–24; G. J. Nolan, "The End of Traditional Budgeting," *Bank Accounting & Finance*, Summer 1998, pp. 29–36; and J. Mariotti, "Surviving the Dreaded Budget Process," *IW*, August 17, 1998, p. 150.
32. S. C. Kavanagh, "Zero-Base Budgeting," The Government Finance Officers Association and the City of Calgary," http://www.gfoa.org/sites/default/files/GFOAZeroBasedBudgeting.pdf2011, 2011.
33. S. Callaghan, K. Hawke, and C. Mignerey, "Five Myths (and Realities) About Zero-Based Budgeting," McKinsey & Company, www.mckinsey.com, October 2014.
34. See, for example, S. Stiansen, "Breaking Even," *Success*, November 1988, p. 16.
35. S. E. Barndt and D. W. Carvey, *Essentials of Operations Management* (Upper Saddle River, NJ: Prentice Hall, 1982), p. 134.
36. E. E. Adam Jr. and R. J. Ebert, *Production and Operations Management*, 5th ed. (Upper Saddle River, NJ: Prentice Hall, 1992), p. 333.
37. See, for instance, C. Benko and F. W. McFarlan, *Connecting the Dots: Aligning Projects with Objectives in Unpredictable Times* (Boston, MA: Harvard Business School Press, 2003); M. W. Lewis, M. A. Welsh, G. E. Dehler, and S. G. Green, "Product Development Tensions: Exploring Contrasting Styles of Project Management," *Academy of Management Journal,* June 2002, pp. 546–564; C. E. Gray and E. W. Larsen, *Project Management: The Managerial Process* (Columbus, OH: McGraw-Hill Higher Education, 2000); J. Davidson Frame, *Project Management Competence: Building Key Skills for Individuals, Teams, and Organizations* (San Francisco, CA: Jossey-Bass, 1999).
38. S. Choudhury, "This Is How Much Tata Motor's Tiago Costs in India," *The Wall Street Journal* online, www.wsj.com, April 6, 2016.
39. For more information, see Project Management Software Directory, www.infogoal.com/pmc/pmcswr.htm.
40. D. Zielinski, "Soft Skills, Hard Truth," *Training,* July 2005, pp. 19–23.
41. The Associated Press, "Canadian, Chinese Companies Sign Deal on Proposed Idaho Mine," *The New York Times* online, www.nytimes.com, June 9, 2016.
42. H. Collingwood, "Best Kept Secrets of the World's Best Companies: Secret 05, Bad News Folders," *Business 2.0,* April 2006, p. 84.
43. R. King, "Companies Need to Apply Disaster Response Planning to Cybersecurity," *The Wall Street Journal* online, www.wsj.com, March 3, 2016; G. Colvin, "An Executive Risk Handbook," *Fortune,* October 3, 2005, pp. 69–70; A. Long and A. Weiss, "Using Scenario Planning to Manage Short-Term Uncertainty," *Outward Insights,* www.outwardinsights.com, 2005; B. Fiora, "Use Early Warning to Strengthen Scenario Planning," *Outward Insights,* www.outwardinsights.com, 2003; L. Fahey, "Scenario Learning," *Management Review,* March 2000, pp. 29–34; S. Caudron, "Frontview Mirror," *Business Finance*, December 1999, pp. 24–30; and J. R. Garber, "What if . . .?," *Forbes*, November 2, 1998, pp. 76–79.
44. S. Caudron, "Frontview Mirror," p. 30.
45. L. Phillips, "EWS Can Stop You From Opening a Bank Account," RebuildCreditScores.com, http://rebuildcreditscores.com/early-warning-services, April 9, 2015.

Managing Operations *Module*

Using millions of parts as small as rivets and as large as five-story buildings, employees at Hyundai Heavy Industries Inc. build as many as 30 ships at one time.[1] *And the "factory" stretches for miles over land and sea. "It's an environment that is too large and complex to be able to keep track of the movement in parts and inventory in real time." Hwang See-young, chief information officer at Hyundai Heavy, knew that production efficiency was limited without real-time data. The solution? High-speed wireless networks that employees can access at any time and anywhere with notebook computers.*

With the new technology, data fly around the shipyard complex at 4 megabits per second. Radio sensors track the movements of parts from fabrication shops to the dry dock and onto a ship being constructed. Also, workers on a ship can access plans using notebook computers or handheld phones. They're also able to hold two-way video conversations with ship designers in the office over a mile away. Eventually, they hope to establish communication capabilities with workers inside a ship that is below ground or at sea level. Now, however, Hyundai Heavy wants to implement the technology in its other construction divisions. Suppose you were in charge of doing this. What would you do?

As the world's largest maker of ships, Hyundai hopes its new technology helps it reduce expenses and streamline production, an important consideration in today's environment. You've probably never given much thought to how organizations "produce" the goods and services that you buy or use. But it's an important process. Without it, you wouldn't have a car to drive or McDonald's fries to snack on, or even a hiking trail in a local park to enjoy. Organizations need to have well-thought-out and well-designed operating systems, organizational control systems, and quality programs to survive in today's increasingly competitive global environment. And it's the manager's job to manage those systems and programs.

THE role of operations management

What is **operations management**? The term refers to the transformation process that converts resources into finished goods and services. Exhibit MO-1 portrays this process in a simplified fashion. The system takes in inputs—people, technology, capital, equipment, materials, and information—and transforms them through various processes, procedures, work activities, and so forth into finished goods and services. Because every unit in an organization produces something, managers need to be familiar with operations management concepts in order to achieve goals efficiently and effectively.

operations management
The transformation process that converts resources into finished goods and services

Operations management is important to organizations and managers for three reasons: (1) it encompasses both services and manufacturing; (2) it's important in effectively and efficiently managing productivity; and (3) it plays a strategic role in an organization's competitive success.

Services and Manufacturing

With a menu that offers more than 200 items, The Cheesecake Factory restaurants rely on a finely tuned production system. One food-service consultant says, "They've evolved with this highly complex menu combined with a highly efficient kitchen."[2]

Every organization produces something. Unfortunately, this fact is often overlooked except in obvious cases such as in the manufacturing of cars, cell phones, or lawnmowers. After all, **manufacturing organizations** produce physical goods. It's easy to see the operations management (transformation) process at work in these types of organizations because raw materials are turned into recognizable physical products. But the transformation process isn't as readily evident in **service organizations** that produce nonphysical outputs in the form of services. For instance, hospitals provide medical and health care services that help people manage their personal health, airlines provide transportation services that move people from one location to another, a cruise line provides a vacation and entertainment service, military forces provide defense capabilities, and the list goes on. These service organizations also transform inputs into outputs, although the transformation process isn't as easily recognizable as that in manufacturing organizations. Take a university, for example. University administrators bring together inputs—professors, books, academic journals, technology materials, computers, classrooms, and similar resources—to transform "unenlightened" students into educated and skilled individuals who are capable of making contributions to society.

manufacturing organizations
Organizations that produce physical goods

service organizations
Organizations that produce nonphysical products in the form of services

The reason we're making this point is that the U.S. economy, and to a large extent the global economy, is dominated by the creation and sale of services. Most of the world's developed countries are predominantly service economies. In the United States, for instance, almost 80 percent of all economic activity is services, and in the European Union it's over 71 percent. In lesser-developed countries, the services sector is less important. For instance, in Chad, it accounts for only 30 percent of economic activity; in the Republic of the Congo, 26 percent; and in Timor-Leste, about 17 percent.[3]

Exhibit MO-1
The Operations System

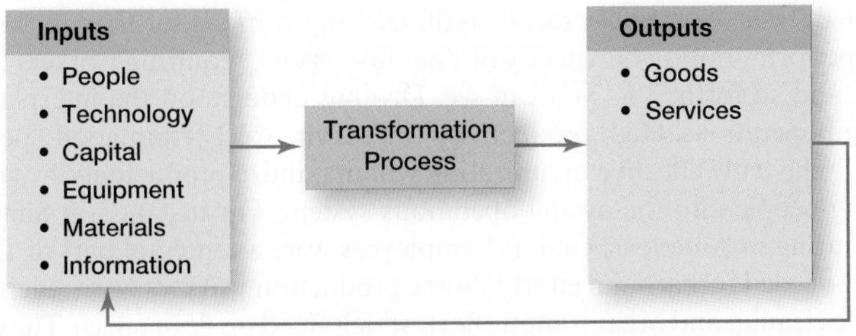

Inputs
- People
- Technology
- Capital
- Equipment
- Materials
- Information

→ Transformation Process →

Outputs
- Goods
- Services

Managing Productivity

One jetliner has roughly 4 million parts. Efficiently assembling such a finely engineered product requires intense focus. Boeing and Airbus, the two major global manufacturers, have copied techniques from Toyota. However, not every technique can be copied because airlines demand more customization than do car buyers and significantly more rigid safety regulations apply to jetliners than to cars.[4] Yet, advances in manufacturing technology are enabling Boeing to significantly increase its ability to turn out custom jetliners. The company plans to increase the production of its 737 model aircraft from 42 planes per month to 57 per month in 2019.[5] At the Evans Findings Company in East Providence, Rhode Island, which makes the tiny cutting devices on dental-floss containers, one production shift each day is run without people.[6] The company's goal is to do as much as possible with no labor. And it's not because they don't care about their employees. Instead, like many U.S. and foreign manufacturers, Evans needed to raise productivity and lower labor costs in order to survive, especially against low-cost competitors. And, some organizations, like Adidas, are planning manufacturing plants that will replace workers with robots altogether.[7] One study estimates that manufacturing facilities that rely on robots will cut labor costs by 33 percent in South Korea and 25 percent in the United States and Taiwan.[8]

Although most organizations don't make products that have 4 million parts and most organizations can't function without people, improving productivity has become a major goal in virtually every organization. For countries, high productivity can lead to economic growth and development. Employees can receive higher wages and company profits can increase without causing inflation. For individual organizations, increased productivity gives them a more competitive cost structure and the ability to offer more competitive prices.

Over the past decade, businesses have made dramatic improvements to increase their efficiency. For example, at Changying Precision Technology Company in China, technology has enabled the company to lower its manufacturing defect rate from 25 percent to 5 percent and increase production capacity from 8,000 units per month to more than 21,000 units.[9] And it's not just in manufacturing that companies are pursuing productivity gains. Les Clos, a French restaurant located in San Francisco, uses a smartphone app called Allset, which enables patrons to book their table, pre-order food, and pay for it. Shortly after adopting Allset, Les Clos saw a 30 percent increase in lunch orders and a 25 percent increase in sales.[10]

Organizations that hope to succeed globally are looking for ways to improve productivity. For example, the Canadian Imperial Bank of Commerce, based in Toronto, automated its purchasing function, saving several million dollars annually.[11] And Skoda, the Czech car company that's a subsidiary of Germany's Volkswagen AG, improved its productivity through an intensive restructuring of its manufacturing process.[12]

Productivity is a composite of people and operations variables. To improve productivity, managers must focus on both. The late W. Edwards Deming, a renowned quality expert, believed that managers, not workers, were the primary source of increased productivity. Some of his suggestions for managers included planning for the long-term future, never being complacent about product quality, understanding whether problems were confined to particular parts of the production process or stemmed from the overall process itself, training workers for the job they're being asked to perform, raising the quality of line supervisors, requiring workers to do quality work, and so forth.[13] As you can see, Deming understood the interplay between people and operations. High productivity can't come solely from good "people management." The truly effective organization will maximize productivity by successfully integrating people into the overall operations system. For instance, at Simplex Nails Manufacturing in Americus, Georgia, employees were an integral part of the company's much-needed turnaround effort.[14] Some production workers were redeployed on a plant-wide cleanup and organization effort, which freed up floor space. The company's sales force was retrained and refocused to sell what customers wanted rather than what was in inventory. The results were dramatic. Inventory was reduced by more than 50 percent, the plant had 20 percent more floor space, orders were more consistent, and employee morale improved. Here's a company that recognized the important interplay between people and the operations system.

Strategic Role of Operations Management

Modern manufacturing originated over 100 years ago in the United States, primarily in Detroit's automobile factories. The success that U.S. manufacturers experienced during World War II led manufacturing executives to believe that troublesome production problems had been conquered. These executives focused, instead, on improving other functional areas, such as finance and marketing, and paid little attention to manufacturing.

However, as U.S. executives neglected production, managers in Japan, Germany, and other countries took the opportunity to develop modern, computer-based, and technologically advanced facilities that fully integrated manufacturing operations into strategic planning decisions. The competition's success realigned world manufacturing leadership. U.S. manufacturers soon discovered that foreign goods were made not only less expensively but also with better quality. Finally, by the late 1970s, U.S. executives recognized they were facing a true crisis and responded. They invested heavily in improving manufacturing technology, increased the corporate authority and visibility of manufacturing executives, and began incorporating existing and future production requirements into the organization's overall strategic plan. Today, successful organizations recognize the crucial role that operations management plays as part of the overall organizational strategy to establish and maintain global leadership.[15]

The strategic role that operations management plays in successful organizational performance can be seen clearly as more organizations move toward managing their operations from a value chain perspective, which we're going to discuss next.

WHAT **is value chain management and why is it important?**

It's 11 P.M., and you're reading a text message from your parents saying they want to buy you a laptop for your birthday this year and that you should order it. You log on to Dell's website and configure your dream machine. You hit the order button and, not long after, your dream computer is delivered to your front door, built to your exact specifications, ready to set up and use immediately to type that management assignment due tomorrow. Or consider Siemens AG's computed tomography manufacturing plant in Forchheim, Germany, which has established partnerships with about 30 suppliers. These suppliers are partners in the truest sense, as they share responsibility with the plant for overall process performance. This arrangement has allowed Siemens to eliminate all inventory warehousing and has streamlined the number of times paper changes hands to order parts from 18 to 1. At the Timken's plant in Canton, Ohio, electronic purchase orders are sent across the street to an adjacent "Supplier City," where many of its key suppliers have set up shop. The process takes milliseconds and costs less than 50 cents per purchase order. And when Black & Decker extended its line of handheld tools to include a glue gun, it totally outsourced the entire design and production to the leading glue gun manufacturer. Why? Because they understood that glue guns don't require motors, which was what Black & Decker did best.[16]

As these examples show, closely integrated work activities among many different players are possible. How? The answer lies in value chain management. The concepts of value chain management have transformed operations management strategies and turned organizations around the world into finely tuned models of efficiency and effectiveness, strategically positioned to exploit competitive opportunities.

WHAT is value chain management?

Every organization needs customers if it's going to survive and prosper. Even a not-for-profit organization must have "customers" who use its services or purchase its products. Customers want some type of value from the goods and services they purchase or use, and these customers decide what has value. Organizations must provide that value to attract and keep customers. **Value** is defined as the performance characteristics, features, and attributes and any other aspects of goods and services for which customers are willing to give up resources (usually money). For example, when you purchase Rihanna's new CD at Best Buy, a new pair of Australian sheepskin Ugg boots online at Zappos, a Wendy's bacon cheeseburger at the drive-through location on campus, or a haircut from your local hair salon, you're exchanging (giving up) money in return for the value you need or desire from these products—providing music during your evening study time, keeping your feet warm *and* fashionable during winter's cold weather, alleviating the lunchtime hunger pangs quickly since your next class starts in 15 minutes, or looking professionally groomed for the job interview you've got next week.

value
The performance characteristics, features, and attributes, and any other aspects of goods and services for which customers are willing to give up resources

How *is* value provided to customers? Through transforming raw materials and other resources into some product or service that end users need or desire when, where, and how they want it. However, that seemingly simple act of turning varied resources into something that customers value and are willing to pay for involves a vast array of interrelated work activities performed by different participants (suppliers, manufacturers, and even customers)—that is, it involves the value chain. The **value chain** is the entire series of organizational work activities that add value at each step from raw materials to finished product. In its entirety, the value chain can encompass the supplier's suppliers to the customer's customer.[17] For instance, consider the value chain from growing macadamia nuts to selling macadamia nut cookies in a grocery store. The chain begins with a farmer who grows the macadamia nuts, picks them from trees, and sells them to a processing plant. The added value is the increase in the farmer's income for selling macadamia nuts and the material and labor costs for growing and picking them. The processing plant removes the shells, discards rotten nuts, and sells the rest to a bakery. The added value created by the processing plant is the difference between the cost of buying the macadamia nuts and the price at which these are sold to the bakery. The bakery adds value by blending the nuts with the cookie dough, baking the cookies, and selling them to the grocery store for a profit. The grocer adds value by buying the cookies from the bakery, transporting them to the store, stocking the shelves, and selling them for a profit.

value chain
The entire series of organizational work activities that add value at each step from raw materials to finished product

Value chain management is the process of managing the sequence of activities and information along the entire value chain. In contrast to supply chain management, which is *internally* oriented and focuses on efficient flow of incoming materials (resources) to the organization, value chain management is *externally* oriented and focuses on both incoming materials and outgoing products and services. Although supply chain management is efficiency oriented (its goal is to reduce costs and make the organization more productive), value chain management is effectiveness oriented and aims to create the highest value for customers.[18] The relationship between Magna International and General Motors illustrates the benefits of improving value chain management. Magna manufactures front and rear bumper covers for GM vehicles. After Magna moved from Ohio to a facility near the GM assembly plant in Michigan, GM saved millions of dollars in purchase costs.[19] By moving closer to GM, Magna no longer needs to maintain a costly storage facility and incur high fuel costs for transport. In turn, the cost savings enables Magna to sell bumper covers to GM at a lower price.

value chain management
The process of managing the sequence of activities and information along the entire value chain

Goal of Value Chain Management

Who has the power in the value chain? Is it the suppliers providing needed resources and materials? After all, they have the ability to dictate prices and quality. Is it the manufacturer who assembles those resources into a valuable product or service? Their contribution in creating a product or service is quite obvious. Is it the distributor that makes sure the product or service is available where and when the customer needs it?

Actually, it's none of these! In value chain management, ultimately customers are the ones with power.[20] They're the ones who define what value is and how it's created and provided. Using value chain management, managers hope to find that unique combination that offers customers solutions to truly meet their unique needs incredibly fast and at a price that can't be matched by competitors.

With these factors in mind then, the goal of value chain management is to create a value chain strategy that meets and exceeds customers' needs and desires and allows for full and seamless integration among all members of the chain. A good value chain involves a sequence of participants working together as a team, each adding some component of value—such as faster assembly, more accurate information, better customer response and service, and so forth—to the overall process.[21] The better the collaboration among the various chain participants, the better the customer solutions. When value is created for customers and their needs and desires are satisfied, everyone along the chain benefits. For example, at Johnson Controls Inc., managing the value chain started first with improved relationships with internal suppliers, then expanded out to external suppliers and customers. As the company's experience with value chain management improved, so did its connection with its customers, which ultimately paid off for all its value chain partners.[22]

Benefits of Value Chain Management

Collaborating with external and internal partners in creating and managing a successful value chain strategy requires significant investments in time, energy, and other resources, and a serious commitment by all chain partners. Given these demands, why would managers ever choose to implement value chain management? A survey of manufacturers noted four primary benefits of value chain management: improved procurement, improved logistics, improved product development, and enhanced customer order management.[23]

MANAGING operations using value chain management

Even though it's the world's largest retailer, Walmart still looks for ways to more effectively and efficiently manage its value chain. Its current efforts involve taking over U.S. transportation services from suppliers in an effort to reduce the cost of transporting goods. The goal is "to handle suppliers' deliveries in instances where Walmart can do the same job for less, then use those savings to reduce prices in stores." Walmart believes it has the size and scale to allow it to ship most products more efficiently than the companies that produce the goods.[24]

Even if you're Walmart, managing an organization from a value chain perspective isn't easy. Approaches to giving customers what they want that may have worked in the past are likely no longer efficient or effective. Today's dynamic competitive environment demands new solutions from global organizations. Understanding how and why value is determined by the marketplace has led some organizations to experiment with a new business model, a concept we introduced in Chapter 9. For example, IKEA transformed itself from a small Swedish mail-order furniture operation into one of the world's largest furniture retailers by reinventing the value chain in that industry. The company offers customers well-designed products at substantially lower prices in return for their willingness to take on certain key tasks traditionally done by manufacturers and retailers—assembling furniture and getting it home.[25] The company's creation of a new business model and willingness to abandon old methods and processes has worked well.

Value Chain Strategy

Exhibit MO-2 shows the six main requirements of a successful value chain strategy: coordination and collaboration, technology investment, organizational processes, leadership, employees, and organizational culture and attitudes.

Exhibit MO-2
Value Chain Strategy Requirement

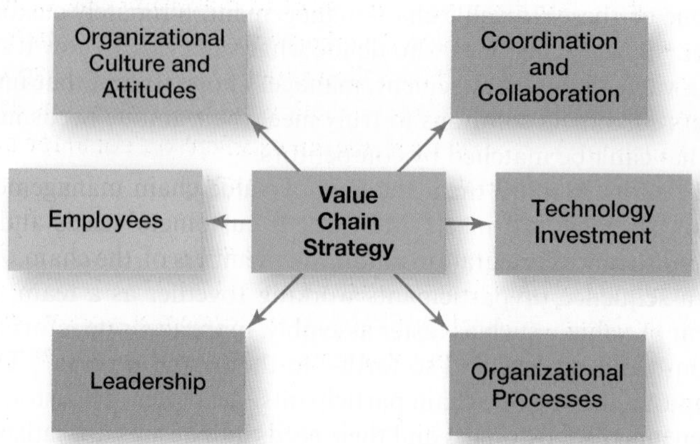

COORDINATION AND COLLABORATION For the value chain to achieve its goal of meeting and exceeding customers' needs and desires, collaborative relationships among all chain participants must exist.[26] Each partner must identify things he or she may not value but that customers do. Sharing information and being flexible as far as who in the value chain does what are important steps in building coordination and collaboration. This sharing of information and analysis requires more open communication among the various value chain partners. For example, Kraft Foods believes that better communication with customers and with suppliers has facilitated timely delivery of goods and services.[27]

TECHNOLOGY INVESTMENT Successful value chain management isn't possible without a significant investment in information technology. The payoff from this investment, however, is that information technology can be used to restructure the value chain to better serve end users. For example, each year the Houston-based food distributor Sysco ships 21.5 million tons of produce, meats, prepared meals, and other food-related products to restaurants, cafeterias, and sports stadiums. To get all that food safely to the right place at the right time, Sysco relies on a complex web of software, databases, scanning systems, and robotics.[28]

ORGANIZATIONAL PROCESSES At Pactiv Corporation, which manufactures consumer and food-service packaging, the company relied on a planning process that included three-year breakthrough goals, which were then translated into one-year goals, annual improvement priorities, and measurable targets. This disciplined approach to planning has helped the company grow and achieve its goals.[29]

organizational processes
The ways that organizational work is done

Value chain management radically changes **organizational processes**—that is, the ways that organizational work is done. When managers decide to manage operations using value chain management, old processes are no longer appropriate. All organizational processes must be critically evaluated from beginning to end to see where value is being added. Non-value-adding activities should be eliminated. Questions such as "Where can internal knowledge be leveraged to improve the flow of material and information?" "How can we better configure our product to satisfy both customers and suppliers?" "How can the flow of material and information be improved?" and "How can we improve customer service?" should be asked for each and every process. For example, when managers at Deere and Company implemented value chain management, a thorough process evaluation revealed that work activities needed to be better synchronized and interrelationships between multiple links in the value chain better managed. They changed numerous work processes division-wide in order to realize greater value.[30]

Three important conclusions can be made about organizational processes. First, better demand forecasting is necessary *and* possible because of closer ties with customers and suppliers. For example, in an effort to make sure that Listerine was on the store shelves when customers wanted it (known in the retail industry as *product replenishment rates*), Walmart and Pfizer's Consumer Healthcare Group collaborated on improving product demand forecast information. Through their mutual efforts, the partners boosted Walmart's sales of Listerine, an excellent outcome for both supplier and retailer. Customers also benefited because they were able to purchase the product when and where they wanted it.

Second, selected functions may need to be done collaboratively with other partners in the value chain. This collaboration may even extend to sharing employees. For instance, Coca-Cola Hellenic Bottling Company places employees in grocery stores where they work with store employees to prepare the merchandising and placement of Coca-Cola products on the shelves.

Finally, new measures are needed for evaluating performance of various activities along the value chain. Because the goal in value chain management is meeting and exceeding customers' needs and desires, managers need a better picture of how well this value is being created and delivered to customers. For example, when Nestlé USA implemented value chain management, it redesigned its metrics system to focus on one consistent set of measurements—including, for instance, accuracy of demand forecasts and production plans, on-time delivery, and customer-service levels—that allowed them to more quickly identify problem areas and take actions to resolve them.[31]

LEADERSHIP Successful value chain management isn't possible without strong and committed leadership. From top organizational levels to lower levels, managers must support, facilitate, and promote the implementation and ongoing practice of value chain management. Managers must seriously commit to identifying what value is, how that value can best be provided, and how successful those efforts have been. A culture where all efforts are focused on delivering superb customer value isn't possible without a serious commitment on the part of the organization's leaders.

Also, it's important that managers outline expectations for what's involved in the organization's pursuit of value chain management. Ideally, managers start with a vision or mission statement that expresses the organization's commitment to identifying, capturing, and providing the highest possible value to customers. For instance, when American Standard began using value chain management, the CEO held dozens of meetings across the United States to explain the new competitive environment and why the company needed to create better working relationships with its value chain partners in order to better serve the needs of its customers.[32]

Then, managers should clarify expectations regarding each employee's role in the value chain. But clear expectations aren't just important for internal partners. Being clear about expectations also extends to external partners. For example, managers at American Standard identified clear requirements for suppliers and were prepared to drop any that couldn't meet them, and did so. The upside, though, was that those suppliers who met the expectations benefited from more business, and American Standard had partners willing to work with them in delivering better value to customers.

EMPLOYEES/HUMAN RESOURCES When new employees at the Thermo Fisher Scientific plant in Marietta, Ohio, have work-related questions, they can consult with a member of the facility's "Tree of Knowledge." The "tree" is actually a bulletin board with pictures of employees who have worked at the plant for decades.[33]

We know from our discussions of management theories throughout this text that employees are an organization's most important resource. Without employees, no products are produced and no services are delivered—in fact, no organized efforts in the pursuit of common goals would be possible. So not surprisingly, employees play an important role in value chain management. The three main human resource requirements for value chain management are flexible approaches to job design, an effective hiring process, and ongoing training.

Flexibility is the key to job design in value chain management. Traditional functional job roles—such as marketing, sales, accounts payable, customer service, and so forth—won't work. Instead, jobs must be designed around work processes that create and provide value to customers. It takes flexible jobs and flexible employees. For instance, at Nordson Corporation's facility in Swainsboro, Georgia, workers are trained to do several different tasks, which isn't all that uncommon in many manufacturing plants. What's unique about this facility is that even salaried employees are expected to spend four hours every month building products on the shop floor.[34]

In a value chain organization, employees may be assigned to work teams that tackle a given process and may be asked to do different things on different days depending on need. In such an environment, where customer value is best delivered through collaborative relationships that may change as customer needs change and where processes or job descriptions are not standardized, an employee's ability to be flexible is critical. Therefore, the organization's hiring process must be designed to identify those employees who have the ability to learn and adapt.

Finally, the need for flexibility also requires a significant investment in continual and ongoing employee training. Whether that training involves learning how to use information technology software, how to improve the flow of materials throughout the chain, how to identify activities that add value, how to make better decisions faster, or how to improve any other number of potential work activities, managers must see to it that employees have the knowledge and tools they need to do their jobs efficiently and effectively.

ORGANIZATIONAL CULTURE AND ATTITUDES The last requirement for value chain management is having a supportive organizational culture and attitudes. From our extensive description of value chain management, you could probably guess the type of organizational culture that's going to support its successful implementation! Those cultural attitudes include sharing, collaborating, openness, flexibility, mutual respect, and trust. These attitudes encompass not only the internal partners in the value chain, but extend to external partners as well.

Obstacles to Value Chain Management

As desirable as these benefits may be, managers must tackle several obstacles in managing the value chain, including organizational barriers, cultural attitudes, required capabilities, and people (see Exhibit MO-3).

ORGANIZATIONAL BARRIERS At General Cable's manufacturing facility in Manchester, New Hampshire, one of the most interesting challenges faced by managers and employees in maintaining its world-class competitiveness is the 23 different nationalities that speak 12 languages besides English. Multiple languages make getting new messages out about anything that comes up especially tricky. But they've made it work using visual cues throughout the plant.[35]

Exhibit MO-3
Obstacles to Value Chain Management

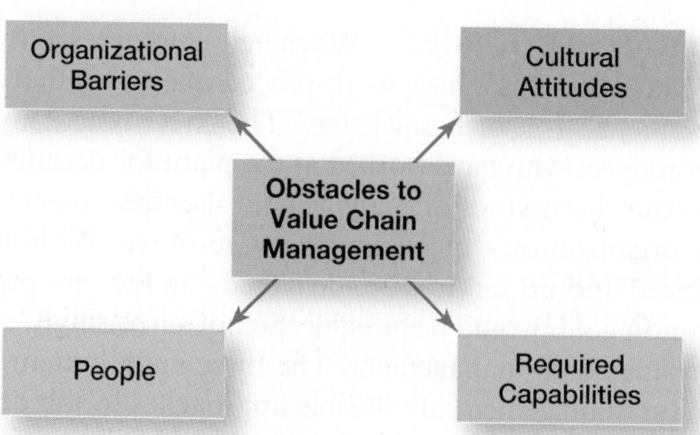

Organizational barriers are among the most difficult obstacles to handle. These barriers include refusal or reluctance to share information, reluctance to shake up the status quo, and security issues. Without shared information, close coordination and collaboration is impossible. And the reluctance or refusal of employees to shake up the status quo can impede efforts toward value chain management and prevent its successful implementation. Finally, because value chain management relies heavily on a substantial information technology infrastructure, system security and Internet security breaches are issues that need to be addressed.

CULTURAL ATTITUDES Unsupportive cultural attitudes—especially trust and control—also can be obstacles to value chain management. The trust issue is a critical one, both lack of trust and too much trust. To be effective, partners in a value chain must trust each other. A mutual respect for, and honesty about, each partner's activities all along the chain is essential. When that trust doesn't exist, the partners will be reluctant to share information, capabilities, and processes. But too much trust also can be a problem. Just about any organization is vulnerable to theft of **intellectual property**—that is, proprietary information that's critical to an organization's efficient and effective functioning and competitiveness. You need to be able to trust your value chain partners so your organization's valuable assets aren't compromised.[36] Another cultural attitude that can be an obstacle is the belief that when an organization collaborates with external and internal partners, it no longer controls its own destiny. However, this lack of control just isn't the case. Even with the intense collaboration that's important to value chain management, organizations still control critical decisions such as what customers value, how much value they desire, and what distribution channels are important.[37]

intellectual property
Proprietary information that's critical to an organization's efficient and effective functioning and competitiveness

REQUIRED CAPABILITIES We know from our earlier discussion of requirements for the successful implementation of value chain management that value chain partners need numerous capabilities. Several of these capabilities—coordination and collaboration, the ability to configure products to satisfy customers and suppliers, and the ability to educate internal and external partners—aren't easy, but they're essential to capturing and exploiting the value chain. Many of the companies we've described throughout this section endured critical, and oftentimes difficult, self-evaluations of their capabilities and processes in order to become more effective and efficient at managing their value chains.

PEOPLE The final obstacles to successful value chain management can be an organization's people. Without their unwavering commitment to do whatever it takes, value chain management won't be successful. If employees refuse to be flexible in their work—how and with whom they work—collaboration and cooperation throughout the value chain will be hard to achieve.

In addition, value chain management takes an incredible amount of time and energy on the part of an organization's employees. Managers must motivate those high levels of effort from employees, which is not an easy thing to do.

Finally, a major human resource problem is the lack of experienced managers who can lead value chain management initiatives. It's not that widespread, so there aren't a lot of managers who've done it successfully. However, progressive organizations see the benefits to be gained from value chain management and pursue it despite obstacles.

CURRENT **issues in managing operations**

Rowe Furniture had an audacious goal: make a sofa in 10 days. It wanted to "become as efficient at making furniture as Toyota is at making cars." Reaching that goal, however, required revamping its operations management process to exploit technology *and* maintain quality.[38] Rowe's actions illustrate three of today's most important operations management issues: technology, quality, and mass customization and lean organizations.

Technology's Role in Operations Management

Global positioning systems (GPS) are changing a number of enterprises from shipping to shopping, from health care to law enforcement, and even farming.[39] Like many other technologies, GPS was invented for military use to track weapons and personnel as they moved. Now GPS is being used to track shipping fleets, revitalize consumer products such as watches or photos, and monitor parolees or sex offenders.

As we know from our previous discussion of value chain management, today's competitive marketplace has put tremendous pressure on organizations to deliver products and services that customers value in a timely manner. Smart companies are looking at ways to harness technology to improve operations management. Many fast-food companies are competing to see who can provide faster and better service to drive-through customers. With drive-through now representing a huge portion of sales, faster and better delivery can be a significant competitive edge. For instance, Wendy's has added awnings to some of its menu boards and replaced some of the text with pictures. Others use confirmation screens, a technology that helped McDonald's boost accuracy by more than 11 percent. Technology used by two national chains tells managers how much food they need to prepare by counting vehicles in the drive-through line and factoring in demand for current promotional and popular staple items. Even Domino's is using a new point-of-sale system to attract customers and streamline online orders.[40]

Although an organization's production activities are driven by the recognition that the customer is king, managers still need to be more responsive. For instance, operations managers need systems that can reveal available capacity, status of orders, and product quality while products are in the process of being manufactured, not just after the fact. To connect more closely with customers, production must be synchronized across the enterprise. To avoid bottlenecks and slowdowns, the production function must be a full partner in the entire business system.

What's making such extensive collaboration possible is technology. Technology is also allowing organizations to control costs, particularly in the areas of predictive maintenance, remote diagnostics, and utility cost savings. For instance, new Internet-compatible equipment contains embedded Web servers that can communicate proactively—that is, if a piece of equipment breaks or reaches certain preset parameters indicating that it's about to break, it asks for help. But technology can do more than sound an alarm or light up an indicator button. For instance, some devices have the ability to initiate e-mail or signal a pager at a supplier, the maintenance department, or contractor describing the specific problem and requesting parts and service. How much is such e-enabled maintenance control worth? It can be worth quite a lot if it prevents equipment breakdowns and subsequent production downtime.

Managers who understand the power of technology to contribute to more effective and efficient performance know that managing operations is more than the traditional view of simply producing the product. Instead, the emphasis is on working together with all the organization's business functions to find solutions to customers' business problems. Even service providers understand the power of technology for these tasks. For example, Southwest Airlines upgraded its cockpit software, enabling its pilots (who have been extensively trained) to fly precise satellite-based navigation approaches to airports, thus saving fuel, reducing delays, and cutting noise.[41]

Quality Initiatives

Quality problems are expensive. For example, even though Apple has had phenomenal success with its iPod, the batteries in the first three versions died after 4 hours instead of lasting the up-to-12 hours that buyers expected. Apple's settlement with consumers cost close to $100 million. At Schering-Plough, problems with inhalers and other pharmaceuticals were traced to chronic quality control shortcomings, for which the company eventually paid a $500 million fine. And the auto industry paid $14.5 billion to cover the cost of warranty and repair work in one year.[42]

Many experts believe that organizations unable to produce high-quality products won't be able to compete successfully in the global marketplace. What is quality? When you consider a product or service to have quality, what does that mean? Does it mean that the product doesn't break or quit working—that is, that it's reliable? Does it mean that the service is delivered in a way that you intended? Does it mean that the product does what it's supposed to do? Or does quality mean something else? We're going to define **quality** as the ability of a product or service to reliably do what it's supposed to do and to satisfy customer expectations.

quality
The ability of a product or service to reliably do what it's supposed to do and to satisfy customer expectations

How is quality achieved? That's an issue managers must address. A good way to look at quality initiatives is with the management functions—planning, organizing, leading, and controlling—that need to take place.

PLANNING FOR QUALITY Managers must have quality improvement goals and strategies and plans to achieve those goals. Goals can help focus everyone's attention toward some objective quality standard. For instance, the *Forbes Travel Guide* rates hotels on a star system with five stars representing the highest quality. Hotels must earn high ratings on 800 standards to earn the five stars highest rating. Bruce Wallin, editorial director of luxury lifestyle magazine *Robb Report*, believes that top service and surprise distinguish five-star hotels from the others. Wallin said, "In Milan there's a hotel where, every afternoon, you get a knock on your door, and instead of house-cleaning it's a cocktail cart. . . . [T]hey'll make whatever drink you want, right in your room."[43] Goals may be specific and challenging, thus managers and employees are partnering together to pursue well-designed strategies to achieve the goals and are confident they can do so.

ORGANIZING AND LEADING FOR QUALITY Because quality improvement initiatives are carried out by organizational employees, it's important for managers to look at how they can best organize and lead them. For instance, at the Moosejaw, Saskatchewan, plant of General Cable Corporation, every employee participates in continual quality assurance training. In addition, the plant manager believes wholeheartedly in giving employees the information they need to do their jobs better. He says, "Giving people who are running the machines the information is just paramount. You can set up your cellular structure, you can cross-train your people, you can use lean tools, but if you don't give people information to drive improvement, there's no enthusiasm." Needless to say, this company shares production data and financial performance measures with all employees.[44]

Organizations with extensive and successful quality improvement programs tend to rely on two important people approaches: cross-functional work teams and self-directed or empowered work teams. Because achieving product quality is something that all employees from upper to lower levels must participate in, it's not surprising that quality-driven organizations rely on well-trained, flexible, and empowered employees.

CONTROLLING FOR QUALITY Quality improvement initiatives aren't possible without having some way to monitor and evaluate their progress. Whether it involves standards for inventory control, defect rate, raw materials procurement, or other operations management areas, controlling for quality is important. For instance, at the Northrup Grumman Corporation plant in Rolling Meadows, Illinois, several quality controls have been implemented, such as automated testing and IT that integrates product design and manufacturing and tracks process quality improvements. Also, employees are empowered to make accept/reject decisions about products throughout the manufacturing process. The plant manager explains, "This approach helps build quality into the product rather than trying to inspect quality into the product." But one of the most important things they do is "go to war" with their customers—soldiers preparing for war or in live combat situations. Again, the plant manager says, "What discriminates us is that we believe if we can understand our customer's mission as well as they do, we can help them be more effective. We don't wait for our customer to ask us to do something. We find out what our customer is trying to do and then we develop solutions."[45]

These types of quality improvement success stories aren't just limited to U.S. operations. For example, at a Delphi assembly plant in Matamoros, Mexico, employees worked hard to improve quality and made significant strides. Their customer rejection rate on shipped products is now 10 ppm (parts per million), down from 3,000 ppm—an improvement of almost 300 percent.[46] Quality initiatives at several Australian companies, including Alcoa of Australia, Wormald Security, and Carlton and United Breweries, have led to significant quality improvements.[47] And at Valeo Klimasystemme GmbH of Bad Rodach, Germany, assembly teams build different climate-control systems for high-end German cars, including Mercedes and BMW. Quality initiatives by Valeo's employee teams have led to significant improvements in various quality standards.[48]

Quality Goals

To publicly demonstrate their quality commitment, many organizations worldwide have pursued challenging quality goals—the two best-known being ISO 9000 and Six Sigma.

ISO 9000
A series of international quality management standards that set uniform guidelines for processes to ensure products conform to customer requirements

ISO 9000 **ISO 9000** is a series of international quality management standards established by the International Organization for Standardization (www.iso.org), which set uniform guidelines for processes to ensure that products conform to customer requirements. These standards cover everything from contract review to product design to product delivery. The ISO 9000 standards have become the internationally recognized standard for evaluating and comparing companies in the global marketplace. In fact, this type of certification can be a prerequisite for doing business globally. Achieving ISO 9000 certification provides proof that a quality operations system is in place.

Almost 40,000 U.S. businesses are ISO 9000 certified. In China, over 200,000 firms have received certification.[49] And those numbers are rising. In 2014 alone, more than 1.6 million certifications were awarded to organizations worldwide.[50]

Six Sigma
A quality program designed to reduce defects and help lower costs, save time, and improve customer satisfaction

SIX SIGMA Motorola popularized the use of stringent quality standards more than 30 years ago through a trademarked quality improvement program called Six Sigma.[51] Very simply, **Six Sigma** is a quality program designed to reduce defects to help lower costs, save time, and improve customer satisfaction. It's based on the statistical standard that establishes a goal of no more than 3.4 defects per million units or procedures. What does the name mean? Sigma is the Greek letter that statisticians use to define a standard deviation from a bell curve. The higher the sigma, the fewer the deviations from the norm—that is, the fewer the defects. At One Sigma, two-thirds of whatever is being measured falls within the curve. Two Sigma covers about 95 percent. At Six Sigma, you're about as close to defect-free as you can get.[52] It's an ambitious quality goal! Although it is an extremely high standard to achieve, many quality-driven businesses are using it and benefiting from it. For instance, General Electric estimates that it has saved $12 billion in costs over a five-year period.[53] Other well-known companies pursuing Six Sigma include ITT Industries, Dow Chemical, 3M Company, American Express, Sony Corporation, Nokia Corporation, and Johnson & Johnson. Although manufacturers seem to make up the bulk of Six Sigma users, service companies such as financial institutions, retailers, and health care organizations are beginning to apply it. What impact can Six Sigma have? Let's look at two examples.

It used to take Wellmark Blue Cross & Blue Shield, a managed-care health care company, 65 days or more to add a new doctor to its medical plans. Now, thanks to

Six Sigma, the company discovered that half the processes they used were redundant. With those unnecessary steps gone, the job now gets done in 30 days or less and with reduced staff. The company also has been able to reduce its administrative expenses by $3 million per year, an amount passed on to consumers through lower health care premiums.[54] McKesson, a health care information technology company, saved $150 million and achieved 99.98 percent order accuracy through operations management improvements.[55]

Although it's important for managers to recognize that many positive benefits come from reaching Six Sigma or obtaining ISO 9000 certification, the key benefit comes from the quality improvement journey itself. In other words, the goal of quality certification should be having work processes and an operations system in place that enable organizations to meet customers' needs and employees to perform their jobs in a consistently high-quality way.

Mass Customization and Lean Organization

The term *mass customization* seems an oxymoron. However, the design-to-order concept is becoming an important operations management issue for today's managers. **Mass customization** provides consumers with a product when, where, and how they want it.[56] Companies as diverse as BMW, Ford, Levi Strauss, Wells Fargo, Mattel, and Dell are adopting mass customization to maintain or attain a competitive advantage. Mass customization requires flexible manufacturing techniques and continual customer dialogue.[57] Technology plays an important role in both.

mass customization
Providing customers with a product when, where, and how they want it

With flexible manufacturing, companies have the ability to quickly readjust assembly lines to make products to order. Using technology such as computer-controlled factory equipment, intranets, industrial robots, barcode scanners, digital printers, and logistics software, companies can manufacture, assemble, and ship customized products with customized packaging to customers in incredibly short timeframes. Dell is a good example of a company that uses flexible manufacturing techniques and technology to custom-build computers to customers' specifications.

Technology also is important in the continual dialogue with customers. Using extensive databases, companies can keep track of customers' likes and dislikes. And the Internet has made it possible for companies to have ongoing dialogues with customers to learn about and respond to their exact preferences. For instance, on Amazon's website, customers are greeted by name and can get personalized recommendations of books and other products. The ability to customize products to a customer's desires and specifications starts an important relationship between the organization and the customer. If the customer likes the product and it provides value, he or she is more likely to be a repeat customer.

An intense focus on customers is also important in order to be a **lean organization**, which is an organization that understands what customers want, identifies customer value by analyzing all activities required to produce products, and then optimizes the entire process from the customer's perspective.[58] Lean organizations drive out all activities that do not add value in customers' eyes. For instance, companies like United Parcel Service, LVMH Moet Hennessy Louis Vuitton, and Harley-Davidson have pursued lean operations. "Lean operations adopt a philosophy of minimizing waste by striving for perfection through continuous learning, creativity, and teamwork."[59] As more manufacturers and service organizations adopt lean principles, they must realize that it's a never-ending journey toward being efficient and effective.

lean organization
An organization that understands what customers want, identifies customer value by analyzing all activities required to produce products, and then optimizes the entire process from the customer's perspective

Pearson **MyLab** Management

Go to **mymanagementlab.com** to complete the problems marked with this icon ✪.

✪ REVIEW AND DISCUSSION QUESTIONS

MO-1. What is operations management?

MO-2. Do you think that manufacturing or service organizations have the greater need for operations management? Explain.

MO-3. What is a value chain, and what is value chain management? What is the goal of value chain management? What are the benefits of value chain management?

MO-4. What is required for successful value chain management? What obstacles exist to successful value chain management?

MO-5. How could you use value chain management in your everyday life?

MO-6. How does technology play a role in manufacturing?

MO-7. What are ISO 9000 and Six Sigma?

MO-8. Describe lean management and explain why it's important.

MO-9. How might operations management apply to other managerial functions besides control?

MO-10. Which is more critical to success in organizations: continuous improvement or quality control? Support your position.

ENDNOTES

1. K. Baxter, "Seoul Showcases Its Talent," *MEED: Middle East Economic Digest,* May 14, 2010, pp. 13–24; E. Ramstad, "High-Speed Wireless Transforms a Shipyard," *Wall Street Journal,* March 16, 2010, p. B6; and Datamonitor, "Company Profile: Hyundai Heavy Industries Co., Ltd.," www.datamonitor.com, November 27, 2009.
2. D. McGinn, "Faster Food," *Newsweek,* April 19, 2004, pp. E20–E22.
3. *World Factbook 2015-2016,* available online at https://www.cia.gov/library/publications/the-world-factbook/, 2016.
4. D. Michaels and J. L. Lunsford, "Streamlined Plane Making," *Wall Street Journal,* April 1, 2005, pp. B1+.
5. J. Dwyer-Lindgren, "Boeing Will Boost 737 Production, Slow 777 Rates," *USA Today* online, www.usatoday.com, January 28, 2016.
6. T. Aeppel, "Workers Not Included," *Wall Street Journal,* November 19, 2002, pp. B1+.
7. M. Sheahan, "Adidas Aims to Open Automated Shoe Factory in Germany in 2016," *Reuters* online, www.reuters.com, October 20, 2015.
8. Associated Press, "Robots Replacing Human Factory Workers at Faster Place," *The Los Angeles Times* online, www.latimes.com, February 10, 2015.
9. PTI, "China Sets Up First Unmanned Factory; All Processes Are Operated by Robots," *The Economic Times* online, www.economictimes.indiatimes.com, July 27, 2015.
10. A. J. Agrawal, "How Retain and Restaurants Can Use Apps to Effectively Market Their Business," *Forbes* online, www.forbes.com, December 30, 2015.
11. C. Fredman, "The Devil in the Details," *Executive Edge,* April–May 1999, pp. 36–39.
12. Information from http://new.skoda-auto.com/Documents/AnnualReports/skoda_auto_annual_report_2007_%20EN_-FINAL.pdf, July 8, 2008; and T. Mudd, "The Last Laugh," *Industry Week,* September 18, 2000, pp. 38–44.
13. W. E. Deming, "Improvement of Quality and Productivity Through Action by Management," *National Productivity Review,* Winter 1981–1982, pp. 12–22.
14. T. Vinas, "Little Things Mean a Lot," *Industry Week,* November 2002, p. 55.
15. J. Hagel III, J. Seely Brown, D. Kulasooriya, C. Giffi, and M. Chen, "The Future of Manufacturing: Making Things in a Changing World," Deloitte Development, LLC, http://dupress.com/articles/future-of-manufacturing-industry/, March 31, 2015; "The Future of Manufacturing 2009," *Industry Week,* November 2009, pp. 25–31; T. D. Kuczmarski, "Remanufacturing America's Factory Sector," *BusinessWeek* online, September 9, 2009.
16. T. Laseter, K. Ramdas, and D. Swerdlow, "The Supply Side of Design and Development," *Strategy+Business,* Summer 2003, p. 23; J. Jusko, "Not All Dollars and Cents," *Industry Week,* April 2002, p. 58; and D. Drickhamer, "Medical Marvel," *Industry Week,* March 2002, pp. 47–49.
17. J. H. Sheridan, "Managing the Value Chain," *Industry Week,* www.industryweek.com, September 6, 1999, pp. 1–4.
18. Ibid., p. 3.
19. D. Sedgwick, "Suppliers Start Moving Closer to GM Plants," *Auto News* online, www.autonews.com, November 17, 2014.
20. J. Teresko, "Forward, March!" *Industry Week,* July 2004, pp. 43–48; D. Sharma, C. Lucier, and R. Molloy, "From Solutions to Symbiosis: Blending with Your Customers," *Strategy+Business,* second quarter 2002, pp. 38–48; and

S. Leibs, "Getting Ready: Your Suppliers," *Industry Week*, www.industryweek.com, September 6, 1999.

21. D. Bartholomew, "The Infrastructure," *Industry Week*, www.industryweek.com, September 6, 1999, p. 1.
22. T. Stevens, "Integrated Product Development," *Industry Week*, June 2002, pp. 21–28.
23. T. Vinas, "A Map of the World: IW Value-Chain Survey," *Industry Week*, September 2005, pp. 27–34.
24. C. Burritt, C. Wolf, and M. Boyle, "Why Wal-Mart Wants to Take the Driver's Seat," *Bloomberg BusinessWeek*, May 31–June 6, 2010, pp. 17–18.
25. R. Normann and R. Ramirez, "From Value Chain to Value Constellation," *Harvard Business Review on Managing the Value Chain* (Boston, MA: Harvard Business School Press, 2000), pp. 185–219.
26. "Collaboration Is the Key to Reducing Costs," *Industry Week*, October 2009, p. 35; J. Teresko, "The Tough Get Going," *Industry Week*, March 2005, pp. 25–32; D. M. Lambert and A. M. Knemeyer, "We're in This Together," *Harvard Business Review*, December 2004, pp. 114–122; and V. G. Narayanan and A. Raman, "Aligning Incentives in Supply Chains," *Harvard Business Review*, November 2004, pp. 94–102.
27. D. Drickhamer, "Looking for Value," *Industry Week*, December 2002, pp. 41–43.
28. J. L. Yang, "Veggie Tales," *Fortune*, June 8, 2009, pp. 25–30.
29. J. Jusko, "Focus. Discipline. Results," *Industry Week*, June 2010, pp. 16–17.
30. J. H. Sheridan, "Managing the Value Chain," p. 3.
31. G. Taninecz, "Forging the Chain," *Industry Week*, May 15, 2000, pp. 40–46.
32. S. Leibs, "Getting Ready: Your Customers," *Industry Week*, www.industryweek.com, September 6, 1999, p. 1.
33. J. Katz, "Empowering the Workforce," *Industry Week*, January 2009, p. 43.
34. D. Blanchard, "In the Rotation," *Industry Week*, January 2009, p. 42.
35. N. Zubko, "Mindful of the Surroundings," *Industry Week*, January 2009, p. 38.
36. "Top Security Threats and Management Issues Facing Corporate America: 2003 Survey of *Fortune* 1000 Companies," ASIS International and Pinkerton, www.asisonline.org.
37. J. H. Sheridan, "Managing the Value Chain," p. 4.
38. R. Russell and B. W. Taylor, *Operations Management*, 5th ed. (New York: Wiley, 2005); C. Liu-Lien Tan, "U.S. Response: Speedier Delivery," *Wall Street Journal*, November 18, 2004, pp. D1+; and C. Salter, "When Couches Fly," *Fast Company*, July 2004, pp. 80–81.
39. D. Joseph, "The GPS Revolution: Location, Location, Location," *BusinessWeek* online, May 27, 2009.
40. J. Jargon, "Domino's IT Staff Delivers Slick Site, Ordering System," *Wall Street Journal*, November 24, 2009, p. B5; and S. Anderson, The Associated Press, "Restaurants Gear Up for Window Wars," *Springfield, Missouri, News-Leader*, January 27, 2006, p. 5B.
41. S. McCartney, "A Radical Cockpit Upgrade Southwest Fliers Will Feel," *Wall Street Journal*, April 1, 2010, p. D1.
42. D. Bartholomew, "Quality Takes a Beating," *Industry Week*, March 2006, pp. 46–54; J. Carey and M. Arndt, "Making Pills the Smart Way," *BusinessWeek*, May 3, 2004, pp. 102–103; and A. Barrett, "Schering's Dr. Feelbetter?" *BusinessWeek*, June 23, 2003, pp. 55–56.
43. S. Herships, "How a Hotel Earns Five Stars: The Checklist," *Marketplace* online, www.marketplace.org, July 2, 2014.
44. J. S. McClenahen, "Prairie Home Companion," *Industry Week*, October 2005, pp. 45–46.
45. T. Vinas, "Zeroing In on the Customer," *Industry Week*, October 2004, pp. 61–62.
46. W. Royal, "Spotlight Shines on Maquiladora," *Industry Week*, October 16, 2000, pp. 91–92.
47. See B. Whitford and R. Andrew, eds., *The Pursuit of Quality* (Perth: Beaumont Publishing, 1994).
48. D. Drickhamer, "Road to Excellence," *Industry Week*, October 16, 2000, pp. 117–118.
49. J. Heizer and B. Render, *Operations Management*, 10th ed. (Upper Saddle River, NJ: Prentice Hall, 2011), p. 193.
50. International Organization for Standardization, "The ISO Survey of Management System Standard Certifications—2014," http://www.iso.org/iso/iso-survey, accessed June 12, 2016.
51. G. Hasek, "Merger Marries Quality Efforts," *Industry Week*, August 21, 2000, pp. 89–92.
52. M. Arndt, "Quality Isn't Just for Widgets," *BusinessWeek*, July 22, 2002, pp. 72–73.
53. "Six Sigma Costs and Savings," *iSixSigma* online, https://www.isixsigma.com/implementation/financial-analysis/six-sigma-costs-and-savings/, accessed June 12, 2016.
54. M. Arndt, "Quality Isn't Just for Widgets."
55. "The Healthcare Supply Chain Top 25 for 2015," *Gartner*, www.gartner.com, November 18, 2015.
56. S. McMurray, "Ford's F-150: Have It Your Way," *Business 2.0*, March 2004, pp. 53–55; "Made-to-Fit Clothes Are on the Way," *USA Today*, July 2002, pp. 8–9; and L. Elliott, "Mass Customization Comes a Step Closer," *Design News*, February 18, 2002, p. 21.
57. E. Schonfeld, "The Customized, Digitized, Have-It-Your-Way Economy," *Fortune*, October 28, 1998, pp. 114–120.
58. Heizer and Render, *Operations Management*, p. 636; and S. Minter, "Measuring the Success of Lean," *Industry Week*, February 2010, pp. 32–35.
59. Heizer and Render, *Operations Management*, p. 636.

PART 6 Management Practice

A Manager's Dilemma

Vancouver, Canada–based Lululemon Athletica Inc. is a well-known manufacturer of yoga and athletic apparel, which is sold in over 250 stores, mostly in North America but also in Australia and New Zealand. Lululemon has built a loyal, almost obsessive/cult-like, customer base. (One customer commented that, "Once you go Lululemon, you never go back."). Others have credited the company's apparel as the reason they started—or continued to—exercise. Retail experts portray the brand positioning to be as much about selling a way of life as selling cute and colorful yoga pants. Customers can take a free yoga class at the stores and be assisted by cheery, knowledgeable employees. All seemed to be well and good, even fantastic, in Lululemon's world. Then, a batch of too-sheer stretchy pants—one of the company's core products—happened. This problem was the company's fourth quality control issue in the span of a year. And for a company that built a billion-dollar business selling premium yoga gear at high prices, this particular problem was a costly stumble. The company responded by recalling the batch of sheer, too-revealing black yoga pants and commenting that, "This event is not the result of changing manufacturers or quality of ingredients." The recall of its top-selling pants proved to be expensive and embarrassing to the company, which had long hyped itself as a premium brand.

Pretend you're part of the management team. Using what you've learned in this Part on monitoring and controlling, what five things would you suggest the team focus on? Think carefully about your suggestions to the team.

Global Sense

This is a story about the global economy. It's about markets, politics, and public opinion. And as jobs—especially white-collar and professional jobs—continue to be outsourced and offshored, the story hits closer and closer to home. Although the terms *offshoring* and *outsourcing* are often used interchangeably, they do mean different things. *Offshoring* is relocating business processes (production and services) from one country to another. *Outsourcing* is moving noncore activities from being done internally to being done externally by an entity that specializes in that activity.

One of the realities of a global economy is that to be competitive, strategic decision makers must look for the best places to do business. If a car can be made more cheaply in Mexico, maybe it should be. If a telephone inquiry can be processed more cheaply in India or the Philippines, maybe it should be. And if programming code can be written more cheaply in China or Russia, maybe it should be. Almost any professional job that can be done outside the organization is up for grabs. There's nothing political or philosophical about the reason for shipping jobs elsewhere. The bottom line is that it can save companies money. But there's a price to be paid in terms of angry and anxious employees. So are offshoring and outsourcing bad?

Critics say "yes." It's affecting jobs once considered "safe" across a wider range of professional work activities. And the offshoring and outsourcing have taken place at a breathtaking pace. What this means is that the careers college students are preparing for probably won't sustain them in the long run. This structural change in the U.S. economy also means that the workforce is likely to face frequent career changes and downward pressures on wages.

Proponents say "no." Their argument is based on viewing economic development as a ladder with every country trying to climb to the next rung. And it's foolish to think that in the United States we've reached the top of the ladder and there's nowhere else to go. Although people fear that educated U.S. workers will face the same fate as blue-collar workers whose jobs shifted to lower-cost countries, the truth is that the United States currently still has a competitive advantage in innovation; although, as discussed earlier, that may be in jeopardy. The biggest danger to U.S. workers isn't overseas competition; it's worrying too much about other countries climbing up the economic ladder and not worrying enough about finding that next higher rung.

Finally, economic forces at work in the latest global recession that led to rapidly rising labor rates in those geographic areas where costs had been low, coupled with higher materials and shipping costs and attractive tax incentives from various U.S. states, may combine to lure back U.S. firms.

Who's right? We probably can't answer that question just yet. Only time will tell. However, we do know that what we're seeing with offshoring and outsourcing is another example of why decision makers need to be aware of the context within which their organizations are doing business.

Discuss the following questions in light of what you learned in Part 6:

- *How are offshoring and outsourcing similar? How are they different?*
- *What arguments do critics use to say offshoring and outsourcing are bad?*
- *What arguments do proponents use to say offshoring and outsourcing are not bad?*
- *How does the decision to offshore and outsource affect monitoring and controlling activities?*
- *Is it just manufacturers that deal with these decisions/issues? Discuss.*

Sources: H. Malcom, "Lulu's No Downward Dog," USA Today, *March 20, 2013, p. 1B+; ("Black Luon Pants Shortage Expected," Lululemon Athletica, Press Release March 18, 2003; D. Searcey, "Judges Turn to Outsourcing as Cases Get More Complex,"* Wall Street Journal, *September 30, 2013; A. Fisher, "Got a Back-Office Job? It May Be Headed Overseas,"* management.fortune.cnn.com, *September 12, 2013; S. Cendrowski, "Can Outsourcing Be Improved?"* Fortune, *June 10, 2013, pp. 14–17; A. Fox, "America Inc.,"* HR Magazine, *May 2013, pp. 44–48; K. O'Sullivan, "Practiced, But Not Perfect,"* CFO, *March 2013, pp. 52–53; J. Bussey, "Will Costs Drive Firms Home?"* Wall Street Journal, *May 5, 2011, pp. B1+; D. Wessel, "Big U.S. Firms Shift Hiring Abroad,"* Wall Street Journal, *April 19, 2011, pp. B1+; P. Engardio, M. Arndt, and D. Foust, "The Future of Outsourcing,"* BusinessWeek, *January 30, 2006, pp. 50–58; J. Thottam, "Is Your Job Going Abroad?,"* Time, *March 1, 2004, pp. 26–36; L. D. Tyson, "Outsourcing: Who's Safe Anymore?"* BusinessWeek, *February 23, 2004, p. 26; A. Fisher, "Think Globally, Save Your Job Locally,"* Fortune, *February 23, 2004, p. 60; "The New Job Migration,"* The Economist, *February 21, 2004, p. 11; O. Thomas, "The Outsourcing Solution,"* Business 2.0, *September 2003, pp. 159–160; and K. Madigan and M. J. Mandel, "Outsourcing Jobs: Is It Bad?"* BusinessWeek, *August 25, 2003, pp. 36–38.*

Continuing Case

Starbucks—Controlling

Once managers have established goals and plans and organized and structured to pursue those goals, the manager's job isn't done. Quite the opposite! Managers must now monitor work activities to make sure they're being done as planned and correct any significant deviations. At Starbucks, managers control various functions, activities, processes, and procedures to ensure that desired performance standards are achieved at all organizational levels.

These young men and women just completed a Starbucks apprenticeship, a 12-month Barista Mastery and Customer Service training program launched in the United Kingdom. The apprentice program is an employee control that ensures partners learn and follow proper procedures relating to the storage, handling, preparation, and service of Starbucks' products and provide customers with exemplary service and treat them with respect.
Source: Nick Ansell/PA Wire/Press Association via AP Images

Controlling the Coffee Experience

Why has Starbucks been so successful? Although many factors have contributed to its success, one significant factor is its ability to provide customers with a unique product of the highest quality delivered with exceptional service. Everything that each Starbucks partner does, from top level to bottom level, contributes to the company's ability to do that efficiently and effectively. And managers need controls in place to help monitor and evaluate what's being done and how it's being done. Starbucks' managers use different types of controls to ensure that the company meets its goals. These controls include transactions controls, security controls, employee controls, and organizational performance controls.

A legal recruiter stops by Starbucks on her way to her office in downtown Chicago and orders her daily Caffè Mocha tall. A construction site supervisor pulls into the drive-through line at the Starbucks store in Rancho Cucamonga, California, for a cinnamon chip scone and Tazo tea. It's 11 P.M. and, needing a break from studying for her next-day's management exam, a student heads to the local Starbucks for a tasty treat—a Raspberry Pomegranate Starbucks Refresher. Now she's ready again to tackle that chapter material on managerial controls.

Every month, an average 75 million customers make purchases at a Starbucks store. The average dollar sale per transaction differs by city, ranging from $6.87 in New York City to $8.76 in Boston. These transactions between partners (employees) and customers—the exchange of products for money—are the major source of sales revenue for Starbucks. Measuring and evaluating the efficiency and effectiveness of these transactions for both walk-in customers and customers at drive-through windows is important. As Starbucks has been doing walk-in transactions for a number of years, numerous procedures and processes are in place to make those transactions go smoothly. However, as Starbucks adds more drive-through windows, the focus of the transaction is on being fast as well as on quality—a different metric than for walk-in transactions. When a customer walks into a store and orders, he can step aside while the order is being prepared; that's not possible in a drive-through line. Recognizing these limitations, the company is taking steps to improve its drive-through service. For instance, digital timers are placed where employees can easily see them to measure service times; order confirmation screens are used to help keep accuracy rates high; and additional pastry racks have been conveniently located by the drive-through windows.

Security is also an important issue for Starbucks. Keeping company assets (such as people, equipment, products, financial information, and so forth) safe and secure requires security controls. The company is committed to providing all partners with a clean, safe, and healthy work environment. All partners share the responsibility to follow all safety rules and practices; to cooperate with officials who enforce those rules and practices; to take necessary steps to protect themselves and other partners; to attend required safety training; and to report immediately all accidents, injuries, and unsafe practices or conditions. When hired, each partner is provided with a manual that covers safety, security, and health standards and is trained on the requirements outlined in the manual. In addition, managers receive ongoing training about these issues and are expected to keep employees trained and up-to-date on any changes. And at any time, any partner can contact the Partner & Asset Protection Department for information and advice.

One security area that has been particularly important to Starbucks has been its gift cards, an area in which it does an enormous volume of business. With gift cards, there are lots of opportunities for an unethical employee to "steal" from the company. The company's director of compliance has said that detecting such fraud can be difficult because it's often not apparent from an operations standpoint. However, Starbucks uses transactional data analysis technology to detect multiple card redemptions in a single day and has identified other "telltale" activities that pinpoint possible fraud. When the company's technology detects transaction activity outside the norm, Starbucks' corporate staff is alerted and a panel of company experts reviews the data. Investigators have found individuals at stores who confess to stealing as much as $42,000. When smaller exceptions are noted, the individuals are sent letters asking them to explain what's going on. Employees who have been so "notified" often quit.

Although Starbucks' control methods are well thought out, some theft is not easily detected. For instance, a Starbucks partner admitted to stealing a customer's credit card number and later using it to rack up purchases amounting to $200 in a grocery store. The customer later returned to the store to confront the employee. Shortly afterwards, Starbucks management terminated the partner's employment and a company representative said the following: "We value our customers' trust and have internally taken immediate steps to address and respond to this issue."

Protecting the company and customers from employee theft is a financial security concern. Vulnerabilities have been found with the Starbucks mobile app, creating additional security concerns. For instance, several customers reported large unauthorized charges to their accounts after using the app to make purchases. One victim reported receiving 10 automated e-mails from Starbucks within a five-minute period for transactions that he did not make. Since then, Starbucks has been finding ways to make mobile app transactions more secure.

Starbucks' part-time and full-time hourly partners are the primary—and most important—source of contact between the company and the customer, and exemplary customer service is a top priority at Starbucks. Partners are encouraged to strive to make every customer's experience pleasant and fulfilling and to treat customers with respect and dignity. What kinds of employee controls does Starbucks use to ensure that this happens? Partners are trained in and are required to follow all proper procedures relating to the storage, handling, preparation, and service of Starbucks' products. In addition, partners are told to notify their managers immediately if they see anything that suggests a product may pose a danger to the health or safety of themselves or of customers. Partners also are taught the warning signs associated with possible workplace violence and how to reduce their vulnerability if faced with a potentially violent situation. In either circumstance where product or partner safety and security are threatened, store managers have been trained as far as the appropriate steps to take if such a situation occurs.

Starbucks recognizes that its investments in store partner development do not pay off unless partners attend work on time. The company studied the causes of irregular attendance and tardiness and learned that unreliable public transportation accounted for much of the truancy problem. So Starbucks is experimenting with ways to help get store partners to work on time. It is teaming up with rideshare service Lyft to increase attendance. It's too soon to know whether this initiative will be successful, but it illustrates how Starbucks has taken control by addressing the cause of the problem.

The final types of control that are important to Starbucks' managers are the organizational performance and financial controls. Starbucks uses the typical financial control measures, but also looks at growth in sales at stores open at least one year as a performance standard. One continual challenge is trying to control store operating costs. There's a fine balance the company has to achieve between keeping costs low and keeping quality high. However, there are steps the company has taken to control costs. For instance, new, thinner garbage bags will save the company half a million dollars a year.

While Starbucks has found ways to effectively control some operating costs, other costs are beyond the company's control (for example, the rising costs of rent and coffee beans). The company manages substantial cost increases by charging higher prices. But, they don't make these decisions lightly. A Starbucks spokesperson said the company evaluates pricing to "balance the need to run our business profitably while continuing to provide value to our loyal customers and to attract new customers.

In addition to the typical financial measures, corporate governance procedures and guidelines are an important part of Starbucks' financial controls, as they are at any public corporation that's covered by Sarbanes-Oxley legislation. The company has identified guidelines for its board of directors with respect to responsibilities, processes, procedures, and expectations.

Starbucks' Value Chain: From Bean to Cup

The steaming cup of coffee placed in a customer's hand at any Starbucks store location starts as coffee beans (berries) plucked from fields of coffee plants. From harvest to storage to roasting to retail to cup, Starbucks understands the important role each participant in its value chain plays.

Starbucks offers a selection of coffees from around the world, and its coffee buyers personally travel to the coffee-growing regions of Latin America, Africa/Arabia, and Asia/Pacific in order to select and purchase the highest-quality *arabica* beans. Once the beans arrive at any one of the five roasting facilities in the United States and three global facilities, Starbucks' master professional roasters take over. These individuals know coffee and do their "magic" in creating the company's rich signature roast coffee in a process that brings balance to all of its flavor attributes. There are many potential challenges to "transforming" the raw material into the quality product and experience that customers have come to expect at Starbucks. Weather, shipping and logistics, technology, political instability, and so forth all could potentially impact what Starbucks is in business to do.

One issue of great importance to Starbucks is environmental protection. Starbucks has taken actions throughout its entire supply chain to minimize its "environmental footprint." For instance, suppliers are asked to sign a code of conduct that deals with certain expectations in business standards and practices. Even company stores are focused on the environmental impact of their store operations. For instance, partners at stores around the world have found innovative ways to reuse coffee grounds. In Japan, for example, a team of Starbucks partners realized that coffee grounds could be used as an ingredient to make paper. A local printing company uses this paper to print the official Starbucks Japan newsletter. In Bahrain, partners dry coffee grounds in the sun, package them, and give them to customers as fertilizer for house plants.

Discussion Questions

P6-1. What companies might be good benchmarks for Starbucks? Why? What companies might want to benchmark Starbucks? Why?

P6-2. Describe how the following Starbucks managers might use forecasting, budgeting, and scheduling (be specific): (a) a retail store manager; (b) a regional marketing manager; (c) the manager for global development; and (d) the CEO.

P6-3. What control criteria might be useful to a retail store manager? To a barista at one of Starbucks's walk-in-only retail stores? How about for a store that has a drive-through?

P6-4. What types of feedforward, concurrent, and feedback controls does Starbucks use? Are there others that might be important to use? If so, describe.

P6-5. What "red flags" might indicate significant deviations from standard for (a) an hourly partner, (b) a store manager, (c) a district manager, (d) the executive vice president of finance, and (e) the CEO? Are there any similarities? Why or why not?

P6-6. Evaluate the control measures Starbucks is using with its gift cards from the standpoint of the three steps in the control process.

P6-7. Using the company's most current financial statements, calculate the following financial ratios: current, debt to assets, inventory turnover, total asset turnover, profit margin on sales, and return on investment. What do these ratios tell managers?

P6-8. Would you describe Starbucks' production/operations technology in its retail stores as unit, mass, or process? How about in its roasting plants? (Hint: you might need to review material in Chapter 11, as well, in order to answer this question.)

P6-9. Can Starbucks manage the uncertainties in its value chain? If so, how? If not, why not?

P6-10. Go to the company's website, www.starbucks.com. Find the information on the company's environmental activities from bean to cup. Select one of the steps in the chain (or your professor may assign you one). Describe and evaluate what environmental actions it's taking. How might these affect the planning, organizing, and controlling taking place in these areas?

P6-11. Look at the company's mission and guiding principles on its website. How might these affect the way Starbucks controls? How do the ways Starbucks controls contribute to the attainment or pursuit of these?

Notes for the Part 6 Continuing Case

Information from Starbucks Corporation 2015 Annual Report, www.investor.starbucks.com, June, 2016; B. Levisohn, "Starbucks 'Will Transform the Tea Market' Just Like It Did Coffee," *Barrons*, online, www.blogs.barrons.com, June 3, 2016; P. Wahba, "Why Starbucks Is Overhauling Its Loyalty Rewards Program," *Fortune* online, www.fortune.com, February 22, 2016; "Profanity-Laced Viral Video Shows Woman Accusing Starbucks Employee of Credit Card Fraud," *Fox News*, online, www.foxnews.com, January 4, 2016; A. Madhani, "Starbucks Eyes Lyft as Way to Ease Worker Commutes," *USA Today* online, www.usatoday.com, July 22, 2015; "Starbucks Drinks to Cost Up to 20 Cents More," *USA Today* online, www.usatoday.com, July 7, 2015; J. Pagliery, "Thieves Are Stealing Money from People's Credit Cards, Bank and PayPal Accounts—By First Tapping into Their Starbucks Mobile App," *CNN Money* online, www.money.cnn.com, May 14, 2015; K. Shah, "Starbucks or Dunkin' Donuts? Where America's Coffee Loyalty Lies," *Eater* online, www.eater.com, January 15, 2015; Company website, www.starbucks.com; C. Cain Miller, "Starbucks and Square to Team Up," *New York Times online,* August 8, 2012; R. Ahmed, "Tata Setting Up Starbucks Coffee Roasting Facility," www.online.wsj.com, July 26, 2012; B. Horovitz, "Starbucks Rolling Out Pop with Pep," *USA Today,* March 22, 2012, p. 1B; Starbucks News Release, "Starbucks Spotlights Connection Between Record Performance, Shareholder Value, and Company Values at Annual Meeting of Shareholders," news.starbucks.com, March 21, 2012; D. A. Kaplan, "Strong Coffee," *Fortune,* December 12, 2011, pp. 100–116; J. A. Cooke, ed., "From Bean to Cup: How Starbucks Transformed Its Supply Chain," www.supplychainquarterly.com, quarter 4, 2010; R. Ruggless, "Starbucks Exec: Security from Employee Theft Important When Implementing Gift Card Strategies," *Nation's Restaurant News,* December 12, 2005, p. 24; and R. Ruggless, "Transaction Monitoring Boosts Safety, Perks Up Coffee Chain Profits," *Nation's Restaurant News,* November 28, 2005, p. 35.

Glossary

A

Absenteeism The failure to show up for work

Active listening Listening for full meaning without making premature judgments or interpretations

Activities The time or resources needed to progress from one event to another in a PERT network

Adjourning The final stage of group development for temporary groups during which group members are concerned with wrapping up activities rather than task performance

Affective component That part of an attitude that's the emotional or feeling part

Affirmative action Organizational programs that enhance the status of members of protected groups

Angel investors A private investor (or group of private investors) who offers financial backing to an entrepreneurial venture in return for equity in the venture

Association of Southeast Asian Nations (ASEAN) A trading alliance of 10 Southeast Asian nations

Assumed similarity The assumption that others are like oneself

Attitude surveys Surveys that elicit responses from employees through questions about how they feel about their jobs, work groups, supervisors, or the organization

Attitudes Evaluative statements, either favorable or unfavorable, concerning objects, people, or events

Attribution theory A theory used to explain how we judge people differently depending on what meaning we attribute to a given behavior

Authentic leadership Leaders who know who they are, know what they believe in, and act on those values and beliefs openly and candidly

Authority The rights inherent in a managerial position to tell people what to do and to expect them to do it

Autocratic style A leader who dictates work methods, makes unilateral decisions, and limits employee participation

Autonomy The degree to which a job provides substantial freedom, independence, and discretion to the individual in scheduling work and determining the procedures to be used in carrying it out

B

Balanced scorecard A performance measurement tool that looks at more than just the financial perspective

Basic corrective action Corrective action that looks at how and why performance deviated before correcting the source of deviation

BCG matrix A strategy tool that guides resource allocation decisions on the basis of market share and growth rate of SBUs

Behavior The actions of people

Behavioral component That part of an attitude that refers to an intention to behave in a certain way toward someone or something

Behavioral theories Leadership theories that identify behaviors that differentiate effective leaders from ineffective leaders

Benchmark The standard of excellence against which to measure and compare

Benchmarking The search for the best practices among competitors or noncompetitors that lead to their superior performance

Bias A tendency or preference toward a particular perspective or ideology

Big data The vast amount of quantifiable information that can be analyzed by highly sophisticated data processing

Big Five Model Personality trait model that includes extraversion, agreeableness, conscientiousness, emotional stability, and openness to experience

Board representatives Employees who sit on a company's board of directors and represent the interests of the firm's employees

Body language Gestures, facial configurations, and other body movements that convey meaning

"Boiled frog" phenomenon A perspective on recognizing performance declines that suggests watching out for subtly declining situations

Boundaryless organization An organization whose design is not defined by, or limited to, the horizontal, vertical, or external boundaries imposed by a predefined structure

Bounded rationality Decision making that's rational, but limited (bounded) by an individual's ability to process information

Breakeven analysis A technique for identifying the point at which total revenue is just sufficient to cover total costs

Budget A numerical plan for allocating resources to specific activities

Budgeting The process of allocating resources to pay for designated future costs

Bureaucracy A form of organization characterized by division of labor, a clearly defined hierarchy, detailed rules and regulations, and impersonal relationships

Business intelligence Data that managers can use to make more effective strategic decisions

Business model How a company is going to make money

Business plan A written document that summarizes a business opportunity and defines and articulates how the identified opportunity is to be seized and exploited

C

Capabilities An organization's skills and abilities in doing the work activities needed in its business

Centralization The degree to which decision making is concentrated at upper levels of the organization

Certainty A situation in which a manager can make accurate decisions because all outcomes are known

Chain of command The line of authority extending from upper organizational levels to the lowest levels, which clarifies who reports to whom

Change agent Someone who acts as a catalyst and assumes the responsibility for managing the change process

Channel The medium a message travels along

Charismatic leader An enthusiastic, self-confident leader whose personality and actions influence people to behave in certain ways

Classical approach First studies of management, which emphasized rationality and making organizations and workers as efficient as possible

Classical view The view that management's only social responsibility is to maximize profits

Closed systems Systems that are not influenced by and do not interact with their environment

Closely held corporation A corporation owned by a limited number of people who do not trade the stock publicly

Cloud computing Refers to storing and accessing data on the Internet rather than on a computer's hard drive or a company's network

Code of ethics A formal statement of an organization's primary values and the ethical rules it expects its employees to follow

Coercive power The power a leader has to punish or control

Cognitive component That part of an attitude that's made up of the beliefs, opinions, knowledge, or information held by a person

Cognitive dissonance Any incompatibility or inconsistency between attitudes or between behavior and attitudes

Commitment concept Plans should extend far enough to meet those commitments made when the plans were developed

Communication networks The variety of patterns of vertical and horizontal flows of organizational communication

Communication process The seven elements involved in transferring meaning from one person to another

Communication The transfer and understanding of meaning

Competitive advantage What sets an organization apart; its distinctive edge

Competitive strategy An organizational strategy for how an organization will compete in its business(es)

Competitor intelligence Gathering information about competitors that allows managers to anticipate competitors' actions rather than merely react to them

Compressed workweek A workweek where employees work longer hours per day but fewer days per week

Conceptual skills The ability to think and to conceptualize about abstract and complex situations

Concurrent control Control that takes place while a work activity is in progress

Conflict Perceived incompatible differences that result in interference or opposition

Consideration The extent to which a leader has work relationships characterized by mutual trust and respect for group members' ideas and feelings

Contingency approach A management approach that recognizes organizations as different, which means they face different situations (contingencies) and require different ways of managing

Contingent workers Temporary, freelance, or contract workers whose employment is contingent on demand for their services

Control process A three-step process of measuring actual performance, comparing actual performance against a standard, and taking managerial action to correct deviations or inadequate standards

Controlling Management function that involves monitoring, comparing, and correcting work performance

Core competencies The organization's major value-creating capabilities that determine its competitive weapons

Corporate governance The system used to govern a corporation so that the interests of corporate owners are protected

Corporate strategy An organizational strategy that determines what businesses a company is in or wants to be in, and what it wants to do with those businesses

Corporation A legal business entity that is separate from its owners and managers

Counterproductive workplace behavior Any intentional employee behavior that is potentially damaging to the organization or to individuals within the organization

Creativity The ability to combine ideas in a unique way or to make unusual associations between ideas

Credibility The degree to which followers perceive someone as honest, competent, and able to inspire

Critical path The longest sequence of activities in a PERT network

Cross-functional team A work team composed of individuals from various functional specialties

Cultural intelligence Cultural awareness and sensitivity skills

D

Decentralization The degree to which lower-level employees provide input or actually make decisions

Decision A choice among two or more alternatives

Decision criteria Criteria that define what's important or relevant to resolving a problem

Decisional roles Managerial roles that revolve around making choices

Decoding Retranslating a sender's message

Decruitment Reducing an organization's workforce

Deep-level diversity Differences in values, personality, and work preferences

Democratic style A leader who involves employees in decision making, delegates authority, and uses feedback as an opportunity for coaching employees

Departmentalization The basis by which jobs are grouped together

Design thinking Approaching management problems as designers approach design problems

Diagonal communication Communication that cuts across work areas and organizational levels

Digital tools Technology, systems, or software that allow the user to collect, visualize, understand, or analyze data

Directional plans Plans that are flexible and set out general guidelines

Disciplinary actions Actions taken by a manager to enforce the organization's work standards and regulations

Discrimination When someone acts out their prejudicial attitudes toward people who are the targets of their prejudice

Disruptive innovation Innovations in products, services or processes that radically change an industry's rules of the game

Distributive justice Perceived fairness of the amount and allocation of rewards among individuals

Diversity skills training Specialized training to educate employees about the importance of diversity and teach them skills for working in a diverse workplace

Division of labor (job specialization) The breakdown of jobs into narrow and repetitive tasks

Divisional structure An organizational structure made up of separate, semiautonomous units or divisions

Downsizing The planned elimination of jobs in an organization

Downward communication Communication that flows downward from a manager to employees

Dysfunctional conflicts Conflicts that prevent a group from achieving its goals

E

Effectiveness Doing the right things, or doing those work activities that will result in achieving goals

Efficiency Doing things right, or getting the most output from the least amount of inputs

Ego strength A personality measure of the strength of a person's convictions

Emotional intelligence (EI) The ability to notice and to manage emotional cues and information

Emotions Intense feelings that are directed at someone or something

Employee empowerment Giving employees more authority (power) to make decisions

Employee engagement When employees are connected to, satisfied with, and enthusiastic about their jobs

Employee productivity A performance measure of both efficiency and effectiveness

Employee recognition programs Personal attention and expressing interest, approval, and appreciation for a job well done

Employee resource groups Groups made up of employees connected by some common dimension of diversity

Employee theft Any unauthorized taking of company property by employees for their personal use

Encoding Converting a message into symbols

Entrepreneurial ventures Organizations that pursue opportunities, are characterized by innovative practices, and have growth and profitability as their main goals

Entrepreneurship The process of starting new businesses, generally in response to opportunities

Environmental complexity The number of components in an organization's environment and the extent of the organization's knowledge about those components

Environmental scanning Screening information to detect emerging trends

Environmental uncertainty The degree of change and complexity in an organization's environment

Equity theory The theory that an employee compares his or her job's input-outcomes ratio with that of relevant others and then corrects any inequity

Escalation of commitment An increased commitment to a previous decision despite evidence it may have been wrong

Esteem needs A person's needs for internal factors such as self-respect, autonomy, and achievement, and external factors such as status, recognition, and attention

Ethical communication Communication that includes all relevant information, is true in every sense, and is not deceptive in any way

Ethics Principles, values, and beliefs that define what is right and wrong behavior

Ethnicity Social traits (such as cultural background or allegiance) that are shared by a human population

Ethnocentric attitude The parochial belief that the best work approaches and practices are those of the home country

Euro A single common European currency

European Union (EU) A union of 28 European nations created as a unified economic and trade entity

Events End points that represent the completion of major activities in a PERT network

Evidence-based management (EBMgt) The systematic use of the best available evidence to improve management practice

Expectancy theory The theory that an individual tends to act in a certain way based on the expectation that the act will be followed by a given outcome and on the attractiveness of that outcome to the individual

Expert power Power that's based on expertise, special skills, or knowledge

Exporting Making products domestically and selling them abroad

External environment Those factors and forces outside the organization that affect its performance

F

Feasibility study An analysis of the various aspects of a proposed entrepreneurial venture designed to determine its feasibility

Feedback control Control that takes place after a work activity is done

Feedback The degree to which carrying out work activities required by a job results in the individual's obtaining direct and clear information about his or her performance effectiveness

Fiedler contingency model A leadership theory proposing that effective group performance depends on the proper match between a leader's style and the degree to which the situation allows the leader to control and influence

Filtering The deliberate manipulation of information to make it appear more favorable to the receiver

First mover An organization that's first to bring a product innovation to the market or to use a new process innovation

First-line (frontline) managers Managers at the lowest level of management who manage the work of non-managerial employees

Flextime (or flexible work hours) A scheduling system in which employees are required to work a specific number of hours a week but are free to vary those hours within certain limits

Forecasts Predictions of outcome

Foreign subsidiary Directly investing in a foreign country by setting up a separate and independent production facility or office

Formal communication Communication that takes place within prescribed organizational work arrangements

Formal planning department A group of planning specialists whose sole responsibility is helping to write organizational plans

Formalization How standardized an organization's jobs are and the extent to which employee behavior is guided by rules and procedures

Forming stage The first stage of group development in which people join the group and then define the group's purpose, structure, and leadership

Franchising An organization gives another organization the right to use its name and operating methods

Free market economy An economic system in which resources are primarily owned and controlled by the private sector

Functional conflicts Conflicts that support a group's goals and improve its performance

Functional strategy A strategy used by an organization's various functional departments to support the competitive strategy

Functional structure An organizational design that groups together similar or related occupational specialties

Fundamental attribution error The tendency to underestimate the influence of external factors and overestimate the influence of internal factors when making judgments about the behavior of others

G

Gantt chart A scheduling chart developed by Henry Gantt that shows actual and planned output over a period of time

General administrative theory An approach to management that focuses on describing what managers do and what constitutes good management practice

General partnership A form of legal organization in which two or more business owners share the management and risk of the business

Geocentric attitude A world-oriented view that focuses on using the best approaches and people from around the globe

Glass ceiling The invisible barrier that separates women and minorities from top management positions

Global company An MNC that centralizes management and other decisions in the home country

Global Leadership and Organizational Behavior Effectiveness (GLOBE) program The research program that studies cross-cultural leadership behaviors

Global mind set Attributes that allow a leader to be effective in cross-cultural environments

Global sourcing Purchasing materials or labor from around the world wherever it is cheapest

Goal-setting theory The proposition that specific goals increase performance and that difficult goals, when accepted, result in higher performance than do easy goals

Goals (objectives) Desired outcomes or targets

Grapevine The informal organizational communication network

Green management Managers consider the impact of their organization on the natural environment

Group cohesiveness The degree to which group members are attracted to one another and share the group's goals

Group Two or more interacting and interdependent individuals who come together to achieve specific goals

Groupthink When a group exerts extensive pressure on an individual to align his or her opinion with others' opinions

Growth strategy A corporate strategy that's used when an organization wants to expand the number of markets served or products offered, either through its current business(es) or through new business(es)

H

Halo effect A general impression of an individual based on a single characteristic

Harvesting Exiting a venture when an entrepreneur hopes to capitalize financially on the investment in the venture

Hawthorne Studies A series of studies during the 1920s and 1930s that provided new insights into individual and group behavior

Heuristics Rules of thumb that managers use to simplify decision making

Hierarchy of needs theory Maslow's theory that human needs—physiological, safety, social, esteem, and self-actualization—form a sort of hierarchy

High-involvement work practices Work practices designed to elicit greater input or involvement from workers

High-performance work practices Work practices that lead to both high individual and high organizational performance

High–high leader A leader high in both initiating structure and consideration behaviors

Human relations view of conflict The view that conflict is a natural and inevitable outcome in any group

Human resource planning Ensuring that the organization has the right number and kinds of capable people in the right places and at the right times

Hygiene factors Factors that eliminate job dissatisfaction, but don't motivate

I

Idea champion Individual who actively and enthusiastically supports new ideas, builds support, overcomes resistance, and ensures that innovations are implemented

Immediate corrective action Corrective action that corrects problems at once to get performance back on track

Importing Acquiring products made abroad and selling them domestically

Incremental budgeting Process starting with the current budget from which managers decide whether they need additional resources and the justification for requesting them

Industrial revolution A period during the late eighteenth century when machine power was substituted for human power, making it more economical to manufacture goods in factories than at home

Informal communication Communication that is not defined by the organization's structural hierarchy

Information overload When information exceeds our processing capacity

Informational roles Managerial roles that involve collecting, receiving, and disseminating information

Initial public offering (IPO) The first public registration and sale of a company's stock

Initiating structure The extent to which a leader defines his or her role and the roles of group members in attaining goals

Innovation Taking creative ideas and turning them into useful products or work methods

Intellectual property Proprietary information that's critical to an organization's efficient and effective functioning and competitiveness

Interactionist view of conflict The view that some conflict is necessary for a group to perform effectively

International Monetary Fund (IMF) An organization of 188 countries that promotes international monetary cooperation and provides advice, loans, and technical assistance

Internet of Things Allows everyday "things" to generate and store and share data across the Internet

Interpersonal communication Communication between two or more people

Interpersonal roles Managerial roles that involve people and other duties that are ceremonial and symbolic in nature

Interpersonal skills The ability to work well with other people individually and in a group

Intuitive decision making Making decisions on the basis of experience, feelings, and accumulated judgment

ISO 9000 A series of international quality management standards that set uniform guidelines for processes to ensure products conform to customer requirements

J

Jargon Specialized terminology or technical language that members of a group use to communicate among themselves

Job analysis An assessment that defines jobs and the behaviors necessary to perform them

Job characteristics model (JCM) A framework for analyzing and designing jobs that identifies five primary core job dimensions, their interrelationships, and their impact on outcomes

Job depth The degree of control employees have over their work

Job description (position description) A written statement that describes a job

Job design The way tasks are combined to form complete jobs

Job enlargement The horizontal expansion of a job by increasing job scope

Job enrichment The vertical expansion of a job by adding planning and evaluating responsibilities

Job involvement The degree to which an employee identifies with his or her job, actively participates in it, and considers his or her job performance to be important to self-worth

Job satisfaction An employee's general attitude toward his or her job

Job scope The number of different tasks required in a job and the frequency with which those tasks are repeated

Job sharing The practice of having two or more people split a full-time job

Job specification A written statement of the minimum qualifications a person must possess to perform a given job successfully

Joint venture A specific type of strategic alliance in which the partners agree to form a separate, independent organization for some business purpose

Labor union An organization that represents workers and seeks to protect their interests through collective bargaining

Laissez-faire style A leader who lets the group make decisions and complete the work in whatever way it sees fit

L

Lateral communication Communication that takes place among any employees on the same organizational level

Leader Someone who can influence others and who has managerial authority

Leader–member exchange theory (LMX) The leadership theory that says leaders create in-groups and out-groups and those in the in-group will have higher performance ratings, less turnover, and greater job satisfaction

Leader–member relations One of Fiedler's situational contingencies that describes the degree of confidence, trust, and respect employees have for their leader

Leadership A process of influencing a group to achieve goals

Leading Management function that involves working with and through people to accomplish organizational goals

Lean organization An organization that understands what customers want, identifies customer value by analyzing all activities required to produce products, and then optimizes the entire process from the customer's perspective

Learning Any relatively permanent change in behavior that occurs as a result of experience

Least-preferred coworker (LPC) questionnaire A questionnaire that measures whether a leader is task or relationship oriented

Legitimate power The power a leader has as a result of his or her position in the organization

Licensing An organization gives another organization the right to make or sell its products using its technology or product specifications

Limited liability company (LLC) A form of legal organization that's a hybrid between a partnership and a corporation

Limited liability partnership (LLP) A form of legal organization consisting of general partner(s) and limited liability partner(s)

Line authority Authority that entitles a manager to direct the work of an employee

Linear programming A mathematical technique that solves resource allocation problems

Load chart A modified Gantt chart that schedules capacity by entire departments or specific resources

Locus of control A personality attribute that measures the degree to which people believe they control their own fate

Long-term plans Plans with a time frame beyond three years

M

Machiavellianism A measure of the degree to which people are pragmatic, maintain emotional distance, and believe that ends justify means

Management by objectives (MBO) A process of setting mutually agreed-upon goals and using those goals to evaluate employee performance

Management by walking around A term used to describe when a manager is out in the work area interacting directly with employees

Management Coordinating and overseeing the work activities of others so their activities are completed efficiently and effectively

Management information system (MIS) A system used to provide management with needed information on a regular basis

Manager Someone who coordinates and oversees the work of other people so organizational goals can be accomplished

Managerial grid A two-dimensional grid for appraising leadership styles

Managerial roles Specific actions or behaviors expected of and exhibited by a manager

Manufacturing organizations Organizations that produce physical goods

Mass customization Providing customers with a product when, where, and how they want it

Mass production The production of items in large batches

Matrix structure An organizational structure that assigns specialists from different functional departments to work on one or more projects

Means-ends chain An integrated network of goals in which the accomplishment of goals at one level serves as the means for achieving the goals, or ends, at the next level

Mechanistic organization An organizational design that's rigid and tightly controlled

Mentoring A process whereby an experienced organizational member (a mentor) provides advice and guidance to a less experienced member (a protégé)

Message A purpose to be conveyed

Middle managers Managers between the lowest level and top levels of the organization who manage the work of first-line managers

Mission The purpose of an organization

Motivation The process by which a person's efforts are energized, directed, and sustained toward attaining a goal

Motivators Factors that increase job satisfaction and motivation

Multidomestic corporation An MNC that decentralizes management and other decisions to the local country

Multinational corporation (MNC) A broad term that refers to any and all types of international companies that maintain operations in multiple countries

N

National culture The values and attitudes shared by individuals from a specific country that shape their behavior and beliefs about what is important

Need for achievement (nAch) The drive to succeed and excel in relation to a set of standards

Need for affiliation (nAff) The desire for friendly and close interpersonal relationships

Need for power (nPow) The need to make others behave in a way that they would not have behaved otherwise

Noise Any disturbances that interfere with the transmission, receipt, or feedback of a message

Nonprogrammed decisions Unique and nonrecurring decisions that require a custom-made solution

Nonverbal communication Communication transmitted without words

Norming stage The third stage of group development, characterized by close relationships and cohesiveness

Norms Standards or expectations that are accepted and shared by a group's members

North American Free Trade Agreement (NAFTA) An agreement among the Mexican, Canadian, and U.S. governments in which barriers to trade have been eliminated

O

Omnipotent view of management The view that managers are directly responsible for an organization's success or failure

Open innovation Opening up the search for new ideas beyond the organization's boundaries and allowing innovations to easily transfer inward and outward

Open systems Systems that interact with their environment

Open workplaces Workplaces with few physical barriers and enclosures

Open-book management A motivational approach in which an organization's financial statements (the "books") are shared with all employees

Operant conditioning A theory of learning that says behavior is a function of its consequences

Operating agreement The document that outlines the provisions governing the way an LLC will conduct business

Operational plans Plans that encompass a particular operational area of the organization

Operations management The transformation process that converts resources into finished goods and services

Opportunities Positive trends in the external environment

Organic organization An organizational design that's highly adaptive and flexible

Organization A deliberate arrangement of people to accomplish some specific purpose

Organization for Economic Cooperation and Development (OECD) An international economic organization that helps its 34 member countries achieve sustainable economic growth and employment

Organizational behavior (OB) The study of the actions of people at work

Organizational change Any alteration of people, structure, or technology in an organization

Organizational chart The visual representation of an organization's structure

Organizational citizenship behavior (OCB) Discretionary behavior that is not part of an employee's formal job requirements, but which promotes the effective functioning of the organization

Organizational commitment The degree to which an employee identifies with a particular organization and its goals and wishes to maintain membership in that organization

Organizational communication All the patterns, networks, and systems of communication within an organization

Organizational culture The shared values, principles, traditions, and ways of doing things that influence the way organizational members act and that distinguish the organization from other organizations

Organizational design Creating or changing an organization's structure

Organizational development (OD) Change methods that focus on people and the nature and quality of interpersonal work relationships

Organizational effectiveness A measure of how appropriate organizational goals are and how well those goals are being met

Organizational performance The accumulated results of all the organization's work activities

Organizational processes The ways that organizational work is done

Organizational structure The formal arrangement of jobs within an organization

Organizing Management function that involves arranging and structuring work to accomplish the organization's goals

Orientation Introducing a new employee to his or her job and the organization

P

Parochialism Viewing the world solely through your own perspectives, leading to an inability to recognize differences between people

Path-goal theory A leadership theory that says the leader's job is to assist followers in attaining their goals and to provide direction or support needed to ensure that their goals are compatible with the goals of the group or organization

Pay-for-performance programs Variable compensation plans that pay employees on the basis of some performance measure

Perceived organizational support Employees' general belief that their organization values their contribution and cares about their well-being

Perception A process by which we give meaning to our environment by organizing and interpreting sensory impressions

Performance management system Establishes performance standards used to evaluate employee performance

Performance The end result of an activity

Performing stage The fourth stage of group development when the group is fully functional and works on group task

Personality The unique combination of emotional, thought, and behavioral patterns that affect how a person reacts to situations and interacts with others

Persuasion skills Skills that enable a person to influence others to change their minds or behavior

PERT network A flowchart diagram showing the sequence of activities needed to complete a project and the time or cost associated with each

Physiological needs A person's needs for food, drink, shelter, sexual satisfaction, and other physical needs

Planned economy An economic system in which economic decisions are planned by a central government

Planning Management function that involves setting goals, establishing strategies for achieving those goals, and developing plans to integrate and coordinate work activities

Plans Documents that outline how goals are going to be met

Policy A guideline for making decisions

Polycentric attitude The view that the managers in the host country know the best work approaches and practices for running their business

Position power One of Fiedler's situational contingencies that describes the degree of influence a leader has over activities such as hiring, firing, discipline, promotions, and salary increases

Prejudice A preconceived belief, opinion, or judgment toward a person or a group of people

Principles of management Fundamental rules of management that could be applied in all organizational situations and taught in schools

Proactive personality A personality trait that describes individuals who are more prone to take actions to influence their environments

Proactive perspective of work design An approach to job design in which employees take the initiative to change how their work is performed

Problem An obstacle that makes it difficult to achieve a desired goal or purpose

Problem-solving team A team from the same department or functional area that's involved in efforts to improve work activities or to solve specific problems

Procedural justice Perceived fairness of the process used to determine the distribution of rewards

Procedure A series of sequential steps used to respond to a well-structured problem

Process conflict Conflict over how work gets done

Process production The production of items in continuous processes

Productivity The amount of goods or services produced divided by the inputs needed to generate that output

Programmed decision A repetitive decision that can be handled by a routine approach

Progressive disciplinary action An approach to ensure that the minimum penalty appropriate to the offense is imposed

Project A one-time-only set of activities that has a definite beginning and ending point in time

Project management The task of getting a project's activities done on time, within budget, and according to specifications

Project structure An organizational structure in which employees continuously work on projects

Q

Qualitative forecasting Forecasting that uses the judgment and opinions of knowledgeable individuals to predict outcomes

Quality The ability of a product or service to reliably do what it's supposed to do and to satisfy customer expectations

Quantitative approach The use of quantitative techniques to improve decision making

Quantitative forecasting Forecasting that applies a set of mathematical rules to a series of past data to predict outcomes

R

Race The biological heritage (including skin color and associated traits) that people use to identify themselves

Range of variation The acceptable parameters of variance between actual performance and the standard

Rational decision making Describes choices that are logical and consistent and maximize value

Readiness The extent to which people have the ability and willingness to accomplish a specific task

Reading skills Skills that entail an understanding of written sentences and paragraphs in work-related documents

Real goals Goals that an organization actually pursues, as defined by the actions of its members

Realistic job preview (RJP) A preview of a job that provides both positive and negative information about the job and the company

Recruitment Locating, identifying, and attracting capable applicants

Referent power Power that arises because of a person's desirable resources or personal traits

Referents The persons, systems, or selves against which individuals compare themselves to assess equity

Reinforcement theory The theory that behavior is a function of its consequences

Reinforcers Consequences immediately following a behavior, which increase the probability that the behavior will be repeated

Relational perspective of work design An approach to job design that focuses on how people's tasks and jobs are increasingly based on social relationships

Relationship conflict Conflict based on interpersonal relationships

Renewal strategy A corporate strategy designed to address declining performance

Resilience An individual's ability to overcome challenges and turn them into opportunities

Resources An organization's assets—including financial, physical, human, intangible, and structural/cultural—that are used to develop, manufacture, and deliver products to its customers

Responsibility The obligation or expectation to perform any assigned duties

Reward power The power a leader has to give positive rewards

Risk A situation in which the decision maker is able to estimate the likelihood of certain outcomes

Role ambiguity When role expectations are not clearly understood

Role Behavior patterns expected of someone occupying a given position in a social unit

Role conflicts Work expectations that are hard to satisfy

Role overload Having more work to accomplish than time permits

Rule An explicit statement that tells managers what can or cannot be done

S

S corporation A specialized type of corporation that has the regular characteristics of a C corporation but is unique in that the owners are taxed as a partnership as long as certain criteria are met

Safety needs A person's needs for security and protection from physical and emotional harm

Satisfice Accept solutions that are "good enough"

Scenario A consistent view of what the future is likely to be

Scheduling Detailing what activities have to be done, the order in which they are to be completed, who is to do each, and when they are to be completed

Scientific management An approach that involves using the scientific method to find the "one best way" for a job to be done

Selection Screening job applicants to ensure that the most appropriate candidates are hired

Self-actualization needs A person's need to become what he or she is capable of becoming

Self-efficacy An individual's belief that he or she is capable of performing a task

Self-employment Individuals who work for profit or fees in their own business, profession, trade, or farm

Self-esteem An individual's degree of like or dislike for himself or herself

Self-managed work team A type of work team that operates without a manager and is responsible for a complete work process or segment

Self-monitoring A personality trait that measures the ability to adjust behavior to external situational factors

Self-serving bias The tendency for individuals to attribute their own successes to internal factors while putting the blame for failures on external factors

Service organizations Organizations that produce nonphysical products in the form of services

Service profit chain The service sequence from employees to customers to profit

Sexual harassment Any unwanted action or activity of a sexual nature that explicitly or implicitly affects an individual's employment, performance, or work environment

Shaping behavior The process of guiding learning in graduated steps using reinforcement or lack of reinforcement

Sharing economy Business arrangements that are based on people sharing something they own or providing a service for a fee

Short-term plans Plans covering one year or less

Simple structure An organizational design with little departmentalization, wide spans of control, centralized authority, and little formalization

Single-use plan A one-time plan specifically designed to meet the needs of a unique situation

Situational leadership theory (SLT) A leadership contingency theory that focuses on followers' readiness

Six Sigma A quality program designed to reduce defects and help lower costs, save time, and improve customer satisfaction

Skill variety The degree to which a job requires a variety of activities so that an employee can use a number of different skills and talents

Skill-based pay A pay system that rewards employees for the job skills they can demonstrate

Skunk works A small group within a large organization, given a high degree of autonomy and unhampered by corporate bureaucracy, whose mission is to develop a project primarily for the sake of radical innovation

Slack time The amount of time an individual activity can be delayed without delaying the whole project

Small business An organization that is independently owned, operated, and financed; has fewer than 100 employees; doesn't necessarily engage in any new or innovative practices; and has relatively little impact on its industry

Social entrepreneur An individual or organization that seeks out opportunities to improve society by using practical, innovative, and sustainable approaches

Social learning theory A theory of learning that says people can learn through observation and direct experience

Social loafing The tendency for individuals to expend less effort when working collectively than when working individually

Social media Forms of electronic communication through which users create online communities to share ideas, information, personal messages, and other content

Social needs A person's needs for affection, belongingness, acceptance, and friendship

Social network structure The patterns of informal connections among individuals within a group

Social obligation When a firm engages in social actions because of its obligation to meet certain economic and legal responsibilities

Social responsibility A business's intention, beyond its legal and economic obligations, to do the right things and act in ways that are good for society

Social responsiveness When a firm engages in social actions in response to some popular social need

Social screening Applying social criteria (screens) to investment decisions

Socialization The process that helps employees adapt to the organization's culture

Socioeconomic view The view that management's social responsibility goes beyond making profits to include protecting and improving society's welfare

Sole proprietorship A form of legal organization in which the owner maintains sole and complete control over the business and is personally liable for business debts

Span of control The number of employees a manager can efficiently and effectively manage

Speaking skills Skills that refer to the ability to communicate information and ideas in talking so others will understand

Specific plans Plans that are clearly defined and leave no room for interpretation

Stability strategy A corporate strategy in which an organization continues to do what it is currently doing

Staff authority Positions with some authority that have been created to support, assist, and advise those holding line authority

Stakeholders Any constituencies in the organization's environment that are affected by an organization's decisions and actions

Standing plans Ongoing plans that provide guidance for activities performed repeatedly

Stated goals Official statements of what an organization says, and what it wants its various stakeholders to believe, its goals are

Status A prestige grading, position, or rank within a group

Stereotyping Judging a person based on a perception of a group to which that person belongs

Storming stage The second stage of group development, characterized by intragroup conflict

Strategic alliance A partnership between an organization and foreign company partner(s) in which both share resources and knowledge in developing new products or building production facilities

Strategic business unit (SBU) The single independent businesses of an organization that formulate their own competitive strategies

Strategic flexibility The ability to recognize major external changes, to quickly commit resources, and to recognize when a strategic decision was a mistake

Strategic leadership The ability to anticipate, envision, maintain flexibility, think strategically, and work with others in the organization to initiate changes that will create a viable and valuable future for the organization

Strategic management process A six-step process that encompasses strategic planning, implementation, and evaluation

Strategic management What managers do to develop the organization's strategies

Strategic plans Plans that apply to the entire organization and establish the organization's overall goals

Strategies The plans for how the organization will do what it's in business to do, how it will compete successfully, and how it will attract and satisfy its customers in order to achieve its goals

Strengths Any activities the organization does well or its unique resources

Stress The adverse reaction people have to excessive pressure placed on them from extraordinary demands, constraints, or opportunities

Stressors Factors that cause stress

Strong cultures Organizational cultures in which the key values are intensely held and widely shared

Structured problems Straightforward, familiar, and easily defined problems

Surface-level diversity Easily perceived differences that may trigger certain stereotypes, but that do not necessarily reflect the ways people think or feel

Sustainability A company's ability to achieve its business goals and increase long-term shareholder value by integrating economic, environmental, and social opportunities into its business strategies

Sustaining innovation Small and incremental changes in established products rather than dramatic breakthroughs

SWOT analysis An analysis of the organization's strengths, weaknesses, opportunities, and threats

Symbolic view of management The view that much of an organization's success or failure is due to external forces outside managers' control

System A set of interrelated and interdependent parts arranged in a manner that produces a unified whole

T

Task conflict Conflicts over content and goals of the work

Task force (or ad hoc committee) A temporary committee or team formed to tackle a specific short-term problem affecting several departments

Task identity The degree to which a job requires completion of a whole and identifiable piece of work

Task significance The degree to which a job has a substantial impact on the lives or work of other people

Task structure One of Fiedler's situational contingencies that describes the degree to which job assignments are formalized and structured

Team structure An organizational structure in which the entire organization is made up of work teams

Technical skills Job-specific knowledge and techniques needed to proficiently perform work tasks

Telecommuting A work arrangement in which employees work at home and are linked to the workplace by computer

Theory X The assumption that employees dislike work, are lazy, avoid responsibility, and must be coerced to perform

Theory Y The assumption that employees are creative, enjoy work, seek responsibility, and can exercise self-direction

Therbligs A classification scheme for labeling basic hand motions

Threats Negative trends in the external environment

Three-needs theory The motivation theory that says three acquired (not innate) needs—achievement, power, and affiliation—are major motives in work

Top managers Managers at or near the upper levels of the organization structure who are responsible for making organization-wide decisions and establishing the goals and plans that affect the entire organization

Total quality management (TQM) A philosophy of management that is driven by continuous improvement and responsiveness to customer needs and expectations

Town hall meeting Informal public meetings where information can be relayed, issues can be discussed, or employees can be brought together to celebrate accomplishments

Traditional goal-setting An approach to setting goals in which top managers set goals that then flow down through the organization and become subgoals for each organizational area

Traditional view of conflict The view that all conflict is bad and must be avoided

Transactional leaders Leaders who lead primarily by using social exchanges (or transactions)

Transformational leaders Leaders who stimulate and inspire (transform) followers to achieve extraordinary outcomes

Transnational or borderless organization An MNC in which artificial geographical barriers are eliminated

Trust The belief in the integrity, character, and ability of a leader

Turnover The voluntary and involuntary permanent withdrawal from an organization

Two-factor theory (motivation-hygiene theory) The motivation theory that intrinsic factors are related to job satisfaction and motivation, whereas extrinsic factors are associated with job dissatisfaction

Type A personality People who have a chronic sense of urgency and an excessive competitive drive

Type B personality People who are relaxed and easygoing and accept change easily

U

Uncertainty A situation in which a decision maker has neither certainty nor reasonable probability estimates available

Unit production The production of items in units or small batches

Unity of command The management principle that each person should report to only one manager

Universality of management The reality that management is needed in all types and sizes of organizations, at all organizational levels, in all organizational areas, and in organizations no matter where located

Unstructured problems Problems that are new or unusual and for which information is ambiguous or incomplete

Upward communication Communication that flows upward from employees to managers

V

Value chain management The process of managing the sequence of activities and information along the entire value chain

Value chain The entire series of organizational work activities that add value at each step from raw materials to finished product

Value The performance characteristics, features, and attributes, and any other aspects of goods and services for which customers are willing to give up resources

Values Basic convictions about what is right and wrong

Values-based management The organization's values guide employees in the way they do their jobs

Variable pay A pay system in which an individual's compensation is contingent on performance

Venture capitalists External equity financing provided by professionally managed pools of investor money

Verbal intonation An emphasis given to words or phrases that conveys meaning

Virtual organization An organization that consists of a small core of full-time employees and outside specialists temporarily hired as needed to work on projects

Virtual team A type of work team that uses technology to link physically dispersed members in order to achieve a common goal

Visionary leadership The ability to create and articulate a realistic, credible, and attractive vision of the future that improves upon the present situation

W

Weaknesses Activities the organization does not do well or resources it needs but does not possess

Whistle-blower Individual who raises ethical concerns or issues to others

Work councils Groups of nominated or elected employees who must be consulted when management makes decisions involving personnel

Work specialization Dividing work activities into separate job tasks

Work teams Groups whose members work intensely on a specific, common goal using their positive synergy, individual and mutual accountability, and complementary skills

Workforce diversity The ways in which people in an organization are different from and similar to one another

World Bank Group A group of five closely associated institutions that provides financial and technical assistance to developing countries

World Trade Organization (WTO) A global organization of 161 countries that deals with the rules of trade among nations

Writing skills Skills that entail communicating effectively in text as appropriate for the needs of the audience

Z

Zero-base budgeting (ZBB) Process starting with an established point of zero rather than using the current budget as the basis for adding, modifying, or subtracting resources

Name Index

C

D

E

H

L

M

N

O

S

T

U

V

Organization Index

Subject Index

D

E

P

Q

R

Y

Z